THEORY AND PRACTICE OF THE EUROPEAN CONVENTION ON HUMAN RIGHTS

Fifth edition

Edited by

Pieter van Dijk
Fried van Hoof
Arjen van Rijn
Leo Zwaak

intersentia

Cambridge – Antwerp – Portland

Intersentia Ltd
Sheraton House | Castle Park
Cambridge | CB3 0AX | United Kingdom
Tel.: +44 1223 370 170 | Fax: +44 1223 370 169
Email: mail@intersentia.co.uk
www.intersentia.com | www.intersentia.co.uk

Distribution for the UK and Ireland:
NBN International
Airport Business Centre, 10 Thornbury Road
Plymouth, PL6 7 PP
United Kingdom
Tel.: +44 1752 202 301 | Fax: +44 1752 202 331
Email: orders@nbninternational.com

Distribution for Europe and all other countries:
Intersentia Publishing nv
Groenstraat 31
2640 Mortsel
Belgium
Tel.: +32 3 680 15 50 | Fax: +32 3 658 71 21
Email: mail@intersentia.be

Distribution for the USA and Canada:
International Specialized Book Services
920 NE 58th Ave. Suite 300
Portland, OR 97213
USA
Tel.: +1 800 944 6190 (toll free) | Fax: +1 503 280 8832
Email: info@isbs.com

Theory and Practice of the European Convention on Human Rights
© The editors and contributors severally 2018

ISBN 978-1-78068-493-2 (hardback)
ISBN 978-1-78068-494-9 (paperback)
D/2018/7849/2
NUR 828

British Library Cataloguing in Publication Data. A catalogue record for this book is available from the British Library.

PREFACE TO THE FIFTH EDITION

The publication of this fifth edition of *Theory and Practice of the European Convention on Human Rights* is again a cause of great satisfaction and gratitude. However, there is also sorrow. In 2015 Fried van Hoof, one of the two co-founders of this book, passed away after a battle against an illness he could not win. Every day we are missing his inspiration and engagement for the cause of human rights which, amongst many other human rights activities, was reflected in the preceding editions of this book. We are grateful for all Fried van Hoof gave to us in the many years we shared. Therefore, we dedicate this edition especially to him. Also, we dedicate this edition to Pieter van Dijk, the second co-founder of this book. In 2013, after a long and successful career as a human rights university professor, a judge in the European Court of Human Rights and a member of the Council of State of the Netherlands, he retired and chose not to participate in the next edition anymore. We are also missing his inspiring engagement. At the same time, we are grateful that we could learn so much from his passionate attitude towards the human rights cause and from his detailed knowledge in all respects. It is our ambition to pursue this book in the founders' spirit.

This book's lasting ambition is to give an overview of the case law of the European Court of Human Rights in respect to the rights protected by the European Convention on Human Rights and Fundamental Freedoms and its Protocols, and to do this in such manner that an added value in relation to the existing online databases can be demonstrated. In this perspective, developments in case law since 2006 have been incorporated in the fifth edition. In addition, we have strived for further improvements in presenting the issues at stake. The sheer amount of case law is tremendous and ever growing. Finding ways to cope with this is an ongoing process. In light of this, we are also planning to present interim online updates of the case law concerning individual articles of the Convention on an annual basis.

Theory and Practice of the European Convention on Human Rights has a history which goes back to 1979. The first editions were written by their founders Pieter van Dijk and Fried van Hoof. On behalf of the third edition (1998) the team of authors was extended with Aalt Willem Heringa, Jeroen Schokkenbroek, Ben Vermeulen, Marc Viering and Leo Zwaak. In addition, Yutaka Arai, Edwin Bleichrodt, Kees Flinterman and Arjen van Rijn joined the authors' team for the fourth edition (2006).

This fifth edition is again the result of the joint commitment of many people. A large team of specialised and experienced authors have written and revised the book's individual chapters. We thank them for their willingness, dedication and patience. In particular, we would like to thank Janneke Gerards and Antoine Buyse for their commitment as co-editors in the first phase of the preparations for the fifth edition. We are grateful to Bas van Bockel, Hansko Broeksteeg and Stefan Sottiaux for their willingness not only to act as authors but as reviewers as well. We express special words of acknowledgment to Linus Hesselink, desk editor and coordinator during the second phase of the preparations for the fifth edition. In particular, he was assigned the task to drive the flock through the gate in time, which he managed extraordinarily well, never despairing. Further, we would like to thank Dylan Helmich for his committed research assistance. Last but not least, we express great thanks to our publisher Kris Moeremans for whom, as a strong believer, no effort was ever too big to make this edition a success. Without his commitment and generosity, and without the dedicated engagement of his staff, we would not have been able to succeed.

Arjen van Rijn
Leo Zwaak

July 2017

TABLE OF ARTICLES

CONTENTS

ABOUT THE AUTHORS

Yutakaka Arai (1969), PhD, professor of International Law and International Human Rights Law at University of Kent, Brussels (BSIS), Belgium. He has published extensively in the field of international humanitarian law and human rights law

Sjoerd Bakker (1973), PhD, attorney at law at Spigt Dutch Caribbean in Willemstad, Curaçao and assistant professor of Contract Law at VU University Amsterdam, the Netherlands. His thesis (2012) dealt with the topic of good faith as a norm of conduct. He has published extensively on issues in the field of contract law and liability law.

Tom Barkhuysen (1968), PhD, lawyer and partner at the law firm Stibbe in Amsterdam, with specialisation in constitutional and administrative law. He is also a professor of Constitutional and Administrative Law at Leiden University, the Netherlands. His thesis (1998) dealt with the right to effective legal protection in case of human rights violations. He has published extensively in the fields of administrative and constitutional law as well as human rights law.

Hemme Battjes (1970), PhD, professor of European Asylum Law at the Vrije Universiteit Amsterdam, the Netherlands. His thesis (2006) dealt with the relation between European and international asylum law. He has published extensively in the fields of migration law and human rights law.

Maya Beeler-Sigron (1983), PhD, is a lawyer and currently working for the International Human Rights Unit of the Swiss Federal Office of Justice. Previously, she was a court clerk with the Administrative Court of the canton of Zurich and worked as an independent partner in a private law firm in the canton of Grisons. Her award-wining thesis (2013) dealt with legitimate expectations under article 1 of Protocol No. 1 to the European Convention on Human Rights. She has mainly published in the field of human rights law.

Edwin Bleichrodt (1968), PhD, Advocate General at the Dutch Supreme Court and professor of Criminal Law and Criminal Procedure Law at Erasmus University Rotterdam, the Netherlands. His thesis (1996) dealt with the conditional sentences and other conditional modalities in Dutch criminal law.

He has published extensively on issues in the field of criminal law and penal sanctions.

Bas van Bockel, (1973) PhD, senior lecturer of EU Law at Utrecht University, the Netherlands, visiting professor at the University of Venice Ca' Foscari, Italy, and honorary judge at the district court of Amsterdam, the Netherlands. He has published extensively on the European system of protection of fundamental rights, and co-edits several periodicals including the Nederlands Tijdschrift voor de Mensenrechten and European Human Rights Cases. Amongst other things he was formerly lecturer of EU Law at Leiden University, the Netherlands, visiting professor of EU Law at Saarland University, Germany and Head of the Master in European Union Studies at Leiden University.

Hansko Broeksteeg (1974), PhD, senior lecturer at Radboud University in Nijmegen, the Netherlands, and deputy judge at the Utrecht District Court. His thesis (2004) dealt with the criminal and financial accountability of politicians. He has published extensively in the fields of constitutional and administrative law and human rights law.

Antoine Buyse (1977), PhD, professor of Human Rights in a Multidisciplinary Perspective and director of the Netherlands Institute of Human Rights (SIM) at Utrecht University, the Netherlands. He is editor-in-chief of the Netherlands Quarterly of Human Rights and he hosts a weblog about the European Convention on Human Rights. His PhD thesis (2008) dealt with post-conflict housing restitution. He has published extensively on the ECHR, including on pilot judgments, the freedom of expression and the abuse of rights.

Karin de Vries (1981), PhD, assistant professor of Constitutional and Administrative Law at the Vrije Universiteit Amsterdam, the Netherlands, where she specialises in migration, citizenship and human rights law. Her thesis (2012) dealt with integration requirements in international and European immigration law. She publishes regularly on human rights topics including the rights of migrants under the ECHR.

Masha Fedorova (1980), PhD, associate professor of Criminal Law and Criminal Procedure at the Radboud University, Nijmegen, the Netherlands. Her thesis (2012) dealt with the right to a fair trial in international criminal proceedings. She has published extensively in the field of criminal law and procedure and human rights law.

Kees Flinterman (1944), PhD, professor emeritus of Human Rights at Maastricht University and Utrecht University, the Netherlands, and former director of the Netherlands Institute for Human Rights and the Netherlands School for

Human Rights Research. He has further been, inter alia, an alternate member of the United Nations Sub-Commission on the Prevention of Discrimination and Protection of Minorities and a member of the United Nations Committee on the Elimination of Discrimination Against Women and the United Nations Human Rights Committee. His thesis (1981) dealt with the Act of State Doctrine in a comparative perspective. He has published extensively in the fields of international human rights law and comparative public law.

Janneke Gerards (1976), PhD, professor of Fundamental Rights Law at Utrecht University, the Netherlands. Based at the department of Jurisprudence, Constitutional and Administrative Law, she is affiliated to the university's research programme *Institutions for Open Societies and the Montaigne Centre for Courts and Rule of Law*. Her research focuses on fundamental rights, judicial review and constitutional law. She has published widely in these areas. Janneke Gerards is also a deputy judge in the Appeals Court of The Hague, a member of the Human Rights Commission of the Dutch Advisory Council on International Affairs, and a member of the Royal Netherlands Academy of Arts and Sciences.

Yves Haeck (1968), PhD, professor of International Human Rights Law at Ghent University, Belgium. He is a former associate professor at Utrecht University, the Netherlands and a visiting professor at the University of Malta. His research interests concern the European Convention on Human Rights and the European Court of Human Rights, with a comparative focus on the Inter-American System, topics on which he has published and lectured widely.

Clara Burbano Herrera (1975), PhD, postdoctoral research fellow at Ghent University, Belgium and postdoctoral research associate at the University of Bergen, Norway, editor-in-chief of the Inter-American and European Human Rights Journal. She has been a fulbright scholar at Harvard University, USA and a professor at the Universidad de Los Andes, Colombia. Her academic work is situated on the intersection between international law and human rights law, related to the role of regional human rights organs in the prevention of human rights violations.

Oswald Jansen (1967), PhD, lawyer and partner at the law firm Resolucíon in The Hague, lawyer and legal counsel of the City of The Hague and professor of European Administrative Law and Public Administration at Maastricht University, the Netherlands. His thesis (1999) entails a comparison of administrative and criminal law for the powers of inspection and criminal investigation. He has published extensively on international, European and comparative administrative law and on administrative sanctions and defence rights.

Laurens Lavrysen (1987), PhD, postdoctoral researcher at the Human Rights Centre of Ghent University, Belgium. His thesis (2016) dealt with the positive obligations doctrine in the jurisprudence of the European Court of Human Rights. He is currently working on a research project concerning the history of the European Convention on Human Rights in Belgium.

Koen Lemmens (1976), PhD, attorney at the Brussels bar, specialised in proceedings before the European Court of Human Rights, associate professor of Human Rights law at KU Leuven and Press Law at Vrije Universiteit Brussel, Belgium. He is the Belgian national director of the European Masters in Human Rights and Democratization Program (European Inter-University Centre, Venice). His work is mainly focused on freedom of expression, the European Convention on Human Rights and (comparative) constitutional law.

Joachim Meese (1973), PhD, professor of Criminal Law and Criminal Procedure at the University of Antwerp, Belgium and managing partner at the law firm Van Steenbrugge Advocaten. His thesis (2005) dealt with the length of criminal procedures. He has published extensively in the field of criminal law and criminal procedural law and he is lecturer at numerous seminars and conferences in Belgium and abroad.

Stefan Sottiaux (1976), PhD, professor of Constitutional Law at the University of Leuven, Belgium and partner at the law firm Demos Public and European Law. His thesis (2006) dealt with the relationship between terrorism and human rights. He has published extensively on constitutional and human rights issues, with a specific focus on the rights to freedom of expression and association and the principle of equality and non-discrimination.

Frederik Swennen (1973), PhD, professor of Family Law and Kinship Studies at the University of Antwerp, Belgium and of counsel in the law firm Greenille by Laga, NIAS Fellow 2017-18. Previously, he worked as a legal clerk in the Belgian Supreme Court. He has published extensively on various topics in the law of persons and family law, particularly on post-modern families. His methodological focus is on socio-legal studies.

Michiel van Emmerik (1965), PhD, associate professor of Constitutional and Administrative Law at Leiden University, the Netherlands and deputy judge at the Midden-Nederland District Court (section administrative law). Previously, he was employed with the Constitutional and Legislative Affairs Division, Ministry of the Interior, The Hague. His thesis (1997) dealt with the right to compensation in cases of human rights violations. He has published extensively in the fields of administrative and constitutional law as well as human rights law.

Arjen van Rijn (1956), PhD, lawyer and partner at the law firm De Clercq in Leiden and The Hague and professor of Constitutional Law and Constitutional Renewal at the University of Curaçao Dr. Moises da Costa Gomez. His thesis (1985) entails a comparison of the freedom of expression in the democratic system of the Federal Republic of Germany and the communist system of the (former) German Democratic Republic. He has published extensively on constitutional and other public law issues.

Marjolein van Roosmalen (1975), PhD, secretary to the Constitutional Law Committee of the Council of State of the Netherlands and co-president of the Joint Council on Constitutional Justice. Her thesis (2007) dealt with state liability in England and the Netherlands. She has authored many publications in the fields of (comparative) constitutional and administrative law.

Ben Vermeulen (1957), PhD, professor of Education Law at the Free University Amsterdam and the Radboud University Nijmegen, the Netherlands, member of and judge in the Dutch Council of State, member of the Venice Commission. His thesis (1989) dealt with the freedom of conscience. He has published extensively on human rights issues such as asylum law, the right to education, the freedom of conscience and religion and the separation of church and state, as well as general issues of constitutional law.

Cornelis Wouters (1970), PhD, senior refugee law advisor with the Division of International Protection of the United Nations High Commissioner for Refugees (UNHCR). His thesis (2009) dealt with the interpretation of the principle of non-refoulement in international treaty law. He has published extensively on international refugee law matters. The views he has expressed in this chapter are not necessarily the views of the United Nations or of UNHCR.

Leo Zwaak (1947), LLM, associate professor at the Law School of Utrecht University, the Netherlands, senior researcher at the Netherlands Institute of Human Rights (SIM). Visiting professor at Washington College of Law at the American University, Washington DC, USA. Co-editor of the Netherlands Quarterly of Human Rights. He has published extensively in the field of European Human Rights Law. He has been retired since 2012.

LIST OF ABBREVIATIONS

A.	Publications of the European Court of Human Rights; Judgments and Decisions, Series A
AJIL	American Journal of International Law
Appl(s)	Application(s) lodged with the Commission under Article 24 of the Convention
B.	Publications of the European Court of Human Rights; Pleadings, Oral Arguments and Documents, Series B
Coll.	Collection of Decisions of the European Commission of Human Rights
Cons. Ass.	Consultative Assembly of the Council of Europe
D&R	Decisions and Reports of the European Commission of Human Rights
HRLJ	Human Rights Law Journal
ICJ Reports	International Court of Justice, Reports of Judgments, Advisory Opinions and Orders
ILM	International Legal Materials
ILO	International Labour Organization
Para(s)	Paragraph(s)
Parl. Ass.	Parliamentary Assembly of the Council of Europe
RCADI	Recueil des Cours de l'Académie de Droit International de la Haye
Reports	Reports of Judgments and Decisions. Publication of the case-law of the Commission and the Court (as from 1996)
Res.	Resolution
UN	United Nations
UN Doc.	United Nations Documents
UNHCR	United Nations High Commissioner for Refugees
UNTS	United Nations Treaty Series
Yearbook	Yearbook of the European Convention on Human Rights

CHAPTER 1

GENERAL SURVEY OF THE CONVENTION

Koen Lemmens*

CONTENTS

---

* In the fourth edition this chapter was revised and updated by Leo Zwaak.

1.   GENESIS OF THE CONVENTION

The European Convention for the Protection of Human Rights and Fundamental Freedoms is a product of the period shortly after the Second World War, when the issue of international protection of human rights attracted a great deal of attention. These rights had been crushed by the atrocities of National Socialism, and the guarantee of their protection at the national level had proved completely inadequate.

As early as 1941 Churchill and Roosevelt, in the Atlantic Charter, launched their four freedoms: freedom of life, freedom of religion, freedom from want and freedom from fear. After the Second World War the promotion of respect for human rights and fundamental freedoms became one of the purposes of the United Nations. Within that framework the Universal Declaration of Human Rights, adopted by the General Assembly of the United Nations on 10 December 1948, became a significant milestone.

Meanwhile, preliminary steps were also taken at the European level. In May 1948, the International Committee of the Movements for European Unity organised a 'Congress of Europe' at The Hague. This initiative gave the decisive impetus to the foundation of the Council of Europe in 1949. In August of the same year, the Consultative Assembly charged its Committee on Legal and Administrative Questions to consider in more detail the matter of a collective guarantee of human rights.

From that moment onwards, the Convention was drafted in a comparatively short period of time. The Committee completed its work in the spring of 1950. It had made considerable headway, but had failed to find a solution to a number of political problems. The subsequently appointed Committee of Senior Officials also had to leave the ultimate decision on a number of matters to the Committee of Ministers, even though it reached agreement on the greater part of the text of the Committee of Experts.

On 7 August 1950, the Committee of Ministers approved a revised draft text, which was less far-reaching than the original proposals on a number of points. For example, the system of individual applications and the jurisdiction of the Court were made optional. This draft text was not substantially altered afterwards.

On 4 November 1950, the Convention, which according to its Preamble was framed 'to take the first steps for collective enforcement of certain rights stated in the Universal Declaration', was signed in Rome.[1] It entered into force on 3 September 1953 and to date (November 2016) has been ratified by the 47 member states of the Council of Europe. To date, 16 Protocols have been added to the Convention,[2] but not all of them have been ratified by all the Contracting States.[3] As a result of the entry into force of Protocol No. 11, Protocols Nos 8, 9 and 10 were repealed. Protocol No. 2, conferring the competence upon the Court to give advisory opinions, has been included almost in its entirety in Protocol No. 11 and has thus become part of the Convention.[4] Protocol No. 12, which contains a general prohibition of discrimination (*viz.* it concerns therefore the enjoyment of any right and not only those protected by the Convention) has only been ratified by 20 High Contracting Parties. This is probably due to risk of extending the scope of the jurisdiction of the Court to any right protected by

---

[1]   213 UNTS, No. 2889, p. 221; Council of Europe, *European Treaty Series*, No. 5, 4 November 1950; see <http://conventions.coe.int>.
[2]   See App. I.
[3]   See App. I.
[4]   Art. 47 of the Convention.

domestic law. This example shows that although the Protocols tend to reform or to complete the Convention, not all Parties do ratify them.[5] Protocol No. 13 abolishes the death penalty in all circumstances. Protocol Nos 15 and 16 have not (yet) entered into force.

2. SCOPE

The aim which the Contracting States wished to achieve was 'to take the first steps for the collective enforcement of certain of the Rights stated in the Universal Declaration'. The purpose of the Convention was therefore, within the framework of the Council of Europe, to lay down certain human rights, proclaimed in 1948 by the United Nations in the Universal Declaration of Human Rights, in a binding agreement, and at the same time to provide for supervision of the observance of those human rights provisions.

Only certain rights were included in these 'first steps'. A comparison with the Universal Declaration discloses that not all the rights mentioned there have been laid down in the Convention. It covers mainly those rights which would be referred to, in the later elaboration of the Universal Declaration in the two Covenants, as 'civil and political rights', and not even all of those. The principle of equality before the law, the right to freedom of movement and residence, the right to seek and to enjoy asylum in other countries from persecution, the right to a nationality, the right to own property and the right to take part in the government, which are included in the Universal Declaration,[6] are not to be found in the Convention.

However, in that respect subsequent steps have been taken within the framework of the Council of Europe, both in the form of additional Protocols to the Convention[7] and in the form of other conventions, including in particular the European Social Charter of 1961.

The drafters concentrated on those rights which were considered essential elements of the foundation of European democracies and with regard to which one might expect that an agreement could easily be reached about their formulation and about the international supervision of their implementation, since they could be deemed to have been recognised in the member states of the Council of Europe. On the other hand, both the detailed formulation of these rights, with the possibilities of limitations and the creation of a supervisory mechanism in a binding treaty, were novel and revolutionary.[8]

---

5   S. Smis, Chr. Janssens, S. Mirgaux and K. Van Laethem, *Handboek Mensenrechten*, Intersentia: Antwerp, 2011, p. 276.

6   Arts. 7, 13, 14, 15, 17 and 21 respectively of the Universal Declaration.

7   For ratifications, see App. I.

8   In view of the emphasis placed by the drafters on democracy it may be a matter of surprise that no provision was included on the right of participation in government and on free

It was precisely these two points – the formulation of the rights and freedoms and the supervisory mechanism – which were used as arguments for separate regulation of, on the one hand, civil and political rights, and, on the other hand, economic, social and cultural rights; a solution which was ultimately also chosen within the framework of the UN. The first category of rights was considered to concern the sphere of freedom of the individual *vis-à-vis* the government. These rights and liberties and their limitations would lend themselves to detailed regulation, while the implementation of the resulting duty on the part of the government to abstain from interference could be reviewed by national and/or international bodies. The second category, on the other hand, was considered to consist not of legal rights but of programmatic rights, the formulation of which necessarily is much vaguer and for the realisation of which the states must pursue a given policy, an obligation which does not lend itself to incidental review of government action for its lawfulness.[9]

It is undeniable that there are differences, roughly speaking, between the two categories of rights with respect to their legal character and their implementation. However, such differences also present themselves *within* those categories. Thus, the right to a fair trial and the right to periodic elections by secret ballot call not only for abstention but also for action on the part of the governments. And in the other category the right to strike has less the character of a programmatic right than has the right to work. In the modern welfare state which is typical for most of the member states of the Council of Europe, the civil rights and liberties are being 'socialised' increasingly, while the social, economic and cultural rights are becoming more concrete as to their content. Therefore, a stringent distinction between the two categories becomes much less justified, while too strict a distinction entails the risk of the necessary connection between the two categories of rights being misunderstood. This connection was emphasised in the Proclamation of Teheran of 1968[10] and reaffirmed in the Vienna Declaration and Programme of Action of 1993, where it has been set forth that 'All human rights are universal, indivisible and interdependent and interrelated. The international community must treat human rights globally in a fair and equal manner, on the same footing, and with the same emphasis. While the significance of national and regional particularities and various historical, cultural and religious backgrounds must

---

elections. Evidently the matter was considered too complex and would have delayed the signing of the Convention. The issue of free elections was covered by the First Additional Protocol soon thereafter (Art. 3).

[9]   See 'Annotations on the text of the draft International Covenant on Human Rights, prepared by the Secretary-General', Document A/2929, pp. 7–8. See also the statement of Henri Rolin, member of the Consultative Assembly, before the Belgian Senate, quoted in H. Golsong, *'Implementation of International Protection of Human Rights'*, RCADI 110, 1963-III, p. 58.

[10]   Text of the Proclamation in Res. 2442(XLII) of the General Assembly of the United Nations, 19 December 1968.

be borne in mind, it is the duty of States, regardless of their political, economic and cultural systems, to promote and protect all human rights and fundamental freedoms.'[11]

This connection, and the recognition of the relative value of the distinction between the two categories of rights, also led the Council of Europe to investigate whether certain economic and social rights should be added to the Convention, and, if so, which ones. The investigation led to Protocol No. 7. The original aim of this Protocol, as recommended by the Parliamentary Assembly in 1972, was 'to insert as many as possible of the substantive provisions of the Covenant on Civil and Political Rights in the Convention'.[12] However, the Committee of Experts which prepared the draft of the Protocol, followed a more restrictive approach, keeping in mind 'the need to include in the Convention only such rights as could be stated in sufficiently specific terms to be guaranteed within the framework of the system of control instituted by the Convention'.[13] Although the idea of such an extension was born in the early 1970s, it was only in 1988 that sufficient states had ratified the Protocol for it to enter into force.[14]

Enthusiasm for Protocol No. 7 appears not to be very great. This has to do with the fact that the original aim of the Protocol can hardly be said to have been achieved. In a comparative report[15] a series of rights had been enumerated which were included in the UN Covenant on Civil and Political Rights but not in the Convention. Only some of these rights are now included in this Protocol. A clarification of the reasons for it, other than the above-mentioned general viewpoint of the Committee of Experts, is not to be found in the Explanatory Report. Furthermore, the rights that have been incorporated are, on the whole, formulated rather narrowly. Most of the rights are framed in more restricted terms than their counterparts in the UN Covenant on Civil and Political Rights.

From Chapter 6 onwards, the rights and freedoms laid down in the Convention and in its Protocols Nos 1, 4, 5, 6, 7, 12, 13 and 14 are discussed by reference to the Decisions and Reports of the former Commission and the case law of the Court. As indicated above, although a number of provisions of the International Covenant on Civil and Political Rights may entail for those Contracting States which have also ratified that Covenant[16] more far-reaching

---

[11]   UN Doc. A/Cont.157/23, para. 5.

[12]   Explanatory Report on Protocol No. 7 to the Convention for the Protection of Human Rights and Fundamental Freedoms, Council of Europe, Strasbourg, 1985, p. 5.

[13]   *Ibid.*, p. 6.

[14]   Protocol No. 7 entered into force on 1 November 1988. For the state of ratifications, see App. I.

[15]   Problems arising from the co-existence of the United Nations Covenants on Human Rights and the European Convention on Human Rights, Doc. H(70)7, Strasbourg 1970, pp. 4–5.

[16]   These are all Contracting States.

obligations than rest on them under the Convention,[17] such obligations are left intact by virtue of Article 53 of the Convention.[18]

3.   STRUCTURE

3.1.   RIGHTS AND FREEDOMS

After Article 1, which deals with the scope of the Convention and will be discussed in section 4, the Convention lists the rights and freedoms that it guarantees.

Section I of the Convention contains the following rights and freedoms:

Article 2:   right to life;

Article 3:   freedom from torture and inhuman or degrading treatment or punishment;

Article 4:   freedom from slavery and forced or compulsory labour;

Article 5:   right to liberty and security of the person;

Article 6:   right to a fair and public trial within a reasonable time;

Article 7:   freedom from retrospective effect of penal legislation;

Article 8:   right to respect for private and family life, home and correspondence;

Article 9:   freedom of thought, conscience and religion;

Article 10:   freedom of expression;

Article 11:   freedom of assembly and association;

Article 12:   right to marry and found a family.

Protocol No. 1 has added the following rights:

Article 1:   right to peaceful enjoyment of possessions;

Article 2:   right to education and free choice of education;

Article 3:   right to free elections by secret ballot.

---

[17]   See the report of the Committee of Experts on Human Rights to the Committee of Ministers, *Problems arising from the Co-Existence of the United Nations Covenants on Human Rights and the European Convention on Human Rights*, Doc. H(70)7, Strasbourg, 1970. In Protocol No. 7 the differences between the obligations resulting from the Covenant and those resulting from the Convention have been partly removed. This Protocol entered into force on 1 November 1988.

[18]   On this, see *infra* 3.4.

Protocol No. 4 has added the following rights and freedoms:

Article 1:   prohibition of deprivation of liberty on the ground of inability to fulfil a contractual obligation;

Article 2:   freedom to move within and choose residence in a country;

Article 3:   prohibition of expulsion of nationals and right of nationals to enter the territory of the State of which they are nationals;

Article 4:   prohibition of collective expulsion of aliens.

Protocol No. 6 has added the prohibition of the condemnation to and execution of the death penalty (Article 1).

Protocol No. 7 has added the following rights and freedoms:

Article 1:   procedural safeguards in case of expulsion of aliens lawfully resident in the territory of a State;

Article 2:   right of review by a higher tribunal in criminal cases;

Article 3:   right to compensation of a person convicted of a criminal offence, on the ground that a new or newly discovered fact shows that there has been a miscarriage of justice;

Article 4:   prohibition of a second trial or punishment for offences for which one has already been finally acquitted or convicted (*ne bis in idem*);

Article 5:   equality of rights and responsibilities between spouses.

Protocol No. 12 enlarges the scope of the prohibition of discrimination of Article 14 to the effect that the prohibition is no longer limited to the rights and freedoms enshrined in the Convention, but is extended to 'any right set forth by law'.[19]

Protocol No. 13 prescribes the abolition of the death penalty in all circumstances.

3.2.   ENJOYMENT, PROTECTION AND LIMITATION

After the articles guaranteeing substantive rights, the drafters have paid attention to the ways these rights have to be protected, ensured and exercised. Article 13 stipulates that everyone whose rights and freedoms set forth in the Convention are violated shall have an effective remedy before a national authority, notwithstanding that the violation has been committed by persons acting in an official capacity. Article 14 obliges the Contracting States to secure

---

[19]   Protocol No. 12 entered into force on 1 April 2005.

the rights and freedoms set forth in the Convention without discrimination on any ground. Article 15 allows states to derogate from a number of provisions of the Convention in time of war or other public emergency threatening the life of the nation. Under Article 16, states are allowed to impose restrictions on the political activity of aliens notwithstanding Articles 10, 11 and 14 of the Convention. Article 17 provides that nothing in the Convention may be interpreted as implying for any state, group or person any right to engage in any activity or perform any act aimed at the destruction of any of the rights and freedoms set forth in the Convention or at their limitation to a greater extent than is provided for in the Convention. Finally, Article 18 implies a prohibition of misuse of power (*détournement de pouvoir*) as to the right of Contracting States to impose restrictions on the rights and freedoms guaranteed by the Convention.

3.3. ENSURING OBSERVANCE

Besides the above-mentioned substantive provisions, the European Convention also contains a number of provisions to ensure the observance by the Contracting States of their obligations under the Convention.[20] The responsibility for the implementation of the Convention rests primarily with the national authorities, in particular the national courts (at least in states where the courts are allowed to directly apply the Convention).[21] This is also implied in Article 13 where, in connection with violations of the rights and freedoms set forth in the Convention, reference is made to an 'effective remedy before a national authority'. For those cases where a national procedure is not available or does not provide for an adequate remedy, or in the last resort has not produced a satisfactory result in the opinion of the injured party or of any of the other Contracting States, the Convention itself provides for a supervisory mechanism on the basis of individual and state complaints. In addition, the Secretary-General of the Council of Europe may take part in the supervision of the observance of the Convention (Article 52).

3.4. FINAL PROVISIONS

Section III contains miscellaneous provisions (Articles 52 to 59). Article 52, relating to inquiries by the Secretary-General, will be discussed separately. The same goes for Article 56, concerning territorial scope, and Article 58, which

---

[20] Essentially covered by section II of the Convention, which establishes the Court and deals, inter alia, with the binding force of the judgments (Art. 46).

[21] On this, see *infra* 6 and Chapter 2.

deals with denunciation of the Convention. Article 57, concerning reservations, will be dealt with separately in Chapter 38.

Article 53 embodies what has become a general rule of international human rights law, *viz.* that a legal obligation implying a more far-reaching protection takes priority over any less far-reaching obligation. The article provides that nothing in the Convention may be construed as limiting or derogating from any of the human rights and fundamental freedoms which may be ensured under the laws of any Contracting State or under any other agreement to which the latter is a party.

Article 54 stipulates that the Convention shall not prejudice the powers conferred on the Committee of Ministers by the Statute of the Council of Europe.

Article 55 is aimed at leaving the supervision of the observance of the Convention at the international level exclusively in the hands of the organs designated by the Convention. The article, which is only extremely rarely discussed, provides that the Contracting States, except by special agreement, will not avail themselves of treaties, conventions or declarations in force between them for the purpose of submitting, by way of petition, a dispute arising out of the interpretation and application of this Convention to a means of settlement other than those provided for in this Convention. Article 55 applies in those instances where the Convention is expressly invoked. With respect to disputes where this is not the case, but where nevertheless a right is at issue that is also protected by the Convention, the rationale for such an exclusive competence is much less self-evident. It is submitted that the text of Article 55 does not dictate the exclusivity of the procedure provided for in the Convention as far as those latter cases are concerned. There is, however, still some difference of opinion as to the exact scope of the obligation of the Contracting States under Article 55.

In the Case of *Cyprus v. Turkey*, the Commission confirmed that Article 62 (now: 55) starts from a monopoly of the Convention institutions for deciding disputes arising out of the interpretation and application of the Convention. Only exceptionally is a departure from this principle permitted, subject to the existence of a 'special agreement' between the High Contracting Parties concerned, permitting the submission of a dispute concerning 'the interpretation or application of the Convention' to an alternative means of settlement 'by way of petition'. The conditions for invoking such a special agreement were not fulfilled in the present case though, particularly it appeared from the application that Cyprus had not consented to the withdrawal of the case from the jurisdiction of the Convention organs.[22]

Finally, Article 59 contains a number of provisions about the ratification and the entry into force of the Convention.

---

[22]   *Cyprus v. Turkey*, EComHR 28 June 1996 (dec.), appl. no. 25781/94.

4. PERSONAL AND TERRITORIAL SCOPE

4.1. EVERYONE WITHIN PARTIES' JURISDICTION

Under Article 1 of the Convention the Contracting States are bound to secure to everyone within their jurisdiction the rights and freedoms set forth in section I of the Convention. To the extent that a state has ratified any of the Protocols Nos. 1, 4, 6, 7, 12 and 13, this obligation also applies to the rights and freedoms laid down in these Protocols, since the latter are considered to contain additional provisions of the Convention, to which all the provisions of the Convention apply accordingly.[23]

Under Article 1 of the Convention, the state is required to 'secure' the Convention rights to everyone within its jurisdiction. This means that public authorities must not only refrain from arbitrary interference with the rights protected by the Convention (negative obligation), but they also have positive obligations.[24] States are indeed under the duty to secure rights through adopting an adequate legal framework.[25] In case of violations of Articles 2 and 3, they also have procedural obligations: they must conduct an effective inquiry into the facts that led to the violations and punish the persons responsible for the misconduct.[26]

The Contracting States must secure these rights and freedoms to 'everyone within their jurisdiction'. These words do not imply any limitation as to nationality. Even those alleged victims who are neither nationals of the state concerned nor of any of the other Contracting States are entitled to protection when they are in some respect subject to the jurisdiction of the state from which they claim that guarantee.[27] Furthermore, it is irrelevant whether they have their residence inside or outside the territory of that state.[28] Moreover, in several cases

---

[23]   See Art. 5 of Protocol No. 1, Art. 6(1) of Protocol No. 4, Art. 6 of Protocol No. 6, Art. 7(1) of Protocol No. 7, Art. 3 of Protocol No. 12 and Art. 5 of Protocol No. 13.

[24]   Grabenwarter identifies these positive obligations with respect to the great majority of rights. Chr. Grabenwarter, *European Convention on Human Rights. Commentary*, Munich: Beck/Hart/Nomos, 2014. On the distinction, see ch. 4.

[25]   See, e.g., *Söderman v. Sweden*, ECtHR (GC) 12 November 2013, appl. no. 5786/08, para. 117.

[26]   See, for an extensive overview of the State's procedural obligations in case of lethal violence, *Armani da Silva v. The United Kingdom*, ECtHR (GC) 30 March 2016, appl. no. 5878/08, paras. 229–239.

[27]   See, e.g., *Austria v. Italy*, EComHR 11 January 1961, appl. no. 788/60, Yearbook IV (1961), p. 116 (138 and 140): 'Whereas, therefore, in becoming a Party to the Convention, a State undertakes, *vis-à-vis* the other High Contracting Parties, to secure the rights and freedoms defined in Section I to every person within its jurisdiction, regardless of their nationality or status; whereas, in short, it undertakes to secure these rights and freedoms not only to its own nationals and those of other High Contracting Parties, but also to nationals of States not parties to the Convention and to stateless persons.'

[28]   The Consultative Assembly had proposed in the draft of the Convention the words 'all persons residing within the territories of the signatory States', but these were changed by the

the Commission and the Court held that although Article 1 sets limits on the scope of the Convention, the concept of 'jurisdiction' under this provision does not imply that the responsibility of the Contracting Parties is restricted to acts committed on their territory.

In the same vein, the Court held that the extradition or expulsion of a person by a Contracting Party to a country where there is a serious risk of torture or inhuman or degrading treatment or punishment, may give rise to an issue under Article 3, and hence engage responsibility of that state under the Convention.[29] In cases where provisions other than Article 3 are at stake, the extraditing state may equally be held responsible for acts which take place thereafter in another country.[30]

There is a presumption of territorial competence since, as a general rule, the notion of 'jurisdiction' within the meaning of Article 1 of the Convention must be considered as reflecting the position under public international law. That notion is indeed 'primarily' or 'essentially' territorial.[31]

In the *Assanidze* case, the Georgian State accepted that the Ajarian Autonomous Republic was an integral part of Georgia and that the matters complained of were within the jurisdiction of the State. However, consideration should be given to the difficulties encountered by the central State authorities in exercising their jurisdiction in the Ajarian Autonomous Republic. The Court noted, first, that Georgia had ratified the Convention for the whole of its territory. Furthermore, it was common ground that the Ajarian Autonomous Republic had no separatist aspirations and that no other state exercised effective overall control there. On ratifying the Convention, Georgia did not make any specific reservation under Article 57 of the Convention with regard to the

---

Committee of Experts in the sense mentioned. See report of the Committee of Experts to the Committee of Ministers, Council of Europe, *Collected Edition of the 'Travaux Préparatoires' of the European Convention on Human Rights*, Vol. IV, The Hague, 1977, p. 20:

'It was felt that there were good grounds for extending the benefits of the Convention to all persons in the territories of the signatory States, even those who could not be considered as residing there in the legal sense of the word.'

See also *X v. Federal Republic of Germany*, EComHR 25 September 1965, appl. no. 1611/62, Yearbook VIII (1965), p. 158 (168), where the Commission held: 'in certain respects the nationals of a Contracting State are within its jurisdiction even when domiciled or resident abroad.' See also *infra* 4.3.

29   *Soering v. The United Kingdom*, ECtHR 7 July 1989, appl. no. 14038/88, para. 90; *Cruz Varas and Others v. Sweden*, ECtHR 20 March 1991, appl. no. 15576/89, para. 69; *Vilvarajah and Others v. The United* Kingdom, ECtHR 30 October 1991, appl. nos. 13163/87, 13164/87, 13165/87, 13447/87, 13448/87, para. 103; *Loizidou v. Turkey*, ECtHR (GC) 23 March 1995, appl. no. 15318/89, para. 62. See also *infra* 7.6.

30   *C. v. the United Kingdom*, EComHR 12 May 1986, appl. no. 10427/83, D&R 47 (1986), p. 85 (95–96), where the applicant, a suspected deserter from the Indian army, had been extradited to India and claimed that he had been deprived of a fair trial within a reasonable time.

31   *Banković and Others v. Belgium and Others*, ECtHR (GC) 12 December 2001, appl. no. 52207/99, paras. 59–61.

Ajarian Autonomous Republic or to difficulties in exercising its jurisdiction over that territory.[32]

In the *Ilaşcu* case, the Court considered that the Moldovan Government, the only legitimate government of the Republic of Moldova under international law, did not exercise authority over part of its territory, namely that part which was under the effective control of the 'MRT'. However, even in the absence of effective control over the Transdniestrian region, Moldova still had positive obligations under Article 1 of the Convention to secure the rights guaranteed by the Convention. These related both to the measures needed to re-establish its control over Transdniestrian territory and to measures to ensure respect for the applicants' rights, including attempts to secure their release. Consequently, the applicants were within the jurisdiction of the Republic of Moldova for the purposes of Article 1. The Court did not have any evidence that since Mr Ilaşcu's release in May 2001 effective measures had been taken to put an end to the continuing infringements of their Convention rights complained of by the other applicants. It accordingly concluded that Moldova's responsibility was capable of being engaged on account of its failure to discharge its positive obligations with regard to the acts complained of which had occurred after May 2001.

With respect to the Russian Federation, the Court observed that throughout the clashes between the Moldovan authorities and the Transdniestrian separatists the leaders of the Russian Federation supported the separatist authorities through political declarations. The Russian Federation drafted the main lines of the ceasefire agreement of 21 July 1992, and moreover signed it as a party.

Therefore, in the light of all these circumstances the Court considered that the Russian Federation's responsibility was engaged in respect of the unlawful acts committed by the Transdniestrian separatists. In acting thus the authorities of the Russian Federation contributed both militarily and politically to the creation of a separatist regime in the region of Transdniestria, The Court considered that on account of these events the applicants came within the jurisdiction of the Russian Federation within the meaning of Article 1 of the Convention, although at the time when these events occurred the Convention was not in force with regard to the Russian Federation. The events which gave rise to the responsibility of the Russian Federation must be considered to include not only the acts in which the agents of that State participated, like the applicants' arrest and detention, but also their transfer into the hands of the Transdniestrian police and regime, and the subsequent ill-treatment inflicted on them by the police, since in acting in that way the agents of the Russian Federation were

---

[32]   *Assanidze v. Georgia*, ECtHR (GC) 8 April 2004, appl. no. 71503/01. Such a reservation would in any event have been ineffective, as the case law precludes territorial exclusions other than in the instance referred to in Art. 56(1) of the Convention (dependent territories); see *Matthews v. The United Kingdom*, ECtHR (GC) 18 February 1999, appl. no. 24833/94, para. 29.

fully aware that they were handing them over to an illegal and unconstitutional regime. The Court considered that there was a continuous and uninterrupted link of responsibility on the part of the Russian Federation for the applicants' fate. In conclusion, the applicants came within the 'jurisdiction' of the Russian Federation for the purposes of Article 1 of the Convention and its responsibility was engaged with regard to the acts complained of.[33] A similar conclusion was reached in the *Al Nashiri* case, in which Poland was held responsible for the violation of Article 3 by CIA agents who detained terrorist suspects on Polish territory. The Court found out that Poland had participated in the rendition and must have known that the suspects ran the risk of maltreatment.[34]

A Contracting State is responsible for acts or omissions on its territory only to the extent that those are the responsibility of its own organs. Thus it was decided that the alleged violations of the Convention by the Supreme Restitution Court could not be held against the Federal Republic of Germany, even though this tribunal held its sessions on West German territory. It was to be considered as an international tribunal, in respect of which Germany had neither legislative nor supervisory powers.[35]

4.2. TERRITORY

Article 56 contains a historical *lex specialis* in respect of the principle of Article 1 according to which the Convention is applicable to everyone within the jurisdiction of the Contracting States. According to general international law a treaty is applicable to the whole territory of a Contracting State, including those territories for whose international relations the state in question is responsible.[36] This is different only when a reservation has been made for one or more of those territories in the treaty itself, or at the time of its ratification. Under Article 56(1), however, the European Convention applies to the latter territories only when the Contracting State concerned has agreed to this via a declaration to that effect addressed to the Secretary-General of the Council of Europe. Such declarations were made in due course by Denmark with respect to Greenland,[37] by the

---

33   *Ilascu and Others v. The Republic of Moldova and Russia*, ECtHR 8 July 2004, appl. no. 48787/99, paras. 380–385. This view is confirmed in the recent case: *Mozer v. The Republic of Moldova and Russia*, ECtHR (GC) 23 February 2016, appl. no. 11138/10.

34   *Al Nashiri v. Poland*, ECtHR 24 July 2014, appl. no. 28761/11, paras. 442 and 452.

35   *X v. Sweden, Federal Republic of Germany and other States*, EComHR 15 July 1965, appl. no. 2095/63, Yearbook VIII (1965), p. 272 (282). See also *X v. Federal Republic of Germany*, EComHR 10 June 1958, appl. no. 235/56, Yearbook II (1958–1959), p. 256 (304), where the Commission reached the same conclusion with respect to the American Court of Restitution Appeals in Germany.

36   See Art. 29 of the 1969 Vienna Convention on the Law of Treaties, ILM 8, (1969), p. 679.

37   Since 1953 Greenland has been an integral part of Denmark.

Netherlands with respect to Suriname[38] and the Netherlands Antilles[39] and by the United Kingdom with respect to most of the non-self-governing territories belonging to the Commonwealth.[40]

The question of what has to be understood by the words 'territory for whose international relations a State is responsible' was raised in a case concerning the former Belgian Congo. The applicants submitted that their complaint related to a time when this area formed part of the national territory of Belgium, and that accordingly the Convention, including the Belgian declaration under Article 25 [the present Article 34], was applicable to the Belgian Congo even though Belgium had not made any declaration as referred to in Article 56 with reference thereto. The Commission, however, held that the Belgian Congo had to be regarded as a territory for whose international relations Belgium was responsible in the sense of Article 56. It reached the conclusion that the complaint was not admissible *ratione loci*, since Belgium had not made any declaration under Article 56 with reference to this territory.[41]

According to paragraph 3, the provisions of the Convention are applied to the territories referred to in Article 56 [former Article 63] with due regard to local requirements. In the *Tyrer* case, the UK Government submitted in this context that corporal punishment on the Isle of Man was justified as a preventive measure based on public opinion on the island. The Court, however, held that 'for the application of Article 63(3), more would be needed: there would have to be positive and conclusive proof of a requirement, and the Court could not regard beliefs and local 'public' opinion on their own as constituting such proof'.[42]

In the *Piermont* case, a German member of the European Parliament had been expelled from French Polynesia and had been prohibited from returning, while a decision was taken prohibiting her from entering New Caledonia, because of certain statements which she had made at a demonstration in Tahiti. The applicant complained that these orders infringed, amongst others, her right to freedom of expression. The French Government submitted that the 'local requirements' of French Polynesia made the interference legitimate. According to the Government the 'local requirements' were the indisputable special features of protecting public order in the Pacific territories, namely their island

---

38 Suriname became independent in 1975.
39 The reservation made with respect to the Netherlands Antilles with reference to Art. 6(3)(c) has since been withdrawn.
40 See Council of Europe, *Collected Texts*, Strasbourg, 1994, p. 88.
41 *X. v. Belgium*, EComHR 30 May 1961, appl. no. 1065/61, Yearbook IV (1961), p. 260 (266–268).
42 *Tyrer v. The United Kingdom*, ECtHR 25 April 1978, appl. no. 5856/72, paras. 36–40, from which it likewise appears that, even apart from the correctness of public opinion, the Court does not wish to regard corporal punishment itself, intended as a preventive measure, as a local requirement in the sense of Article 63(3), which would have to be taken into account in the application of Article 3. See also *Wiggins v. The United Kingdom*, EComHR 8 February 1978 (dec.), appl. no. 7456/76, D&R 13 (1979), p. 40 (48).

status and distance from metropolitan France and also the especially tense political atmosphere. The Court noted that the arguments put forward by the Government related essentially to the tense local political atmosphere taken together with an election campaign and, therefore, emphasised circumstances and conditions rather than requirements. A political situation, which admittedly was a sensitive one but also one which could occur in the mother country, did not suffice to interpret the phrase 'local requirements' as justifying an interference with the right secured in Article 10.[43]

When territories become independent, a declaration under Article 56 automatically ceases to apply because the Contracting State which made it is no longer responsible for the international relations of the new state.[44] This new state does not automatically become a party to the Convention. In the majority of cases[45] it will not even be able to become a party, since Article 59(1) makes signature possible only for member states of the Council of Europe and membership of the latter organisation is open only to European states.[46]

4.3. RESPONSIBILITY OUTSIDE TERRITORY

The fact that the Convention is applicable only to the territory of the Contracting States does not imply that a Contracting State cannot be responsible under the Convention for acts of its organs that have been committed outside its territory. In the *Al Skeini* case, the Court enlisted the situations in which states can be held liable for extra-territorial acts.[47] Two hypotheses can be distinguished.[48]

First, there is the situation of effective control over an area outside the national territory.

In the *Loizidou* case, the Court held Turkey responsible for alleged violations of Article 8 of the Convention and Article 1 of Protocol No. 1, which took place in the northern part of Cyprus, because that part was under control of Turkish forces in Cyprus which exercised overall control in that area. The Court held that the responsibility of a Contracting Party might indeed arise when as a consequence of military action, 'whether lawful or unlawful', it exercises effective control of an area outside its national territory. The obligation to secure, in such an area, the rights and freedoms set out in the Convention, derives from

---

43 *Piermont v. France*, ECtHR 27 April 1995, appl. nos. 15773/89, 15774/89, para. 59.

44 See, *e.g., X v. The Netherlands*, EComHR 4 October 1976, appl. no. 7230/75, D&R 7 (1977), p. 109 (110–111).

45 This was different in the cases of Cyprus and Malta only, which after their independence, became members of the Council of Europe and parties to the Convention.

46 Art. 4 of the Statute of the Council of Europe.

47 *Al-Skeini and Others v. the United Kingdom*, ECtHR (GC) 7 July 2011, appl. no. 55721/07, paras. 130–141. See, as well, *Grabenwarter v. Austria*, EComHR 28 February 1995, appl. no. 21640/93, p. 7–10.

48 F. Jacobs, R. White, Cl. Ovey, *The European Convention on Human Rights*, Oxford: Oxford University Press, 2014, p. 93.

the fact of such control whether it is exercised directly, through its armed forces, or through a subordinate local administration.[49]

In *Cyprus v. Turkey*, the Court held more generally that: 'It is of course true that the Court in the *Loizidou* Case was addressing an individual's complaint concerning the continuing refusal of the authorities to allow her access to her property. However, it is to be observed that the Court's reasoning is framed in terms of a broad statement of principle as regards Turkey's general responsibility under the Convention for the policies and actions of the "TRNC" authorities. Having effective overall control over Northern Cyprus, its responsibility cannot be confined to the acts of its own soldiers or officials in Northern Cyprus but must also be engaged by virtue of the acts of the local administration which survives by virtue of Turkish military and other support. It follows that, in terms of Article 1 of the Convention, Turkey's "jurisdiction" must be considered to extend to securing the entire range of substantive rights set out in the Convention and those additional Protocols which she has ratified, and that violations of those rights are imputable to Turkey.'[50]

The second cluster of cases concerns cases involving state agent authority and control. This situation deals with a variety of cases. Obviously, states can be held liable for the actions of their diplomats and consular agents, present on the territory of foreign states further to the provisions of international law, and exercising authority and control over others.[51] In the *Bankovic'* case, the Court held that recognised instances of the extra-territorial exercise of jurisdiction by a state include cases involving the activities of its diplomatic or consular agents abroad and on board aircraft and vessels registered in, or flying the flag of, that state. In these specific situations, customary international law and treaty provisions have recognised the extra-territorial exercise of jurisdiction by the relevant state.[52] In contrast, the Court fairly found that the participation of a state in the defence of proceedings against it in another state does not, without more, amount to an exercise of extra-territorial jurisdiction. The Court considered that, in the particular circumstances of the case, the fact that the United Kingdom Government raised the defence of sovereign immunity before the Irish courts, where the applicant had decided to sue, does not suffice to bring them within the jurisdiction of the United Kingdom within the meaning of Article 1 of the Convention.[53]

---

[49]   *Loizidou v. Turkey*, ECtHR (GC) 23 March 1995, appl. no. 15318/89, para. 62. See in this respect also *Ilaşcu and Others v. The Republic of Moldova and Russia*, ECtHR 8 July 2004, appl. no. 48787/99, paras. 386–394.

[50]   *Cyprus v. Turkey*, ECtHR (GC) 10 May 2001, appl. no. 25781/94, para. 77.

[51]   *Al-Skeini and Others v. the United Kingdom*, ECtHR (GC) 7 July 2011, appl. no. 55721/07, *supra* n. 47, para. 134.

[52]   *Banković and Others v. Belgium and Others*, ECtHR (GC) 12 December 2001, appl. no. 52207/99, *supra* n. 31, para. 73.

[53]   *McElhinney v. Ireland and the United Kingdom*, ECtHR (GC) 21 November 2001, appl. no. 31253/96, para. 39.

Next, a state can have jurisdiction on the territory of another state by exercising all or some of the public powers normally exercised by the latter because it was invited to do so, or because the other state consented or acquiesced.[54]

Finally, 'in certain circumstances, the use of force by a State's agents operating outside its territory may bring the individual thereby brought under the control of the State's authorities into the State's Article 1 jurisdiction. This principle has been applied where an individual is taken into the custody of State agents abroad.'[55]

This was, for instance, true in the *Öcalan* case, where the applicant was arrested by members of the Turkish security forces inside an aircraft in the international zone of Nairobi Airport. Directly after he had been handed over by the Kenyan officials to the Turkish officials the applicant was effectively under Turkish authority and was, therefore, brought within the 'jurisdiction' of that State for the purposes of Article 1 of the Convention, even though in this instance Turkey exercised its authority outside its territory.[56] A similar reasoning applies 'to the buildings, aircraft or ship in which individuals are held. What is decisive in such cases is the exercise of physical power and control over the person in question'.[57]

4.4. CONFLICTING OBLIGATIONS

In the multi-layered global order, states ratify many international treaties and they are party to numerous international organisations. In case of the High Contracting Parties to the ECHR, it is easy to see that they are as well members of the UN and that, to date, 28 of them are Member States the European Union. The question then is what should happen whenever obligations stemming from other treaties risk interfering with obligations under the ECHR.

At this point, the most obvious conflicts arise whenever EU Member States have obligations under EU law which are subsequently questioned from an ECHR perspective. The accession of the EU to the ECHR could be an important factor in avoiding such conflicts. However, since CJEU Opinion 2/2013 on the

---

[54] *Banković and Others v. Belgium and Others*, ECtHR (GC) 12 December 2001, appl. no. 52207/99, *supra* n. 31, para. 71.

[55] *Al-Skeini and Others v. the United Kingdom*, ECtHR (GC) 7 July 2011, appl. no. 55721/07, *supra* n. 47, para. 136.

[56] *Öcalan v. Turkey*, ECtHR (GC) 12 March 2003, appl. no. 46221/99, paras. 93–94; see also *Issa and Others v. Turkey*, ECtHR 30 March 2005, appl. no. 31821/96, para. 38.

[57] *Al-Skeini and Others*, ECtHR (GC) 7 July 2011, appl. no. 55721/07, *supra* n. 47, para. 136. References to *Medvedyev and Others v. France*, ECtHR (GC) 29 March 2010, appl. no. 3394/03 (concerning ships, see also *Hirsi Jaama and Others v. Italy*, ECtHR (GC) 23 February 2012, appl. no. 27765/09) and *Al-Saadoon and Mufdhi v. The United Kingdom*, ECtHR 2 March 2010, appl. no. 61498/08 (military prisons under British control in Iraq).

accession of the EU to the ECHR, delivered on 18 December 2014, it is clear that this accession will not take place soon. In the meantime, potential conflicts can be solved based on the ECtHR's case law.

When it comes to the relation between EU law and the ECHR, the *Bosphorus* case is a milestone.[58] The UN had imposed sanctions against the Federal Republic of Yougoslavia. These sanctions were implemented by the then European (Economic) Community through Regulations which in turn where transposed in the national law of the Member States. On 8 June 1993, the Irish authorities impounded, further to these rules, an aircraft, leased by the Turkish Company Bosphorus Hava Yolları Turizm from Yougoslavia Airlines which was stationed in Dublin. Before the ECtHR, Bosphorus complained that the Irish authorities had acted in violation of Article 1 of the First Protocol to the Convention (protection of property rights). Clearly, the Irish State was in an uncomfortable position: in complying with its EU (and UN) obligations, it risked violating the ECHR. However, the Court found a way out. Its reasoning is sound, although not uncontested.[59]

The first, preliminary, question concerns the character of the authorities at the origins of the behaviour complained of. If the interference with fundamental rights is attributable to an international organisation, the complaint will be inadmissible.[60] If, on the contrary, national authorities are accountable, the complaints will be admissible and the merits can be assessed.

When it comes to the merits of the case, the Court insists on one fundamental aspect: the states' discretionary power.[61] Whenever states have some leeway in complying with their international obligations, their responsibility under the ECHR can be entirely assessed by the Court. Things are more complicated, though, when states do not have any discretionary power. In this hypothesis, the Court has developed the idea that the states can comply with their international obligations, as long the other international legal system offers a protection of fundamental rights, both substantively and procedurally, equivalent to the ECHR. In such cases, there is a presumption that the state has complied with its obligations under the Convention. The Court will not have to verify separately

---

[58] *Bosphorus Hava Yolları Turizm ve Ticaret Anonim Şirketi v. Ireland*, ECtHR (GC) 30 June 2005, appl. no. 45036/98.

[59] C. Costello, 'The Bosphorus Ruling of the European Court of Human Rights: Fundamental Rights and Blurred Boundaries in Europe', 6 *Human Rights Law Review*, 2006, 87–130; K. Kuhnert, 'Bosphorus – Double Standards in European Human Rights Protection', 2 *Utrecht Law* Review, 2006, 177–189; T. Lock, 'Beyond Bosphorus: The European Court of Human Rights' Case Law on the Responsibility of Member States of International Organisations Under the European Convention on Human Rights', 10 *Human Rights Law Review*, 2010, 529–545.

[60] *Behrami and Behrami v. France and Saramati v. France, Germany and Norway*, ECtHR (GC) 2 May 2007, appl. nos. 71412/01 and 78166/01.

[61] J. Gerards and L. Glas, 'De verhouding tussen het EHRM en het HvJ EU na toetreding van de EU tot het EVRM, *Ars Aequi*, 2012, 524–525.

whether the Conventionally-protected right has been violated. However, this presumption can be rebutted whenever the protection of the Convention rights was manifestly deficient. The *Bosphorus* presumption has been confirmed by later case law.[62]

Problems may arise as well whenever a state's act or omission is inspired by UN rules. It follows from the Court's case law that its reasoning is similar to that developed in the *Bosphorus* case. In the *Nada* case, the Court found out that the UN Resolution at stake left some discretionary powers to the national authorities. Their acts could therefore be assessed in the light of the Convention.[63] In the case of *Al-Dulimi and Montana*, the Court concluded even that there was no conflict of obligations, since the wording of the UN Security Council at stake did not exclude a domestic judicial control of the sanctions national states were supposed to impose. Therefore, the Swiss authorities had to comply with Article 6 ECHR.[64]

5. TEMPORAL SCOPE

5.1. INTRODUCTION

By virtue of a generally accepted principle of international law a treaty is not applicable to acts or facts that have occurred, or to situations that have ceased to exist, before the treaty entered into force and was ratified by the state in question.[65] This also applies to the European Convention.[66] In the *Pfunders* case, the Commission inferred from the nature of the obligations under the Convention that the fact that the respondent State (in this case Italy) was a party to the Convention at the time of the alleged violation was decisive, without it being necessary for the applicant State (in this case Austria) to have ratified the Convention at that time.[67] However, these principles must be somewhat refined. If evidence is obtained under torture which took place before the entry into force of the Convention, an applicant can still file a complaint about the use of

---

[62]   E.g. *Avotiņš v. Latvia*, ECtHR (GC) 23 May 2016, appl. no. 17502/07; *M.S.S. v. Belgium and Greece*, ECtHR (GC) 21 January 2011, appl. no. 30696/09; *Michaud v. France*, ECtHR 6 December 2012, appl. no. 12323/11.

[63]   *Nada v. Switzerland*, ECtHR (GC) 12 September 2012, appl. no. 10593/08.

[64]   *Al-Dulimi and Montana Managemant Inc. v. Switzerland*, ECtHR (GC) 21 June 2016, appl. no. 5809/08.

[65]   See Art. 28 of the Vienna Convention on the Law of Treaties, ILM 8 (1969), p. 679.

[66]   *Proszak v. Poland*, ECtHR 16 December 1997, appl. no. 25086/94, para. 31; *Ilascu and Others v. The Republic of Moldova and Russia*, ECtHR 8 July 2004, appl. no. 48787/99, *supra* n. 33, para. 400; *Dimitrov v. Bulgaria*, ECtHR 23 September 2004, appl. no. 47829/99, para. 54.

[67]   *Austria v. Italy*, EComHR 11 January 1961, appl. no. 788/60, Yearbook IV (1961), *supra* n. 27, p. 116 (142).

this evidence in a criminal procedure subsequent to the entry into force of the Convention.[68]

In the case of *Blečić v. Croatia*, the Court explicitly mentioned that is of utmost importance to assess *the critical moment*, when the alleged interference took place. In the case at hand, the interference concerned the termination of a tenancy. A Supreme Court's decision of 15 February 1996 lay at the origin of this termination, but it dated back to a moment in time prior to the entry into force of the Convention in Croatia. The complaint was inadmissible *ratione temporis*.[69] If, however, persons die before the entry into force of the Convention, but the criminal and civil proceedings are still running after the entry into force of the Convention, a complaint based on the procedural obligations stemming from Article 2 (or Article 3)[70] will be admissible *ratione temporis*.[71] In the *Janowiec and Others* case, the Grand Chamber clarified its case law, in three main lines.[72] If the death occurs before the critical date, the Court will only be able to deal with the procedural acts and omissions subsequent to that date. Second, there has to be a 'genuine connection' between the date of death and the entry into force of the Convention. This means that the lapse of time between the event and the entry into force of the Convention must be reasonably short and a major part of the investigation must have been done, or ought to have been done, after the entry into force of the Convention.[73] Finally, even if a connection is not 'genuine', the Court may have competence *ratione temporis* if this is needed to ensure the effective and real protection of the guaranties and values protected by the Convention.[74]

5.2. CONTINUING VIOLATIONS

Of particular note is the case law developed by the Commission concerning complaints which relate to a continuing situation, i.e. to violations of the Convention which are caused by an act committed at a given moment, but which continue owing to the consequences of the original act. Such a case occurred with respect to a Belgian national who lodged a complaint concerning a conviction by a Belgian court for treason during the Second World War. The verdict had been pronounced before Belgium had ratified the Convention, but the situation complained about, *viz.* the punishment in the form of, *inter alia*, a limitation of the right of free expression, continued after the Convention had

---

[68] *Harutyunyan v. Armenia*, ECtHR 28 June 2007, appl. no. 36549/03, para. 50.
[69] *Blečić v. Croatia*, ECtHR (GC) 8 March 2006, appl. no. 59532/00.
[70] As to Article 3, see, e.g., *Yatsenko v. Ukraine*, ECtHR 16 February 2012, appl. no. 75345/01.
[71] *Šilih v. Slovenia*, ECtHR (GC) 9 April 2009, appl. no. 71463/01.
[72] *Janowiec and Others v. Russia*, ECtHR (GC) 21 October 2013, appl. no. 55508/07, 29520/09, para. 142.
[73] *Ibid.*, para. 148.
[74] *Ibid.*, paras. 149–151.

become binding upon Belgium. According to the Commission the latter fact was decisive and the complaint accordingly was declared admissible.[75]

Similarly, the Court held in the *Papamichalopoulos* case that the expropriation of land amounted to a continuing violation of Article 1 of Protocol No. 1. The alleged violations had begun in 1967. At that time Greece had already ratified the Convention and Protocol No. 1, and their denunciation by Greece from 13 June 1970 until 28 November 1974 during the military regime had not released it from its obligations under them 'in respect of any act which, being capable of constituting a violation of such obligations, [might] have been performed by it' earlier, as stated in Article 58(2) of the Convention. Greece had, however, not recognised the Commission's competence to receive individual petitions until 20 November 1985 and then only in relation to acts, decisions, facts and events subsequent to that date. However, the Government had not raised any preliminary objection in that regard and the Court held that the question did not call for consideration by the Court on its own motion. The Court merely noted that the applicants' claim related to a continuing situation.[76] Along the same lines, the Court may find that a measure of expropriation is an instantaneous act, subject therefore to the six-month rule, whereas the refusal to pay compensation is a continuing situation.[77]

In the case of *Varnava*, the Court made a distinction between cases of suspicious disappearance and suspicious death. Disappearances are continuing situations, in that they are characterised by ongoing worries about what happened to the missing person(s), usually accompanied by long-lasting torment of the victims' relatives.[78]

It further noted that not all continuing situations are equal. Precisely because of the problems caused by the passage of time (memories fading, evidence disappearing, witnesses passing away, ...) applicants cannot wait infinitely to bring their case to Strasbourg. When it comes to disappearances, applicants will have to be diligent and act within a reasonable lapse of time.[79]

---

[75]   *De Becker v. Belgium*, ECtHR 27 March 1962, appl. no. 214/56, Yearbook II (1958–1959), p. 214 (244). See also *X. v. Switzerland*, EComHR 12 July 1976, appl. no. 7031/75, D&R 6 (1977), p. 124; *X. v. the United Kingdom*, EComHR 29 September 1976, appl. no. 7202/75, D&R 7 (1977), p. 102; and *X. v. Belgium*, EComHR 3 December 1979, appl. no. 8701/79, D&R 18 (1980), p. 250 (251) concerning disfranchisement. See, however, the decision of the Commission on *X and Y v. Portugal*, EComHR 3 July 1979, appl. nos. 8560/79 and 8613/79, D&R 16 (1979), p. 209 (211–212), in which two servicemen complained that their transfer had taken place in contravention of Art. 6.

[76]   *Papamichalopoulos and Others v. Greece*, ECtHR 24 June 1993, appl. no. 14556/89, para. 40; *Vasilescu v. Romania*, ECtHR 22 May 1998, appl. no. 27053/95, para. 49; *Cyprus v. Turkey*, ECtHR (GC) 10 May 2001, appl. no. 25781/94, para. 189; *Eugenia Michaelidou Developments Ltd. and Michael Tymvios v. Turkey*, ECtHR 31 July 2003, appl. no. 16163/90, para. 31.

[77]   *Almeida Garrett, Mascarenhas Falcão and Others v. Portugal*, ECtHR 11 January 2000, appl. nos. 29813/96 and 30229/96.

[78]   *Varnava and Others v. Turkey*, ECtHR (GC) 18 September 2009, appl. nos. 16064/90, 16065/90, 16066/90, 16068/90, 16069/90, 16070/90, 16071/90, 16072/90 and 16073/90, para. 148.

[79]   *Ibid.*, para. 161.

5.3. DENUNCIATION

Even after a state has denounced the Convention in accordance with Article 58(1), the Convention remains fully applicable to that state for another six months (Article 58(2)). A complaint submitted between the date of denunciation of the Convention and that on which that denunciation becomes effective thus falls within the scope of the Convention *ratione temporis*. This occurred in the case of the second complaint, of April 1970, by Denmark, Norway and Sweden against Greece. On 12 December 1969 Greece had denounced the Convention. This denunciation was, therefore, to become effective on 13 June 1970. The Commission decided that in virtue of Article 65(2) [the present Article 58(2)] Greece was still bound, at the time of the complaint, to comply with the obligations ensuing from the Convention, and that consequently the Commission could examine the complaint.[80]

6. EFFECT WITHIN NATIONAL LEGAL SYSTEMS

It is primarily the task of the national authorities to secure the rights and freedoms set forth in the Convention. The basic idea is that the Court has a subsidiary role: only when national authorities fail to comply with their obligations under the ECHR, does the Court have the competence to assess a possible complaint. Furthermore, the Court itself stressed this subsidiary role when it created 'the margin of appreciation'. National authorities will be normally better placed to make policy choices or to protect human rights in a way that fits best in the national constitutional traditions. Obviously, this margin of appreciation or leeway is not unlimited and goes together with European supervision.[81] Protocol No. 15 will integrate the margin of appreciation in the Preamble to the Convention.

To what extent the national courts can play a part in this, by reviewing the acts and omissions of those national authorities, depends mainly on the question of whether the provisions of the Convention are directly applicable in proceedings before those national courts. The answer to this question depends in turn on the effect of the Convention within the national legal system concerned. The Convention does not impose upon the Contracting States the obligation

---

[80]   *Denmark, Norway and Sweden v. Greece*, EComHR 16 July 1970, appl. no. 4448/70, Yearbook XIII (1970), p. 108 (120). After the admissibility declaration, the Commission desisted from further examination. However, on 18 November 1974 Greece became a party again to the Convention, and the Commission then resumed its examination of the complaint. Finally, on 4 October 1976, after both the applicant States and the respondent State had intimated that they were no longer interested in proceeding with the case, the Commission struck the case off the list; D&R 6 (1977), p. 6 (8).

[81]   *Handyside v. The United Kingdom*, ECtHR 7 December 1976, appl. no. 5493/72, para. 49.

to make the Convention part of domestic law or otherwise to guarantee its domestic applicability and supremacy over national law.[82]

In the context of the relationship between international law and municipal law there are two contrasting views. According to the so-called *dualistic* view the international and the national legal system form two separate legal spheres and international law has effect within the national legal system only after it has been 'transformed' into national law via the required procedure. The legal subjects depend on this transformation for the protection of the rights laid down in international law; their rights and duties exist only under national law. This is the case, for instance, in the United Kingdom; only in 1998 has the Convention been incorporated, under the Human Rights Act. However, under this Human Rights Act, the UK courts are not allowed to disapply an (other) Act of Parliament, which they consider to conflict with the Convention/Human Rights Act. They can only go so far as to give a declaratory judgment, leaving it to the legislature to remedy the situation of conflict between the two Acts of Parliament. In another dualistic system, that of the Federal Republic of Germany, the Convention has been transformed by a federal law (*Zustimmungsgesetz*) according to Article 59(2) of the Constitution, thereby becoming part of the domestic law of the Federal Republic.

In a dualistic system, after the Convention has been approved and transformed into domestic law, the question remains as to what status it has within the national legal system. The answer to this question is to be found in national constitutional law and practice. Under German constitutional law, for instance, the Convention has no priority over the Federal Constitution nor is it of equal rank. It has, however, the rank of a federal statute. The consequences of this have been mitigated by interpreting German statutes in line with the Convention; the German *Bundesverfassungsgericht* has even decided that priority should be given to the provisions of the Convention over subsequent legislation unless a contrary intention of the legislature could be clearly established. Even provisions of the Federal Constitution have to be interpreted in light of the Convention. As pointed out above, the UK courts cannot disapply Acts of Parliament considered not to be in conformity with the Human Rights Act. However, it can be safely assumed that many discrepancies can and will be resolved by interpreting the conflicting Act of Parliament in conformity with the Human Rights Act, meaning conformity with the Convention and the accompanying case law of the Court.

According to the so-called *monistic* view, on the other hand, the various domestic legal systems are viewed as elements of the all-embracing international legal system, within which the national authorities are bound by international

---

[82] See J. Gerards and J. Fleuren (eds.), *Implementation of the European Convention on Human Rights and of the Judgments of the ECtHR in National Case-law. A Comparative Analysis*, Cambridge: Intersentia, 2014.

law in their relations with individuals as well, regardless of whether or not the rules of international law have been transformed into national law. In this view, the individual derives rights and duties directly from international law, so that in national proceedings he may directly invoke rules of international law, which must be applied by the national courts and to which the latter must give priority over any national law conflicting with it.

However, even among the monistic systems many differences exist, not the least because of the problem of the hierarchy of norms. Although as a general rule they accept the domestic legal effect of (approved) international treaties, the scope of this acceptance varies considerably. In the Netherlands, self-executing provisions of treaties and of decisions of international organisations (i.e. written international law) may be invoked before domestic courts and may set aside conflicting (*anterior* and *posterior*) statutory law, including provisions in the Constitution. In fact, the Dutch courts have actively made use of the Convention in setting aside or interpreting Acts of Parliament. In France the *Cour de Cassation*, relying upon Article 55 of the French Constitution, has accepted the prevalence of treaties (including EC law) over national *lois* since 1975. The *Conseil d'Etat* has been much more hesitant, but finally, in 1989, accepted the supremacy of treaties over domestic legislation.

The prevailing opinion is that the system resulting from the monistic view is not prescribed by international law at its present stage of development. International law leaves the states full discretion to decide for themselves in what way they will fulfil their international obligations and implement the pertinent international rules within their national legal system; they are internationally responsible only for the ultimate result of this implementation. This holds good for the European Convention as well,[83] although the Court indicated that the system according to which the Convention has internal effect is a particularly faithful reflection of the intention of the drafters.[84] The consequence is that there is no legal obligation to assign internal effect to the Convention nor to afford it prevalence over national law. However, the great majority of Contracting States have provided for internal effect; many also accept that the Convention prevails over national legislation.

In states in which the Convention has internal effect one must ascertain for each provision separately whether it is directly applicable (i.e. is self-executing),

---

[83] See *Swedish Engine Drivers' Union v. Sweden*, ECtHR 6 February 1976, appl. no. 5614/72, para. 50, in which the Court held that 'neither Article 13 nor the Convention in general lays down for the Contracting States any given manner for ensuring within their internal law the effective implementation of any of the provisions of the Convention'. Similarly, see *Belgian Linguistics Case v. Belgium (No. 2)*, ECtHR 23 July 1968, appl. nos. 1474/62, 1677/62, 1691/62, 1994/63 and 2126/64, section 2, para. 11 and *National Union of Belgian Police v. Belgium*, ECtHR 27 October 1975, appl. no. 4464/70, para. 38. See also the dissenting opinion of the Commission members Sperduti and Opsahl in the report of the Commission in *Ireland v. the United Kingdom*, ECtHR 18 January 1978, appl. no. 5310/71, B.23-I (1980), pp. 503–505.

[84] *Ireland v. the United Kingdom*, ECtHR (GC) 18 January 1978, appl. no. 5310/71, para. 239.

so that individuals may directly invoke such a provision before the national courts. The self-executing character of a Convention provision may generally be presumed when the content of such a provision can be applied in a concrete case without there being a need for supplementary measures on the part of the national legislative or executive authorities.

7. DRITTWIRKUNG

Horizontal effect or *Drittwirkung* is a complicated phenomenon about which there are widely divergent views. Hereafter, in the discussion of the separate rights and freedoms, certain aspects of *Drittwirkung* will be discussed insofar as the Strasbourg case law calls for it. For a detailed treatment of *Drittwirkung*, in particular also as to its recognition and effect under national law, reference may be made to the literature.[85]

What does the term *Drittwirkung* mean? Two views in particular must be distinguished. According to the first view, *Drittwirkung* of provisions concerning human rights means that these provisions also *apply* to legal relations between private parties and not only to legal relations between an individual and the public authorities. According to the second view, *Drittwirkung* of human rights provisions is defined as the possibility for an individual to *enforce* these rights against another individual. Advocates of the latter view consider that *Drittwirkung* of human rights is present only if an individual in his legal relations with other individuals is able to enforce the observance of the law concerning human rights via some procedure or other.

As to the latter view it may at once be pointed out that no *Drittwirkung* of the rights and freedoms set forth in the Convention can be directly effectuated

---

[85]   See, e.g., E.A. Alkema, 'The Third-party Applicability or "Drittwirkung" of the ECHR', in *Protecting Human Rights; The European Dimension*, Cologne, 1988, pp. 33–45; A. Clapham, 'The "Drittwirkung" of the Convention', in R.St.J. McDonald, F. Matscher, H. Petzold (eds.), *The European System for the Protection of Human Rights*, Dordrecht/Boston/London, 1993, pp. 163–206; B.J. De Vos, *Horizontale werking van grondrechten. Een kritiek.* [Horizontal Application of Fundamental Rights. A Critique], Antwerp, 2010; A. Drzemczewski, 'The Domestic Status of the European Convention on Human Rights; New Dimensions', 1 *Legal Issues of European Integration*, 1977, pp. 1–85; M.A. Eissen, 'La convention et les devoirs des individus', in *La protection des droits de l'homme dans le cadre européen*, Paris, 1961, pp. 167–194; H. Guradze, 'Die Schutzrichtung der Grundrechtsnormen in der Europäischen Menschenrechts-konvention', *Festschrift Nipperdy*, Vol. II, 1965, pp. 759–769; M.M. Hahne, *Das Drittwirkungsproblem in der Europäischen Konvention zum Schutz der Menschenrechte und Grundfreiheiten*, Heidelberg, 1973; D.J. Harris, M. O'Boyle, C. Warbrick, *Law of the European Convention of Human Rights*, Oxford, 2014, pp. 21–24; E. Engle, 'Third Party Effect of Fundamental Rights', 5 *Hanse Law Review*, 2009, pp. 165–173; D.H.M. Meuwissen, *De Europese Conventie en het Nederlandse Recht* [The European Convention and Dutch Law], Leyden, 1968, pp. 201 – 11; J. Van der Walt, *The Horizontal Effect Revolution and the Question of Sovereignty*, Berlin, 2014, 201–232.

via the procedure set up by the Convention. In fact, in Strasbourg it is possible to lodge complaints only about violations of the Convention by one of the Contracting States; a complaint directed against an individual is inadmissible for reason of incompatibility with the Convention *ratione personae*. This follows from Articles 19, 32, 33 and 34 of the Convention and has also been confirmed by the Strasbourg case law.[86] As a consequence, an individual can bring up an alleged violation of his fundamental rights and freedoms by other individuals in Strasbourg only indirectly, *viz.* when a Contracting State can be held responsible for the violation in one way or another.[87] For instance, cases have been brought to the Court concerning the interpretation of wills[88], or the lack of protection of workers against their employers.[89] Similarly, the interdiction imposed on tenants of a flat to install a satellite dish has led to a case to the Court.[90]

In such cases the supervision in the Strasbourg procedure concerns the responsibility of the state and not that of the private actor. It is, therefore, no surprise that the Strasbourg case law provides little clarity as far as *Drittwirkung* is concerned. Any urgency for a more straightforward approach is not felt. In the *Verein gegen Tierfabriken* case the Court even explicitly stated that it does not consider it desirable, let alone necessary, to elaborate a general theory concerning the extent to which the Convention guarantees should be extended to relations between private individuals *inter se*.[91] At best a kind of 'indirect *Drittwirkung*'[92] is recognised in cases where from a provision of the Convention – notably Articles 3, 10 and 11 – rights are inferred for individuals which, on the basis of a positive obligation on the part of Contracting States to take measures in order to make their exercise possible, must also be enforced *vis-à-vis* private third parties.[93]

The fact that in Strasbourg no complaints can be lodged against individuals need not, however, bar the recognition of *Drittwirkung* of the Convention, not even in the second sense referred to above. The possibility of enforcement, which in this view is required, does not necessarily have to be enforcement under international law, but may also arise from national law.[94] In that context two situations must be distinguished. In the first place, there are states where those rights and freedoms included in the Convention, which are self-

---

[86]   See *infra* Chapter 2.
[87]   As a rule, a state is not internationally responsible for the acts and omissions of its nationals or of individuals within its jurisdiction; on this, see *infra* Chapter 2.
[88]   *Pla and Puncernau v. Andorra*, ECtHR 13 July 2004, appl. no. 69498/01.
[89]   *Heinisch v. Germany*, ECtHR 21 July 2011, appl. no. 28274/08.
[90]   *Khurshid Mustafa and Tarzibachi v. Sweden*, ECtHR 16 December 2008, appl. no. 23883/06.
[91]   *VgT Verein gegen Tierfabriken v. Switzerland*, ECtHR 28 June 2001, appl. no. 24699/94, para. 40.
[92]   See Alkema, *supra* n. 84, p. 33.
[93]   For an elaborate survey of such cases of 'indirect *Drittwirkung*' and other comparable cases of 'private abuse of human rights', see Clapham, *supra* n. 85.
[94]   See Hahne, *supra* n. 85, pp. 81–94.

executing, can be directly applied by the national courts.[95] In those states the relevant provisions of the Convention can be directly invoked by individuals against other individuals insofar as their *Drittwirkung* is recognised by the national courts. Judgments of these national courts which conflict with the Convention, for which indeed the Contracting State concerned is responsible under the Convention, may then be submitted to the Strasbourg Court via the procedure under Article 34 or via the procedure under Article 33. In addition, there are those states in whose national legal systems the provisions of the Convention are not directly applicable. Those states are also obliged under the general guarantee clause of Article 1 of the Convention to secure the rights and freedoms set forth in the Convention. If one starts from the principle of *Drittwirkung*, such states also have to secure protection for individuals against violations of their fundamental rights by other individuals in their national legal system. If the competent national authorities default in this respect or if the applicable provisions of national law are not enforced, responsibility arises for the state concerned, a responsibility which may be invoked via the procedure under Article 34 or Article 33 of the Convention.[96]

At the same time, the existence of a supervisory system as described above does not in itself imply *Drittwirkung*. It does not necessarily imply that the Convention is applicable to legal relations between private parties if, in a given state, individuals may directly invoke the Convention before the courts. And the nature of the obligation arising from Article 1 of the Convention for those states in whose legal system the Convention is not directly applicable, is also in itself not decisive for the question concerning that type of *Drittwirkung*. In fact, one cannot deduce from Article 1 whether the Contracting States are obliged to secure the rights and freedoms only in relation to the public authorities or also in relation to other individuals. For a possible *Drittwirkung*, therefore, other arguments have to be put forward.

What arguments for *Drittwirkung* can be inferred from the Convention itself? It is beyond doubt that the issue of *Drittwirkung* was not taken into account when the Convention was drafted, if it played any part at all in the discussions. One can infer from the formulation of various provisions that they were not written with a view to relations between private parties. On the other hand, the subject matter regulated by the Convention – fundamental rights and freedoms – lends itself eminently to *Drittwirkung*. It is precisely on account of the fundamental character of these rights that it is difficult to appreciate why they should deserve protection in relation to public authorities, but not in relation to private parties.

---

[95]   That this so-called 'internal effect' of the Convention does not necessarily follow from international law according to its present state, has been explained *supra* 1.6.

[96]   For the above, see Hahne, *supra* n. 85, pp. 89–90.

It is submitted that it is not very relevant whether the drafters of the Convention had *Drittwirkung* in mind. Of greater importance is what conclusions may be drawn for the present situation from the principles set forth in the Convention, and specifically in its Preamble. In the Preamble, the drafters of the Convention gave evidence of the great value they attached to general respect for the fundamental rights and freedoms.[97] From this emphasis on general respect an argument pro rather than contra *Drittwirkung* can be inferred. But, as has been observed above, the drafters did not make any pronouncement on this.

Neither do the separate provisions of the Convention provide any clear arguments for or against *Drittwirkung*. Article 1 has already been discussed above. Article 13 is also mentioned in this context. From the last words of this article, *viz.* 'notwithstanding that the violation has been committed by persons in their official capacity', it is inferred by some that the Convention evidently also intends to provide a remedy against violations by individuals,[98] whereas others assert that those words merely indicate that the state is responsible for violations committed by its officials,[99] or that Article 13 does not afford an independent argument for *Drittwirkung*.[100] In addition, it is sometimes inferred from Article 17 that the Convention has *Drittwirkung*. It is, however, doubtful whether such a general conclusion may be drawn from Article 17.[101] That provision forbids not only public authorities, but also individuals from invoking the Convention for the justification of an act aimed at the destruction of fundamental rights of other persons. Such a prohibition of abuse of the Convention is quite another matter than a general obligation for individuals to respect the fundamental rights of other persons in their private legal relationships.

In summary, one may conclude that *Drittwirkung* does not imperatively ensue from the Convention. On the other hand, nothing in the Convention prevents the states from conferring *Drittwirkung* upon the rights and freedoms laid down in the Convention within their national legal systems insofar as they lend themselves to it. In some states *Drittwirkung* of the rights and freedoms guaranteed by the Convention is already recognised, whilst in other states this *Drittwirkung* at least is not excluded in principle.[102] Some have adopted the view that it may be inferred from the changing social circumstances and legal opinions that the purport of the Convention is *going to be* to secure a certain

---

[97] It states, among other things, that the Universal Declaration, of which the Convention is an elaboration, 'aims at securing universal and effective recognition and observance of the rights therein declared', while the Contracting States affirm 'their profound belief in those Fundamental Freedoms which are the foundation of justice and peace in the world'.

[98] See Eissen, *supra* n. 85, pp. 177 et seq.

[99] See Guradze, *supra* n. 85, p. 764.

[100] See Meuwissen, *supra* n. 85, p. 210.

[101] *Ibid.*

[102] See Drzemczewski, *supra* n. 85, p. 63 et seq.

minimum guarantee for the individual as well as in his relations with other persons.[103] It would seem that with regard to the spirit of the Convention a good deal may be said for this view, although in the case of such a subsequent interpretation one must ask oneself whether one does not thus assign to the Convention an effect which may be unacceptable to (a number of) the Contracting States, and consequently is insufficiently supported by their implied mutual consent.

At the same time, whether *Drittwirkung* can be assigned to the Convention at all also depends, in particular, on the nature and formulation of each separate right embodied in the Convention. In this context Alkema warns us that the nature of the legal relations between private parties may be widely divergent and that consequently *Drittwirkung* is a multiform phenomenon about which general statements are hardly possible.[104]

8. SUPERVISORY MECHANISM UNTIL 1998

8.1. BEFORE PROTOCOL No. 11

In order to ensure the rights and freedoms laid down in the Convention, two bodies were originally established: the European Commission of Human Rights and the European Court of Human Rights. Furthermore, the Committee of Ministers of the Council of Europe and the Secretary-General of the Council of Europe played a part in the supervisory mechanism. The European Commission of Human Rights and the European Court of Human Rights were set up specifically to ensure the observance of the engagements undertaken by the Contracting States under the Convention (Article 19 old). The other two organs were established by the Statute of the Council of Europe and not by the Convention.

8.2. EUROPEAN COMMISSION ON HUMAN RIGHTS

Under the old system, the individual complaints procedure covered the following two separate phases:

1. *The decision on admissibility.* After the Secretariat of the Commission had decided to register an application, the Commission examined the admissibility of the complaint. If the application was ruled inadmissible, the procedure ended.

---

[103] See Meuwissen, *supra* n. 85, p. 211; and Clapham, *supra* n. 85, in particular pp. 200–206.
[104] See Alkema, *supra* n. 85, pp. 254–255.

2. *The examination of the merits.* If the application was declared admissible, the Commission examined the merits of the case. The procedure could, at this point, end in a friendly settlement or some other arrangement. If no settlement was reached, the Commission stated its opinion in a report. The case could subsequently be submitted to the Court,[105] which then gave the final decision on the merits. If a case was not submitted to the Court, the Committee of Ministers gave the final decision on the merits.

The most important decisions of the Commission on admissibility as well as the great majority of its reports have been published.[106]

8.3. EUROPEAN COURT OF HUMAN RIGHTS

As with the Commission, the European Court of Human Rights was specifically set up to supervise the observance by the Contracting States of their engagements arising from the Convention (under the old Article 19).

For the consideration of each case a Chamber composed of nine judges was constituted from the Court (under the old Article 43). Persons sitting as *ex officio* members of the Chambers were those judges who were elected in respect of the States Parties to the case. If such a judge was not available, the place was taken by a judge *ad hoc*; a person chosen by the state in question. In addition, either the

---

[105] According to Art. 48 (old) of the Convention:

'The following may bring a case before the Court, provided that the High Contracting Party concerned, if there is only one, or the High Contracting Parties concerned, if there is more than one, are subject to the compulsory jurisdiction of the Court, failing that, with the consent of the High Contracting Parties concerned, if there is only one, or of the High Contracting Parties concerned if there is more than one:

(a) the Commission;

(b) a High Contracting Party whose national is alleged to be a victim;

(c) a High Contracting Party which referred the case to the Commission;

(d) a High Contracting Party against which the complaint has been lodged.'

[106] The publication system of the Commission was rather complicated and therefore requires some elucidation. Not all decisions of the Commission were published, especially not those taken after summary proceedings. A number of the decisions concerning admissibility are to be found in the *Yearbook of the European Convention on Human Rights* and in the *Collection of Decisions*, continued after 1975 as *Decisions and Reports*. The reports of the Commission were published separately; in addition, they were sometimes included in the *Yearbooks* and in the *Decisions and Reports*. Sometimes a decision was included in the *Yearbooks* but not in the *Collection of Decisions/Decisions and Reports* and vice versa. In the *Digest of Strasbourg case-law relating to the European Convention on Human Rights*, published by Carl Heymans Verlag, the case law of the Commission and the Court has been incorporated. For those cases that were referred to the Court, the main parts of the reports of the Commission were since 1985 also published as an Annex to the judgment of the Court (Series A), while before 1985 they were included in the materials published in Series B. As from 1996 the case law of the Commission was and that of the Court still is published in *Reports of Judgments and Decisions*.

President or the Vice-President sat as an *ex officio* member of the Chamber. The other members of the Chamber were chosen by lot. For that purpose, the judges were divided into three regional groups. The Chamber thus constituted was able, or was obliged, under certain conditions, to relinquish jurisdiction in favour of, originally, the plenary Court, and later a Grand Chamber of 17 judges.[107] To prevent inconsistencies in the case law, the Court, in its Rules,[108] had assigned to the Chambers the right to relinquish jurisdiction in favour of the plenary Court/ Grand Chamber when a case pending before a Chamber raised serious questions affecting the interpretation of the Convention. A Chamber was obliged to do so where the resolution of such questions might have a result inconsistent with a judgment previously delivered by a Chamber or by the plenary Court/Grand Chamber. According to Rule 51(5) of the old Rules of Court the Grand Chamber could exceptionally, when the issues raised were particularly serious or involved a significant change of existing case law, relinquish jurisdiction in favour of the plenary Court.

No case could be brought before the Court unless it had been declared admissible by the Commission, and the Commission had stated its opinion on the merits in a report.

All the judgments of the Court were published, as were the documents relating to the proceedings, including the report of the Commission, but excluding any document which the President considered unnecessary to publish.[109]

8.4. COMMITTEE OF MINISTERS OF THE COUNCIL OF EUROPE

Unlike the Commission and the Court, the Committee of Ministers was not set up by the Convention. Here a supervisory function had been entrusted to an already existing body of the Council of Europe. Accordingly, the composition, organisation and general functions and powers of the Committee of Ministers

---

[107] On 27 October 1993, the Court decided to establish a Grand Chamber to exercise the jurisdiction of the plenary Court in most cases.

[108] Further to Art. 25 of the Convention, the Plenary Court adopts the rules of the Court. Those rules essentially deal with the functioning of the Court and practical aspects of the proceedings.

[109] The judgments and decisions of the Court were published in the *Publications of the European Court of Human Rights, Series A*. The documents of the case, including the report of the Commission, were published in the *Publications of the European Court of Human Rights, Series B*. Since 1985, the main parts of reports of the Commission were also published as an annex to the Court judgments in Series A. In addition, a summary was published in the *Yearbook of the European Convention on Human Rights*. In 1996 the Series A ceased to exist. Subsequently the judgments of the Court were published in *Reports of Judgments and Decisions*.

are not regulated in the Convention, but by the Statute of the Council of Europe.[110]

The function assigned to the Committee of Ministers in the Convention was the result of a compromise. On the one hand, during the drafting of the Convention there was a body of opinion which wished to institute, in addition to the Commission, a Court with compulsory jurisdiction. Others, however, held that it was preferable to entrust supervision, apart from the Commission, only to the Committee of Ministers. Ultimately the two alternatives were combined by making the jurisdiction of the Court optional and granting the Committee the power, in those cases that were not, or could not be, submitted to the Court, to decide on the question of whether there had been a violation of the Convention.

9. SUPERVISORY MECHANISM SINCE 1998

9.1. UNDER PROTOCOL No. 11

One of the most important reasons that prompted the revision of the supervisory system was the increasing workload of the existing institutions. This was due to the fact that, in the 1990s in the aftermath of the disappearance of the East Bloc, an important number of Central and Eastern European States became party to the Convention. As of that period, potentially 800 million Europeans could file a complaint. Not surprisingly, the number of complaints did increase dramatically. For example, the yearly number of individual applications registered grew from 1,013 in 1988 to 4,721 in 1997, and the number of judgments – including decisions rejecting applications submitted under Protocol No. 9 – delivered by the Court rose from 19 in 1988 to 150 in 1997. Another important reason was the increasing length of time needed to deal with applications.

The entry into force of Protocol No. 11 on 1 November 1998 meant a considerable alteration of the supervisory mechanism under the Convention. A new, permanent Court took the place of the European Commission of Human Rights and the European Court of Human Rights. In addition, the role of the Committee of Ministers of the Council of Europe in the individual complaint procedure was dropped. Under Article 46, paragraph 2, the Committee of Ministers has, however, retained its supervisory role with respect to the execution of the Court's judgments.

Another important change was that the individual right of complaint was no longer dependent on the optional recognition by the State. Henceforth ratification of the Convention automatically entailed recognition of the individual right of complaint.[111] Acceptance of the Court's jurisdiction by the

---

[110] See Arts. 13–21 of the Statute of the Council of Europe.
[111] Art. 34 of the Convention.

state was also no longer required. The new system provides for the Court's jurisdiction as the only and compulsory jurisdiction. The state's right of complaint continues to exist in addition to that of the individual.[112]

9.2. UNDER PROTOCOL No. 14

The reform under Protocol No. 11 has, however, proven to be insufficient to cope with the prevailing situation. Since 1998, the number of applications has dramatically increased. As a result of the massive increase of individual applications, the effectiveness of the system and thus the credibility and authority of the Court were seriously endangered.

In order to cope with this problem, Protocol No. 14 was drafted to amend the control system of the Convention. Unlike Protocol No.11, Protocol 14 made no radical changes to the control system. The changes related more to the functioning of the system rather than to its structure. Its main purpose was to improve the system, giving the Court the procedural means and flexibility it needs to process all applications in a timely fashion, while allowing it to concentrate on the most important cases that require in-depth examination.

The amendments concerned the following aspects: (1) reinforcement of the Court's filtering capacity in respect of the flux of unmeritorious applications; (2) a new admissibility criterion concerning cases in which the applicant has not suffered a significant disadvantage; (3) measures for dealing with repetitive cases. Together these elements of the reform sought to reduce the time spent by the Court on clearly inadmissible, repetitive and less important applications, in order to enable the Court to concentrate on those cases that raise important human rights issues.[113]

9.3. EUROPEAN COURT OF HUMAN RIGHTS

The European Court of Human Rights is now composed of a number of judges equal to that of the Contracting States.[114] The Court functions on a permanent basis. Judges sit on the Court in their individual capacity and do not represent any state. In fact, they do not even have to be citizen of the state in respect of which they have been elected. They cannot engage in any activity which is incompatible with their independence or impartiality or with the demands of full-time office.

The purpose of Protocol Nos. 11 and 14 was to streamline procedures rather than to change substantive matters. Thus, the Court now also exercises the filter function that in the past was performed by the Commission. In order to

---

[112]   Art. 33 of the Convention.
[113]   See *infra* 9.6.
[114]   Art. 20 of the Convention.

perform all its missions, the Court is made up of various judicial formations. Those formations have, as will be explained, different tasks and are made up of a varying number of judges. The Court consists indeed of single-judge formations, Committees, Chambers and the Grand Chamber (Article 26).

Further to Article 27, *single judges* will declare inadmissible or strike out of the list of cases those applications that need no further examination. This means that the judge will take such decisions only in clear-cut cases, where the inadmissibility of the application is manifest from the outset. The single-judge formations will be assisted by rapporteurs from the Registry with knowledge of the language and the legal system of the respondent party concerned (Article 24(2)). The decision itself remains the sole responsibility of the judge. If a single judge decides not to take such a decision, the case will be send to a Committee or to a Chamber (Article 27(3)). The decisions of a single judge are final. In order to avoid any bias, a single judge cannot treat applications against the State in which respect he has been elected (Article 26(3)).

Committees of three judges can as well declare applications inadmissible or strike them out of the list of case, if no further examination is needed (Article 28 (1a). Moreover, on the basis of Article 28 (1b), the Committee may also, in a joint decision, declare individual applications admissible and decide on their merits, when the questions they raise concerning the interpretation or application of the Convention are covered by well-established case law of the Court. The Committees may rule on all aspects of the case (admissibility, merits, just satisfaction) in a single judgment or decision. Unanimity is required on each aspect. Failure to reach a unanimous decision counts as no decision, in which event the Chamber procedure applies (Article 29). It will then fall to the Chamber to decide whether all aspects of the case should be covered in a single judgment. Even when the Committee initially intends to apply the procedure provided for in Article 28(1)(b), it may declare an application inadmissible under Article 28(1)(a). This may happen, for example, if the respondent Party has persuaded the Committee that domestic remedies have not been exhausted.

When a three-judge Committee gives a judgment on the merits, the judge elected in respect of the High Contracting Party concerned will not be an *ex officio* member of the decision-making body. However, paragraph 3 of Article 28 provides that a Committee may invite the judge elected in respect of the High Contracting Party concerned to replace one of its members. In certain circumstances it may, in particular, be useful to do so if questions relating to the domestic legal system concerned need to be clarified.

The competence of the *Chambers* composed of seven judges is laid down in Article 29. Its first paragraph reads as follows:

'If no decision is taken under Article 27 or 28, or no judgment rendered under Article 28, a Chamber shall decide on the admissibility and merits of individual applications submitted under Article 34. The decision on admissibility may be taken separately.'

Paragraph 2 of Article 29 deals with inter-state applications:

'A Chamber shall decide on the admissibility and merits of inter-State applications submitted under Article 33. The decision on admissibility shall be taken separately unless the Court, in exceptional cases, decides otherwise.'

Finally, Arts. 30 and 31 of the Convention deal with the competences of the *Grand Chamber*, composed of 17 judges. Further to Article 30, a Chamber can relinquish jurisdiction to the Grand Chamber, unless a party opposes it, whenever a pending case raises a serious question of interpretation of the Convention or the Protocols. Relinquishment is also possible whenever there is a risk that the outcome of the case is inconsistent with previous judgments. Further to Article 43, each party can ask within a delay of three months after the date of the judgment, to refer the case to the Grand Chamber. A panel of five judges of the Grand Chamber will decide on the request: referrals are accepted in case of serious questions of interpretation of the Convention or the Protocols or in case of serious issues of general importance.

Apart from these contentious competences, Article 31 foresees that the Grand Chamber also gives advisory opinions requested by the Committee of Ministers on the basis of Article 47. The Grand Chamber also decides on questions expedited by the Committee of Ministers on the execution of final judgments by the states that have been found in violation of the Conventions or the Protocols (Article 46).

9.4. ELECTION OF COURT MEMBERS

For the election of the judges every member of the Council of Europe nominates three candidates of whom at least one must be of the opposite sex of the other candidate, save in exceptional circumstances.[115] From the list thus produced the Parliamentary Assembly ultimately elects the members of the Court by a majority of the votes cast (Article 22).

According to Article 23 judges will be elected for a period of nine years, and may be not be re-elected. The term of office of the judges shall expire when they reach the age of 70. Article 2 of Protocol No. 15 clearly indicates that judges may not be older than 65 years the day the list of three candidates is requested by the Parliamentary Assembly. The members of the Court hold office until replaced. After having been replaced they continue to deal with such cases as they already

---

[115] Committee on the Election of Judges to the European Court of Human Rights Procedure for electing judges to the European Court of Human Rights AS/Cdh/Inf (2017)01 rev 4. On the elections: K. Lemmens, "(S)electing Judges for Strasbourg. A (Dis)appointing Process?" in M. Bobek (ed.), *Selecting Europe's Judges*, Oxford, 2015, pp. 95–119.

had under consideration (Article 23(3)). No judge may be dismissed from office unless the other judges decide by a majority of two-thirds that that judge has ceased to fulfil the required conditions (Article 23(4)).

The Court functions on a permanent basis.[116] The judges have a full-time office (Article 21(3)), and have their home basis in Strasbourg.

The Plenary Court elects its President, two Vice-Presidents and the Presidents of the Chambers of the Court (Article 25).

9.5. REQUIREMENTS FOR MEMBERSHIP

The Convention lays down certain requirements for members of the Court. Candidates must be of high moral character and must either possess the qualifications required for appointment to high judicial office or be jurisconsults of recognised competence (Article 21(1)). The judges shall sit on the Court in their individual capacity (Article 21(2)). During their term of office the judges shall not engage in any activity which is incompatible with their independence, impartiality, or with the demands of a full-time office (Article 21(3)). According to Rule 3 of the Rules of Court,[117] before taking up their duties, the judges must take an oath or make a declaration to the effect that they will exercise their function independently and impartially. Similarly, a judge may not exercise his function when he is a member of a government or holds a post or exercises a profession which is incompatible with his independence and impartiality (Rule 4 of the Rules of Court).

Article 51 of the Convention provides that the members of the Court, during the exercise of their functions, are entitled to the privileges and immunities provided for in Article 40 of the Statute of the Council of Europe and in the agreements made thereunder,[118] which furthers the independent exercise of their function.

9.6. SESSIONS OF THE COURT

The seat of the Court is in Strasbourg, but if it considers it expedient, the Court may exercise its functions elsewhere in the territories of the member states of the Council of Europe (Rule 19 of the Rules of Court). Rule 20 of the Rules of Court provides that the President convenes the Court whenever the performance of its functions under the Convention and under these Rules so requires in a plenary session and also at the request of at least one-third of the members. The quorum

---

[116] Art. 19.
[117] < www.echr.coe.int/Documents/Rules_Court_ENG.pdf >.
[118] See Sixth Protocol to the General Agreement on Privileges and Immunities of the Council of Europe, Strasbourg, 5 March 1996, ETS, No. 162.

for the sessions of the plenary Court is two-thirds of the judges (Rule 20(2) of the Rules of Court).

In order to consider cases brought before it, the Court shall sit in single-judge formations, Committees of three judges, Chambers and the Grand Chamber.[119] In plenary the Court will only deal with administrative matters, such as the election of the President, the Vice-Presidents and the Presidents of the Chambers, and the adoption of the Rules of Procedure (Article 25). Under Article 26(2) the Committee of Ministers may, by a unanimous decision and for a fixed period, at the request of the plenary Court, reduce the number of judges of the Chambers to five.

The Chambers, consisting of seven judges, as provided for in Article 25(b) of the Convention, shall be set up by the plenary Court. In fact, the Court divides its membership into Sections. There shall be at least four Sections. Each judge shall be a member of a Section. The composition of the Sections shall be geographically and gender balanced and shall reflect the different legal systems of the Contracting Parties. On the basis of a proposal by the President the plenary Court may constitute an additional Section (Rule 25).

The Committees, as provided for in Article 26(1) of the Convention, are composed of three judges belonging to the same Section. The Committees are constituted for a period of 12 months by rotation among the members of each Section, excepting the President of the Section.[120]

The Grand Chamber, consisting of 17 judges, includes the President of the Court, the Vice-Presidents, the Presidents of the Chambers and other judges chosen in accordance with the Rules of Court. There shall sit as an *ex officio* member of the Chamber and the Grand Chamber the judge elected in respect of the State Party concerned or, if there is none or if he or she is unable to sit, a person of that state's choice. To make sure that the Grand Chamber looks into the matter afresh when it examines a case referred to it under Article 43, judges from the Chamber which rendered the judgment are excluded, with the exception of the President of the Chamber and the judge who sat in respect of the state concerned (Article 26).

For the consideration of a case a Chamber is constituted from the Section (Article 26(1) and Rule 26(1)). Persons sitting as *ex officio* members of the Chambers are the President of the Section and those judges who are elected in respect of any State Party to the case. If such a judge is unable to sit or withdraws, the President of the Chamber shall appoint an *ad hoc* judge, chosen from a list with three to five candidates designated by the Contracting States as persons being able to serve as *ad hoc judge* (Rule 29). The other members of the Chamber are chosen by designation by the President of the Section (Rule 26 of the Rules of Court).

---

[119]   Art. 26(1) of the Convention.
[120]   Rule 27 of the Rules of Court.

Judges may not take part in the consideration of any case in which they have a personal interest or with respect to which they have previously acted as agent, advocate, or adviser of a party or of a person having an interest in the case, or as a member of a tribunal or commission of enquiry, or in any other capacity. If a judge considers that he or she should not take part in the consideration of a particular case, he or she informs the President, who shall exempt the judge concerned from sitting. The initiative may also be taken by the President, when the latter considers that such a withdrawal is desirable. In case of disagreement the Court decides (Rule 28(2), (3) and (4) of the Rules of Court).

The hearings of the Court are public, unless the Court decides otherwise in exceptional circumstances (Rule 63 of the Rules of Court). This publicity is a logical implication of the judicial character of the procedure. The deliberations of the Court, on the other hand, are in private (Rule 22 of the Rules of Court).

The Court takes its decisions by a majority of votes of the judges present. If the voting is equal, the President of the (Grand) Chamber has a casting vote (Rule 23 of the Rules of Court).

In accordance with Article 44(3) of the Convention final judgments of the Court shall be published, under the responsibility of the Registrar, in an appropriate form. The Registrar shall in addition be responsible for the publication of official reports of selected judgments and decisions and of any document which the President of the Court considers useful to publish.[121]

10. COMMITTEE OF MINISTERS

10.1. INTRODUCTION

Unlike the Court, the Committee of Ministers was not set up by the Convention. Here a function was entrusted to an already existing body of the Council of Europe. Accordingly, the composition, organisation, general functions and powers, and procedure of the Committee of Ministers are not regulated by the Convention, but by the Statute of the Council of Europe.[122] After the entry into force of Protocol No. 11, under Article 46(2) the Committee of Ministers retained its function of supervising the execution of judgments of the Court, while its power under former Article 32 in respect of individual applications was abolished.

Article 46(3) grants the Committee of Ministers the right to ask the Court to interpret a final judgment, for the purpose of facilitating the supervision of its execution. The Court's reply will settle any argument concerning a judgment's exact meaning. According to Article 46(3) a referral decision shall

---

[121]   Rule 78 of the Rules of Court.
[122]   See Arts. 13–21 of the Statute of the Council of Europe.

require a majority vote of two-thirds of the representatives entitled to sit on the Committee. According to the Explanatory Report to this Protocol the aim of the new paragraph 3 is to enable the Court to give an interpretation of a judgment, not to pronounce on the measures taken by the High Contracting Parties to comply with that judgment. No time-limit will be set for making requests for interpretation, since a question of interpretation may arise at any time during the Committee of Ministers' examination of the execution of a judgment.[123]

Paragraphs 4 and 5 of Article 46 empower the Committee of Ministers to bring infringement proceedings before the Court. On the basis of paragraph 4 the Committee of Ministers may – if it considers that a High Contracting Party has refused to abide by a final judgment in a case to which it is a party, after serving formal notice on that party and by decision adopted by a majority vote of two-thirds of the representatives entitled to sit on the Committee – refer to the Court the question of whether that Party has failed to fulfil its obligation under paragraph 1. If the Court finds a violation of paragraph 1, it shall refer the case to the Committee of Ministers for consideration of the measures to be taken. If the Court finds no violation of paragraph 1, it shall return the case to the Committee of Ministers, which shall close its examination of the case.[124] Article 46 thus introduces a wider range of measures of bringing pressure to secure execution of judgments. Before the introduction of this possibility, the ultimate measure available to the Committee of Ministers was recourse to Article 8 of the Statute of the Council of Europe (suspension of voting rights in the Committee of Ministers or even expulsion from the Council of Europe), which in most cases would be an overkill.

10.2. COMPOSITION

The Committee of Ministers consists of one representative from each Member State of the Council of Europe – as a rule the Minister for Foreign Affairs. In case of the latter's inability to be present, or if other circumstances make it desirable, an alternate may be nominated, who shall, whenever possible, be a member of government (Article 14 of the Statute). In practice, the Committee has one session annually at the level of the Ministers. In the intervening periods its duties are discharged by the so-called 'Committee of the Ministers' Deputies', consisting of high officials who are generally the permanent representatives of their governments to the Council of Europe and who meet weekly.[125] Every representative on the Committee of Ministers appoints an alternate (Rule 14 of the Rules of the Committee of Ministers).

---

[123] Explanatory Report to Protocol No. 14, para. 97.
[124] Art. 46(5) of the Convention.
[125] <www.coe.int/en/web/cm>.

10.3. SESSIONS

The sessions of the Committee of Ministers are not public, unless the Committee decides otherwise (Article 21(a) of the Statute). In principle, the rules of procedure that apply to the Committee as executive organ of the Council of Europe are equally applicable to its functions within the context of the Convention.

11. SECRETARY-GENERAL OF THE COUNCIL OF EUROPE

The Secretary-General of the Council of Europe also plays a part within the framework of the Convention. The Secretary-General is the highest official of the Council of Europe and is elected for a once renewable period of five years by the Parliamentary Assembly from a list of candidates which is drawn up by the Committee of Ministers (Article 36 of the Statute of the Council of Europe).

The Secretary-General is involved in the Convention system in various ways, on the one hand by reason of his administrative functions as they result from the Statute of the Council of Europe, and on the other hand in connection with a specific supervisory task created by the Convention.

Ratifications of the Convention must be deposited with the Secretary-General (Article 59(1)), who has to notify the Members of the Council of Europe of the entry into force of the Convention and keep them informed of the names of the states which have become parties to the Convention (Article 59(5)).[126] A denunciation of the Convention must also be notified to the Secretary-General, who informs the other Contracting States (Article 58). Deposition with the Secretary-General is also required for the notification by which a state declares that the Convention extends to a territory for whose international relations that state is responsible (Article 56(1)).

Moreover, the Secretary-General fulfils an important administrative function under Article 15(3) of the Convention. Any state availing itself under Article 15 of the right to derogate from one or more provisions of the Convention in time of war or another emergency threatening the life of the nation, must keep the Secretary-General fully informed of the measures taken in that context and the reasons therefor. It must also inform him when such measures have ceased to operate.

The most important function assigned to the Secretary-General in the Convention, however, is of quite a different nature. Under Article 52 he has the task of supervising the effective implementation by the Contracting States of the provisions of the Convention. This supervisory task of the Secretary-General will be dealt with in Chapter 4.

---

[126]   The same applies for Protocols to the Convention.

12. RIGHT OF COMPLAINT OF STATES

12.1. INTRODUCTION

What is called here the 'right of complaint' under the Convention is the right to take the initiative for the supervisory procedure provided for in the Convention on the ground that the Convention has allegedly been violated by a Contracting State. The Convention differentiates between the right of complaint for states on the one hand (Article 33) and that for individuals on the other hand (Article 34).

When the Convention enters into force for a state, that state acquires the right to lodge, through the Secretary-General, an application with the Court on the ground of an alleged violation of one or more provisions of the Convention by another Contracting State.[127]

12.2. OBJECTIVE CHARACTER

This right of complaint for states constitutes an important divergence from the traditional principles of international law concerning inter-state action. According to these principles a state can bring an international action against another state only when a right of the former is at stake, or when that state takes up the case of one of its nationals whom it considers to have been treated by the other state in a way contrary to the rules of international law – so-called 'diplomatic protection'.

Under the Convention a state may also lodge a complaint about violations committed against persons who are not its nationals or against persons who are not nationals of any of the Contracting States or are stateless, and even about violations against nationals of the respondent state. States may equally lodge a complaint about the incompatibility with the Convention of legislation or an administrative practice of another state without having to allege a violation of a right of any specified person – the so-called 'abstract applications'. Thus, the right of complaint for states assumes the character of an *actio popularis*: any Contracting State has the right to lodge a complaint about any alleged violation of the Convention, regardless of whether there is a special relationship between the rights and interests of the applicant state and the alleged violation.

In the *Pfunders* case between Austria and Italy, the Commission stressed that a state which brings an application under Article 33, 'is not to be regarded as exercising a right of action for the purpose of enforcing its own rights, but

---

[127]   For an overview: <www.echr.coe.int/Documents/InterStates_applications_ENG.pdf>.

rather as bringing before the Commission an alleged violation of the public order of Europe'.[128] The Court similarly held that, unlike international treaties of the classic kind, 'the Convention comprises more than mere reciprocal engagements between Contracting States. It creates, over and above a network of mutual, bilateral undertakings, objective obligations which, in the words of the Preamble, benefit from a "collective enforcement"'.[129] The supervisory procedure provided for in the Convention, therefore, has an objective character; its aim is to protect the fundamental rights of individuals against violations by the Contracting States, rather than to implement mutual rights and obligations between those states. This objective character of the procedure is also reflected in other respects, which will be mentioned later.[130]

Clear examples of inter-state applications within the framework of the 'collective enforcement' mentioned by the Court are the applications of Denmark, Norway, Sweden and the Netherlands of September 1967 and the joint application of the three Scandinavian countries of April 1970 against Greece,[131] and the application of the Scandinavian countries, France and the Netherlands of July 1982 against Turkey.[132] The complaints against Greece were in fact lodged at the instance of the Parliamentary Assembly[133], which considered it the duty of the Contracting States to lodge an application under Article 33 in the case of an alleged serious violation.[134]It illustrates to what extent the Parliamentary Assembly was concerned about the situation in Greece and believed that the mechanism of collective guarantees of human rights had to be used if it did not wanted to become 'meaningless'.[135]

---

[128] *Austria v. Italy*, EComHR 11 January 1961, appl. no. 788/60, Yearbook VI (1961), *supra* n. 27, p. 116 (140). See also *France, Norway, Denmark, Sweden and the Netherlands v. Turkey*, EComHR 6 December 1983, appl. nos. 9940–9944/82, D&R 35 (1984), p. 143 (169); *Chrysostomos, Papachrysostomou* and *Loizidou v. Turkey*, EComHR 4 March 1991, appl. nos. 15299/89, 15300/89 and 15318/89, D&R 68 (1991), p. 216 (242).

[129] *Ireland v. the United Kingdom*, ECtHR (GC) 18 January 1978, appl. no. 5310/71, *supra* n. 83, para. 239; report of *Cyprus v. Turkey*, EComHR 4 October 1983, appl. no. 8007/77, D&R 72 (1992), p. 5 (19), where the Commission further noted that a government cannot avoid this collective enforcement by not recognising the government of the applicant state.

[130] See *infra* 13.3.

[131] *Denmark, Norway, Sweden and the Netherlands v. Greece*, EComHR 31 May 1968 (dec.), appl. nos. 3321–3323/67 and 3344/67 Yearbook XI (1968), p. 690, and *Denmark, Norway and Sweden v. Greece*, EComHR 16 July 1970, appl. no. 4448/70, Yearbook XIII (1970), *supra* n. 70, p. 108.

[132] *France, Norway, Denmark, Sweden and the Netherlands v. Turkey*, EComHR 6 December 1983, appl. nos. 9940–9944/82, D&R 35 (1984), *supra* n. 127, p. 143.

[133] Res. 346 (1967), 'On the situation in Greece', Council of Europe, Cons. Ass., Nineteenth Ordinary Session, Second Part, 25–28 September 1967, *Texts Adopted*.

[134] See also: Y. Tyagi, 'The Denunciation of Human Rights Treaties', *British Yearbook on International Law 2008*, Oxford: Oxford University Press, 2009, pp. 157–160.

[135] Res. 346 (1967), 'On the situation in Greece', Council of Europe, Cons. Ass., Nineteenth Ordinary Session, Second Part, 25–28 September 1967, Texts Adopted.

12.3. CASES OF SPECIAL INTEREST TO CONTRACTING STATES

The Convention, of course, at the same time protects the particular interests of the Contracting States when they claim that the rights set forth in the Convention must be secured to their nationals coming under the jurisdiction of another Contracting State. And even though states have the right to initiate a procedure in which they have no special interest, in practice they will more readily be inclined to bring an application when there has been a violation against persons who are their nationals or with whom they have some other special link.

A case in which the applicant state's own nationals were involved occurred for the first time when Cyprus brought applications against Turkey concerning the treatment of nationals of Cyprus during the Turkish invasion and the subsequent occupation of that island.[136] In total, three applications emanated from this dispute.[137] In November 1994, Cyprus lodged another complaint against Turkey. The Court found that several articles of the Convention had been violated.[138] A complaint filed by Denmark against Turkey in 1997 was struck out of the list in 2000. Recent examples of inter-state applications concern Russia. Georgia has lodged applications against Russia[139] and so did Ukraine.[140] In both cases, the complaints have arisen due to the political and military tensions between Russia and its neighbours.

Examples of applications concerning persons with whom the applicant state had a special relationship other than the link of nationality are the applications of Greece against the United Kingdom, which concerned the treatment of Cypriots of Greek origin.[141] Further, Austria lodged a complaint in the so-called *Pfunders* case in connection with the prosecution of six young men by Italy for the murder of an Italian customs officer in the boundary region of Alto Adige (South Tyrol) disputed by both States.[142] Finally, the applications of Ireland against the United Kingdom concerned the treatment of, and the legislation

---

[136]   *Cyprus v. Turkey*, EComHR 26 May 1975 (dec.), appl. nos. 6780/74 and 6950/75, Yearbook XVIII (1975), p. 82.

[137]   See also *Cyprus v. Turkey*, EComHR 4 October 1983, appl. no. 8007/77, Yearbook XX (1977), p. 98.

[138]   *Cyprus v. Turkey*, ECtHR (GC) 10 May 2001, appl. no. 25781/94, *supra* n. 50.

[139]   *Georgia v. Russia (No. 1)*, ECtHR (GC) 3 July 2014, appl. nos. 13255/07, 38263/08 and 61186/09.

[140]   *Ukraine v. Russia*, ECtHR 1 September 2015, appl. nos. 20958/14, 43800/14, 49537/14 and 42410/15.

[141]   *Greece v. the United Kingdom*, EComHR 2 June 1956 (dec.), appl. nos. 176/56 and 299/57, Yearbook II (1958–1959), pp. 182 and 186, respectively.

[142]   *Austria v. Italy*, EComHR 11 January 1961, appl. no. 788/60, Yearbook IV (1961), *supra* n. 27, p. 116.

concerning Roman Catholics in Northern Ireland, who aspire for union with the Irish Republic.[143]

12.4. ADMISSIBILITY

In order for state complaints to be admissible hardly any *prima facie* evidence is required. The Commission deduced from the English text (alleged breach) and from the French wording (*qu'elle croira pouvoir être imputé*) that the mere allegation of such a breach was, in principle, sufficient under this provision (Article 24; the present Article 33).[144] The Commission based this point of view on the fact that the provisions of Article 27(2) [the present Article 34(3)] 'empowering it to declare inadmissible any petition submitted under Article 25 [the present Article 34], which it considers either incompatible with the provisions of the Convention or "manifestly ill-founded" apply, according to their express terms, to individual applications under Article 25 [the present Article 34] only, and that, consequently, any examination of the merits of State applications must in such cases be entirely reserved for the post-admissibility stage.'[145]

On the other hand, the Commission was of the opinion that Article 27 [the present Article 35] did not exclude the application of the general rule according to which an application under Article 24 [the present Article 33] may be declared inadmissible if it is clear from the outset that it is wholly unsubstantiated or otherwise lacking the requirements of a genuine allegation in the sense of Article 24 [the present Article 33] of the Convention.[146]

The Commission held, on the other hand, that the rule requiring the exhaustion of domestic remedies applied not only to individual applications lodged under Article 34 but also to cases brought by states under Article 33 of the Convention.[147]

12.5. PRACTICE

Up to December 2016 a total of 27 applications had been lodged by states. Even this very low number provides a distorted picture. In fact, only six situations in different states have been put forward in Strasbourg by means of an inter-state

---

[143] *Ireland v. the United Kingdom*, EComHR 1 October 1972, appl. nos. 5310/71 and 5451/72, Yearbook XV (1972), p. 76.

[144] *France, Norway, Denmark, Sweden and the Netherlands v. Turkey*, EComHR 6 December 1983, appl. nos. 9940–9944/82, D&R 35 (1984), *supra* n. 127, p. 143 (161).

[145] *Ibid.*

[146] *Ibid.*, p. 162.

[147] *Cyprus v. Turkey*, EComHR 28 June 1996 (dec.), appl. no. 25781/94, D&R 86-B (1996), p. 104 (139).

application. In the 1950s Greece complained twice about the conduct of the United Kingdom in Cyprus; Austria filed a complaint in 1960 about the course of events during proceedings against South Tyrolean activists in Italy; the five applications of the Scandinavian countries and the Netherlands concerned the situation in Greece during the military regime; Ireland lodged two applications against the United Kingdom about the activities of the military and the police in Ulster; and all four applications of Cyprus were connected with the Turkish invasion of that island, while the five applications in 1982 all related to the situation in Turkey under the military regime. The complaint by Denmark against Turkey concerned the treatment of a Danish citizen in a Turkish prison. The more recent complaints concern, as indicated before, the difficult relations between Russia and some of its neighbouring States (three by Georgia, and four by Ukraine).

Given the number of violations that have occurred during the more than 50 years that the Convention has been in force, it is evident that the right of complaint of states has not proved to be a very effective supervisory tool. The idea contained in the Preamble – as it was also formulated by the Commission in the *Pfunders* case and by the Court in *Ireland v. the United Kingdom*, *viz.* that the Contracting States were to guarantee the protection of the rights and freedoms collectively – has hardly materialised. Save for two instances,[148] the Contracting States have not been willing to lodge complaints about situations in other states where no special interest of their own was involved. Such a step is generally considered to run counter to their interest in that charging another state with violating the Convention is bound to be considered an unfriendly act by the other party, with all the political repercussions that may be involved. Moreover, an application by a state that does have a special interest of its own may create negative effects in that it may stir up the underlying conflict.

In comparison with inter-state applications individual complaints have the advantage that in general political considerations will not play as important a part.[149] For this reason as well it is of the utmost importance that individual complaints may now be lodged against all Contracting States. At the time when some Contracting States had not recognised the individual right of complaint, the inter-state procedure – apart from the remedy of Article 52, which so far has not functioned very adequately – was the only mechanism for supervising the observance by all Contracting States of their obligations under the Convention. That situation was far from satisfactory.

---

[148] The applications of the Scandinavian countries and the Netherlands against Greece in 1967 and 1970 and the applications of France, the Netherlands and the Scandinavian countries against Turkey in 1982.

[149] Here, too, political motives may sometimes constitute the real incentive for an application, while even if that is not the case, the application may have some political implications.

13. RIGHT OF COMPLAINT OF INDIVIDUALS

13.1. INTRODUCTION

Article 34 undoubtedly constitutes the most progressive provision of the Convention. It has removed the principal limitation by which the position of the individual in international law was traditionally characterised. One improvement as compared to the traditional practice of diplomatic protection was brought about by the elimination of the condition of the link of nationality in the case of an action by a state. However, the individual right of complaint, despite its limitations, constituted an even greater improvement over the classic system. It is precisely because states are generally reluctant to submit an application against another state that the individual right of complaint constitutes a necessary expedient for achieving the aim of the Convention, to secure the rights and freedoms of individuals against the states.

The importance of the individual right of complaint for the functioning of the supervisory system under the European Convention becomes clear from the large number of individual applications that have been submitted. In 2016, 53,500 applications were assigned to either a single judge, a Committee or a Chamber. However, to put these figures in context, it is worth highlighting that in that same year 38,505 applications were decided by the Court: 36,579 were declared inadmissible or struck out and 1,926 were decided by judgement. On 31 December 2016, a total of 79,750 applications were pending before the Court.[150] Although this is a considerable number, it is a significant decrease with regard of the backlog of 151,600 applications pending in 2012.

13.2. REQUIREMENTS

Anyone who in a relevant respect is subject to the jurisdiction of a State Party and is allegedly a victim of a violation of the Convention by that state may lodge an application. The nationality of the applicant is irrelevant. This means that the right of complaint is conferred not only on the nationals of the state concerned, but also on those of other Contracting States, on the nationals of states which are not parties to the Convention, and on stateless persons, provided that they satisfy the condition referred to in Article 1. This entails that they were subject to the jurisdiction of the respondent state at the moment the violation allegedly took place. Lack of legal capacity does not affect the natural person's right of complaint. In several cases, the Court held that minors have the right, of their own accord and without being represented by their guardians, to

---

[150]   <www.echr.coe.int/Documents/Stats_analysis_2016_ENG.pdf>.

lodge a complaint.[151] In the *Scozzari and Giunta* case, the Court held that 'In particular, minors can apply to the Court even, or indeed especially, if they are represented by a mother who is in conflict with the authorities and criticizes their decisions and conduct as not being consistent with the rights guaranteed by the Convention. Like the Commission, the Court considers that in the event of a conflict over a minor's interests between a natural parent and the person appointed by the authorities to act as the child's guardian, there is a danger that some of those interests will never be brought to the Court's attention and that the minor will be deprived of effective protection of his rights under the Convention. Consequently, as the Commission observed, even though the mother has been deprived of parental rights – indeed that is one of the causes of the dispute which she has referred to the Court – her standing as the natural mother suffices to afford her the necessary power to apply to the Court on the children's behalf, too, in order to protect their interests.'[152] The same applies to persons who have lost their legal capacity after being committed to a psychiatric hospital.[153]

Besides individuals, non-governmental organisations and groups of persons may also file an application. With respect to the last-mentioned category the Commission decided during its first session that these must be groups which have been established in a regular way according to the law of one of the Contracting States. If that is not the case, the application must have been signed by all the persons belonging to the group.[154] As to the category of non-governmental organisations, the Commission decided that they must be *private* organisations, and that municipalities, for instance, cannot be considered as such.[155] In the *Danderyds Kommun* case, the Court held in this respect that it is not only the central organs of the state that are clearly governmental organisations, as opposed to non-governmental organisations, but also decentralised authorities that exercise public functions, notwithstanding the extent of their autonomy *vis-à-vis* the central organs. This is the case even

---

151 See, *e.g.*, *Nielsen v. Denmark*, ECtHR 28 November 1988, appl. no. 10929/84, para. 58.

152 *Scozzari and Giunta v. Italy*, ECtHR (GC) 13 July 2000, appl. nos. 39221/98 and 41963/98, para. 138; *Covezzi and Morselli v. Italy*, ECtHR 24 January 2002, appl. no. 52763/99, paras. 103–105. Persons lacking legal capacity under domestic law may can have standing before the ECHR without the approval of their guardian. *Zehentner v. Austria*, ECtHR 16 July 2009, appl. no. 20082/02, paras. 39–40.

153 *Winterwerp v. The Netherlands*, ECtHR 24 October 1979, appl. no. 6301/73, para. 10; *Van der Leer v. The Netherlands*, ECtHR 21 February 1990, appl. no. 11509/85, para. 6; *Herczegfalvy v. Austria*, ECtHR 24 September 1992, appl. no. 10533/83, para. 13; *Croke v. Ireland*, ECtHR 15 June 1999, appl. no. 33267/96; *Valle v. Finland*, ECtHR 16 March 2000, appl. no. 28808/95.

154 See the report of the session: DH(54)3, p. 8.

155 *Sixteen Austrian Communes and some of their Councillors v. Austria*, EComHR 31 May 1974, appl. nos. 5767/72, 5922/72, 5929–5931/72, 5953–5957/72, 5984–5988/73 and 6011/73, Yearbook XVII (1974), p. 338 (352); *Ayuntamiento M. v. Spain*, EComHR 7 January 1991, appl. no. 15090/89, D&R 68 (1991), p. 209 (214); *Consejo General de Colegios Oficiales de Economistas de Espaòa v. Spain*, EComHR 28 June 1995, appl. nos. 26114/95 and 26455/95, D&R 82 (1995), p. 150.

if the municipality is claiming that in this particular situation it is acting as a private organ.[156] *Radio France*, however, was considered a non-governmental organisation, notwithstanding its public service mission and its public funding, because of its organic independence and the pluralist media landscape in which it operates.[157]

A wide range of organisations, such as newspapers,[158] churches and other religious institutions,[159] associations,[160] political parties[161] and companies[162] have submitted applications. Although the rights and freedoms laid down in the Convention apply to individuals as well as to non-governmental organisations, some of the rights and freedoms are by their nature not susceptible of being exercised by a legal person. Insofar as Article 9 is concerned, the Strasbourg organs have made a distinction between the freedom of conscience and the freedom of religion. In contrast to freedom of religion,[163] freedom of conscience cannot be exercised by a legal person.[164] The right not to be subjected to degrading treatment and punishment can also not be exercised by a legal person[165] and the same holds good for respect to the right to education.[166] The Court and the Commission have also examined complaints brought by a trade union concerning collective aspects of trade union freedom[167] including strike action.[168]

---

[156]   *Danderyds Kommun v. Sweden*, ECtHR 7 June 2001, appl. no. 52559/99.

[157]   *Radio France and Others v. France*, ECtHR 30 March 2004, appl. no. 53984/00.

[158]   *Association Ekin v. France*, ECtHR 17 July 2001, appl. no. 39288/98, para. 38; *Alithia Publishing Company v. Cyprus*, ECtHR 11 July 2002, appl. no. 53594/99, para. 1.

[159]   *Christian Association Jehovah's Witnesses v. Bulgaria*, EComHR 3 July 1997, appl. no. 28626/95; *The Holy Monasteries v. Greece*, ECtHR 9 December 1994, appl. nos. 13092/87 and 13984/88, paras. 48–49; *Metropolitan Church of Bessarabia and Others v. Moldova*, ECtHR 13 December 2001, appl. no. 45701/99, para. 101.

[160]   *Wilson, National Union of Journalists and Others v. The United Kingdom*, ECtHR 2 July 2002, 30668/96, 30671/96 and 30678/96, para. 41.

[161]   *Freedom and Democracy Party (Özdep) v. Turkey*, ECtHR (GC) 8 December 1999, appl. no. 23885/94; *Refah Partisi (The Welfare Party) and Others v. Turkey*, ECtHR (GC) 31 July 2001, appl. nos. 41340/98, 41342/98, 41343/98 and 41344/98.

[162]   *AGOSI v. The United Kingdom*, ECtHR 24 October 1986, appl. no. 9118/80, para. 25; *Tre Traktörer Aktiebolag v. Sweden*, ECtHR 7 July 1989, appl. no. 10873/84, para. 35.

[163]   *Metropolitan Church of Bessarabia and Others v. Moldova*, ECtHR 13 December 2001, appl. no. 45701/99, *supra* n. 158, para. 101; *Cha'are Shalom Ve Tsedek v. France*, ECtHR (GC) 27 June 2000, appl. no. 27417/95, para. 72.

[164]   *Verein 'Kontakt-Information-Therapie' (KIT) and Hagen v. Austria*, EComHR 12 October 1988 (dec.), appl. no. 11921/86, D&R 57 (1988), p. 81 (88).

[165]   *Idem*; *Identoba and Others v. Georgia*, ECtHR 12 May 2015, appl. no. 73235/12.

[166]   *Ingrid Jordebo Foundation of Christian Schools and Ingrid Jordebo v. Sweden*, EComHR 6 March 1987 (dec.), appl. no. 11533/85, D&R 51 (1987), p. 125 (128).

[167]   *National Union of Belgian Police v. Belgium*, ECtHR 27 October 1975, appl. no. 4464/70, paras. 38–42; *Swedish Engine Drivers' Union v. Sweden*, ECtHR 6 February 1976, appl. no. 5614/72, *supra* n. 82, paras. 35–43; *Federation of Offshore Workers' Trade Union and Others v. Norway*, ECtHR 27 June 2002, appl. no. 38190/97.

[168]   *UNISON v. the United Kingdom*, ECtHR 10 January 2002, appl. no. 53574/99.

In other cases, too, it was stressed that some of the rights and freedoms included in the Convention apply only to natural persons. In the case of *X Union v. France* the Commission stated: 'In the present case, the applicant union as a legal person does not itself claim to be the victim of an infringement of the right to free choice of residence guaranteed by Article 2 of Protocol No. 4, since the legislative restrictions in question are only applicable to natural persons. (...) It might however be considered that the application really emanates from the members of the union, which is empowered (...) to initiate proceedings on behalf of its members. (...) However, it is noted in this context that the petition does not mention any specific case of one or more teachers alleged to be subjected to a measure constituting an infringement.'[169]

Obviously, other rights or freedoms are clearly applicable to legal persons. In the case of *A. Association and H v. Austria*, lodged by a political party and its chairman/legal representative alleging violation of Article 11 because of the prohibition of a meeting, the Commission held that, as the right invoked could be exercised by both the organiser of a meeting, even if it is a legal person as in the present case, and by individual participants, both applicants could claim to be victims of a violation of their rights under Article 11.[170]

13.3. VICTIM

a. Introduction

Whereas states may complain about 'any alleged breach of the provisions of the Convention and the Protocols thereto by another High Contracting Party' (Article 33), and consequently also about national legislation or administrative practices *in abstracto*, individuals must claim 'to be the victim of a violation by one of the High Contracting Parties of the rights set forth in this Convention and the Protocols thereto' (Article 34). Further to the Court's well-established case law, the concept of 'victim' must be 'interpreted autonomously and irrespective of domestic concepts such as those concerning an interest or capacity to act'.[171]

The special relationship required is that the individual applicant himself is the victim of the alleged violation.[172] He may not bring an *actio popularis*, nor

---

[169]   *X. Union v. France*, EComHR 4 May 1983, appl. no. 9900/82, D&R 32 (1983), p. 261 (264).

[170]   *A. Association and H. v. Austria*, EComHR 15 March 1984, appl. no. 9905/82, D&R 36 (1984), p. 187 (191–192).

[171]   *Gorraiz Lizarraga and Others v. Spain*, ECtHR 27 April 2004, appl. no. 62543/00, para. 35; *Vallianatos and Others v. Greece*, ECtHR (GC) 7 November 2013, appl. nos. 29381/09 and 32684/09, para. 47.

[172]   This question remains relevant throughout the examination of the application: *D. v. Federal Republic of Germany*, EComHR 15 March 1984, appl. no. 9320/81, D&R 36 (1984), p. 24 (30–31).

may he submit abstract complaints.[173] The Commission held that the mere fact that trade unions considered themselves as guardians of the collective interests of their members, did not suffice to make them victims within the meaning of Article 34, of measures affecting those members.[174]

However, sometimes situations can be more nuanced. An individual application may be concerned not only with the personal interest of the applicant, but also with the public interest. A good example are cases concerning environmental pollution and nuisances, which can affect the applicant parties as well as other people living in the same places or even wider regions.[175]

Consequently, the procedure that originates from an individual complaint may in some respects also assume an objective character. Thus, the Commission adopted the view that, on the ground of the general function assigned to it in Article 19 [old] 'to ensure the observance of the engagements undertaken by the High Contracting Parties in the present Convention', it was competent to examine *ex officio*, also in case of an application by an individual, whether there had been a violation. It did not need to confine itself to an examination of the violations expressly alleged by the applicant.[176] The Court followed this approach, stressing that it is master of the 'characterisation' of the complaint.[177]

Another implication of this objective character was manifested in the Commission's view that, when an applicant withdraws his or her application or no longer shows any interest in the case, the procedure does not necessarily come to an end, but might be pursued in the public interest. Thus, in its decision in the *Gericke* case, the Commission expressly held 'that the interests served by the protection of human rights and fundamental freedoms guaranteed by the Convention extend beyond the individual interests of the persons concerned; (…) whereas, consequently, the withdrawal of an application and the respondent

---

173   *Klass and Others v. Germany*, ECtHR (GC) 6 September 1978, appl. no. 5029/71, para. 33; *Marckx v. Belgium*, ECtHR 13 June 1979, appl. no. 6833/74, para. 27; *Di Lazzaro v. Italy*, EComHR 10 July 1997, appl. no. 31924/96, D&R 90, p. 134; *İlhan v. Turkey*, ECtHR (GC) 27 June 2000, appl. no. 22277/93, para. 52; *Christian Federation of Jehova's Witnesses of France v. France*, ECtHR 6 November 2001, appl. no. 53430/99. *Burden v. The United Kingdom*, ECtHR (GC) 29 April 2008, appl. no. 13378/05, par. 23; *Roman Zakharov v. Russia*, ECtHR (GC) 4 December 2015, appl. no. 47143/06, par. 164; *G.J. v. Spain*, ECtHR 21 June 2016, appl. no. 59172/12.

174   *Purcell v. Ireland*, EComHR 16 April 1991, appl. no. 15404/89, D&R 70 (1991), p. 262 (273); *Greek Federation of Customs Officers, Gialouris and Others v. Greece*, EComHR 6 April 1995 (dec.), appl. no. 24581/94, D&R 81, p. 123.

175   *López Ostra v. Spain*, ECtHR 9 December 1994, appl. no. 16798/90, para. 42; *Di Sarno and Others v. Italy*, ECtHR 10 January 2012, appl. no. 30765/08, para. 81.

176   See, e.g., *X. v. Belgium*, EComHR 28 September 1956, appl. no. 202/56, Yearbook I (1955–1957), p. 190 (192) and *Foti, Lentini and Cenerini and Others v. Italy*, ECtHR 10 December 1982, appl. nos. 7604/76, 7719/76 and 7781/77, D&R 14 (1979), p. 133 (143).

177   *Lupeni Greek Catholic Parish and Others v. Romania*, ECtHR (GC) 29 November 2016, appl. no. 76943/11, para. 67; *Karrer v. Romania*, ECtHR 21 February 2012, appl. no. 16965/10, para. 25.; *Guerra and Others v. Italy*, ECtHR (GC) 19 February 1998, appl. no. 14967/89, para. 44.

Government's agreement thereto cannot deprive the Commission of the competence to pursue its examination of the case.'[178]

A similar reasoning was developed in the *Karner* case.[179]

For his application to be admissible the applicant is not required to *prove* that he is the victim of the alleged violation. Article 34 only provides that the applicant must be a person 'claiming to be the victim' (*qui se prétend victime*).[180] However, this does not mean that the mere submission of the applicant that he is a victim is in itself sufficient. The test is whether, assuming that the alleged violation has taken place, it is to be deemed plausible that the applicant is a victim, on the basis of the facts submitted by the applicant and the facts, if any, advanced against them by the defendant state. If this is not the case, the application is declared 'incompatible with the provisions of the present Convention' and, on the ground of Article 27(2) [the present Article 35(2)], pronounced inadmissible.[181] On the other hand, even if the applicant does not expressly submit that he is the victim of the challenged act or omission, the application may still be declared admissible if there appears to be sufficient ground for this.[182]

In the *Gayduk* case, the applicants alleged a violation of Article 1 of Protocol I. However, the Court held that it did not appear from the material in the case file that any of them had sought to exercise a property right. On the contrary, some of the applicants had stated that they had no need of the initial deposits and had emphasised that the main purpose of their applications was to recover the indexed amounts. In these circumstances, and insofar as the applications concerned repayment of the deposits themselves, the Court found that the

---

[178] *Gericke v. Federal Republic of Germany*, ECtHR 16 December 1964, appl. no. 2294/64, Yearbook VIII (1965), p. 314 (320). See also *Heinz Kornmann v. Federal Republic of Germany*, EComHR 24 May 1966, appl. no. 2686/65, Yearbook IX (1966), p. 494 (506–508).

[179] *Karner v. Austria*, ECtHR 24 July 2003, appl. no. 40016/98, para. 27.

[180] An amendment to replace these words by 'which has been the victim', tabled at the Consultative Assembly, was withdrawn after discussion, because it was recognised that this was a 'right to complain from the point of view of procedure' and not a 'substantial right of action': Council of Europe, Cons. Ass., First Session, Fourth Part, *Reports*, 1949, pp. 1272–1274.

[181] See, *e.g.*, *X. v. the Netherlands*, ECtHR 13 December 1965, appl. no. 1983/63, Yearbook IX (1966), p. 286 (304). In a few cases the Commission declared the application 'manifestly ill-founded' because in its view the applicant could not be regarded as a victim: see, *e.g.*, *X. v. Austria*, EComHR 1 June 1967, appl. no. 2291/64, Coll. 24 (1967), p. 20 (33 and 35); and *X v. Federal Republic of Germany*, EComHR 1 April 1974, appl. no. 4653/70, Yearbook XVII (1974), p. 148 (178). This also leads to a declaration of inadmissibility, but the ground was indicated wrongly here, since the question of whether the application is well-founded depends on whether there has been a violation of the Convention, not on the question of the effect of such a violation, if any, for the applicant. See also the decision of *Očić v. Croatia*, ECtHR 25 November 1999, appl. no. 46306/99 where the Court observed that there was no sufficiently direct connection between the applicant as such and the injury he maintained he suffered as a result of the alleged breach of the Convention.

[182] See, *e.g.*, *X v. Federal Republic of Germany*, EComHR 17 December 1955, appl. no. 99/55, Yearbook I (1955–1957), p. 160 (161).

applicants could not claim to have standing as 'victims' within the meaning of Article 34 of the Convention.[183]

In the *Lacko* case, the applicants complained that by publicly and formally referring to certain persons as *Roma*, i.e. their ethnic identity, by singling out such persons for special treatment, by prohibiting them from entering and settling in the respective municipalities and by publicly threatening to enforce such exclusion orders through physical expulsion the Slovakian authorities discriminated against them on the grounds of their race and ethnicity in a manner which constituted degrading treatment. The Court noted that the third applicant had not alleged that he lived or intended to live in the settlements and it did not appear from the documents submitted that he needed to visit those municipalities and was prevented from doing so. In these circumstances, the Court considered that the third applicant could not claim to be a victim of a violation of his rights under Article 2 of Protocol No. 4, taken alone or in conjunction with Article 14 of the Convention.[184] In any event, mere suspicion and conjecture will be insufficient as to 'prove' victimhood.[185]

b. Personally affected

The requirement of 'victim' implies that the violation of the Convention must have *affected* the applicant in some way. According to the Court's well-established case law 'the word "victim" in Article 34 refers to the person directly affected by the act or omission at issue'.[186] To this the Court usually adds, however, a phrase of the sort that 'the existence of a violation being conceivable even in the absence of prejudice; prejudice is relevant only in the context of Article 41'.[187] In the *Gayduk* case, the Court held that the issue of whether an applicant may claim to be a 'victim' within the meaning of Article 34 of the

---

[183] *Gayduk and Others v. Ukraine*, ECtHR 2 July 2002, appl. nos. 45526/99, 46099/99, 47088/99, 47176/99, 47177/99, 48018/99, 48043/99, 48071/99, 48580/99, 48624/99, 49426/99, 50354/99, 51934/99, 51938/99, 53423/99, 53424/99, 54120/00, 54124/00, 54136/00, 55542/00 and 56019/00.

[184] *Gayduk and Others v. Ukraine*, ECtHR 2 July 2002, appl. nos. 45526/99, 46099/99, 47088/99, 47176/99, 47177/99, 48018/99, 48043/99, 48071/99, 48580/99, 48624/99, 49426/99, 50354/99, 51934/99, 51938/99, 53423/99, 53424/99, 54120/00, 54124/00, 54136/00, 55542/00 and 56019/00.

[185] *Senator Lines GmbH v. Austria, Belgium, Denmark, Finland, France, Germany, Greece, Ireland, Italy, Luxembourg, The Netherlands, Portugal, Spain, Sweden and The United Kingdom*, ECtHR (GC) 10 March 2004, appl. no. 55672/00; *Segi and Others & Gestoras Pro-Amnistia and Others v. 15 states of the European Union*, 23 May 2002, appl. nos. 6422/02 and 9916/02.

[186] *Lüdi v. Switzerland*, ECtHR 15 June 1992, appl. no. 12433/86, para. 34. See also the judgment of *Groppera Radio AG and Others v. Switzerland*, ECtHR 28 March 1990, appl. no. 10890/84, para. 47; *Buckley v. The United Kingdom*, ECtHR 25 September 1996, appl. no. 20348/92, paras. 56–59; *Valmont v. The United Kingdom*, ECtHR 23 March 1999, appl. no. 36385/97; *Skubenko v. Ukraine*, ECtHR 6 April 2004, appl. no. 41152/98.

[187] *İlhan v. Turkey*, ECtHR (GC) 27 June 2000, appl. no. 22277/93, *supra* n. 172, para. 52.

Convention does not turn on the substance or content of the right in issue, but solely on the question of whether it is linked to the person who relies on it.[188]

The requirement that the applicant be *personally* affected by the alleged violation was stressed by the Commission right from the beginning. Thus, an application in which it was submitted that the Norwegian legislation concerning *abortus provocatus* conflicted with Article 2(1) of the Convention, was declared inadmissible because of the fact that the applicant had not alleged that he himself was the victim of this legislation, but had lodged his application "on behalf of parents who without their own consent or knowledge (...) have or will have their offspring taken away by abortus provocatus, and on behalf of those taken away by such operations".[189]

The 'personal' link may be open to debate in cases in which the victim dies during the procedure in Strasbourg. The Court accepts that, as a general rule, heirs may continue a pending procedure as long as they have an interest in it and have expressed the wish to continue.[190] However, there are exceptions to this principle. In the *Levi* case, the Court stressed that heirs of applicants cannot be seen as victims of a violation of Article 6 of the Convention, unless they were party themselves to the domestic proceedings or already involved in those proceedings as heirs.[191]

c. *Potential and future victim*

The Commission and the Court have accepted as victims in the sense of Article 34 a category of persons of whom it could not be ascertained with certainty that they had suffered an injury. The reason for this acceptance was due to the fact that the applicants could not know whether the challenged legislation had or had not been applied to them. This matter came up in the *Klass* case. Three lawyers, a judge and a public prosecutor alleged violation of the secrecy of their mail and telecommunications by the authorities. The measures concerned were secret insofar that the persons in question were not informed of them in all cases, and if they were informed, then only afterwards. The Court concluded that 'an individual may, *under certain conditions*, claim to be the victim of a violation occasioned by the mere existence of secret measures or of legislation permitting secret measures, without having to allege that such measures were in fact applied to him'.[192] The principle of effectiveness (*l'effet utile*), according to the

---

[188]   *Gayduk and Others v. Ukraine*, ECtHR 2 July 2002, appl. nos. 45526/99, 46099/99, 47088/99, 47176/99, 47177/99, 48018/99, 48043/99, 48071/99, 48580/99, 48624/99, 49426/99, 50354/99, 51934/99, 51938/99, 53423/99, 53424/99, 54120/00, 54124/00, 54136/00, 55542/00 and 56019/00.

[189]   *X. v. Norway*, EComHR 29 May 1961, appl. no. 867/60, Yearbook IV (1961), p. 270 (276).

[190]   *Malhous v. Czech Republic*, ECtHR (GC) 13 December 2000 (dec.), appl. no. 33071/96.

[191]   *Levi and Others v. Bulgaria*, ECtHR 23 September 2014, appl. no. 23474/06.

[192]   *Klass and Others v. Germany*, ECtHR (GC) 6 September 1978, appl. no. 5029/71, *supra* n. 172, para. 34.

Court, justifies this approach. This implies that the procedural provisions of the Convention are to be applied in such a way as to contribute to the effectiveness of the system of individual applications.

The Court's reasoning in *Klass* may be summarised to imply that in case of the existence of secret measures (whether based on legislation or not) the victim-requirement under Article 34 may already be satisfied when the applicant is a *potential* victim. A comparable line of reasoning was followed by the Commission in the *Malone* case, in which it found that the 'applicant is directly affected by the law and practice in England and Wales (...) under which the secret surveillance of postal and telephone communications on behalf of the police is permitted and takes place. His communication has at all relevant times been liable to such surveillance without his being able to obtain knowledge of it. Accordingly (...) he is entitled to claim (...) to be a victim (...) irrespective of whether or to what extent he is able to show that it has actually been applied to him.'[193]

Shortly afterwards, in the *Marckx* case, the Court adopted the same approach by express reference to the *Klass* case. In the *Marckx* case, it had been advanced that the Belgian legislation concerning illegitimate children conflicted with the Convention. The Belgian Government submitted that this was in reality an abstract complaint, since the challenged legislation had not been applied to the applicant. The Court held that: 'Article 25 [the present Article 34] of the Convention entitles individuals to contend that a law violates their rights by itself, in the absence of an individual measure of implementation, if they run the risk of being directly affected by it.'[194] This was considered to be the case here. According to the Court the question of whether the applicant has actually been placed in an unfavourable position is not a criterion of the victim-requirement: 'the question of prejudice is not a matter for Article 25 [the present Article 34] which, in its use of the word "victim", denotes "the person directly affected by the act or omission which is in issue".'[195]

In the *Dudgeon* case, and later in the *Norris* case and the *Modinos* case, the applicants complained about the existence of laws which had the effect of making certain homosexual acts, between consenting adult males, criminal offences. The Court held that 'in the personal circumstances of the applicant, the very existence of this legislation continuously and directly affects his private life'.[196]

---

[193] Report of *Malone v. The United Kingdom*, ECommHR 17 December 1982, appl. no. 8691/79, para. 114. See also *Hewitt and Harman v. the United Kingdom*, ECommHR 9 May 1989, appl. no. 12175/86, D&R 67 (1991), p. 89 (98); *Radio X., S., W. & A. v. Switzerland*, ECommHR 17 May 1984, appl. no. 10799/84, D&R 37 (1984), p. 236 (239).

[194] *Marckx v. Belgium*, ECtHR 13 June 1979, appl. no. 6833/74, *supra* n. 172, para. 27.

[195] *Ibid.*

[196] *Dudgeon v. The United Kingdom*, ECtHR (GC) 22 October 1981, appl. no. 7525/76, para. 41; *Norris v. Ireland*, ECtHR 26 October 1988, appl. no. 10581/83, paras. 31–34; *Modinos v. Cyprus*, ECtHR 22 April 1993, appl. no. 15070/89, para. 24. See also *Bowman v. The United Kingdom*, ECtHR (GC) 19 February 1998, appl. no. 24839/24, para. 29; *S.L. v. Austria*, ECtHR

In the *Rekvényi* case, a police officer complained about a constitutional prohibition preventing members of the police force from joining political parties or engaging in political activities. The Government submitted that the applicant had failed to specify the political activities which he felt he was prevented from pursuing. In its view, the applicant had thus failed to substantiate his complaint for the purposes of admissibility. In these circumstances, the Government raised the question of whether the applicant could claim to be a victim of any breach of his Convention rights, within the meaning of Article 25 [the present Article 34] of the Convention. The Commission held that it was true that, notwithstanding the impugned provision of the Constitution, in the relevant period the applicant was not completely prevented from engaging in political activities. However, the Commission, having regard to the limited nature of these possibilities to articulate political preferences and, in particular, to the circular letters issued by the Head of the National Police, considered that the applicant could be reasonably concerned by the consequences of his expression of political views. In these circumstances, the Commission found that the applicant could claim to be a victim within the meaning of Article 34 of the Convention.[197]

In the *Segi* case, the applicant organisations complained that they had been described by the 15 Member States of the European Union as terrorist organisations. The Court considered that the mere fact that the names of two of the applicants (*Segi* and *Gestoras Pro-Amnistía*) appeared in the list referred to in that provision as 'groups or entities involved in terrorist acts' might be embarrassing, but the link was much too tenuous to justify application of the Convention. Consequently, the Court considered that the situation complained of did not give the applicant associations, and *a fortiori* their spokespersons, the status of victims of a violation of the Convention within the meaning of Article 34 of the Convention.[198]

In general, it can be said that even if persons are not (yet) affected by the implementation of an individual measure, they can nevertheless argue that they are victims of a violation of the Convention if the abstract legislation forces them to change their behaviour, makes them possibly subject to prosecution or targets a class of people to which they belong.[199]

The question of whether applicants having a *future* interest may also be considered victims in the sense of Article 34.

In the *Kirkwood* case, such a situation was at stake. The case concerned a man who complained that his envisaged extradition from the United

---

22 November 2001, appl. no. 45330/99; *Bland v. The United Kingdom*, ECtHR 19 February 2002, appl. no. 52301/99.

[197] *Rekvényi v. Hungary*, ECtHR (GC) 20 May 1999, appl. no. 25390/94, D&R 89 (1997), p. 47 (51–52).

[198] *Segi and Others & Gestoras Pro-Amnistia v. 15 states of the European Union*, ECtHR 23 May 2002, appl. nos. 6422/02, *supra* n. 184.

[199] *Tănase v. Moldova*, ECtHR (GC) 27 April 2010, appl. no. 7/08, para. 104; *Burden v. The United Kingdom*, ECtHR (GC) 29 April 2008, appl. no. 13378/05, paras. 33–34.

Kingdom to California would amount to inhuman and degrading treatment contrary to Article 3 of the Convention since, if extradited, he would be tried for two accusations of murder and one of attempt to murder, and would very probably be sentenced to death. He argued that the circumstances surrounding the implementation of such a death penalty would constitute inhuman and degrading treatment. He referred in particular to the 'death row' phenomenon of excessive delay due to a prolonged appeal procedure which might last several years, during which he would be gripped with uncertainty as to the outcome of his appeal and, therefore, as to his fate. The Commission held as follows with respect to the victim-requirement: 'In these circumstances, faced with an imminent act of the executive, the consequences of which for the applicant will allegedly expose him to Article 3 treatment, the Commission finds that the applicant is able to claim to be a victim of an alleged violation of Article 3.'[200]

In several cases where a decision had been taken to expel a person to a country where he claimed he risked being treated contrary to Article 3, the Commission has held that a person who is about to be subjected to a violation of the Convention may claim to be a victim.[201] If, however, the order to leave the territory of the state concerned is not enforceable, the person concerned may not yet claim to be a victim. Only the notification of an expulsion order to him, with reference to the country of destination, can confer on him the status of victim, provided that domestic remedies have been exhausted. Thus, in the *Vijayanthan and Pusparajah* case, the Court made a distinction between, on the one hand, the *Soering* case, where the Home Secretary had signed the warrant for the applicant's extradition, and that of *Vilvarajah,* where the deportation of the applicants to Sri Lanka had taken place during the proceedings before the Commission and, on the other hand, that of *Vijayanthand and Pusparajah*. In respect of the latter case, the Court found that, despite the direction to leave French territory, not enforceable in itself, and the rejection of their application for exceptional leave to remain, no expulsion order had been made with respect to the applicants. If the Commissioner of Police were to decide that they should be removed, the appeal provided for in French law would be open to the applicants, with all its attendant safeguards, but at the moment here at issue such an appeal would probably have been declared inadmissible as premature or devoid of purpose by the competent court. The applicants could not, as matters stood, claim 'to be the victim(s) of a violation' within the meaning of Article 25(1) [the present Article 34].[202]

---

[200] *Kirkwood v. The United Kingdom*, EComHR 12 March 1984, appl. no. 10479/83, D&R 37 (1984), p. 158 (182). Similar reasoning in the famous Soering Case, *Soering v. The United Kingdom*, ECtHR 7 July 1989, appl. no. 14038/88, paras. 90–91.

[201] *A. v. France*, EComHR 27 February 1991, appl. no. 17262/90, D&R 68 (1991), p. 319 (334); *Vijanathan and Pusparajah v. France*, ECtHR 27 August 1992, appl. nos. 17550/90 and 17825/91, D&R 70 (1991), p. 298 (314); *Voulfovitch and Oulianova v. Sweden*, EComHR 13 January 1992, appl. no. 19373/92 D&R 74 (1993), p. 199 (207).

[202] *Vijanathan and Pusparajah v. France,* ECtHR 27 August 1992, appl. nos. 17550/90 and 17825/91, para. 46.

In a case where the applicants complained about the decision of the French President to resume nuclear testing on Mururoa and Fangataufa atolls in French Polynesia, which allegedly violated their rights under Articles 2, 3 and 8 of the Convention and Article 1 of Protocol No. 1, the Commission found the consequences, if any, of the resumption of the tests at issue too remote to affect the applicants' personal situation directly. Therefore, they could not claim to be a victim under Article 25 [the present Article 34].[203] In a case where the complaint concerned restrictions on the exercise of the right of ownership the Commission held that the only subject of the proceedings was whether or not a particular prefectoral order was lawful. The Commission recalled that is was only in highly exceptional circumstances that an applicant may claim to be a victim of a violation of the Convention owing to the risk of a future violation. An example of this would be a piece of legislation which, while not having been applied to the applicant personally, subjects him to the risk of being directly affected in specific circumstances of his life. In the instant case, the Commission noted that the applicants, taken individually, had not submitted any evidence in support of their allegations, such as their title-deeds to property or documents relating to the consequences or losses they had allegedly suffered as a result of the implementation of the prefectoral order.[204]

In the case of *Asselbourg and 78 Others and Greenpeace Association*, the Court considered that the mere mention of the pollution risks inherent in the production of steel from scrap iron was not enough to justify the applicants' assertion that they were the victims of a violation of the Convention. They should be able to assert, arguably and in a detailed manner, that for lack of adequate precautions taken by the authorities the degree of probability of the occurrence of damage was such that it could be considered to constitute a violation, on condition that the consequences of the act complained of were not too remote. In the Court's opinion, it was not evident from the file that the conditions of operation imposed by the Luxembourg authorities and, in particular, the norms dealing with the discharge of air-polluting wastes were so inadequate as to constitute a serious infringement of the principle of precaution.[205]

It can be concluded that, whenever an applicant complains about future victimhood, this implies that the risk is 'sufficiently real'.[206]

---

[203] *Tauira and 18 Others v. France*, EComHR 4 December 1995, appl. no. 28204/95, D&R 83 (1995), p. 112 (131–133). See also *Christian Federation of Jehova's Witnesses of France v. France*, ECtHR 6 November 2001, appl. no. 53430/99 *supra* n. 172.

[204] *Association des Amis de Saint Raphaël et de Fréjus and Others v. France*, EComHR 1 July 1998, appl. no. 38912/97, D&R 94 (1998), p. 124 (132).

[205] *Asselbourg and Others v. Luxembourg*, ECtHR 29 June 1999, appl. no. 29121/95.

[206] *M.T. v. Sweden*, ECtHR 26 February 2015, appl. no. 1412/12, para. 58; *Bensaid v. The United Kingdom*, ECtHR 6 February 2001, appl. no. 44599/98, para. 40.

d. Indirect victim

It is conceivable that an individual may experience a personal injury owing to a violation of the Convention against another person. Indeed, as the Court puts it, 'Article 34 concerns not just the direct victim or victims of the alleged violation, but also any indirect victims to whom the violation would cause harm or who would have a valid and personal interest in seeing it brought to an end.'[207] Under certain circumstances, therefore, an individual may lodge an application on his own account concerning a violation of the Convention against another person, without the applicant himself having directly suffered a violation of one of his rights or freedoms. In such a case, the applicant must have so close a link with the direct victim of the violation that he himself is also to be considered a victim. On that basis the Commission and the Court developed in its case law the concept of 'indirect victim', meaning that a near relative of the victim or certain other third parties can refer the matter to Strasbourg on their own initiative insofar as the violation concerned is (also) prejudicial to them or insofar as they have a personal interest in the termination of that violation.[208] Thus, a spouse was considered a victim in view of the fact that she had suffered financial and moral injury in consequence of a violation of the Convention committed against her husband.[209] Another applicant was regarded as an indirect victim because he had submitted that his twin brother had wrongfully been detained in a state institution, in which he had later died.[210] That a purely non-material interest is sufficient for the admissibility of the action of an applicant as the indirect victim becomes evident, for example, from the decision by the Commission that a complaint of a mother about the treatment of her detained son was admissible.[211] And in the Case of X, *Cabales and Balkandali* the Commission held: 'When the alleged violation concerns a refusal of a leave to remain or an entry clearance, the spouse of the individual concerned can claim to be a victim, even if the individual concerned is in fact staying with her, but unlawfully and under constant threat of deportation.'[212]

The father of a hostage-taker killed by special police was considered as an indirect victim of an alleged violation of Article 2. The same applied to the deceased's sister, notwithstanding the fact that under national law the

---

[207]   *Vallianatos and Others v. Greece,* ECtHR (GC) 7 November 2013, appl. nos. 29381/09 and 32684/09, *supra* n. 170, para. 47.

[208]   *X v. Federal Republic of Germany,* EComHR 31 May 1956, appl. no. 100/55, Yearbook I (1955–1957), p. 162 (162–163); *Hibbert v. The Netherlands,* ECtHR 26 January 1999, appl. no. 38087/97; *Çelikbilek v. Turkey,* ECtHR 22 June 1999, appl. no. 27693/95.

[209]   *Lucienne Koolen v. Belgium,* ECtHR 18 December 1963, appl. no. 1478/62, Yearbook VI (1963), p. 590 (620).

[210]   *X. v. Belgium,* EComHR 13 December 1976, appl. no. 7467/76, D&R 8 (1978), p. 220 (221).

[211]   *Y. v. Austria,* EComHR 14 December 1961, appl. no. 898/60, Coll. 8 (1962), p. 136.

[212]   *Abdulaziz, Cabales and Balkandali v. the United Kingdom,* ECtHR 28 May 1985, appl. nos. 9214/80, 9473/81 and 9474/81, D&R 29 (1982), p. 176 (182).

deceased's children, who were not among the applicants, were his heirs.[213] On the other hand, an applicant was not admitted who submitted that his sisters had wrongfully failed to receive compensation for their sufferings during the Nazi regime and who now claimed this in his own name. This compensation related only to the sufferings of the sisters, not to those of the applicant, so that the latter could not be considered as a victim himself.[214] In the case of *Becker v. Denmark*, a German journalist, who was director of a body called Project Children's Protection & Security International, challenged the repatriation of 199 Vietnamese children, proposed by the Danish Government, as contrary to Article. 3 of the Convention. It was held that he was not a direct victim but considered to be an indirect victim because the children depended on him and he had been entrusted with at least the care of the children by the Vietnamese authorities on behalf of their parents.[215]

It is not easy to summarise the Court's case law on this point. In the Grand Chamber Case *Centre for Legal Resources on behalf of Mr Valentin Câmpeanu*, an overview was proposed. Whenever applications are related to the death or disappearances of victims before a complaint was lodged, the Court will accept the application by relatives or a next-of-kin, either because the case raises a question of general human rights protection and the applicants had an interest in pursuing the application, either because of the own rights of the applicants as indirect victims.[216] The Court is more flexible in cases related to the death or disappearance of persons in circumstances prone to engage the responsibility of the state. However, in some cases on assisted suicide, involving non-transferrable rights protected by Articles 2, 3, 5, 8, 9, and 14, the Court was not willing to accept the idea of indirect victimhood.[217] In another case, *Koch,* it did recognise that a husband was affected by the refusal to let his wife acquire a lethal dose of pentobarbital of sodium.[218] If, for instance, under Articles 5, 6 or 8 transferrable rights may be at stake, and close relatives can be awarded victim status if they have a (moral) interest in having the direct victim be found not-guilty, if their own reputation or that of the family is at stake, or if they have a pecuniary interest.[219]

---

[213] *Andronicou and Constantinou v. Cyprus*, ECtHR (GC) 9 October 1997, app. 25052/94, D&R 85-A (1996), p. 102. See also, as far as Art. 2 is concerned, *Giuliani and Gaggio v. Italy*, ECtHR (GC) 24 March 2011, appl. no. 23458/02 (parents and sister of a demonstrator killed by police force bringing a claim to the Court).

[214] *X v. Federal Republic of Germany*, EComHR 30 May 1956, appl. no. 113/55, Yearbook I (1955–1957), p. 161 (162). See also *B., R. and J. v. Federal Republic of Germany*, EComHR 15 March 1984, appl. no. 9639/82 D&R 36 (1984), p. 139.

[215] *Becker v. Denmark*, EComHR 3 October 1975 (dec.), appl. no. 7011/75, Yearbook XIX (1976), p. 416 (450).

[216] *Centre for Legal Resources on behalf of Valentin Câmpeanu v. Romania*, ECtHR (GC) 17 July 2014, appl. no. 47848/08, para. 98.

[217] *Sanles Sanles v. Spain*, ECtHR 26 October 2000, appl. no. 48335/99.

[218] *Koch v. Germany*, ECtHR 19 July 2012, appl. no. 497/09.

[219] *Centre for Legal Resources on behalf of Valentin Câmpeanu v. Romania*, ECtHR (GC) 17 July 2014, appl. no. 47848/08, *supra* n. 215, para. 100.

Finally, it should be mentioned that in certain cases shareholders can be considered as victims of alleged violations of rights and freedoms of the company. The Court holds that disregarding an applicant company's legal personality can be justified only in exceptional circumstances, in particular where it was clearly established that it was impossible for the company to apply to the Convention institutions through the organs set up under its articles of incorporation or – in the event of liquidation – through its liquidators, as in the *Agrotexim Hellas* case.[220]

e. Loss of victim status

Cases may occur in which the violation complained of has meanwhile been terminated or at least no longer exists at the moment the Court examines the case. The applicant will then not be admitted, because he can no longer allege to be a victim.[221] The status of victim must exist during all relevant stages of the proceedings before the Court.[222]

If, for instance, in the meantime the violation of the Convention complained of has been recognised by the authorities and the applicant has received sufficient redress, he can no longer claim to be a victim of that violation.[223] In the *Amuur* case, the Court considered that the notion of 'victim' within the meaning of Article 34 of the Convention denotes the person directly affected by the act or omission in issue, the existence of a violation of the Convention being conceivable even in the absence of prejudice; prejudice is relevant only in the context of Article 41 of the Convention. Consequently, a decision or measure favourable to the applicant is not in principle sufficient to deprive him of his status as 'victim', unless the national authorities have acknowledged, either expressly or in substance and have afforded redress for,

---

[220] *Lebedev v. Russia*, ECtHR 25 November 2004, appl. no. 4493/04. Along the same lines: *Centro Europa 7 S.R.L. and Di Stefano v. Italy*, ECtHR (GC) 7 June 2012, appl. no. 38433/09, paras. 90–95. *Agrotextim Hellas S.A. v. Greece*, EComHR 10 March 1994, appl. no. 14807/89, D&R., 72 (1992).

[221] See, *e.g.*, the report *Foti, Lentini and Cenerini and Others v. Italy*, ECtHR 15 October 1980, appl. nos. 7604/76, 7719/76 and 7781/77, B.48 (1986), p. 30; *Dores and Silveira v. Portugal*, CM 6 July 1983, appl. nos. 9345/81 and 9346/81, D&R 41 (1985), p. 60 (19–20); *Farragut v. France*, EComHR 6 July 1984, appl. no. 10103/82, D&R 39 (1984), p. 186 (207); *Gulsen and Halil Yasin Ketenoglou v. Turkey*, ECtHR 25 September 2001, appl. nos. 29360/95 and 29361/95, paras. 36–37.

[222] *Centro Europa 7 S.R.L. and Di Stefano v. Italy*, ECtHR (GC) 7 June 2012, appl. no. 38433/09, *supra* n. 219, para. 80.

[223] *Verband Deutscher Flugleiter and Others v. Federal Republic of Germany*, EComHR 10 July 1981, appl. no. 8865/80, D&R 25 (1982), p. 252 (254–255); *Baraona v. Portugal*, ECtHR 8 July 1987, appl. no. 10092/82 D&R 40 (1985), p. 118 (137); *Anca and Others v. Belgium*, EComHR 10 December 1984, appl. no. 10259/83 D&R 40 (1985), p. 170 (177–178); *Byrn v. Denmark*, EComHR 1 July 1992, appl. no. 13156/87, D&R 73 (1993), p. 5 (9), and as regards 'reasonable time': *G. v. Federal Republic of Germany*, EComHR 6 July 1983, appl. no. 8858/80, D&R 33 (1983), p. 5 (6–7).

the breach of the Convention.[224] States must offer 'appropriate and sufficient redress'.[225] To what extent redress is sufficient and appropriate depends on all the specific circumstances of the case, taking into account the rights that have been violated.[226] In any event, redress has to be offered within a reasonable delay.[227]

In the case of *Aydin and 10 Others*, the first applicant submitted that the *ex gratia* financial aid he had received had no connection with the disappearance of his father and, therefore, could not form a basis of a finding that he could no longer claim to be a victim within the meaning of Article 34 of the Convention. The Court held that since it did not appear that the financial aid, which had in fact been paid to the first applicant, was based on an acknowledgement, either expressly or in substance, and since the first applicant's rights under the Convention had been disrespected by the authorities, the financial aid at issue could not be regarded as sufficient for a deprivation of the first applicant's status as a 'victim' in respect of his material losses. The Court, therefore, accepted that the first applicant could claim to be a victim.[228]

In the *Burdov* case, the Court held that a decision or measure favourable to the applicant was in principle not sufficient to deprive him of his status as a 'victim' unless the national authorities have acknowledged, either expressly or in substance, and then afforded redress for, the breach of the Convention.[229] In the *Doubtfire* case, the Court noted that the applicant's conviction was quashed on the grounds that the proceedings had been unfair because of the lack of full disclosure by the prosecution. It was open to the applicant to apply for compensation in respect of his conviction and imprisonment. In these circumstances, the applicant could no longer claim to be a victim of the alleged violation of Article 6 of the Convention.[230]

As to the question of whether the applicant may continue to claim to be a victim of a violation of Article 6(1) of the Convention on the grounds of the length of the criminal proceedings against him, the Court has held that the mitigation of a sentence on the ground of the excessive length of proceedings does not in principle deprive the individual concerned of his status as a victim within the meaning of Article 34 of the Convention. However, according to the Court, this general rule is subject to an exception when the national authorities have acknowledged in a sufficiently clear way the failure to observe the

---

224 *Amuur v. France*, ECtHR 25 June 1996, appl. no. 19776/92, para. 36; *Nada v. Switzerland*, ECtHR (GC) 12 September 2012, appl. no. 10593/08, para. 128.

225 *Gäfgen v. Germany*, ECtHR (GC) 1 June 2010, appl. no. 22978/05, para. 116.

226 *Ibid.*

227 *Sartory v. France*, ECtHR 24 September 2009, appl. no. 40589/07, para. 27.

228 *Aydin and Others v. Turkey*, ECtHR 1 February 2000, appl. nos. 28293/95, 29494/95 and 30219/96.

229 *Burdov v. Russia*, ECtHR 7 May 2002, appl. no. 59498/00, para. 31. See also *Skubenko v. Ukraine*, ECtHR 6 April 2004, appl. no. 41152/98.

230 *Doubtfire v. The United Kingdom*, ECtHR 23 April 2002, appl. no. 31825/96.

reasonable time requirement and have afforded redress by reducing the sentence in an express and measurable manner.[231]

In a case where the applicants submitted that the authorities' recording of their telephone conversations with counsel was contrary to the Convention, the records in question had since been destroyed. In view of this the German Government advanced that the alleged violation had become a moot point. The Commission, however, decided that since the destruction had not taken place in response to a request from the applicants and the latter had not received reparation otherwise, 'the applicants still have to be considered as victims although the records in question no longer exist'.[232] In a case where a settlement between the parties had been reached which disposed of previous applications to the Commission and the Court concerning criminal proceedings against the applicant, the Commission found that the declaration made by the applicant in the context of those applications were unequivocal in that it was intended to prevent him from bringing further applications before the Convention organs.[233]

In the *Caraher* case, the Court held that the possibility of obtaining compensation for the death of a person will generally, and in normal circumstances, constitute an adequate and sufficient remedy for a substantive complaint of an unjustified use of lethal force by a state agent in violation of Article 2 of the Convention. Separate procedural obligations may also arise under Article 2 concerning the provision of effective investigations into the use of lethal force. Where a relative accepts a sum of compensation in settlement of civil claims and renounces further use of local remedies, he or she will generally no longer be able to claim to be a victim in respect of those matters.[234] However, in the case of *Z.W. v. the United Kingdom*, the Court observed that the compensation accepted by the applicant was not in settlement of her civil claims and not part of the process of exhaustion of domestic remedies. Her claims in the civil court were struck out and the award of GBP 50,000 was made as compensation for criminal injuries. This statutory scheme was not concerned with any alleged failings by the local authority in its duty to protect the applicant, which was the essence of the complaint raised by her under Article 3 of the Convention, but rather with the injuries attributable to her as a victim of a criminal offence committed by her foster parents. The Court, therefore, found that the applicant might still claim to be a victim of a violation of Article 3 of the Convention in respect of her complaints against the local authority.[235]

---

[231] *Beck v. Norway*, ECtHR 26 June 2001, appl. no. 26390/95, para. 27; *Jensen v. Denmark*, ECtHR 20 September 2001, appl. no. 48470/99; *Wejrup v. Denmark*, ECtHR 7 March 2002, appl. no. 49126/99.

[232] *A, B, C and D v. Federal Republic of Germany*, EComHR 13 December 1979, appl. no. 8290/78, D&R 18 (1980), p. 176 (180).

[233] *Mlynek v. Austria*, EComHR 31 August 1994, appl. no. 22634/93, D&R 79 (1994), p. 103 (107).

[234] *Caraher v. The United Kingdom*, ECtHR 11 January 2000, appl. no. 24520/94.

[235] *Z.W. v. The United Kingdom*, ECtHR 27 November 2001, appl. no. 34962/97.

In the cases of *Van den Brink* and *Zuiderveld and Klappe*, the respondent Government contended before the Court that the applicants could not claim to be victims of a breach of Article 5(3) as the time each one spent in custody on remand was deducted in its entirety from the sentence ultimately imposed on them. According to the Court the relevant deduction did not *per se* deprive the individual concerned of his status as an alleged victim within the meaning of Article 34 of a breach of Article 5(3). The Court added that 'the position might be otherwise if the deduction from sentence had been based upon an acknowledgement by the national courts of a violation of the Convention'.[236]

Again, it must be noted that even when applicants cannot longer claim to be victims, the Court may still decide to consider the case whenever the issues at stake involve general questions of public interest.[237]

13.4. REPRESENTATION AND SUBSTITUTION

The requirement that the violation of the Convention must have caused the applicant a personal injury does not, of course, prevent an application from being lodged by his representative.[238] Furthermore, if the victim himself is not able, or is not adequately able, to undertake an action – for example a detained person, a patient in a mental clinic, a very young person – a close relative, a guardian, a curator, or another person may act on his behalf. In that case the name of the victim must be made known and, if possible, he must have given his consent to lodging the application.[239]

Articles 36 and 45 of the Rules of Court specify under which conditions an applicant can be represented by an attorney. It is essential that a power of attorney or written authority to act be supplied together with a signed application. The representative must be able to prove that (s)he received specific and precise information to lodge a complaint on behalf of the victim.[240] The power in itself is not subject to specific requirements and can therefore be drafted in a rather simple way, as long as not has been shown that it was made up without the applicant's knowledge and consent.[241]

---

[236] *Van der Sluijs, Zuiderveld and Klappe v. The Netherlands*, ECtHR 22 May 1984, appl. nos. 9362/81, 9363/81 and 9387/81, para. 41 and para. 37 respectively.

[237] *Konstantin Markin v. Russia*, ECtHR (GC) 22 March 2012, appl. no. 30078/06, paras. 89–90.

[238] *X. v. Federal Republic of Germany*, EComHR 13 July 1970, appl. no. 282/57, Yearbook I (1955–1957), p. 164 (166).

[239] See, *e.g., X v. the United Kingdom*, EComHR 31 May 1972, appl. no. 5076/71, Coll. 40 (1972), p. 64 (66); *Saniewski v. Poland*, ECtHR 26 June 2001, appl. no. 40319/98.

[240] *Post v. the Netherlands*, ECtHR 20 January 2009, appl. no. 21727/08.

[241] *Hirsi Jaama and Others v. Italy*, ECtHR (GC) 23 February 2012, appl. no. 27765/09, para. 52. Concerning discussions on the validity of signatures, see: *Hussun and Others v. Italy*, ECtHR 19 January 2010, appl. nos. 10171/05, 10601/05, 11593/05 and 17165/05.

In case of the death of the victim his heir may lodge an application or uphold a previously lodged application only if the allegedly violated right forms part of the estate or if on other grounds he himself is to be considered the (direct or indirect) victim.[242] In the *Kofler* case, the Commission stated that 'the heirs of a deceased applicant cannot claim a general right that the examination of the application introduced by the *de cujus* be continued by the Commission'. The nature of the complaint (which concerned the duration of the proceedings that resulted in the applicant's conviction and sentence) did not allow that complaint to be considered as transferable because the complaint was closely linked with the late applicant personally and his heirs 'cannot now claim (…) to have themselves a sufficient legal interest to justify the further examination of the application on their behalf'.

Accordingly, the issue is whether the widow(er) or heir can claim that the applicant's original interest in having the alleged violation of the Convention established might be considered as an interest vested in them. Such an interest was found to exist in a case where the deceased applicant had complained about his criminal conviction. In particular, he had claimed that he had not had a 'fair hearing' nor had he benefited from the 'presumption of innocence'. The Commission emphasised that, by their very nature, complaints relating to Article 6 were closely linked to the person of the deceased applicant. However, the Commission continued by saying that 'this link is not exclusive and it cannot be claimed that they have no bearing at all on the person of the widow'. The widow could claim to be a victim, since she suffered the effects of the decisions concerning the seizure of property and a daily fine and civil imprisonment, both of which were enforceable against her.[243] In *X v. France*, the Court took an even more liberal position. In this case, the applicant, who was given a number of blood transfusions, was found to have been infected with HIV. The applicant died shortly after the referral of his case to the Court, but his parents expressed the wish to continue the proceedings. The Court accepted that they were entitled to take Mr X's place in the proceedings before it.[244] Also, in other cases concerning the length of proceedings the Court, without restrictions, showed

---

[242] See, on the one hand, *X. v. Federal Republic of Germany*, EComHR 13 July 1970, appl. no. 282/57, Yearbook I (1955–1957), *supra* n. 237, p. 164 (166), and on the other hand *X v. Austria*, EComHR 4 October 1966, appl. no. 1706/62, Yearbook IX (1966), p. 112 (124). See also *Ensslin, Baader and Raspe v. Federal Republic of Germany*, EComHR 8 July 1978, appl. nos. 7572/76, 7586/76 and 7587/76, Yearbook XXI (1978), p. 418 (452). See, however, *Baader, Meins, Meinhof, Grundmann v. Federal republic of Germany*, EComHR 30 May 1975, appl. no. 6166/73, Yearbook XVIII (1975), p. 132 (142); *Björkgren and Ed v. Sweden*, EComHR 7 January 1991, appl. no. 12526/86, D&R 68 (1991), p. 104 (105), where the Commission recognised the right of action of a widow and sole heir with regard to an action relating to property; *Dujardin v. France*, EComHR 2 September 1991, appl. no. 16734/90 D&R 72 (1992), p. 236 (243).

[243] *Funke v. France*, ECtHR 25 February 1993, appl. no. 10828/84, D&R 57 (1988), p. 5 (25–26).

[244] *X. v. France*, ECtHR 31 March 1992, appl. no. 18020/91, para. 26.

itself to be willing to continue the proceedings at the wish of the heirs of the deceased applicant.[245]

If the death of the direct victim is the result of the alleged violation, for example in the case of torture, his relatives will as a rule qualify as indirect victims.[246] This was, however, different in the *Scherer* case where the applicant's executor had not expressed any intention whatsoever of seeking, on Mr Scherer's behalf, to have the criminal proceedings reopened in Switzerland or to claim compensation for non-pecuniary damage in Strasbourg. Under these circumstances Mr Scherer's death could be held to constitute a 'fact of a kind to provide a solution of the matter'.[247]

In the *Scozzari and Giunta* case, the Italian Government contested the first applicant's standing to also act on behalf of her children, because, as her parental rights had been suspended, there was a conflict of interest between her and the children, and criminal proceedings were pending against her for offences against her children. The Court pointed out that in principle a person who is not entitled under domestic law to represent another may nevertheless, in certain circumstances, act before the Court in the name of the other person. In particular, minors can apply to the Court even, or indeed especially, if they are represented by a mother who is in conflict with the authorities and criticises their decisions and conduct as not being consistent with the rights guaranteed by the Convention. The Court considered that in the event of a conflict over a minor's interests between a natural parent and the person appointed by the authorities to act as the child's guardian, there is a danger that some of those interests will never be brought to the Court's attention and that the minor will be deprived of effective protection of his rights under the Convention. Consequently, even though the mother had been deprived of parental rights – indeed that was one of the causes of the dispute which she had referred to the Court – her standing as the natural mother sufficed to afford her the necessary power to apply to the Court on the children's behalf as well, in order to protect their interests. Moreover, the conditions governing individual applications are not necessarily the same as national criteria relating to *locus standi*. National rules in this respect may serve different purposes from those contemplated by Article 34 of the Convention and, whilst those purposes may sometimes be analogous, they

---

[245] *Vocaturo v. Italy*, ECtHR 24 May 1991, appl. no. 11891/85, para. 2 and *G. v. Italy*, 27 February 1992, appl. no. 12787/87, paras. 2–3. See also *Prisca and De Santis v. Italy*, EComHR 10 October 1991, appl. no. 14660/89, D&R 72 (1992), p. 141 (147).

[246] *Vocaturo v. Italy*, ECtHR 24 May 1991, appl. no. 11891/85, *supra* n. 244, para. 2; *G. v. Italy*, ECtHR 27 February 1992, appl. no. 12787/87, *supra* n. 244, para. 2; *Raimondo v. Italy*, ECtHR 22 February 1994, appl. no. 12954/87, para. 2; *Yasa v. Turkey*, ECtHR 2 September 1998, appl. no. 22495/93, para. 66; *Aytekin v. Turkey*, ECtHR 23 September 1998, appl. no. 22880/93, *Kakoulli v. Turkey*, ECtHR 4 September 2001, appl. no. 38595/97.

[247] *Scherer v. Switzerland*, ECtHR 25 March 1993, appl. no. 17116, paras. 31–32.

need not always be so.[248] On the basis of this argument, the Court has accepted that a parent can bring a claim to the Court on behalf of her minor children, even if she has no exclusive parental authority and even in the absence of an agreement with the other parent.[249]

In the case of *P., C. and S. v. the United Kingdom*, the applicants P and C complained on behalf of their daughter S concerning the failure to make post-adoption provision for any form of direct contact with her and the reduction in indirect contact. The Government disputed that the applicants – the natural parents – could claim to bring an application on behalf of S as they retained no residual parental authority over her and had no standing domestically to represent S. The Court found that the key consideration in such a case is that any serious issues concerning respect for a child's rights should be examined. It was claimed on behalf of S that since the freeing for adoption proceedings she had been deprived of the opportunity to maintain a meaningful relationship with her birth parents. It could not be disputed that this was a right which S should enjoy without unjustified interference. The adoptive parents had, according the Government, objected to direct contact between P and C and S, and it was their decision to restrict indirect contact to one letter per year. In the circumstances, it could not be expected that they introduce an application on behalf of S raising the point. Therefore, given the issues raised in this application and the standing of P and C as S's natural parents, P and C might apply to the Court on her behalf in order to protect her interests.[250]

In the case of *Lambert v. France*, on the question whether the withdrawal of artificial nutrition of a person in a chronic vegetative state would constitute a violation of the Convention, the Court summarised its case law.[251] In cases where the death or disappearance of a victim took place in circumstances that could engage the responsibility of the state, a next-of-kin can file a complaint. The Court also pays attention to victims in a vulnerable position (on account of criteria such as age, sex, disability) who may not be able to lodge a complaint: other persons may then file an application if there is a close link with the victim. Exceptionally, if no legal representatives are known and no next-of-kin either, an NGO may intervene.[252] In the specific case at hand, the Court decided that the relatives could not act on behalf of the person in vegetative state, but that they had standing on their own behalf.

---

[248] *Scozzari and Giunta v. Italy*, ECtHR (GC) 13 July 2000, appl. nos. 39221/98 and 41963/98, *supra* n. 151, paras. 135–139.

[249] *Diamante and Pelliccioni v. San Marino*, ECtHR 27 September 2011, appl. no. 32250/08, paras. 146–147; *Raw and Others v. France*, ECtHR 7 March 2013, appl. no. 10131/11, para. 52.

[250] *P., C. and S. v. The United Kingdom*, ECtHR 11 December 2001, appl. no. 56547/00; *Sylvester v. Austria*, ECtHR 26 September 2002, appl. nos. 36812/97 and 40104/98.

[251] *Lambert and Others v. France*, ECtHR (GC) 5 June 2015, appl. no. 46043/14, paras. 89–95.

[252] *Centre for Legal Resources on behalf of Valentin Câmpeanu v. Romania*, ECtHR (GC) 17 July 2014, appl. no. 47848/08, paras. 104–114.

13.5. OBLIGATION OF NON-INTERFERENCE

According to the last sentence of Article 34 the Contracting States undertake not to interfere in any way with the exercise of the individual right of complaint. In this respect, the Court held in the *Cruz Varas* case that Article 25 [the present Article 34] imposes an obligation not to interfere with the right of the individual to effectively present and pursue his complaint with the Commission. Although such a right is of a procedural nature distinguishable from the substantive rights contained in the Convention, it must be open to individuals to complain of alleged infringements of it in Convention proceedings. In this respect also the Convention must be interpreted as guaranteeing rights which are practical and effective as opposed to theoretical and illusory.[253] It can be argued that the respondent state has three kinds of obligations in this respect.[254]

In the first place, the state must *refrain from hindering* the applicants communicating with the Court or putting them under pressure not to lodge an application, to modify it or to withdraw it.[255] No intimidation on the applicants can be accepted, since this would entail a chilling effect on (future) applicants and their representatives.[256]

In the *Akdivar* case concerning the alleged burning of houses by security forces in South-East Turkey, the question arose whether the Turkish authorities had hindered the effective exercise of the right of individual petition. Some of the applicants, or persons thought to be applicants, had been directly interrogated by the Turkish authorities about their applications to the Commission and had been asked to sign statements declaring that no such applications had been made. Furthermore, in the case of two of the applicants the interview had been filmed. The Court found a violation of Article 25(1) [the present Article 34] in this respect. It held that the applicants must be able to communicate freely with the Commission without being subjected to any form of pressure from the authorities to withdraw or modify their complaints. Given their vulnerable position and the reality that in South-East Turkey complaints against the authorities might well give rise to a legitimate fear of reprisals, the matters complained of amounted to a form of illicit and unacceptable pressure on the applicants to withdraw their applications. Moreover, it could not be excluded that the filming of the two persons, who were subsequently declared not to be applicants, could have contributed to this pressure. The Court also held that the

---

[253] *Cruz Varas and Others v. Sweden*, ECtHR 20 March 1991, appl. no. 15576/89, *supra* n. 29, para. 99. See also *Agrotextim Hellas S.A. v. Greece*, EComHR 10 March 1994, appl. no. 14807/89, D&R 72 (1992) *supra* n. 219, p. 148 (156).

[254] See as well, <www.echr.coe.int/Documents/Admissibility_guide_ENG.pdf>, pp. 18–21.

[255] *Mamatkulov and Askarov v. Turkey*, ECtHR (GC) 4 February 2005, appl. nos. 46827/99 and 46951/99, para. 102.

[256] *Mechenkov v. Russia*, ECtHR 7 February 2008, appl. no. 35421/05, para. 116; *Lopata v. Russia*, ECtHR 13 July 2010, appl. no. 72250/01, paras. 150–151.

fact that the applicants actually pursued their application to the Commission did not prevent such behaviour on the part of the authorities from amounting to a hindrance in respect of the applicants in breach of this provision.[257]

In the *Kurt* case, the Court held that the threat of criminal proceedings against an applicant's lawyer concerning the contents of a statement drawn up by him must be considered as interfering with the exercise of the applicant's right of petition.[258] The same was the case as regards the institution of criminal proceedings against a lawyer involved in the preparation of an application to the Commission.[259] In the *McShane* case, the Court considered that the threat of disciplinary proceedings may also infringe this guarantee of free and unhindered access to the Convention system.[260]

In practice, difficulties arise particularly with respect to persons who have been deprived of their liberty in one way or another. The Court does not regard every form of monitoring of the mail of detained persons addressed to it as unlawful, although it considers it more in conformity with the spirit of the Convention that the letters are forwarded unopened. According to the Court there is a conflict with Article 34 only when an applicant cannot freely submit his grievances in a complete and detailed way. In the *Manoussos* case, the applicant complained that he was not allowed to send telegrams or make telephone calls to the Court's Registry, and that letters sent to him by the latter were opened on several occasions. The Court considered that such complaints fell to be examined under Article 8 of the Convention rather than under Article 34. In particular, the voluminous correspondence which the applicant had sent to the Court confirmed that he was able to submit all his complaints to the Court by ordinary mail, and there was no indication that the correspondence between the Court and the applicant was unduly delayed or tampered with. Finally, the Court noted that the applicant was granted free legal aid under the legal aid scheme funded by the Council of Europe, and that the Czech Bar Association recommended a lawyer who was willing to represent the applicant in the proceedings before the Court following his failure to appoint a lawyer. However, the applicant declined the lawyer's assistance for reasons which the Court considered groundless. Accordingly, he bore full responsibility for any alleged inadequacies in the presentation of his case to the Court. In view of the above facts and considerations the Court found that the alleged violation of Article 34 of the Convention had not been established.

---

[257] *Akdivar and Others v. Turkey*, ECtHR (GC) 16 September 1996, appl. no. 21893/93, para. 105; *Kurt v. Turkey*, ECtHR 25 May 1998, appl. no. 24276/94, para. 165; *Orhan v. Turkey*, ECtHR 18 June 2002, appl. no. 25656/94, para. 406; *Dulas v. Turkey*, ECtHR 30 January 2001, appl. no. 25801/94 para. 79.

[258] *Kurt v. Turkey*, ECtHR 25 May 1998, appl. no. 24276/94, *supra* n. 256, paras. 164–165.

[259] *Şarli v. Turkey*, ECtHR 22 May 2001, appl. no. 24490/94, paras. 85–86; *Elci and Others v. Turkey*, ECtHR 13 November 2003, appl. nos. 23145/93 and 25091/94, para. 711.

[260] *McShane v. The United Kingdom*, ECtHR 28 May 2002, appl. no. 43290/98, para. 149.

In this context, the European Agreement relating to persons participating in proceedings before the European Court of Human Rights is also of interest. In Article 3(2) of this Agreement, states undertake to guarantee also to detained persons the right to free correspondence with the Court. This means that, if their correspondence is at all examined by the competent authorities, this may not entail undue delay or alteration of the correspondence. Nor may detained persons be subjected to disciplinary measures on account of any correspondence with the Court. Finally, they have a right to speak, out of hearing of other persons, with their lawyer concerning their application to the Court, provided that the lawyer is qualified to appear as a barrister before the courts of the state concerned. With respect to these provisions the authorities may impose limitations only insofar as they are in accordance with the law and are necessary in a democratic society in the interests of national security, for the detection and prosecution of a crime, or for the protection of health. Despite the fact that individuals cannot rely directly on this Agreement in the form of separate application, it is of importance for the promotion of an undisturbed exercise of the individual right of complaint, because the Court can take its provisions into account in connection with Article 34. The scope of the state's obligation under Article 34, however, is not necessarily confined to the provisions of this Agreement.

In the *Klyakhin* case, the issue concerned the alleged refusal of the prison authorities to forward the applicant's letters to the Court, delays in posting the letters and an alleged failure of the authorities to give the incoming letters from the Court to the applicant. While there was no allegation of undue pressure, interception of letters by prison authorities can hinder applicants in bringing their cases to the Court. As to exhaustion of domestic remedies in this respect, the Court observed that Article 34 of the Convention imposes an obligation on the Contracting States not to interfere with the right of the individual effectively to present and pursue his application before the Court. Such an obligation confers upon the applicant a right distinguishable from the rights set out in Section I of the Convention or its Protocols. In view of the nature of this right the requirement to exhaust domestic remedies does not apply to it. Given the importance attached to the right of individual petition it would be unreasonable to require the applicant to make recourse to a normal judicial procedure within the domestic jurisdiction in every event where the prison authorities interfere in his correspondence with the Court. In these circumstances, the Court considered that the applicant's complaint under Article 34 could not be rejected for failure to exhaust domestic remedies. It found that this part of the application raised complex questions of fact and law, the determination of which should depend on an examination of the merits. Finally, it deserves attention that neither the Convention nor the above-mentioned European Agreement impose an obligation on the Contracting States to inform private parties of the possibility of filing an application with the Court after they have exhausted the domestic remedies. At any rate, according to the Commission, such an obligation could not be inferred from the words 'not to hinder in any way the effective exercise of this right' of Article 25 [present Article 34]. Considering the text of Article 34 this interpretation is not incomprehensible. Still, it would be in keeping with the spirit of the Convention if, in appropriate cases, after the domestic remedies have been exhausted, the attention of individuals was drawn to the possibility of lodging a complaint with the Court. After all, a state, which by becoming a party to the Convention recognises the right of complaint under Article 34, may be expected to assure the effective exercise of this right by giving adequate publicity to the existence of the right of complaint.

Correspondence with the Court in which the applicants complain about interference with the exercise of the right of complaint is not considered as a separate 'application' or '*requête*' to which the rules of admissibility are applicable. As a rule, the case will be settled between the Court and the Contracting State concerned on an administrative basis, the applicant being permitted to react to any observations which a state may make. However, if along with another complaint such a complaint is also lodged, the Court appears to be prepared to examine the latter together with the first complaint.

In the *Salman* case, the Court found that the document recording the first interview showed that the applicant was questioned, not only about her declaration of means, but also about how she introduced her application to the Commission and with whose assistance. Furthermore, the Government had not denied that the applicant was blindfolded while at the Adana anti-terrorism branch headquarters. The Court found that blindfolding had increased the applicant's vulnerability, causing her anxiety and distress, and disclosed, in the circumstances of this case, oppressive treatment. Furthermore, there was no plausible explanation as to why the applicant was questioned twice about her legal aid application and, in particular, why the questioning was conducted on the first occasion by police officers of the anti-terrorism branch, whom the applicant had claimed were responsible for the death of her husband. The applicant must have felt intimidated by these contacts with the authorities. This constituted undue interference with her petition to the Convention organs.[261]

Second, states are under *the duty to collaborate* with the Court, allowing the judges to examine the case, knowing all the relevant facts. In the *Tanrikulu* case, the Court observed that it was of the utmost importance for the effective operation of the system of individual petition instituted under Article 34, not only that applicants or potential applicants should be able to communicate freely with the Convention organs without being subject to any form of pressure from the authorities, but also that states should furnish all necessary facilities to make possible a proper and effective examination of applications. According

---

[261] *Salman v. Turkey*, ECtHR (GC) 27 June 2000, appl. no. 21986/93, paras. 131–132.

to the Court it is inherent in proceedings relating to cases of this nature, where an individual applicant accuses state agents of violating rights under the Convention – his own or someone else's – that in certain instances solely the respondent government have access to information capable of corroborating or refuting these allegations. A failure on a government's part to submit such information which is in their hands without a satisfactory explanation may not only give rise to the drawing of inferences as to the well-foundedness of the applicant's allegations, but may also reflect negatively on the level of compliance by a respondent state with its obligations under Article 38 of the Convention.[262] The same applies to delays by the state in submitting information which prejudices the establishment of facts in a case.[263] If domestic courts refuse to give photocopies of case files to vulnerable applicants, who cannot obtain the information without state support, jeopardising thus the possibility to lodge a complaint with the Court, the state fails to comply with its obligations under Article 34.[264]

In the *Tepe* case, the Court concluded that the Government had failed to provide any convincing explanation for its delays and omissions in response to the Court's requests for relevant documents, information and witnesses. The Court considered, therefore, that it could draw inferences from the Government's conduct in the instant case. Bearing in mind the difficulties arising from a fact-finding exercise of this nature and in view of the importance of a respondent government's co-operation in Convention proceedings, the Court found that the Government had failed to furnish all necessary facilities to the Court in its task of establishing the facts within the meaning of the then Article 38(1) (a) of the Convention. Accordingly, it did not consider it necessary to also examine these matters under Article 34 of the Convention.[265] A government cannot, in any event, simply invoke national security reasons not to collaborate with the Court.[266]

Finally, the respondent states have the *obligation to respect the binding nature of interim measures.*

In the *Cruz Varas* case, the question arose of whether the failure on the part of the respondent State to comply with the Commission's indication of provisional measures under Rule 36 of the Rules of Procedure of the Commission[267]

---

[262] *Tanrikulu v. Turkey*, ECtHR (GC) 8 July 1999, appl. no. 23763/94, paras. 66 and 70; *Maslova en Nalbandov v. Russia*, ECtHR 24 January 2008, appl. no. 839/02, paras. 128–131.

[263] *Orhan v. Turkey*, ECtHR 18 June 2002, appl. no. 25656/94, *supra* n. 256, para. 266; *Aktas v. Turkey*, ECtHR 24 April 2003, appl. no. 24351/94, para. 341.

[264] *Cano Moya v. Spain*, ECtHR 11 October 2016, appl. no. 3142/11, paras. 43–52.

[265] *Tepe v. Turkey*, ECtHR 9 May 2003, appl. no. 27244/95, para. 135; See also *Tahsin Acar v. Turkey*, ECtHR 8 April 2004, appl. no. 26307/92, para. 254; *Shamayev and Others v. Georgia and Russia*, ECtHR 12 April 2005, appl. no. 36378/02, para. 504.

[266] *Janowiec and Others v. Russia*, ECtHR (GC) 21 October 2013, appl. no. 55508/07, 29520/09, *supra* n. 71, paras. 202–216.

[267] See 2.2.8.2.

amounted to a violation of the obligation not to hinder the effective exercise of the right of individual petition. The Court took the position that the Convention did not contain any provision empowering the Convention organs to order interim measures. In the absence of a specific provision for such a power a Rule 36 indication could not give rise to a binding obligation.[268] In the subsequent cases of *Öcalan*[269] and *Mamatkulov and Abdurasulovic*,[270] the Court changed its position and held that its interim measures under Rule 39 of the Rules of Court are legally binding. That position was confirmed by the Grand Chamber after a referral (by virtue of Article 43 of the Convention).[271]

The Court held that when there is a 'plausibly asserted' risk of 'irreparable damage' to one the core rights of the Convention, interim measures aim at preserving and protecting the rights of the applicants during the procedure.[272] Usually, interim measures will be asked for in cases of alleged violations of Article 2 or 3. Not surprisingly, most demands concern situations where extradition or deportation are at stake.[273] Exceptionally, claims under Articles 6[274] and 8[275] may lead to the application of interim measures.

Interim measures can be imposed for the length of the procedure, but a shorter period is possible. They also may be discontinued.[276] A Practice Direction has been taken by the President of the Court on the procedure to be followed when an applicant calls for an interim measure. There is no appeal against the Court's decision to refuse such measures.[277]

13.6. THE EUROPEAN CONVENTION AND THE COVENANT ON CIVIL AND POLITICAL RIGHTS

The co-existence of the possibilities of an individual right of complaint under the UN Covenant on Civil and Political Rights and the Convention raises two questions in particular. Is an individual, when he considers that one or more of his rights and freedoms, laid down in both treaties, has been violated, allowed to choose which action to institute? And may he also bring both actions for the same matter, either simultaneously or successively?

---

[268] See *Cruz Varas and Others v. Sweden*, ECtHR 20 March 1991, appl. no. 15576/89, para. 98.

[269] *Öcalan v. Turkey*, ECtHR (GC) 14 December 2000, appl. no. 46221/99.

[270] *Mamatkulov and Abdurasulovic v. Turkey*, ECtHR 3 February 2003, appl. nos. 46827/99 and 46951/99, paras. 94–96.

[271] See 2.2.8.2.

[272] *Paladi v. Moldova*, ECtHR (GC) 10 March 2009, appl. no. 39806/05, para. 89.

[273] <www.echr.coe.int/Documents/PD_interim_measures_intro_ENG.pdf>. As to Art. 2, e.g.: *Lambert and Others v. France*, ECtHR (GC) 5 June 2015, appl. no. 46043/14; On Art. 3, e.g., *Y.P and L.P. v. France*, ECtHR 2 September 2010, appl. no. 32476/06.

[274] *Othman v. The United Kingdom*, ECtHR 17 January 2012, appl. no. 8139/09.

[275] *Eskinazi and Chelouche v. Turkey*, ECtHR 6 December 2005, appl. no. 14600/05.

[276] <www.echr.coe.int/Documents/PD_interim_measures_intro_ENG.pdf>.

[277] <www.echr.coe.int/Documents/PD_interim_measures_intro_ENG.pdf>.

The first question may at once be answered in the affirmative. An individual who regards himself as the victim of a violation of one of the rights and freedoms guaranteed in the Convention as well as in the UN Covenant on Civil and Political Rights, must be considered free to use the procedure which he regards as the most favourable for his case, since neither of the two treaties prohibits this choice.[278] This is all the more so since the scope of a fundamental right may be different. This freedom of choice does not apply with respect to inter-state complaints, since Article 55 of the Convention provides that the Contracting Parties agree that, except by special agreement, they will not avail themselves of treaties, conventions or declarations in force between them for the purpose of submitting, by way of petition, a dispute arising out of the interpretation or application of the Convention to a means of settlement other than those provided for in the Convention.

With respect to the second question, three situations may arise: (1) identical applications are lodged at the same time under both instruments; (2) the applicant first tries the procedure of the UN Covenant on Civil and Political Rights and then, if he is not satisfied with the outcome, that of the Convention; and (3) the applicant applies first to the European Court and subsequently, if he is not satisfied with the outcome, to the Human Rights Committee.

In the first case, the applicant incurs the risk of being received by neither the Court nor the Committee. According to Article 35(2)(b) the Court cannot consider an application which is substantially the same as a matter which has already been submitted to another procedure of international investigation or settlement and if it contains no relevant new information.[279] For its part, Article 5(2) of the Optional Protocol of the UN Covenant on Civil and Political Rights provides that the Committee shall not consider any communication from an individual unless it has ascertained that the same matter is not being examined under another procedure of international investigation or settlement. From these provisions it appears that there is a real possibility that the application may be rejected by both organs. Such a highly unsatisfactory situation may be avoided if the Commission and the Committee pursue a flexible policy on this point. They might postpone consideration so as to enable the applicant to withdraw one of the two complaints. However, the situation where two applications are lodged at the same moment is likely to occur only rarely.

It is more likely that applications in Geneva and Strasbourg are lodged successively. If, as in the case mentioned above under (2), the second application is lodged in Strasbourg, this leads to its being declared inadmissible under Article 35(2)(b), unless relevant new information is put forward. In the opposite

---

[278] See *Secretariat Memorandum prepared by the Directorate of Human Rights on the effects of the various international human rights instruments providing a mechanism for individual communications on the machinery of protection established by the European Convention on Human Rights*, H(85)3, No. 23, p. 9.

[279] On this, see 2.2.12.4.

case, that of (3), such a conclusion does not follow imperatively from the text of Article 5(2)(a) of the Protocol. This provision provides for inadmissibility of a matter which is 'being examined under another procedure'. It is thus only the fact that the matter *is being* examined elsewhere which bars its admissibility, not the fact that the matter *has been* examined elsewhere. The Human Rights Committee, therefore, has actually taken the view that no complaint submitted to it is inadmissible merely on account of the fact that this case has already been examined in another procedure.[280]

It is questionable whether it is desirable that cases dealt with in Strasbourg may afterwards be brought up before the Committee again. An argument against this is that such a form of 'appeal' against decisions of the Strasbourg organs is contrary to the intention of the drafters of the Convention that the outcome of the procedure provided there is final. This intention may be inferred from Articles 35 and 42 of the Convention. Moreover, reasons of procedural economy may be advanced against renewed consideration of the same case by the Human Rights Committee. In general, it takes a number of years for a case to pass through the Strasbourg procedure and the preceding national procedures. One may well wonder whether after such a long procedure the case should be reopened again.

In any event the Committee of Ministers of the Council of Europe has answered that question in the negative. In 1970 it urged those Contracting States, which were to ratify the Optional Protocol to the UN Covenant on Civil and Political Rights, to attach to their ratification a declaration denying the competence of the Human Rights Committee to receive communications from individuals concerning matters which have already been or are being examined in a procedure under the Convention, unless rights or freedoms not set forth in the Convention are invoked in such communications.[281] Several of the Contracting States which are also parties to the Protocol, have followed up this suggestion by making a declaration or a reservation. The Netherlands, however, has refrained from making such a declaration or reservation. In the opinion of the Dutch Government there are indeed some practical objections to possible double procedures concerning the same matter, but they constitute an insufficient argument for preventing individuals from applying to the Human Rights Committee after having done so to the European Commission on Human Rights/Court. Moreover, the Dutch Government submits that the Committee and the Commission/Court have different powers in a number of respects. Finally, the making of declarations as suggested by the Committee of Ministers might be imitated in other regional arrangements, which might be detrimental to the worldwide system for the protection of human rights.[282] For individuals

---

[280]   See *Report of the Human Rights Committee of 1978*, General Assembly Official Records (A/33/40), p. 100.

[281]   See Yearbook XIII (1970), pp. 74–76.

[282]   Second Chamber, Session 1975–76, 13 932 (R 1037), Nos 1–6, p. 42.

subject to the jurisdiction of the Netherlands, therefore, it is possible to initiate, after the Strasbourg procedure, the procedure provided for in the Optional Protocol to the UN Covenant on Civil and Political Rights.

As regards the relevant practice of the two bodies concerned, the following may be observed. Only a few cases have been rejected by the European Commission on Human Rights and the Court under Article 35(2)(b) of the European Convention. The Secretariat usually prevents this by advising an applicant, who lodges a complaint already brought before the Committee, about the content of Article 35(2)(b). In a case where two members of the *Grapo* (an anti-fascist revolutionary group) had brought a complaint before the Commission, the Commission noted that it appeared from their letters to the Commissions that, before bringing his complaint in Strasbourg, the first applicant had brought a communication to the Human Rights Committee. The second applicant had joined this individual communication after having brought his complaint before the Commission. The Commission noted that in the relevant part of their application form the applicants omitted to mention the existence of the communication in question, then pending before the Human Rights Committee. Therefore, the Commission took the view that a situation of this type was incompatible with the spirit and letter of the Convention, which seeks to avoid a plurality of international proceedings relating to the same cases. According to the Commission the application was substantially the same as the petition submitted by the applicants to the Human Rights Committee, which was still pending before that Committee and was, therefore, inadmissible under Article 27(1)(b) [new Article 35(2)(b)].[283] The Commission also noted that a request for suspension of the proceedings before an international body (the applicants had requested the Human Rights Committee to grant such a suspension) did not have the same effect as a complete withdrawal of the application, which was the only step allowing the Commission to examine an application also brought before it.[284]

An interesting issue came up in the case of *A.N. v. Denmark*. Denmark had made a reservation, with reference to Article 5(2)(a) of the Optional Protocol, in respect of the competence of the Committee to consider a communication from an individual if the matter has already been considered under other procedures of international investigation. The author of the communication had already filed an application concerning the same matter with the Commission, which was declared inadmissible as manifestly ill-founded. On the basis of these facts but without any further argument the Committee concluded that it was not competent to consider the communication. It thus implicitly dismissed the position taken by one of its members in his individual opinion, who argued

---

[283] *Calcerrada Fornieles and Cabeza Mato v. Spain*, EComHR 6 July 1992, appl. no. 17512/90, D&R 73 (1992), p. 214 (223–224).

[284] *Ibid.*, p. 224.

that an application that had been declared inadmissible had not, in the meaning of the Danish reservation, been 'considered' in such a way that the Human Rights Committee was precluded from it. According to this point of view, the reservation aims at preventing a review of cases but does not seek to limit the competence of the Human Rights Committee merely on the ground that the rights of the UN Covenant on Civil and Political Rights allegedly violated may also be covered by the European Convention and its procedural requirements since it concerns a separate and independent international instrument.[285] In the *Wackenheim* case, the Committee declared a communication admissible, although the complaint had already been dealt with by the European Commission (who declared it inadmissible),[286] and notwithstanding the French reservation to Article 52(a), since the French State had not referred to this reservation.[287]

In the case of *Pauger*, the Committee decided that, irrespective of whether the State Party has invoked its reservation to Article 5(2)(a) of the Optional Protocol or not, the European Court has based the decision of inadmissibility solely on procedural grounds, rather than on reasons that include a certain consideration of the merits of the case. This meant that the same matter had not been 'examined' within the meaning of the Austrian reservation to Article 5(2)(a) of the Optional Protocol.[288] In the case of *Franz and Maria Deisl*, the Committee noted that the European Court declared the authors' application inadmissible for failure to comply with the six-month rule, and that no such procedural requirement existed under the Optional Protocol. In the absence of an 'examination' of the same matter by the European Court, the Committee concluded that it was not precluded from considering the authors' communication by virtue of the Austrian reservation to Article 52(a), of the Optional Protocol.[289]

In the case of *Rupert Althammer*, the Committee recalled that it on earlier occasions had already decided that the independent right to equality and non-discrimination embedded in Article 26 of the Covenant provides a greater protection than the accessory right to non-discrimination contained in

---

[285] *Report of the Human Rights Committee of 1982*, General Assembly Official Records (A/37/40), p. 213, and the individual opinion of the East German expert, Mr Graefrath, appended to this decision, p. 214. See also Communication No. 168/1984, *Report of the Human Rights Committee of 1985*, General Assembly Official Records (A/40/40), p. 235; see also Communication No. 744/1997, *Linderholm*, decision on admissibility adopted on 23 July 1999, UN Doc. CCPR/C/66/D/744/1997, at para. 4.2. where the Committee decided in the same way.

[286] *Wackenheim v. France*, EComHR 16 October 1996, appl. no. 29961/96.

[287] Communication No. 854/1999, Views adopted on 26 July 2002, para. 6.2.

[288] Communication No. 716/1996, *Pauger*, Views adopted on 25 March 1999, at para. 6.4. See, as well: Communication No. 1504/2006; *Vincent*, Views adopted on 31 October 2007, at para. 7.2.

[289] Communication No. 1069/202, Views adopted on 27 July 2004 at para. 10.2.

Article 14 of the European Convention. The Committee had taken note of the decision taken by the European Court on 12 January 2001 rejecting the authors' application as inadmissible as well as of the letter from the Secretariat of the European Court explaining the possible grounds of inadmissibility. It noted that the authors' application was rejected because it did not disclose any appearance of a violation of the rights and freedoms set out in the Convention or its Protocols as it did not raise issues under the right to property protected by Article 1 of Protocol No. 1. As a consequence, in the absence of an independent claim under the Convention or its Protocols, the Court could not have examined whether the authors' accessory rights under Article 14 of the Convention had been breached. In the circumstances of the case, therefore, the Committee concluded that the question of whether or not the authors' rights to equality before the law and non-discrimination had been violated under Article 26 of the Covenant was not the same matter that was before the European Court. The Committee, therefore, decided that the communication was admissible.[290] The outcome will now be different in respect of those states which have ratified Protocol No. 12.

---

[290] Communication No. 998/2001, Views adopted on 8 August 2003 at para. 7.1.

CHAPTER 2
PROCEDURE BEFORE THE COURT

Leo Zwaak, Yves Haeck and Clara Burbano Herrera[*]

CONTENTS

---

[*] In the fourth edition this chapter was revised and updated by Leo Zwaak.

1. EXAMINATION OF ADMISSIBILITY OF AN APPLICATION

1.1. REGISTRATION

A complaint usually reaches the Registry of the Court by way of a letter. As a rule, such letters have the character of a first contact and not of a formal application. Applicants may approach the Registry by sending a letter by facsimile ('fax'). However, they must send the signed original by post within five days following the dispatch by fax. It is in the interest of the applicant to be diligent in conducting the correspondence with the Registry. Any delay in replying or failure to reply is likely to be regarded as a sign that the applicant is not or no longer interested in having his case dealt with. Thus, if he does not answer a letter sent to him by the Registry within one year of its dispatch to him, his file will be destroyed.

The applicant receives a form for him to fill out which should be returned to the Registry within six weeks at the latest. He may also submit documents in addition to this form. The application, which must bear his signature, must contain: the name, age, occupation and address of the applicant; the name, occupation and address of his representative, if any; the name of the Contracting State against which the application is lodged; as specifically as possible, the object of the application and the provision of the Convention allegedly violated; a statement of the facts and arguments on which the application is based; and finally any relevant documents, and in particular any judgment or other act relating to the object of the application.[1] Moreover, in his application the applicant must provide information showing that the conditions laid down in Article 35(1) concerning the exhaustion of domestic remedies and the six-month time-limit for filing the application have been complied with.

If the above-mentioned requirements are satisfied and the complaint, *prima facie*, discloses a violation of the Convention, it will in general be entered in the official register of the Court. Registration has no other meaning than that the complaint is pending before the Court; no indications as to its admissibility may be inferred from it.

Until 1 January 2014, registration of a complaint – save in the event of failure to supply certain documents or information – was not refused if the party submitting it insisted on registration. Nevertheless, only a small part of all complaints received was actually registered. The other cases were withdrawn during the phase of the first correspondence with the Registry of the Court. The Registry had been instructed to draw the attention of potential applicants to the possibility of rejection of the complaint in cases where the existing case law pointed in that direction. The Registry did so by means of standard letters. At present, however, in the interest of efficiency, the Court has decided to do away with the warning letter. In accordance with Rule 49(1) of the Rules of Court where the material submitted by the applicant is on its own sufficient to disclose that the application is inadmissible or should be struck out of the list, the application shall be considered by a single-judge formation unless there is some special reason to the contrary. Rule 49(2) provides that once the case is ready to be examined, the President of the Section to which the case is assigned shall designate a judge as rapporteur, who will examine the application and decide whether it should be considered by a Committee or a Chamber.[2]

1.2. LANGUAGES

The official languages for the Court are English and French, however, you may write in an official language of one of the states that has ratified the Convention.

In connection with individual complaints, and for as long as no Contracting Party has been given notice of such an application, all communications with and oral and written submissions by applicants or their representatives, if not in one of the Court's official languages, will be in one of the official languages

---

[1] Rule 47(1) of the Rules of Court of the European Court of Human Rights, Strasbourg, as amended by the Court on 17 June and 8 July 2002, 11 December 2007, 22 September 2008 and May 2013 (amended on 19 September 2016) (the Rules of Court). See <www.echr.coe.int/Documents/Report_Rule_47_ENG.pdf>.

[2] See in this respect Reflection Group on the Reinforcement of the Human Rights Protection Mechanism, CDDH-GDR (2001)010, 15 June 2001, p. 9.

of the Contracting Parties.[3] If a Contracting Party is informed or given notice of an application, the application and any accompanying documents will be communicated to that state in the language in which they were lodged with the Registry by the applicant. In practice, this means that the parties may also use any of the other languages of the Contracting States, and that the correspondence may also be conducted in those languages.

All communications with and pleadings by such applicants or their representatives in respect of a hearing, or after a case has been declared admissible, will be in one of the Court's official languages, unless the President of the Chamber authorises the continued use of the official language of a Contracting Party. If such leave is granted, the Registrar will make the necessary arrangements for the interpretation and translation into English or French of the applicant's oral and written submissions respectively, in full or in part, where the President of the Chamber considers it to be in the interests of the proper conduct of the proceedings.[4] Exceptionally the President of the Chamber may make the grant of leave subject to the condition that the applicant bears all or part of the costs of making such arrangements. Unless the President of the Chamber decides otherwise, any decision made in this respect will remain valid in all subsequent proceedings in the case, including those in respect of requests for referral of the case to the Grand Chamber and requests for interpretation or revision of a judgment.

The President of the Chamber may direct that a Contracting Party which is a party to the case will, within a specified time, provide a translation into, or a summary in, English or French of all or certain annexes to its written submissions or of any other relevant document, or of extracts therefrom. The President of the Chamber may invite the respondent Contracting Party to provide a translation of its written submissions in the, or an, official language of that Party in order to facilitate the applicant's understanding of those submissions. Any witness, expert or other person appearing before the Court may use his or her own language if he or she does not have sufficient knowledge of either of the two official languages. In that event the Registrar shall make the necessary arrangements for interpreting or translation.[5]

1.3. REPRESENTATION

States are represented before the Court by their agents, who may be assisted by advocates or advisers.[6] Individuals, non-governmental organisations, or groups of

---

[3]   Rule 34(3)(a) Rules of the Court.
[4]   Rule 34(3) (b) Rules of the Court.
[5]   Rule 34(6) of the Rules of Court.
[6]   Rule 35 of the Rules of Court.

individuals may present and conduct applications before the Court on their own behalf, but may also be represented or assisted by an advocate authorised to practise in any of the Contracting Parties and residing in the territory of one of them, or any other person approved by the President of the Chamber. The President of the Chamber may, where representation would otherwise be obligatory, grant leave to the applicant to present his or her own case, subject, if necessary, to being assisted by an advocate or other approved representative. In exceptional circumstances and at any stage of the procedure, the President of the Chamber may, where he or she considers that the circumstances or the conduct of the advocate or other person appointed so warrant, direct that the latter may no longer represent or assist the applicant and that the applicant should seek alternative representation.[7] The advocate or other approved representative, or the applicant in person who seeks leave to present his or her own case, must have an adequate understanding of one of the Court's official languages, even if leave is granted to use one of the (other) languages of the Contracting States. In case he or she does not have sufficient proficiency to express himself or herself in the Court's official languages, leave may be given to use one of the official languages of the Contracting States.[8]

1.4. COSTS OF PROCEEDINGS

The procedure before the Court is free of charge for the parties; the expenses are accounted for by the Council of Europe.[9] Where a witness, expert or other person is summoned at the request or on behalf of a Contracting Party, the costs of their appearance shall be borne by that party unless the Chamber decides otherwise. The costs of the appearance of any such person who is in detention in the Contracting Party on whose territory on-site proceedings before a delegation takes place, shall be borne by that party unless the Chamber decides otherwise. In all other cases, the Chamber shall decide whether such costs are to be borne by the Council of Europe or awarded against the applicant or third party at whose request or on whose behalf the person appears.[10] In all cases, such costs will be taxed by the President of the Chamber.[11] Finally, in every stage of the procedure, after the written observations of the respondent government concerning the admissibility have been received or the time-limit for this has expired, the President of the Chamber may grant the applicant free legal aid if he deems this necessary for the proper conduct of the case before the Chamber and the applicant does not have sufficient means.[12]

---

[7]   Rule 36(4)(b) of the Rules of Court.
[8]   Rule 36(5) of the Rules of Court.
[9]   Art. 50 ECHR.
[10]   Rule A5 of the Rules of the Court.
[11]   Rule A5(6) of the Annex to the Rules of Court.
[12]   Rules 100–105 of the Rules of Court.

The President of the Chamber will conclude that free legal aid is necessary when it is evident that the applicant has had no legal training, or when it appears from the written documents submitted by him that he is unable to defend his case adequately before the Court.[13] In order to establish that he does not have sufficient means, the applicant must submit a declaration to that effect, certified by the appropriate domestic authorities.[14] Free legal aid may comprise not only lawyer's fees but also the travelling and subsistence expenses and any other necessary expenses incurred by the applicant and his lawyer.[15]

1.5. HANDLING OF CASE AFTER RECEIVAL OF APPLICATION

Any individual application will be assigned to a Section of a Chamber by the President of the Court. If the application is brought by a state, the President gives notice of the application to the state against which the claim is made and assigns the application to one of the Sections. The President of the Section constitutes the Chamber and invites the respondent state to submit written observations on the admissibility.[16] Where the material submitted by the applicant is on its own sufficient to disclose that the application is inadmissible or should be struck out of the list, the application shall be considered by a single-judge formation unless there is some special reason to the contrary.[17] Where an application is made under Article 34 of the Convention and its examination by a Chamber or a Committee exercising the functions attributed to it under Rule 53(2) seems justified, the President of the Section to which the case has been assigned shall designate a judge as judge-rapporteur, who shall examine the application.[18] In their examination of applications, judge-rapporteurs (1) may request the parties to submit, within a specified time, any factual information, documents or other material which they consider to be relevant; (2) shall, subject to the President of the Section directing that the case be considered by a Chamber or a Committee, decide whether the application is to be considered by a single-judge formation, by a Committee or by a Chamber; (3) shall submit such reports, drafts and other documents as may assist the Chamber or the Committee or the respective President in carrying out their functions.[19]

This procedure is known as the 'summary procedure', by which the Committee of three, by unanimous vote ('global formula'), may declare an

---

13   Rule 100 of the Rules of the Court.
14   Rule 102 of the Rules of Court.
15   Rule 103 of the Rules of Court.
16   Rule 48 of the Rules of Court.
17   Rule 49(1) of the Rules of the Court.
18   Rule 49(2) of the Rules of the Court.
19   Rule 49(3) of the Rules of the Court.

application inadmissible or strike it off the list, when such a decision can be taken without further examination.[20] In 2016 53,500 applications were allocated to a judicial formation, an overall increase of 32 per cent compared with 2015 (40,550). 27,300 of these were identified as single-judge cases likely to be declared inadmissible (a decrease of 1 per cent in relation to 2015). 26,200 were identified as probable Chamber or Committee cases (an increase of 100 per cent).[21]

Since January 2002 the applicant no longer receives a copy of the decision. He or she will receive a letter from the Registry stating that the application has been declared inadmissible and a brief outline in general terms of the grounds ('the global formula'). The letter states that the Registry is not able to give any further information or reasons in connection with the decision. This decision is final.[22]

If the application has not been declared inadmissible by unanimous vote of the Committee of three, the case will be examined by a Chamber. It is for the judge-rapporteur to prepare a report summarising the facts of the case, indicating the issues which it raises and making a proposal as to the procedure to be followed. The Chamber may request additional relevant information from the applicant or the state concerned and/or give notice of the application to the state and invite the state to present written observations on the admissibility of the application.[23] The information and/or observations of the state are communicated to the applicant, so that the latter may comment on it. The same holds true with respect to the information and/or observations obtained from the applicant, which will be communicated to the respondent state. After receipt of the observations of the state against which the application is brought, the application is examined by the judge-rapporteur. Before deciding upon the latter's report on admissibility, the Chamber may invite the parties to submit further observations in writing or orally.[24] If the Chamber decides to hold a hearing in this phase, the parties are invited to plead also on the merits. Such a combined procedure is intended to save time.[25]

A state may be assumed not to lodge an application lightly, on account of the political complications which such a step may involve. In the case of individual applications the chances for this to happen are greater. It would therefore not be right to communicate for comments to the governments concerned also those numerous applications which, *prima facie*, fail to satisfy the admissibility conditions. Nor does it appear to be objectionable that among individual applications a first selection is made *via* a simplified procedure, provided that the legal position of the applicant is not negatively affected by such a procedure. It is therefore of the greatest importance that the rapporteur be obliged to transmit

---

[20] Rule 53(2) of the Rules of Court.
[21] Analysis of statistics 2016 <www.echr.coe.int/Documents/Stats_analysis_2016_ENG.pdf>.
[22] Art. 28 ECHR.
[23] Rule 54(2) of the Rules of Court.
[24] Rule 54(2) (c) of the Rules of Court.
[25] Rules 54(3) and 54 A of the Rules of Court.

any information he obtains from a government to the applicant, upon which the latter may comment. Thus, the equality of the parties is properly secured.

It is less satisfactory, in our opinion, that the outcome of the simplified procedure is not communicated to the applicant in the form of a decision, signed by the president of the Committee concerned, with a specification of the ground(s) of inadmissibility, but by a Registrar's letter. The letter, signed by a member of the Registry, and which is not in the applicant's own language, does not do justice to the public character of the decision and is often experienced as a denial of justice.

In the case that the application is handled by a Chamber, the latter decides on the admissibility and merits.[26] At this stage of the proceedings, an oral hearing will be held if necessary. The Chamber may declare the case inadmissible at any stage of the proceeding, even if the case was initially declared admissible.[27] The decision on admissibility must be reasoned and as a rule is taken separately.[28] According to the Explanatory Report to Protocol 11, in its decision declaring the application admissible the Chamber may give the parties an indication of its opinion on the merits. A separate decision on admissibility is important to the parties if they are considering starting negotiations to reach a friendly settlement. There may, however, be situations in which the Court, in exceptional cases, might not take a separate admissibility decision. This could occur, for example, where a state does not object that a case be declared admissible.[29]

The main aim of Protocol No. 14 was to reduce the time spent by the Court on clearly inadmissible applications and repetitive applications. The filtering capacity has been increased by making a single judge competent to declare inadmissible or to strike out an individual application. This mechanism maintains the judicial character of the decision-making on admissibility. The single judges will be assisted by non-judicial rapporteurs, who will be staff members of the Registry. The work of rapporteurs will be carried out by other persons than judges, in order to achieve a significant potential increase in the filtering capacity which the institution of single-judge formations aims at. According to Article 26(3) the single judge shall not sit in cases concerning the High Contracting Party in respect of which he or she has been elected. The establishment of this system has led to a significant increase in the Court's filtering capacity.

Article 26(1) sets out the competence of the single-judge formations. Their competence will be limited to taking decisions of inadmissibility and decisions to strike a case out of the list 'where such a decision can be taken without further examination'. The purpose of this amendment is to provide the Court with an

---

[26]   Art. 29(1) ECHR.
[27]   Art. 35(4) ECHR.
[28]   Art. 45(1) ECHR.
[29]   Protocol No. 11 to the European Convention on Human Rights and Explanatory Report, paras. 77 and 78, Council of Europe, Strasbourg May 1994, H(94)5 (Explanatory Report).

additional tool which should assist it in its filtering work and allow it to devote more time to cases which warrant examination on the merits, whether seen from the perspective of the legal interest of the individual applicant or considered from the broader perspective of the law of the Convention and the European public order to which it contributes. The latter point is important with regard to the new admissibility criterion that the Court shall declare inadmissible where the applicant has not suffered a significant disadvantage, introduced in Article 35, in respect of which the Court's Chambers and Grand Chamber will first have to develop case law. In case of doubt as to the admissibility, the judge will refer the application to a Committee or Chamber.

Under the rule contained in Article 26(4), each High Contracting Party will be required to draw up a reserve list of *ad hoc* judges from which the President of the Court shall choose someone when the need arises to appoint an *ad hoc* judge. It is understood that the list of potential *ad hoc* judges may include names of judges elected in respect of other High Contracting Parties. More detailed rules on the implementation of this new system may be included in the Rules of Court.

Paragraphs 1 and 2 of Article 28 extend the powers of three-judge Committees. Under paragraph 28(1)(b), they may also, in a joint decision, declare individual applications admissible and decide on the merits, when the questions raised concerning the interpretation and application of the Convention are covered by well-established case law of the Court. 'Well-established case law' normally means case law which has been consistently applied by a Chamber. Exceptionally, however, it is conceivable that a single judgment on a question of principle may constitute 'well-established case law', particularly when rendered by the Grand Chamber. This new competence will apply, in particular, to repetitive cases, which account for a significant proportion of the Court's judgments. Parties may, of course, contest the 'well-established' character of the case law before the Committee.[30]

The new procedure concerning repetitive cases will be both simplified and accelerated, although it preserves the adversarial character of proceedings and the principle of judicial and collegiate decision-making on the merits. It will be simplified in that the Court will bring the case (possibly a group of similar cases) to the attention of the respondent party, pointing out that it concerns an issue which is already the subject of well-established case law. Should the respondent party agree with the Court's position, the latter will be able to give its judgment very rapidly. The respondent party may contest the application, for example, if it considers that domestic remedies have not been exhausted or that the case at issue differs from applications which have resulted in well-established case law.[31]

However, it may not veto the use of this procedure which lies within the Committee's sole competence. The Committee will rule on all aspects of

---

[30]   *Ibid.*, para. 68.
[31]   <www.echr.coe.int/Documents/Pilot_judgment_procedure_ENG.pdf>.

the case (admissibility, merits and just satisfaction) in a single judgment or decision. The procedure still requires unanimity on each aspect. Failure to reach a unanimous decision counts as no decision, in which event the Chamber procedure will apply.[32] It will then fall to the Chamber to decide whether all aspects of the case should be covered in a single judgment. Even when the Committee initially intends to apply the procedure provided for in Article 28(1)(b), it may still declare an application inadmissible under Article 28(1)(a). This may happen, for example, if the respondent party has persuaded the Committee that domestic remedies have not been exhausted. The implementation of the new procedure will increase substantially the Court's decision-making capacity and effectiveness, since many cases can be decided by three judges, instead of the seven currently required for admissible applications.

Even when a three-judge Committee gives a judgment on the merits, the judge elected in respect of the High Contracting Party concerned will not be an *ex officio* member of the Committee, in contrast with the situation with regard to judgments on the merits under the Convention as it stands. The presence of this judge would not appear necessary, since the Committee will deal with cases on which well-established case law exists. However, a Committee may invite the judge elected in respect of the High Contracting Party concerned to replace one of its members, if it deems the presence of this judge to be useful. For example, it may be felt that this judge, who is familiar with the legal system of the respondent party, should join in taking the decision, in particularly when such questions as exhaustion of domestic remedies need to be clarified. One of the factors which a Committee may consider relevant in this respect is whether the respondent party has contested the applicability of Article 28(1)(b).[33] According to the Explanatory Report to the Convention the reason why this factor has been explicitly mentioned in Article 28(3) is that it was considered important to have at least some reference in the Convention itself to the possibility for respondent parties to contest the application of the simplified procedure.[34] A respondent party may contest the new procedure, for example, on the basis that the case in question differs in some material respect from the established case law cited. It is likely that the expertise the national judge will have in domestic law and practice will be relevant to this issue and therefore helpful to the Committee. Should this judge be absent or unable to sit, the procedure provided for in Article 26(4) *in fine* will apply.[35]

While separate decisions on admissibility were the rule before the entry into force of Protocol No. 11, joint decisions are now commonly taken on the admissibility and merits of individual applications, which allows the Registry

---

32   Art. 29 (1) ECHR.
33   Art. 28(3) ECHR.
34   Explanatory Report to Protocol No. 14, CETS 194, para. 71.
35   'If there is none or if the judge is unable to sit, a person chosen by the President of the Court from a list submitted in advance by that Party shall sit in the capacity of judge.'

and judges to process faster while respecting fully the principle of adversarial proceedings. This practice has been formalised in Article 29. However, the Court may always decide that it prefers to take a separate decision on the admissibility of a particular application. According to the second paragraph of Article 29 separate decisions are the rule in the case of inter-state applications.

1.6. RELINQUISHMENT OF JURISDICTION IN FAVOUR OF THE GRAND CHAMBER

Where cases pending before a Chamber raise serious questions affecting the interpretation of the Convention or its Protocols, or where the resolution of a question before the Chamber might have a result inconsistent with a judgment previously delivered by the Court, the Chamber may, at any time before it has rendered its judgment, relinquish jurisdiction in favour of the Grand Chamber, unless one of the parties to the case objects.[36] The Chamber may take this decision of its own motion and does not have to give reasons for it. The Registrar notifies the parties of the Chamber's intention to relinquish jurisdiction. The parties will have one month from the date of that notification within which to file at the Registry a duly reasoned objection. An objection which does not fulfil these conditions will be considered invalid by the Chamber.[37] Article 30 ECHR will be amended once Protocol No. 15 ECHR enters into force.[38] According to Article 3 of this Protocol the right of the parties to a case to object to relinquishment of jurisdiction over it by a Chamber in favour of the Grand Chamber will be removed.

1.7. PUBLIC CHARACTER OF PROCEEDINGS

In accordance with Rule 63 of the Rules of the Court the hearings are public unless, in accordance with paragraph 2 of that Rule, the Chamber in exceptional circumstances decides otherwise, either of its own motion or at the request of a party or another person concerned. Paragraph 2 provides that the press and the public may be excluded from all or part of a hearing in the interests of morals, public order or national security in a democratic society, where the interests of juveniles or the private life of the parties so require, or to the extent strictly necessary in the opinion of the Chamber in special circumstances where

---

[36]   Art. 30 ECHR.
[37]   Rule 72(2) of the Rules of Court.
[38]   Protocol No. 15 Amending the Convention for the Protection of Human Rights and Fundamental Freedoms, 24 June 2013, ECTS No. 213. The Protocol will enter into force 3 months after all parties to the Convention have ratified it.

publicity would prejudice the interests of justice. In accordance with paragraph 3, any request for a hearing to be held in camera must include reasons and specify whether it concerns all or only part of the hearing.

Rule 33 provides that all documents deposited with the Registry in connection with an application, with the exception of those deposited within the framework of friendly-settlements negotiations, must be accessible to the public unless the President of the Chamber decides otherwise, either of its own motion or at the request of a party or another person concerned. According to its paragraph 2, public access to a document or to any part of it may be restricted in the interests of morals, public order or national security in a democratic society, where the interests of juveniles or the protection of the private life of the parties so require, or to the extent strictly necessary in the opinion of the President in special circumstances where publicity would prejudice the interests of justice.

Decisions and judgments given by a Chamber are always accessible to the public.[39] The Court periodically makes accessible to the public general information about decisions taken by the Committees.[40] According to Rule 77(2) the judgment may be read out at a public hearing.

1.8. INTERIM MEASURES

a. Scope

In cases where there is plausibly asserted to be a risk of irreparable damage to the enjoyment by the applicant of one of the core rights under the Convention, the object of an interim measure is, first, to ensure the continued existence of the matter that is the subject of the application and therefore to allow the Court to properly examine the application; and secondly, the preservation of the asserted rights of the applicant before irreparable damage is done to it.[41]

While the Court has never truly identified the rights with regard to which it can issue an interim measure, it has held that requests for its application usually concern the right to life (Article 2), the right not to be subjected to torture, inhuman or degrading treatment or punishment (Article 3) and, exceptionally, the right to respect for private and family life (Article 8) or other rights guaranteed by the Convention.[42]

---

[39]   The case law of the European Court of Human Rights can be found in HUDOC, <www.echr. coe.int/Pages/home.aspx?p=home&c=>.

[40]   Rule 33(4) of the Rules of Court.

[41]   *Mamatkulov and Askarov v. Turkey*, ECtHR (GC) 4 February 2005, appl. nos. 46827/99, 46959/99, paras. 124–125; see also *Paladi v. Moldova*, ECtHR (GC) 10 March 2009, appl. no. 39808/05, para. 89; *Makharadze and Sikharulidze v. Georgia*, ECtHR 22 November 2011, appl. no. 35254/07, para. 98.

[42]   *Mamatkulov and Askarov v. Turkey, supra* n. 41, para. 104.

Today, interim measures are essentially issued to temporarily halt the deportation or extradition of an applicant owing to danger for his integrity or life upon arrival in the receiving country.[43] This was for example the case regarding an extradition of a convicted terrorist to Morocco[44] or the extradition of a Tajik and an Uzbek to Tajikistan on account of presumed membership of a terrorist organisation.[45] On occasions a state is requested through an interim measure to provide a prisoner with adequate medical treatment in an appropriate medical establishment.[46] An interim measure has also, albeit very exceptionally, been issued to suspend the deportation to prevent a violation of the right to family life.[47] And the same can be said about measures issued to prevent the violation of the right to a fair trial.[48] On one occasion, the murder of an applicant during the Strasbourg proceedings itself has led to the adoption of an interim measure to the State not to hinder the right of petition of the remaining applicant in the case pending in Strasbourg,[49] and in another case a measure was indicated to a government to appoint a lawyer to represent a woman who had been divested of her legal capacity, and had not been able to participate in the adoption proceedings of her own daughter, before the European Court.[50]

b. Legal character

Originally, i.e. in the *Cruz Varas and Others* case, the Court took the position that the Convention did not contain any provision empowering the Convention organs to order interim measures.[51] The Court further noted that the practice of states revealed almost total compliance with the indications of interim measures. Subsequent practice could indeed be taken as establishing the agreement of states regarding the interpretation of a Convention provision, but not to create new rights and obligations which were not included in the Convention at the outset. The practice of complying with Rule 39 was rather based on good faith co-operation. Furthermore, no assistance could be derived from general principles of international law since no uniform legal rule existed on the matter.

---

[43] For an overview: C. Burbano Herrera and Y. Haeck, 'Staying the Return of Aliens from Europe through Interim Measures: the Case-law of the European Commission and the European Court of Human Rights', 13(1) *European Journal of Migration and Law*, 2011, pp. 31–51.

[44] *Ouabour v. Belgium*, ECtHR 2 June 2015, appl. no. 26417/10, para. 37.

[45] *Khodzhayev v. Russia*, ECtHR 12 May 2010, appl. no. 52466/08, para. 3.

[46] *Makharadze and Sikharulidze v. Georgia*, supra n. 41, para. 35; *Salakhov and Islyamova v. Ukraine*, ECtHR 14 March 2013, appl. no. 28005/08, para. 215.

[47] *Neulinger and Shuruk v. Switzerland*, ECtHR (GC) 6 July 2010, appl. no. 41615/07.

[48] *Öcalan v. Turkey*, ECtHR 30 November 1999, appl. no. 46221/99, Press Release 683 of 30 November 1999; Information Note No. 12, p. 23; *Bilasi-Ashri v. Austria*, ECtHR 26 November 2002, appl. no. 3314/02.

[49] *Bitiyeva and X. v. Russia*, ECtHR 21 June 2006 appl. nos. 57953/00, 37392/03.

[50] *X. v. Croatia*, ECtHR 17 July 2008, appl. no. 11223/04.

[51] *Cruz Varas and Others v. Sweden*, ECtHR 20 March 1991, appl. no. 15576/89, para. 102.

Accordingly, the Court found that the power to order binding interim measures could not be inferred from Article 34 or from other sources. According to the Court, it was within the province of the Contracting Parties to decide whether it was expedient to remedy this situation. However, the Court observed that where a state decided not to comply with a Rule 39 indication, it knowingly assumed the risk of being found in breach of Article 3 of Protocol No. 4 by the Convention organs.[52] This interpretation by the Court of Article 34, was confirmed in the case of *Conka*.[53]

In subsequent case law, inter alia in the *Mamatkulov and Askarov* case, however, the Court changed its view and held that its interim measures under Rule 39 of the Rules of Court are legally binding. In the aforementioned case, the Court held for the first time that by virtue of Article 34 ECHR member states undertake to refrain from any act or omission that may hinder the effective exercise of an individual applicant's right of application, and that a failure by a member state to comply with interim measures is to be regarded as preventing the Court from effectively examining the applicant's complaint and as hindering the effective exercise of his or her right and, accordingly, as a violation of Article 34 ECHR.[54] In order to come to this conclusion, the Court referred to the principle of effectivity, as well as the case law of the International Court of Justice, the Inter-American Court of Human Rights, the Human Rights Committee and the UN Committee against Torture, which, although operating under different treaty provisions to those of the Court, have confirmed that the preservation of the asserted rights of the parties in the face of the risk of irreparable damage represents an essential objective of interim measures in international law, the fact that a failure by a respondent state to comply with interim measures would undermine the effectiveness of the right of individual application under Article 34 and the state's formal undertaking in Article 1 ECHR to protect the ECHR rights and freedoms. The Court also referred to the fact that interim measures permit it not only to carry out an effective examination of the application but also to ensure that the protection afforded to the applicant by the Convention is effective; such indications also subsequently allow the Committee of Ministers to supervise execution of the final judgment. Such measures thus enable the state concerned to discharge its obligation to comply with the final judgment of the Court, which is – unlike the decisions and reports of the former Commission – legally binding under Article 46 ECHR.[55]

Nowadays, pursuant to the Court's vision itself, its interim measures are clearly binding upon states and have to be complied with,[56] and their non-

---

[52]   *Ibid.*, para. 103.
[53]   *Çonka v. Belgium,* ECtHR 13 March 2001 (dec.), appl. no. 51564/99.
[54]   *Mamatkulov and Askarov v. Turkey, supra* n. 41, para. 128.
[55]   *Ibid.*, paras. 108–127.
[56]   *Aoulmi v. France*, ECtHR 17 January 2006, appl. no. 50278/99; *Shtukaturov v. Russia*, ECtHR 27 March 2008, appl. no. 44009/05.

observance by a state will lead to an autonomous and almost automatic violation of the right to application (Article 34, *in fine* ECHR), under which a state may not hinder that right of petition.[57] A delay in the enforcement of an interim measure may also lead to a violation of Article 34. For example, a delay of four days due to the failure of the government and the domestic courts to enforce an interim measure in a particular case was deemed sufficient to establish a violation of Article 34 ECHR[58]

The fact that the damage which the measure aims to prevent subsequently turns out not to have occurred in spite of the state's failure to act in full compliance with the measure, is irrelevant for the appraisal of whether a state has complied with its obligations under Article 34. Therefore, no actual damage needs to be established.[59]

A state can exceptionally escape its responsibility for non-compliance/ late compliance, when it shows that there was an objective impediment which prevented (early) compliance, that it took all reasonable steps to remove the impediment and that it has kept the Court informed about the situation.[60]

c. Practice

Between 2006 and 2010 we see an increase of over 4,000 per cent in the number of requests for interim measures. Whilst in 2006 only 112 requests were received, by 2010, that figure had risen to 4,786. Meanwhile, the amount has once again decreased. In 2016 2,286 requests have been submitted while only 129 have been granted. While in recent years non-compliances have been on the increase[61], in the majority of cases the interim measures are taken seriously by the national authorities. In fact, it is only in cases of extreme urgency that interim measures are indicated: the facts must *prima facie* point to a violation of the Convention, and the omission to take the proposed measures must result or threaten to result in irreparable injury to certain vital interests of the parties or to the progress

---

[57]   *Olaechea Cahuas v. Spain*, ECtHR 10 August 2006, appl. no. 24668/03. See Y. Haeck, C. Burbano Herrera and L. Zwaak, 'Interim Measures in the Case-Law of the European Court for the Protection of Human Rights', *European Constitutional Law Review*, 2008, 41–63; C. Harby, 'The Changing Nature of Interim Measures before the European Court of Human Rights', 1 *European Human Rights Law Review*, 2010, 73–84.

[58]   *Paladi v. Moldova*, *supra* n. 41, paras. 84–106.

[59]   *Ibid.*, paras. 89, 104. But see Partly dissenting opinion of Judges Malinverni, Costa, Jungwiert, Myjer, Sajo, Lazarova Trajkovska and Karakas under *Paladi v. Moldova*, *supra* n. 58 and Partly dissenting opinion of Judge Bratza under *Paladi v. Moldova*, ECtHR 10 July 2007, appl. no. 39806/05.

[60]   *Paladi v. Moldova*, *supra* n. 41.

[61]   For an overview, see Y. Haeck, C. Burbano Herrera and L. Zwaak, 'Strasbourg's Interim Measures under Fire: Does the Rising Number of State Incompliances with Interim Measures Pose a Threat to the European Court of Human Rights?', *European Yearbook of Human Rights*, 2011, 375–403. Some very recent cases are: *Amirov v. Russia*, ECtHR 27 November 2014, appl. no. 51857/13 and *Kondrulin v. Russia*, ECtHR 20 September 2016, appl. no. 12987/15.

of the examination. Such would be the case, for instance, if an expulsion threatens to constitute a violation of Article 3 ECHR, in view of a serious risk that the person concerned will be exposed to torture or inhuman treatment or punishment. In that case, a stay of expulsion may be requested until the Court has had the opportunity to investigate the case. However, it will do so only if there is a high degree of probability that a violation of Article 3 is likely to occur.[62] This requires that the applicant states his case in a convincing manner and possibly also presents some evidence showing the danger to life or limb to which he may be exposed if expelled or extradited to a particular country. It is not sufficient for the applicant to provide information about the danger or uncertain situation in his country of origin and/or his being an opponent of the ruling government.

In what follows a few examples will be given of cases in which the European Court had to decide whether the respondent state concerned had abided by the interim measures issued.

In the *Soering* case, the applicant argued that, notwithstanding the assurance given to the United Kingdom Government, there was a serious likelihood that he would be sentenced to death if extradited to the United States of America. He maintained that in the circumstances and, in particular, having regard to the 'death row phenomenon', he would thereby be subjected to inhuman and degrading treatment and punishment contrary to Article 3 ECHR. He also submitted that his extradition to the United States would constitute a violation of Article 6(3)(c), because of the absence of legal aid in the State of Virginia to pursue various appeals. Finally, he claimed that, in breach of Article 13, he had no effective remedy under United Kingdom law in respect of his complaint under Article 3. The President of the Commission indicated to the United Kingdom Government, in accordance with Rule 39, that it was desirable, in the interests of the parties and the proper conduct of the proceedings, not to extradite the applicant to the United States until the Commission had had an opportunity to examine the application. This indication was subsequently prolonged by the Commission on several occasions until the case was referred to the Court, which on its turn indicated an interim measure.[63]

In June 2010, Turkey was also able to escape its responsibility under Article 34 in a case (*M.B. and Others*) where an Iranian family of four were deported to Iran on 30 July 2008 where they allegedly could face ill-treatment incompatible with Article 3 despite an interim measure issued by the Court to the contrary some hours earlier.[64] While the applicants alleged that their lawyer had been informed of the interim measure at around 1 p.m. and that they had been deported at 4 p.m., the Government maintained it had not failed to comply

---

[62] *Jabari v. Turkey*, ECtHR 11 July 2000, appl. no. 40035/98, para. 6.
[63] *Soering v. United Kingdom*, ECtHR 7 July 1989, appl. no. 14038/88, paras. 4, 77.
[64] *M.B. and Others v. Turkey*, ECtHR 15 June 2010, appl. no. 36009/08, paras. 3–4, 6, 10–15.

with the interim measure,[65] and the Court stated that that the letter addressed to the Turkish Government containing the interim measure was faxed to the Permanent Representative of Turkey to the Council of Europe at 12.47 p.m. (Strasbourg local time) and that the letter addressed to the applicants' lawyer was faxed at 1.06 p.m. (Strasbourg local time) (2.06 p.m. Turkish local time) and that, according to the document submitted by the Government regarding the deportation of the applicants signed by three Turkish and two Iranian police officers, the applicants were deported at 1 p.m. (Strasbourg local time). Therefore, the deportation took place only 13 minutes after Turkey was informed of the interim measure. So, taking into account the short time that elapsed between the receipt of the fax by the Government and the deportation of the applicants, the Court considered that it had not been established that Turkey had failed to demonstrate the necessary diligence in complying with the measure indicated by the Court.[66] However, only one month later Turkey was convicted of failing to comply with an interim measure and therefore violating Article 34 ECHR in the *D.B.* case. On 26 August 2008, the European Court decided to request the Turkish Government, under Rule 39, to allow, before 3 October 2008, the applicant's representative (or another advocate) to have access to the applicant in the Foreigners' Detention Centre where he was held with a view to obtaining a power of attorney and information concerning the alleged risks that the applicant would face if deported to Iran, i.e. after two lawyers instructed by the applicant's representative were not authorised to do so by the respective administrations.[67] The Government informed the Court, 13 days after the deadline given by the Court, that the competent authorities had been instructed to authorise the applicant to meet a lawyer. Only on 21 October 2008, 18 days after the deadline, was the applicant able to meet an advocate and sign an authority form. This led the Court to conclude that the Government had failed to comply with necessary diligence with the interim measure. Moreover, according to the Court, there were no objective impediments which prevented Turkey from complying with the interim measure in due time. In this connection, the Court wouldn't accept the argument put forward by Turkey that the beneficiary could not meet a lawyer in order to provide a power of attorney for the Court because that lawyer did not have a power of attorney to meet the beneficiary in the first place. Because of that initial administrative obtuseness, the Court held that the application had been put in jeopardy, since the applicant could not sign a power of attorney and provide more detailed information concerning the alleged risks that he would face in Iran. The applicant's effective representation before the Court had been seriously hampered. The fact that he had subsequently been able to meet a lawyer, sign the authority form and provide the information regarding

---

65   *Ibid.*, paras. 46–47.
66   *Ibid.*, paras. 48.
67   *D.B. v. Turkey*, ECtHR 13 July 2010, appl. no. 33526/08.

his situation in Iran had not altered the lack of timely action by the authorities, which had been incompatible with Turkey's obligations.[68]

Italy, albeit under the Berlusconi administration, has on a number of occasions blatantly refused to abide by an interim measure issued by the European Court. This implied that the beneficiaries of the provisional measures were effectively deported to Tunisia, notwithstanding the respective interim measures issued by the Court. In *Ben Khemais*, the beneficiary was a Tunisian national who was to be expelled by the Italian authorities back to his country of origin, where he had allegedly been sentenced *in absentia* to 10 years' imprisonment for being a member of a terrorist organisation. Out of fear of being denied justice if sent back, and thus of an increase of his sentence without a proper trial, and of being subjected to ill-treatment or even tortured, he applied to the European Court for an interim measure. On 29 March 2007, Italy was invited not to expel the applicant pending a decision on the merits.[69] The Italian Government nonetheless decided to ignore the provisional measure and deported the Tunisian on 3 June 2008. In a fax of 11 June 2008, the Court was informed by Italy that a deportation order had been issued on 31 May 2008 (thus after the interim measure) for the role the applicant had played in the activities of Islamic extremists, and an Italian criminal court had given its authorisation to the expulsion by observing that the person presented a threat to state security because he was in a position to renew contracts aimed at resuming terrorist activities.[70] In Strasbourg, Italy advanced a number of reasons for not holding it responsible for the events: first, the interim measure was taken on an erroneous factual basis, given that the expulsion was not based on a criminal court order, as indicated in the statement of facts accompanying the case communicated to the Government; secondly, the applicant had not exhausted all domestic remedies, as the judicial decision confirming the expulsion issued by the Milan Court of Appeal had not been not final; thirdly, given that the expulsion was based on a ministerial order after Italy had obtained diplomatic guarantees from Tunisia as to the treatment of the applicant, the non-abidance with the provisional measure did not breach any Convention interest; and fourthly, given that non-compliance with an interim measure did not automatically lead to a violation of Article 34, it was held that owing to the fact that the expulsion had only taken place almost one year after the exchange of the conclusions between the parties in Strasbourg, and the case was thus ready to be decided, neither the right of complaint nor the effective examination of the case by the Court were hindered.[71] On account of its failure to abide by the measure, Italy was nonetheless convicted for violating Article 34 ECHR.[72] The Court held that, regardless of whether the expulsion was

---

[68]   *Ibid.*, para. 67.
[69]   *Ben Khemais v. Italy*, ECtHR 24 February 2009, appl. no. 246/07, para. 18.
[70]   *Ibid.*, para. 23.
[71]   *Ibid.*, paras. 73–77.
[72]   *Ibid.*, para. 82.

carried out after the exchange of observations between the parties, by deporting the applicant to a third country the level of protection of the rights enshrined in Articles 2 and 3 had been irreversibly undermined. Moreover, the applicant had lost all contact with his lawyer – the latter being denied the possibility to visit his client. So, the normal procedure used by the European Court to examine a case, which is part of the effectivity of the right to application, was no longer possible.[73] In addition, Italy, before expelling the applicant, had not requested the lifting of the provisional measure – which was therefore still in force – and had proceeded with the expulsion even before obtaining diplomatic assurances from Tunisia that Italy had relied on in its comments.[74] Finally, the applicant's removal from the jurisdiction of Italy was a serious obstacle that could prevent Italy from fulfilling its obligations (under Articles 1 and 46 ECHR) to safeguard the applicant's rights and erase the consequences of eventual violations found, which could be labelled as a hindrance to the effective exercise by the applicant's right under Article 34 – in fact that right had been reduced to nil in the eyes of the Strasbourg Court.[75]

The case of *Al-Saadoon and Mufdhi*, a British case, concerns events that have taken place in Iraq in 2008. On 30 December 2008, the European Court tried – in vein – to halt the imminent transfer of two Iraqi nationals accused of murdering British soldiers, to the Iraqi authorities by the British forces in Iraq (whose UN Mandate was to expire on 31 December 2008) through applying Rule 39. This measure was issued following allegations that the beneficiaries would run a real risk of being killed in violation of their right to life (Article 2 ECHR) or the abolition of the death penalty (Article 1 of Protocol No. 13), being ill-treated in violation of the prohibition of torture (Article 3 ECHR) or receiving an unfair trial (Article 6 ECHR) upon being transferred. *In casu*, on 22 December 2008 the applicants requested an interim measure with the European Court. Following a ruling by the Court of Appeal in London on Tuesday 30 December 2008 that the handover should go ahead and, despite the European Court's provisional measure indicated the same day (shortly after it had been informed of the ruling of the Court of Appeal) to the UK Government that the applicants should not be removed or transferred from their custody until further notice, and despite also a subsequent High Court order dating from the night of the same day requiring the British authorities to honour the Strasbourg interim measure if the applicants were still under British control, the Iraqis were handed over to the Iraqi authorities on 31 December 2009. On the afternoon of 31 December, the Court was informed that the applicants had been transferred. By a letter dated 31 December, the UK informed the European Court that, principally because

---

[73] *Ibid.*, paras. 84–85.
[74] *Ibid.*, para. 86.
[75] *Ibid.*, para. 87. For some other cases: *Ali Toumi v. Italy*, ECtHR 5 April 2011 appl. no. 25719/09; *Trabelsi v. Italy*, ECtHR 13 April 2010, appl. no. 50163/08.

the UN Mandate which authorised the role of British forces in arrest, detention and imprisonment tasks in Iraq was due to expire, they could exceptionally not comply with the Court's measure.[76] Indeed, the letter to the Court stated that '(…) the Government took the view that, exceptionally, it could not comply with the measure (…); and (…) this action should not be regarded as a breach of Article 34 in this case. The Government regard the circumstances of this case as wholly exceptional. It remains the Government policy to comply with Rule 39 measures indicated by the Court as a matter of course where it is able to do so.'[77]

The objective impediments under UK law or legal obligations towards Iraq, claimed by the Government, for not complying with the measure, such as the absence, on 31 December 2008, of any available course of action consistent with respect for Iraqi sovereignty other than the transfer of the applicants, was deemed by the European Court to be of the respondent State's own making, and was therefore dismissed. The Court did not consider that the UK had taken all steps which could reasonably have been taken in order to comply with the interim measure taken by the Court. The failure to comply with the interim measure and the transfer of the applicants out of the UK's jurisdiction exposed them to a serious risk of grave and irreparable harm and amounted to a violation of Article 34 ECHR.[78]

As regards the manner in which requests under Rule 39 are to be presented, it is important to follow the indications found in the relevant Practice direction issued by the President of the Court.[79] It is useful to mention the following essential points. Firstly, the request should be submitted as soon as the final domestic decision has been taken, and sufficiently in advance of the execution of the decision, for instance an expulsion order, so that an intervention by the Court is still possible. The Court may not be able to deal with requests in removal cases received less than a working day before the planned time of removal. Indeed, a certain time is required for the Registry to prepare the case and, when necessary, to communicate or to obtain information on the matter, for instance by contacting the Agent of the Government to inquire about the Government's intentions. For these reasons, making a conditional request under Rule 39 pending the decision of the domestic authorities or courts might be advisable. In that case, one must indicate clearly the date on which the domestic decision will be taken and also mention that the request is subject to the final domestic

---

[76]   *Al-Saadoon and Mufdhi v. United Kingdom*, ECtHR 2 March 2010, appl. no. 61498/08, paras. 78–81.

[77]   *Ibid.*, para. 81.

[78]   *Ibid.*, paras. 162–165.

[79]   Practice direction issued by the President of the Court in accordance with Rule 32 of the Rules of Court on 5 March 2003 and amended on 16 October 2009 and on 7 July 2011. On the procedure, see also Y. Haeck and C. Burbano Herrera, 'Interim Measures in the Case Law of the European Court of Human Rights', 21(4) *Netherlands Quarterly of Human Rights*, 2003, 625–675.

decision being negative. Beware, an indication under Rule 39 will not be given if it is still possible to apply for domestic remedies with suspensive effect.

Secondly, the request must be in writing and should contain the required information. A telephone conversation might serve as an announcement of the request, but it cannot as such set in motion the procedure under Rule 39. On the other hand, communication by fax (or post) is sufficient provided it contains adequate information. In this connection, it is also very important to provide the Court with copies of relevant national judgments and decisions showing the arguments which have been put before the domestic authorities and courts and the reasons for the refusal to grant the claim.

Thirdly, people requesting an interim measure must always reply to correspondence from the Registry. In case of a rejection of an interim measure, they must inform the Court whether they wish to pursue the application. In case an interim measure has been indicated, they must keep the Court informed about the state of any continuing domestic proceedings.

d. Urgent notification

According to Rule 40, in case of urgency, the Registrar, with the authorisation of the President of the Chamber, may inform the respondent state of the introduction of the application and of a summary of its objects. The purpose of this provision is to prevent surprise on the part of the Contracting State concerned if afterwards any interim measures prove desirable.

e. Case priority

According to Rule 41 of the Rules of Court the Chamber shall deal with applications in the order in which they become ready for examination. It may, however, decide to give priority to a particular application. In the case of *X v. France*, the applicant was a haemophiliac who had undergone several blood transfusions and of whom it was discovered that he was HIV positive. He started proceedings for indemnity. He lodged his application with the Commission on 19 February 1991, alleging that his case had not been heard within a reasonable time as required under Article 6(1) ECHR. The Commission found a violation of Article 6(1) on 17 October 1991. The Court was prepared to give priority to the case and delivered its judgement on 31 March 1992, finding a violation of Article 6(1).[80] However, in February 1992 the applicant died.

In the case of *D. v. United Kingdom*, the applicant, who suffered from AIDS, maintained that his removal from the United Kingdom to St Kitts would expose him to inhuman and degrading treatment. His case was dealt with by the

---

[80] *X v. France*, ECtHR 31 March 1992, appl. no. 18020/91.

Court with priority.[81] In a case against Moldova and the Russian Federation concerning the responsibility for violations of the Convention in Transdniestria, a region which was separated from Moldova and was under the control of the Russian Federation, the Court decided to give priority to the examination.[82]

The *Pretty* case concerned an applicant who was dying of motor neurone disease, a degenerative disease affecting the muscles, for which there is no cure. The disease was at an advanced stage and the applicant's life expectancy was very poor. Given that the final stages of the disease were distressing and undignified, she wished to be able to control how and when she would die and be spared suffering and indignity. Although it is not a crime to commit suicide in English law, the applicant was prevented by her disease from taking such a step without assistance. It is, however, a crime to assist another to commit suicide under section 2(1) of the Suicide Act 1961. Ms Pretty wished to be assisted by her husband, but the Director of Public Prosecutions had refused her request to guarantee her husband freedom from prosecution if he did so. Her appeals against that decision were unsuccessful. The applicant complained of a violation amongst others of Articles 2 and 3 ECHR. The application was registered on 18 January 2002. On 22 January 2002, the Court decided to apply Rule 41 and to give the case priority, and to apply Rule 40 concerning an urgent notification to the application to the respondent Government. On 29 April 2002, the Court gave its judgment in the case and found no violation of the Convention.[83] Ms Pretty afterwards died in a natural way.

1.9. ADMISSIBILITY CRITERIA

Two of the admissibility conditions set forth in the Convention apply to applications submitted by states as well as to those submitted by individuals. These are the condition that all remedies within the legal system of the respondent state must have been exhausted before the case is submitted to the Court, and the condition that the application must have been submitted within a period of six months from the date on which the final national decision was taken (Article 35(1)). For the admissibility of an individual application additional requirements are that the application is not anonymous; that the application is not substantially the same as a matter that has already been examined by the Court or has already been submitted to another procedure of international investigation or settlement and contains no relevant new information; that the application is not incompatible with the provisions of the Convention or the

---

[81]   *D v. United Kingdom*, ECtHR 2 May 1997, appl. no. 30240/96.
[82]   *Ilaşcu and Others v. Moldova and the Russian Federation,* ECtHR (GC) 4 July 2001 (dec.), appl. no. 48787/99.
[83]   *Pretty v. United Kingdom*, ECtHR 29 April 2002, appl. no. 2346/02, para. 42.

Protocols thereto; that the application is not manifestly ill-founded; and that the application does not constitute an abuse of the right to lodge an application (Article 35(2) and (3)).

Paragraph 4 of Article 35 provides that the Court may reject the application which it considers inadmissible under this Article at any stage of the proceedings. Thus, it may do so also after having declared the case admissible at an earlier stage. Strictly speaking, one ought to differentiate between applications which are inadmissible and applications falling outside the competence of the Court, even though the Convention does not provide a clear basis for such a distinction. Applications by states may only be rejected on the grounds mentioned in Article 35(1), and not on the ground of incompatibility with the Convention mentioned in Article 35(2). All the same, it is evident that applications by states may also fall outside the jurisdiction of the Court, for instance when the application relates to a period in which the Convention was not yet binding upon the respondent state. The Court will have to reject such an application, but in this case, properly speaking, on account of lack of jurisdiction, not on account of inadmissibility, the grounds for which are enumerated exhaustively in the Convention. The practice concerning individual applications, however, shows that the Court usually rejects applications outside its competence *ratione personae, ratione materiae, ratione loci* or *ratione temporis* on account of inadmissibility. That is why issues relating to the jurisdiction of the Court will be discussed below under the heading of admissibility conditions.

In practice, the Court applies a particular sequence in the admissibility conditions by reference to which an application is examined. This sequence is based partly on logical, partly on practical grounds. But on the ground of practical considerations the case law of the Court diverges from this sequence on numerous occasions. Especially the use of the so-called 'global formula' is striking.[84] The Court uses this formula for rejecting an application which contained various separate complaints, as a whole on account of its manifestly ill-founded character, although the separate complaints might be inadmissible on different grounds. The Court based this approach on the fact that it did not consider it necessary in such a case to make a detailed examination of the separate elements of the application. Although according to Article 45(1), reasons must be given for judgments in which an application is declared admissible or inadmissible, the Explanatory Report points out that such reasons can be given in summary form.[85]

Protocol No. 14, which entered into force on 1 June 2010 changed the procedure considerably. This Protocol introduced a new admissibility criterion

---

[84]   This is often formulated as follows: 'An examination by the Court of this complaint as it has been submitted does not disclose any appearance of a violation of the rights and freedoms set out in the Convention.'

[85]   Explanatory Report, para. 105.

to the criteria laid down in Article 35. According to Article 35(3) the Court shall declare inadmissible any individual application submitted under Article 34 if it considers that the application is incompatible with the provisions of the Convention or the Protocols thereto, manifestly ill-founded, or an abuse of the right of individual application or the applicant has not suffered a significant disadvantage, unless respect for human rights as defined in the Convention and the Protocols thereto requires an examination of the application on the merits and provided that no case may be rejected on this ground which has not been duly considered by a domestic tribunal.

This new admissibility requirement provides the Court with an additional tool which should assist it in concentrating on cases which warrant an examination on the merits, by employing it to declare inadmissible applications where the applicant has not suffered any significant disadvantage, and which in the terms of respect for human rights, do not otherwise require an examination on the merits by the Court. Furthermore, the new admissibility criterion contains an explicit exception to ensure that it does not lead to the rejection of cases which have not been duly considered by a domestic tribunal. In the Explanatory Report to Protocol 14 it is stressed that the new criterion does not restrict the right of individuals to apply to the Court or alter the principle that all individual applications are examined on their admissibility. While the Court alone is competent to interpret the new admissibility requirement and decide on its application, its terms should ensure that rejection of cases requiring an examination on the merits is avoided. The latter will notably include cases which, notwithstanding their trivial nature, raise serious questions affecting the application or interpretation of the Convention or important questions concerning national law.[86]

The new criterion is meant as a tool for the Court in its filtering capacity. It was introduced in Protocol No. 14 to allow the Court to devote more time to cases which warrant examination on the merits. Its introduction was considered necessary in view of the ever-increasing caseload of the Court. According to the Explanatory Report to Protocol No. 14 it was necessary to give the Court some degree of flexibility in addition to that already provided for by the existing admissibility criteria. The interpretation of these criteria has been established in the case law that has been developed over several decades and is therefore difficult to be changed. It further pointed out that it is very likely that the numbers of individual applications to the Court will continue to increase, up to a point where other measures set out in this Protocol may well prove insufficient to prevent the Convention system from becoming totally paralysed, unable to fulfil its central mission of providing legal protection of human rights at the European level, rendering the right of individual application illusory

---

[86]   Explanatory Report to Protocol No. 14, CETS 194, para. 39.

in practice.[87] See in this respect the decision as to admissibility in the case of *Korolev* where the Court stated that Article 35(3)(b) does not allow the rejection of an application on the ground of the new admissibility requirement if the case has not been duly considered by a domestic tribunal. Qualified by the drafters as a second safeguard clause, its purpose is to ensure that every case receives a judicial examination whether at the national level or at the European level, in other words, to avoid a denial of justice. The clause is also consistent with the principle of subsidiarity, as reflected notably in Article 13 ECHR, which requires that an effective remedy against violations be available at the national level.[88]

In our opinion, the new criterion may have a filtering effect only after the Court has developed clear-cut jurisprudential criteria of an objective character capable of straightforward application. The terms 'has not suffered a significant disadvantage' are open to interpretation. Like many other terms used in the Convention, they are legal terms capable of, and requiring, interpretation establishing objective criteria through gradual development of the case law of the Court. According to the Explanatory Report, even in case the applicant has not suffered any significant disadvantage, the application will not be declared inadmissible if respect for human rights as defined in the Convention or the Protocols thereto requires an examination on the merits.[89] Furthermore, it will never be possible for the Court to reject an application on account of its trivial nature if the case has not been duly considered by a domestic tribunal.[90] It might be questioned if this element of subsidiarity could ever be applied in a consistent and well-balanced way, given the considerable differences between the domestic legal systems and judicial practices of the High Contracting Parties. In any case, it is to be expected that examination of whether this exception clause does apply, will require a thorough examination of the part of the file concerning domestic proceedings, and consequently reduce the gain of time that the application of the new criteria is meant to produce. On the other hand, the psychological costs on the part of the applicant of seeing his or her application being declared inadmissible for lack of significant disadvantage should not be underestimated. So far, this new admissibility ground has not led to dramatic decisions. Applications concerning claims of EUR 90, EUR 150 and a penalty of EUR 22, together with the deduction of a point for a traffic sanction have been declared inadmissible.[91] Finally, in the decision as to the admissibility in the case of *Gaftoniuc v. Romania*, the Court held in the circumstances of the case, it was conscious that the impact of a pecuniary loss must not be measured in abstract terms; even modest pecuniary damage may be significant in the light of the

---

[87] *Ibid.*, para. 78.
[88] *Korolev v. Russia*, ECtHR 1 July 2010 (dec.), appl. no. 25551/05.
[89] See in this respect Art. 37(1) ECHR.
[90] Explanatory Report to Protocol No. 14, CETS 194, paras. 81–82.
[91] *Ionescu v. Romania*, ECtHR 1 June 2010 (dec.), appl. no. 36659/04; *Rinck v. France*, ECtHR 7 July 2010 (dec.), appl. no. 18774/09.

person's specific condition and the economic situation of the country or region in which he or she lives. However, even taking into consideration the applicant's personal situation, i.e. a teacher within a public school and a single mother, the Court found that in the light of the minor nature of the award, roughly equal, to EUR 25 the applicant did not suffer a significant disadvantage within the meaning of Article 35(3)(b).[92]

Protocol No. 14 also amends Article 38 ECHR, which according to its wording was intended to apply after a case had been declared admissible. In its new wording, the text will read as follows: 'The Court shall examine the case together with the representatives of the parties and, if need be, undertake an investigation, for the effective conduct of which the High Contracting Parties concerned shall furnish all necessary facilities.'

The changes are intended to allow the Court to examine cases together with the parties' representatives, and to undertake an investigation, not only when the decision on admissibility has been taken, but at any stage of the proceedings. Since this provision even applies before the decision on admissibility has been taken, High Contracting Parties are required to provide the Court with all necessary facilities prior to that decision. Any problem which the Court might encounter in this respect can be brought to the attention of the Committee of Ministers so that the latter can take any step it deems necessary.[93]

The separate admissibility conditions are discussed here in the sequence referred to above.

1.10. EXHAUSTION OF DOMESTIC REMEDIES – ARTICLE 35(1)

a. Introduction

Article 35(1) provides that the Court may only deal with the matter after all domestic remedies have been exhausted, according to the generally recognised rules of international law, and within a period of six months from the date on which the final decision was taken. Article 35(1) will be amended once Protocol 15 to the Convention enters into force.[94] According to Article 4 of this Protocol the period within which an application must be made to the Court will be shortened from six to four months.

First, this article entails the so-called rule of the 'exhaustion of local remedies' (*épuisement des voies de recours internes*) (hereafter: the local remedies

---

[92]   *Gaftoniuc v. Romania*, ECtHR 22 February 2011 (dec.), appl. no. 30934/05.
[93]   Explanatory Report to Protocol No. 14, CETS 194, para. 90.
[94]   Protocol No. 15 Amending the Convention for the Protection of Human Rights and Fundamental Freedoms, 24 June 2013, ECTS No. 213. The Protocol will enter into force 3 months after all parties to the Convention have ratified it.

rule), which is to be regarded as a general rule of international procedural law.

It should be mentioned at the outset that the local remedies rule does not apply to procedures for affording satisfaction under Article 41 ECHR.[95] In fact, such procedures do not ensue from a new application, but constitute a continuation of the original application after a violation has been found by the Court. Questions of admissibility are not involved there at all.[96] Article 35(1) refers expressly to the general rules of international law in the matter, and in its case law the Court was indeed frequently guided by international judicial and arbitral decisions with respect to this rule. It, for instance, referred expressly, to the judgment of the International Court of Justice in the *Interhandel* case concerning the rationale of the local remedies rule.[97]

In the *Akdivar* case, the Court recalled that the rule of exhaustion of domestic remedies obliges those seeking to bring their case against the state before an international judicial or arbitral organ to use first the remedies provided by the national legal system. Consequently, states are dispensed from answering before an international body for their acts before they have had an opportunity to put matters right through their own legal systems. The rule is based on the assumption, reflected in Article 13 ECHR – with which it has close affinity –, that there is an effective remedy available in respect of the alleged breach in the domestic system whether or not the provisions of the Convention are incorporated in national law. In this way, it is an important aspect of the principle that the machinery of protection established by the Convention is subsidiary to the national systems safeguarding human rights.[98] It applies regardless of whether the provisions of the Convention have been incorporated into national law.[99] In the decision as to admissibility in the case of *Demospoulos and Others v. Turkey*, the Court reiterated that the rule of exhaustion of domestic remedies is an indispensable part of the functioning of the protection system under the Convention and that this is a basic principle.[100]

The local remedies rule applies in principle to applications by states as well as to individual applications. This ensues from the wording of Article 35(2) and (3) as compared to that of Article 35(1). The second and third paragraphs of Article 35 expressly declare the admissibility conditions mentioned therein to be

---

[95] On this, see *infra* section 5.
[96] *De Wilde, Ooms and Versyp v. Belgium ('Vagrancy' Cases)*, ECtHR 10 March 1972, appl. nos. 2832/66 2835/66 2899/66, para. 16.
[97] *ICJ Reports*, 1959, p. 6 (27).
[98] *Akdivar and Others v. Turkey*, ECtHR (GC) 16 September 1996, appl. no. 21893/93, para. 65; *Aksoy v. Turkey* ECtHR 18 December 1996, appl. no. 21987/93, para. 51; *İlhan v. Turkey*, ECtHR (GC) 27 June 2000, appl. no. 22277/93, para. 61; *D.H. and Others v. the Czech Republic*, ECtHR (GC) 13 November 2007, appl. no. 57325/00, para. 116.
[99] *Eberhard and M. v. Slovenia*, ECtHR 1 December 2009, appl. nos. 8673/05 and 9733/05, para. 103.
[100] *Demospoulos and Others v. Turkey*, ECtHR (GC) 19 May 2009, appl. nos. 46113/99, para.69.

applicable only to applications lodged under Article 4, while the first paragraph of Article 35, where the local remedies rule is laid down, is formulated in a general way and is therefore also applicable to applications by states. The same conclusion flows from the fact that the local remedies rule is a general rule of international procedural law.

While in the case of an individual application the local remedies must have been exhausted by the applicant himself, with respect to applications by states the rule implies that the local remedies must have been exhausted by those individuals in respect of whom, according to the allegation of the applicant state, the Convention has been violated.[101]

The local remedies rule is not an admissibility condition of an *absolute* character. In the *Aksoy* case, the Court held that the rule of exhaustion is neither absolute nor capable of being applied automatically.[102] On the basis of the reference in Article 35(1) to the 'generally recognised rules of international law', this rule is applied with flexibility.[103] Point of departure is that each concrete case should be judged 'in the light of its particular facts'. According to the Court this means, amongst other things, that it must take realistic account not only of the existence of formal remedies in the legal system of the Contracting Party concerned but also of the general legal and political context in which they operate as well as the personal circumstances of the applicants.[104] In this respect the Court noted in the *Akdivar* case that the situation existing in South-East Turkey at the time of the applicants' complaints was – and continued to be – characterised by significant civil strife due to the campaign of terrorist violence waged by the PKK and the counter-insurgency measures taken by the Government in response to it. In such a situation, it must be recognised that there may be obstacles to the proper functioning of the system of the administration of justice. In particular, the difficulties in securing probative evidence for the purposes of domestic legal proceedings, inherent in such a troubled situation, may make the pursuit of judicial remedies futile and the administrative inquiries on which such remedies depend may be prevented from

---

[101] The condition applies in international law only when the action of a state is concerned with the treatment of individuals. If a state puts forward its own legal position, the condition is not applied, since as a rule a state cannot be subjected against its will to the jurisdiction of another state.

[102] *Aksoy v. Turkey, supra* n. 98, para. 53; *Selmouni v. France*, ECtHR (GC) 28 July 1999, appl. no. 25803/94, para. 77.

[103] The Court has frequently stated that Art. 35 must be applied with some degree of flexibility and without excessive formalism. See, e.g., *Cardot v. France*, ECtHR 19 March 1991, appl. no. 11069/84, para. 36; *Akdivar v. Turkey, supra* n. 98, para. 69; judgment of 29 August 1997, *Ilhan v. Turkey, supra* n. 98, para. 51; *Kozacıoğlu v. Turkey*, ECtHR (GC) 19 February 2009, appl. no. 2334/03, para.40.

[104] *Akdivar v. Turkey, supra* n. 98, para. 69; *Financial Times Ltd and Others v. the United Kingdom*, ECtHR 15 December 2009, appl. no. 821/03, para. 42; *Saghinadze and Others v. Georgia*, ECtHR 27 May 2010, appl. no. 18768/05, para. 80.

taking place.[105] However, making use of the available remedies in accordance with domestic procedure and complying with the formalities laid down in national law are especially important where considerations of legal clarity and certainty are at stake.[106]

b.   Non-applicability of domestic remedies rule

1.   Inter-state complaints

The rule does not apply when a state brings up the legislation or administrative practice of another state without the complaint being related to one or more concrete persons as victims of this legislation or administrative practice (the so-called 'abstract' complaints). In such a case, there are no individuals who must have exhausted the local remedies, while the applicant state itself cannot be expected to institute proceedings before the national authorities of the respondent state. An example is the first *Cyprus* case, where Greece submitted that a number of emergency acts which were in force in Cyprus at that time, conflicted with the provisions of the Convention. In this case the Commission decided that the provision of 'Article 26 [the present Article 35(1)] concerning the exhaustion of domestic remedies (…) does not apply to the present application, the scope of which is to determine the compatibility with the Convention of legislative measures and administrative practices in Cyprus'.[107]

Later case law concerning inter-state applications confirmed this position.[108] According to the case law, an administrative practice comprises two elements: repetition of acts and official tolerance. The first element is defined as an accumulation of identical or analogous breaches which are sufficiently numerous and interconnected to amount not merely to isolated incidents or exceptions but to a pattern or system.[109] By official tolerance is meant 'that though acts of torture or ill-treatment are plainly illegal, they are tolerated in the sense that the superiors of those immediately responsible, though cognisant of such acts, take no action to punish them or to prevent their repetition; or that a higher

---

[105]   *Akdivar v. Turkey, supra* n. 98, para. 70; see also, *Mentes v. Turkey*, ECtHR 28 November 1997 appl. no. 23186/94, para. 58; *Dulas v. Turkey*, ECtHR 30 January 2001, appl. no. 25801/94, para. 45; *Ayder v. Turkey*, ECtHR 8 January 2004, appl. no. 23656/94, para. 89.

[106]   *Saghinadze and Others v. Georgia, supra* n. 104, para. 83.

[107]   *Greece v. United Kingdom*, EComHR 2 June 1956 (dec.), appl. no. 176/56, Yearbook II (1958–1959), p. 182 (184).

[108]   See, e.g., *Ireland v. United Kingdom*, EComHR 1 October 1972 (dec.), appl. no. 5310/71, Yearbook XV (1972), p. 76 (242); *Second Greek Case*, EComHR 16 July 1970 (dec.), appl. no. 4448/70, Yearbook XIII (1970), p. 108 (134–136); and *France, Norway, Denmark, Sweden and Netherlands v. Turkey*, EComHR 6 December 1983 (dec.), appl. nos. 9940–9944/82 D&R 35 (1984), p. 143 (162–163); *Cyprus v. Turkey*, EComHR 28 June 1996, (dec.), appl. no. 25781/94D & R 86A p. 104(138). See also *Akdivar v. Turkey, supra* n. 98, para. 67.

[109]   *Ireland v. United Kingdom*, ECtHR (GC) 18 January 1978, appl. no. 5310/71, para. 159; *Akdivar v. Turkey, supra* n. 98, para. 67.

authority, in face of numerous allegations, manifests indifference by refusing any adequate investigation of their truth or falsity, or that in judicial proceedings a fair hearing of such complaints is denied.'[110]

In the case of *France, Norway, Denmark, Sweden and Netherlands v. Turkey,* the Commission added that for it to reach the conclusion that there was no official tolerance, 'any action taken by the higher authority must be on a scale which is sufficient to put an end to the repetition of acts or to interrupt the pattern or system'.[111]

A condition is always that the applicant state should give 'substantial evidence' of the existence of the national legislation or administrative practice concerned. This requirement of 'substantial evidence' may take on a different meaning depending on whether the admissibility stage or the examination of the merits is concerned. According to the Commission: 'The question whether the existence of an administrative practice is established or not can only be determined after an examination of the merits. At the stage of admissibility *prima facie* evidence, while required, must also be considered as sufficient. (…) There is *prima facie* evidence of an alleged administrative practice where the allegations concerning individual cases are sufficiently substantiated, considered as a whole and in the light of the submissions of the applicant and the respondent Party. It is in this sense that the term "substantial evidence" is to be understood.'[112]

If the applicant state does not succeed in doing so, the local remedies rule applies.

2.   Individual complaints

In the case of individual applicants there can be no question of a completely abstract complaint about an administration practice. The applicant must submit that he is the victim of the alleged violation, which means that he is at the same time the person who must have exhausted all available local remedies.

As has been mentioned above, however, a legislative measure or administrative practice may indeed be challenged by an individual applicant, provided that he proves satisfactorily that he himself is the victim of it. A legislative measure or administrative practice may be of such a nature as to justify the presumption that the remedies of the state in question offer no prospects of effective redress. This is clearly the case if the situation complained of precisely consists of the absence of an effective judicial remedy required by one of the provisions of the Convention. The rationale for the exhaustion rule

---

[110]   *Greek* Case, EComHR 5 November 1969 (rep.), appl. nos. 9940–9944/82, Yearbook XII (1969), p. 196.

[111]   *France, Norway, Denmark, Sweden and Netherlands v. Turkey, supra* n. 108, p. 143 (164).

[112]   *Ibid.*, pp. 164–165.

is to afford the national authorities, primarily the courts, the opportunity to prevent or put right the alleged violations of the Convention. It is based on the assumption, reflected in Article 13, that the domestic legal order will provide an effective remedy for violations of Convention rights. This is an important aspect of the subsidiary nature of the Convention machinery.[113]

Ineffectiveness of remedies may particularly occur in the case of practices of torture and inhuman treatment. On that ground, in the *Donnelly* case, the Commission took the view that in such a situation the local remedies rule is not applicable, provided that the applicant gives *prima facie* evidence that such a practice has occurred and that he was the victim of it.[114] Several cases have been submitted by Kurdish citizens alleging that an administrative practice existed on the part of the Turkish authorities of tolerating abuses of human rights in relation to persons in police custody.[115] In one case the applicant had been killed following the submission of his application to the Commission and there were indications that to pursue the available remedies might have entailed serious risks for the other applicants. The Commission held that in these circumstances it was not necessary to resolve the question if there existed an administrative practice, because the applicants had done all that could be expected in the circumstances in relation to the local remedies. In the *Aksoy* case, the Commission noted the applicant's declaration that he had told the public prosecutor that he had been tortured. Moreover, when asked to sign a statement, he had answered that he could not sign because he could not move his hands. Although it was found not possible to establish in detail what happened during the applicant's meeting with the public prosecutor, the Commission found no reason to doubt that during their conversation there were elements which should have made the public prosecutor initiate an investigation or, at the very least, try to obtain further information from the applicant about his state of health or about the treatment to which he had been subjected. The Commission further noted that, after his detention, the applicant was in a vulnerable position, if he had, as he stated, been subjected to torture during his detention. The threats to which the applicant claimed to have been exposed after he had complained to the Commission, as well as his tragic death in circumstances which had not been fully clarified, were further elements which could at least support the view that the pursuance of remedies was not devoid of serious risks. The applicant could be said to have complied with the domestic remedies rule.[116] The Court accepted the facts as they had been established by the Commission and, on that basis, held

---

[113]   *Selmouni v. France, supra* n. 102, para. 152; *Kudla v.* Poland, ECtHR (GC), 26 October 2001, appl. no. 30210/96, para. 152.

[114]   *Donnelly and Others v. United Kingdom,* EComHR 5 April 1973 (dec.), appl. nos. 5577–5583/72, Yearbook XVI (1973), p. 212 (262). See also *Greek* Case, *supra* n. 110, p. 194.

[115]   *Aksoy v. Turkey,* EComHR 19 October 1994 (dec.), appl. no. 21987/93, D&R 79-A (1994), p. 60 (70–71); *Akdivar and Others v. Turkey,* EComHR 19 October 1994 (dec.), appl. no. 21893/93.

[116]   *Aksoy v. Turkey,* EComHR 19 October 1994 (dec.), *supra* n. 115, p. 60 (70–71).

that these constituted special circumstances which absolved Mr Aksoy from the obligation to exhaust the local remedies. Having reached that conclusion, the Court did not find it necessary to pronounce on whether there existed an administrative practice obstructing applications being made.[117]

At an earlier occasion, three applicants who had been placed in police custody, suspected of an offence coming within the jurisdiction of the State Security Council, alleged violations of Article 3 in that they were subjected to torture while held *incommunicado* in police custody. The Commission held that the Government had not mentioned any domestic remedy available to the applicants with regard to their detention *incommunicado* by the police, as such. Apparently, this particular form of detention was an administrative practice.[118] In the *Akdivar* case, the applicants maintained their allegations before the Court, which they had already made before the Commission, that the destruction of their homes was part of a State-inspired policy. That policy, in their submissions, was tolerated, condoned and possibly ordered by the highest authorities in the State aimed at massive population displacement in the emergency region of South-East Turkey. There was thus an administrative practice which rendered any remedies illusory, inadequate and ineffective. The Court concluded that there were special circumstances absolving the applicants from the obligation to exhaust their domestic remedies. The Court also emphasised that its ruling was confined to the particular circumstances of that case. It was not to be interpreted as a general statement that remedies were ineffective in that area of Turkey.[119]

c. Available remedies

In connection with the local remedies rule it is in the first place important to know what remedies are available. That question is to be answered on the basis of national law. It is for the respondent state to introduce any objection that the applicant has not exhausted domestic remedies[120] and to meet the burden of proving the existence of available and sufficient domestic remedies.[121] The respondent state also has the burden of proving that the existing remedies are effective, albeit only in cases where there is 'serious doubt'.[122]

---

117   *Aksoy v. Turkey, supra* n. 98, paras. 55–57.

118   *Hazar and Acik v. Turkey*, EComHR 11 October 1991 (dec.), appl. nos. 16311/90 16312/90 16313/90 D&R 72 (1992), p. 200 (208).

119   *Akdivar v. Turkey, supra* n. 98, para. 77.

120   *Selmouni v. France, supra* n. 102, para. 76: *A, B and C v. Ireland*, ECtHR (GC) 16 December 2010, appl. no. 25579/05, para. 142.

121   *Farrel v. United Kingdom*, EComHR 11 December 1982 (dec.), appl. no. 9013/80, D&R 30 (1983), p. 96 (101–102); *Stran Greek Refineries and Stratis Andreadis v. Greece*, ECtHR 9 December 1994, appl. no. 13427/87, para. 35; *Akdivar v. Turkey, supra* n. 98, para. 68 *Djavit v. Turkey*, ECtHR 20 February 2003, appl. no. 20652/92, para. 29.

122   *Dalia v. France*, ECtHR 19 February 1998, appl. no. 26102/95, para. 38; *McFarlane v. Ireland*, ECtHR (GC) 10 September 2010, appl. no. 31333/06, para. 107.

No definition of the term 'remedy' is to be found in the case law. In various places there are, however, indications as to its meaning. The concept of 'remedy' at all events does not cover those procedures in which one does not claim a right, but attempts to obtain a favour. The existence of remedies must be sufficiently certain not only in theory but also in practice. In determining whether any particular remedy meets the criteria of availability and effectiveness, regard must be had to the particular circumstances of the individual case. The position taken by the domestic courts must be sufficiently consolidated in the national legal order. Thus, the Court has held that recourse to a higher court ceases to be 'effective' on account of divergences in that court's case law, as long as these divergences continue to exist.[123] The Court has held that where an applicant complains about conditions of detention after the detention has already ended, a compensatory remedy that is available and sufficient – that is to say, one which offers reasonable prospects of success – is a remedy that has to be used for the purposes of Article 35(1).[124]

It is not only the *judicial* remedies which must be sought, but every remedy available under national law which may lead to a decision that is binding on the authorities,[125] including the possibility of appeal to administrative bodies, provided that the remedy concerned is adequate and effective.[126] The Court must take realistic account not only of formal remedies available in the domestic legal system, but also of the general legal and political context in which they operate as well as the personal circumstances of the applicant.[127]

The question of whether extraordinary remedies must also have been sought cannot be answered in a general way.[128] Discretionary or extraordinary remedies need not be used, for example requesting a court to review its decision,[129] or requesting the reopening of proceedings, except in special circumstances where, for example, it is established under domestic law that such a request does in fact constitute an effective remedy,[130] or where the quashing of a judgment that has acquired legal force is the only means by which the respondent state can put

---

[123]   *Ferriera Alves v. Portugal (No. 6)*, ECtHR 13 April 2010, appl. no. 46436/06 and 55676/08, paras. 28–29.
[124]   *Lienhardt v. France*, ECtHR 13 September 2011 (dec.), appl. no. 12139/10; *Rahzali and Others v. France*, ECtHR 10 April 2012 (dec.), appl. no. 37568/09; *Ignats v. Latvia*, ECtHR 24 September 2013 (dec.), appl. no. 38494/05.
[125]   *Selmouni v. France, supra* n. 102, para. 75.
[126]   *D.H and Others v. Czech Republic, supra* n. 98, para. 115.
[127]   *Akdivar and Others v. Turkey, supra* n. 98, paras. 68–69; *Khashiyev and Akayeva v. Russia*, ECtHR 24 February 2005, appl. no. 57942/00 and 57945/00, paras. 116–117.
[128]   *Kustannus Oy Vapaa Ajattelija and Others v. Finland*, EComHR 15 April 1996 (dec.), appl. no. 20471/92D& R 85 A (1996), p. 29(39).
[129]   *Prystavska v. Ukraine*, ECtHR 17 December 2012 (dec.), appl. no. 21287/02; *Cinar v. Turkey*, ECtHR 13 November 2003 (dec.), appl. no. 28602/95.
[130]   *K.S and K.S. AG v. Switzerland*, EComHR 12 January 1994 (dec.).

matters right through its own legal system.[131] Similarly, an appeal to a higher authority does not constitute an effective remedy.[132] Nor does a remedy that is not directly accessible to the applicant but is dependent on the exercise of discretion by an intermediary.[133] Lastly, a domestic remedy which is not subject to any precise time-limit and thus creates uncertainty cannot be regarded as effective.[134] Whether an individual application to the Constitutional Court is required by Article 35(1) will depend largely on the particular features of the respondent state's legal system and the scope of its Constitutional Court's jurisdiction. Thus, in a state where this jurisdiction is limited to reviewing the constitutionality of legal provisions and their compatibility with provisions of superior legal force, applicants will be required to avail themselves of a complaint to the Constitutional Court only if they are challenging a provision of a statute or regulation as being in itself contrary to the Convention.[135] However, this will not be an effective remedy where the applicant is merely complaining of the erroneous application or interpretation of statutes or regulations which are not unconstitutional *per se*.[136] An application for retrial or similar extraordinary remedies cannot, as a general rule, be taken into account for the purpose of applying Article 35 ECHR.[137] In the case of *Jilicic v. Bosnia*, the Court held that when a remedy has been pursued, use of another remedy which has essentially the same objective is not required. It is for the Court to determine whether a particular body is domestic or international in character having regard to all relevant factors including the legal character, its founding instrument, its competence, its place (if any) in an existing legal system and its funding.[138]

The interpretation and application of the relevant provisions of national law in principle belong to the competence of the national authorities concerned. The Court, on the other hand, is competent to judge whether, as a result of such an interpretation or application, the applicant would become the victim of a denial of justice. In the *Akdivar* case, the Court held that this means amongst other things that it must take realistic account not only of the existence of formal remedies in the legal system of the Contracting Party concerned but also of the general legal and political context in which they operate as well as the personal circumstances of the applicants.[139]

---

[131] *Kiiskinen and Kovalainen v. Finland*, ECtHR 1 June 1999 (dec.), appl. no. 26323/95; *Nikula v. Finland*, ECtHR 30 November 2000 (dec.), appl. no. 31611/96.

[132] *Horvath v. Croatia*, ECtHR 26 July 2001, appl. no. 51585/99, para. 47; *Hartman v. Czech Republic*, ECtHR 10 July 2003, appl. no. 53341/99, para. 66.

[133] *Tănase v. Moldova*, ECtHR (GC) 27 April 2010, appl. no. 7/08, para. 122.

[134] *Williams v. United Kingdom*, ECtHR 17 February 2009 (dec.), appl. no. 32567/06.

[135] *Grišankova and Grišankovs v. Latvia*, ECtHR 13 February 2003 (dec.), appl. no. 36117/02; *Liepājnieks v. Latvia*, ECtHR 2 November 2010 (dec.), appl. no. 37586/06.

[136] *Smirnov v. Russia*, ECtHR 6 July 2006 (dec.), appl. no. 14085/04.

[137] *Tumilovich v. Russia*, ECtHR 29 January 2004 (dec.), appl. no. 47033/99.

[138] *Jilicic v. Bosnia*, ECtHR 15 November 2005 (dec.), appl. no. 41183/02.

[139] *Akdivar v. Turkey*, supra n. 98, para. 69; see also *Selmouni v. France*, supra n. 102, para. 77.

A question which for a long time had been left undecided in the case law is what an applicant should do when different remedies are open to him. Must he pursue them all or may he confine himself to bringing the action which in his view is most likely to be successful? The text of Article 35(1) appears to suggest the former, for it refers to 'all domestic remedies'.   In the decision as to the admissibility in the case of *Aquilina v. Malta,* the Court held that if more than one potentially effective remedy is available, the applicant is only required to have used one of them.[140]

In the *Airey* case, the Court held that it was primarily for the applicant to select which legal remedy to pursue.[141] It is up to the applicant in those cases to indicate which remedy he has chosen and for what reasons. These grounds have to be objective and reasonable.[142] In the case of *A, B and C v. Ireland*, the third applicant had a rare form of cancer. When she discovered she was pregnant she feared for her life as she believed that her pregnancy increased the risk of her cancer returning and that she would not obtain treatment for that cancer in Ireland while pregnant. The Court considered that the establishment of any such relevant risk to her life caused by her pregnancy clearly concerned fundamental values and essential aspects of her right to respect for her private life. The Court considered that the only non-judicial means for determining such a risk on which the Government relied, the ordinary medical consultation between a woman and her doctor, was ineffective. The uncertainty surrounding such a process was such that it was evident that the criminal provisions of the 1861 Act constituted a significant chilling factor for women and doctors as they both ran a risk of a serious criminal conviction and imprisonment if an initial doctor's opinion that abortion was an option as it posed a risk to the woman's health was later found to be against the Irish Constitution. Neither did the Court consider recourse by the third applicant to the courts (in particular, the constitutional courts) to be effective, as the constitutional courts were not appropriate for the primary determination of whether a woman qualified for a lawful abortion. It was likewise inappropriate to ask women to pursue such complex constitutional proceedings when their right to have an abortion if pregnancy posed a threat to their life was not disputed. In any event, it was unclear how the courts were to enforce any mandatory order requiring doctors to carry out an abortion, given the lack of clear information from the Government to the Court as regards lawful abortions currently carried out in Ireland. The Court concluded that neither the medical consultation nor litigation options, relied on by the Irish Government, constituted effective and accessible procedures which allowed the

---

[140]   *Aquilina v. Malta*, ECtHR (GC) 29 April 1999, appl. no. 25642/94, para. 39; *Moreira Barbosa v. Portugal*, ECtHR 29 April 2004 (dec.), appl. no. 65681/01; *Jeličić v. Bosnia and Herzegovina, supra* n. 138; *Karakó v. Hungary*, ECtHR 28 April 2009, appl. no. 39311/05, para. 14.

[141]   *Airey v. Ireland*, ECtHR 9 October 1979, appl. no. 6289/73, para. 23.

[142]   *Idem.*

third applicant to establish her right to a lawful abortion in Ireland. Moreover, there was no explanation why the existing constitutional right had not been implemented to date.[143]

d. Dispensation

Another important question in connection with Article 35(1) is whether all the available legal remedies must have been pursued. Here, too, a good deal depends on the relevant national law, and the answer to this question can only be given on a case-by-case basis. The Court held that the rule of exhaustion of domestic remedies referred to in Article 35(1) obliges those seeking to bring their case against the state before an international judicial or arbitral organ to use first the remedies provided by the national legal system. Consequently, states are dispensed from answering before an international body for their acts before they have had an opportunity to put matters right through their own legal systems. The rule is based on the assumption, reflected in Article 13 – with which it has close affinity –, that there is an effective remedy available in respect of the alleged breach in the domestic system whether or not the provisions of the Convention are incorporated in national law. In this way, it is an important aspect of the principle that the machinery of protection established by the Convention is subsidiary to the national systems safeguarding human rights. Under Article 35(1), normal recourse should be had by an applicant to remedies which are available and sufficient to afford redress in respect of the breaches alleged. The existence of the remedies in question must be sufficiently certain not only in theory but in practice, failing which they will lack the requisite accessibility and effectiveness. However, there is no obligation to have recourse to remedies which are inadequate or ineffective. In addition, according to the 'generally recognised rules of international law' to which Article 35(1) makes reference, there may be special circumstances which absolve the applicant from the obligation to exhaust the domestic remedies at his disposal. The rule is also inapplicable where an administrative practice consisting of a repetition of acts incompatible with the Convention and official tolerance by the state authorities has been shown to exist, and is of such a nature as to make proceedings futile or ineffective.[144]

From the very voluminous and rather casuistic case law the following trends may be inferred.

---

[143] *A, B and C v. Ireland*, ECtHR (GC) 16 December 2010, appl. nos. 25579/05, paras. 256–258.
[144] *Aksoy v. Turkey*, ECtHR 18 December 1996, appl. no. 21987/93, paras. 51–52; *Akdivar v. Turkey, supra* n. 98, paras. 65–67.

1.   Effective and adequate remedies

Applicants are only obliged to exhaust domestic remedies which are available in theory and in practice at the relevant time and which they can directly institute themselves – that is to say, remedies that are accessible, capable of providing redress in respect of their complaints and offering reasonable prospects of success[145] Recourse to an organ which supervises the administration but cannot take binding decisions, such as an Ombudsman, does not constitute an adequate and effective remedy in the sense of Article 35(1).[146]

The existence of remedies must be sufficiently certain not only in theory but also in practice. In determining whether any particular remedy meets the criteria of availability and effectiveness, regard must be had to the particular circumstances of the individual case. The position taken by the domestic courts must be sufficiently consolidated in the national legal order. Thus, the Court has held that recourse to a higher court ceases to be 'effective' on account of divergences in that court's case law, as long as these divergences continue to exist.[147] Where the national authorities remain passive in the face of serious allegations of misconduct or infliction of harm by state agents, this is a relevant criterion in absolving the applicant from the obligation to exhaust domestic remedies. The speed with which a remedy can be exercised may also be a relevant factor in assessing its effectiveness.[148]

In the *Tsomtsos* case, the Court reiterated that the only remedies Article 35 ECHR requires to be exhausted are those that are available and sufficient and relate to the breaches alleged.[149] In the *Iatridis* case, the Court considered that an action for damages might sometimes be deemed a sufficient remedy, in particular where compensation is the only means of redressing the wrong suffered. In the instant case, however, compensation would not have been an alternative to the measures which the Greek legal system should have afforded the applicant to overcome the fact that he was unable to regain possession of the cinema despite a court decision quashing the eviction order. Furthermore, the various proceedings pending in the Athens Court of First Instance were decisive only in respect of an award of just satisfaction under Article 41 ECHR. As to the third limb of the objection, the Court reiterated that Article 35 requires the exhaustion only of remedies that relate to the breaches alleged: suing a private individual cannot be regarded as such a remedy in respect of an act on the part

---

145   *Sejdovic v. Italy*, ECtHR (GC) 1 March 2006, appl. no. 56591/00, para. 46; *Paksas v. Lithuania*, ECtHR (GC), 6 January 2011, appl. no. 34932/04, para. 75.

146   *Denizci and Others v. Turkey*, ECtHR 23 May 2001, appl. nos. 25316/94 25317/94 25318/94, para. 362.

147   *Fereira Alvez v. Portugal (No. 6)*, *supra* n. 123, paras. 28–29.

148   *Selmouni v. France*, EComHR 25 November 1996, appl. nos. 25803/94, D & R 88 B (1997), p. 55 (62–63).

149   *Tsomtsos v. Greece*, ECtHR 15 November 1996, appl. no. 20680/92, para. 32.

of the state, in this instance the refusal to implement a judicial decision and return the cinema to the applicant.[150] In addition, any procedural means which might have prevented a breach of the Convention should have been used.[151] An applicant may of course refrain from an appeal if the tribunal in question is not competent in the matter of his claim.[152] In the Slovak Republic a petition to the Constitutional Court is not an effective remedy, insofar as the formal institution of the proceedings depends on a decision of the court and the court cannot interfere with or quash decisions of the ordinary courts.[153]

In the *Boyle and Rice* case, the Court held that recourse to the administrative bodies could be considered an effective remedy in respect of complaints concerning the application or implementation of prison regulations.[154] In the *Brozicek* case, the Court observed that in the Italian legal system an individual was not entitled to apply directly to the Constitutional Court for review of a law's constitutionality. Only a court trying the merits of a case has the right to make a reference to the Constitutional Court, either of its own motion or at the request of a party. Accordingly, such an application cannot be a remedy whose exhaustion is required under Article 35 ECHR.[155] However, in the *Cenbauer* case, the Court considered that it had not been demonstrated that an appeal to the administrative bodies or to a judge responsible for supervising the execution of sentences offered the applicant the possibility of securing redress for his complaints. In particular, the Court notes that section 15(1) of the amended Act on Enforcement of Prison Terms refers to a complaint concerning the 'acts or decisions of a prison employee' and, accordingly, did not provide a remedy in respect of complaints relating to the general conditions in prison.[156] In the *Tumilovich* case, the Court held that an application for retrial or similar extraordinary remedies could not, as a general rule, be taken into account for the purpose of applying Article 35 ECHR.[157] With regard to the right to have a court decide speedily on the lawfulness of detention, an action for damages against the state is not a remedy which has to be exhausted, because the purpose of an action for damages on the ground of the defective operation of the machinery of justice is to secure compensation for the prejudice caused

---

150 *Iatridis v. Greece*, ECtHR (GC) 19 October 2000, appl. no. 31107/96, para. 47.

151 *Barberà, Messegué and Jabardo v. Spain*, ECtHR (GC) 6 December 1988, appl. no. 10590/83, para. 59; *Cardot v. France, supra* n. 103, para. 36.

152 *Guzzardi v. Italy*, ECtHR 6 November 1980, appl. no. 7367/76, para. 69.

153 *Šamková v. Slovak Republic*, EComHR 28 June 1996 (dec.), appl. no. 26384/95, D & R 86 A (1997) p. 43 (151–152).

154 *Boyle and Rice v. United Kingdom*, ECtHR 27 April 1988, appl. nos. 9659/82, 9658/82, para. 65.

155 *Brozicek v. Italy*, ECtHR (GC) 19 December 1989, appl. no. 10964/84, para. 34; *De Jorio v. Italy*, ECtHR 6 March 2003 (dec.), appl. no. 73936/01.

156 *Cenbauer v. Croatia*, ECtHR 5 February 2004 (dec.), appl. no. 73786/01.

157 *Tumilovich v. Russia, supra* n. 137; *Berdzenishvili v. Russia*, ECtHR 29 January 2004 (dec.), appl. no. 31697/03; *Denisov v. Russia*, ECtHR 6 May 2004 (dec.), appl. no. 33408/03.

by deprivation of liberty, not to assert the right to have the lawfulness of that deprivation of liberty decided speedily by that court.[158]

In the *Akdivar* case, the applicants alleged that there was no effective remedy available for obtaining compensation before the administrative courts in respect of injuries or damage to property arising out of criminal acts of members of the security forces. In order to demonstrate that the available remedies were not ineffective, the Turkish Government referred to a number of judgments of the administrative courts. Some of these decisions concerned cases in which the State Council had awarded compensation to individuals for damage inflicted by public officials or by terrorists, or suffered in the course of confrontations between the Government, the public and the PKK. According to the Government, claims for compensation could also have been lodged in the ordinary civil courts. The Court considered it significant that the Government, despite the extent of the problem of village destruction, had not been able to point to examples of compensation being awarded in respect of allegations that property had been purposely destroyed by members of the security forces or to prosecutions having been brought against them in respect of such allegations. In this connection, the Court noted the evidence referred to by the Delegate of the Commission as regards the general reluctance of the authorities to admit that this type of illicit behaviour by members of the security forces had occurred. It further noted the lack of any impartial investigation, any offer to co-operate with a view to obtaining evidence or any *ex gratia* payments made by the authorities to the applicants. Moreover, the Court did not consider that a remedy before the administrative courts could be regarded as adequate and sufficient in respect of the applicants' complaints, since it was not satisfied that a determination could be made in the course of such proceedings concerning the claim that their property was destroyed by members of the gendarmerie.[159] As regards the civil remedy invoked by the respondent Government, the Court attached particular significance to the absence of any meaningful investigation by the authorities into the applicants' allegations and of any official expression of concern or assistance notwithstanding the fact that statements by the applicants had been given to various State officials. It appeared to have taken two years before statements were taken from the applicants by the authorities about the events complained of, probably in response to the communication of the complaint by the Commission to the Government.[160]

In the *Egmez* case, the applicant made a complaint to the Ombudsman which resulted in a report naming some of the officers responsible for the alleged ill-treatment of the applicant. Having regard to the Attorney-General's refusal

---

[158]   *Tomasi v. France*, ECtHR 27 August 1992 appl. no. 12850/87, para. 81: *Navarra v. France*, ECtHR 23 November 1993, appl. no. 13190/87, para. 24.
[159]   *Akdivar v. Turkey, supra* n. 98, paras. 71–72.
[160]   *Ibid.*, para. 73.

to take any action, the Court decided that the applicant's complaint to the Ombudsman had not discharged the authorities of the Republic of Cyprus of the duty to 'undertake an investigation capable of leading to the punishment (as opposed to the mere identification) of those responsible'.[161] The same was true in the *Denizci case*, where the Attorney-General refrained from taking any action despite the power he had to conduct an *ex officio* enquiry and where, under Cypriot law, the Ombudsman would have had no power to order any measures or impose any sanctions. In those circumstances, the Court considered that the applicants were justified in considering that no other legal remedy on the national level would be effective in respect of their complaints.[162] In the *Yasa* case, the Court held that with respect to an action in administrative law under Article 125 of the Turkish Constitution based on the authorities' strict liability, that a Contracting State's obligation under Articles 2 and 13 of the Convention to conduct an investigation capable of leading to the identification and punishment of those responsible in cases of fatal assault might be rendered illusory if in respect of complaints under those articles an applicant were to be required to exhaust an administrative law action leading only to an award of damages. Consequently, the applicant was not required to bring the administrative proceedings in question.[163]

In the *Doğan* case, the Court stated that, when an individual formulates an arguable claim in respect of forced eviction and destruction of property involving the responsibility of the state, the notion of an 'effective remedy', in the sense of Article 13 ECHR, entails, in addition to the payment of compensation where appropriate, a thorough and effective investigation capable of leading to the identification and punishment of those responsible and including effective access by the complainant to the investigative procedure. Otherwise, if an action based on the state's strict liability were to be considered a legal action that had to be exhausted in respect of complaints under Article 8 ECHR or Article 1 of Protocol No. 1, the state's obligation to pursue those guilty of such serious breaches might thereby disappear. As regards a civil action for redress for damage sustained through illegal acts or patently unlawful conduct on the part of state agents, the Court recalled that a plaintiff must, in addition to establishing a causal link between the tort and the damage he had sustained, identify the person believed to have committed the tort. In the instant case, however, those responsible for the forced eviction of the applicants from their village were still unknown. Accordingly, the Court did not consider that a remedy before the administrative or civil courts could be regarded as adequate and effective in respect of the applicants' complaints, since it was not satisfied that a determination could be

---

[161]   *Egmez v. Cyprus*, ECtHR 21 December 2000, appl. no. 30873/96, para. 67.
[162]   *Denizci and Others v. Cyprus, supra* n. 146, paras. 362–363.
[163]   *Yasa v. Turkey*, ECtHR 2 September 1998, appl. no. 22495/93, para. 74.

made in the course of such proceedings concerning the allegations that villages were forcibly evacuated by members of the security forces.[164]

In the *Hobbs* case, the Court held that a declaration of incompatibility issued by a British court to the effect that a particular legislative provision infringed the Convention cannot be regarded as an effective remedy within the meaning of Article 35(1). It stated: 'In particular, a declaration is not binding on the parties to the proceedings in which it is made. Furthermore, by virtue of section 10(2) of the 1998 Act, a declaration of incompatibility provides the appropriate minister with a power, not a duty, to amend the offending legislation by order so as to make it compatible with the Convention. The minister concerned can only exercise that power if he considers that there are 'compelling reasons' for doing so.'[165]

Thus, a remedy which is not enforceable or binding, or which is dependent on the discretion of the executive, falls outside the concept of effectiveness as established in the Convention case law, notwithstanding that it may furnish adequate redress in cases in which it has a successful outcome.[166]

In a case against Ireland, the Court held that in a legal system providing constitutional protection for fundamental rights, it is incumbent on the aggrieved individual to test the extent of that protection and, in a common-law system, to allow the domestic courts to develop those rights by way of interpretation. In this respect, it was recalled that a declaratory action before the High Court, with a possibility of an appeal to the Supreme Court, constitutes the most appropriate method under Irish law of seeking to assert and vindicate constitutional rights.[167]

In the *Horvat* case, the Court noted that proceedings pursuant to section 59(4) of the Hungarian Constitutional Court Act are considered as being instituted only if the Constitutional Court, after a preliminary examination of the complaint, decides to admit it. Thus, although the person concerned can lodge a complaint directly with the Constitutional Court, the formal institution of proceedings depends on the latter's discretion.

In the *Said* case, the Government argued that the applicant had failed to exhaust domestic remedies, in view of the fact that he had independently and voluntarily withdrawn his application for a provisional measure in the proceedings before the Administrative Jurisdiction Division of the Council of State. The Court noted that according to the case law of the President of the

---

[164]   *Doğan and Others v. Turkey*, ECtHR 18 November 2004, appl. nos. 8803/02 8804/02 8805/02, paras. 106–108.

[165]   *Hobbs v. United Kingdom*, ECtHR 6 June 2002 (dec.), appl. no. 63684/00; *Walker v. United Kingdom*, ECtHR 16 March 2004 (dec.), appl. no. 37212/02; *Pearson v. United Kingdom*, ECtHR 27 April 2004 (dec.), appl. no. 8374/03; *Varnava and Others v. Turkey*, ECtHR (GC) 18 September 2009, appl. nos. 16064/90–16066/90, 16068/90–16073/90, para. 157.

[166]   *B. and L. v. United Kingdom*, ECtHR 29 June 2004 (dec.), appl. no. 36536/02.

[167]   *Independent News and Media plc and Independent Newspapers (Ireland) Limited v. Ireland*, ECtHR 19 June 2003 (dec.) appl. no. 55120/00.

Administrative Jurisdiction Division, a request for a provisional measure will be declared inadmissible if the date for the expulsion has not yet been made known. No reproach could therefore be made of the applicant for withdrawing his request.[168]

2.   Remedy and real chances of success

A remedy is ineffective and does not therefore have to be sought if, considering well-established case law, it does not offer any real chance of success.[169] In that case, however, the applicant must give some evidence of the existence of such case law. Particularly in a common-law system, where the courts extend and develop principles through case law, it is generally incumbent on an aggrieved individual to allow the domestic courts the opportunity to develop existing rights by way of interpretation.[170]

For a situation where reliance on standing case law was honoured reference may be made to the decision of the Commission in the so-called '*Vagrancy*' cases, where three Belgians claimed that they had been unlawfully detained for vagrancy.[171] Up to the moment at which the applications were lodged it had been established case law of the Belgian Council of State that the latter had no jurisdiction with respect to an appeal against such detention. After the applications had been declared admissible, the Council of State reversed its approach. According to the Commission, this was no reason for declaring the applications as yet inadmissible because of non-exhaustion of an effective local remedy.[172]

3.   Length of proceedings

Effectiveness is also considered to be lacking when the procedure is exceptionally protracted. In the *Plaskin* case, the Court noted that according to the Convention organs' constant case law, complaints concerning length of procedure could be brought before it before the final termination of the proceedings in question.[173]

---

[168]   *Said v. the Netherlands*, ECtHR 5 October 2004 (dec.), appl. no. 2345/02.

[169]   *Vernillo v. France*, ECtHR 19 February 1998, appl. no. 11889/85, para. 27; *Dalia v. France*, *supra* n. 122, para. 38; *Merger and Cros v. France*, ECtHR 11 March 2004 (dec.), appl. no. 68864/01.

[170]   *Whiteside v. United Kingdom*, EComHR 7 March 1994 (dec.), appl. no. 20357/92, D&R 76-A (1994), p. 80 (88); *Martin v. United* Kingdom, ECtHR 27 March 2003 (dec.), appl. no. 63608/00.

[171]   *De Wilde, Ooms and Versyp v. Belgium*, EComHR 7 April 1967 (dec.), appl. nos. 2832, 2835 and 2899/66, Yearbook X (1967), p. 420.

[172]   *De Wilde, Ooms and Versyp v. Belgium ('Vagrancy' Cases)*, EComHR 19 July 1969 (rep.), appl. nos. 2832, 2835 and 2899/66, B.10 (1971), p. 94. See also *Öztürk v. Germany*, EComHR 15 December 1981 (dec.), appl. no. 8544/79D&R 26 (1982), p. 55 (69).

[173]   *Plaskin v. Russia*, ECtHR 29 April 2004, appl. no. 14949/02, para. 35; *Todorov v. Bulgaria*, ECtHR 18 January 2005, appl. no. 39832/98, para. 59.

However, that is only the case if a given procedure is structurally protracted, i.e. in all cases.[174] The fact that a given procedure is very lengthy in a concrete case does not in itself set aside the condition of the Convention that a remedy in such a procedure must be sought. In fact, in that case the applicant will first of all have to seek redress against that long duration within the national legal system concerned.

In cases where requiring the applicant to use a particular remedy would be unreasonable in practice and would constitute a disproportionate obstacle to the effective exercise of the right of individual application under Article 34, the Court has concluded that the applicant was dispensed from that requirement[175]

4.   Independence of court

The prior exhaustion of local remedies is not required if the competent court is not fully independent, thus that the necessary guarantees for a fair trial are not present. In the first *Greek* case, where Denmark, Norway, Sweden and the Netherlands complained about the torture of political prisoners in Greece, the applicant States alleged the existence of an administrative practice to which the local remedies rule was not applicable. In the Commission's opinion, however, the applicant States had not given 'substantial evidence' for the existence of such a practice. Nevertheless, the applications were not rejected under Article 26 [the present Article 35(1)]. The Greek Government had discharged several judges for political reasons. Under those circumstances the Commission found that there was insufficient independence of the judiciary. It concluded that the judicial procedures provided for under Greek law no longer constituted effective remedies which should have been exhausted.[176]

A comparable situation arose as a result of the Turkish military action in Cyprus. According to the Commission the action had 'deeply and seriously affected the life of the population in Cyprus and, in particular, that of the Greek Cypriots'.[177] The circumstances were such that the existing remedies available in domestic courts in Turkey or before Turkish military courts in Cyprus' could be considered as effective remedies which had to be exhausted according to Article 35(1) with respect to complaints of inhabitants of Cyprus only 'if it were shown that such remedies are both practicable and normally functioning in such cases'.[178] The Commission found that this had not been proved by the Turkish Government.

In the *Yöyler* case, the Court considered that a complaint to the chief public prosecutor's office could in principle provide redress for the kind of violations

---

[174]   *Plaskin v. Russia, supra* n. 173.

[175]   *Gaglione and Others v. Italy*, ECtHR 21 December 2010, appl. no. 45667/07, para. 22.

[176]   *Denmark, Norway, Sweden and Netherlands v. Greece*, EComHR 31 May 1968 (dec.), appl. nos. 3321–3323 and 3344/67, Yearbook XI (1968), p. 730 (774).

[177]   *Cyprus v. Turkey*, EComHR 26 May 1975 (dec.), appl. nos. 6780/74 and 6950/75, D&R 2 (1975), p. 125 (137).

[178]   *Ibid.*, pp. 137–138.

alleged by the applicants. However, any prosecutor who receives a complaint alleging a criminal act by a member of the security forces must decline jurisdiction and transfer the file to the Administrative Council. On that account, the Court reiterated that it has already found in a number of cases that the investigation carried out by the latter body cannot be regarded as independent since it is composed of civil servants, who are hierarchically dependent on the governor, and an executive officer is linked to the security forces under investigation.[179] In the *Doğan* case, the Court noted in this connection that the applicants filed petitions with various administrative authorities complaining about the forced evacuation of their village by the security forces. These proceedings did not result in the opening of a criminal investigation or any inquiry into the applicants' allegations. The Court was therefore of the opinion that the applicants were not required to make a further explicit request to this effect by filing a criminal complaint with the chief public prosecutor's office as this would not have led to any different result.[180]

e.   Submission in substance to national authorities

The local remedies rule is considered to be complied with only if the points on which an application is lodged in Strasbourg have also been put forward in the relevant national procedure.[181] This means that if the applicant has not relied on the provisions of the Convention, he or she must have raised arguments to the same or like effect on the basis of domestic law, in order to have given the national courts the opportunity to redress the alleged breach in the first place.[182]

In the *Van Oosterwijck* case, the Court held in this respect: 'The fact that the Belgian courts might have been able, or even obliged, to examine the case of their own motion under the Convention cannot be regarded as having dispensed the applicant from pleading before them the Convention or arguments to the same or like effect.'[183]

The formula used in the case law requires that the point concerned must have been submitted 'in substance' to the national authorities.[184] The precise implications of this requirement will depend on the concrete circumstances of the case. In general, the applicant will not be required to have explicitly referred

---

[179]   *Yöyler v. Turkey*, ECtHR 24 July 2003, appl. no. 26973/95, para. 93; *İpek v. Turkey*, ECtHR 17 February 2004, appl. no. 25760/94, para. 207.

[180]   *Doğan v. Turkey*, ECtHR 18 November 2004, appl. no. 42831/98, para. 109.

[181]   *Ahmed Sadik v. Greece*, ECtHR 15 November 1996, appl. no. 18877/91, para. 30; *Selmouni v. France*, supra n. 102, para. 74; *Azinas v. Cyprus*, ECtHR 28 April 2004, appl. no. 56679/00, paras. 40–41.

[182]   *Gäfgen v. Germany*, ECtHR 1 June 2010, appl. no. 22978/05, paras. 142 and 144; *Karapanagiotou v. Greece,* ECtHR 26 October 2010, appl. no. 1571/08, para. 29.

[183]   *Van Oosterwijck v. Belgium,* ECtHR 6 November 1980, appl. no. 7654/76, para. 39.

[184]   *Glasenapp v. Germany*, ECtHR (GC) 28 August 1986, appl. no. 8228/80, para. 44; *Akdıvar v. Turkey, supra* n. 98, paras. 65–67 and *Aksoy v. Turkey, supra* n. 98, paras. 51–52.

to the relevant articles of the Convention in the national procedure.[185] In the case of *Gasus Dosier- und Fördertechnik GmbH,* the Court observed that it was true that Article 1 of Protocol No. 1 was referred to for the first time by the Tax Collector, and that the applicant company consistently denied its applicability and argued it before the Supreme Court only in an alternative submission. Nevertheless, in the event both the Court of Appeal and the Supreme Court were able to deal with the allegation of a violation of that provision and in fact did so. Accordingly, the applicant company did provide the Dutch courts, and more particularly the Netherlands Supreme Court, with the opportunity of preventing or putting right the alleged violation of Article 1 of Protocol No. 1.[186]

In the *Cajella* case, the applicant lodged a constitutional application, in accordance with the relevant domestic rules, in which he alleged a violation of Article 5(3) and Article 6(1) ECHR on account of the length of his detention on remand and of the criminal proceedings concerning the charge of complicity in attempted murder. The application was examined both by the First Hall of the Civil Court and by the Constitutional Court. In the Court's view, by raising the 'reasonable time' issue before the competent domestic courts, the applicant invited them to examine the length of his trial and of his deprivation of liberty in the light of the Court's case law and to determine whether, during the relevant periods, there had been excessive delays for which the authorities might be held responsible. By doing so, he complied with his obligation to make normal use of the available domestic remedies. Against this background, it was of little relevance that the applicant might not have explicitly drawn the attention of the Civil Court and of the Constitutional Court to the shortcomings which, according to him, had occurred during a specific stage of the proceedings.[187]

Express reference to provisions of the Convention may, however, be necessary in certain cases: 'In certain circumstances it may nonetheless happen that express reliance on the Convention before the national authorities constitutes the sole appropriate manner of raising before those authorities first, as is required by Article 26, an issue intended, if need be, to be brought subsequently before the European review bodies.'[188]

In other words, express reference to the provisions of the Convention is necessary if there is no other possibility of submitting the issue 'in substance' in the appropriate way to the national organs.[189]

---

[185] Thus, the Court in *Van Oosterwijck v. Belgium, supra* n. 183, para. 39.
[186] *Gasus Dosier- und Fördertechnik GmbH, v. Netherlands,* ECtHR 23 January 1995, appl. no. 15375/89, para. 49.
[187] *Calleja v. Malta,* ECtHR 18 March 2004, appl. no. 75274/01 (dec.).
[188] *Van Oosterwijck v. Belgium, supra* n. 183, para. 37.
[189] See *Guzzardi v. Italy, supra* n. 152, para. 72, where it was held: 'However, a more specific reference was not essential in the circumstances since it did not constitute the sole means of achieving the aim pursued (…). He [the applicant] (…) derived from the Italian legislation

The above exposé holds true for those Contracting States where the Convention has internal effect. Things are different, of course, in Contracting States where the Convention has no domestic status and has not been incorporated. Indeed, in such a case directly invoking the Convention before the national authorities will in most cases be of no avail. Consequently, the Commission decided in a case against the United Kingdom: 'Before lodging this application the applicant lodged an appeal against her conviction and sentence. Although in the appeal proceedings she did not invoke the rights guaranteed in Articles 5, 9 and 10, she has to be considered to have exhausted domestic remedies because the Convention which guarantees the said rights is not binding law for the British courts and it is doubtful whether the rights and liberties in question constitute general principles which could successfully be invoked by the defence in criminal proceedings before the British courts.'[190]

Here again, however, it may be required that the applicant has invoked legal rules or principles of domestic law which are 'in substance' the same as the relevant provisions of the Convention.[191]

f. Burden of proof

Where the government claims non-exhaustion of domestic remedies, it bears the burden of proving that the applicant has not used a remedy that was both effective and available.[192] The availability of any such remedy must be sufficiently certain in law and in practice.[193] The remedy's basis in domestic law must therefore be clear.[194] The remedy must be capable of providing redress in respect of the applicant's complaints and of offering reasonable prospects of success.[195] The development and availability of a remedy said to exist, including its scope and application, must be clearly set out and confirmed or complemented by practice or case law.[196] This applies even in the context of a common law-inspired system with a written constitution implicitly providing for the right relied on by the applicant concerning a remedy that had been available in theory for almost 25 years but had never been used.[197] In general, the Court is well informed about the remedies available under the different national systems of law and, in dubious cases, may ascertain their existence via its Registry. If the Court has established

---

pleas equivalent, in the Court's view, to an allegation of a breach of the right guaranteed by Article 5 of the Convention.'

[190] *Arrowsmith v. United Kingdom*, EComHR 16 May 1975 (dec.), appl. no. 7050/75.
[191] *Geouffre de la Pradelle v. France*, ECtHR 16 December 1992, appl. no. 12964/87, para. 26.
[192] *Dalia v. France, supra* n. 122, para. 38; *McFarlane v. Ireland, supra* n. 122, para. 107.
[193] *Vernillo v. France, supra* n. 169, para. 27.
[194] *Scarvuzzo-Hager and Others v. Switzerland*, ECtHR 30 November 2004 (dec.), appl. no. 41773/98; *Norbert Sikorski v. Poland*, ECtHR 22 October 2009, appl. no. 17599/05, para. 117.
[195] *Scoppola v. Italy (No. 2)*, ECtHR 17 September 2009, appl. no. 10249/03, para. 71.
[196] *Mikolaiová v. Slovakia*, ECtHR 18 January 2011, appl. no. 4479/03, para. 34.
[197] *McFarlane v. Ireland, supra* n. 122, para. 117.

which remedies exist under national law, it is for the applicant to prove that these remedies have been exhausted or that they are not effective or adequate.

The main source of information in that respect is the respondent state. However, the Court investigates *ex officio* whether the local remedies rule has been complied with. In many cases of individual applications which were declared inadmissible under this rule, that conclusion was reached on the basis of such an *ex officio* investigation, without the application first having been transmitted to the state against which it was directed. If the application is transmitted to the state concerned – and with inter-state applications this is always the case (Rule 51 of the Rules of Court) –, the burden of proof with respect to the local remedies rule is divided as follows: the respondent state which relies on the rule must prove that certain effective and adequate remedies exist under its system of law which should have been sought.[198] In the *Bozano* case, the Court held that the Government had to indicate in a sufficiently clear way the remedies that were open to the applicant: 'it is not for the Convention bodies to cure of their own motion any want of precision or shortcomings in respondent States' arguments.'[199] If the state succeeds in proving its plea, subsequently it is for the applicant to prove that those remedies have been exhausted, or that they are not effective or adequate. The government's arguments will clearly carry more weight if examples from national case law are supplied.[200] Where the government argues that the applicant could have relied directly on the Convention before the national courts, the degree of certainty of such a remedy will need to be demonstrated by concrete examples.[201] In the *Akdivar* case, the Court elaborated this rule of the burden of proof by indicating that there may be special circumstances absolving the applicant from the requirement of exhaustion of domestic remedies. According to the Court, one such reason may be constituted by the national authorities remaining totally passive in the face of serious allegations of misconduct or infliction of harm by state agents, for example where they failed to undertake investigations or offer assistance. In such circumstances, it can be said that the burden of proof shifts once again, so that it becomes incumbent on the respondent government to justify its response in relation to the scale and seriousness of the matters complained of.[202]

---

[198] *De Wilde, Ooms and Versyp v. Belgium ('Vagrancy' Cases)*, ECtHR 18 June 1971, appl. nos. 2832/66, 2835/66, 2899/66, para. 16; *Deweer v. Belgium*, ECtHR 27 February 1980, appl. no. 6903/75, para. 29; *Akdivar v. Turkey, supra* n. 98, para. 68; *Mentes, supra* n. 105, para. 57; judgment of 29 April 2003, *Dankevich v. Ukraine*, appl. no. 40679/98, para. 107; *Doğan v. Turkey, supra* n. 180, para. 102; *Nada v. Switzerland*, ECtHR (GC) 12 September 2012, appl. no. 10593/08, para. 141.

[199] *Bozano v. Italy*, ECtHR 18 December 1986, appl. no. 9990/82, para. 46.

[200] *Doran v. Ireland*, ECtHR 28 February 2002 (dec.), appl. no. 50389/99; *Andrášik and Others v. Slovakia*, 22 October 2002 (dec.), appl. no. 57984/00.

[201] *Slavgorodski v. Estonia*, ECtHR 9 March 1999 (dec.), appl. no. 37043/97.

[202] *Akdivar v. Turkey, supra* n. 98, para. 68; *Aksoyv Turkey, supra* n. 98, paras. 56–57; *Stran Greek Refineries and Stratis Andreadis v. Greece, supra* n. 121, para. 35; *Cenbauer v. Croatia, supra* n. 156.

g. *Time of preliminary objection*

The Court takes cognisance of preliminary objections concerning the exhaustion of local remedies only insofar as the respondent state has raised them at the stage of the initial examination of admissibility, if their character and the circumstances permitted the state to do so at that moment.[203] The latter qualification was at issue in the *Campbell and Fell* case. Here, the Government raised the plea of non-exhaustion in its observations on the merits after the case had been declared admissible, because new developments had taken place in the relevant English case law only a few days before the Government had submitted its observations on admissibility. According to the Court, the Government could not reasonably have been expected to raise the plea of non-exhaustion at an earlier stage. There was, therefore, no estoppel on its part to do so at this stage of the proceedings. On the other hand, the Court held that it would be unjust now to find these complaints inadmissible for failure to exhaust domestic remedies, because after the Government had raised the issue the Commission had decided on the basis of former Article 29 not to reject the application on this ground. Consequently, the applicant was justified in relying on the Commission's decision by pursuing his case under the Convention instead of applying to the domestic courts.[204]

The question may be raised as to whether the Court should institute *ex officio* an inquiry into the compliance with the local remedies rule after the case has been transmitted to the state in case the respondent government has not raised an exception as to the admissibility under Article 35(1). In the *Kurt* case, the Court noted that the Government's objection was not raised in their memorial but only at the hearing and therefore outside the time-limit prescribed in Rule 48(1) of Rules of Court A [*cf.* the present Rule 55 new], which stipulated: 'A Party wishing to raise a preliminary objection must file a statement setting out the objection and the grounds therefore not later than the time when that Party informs the President of its intention not to submit a memorial or, alternatively, not later than the expiry of the time-limit laid down in Rule 37 §1 for the filing of its first memorial.' The objection was therefore dismissed.[205]

In the *Malama* case, the Court pointed out that according to Rule 55 of the Rules of Court, '[a]ny plea of inadmissibility must, in so far as its character and the circumstances permit, be raised by the respondent Contracting Party in its written or oral observations on the admissibility of the application'. It was clear from the case file that that condition had not been satisfied in the instant case.

---

[203] See, *inter alia*, *De Wilde, Ooms and Versyp v. Belgium ('Vagrancy' Cases)*, *supra* n. 198, para. 60; *Artico v. Italy*, ECtHR 13 May 1980, appl. no. 6694/74, para. 27; *Guzzardi v. Italy*, *supra* n. 152, para. 63; and *Foti, Lentini and Cenerini and Others v. Italy*, ECtHR 10 December 1982, appl. no. 7604/76, para. 44.

[204] *Campbell and Fell v. United Kingdom*, ECtHR 28 June 1984, appl. nos. 7819/77 and 7878/77, para. 58–63.

[205] *Kurt v. Turkey*, ECtHR 25 May 1998, appl. no. 24276/94, para. 81.

The Government was consequently estopped from raising this objection. Nor could the Court accept that the applicant had altered the subject matter of her application, since her complaints had manifestly always concerned the absence of fair compensation for the expropriation of her land. The subsequent payment of an amount of compensation contested by the applicant was, admittedly, a new fact, but one which was linked to her original complaints.[206]

h. Time of exhaustion of local remedies

The assessment of whether domestic remedies have been exhausted is normally carried out with reference to the state of the proceedings on the date on which the application was lodged with the Court. This rule is, however, subject to exceptions following the creation of new remedies.[207] The Court has departed from this rule in particular in cases concerning the length of proceedings.[208]

In the *Baumann* case, the Court held that the assessment of whether domestic remedies have been exhausted is normally carried out with reference to the date on which the application was lodged with it.[209] Nevertheless, this rule is subject to exceptions, which may be justified by the particular circumstances of a case. Thus, after the Italian Parliament passed a special act designed to provide a domestic remedy for alleged violations of the 'reasonable-time' requirement ('the Pinto Act'), the Court found a departure from that general principle justified because the growing number of identical applications threatened to 'affect the operation, at both national and international level, of the system of human-rights protection set up by the Convention'.[210] Where the government intends to lodge a non-exhaustion plea, it must do so, insofar as the character of the plea and the circumstances permit, in its observations prior to adoption of the admissibility decision, though there may be exceptional circumstances dispensing it from that obligation.[211]

i. Effect of declaration of inadmissibility

The effect of a declaration of inadmissibility on account of non-exhaustion of the local remedies is generally of a *dilatory* character. The applicant may submit his

---

206 *Malama v. Greece*, ECtHR 1 March 2001, appl. no. 43622/98, para. 40.

207 *İçyer v. Turkey*, ECtHR 12 January 2006 (dec.), appl. no. 18888/02, para. 72.

208 *Predil Anstalt v. Italy*, ECtHR 14 March 2002 (dec.), appl. no. 31993/96; *Bottaro v. Italy*, ECtHR 23 May 2002 (dec.), appl. no. 56298/00; *Andrášik and Others v. Slovakia*, *supra* n. 200; *Techniki Olympiaki A.E. v. Greece*, ECtHR 1 October 2013 (dec.), appl. no. 40547/10.

209 *Baumann v. France*, ECtHR 22 May 2001, appl. no. 33917/98, para. 47; *Sellier v. France*, ECtHR 23 September 2003, appl. no. 60992/00, para. 18; *Csikos v. Hungary*, ECtHR 5 December 2005, appl. no. 37251/04, para. 17.

210 *Giacometti v. Italy*, ECtHR 8 November 2001 (dec.), appl. no. 34939/97; *Karoussiotis v. Portugal*, ECtHR 1 February 2011, appl. no. 23205/08, para. 57.

211 *Mooren v. Germany*, ECtHR 9 July 2009, appl. no. 11364/03, para. 57.

case again to the Court after having obtained a decision of the highest national court. In fact, such a decision is considered as relevant new information by the Court, so that the application will not be rejected as being substantially the same as a matter already examined by the Court in the sense of Article 35(2)(b). The question of whether the local remedies rule must also be applied if meanwhile the national time-limits for appeal have expired, so that in fact local remedies are no longer available, will have to be decided on a case-by-case basis. Application of the rule in such a case has *peremptory* effect, since both the national and the international procedure are then barred. Such a consequence appears justified only when the individual in question is to be blamed for having allowed the time-limit to expire. A cut-and-dried answer to this as well as several other questions concerning the application of the local remedies rule cannot be given *in abstracto*. For guidance, use may be made of the general starting point that what can be demanded of the individual is not 'what is impossible or ineffective, but only what is required by common sense, namely 'the diligence of a bonus pater familias'.[212]

j. Special circumstances absolving from exhaustion obligation

The Court has accepted the possibility that according to the generally recognised rules of international law there may be special circumstances in which even effective and adequate remedies may be left unutilised.[213] The following special circumstances have been invoked by applicants: doubts on the part of the applicant regarding the effectiveness of a particular remedy will not absolve him or her from the obligation to try it;[214] lack of knowledge on his part as to (the existence of) a particular remedy;[215] non-admittance of an appeal because of a procedural mistake by the applicant;[216] poor financial position of the applicant or the high costs of the procedure;[217] lack of free legal aid;[218] fear of repercussions;[219] errors or wrong advice by counsel or by the authorities;[220] the

---

[212] Thus Judge Tanaka in his separate opinion in the *Barcelona Traction* Case, *ICJ Reports*, 1970, p. 148.

[213] *Kiiskinen v. Finland, supra* n. 131.

[214] *Epözdemir v. Turkey*, ECtHR 31 January 2002 (dec.), appl. no. 57039/00; *Milošević v. the Netherlands*, ECtHR 19 March 2002 (dec.), appl. no. 77631/01; *Pellegriti v. Italy*, ECtHR 26 May 2005 (dec.), appl. no. 77363/01; *MPP Golub v. Ukraine*, ECtHR 11 February 2005 (dec.), appl. no. 5778/05.

[215] *Botta v. Italy*, EComHR 15 March 1996 (dec.) 21439/93D & R 80 (1995), p. 14.

[216] *Gäfgen v. Germany, supra* n. 182, para. 143.

[217] *Van Oosterwijck v. Belgium, supra* n. 183, para. 38.

[218] *Granger v. United Kingdom*, ECtHR 28 March 1990, appl. no. 11932/86, para. 47.

[219] *Akdivar v. Turkey, supra* n. 98, para. 68; *Isayeva, Yusupova and Bazayeva v. Russia*, ECtHR 24 February 2005, appl. nos. 57947/00, 57948/00 and 57949/00, paras. 157–159, 160–161, 224.

[220] *Steglich-Petersen v. Denmark*, EComHR 21 October 1998 (dec.), appl. no. 41250/98, D & R 94 (1998), p. 163. See, however, the Court's judgment of *Artico v. Italy, supra* n. 203, para. 27. In *H. v. United Kingdom*, EComHR 4 July 1983 (dec.), appl. no. 10000/82D&R 33 (1983),

fact that two applicants had filed the same complaint, while only one applicant has exhausted the domestic remedies.[221] So far, special circumstances justifying the non-exhaustion have been recognised only exceptionally in the case law.

In the *Akdivar* case, the Court took account of the fact that the events complained of took place in an area of Turkey subject to martial law and characterised by severe civil strife. In such a situation the Court was of the opinion that it must bear in mind the insecurity and vulnerability of the applicants' position following the destruction of their homes and the fact that they must have become dependent on the authorities in respect of their basic needs. Against such a background the prospects of success of civil proceedings based on allegations against the security forces must be considered to be negligible in the absence of any official inquiry into their allegations, even assuming that they would have been able to secure the services of lawyers willing to press their claims before the courts. In this context, the Court found particularly striking the Commission's observation that the statements made by villagers following the events complained of gave the impression of having been prepared by the gendarmes. Nor could the Court exclude from its considerations the risk of reprisals against the applicants or their lawyers if they had sought to introduce legal proceedings alleging that the security forces were responsible for burning down their houses as part of a deliberate state policy of village clearance. Therefore, the Court considered that, in the absence of convincing explanations from the Government in rebuttal, the applicants had demonstrated the existence of special circumstances which dispensed them at the time of the events complained of from the obligation to exhaust the domestic remedies.[222] In the *Selmouni* case, the Commission had previously held that where the national authorities remained passive in the face of serious allegations of misconduct or infliction of harm by state agents, this was a relevant criterion in absolving the applicant from the obligation to exhaust domestic remedies.[223]

In the *Bahaddar* case, the Government maintained that the applicant had not exhausted the domestic remedies available to him. The Deputy Minister of Justice had rejected the application for revision of his refusal to recognise the applicant's refugee status or, in the alternative, to grant him a residence permit on humanitarian grounds. The applicant's lawyer had appealed against this decision to the Judicial Division of the Council of State, stating that the grounds

---

p. 247 (253), the Commission accepted that all domestic remedies were exhausted, since the applicant had received counsel's advice that a domestic remedy would have no prospects of success.

[221] *A. Association and H v. Austria*, EComHR 15 March 1984 (dec.), appl. no. 9905/82, D&R 36 (1984), p. 187 (192) where the Commission considered also the second applicant to be admissible.

[222] *Akdivar v. Turkey, supra* n. 98, paras. 73–75; *Selçuk and Asker v. Turkey*, ECtHR 24 April 1998 appl. nos. 23184/94 and 23185/94, para. 65; *Ayder v. Turkey, supra* n. 105, para. 91.

[223] *Selmouni v. France*, EComHR 11 December 1997 (dec.), appl. no. 25803/94, D & R 88 B (1997), p. 55 (62–63).

for the appeal would be submitted as soon as possible. The lawyer had been reminded by the Judicial Division three months later that no such grounds had yet been received, and was invited to submit them within a month. This she had failed to do, submitting her grounds of appeal only three months later; she had not asked for an extension of the time-limit, as she might have done. The Court held that even in cases of expulsion to a country where there is an alleged risk of ill-treatment contrary to Article 3, the formal requirements and time-limits laid down in domestic law should normally be complied with, such rules being designed to enable the national jurisdictions to discharge their caseload in an orderly manner. Whether there are special circumstances which absolve an applicant from the obligation to comply with such rules will depend on the facts of each case. It should be borne in mind in this regard that in the case of applications for recognition of refugee status it may be difficult, if not impossible, for the person concerned to supply evidence within a short time, especially if – as in the present case – such evidence must be obtained from the country from which he or she claims to have fled. Accordingly, time-limits should not be so short, or applied so inflexibly, as to deny an applicant for recognition of refugee status a realistic opportunity to prove his or her claim.[224]

In the case of *R.M.D. v. Switzerland*, the applicant complained about the fact that he had been detained for two months in seven different cantons, which had deprived him of any possibility of having the lawfulness of his detention reviewed by a court as required by Article 5(4) ECHR. Regarding the question of whether the applicant had fulfilled the requirement of exhaustion of domestic remedies, the Court noted that it must take realistic account not only of the *existence of formal remedies* in the legal system of the Contracting Parties concerned, but also of the *context* in which they operate and the *personal circumstances* of the applicant. In this case, the applicant was transferred to different cantons of Switzerland in a short period of time. The applicant filed a complaint about his detention at the court in the first county, but when he was transferred, that court declared itself unable to decide on the matter. The applicant did not file another complaint at any of the other counties. According to the Court, the applicant could not be blamed for failing to avail himself of the remedies available in the other counties, since he was in a position of great legal uncertainty, because he could be transferred to another county soon. Furthermore, he had many practical difficulties in arranging effective representation, as many detained persons have. The problem in this case was not that remedies were unavailable in each of the cantons, but that they were ineffective in the applicant's particular situation. Because of the constant transfers, he was unable to obtain a decision on his detention from a court as he was entitled to under Article 5(4).[225]

---

224   *Bahaddar v. the Netherlands,* ECtHR 19 February 1998, appl. no. 25894/94, para. 45.
225   *R.M.D. v. Switzerland,* ECtHR 26 September 1997, appl. no. 19800/92, paras. 43–45.

In the *Ayder* case, where an unqualified undertaking was given by a senior public official that all property owners would be compensated for the damage sustained, and damage assessment reports were thereafter prepared in respect of each property, the Court found that, in the absence of a clear indication to the contrary, property owners could legitimately expect that compensation would be paid without the necessity of their commencing proceedings in the administrative courts. The Court did not consider that it has been shown that the need for each property owner to bring separate judicial proceedings was made sufficiently clear. In the light of the foregoing, the Court concluded that there existed special circumstances which dispensed the applicants from the obligation to exhaust domestic remedies.[226]

1.11. SIX MONTHS PERIOD – ARTICLE 35(1)

Being the second admissibility criterion set forth in Article 35(1), the six-month time-limit serves to prevent that the compatibility of a national decision, action or omission with the Convention might still be questioned after a considerable lapse of time by the submission of an application to the Court. Its purpose is to maintain reasonable legal certainty and ensure that cases raising issues under the Convention are examined within a reasonable time. It ought also to prevent the authorities and other persons concerned from being kept in a state of uncertainty for a long period of time. Lastly, the rule is designed to facilitate establishment of the facts of the case, which otherwise, with the passage of time, would become more and more difficult, and a fair examination of the issue raised under the Convention would thus become problematic. On the other hand, the period of six months is considered to leave the person concerned with sufficient time to evaluate the desirability of submitting an application to the Commission and to decide on the content thereof.[227]

The purpose of the six-month rule is to promote security of the law and to ensure that cases raising issues under the Convention are dealt with within a reasonable time. Furthermore, it serves also to protect the authorities and other persons concerned from being under any uncertainty for a prolonged period of time. Finally, it should ensure the possibility of ascertaining the facts of the case before that possibility fades away, making a fair examination of the question at issue next to impossible[228] That rule marks out the temporal limit of the supervision exercised by the Court and signals, both to individuals and state authorities, the period beyond which such supervision is no longer possible. It reflects the wish of the High Contracting Parties to prevent past judgments

---

226   *Ayder v. Turkey, supra* n. 105, paras. 101–102.
227   *Sabri Güneş v. Turkey*, ECtHR (GC) 29 June 2012, appl. no. 27396/06, para. 39.
228   *Berdzehnishvili v. Russia, supra* n. 157.

being constantly called into question and constitutes a legitimate concern for order, stability and peace.[229]

The introduction of the application, and not its registration by the Registry to the Court, has to take place within a period of six months from the final decision.[230] The six-month rule cannot require an applicant to lodge his or her complaint with the Court before his or her position in connection with the matter has been finally settled at the domestic level.[231]

The six-month rule is an admissibility condition which applies to applications by States as well as individuals.

a. Final decision

By virtue of Article 35(4), the Court may declare a complaint inadmissible at any stage of the proceedings and the six-month rule is a mandatory one which the Court has jurisdiction to apply of its own motion.[232] Moreover, it is not open to the Court to set aside the application of the six months' rule solely because a government has not made a preliminary objection based on it.[233]

The six-month period runs from the final decision in the process of exhaustion of domestic remedies.[234] The applicant must have made normal use of domestic remedies which are likely to be effective and sufficient.[235] The object of the six-month time limit is to promote legal certainty, by ensuring that cases raising issues under the Convention are dealt with in a reasonable time and that past decisions are not continually open to challenge. The rule also affords the prospective applicant time to consider whether to lodge an application and, if so, to decide on the specific complaints and arguments to be raised.[236]

There is a close relation between the admissibility condition of the six-month period and the one concerning the exhaustion of local remedies.[237] Only remedies which are normal and effective can be taken into account as an applicant cannot extend the strict time-limit imposed by the Convention by seeking to make inappropriate or misconceived applications to bodies or institutions which have no power or competence to offer effective redress

---

[229] *Idalov v. Russia*, ECtHR (GC) 22 May 2012, appl. no. 5826/03, para. 128; *Sabri Günes v. Turkey, supra* n. 227, para. 40.

[230] *Belchev v. Bulgaria*, ECtHR 6 February 2003 (dec.), appl. no. 39084/97.

[231] *Varnava and Others v. Turkey, supra* n. 165, para. 157; *Chapman v. Belgium*, ECtHR 5 March 2013 (dec.), appl. no. 39619/06, para. 34.

[232] *Assanidze v. Georgia*, ECtHR (GC) 8 April 2004, appl. no. 71503/01, para. 160; *Benet Praha, Spol. S.R.O. v. Czech Republic*, ECtHR 28 September 2010 (dec.), appl. no. 38354/06.

[233] *Walker v. the United Kingdom*, ECtHR 25 January 2000 (dec.), appl. no. 34979/97; *Benet Praha, Spol. S.R.O. v. Czech Republic, supra* n. 232.

[234] *Paul and Audrey Edwards v. the United Kingdom*, ECtHR 7 June 2001 (dec.), appl. no. 46477/99.

[235] *Moreira Barbosa v. Portugal, supra* n. 140.

[236] *Worm v. Austria*, ECtHR 29 August 1997, appl. no. 22714/93, paras. 32–33.

[237] *Berdzenishvili v. Russia, supra* n. 157.

for the complaint in issue under the Convention.[238] Account cannot be taken of remedies the use of which depends on the discretionary powers of public officials and which are, as a consequence, not directly accessible to the applicant. Similarly, remedies which have no precise time-limits create uncertainty and render nugatory the six-month rule contained in Article 35(1).[239]

As a rule Article 35(1) does not require applicants to have applied for the reopening of proceedings or to have used similar extraordinary remedies and does not allow the six-month time-limit to be extended on the grounds that such remedies have been used.[240] However, if an extraordinary remedy is the only judicial remedy available to the applicant, the six-month time-limit may be calculated from the date of the decision given regarding that remedy.[241] An application in which an applicant submits his or her complaints within six months of the decision dismissing his or her request for reopening of the proceedings is inadmissible because the decision is not a 'final decision'.[242] However, the Court has also accepted that situations in which a request to reopen the proceedings is successful and actually results in a reopening may be an exception to this rule.[243] In cases where proceedings are reopened or a final decision is reviewed, the running of the six-month period in respect of the initial set of proceedings or the final decision will be interrupted only in relation to those Convention issues which served as a ground for such a review or reopening and were the subject of examination before the extraordinary appeal body.[244]

b.   *Starting point time-limit*

The six-month rule is autonomous and must be construed and applied to the facts of each individual case, so as to ensure the effective exercise of the right to individual petition. While taking account of domestic law and practice is an important aspect, it is not decisive in determining the starting point of the six-month period.[245] If a judgment is not delivered at a public hearing, the six-month period starts at the moment it was served on the applicant.[246] In the *Worm* case, the Court noted that, under domestic law and practice, the applicant was entitled to be served *ex officio* a written copy of the Court of Appeal's judgment, and that the long delay for this service was exclusively the responsibility of the judicial authorities. The said judgment, which in its final version ran to over

---

238   *Fernie v. United Kingdom*, ECtHR 5 January 2006 (dec.), appl. no. 14881/04.
239   *Williams v. United Kingdom*, *supra* n. 134.
240   *Berdzenishvili v. Russia*, *supra* n. 157; *Tucka v. United Kingdom*, ECtHR 18 January 2011 (dec.), appl. no. 34586/10.
241   *Ahtinen v. Finland*, ECtHR 31 May 2005 (dec.), appl. no. 48907/99.
242   *Sapeyan v. Armenia*, ECtHR 13 January 2009 (dec.), appl. no. 35738/03, para. 23.
243   *Korkmaz v. Turkey*, ECtHR 17 January 2006 (dec.), appl. no. 42576/98.
244   *Sapeyan v. Armenia*, *supra* n. 242, para. 24.
245   *Sabri Günes v. Turkey*, *supra* n. 227, paras. 52 and 55.
246   *Venkadajalasarma v. Netherlands*, ECtHR 9 July 2002 (dec.), appl. no. 58510/00.

nine pages, contained detailed legal reasoning. In these circumstances, the Court shared the Commission's view that the object and purpose of Article 26 [the present Article 35(1)] were best served by counting the six-month period as running from the date of service of the written judgment. Moreover, this was the solution adopted by Austrian law in respect of time-limits for lodging domestic appeals.[247] The six-month period starts running from the date on which the applicant and/or his or her representative has sufficient knowledge of the final domestic decision.[248] It is for the state which relies on the failure to comply with the six-month time-limit to establish the date when the applicant became aware of the final domestic decision.[249] Where an applicant is entitled to be served automatically with a copy of the final domestic decision, the object and purpose of Article 35(1) of the Convention are best served by counting the six-month period as running from the date of service of the copy of the decision.[250] The six-month period runs from the date on which the applicant's lawyer became aware of the decision completing the exhaustion of the domestic remedies, notwithstanding the fact that the applicant only became aware of the decision later.[251] Where the domestic law does not provide for service, it is appropriate to take the date the decision was finalised as the starting point, that being when the parties were definitely able to find out its content.[252] The applicant or his or her lawyer must show due diligence in obtaining a copy of the decision deposited with the court's Registry.[253] Where it is clear from the outset that the applicant has no effective remedy, the six-month period runs from the date on which the act complained of took place or the date on which the applicant was directly affected by or became aware of such an act or had knowledge of its adverse effects.[254] Where an applicant avails himself or herself of an apparently existing remedy and only subsequently becomes aware of circumstances which render the remedy ineffective, it may be appropriate to take the start of the six-month period from the date when the applicant first became or ought to have become aware of those circumstances.[255]

In the *Papageorgiou* case, the Court held that an application is lodged on the date of the applicant's first letter, provided the applicant has sufficiently indicated the purpose of the application. Registration – which is effected when the Secretary to the Commission receives the full case file relating to the application – has only one practical consequence: it determines the order in which applications will be

---

[247] *Worm v. Austria, supra* n. 236, para. 33.

[248] *Koç and Tosun v. Turkey,* ECtHR 13 November 2008 (dec.), appl. no. 23852/04.

[249] *Şahmo v. Turkey,* ECtHR 1 April 2003 (dec.), appl. no. 37415/97.

[250] *Worm v. Austria, supra* n. 236, para. 33.

[251] *Çelik v. Turkey,* ECtHR 23 September 2004 (dec.), appl. no. 52991/99.

[252] *Papachelas v. Greece,* ECtHR 25 March 1999 (dec.), appl. no. 31423/96, para. 30.

[253] *Ölmez v. Turkey,* ECtHR 1 February 2005 (dec.), appl. no. 39464/98.

[254] *Dennis and Others v. the United Kingdom,* ECtHR 2 July 2002 (dec.), appl. no. 76573/01; *Varnava and Others v. Turkey, supra* n. 165, para. 157.

[255] *Varnava and Others v. Turkey, supra* n. 165, para. 158.

considered. As to the applicant's alleged negligence, the Court considered that parties to proceedings could not be required to enquire day after day whether a judgment that has not been served on them has been delivered.[256]

In the *Monory* case, the Court recalled that it had previously stated that when the reasons for a decision are necessary for the introduction of an application, the six-month period ordinarily runs not from the date of notification of the operative part of the decision but from the date on which the full reasons for the decision were given.[257] It recalled that according to its case law, if the applicant or his representative fails to make reasonable efforts to obtain a copy of the final decision, the delay in the lodging of the application with the Court is deemed to be due to their own negligence.[258]

c. Continuing situation

A special starting date for the time-limit applies to cases of a so-called 'continuing situation', where the violation is not (only) constituted by an act performed or a decision taken at a given moment, but (also) by its consequences, which continue and thus repeat the violation day by day. As long as that situation exists, the six-month period does not commence, since it serves to make acts and decisions *from the past* unassailable after a given period.[259]

A well-known example is the *De Becker* case. De Becker had been sentenced to death in 1946 for treason during the Second World War. Later this sentence was converted to imprisonment, and in 1961 he was released under certain conditions. Under Belgian criminal law, such a sentence resulted in the limitation of certain rights – including the right to freedom of expression – which limitation continued to apply after the release.[260] The concept of a 'continuing situation' refers to a state of affairs which operates by continuous activities by or on the part of the state to render the applicants victims. The fact that an event has significant consequences over time does not mean that the event has produced a 'continuing situation'.[261]

Normally, the six-month period runs from the final decision in the process of exhaustion of domestic remedies. Where it is clear from the outset however that no effective remedy is available to the applicant, the period runs from the date of the acts or measures complained of.[262] In the case of *Koval v. Ukraine*, the

---

[256] *Papageorgiou v. Greece*, ECtHR 22 October 1997, appl. no. 24628/94, para. 32.

[257] *Monory v. Hungary and Romania*, ECtHR 17 February 2004 (dec.), appl. no. 71099/01.

[258] *Züleyha Yilmaz v. Turkey*, ECtHR 9 April 2002 (dec.), appl. no. 27532/95.

[259] See in this respect: *Iatridis v. Greece*, ECtHR (GC) 25 March 1999, appl. no. 31107/96, para. 50; *Malama v. Greece, supra* n. 206, para. 35.

[260] *De Becker v. Belgium*, ECtHR 27 March 1962, appl. no. 214/56, Yearbook II (1958–1959), p. 214 (230–234). See also appl. no. 4859/71, *X v. Belgium*, Coll. 44 (1973), p. 1 (18).

[261] *Iordache v. Romania*, ECtHR 14 October 2008, appl. no. 6817/02, para. 49.

[262] *D.P. and J.C. v. the United Kingdom*, ECtHR 26 June 2001 (dec.), appl. no. 38719/97.

Court held that since the applicant referred to specific events which occurred on identifiable dates, they could not be construed as a 'continuing situation'.[263]

Where the alleged violation constitutes a continuing situation against which no domestic remedy is available, it is only when the situation ends that the six-month period starts to run.[264] The case of *Varnava and Others v. Turkey,* for example, concerned the enforced disappearance of Greek Cypriots in Northern Cyprus. The applicants submitted their complaints in this case 15 years after the disappearance of their relatives. The Court formulated in this case the following general principles: applications can be rejected as out of time in disappearance cases where there has been excessive or unexplained delay on the part of applicants once they have, or should have, become aware that no investigation has been instigated or that the investigation has lapsed into inaction or become ineffective and, in any of those eventualities, there is no immediate, realistic prospect of an effective investigation being provided in the future. Where there are initiatives being pursued in regard to a disappearance situation, applicants may reasonably await developments which could resolve crucial factual or legal issues. Indeed, as long as there is some meaningful contact between families and authorities concerning complaints and requests for information, or some indication, or realistic possibility, of progress in investigative measures, considerations of undue delay will not generally arise. However, where there has been a considerable lapse of time, and there have been significant delays and lulls in investigative activity, there will come a moment when the relatives must realise that no effective investigation has been, or will be provided. When this stage is reached will depend, unavoidably, on the circumstances of the particular case.'[265] This shows that the Court has no infinite patience: it will also be a complaint at some point in continuing violations. The fact that the complainants in this case had waited 15 years before the filing of their complaint, however, according to them, the Court could not be invoked so that their complaint could be declared admissible. In the cases *E.R. v. Turkey*[266] and *Bozkir v. Turkey,*[267] for example, the Court considered the submission of an application 10 and eight years after the disappearance of their relatives in time. In these cases, the national authorities carried out continuous – though sporadic – research. In other cases, by contrast, where the applicant until more than 10 years after the event got to the European Court, although the national authorities for years no longer gave evidence to conduct any investigation, the Court considered that the time limit expired.

In the case of *Otto,* the Court held that the time starts to run on the day following the date on which the final decision has been pronounced in public,

---

[263]   *Koval v. Ukraine,* ECtHR 30 March 2004 (dec.), appl. no. 65550/01.
[264]   *Sabri Güneş v. Turkey,* ECtHR (GC) 29 June 2012, appl. no. 27396/06, para. 54.
[265]   *Varnava and Others v. Turkey, supra* n. 165, para. 165.
[266]   *E.R. v. Turkey,* ECtHR 31 July 2012, appl. no. 23016/04.
[267]   *Bozkir v. Turkey,* ECtHR 26 February 2013, appl. no. 24589/04.

or on which the applicant or his/her representative was informed of it, and expires six calendar months later, regardless of the actual duration of those calendar months.[268] Compliance with the six-month deadline is determined using criteria specific to the Convention, not those of each respondent state's domestic legislation.[269] In the case of *Sabri Güneş v. Turkey*, the Court held that the application by the Court of its own criteria in calculating time-limits, independently of domestic rules, tends to ensure legal certainty, proper administration of justice and, thus, the practical and effective functioning of the Convention mechanism.[270] In this case, the issue was whether or not, when the *dies ad quem* of the time-limit was an official holiday or a day considered to be an official holiday, the time-limit would be extended to include the first working day thereafter. The established case law of the Commission was that the six-month time-limit started to run on the day following delivery of the final domestic decision and that it expired six calendar months later. That method had been used in several cases examined by the Commission and the Court had specifically followed that approach subsequently. However, the question was what approach to adopt when the last day of the six-month time-limit was a non-working day. While the Chamber had referred to the decision in the case of *Fondation Croix-Etoile, Baudin and Delajoux v. Switzerland*, in which the Commission considered that the deadline should be extended to the next working day, the Court in its case law had not taken non-working days into account when determining the expiry date of the time-limit. The Court had confirmed on several occasions the principle that compliance with the six-month time-limit must satisfy the Convention criteria and not the arrangements laid down by the domestic law of each respondent state. Therefore, the six-month time-limit started to run on the date of service of a copy of the final domestic judgment or decision. The fact that the last day of the six-month period falls on a Saturday, a Sunday or an official holiday and that in such a situation, under domestic law, time-limits are extended to the following working day, does not affect the determination of the *dies ad quem*.[271]

d. Special circumstances absolving from six-month requirement

With respect to the six-month rule, too, the Commission has admitted that special circumstances might occur in which the applicant need not satisfy this requirement. The case law on this point is almost identical with that regarding special circumstances in connection with the local remedies rule. In the *Toth* case, the Court joined the liberal approach taken by the Commission and

---

[268]   *Otto v. Germany*, ECtHR 10 November 2009 (dec.), appl. no. 21425/06.
[269]   *Benet Praha, spol. s.r.o., v. the Czech Republic, supra* n. 232.
[270]   *Sabri Güneş v. Turkey, supra* n. 264, para. 56.
[271]   *Ibid.*, paras. 43 and 61.

held that it was hardly realistic to expect a detainee without legal training to understand fully the complexity of the case concerned and in particular the difference of the two types of procedure involved. The applicant was therefore excused for, strictly speaking, not complying with the six-month rule.[272]

Special considerations could apply in exceptional cases where an applicant first avails himself of a domestic remedy and only at a later stage becomes aware, or should have become aware, of the circumstances which make that remedy ineffective. In such a situation, the six-month period might be calculated from the time when the applicant becomes aware, or should have become aware, of these circumstances.[273]

1.12. ANONYMOUS APPLICATIONS – ARTICLE 35(2)(a)

The applicant must be duly identified in the application form.[274] The Court may decide that the applicant's identity should not be disclosed to the public;[275] in that case, the applicant will be designated by his or her initials or simply by a letter. In the case of *Shamayev and Others*, the Court reiterated, as clearly as possible, that it alone is competent to decide on its jurisdiction to interpret and apply the Convention and its Protocols, in particular with regard to the issue of whether the person in question is an applicant within the meaning of Article 34 of the Convention and whether the application fulfils the requirements of that provision. Unless they wish their conduct to be declared contrary to Article 34 of the Convention, a government which has doubts as to the authenticity of an application must inform the Court of its misgivings, rather than deciding itself to resolve the matter.[276]

This condition makes it possible to bar applications which have been lodged for purely political or propagandistic reasons, although cases are also conceivable in which an applicant wishes to remain anonymous for fear of repercussions. However, after having lodged his complaint, the applicant is asked if he objects to his identity being disclosed. If he objects, his identity will not be disclosed during the procedure before the Court nor in the judgment or decision.[277]

For obvious reasons, the condition does not apply to inter-state applications. The Court is rather flexible with respect the *condition* that the application may not be anonymous. In the case of *Kuznetsova*, the Court observed that, though unsigned, the application form contained the applicant's personal details

---

[272] *Toth v. Austria*, ECtHR 12 December 1991, appl. no. 11894/85, para. 82.
[273] *Doğan v. Turkey*, ECtHR 28 November 2004, appl. no. 49593/99, para.113.
[274] Rule 47(1) (a) Rules of Court.
[275] Rule 47(4) Rules of Court.
[276] *Shamayev and Others v. Georgia and Russia*, ECtHR 12 April 2005, appl. no. 36378/02, para. 293; *Sindicatul Păstorul cel Bun v. Romania*, ECtHR (GC) 9 July 2013, appl. no. 2330/09, para. 69.
[277] Rule 47(3) Rules of Court.

sufficient to erase any doubt as to her identity, and that all the subsequent correspondence to the Court was duly signed by the applicant's representatives. In such circumstances, the Court had no grounds to consider the application as anonymous. Accordingly, the Government's objection must be dismissed.[278]

An application to the Court is regarded as anonymous where the case file does not indicate any element enabling the Court to identify the applicant.[279] None of the forms or documents submitted contains a mention of the name, but only a reference and aliases, and the power of attorney is signed 'X': the identity of the applicant is not disclosed.

Article 35(2)(a) is not applicable where applicants have submitted factual and legal information enabling the Court to identify them and establish their links with the facts in issue and the complaint raised.[280] Individuals using pseudonyms and explaining to the Court that the context of an armed conflict obliged them not to disclose their real names in order to protect their family members and friends. Finding that 'behind the tactics concealing their real identities for understandable reasons were real people identifiable from a sufficient number of indications, other than their names' and 'the existence of a sufficiently close link between the applicants and the events in question', the Court did not consider that the application was anonymous.[281]

1.13. SUBSTANTIALLY THE SAME APPLICATIONS – ARTICLE 35(2)(b)

a. Introduction

The purpose of the first limb of Article 35(2)(b) is to ensure the finality of the Court's decisions and to prevent applicants from seeking, through the lodging of a fresh application, to appeal previous judgments or decisions of the Court.[282] In the case of *Ivantoc and Others v. Moldova and Russia*, the Moldovan Government considered that the Court was not competent to deal with allegations of non-enforcement of a judgment, a task which was within the competence of the Committee of Ministers.[283] The Court recalled that an application is considered as being 'substantially the same' where the parties, the complaints and the facts are identical.[284] The concept of complaint is characterised by the facts alleged

---

[278] *Kuznetsova v. Russia*, ECtHR 19 January 2006 (dec.), appl. no. 67579/01.

[279] *'Blondje' v. the Netherlands*, ECtHR 15 September 2009 (dec.) appl. no. 7245/09.

[280] *Sindicatul Păstorul cel Bun v. Romania*, supra n. 277, para.71.

[281] *Shamayev and Others v. Georgia and Russia*, supra n. 277, para. 275.

[282] *Kafkaris v. Cyprus*, ECtHR 21 June 2011 (dec.), appl. no. 9644/09, para. 67.

[283] *Ivantoc and Others v. Moldova and Russia*, ECtHR 15 November 2011, appl. no. 23687/05, para. 83.

[284] *Verein gegen Tierfabriken Schweiz (VgT) v. Switzerland (No. 2)*, ECtHR 30 June 2009, appl. no. 32772/02, para. 63.

in it and not merely by the legal grounds or arguments relied on.[285] Where the applicant submits new information, the application will not be essentially the same as a previous application.[286]

Accordingly, the powers assigned to the Committee of Ministers by Article 46 to supervise the execution of the Court's judgments and evaluate the implementation of the measures taken by the states under this article will not be encroached upon where the Court has to deal with relevant new information in the context of a fresh application. Moreover, in the specific context of a continuing violation of a Convention right following adoption of a judgment in which the Court has found a violation of that right during a certain period of time, it is not unusual for the Court to examine a second application concerning a violation of that right in the subsequent period.[287]

This ground of inadmissibility does also not apply with respect to inter-State complaints. This does not exclude, however, that the Court will have to consider at the merits stage whether and, if so, to what extent an inter-state application is substantially the same as a previous one. As the Commission observed in its Report on the case of *Cyprus v. Turkey*,[288] Article 27(1)(b) [the present Article 35(2)(b)] reflects a basic legal principle of procedure which arises in inter-state cases during the examination of the merits. The Commission stated that it could not be its task to investigate complaints already examined in a previous case, and a state could not therefore, except in specific circumstances, claim an interest to have new findings made where the Commission has already adopted a Report under former Article 31 ECHR concerning the same matter.[289] The same holds good for Court judgments.

In practice, declarations of inadmissibility on the ground of the identical character of two or more applications do not occur frequently. In the case of *Cyprus v. Turkey* (the fourth inter-state complaint) the Commission recalled that in its Report of 10 July 1976 concerning applications Nos. 6780/74 and 6950/75, *Cyprus v. Turkey* (the first and second inter-state cases), it had considered that the evidence before it did not allow a definitive finding with regard to the fate of Greek Cypriots declared to be missing. Although in its Report of 4 October 1983 concerning application No. 8007/77, *Cyprus v. Turkey* (the third inter-state case), the Commission had considered that it had found sufficient indications, in an indefinite number of cases, that Greek Cypriots who were still missing at the time had been unlawfully deprived of their liberty, it could not be established with any certainty that this finding also concerned the cases in the present

---

[285]   *Powell and Rayner v. the United Kingdom*, ECtHR 21 February 1990, appl. no. 9310/81, para. 29; *Guerra and Others v. Italy*, ECtHR (GC) 19 February 1998, appl. no. 14967/89, para. 44.

[286]   *Patera v. the Czech Republic*, ECtHR 10 January 2006 (dec.), appl. no. 25326/03.

[287]   *Ivantoc and Others v. Moldova and Russia, supra* n. 284, paras. 86–87.

[288]   *Cyprus v. Turkey*, EComHR 4 October 1983 (rep.), appl. nos. 6780/74 and 6950/75, D&R 72 (1992), p. 5 (23).

[289]   *Cyprus v. Turkey, supra* n. 108, p. 104 (132–133).

applications. Finally, the Commission recalled that an examination of the merits of application No. 25781/94, *Cyprus v. Turkey* (the fourth inter-state case) still remained to be carried out. In these circumstances, the Commission reserved the question of whether the present applications did concern a 'matter' which had 'already been examined' by the Commission in the context of one of the inter-state cases. For the same reason, the Commission postponed to the merits stage the Government's arguments about the *res judicata* effect of the Committee of Ministers' resolution in the third inter-state case.[290] In the *Oberschlick* case, the applicant complained under Article 10 ECHR that his right to freedom of expression had been violated because the Supreme Court had dismissed the plea of nullity for the preservation of the law as regards his conviction for defamation, which the European Court of Human Rights had found to be in violation of Article 10 ECHR. The Commission found that the applicant did not complain about his previous conviction, but about the Supreme Court's decision of 17 September 1992, which was taken after the European Court of Human Rights had given its *Oberschlick* judgment on 23 May 1991.[291] Consequently, the application was not identical.

b. Same matter

An application or a complaint is declared inadmissible if it 'is substantially the same as a matter that has already been examined by the Court … and contains no relevant new information'. This includes cases where the Court has struck the previous application from its list of cases on the basis of a friendly-settlement procedure.[292] However, if a previous application has never formed the subject of a formal decision, the Court is not precluded from examining the recent application.[293] The Court examines whether the two applications brought before it by the applicants relate essentially to the same persons, the same facts and the same complaints.[294] However, for an application to be substantially the same as another which has already been examined by the Court or other procedure of international investigation or settlement for the purposes of Article 34(2)(b), it must concern substantially not only the same facts and complaints but be introduced by the same persons.[295] An inter-state application does not deprive individual applications of the possibility of introducing, or pursuing their own

---

[290] *Ibid.*, p. 104 (133–134).

[291] *Oberschlick v. Austria*, EComHR 16 May 1995 (dec.), appl. no. 19255/92 and 21655/93, D & R 81 A (1995), p. 5(10).

[292] *Kezer and Others v. Turkey*, ECtHR 5 October 2004 (dec.) appl. no. 58058/00.

[293] *Sürmeli v. Germany*, ECtHR 29 April 2004 (dec.), appl. no. 75529/01.

[294] *Verein gegen Tierfabriken Schweiz (VgT) v. Switzerland (No. 2)*, *supra* n. 285 para. 63; *Vojnović v. Croatia*, ECtHR 26 June 2012 (dec.), appl. no. 48139/10, para. 28.

[295] *Folgerø and Others v. Norway*, ECtHR 14 February 2006 (dec.), appl. no. 15472/02; *Malsagova and Others v. Russia*, ECtHR 6 March 2008 (dec.), appl. no. 27244/03.

claims.[296] An application will generally fall foul of this article where it has the same factual basis as a previous application. It is insufficient for an applicant to allege relevant new information where he has merely sought to support his past complaints with new legal arguments[297]or provided supplementary information on domestic law incapable of altering the reasons for the dismissal of his/her previous application.[298] In order for the Court to consider an application which relates to the same facts as a previous application, the applicant must genuinely advance a new complaint or submit new information which has not been previously considered by the Court.[299]

In the case of *Cyprus v. Turkey*, mentioned above, although the Commission decided that Article 35(2)(b) did not apply with respect to inter-state complaints, it did not exclude that it would have to consider at the merits stage whether and, if so, to what extent the present inter-state application was substantially the same as a previous one.[300] The Commission, therefore, reserved the question whether and, if so, to what extent the applicant Government could have a valid legal interest in the determination of the alleged continuing violations of the Convention insofar as they had already been dealt with in previous Reports of the Commission. The Commission noted, in this context, that at least some of the complaints raised did not seem to be covered by definitive findings in earlier Reports, and some others seemed to concern entirely new facts.

For an answer to the question of whether a concrete case concerns a matter which is substantially the same as a matter which has already been examined by the Court, it is decisive whether new facts have been put forward in the application. These facts must be of such a nature that they cause a change in the legal and/or factual data on which the Court based its earlier decision. The mere submission of one or more new legal arguments is therefore insufficient, if the facts on which the application is based are the same.[301]

A new fact is indeed involved when an applicant whose earlier application has been declared inadmissible on account of non-exhaustion of local remedies, has afterwards obtained a decision in the last resort in the national legal system.[302]

In the case of *Massuero v. Italy* the Court noted that another application though relating to the same set of proceedings, was lodged by a different applicant, namely by Mr Francesco Nobili Massuero, the father of the actual applicant. Consequently, the present application could not be regarded as being

---

[296]   *Varnava and Others* v. *Turkey*, *supra* n. 165, para. 118.

[297]   *I.J.L. v. the United Kingdom*, ECtHR 6 July 1999 (dec.), appl. no. 30029/97; *Mann v. United Kingdom and Portugal*, ECtHR 1 February 2011 (dec.), appl. no. 360/10.

[298]   *X v. United Kingdom*, EComHR 10 July 1981 (dec.), appl. no. 8206/78.

[299]   *Kafkaris v. Cyprus*, *supra* n. 283, para. 68.

[300]   *Cyprus v. Turkey*, *supra* n. 108, p. 104 (134).

[301]   *Ferme, Ferme and Kostrevc v. Slovenia*, ECtHR 9 January 2001 (dec.), appl. no. 47869/99; *Timar v. Hungary*, ECtHR 3 May 2001 (dec.), appl. no. 36186/97.

[302]   *Buscarini v. San Marino*, ECtHR 4 May 2000 (dec.), appl. no. 31657/96.

substantially the same of the previous one.[303] In the case of *Riener v. Bulgaria*, some of the events complained of were the subject matter of an application declared inadmissible by the former Commission. However, the present case concerned essentially a continuous situation and the new developments since 1997 constituted 'relevant new information' within the meaning of Article 35(2)(b) ECHR.[304]

In the case of *I.J.L v. United Kingdom*, the applicant complained about a report prepared by Inspectors appointed by the Department of Trade and Industry to investigate allegations of an unlawful share support operation at the time of the takeover by Guinness PLC of the Distillers Company PLC. The Court noted that the applicant in a separate application (no. 29522/95) complained, *inter alia*, that the Inspectors' investigation, his trial and conviction and the resultant publicity blighted his reputation and led to the annulment of his knighthood. The Commission had found as a result that the applicant's complaint was inadmissible as being manifestly ill-founded. For the Court, the publication of the Report could not be said to have caused the applicant any further prejudice to his private life including reputation over and above that attendant on his conviction following a lengthy jury trial. It further considered that in the circumstances the applicant's new application had the same factual basis as that of his previously rejected complaint under Article 8 notwithstanding that he had sought to support it with a new legal argument. Since the application was substantially the same as a matter that has previously been examined by the Convention institutions, it was inadmissible within the meaning of Article 35(2)(b) and (4) ECHR.[305]

c. Same applicant

From the formulation of Article 35(2)(b) it could be inferred that the words 'substantially the same matter' also cover an application that is otherwise identical but is lodged by another applicant. The provision is, however, to be interpreted in the sense that it is only directed against identical applications by the same applicant. It would not be in conformity with the purpose of the Convention to provide individual legal protection, if an application from X, who considers himself to be the victim of a violation of the Convention, would not be admitted on the ground of the fact that an identical violation in relation to Y is already being examined or has already been examined. As appeared from its case law, the Commission did not object to identical applications from different applicants, although it then joined such cases, if possible.[306]

---

303 *Massuero v. Italy*, ECtHR 1 April 2004 (dec.), appl. no. 58587/00.
304 *Riener v. Bulgaria*, ECtHR 23 May 2006, appl. no. 46343/99, para. 103.
305 *I.J.L v. United Kingdom*, ECtHR 6 July 1999 (dec.), appl. no. 39029/97.
306 See, e.g., the successive *Le Compte v. Belgium*, EComHR 6 October 1979 (dec.), appl. no. 6878/75, D&R 6 (1977), p. 79 and *Van Leuven and De Meyere v. Belgium*, EComHR 10 March

The question of identical complaints may also arise in connection with the lodging of a complaint by a state as well as by an individual. Thus, in the applications of a number of Northern Irishmen, matters were denounced which had already formed the subject of the application of the Irish Government against United Kingdom. The latter application had meanwhile been declared admissible, but the examination of the merits was still pending. The Commission did not decide on the question of whether the individual applications were now to be rejected on account of their having the same character as the application by a state, because 'the relevant part of the inter-State case has (…) not yet been examined within the meaning of Article 35(2)(b) ECHR'.[307] This result in itself may be welcomed, but the reasoning on which it is based is less satisfactory. Indeed, the argument followed by the Commission leaves wide open the possibility that in similar cases, where the examination has already been completed, the Commission may decide differently. On the ground of the emphasis which the Convention puts on individual legal protection this would be regrettable since it might discourage individual applicants. The application of a state and that of an individual are distinctly different, both in character and as to the interests involved. The latter specially concerns the personal interests of the individual applicant, while the former is aimed much more at denouncing a general situation concerning 'European public order'. It is therefore questionable whether in the case of a succession of two applications of so different a character it is still possible to speak of 'a matter which is substantially the same'.

In the *Peltonen* case, the applicant complained about a refusal to issue a passport. The Government drew the Commission's attention to the fact that the applicant's brother had submitted a communication with similar contents to the Human Rights Committee under the Optional Protocol to the Covenant on Civil and Political Rights. The Commission held that it was true that the freedom guaranteed by Article 2(2) of Protocol No. 4 resembled that protected by Article 12 of the International Covenant on Civil and Political Rights. The Commission recalled, however, that if the complainants before the Commission and, for instance, the United Nations Human Rights Committee were not identical, the complaint to the Commission could not be considered as being substantially the same as the communication to the Committee.[308] In the

---

1977 (dec.), appl. no. 7238/75, D&R 8 (1977), p. 140. In its decision in the last-mentioned case the Commission held (p. 160): 'In view of all the similarities between the two applications it is desirable that they should be examined together.' The same conclusion can also be drawn from the opinion of the Commission in the case of *Donnelly and Others v. United Kingdom*, *supra* n. 114, p. 212 (266) that 'apart from the fact that the applicants are different in each case (…) this complaint could still not be rejected under Article 27(1)(b) of the Convention'.

[307] *Donnelly and Others v. United Kingdom*, *supra* n. 114, p. 212 (266).

[308] *Peltonen v. Finland*, EComHR 20 February 1995 (dec.), appl. no. 19583/92, D & R 80 A (1995), p. 38(43).

case of *Smirnova and Smirnova v. Russia*, the Court recalled that Article 35(2) (b) is intended to avoid the situation where several international bodies would be simultaneously dealing with applications which are substantially the same. A situation of this type would be incompatible with the spirit and the letter of the Convention, which seeks to avoid a plurality of international proceedings relating to the same cases. The Court noted, first, that a communication pending before the Human Rights Committee was lodged by and concerned only the first applicant, and its effects could not for this reason be extended to the second applicant. Next, the first applicant's complaints in that case were directed against her arrest on 26 August 1995 and, in particular, the question whether this arrest was justified, the impossibility to challenge it in the courts, and the alleged inadequate conditions of detention. The scope of the factual basis for the first applicant's application to the Court, although going back to the arrest of 26 August 1995, was significantly wider. It extended to the whole of the proceedings which terminated in 2002, and included the first applicant's arrest on three more occasions since 26 August 1995. It followed that the first applicant's application was not substantially the same as the petition pending before the Human Rights Committee, and that being so, it fell outside the scope of Article 35(2)(b).[309]

d. Submission to another international procedure or settlement

In the case of *OAO Neftyanaya Kompaniya Yukos v. Russia*, the Court recalled that the purpose of the second limb of Article 35(2)(b) was to avoid the situation where several international bodies would be simultaneously dealing with applications which are substantially the same. A situation of this type would be incompatible with the spirit and the letter of the Convention, which seeks to avoid a plurality of international proceedings relating to the same cases.[310] The Court further noted that the present case has been introduced and maintained by the applicant company in its own name. Although these entities could arguably be seen as having been affected by the events leading to the applicant company's liquidation, they had never taken part, either directly or indirectly, in the Strasbourg proceedings. The Court reiterated that in November 2007 the applicant company was liquidated and that despite this fact in its admissibility decision of 29 January 2009 it nevertheless accepted the application 'because the issues raised by the case transcend[ed] the person and the interests of the applicant [company]' and '(…) striking the application out of the list under such circumstances would undermine the very essence

---

[309] *Smirnova and Smirnova v. Russia*, ECtHR 3 October 2002 (dec.), appl. nos. 46133/99 and 46183/99.

[310] *OAO Neftyanaya Kompaniya Yukos v. Russia*, ECtHR 20 September 2011, appl. no. 14902/04, para. 520; *Eğitim ve Bilim Emekçileri Sendikası v. Turkey*, ECtHR 25 September 2012, appl. no. 20641/05, para. 37.

of the right of individual applications by legal persons, as it would encourage governments to deprive such entities of the possibility to pursue an application lodged at a time when they enjoyed legal personality(…)', which showed that the Court had throughout placed emphasis on the applicant company in its own right. In these circumstances, the Court found that the parties in the above-mentioned arbitration proceedings and in the present case were different and therefore the two matters were not 'substantially the same' within the meaning of Article 35(2)(b) ECHR.[311] In determining whether its jurisdiction is excluded by virtue of this Convention provision the Court would have to decide whether the case before it is substantially the same as a matter that has already been submitted to a parallel set of proceedings and, if that is so, whether the simultaneous proceedings may be seen as 'another procedure of international investigation or settlement' within the meaning of Article 35(2)(b) ECHR.[312] The Court has underlined that it is not the date of submission to a parallel set of proceedings that is decisive, but whether a decision on the merits has already been taken in those proceedings by the time it examines the case.[313]

So far very few decisions have been published in which an application was declared inadmissible on the ground that a matter had already been submitted to another international body for investigation or settlement. In view of the small number of international organs charged with the supervision of the implementation of human rights obligations this is not surprising. It *is*, however, somewhat surprising in connection with the UN Covenant on Civil and Political Rights and the Optional Protocol accompanying it.[314] This Protocol confers on individuals the right to submit an application ('communication') to the Human Rights Committee,[315] so that a case referred to in Article 35(2)(b) is quite conceivable. The Commission held that it would be against the letter and spirit of the Convention if the same matter was simultaneously submitted to two international institutions. Article 35(2)(b) ECHR aims at avoiding the plurality of international procedures concerning the same case.[316] The assessment of similarity of the cases would usually involve the comparison of the parties in the respective proceedings, the relevant legal provisions relied on by them, the scope of their claims and the types of the redress sought.[317] The Court therefore verifies, as is the case with the first limb of Article 35(2)(b) mentioned above,

---

[311] *OAO Neftyanaya Kompaniya Yukos v. Russia, supra* n. 311, para. 521.

[312] *Ibid.,* para. 520.

[313] *Peraldi v. France*, ECtHR 7 April 2009 (dec.), appl. no. 2096/05.

[314] The UN Covenant on Civil and Political Rights and the Optional Protocol belonging thereto entered into force on 26 March 1976.

[315] See Art. 1 of the Protocol.

[316] *Calcerrada Fornieles and Cabeza Mato v. Spain*, EComHR 6 July 1992 (dec.), appl. no. 17512/90D&R 73 (1992), p. 214 (223).

[317] *OAO Neftyanaya Kompaniya Yukos v. Russia, supra* n. 311, para. 521; *Greek Federation of Bank Employee Unions v. Greece*, ECtHR 6 December 2011 (dec.), appl. no. 72808/10.

whether the applications to the different international institutions concern substantially the same persons, facts and complaints.[318]

In order not to run the risk of being declared inadmissible by the Court under Article 35(2)(b), the applicant has to withdraw his application lodged with the other body. It is not sufficient to request a suspension of the proceedings pending before that body, because this does not have the same effect as a complete withdrawal of the application, which is the only step allowing the Court to examine an application also brought before it.[319] New events subsequent to the introduction of an application but directly related to the facts adverted to therein will be taken into account by the Court at the time of the examination of the application. Therefore, an application introduced before the Commission by two applicants, which had the same object as the application submitted to the Human Rights Committee by one of the applicants and joined by the second after the introduction of the application before the Commission, was considered to be substantially the same as the one submitted to the Human Rights Committee.[320]

In a case where the application had been submitted by the Council of Civil Service Unions and six individuals, the Commission held that these applicants were not identical with the complainant before the ILO organs concerned. The complaints before the ILO were brought by the Trade Union Congress, through its General Secretary, on its own behalf. The six individual applicants before the Commission would not have been able to bring such complaints since the Committee on Freedom of Association only examines complaints from organisations of workers and employees. Accordingly, the application could not be regarded as being substantially the same as the complaints before the ILO.[321]

In the *Lukanov* case, the applicant complained about the conditions of detention. In the same case the Human Rights Committee of the Inter-Parliamentary Union examined in particular the conditions of the applicant's detention. On 12 September 1992, at the 88th Conference of the Inter-Parliamentary Council, the Committee issued a Report on the applicant's case. The matter was still under consideration by the Union. The Commission observed that the Inter-Parliamentary Union was an association of parliamentarians from all over the world, set up *inter alia* to unite parliamentarians in common action and to advance international peace and co-operation. The Union is a non-governmental organisation. The organs of the Union may adopt resolutions which are communicated by the parliamentarians concerned to the national parliaments and to international organisations. The Commission considered that the term 'another procedure' referred to judicial or quasi-judicial proceedings similar to those set up by the Convention. Moreover, the term 'international

---

[318]   *Karoussiotis v. Portugal, supra* n. 210, para. 63.
[319]   *Ibid.*, p. 224.
[320]   *Ibid.*
[321]   *Council of Civil Service Unions v. United Kingdom*, EComHR 20 January 1987 (dec.), appl. no. 11603/85, D&R 50 (1987), p. 228 (237).

investigation or settlement' refers to institutions and procedures set up by states, thus excluding non-governmental bodies. The Commission considered that the Inter-Parliamentary Union constituted a non-governmental organisation, whereas Article 35(2)(b) referred to inter-governmental institutions and procedures. It followed that the procedures of the Inter-Parliamentary Union did not constitute 'another procedure of international investigation or settlement' within the meaning of Article 35(2)(b) ECHR.[322]

In the *Hill* case, the Court noted that it appeared from the file that the applicant and his brother had introduced an application with the UN Human Rights Committee set up under the International Covenant on Civil and Political Rights complaining that their right to a fair trial had been breached by the Spanish courts, namely the Provincial High Court of Valencia. The Court observed that, on 2 April 1997, the Human Rights Committee had given its view on the case, finding Spain to be in breach of several provisions of the Covenant. In order to execute this decision, the applicant had instituted two separate sets of proceedings before the Spanish authorities which had still not ended. The Court noted that the application did not concern the breach of the applicant's right to a fair trial guaranteed by Article 6 ECHR in the framework of the criminal proceedings against him in the Provincial High Court of Valencia. The complaints submitted to the Court concerned the execution of the decision of the UN Human Rights Committee finding a violation of several rights guaranteed by the International Covenant. However, the Court did not need to decide whether the application could be rejected as being substantially the same as those submitted to the Human Rights Committee, as it was in any case inadmissible *ratione materiae*.[323] In the *Smirnova* case, the Court ascertained to what extent the proceedings before it overlapped with those before the United Nations Human Rights Committee. The Court noted, first, that the communication pending before the Human Rights Committee was lodged by and concerned only the first applicant, and its effects could not for this reason be extended to the second applicant. Next, the first applicant's complaints in that case were directed against her arrest on 26 August 1995 and, in particular, the question whether this arrest was justified, the impossibility to challenge it in the courts, and the alleged inadequate conditions of detention. The scope of the factual basis for the first applicant's application to the Court, although going back to the arrest of 26 August 1995, was significantly wider. It extended to the whole of the proceedings which terminated in 2002, and included the first applicant's arrest on three more occasions since 26 August 1995. It followed that the first applicant's application was not substantially the same as the petition pending before the Human Rights Committee, and that being so, it fell outside the scope

---

[322]   *Lukanov v. Bulgaria*, EComHR 12 January 1995 (dec.), appl. no. 21915/93, D & R 80 A (1995), p. 108 (123–124).

[323]   *Hill v. Spain*, ECtHR 4 December 2001 (dec.), appl. no. 61892/00.

of Article 35(2)(b) ECHR and could not be rejected pursuant to that provision.[324] In the case of *Kovačić, Mrkonjić and Golubović*, the Court acknowledged that the Convention institutions have interpreted the concept of 'substantially the same application' very restrictively. They have found themselves prevented from dealing with an application if the applicant in the other international procedure was the same as the applicant who lodged the application to the Commission or to the Court.[325] The Court continued that, even assuming that arbitration proceedings before the International Monetary Fund and mediation proceedings under the auspices of the Bank for International Settlement in the framework of succession negotiations were pending and that their subject matter were the same as that in the present cases, that the parties to the IMF and BIS procedures were not the same as those to the proceedings before the Court. It followed that it had not been shown that an application identical to, or substantially the same, as those before the Court in the present cases had already been submitted to another procedure of international investigation or settlement.[326]

The Court of Justice of the European Communities has also jurisdiction to deal with human rights issues within the Community context.[327] The applicable human rights issues may be identical to issues covered by the Convention. This will be even more so after the EU Charter of Fundamental Human Rights will have become binding. This raises the question of whether the examination of those issues by the Court of Justice has to be considered 'another procedure of international investigation or settlement' in the sense of Article 35(2)(b) ECHR. Leaving apart the fact that in most of the procedures the issues raised before the two Courts will not be 'substantially the same',[328] since all the Member States of the EU are also parties to the Convention and the European Court of Human Rights considers itself competent to also deal with complaints against Member States of the EU that have a community context,[329] it may be expected that the Court will consider the procedure before the Court of Justice as a

---

[324]   *Smirnova and Smirnova v. Russia, supra* n. 310.

[325]   *Council of Civil Service Unions and Others v. United Kingdom, supra* n. 322, p. 228 (236–237).

[326]   *Kovačić, Mrkonjić and Golubović v. Slovenia*, ECtHR 9 October 2003 (dec.), appl. nos. 44574/98 45133/98 48316/99.

[327]   Standing case law since Case 11/70, *Internationale Handelsgesellschaft* [1970] ECR 1125 at p. 1134.

[328]   *Matthews v. United Kingdom*, ECtHR 18 February 1999, appl. no. 24833/94, paras. 33–35.

[329]   An example of this is *Sacchi v. Italy*, EComHR 12 March 1976, appl. no. 6452/74 D&R 5 (1976), p. 43, the core of which was also discussed by the Court of Justice in Luxembourg, of which the court of *Biella* had requested a preliminary ruling in Case 155/73 *Sacchi* [1974] ECR 09. Mr Sacchi, operator of a cable television firm (Telebiella) without a licence, refused to pay the contribution for the TV receiving sets, which was punishable under Italian law. Upon this, he was convicted. A request for a licence for transmission via a cable system was refused. A presidential decree of 29 March 1973 assimilated cable TV equipment to radio and TV equipment, thus making it subject to the RAI/TV monopoly. Sacchi lodged a complaint with the Commission in Strasbourg about violation of Art. 10(1) of the Convention. Questions were submitted to the Court in Luxembourg, *inter alia*, about free movement of goods and services, competition and national monopolies of a commercial nature.

'domestic remedy'. This will certainly be the case after the EU has acceded to the Convention.

1.14. INCOMPATIBILITIES – ARTICLE 35(3)(a)

Incompatibility with the Convention was concluded at in the case law of the Commission: (1) if the application fell outside the scope of the Convention *ratione personae, ratione materiae, ratione loci*, or *ratione temporis*; (2) if the individual applicant did not satisfy the condition of Article 34; and (3) if the applicant, contrary to Article 17, aimed at the destruction of one of the rights and freedoms guaranteed in the Convention.

In relation to the categories referred to in (1), it has been observed above that the Commission did not differentiate clearly between its competence and the admissibility of the application. Of these categories the territorial and the temporal scope of the Convention have already been discussed. In the case of *Cyprus v. Turkey*, the Commission held that an inter-state complaint could not be rejected as being incompatible with the provisions of the Convention.[330]

a.   Jurisdiction ratione personae

Whether an application falls within the scope of the Convention *ratione personae* is determined by the answer to the question who may submit an application to the Court (active legitimation) and against whom such an application may be lodged (passive legitimation). This question has been answered above throughout. An application may be lodged by any of the Contracting States as well as by those natural persons, non-governmental organisations and groups of individuals who are within the jurisdiction of the state against which the complaint is directed. With respect to applications by states it is also to be noted that they must be lodged by a national authority competent to act on behalf of the state in international relations. In that respect, regard must be had not only to the text of the Constitution but also to the practice under it.[331]

The Court cannot receive applications directed against a state which is not a party to the Convention[332] or, as the case may be, to the Protocols relied upon in the application.[333] In the case of *Stephens v. Cyprus, Turkey and the United Nations* the Court held that to the extent that the applicant's complaint was

---

[330]   *Cyprus v. Turkey, supra* n. 108, p. 104(135).

[331]   *Cyprus* v. *Turkey, supra* n. 177, p. 82 (116).

[332]   For some of the numerous examples, see, *Confédération Française Démocratique du Travail v. European Communities*, EComHR 10 July 1978 (dec.), appl. no. 8030/77 Yearbook XXI (1978), p. 530 (536–538); *Heinz v. Contracting States also Parties to the European Patent Convention*, EComHR 10 January 1994 (dec.), appl. no. 21090/92, D&R 76-A (1994), p. 125 (127).

[333]   See *De Saedeleer v. Belgium*, ECtHR, 24 July 2007, appl. no. 27535/04, para. 68.

directed against the UN, the Court noted that United Nations Peacekeeping Force in Cyprus (UNFICYP), which has control over the buffer zone, is a subsidiary organ of the UN created under the UN Charter and is under the exclusive control and command of the UN. Consequently, its actions and inactions were in principle attributable to the UN. The Court reiterated that the UN has a legal personality separate from that of its member states and is not a Contracting Party to the Convention.[334]

Compatibility *ratione personae* requires the alleged violation of the Convention to have been committed by a Contracting State or to be in some way attributable to it. Even where the respondent state has not raised any objections as to the Court's jurisdiction *ratione personae*, this issue calls for consideration by the Court of its own motion.[335] Fundamental rights protected by international human rights treaties should be secured to individuals living in the territory of the State Party concerned, notwithstanding its subsequent dissolution or succession.[336] A state-owned company must enjoy sufficient institutional and operational independence from the state for the latter to be absolved of responsibility under the Convention for its acts and omissions.[337] Applications will be declared incompatible *ratione personae* with the Convention if the applicant lacks standing as regards Article 34 ECHR.[338] Furthermore, an application will be declared inadmissible *ratione personae* if the alleged violation does not come under the responsibility of the respondent state. In general, a state is internationally responsible for the acts of its legislative, executive and judicial branch of government. The question may arise as to whether a particular organ or person can be considered to belong to these government organs for the purpose of the Convention. The case has already been mentioned of a foreign or international organ which is active in the territory of a Contracting State, but does not fall under its responsibility.[339] Thus, an application brought in substance against the European Patent Office falls outside the scope of the Court's jurisdiction *ratione personae*.[340] In the *Calabro* case, the Court held that, insofar as the applicants' complaint concerned the Greek authorities' apparent

---

[334] *Stephens v. Cyprus, Turkey and the United Nations*, ECtHR 11 December 2008 (dec.), appl. no. 45267/06.

[335] *Sejdić and Finci v. Bosnia and Herzegovina*, ECtHR (GC) 22 December 2009, appl. nos. 27996/06 and 34806/06, para. 27.

[336] *Bijelić v. Montenegro and Serbia*, ECtHR 28 April 2009, appl. no. 11890/05, para. 69.

[337] *Mykhaylenky and Others v. Ukraine*, ECtHR 30 November 2004, appl. nos. 35091/02 and Others, pars. 43–45; *Cooperativa Agricola Slobozia-Hanesei v. Moldova*, ECtHR 3 April 2007, appl. no. 39745/02, para. 19.

[338] *Municipal Section of Antilly v. France*, ECtHR 23 November 1999 (dec.), appl. no. 45129/98; *Döşemealtı Belediyesi v. Turkey*, ECtHR 23 March 2010 (dec.) appl. no. 50108/06; *Moretti and Benedetti v. Italy*, ECtHR 27 April 2010 (dec.), appl. no. 16318/07.

[339] For the special position of the British Judicial Committee of the Privy Council, see *X v. United Kingdom*, EComHR, appl. no. 3813/68, Yearbook XIII (1970), p. 586 (598–600).

[340] *Heinz v. Contracting States also Parties to the European Patent Convention*, *supra* n. 332, p. 125 (127).

reluctance to co-operate with their Hungarian counterparts, it was competent to assure the respect of the text of the European Convention on Human Rights and not that of any other international agreement.[341]

Furthermore, the situation may arise where a state is responsible for the international relations of a given territory, without it being possible that an application is lodged against it on account of the acts of the authorities in those territories. Indeed, the Convention is only applicable to those territories if the state in question has made a declaration as referred to in Article 56(1).

Applications may be directed only against *states*, and consequently not against individuals or groups of individuals. Applications against individuals are therefore declared inadmissible *ratione personae*.[342] In practice, a number of complaints are directed against the most varied categories of individuals and organisations, such as judges and lawyers in their personal capacity, employers, private radio and TV stations and banks. It appears from its case law, however, that the Commission did investigate whether a violation of the Convention by an individual may involve the responsibility of a state. Under international law a state is responsible for acts of individuals to the extent that the state has urged the individuals to commit the acts in question, has given its consent to them, or in violation of its international obligations has neglected to prevent those acts, to punish the perpetrators, or to impose an obligation to redress the injury caused.[343] These principles also apply within the framework of the European Convention, albeit that Article 1 creates that responsibility with respect to the treatment of 'everyone within their jurisdiction', and not only of foreigners. The Court has also held that a state cannot absolve itself from this responsibility by delegating its obligations to private bodies or individuals.[344]

States may be held responsible for acts of their authorities, whether performed within or outside national boundaries, which produce effects outside their own territory.[345] However, this will occur only exceptionally,[346] namely

---

[341]   *Calabró v. Italy and Germany*, ECtHR 21 March 2002 (dec.), appl. no. 59895/00; See also *Karalyos and Huber v. Hungary and Greece*, ECtHR 6 April 2004, appl. no. 75116/00, para. 40, where the question concerned the European Convention on Information on Foreign Law.

[342]   See *X v. United Kingdom*, EComHR 10 December 1976 (dec.), appl. no. 6956/75, D&R 8 (1978), p. 103 (104); *Durini v. Italy*, EComHR 12 January 1994 (dec.), appl. no. 19217/91, D&R 76-A (1994), p. 76 (79), where the complaints concerning the contents of a will were directed against the testator and did not engage the responsibility of the State.

[343]   See I. Brownlie, *Principles of Public International Law*, Oxford, 1990, pp. 444–476.

[344]   *Van der Mussele v. Belgium*, ECtHR 23 November 1983, appl. no. 8919/80, para. 29.

[345]   *Drozd and Janousek v. France and Spain*, ECtHR 26 June 1992, appl. no. 12747/87, para. 91; *Loizidou v. Turkey* (preliminary objections), ECtHR (GC) 23 March 1995, appl. no. 15318/89, para. 62.

[346]   *Banković and Others v. Belgium and Others*, ECtHR (GC) 12 December 2001, appl. no. 52207/99, para. 71; *Ilaşcu and Others v. Moldova and Russia*, appl. no. 48787/99 supra n. 82, para. 314; 40; *Medvedyev and Others v. France*, ECtHR (GC) 29 March 2010, appl. no. 3394/03, paras. 63–64.

where a Contracting State is in effective control over an area or has at the very least a decisive influence over it.[347]

A state may be held accountable for violations of the Convention rights of persons who are in the territory of another state but who are found to be under the former state's authority and control through its agents operating – whether lawfully or unlawfully – in the latter state.[348] In the case of *Al-Skeini v. the United Kingdom*, the Court held that following the removal from power of the Ba'ath regime and until the accession of the interim Iraqi Government, the United Kingdom (together with the United States of America) assumed in Iraq the exercise of some of the public powers normally to be exercised by a sovereign government. In particular, the United Kingdom assumed authority and responsibility for the maintenance of security in South-East Iraq.[349] Acts committed by troops of the United Nations Multinational Forces can only be attributed to the international organisation when it has no effective control nor ultimate authority over that conduct.[350]

In these cases, the national authorities carried out continuous – though sporadic – research. In other cases, by contrast, where the applicant until more than 10 years after the event got to the European Court, although the national authorities for years no longer gave evidence to conduct any investigation, the Court considered that the time limit expired. For territories which are legally within the jurisdiction of a Contracting State but not under the effective authority/control of that state, applications may be considered incompatible with the provisions of the Convention.[351] However, regard must be had to the state's positive obligations under the Convention.[352]

There are exceptions to the principle that an individual's physical presence in the territory of one of the Contracting Parties has the effect of placing that individual under the jurisdiction of the state concerned, for example where a state hosts the headquarters of an international organisation against which the applicant's complaints are directed. The mere fact that an international criminal tribunal has its seat and premises in the Netherlands is not a sufficient ground for attributing to that State any alleged acts or omissions on the part of the

---

[347] *Al-Skeini and Others v. the United Kingdom*, ECtHR (GC) 7 July 2011, appl. no. 55721/07, paras. 138–140; *Catan and Others v. Moldova and Russia*, ECtHR (GC) 19 October 2012, appl. nos. 43370/04, 8252/05 and 18454/06, paras. 106–107.

[348] *Issa and Others v. Turkey*, ECtHR 16 November 2004, appl. no. 31821/96, para. 71; *Öcalan v. Turkey, supra* n. 48, para. 91; *Medvedyev and Others v. France, supra* n. 348, paras. 66–67.

[349] *Al-Skeini and Others v. the United Kingdom, supra* n. 347, para. 149.

[350] *Al-Jedda v. the United Kingdom*, ECtHR (GC) 7 July 2011, appl. no. 27021/08, paras. 84–85. With regard to acts taking place in a UN buffer zone, see *Issaak and Others v. Turkey*, ECtHR 28 September 2006 (dec.), appl. no. 44587/98.

[351] *An and Others v. Cyprus*, EComHR 8 October 1991 (dec.), appl. no. 18270/99.

[352] *Ilaşcu and Others v. Moldova and Russia, supra* n. 82, paras. 312–313; *Ivantoc and Others v. Moldova and Russia, supra* n. 284, paras. 105–106; *Catan and Others v. Moldova and Russia, supra* n. 347, paras. 109–110.

international tribunal in connection with the applicant's conviction.[353] The mere participation of a state in proceedings brought against it in another state does not in itself amount to an exercise of extra-territorial jurisdiction.[354]

In the *Campbell and Cosans* case, the Court held the Government of the United Kingdom responsible for acts occurring at state schools, since the State had assumed responsibility for formulating general school policy.[355] Functions relating to the internal administration of a school, such as discipline, could not be said to be ancillary to the educational process. In this respect, the Court noted that a school's disciplinary system fell within the ambit of the right to education which has also been recognised in Article 28 of the UN Convention on the Rights of the Child. Secondly, it held that in the United Kingdom, independent schools co-existed with a system of public education. The fundamental right of everyone to education was a right guaranteed equally to pupils in state schools and independent schools, no distinction being made between the two. Finally, the Court referred to the above-mentioned *Van der Mussele* judgment where it held that a state could not absolve itself from responsibility by delegating its obligations to private bodies or individuals.[356]

In the *Nielsen* case, the Government argued that the placement of a minor in a psychiatric hospital was the sole responsibility of the mother. The majority of the Commission found, however, that the final decision on the question of hospitalisation of the applicant was not taken by the holder of parental rights but by the Chief Physician of the Child Psychiatric Ward of the State Hospital, thus engaging the responsibility of the State under Article 5(1).[357] The Court disagreed with the Commission and held that the decision on the hospitalisation was in fact taken by the mother in her capacity as holder of parental rights.[358]

In the *Ciobanu* case, the Court noted that the applicants' representatives failed to submit to the Court all information of relevance to the case under the Convention by introducing a complaint in the name of a deceased person, by signing the power of attorney on behalf of the deceased applicant and by omitting to inform the Court of the applicant's death. The Court further noted that the applicant died on 31 December 1996, i.e. before the submission of his complaint

---

[353] *Galić v. the Netherlands*, ECtHR 9 June 2009 (dec.), appl. no. 22617/07; *Blagojević v. the Netherlands*, ECtHR, 9 June 2009 (dec.), appl. no. 49032/07; *Djokaba Lambi Longa v. the Netherlands*, ECtHR 9 October 2012 (dec.), appl. no. 33917/12. For the acceptance of an international civil administration in the respondent state's territory, see *Berić and Others v. Bosnia and Herzegovina*, ECtHR 16 October 2007 (dec.), appl. nos. 36357/04, para. 30.

[354] *McElhinney v. Ireland and the United Kingdom*, ECtHR (GC) 9 February 2000 (dec.), appl. no. 31253/96; *Manoilescu and Dobrescu v. Romania and Russia*, ECtHR 3 March 2005 (dec.), appl. no. 60861/00, paras. 99–11; *Treska v. Albania and Italy*, ECtHR 29 June 2006 (dec.), appl. no. 26937/04.

[355] *Campbell and Cosans v. United Kingdom*, ECtHR 25 February 1982, appl. nos. 7511/76 7743/76, para. 26.

[356] *Van der Mussele v. Belgium*, ECtHR 25 March 1993, appl. no. 8919/80 para. 30.

[357] *Nielsen v. Denmark*, EComHR 12 March 1987 (rep.), appl. no. 10929/84, A.144, p. 38.

[358] *Nielsen v. Denmark*, ECtHR 28 November 1988, appl. no. 10929/84, para. 73.

to the Court. Therefore, the applicant had not expressed any intention to lodge such a complaint, nor claimed to be a victim, as required by Article 34 ECHR, on the date of the application. Accordingly, it found that the case was not legally brought before it as regards the applicant who, as a consequence, lacked *locus standi*. Moreover, it recalled that the representatives did not lodge any complaint to the Court in their own name, nor did they manifest their intention to continue the case of the deceased in their own capacity. It followed from this that the representatives also lacked *locus standi* for the purpose of the proceedings before the Court. Accordingly, the application was incompatible *ratione personae*.[359]

In the *Mykhaylenky* case, the issue arose whether the State was liable for the debts of a state-owned company which was a separate legal entity, and could be held responsible for the ultimate failure to pay the applicants the amounts awarded to them in the judgments against that company. The Court considered that the Government had not demonstrated that the company enjoyed sufficient institutional and operational independence from the State as to absolve the State from responsibility under the Convention for its acts and omissions. The Court noted that it was not suggested by the Government or by the materials in the case file that the State's debts to the company had ever been paid in full or in part, which implied the State's liability as regards the ensuing debts of the company. The debtor company had operated in the highly regulated sphere of nuclear energy and conducted its construction activities in the Chernobyl zone of compulsory evacuation, which was placed under strict governmental control due to environmental and public health considerations. This control even extended to the applicants' terms of employment by the company, including their salaries. The State had prohibited the attachment of the company's property due to possible contamination. Moreover, the management of the company was transferred to the Ministry of Energy as of May 1998. In the Court's opinion, these elements confirmed the public nature of the debtor enterprise, regardless of its formal classification under domestic law. Accordingly, the Court concluded that there were sufficient grounds to deem the State liable for the debts of the company to the applicants in the special circumstances of the case, despite the fact that the company was a separate legal entity. The Court found, therefore, that the applicants' complaint was compatible *ratione personae* with the provisions of the Convention.[360]

b. *Jurisdiction ratione materiae*

In order to answer the question of whether an application falls within the scope of the Convention *ratione materiae*, it is necessary to differentiate between state applications and individual applications.[361]

---

[359]   *Ciobanu v. Romania,* ECtHR 16 December 2003 (dec.) appl. no. 52414/99.

[360]   *Mykhaylenky and Others v. Ukraine, supra* n. 338, paras. 43–45; *Cooperativa Agricola Slobozia-Hanesei v. Moldova,* ECtHR 3 July 2007, appl. no. 39745/02, para. 19.

[361]   Strictly speaking, inter-state applications cannot be rejected on this ground.

Article 33, which permits the Contracting States to lodge applications on 'any alleged breach of the provisions of the Convention by another High Contracting Party', leaves open the possibility for states to submit applications which relate to provisions of the Convention other than the articles of Section I. Articles that might be considered as such, for instance, are Article 1 concerning the obligation for a Contracting State to secure to everyone within its jurisdiction the rights and freedoms of Section I of the Convention, and Article 34 in case of interference with the exercise of the individual right of complaint. The same applies to Article 46 in case of refusal to give effect to a judgment of the Court, and Article 52 in case of refusal to furnish the requested information to the Secretary General of the Council of Europe concerning the implementation of the provisions of the Convention. So far, the Contracting States have not availed themselves of this wider right of action, except where Article 1 is concerned.

The right of complaint of individuals has a somewhat more limited character. It appears from Article 34 that individuals may lodge complaints only about 'the rights set forth in this Convention', which implies that their complaints may relate only to the articles of Section I and the articles of the Protocols containing additional rights. The question does arise whether an exception must be made for Article 34; in other words, whether the right of complaint itself, the exercise of which the Contracting States have undertaken not to hinder, may be considered a 'right'. As a rule the Commission dealt with such a complaint in another way than with a complaint concerning the violation of one of the rights or freedoms of Section I, in that it consulted directly with the government concerned.

It might be argued that, apart from the right of individual complaint under Article 34, if an individual who has been successful before the Court, feels that the judgment has not been complied with, he or she may properly claim to be a victim of a violation of Article 46, which contains the obligation to abide by the judgment of the Court. In the case of *Olsson I*, the main issue was whether the decision of the Swedish authorities to take the children of the applicants into care had given rise to a violation of Article 8 ECHR. The Court found a violation of that provision and awarded the applicants just satisfaction under Article 41 ECHR.[362] In the case of *Olsson II*, the applicants complained that despite the Court's *Olsson I* judgment, the Swedish authorities had continued to hinder their reunion with their children. The applicants had still not been allowed to meet the children under circumstances which would have enabled them to re-establish parent-child relationships. In their view, Sweden had continued to act in breach of Article 8 and had thereby failed to comply with its obligations under Article 46(1) ECHR. The Court referred to Resolution DH (88)18, adopted on 26 October 1988, concerning the execution of the *Olsson I* judgment, where the Committee of Ministers, 'having satisfied itself that the Government of Sweden has paid to the applicants the sums provided for in the judgment', declared that

---

[362]   *Olsson v. Sweden (No. 1)*, ECtHR 24 March 1988, appl. no. 10465/83, para. 84.

the Committee had 'exercised its functions under Article 46(2) ECHR'. The Court held that in the circumstances of the case no separate issue arose under Article 46, since the present complaint raised a new issue which had not been determined by the *Olsson I* judgment.[363] The Court left thus open the possibility that there might be circumstances under which a complaint under Article 46 ECHR could be examined by it. The late Judge Martens has questioned the position that the Committee of Ministers' competence under Article 46(2) ECHR is an exclusive one. He gave two reasons for taking the view that complaints under Article 46(1) should not be decided by the Committee of Ministers but by the Court. In the first place, the interpretation of its judgments is, in the nature of things, better left to the Court than to a gathering of professional diplomats who are not necessarily trained lawyers possessing the qualifications laid down in the Convention. Secondly, the members of the Committee of Ministers are under the direct authority of their national administration and cannot be considered as a 'tribunal' in the sense of the Convention.[364] Under Protocol No. 14, the Committee of Ministers has the possibility to refer to the Court the question whether a Contracting Party has failed to fulfil its obligations under paragraph 4 of Article 46.

The Court cannot deal with complaints about rights or freedoms not set forth in the Convention. Complaints concerning such rights and freedoms are declared inadmissible by the Court as being incompatible with the Convention. In practice, a great many complaints concern a variety of 'rights and freedoms'. From the colourful case law of the Commission the following examples of incompatibility *ratione materiae* may be cited: right to a university degree, right to asylum, right to start a business, right to diplomatic protection, right to a divorce, right to a driving licence, a general right to free legal aid, right to free medical aid, right to adequate housing, right to a nationality, right to a passport, right to a pension, right to a promotion and the right to be recognised as a scholar. In this context it should, however, be borne in mind that a right which is not set forth in the Convention, may find protection *indirectly* via one of the provisions of the Convention. Thus, it is conceivable that, although the right to admission to a country of which one is not a national, has not been included in the Convention, under certain circumstances a person cannot be denied admission to a country if his right to respect for his family life (Article 8) would be violated. Similarly, although the Convention does not recognise a right to a pension, violation of an existing right to a pension may be contrary to Article 1 of Protocol No. 1, in which the right to the enjoyment of one's possessions is protected.

---

[363] *Olsson v. Sweden (No. 2)*, ECtHR 27 November 1992, appl. no. 13441/87, para. 75.
[364] S.K. Martens, 'Individual Complaints under Article 53 of the European Convention on Human Rights', in R. Lawson and M. de Blois (eds.), *The Dynamics of the Protection of Human Rights in Europe. Essays in Honour of Henry G. Schermers*, Vol. III, Dordrecht, 1994, pp. 253–286 (284–286).

Complaints to be equated with those concerning rights not protected in the Convention are complaints concerning rights which are indeed incorporated in the Convention, but with respect to which the respondent state has made a reservation. Complaints relating to such rights are also declared inadmissible on account of incompatibility with the Convention.[365]

The applicant is not required to indicate accurately in his application the rights set forth in the Convention which in his opinion have been violated. The Commission proved prepared to investigate *ex officio*, by reference to the submissions of the applicant, whether there has been a violation of one or more of the provisions of Section I. This approach is in conformity with the above-mentioned objective character of the European Convention.[366] Nevertheless, it remains advisable for an applicant or counsel to raise all important points of fact and law already during the examination of admissibility. The possible consequences if this is not done are apparent from the *Winterwerp* case. The Court held that there was an evident connection between the issue of Article 6 raised before it and the initial complaints. This, in combination with the fact that the Netherlands Government had not raised a preliminary objection on the point, induced the Court to take the alleged violation of Article 6 into consideration,[367] but its observations indicate that the Court would not be prepared to adopt such a lenient attitude in all circumstances.

c. *Victim requirement*

The second of the above-mentioned categories of cases in which the application is not compatible with the provisions of the Convention – those cases where the applicant does not satisfy the condition of Article 34 – concerns the condition which has already been discussed at length, *viz.* that an individual applicant must be able to furnish *prima facie* evidence that he is personally the victim of the violation of the Convention alleged by him, or at least has well-founded reasons for considering himself to be the victim. If he merely puts forward a violation *in abstracto*, or a violation which has done a wrong only to other persons, his application is incompatible with the provisions of the Convention.

---

[365] *Kozlova and Smirnova v. Latvia*, ECtHR 23 October 2001 (dec.), appl. no. 57381/00.

[366] The approach was confirmed expressly by the Court in its judgment of *Guzzardi v. Italy*, *supra* n. 152, para. 106. In that case, the Commission had – wrongly, according to the Italian Government – also considered the complaint in the light of Art. 5, whereas the applicant had not expressly referred to it. On the basis of a detailed motivation the Court held as follows: 'The Commission and the Court have to examine in the light of the Convention as a whole the situation impugned by an applicant. In the performance of this task, they are, notably, free to give to the facts of the case, as found to be established by the material before them (…), a characterisation in law different from that given to them by the applicant' (para. 58).

[367] *Winterwerp v. the Netherlands*, ECtHR 24 October 1979, appl. no. 6301/73, para. 72.

d. Destruction or limitation of a right or freedom

The most obvious case of incompatibility with the provisions of the Convention is the third of the above-mentioned categories. This concerns applications which are directed at the destruction or limitation of one of the rights or freedoms guaranteed in the Convention, and as such conflict with Article 17, which will hereafter be discussed in greater detail. Even if Article 17 had not been written, such applications of course would still be inadmissible, *viz.* on account of abuse of the right of complaint in the sense of Article 35(3), which will be discussed now.

1.15. ABUSE OF THE RIGHT OF COMPLAINT – ARTICLE 35(3)(a)

On this ground, too, in practice very few applications are declared inadmissible. This may probably be accounted for by the fact that it is very difficult to establish such an abuse, since the applicant's motives cannot easily be ascertained, certainly not in so early a stage of the examination. As regards the concept of 'abuse', within the meaning of Article 35(3), it must be understood in its ordinary sense according to general legal theory – namely, the harmful exercise of a right for purposes other than those for which it is designed. Accordingly, any conduct of an applicant that is manifestly contrary to the purpose of the right of individual application as provided for in the Convention and impedes the proper functioning of the Court or the proper conduct of the proceedings before it constitutes an abuse of the right of application.[368]

In the case of *Akdivar and Others v. Turkey*, the Court held that the use of offensive language in proceedings before the Court is undoubtedly inappropriate, the Court considers that, except in extraordinary cases, an application may only be rejected as abusive if it was knowingly based on untrue facts.[369] In the case of *Drijfhout v. the Netherlands*, the Court held in this respect that the submission of an application under a false identity forced the Court to conclude on the facts available that an attempt has been made to pass the applicant off under a false identity. It further found that the applicant persisted in refusing to reveal her true identity.[370] An application may be rejected as abusive under Article 35(3) ECHR, if it was knowingly based on untrue facts.[371] This type of abuse may also be committed by omission, where the applicant fails to inform the Court at the

---

[368] *Petrovic v. Serbia*, ECtHR 18 October 2011 (dec.), appl. no. 58551/11.
[369] *Akdivar and Others v. Turkey, supra* n. 98, paras. 53–55; *Varbanov v. Bulgaria*, ECtHR 5 October 2000, appl. no. 31365/96, para. 36; *S.A.S. v. France*, ECtHR (GC) 1 July 2014, appl. no. 43835/11, para. 67.
[370] *Drijfhout v. the Netherlands*, ECtHR 22 February 2011 (dec.) appl. no. 51721/09, paras. 27–29.
[371] *Bagheri and Maliki v. the Netherlands*, ECtHR 15 May 2007 (dec.), appl. no. 30164/04; *Poznanski and Others v. Germany*, ECtHR 3 July 2007 (dec.), appl. no. 25101/05.

outset of a factor essential for the examination of the case. In the case of *Al-Nashif v. Bulgaria*, the Court, while it considered that an application deliberately grounded on a description of facts omitting events of central importance may in principle constitute an abuse of the right of petition, did not find it established that such a situation obtained in the present case, regard being had to the stage of the proceedings, to the fact that the information allegedly withheld only concerned new developments after the deportation complained of and to the explanation by the applicants' lawyer.[372] If new, important developments occur during the proceedings before the Court and if – despite the express obligation on him or her under the Rules of Court – the applicant failed to disclose that information to the Court, thereby preventing it from ruling on the case in full knowledge of the facts, his or her application may be rejected as being an abuse of application.[373] In the case of *Miroļubovs and Others v. Latvia*, the Latvian Government informed the Court that documents relating to the negotiations with a view to a friendly settlement had been sent to the Latvian Prime Minister via a third party. The Government concluded that the application should be declared inadmissible on the ground of an abuse of the right of petition as there had been a breach of the confidentiality requirement under the friendly-settlement procedure. The Court stressed that the confidentiality requirement was designed to facilitate friendly settlements by protecting the parties and the Court against possible pressure, and that an intentional breach of confidentiality by an applicant could indeed amount to abuse of the right of petition and result in the application being rejected. However, the Court noted the difficulty of monitoring compliance with this requirement and the threat to the applicant's defence rights if it were imposed as an absolute rule. What the parties were prohibited from doing was publicising the information in question, for instance in the media or in correspondence liable to be read by a large number of people. In the instant case, as the Latvian Government had not adduced evidence that all the applicants had consented to the disclosure of the confidential documents, the Court was unable to find that the applicants had abused the right of individual petition.[374] Sometimes judgments and decisions of the Court, and cases still pending before it, are used for the purposes of a political speech at national level in the Contracting States. An application inspired by a desire for publicity or propaganda is not for this reason alone an abuse of the right of application.[375] According to Rule 47(6) of the Rules of Court, applicants, acting in person or through their legal representatives, are under the continuous obligation to keep

---

[372] *Al-Nashif v. Bulgaria*, ECtHR 20 June 2002, appl. no. 50963/99, para. 89.
[373] *Hadrabová and Others v. the Czech Republic*, ECtHR 25 September 2007 (dec.) appl. no. 42165/02; *Predescu v. Romania*, ECtHR 2 December 2008, appl. no. 21447/03, paras. 25–27.
[374] *Miroļubovs and Others v. Latvia*, ECtHR 15 September 2009, appl. no. 798/05, paras. 62–65; *Deceuninck v. France*, ECtHR 13 December 2011 (dec.), appl. no. 47447/08.
[375] *Khadzhialiyev and Others v. Russia*, ECtHR 6 November 2008, appl. no. 3013/04, paras. 66–67.

the Court informed of all important circumstances regarding their pending applications.[376] An application may be rejected as abusive under Article 35(3) if, among other reasons, it was knowingly based on untrue facts.[377] Incomplete and therefore misleading information may also amount to an abuse of the right of application, especially if the information concerns the very core of the case and no sufficient explanation is given for the failure to disclose that information.[378]

An abuse may consist primarily in the object one wishes to attain with the application. Such an abuse of the right of complaint was found to exist in the case of *Ilse Koch*. This wife of the former commandant of the Buchenwald concentration camp had been convicted for violation of the most elementary human rights. She submitted that she was innocent and claimed her release, without invoking a specific provision of the Convention. In her application she voiced a number of accusations and complaints which were not supported in any way by the Convention. The Commission declared her application inadmissible, because her sole aim evidently was to escape the consequences of her conviction, so that her application constituted a 'clear and manifest abuse'.[379] It cannot be the task of the Court, a body which was set up under the Convention to ensure the observance of the engagements undertaken by the High Contracting Parties with respect to the Convention, to deal with a succession of ill-founded and querulous complaints, creating unnecessary work which is incompatible with its real functions.[380]

In the case of *Řehák v. the Czech Republic*, the applicant had sent a number of letters making serious defamatory and groundless accusations about the integrity of certain judges of the Court and members of its Registry. Furthermore, the applicant, who had systematically questioned and contested the impartiality of judges of the Court and members of its Registry, accused Czech members of the Registry of serious political crimes. The Court held that in seeking to ensure the widest possible circulation of his accusations and insults, the applicant had evidenced his determination to harm and tarnish the reputation of the very institution of European Court of Human Rights, its members and staff. The Court recalled that, in principle, an application may only be rejected as abusive under Article 35(3) if it was knowingly based on untrue facts, even if it uses offensive language. The Court was of the opinion that the applicant's allegations were intolerable, exceeding the bounds of normal criticism, albeit misplaced, and amount to contempt of court. Such conduct by

---

[376] *Bekauri v. Georgia*, ECtHR (Preliminary Objection) 10 April 2012, appl. no. 14102/02, paras. 22–25.

[377] *Keretchashvili v. Georgia*, ECtHR 29 April 2010 (dec.), appl. no. 44328/05.

[378] *Pirtskhalaishvili v. Georgia*, ECtHR 29 April 2010 (dec.) appl. no. 44328/05.

[379] *Ilse Koch v. Germany*, EComHR 8 March 1963, appl. no. 1270/61, Yearbook V (1962), p. 126 (134–136); *Petrovic v. Serbia*, *supra* n. 370.

[380] *M v. the United Kingdom*, EComHR 15 October 1987 (dec.), appl. no. 14284/87, D&R 54 (214); *Petrovic v. Serbia*, *supra* n. 370.

the applicant – even supposing that his original application would not be deemed manifestly ill-founded – is contrary to the purpose of the right of individual petition, as provided for in Articles 34 and 35 ECHR. There is no doubt whatsoever that it constitutes an abuse of the right of application within the meaning of Article 35(3) ECHR.[381] The Court has repeatedly held that, although the use of offensive language in proceedings before the Court is undoubtedly inappropriate, except in extraordinary cases, an application may only be rejected as abusive if it is knowingly based on untrue facts.[382]

In the *Klyakhin* case, the Court considered that, although some of the applicant's statements were inappropriate, they did not give rise to such extraordinary circumstances justifying a decision to declare the application inadmissible as an abuse of the right of petition.[383] In the *Manoussos* case, the Court noted, on the one hand, that in some of the applicant's submissions he used insulting expressions about Czech people in general and about certain Czech authorities and found nothing to warrant the use of such a language. On the other hand, the Court took into consideration that such expressions were of rare occurrence in the applicant's voluminous submissions and that they had not recurred since the Section Registrar's letter in which the applicant was advised of the possible consequences of his continued use of insulting language. Considering all circumstances of the case, the Court did not find it appropriate to declare the application inadmissible as being abusive within the meaning of Article 35(3) ECHR.[384] In the *Duringer* case, the Court held that the applicant had sent numerous communications, by letter and e-mail, making serious accusations touching the integrity of certain judges of the Court and members of its Registry. The applicant, who had systematically tried to cast aspersions on judges of the Court, members of its Registry and politicians of the respondent State, accused certain judges in particular of extremely serious crimes. Moreover, in seeking to ensure the widest possible circulation of his accusations and insults the applicant had evidenced his determination to harm and tarnish the image of the institution and its members. The Court noted in addition that the application lodged, by a person who claimed to be called Forest Grunge, contained the same expressions as the applicant used. It noted furthermore, that in most passages the texts of these communications were similar, if not identical, like their presentation and the long lists of their addressees. Even supposing that the name 'Forest Grunge' was not an alias used by the applicant, the Court considered that the remarks repeatedly made, without any foundation, were totally offensive and preposterous,

---

381   *Řehák v. the Czech Republic*, ECtHR 18 May 2004, (dec.), appl. no. 67208/01; *S.A.S. v. France, supra* n. 371, para. 67.

382   *Akdivar v. Turkey, supra* n. 98, paras. 53–54; *Varbanov. V. Bulgaria, supra* n. 371, para. 36; *Duringer and Others and Grunge v. France*, ECtHR 4 February 2003 (dec.), appl. nos 61164/00 and 18589/02.

383   *Klyakhin v. Russia*, ECtHR 14 October 2003 (dec.), appl. no. 46082/99.

384   *Manoussos v. Czech Republic and Germany*, ECtHR 9 July 2002 (dec.), appl. no. 46468/99.

could not fall within the scope of the provisions of Article 34 ECHR. In the Court's opinion, the intolerable conduct of the applicant and Mr Forest Grunge – always supposing that the latter actually existed – was contrary to the purpose of the right of individual petition, as provided for in Articles 34 and 35 ECHR.[385]

The fact that an applicant gives publicity to certain details of the examination of his case, may lead the application being declared inadmissible on account of abuse. In the case of *Khadzhialiyev and Others v. Russia*, the Government submitted that the application had not been lodged in order to restore the allegedly violated rights of the applicants. The actual object and purpose of the application was clearly political as the applicants wanted to 'incriminate the Russian Federation in allegedly adopting a policy infringing upon human rights in the Chechen Republic'. The Court observed that the complaints the applicants brought to its attention concerned their genuine grievances. Nothing in the case file revealed any appearance of an abuse of their right of individual petition.[386]

As was pointed out above, the present admissibility condition does not apply to applications by states. Nevertheless, the case law of the Commission teaches that the Commission did not exclude the possibility that an application by a state might likewise be rejected on account of abuse. This would not be done on the ground of the admissibility condition mentioned in Article 35(2), but on the ground of the general legal principle that the right to bring an action before an international organ must not be abused. Referring to its decision in the first *Greek* case,[387] the Commission stated in the case of *Cyprus v. Turkey* that: 'even assuming that it is empowered on general principle to make such a finding, [the Commission] considers that the applicant Government have, at this stage of the proceedings, provided sufficient particularised information of alleged breaches of the Convention for the purpose of Article 24.'[388]

In its preliminary objection in the case of *Cyprus v. Turkey* before the Court the Turkish Government pleaded that the applicant Government had no legal interest in bringing the application. It argued that Resolutions DH (79) 1 and DH (92) 12, adopted by the Committee of Ministers on the previous inter-state applications constituted *res judicata* in respect of the complaints raised in the instant application which, they maintained, were essentially the same as those which were settled by the aforementioned decisions of the Committee of Ministers. The Court did not agree and it added that this was the first occasion on which it had been seized of the complaints invoked by the applicant Government in the context of an inter-state application, it being observed that, as regards the previous applications, it was not open to the parties or to the Commission to

---

[385] *Duringer and Others and Grunge, supra* n. 384.
[386] *Khadzhialiyev and Others v. Russia*, ECtHR 6 November 2008, appl. no. 3013/04, paras. 66–67.
[387] *Denmark, Norway, Sweden and Netherlands* v. *Greece, supra* n. 110, p. 690 (764).
[388] *Cyprus* v. *Turkey, supra* n. 177 p. 82 (116); *Cyprus* v. *Turkey, supra* n. 108, p. 104 (134).

refer them to the Court under former Article 45 ECHR read in conjunction with former Article 48. The Court continued that, without prejudice to the question of whether and in what circumstances the Court had jurisdiction to examine a case which was the subject of a decision taken by the Committee of Ministers pursuant to former Article 32 ECHR, it should be noted that, in respect of the previous inter-state applications, neither Resolution DH (79) 1 nor Resolution DH(92)12 resulted in a 'decision' within the meaning of Article 32(1). This was clear from the terms of these texts. Indeed, it was to be further observed that the respondent Government accepted in their pleadings on their preliminary objections in the *Loizidou* case that the Committee of Ministers did not endorse the Commission's findings in the previous interstate cases. The Court accordingly concluded that the applicant Government had a legitimate interest in having the merits of the instant application examined by the Court.[389]

1.16. MANIFESTLY ILL-FOUNDEDNESS – ARTICLE 35(3)(a)

This admissibility condition, again, applies only to individual applications. Inter-state applications, which may be assumed to be filed only after extensive deliberation and to have been prepared by expert legal advisers of the government, may in general be expected not to be manifestly ill-founded.

A great many individual applications have been declared inadmissible on the ground of being manifestly ill-founded. The majority of manifestly ill-founded applications are declared inadmissible *de plano* by a single judge or a three-judge committee (Articles 27 and 28 ECHR). However, some applications of this type are examined by a Chamber or even – in exceptional cases – by the Grand Chamber.[390] The term 'manifestly ill-founded' may apply to the application as a whole or to a particular complaint within the broader context of a case. Hence, in some cases, part of the application may be rejected as being of a 'fourth instance' nature, whereas the remainder is declared admissible and may even result in a finding of a violation of the Convention. In principle, and without prejudice to its power to examine the compatibility of national decisions with the Convention, it is not the Court's role to assess itself the facts which have led a national court to adopt one decision rather than another. If it were otherwise, the Court would be acting as a court of third or fourth instance, which would be to disregard the limits imposed on its action.[391]

In the case of *Baumann v. France*, the Court considered that it is not for the Court to act as a court of appeal or, as is sometimes said, as a court of

---

[389] *Cyprus v. Turkey*, ECtHR (GC) 10 May 2001, appl. no. 25781/94, paras. 65–68.
[390] *Gratzinger and Gratzingerova v. the Czech Republic*, ECtHR (GC) 10 July 2002 (dec.), appl. no. 39794/98.
[391] *Kemmache v. France (No. 3)*, ECtHR 24 November 1994, appl. no. 17621/91, para. 44.

fourth instance, from the decisions taken by domestic courts. It is the role of the domestic courts to interpret and apply the relevant rules of procedural or substantive law. Furthermore, it is the domestic courts which are best placed for assessing the credibility of witnesses and the relevance of evidence to the issues in the case.[392] However, in the case of *Sisojeva and Others v. Latvia*, the Court noted at the outset that the applicants considered the NonCitizens Act and the Russian-Latvian agreement of 30 April 1994 to have been incorrectly applied to their case. In that connection it reiterated that, in accordance with Article 19 ECHR, its sole duty is to ensure the observance of the engagements undertaken by the Contracting Parties to the Convention. In particular, it is not its function to deal with errors of fact or law allegedly committed by a national court or to substitute its own assessment for that of the national courts or other national authorities unless and insofar as they may have infringed rights and freedoms protected by the Convention. In other words, the Court cannot question the assessment of the domestic authorities unless there is clear evidence of arbitrariness, which there was not in the instant case.[393]

In practice, applications are declared manifestly ill-founded in particular if the facts about which a complaint is lodged evidently do not indicate a violation of the Convention, or if those facts cannot be proven or are manifestly incorrect. As to the latter, the applicant is required to give *prima facie* evidence of the facts put forward by him.[394] In the case of *Demir and Baykara v. Turkey*, the Court held that in order to determine the meaning of the terms and phrases used in the Convention, the Court is guided mainly by the rules of interpretation provided for in Articles 31 to 33 of the Vienna Convention. In accordance with the Vienna Convention, the Court is required to ascertain the ordinary meaning to be given to the words in their context and in the light of the object and purpose of the provision from which they are drawn. Recourse may also be had to supplementary means of interpretation, either to confirm a meaning determined in accordance with the above steps, or to establish the meaning where it would otherwise be ambiguous, obscure or manifestly absurd or unreasonable.[395] Insofar as the applicant's complaint may be understood to concern assessment of the evidence and the result of the proceedings before the domestic courts, the Court reiterated that, according to Article 19 ECHR, its duty is to ensure the observance of the engagements undertaken by the Contracting Parties to the Convention. In particular, it is not its function to deal with errors of fact or law allegedly committed by a national court unless

---

[392] *Baumann v. France*, ECtHR 22 May 2001, appl. no. 33592/96, para. 49; *Posokhov v. Russia*, ECtHR 9 July 2002 (dec.), appl. no. 63486/00, para. 5.

[393] *Sisojeva and Others v. Latvia*, ECtHR (GC) (Striking out) 15 January 2007, appl. no. 60654/00, para. 89.

[394] *Trofimchuk v. Ukraine*, ECtHR 31 May 2005 (dec.), appl. no. 4241/03; *Baillard v. France*, ECtHR 25 September 2008 (dec.), appl. no. 6032/04.

[395] *Demir and Baykara v. Turkey*, ECtHR (GC) 12 November 2008, appl. no. 34503/97, para. 65.

and insofar as they may have infringed rights and freedoms protected by the Convention. Moreover, while Article 6 ECHR guarantees the right to a fair hearing, it does not lay down any rules on the admissibility of evidence or the way it should be assessed, which are therefore primarily matters for regulation by national law and the national courts.[396] In the *Timar* case, the applicant complained about the outcome of the official liability action and that the Hungarian courts lacked impartiality in these proceedings, also, in breach of Article 6(1). The Court reiterated that, in particular, it is not its function to deal with errors of fact or law allegedly committed by a national court unless and insofar as they may have infringed rights and freedoms protected by the Convention. Moreover, while Article 6 ECHR guarantees the right to a fair hearing, it does not lay down any rules on the admissibility of evidence or the way it should be assessed, which are therefore primarily matters for regulation by national law and the national courts.[397] In cases in which there are conflicting accounts of events, the Court is inevitably confronted, when establishing the facts, with the same difficulties as those faced by any first instance court.[398] The Court is sensitive to the subsidiary nature of its role and must be cautious in taking on the role of a first instance tribunal of fact where this is not rendered unavoidable by the circumstances of a particular case. Nonetheless, where allegations are made under Article 3 ECHR, the Court must apply a particularly thorough scrutiny even if certain domestic proceedings and investigations have already taken place.[399] Although in the majority of cases the Court takes over the facts as set put by national courts, in accordance with the fourth instance doctrine and the subsidiarity principle, the Court has the opportunity to question witnesses and organise fact-finding missions. Where the facts are disputed, especially in cases concerning an alleged violation of Articles 2 and 3 of the ECHR, the Court stated that a special vigilance for proper fact-finding is necessary.[400] According to the Court, it is of the utmost importance in these cases for the effective operation of the system of individual petition instituted under Article 34 ECHR that states should furnish all necessary facilities to make possible a proper and effective examination of applications. This obligation requires the Contracting States to furnish all necessary facilities to the Court, whether it is conducting a fact-finding investigation or performing its general duties as regards the examination of applications. A failure on a government's part to submit such information which is in their hands without a satisfactory explanation may not only give rise to the drawing of inferences as to the well-

---

[396]   *Schenk v. Switzerland*, ECtHR 12 July 1988, appl. no. 10862/84, paras. 45–46; *García Ruiz v. Spain*, ECtHR (GC) 12 January 1999, appl. no. 30544/96, para. 28; *Perlala v. Greece*, ECtHR 22 February 2007, appl. no. 17721/04, para. 25.

[397]   *Timar v. Hyngary, supra* n. 302.

[398]   *El Masri v. Macedonia*, ECtHR (GC), 13 December 2012, appl. no. 39630/09, para. 151.

[399]   *Ibid.,* para. 155.

[400]   *Kashyamakhnov v. Russia*, ECtHR 14 November 2013, appl. no. 29604/12, para. 99.

foundedness of the applicant's allegations, but may also reflect negatively on the level of compliance by a respondent state with its obligations under Article 38 ECHR.[401] In its most extreme case, it already gave rise to a reversal of the burden of proof in favour of the complainant.[402] Moreover, Rule A1 to Rule 8 of the Annex to the Rules of Court, discloses the possible research activities that would enable the Court. This includes the possibility of appointing external experts and on-the-spot investigations to perform. It has mainly been in the context of Turkish and Russian cases that the Court has been compelled to seek out evidence by conducting fact-finding missions in the defendant contracting state and in Strasbourg itself.[403] These cases involve serious human rights violations including enforced disappearances, extra-judicial killings, torture and the destruction of entire villages. In many of these cases, the national authorities failed to conduct an effective investigation into the facts, and there was little or no evidence.

An application is manifestly ill-founded if it does indeed relate to a right protected by the Convention, but a *prima facie* examination discloses that the facts put forward cannot by any means justify the claim of violation, so that an examination of the merits is superfluous. The power to declare an application inadmissible on the ground that it is manifestly ill-founded fits into the screening function which the drafters of the Convention intended the admissibility examination to perform. For a proper discharge of that function no more is needed than the power to reject those applications the ill-founded character of which is actually *manifest*. In several cases, however, the Commission has used this competence in a way which clearly went beyond this.

1.17. NO SIGNIFICANT DISADVANTAGE – ARTICLE 35(3)(b)

A new admissibility criterion was added to the criteria laid down in Article 35 with the entry into force of Protocol No. 14 on 1 June 2010: '(b) the applicant has not suffered a significant disadvantage, unless respect for human rights as defined in the Convention and the Protocols thereto requires an examination of the application on the merits and provided that no case may be rejected on this ground which has not been duly considered by a domestic tribunal.'

In accordance with Article 20 of the Protocol, the new provision will apply to all applications pending before the Court, except those declared admissible. The Court may apply this criterion to all cases in which no decision on

---

[401]   *Janowiec and Others v. Russia*, ECtHR (GC), 21 October 2013, appl. nos. 55508/07 and 29520/09, para. 202.

[402]   *Tangiyeva v. Russia*, ECtHR 29 November 2007, appl. no. 57935/00, para. 77; *Zubayrayev v. Russia*, ECtHR 10 January 2008, appl. no. 67797/01, para. 76.

[403]   *Shamayev and Others v. Georgia and Russia, supra* n. 277, para. 497; *Ipek v. Turkey, supra* n. 179, paras. 114–119.

admissibility was taken at the entry into force of Protocol No. 14, regardless of the date of submission of the application. Accordingly, in the case of *Vistiņš and Perepjolkins v. Latvia*, the Government's preliminary objection raising no significant disadvantage was dismissed because the application was declared admissible in 2006, before the entry into force of Protocol No. 14.[404] In fulfilling this new criterion, the Court formulated the following principles: 'The Court reiterates that the main element contained in the new admissibility criterion is the question of whether the applicant has suffered a "significant disadvantage". Inspired by the above-mentioned general principle *de* minimis non curat praetor, the new criterion hinges on the idea that a violation of a right, however real from a purely legal point of view, should attain a minimum level of severity to warrant consideration by an international court. The assessment of this minimum level is, in the nature of things, relative and depends on all the circumstances of the case. The severity of a violation should be assessed, taking account of both the applicant's subjective perceptions and what is objectively at stake in a particular case.'[405]

Article 35(3)(b) is composed of three distinct elements. First, the admissibility criterion itself: the Court may declare inadmissible any individual application where the applicant has suffered no significant disadvantage. Next come two safeguard clauses. First, the Court may not declare such an application inadmissible where respect for human rights requires an examination of the application on the merits. Secondly, no case may be rejected under this new criterion which has not been duly considered by a domestic authority. It should be mentioned here that according to Article 5 of Protocol No. 15 amending the Convention, which is currently not yet in force, the second safeguard clause is to be removed.[406] Where the three conditions of the inadmissibility criterion are satisfied, the Court declares the complaint inadmissible under Article 35(3)(b) and (4) ECHR.

According to the Court any infringement of the Convention should therefore achieve a certain minimum level of severity in order to be considered. To assess whether an applicant has or has not suffered a significant disadvantage, the Court takes into account the subjective perception of the applicant on the one hand and, on the other, objective grounds.[407] The subjective perception must be justified on objective grounds.[408] The Court ruled that it was not satisfied that requirement in a case where the applicant complained that during an inspection the inspectors of the Labour Inspectorate had entered his garage without his permission. The Court considered that the interference alleged by

---

[404] *Vistiņš and Perepjolkins v. Latvia*, ECtHR (GC) 25 October 2012, appl. no. 71243/01, para.66.

[405] *Ladygin v. Russia*, ECtHR 30 August 2011, appl. no. 35365/05.

[406] In Arti. 35(3)(b) of the Convention, the words 'and provided that no case may be rejected on this ground which has not been duly considered by a domestic tribunal' shall be deleted.

[407] *Korolev v. Russia*, ECtHR 1 July 2010 (dec.), appl. no. 2551/05.

[408] *Ladygin v. Russia, supra* n. 407.

the applicant could have had no more than a minimal impact, if at all, on the applicant's 'home' or 'private life'. Indeed, the applicant did not suggest that it caused him any actual inconvenience whatsoever, nor even that he personally was in any way affected by the inspectors' ingress.[409] In the case of *Giuran*, the Court found that the applicant had suffered a significant disadvantage because the proceedings concerned a question of principle for him, namely his right to respect for his possessions and for his home. This was despite the fact that the domestic proceedings which were the subject of the complaint were aimed at the recovery of stolen goods worth EUR 350) from the applicant's own apartment.[410] Moreover, in evaluating the subjective significance of the issue for the applicant, the Court can take into account the applicant's conduct, for example in being inactive in court proceedings during a certain period which demonstrated that in this case the proceedings could not have been significant to her.[411]

The Court has also decided that the nature of the alleged violated right, the seriousness of the suspected violation[412] and its consequences on the personal circumstances of the applicant are relevant to the determination of substantial disadvantage.[413] The Court seems to go in that direction, as evidenced by its assessment of a complaint about a violation of Article 5(4) of the ECHR because of a lengthy pre-trial detention in poor conditions. Although the Government had argued in this case that there was a lack of significant disadvantage, the Court held that, in view of the great importance of the right to liberty in a democratic society, the criterion of Article 35(3)(b) could not be applied.[414]

A certain remediation by the respondent state of the prejudice suffered can – but need not – lead to inadmissibility for lack of substantial disadvantage. In case of *Gagliano Giorgi*, the Court for the first time dealt with a complaint concerning the length of *criminal* proceedings. Looking at the fact that the applicant's sentence was reduced as a result of the length of the proceedings, the Court concluded that this reduction compensated the applicant or particularly reduced any prejudice which he would encounter as a result of the lengthy proceedings. Accordingly, the Court held that he had not suffered any significant disadvantage.[415] In the case of *Galović*, the Court found that the applicant had actually benefited from the excessive length of *civil* proceedings because she remained in her property for another six years and two months.[416] Two further Dutch cases have also dealt with the length of criminal proceedings and the lack

---

[409] *Zwinkels v. the Netherlands*, ECtHR 9 October 2012 (dec.), appl. no. 16593/10.

[410] *Giuran v. Romania*, ECtHR 20 June 2011, appl. no. 24360/04, paras. 17–25.

[411] *Shefer v. Russia*, ECtHR 13 March 2012 (dec.), appl. no. 45175/04.

[412] *Gaglione and Others v. Italy*, ECtHR 21 December 2010, appl. no. 45667/07 and Others, para. 18.

[413] *Rinck v. France, supra* n. 91; *Giusti v. Italy*. ECtHR 18 October 2011 (dec.), appl. no. 13175/03.

[414] *Bannikov v. Latvia*, ECtHR 11 June 2013, appl. no. 19279/03, para. 58.

[415] *Gagliano Giorgi v. Italy*, ECtHR 6 March 2012, appl. no. 23563/07, para.57.

[416] *Galović v. Croatia*, ECtHR 5 March 2013 (dec.), appl. no. 54388/09, para. 77.

of an effective remedy. In the case of *Çelik* and *Van der Putten* the applicants' complaints concerned solely the length of the proceedings before the Supreme Court as a consequence of the time taken by the Court of Appeal to complete the case file. However, in both cases, the applicants lodged an appeal on points of law to the Supreme Court without submitting any ground of appeal. Finding that no complaint was made about the judgment of the Court of Appeal or about any aspect of the prior criminal proceedings, the Court considered in both cases that the applicants had suffered no significant disadvantage.[417]

The wording of Article 35(3)(b) shows that the Court may not dismiss a case for lack of a significant disadvantage when respect for the rights specified in the Convention and the Protocols require examination of the merits. This condition enables the Court to further investigate a case when questions of a general nature relevant to compliance with the ECHR occur.[418] This may be the case when an important matter of principle itself suggests that the petition concerns a structural deficiency.[419] The Court has already held that respect for human rights does not require it to continue the examination of an application when, for example, the relevant law has changed and similar issues have been resolved in other cases before it.[420] Nor where the relevant law has been repealed and the complaint before the Court is of historical interest only.[421] Similarly, respect for human rights does not require the Court to examine an application where the Court and the Committee of Ministers have addressed the issue as a systemic problem, for example non-enforcement of domestic judgments.[422]

The second element is a safeguard clause to the effect that the application will not be declared inadmissible if respect for human rights as defined in the Convention or the Protocols thereto requires an examination on the merits. A second safeguard clause is added to the first one. It will never be possible for the Court to reject an application on account of its trivial nature if the case has not been duly considered by a domestic tribunal. This clause, which reflects the principle of subsidiarity, ensures that, for the purposes of the application of the new admissibility criterion every case will receive a judicial examination whether at the national level or the European level.[423] In the *Zivic* case, the Court found that even assuming that the applicant had not suffered a significant disadvantage the case raised issues of general interest which required examination. This was

---

417 *Çelik v. the Netherlands*, ECtHR 27 August 2013 (dec.), appl. no. 12810/13; *Van der Putten v. the Netherlands*, ECtHR 27 August 2013 (dec.), appl. no. 15909/13.

418 *Korolev v. Russia*, *supra* n. 409.

419 *Eon v. France*, ECtHR 14 March 2013, appl. no. 26118/10, para. 34.

420 *Léger v. France*, ECtHR (Striking out) 30 March 2009, appl. no. 19324/02, para. 51; *Rinck v. France*, *supra* n. 91.

421 *Ionescu v. Romania*, *supra* n. 91.

422 *Vasilchenko v. Russia*, ECtHR 23 September 2010, appl. no. 34784/02, para. 49; *Gaftoniuc v. Romania*, *supra* n. 92; *Burov v. Moldova*, ECtHR 14 June 2011 (dec.), appl. no. 38875/03; *Guruyan v. Armenia*, ECtHR 24 January 2012 (dec.), appl. no. 11456/05.

423 Explanatory Report to Protocol No. 14, CETS 194, paras. 81–82.

due to the inconsistent case law of the District Court in Belgrade as regards the right to fair wages and equal pay for equal work, that is, payment of the same salary increase granted to a certain category of police officers.[424]

Lastly, Article 35(3)(b) does not allow the rejection of an application under the admissibility requirement if the case has not been duly considered by a domestic tribunal. The purpose of that rule, qualified by the drafters as a 'second safeguard clause' is to ensure that every case receives a judicial examination, either at the national or at the European level. As mentioned above, the second safeguard of Article 35(3)(b) is to be deleted upon the coming into force of Protocol No. 15 amending the Convention. The purpose of the second safeguard clause is thus to avoid a denial of justice for the applicant.[425] The applicant should have had the opportunity of submitting his arguments in adversarial proceedings before at least one level of domestic jurisdiction.[426] If no effective and adequate remedy exists at the national level, this safety net is automatically applied.[427] According to the Court in case of *Vincent Cecchetti*, the clause is also consonant with the principle of subsidiarity, as reflected notably in Article 13 ECHR, which requires that an effective remedy against violations be available at national level. The Court must first examine the notion of 'case', which seems to be distinguished in this provision from the term 'application'. The question is thus whether the due consideration by a domestic tribunal should concern the case (in the sense of request, action or claim) that the applicant brought before that tribunal or the complaints as subsequently submitted to this Court. As to the question whether his case has been 'duly considered', the Court is of the view that this condition should not be interpreted as strictly as the requirements of a fair trial; otherwise it would difficult to understand why the wording of Article 35(3)(b) did not read 'fairly considered'.[428]

1.18. REJECTION OF INADMISSIBLE APPLICATIONS – ARTICLE 35(4)

Under the old system the Commission could, in the course of its examination of the merits of an individual application which it had accepted as admissible, decide to reject the application as inadmissible if, on the basis of these examinations, it reached the conclusion that not all the conditions of admissibility had been complied with (Article 29). Although the wording of Article 35(4) is not exactly

---

[424] *Zivic v. Serbia*, ECtHR 13 September 2011, appl. no. 37204/08, paras. 36–42.
[425] *Korolev v. Russia*, *supra* n. 88; *Gaftoniuc v. Romania*, *supra* n. 92; *Fedotov v. Moldova*, ECtHR 24 May 2011 (dec.), appl. no. 51838/07.
[426] *Ionescu v. Romania*, *supra* n. 91.
[427] *Dudek v. Germany*, ECtHR 23 November 2010 (dec.), appl. nos. 12977/09, 15856/09, 15890/09, 15892/09 and 16119/09.
[428] *Vincent Cecchetti v. San Marino*, ECtHR 9 April 2013 (dec.), appl. no. 40173/08.

the same as the former Article 29 ECHR the Explanatory Report to Protocol No. 11 indicates no significant differences. According to the Explanatory Report, paragraph 4 of Article 35 does not signify that a state is able to raise an admissibility question at any stage of the proceedings, if it could have been raised earlier. However, the Court will be able to reject an application at any stage of the proceedings – even without an oral hearing – if it finds the existence of one of the grounds of non- acceptance provided in Article 35. Copies of all decisions declaring applications inadmissible should be transmitted to the states concerned for information.[429] From the text of Article 35(4) it cannot be inferred that this provision may be applied only if *new* facts have become known to the Court. From the *Schiesser* case one might conclude that the Court was prepared to apply Article 29 even by analogy. In that case the applicant had adduced a violation of Article 5(4), after his complaint concerning Article 5(3) had already been declared admissible by the Commission. In its report the Commission stated that, as regards Article 5(4), the requirement of previous exhaustion of local remedies had not been complied with. When the Swiss Government subsequently requested the Court to declare the application incompatible with the requirements of former Article 26, the latter took the position that it had no jurisdiction to deal with the issue, holding among other things: 'The Court takes the view that, on the point now being considered, the Commission's report amounts, in substance, to an implicit decision of inadmissibility, although it does not expressly refer to Article 29(1) or even to Article 27(3).'[430]

However, there cannot possibly be a question of an implicit decision on the basis of Article 29, since the decision of the Commission had been taken with 11 votes in favour, one against and two abstentions. Since Article 29 (old) explicitly required unanimity, reference by the Court to Article 29(1) would seem to be out of place.

The Court reaffirmed its position in the *Artico* case, where it held with reference to its *Schiesser* judgment, that: 'despite the apparent generality of the wording of Article 29, the respondent State is entitled by analogy to the benefit of the provisions governing the initial stage of the proceedings, in other words to obtain from the Commission, in a supplementary decision, *a* ruling by majority vote (Article 34) on the questions of jurisdiction or admissibility submitted to the Commission by the State immediately it has been led to do so by the change in the legal situation.'[431]

In the case of *K. and T. v. Finland*, the Grand Chamber noted that neither the Convention nor the Rules of Court empowered it to review a decision by the panel to accept a request for a rehearing. What is more, the terms of Article 43(3)

---

[429] Council of Europe, Explanatory Report to Protocol No. 11 to the European Convention of Human Rights and Fundamental Freedoms restructuring the control machinery established thereby, ETS, No. 155 para. 88.
[430] *Schiesser v. Switzerland,* ECtHR 4 December 1979, appl. no. 7710/76, para. 41.
[431] *Artico v. Italy, supra* n. 203, para. 27 (emphasis added).

ECHR (which provides: 'If the panel accepts the request, the Grand Chamber shall decide the case by means of a judgment') make clear that once the panel has accepted a request for a rehearing, the Grand Chamber has no option but to examine the case. Consequently, once the panel has noted that the case raises, or might raise, a serious question or issue within the meaning of Article 43(2), it is the entire 'case', insofar as it has been declared admissible, that is automatically referred to the Grand Chamber, which in principle decides the case by means of a new judgment. However, that does not mean that the Grand Chamber may not be called upon to examine, where appropriate, issues relating to the admissibility of the application in the same manner as is possible in normal Chamber proceedings, for example by virtue of Article 35(4) *in fine* ECHR (which empowers the Court to 'reject any application which it considers inadmissible … at any stage of the proceedings'), or where such issues have been joined to the merits, or where they are otherwise relevant at the merits stage.[432]

The Grand Chamber may likewise be required to apply other provisions of the Convention that enable it to terminate the proceedings by a means other than a judgment on the merits, for example by approving a friendly settlement (Article 39 ECHR) or striking the application out of the list of cases (Article 37). The principle governing proceedings before the Grand Chamber, as before the other Chambers of the Court, is that it must assess the facts as they appear at the time of its decision by applying the appropriate legal solution. Once a case is referred to it, the Grand Chamber may accordingly employ the full range of judicial powers conferred on the Court.[433]

In the *Pisano* case, the Government made a preliminary objection in which they asked the Court to declare the application inadmissible. The Court held that Article 35(4) allows the Court, even at the merits stage, subject to Rule 55 of the Rules of Court, to reconsider a decision to declare an application admissible where it concludes that it should have been declared inadmissible for one of the reasons given in the first three paragraphs of Article 35, including that of incompatibility with the provisions of the Convention (Article 35(3) taken together with Article 34). According to the Court's settled case law, such incompatibility was present *ratione personae* if the applicant could not or could no longer claim to be a victim of the alleged violation. The Court held, however, that in the instant case both at the time when the applicant lodged his application and at the time when the Chamber declared it admissible, the applicant was perfectly entitled to complain of the criminal proceedings in which he had been sentenced to life imprisonment without evidence being heard from a defence witness whom he regarded as crucial. His conviction had become final, as he had exhausted all the remedies available in domestic law for the submission of arguments concerning the failure to call the witness. His complaints to the

---

[432] *K. and T. v. Finland*, ECtHR (GC) 12 July 2001, appl. no. 25702/94, paras. 140–141.
[433] *Pisano v. Italy*, ECtHR 24 October 2002, appl. no. 36732/97, para. 28.

Court on that account under Article 6(1) and (3)(d) ECHR were not manifestly ill-founded, as the Chamber held in its decision on the admissibility of the application, and the panel of the Grand Chamber subsequently agreed, that those complaints raised serious questions affecting the interpretation or application of the Convention. It was true that the applicant failed to inform the Court in good time of his application for a retrial, but, contrary to the Government's assertion, such an application was not a remedy of which he was required to avail himself for the purposes of Article 35(1) ECHR. It remained to be determined whether the application should be rejected as being incompatible *ratione personae* with the provisions of the Convention on the ground that, as a result of his acquittal with final effect after a retrial at which the witness B. gave evidence, the applicant could no longer claim to be the 'victim', within the meaning of Article 34, of a violation of the Convention. In this connection, the Court noted that, although the situation of which the applicant complained had been remedied, the Italian courts dealing with the case had not found a violation of the relevant provisions of the Convention as regards the failure to examine B. during the initial trial. In the absence of such an acknowledgement by the national authorities, the Court considered that it could not, in the light of events which occurred after the initial declaration of admissibility, subsequently declare the application inadmissible and reject it pursuant to Article 35(4) *in fine* ECHR on the ground that the applicant could no longer claim to be the 'victim' of the alleged violation.[434]

In the *Assanidze* case, the Chamber to which the case was originally assigned, declared the whole of the applicant's complaint under Article 5(1) ECHR admissible in its decision on 12 November 2002. At the hearing on 19 November 2003, the applicant complained for the first time about his prosecution in December 1999 and his ensuing detention in the second set of criminal proceedings. The Court held that, by virtue of Article 35(4) ECHR, it might declare a complaint inadmissible 'at any stage of the proceedings' and the six-month rule is a mandatory one which the Court has jurisdiction to apply of its own motion. In the light of the Government's observations and the special circumstances of the case, the Court considered that in it was necessary to take this rule into account when examining the various periods for which the applicant was detained. With regard to the first period of detention it held that the complaint under Article 5(1) was made outside the six-month time-limit, since the applicant lodged his application with the Court on 2 July 2001. It followed that this part of the application had to be declared inadmissible as being out of time. As to the complaint concerning the applicant's prosecution on 11 December 1999 in the second set of criminal proceedings and his detention

---

[434]   *Ibid.*, paras. 34–38; *Odièvre v. France*, ECtHR (GC) 13 February 2003, appl. no. 42326/98, para. 22; *Blečić v. Croatia*, ECtHR (GC) 8 March 2006, appl. no. 59532/00, para. 65; *Ališić and Others v. Bosnia and Herzegovina, Croatia, Serbia, Slovenia and the former Yugoslav Republic of Macedonia*, ECtHR (GC) 16 July 2014, appl. no. 60642/08, para. 78.

between that date and his acquittal, the Court noted that the first occasion it was raised before it was on 23 September and 19 November 2003. Consequently, it had not been dealt with in the admissibility decision of 12 November 2002, which defined the scope of the Court's examination. It followed that this complaint fell outside the scope of the case referred to the Grand Chamber for examination.[435]

2. PROCEDURE AFTER ADMISSION

The decision declaring an application admissible is communicated by the Registrar to the applicant, to the Contracting Party or Parties concerned and to any third party where these have previously been informed of the application.[436] According to Article 37, the Court may at any stage of the proceedings decide to strike an application out of the list of cases where the circumstances lead to the conclusion that one of the situations mentioned there presents itself.

After the Court has declared an application admissible, it subjects the complaint contained therein to an examination of the merits (Article 38(1)(a)). The Court also places itself at the disposal of the parties 'with a view to securing a friendly settlement of the matter on the basis of respect for human rights as defined in the Convention and the Protocols thereto' (Article 38(1)(b)). If no settlement can be reached in the case of an individual application, the President of the Chamber will fix deadlines for the submission of further written observations and the Chamber may decide, either at the request of a party or of its own motion, to hold a hearing on the merits.[437] In the case of an inter-state complaint, the President of the Chamber will, after consulting the Contracting Parties concerned, lay down the time-limits for the filing of written observations on the merits and for the production of any further evidence. A hearing on the merits shall be held if one or more of the Contracting Parties concerned so requests, or if the Chamber so decides on its own motion.[438]

2.1. THIRD-PARTY INTERVENTION

A Contracting Party one of whose nationals is an applicant, has the right to submit written comments and to take part in hearings.[439] When notice of an application is given to the respondent party, a copy of the application will

---

[435] *Assanidze v. Georgia, supra* n. 232, paras. 160–162.
[436] Rule 56(2) Rules of Court.
[437] Rule 59 Rules of Court.
[438] Rule 58 Rules of Court.
[439] Art. 36(1) ECHR; Rule 44 Rules of Court.

at the same time be transmitted to any other Contracting Party one of whose nationals is an applicant in the case. If a Contracting Party wishes to exercise its right to submit written comments or to take part in a hearing, it must so advise the Registrar in writing not later than 12 weeks after the transmission or notification.[440] Another time limit may be fixed by the President of the Chamber for exceptional reasons.[441] In accordance with Article 36(2) ECHR, the President of the Chamber or the Grand Chamber[442] may, in the interests of the proper administration of justice, invite any Contracting Party which is not a party to the proceedings, or any person concerned who is not the applicant, to submit written comments or take part in hearings. The President of a Chamber or the Grand Chamber is left a certain margin of discretion in this respect.

Third-party intervention is only possible before a Chamber or the Grand Chamber, and not before a Committee of three judges.[443] The drafters of Protocol 11 mentioned the possibility for states whose nationals have lodged applications against other States Parties to the Convention, to submit written comments and take part in hearings, only in relation to applications that have been declared admissible.[444] Nevertheless, the Court has admitted third-party intervention in cases where it had not yet decided on the admissibility. In the case of *T.I. v. United Kingdom*, the Court took note of the comments of the German Government and of the United Nations High Commissioner for Refugees, while the German Government also took part in the oral hearing.[445] The interventions were made at the request of the Court and related to the admissibility of the case. In fact, the case finally was declared manifestly ill founded.

Individuals, non-governmental-organisations or group of individuals must have a perceptible interest in the outcome of the case, if they want to intervene.[446] In the cases of *T.* and *V. v. United Kingdom*, concerning the trial and sentencing of two minors who had murdered a child, the President granted leave to the non-governmental organisation Justice and to the parents of the child who had been murdered to submit written comments in connection with the case. The President, furthermore, granted leave to the victim's parents to attend the hearing and to make oral submissions to the Court.[447] In the *Soering* case, which concerned extradition to the United States, where the applicant would run the

---

440   *Soering v. United Kingdom, supra* n. 63; the Government of Germany intervened because the applicant was a German national.

441   Rule 44(1)(2) Rules of Court.

442   From Rule 44(2)(a) it appears that this power of the President is exercised by the President of the (Grand) Chamber.

443   Art. 36(1) ECHR only mentions the Chamber and Grand Chamber.

444   Explanatory Report to Protocol No. 11, para. 48.

445   *T.I. v. United Kingdom*, ECtHR 7 March 2000 (dec.), appl. no. 43844/98.

446   The Explanatory Report to Protocol No. 11 states in this respect in para. 48: 'establishing an interest in the result of any case.'

447   *T. v. United Kingdom*, ECtHR (GC) 16 December 1999, appl. no. 24724/94, para. 4; *V. v. United Kingdom*, ECtHR (GC) 16 December 1999, appl. no. 24888/94, para. 8.

risk of being on 'death row' for a long period of time, Amnesty International was granted leave to intervene.[448] Other examples of non-governmental organisations which were granted leave to intervene are Human Rights Watch, Interights, Article 19, Liberty and Aire.[449] On the other hand, in the *Modinos* case, concerning the prohibition of homosexual activities in Cyprus, the intervention of the International Lesbian and Gay Association was refused. Given the Court's previous judgments in the case of Northern Ireland and United Kingdom, the Court did not see any need for a third-party intervention.[450] In the case of *Slivenko v. Latvia*, third-party comments were received from the Russian Government, having exercised its right to intervene.[451] In the case of *Saadi v. Italy*, third-party comments were received from the Government of the United Kingdom.[452] In some cases, even international bodies or human rights bodies established by a government intervened in a proceeding. For example, the Venice Commission intervened in a case concerning the question whether the alleged violations could be imputed to Serbia and/or Montenegro as a result of the declaration of independence of Montenegro[453] or even on the question whether the Human Rights Chamber of Bosnia-Herzegovina could be considered as an international body within the meaning of Article 35(2)(b) ECHR.[454] The Northern Ireland Human Rights Commission intervened in a case involving a boy who was shot in Belfast by members of the Royal Ulster Constabulary.[455]

Requests for leave for this purpose must be duly reasoned and submitted in one of the official languages, within a reasonable time after the fixing of the written procedure. Any invitation or grant of leave referred to in paragraph 2 of Rule 41 of the Rules of the Court may be subject to any conditions, including time-limits, set by the President of the Chamber. Where such conditions are not complied with, the President may decide not to include the comments in the case file. Written comments have to be submitted in one of the official languages, save where leave to use another language has been granted. They are forwarded by the Registrar to the parties to the case, who are entitled, subject to any conditions,

---

[448]   *Soering v. Germany, supra* n. 63.

[449]   *Jersild v. Denmark,* ECtHR (GC) 23 September 1994, appl. no. 15890/89, para. 5 (Human Rights Watch); *McCann and Others v. United Kingdom,* ECtHR (GC) 27 September 1995, appl. no. 18984/91, para. 5 (Amnesty International, Liberty, the Committee on the Administration of Justice, Inquest, British Irish Rights Watch); *Akdivar v. Turkey, supra* n. 98, para. 7 (Amnesty International); *Saunders v. United Kingdom,* ECtHR (GC) 17 December 1996, appl. no. 19187/91, para. 5 (Liberty); *Chahal v. United Kingdom,* ECtHR (GC) 15 November 1996, appl. no. 22414/93, para. 6 (Amnesty) International, Justice, Liberty, Aire Centre, Joint Council for the Welfare of Immigrants); *Vo v. France,* ECtHR (GC) 8 July 2004, appl. no. 53942/00, paras. 60–73, (*Center for Reproductive Rights*), (*Family Planning Association*).

[450]   *Modinos v. Cyprus,* ECtHR 22 April 1993, appl. no. 15070/89, para. 4.

[451]   *Slivenko v. Latvia,* ECtHR (GC) 9 October 2003, appl. no. 48321/99, para. 6.

[452]   *Saadi v. Italy,* ECtHR (GC) 28 February 2008, appl. no. 37201/06, paras. 117–123.

[453]   *Bijelic v. Montenegro and Serbia, supra* n. 337, para. 9.

[454]   *Jelicic v. Bosnia and Herzegovina, supra* n. 138.

[455]   *Hugh Jordan v. United Kingdom,* ECtHR 4 May 2001, appl. no. 24746/94, para. 7.

including time-limits, set by the President of the Chamber, to file written observations in reply or, where appropriate, to reply at the hearing.[456]

Protocol No. 14 amended Article 36, by adding a third paragraph which reads as follows: 'In all cases before a Chamber or the Grand Chamber, the Council of Europe Commissioner for Human Rights may submit written comments and take part in hearings.'

This provision originates from an express request by the Council of Europe's Commissioner, supported by the Parliamentary Assembly.[457] In the past, it was already possible for the President of the Court to invite the Commissioner on Human Rights to intervene in pending cases. With a view to protecting the general interest more effectively, the third paragraph added to Article 36 for the first time mentions the Commissioner for Human Rights in the Convention text by formally providing that the Commissioner has the right to intervene as third party. The Commissioner's experience may help enlighten the Court on certain questions, particularly in cases which highlight structural or systemic weaknesses in the respondent or other High Contracting Parties.[458] If the Commissioner for Human Rights wishes to exercise the right under Article 36(3) to submit written observations or take part in a hearing, he or she shall so advise the Registrar in writing not later than 12 weeks after transmission of the application to the respondent Contracting Party or notification to it of the decision to hold an oral hearing. Another time-limit may be fixed by the President of the Chamber for exceptional reasons. Should the Commissioner for Human Rights be unable to take part in the proceedings before the Court himself, he or she shall indicate the name of the person or persons from his or her Office whom he or she has appointed to represent him. He or she may be assisted by an advocate.[459] In the case of *M.S.S. v. Belgium and Greece,* apart from the Commissioner for Human Rights there were also interventions by the Office of the United Nations High Commissioner for Refugees, and by the Governments of the Netherlands and the United Kingdom.[460]

2.2. STRIKING OFF LIST OF CASES – ARTICLE 37

Article 37 provides that the Court may at any stage at any stage of the proceedings – i.e. including during its examinations of the merits – decide to strike an application off its list of cases where the circumstances lead to the conclusion that the applicant does not intend to pursue his petition, or that the

---

[456] Rule 44(5) Rules of the Court.
[457] Recommendation 1640(2004), adopted on 26 January 2004.
[458] Explanatory Report to Protocol No. 14, CETS 194, para. 87.
[459] Rule 44(2) Rules of Court.
[460] *M.S.S. v. Belgium and Greece,* ECtHR (GC) 21 January 2011, appl. no. 30696/09.

matter has been resolved, or that for any other reason established by the Court, it is no longer justified to continue the examination of the application.

In the case of an inter-state application, the Chamber may only strike a case off the list if the applicant Contracting Party notifies the Registrar of its intention not to proceed with the case and the other Contracting Party or Parties concerned in the case agree to such discontinuance.[461]

The Chamber will not make such a decision if it holds that any reason of a general character affecting the observance ECHR and the Protocols thereto justifies further examination of the application.

The decision to strike out an application which has been declared admissible, is given in the form of a judgment. The President of the Chamber forwards that judgment, once it has become final, to the Committee of Ministers in order to allow the latter to supervise, in accordance with Article 46(2) ECHR, the execution of any undertakings which may have been attached to the discontinuance, friendly settlement or solution of the matter.[462] When an application has been struck out, the costs are at the discretion of the Court. If an award of costs is made in a decision striking out an application which has not been declared admissible, the President of the Chamber forwards that decision also to the Committee of Ministers.[463]

The Court may also decide to strike a case off its list of cases if the applicant shows a lack of interest by not responding to the request of providing further information. Thus, in a number of cases concerning the length of civil proceedings, a lack of interest was manifested by the applicants in the proceedings pending before the Court, which the Court considered to be an implied withdrawal constituting a 'fact of a kind to provide a solution of the matter'. In the opinion of the Court, there were no reasons of *ordre public* for continuing the proceedings. The Court, therefore, ordered these cases to be struck off the list, subject to the possibility of their being restored thereto in the event of a new situation justifying such a course.[464] In the case of *Pisano v. Italy*, the Court reiterated that, under Article 37(1)(b) ECHR, it may '(...) at any stage of the proceedings decide to strike an application out of its list of cases where the circumstances lead to the conclusion that ... the matter has been resolved (...)'. In order to ascertain whether that provision applies to the present case, the Court must answer two questions in turn: first, whether the circumstances complained of directly by the applicant still obtain and, secondly, whether the effects of a possible violation ECHR on account of those circumstances have

---

[461] Rule 43(2) Rules of Court.

[462] Rule 43(3) of the Rules of Court.

[463] Rule 43(4) Rules of Court.

[464] *Gilberti, Nonnis, Trotto, Cattivera, Seri, Gori, Casadio, Testa, Covitti, Zonetti, Simonetti, Dal Sasso v. Italy*, ECtHR 21 March 2001, appl. nos. 12665/87, 12785/87, 12828/87, 12956/87; *Zhukov v. Russia*, ECtHR 23 April 2002 (dec.), appl. no. 54260/00; *Molotchko v. Ukraine* ECtHR 26 April 2012, appl. no. 12271/10, para. 104.

also been redressed.[465] In the case of *Sisojeva and Others v. Latvia*, the Court noted that, despite repeated reminders on the part of the Directorate, none of the applicants has so far acted on the latter's recommendations. In their submissions to the Grand Chamber, the applicants contended that they did not have all the documents required in order to apply for a residence permit, so that any response on their part would have been futile. However, the Court observed that they had hitherto failed to make any attempt, however small, to get in touch with the authorities and try to find a solution to whatever difficulties may arise. Having regard to the case file as a whole as it currently stood, and in the light of the explanations provided by the Government, the Court saw no indication that the latter had acted in bad faith. Consequently, and in the light of all the relevant circumstances of the case, the Court considered that the options outlined by the Latvian authorities for regularising the applicants' situation were adequate and sufficient to remedy their complaint. The Court found that both conditions for the application of Article 37(1)(b) were met.[466]

According to Article 37(2), the Court may decide to restore an application to its list of cases if it considers that the circumstances justify such a course. It is evident that the same possibility of re-acceptance does not exist with respect to cases which have been declared inadmissible.[467]

In the cases of *Aydin*[468] and *Akman*,[469] the applicants did not agree with a friendly settlement of the case. They stressed, *inter alia,* that the proposed declaration omitted any reference to the unlawful nature of the killing of their son and failed to highlight that he was unarmed at the material time. In the applicants' submission, the terms of the declaration did not determine any of the fundamental human rights questions raised by the application. They urged the Court to proceed with its decision to take evidence in the case with a view to establishing the facts. The Court observed at the outset that the parties were unable to agree on the terms of a friendly settlement of the case. It recalled that, according to Article 38(2) ECHR, friendly-settlement negotiations are confidential. Rule 62(2) of the Rules of Court stipulates in this connection that no written or oral communication and no offer or concession made in the framework of the attempt to secure a friendly settlement may be referred to or relied on in the contentious proceedings. The Court therefore proceeded on the basis of the declaration made outside the framework of the friendly-settlement negotiations by the respondent Government. Having examined

---

[465]   *Pisano v. Italy, supra* n. 435, para. 42; *Sisojeva and Others v. Latvia, supra* n. 395, para. 97; *Borisov v. Lithuania*, ECtHR 14 June 2011, appl. no. 9958/04, para. 107; *Mihailovs v. Latvia* ECtHR 22 January 2013, appl. no. 35939/10, para. 83; *Buchs v. Switzerland*, ECtHR 27 May 2014, appl. no. 9929/12, para. 27.

[466]   *Sisojeva and Others v. Latvia, supra* n. 395, para. 98; *Buchs v. Switzerland, supra* n. 397, para. 29.

[467]   *J. v. France*, EComHR 1 April 1990 (dec.), appl. no. 16542/90 D&R 72 (1992), p. 226 (227).

[468]   *Aydin v. Turkey*, ECtHR 10 July 2001, appl. nos. 28293/95 29494/95 30219/96, para. 32.

[469]   *Akman v. Turkey*, ECtHR 25 October 2001, appl. no. 37453/87, para.25.

carefully the terms of the respondent Government's declaration and having regard to the nature of the admissions contained in the declaration as well as the scope and extent of the various undertakings referred to therein, together with the amount of compensation proposed, the Court considered that it was no longer justified to continue the examination of the application. Moreover, the Court was satisfied that respect for human rights as defined in the Convention and the Protocols thereto did not require it to continue the examination of the application. The Court noted in this regard that it had specified the nature and extent of the obligations which arose for the respondent Government in cases of alleged unlawful killings by members of the security forces under Articles 2 and 13 ECHR. In two other judgments, the cases of *Toğcu* and *T.A. v. Turkey*, both concerning disappearances of the applicants' relatives, the Court based its decision to strike out these cases on a formalistic statement from the Turkish Government, notwithstanding the rejection of a friendly settlement by the applicants.[470] In a dissenting opinion, Judge *Loucaides* opposed this 'striking out' process of the applications in a way which was very similar to the arguments of the applicants. He argued that there was no acceptance by the Government of responsibility for the violations complained of and that there was no undertaking to carry out any investigation of the disappearances. He also disagreed with the Turkish Government's statement: 'The Government consider that the supervision by the Committee of Ministers of the execution of Court judgments concerning Turkey in this and similar cases is an appropriate mechanism for ensuring that improvements will be made in this context.' In his opinion, that seemed to imply that the Government considered the Committee of Ministers as a more appropriate mechanism for ensuring improvements in cases like the one in respect of which the declaration was made than an examination of 'this and similar' cases by the Court. He feared that: 'the solution adopted may encourage a practice by States – especially those facing serious or numerous applications – of "buying off" complaints for violations of human rights through the payment of *ex gratia* compensation, without admitting any responsibility and without any adverse publicity, such payments being simply accompanied by a general undertaking to adopt measures for preventing situations like those complained of, from arising in the future on the basis of unilateral declarations which are approved by the Court even though they are unacceptable to the complainants. This practice will inevitably undermine the effectiveness of the judicial system of condemning publicly violations of human rights through legally binding judgments and, as a consequence, it will reduce substantially the required pressure on those Governments that are violating human rights.'[471]

---

[470] *Toğcu v. Turkey*, ECtHR 9 April 2002, appl. no. 27601/95, para. 32 and *T.A. v. Turkey*, ECtHR 9 April 2002, appl. no. 26307/95.
[471] *Ibid*. Dissenting opinion of Judge Loucaides.

The President of the Chamber, Judge Costa, stated in his concurring opinion that he came close to the views of Judge *Loucaides* and stressed that striking out should not be abused and should only be used in narrowly defined cases.[472] He continued by saying that 'in the circumstances of the present cases, and without calling into question the good faith and sincerity of the respondent State, I am very concerned by the unilateral nature of its undertakings'.[473]

The cases of *Akman* and *Aydin* may be distinguished from the latter two cases because the *Akman* case concerned an alleged instantaneous violation, i.e. murder, and the *Aydin* case concerned a disappearance of a person in respect of which an investigation was still being pursued at the time of the decision of the Court to strike the case out of the list, while the cases of *Toğcu* and *T.A. v. Turkey* concerned an alleged continuing violation, i.e. disappearance of a person. As Judge *Loucaides* pointed out: 'Departure from both decisions is justified for cogent reasons, namely to ensure more effective implementation of the obligations of the High Contracting Parties to the Convention through ceasing to strike cases out as a result of approving the method of compensation proposed by the respondent States on the basis of unilateral declarations unacceptable to the latter, like the one in the present case.'

The *Tahsin Acar* case, concerning the disappearance of the applicant's brother, was referred to the Grand Chamber. The Turkish Government had sent the Court a text of a unilateral declaration expressing regret for the actions that had led to the application and offering to make an *ex gratia* payment of GBP 70,000 to the applicant for any pecuniary and non-pecuniary damage and for costs. The Government requested the Court to strike the case out of the list under Article 37 ECHR. The Grand Chamber considered that, under certain circumstances, it might be appropriate to strike out an application under Article 37(1)(c) ECHR on the basis of a unilateral declaration by the respondent government, even if the applicant wished the examination of the case to be continued. Depending on the particular circumstances of each case, various considerations could come into play in the assessment of a unilateral declaration. It might be appropriate to examine whether the facts are in dispute between the parties, and, if so, to what extent. Other factors that might be taken into account are the nature of the complaints made, whether the Court has ruled on similar issues in previous cases, the nature and scope of any measures taken to enforce judgments delivered in such cases, and the impact of those measures on the case before the Court. The Court should also ascertain, among other things,

---

[472] Such as where the applicant dies and the proceedings are not continued by his heirs: *Gladkowski v. Poland*, ECtHR 14 May 2000 appl. no. 26697/96 or where proceedings are taken over by a legal entity which does not, in that particular case, have a legitimate interest allowing it to pursue the proceedings: *S.G. v. France*, ECtHR 18 September 2001, appl. no. 40669/98.

[473] Judgments of 9 April 2002, concurring opinion of the President of the Chamber Judge Costa. On 9 September 2002, the case of *T.A. v. Turkey* has been referred to the Grand Chamber.

whether in its declaration the government made any admissions concerning the alleged violations of the ECHR and, if so, should determine the scope of such admissions and the manner in which the government intended to provide redress to the applicant. The Grand Chamber held that the unilateral declaration made in the present case did not adequately address the applicant's grievances. In the Chamber's view, where a person had disappeared or had been killed by unknown persons and there was prima facie evidence that supported allegations that the domestic investigation had fallen short of what was necessary under the Convention, a unilateral declaration should at the very least contain an admission to that effect, combined with an undertaking by the respondent government to conduct, under the supervision of the Committee of Ministers, an investigation that fully complied with the requirements of the ECHR as defined by the Court in previous cases of a similar nature. As the Government's unilateral declaration in the present case did not contain any such admission or undertaking, it did not offer a sufficient basis for the Court to hold that it was no longer justified to continue the examination of the application. The Grand Chamber accordingly rejected the Government's request to strike the application out under Article 37(1)(c) ECHR and decided to pursue its examination of the merits of the case.[474]

2.3. EXAMINATION OF MERITS – ARTICLE 29

Article 29 states that, except for cases declared inadmissible by a Committee, the Chamber has to examine the admissibility and the merits of the case. There may, however, be situations in which the Court, will not take a separate admissibility decision. This could occur, for example, where a state does not object that a case be declared admissible.

According to Rule 58(1) of the Rules of Court, once the Chamber has decided to admit an inter-state application, the President of the Chamber will, after consulting the Contracting Parties concerned, lay down the time-limits for the filing of written observations on the merits and for the production of any further evidence. The President may however, with the agreement of the Contracting Parties concerned, direct that a written procedure is to be dispensed with. According to Rule 59(1), in the case of an individual application the Chamber or its President may invite the parties to submit further evidence and written observations.

An application is initially examined by one or more judges as judge-rapporteurs whom the Chamber appoints from among its members[475] and who

---

[474]   *Tahsin Acar v. Turkey*, ECtHR (GC), 6 May 2003, appl. no. 26307/95, paras. 74–82.
[475]   Rule 48(2) with respect to inter-state applications and Rule 49(1) with respect to individual applications.

submit such reports, drafts and other documents as may assist the Chamber in carrying out its functions. The merits of an application will be examined by a Chamber and, exceptionally, by the Grand Chamber. The parties will present their submissions by means of a written procedure. The oral procedure will consist of a hearing at which the applicant, or a State Party in an inter-state case, and the respondent state may present their arguments orally. The President of the Chamber fixes the written and oral procedure.[476]

Article 40 ECHR indicates that oral proceedings are, in principle, to be conducted in public. It also specifies that documents submitted in the written proceedings (memorials and formal written information) are also, in principle, accessible to the public. Thus, documents deposited with the Registrar and not published will be accessible to the public unless otherwise decided by the President, either on his own initiative or at the request of a party or of any other person concerned.

a. Written procedure

According to Rule 38(1) of the Rules of Court no written observations or other documents may be filed after the time-limit set by the President of the Chamber or the judge-rapporteur. For the purposes of observing this time-limit the material date is the certified date of dispatch of the document or, if there is none, the actual date of receipt at the Registry.[477]

According to Rules 17–19 of Practice Direction 3, a time-limit set under Rule 38 may be extended on request from a party. A party must make such a request as soon as it has become aware of the circumstances justifying such an extension and, in any event, before the expiry of the time-limit. It should state the reason for the delay. If an extension is granted, it applies to all parties for which the relevant time-limit is running, including those which have not asked for it. According to Rules 3 and 7 of Practice Direction 3, all pleadings as well as documents should be sent in three copies by post with one copy sent, if possible, by fax. In case of the use of fax the name of the person signing a pleading must also be printed on it so that he or she can be identified.

Concerning the form and contents, Practice Direction 3 in Rule 8 prescribes that a pleading should include: (1) the application number and the name of the case; and (2) a title indicating the nature and content (e.g. observations on admissibility [and the merits]; reply to the government's/the applicant's observations on admissibility [and the merits]; observations on the merits; additional observations on admissibility [and the merits]; memorial etc.). In addition, Rule 9, prescribes that a pleading should normally in addition: (1) be on A4 paper having a margin of not less than 3.5 cm wide; (2) be wholly

---

[476] Rule 59(4) Rules of Court. See in this respect Practice Direction 3 to the Rules of Court.
[477] Rule 38(2) Rules of Court.

legible and, preferably typed; (3) have all numbers expressed as figures; (4) have pages numbered consecutively; (5) be divided into numbered paragraphs; (6) be divided into chapters and/or headings corresponding to the form and style of the Court's decisions and judgments; (7) place any answer to a question by the Court or to the other party's arguments under a separate heading; (8) give a reference to every document or piece of evidence. According to Rule 10, if a pleading exceeds 30 pages, a short summary should also be filed with it. Finally, according to Rule 11, where a party produces documents or other exhibits together with a pleading, every piece of evidence should be listed in a separate annex. Concerning the contents, Rule 13 prescribes that the pleadings should include: (1) a short statement confirming a party's position on the facts of the case as established in the decision on admissibility; (2) legal arguments relating to the merits of the case; and (3) a reply to any specific questions on a factual or legal point put by the Court. An applicant submitting claims for just satisfaction should do so in the written observations on the merits. Itemised particulars of all claims made, together with the relevant supporting documents or vouchers, should be submitted. If the applicant fails in doing so, the Chamber may reject the claim in whole or in part.[478]

b. Oral hearing

The examination of the merits usually takes a good deal of time; apart from exceptional cases, about two years. In some cases this is inevitable, *viz.* if it is difficult to ascertain the facts, or if the attempts to reach a friendly settlement take a long time. On the whole, however, the desirability of shortening the procedure is evident, especially if it is borne in mind that the time which elapses between the moments at which an application is submitted and the date of the decision on admissibility is also rather long in many cases. In this respect, it has to be noted that the Rules of Court have been amended and that the rule which provided that in general an oral hearing has been deleted. Instead, Rule 59(3) of the Rules of Court provides that the Chamber may decide, either at the request of a party or of its own motion, to hold a hearing on the merits if it considers that the discharge of its functions under the Convention so requires. The practice is now that an oral hearing is held in a limited number of cases only.

The applicant must be represented at any hearing decided on by the Chamber, unless the President of the Chamber exceptionally grants leave to the applicant to present his or her own case, subject, if necessary, to being assisted by an advocate or other approved representative.[479] According to Rule 64 of the Rules of Court, the President of the Chamber organises and directs hearings and prescribes the order in which those appearing before the Chamber will be called upon to speak.

---

[478] Rule 60 Rules of Court.
[479] Rule 36(3) Rules of Court.

Where a party or any other person due to appear fails or declines to do so, the Chamber may, provided that it is satisfied that such a course is consistent with the proper administration of justice, nonetheless proceed with the hearing.[480] In the *Diennet* case, the hearing took place although at a preparatory meeting the Court was informed that the applicant's lawyer was stranded in Paris as a result of an airline strike. It decided to hold the hearing at the appointed time and to fax a provisional record of it to the applicant's lawyer so that she could submit any observations in writing before the deliberations.[481]

All communications with and pleadings by individual applicants or their representatives, witnesses or experts in respect of a hearing, or after a case has been declared admissible, shall be in one of the Court's official languages, unless the President of the Chamber authorises the continued use of the official language of a Contracting Party.[482]

c. Investigative measures and inquiry on spot

The Chamber may, at the request of a party or of its own motion, adopt any investigative measures which it considers capable of clarifying the facts of the case. The Chamber may, *inter alia*, invite the parties to produce documentary evidence and decide to hear as a witness or expert or in any other capacity any person whose evidence or statements seem likely to assist it in carrying out its tasks.[483] The Chamber may also ask any person or institution of its choice to express an opinion or make a written report on any matter considered by it to be relevant to the case. According to Rule A1(3) of the Annex to the Rules of Court, after a case has been declared admissible or, exceptionally, before the decision on admissibility, the Chamber may appoint one or more of its members or of the other judges of the Court, as its delegate or delegates, to conduct an inquiry, carry out an on-site investigation or take evidence in some other manner. The Chamber may also appoint any person or institution of its choice to assist the delegation in such manner as it sees fit. Under the Convention the Contracting States are obliged to furnish these facilities (Article 38(1)(a)). In accordance with Rule A1(5) of the Annex to the Rules of Court, proceedings forming part of any investigation by a Chamber or its delegation will be held *in camera*, save insofar as the President of the Chamber or the head of the delegation decides otherwise.

The parties must assist the Chamber, or its delegation, in implementing any measure for taking evidence. The Contracting Party on whose territory on-site proceedings before a delegation take place must extend to the delegation the facilities and co-operation necessary for the proper conduct of the proceedings.

---

[480] Rule 65 Rules of Court.
[481] *Diennet v. France,* ECtHR 26 September 1995, appl. no. 18160/91, para. 5.
[482] Rule 34 Rules of Court.
[483] Rule A1(1) and (2) of the Annex to the Rules of Court.

These include, to the full extent necessary, freedom of movement within the territory and all adequate security arrangements for the delegation, for the applicant and for all witnesses, experts and others who may be heard by the delegation. It is the responsibility of the Contracting Party concerned to take steps to ensure that no adverse consequences are suffered by any person or organisation on account of any evidence given, or of any assistance provided, to the delegation.[484] The Court does not have any means for compelling a witness, expert or other person to appear before it. Rule A3 of the Annex to the Rules of Court provides that, where a party or any other person due to appear fails or declines to do so, the delegation [and the Chamber, as the case may be] may, provided that it is satisfied that such a course is consistent with the proper administration of justice, nonetheless continue with the proceedings. Even without an express provision in the Rules of Procedure it would seem possible for the Court to communicate such failure to the Contracting State concerned. This state will then have to take any appropriate measures necessary to ensure that the persons in question will co-operate. In fact, the Contracting States are obliged to give the Court the necessary assistance in the performance of its duties. This would seem to also ensue by analogy from Article 38(1)(a) ECHR, which provides that, if the Court decides to carry out an inquiry on the spot, 'the States concerned shall furnish all necessary facilities'.

The head of the delegation may request the attendance of witnesses, experts and other persons during on-site proceedings before a delegation. The Contracting Party on whose territory such proceedings are held must, if so requested, take all reasonable steps to facilitate that attendance. In accordance with Rule 37(2), the Contracting Party in whose territory the witness resides is responsible for servicing any summons sent to it by the Chamber for service. In the event of such service not being possible, the Contracting Party must give reasons in writing. The Contracting Party shall further take all reasonable steps to ensure the attendance of persons summoned who are under its authority or control.[485]

The President of the Chamber may, as he or she considers appropriate, invite, or grant leave to, any third party to participate in an investigative measure. The President lays down the conditions of any such participation and may limit that participation if those conditions are not complied with.[486]

As a result of a number of individual complaints against Turkey the Court organised fact-finding missions to Turkey.[487] This concerned allegations of gross violations, such as disappearances, killing and torture in South-East Turkey. In most of these cases the domestic authorities had neither made any effective inquiry into the alleged violations, nor started any serious investigation

---

[484] Rule A 2 of the Annex to the Rules of Court.
[485] Rule A 5(4) of the Annex to the Rules of Court.
[486] Rule A 1(6) of the Annex to the Rules of Court.
[487] *Aksoy v. Turkey, supra* n. 98, para. 23; *Kurt v. Turkey, supra* n. 205, para. 13; *Cakici v. Turkey,* ECtHR (GC) 8 July 1999, appl. no. 23657/94, para. 13.

against the perpetrators of the cruelties.[488] A delegation of three Judges of the Court took evidence from witnesses in Ankara in the *Abdürrezzak İpek* case. The applicant complained about the disappearance of his two sons, who were allegedly last seen by three people taken into detention with them. He also alleged that his family home and property were destroyed by security forces in the course of an operation conducted in his village. The Turkish Government submitted that the investigation carried out by the authorities proved that no operation was conducted in the area by security forces. It further maintained that the applicant's sons were never detained.[489]

On 11 September 2002, the Grand Chamber decided that a delegation of judges should carry out an on-the-spot investigation in Moldova in the *Ilaşcu* case. The Court also decided to ask the parties to provide further clarification in writing about the case. The applicants had been convicted in 1993 for various crimes by a court of the 'Moldovan Republic of Transdniestria' (MRT), a region of Moldova which declared its independence in 1991 but is not recognised by the international community. The first applicant had been sentenced to capital punishment and the other three applicants to prison sentences of between 12 and 15 years. The judgment was subsequently declared unconstitutional by the Supreme Court of Moldova. Three of the applicants were detained in Transdniestria, while the first applicant was released on 5 May 2001 and moved to Romania. The applicants complained of the proceedings which led to their conviction in 1993 and claimed that their detention since then had been unlawful. They also complained of the conditions of their detention and, in substance, of a violation of their right not to be hindered in the effective exercise of the right of individual application. The applicants considered that the Moldovan authorities were responsible under the Convention for the alleged violations of their Convention rights since they had not taken adequate measures to stop them. They further contended that the Russian Federation shared that responsibility as the territory of Transdniestria was and continues to be *de facto* under Russia's control owing to the stationing of its troops and military equipment and its alleged support of the separatist regime.[490]

Article 38(1)(a) ECHR provides for measures to enforce the duty of co-operation on the part of a Contracting State. In cases in which, in the Court's opinion, an inquiry on the spot is absolutely necessary while the Contracting Party refuses to co-operate, it would appear most appropriate for the Court to appeal to the Committee of Ministers. Via a resolution the latter organ may bring pressure to bear on the recalcitrant state to comply with its obligations and to co-operate in making an investigation on its territory possible. In addition, although in practice this is not very likely to occur, another Contracting State

---

[488] *Akdeniz and Others v. Turkey*, EComHR 10 September 1999 (rep.), appl. no. 23954/94, para. 384.
[489] Press release issued by the Registrar, 20 November 2002.
[490] Press release issued by the Registrar, 11 October 2002.

might lodge an application against the recalcitrant state for alleged violation of Article 38. As was stated above, Article 33 permits the Contracting States to complain about 'any alleged breach of the provisions ECHR by another High Contracting Party', so that they need not confine themselves to the rights and freedoms of Section I ECHR and of the Protocols, but may also bring up an article such as Article 38. In the *Timurtas* case, the Court held: 'It is inherent in proceedings relating to cases of this nature, where an individual applicant accuses State agents of violating his rights under the Convention, that in certain instances solely the respondent State has access to information capable of corroborating or refuting these allegations. A failure on a Government's part to submit such information as is in their hands without a satisfactory explanation may not only reflect negatively on the level of compliance by a respondent State with its obligations under Article 38(1)(a) ECHR, but may also give rise to the drawing of inferences as to the well-foundedness of the allegations. In this respect, the Court reiterates that the conduct of the parties may be taken into account when evidence is being obtained.'[491]

In the case of *Husayin (Abu Zubydah) v. Poland*, the Court held that a failure on a government's part to submit such information which is in its hands without a satisfactory explanation may not only give rise to the drawing of inferences as to the well-foundedness of the applicant's allegations, but may also reflect negatively on the level of compliance by a respondent state with its obligations under Article 38 ECHR. In particular, in a case where the application raises issues concerning the effectiveness of the investigation, the documents of the criminal investigation are fundamental to the establishment of the facts and their absence may prejudice the Court's proper examination of the complaint both at the admissibility and at the merits stage.[492]

In the case of *Georgia v. Russia (1)*, the Court held that having regard to the Russian Government's persistent refusal to provide the Court with copies of the two circulars issued by the Internal Affairs Directorate of St Petersburg and by the Russian Ministry of the Interior at the end of September 2006 – stating that they were 'State secret' – the Court considered it appropriate to address the question of whether Russia had complied with its obligation under Article 38. Given that the Russian Government had exclusive access to these documents, capable of corroborating or refuting the allegations in question, its lack of co-operation enabled the Court to draw inferences as to the well-foundedness of those allegations. The Court had already found in other cases relating to documents classified 'State secret' that the Government could not rely on provisions of national law to justify its refusal to comply with the Court's request to provide evidence.

---

[491] *Timurtas v. Turkey*, ECtHR 13 June 2000 appl. no. 23531/94, para. 66. See also *Aktas v. Turkey*, ECtHR 24 April 2003, appl. no. 24351/94, paras. 272–277; *Tepe v. Turkey*, ECtHR 9 May 2003, appl. no. 29422/95, paras. 128–135; and *Tekdag v. Turkey*, ECtHR 15 January 2004, appl. no. 27699/95, paras. 57–61.

[492] *Husayn (Abu Zubaydah) v. Poland*, ECtHR 24 July 2014, appl. no. 7511/13, paras. 352–353.

Furthermore, the Russian Government had failed to give a specific explanation for the secrecy of the circulars. The Court thus found that Russia had fallen short of its obligation to furnish all necessary facilities to the Court in its task of establishing the facts of the case. There had accordingly been a violation of Article 38.[493]

Where a witness, expert or other person is summoned at the request or on behalf of a Contracting Party, the costs of their appearance will be borne by that party unless the Chamber decides otherwise. The costs of the appearance of any such person who is in detention in the Contracting Party on whose territory on-site proceedings before a delegation take place, will be borne by that party unless the Chamber decides otherwise. In all other cases, the Chamber decides whether such costs are to be borne by the Council of Europe or awarded against the applicant or third party at whose request or on whose behalf the person appears. In all cases, such costs are taxed by the President of the Chamber.[494] Rule A 6 lays down the oath or solemn declaration by witnesses and experts heard by a delegation.

Any delegate may put questions to the agents, advocates or advisers of the parties, to the applicant, witnesses and experts, and to any other persons appearing before the delegation. Witnesses, experts and other persons appearing before the delegation may, subject to the control of the head of the delegation, be examined by the agents and advocates or advisers of the parties. In the event of an objection to a question put, the head of the delegation decides. Save in exceptional circumstances and with the consent of the head of the delegation, witnesses, experts and other persons to be heard by a delegation will not be admitted to the hearing room before they give evidence. The head of the delegation may make special arrangements for witnesses, experts or other persons to be heard in the absence of the parties where that is required for the proper administration of justice. The head of the delegation decides in the event of any dispute arising from an objection to a witness or expert. The delegation may hear for information purposes a person who is not qualified to be heard as a witness or expert.[495]

A verbatim record is prepared by the Registrar of any proceedings concerning an investigative measure. If all or part of the verbatim record is in a non-official language, the Registrar arranges for its translation into one of the official languages. The representatives of the parties receive a copy of the verbatim record in order that they may, subject to the control of the Registrar or the head of the delegation, make corrections, but in no case may such corrections affect the sense and bearing of what was said. The Registrar lies down, in accordance with the instructions of the head of the delegation, the time-limits granted for this purpose. The verbatim record, once so corrected, is signed by the head of the delegation and the Registrar and then constitutes certified matters of record.[496]

---

[493] *Georgia v. Russia (No. 1)*, ECtHR (GC) 3 July 2014, appl. no. 13255/07, paras. 104–107.
[494] Rule A5(6) of the Annex to the Rules of Court.
[495] Rule A7 of the Annex to the Rules of Court.
[496] Rule A8 of the Annex to the Rules of Court.

d. Hearing of witnesses or experts

Since the amendment of the Rules of Court the provisions concerning the hearing of witnesses and experts are to be found in the Annex to the Rules of Court concerning investigative measures. The provisions concerning investigative measures by a delegation apply, *mutatis mutandis*, to any such proceedings conducted by the Chamber itself.[497] According to Rule A 1(1) of the Annex to the Rules of Court, the Chamber may, at the request of a party or of its own motion, adopt any investigative measure which it considers capable of clarifying the facts of the case.

Witnesses, experts and other persons to be heard by a Chamber are summoned by the Registrar. The summons has to indicate 1) the case in connection with which it has been issued; (2) the object of the inquiry, expert opinion or other investigative measure ordered by the Chamber or the President of the Chamber; and (3) any provisions for the payment of sums due to the person summoned.[498]

The Chamber may, *inter alia*, invite the parties to produce documentary evidence and decide to hear as a witness or expert or in any other capacity any person whose evidence or statements seem likely to assist it in carrying out its tasks.[499] The Chamber may also ask any person or institution of its choice to express an opinion or make a written report on any matter considered by it to be relevant to the case.[500]

2.4. FRIENDLY SETTLEMENT – ARTICLE 39

From the terms of Article 38 it is clear that the ECHR drafters intended the attempts to reach a friendly settlement to take place simultaneously with the examination of the merits. This makes sense. In fact, on the one hand, a complete examination of the merits is superfluous if a friendly settlement is reached. On the other hand, the Court cannot mediate in an effective way with a view to reaching such a settlement until it has gained some insight into the question of whether or not the application is well-founded.

The friendly settlement is a form of conciliation, one of the traditional methods of peaceful settlement of international disputes. As such, with the method of the friendly settlement a non-legal element was introduced into the procedure. Indeed, this method is not necessarily based on exclusively legal considerations; other factors may also play a part in it. In turn, the legal element

---

[497] Rule A3(3) of the Annex to the Rules of Court.
[498] Rule A5(2) in conjunction with Rule A1(4) of the Annex to the Rules of Court.
[499] Rule A1 of the Annex to the Rules of Court.
[500] Rule A1(2) of the Annex to the Rules of Court.

consists of the fact that a friendly settlement still needs to be approved by the Court on the basis of respect for the rights and freedoms in the Convention. Experience demonstrates the great utility of the conciliation element in Convention proceedings.

Friendly-settlement negotiations could be 'guided', or even encouraged, by a judge (with the help of the Registry of the Court). Also, during friendly-settlement negotiations, parties may call upon the services of the Court's Registry to help them in these negotiations. A member of a Chamber might at any stage assist the parties in settling their case.

The friendly-settlement procedure provides the respondent state with the possibility to solve a dispute with the applicant before the European Court has to pronounce itself on the possible existence of a (number of alleged) human rights violation(s) and/or just satisfaction, and is an illustration of the subsidiarity principle, a central principle underlying the entire Convention system.

With the entry into force of Protocol No. 14, the provisions of Article 39 (new) are taken partly from the present Article 38(1)(b) and (2) and also from the present Article 39. Since under the present Article 38(1)(b), it is only after an application has been declared admissible that the Court places itself at the disposal of the parties with a view to securing a friendly settlement, this procedure will be more flexible. The Court is free to place itself at the parties' disposal at any stage of the proceedings.

Friendly settlements will thus be encouraged, and may prove particularly useful in repetitive cases, and other cases where questions of principle or changes in domestic law are not involved. It goes without saying that these friendly settlements, too, will have to be based on respect for human rights, pursuant to Article 39(1).[501]

Article 39 provides for supervision of the execution of friendly settlements by the Committee of Ministers. This new provision was inserted to reflect a practice which the Court had already developed. In the framework of the text of Article 46(2), the Court used to endorse friendly settlements through *judgments* and not – as provided for in the present Article 39 ECHR – through *decisions*, since their execution was not subject to supervision by the Committee of Ministers. It was recognised, however, that adopting a judgment, instead of a decision, might have negative connotations for respondent parties, and make it harder to secure a friendly settlement. The new procedure will make this easier and thus reduce the Court's workload.[502]

Where the parties to the pilot case reach a friendly-settlement agreement, such agreement shall comprise a declaration by the respondent Contracting Party on the implementation of the general measures identified in the pilot

---

[501] Explanatory Report to Protocol No. 14, CETS 194, para. 93.
[502] *Ibid.*, para. 94.

judgment as well as the redress to be afforded to other actual or potential applicants.[503]

a. Way of securing friendly settlement

The Court has wide discretion as to how it may try to secure a friendly settlement. The Convention does not impose any limitations on the Court in this matter, with the exception of the requirement to be discussed below that the settlement reached must be based on respect for human rights as defined in the Convention.[504]

This flexible and informal character of the procedure enables the Court to create an atmosphere which makes it easier for the parties to reach a compromise. In this context, the fact that the procedure is confidential plays an important part. Furthermore, the fact that it may be attractive for the respondent state to avoid continuation of the procedure, which would lead to a thorough examination of the facts and might result in a public condemnation, helps to create a situation in which states may be willing to accept a compromise. The individual applicant may also benefit from the compromise by having certainty about the outcome of the dispute, and reparation, if any, of the damages incurred, at the earliest possible moment. He or she may, therefore, generally also wish to avoid lengthy proceedings before the Court, involving the risk of an unfavourable judgment. The separate decision on admissibility is important for the parties when considering whether they should start friendly-settlement negotiations.[505]

On the other hand, the procedure of the friendly settlement entails the drawbacks of a non-public procedure. Owing to the fact that it is a compromise, the friendly settlement, without further qualifications, would involve the risk that ultimately an agreement may be reached which does not meet the standards with respect to human rights set by the Convention. However, the concluding words of Article 38(1)(b) require the settlement to be reached 'on the basis of respect for Human Rights as defined in this Convention'. It is the duty of the Court to see to this. Besides the parties concerned, the Court must agree to the content of the settlement. It may happen, for instance, that the victim of a violation is ready to accept a given sum of money with which the government concerned might wish to buy off the violation, while the cause of the violation, for instance in the form of a legal provision or an administrative practice conflicting with the Convention, would continue to exist. In such a case, the Court will have to demand that the Contracting State concerned, in addition to giving compensation to the victim, takes measures to alter the

---

[503]   Rule 61(7) Rules of Court.
[504]   Art. 38(1)(b) ECHR.
[505]   Explanatory Report to Protocol No. 11, para. 78.

law or administrative practice in question. In its attempts to secure a friendly settlement, too, the Court has a duty with respect to the public interest, which constitutes a further indication of the 'objective' character of the procedure provided for in the Convention.

Besides the public interest in the maintenance of the legal order created by the Convention, that of the *Rechtsfrieden* (peace through justice) also plays a part here. Indeed, if the Court would not see to it that the existing violation be ended, there would be considerable risk that repeated applications might be submitted about the same situation conflicting with the Convention in a given Contracting State.

About the actual course of the attempts to reach a friendly settlement and the role of the Court, only a few general remarks can be made, precisely because the procedure is confidential and data about it are therefore scanty.

Article 38 states that the Court places itself at the disposal of the parties. However, in practice, within the Court, it is the Registry – and not the judges themselves – which is the main and proactive player, while in the old days it was rather reticent, mainly functioning as a go-between between the parties.[506] Immediately after a complaint has been declared admissible, the Registrar, acting on instructions of the Chamber or its President invites the parties to state whether they wish to make proposals for a possible settlement. In clone cases, today, the Registry also provides parties with a specific settlement proposal, including a specified sum of money.[507]

A friendly settlement will even be possible after the case has been referred to the Grand Chamber.[508]

Sometimes the Court will first examine the possibilities for a friendly settlement in discussions with one or both of the parties separately. In other cases, it will at once bring the parties into contact with each other because it considers that there are possibilities for a settlement.[509]

The role of the Court will have to be more or less active depending on whether an inter-state application or an individual application is concerned. In the first case, the parties are more or less on equal terms, so that the Court may confine itself to a more passive role. In case of an individual application, on the contrary, it may be true that the parties are formally on equal terms, but the respondent state is generally better equipped to conduct the negotiations within the framework of a friendly settlement than is an individual applicant. Therefore, the latter, in taking a decision on whether or not to agree to a given settlement,

---

[506] H. Keller, M. Forowics and L. Engi, *Friendly Settlements before the European Court of Human Rights. Theory and Practice*, Oxford, 2010, p. 36.
[507] *Ibid.*
[508] *Ibid.*, para. 51. See in this respect, *Pisano v. Italy, supra* n. 435, para. 28.
[509] See in this respect: N. Bratza and M. O'Boyle, 'The Legacy of the Commission to the New Court under the Protocol No. 11', in M. de Salvia and M.E. Villiger (eds.), *The Birth of European Human Rights Law. Liber Amicorum Carl Aage Norgaard*, Baden-Baden, 1998, p. 387.

may be guided by the Court. The Court, owing to its expertise and experience, will often be better able to evaluate the content of the settlement, and by playing a guiding role may to some extent neutralise a factual inequality of the parties to the negotiations. However, the role of the Court should not dominate to such an extent that it is actually the Court which determines the terms of the settlement and imposes it more or less upon the individual applicant. Up to the present, however, there have been no indications of such a situation, although, as has been said, present-day Registry practice is far more proactive than it used to be.

The Court is responsible for the establishment of the facts and may conduct an investigation on the understanding that the parties furnish the Court with all the relevant information. Parties to friendly-settlement proceedings are not at liberty to disclose the nature and content of any communication made with a view to and in connection with a friendly settlement. Material relating to the friendly-settlement negotiations must remain confidential.[510] In accordance with Article 39 ECHR and Rule 62(2) of the Rules of Court, friendly-settlement negotiations are confidential and no written or oral communication and no offer or concession made within the framework of the attempt to secure a friendly settlement may be referred to or relied on in the contentious proceedings. This rule is absolute and does not allow for an individual assessment of how much detail was disclosed.[511] Noting the importance of this principle, the Court further reiterates that it cannot be ruled out that a breach of the rule of confidentiality might, in certain circumstances, justify the conclusion that an application is inadmissible on the ground of an abuse of the right of application.[512] The Court has frequently held that procedural rules in domestic law are designed to ensure the proper administration of justice and compliance with the principle of legal certainty, and that litigants must be entitled to expect those rules to be applied. This principle is also applied in respect of the procedural provisions of the ECHR and of the Rules of Court. Moreover, the rule of confidentiality in respect of friendlysettlement negotiations is especially important because it aims to protect the parties and the Court itself from any political or other kind of pressure. Therefore, it is logical that the intentional breach of this rule constitutes an abuse of procedure. However, the Court notes that the direct responsibility of the party for the disclosure of the confidential information should be clearly established; a simple suspicion is not enough for an application to be declared inadmissible as an abuse of the right of individual application under the ECHR.[513]

---

[510]   Rule 43(3) and 62(2) of the Rules of Court.

[511]   *Balenović v. Croatia*, ECtHR 20 September 2010 (dec.), appl. no. 28369/07; *Abbasov and Others v. Azerbaijan*, ECtHR 28 May 2013, appl. no. 36609/06, para. 28.

[512]   *Popov v. Moldova (No. 1)*, ECtHR 18 January 2005, appl. no. 74153/01, para. 48; *Miroļubovs and Others v. Latvia*, ECtHR 15 September 2009, appl. no. 798/05, para. 66; *Abbasov and Others v. Azerbaijan*, *supra* n. 513, para. 29.

[513]   *Barreau and Others v. France*, ECtHR 13 December 2011 (dec.), appl. no. 24697/09; *Abbasov and Others v. Azerbaijan*, *supra* n. 513, para. 29.

If a friendly settlement in the sense of Article 38 is reached, the Court strikes the case out of its list by means of a decision which is confined to a brief statement of the facts and of the solutions reached.[514] As stated above, the Court now endorses friendly settlements through *judgments* and not – as provided for in Article 39 – through *decisions*, of which execution is not subject to supervision by the Committee of Ministers. If the Court is informed that an agreement has been reached between the applicant and the respondent state, it verifies the equitable nature of the agreement and, where it finds the agreement to be equitable, strike the case out of its list in accordance with Rule 43(3).[515] In general, the Court virtually always agrees with the friendly settlement reached.[516]

In a case where the applicant had agreed to settle his claims and signed an agreement in this respect, but later refused to abide by the terms of the agreement whereby he undertook to withdraw the application from the Court, the Court considered that it was no longer justified to continue the examination of the application under Article 37(1)(c) ECHR. It was satisfied, having regard to the agreement reached, that respect for human rights did not require the continued examination of the application.[517] Article 39(2) ECHR and Rule 62(2) of the Rules of Court prohibit the parties from making public information concerning the friendly-settlement negotiations, either through the media, or by a letter likely to be read by a significant number of people, or by any other means.[518] In the *Paladi* case, however, the Court accepted the applicant's view that the amount of compensation offered no reasonable relationship with the alleged ECHR violations, if these were to be proved. It also noted that the applicant was undoubtedly in a poor state of health, making him unable to attend court hearings. He was, moreover, not assisted by his lawyer, which deprived him of important advice on complex legal matters. The Court concluded that the matter had not been resolved, within the meaning of Article 37(1)(b), nor that 'it is no longer justified to continue the examination of the application' within the meaning of Article 37(1)(c). Indeed, it considered, given the seriousness of the alleged violations, that 'respect for human rights as defined in the Convention and the Protocols thereto' required it to continue the examination of the application.[519]

b. Friendly settlements reached

In a great number of cases, the substance of the settlement consisted merely in that the government concerned paid compensation and/or redressed the

---

[514] Art. 39 ECHR.
[515] Rule 75(4) of the Rules of Court.
[516] For an exception, see *Ukrainian Media Group v. the Ukraine*, ECtHR 29 March 2005, appl. no. 72713/01, para. 7.
[517] *Paritchi v. Moldova*, ECtHR 1 March 2005, appl. no. 54396/00.
[518] *Abbasov and Others v. Azerbaijan, supra* n. 513, para. 30.
[519] *Paladi v. Moldova*, ECtHR 10 July 2007, appl. no. 36806/05.

consequences of the violation for the victim as much as possible, without admitting that and even underscoring that no Convention violation had been committed.[520] A number of settlements are in fact based on judgments of the Court in cases which had raised identical issues. In a case against the United Kingdom, for instance, six applicants complained about their dismissal from employment after refusal to join a trade union. After the Court's judgment in the *Young, James and Webster* case the Government settled the case by offering the applicants compensation in respect of loss of earnings, pension rights and other employment benefits.[521]

In a case where the applicant complained under Articles 8, 13 and 14 ECHR about the investigation and inquiries into his sexual orientation and about his discharge from the RAF by reason of his homosexuality, the Court noted that it considered the issues raised in its judgment in, *inter alia*, *Smith and Grady*, in which violations of Articles 8 and 13 ECHR were found. The Court further observed that following that judgment, the policy of the Ministry of Defence was abandoned and homosexuals had been allowed to serve in United Kingdom armed forces as from 12 January 2000. Furthermore, the respondent State paid a certain amount for compensation.[522]

Many applications received in Strasbourg allege that the length of domestic criminal, civil or administrative court proceedings has exceeded the 'reasonable time' stipulated in Article 6(1) ECHR. A particularly high number of such applications concerned Italy. In a very high number of applications against Turkey the applicants complained in relation to the payment of compensation following the expropriation of their property. They alleged that the compensation they received did not reflect the real increase in inflation during the period between the date the amount was fixed and the date of payment. The great majority of these cases ended by reaching a friendly settlement in which the Turkish Government agreed to pay a certain amount of compensation.

There are also examples of more substantive settlements. In this respect, mention could be made of the settlement in the case of *France, Norway, Denmark, Sweden and Netherlands v. Turkey*, which was accepted by the Commission in 1985. The substantive parts of the settlement included the assurance by the Turkish Government that they would strictly observe their obligations under Article 3 ECHR, a vague promise concerning the granting of amnesty and – as regards the derogations under Article 15 ECHR – a reference to an even vaguer

---

[520] See, e.g., *Köksal v. the Netherlands*, ECtHR 20 March 2001, appl. no. 31725/96, para. 14; *Değerli v. Turkey*, ECtHR 21 May 2001, appl. no. 31896/96, para. 14; *Gawracz v. Turkey*, ECtHR 12 February 2002, appl. no. 32055/96, para. 9; *Samy v. the Netherlands*, ECtHR 18 June 2002, appl. no. 36499/97, para. 14; *Sędek v. Poland*, ECtHR 6 May 2003, appl. no. 67165/01, para. 14; *Binbay v. Turkey*, ECtHR 21 October 2004, appl. no. 24922/94, para. 19.

[521] *Eaton and Others v. United Kingdom*, EComHR 10 December 1984 (rep.), appl. nos. 8476/79–8481/79, D&R 39 (1984), p. 11 (15).

[522] *Brown v. United Kingdom*, ECtHR 29 July 2003, appl. no. 52770/99, para. 13.

declaration by the Turkish Prime Minister of 4 April 1985, stating that 'I hope that we will be able to lift martial law from the remaining provinces within 18 months'.[523] Particularly the acceptance by the applicant States of the latter part of the settlement was striking in view of the fact that, when lodging their complaint, the applicant States upheld that a public emergency threatening the life of the nation did not exist in Turkey in 1982. Although the application, as declared admissible, also included alleged violations of Articles 5, 6, 9, 10, 11 and 17 ECHR, those provisions were not explicitly mentioned in the settlement.

By their rather lenient attitude the applicant Governments had manoeuvred the Commission into a very difficult position. It may even be argued that the Commission was left with no choice but to accept the settlement. Indeed, in the alternative the case would have been decided by the Committee of Ministers – Turkey had not recognised the jurisdiction of the Court yet – in which organ the applicant States and Turkey would obviously have played a prominent if not decisive role. Be this as it may, it does not turn the settlement into one which has been reached 'on the basis of respect for Human Rights as defined in this Convention'. In our view, the Commission should at any rate have insisted on a stricter type of supervision over the observance by Turkey of its commitments under the settlement. With respect to Article 15 as well as to the granting of amnesty there was in fact no supervision at all: the Turkish Government only undertook to keep the Commission informed of further developments. As far as Article 3 was concerned, supervision was confined to a commitment by Turkey to submit three reports under former Article 57 during 1986, a dialogue with the Commission on each of those reports, and a short final report on the implementation of the settlement to be prepared not later than 1 February 1987. All this, moreover, was to be conducted in a confidential manner.[524]

After Turkey had accepted the right of individual petition and the compulsory jurisdiction of the Court in 1989, many applications were brought against Turkey alleging violations of Article 2 and 3 ECHR. Several cases ended in a friendly settlement, sometimes even if the Court had held that the most appropriate remedy in principle would have been a new trial or resumption of proceedings at the applicant's request.[525] In some of those the Court accepted the friendly settlement. The Court stated that, in view of its responsibilities under Article 19 ECHR, it would nevertheless be open to the Court to proceed with its consideration of the case if a reason of public policy (*ordre public*) appeared to necessitate such a course, but that it discerned no such reason.[526] In other cases, the Turkish Government accepted that the use

---

[523] *France, Norway, Denmark, Sweden and Netherlands v. Turkey*, EComHR 7 December 1985, appl. nos. 9940/82–9944/82, D&R 44 (1985), p. 31 (39).

[524] *Ibid.*

[525] *Kavak v. Turkey*, ECtHR 19 May 2009 (dec.), appl. nos. 34719/04 and 37472/05.

[526] *Sur v. Turkey*, ECtHR 3 October 1997, appl. no. 17722/02, para. 31; *Saki v. Turkey*, ECtHR 31 October 2001, appl. no. 29359/95, para. 14; *Toğcu v. Turkey, supra* n. 472, para. 37; *Doğan v.*

of excessive or disproportionate force resulting in death constitutes a violation of Article 2 ECHR and undertook to issue appropriate instructions and adopt all necessary measures to ensure that the right to life – including the obligation to carry out effective investigations – is respected in the future. In fact, new legal and administrative measures were adopted which resulted in a reduction in the occurrence of deaths in circumstances similar to those of the application referred to here, as well as more effective investigations.[527] In the case of *Denmark v. Turkey,* the Court observed that the friendly settlement, *inter alia*, made provision for the payment of a sum of money to the applicant Government, included a statement of regret by the respondent Government concerning the occurrence of occasional and individual cases of torture and ill-treatment in Turkey, emphasised, with reference to Turkey's continued participation in the Council of Europe's police-training project, the importance of the training of Turkish police officers, and provided for the establishment of a new bilateral project in this area. Furthermore, it had been decided to establish a continuous Danish-Turkish political dialogue that would also focus on human rights issues and within which individual cases might be raised. The Court also took note of the changes to the legal and administrative framework which had been introduced in Turkey in response to instances of torture and ill-treatment as well as the respondent Government's undertaking to make further improvements in the field of human rights – especially concerning the occurrence of incidents of torture and ill-treatment – and to continue their co-operation with international human rights bodies, in particular the Committee for the Prevention of Torture. Against that background the Court was satisfied that the settlement was based on respect for human rights as defined in the Convention or its Protocols.[528]

In cases of deportation or extradition a friendly settlement may sometimes lead to an immediate solution.[529] In the case of *Yang Chun Jin Alias Yang Xiaolin v. Hungary*, the applicant alleged that, if extradited to China, he risked having an unfair trial, being detained under harsh conditions, being subjected to torture or being sentenced to death. Noting that the Hungarian Minister of Justice had decided to refuse the applicant's extradition to China and that he had left Hungary for Sierra Leone, the Court found that the applicant was no longer threatened with extradition to China from Hungary and that the matter

---

Turkey, ECtHR 19 June 2003, appl. no. 37033/03, para. 21; *Yavuz and Others v. Turkey*, ECtHR 5 June 2012, appl. no. 40872/07.

[527] *Akman v. Turkey,* ECtHR 26 June 2001, appl. no. 37453/97, para. 31; *Yakar v. Turkey,* ECtHR 26 November 2002, appl. no. 36189/97, para. 32; *Örnek and Eren v. Turkey,* ECtHR 15 July 2004, appl. no. 41306/98, para. 24; *Çelik v. Turkey,* ECtHR 27 July 2004, appl. no. 52991/99, para.16; *Association SOS Attentats and de Boery v. France*, ECtHR 14 October 2006, appl. no. 76642/01, para. 37.

[528] *Denmark v. Turkey,* ECtHR 5 April 2000, appl. no. 34382/97, paras. 24–25.

[529] *Musa and 175 other applicants v. United Kingdom*, ECtHR 26 June 2012, appl. no. 8276/07.

was resolved.[530] In *S.J. v. Belgium*, the applicant, a Nigerian woman about to be expelled, was to be provided with a permanent residence permit, together with her children, as part of the friendly settlement reached with the state.[531]

Friendly settlements can also be found in which there is, apart from a financial compensation, the willingness on the part of the respondent state to amend the legislation which gave rise to the complaint. The case of *Hutten-Czapska* concerned loss of rental income of more than 100,000 Polish landlords due to a restrictive system of rent control. In reaching a friendly settlement adopted by the court, the Polish Government identified various general measures that had been taken to resolve the underlying housing problem. Besides, the Government recognised that it should better balance the interests of the landlords and the general community, although the scale of the problem and the alleged lack of efforts by the Government to solve it led to one concurring and one dissenting opinion.[532]

In the *Selim* case, the applicant wished to contract a civil marriage with a Romanian citizen. The Municipality of Nicosia informed the applicant that section 34 of the Marriage Act did not provide the possibility for a Turkish Cypriot professing the Muslim faith to contract a civil marriage. The applicant was thus forced to marry in Romania without any of his family or friends being able to attend. The case ended in a friendly settlement. The Court took note of the agreement reached between the Government and the applicant. It noted in addition that new legislation had been enacted, which provided for the application of the Marriage Act Cap. 279 to members of the Turkish Community, thus conferring on them the right to marry. It further noted that a new law (The Civil Marriage Act 2002), which would apply to all Cypriots without distinction of origin, was also to be tabled in Parliament for enactment.[533]

c. Other forms of arrangements

Apart from the friendly settlement referred to in Article 37(1)(b), the parties sometimes reach a settlement of the dispute among themselves. In those cases, the applicant withdraws his complaint after having come to some kind of arrangement with the government concerned.[534]

There is also a possibility that the Court may decide to strike the case off the list of cases, if a solution is reached by way of a unilateral declaration. In accordance with Article 37(1)(c) and Rule 62A the Court may at any stage of

---

[530] *Yang Chun Jin Alias Yang Xiaolin v. Hungary*, ECtHR 8 March 2001, appl. no. 58573/00; see also *K.K.C. v. Netherlands*, ECtHR, 21 December 2001 appl. no. 58964/00; *Ahmed v. Austria*, ECtHR 22 February 2007, paras. 20–22.

[531] *S.J. v. Belgium*, ECtHR 19 March 2015, appl. no.70055/10.

[532] *Hutten-Czapska v. Poland,* ECtHR 28 April 2008, appl. no. 35014/97, paras. 37–53.

[533] *Selim v. Cyprus,* ECtHR 16 July 2002, appl. no. 47293/99, para.16.

[534] Rule 43(1) Rules of Court.

the proceedings decide to strike an application off its list of cases where the circumstances lead to the conclusion that it is no longer justified to continue the examination of the application. The Court may, however, decide to restore the case to the list again if new circumstance may justify this.[535]

In the cases of *Aydin*,[536] *Akman*[537] and *Tahsin Acar*[538] the applicants did not agree with a friendly settlement of the case. The Court held that having examined carefully the terms of the respondent Government's declaration and having regard to the nature of the admissions contained in the declaration as well as the scope and extent of the various undertakings referred to therein, together with the amount of compensation proposed, it considered that it was no longer justified to continue the examination of the applications. In the case of *Tahsin Acar,* however, the Grand Chamber held that, under certain circumstances, it might be appropriate to strike out an application under Article 37(1)(c) ECHR on the basis of a unilateral declaration by the respondent Government even if the applicant wished the examination of the case to be continued. It will, however, depend on the particular circumstances whether the unilateral declaration offers a sufficient basis for finding that respect for human rights as defined in the Convention does not require the Court to continue its examination of the case.[539]

As a non-exhaustive list the Court indicated that relevant factors for deciding whether a unilateral declaration is sufficient to decide to strike a case of the list of cases include the nature of the complaints made, the question of whether the issues raised are comparable to issues already determined by the Court in previous cases, the nature and scope of any measures taken by the respondent government in the context of the execution of judgments delivered by the Court in any such previous cases, and the impact of these measures on the case at issue. It may also be material whether the facts are in dispute between the parties, and, if so, to what extent, and what *prima facie* evidentiary value is to be attributed to the parties' submissions on the facts. In that connection, it will be of significance whether the Court itself has already taken evidence in the case for the purposes of establishing disputed facts. Other relevant factors may include the question of whether in its unilateral declaration the respondent government has made any admission(s) in relation to the alleged violations ECHR and, if so, the scope of such admissions and the manner in which it intends to provide redress to the applicant. As to the last-mentioned point, in cases in which it is possible to eliminate the effects of an alleged violation (as, for example, in some property cases) and the respondent government declares its readiness to do so, the intended redress is more likely to be regarded as appropriate for the purposes of striking out the application, the Court, as always, retaining its power to restore

---

[535] *B.B. v. France*, ECtHR 7 September 1998, appl. no. 30930/96, para. 37.
[536] *Aydin v. Turkey, supra* n. 470, para. 15.
[537] *Akman v. Turkey, supra* n. 471, para. 30.
[538] *Tahsin Acar v. Turkey, supra* n. 476, para. 65.
[539] *Ibid.*, para. 75.

the application to its list as provided in Article 37(2) ECHR and Rule 43(5) of the Rules of Court.[540]

The full admission of liability in respect of an applicant's allegations under the Convention cannot be regarded as a condition *sine qua non* for the Court's being prepared to strike an application out on the basis of a unilateral declaration by a respondent government. However, in cases concerning persons who have disappeared or have been killed by unknown perpetrators and where there is *prima facie* evidence in the case file supporting allegations that the domestic investigation fell short of what is necessary under the Convention, a unilateral declaration should at the very least contain an admission to that effect, combined with an undertaking by the respondent government to conduct, under the supervision of the Committee of Ministers in the context of the latter's duties under Article 46(2) ECHR, an investigation that is in full compliance with the requirements of the ECHR.[541]

d. Non-compliance with terms of friendly settlement

The Court may, in accordance with Article 37(2) ECHR decide to restore an application to its list of cases if it considers that the circumstances justify such a course.[542]

It would also seem to be possible that one of the Contracting States submits a complaint concerning non-compliance with a friendly settlement to the Committee of Ministers. In fact, as members of the Council of Europe the Contracting States may take the initiative for the much more far-reaching procedure of expulsion of a Member State from the organisation under Article 8 of the Statute of the Council of Europe, when the latter has seriously violated its engagements concerning human rights and fundamental freedoms. They, therefore, must certainly also be considered authorised to put non-compliance with a friendly settlement before the Committee of Ministers in order to try, through that organ, to induce the state in question to comply with its obligations under the settlement. In view thereof it would be advisable that the Committee of Ministers, when stating that no further steps in the respective case are necessary in view of the settlement reached, were to reserve to itself the right to take appropriate measures at a later date should one of the parties not comply with its obligations.

However, since the entry into force of Protocol No. 11 a practice has been developed by which the Court endorses friendly settlements through *judgments* and not – as provided for in Article 39 ECHR – through *decisions*, whose execution is not subject to supervision by the Committee of Ministers. Under

---

[540]   *Ibid.*, para. 76.
[541]   *Ibid.*, para. 84.
[542]   For an example, see *Katic v. Serbia*, ECtHR 7 July 2009, appl. no. 13920/04, para. 84.

Protocol No. 14, Article 39 expressly provides for supervision of the execution of friendly settlements by the Committee of Ministers. According to the Explanatory Report to Protocol No. 14 this amendment is in no way intended to reduce the Committee's present supervisory powers, particularly concerning the strike-out decisions covered by Article 37. It would be advisable for the Committee of Ministers to distinguish more clearly, in its practice, between its supervision function by virtue of the new Article 39(4) (friendly settlements), on the one hand and that under Article 46(2) (execution of judgments), on the other.[543]

A non-official settlement may also be reached when the Court's examination of the merits is quite complete, or almost so. It must, therefore, be determined for each individual case what the best solution is if such a settlement is not complied with by the Contracting State in question: supervision by the Committee of Ministers or restoration of the application to the list. When a thorough examination of the merits has not yet taken place, it would seem to be most appropriate for the Court to place the case on the list of cases again when 'the circumstances of the case as a whole justify such restoration'. The consequence of this is that the original application as a whole is resuscitated, so that no additional difficulties may arise in connection with the admissibility conditions. Here again, however, the Court will first have to ascertain whether the settlement has really not been complied with, and it will therefore have to give the state concerned an opportunity to prove the contrary.

3. PROCEEDINGS BEFORE THE GRAND CHAMBER

The Grand Chamber has competence both with regard to inter-state applications referred to it under Article 30 or Article 43 ECHR as well as to individual applications when they are referred to it under Article 30 or Article 43. The Grand Chamber is also competent to consider requests for advisory opinions, a function which the plenary Court carried out under the former system.[544] In cases with specified serious implications, a Chamber will be able to relinquish jurisdiction *proprio motu* in favour of the Grand Chamber at any time, as long as it has not yet rendered judgment, unless one of the parties to the case objects.[545] Such relinquishment should also speed up proceedings. Once a judgment has been rendered by a Chamber, any of the parties may request that the case be referred to the Grand Chamber for a rehearing.[546]

---

[543]   *Explanatory Report to Protocol No. 14*, para. 94.
[544]   Rule 88 Rules of Court.
[545]   Rule 72 Rules of Court.
[546]   Rule 73 Rules of Court.

3.1. RELINQUISHMENT OF JURISDICTION BY A CHAMBER

In accordance with Article 30 ECHR, where a case pending before a Chamber raises a serious question affecting the interpretation ECHR or the Protocols thereto or where the resolution of a question before it might have a result inconsistent with a judgment previously delivered by the Court, the Chamber may, at any time before it has rendered its judgment, relinquish jurisdiction in favour of the Grand Chamber, unless one of the parties to the case has objected in accordance with paragraph 2 of this Rule. Reasons need not be given for the decision to relinquish.[547] Conferring a veto right on the parties keeps open the possibility for their case to receive a second handling. However, the objection against relinquishment of jurisdiction has to be duly reasoned; otherwise it will be considered invalid.[548]

3.2. REFERRAL TO THE GRAND CHAMBER

In accordance with Article 43(1) ECHR, within a period of three months from the date of the judgment of the Chamber, any party to the case may, in exceptional cases, request that the case be referred to the Grand Chamber. A rehearing of the case, as envisaged in Article 43, will take place only exceptionally, when a case raises a serious question affecting the interpretation or application ECHR or a serious issue of general importance.[549] The purpose is to ensure the quality and consistency of the Court's case law by allowing for a re-examination of the most important cases. The intention is that these conditions will be applied in a strict sense.[550]

The party must specify in its request the serious question affecting the interpretation or application ECHR or the Protocols thereto, or the serious issue of general importance, which in its view warrants consideration by the Grand Chamber.[551]

According to the Explanatory Report to Protocol No. 11, serious questions affecting the interpretation ECHR are involved when a question of importance not yet decided by the Court is at stake, or when the decision is of importance for future cases and for the development of the Court's case law. Moreover, a serious question may be particularly evident when the judgment concerned is not consistent with a previous judgment of the Court. A serious question concerning the application ECHR may be at stake when a judgment necessitates a substantial

---

[547] Rule 72(1) Rules of Court.
[548] Rule 72(2) Rules of Court.
[549] Art. 43(2) ECHR and Rule 73(2) Rules of Court.
[550] Explanatory Report to Protocol No. 11, para. 99. See in this respect Art. 43(1) ECHR and Rule 73(1) Rules of Court, where the term 'exceptionally' has been used.
[551] Rule 73(1) Rules of Court.

change to national law or administrative practice but does not itself raise a serious question of interpretation ECHR. A serious issue of general importance could involve a substantial political issue or an important issue of policy.[552]

A request for a rehearing may concern the admissibility as well as the merits of a case. A request may also be made if a party to the case has a disagreement with respect to a judgment concerning the award of just satisfaction under Article 41 if the Convention.[553]

In order to ensure that the parties are in a position to observe the time limit of three months from the date of delivery of the judgment, they will be informed about the date on which the judgment is delivered. A panel of five judges of the Grand Chamber decides on the acceptance of the request. If the request is accepted, the Grand Chamber has to make the final determination as to whether the Convention has been violated after written and, if the Court so decides, oral proceedings. If the conditions for a request of referral are not met, the panel rejects the request and the Chamber's judgment becomes final. It will accept the request only if it considers that the case does raise a serious question as defined in Article 43(2). Reasons need not be given for a refusal of the request.[554]

In the *Pisano* case, the Italian Government asked the Grand Chamber to review the decision of the panel of five judges to accept the request for referral. It argued that the request did not satisfy the conditions laid down in Article 43 ECHR. In the Government's submission, the case did not raise any serious questions affecting the interpretation or application of the ECHR, or indeed any serious issues of general importance. It emphasised that the applicant had not produced any evidence to suggest that it did but had merely referred to the dissenting opinion appended to the Chamber judgment. The latter opinion, however, was not sufficient to justify a rehearing of the case as it did not in any way call into question the manner in which Article 6 ECHR had been construed. Lastly, the Government argued that the Grand Chamber, seeing that it had the final say about its own jurisdiction and whether it had been validly seized, was not bound by the opinion of the five judges. The Grand Chamber noted that neither the Convention nor the Rules of Court empowered it to review a decision by the panel to accept a request for a rehearing. What is more, the terms of Article 43(3) ECHR provide as follows: 'If the panel accepts the request, the Grand Chamber shall decide the case by means of a judgment' and thus make it clear that, once the panel has accepted a request for a rehearing, the Grand Chamber has no option but to examine the case.[555]

---

[552] Explanatory Report to Protocol No. 11, paras. 100–102.
[553] *Kingsley v. United Kingdom*, ECtHR 28 May 2002, appl. no. 35605/97, para. 7.
[554] Rule 73(2) Rules of Court.
[555] *Pisano v. Italy, supra* n. 435, para. 26.

3.3. PROCEDURE BEFORE THE GRAND CHAMBER

According to Rule 71(1) of the Rules of Court, any provisions governing proceedings before the Chambers shall apply, *mutatis mutandis*, to proceedings before the Grand Chamber.

Where a case has been submitted to the Grand Chamber either under Article 30 or under Article 43 ECHR, the President of the Grand Chamber designates as judge-rapporteur(s) one or, in the case of an inter-state application, one or more of its members.[556] The judge-rapporteur of the Grand Chamber is always another judge than the judge elected in respect of the respondent party. The proceedings of the Grand Chamber are normally written proceedings but, if the Court so decides, oral proceedings may be held. The powers conferred on a Chamber in relation to the holding of a hearing may, in proceedings before the Grand Chamber, also be exercised by the President of the Grand Chamber.[557] From the text of Article 31(a) ECHR it may be deduced that, if the decision to relinquish jurisdiction in favour of the Grand Chamber before a decision as the admissibility has been taken, the Grand Chamber will also decide on admissibility. After all, in accordance with Article 35(4) ECHR, the Court rejects any application which it considers inadmissible. It may do so at any stage of the proceedings. Also in this stage third-party intervention is possible.[558]

As holds good for the Chambers of the Court, the Grand Chamber must assess the facts as they appear at the time of its decision by applying the appropriate legal solution. Once a case is referred to it, the Grand Chamber deals with the case afresh and may employ the full range of judicial powers conferred on the Court.[559] In this respect the Court held:

'The Court would first note that all three paragraphs of Article 43 use the term "the case" ("*l'affaire*") for describing the matter which is being brought before the Grand Chamber. In particular, paragraph 3 of Article 43 provides that the Grand Chamber is to "decide *the case*" – that is the whole case and not simply the "serious question" or "serious issue" mentioned in paragraph 2 – "by means of a judgment". The wording of Article 43 makes it clear that, whilst the existence of "a serious question affecting the interpretation or application ECHR or the Protocols thereto, or a serious issue of general importance" (paragraph 2) is a prerequisite for acceptance of a party's request, the consequence of acceptance is that the whole "case" is referred to the Grand Chamber to be decided afresh by means of a new judgment (paragraph 3). The same term "the case" ("*l'affaire*") is also used in Article 44 §2 which defines the conditions under which the judgments of a Chamber become final. If a request by a party for referral under

---

556   Rule 50 Rules of Court.
557   Rule 71(2) Rules of Court.
558   Rule 44 (3) Rules of Court.
559   *Pisano v. Italy, supra* n. 435, para. 28.

Article 43 has been accepted, Article 44 can only be understood as meaning that the entire judgment of the Chamber will be set aside in order to be replaced by the new judgment of the Grand Chamber envisaged by Article 43 §3. This being so, the "case" referred to the Grand Chamber necessarily embraces all aspects of the application previously examined by the Chamber in its judgment, and not only the serious "question" or "issue" at the basis of the referral. In sum, there is no basis for a merely partial referral of the case to the Grand Chamber.'[560]

The Grand Chamber may also re-examine, where appropriate, issues relating to the admissibility of the application in the same manner as this is possible in normal Chamber proceedings, for example by virtue of Article 35(4) ECHR *in fine*.[561]

The Grand Chamber may likewise be required to apply other provisions ECHR that enable it to terminate the proceedings by a means other than a judgment on the merits, for example by approving a friendly settlement (Article 39 ECHR) or striking the application out of the list of cases (Article 37).

4. JUDGMENT OF THE COURT

Where the Chamber finds that there has been a violation of the ECHR or the Protocols thereto, it gives in the same judgment a ruling on the application of Article 41 ECHR if that question, after being raised in accordance with Rule 60 of the Rules of Court, is ready for decision. If the question is not ready for decision, the Chamber reserves it in whole or in part and fixes the further procedure.[562]

According to Article 42 in conjunction with Article 44(2) ECHR, judgments of Chambers become final (1) when the parties declare that they will not request that the case be referred to the Grand Chamber; or (2) three months after the date of the judgment, if reference of the case to the Grand Chamber has not been requested; or (3) when the panel of the Grand Chamber rejects the request to refer the case to the Grand Chamber. According to Article 44(1) ECHR, the judgment of the Grand Chamber is final. Judgments will have to be reasoned (Article 45(1)). This article does not concern decisions taken by the panel of five judges of the Grand Chamber in accordance with Article 43, nor Committee decisions on admissibility under Article 28.

The judgment will be transmitted to the parties but will not be published until it has become final (Article 44(3)). Unless the Court decides that a judgment will be given in both official languages, all judgments will be given either in English

---

[560] *K. and T. v. Finland, supra* n. 434, para. 140; *Göcv v. Turkey,* ECtHR 11 July 2002, appl. no. 36590/97, para. 36; *Pisano v. Italy, supra* n. 435, para. 28; *Perna v. Italy,* ECtHR (GC) 6 May 2003, appl. no. 48898/99, para. 23; *Tahsin Acar v. Turkey, supra* n. 476, para. 63.

[561] *Azinas v. Cyprus, supra* n. 181, para. 32.

[562] Rule 75(1) Rules of Court.

or in French.[563] According to Rule 77 of the Rules of Court, the judgment may be read out at a public hearing by the President of the Chamber or by another judge delegated by him or her. The agents and representatives of the parties are informed in due time of the date of the hearing. Final judgments of the Court are published, under the responsibility of the Registrar, in an appropriate form. The Registrar is in addition responsible for the publication of official reports of selected judgments and decisions and of any document which the President of the Court considers it useful to publish.[564]

According to Article 46, the High Contracting Parties undertake to abide by the final judgment of the Court in any case to which they are parties. The final judgment is transmitted to the Committee of Ministers, which will supervise its execution.

With respect to the binding force and execution of judgments, Protocol No. 14 amended Article 46 ECHR. Three new paragraphs have been added to Article 46. Article 46, in its paragraph 3, empowers the Committee of Ministers to ask the Court to interpret a final judgment, for the purpose of facilitating the supervision of its execution. The Committee of Ministers' experience of supervising the execution of judgments shows that difficulties are sometimes encountered owing to disagreement as to the interpretation of judgments. The Court's reply settles any argument concerning a judgement's exact meaning. The qualified majority vote required on the part of the Committee of Ministers by the last sentence of paragraph 3 shows that the Committee of Ministers should use this possibility sparingly, to avoid overburdening the Court. The aim of paragraph 3 is to enable the Court to give an interpretation of a judgment, not to pronounce on the measures taken by a High Contracting Party to comply with that judgment. No time-limit has been set for making requests for interpretation, since a question of interpretation may arise at any time during the Committee of Ministers' examination of the execution of a judgment.

The Court is free to decide on the manner and form in which it wishes to reply to the request. Normally, it would be for the formation of the Court which delivered the original judgment to rule on the question of interpretation. More detailed rules governing this new procedure may be included in the Rules of Court.[565]

Paragraphs 4 and 5 of Article 46 empower the Committee of Ministers to bring infringement proceedings in the Court. The Court will sit as a Grand Chamber,[566] having first served the state concerned with notice to comply. The Committee of Ministers' decision to do so requires a qualified majority of two-thirds of the representatives entitled to sit on the Committee. This infringement

---

[563] Rule 76 Rules of Court.
[564] Rule 78 Rules of Court.
[565] Explanatory Report to Protocol No. 14, CETS 194, paras. 96–97.
[566] Art. 31(b).

procedure does not aim to reopen the question of violation, already decided in the Court's first judgment. Nor does it provide for payment of a financial penalty by a High Contracting Party found in violation of Article 46, paragraph 1. It is felt that the political pressure exerted by proceedings for non-compliance in the Grand Chamber and by the latter's judgment should suffice to secure execution of the Court's initial judgment by the state concerned.[567]

In fulfilling its supervisory task, the Committee of Ministers invited the Court as far as possible, to identify, in its judgments finding a violation ECHR, what it considers to be an underlying systemic problem and the source of this problem, in particular when it is likely to give rise to numerous applications, so as to assist states in finding the appropriate solution and the Committee of Ministers in supervising the execution of judgments.[568]

In this respect, the Court held in the *Broniowski* case, that above all, the measures adopted must be such as to remedy the systemic defect underlying the Court's finding of a violation so as not to overburden the Convention system with large numbers of applications deriving from the same cause. Such measures should therefore include a scheme which offers redress to those affected by the Convention violation identified in the instant judgment in relation to the present applicant. In this context, the Court's concern is to facilitate the most speedy and effective resolution of a dysfunction established in national human rights protection. Once such a defect has been identified, it falls to the national authorities, under the supervision of the Committee of Ministers, to take, retroactively if appropriate, the necessary remedial measures in accordance with the subsidiary character of the ECHR, so that the Court does not have to repeat its finding in a lengthy series of comparable cases. The Court held that, with a view to assisting the respondent State in fulfilling its obligations under Article 46, the Court had sought to indicate the type of measure that might be taken by the Polish State in order to put an end to the systemic situation identified in the present case. The Court was not in a position to assess whether the December 2003 Act could be treated as an adequate measure in this connection since no practice of its implementation had been established as yet. In any event, this Act did not cover persons who – like Mr Broniowski – had already received partial compensation, irrespective of the amount of such compensation. Thus, it was clear that for this group of Bug River claimants the Act could not be regarded as a measure capable of putting an end to the systemic situation identified in the present judgment as adversely affecting them. Nevertheless, as regards general measures to be taken, the Court considered that the respondent State must, primarily, either remove any hindrance to the implementation of the right of the numerous persons affected by the situation found, in respect of the applicant, to

---

[567] Explanatory Report to Protocol No. 14, CETS 194, para. 98.
[568] Resolution Res. (2004) 3 of 12 May 2004 on judgments revealing an underlying systemic problem.

have been in breach the ECHR, or provide equivalent redress in lieu. As to the former option, the respondent State should, therefore, through appropriate legal and administrative measures, secure the effective and expeditious realisation of the entitlement in question in respect of the remaining Bug River claimants, in accordance with the principles for the protection of property rights laid down in Article 1 of Protocol No. 1, having particular regard to the principles relating to compensation.[569] Since the applicant belonged to a fairly large group of victims of similar violations, the Court on 4 July 2004 for the first time has used the 'leading case' procedure, whereby examination of the many similar cases was suspended until the required measures had been taken. This procedure is one of the means chosen to reduce the Court's workload.[570]

In the *Sejdovic* case, the Court held that the infringement of the applicant's right to a fair trial had originated in a problem resulting from Italian legislation on the question of trial *in absentia* and had been caused by the wording of the provisions of the CCP relating to the conditions for lodging an application for the lifting of a procedural bar. There was a shortcoming in the Italian legal system which meant that every person convicted *in absentia* who had not been effectively informed of the proceedings against him could be deprived of a retrial. The Court considered that the shortcomings of domestic law and practice revealed in the present case could lead in the future to a large number of well-founded applications. Italy had a duty to remove every legal obstacle that might prevent either the reopening of the time allowed for an appeal or a retrial in the case of every person convicted by default who, not having been effectively informed of the proceedings against him, had not unequivocally waived the right to appear at his trial. Such persons would thus be guaranteed the right to obtain a new ruling on the charges brought against them from a court which had heard them in accordance with the requirements of Article 6 ECHR. Consequently, Italy should take appropriate measures to make provision for and regulate further proceedings capable of effectively securing the right to the reopening of proceedings, in accordance with the principles of the protection of the rights enshrined in Article 6 ECHR.[571]

According to the Explanatory Report to Protocol No. 14, the Committee of Ministers will bring infringement proceedings only in exceptional circumstances. Nonetheless, it appeared necessary to give the Committee of Ministers, as the competent organ for supervising execution of the Court's judgments, a wider range of means of pressure to secure execution of judgments. Currently the ultimate measure available to the Committee of Ministers is recourse to Article 8 of the Council of Europe's Statute (suspension of voting rights in the Committee of Ministers, or even expulsion from the Organisation).

---

[569] *Broniowski v. Poland,* ECtHR 12 May 2004, appl. no. 31443/96, paras. 193–194.
[570] Human Rights Information Bulletin, H Inf(2005)1, p. 23.
[571] *Sejdovic v. Italy,* ECtHR 10 November 2004, appl. no. 56581/00, paras. 46–47.

This is an extreme measure, which would prove counter-productive in most cases; indeed, the High Contracting Party which finds itself in the situation foreseen in paragraph 4 of Article 46 continues to need the discipline of the Council of Europe. The new Article 46, therefore, adds further possibilities of bringing pressure to bear to the existing ones. The procedure's mere existence, and the threat of using it, should act as an effective new incentive to execute the Court's judgments. It is foreseen that the outcome of infringement proceedings will be expressed in a judgment of the Court.

PILOT-JUDGMENT PROCEDURE

Many of the cases pending before the European Court of Human Rights are so-called 'repetitive cases', which derive from a common dysfunction at the national level. The pilot-judgment procedure was developed as a technique of identifying the structural problems underlying repetitive cases against many countries and imposing an obligation on states to address those problems. Where the Court receives several applications that share a root cause, it can select one or more for priority treatment under the pilot procedure. In a pilot judgment, the Court's task is not only to decide whether a violation of the ECHR occurred in a specific case but also to identify the systemic problem and to give the government clear indications of the type of remedial measures needed to resolve it. A key feature of the pilot procedure is the possibility of adjourning, or 'freezing', related cases for a period of time on the condition that the Government act promptly to adopt the national measures required to satisfy the judgment. The Court can, however, resume examining adjourned cases whenever the interests of justice so require.[572]

The case of *Broniowski v. Poland* was the first pilot judgment on the subject of properties situated beyond the Bug River – which concerned some 80,000 people. After Poland's eastern border had been redrawn in the aftermath of the Second World War, Poland undertook to compensate Polish citizens who had been repatriated and had had to abandon their property situated beyond the Bug River and now in Ukrainian, Belarusian or Lithuanian territory. Following an application by a Polish national who complained that he had not received the compensatory property to which he was entitled, the Court found that the case disclosed the existence, within the Polish legal order, of a structural deficiency which denied a whole class of individuals the peaceful enjoyment of their possessions. The Court requested to ensure, through appropriate legal and administrative measures, the implementation of a property right in respect of the remaining Bug River claimants or provide them with

---

[572] Rule 61 of Rules of Court.

equivalent redress in lieu.[573] On 6 July 2004, having regard to the fact that the substantive examination of the remaining cases was linked to the execution of the *Broniowski* judgment and the implementation of the measures indicated by the Court to the Polish Government, the Court decided that all similar applications – including future applications – should be adjourned pending the outcome of the leading case and the adoption of the measures to be taken at national level. It also decided that the Polish Government and the Committee of Ministers of the Council of Europe should be informed of the adjournment and supplied with a list of the adjourned pending cases. The applicants were informed accordingly.[574] Following this judgment Poland passed in July 2005 a new law providing for financial compensation for properties abandoned beyond the Bug River. The Court, having found that the new law and the compensation scheme were effective in practice, struck out in 2007 and 2008 more than 200 similar applications which had been adjourned and decided that the continued application of the pilot-judgment procedure in the case was no longer justified.[575] The case of *Hutten-Czapska v. Poland* also concerned the violation of property rights. The system imposed a number of restrictions on landlords' rights, in particular setting a ceiling on rent levels which was so low that landlords could not even recoup their maintenance costs, let alone make a profit. The Court estimated that about 100,000 landlords were potentially concerned. The Court considered that the Polish State had to, above all, through appropriate legal and/or other measures, secure in its domestic legal order a mechanism maintaining a fair balance between the interests of landlords, including their entitlement to derive profit from their property, and the general interest of the community – including the availability of sufficient accommodation for the less well-off – in accordance with the principles of the protection of property rights under the Convention. It was not for the Court to specify what would be the most appropriate way of setting up such remedial procedures or how landlords' interest in deriving profit should be balanced against the other interests at stake. However, the Court observed in passing that the many options open to the State certainly included the measures indicated by the Constitutional Court in its June 2005 Recommendations, setting out the features of a mechanism balancing the rights of landlords and tenants and criteria for what might be considered a 'basic rent', 'economically justified rent' or 'decent profit'.[576] The Court decided in March 2011 to close its special procedure for dealing with systemic or structural human rights violations which had been applied to these 'rent-control' cases. The Court was satisfied that Poland has changed its laws and procedures such that landlords

---

[573]   *Broniowski v. Poland*, *supra* n. 571, para. 194.
[574]   ECtHR Press Release 31 August 2004.
[575]   ECtHR Press Release 16 October 2008.
[576]   *Hutten-Czapska v. Poland*, ECtHR (GC) 19 June 2006, appl. no.35014/97, para. 239.

could now: recover the maintenance costs for their property; include in the rent charged a gradual return for capital investment and make a 'decent profit'; and, have a reasonable chance of receiving compensation for past violations of their property rights.[577] In the case of *Suljagić v. Bosnia and Herzegovina*, the Court noted that the case concerned a systemic problem, namely the shortcomings of the repayment scheme for foreign currency deposited before the dissolution of the SFRY. This problem lay behind more than 1,350 similar applications currently pending before the Court.[578] In November 2010, having concluded that the matter had been resolved, the Court closed the pilot-judgment procedure in question.[579] The pilot-judgment procedure, which the Court decided to apply to the case of *Maria Atanasiu and Others v. Romania*, was designed to assist the member states in fulfilling their role in the Convention system by resolving structural problems speedily at national level. That entailed an assessment by the Court extending beyond the case of the individual applicant, in the interests of other potentially affected persons. The Court decided that general measures should be put in place, within 18 months from the date on which the judgment became final, to secure effective and rapid protection of the right to restitution. Pending the introduction of those measures, the Court adjourned the examination of all applications stemming from the same problem.[580] In April 2012 the Romanian Government requested that the time-limit be extended by nine months. In June 2012, the Court decided to grant the request and deferred the deadline until 12 April 2013. A further one-month extension of the time-limit was granted to the Romanian Government in April 2013. On 16 May 2013, the Romanian Parliament passed a law on finalisation of the process of physical restitution or alternative compensation in respect of immovable property that wrongly passed into state ownership during the communist regime.[581] In the case of *Manushaqe Puto and others v. Albania,* the Court recalled, as it had stated in previous similar cases, that the violations it had found originated in a widespread problem affecting a large number of people. It noted with concern that it had found those violations despite having indicated in its previous judgments in 2007, 2009 and 2011 that Albania take general measures to remedy the problem. There were 80 similar cases pending before the Court. The Court in particular urged the authorities, as a matter of priority, to start making use of other alternative forms of compensation as provided for by Albanian legislation in 2004, instead of relying heavily on financial compensation. It was important

---

[577]   ECtHR Press Release No. 284, 31 March 2011.

[578]   *Suljagić v. Bosnia and Herzegovina*, ECtHR 3 November 2009, appl. no. 27912/02, para. 63.

[579]   *Zadric v. Bosnia and Herzegovina*, ECtHR 16 November 2010 (dec.), appl. no. 18804/04.

[580]   *Maria Atanasiu and Others v. Romania*, ECtHR 12 October 2010, appl. nos. 30767/05 and 33800/06, paras. 210–212.

[581]   ECtHR Press Release 099, 3 April 2013.

to set realistic, statutory and binding time-limits in respect of every step of the compensation process.[582] The Court adjourned proceedings concerning all new applications lodged with it after the delivery of the present judgment in which the applicants raised arguable complaints relating solely to the prolonged nonenforcement of final property decisions for the execution of which the State was responsible, including applications in which complaints alleging a lack of effective remedies in respect of such non-enforcement were also raised. The adjournment was effective for a period of 18 months after the judgment became final. The applicants in such cases were informed accordingly. The Court decided, however, to follow a different course in respect of applications lodged before the delivery of the judgment. Proceedings in respect of all registered cases were not adjourned. They continued to be examined after the judgment became final, without prejudice to the Court's power at any moment to declare inadmissible any such case or to strike it out of its list following a friendly settlement between the parties or the resolution of the matter by other means in accordance with Articles 37 or 39 ECHR or Rule 62A of the Rules of Court.[583]

A number of cases concerned the excessive length of proceedings and lack of domestic remedy.[584] From 1959 to 2009, the Court had delivered judgments in more than 40 cases against Germany finding repetitive violations of the ECHR on account of the excessive length of civil proceedings. In 2009 alone, 13 such violations of the reasonable time requirement of Article 6(1) had been found. In another judgment, delivered in 2006, the Court had already pointed out the lack of an effective remedy against excessively long court proceedings and drawn the German Government's attention to its obligation to select, subject to supervision by the Committee of Ministers, the general measures to be adopted to put an end to the violation found by the Court and to redress so far as possible the effects.[585] The Court requested the introduction of, at the latest within one year from the date on which the judgment became final, an effective domestic remedy capable of affording redress for excessively long court proceedings before the administrative courts.[586] The Court accepted that the Remedy Act had been enacted to address the issue of excessive length of domestic proceedings in an effective manner, taking account of ECHR requirements. In particular, compensation was to be determined with regard to the individual circumstances of the case, the length of the protraction and the significance of its consequences

---

[582] *Manushaqe Puto and Others v. Albania*, ECtHR 31 July 2012, appl. nos. 604/07, 43628/07, 46684/07 and 34770/09, para. 102.

[583] *Ibid.*, paras. 120–121.

[584] See, e.g., *Athanasiou and Others v. Greece*, ECtHR 21 December 2010, appl. no. 50973/08; *Dimitrov and Hamanov v. Bulgaria*, ECtHR 10 May 2011, appl. nos. 48059/06 and 2708/09; *Finger v. Bulgaria*, ECtHR 10 May 2011, appl. no. 37346/05.

[585] *Rumpf v. Germany*, ECtHR 2 September 2010, appl. no. 46344/06, para. 64.

[586] *Ibid.*, para. 72.

for the applicant. Finally, compensation was to be awarded irrespective of an establishment of fault.[587] In the case of *Ümmühan Kaplan v. Turkey*, the Court noted that the violation of the applicant's rights arose out of a structural problem in Turkey. As of 31 December 2011, over 2,700 applications stemming from the same issue had been pending before it (of which 2,373 had not been communicated to the Turkish Government and 330 had been communicated). Against that background, the Court decided to apply the pilot-judgment procedure, in view of the growing number of applicants and potential judgments finding a violation.[588] Following the pilot-judgment procedure applied in this judgment, the Turkish Grand National Assembly enacted a law on the settlement – by a compensation award – of 'length of proceedings' applications not yet communicated to the Turkish Government and lodged with the Court before 23 September 2012.[589]

The case of *Greens and M.T. v. the United Kingdom*, concerned the legislation in the United Kingdom which imposes a blanket ban on voting for convicted prisoners in detention. The Court observed that the United Kingdom had still not amended its legislation five years after the *Hirst (No. 2) v. the United Kingdom* judgment of 6 October 2005. The Court had received 2,500 similar applications. Applying its pilot-judgment procedure, the Court has given the United Kingdom Government six months from the date when *Greens and M.T.* becomes final to introduce legislative proposals to bring the disputed law/s in line with the Convention. The Government is further required to enact the relevant legislation within any time frame decided by the Committee of Ministers, the executive arm of the Council of Europe, which supervises the execution of the Court's judgments. The Court has also decided that it will not examine any comparable cases pending new legislation and proposes to strike out all such registered cases once legislation has been introduced.[590] In the case of *Scoppola v. Italy (No. 3)*,[591] the Court has confirmed *Hirst (No. 2) v. the United Kingdom*,[592] again holding that general, automatic and indiscriminate disenfranchisement of all serving prisoners, irrespective of the nature or gravity of their offences, is incompatible with Article 3 of Protocol No. 1. However, it accepted the United Kingdom Government's argument that each state has a wide discretion as to how it regulates the ban, both as regards the types of offence that should result in the loss of the vote and as

---

[587] *Taron v. Germany and Garcia Cancio v. Germany*, ECtHR 1 June 2012 (dec.), appl. nos. 53126/09 and 19488/09.

[588] *Ümmühan Kaplan v. Turkey*, ECtHR 20 March 2012, appl. no. 24240/07.

[589] *Müdür Turgut and Others v. Turkey*, ECtHR 26 March 2013 (dec.), appl. no. 4860/09; *Demiroğlu and Others v. Turkey*, ECtHR 14 June 2013 (dec.), appl. no. 56125/10.

[590] *Greens and M.T. v. the United Kingdom*, ECtHR 23 November 2010, appl. nos. 60041/08 and 60054/08, paras. 120–122.

[591] *Scoppola v. Italy (No. 3)*, ECtHR (GC) 22 May 2012, appl. no. 126/05.

[592] *Hirst v. the United Kingdom (No. 2)*, ECtHR (GC) 6 October 2005, appl. no. 74025/01.

to whether disenfranchisement should be ordered by a judge in an individual case or should result from general application of a law. The consideration of the approximately 2,000 pending cases against the United Kingdom was further adjourned until, at the latest, 30 September 2013. On 24 September 2013, the Court decided not to further adjourn its proceedings in the 2,281 pending applications and to process them in due course.[593]

In the case of *Kurić and Others v. Slovenia*, concerned applicants who belonged to a group of persons known as the 'erased', who on 26 February 1992 lost their status as permanent residents following Slovenia's declaration of independence in 1991, and faced almost 20 years of extreme hardship. The number of 'erased' people in 1991 amounted to 25,671. The Court held in particular that, despite the efforts made since 1999, the Slovenian authorities had failed to remedy comprehensively and with the requisite promptness the grave consequences for the applicants of the erasure of their names from the Slovenian Register of Permanent Residents. The Court also decided to apply the pilot-judgment procedure, holding that the Government should, within one year, set up a compensation scheme for the 'erased' in Slovenia. It decided it would adjourn examination of all similar applications in the meantime.[594] In its judgment on just satisfaction in this case the Court decided the question of pecuniary damage. It held, unanimously, that the Slovenian Government was to pay the six applicants whose rights under the Convention had been violated amounts between EUR 29,400 and EUR 72,770 each.[595]

The case of *Ananyev and Others v. Russia* concerned the applicants' complaints that they had been detained in inhuman and degrading conditions in remand centres awaiting criminal trials against them. Under Article 46, the Court held that the Russian Government had to: improve the material conditions of detention, by shielding the toilets in cells, removing thick netting from cell windows and increasing the frequency of showers; change the applicable legal framework, as well as practices and attitudes; ensure that pre-trial detention is only used in absolutely necessary cases; establish maximum capacity for each remand prison; and, ensure that victims can complain effectively about inadequate conditions of detention and that they obtain appropriate compensation. And to produce, in co-operation with the Council of Europe Committee of Ministers, within six months from the date on which the judgment became final, a binding time frame for implementing preventive and compensatory measures in respect of the allegations of violations of Article 3 ECHR.[596] The case of *Torreggiani and Others v. Italy* concerned the issue of overcrowding in Italian prisons. This structural problem has now been acknowledged at national level.

---

[593]   ECtHR Press Release 24 September 2013.
[594]   *Kurić and Others v. Slovenia*, ECtHR (GC) 26 June 2012, appl. no. 26828/06.
[595]   *Kurić and Others v. Slovenia*, ECtHR (GC) 12 March 2014, appl. no. 26828/06.
[596]   *Ananyev and Others v. Russia*, ECtHR 10 January 2012, appl. nos. 42525/07 and 60800/08.

The Court called on the authorities to put in place, within one year, a remedy or combination of remedies providing redress in respect of violations of the ECHR resulting from overcrowding in prison. The Court decided to apply the pilot-judgment procedure in view of the growing number of persons potentially concerned in Italy and of the judgments finding a violation liable to result from the applications in question.[597] Following the application of the pilot-judgment procedure, the Italian State enacted a number of legislative measures aimed at resolving the structural problem of overcrowding in prisons, reformed the law to allow detained persons to complain to a judicial authority about the material conditions of detention and introduced a compensatory remedy providing for damages to be paid to persons who had been subjected to detention contrary to the European Convention on Human Rights.[598]

A number of cases have concerned the recurring practice consistently highlighted by the Court since 2002 in more than 200 cases in which the Russian State failed to execute judgment debts. In this case, the applicant complained of the authorities' failure to execute domestic judgments awarding him social benefits. In the case of *Burdov v. Russia (No. 2),* the Court requested in particular, to set up, within six months from the date on which the judgment became final, an effective domestic remedy or combination of such remedies which would secure adequate and sufficient redress for non-enforcement or delayed enforcement of domestic judgments.[599] Following this pilot judgment, Russia passed two laws which came into force on 4 May 2010 and provided that an application could be made to the domestic courts for compensation for delayed enforcement of judgments delivered against the State and for the excessive length of judicial proceedings.[600] In the cases of *Ilyushkin and Others v. Russia and Kalinkin and Others v. Russia,* the Court considered that the new legislation did not resolve the problem of failure to enforce judgments ordering the provision of housing to members of the Russian armed forces. The Court noted with regret that there was still no remedy available in Russia by which to complain of such delays where the judicial decisions in question imposed obligations in kind on the Russian State. That problem, in the Court's view, remained unresolved despite the Compensation Act enacted in 2010 following the *Burdov (No. 2)* judgment. The Court therefore considered that an application before it continued to be the only means by which these applicants could assert their rights and obtain effective redress for the clear violations of their Convention rights.[601] In the case of *Olaru and Others v. the Republic of Moldova,*

---

[597] *Torreggiani and Others v. Italy,* ECtHR 8 January 2013, appl. no. 43517/09.
[598] ECHR, Press Release 007, 8 January 2013.
[599] *Burdov v. Russia (No. 2),* ECtHR 15 January 2009, appl. no. 33509/04.
[600] ECtHR Press Release 24, 15 January 2009.
[601] *Ilyushkin and Others v. Russia,* ECtHR 17 April 2012, appl. no. 5734/08: *Kalinkin and Others v. Russia,* ECtHR 17 April 2012, appl. no. 16967/10; *Gerasimov and Others v. Russia,* ECtHR 1 July 2014, appl. no. 29920/05, para. 190.

the Court noted that non-enforcement, particularly in social housing cases, was Moldova's prime problem in terms of the number of applications pending before the Court and reflected a persistent structural dysfunction and a practice that was incompatible with the Convention. It therefore decided to adopt a pilot-judgment procedure. Following its approach in *Burdov v. Russia (No. 2)*, it ruled that the State must, within six months of the Court's judgment in the applicants' case becoming final, set up an effective domestic remedy securing adequate and sufficient redress for the non-enforcement or delayed enforcement of final domestic judgments concerning social housing and, within one year, grant such redress to all victims in applications lodged before the delivery of its judgment. Proceedings in applications lodged after delivery would be adjourned for one year and applicants in such cases could be required to resubmit their grievances to the domestic authorities.[602]

The recurring practice is consistently highlighted by the Court since 2004 in more than 300 cases in which Ukraine failed to honour judgment debts. In the case of *Yuriy Nikolayevich Ivanov v. Ukraine*, an army veteran complained of the prolonged non-enforcement of judgments ordering the authorities to pay him retirement payment arrears. The Court had requested in particular, the introduction, within one year from the date on which the judgment became final, one or more effective remedies capable of affording adequate and sufficient redress for non-enforcement or delayed enforcement of domestic judgments.[603] Having stayed its examination of more than 2,000 similar applications pending before it, the Court noted on 21 February 2012 that, although a number of cases had been dealt with, Ukraine had not adopted the required general measures to solve the issues of non-enforcement at domestic level. Accordingly, the Court decided to resume the examination of applications raising similar issues.[604]

5. AWARD OF COMPENSATION – ARTICLE 41

5.1. INTRODUCTION

When the Court finds that a violation of ECHR by a Contracting State has taken place, under Article 41 it may afford just satisfaction to the injured party, provided that the consequences of the violation cannot be fully repaired according to the internal law of the state concerned. The initiative for having the claim for just satisfaction determined lies with the original applicant as

---

[602] *Olaru and Others v. the Republic of Moldova*, ECtHR 28 July 2009, appl. nos. 476/07. 22539/05, 17911/08; see also *Balan v. the Republic of Moldova*, ECtHR 10 February 2012 (dec.), appl. no. 44746/08.

[603] *Yuriy Nikolayevich Ivanov v. Ukraine*, ECtHR 15 October 2009, appl. no. 40450/04.

[604] ECtHR Press Release 29 February 2012.

the injured person.[605] According to Rule 75(1) of the Rules of the Court, where the Chamber finds that there has been a violation ECHR or the Protocols thereto, it gives in the same judgment a ruling on the application of Article 41 ECHR if that question, after being raised in accordance with Rule 60 of the Rules of Court, is ready for decision; if the question is not ready for decision, the Chamber reserves it in whole or in part and fixes the further procedure. In that case, and also in the case that the claim by the applicant is brought after the judgment on the merits, the Chamber which rules on the application of Article 41 will, as far as possible, be composed of those judges who sat to consider the merits of the case. Where it is not possible to constitute the original Chamber, the President of the Court completes or composes the Chamber by drawing lots (Rule 75(2) of the Rules of Court). This would seem appropriate from the viewpoint of procedural economy. These judges are best informed of the different aspects of the case, and for that reason most competent to determine the amount of compensation to be awarded, if any. Any claim which the applicant Contracting Party or the applicant may wish to make for just satisfaction under Article 41 ECHR must, unless the President of the Chamber directs otherwise, be set out in the written observations on the merits or, if no such written observations are filed, in a special document filed no later than two months after the decision declaring the application admissible. Thus, in the *Nasri* case, despite several reminders, counsel for the applicant did not file any claims for just satisfaction. The Court, for its part, saw no ground for examining this question of its own motion.[606]

The Court specifies in its judgment the period, usually three months, within which the specified sum must have been paid to the individual.[607] And in accordance with Rule 75(3) of the Rules of Court the Chamber may, when affording just satisfaction under Article 41 ECHR, direct that if settlement is not made within a specified time, interest is to be payable on any sums awarded. It is subsequently up to the Committee of Ministers under Article 54 to determine if the specified sum has been paid within the time-limit set by the Court.

The Court will award financial compensation under Article 41 only where it is satisfied that the loss or damage complained of was actually caused by the violation it has found, since the state cannot be required to pay damages in respect of losses for which it is not responsible.[608]

---

[605] See Rule 60 Rules of Court.

[606] *Nasri v. France*, ECtHR 13 July 1995, appl. no. 19465/92, para. 49; *Schöps v. Germany*, ECtHR 13 February 2001, appl. no. 25116/94, para. 57.

[607] See, e.g., *Moreira de Azevedo v. Portugal*, ECtHR 28 August 1991, appl. no. 11296/84; *Platakou v. Greece*, ECtHR 11 January 2001, appl. no. 38460/97; *Västberga Taxi Aktiebolag and Vulic v. Sweden*, ECtHR 23 July 2002 appl. no. 36985/97.

[608] *Kingsley v. United Kingdom, supra* n. 555, para. 40; *Muñoz Díaz v. Spain*, ECtHR 8 December 2009, appl. no. 49151/07, para. 85; *Vilnes and Others v. Norway*, ECtHR 5 December 2013, appl. nos 52806/09 and 22703/10, para. 269.

In the case of *Cyprus v. Turkey*, the Court considered that bearing in mind the specific nature of Article 41 in relation to the general rules and principles of international law, the Court could not interpret that provision in such a narrow and restrictive way as to exclude inter-state applications from its scope. The overall logic of Article 41 ECHR was not substantially different from the logic of reparations in public international law. Accordingly, the Court considered that Article 41 did, as such, apply to inter-state cases. However, according to the very nature of the ECHR, it was the individual and not the state who was directly or indirectly harmed and primarily 'injured' by a violation of one or several Convention rights. If just satisfaction was afforded in an inter-state case, it always had to be done for the benefit of individual victims.[609]

5.2. NON-INDEPENDENCE OF COMPENSATION PROCEDURE

From the Court's case law it becomes clear that an application for compensation on the basis of Article 41 is not considered as an independent procedure, but is dealt with as an element of a larger whole, of which the examination of the merits forms the first part. In the '*Vagrancy*' cases the Court stated that the application for compensation is closely linked to the proceedings concerning the merits before the Court, and cannot therefore be regarded as a new complaint, to which Articles 34 and 35 ECHR apply. For that reason, the original applicant did not need to exhaust once more the local remedies with respect to his application for compensation.[610] In the *Barberà, Messegué and Jabardo* case, the Court noted that there existed under Spanish law a remedy making it possible to obtain compensation in the event of the malfunctioning of the system of justice. However, referring to the aforementioned '*Vagrancy*' cases, it did not consider itself bound to stay the proceedings relating to the applicants' claims.[611]

In the *Anguelova* case, the Bulgarian Government argued that, since Article 362 §1 (4) of the Bulgarian Code of Criminal Procedure provided for the possibility of reopening criminal proceedings in cases where the European Court of Human Rights had found a violation of the Convention the applicant

---

[609] *Cyprus v. Turkey, supra* n. 391, paras. 39–47.

[610] *De Wilde, Ooms and Versyp v. Belgium ('Vagrancy' Cases), supra* n. 96, para. 20. See also *Guzzardi v. Italy, supra* n. 152, para. 113; *Rotaru v. Romania*, ECtHR (GC) 4 May 2000, appl. no. 28341/95, para. 83; *Ilijkov v. Bulgaria*, ECtHR 21 July 2001, appl. no. 33977/96, para. 123; *Anguelova v. Bulgaria*, ECtHR 13 June 2002, appl. no. 38361/97, para. 172.

[611] *Barberà, Messegué and Jabardo v. Spain*, ECtHR 13 June 1994, appl. nos. 10588/83 10589/83 10590/83, para. 17; *Berktay v. Turkey*, ECtHR 1 March 2001, appl. no. 22493/93, para. 215; *Bykov v. Russia*, ECtHR (GC) 10 March 2009, appl. no. 4378/02, para.110; *E.R. and Others v. Turkey, supra* n. 266, para. 118.

should, if the Court found a violation in the present case, submit a civil claim for damages once the criminal proceedings were reopened. The Court noted that the provision of the Code of Criminal Procedure referred to by the Government concerned the reopening of criminal proceedings which were ended by a judicial decision, whereas the investigation in the applicant's case was terminated by a decision of the prosecuting authorities. It was, therefore, unclear whether the Code of Criminal Procedure required the reopening of the investigation after the Court's findings in the present case. Furthermore, the Court held that Article 41 ECHR does not require applicants to exhaust domestic remedies a second time in order to obtain just satisfaction if they have already done so in vain in respect of their substantive complaints. In this connection, the Court considered that the hypothetical possibility that the investigation might be resumed, many years after the death of the applicant's son in police custody and after the first ineffective investigation, and that the applicant might then have the opportunity to bring a civil claim, which would only be successful if the fresh investigation produced results, could not reasonably be interpreted as *restitutio in integrum* under domestic law.[612] In the case of *Mikheyev v. Russia*, the Court considered that the fact that the applicant may still receive an award in respect of pecuniary damage under the domestic legal proceedings did not deprive him of his right to claim compensation under Article 41. The Court may examine this issue even if domestic proceedings of a similar nature are still pending; any other interpretation of Article 41 would make this provision ineffective.[613]

5.3. NON-READINESS FOR DECISION

Article 41 appears to imply that the decision on an award of compensation must be given together with the judgment on the merits. Rule 75 of the Rules of Court, however, leaves the moment of the decision on an award of compensation entirely open. If the Chamber of the Court which deals with the case finds that there is a violation of the ECHR, the Chamber gives a decision on the application of Article 41 in the same judgment only if the question, after having been raised under Rule 75, is ready for decision. As an example, reference could be made to the judgment in the *Golder* case, in which the Court, after having found that there had been a violation of Article 6(1) and Article 8, decided that in the circumstances of the case it was not necessary to afford to the applicant any just satisfaction other than that resulting from the finding of a violation

---

[612]   *Anguelova v. Bulgaria, supra* n. 612, para. 172.
[613]   *Mikheyev v. Russia*, ECtHR 26 January 2006, appl. no. 77617/01, para. 155.

of his rights.[614] The majority of the decisions concerning Article 41 are made simultaneously with the judgment on the merits.

If the question of compensation has been raised, but is not yet ready for decision, the Chamber reserves it in whole or in part and fixes the ensuing procedure. If the question of the compensation has not been raised, the Chamber lays down a time-limit within which this may be done by the original applicant.[615] Thus the possibilities for raising the question of compensation have been left as wide as possible. At the same time, the interests of the respondent states are served in this way because, as the Court formulated it: 'they may be reluctant to argue the consequences of a violation the existence of which they dispute and they may wish, in the event of a finding of a violation, to maintain the possibility of settling the issue of reparation directly with the injured party without the Court being further concerned.'[616]

In a number of cases the applicants complained that as a consequence of the length of domestic proceedings they were deprived of the enjoyment of their property, thereby relying on Article 1 of Protocol No. 1. Since the Court already found a violation of Article 6(1), it did not find it necessary to examine the complaint based on Article 1 of Protocol No. 1. Nevertheless, in the *Brigandi* case, where the applicant had sought compensation for loss of enjoyment, the Court found that the measures already taken by the national courts – which included compensation for loss of enjoyment – had not made full reparation for the consequences of the breach found. The Court therefore awarded the applicant a specified sum on an equitable basis.[617] In the *Zanghì* case, the applicant had only claimed compensation in respect of damage resulting from the alleged violation of Article 1 of Protocol No. 1. In its judgment of the same day as that in the *Brigandi* case and concerning the same respondent State and in connection with the same type of violation, the Court observed that it was still possible that the national courts before which the applicant's action remained pending, might make reparation for the final consequences of the failure to try the case within a reasonable time. Therefore, as matters stood, it dismissed the applicant's claim for compensation of damage.[618] After having obtained a final domestic decision, Mr Zanghì again requested compensation for the financial consequences of the failure to try the case within a reasonable time. The Court decided to re-enter the case on its list. This means that the dismissal of the claim for just satisfaction 'as the matter stood' in the Court's earlier judgment was only provisional. It also means, by implication, that the applicant was not

---

[614]   *Golder v. United Kingdom*, ECtHR (GC) 21 February 1975, appl. no. 4451/70, para. 46; *Morris v. United Kingdom*, ECtHR 26 February 2002, appl. no. 38784/97, para. 98; *Niederböster v. Germany*, ECtHR 27 February 2003, appl. no. 39547/98, para. 49.

[615]   See, e.g., *König v. Germany*, ECtHR 28 June 1978, appl. no. 39753/73, para. 140.

[616]   *Ringeisen v. Austria*, ECtHR 22 June 1972, appl. no. 2614/65, para. 18.

[617]   *Brigandi v. Italy*, ECtHR 19 February 1991, appl. no. 1146/85, para. 33.

[618]   *Ibid.*, para. 9.

estopped, because he relied the first time, in support of his claim, on Article 1 of Protocol No. 1 and not on Article 6 ECHR. The Court found, however, that, as it held it unnecessary to rule on the complaint based on Article 1 of Protocol No. 1, the financial consequences of an infringement of the applicant's right to the peaceful enjoyment of his possessions could not be taken into consideration. As to the consequences of the breach of Article 6(1) ECHR, which was found by the Court on 19 February 1991, it noted at the time, even though no claim for just satisfaction had been made under that head, that it was still possible that the national courts might make reparation for them. The final domestic decision, in the opinion of the Court, was not of such a nature as to call for a reconsideration of the decision delivered on 19 February 1991.[619] Thus for the second time, and this time finally, the applicant's claim for compensation was dismissed. In its final judgment, the Court did not it make clear, in which way and to what extent the final domestic decision compensated the applicant in respect of the alleged violation of Article 6, nor did it indicate how its final judgment in the *Zanghi* case was to be reconciled with that in the *Brigandi* case.

In the *Vogt* case, the Court was of the opinion, that the question of reparation was not ready for decision. It was accordingly necessary to reserve it and to fix the further procedure, account being taken of the possibility of an agreement between the respondent State and the applicant.[620] In the *Papamichalopoulos* case, the Court invited the Government and the applicants to submit, within two months, the names and positions of experts chosen by agreement for the purpose of valuing the disputed land and to inform it, within eight months from the expiry of that period, of any friendly settlement that they might reach before the valuation.[621]

5.4. SUPERVISION BY THE COURT OF AGREEMENT ON COMPENSATION

Even if an agreement is reached between the injured party and the state found to be liable of a violation, the Court is still involved in the matter. In fact, according to Rule 75(4) of its Rules of Court, the Court will have to verify the equitable nature of such agreement and, when it finds the agreement to be equitable, will strike the case off the list by means of a judgment. Such a supervision of the equitable nature of the agreement on compensation was exercised by the Court

---

[619] *Zanghi v. Italy,* ECtHR 10 February 1993, appl. no. 11491/85, para. 8.

[620] *Vogt v. Germany,* ECtHR 26 February 1995, appl. no. 17851/91, para. 74. See also *Carbonara and Ventura v. Italy,* ECtHR 30 May 2000, appl. no. 24638/94, para. 79; *Scordino v. Italy (No. 3),* ECtHR 6 March 2007, appl. no. 43662/98, para.18; *Guiso-Gallisay v. Italy* (Just satisfaction), ECtHR (GC) 22 December 2009, appl. no. 58858/00, para. 101.

[621] *Papamichalopoulos and Others v. Greece,* ECtHR 31 October 1995, appl. no. 14556/89, para. 3.

in, for example, the *Luedicke, Belkacem and Koç* case,[622] the *Airey* case,[623] the *Malone* case,[624] the *Kostovski* case[625] and the *Katikaridis* case.[626]

In the *Winterwerp* case, the judgment under Article 41 consisted in the unanimous decision of the Court to strike the case off the list. The reason for this was that meanwhile an arrangement had been made between the Netherlands Government and Winterwerp, which agreement was judged for its equitable nature by the Court.[627]

Sometimes the agreement concerns only a part of the claim of the applicant and the Court has to decide about the rest of the claim. Thus, in the *Barthold* case, the settlement only concerned the claims for fees and expenses and for loss of earnings.[628] The Court took note of this agreement and considered it appropriate to strike the case off the list as far as those claims were concerned.

5.5. *RESTITUTIO IN INTEGRUM*

As to the merits of the procedure for compensation under Article 41, it is the passage 'if the internal law of the said Party allows only partial reparation to be made for the consequences of this decision or measure' which has particularly caused problems.

In the *'Vagrancy'* cases, the Belgian Government submitted that the application for compensation was ill-founded, because under Belgian law compensation could be obtained from the State for damage caused by an unlawful situation for which the State was responsible under national or international law. Those who claimed compensation before the Court therefore ought to have applied first to the national court.[629] The Court held that the treaties from which the text of Article 41 has been derived, undoubtedly related in particular to cases where the nature of the injury would make it possible to wipe out entirely the consequences of a violation but where the internal law of the state involved precludes this being done. However, according to the Court, this did not alter the fact that Article 41 is also applicable to cases in which such a *restitutio in integrum* is not possible precisely on account of the nature of the injury concerned.[630] The Court added the following: 'indeed, common sense

---

[622]   *Luedicke, Belkacem and Koç v. Germany*, ECtHR 10 March 1980, appl. nos. 6210/73 6877/75 7132/75, para. 13.

[623]   *Airey v. Ireland*, ECtHR 6 February 1981, appl. no. 6289/73, para. 10.

[624]   *Malone v. United Kingdom*, ECtHR 26 April 1985, appl. no. 8691/79, para. 9.

[625]   *Kostovski v. the Netherlands*, ECtHR 29 March 1990, appl. no. 11454/85, para. 7.

[626]   *Katikaridis v. Greece*, ECtHR 31 March 1998, appl. no. 19385/92, para. 11.

[627]   *Winterwerp v. the Netherlands*, ECtHR 27 November 1981 appl. no. 6301/73.

[628]   *Barthold v. Germany*, ECtHR 31 January 1986, appl. no. 8734/79, para. 9.

[629]   *De Wilde, Ooms and Versyp v. Belgium ('Vagrancy' Cases)*, supra n. 96, para. 15.

[630]   *Ibid.*, para. 20. See in this respect a.o. *Papamichalopoulos and Others v. Greece*, supra n. 623, para. 34; *Brumărescu v. Romania*, ECtHR 23 January 2001, appl. no. 28342/95, para. 20; *Agrokompleks v. Ukraine*, ECtHR 25 July 2013, appl. no. 23465/03, para. 75.

suggests that this must be so *a fortiori*.[631] The Court distinguished here between those cases in which, considering the nature of the injury, *restitutio in integrum* is possible and those in which it is not, and considered it has jurisdiction in both cases; in the first case, however, only when such *restitutio in integrum* is precluded under national law. Thus, in the '*Vagrancy*' cases, which according to the Court belonged to the second category, the Court declared that it had jurisdiction to award compensation. It held, however, that the applicants' claims for damages were not well-founded. Although in this case the decision not to grant compensation was taken unanimously, there were considerable differences of opinion within the Court on the argument described above.

In its judgment in the '*Vagrancy*' cases as well as in the subsequent *Ringeisen* case the Court did take into account the fact that the Belgian and the Austrian Government, respectively, had refused compensation to the applicant.[632] But in the '*Vagrancy*' cases it immediately added: 'The mere fact that the applicants could have brought and could still bring their claims for damages before a Belgian Court does not therefore require the Court to dismiss their claims as being ill-founded any more than it raises an obstacle to their admissibility.'[633]

In the *Ringeisen* case, the Court was even more explicit. The necessity to apply Article 41 exists 'once a respondent government refuses the applicant reparation to which he considers he is entitled'.[634]

In the *Barberà, Messegué and Jabardo* case, the Spanish Government submitted that the Court's principal judgment[635] had been executed in Spain in the fullest possible manner. The Constitutional Court's judgment quashing the convictions and ordering that the proceedings in the *Audiencia Nacional* be reopened, represented an innovation for the Spanish legal system, under which previously the finding of a violation by the European Court of Human Rights could not constitute a ground for reopening proceedings. In the subsequent proceedings all the guarantees laid down in Article 6 had been scrupulously complied with and they therefore afforded the most complete *restitutio in integrum* that could be obtained from the point of view of Article 41. However, the Court observed that it could not speculate as to what the outcome of the proceedings would have been had the violation of the ECHR not occurred. At any rate, the applicants were kept in prison as a direct consequence of the trial found by the Court to be in violation ECHR. There was thus, in the opinion of the Court, a clear causal connection between the damage claimed by the

---

631 *De Wilde, Ooms and Versyp v. Belgium ('Vagrancy' Cases), supra* n. 96, para. 20.
632 *Ringeisen v. Austria*, ECtHR 10 March 1972, appl. no. 2614/65, para. 16.
633 *Ibid.*, para. 20.
634 *Ibid.*
635 *Barberà, Messegué and Jabardo v. Spain, supra* n. 613, para. 2, where the Court found a violation of Art. 6(1) based above all on 'the fact that very important pieces of evidence were not adequately adduced and discussed at the trial in the applicants' presence and under the watchful eye of the public'.

applicants and the violation of the ECHR. In the nature of things the subsequent release and acquittal of the applicants could not in themselves afford *restitutio in integrum* or complete reparation for damage derived from their detention.[636] Accordingly, the Court considered that the question to be decided was the level of just satisfaction, in respect of both past and future pecuniary loss, which it was necessary to award to each applicant, the matter to be determined by the Court at its discretion, having regard to what was equitable.[637]

In the *Papamichalopoulos* case, the Court found a violation on the basis of an irregular *de facto* expropriation (occupation of land by the Greek Navy since 1967) which had lasted more than 25 years by the date of the principal judgment of 24 June 1993. In its judgment on just satisfaction, the Court held: 'the unlawfulness of such a dispossession inevitably affects the criteria to be used for determining the reparation owed by the respondent State, since the pecuniary consequences of a lawful expropriation cannot be assimilated to those of an unlawful dispossession.'[638]

Consequently, the Court ordered the Greek State to pay the applicants 'for damage and loss of enjoyment since the authorities took the possession of the land in 1967, the current value of the land, increased by the appreciation brought about by the existence' of certain buildings which had been erected on the land since the occupation, as well as the construction costs of those buildings.[639] In the *Iatridis* case, the applicant owned a cinema but did not own the land on which the cinema that he ran was situated. The ownership of the cinema site has been a matter of dispute between the lessors of the cinema and the State since 1953, and this dispute had still not been resolved by the date of adoption of this judgment. In its principal judgment in the case the Court held that 'on 23 October 1989 the Athens Court of First Instance heard the case under summary procedure and quashed the eviction order on the grounds that the conditions for issuing it had not been satisfied. No appeal lay against that decision. From that moment on, the applicant's eviction thus ceased to have any legal basis and Ilioupolis Town Council became an unlawful occupier and should have returned the cinema to the applicant, as was indeed recommended by all the bodies from whom the Minister of Finance sought an opinion, namely the Ministry of Finance, the State Legal Council and the State Lands Authority.'[640]

Consequently, the Court considered that the manifest unlawfulness under Greek law of the interference complained of would justify awarding the applicant full compensation. Nothing short of returning the use of the cinema to the

---

[636]   *Barberà, Messegué and Jabardo v. Spain*, *supra* n. 613, para. 17.
[637]   *Idem.* In the same sense *Smith and Grady v. United Kingdom*, ECtHR 25 July 2000, appl. nos. 33985/96 33986/96, paras. 18–19.
[638]   *Papamichalopoulos and Others v. Greece*, ECtHR 31 October 1995, appl. no. 14556/89, para. 36; *Guiso-Gallisay v. Italy*, *supra* n. 622, para. 98.
[639]   *Ibid.*, para. 39. See also the judgment of 10 June 2003, *Serghides,* appl. no. 31515/04 para. 23.
[640]   *Iatridis v. Greece*, *supra* n. 259, para. 61.

applicant would put him, as far as possible, in a situation equivalent to the one in which he would have found himself had there not been a breach of Article 1 of Protocol No. 1. The Court pointed out that the applicant did not own the land on which the cinema that he ran was situated. He rented that land from a third party, under a lease valid until 30 November 2002. The issue of the ownership of the land was at the material time the subject of proceedings in the national courts. In all the circumstances, the Court considered that the applicant should be awarded only compensation that would cover loss of the earnings that he could have derived from running the cinema until the end of the current lease (30 November 2002).[641]

In the principal judgment in the case of the *Former King of Greece*, the Court held that the interference in question satisfied the requirement of lawfulness and was not arbitrary. The act of the Greek Government which the Court held to be contrary to the Convention was an expropriation that would have been legitimate but for the failure to pay any compensation. The lawfulness of such a dispossession inevitably affects the criteria to be used for determining the reparation owed by the respondent State, since the pecuniary consequences of a lawful taking cannot be assimilated to those of an unlawful dispossession. In this connection, the Court noted that international case law, of courts or arbitration tribunals, gave the Court valuable guidance; although that case law concerned more particularly the expropriation of industrial and commercial undertakings, the principles identified in that field were valid for situations such as the one in the instant case. In the *Amoco International Finance Corporation* Case, the Iran-United States Claims Tribunal stated, referring to the judgment of the Permanent Court of International Justice in the *Case Concerning the Factory at Chorzów*, that 'a clear distinction must be made between lawful and unlawful expropriations, since the rules applicable to the compensation to be paid by the expropriating State differ according to the legal characterisation of the taking.' (Amoco International Finance Corporation v. Iran, Interlocutory Award of 14 July 1987, Iran–U.S. Claims Tribunal Reports (1987–II), §192).[642]

In view of the above, the Court was of the opinion that in the present case the nature of the breach found in the principal judgment did not allow the Court to proceed on the basis of the principle of *restitutio in integrum*. That said, the Government was of course free to decide on its own initiative to return all or part of the properties to the applicants. In conclusion, the Court held that, unless the Government would decide on its own initiative to return the properties to the applicants, it deemed it appropriate to fix a lump sum based,

---

[641]   *Iatridis v. Greece* (Art. 41), *supra* n. 150, para. 37; *Guiso-Gallisay v. Italy*, *supra* n. 622, para. 105; *Vriani and Others v. Albania*, ECtHR 7 December 2010, appl. nos. 35720/04 and 42832/06, para. 27; *De Luca v. Italy* ECtHR 24 September 2013, appl. no. 43870/04, para. 80; *Vistiņš and Perepjolkins v. Latvia*, *supra* n. 406, para. 33.

[642]   *Former King of Greece v. Greece*, ECtHR (GC) 28 November 2002, appl. no. 25701/4, paras. 74–75; *Vistiņš and Perepjolkins v. Latvia*, *supra* n. 406, para. 36.

as far as possible, on an amount 'reasonably related' to the value of the property taken, i.e. an amount which the Court would have found acceptable under Article 1 of Protocol No. 1, had the Greek State compensated the applicants. In determining this amount the Court took into account the claims of each applicant, the question of the movable property, the valuations submitted by the parties and the possible options for calculating the pecuniary damage, as well as the lapse of time between the dispossession and the present judgment. The Court considered that in the unique circumstances of the present case recourse to equitable considerations was particularly called for.[643] Restitution of the land not being possible, the Court awarded for pecuniary damage sums that took into consideration the current value of the land in relation to the property market on the date that its judgment was delivered. In addition, it sought to compensate losses that would not be covered by payment of that amount, by taking account of the potential of the land in question, calculated, where appropriate, on the basis of the construction costs of the buildings erected by the State.[644] In the case of *Kozacıoğlu v. Turkey*, the Court held that in determining the appropriate amount of compensation, the Court must have regard to the general criteria laid down in its case law concerning Article 1 of Protocol No. 1. This provision says that he taking of property without payment of an amount reasonably related to its value will normally constitute a disproportionate interference under Article 1 of Protocol No. 1. In addition, it had just found that legitimate 'public interest' aims, such as those pursued by measures for the conservation of a country's historical or cultural heritage, may call for less than reimbursement of the full market value of the expropriated properties. Nevertheless, the Court considered that the level of compensation must take into account the value arising from the expropriated building's specific features.[645] In the case of *Guiso-Gallisay v. Italy*, the Court was of the opinion that the particular features of the *Papamichalopoulos* case made it inappropriate to apply the principles laid down in it to cases of constructive expropriation. While acknowledging that the applicants were entitled to receive the full value of the property, the Court considered, on the one hand, that the date to be taken into consideration in assessing the pecuniary damage should not be that on which the Court's judgment was delivered, but the date on which they lost ownership of the land. The former approach could in fact open the door to a margin of uncertainty or even arbitrary decisions. At the same time, the Court considered that automatically assessing the losses sustained by the applicants as the equivalent of the gross value of the buildings erected by the State could not be justified. Such a method could lead to disparities in the treatment of applicants, depending

---

[643] *Idem*, para. 79.
[644] *Scordino v. Italy (No. 1)*, ECtHR (GC) 29 March 2006, appl. no. 36813/97, paras. 250–254; *Pasculli v. Italy (Just satisfaction)*, ECtHR 14 December 2007, appl. no. 36818/97, para. 34; *Guiso-Gallisay v. Italy*, *supra* n. 622, para. 100; *Kurić v. Slovinia*, *supra* n. 597, para. 80.
[645] *Kozacıoğlu v. Turkey*, *supra* n. 103, para. 82.

on the nature of the public works undertaken by the authorities, something that was not necessarily related to the land's original potential. In addition, such a compensation method would be to assign a punitive or dissuasive role to compensation for pecuniary damage *vis-à-vis* the respondent State, rather than a compensatory role *vis-à-vis* the applicants.[646] The Court pointed out that, in the event of unlawful dispossession of property, the compensation ought to reflect the idea of a total elimination of the consequences of the impugned interference. It noted that the nature of the violation found in the principal judgment enabled it to work from the principle of *restitutio in integrum* and that, specifically, restitution of the impugned land, including the existing buildings, would have placed the applicants in the closest situation to that in which they would have found themselves had there not been a breach of the requirements of Article 1 of Protocol No. 1. The Court decided that, where restitution was impossible, the State was to pay the applicants a sum corresponding to the current value of the land, increased by an amount reflecting the appreciation brought about by the existence of buildings.[647] In the case of *Vrioni and Others v. Albania*, the Court noted that *restitutio in integrum* could not be effected in view of the findings of the domestic courts. It was for this reason that the domestic courts ordered compensation to be paid to the applicants in accordance with the Property Act. The Court could not accept the respondent State's proposal to apply the method of calculation of pecuniary damage as adopted by the Grand Chamber of the Court in the case of *Guiso-Gallisay*. Contrary to *Guiso-Gallisay*, the present case did not relate to such constructive expropriation. The Court noted that it was the failure to pay compensation and not the inherent unlawfulness of the taking of land, as in *Guiso-Gallisay*. The Court noted with interest that the authorities had adopted property valuation maps in respect of the entire territory of Albania. The reference price, as stated by the Government, reflected the real market value and was interest-and inflation-indexed at the time of adoption of the maps. The Court therefore based its findings for the calculation of pecuniary damage on the property valuation maps adopted in respect of the Tirana region in 2008. The Court rejected the applicants' claim for compensation for the damage resulting from the impossibility of using and enjoying the plot of land. It noted that the domestic courts' findings were clear as regards the applicants' entitlement to compensation in lieu of the restitution of land and the applicants could not interpret those judgments as giving rise to an expectation that they would lease the plot of land or construct a building on it.[648] In the case of *Vistiņš and Perepjolkins v. Latvia*, the Court observed that, prior to their expropriation, the plots of land had undergone three successive valuations: in 1994, in 1996 and in 1997. The first valuation, carried out when the

---

[646]   *Guiso-Gallisay v. Italy, supra* n. 622, para. 103; *Vrioni and Others v. Albania supra* n. 643, para. 34.

[647]   *Guiso-Gallisay v. Italy, supra* n. 622, para. 101.

[648]   *Vrioni and Others v. Albania, supra* n. 643, paras. 33–37.

land was acquired by donation, was never relied upon during the proceedings concerning expropriation and compensation. As to the third, it produced values that the Court found insufficient for the purposes of Article 1 of Protocol No. 1. According to the Government's explanations, which were not disputed by the applicants, the cadastral value of the real estate at the time was calculated according to purely urban-planning criteria and did not reflect its actual market value. Consequently, the Court did not find it appropriate to use it as the basis for calculating the pecuniary damage.[649]

5.6. MEASURES OF REDRESS

In several cases the Court has noted that it is well established that the principle underlying the provision of just satisfaction for a breach of the ECHR is that the applicant should as far as possible be put in the position he would have enjoyed had the proceedings complied with the Convention's requirements.[650]

The Court has indicated that, in the context of the execution of judgments in accordance with Article 46 ECHR, a judgment in which it finds a breach imposes on the respondent state a legal obligation under that provision to put an end to the breach and make reparation for its consequences in such a way as to restore as far as possible the situation existing before the breach. If, on the other hand, national law does not allow – or allows only partial – reparation to be made for the consequences of the breach, Article 41 empowers the Court to afford the injured party such satisfaction as appears to it to be appropriate. It follows, *inter alia*, that a judgment in which the Court finds a violation of the ECHR or its Protocols imposes on the respondent state a legal obligation not just to pay those concerned the sums awarded by way of just satisfaction, but also to choose, subject to supervision by the Committee of Ministers, the general and/ or, if appropriate, individual measures to be adopted in its domestic legal order to put an end to the violation found by the Court and to redress so far as possible the effects.[651] Furthermore, it follows from the Convention, and from Article 1 in particular, that in ratifying the Convention the Contracting States undertake to ensure that their domestic legislation is compatible with it. Consequently, it is for the respondent state to remove any obstacles in its domestic legal system that might prevent the applicant's situation from being adequately redressed.[652]

---

[649] *Vistiņš and Perepjolkins v. Latvia, supra* n. 406, para. 37.

[650] See, e.g., *Piersack v. Belgium*, ECtHR 1 October 1982, appl. no. 8692/79, para. 12; *Kingsley v. United Kingdom, supra* n. 555, para. 40; *Plotnikovy v. Russia*, ECtHR 24 February 2005, appl. no. 43833/02, para. 33; *Sace Elektrik Ticaret ve Sanayi A.Ş. v. Turkey*, ECtHR 22 October 2013, appl. no. 20577/05, para. 33.

[651] *Scozzari and Giunta v. Italy*, ECtHR (GC) 13 July 2000, appl. nos. 39221/98 41963/98, para. 249; para. 43; *Haase v. Germany*, ECtHR 8 April 2004, appl. no. 11057/02, para. 115.

[652] *Meastri v. Italy*, ECtHR 17 February 2004, appl. no. 39748/98, para. 47.

5.7. INJURED PARTY

The term 'injured party' is fairly clear in the Court's view. 'Injured party' is a synonym for 'victim' in Article 34, and as such may be considered 'the person directly affected by the failure to observe the Convention'.[653] This also includes legal persons.[654] From this it follows, for instance, that counsel for the applicant cannot bring his fee directly under the claim for reparation pursuant to Article 41, although it may after all form part of the reparation awarded to the applicant. In the *Belkacem* case, the applicant had received free legal aid with respect to the Strasbourg proceedings and had not stated that he owed his counsel any additional amount. When the latter nevertheless claimed a supplementary fee, the Court decided that a lawyer 'cannot rely on Article 50 to seek just satisfaction on his own account'.[655]

In the *Pakelli* case, counsel had not claimed an immediate payment of his fee because of the financial situation of his client. Reparation of costs for legal assistance was nevertheless awarded, because counsel had not waived his right to reparation of his costs (as the Government suggested). The Court noted that 'in a human rights case a lawyer will be acting in the general interest if he agrees to represent or assist a litigant even if the latter is not in a position to pay him immediately'[656] and brought the payment under the reparation.

In *X v. France*, the applicant had died during the proceedings before the Court. His parents, however, had expressed their wish to continue the proceedings. The Court decided that the parents were entitled to take his place. The applicant had claimed FRF 150,000 for non-pecuniary damage. The case concerned the length of compensation proceedings brought by a haemophiliac inflicted with the AIDS virus following a blood transfusion. The applicant had claimed that the length of proceedings had prevented him from obtaining the compensation which he had hoped for, and thus from being able to live independently and in better psychological conditions for the remaining period of his life. Without further observation the Court found that the applicant had sustained non-pecuniary damage and held that France was to pay the applicant's parents the entire sum sought.[657]

---

653 *The Sunday Times v. United Kingdom*, ECtHR 6 November 1980, appl. no. 6538/74, para. 13. See also *Gillow v. United Kingdom*, ECtHR 14 September 1987, appl. no. 9063/80, para. 23: 'Since this case relates to events and their consequences which were experienced by Mr and Mrs Gillow together, the Court considers it equitable that all sums awarded in this judgment should be paid to the survivor of them, Mrs Gillow.'

654 *Unión Alimentaria Sanders S.A v. Spain*, ECtHR 7 July 1989, appl. no. 11681/85, para. 45; *Société industrielle d'Entretien et de Service (SIESO) v. France*, ECtHR 19 March 2002, appl. no. 56198/00, paras. 18–24.

655 *Luedicke Belkacem and Koç, supra* n. 624, para. 15. See also *Artico v. Italy, supra* n. 203, para. 40; *Delta v. France* ECtHR 19 December 1990, appl. no. 11444/85, para. 47; *Former King of Greece v. Greece, supra* n. 644, para. 105.

656 *Pakelli v. Italy*, ECtHR 25 April 1983, appl. no. 8398/78, para. 47.

657 *X v. France, supra* n. 80, para. 54.

Frequently, the Court has been requested to award damages to the relatives of a person who was unlawfully killed by agents of the state or had disappeared and for whose disappearance the respondent state was held responsible.[658] In the *Kurt* case, the applicant maintained that both she and her son had been victims of specific violations of the ECHR as well as a practice of such violations. She requested the Court to award a total amount of GBP 70,000 which she justified as follows: GBP 30,000 for her son in respect of his disappearance and the absence of safeguards and effective investigative mechanisms in that regard; GBP 10,000 for herself to compensate for the suffering to which she had been subjected on account of her son's disappearance and the denial of an effective remedy with respect to his disappearance; and GBP 30,000 to compensate both of them on account of the fact that they were victims of a practice of 'disappearances' in South-East Turkey. The Court recalled that it had found the respondent State in breach of Article 5 in respect of the applicant's son. It considered that an award of compensation should be made in his favour having regard to the gravity of the breach in question. It awarded the sum of GBP 15,000, which amount was to be paid to the applicant and held by her for her son and his heirs. Moreover, given that the authorities had not assisted the applicant in her search for the truth about the whereabouts of her son, which had led it to find a breach of Articles 3 and 13 in her respect, the Court considered that an award of compensation was also justified in her favour. It accordingly awarded the applicant the sum of GBP 10,000.[659]

If the Court decides that there has been a violation of the ECHR, this does not mean that the next-of-kin will be automatically awarded compensation. First of all, there should be a causal link between the violation found and the damage alleged. Secondly, the alleged damage should be substantiated. In the *Ogur* case, the Court noted that, as regards pecuniary damage, the file contained no information on the applicant's son's income from his work as a night-watchman, the amount of financial assistance he gave the applicant, the composition of her family or any other relevant circumstances. That being so, the Court could not allow the compensation claim submitted under this head in accordance with Rule 60(2) of the Rules of Court.[660] In most of the cases only non-pecuniary damage was taken into consideration.[661] In the case of *McCann, Farrell and*

---

[658]   *McCann, Farrell and Savage v. United Kingdom,* ECtHR 27 September 1995, appl. no. 18984/91, para. 142; *Andronicou and Constantinou v. Cyprus,* ECtHR (GC) 9 October 1997, appl. no. 25052/94, para. 153; *Kaya v. Turkey,* ECtHR 19 February 1998, appl. no. 22729/93, para. 1; *Kurt v. Turkey supra* n. 205, para. 73; *Cakici v. Turkey, supra* n. 489, para. 8.

[659]   *Kurt v. Turkey, supra* n. 205, para. 321.

[660]   *Oğur v. Turkey,* ECtHR 20 May 1999, appl. no. 21594/93, para. 98; *Cakici v. Turkey, supra* n. 489, para. 127: *Vrountou v. Cyprus,* ECtHR 13 October 2015, appl. no. 33631/06, para. 95.

[661]   *Kaya v. Turkey, supra* n. 660, para. 122; *Oğur v. Turkey, supra* n. 662, para. 98.

Savage, the Court held in this respect that, having regard to the fact that the three terrorist suspects who were killed had been intending to plant a bomb in Gibraltar, the Court did not consider it appropriate to make an award under this head. It therefore dismissed the applicants' claim for damages.[662]

In the *Haase* case, the applicants claimed non-pecuniary damage on behalf of the children. The Court pointed out that in principle a person who is not entitled under domestic law to represent another may nevertheless, in certain circumstances, act before the Court in the name of the other person.[663]

The Court referred in this respect to the *Aksoy* case, where the pecuniary claims made by the applicant prior to his death for loss of earnings and medical expenses arising out of detention and torture were taken into account by the Court in making an award to the applicant's father who had continued the application.[664]

In the event of a conflict over a minor's interests between a natural parent and the person appointed by the authorities to act as the child's guardian, there is a danger that some of those interests will never be brought to the Court's attention and that the minor will be deprived of effective protection of his rights under the Convention. Consequently, even though the parents had been deprived of parental rights – indeed that was one of the causes of the dispute which they had referred to the Court – their standing sufficed to afford them the necessary power to apply to the Court on the children's behalf, too, in order to protect their interests.[665] In the case of *Fadeyeva v. Russia*, the Court noted that the applicant did not present any written agreement between her and her lawyers. However, this did not mean that such an agreement did not exist. Russian legislation provides that a contract on consulting services may be concluded in an oral form (Article 153 read in conjunction with Article 779 of the Civil Code of the Russian Federation), and nothing indicated that this was not the case in respect of the applicant and her representatives. In any event, the Government had not presented any argument to the contrary. Therefore, the lawyers' fees were recoverable under domestic law, and, from the standpoint of the ECHR, real. The fact that the applicant was not required to cover these fees in advance did not affect this conclusion.[666]

---

[662] *McCann, Farrell and Savage v. United Kingdom, supra* n. 666, para. 218; *Pitsayeva and Others v. Russia*, ECtHR 9 January 2014, appl. no. 53036/08, para. 539; *Jelić v. Croatia*, ECtHR 12 June 2014, appl. no. 57856/11, para. 125.

[663] *Haase v. Germany, supra* n. 653.

[664] *Aksoy v. Turkey, supra* n. 98, para. 113.

[665] *Tahsin Acar v. Turkey, supra* n. 472, para. 120.

[666] *Fadeyeva v. Russia*, ECtHR 9 June 2005, appl. no. 55723/00, para. 147; *Tsintsabadze v. Georgia*, ECtHR 15 February 2011, appl. no. 35403/06, para. 105; *Kakabadze and Others v. Georgia*, ECtHR 2 October 2012, appl. no. 1484/07, para. 108; *Jelić v. Croatia*, ECtHR 13 October 2014, appl. no. 57856/11, para. 125.

5.8. JUST SATISFACTION

As to the term 'just satisfaction', the formulation of Article 41 makes it plain in the first place that the Court has a certain discretion in determining it: 'as is borne out by the adjective "just" and the phrase "if necessary", the Court enjoys a certain discretion in the exercise of the power conferred by Article 41'.[667] Taking this as a point of departure, the Court strictly upholds that the only element qualifying for satisfaction is the injury due to the previously found violation of the ECHR. Injury which is connected therewith, but which in fact is due to other causes, does not qualify for satisfaction.[668] The Court therefore requires a causal link between the injury and the violation.[669] In the *Quaranta* case, the applicant had claimed compensation in respect of the main complaint, concerning the right to liberty under Article 5, whereas the Court had only found a violation in relation to one of the subsidiary complaints. The Court rejected the compensation claim for lack of causal link.[670] In cases where the Court finds a violation of the reasonable time requirement of Article 6, it usually does not find that there exists a causal link between the violation and the alleged damage.[671]

In the *Albert and Le Compte* case, the first claim concerned a request to the Court to direct the State to annul the disciplinary sanctions imposed on the applicants. The Court decided that, even when leaving aside the fact that the Court is not empowered to do this: 'the disciplinary sanctions, which were the outcome of proceedings found by the Court not to have complied with one of the rules of Article 6 (1) ECHR, cannot on that account alone be regarded as the consequences of that breach. As for the criminal sentence, there is no connection whatsoever between them and the violation (…) As for the applicant's second series of claims (…), the Court considers it proper to distinguish here, as in the Case of *Le Compte, Van Leuven and De Meyere* (…), between damage caused by a violation ECHR and the costs incurred by the applicant.'[672]

In the *Canea Catholic Church* case, the Court held that in holding that the applicant church had no capacity to take legal proceedings, the Court of

---

[667]   *Guzzardi v. Italy, supra* n. 152, para. 114.

[668]   *König v. Germany* ECtHR 10 March 1980, appl. no. 6273/73, para. 18; *Airey v. Ireland, supra* n. 625, para. 12.

[669]   *Benthem v. the Netherlands*, ECtHR 23 October 1985, appl. no. 8848/80, para. 46; *Bönisch v. Austria*, ECtHR 2 June 1986, appl. no. 8658/79, para. 11; *Cöeme v. Belgium*, ECtHR 22 June 2000, appl. nos. 32492/96 32547/96 32548/96, para. 155; *Meastri v. Italy, supra* n. 654, para. 47, para. 46.

[670]   *Quaranta v. Switzerland*, ECtHR 24 May 1991, appl. no. 12744/88, para. 43.

[671]   *Kutic v. Croatia*, ECtHR 1 March 2002, appl. no. 48778/99, para. 39; *Marques Francisco v. Portugal*, ECtHR 6 June 2002, appl. no. 47833/99, para. 27; *Mereu and S. Maria Navarrese S.R.L v. Italy*, ECtHR 13 June 2002, appl. no. 38594/97, para. 19.

[672]   *Albert and Le Compte v. Belgium*, ECtHR 24 October 1983, appl. no. 7299/75, 7496/76, para. 9. See on the said distinction also, e.g., *The Sunday Times v. United Kingdom, supra* n. 655, para. 16; *Le Compte, Van Leuven and De Meyere v. Belgium, supra* n. 307, para. 13; *Van Droogenbroeck v. Belgium*, ECtHR 25 April 1983, appl. no. 7906/77, para. 13.

Cassation did not only penalise the failure to comply with a simple formality necessary for the protection of public order, as the Government maintained. It also imposed a real restriction on the applicant church preventing it on this particular occasion and for the future from having any dispute relating to its property rights determined by the courts. Such a limitation impaired the very substance of the applicant church's 'right to a court' and therefore constituted a breach of Article 6(1) ECHR. Making its assessment on an equitable basis, the Court awarded the applicant church the whole of the sum sought for the pecuniary damage it sustained on account of its inability to take legal proceedings.[673] In the *Akdeniz* case, the Court held that a precise calculation of the sums necessary to make complete reparation in respect of the pecuniary losses suffered by an applicant may be prevented by the inherently uncertain character of the damage flowing from the violation. An award may still be made notwithstanding the large number of imponderables involved in the assessment of future losses, though the greater the lapse of time involved the more uncertain the link between the breach and the damage becomes. The question to be decided in such cases is the level of just satisfaction, in respect of either past and future pecuniary loss, which it is necessary to award to an applicant, the matter to be determined by the Court at its discretion, having regard to what is equitable.[674] In the case of *Varnava v. Turkey,* the Court observed that there was no express provision for non-pecuniary or moral damage. Evolving case by case, the Court's approach in awarding just satisfaction had distinguished situations where the applicant had suffered evident trauma, whether physical or psychological, pain and suffering, distress, anxiety, frustration, feelings of injustice or humiliation, prolonged uncertainty, disruption to life, or real loss of opportunity and those situations where the public vindication of the wrong suffered by the applicant, in a judgment binding on the Contracting State, was a powerful form of redress in itself. In many cases where a law, procedure or practice had been found to fall short of Convention standards this was enough to put matters right.[675] In some situations, however, the impact of the violation could be regarded as being of a nature and degree as to have impinged so significantly on the moral well-being of the applicant as to require something further. Such elements did not lend themselves to a process of calculation or precise quantification. Nor was it the Court's role to function akin to a domestic tort mechanism court in apportioning fault and compensatory damages between civil parties. Its guiding principle was equity, which above all involves flexibility and an objective consideration of what was just, fair and reasonable in all the circumstances of the case, including not only the position of the applicant but the overall context in which the breach occurred. Its non-pecuniary awards served to give

---

673   *Canea Catholic Church v. Greece*, ECtHR 16 December 1997, appl. no. 25528/94, para. 55.
674   *Akdeniz and Others v. Turkey*, ECtHR 31 May 2001, appl. no. 23954/94, paras. 128 and 130.
675   *Varnava v. Turkey, supra* n. 165, para. 222; *Cyprus v. Turkey, supra* n. 391, para. 56.

recognition to the fact that moral damage occurred as a result of a breach of a fundamental human right and reflect in the broadest of terms the severity of the damage; they were not, nor should they be, intended to give financial comfort or sympathetic enrichment at the expense of the Contracting Party concerned. It was therefore not the case that there were specific scales of damages that should be awarded in disappearance cases as the applicants had sought to deduce from the past cases involving disappearances in Russia and Turkey. Neither could the Court agree that the Chamber erred in taking into account the background of the case and the ongoing executions process before the Committee of Ministers. As the applicants' own submissions made plain, their principal concern was for the uncertainty to be brought to an end by the provision of information about what happened to their relatives so long ago.[676]

a. Relevant factors

The reparation under Article 41 is intended to place the applicant as far as possible in the position he would have been, had the violation of the ECHR not taken place.[677] Whether and to what extent satisfaction will be awarded by the Court depends on the circumstances of the case.

In the *Neumeister* case, there had been a violation of Article 5(3) and the Court awarded the applicant compensation, amounting to Austrian Sch. 30,000. An important factor in the determination of the amount was the degree to which the detention under remand had exceeded reasonable limits. In this case, however, there were a number of circumstances which induced the Court to decide that compensation for material injury was not necessary. Especially, the duration of the detention under remand counted towards the ultimately imposed imprisonment. For the remainder he had been granted a pardon. These factors also amply counterbalanced, in the Court's opinion, the moral injury which Neumeister had sustained. Even though this did not, according to the Court, constitute a genuine *restitutio in integrum*, it approached this very closely. The sum of money was therefore awarded to him as compensation for the damage he had incurred in the form of costs in the matter of legal assistance in his attempts to prevent the violation of the ECHR, subsequently to request the Commission and the Court to establish this violation, and finally to obtain compensation.[678]

In the *Guincho* case, the Court found a violation of the reasonable time requirement of Article 6(1), which stemmed from two periods of almost total inactivity on the part of the State. The resultant lapse of time, totalling more than two years, did not only 'reduce the effectiveness of the action brought, but it also placed the applicant in a state of uncertainty which still persists and in

---

[676] *Ibid.*, para. 225.
[677] *Piersack v. Belgium*, ECtHR 1 October 1982, appl. no. 8692/79, para. 12.
[678] *Neumeister v. Austria*, ECtHR 7 May 1974, appl. no. 1936/63, paras. 30–31.

such a position that even a final decision in his favour will not be able to provide compensation for the lost interest'. Accordingly, the Court awarded the applicant a compensation of 150,000 Escudos.[679]

Other factors can also play a part in the awarding of reparation of costs and expenses. In the *Airey* case, for instance, it seems to have been an important factor that the UK Government had already declared itself prepared before the proceedings started to award a given amount.[680] On the other hand, no compensation is awarded if the fees are borne by an insurance company, since in that case 'there is no prejudice capable of being the subject of a claim for restitution'.[681] The same argument applies, if the applicant has received free legal aid.[682] In the *Wassink* case, the applicant also sought a specified amount for the expenses and fees of the lawyer who represented him before the Commission and the Court. The Dutch Government argued that the applicant, who had received legal aid in Strasbourg, had not shown that he had to pay his lawyer additional fees whose reimbursement he was entitled to request. In the Court's view, the mere fact that the applicant was granted legal aid did not mean that he was not under an obligation to pay the fee note drawn up by his counsel and attached to the claim submitted under Article 41. In the absence of proof to the contrary, the Court must accept that the applicant was required to pay his lawyer the amount set out in the fee note, from which the sums received from the Council of Europe were to be deducted.[683] The fact that an applicant has accepted an out-of-court settlement does not exclude the award of compensation. In the *Silva Pontes* case, where the applicant had concluded an agreement with the defendant private party, the Court held that the agreement concerned the consequences of a road accident and not those, for which the State could be held responsible, flowing from the failure to comply with the reasonable time requirement. The Court, therefore, awarded the applicant a specified sum for pecuniary and non-pecuniary damage.[684]

The Court also takes into consideration, whether the finding of a violation has effects beyond the confines of a particular case. The respondent state is then under the obligation to take the necessary measures in its domestic legal system to ensure the performance of its obligations under Article 46 ECHR.

---

[679] *Guincho v. Portugal*, ECtHR 10 July 1984, appl. no. 8990/80, paras. 29–30. See also, *inter alia*, *Campbell and Cosans v. United Kingdom*, ECtHR 25 February 1982, appl. nos. 7511/76, 7743/76, paras. 12–14 and *Gillow v. United Kingdom*, *supra* n. 655, para. 11.

[680] *Airey v. Ireland*, *supra* n. 625, para. 10.

[681] *Öztürk v. Germany*, ECtHR 23 October 1984, appl. no. 8544/79, para. 9.

[682] *Johnston and Others v. Ireland*, ECtHR 18 December 1986, appl. no. 9697/82, para. 86; *Baggetta v. Italy*, ECtHR 25 June 1987, appl. no. 10256/83, para. 28; *Feldbrugge v. the Netherlands*, ECtHR 27 July 1987, appl. no. 8562/79, para. 18.

[683] *Wassink v. the Netherlands*, ECtHR 27 September 1990, appl. no. 12535/86, para. 42. In the same sense, see *Koendjbiharie v. the Netherlands*, ECtHR 25 October 1990, appl. no. 11487/85, para. 35.

[684] *Silva Pontes v. Portugal*, ECtHR 23 March 1994, appl. no. 14940/89, para. 46.

Thus, in the *Norris* case, the Court took into account that Ireland had to take the necessary steps to ensure its obligations under Article 46. In this respect, the Court referred to the change in the law, which had been effected with regard to Northern Ireland in compliance with the Court's finding of a violation in the *Dudgeon* case. This lead the Court to the decision that its finding of a violation constituted adequate just satisfaction for the purposes of Article 41.[685] However, the Court held in the *Dudgeon* case that changes in the contested legislation or practice after finding of a violation cannot constitute *per se* just satisfaction in respect of facts that had occurred previously, although they may be taken into account for the award of non-pecuniary damage.[686] Moreover it may take several years before the respondent state has made the necessary changes. In fact, in Ireland it took almost four years before the Criminal Law (Sexual Offences) Act 1993 modified Irish Law to decriminalise consensual homosexual acts between adult males.[687] In the case of *S. L. v. Austria,* the Court noted that these judgments were given between 20 and 10 years previously. The Court considered it now appropriate to award just satisfaction for non-pecuniary damage in a case like the present one, even though the Criminal Code in this respect had recently been repealed and the applicant has therefore achieved in part the objective of his application. In fact, the Court attached weight to the fact that the applicant was prevented from entering into relations corresponding to his disposition until he reached the age of 18.[688]

A trend appears to have developed in the case law of the Court to the effect that injury pursuant to Article 41 can be made good as far as it was 'incurred by the applicants in order to try to prevent the violation found by the Court or to obtain redress therefore' and only if it fulfils specifically three criteria: costs and expenses susceptible of satisfaction must have been (1) 'actually incurred', (2) 'necessarily incurred' and (3) 'reasonable as to quantum'.[689] These criteria apply to costs described as material damage as well as to costs referable to proceedings.[690] In the case of *Dacia S.R.L. v. Moldova,* the Court was aware of the

---

[685] *Norris v. Ireland*, ECtHR 26 October 1988, appl. no. 10581/83, para. 50.

[686] *Dudgeon v. United Kingdom*, ECtHR 24 February 1983, appl. no. 7525/76, para. 14.

[687] D.J. Harris, M. O'Boyle and C. Warbrick, *Law of the European Convention on Human Rights*, London, 1995, p. 30.

[688] *S.L. v. Austria*, ECtHR 9 January 2003, appl. no. 45330/98, para. 52. See also *B.B. v. United Kingdom*, ECtHR 10 February 2004, appl. no. 53760/00, para. 34.

[689] *Le Compte, Van Leuven and De Meyere, supra* n. 307, para. 14; *Baranowski v. Poland*, ECtHR 28 March 2000, appl. no. 28358/95, para. 82; *Sabeur Ben Ali v. Malta*, ECtHR 29 June 2000, appl. no. 35892/97, para.49; *Ilijkov v. Bulgaria, supra* n. 612, para. 124; *I.J.L. and Others v. the United Kingdom*, ECtHR 25 September 2001, appl. nos. 29522/95, 30056/96 and 30574/96, para. 18; *Fleri Soler and Camilleri v. Malta*, ECtHR 17 July 2008, appl. no. 35349/05, para. 18; *Bykov v. Russia, supra* n. 613, para. 114; *Zammit and Attar Cassar v. Malta*, ECtHR 30 July 2015, appl. no. 1946/12, para. 75.

[690] See, e.g., *The Sunday Times v. United Kingdom, supra* n. 655, paras. 23–42; *Dudgeon v. United Kingdom supra* n 694, paras. 19–22; 43; *Punzelt v. Czech Republic*, ECtHR 25 April 2000, appl. no. 31315/98, para. 106; *Coëme v. Belgium* ECtHR, *supra* n. 671, para. 155; *Driza v. Albania*, ECtHR 13 November 2007, appl. no. 33771/02, para. 141.

---

difficulties in calculating lost profits in circumstances where such profits could fluctuate owing to a variety of unpredictable factors. However, it agreed with the applicant company that in the present case it was rather simple to determine the hotel's profits in a precise manner during the reference period, since it continued to operate without much change, except for the replacement of the owner and the administration in 2003. The failure to submit information regarding the actual profits made or losses incurred since 2003 was fully attributable to the respondent Government, which alone had access to it, and prevented the Court from verifying the applicant company's estimations. While the applicant company was eventually given access to the hotel's documents, the observations requested from the parties at that stage were expressly limited to the issue of the value of the hotel. The Court also considered that the applicant company's calculations ware not excessive, considering what it could have claimed based on the latest financial results of the hotel before its transfer to the State. In such circumstances, and considering the absence of any assistance from the Government in its task of calculating the lost profits owed to the applicant company, the latter's claims in this respect were accepted in full.[691] In the case of *Tebieti Mühafize Cemiyyeti and Israfilov v. Azerbaijan,* the Court noted with respect to the legal fees incurred in the Convention proceedings, that in the contract for legal services signed with his counsel, the work to be done by the lawyer was broken down into separate stages and the total amount of fees was broken down accordingly for each stage. Among others, the contract stipulated specific amounts to be paid for the lawyer's work in connection with 'submissions on friendly settlement', 'assistance in friendly-settlement negotiations' and 'participation in oral hearings'. As there had been no formal friendly-settlement proposals or oral hearings in the present case, the part of the total amount covering this portion of the claimed legal fees must be rejected. As for the remainder of the claim, the Court noted that, although the applicants had not yet actually paid the legal fees, they were bound to pay them pursuant to a contractual obligation to his counsel. Accordingly, insofar as his counsel was entitled to seek payment of his fees under the contract, the legal fees were 'actually incurred'.[692]

b. Costs of proceedings

Legal costs are only recoverable insofar as they relate to the violation found.[693] Concerning the domestic proceedings, the Court has held that according to its long-established practice, where an applicant has, in such proceedings, incurred

---

[691]   *Dacia S.R.L. v. Moldova,* ECtHR 24 February 2009, appl. no. 3052/04, para. 47.
[692]   *Tebieti Mühafize Cemiyyeti and Israfilov v. Azerbaijan,* ECtHR 8 October 2009, appl. no. 37803/03, para. 106; *L.H. v. Latvia* ECtHR 29 April 2014, appl. no. 52019/07, para. 69.
[693]   *Pham Hoang v. France,* ECtHR 25 September 1992 appl. no. 13191/87, para. 45; *Former King of Greece v. Greece, supra* n. 644, para. 105; *Serghides v. Poland,* ECtHR 10 June 2003, appl. no. 31515/04, para. 38.

costs as a direct result of seeking redress for, or to prevent a, breach of his or her rights, these may be regarded as a financial loss flowing from that breach and thus recoverable in Strasbourg proceedings, regardless of whether these could have been reimbursed at the domestic level.[694]

In the *Eckle* case, the Court extensively went into the matter of restitution of costs of proceedings. The Court held that an applicant is entitled to an award of costs and expenses under Article 41, when these costs are incurred in order to seek, through the domestic legal order, prevention or redress of a violation, to have the same established by the Commission and later by the Court, or to obtain reparation therefor, and when they 'were actually incurred, were necessarily incurred and were also reasonable as to quantum'. Considering, however, the proceedings in which the costs were incurred in this case, the claim for restitution of costs and expenses incurred in the proceedings before the Koblenz Court of Appeal was rejected.[695]

In relation to the claims for restitution of costs incurred in the 'review' procedure before the Regional Court of Trier, the Court considered that 'in view of his not having raised the issue of "reasonable time" himself the applicant cannot recover in full Mr von Stackelberg's fees and disbursements'.[696]

On the other hand, in the *Campbell and Fell* case,[697] the restitution of costs and expenses was made conditional on the degree to which the complaints were successful.

The costs made with respect to the Strasbourg proceedings must have been made with a view to establishing the violation of the ECHR by the Court. Just satisfaction may be afforded for costs incurred at all stages of the proceedings. The reimbursement may cover the costs and fees of the lawyer as well as travel and subsistence expenses. The Court will also take other costs, such as services of experts and photocopying and postal costs and translation fees, into consideration, as long as these costs are necessarily incurred. However, the applicant must seek the reimbursement of these costs himself, because according to the Court, this is not a matter which it has to examine of its own motion.[698] In the *Brogan* case, the applicants did not submit any claim for reimbursement of costs and expenses and the Court held that the question of the application of Article 41 was not ready for decision in relation to the claim for compensation for prejudice suffered.[699] When the Court had to deal with the question of

---

[694] *Associated Society of Locomotive Engineers & Firemen (ASLEF) v. the United Kingdom*, ECtHR 27 February 2007, appl. no. 11002/05, para. 59.

[695] *Eckle v. Germany*, ECtHR 21 June 1983, appl. no. 8130/78, para. 30.

[696] *Ibid.*, para. 28.

[697] *Campbell and Fell v. United Kingdom*, *supra* n. 204, para. 146. See also *Johnston v. Ireland*, *supra* n. 684, para. 86.

[698] *Huvig v. France*, ECtHR 24 April 1990, appl. no. 11105/84, para. 38; *Colacioppo v. Italy*, ECtHR 19 February 1991, appl. no. 13593/88, para. 16.

[699] *Brogan and Others v. United Kingdom* ECtHR 29 November 1988, appl. nos. 11209/84, 11234/84, 11266/84, para. 71.

compensation under Article 41, the applicants sought not only compensation for prejudice sustained but also for reimbursement of costs and expenses incurred before the Convention organs. However, the Court stated that it had held that in its principal judgment there was no call to examine the application of Article 50 (the present Article 41) in relation to reimbursement of any costs or expenses incurred. The Court referred to Article 52 [the present Article 42] according to which the earlier decision was final. Therefore, the Court could not entertain the applicants' subsequent claim in this respect.[700] In the *Akdivar* case, the applicants complained that notwithstanding the order in the principal judgment for costs to be paid in pounds sterling, the respondent Government had paid only part of the costs owed, in equal divisions, into bank accounts opened by the authorities on behalf of each of the applicants. The sums had been paid in Turkish lira some four months after the delivery of the principal judgment, on 13 January 1997. As a result, the applicants stated that there was a shortfall of GBP 5,681.89 as of 13 January 1997, which sum had accumulated 8 per cent interest since. The Court pointed out that by Article 53 [the present Article 46] ECHR the High Contracting Parties undertake to abide by the decision of the Court in any case to which they are parties. Furthermore, it considered that the issue of a shortfall in the payment of costs ordered in the principal judgment is a matter which concerns the proper execution of a judgment of the Court by the respondent state. Accordingly, it is a question which falls to be decided by the Committee of Ministers of the Council of Europe.[701]

In the case of *L. and V. v. Austria*, the applicants asserted that following the Court's judgment further costs had to be incurred in order to remove the consequences flowing from the violation of the ECHR. They argued in particular that – in case of a finding of a violation by the Court – they would be entitled, pursuant to Article 363a of the Code of Criminal Procedure, to have the criminal proceedings reopened in order to have their convictions set aside and to have them removed from their criminal records. The applicants therefore requested the Court to rule that the respondent State was obliged to pay any future costs necessary for removing the consequences of the violation at issue and to reserve the fixing of the exact amount to a separate decision. The Court considered that such a claim was speculative. The Court noted, in particular, that both applicants were sentenced to a prison term suspended on probation in 1997 and that the three-year probationary period had already expired. What remained was the entry of their convictions in their criminal records. In this situation it was open to doubt whether there would be any need for the applicants to have the criminal proceedings against them reopened, as the respondent State might well choose other means to have their convictions expunged. The respondent State might for instance decide to grant the applicants a pardon and have their convictions

---

[700] *Ibid.*, para. 7.
[701] *Akdivar v. Turkey, supra* n. 98, para. 59.

removed from their criminal records. Having regard to these circumstances, the Court dismissed the applicants' claim for future costs.[702]

c.   Other damages

What other kind of damage may be compensated in addition to direct costs of proceedings? In the *König* case, according to the Court, the extent to which the 'reasonable time' had been exceeded had left the applicant in prolonged uncertainty as to the possibilities of his career, which in the Court's opinion ought to be compensated in the form of DM 30,000 of damages.[703] In the *Goddi* case, the applicant maintained that, if he had had an opportunity of having his defence adequately presented, he would certainly have received a lighter sentence. The Court did not accept so categorical an allegation. However, it held that the outcome might possibly have been different if the applicant had had the benefit of a practical and effective defence and that, therefore, such a loss of real opportunities warranted the award of just satisfaction.[704] A similar reasoning was followed by the Court in the *Colozza* case, where it had found a violation of Article 6(1) ECHR, since the applicant was never heard in his presence by a 'tribunal' which was competent to determine all the aspects of the matter. The Court noted that an award of just satisfaction could only be based on the fact that the applicant had not had the benefit of the guarantees of Article 6 and awarded a just satisfaction to the applicant's widow for loss of real opportunities.[705] Reparation of loss of earnings is also possible,[706] as well as the repayment of fines and costs unjustly awarded against the applicant,[707] and reimbursement of the travel and subsistence expenses met by the applicant in attending the hearings before the Commission and the Court.[708] Reparation of immaterial damage can be awarded for suffered uncertainty,[709] feeling of unequal treatment,[710] unjust imprisonment[711] and feeling of frustration.[712]

---

[702]   *L. and V. v. Austria* ECtHR 9 January 2003, appl. nos. 39392/98, 39829/98, para. 68.

[703]   *König v. Germany, supra* n. 670, para. 19.

[704]   *Goddi v. Italy,* ECtHR 9 April 1984, appl. no. 8966/80, para. 35.

[705]   *Colozza v. Italy,* ECtHR 12 February 1985, appl. no. 9024/80, para. 38. See also *Bönisch v. Austria supra* n. 671, para. 13; *Lingens v. Austria,* ECtHR 8 July 1986, appl. no. 9815/82, para. 50; *Inze v. Austria,* ECtHR 28 October 1987, appl. no. 8695/79, para. 47.

[706]   *Unterpertinger v. Austria,* ECtHR 24 November 1986, appl. no. 9120/80, para. 35; *Berrehab v. the Netherlands,* ECtHR 21 June 1988, appl. no. 10730/84, para. 34, where, however, no reparation of loss of earnings was awarded because of the lack of a causal link.

[707]   *Deweer v. Belgium, supra* n. 198, para. 60; *Lingens v. Austria, supra* n. 707, para. 53.

[708]   *Corigliano v. Italy,* ECtHR 10 December 1982, appl. no. 8304/78, para. 53.

[709]   *Guincho v. Portugal, supra* n. 681, para. 44.

[710]   *Bönisch v. Austria, supra* n. 671, para. 11; *Lechner and Hess v. Austria,* ECtHR 23 April 1987, appl. no. 9316/81, para. 65; *Baraona v. Portugal,* ECtHR 8 July 1987, appl. no. 10092/82, para. 61.

[711]   *Unterpertinger v. Austria, supra* n. 708, para. 35.

[712]   *Keegan v. United Kingdom,* ECtHR 26 May 1994, appl. no. 16969/90, para. 68; *Papamichalopoulos and Others v. Greece, supra* n. 623, para. 36.

Several factors can play a part in the determination of the amount of such kinds of compensation. In the *Ringeisen* case,[713] the Court had found that there had been a violation of Article 5(3). The Court awarded the applicant a compensation of DM 20,000, and in fixing the amount of this sum, took into account the following factors. First, the fact that the detention under remand had exceeded reasonable limits by 22 months. Although the period of imprisonment to which he had ultimately been condemned was reduced by the duration of the detention under remand, he had always maintained that he was innocent, and on that account had undoubtedly felt so long a detention under remand as unjust. Secondly, the fact that his detention had been hard on him, since it had been impossible for him to undertake anything to avoid bankruptcy.

In the *Artico* case, the Court took three elements into consideration, *viz.* the imprisonment actually served, the additional imprisonment which the applicant had possibly incurred in consequence of the lack of effective legal aid, and the isolated position in which he had been placed as a result of this.[714]

In the *Sporrong and Lönnroth* case, the Court had found a violation of Article 1 of Protocol No. 1 ECHR. In order to decide whether or not the applicants had been prejudiced, the Court had to determine during which periods the continuation of the measures complained of had been in violation of Protocol No. 1, and then which constituent elements of damage warranted examination. The Court found it reasonable that a municipality should, after obtaining an expropriation permit, require some time to undertake and complete the planning needed to prepare the final decision on the expropriation contemplated. Whilst a comparison between the beginning and the end of the periods of damage did not show that the applicants were prejudiced in financial terms, the Court nevertheless did not conclude that there was no loss within that period. There were, in fact, other factors which also warranted attention. First, there were limitations on the utilisation of the properties. In addition, during the periods of damage the value of the properties in question fell. Furthermore, there were difficulties in obtaining loans, secured by way of mortgage. Above all, the applicants were left in prolonged uncertainty as they did not know what the fate of their properties would be. To these factors had to be added the non-pecuniary damage occasioned by the violation of Article 6(1) ECHR: the applicants' case could not be heard by a tribunal competent to determine all the aspects of the matter. The applicants thus suffered damage for which reparation

---

[713] *Ringeisen v. Austria, supra* n. 618, paras. 25–26. The Court did not exclude that a third factor – the deteriorated health due to the detention – could also have played a role, but Ringeisen had not advanced any evidence for that fact while from medical reports the contrary could be inferred.

[714] *Artico v. Italy, supra* n. 203, para. 48. See further *Eckle v. Germany, supra* n. 697, para. 14; and particularly *Sporrong and Lönnroth v. Sweden*, ECtHR 18 December 1984, appl. nos. 7151/75 7152/75, paras. 19–21.

was not provided by the withdrawal of the expropriation permits.[715] As regards claims for loss of earnings, the Court's case law establishes that there must be a clear causal connection between the damage claimed by the applicant and the violation of the ECHR and that this may, in the appropriate case, include compensation in respect of loss of earnings.[716]

In the *Bozano* case, the applicant claimed just satisfaction for the violation of Article 5(1) ECHR. The Court stated that the applicant's detention in France involved a serious breach of the ECHR, which inevitably caused him substantial non-pecuniary damage. With regard to his subsequent detention in Switzerland and Italy the Court found that it had no jurisdiction to review the compatibility of that detention with the Convention, since the Commission had either declared the applicant's complaints against those two States inadmissible or struck them off its list. Nonetheless, there was a need to have regard to the applicant's detention as it was prior to the enforcement of the deportation order. In the Court's view, the real damage was that sustained as a consequence of the process of enforcing the deportation order and of the unlawful and arbitrary deprivation of liberty.[717]

If the damage or the costs do not lend themselves to a process of calculation or the calculation presented to the Court is unreasonable, the Court fixes them on an equitable basis.[718] In the *Young, James and Webster* case, there was no dispute that all three applicants had incurred pecuniary and non-pecuniary losses and also liability for legal costs and expenses referable to the Strasbourg proceedings, but certain claims exceeded as to their quantum the sums offered by the UK Government during unsuccessful friendly-settlement negotiations.[719]

During the settlement negotiations, the UK Government offered to have the costs in question independently assessed or 'taxed' by a Taxing Master. In the opinion of the Court, this would have been a reasonable method of assessment. However, the applicants did not take up this offer. In these circumstances, the Court accepted the figure of GBP 65,000 offered by the Government in respect of all legal costs and expenses.[720]

A claim for compensation will be rejected, when there is nothing to suggest with reasonable certainty that without the violation the result would have been different.[721] Other possible reasons for rejection of reparation claims are: the

---

[715]   *Sporrong and Lönnroth v. Sweden supra* n. 716, para. 26.

[716]   *Barberà, Messegué and Jabardo v. Spain supra* n. 613, paras. 16–20; *Cakici v. Turkey, supra* n. 489, para. 127; *Tanli v. Turkey*, ECtHR 10 April 2001, appl. no. 26129/95, para. 181.

[717]   *Bozano v. Italy supra* n. 199, para. 9.

[718]   *Artico v. Italy, supra* n. 203, para. 48; *Young, James and Webster v. United Kingdom*, ECtHR 18 October 1982, appl. nos 7601/76 7806/77, para. 11; *Bönisch v. Austria, supra* n. 671, para. 11.

[719]   *Young, James and Webster v. United Kingdom*, ECtHR 18 October 1982, appl. nos. 7601/76, 7806/77, para. 11.

[720]   *Ibid.*, para. 12.

[721]   *De Wilde, Ooms and Versyp v. Belgium ('Vagrancy' Cases), supra* n. 96, para. 20; *Luberti v. Italy*, ECtHR 23 February 1984, appl. no. 9019/80, para. 40.

Court's finding that, by holding that the violation has occurred, its judgment has already furnished sufficient satisfaction for the purposes of Article 50;[722] the conclusion that the applicants did not suffer any damage;[723] the fact that the domestic court has imposed a sentence identical to that given before the judgment of the Court, but now after a trial attended by all the guarantees laid down by the Convention;[724] the circumstance that the applicant has adduced insufficient evidence or information in support of his claim;[725] or the Court's holding that the 'claims stem from matters in respect of which it has found no violation'.[726]

In the case of *Abdulaziz, Cabales and Balkandali*, the applicants sought 'substantial', but unquantified, compensation for non-pecuniary damage in the form of distress, humiliation and anxiety. They stated that the interference complained of concerned a vital element in society, namely family life; that sexual discrimination was universally condemned; and that the existence of a practice in breach of the ECHR was an aggravating factor. The Court held that by reason of its very nature, non-pecuniary damage of the kind alleged could not always be the object of concrete proof. However, it is reasonable to assume that persons who, like the applicants, find themselves faced with problems relating to the continuation or inception of their married life may suffer distress and anxiety. The Court, however, considered that in the circumstances of these cases its findings of violation of themselves constitute sufficient just satisfaction. The applicants' claim for monetary compensation could not therefore be accepted.[727]

In the case of *A.D.T. v. United Kingdom*, concerning a conviction for homosexual acts with a number of consenting adults, the Court awarded GBP 10,000 in respect of non-pecuniary damage.[728] In the *Smith and Grady* case, the applicants submitted that both the investigation of their sexual orientation and their consequent discharge from the armed forces on the sole ground of their homosexuality were profoundly degrading and humiliating events. Moreover, and as a result, they could not now pursue a career in a profession which they enjoyed and in which they excelled.[729] The Court recalled that, in its principal

---

[722] *Le Compte, Van Leuven and De Meyere v. Belgium, supra* n. 307, para. 12; *F. v. Switzerland*, ECtHR 18 December 1987, appl. no. 11329/85, para. 45; *Modinos v. Cyprus, supra* n. 452, para. 30.

[723] *Engel and Others v. the Netherlands*, ECtHR 23 November 1976, appl. nos. 5100/71, 5101/71 and 5102/71, para. 10.

[724] *Piersack v. Belgium, supra* n. 652, para. 15; *Windisch v. Austria*, ECtHR 28 June 1993, appl. no. 12489/86, para. 11.

[725] *Foti and Others v. Italy*, ECtHR 21 November 1983, appl. nos. 7604/76 7719/76 7781/77, para. 18; *Deumeland v. Germany*, ECtHR (GC) 29 May 1986, appl. no. 9384/81, para. 98; *Gillow v. United Kingdom, supra* n. 655, para. 14.

[726] *Johnston v. Ireland, supra* n. 684, para. 85.

[727] *Abdulaziz, Cabales and Balkandali v. United Kingdom*, ECtHR 28 May 1985, appl. nos. 9214/80 9473/81 9474/81, para. 96.

[728] *A.D.T. v. United Kingdom*, ECtHR 31 July 2000, appl. no. 35765/97, paras. 43–45.

[729] *Smith and Grady v. United Kingdom, supra* n. 639, para. 10.

judgment, it had found that both the investigations and consequent discharges constituted 'especially grave' interferences with the applicants' private lives for three reasons. In the first place, the Court considered that the investigation process was of an 'exceptionally intrusive character', noting that certain lines of questioning were 'particularly intrusive and offensive'. Secondly, the Court considered that the discharge of the applicants had a 'profound effect on their careers and prospects' and, thirdly, it found the absolute and general character of the policy striking, leading as it did to the discharge of the applicants on the ground of an innate personal characteristic irrespective of their conduct or service records. The principal judgment had also noted that the High Court, in its judgment delivered on 7 June 1995 in the domestic judicial review proceedings, had described the applicants' service records as 'exemplary' and had found that they had been 'devastated' by their discharge. Although not found to give rise to a violation of Article 3, these events were described in that context as having been 'undoubtedly distressing and humiliating for each of the applicants'. The Court considered it clear that the investigations and discharges described in the principal judgment were profoundly destabilising events in the applicants' lives which had and, it cannot be excluded, continue to have a significant emotional and psychological impact on each of them. The Court therefore awarded, on an equitable basis, GBP 19,000 to each applicant in compensation for non-pecuniary damage.[730] With respect to the pecuniary damages the Court referred to the *Vogt* case and recalled that one of the reasons why it considered Mrs Vogt's dismissal from her post as a schoolteacher to be a 'very severe measure', was the finding that schoolteachers in her situation would 'almost certainly be deprived of the opportunity to exercise the sole profession for which they have a calling, for which they have been trained and in which they have acquired skills and experience'.[731] In the present case, the Court was of the opinion that the significant differences between service and civilian life and qualifications, together with the emotional and psychological impact of the investigations and of the consequent discharges, rendered it difficult for the applicants to find civilian careers which were, and would continue to be, equivalent to their service careers. Both applicants had access to certain armed forces' resettlement services. However, the first applicant submitted that she was too psychologically affected by the events surrounding her discharge to take immediate and full advantage of those services. The second applicant did participate in a resettlement programme and he received a resettlement grant of GBP 5,583.[732] Moreover, the Court considered significant the loss to the applicants of the non-contributory service pension scheme. The lump sum and service pension which the first applicant would receive on retirement

---

[730] *Ibid.*, paras. 12–13.
[731] *Vogt v. Germany, supra* n. 622, para. 60.
[732] *Smith and Grady v. United Kingdom, supra* n. 639, para. 20.

were substantially less than the amounts she would have received had she not been discharged, even if she had not achieved her predicted promotions before retirement. The same held true, but to a lesser extent, for the second applicant. In such circumstances, and making its assessment on an equitable basis, the Court awarded compensation (inclusive of interest claimed) to the applicants in respect of past loss of earnings, for future loss of earnings and for the loss of the benefit of the non-contributory service pension scheme.[733]

In the *Davies* case, the Government contended that the applicant was not entitled to any compensation because he had not shown that he had suffered any stress or distress as a result of the violation. The Court observed that some forms of non-pecuniary damage, including emotional distress, by their very nature cannot always be the object of concrete proof. This did not prevent the Court from making an award if it considered that it was reasonable to assume that an applicant had suffered injury requiring financial compensation. It was reasonable to assume that the applicant suffered distress, anxiety and frustration exacerbated by the unreasonable length of the proceedings. The Court awarded the applicant EUR 4,500.[734]

In the *Stran Greek Refineries and Stratis Andreadis* case, the Court held that the adequacy of compensation might be diminished if it is paid without reference to various circumstances likely to reduce its value, such as the lapse of a considerable period of time.[735] In the *Guillemin* case, the Court took note of the excessive and continuing duration of the proceedings the applicant had brought to secure compensation for an expropriation which the Court of Cassation had held to be unlawful. The Court observed that since the principal judgment was given, the proceedings in the national courts, which were still pending, had deprived the applicant of the compensation to which she was entitled and would doubtless continue to deprive her of it, at least until the Court of Cassation would give judgment. The Court considered it appropriate, without prejudice to the amount that would finally be paid to the applicant at the end of the proceedings in the Court of Cassation, to award her compensation for the loss of availability of the sum already awarded in the judgment of the Evry *tribunal de grande instance* on 26 May 1997 that has been caused by the town council's refusal to comply with that judgment.[736]

The Court is rewarding damages, and even to large amounts, if this is justified by the case. In cases where the damage amount is not clearly established, the Court itself estimates the damage amount based on the evidence in the case. The Court's damage awards are made for violations under different provisions

---

[733] *Ibid.*, paras. 20–25.

[734] *Smith and Grady v. United Kingdom, supra* n. 639, para. 38. In the same sense, see *Peck v. United Kingdom*, ECtHR 28 January 2003, appl. no. 44647/98, para. 119.

[735] *Stran Greek Refineries and Stratis Andreadis v. Greece*, ECtHR 9 December 1998, *supra* n. 121, para. 82; *De Luca v. Italy*, ECtHR 24 September 2013, appl. no. 43870/04, para. 80.

[736] *Guillemin v. France*, ECtHR 2 September 1998, appl. no. 19632/92, paras. 24–25.

of ECTHR law, as every case has different circumstances in connection with the damage suffered and the violations committed. In the case of *Centro Europa 7 S.R.L. and Di Stefano v. Italy*, the Court awarded pecuniary damages of EUR 10 million plus EUR 100,000 for costs and expenses, to the company.[737]

In the *Selim Sadak* case, the applicants alleged that they had sustained pecuniary damage corresponding to what they would have earned as members of parliament had they not been forced to vacate their seats and the loss of earnings they endured as a result of the restrictions to their civic rights. The Court considered that, irrespective of the dissolution of the Democratic Party (DEP), because of the forfeiture of their parliamentary seats the applicants undoubtedly sustained pecuniary damage, which, however, could not be assessed with precision. To that must be added non-pecuniary damage, which the finding of a violation in this judgment was not sufficient to make good.[738]

In the *Teixeira de Castro* case, the applicant claimed, firstly, compensation for loss of earnings during the three years of his six-year sentence he spent in prison, on the ground that without the two police officers' intervention he would not have been convicted. He also requested compensation for loss of earnings because, when he came out of prison he had been dismissed and was unable to find another job as he was labelled a drug trafficker. Owing to the fact that he had been in prison and had consequently had no earnings, his wife and son had gone hungry and had known periods of intense anxiety. Since his conviction, their life had been a series of humiliations; he had lost friends and become estranged from members of his family. The Court held that the documents in the case file suggested that the term of imprisonment complained of would not have been imposed if the two police officers had not intervened. The loss by the applicant both of his earnings while he was deprived of his liberty and of opportunities when he came out of prison were actual and entitled him to an award of just satisfaction.[739] However, in cases of deprivation of liberty, too, compensation for pecuniary damages will not be given if there does not exist a causal link between the violation found and the claimed damages.[740]

d. No jurisdiction to impose certain measures

Repeatedly the Court has declared that it lacked jurisdiction to direct the States to take certain measures, for instance to abolish the violation found by the Court, etc. The Court notes regularly that it is left to the state concerned to

---

[737] *Centro Europa 7 S.R.L. and Di Stefano v. Italy*, ECtHR (GC) 7 June 2012, appl. no. 38433/09; *Anonymos Touristiki Etaira Xenodocheia Kritis v. Greece*, ECtHR 2 December 2010, appl. no. 35332/05; *Theodoraki and Others v. Greece*, ECrHR 2 December 2010, appl. no. 9368/06.

[738] *Selim Sadak v. Turkey (No. 2)*, ECtHR 11 June 2002, appl. no. 25144/94, para. 56.

[739] *Teixeira de Castro v. Portugal*, ECtHR 9 June 1998 appl. no. 25829/94, para. 49.

[740] *Yagmurdereli v. Turkey*, ECtHR 4 June 2002, appl. no. 29590/96, para. 69.

choose the means within its domestic legal system to give effect to its obligations under Article 53.[741]

In the *Corigliano* case, the Court declared the claim inadmissible to order the State to make certain articles of the Penal Code inapplicable to 'political and social trials'. This 'falls outside the scope of the case brought before the Court', according to the Court.[742] Also the request to publish a summary of the Court's judgment in local newspapers or the removal of any reference to the applicant's conviction in the central criminal records, falls outside the scope of the jurisdiction of the Court.[743]

In the *Bozano* case, the applicant had requested the Court to recommend the French Government to approach the Italian authorities through diplomatic channels, with a view to securing either a 'presidential pardon' – leading to his 'rapid release' – or a reopening of the criminal proceedings taken against him in Italy from 1971 to 1976. The Government argued that the Court did not have the power to take such a course of action. Furthermore, it maintained that it would in any case be unconnected with the subject matter of the dispute, since it would amount to recommending France to intervene in the enforcement of final decisions of the Italian courts. The Court did not go into these arguments. It merely pointed out that Mr Bozano's complaints against Italy were not in issue before it, as the Commission had declared them inadmissible.[744] One cannot escape the impression that the Court did not want to enter into the issue whether or not it had the power to make a recommendation as requested by the applicant. It might be argued that in cases where *restitutio in integrum* is impossible, as in the present case, the Court had nothing left than to award just satisfaction. However, what Mr Bozano in addition requested from the Court was only a *recommendation* and such a recommendation should, in general, not be deemed inappropriate, comparable as it would seem to be with the recommendation of provisional measures, for which there is also no express basis in the Convention.

In the *Akdivar* case, the applicants claimed, *inter alia*, compensation under this provision for the losses incurred as a result of the destruction of their houses by the security forces which forced them to abandon their village. They further submitted that the Court should confirm, as a necessary implication of an award of just satisfaction, that the Government should (1) bear the costs of necessary repairs in their village to enable the applicants to continue their way of life there; and (2) remove any obstacle preventing the applicants from returning to their village. The Court held that, if *restitutio in integrum* is in practice impossible,

---

[741] *Saïdi v. France*, ECtHR 20 September 1993, appl. no. 14647/89, para. 47; *Tolstoy Miloslavsky v. United Kingdom*, ECtHR 13 July 1995, appl. no. 18139/91, paras. 69–72; *Papamichalopoulos and Others v. Greece, supra* n. 623, para. 34; *Akdivar v. Turkey, supra* n. 98, para. 62.

[742] *Corigliano v. Italy, supra* n. 710, para. 51.

[743] *Manifattura FL v. Italy*, ECtHR 27 February 1992, appl. no. 12407/86, para. 26; *Castells v. Spain*, ECtHR 23 April 1992, appl. no. 11798/85, para. 54.

[744] *Bozano v. France, supra* n. 199, para. 65.

the respondent States are free to choose the means whereby they will comply with a judgment in which the Court has found a breach, and the Court will not make consequential orders or declaratory statements in this regard. It falls to the Committee of Ministers acting under Article 54 ECHR, to supervise compliance in this respect.[745]

In the *Papamichalopoulos* case, the Court held that 'the loss of all ability to dispose of the land in issue, taken together with the failure of the attempts made [up to then] to remedy the situation complained of, [had] entailed sufficiently serious consequences for the applicants de facto to have been expropriated in a manner incompatible with their right to the peaceful enjoyment of their possessions.'

The act of the Greek Government which the Court held to be contrary to the Convention, was not an expropriation that would have been legitimate but for the failure to pay fair compensation; it was a taking by the State of land belonging to private individuals, which has lasted 28 years, the authorities ignoring the decisions of national courts and their own promises to the applicants to redress the injustice committed in 1967 by the dictatorial regime.[746] Consequently, the Court considered that the return of the land in issue, – as defined in 1983 by the Athens second Expropriation Board – would put the applicants as far as possible in a situation equivalent to the one in which they would have been if there had not been a breach of Article 1 of Protocol No. 1; the award of the existing buildings would then fully compensate them for the consequences of the alleged loss of enjoyment. The Court held that if the respondent State did not make such restitution within six months from the delivery of this judgment, the Court held that it was to pay the applicants, for damage and loss of enjoyment since the authorities took possession of the land in 1967, the current value of the land, increased by the appreciation brought about by the existence of the buildings, and the construction costs of the latter.[747]

In the *Velikova* case, the applicant claimed FRF 100,000 in compensation for the pain and suffering resulting from violations of the ECHR. She asked for an order of the Court that this amount be paid directly to her in full, free of taxes or of any claim or attachment by the Government or by third persons. The applicant also requested the Court to order that there should be no negative consequences for her, such as reduction in social benefits due to her, as a result of the receipt of the above amount. The Court considered that the compensation fixed pursuant to Article 41 and due by virtue of a judgment of the Court should be exempted from attachment. It held, that it would be incongruous to award the applicant an amount in compensation for, *inter alia*, deprivation of life constituting a

---

[745] *Akdivar v. Turkey, supra* n. 98, para. 62; *Selçuk and Asker v. Turkey, supra* n. 222, para. 154; *Mentes and Others v. Turkey*, ECtHR 24 July 1998, appl. no. 23186/94, para. 423.

[746] *Papamichalopoulos and Others v. Greece, supra* n. 623, para. 45.

[747] *Ibid.*, paras. 38–40.

violation of Article 2, if the State itself were then allowed to attach this amount. The purpose of compensation for nonpecuniary damage would inevitably be frustrated and the Article 41 system perverted, if such a situation were to be deemed satisfactory. However, the Court held that it had no jurisdiction to make an order exempting compensation from attachment. It therefore left this point to the discretion of the Bulgarian authorities.[748]

Where the choice of measures is in practice theoretical, since it is constrained by the nature of the violation, the Court can itself directly require certain steps to be taken. To date, it has made use of this possibility on two occasions only. In the *Assanidze* case, the Court ordered the release of the applicant, who was being arbitrarily detained in breach of Article 5 ECHR. It held that as regards the measures which the Georgian State must take, subject to supervision by the Committee of Ministers, in order to put an end to the violation that had been found, its judgments are essentially declaratory in nature and that, in general, it is primarily for the state concerned to choose the means to be used in its domestic legal order in order to discharge its legal obligation under Article 46 ECHR, provided that such means are compatible with the conclusions set out in the Court's judgment. This discretion as to the manner of execution of a judgment reflects the freedom of choice attaching to the primary obligation of the Contracting States under the Convention to secure the rights and freedoms guaranteed. However, by its very nature, the violation found in the instant case did not leave any real choice as to the measures required to remedy it. In these conditions, having regard to the particular circumstances of the case and the urgent need to put an end to the violation of Article 5(1) and Article 6(1) ECHR, the Court considered that the respondent State must secure the applicant's release at the earliest possible date.[749] In the *Ilascu* case, the Court considered that any continuation of the unlawful and arbitrary detention of the three applicants would necessarily entail a serious prolongation of the violation of Article 5 found by the Court and a breach of the respondent States' obligation under Article 46(1) ECHR to abide by the Court's judgment. Regard being had to the grounds on which the respondent States had been found by the Court to be in violation of the ECHR, they must take every measure to put an end to the arbitrary detention of the applicants still detained and to secure their immediate release.[750]

In this respect, it should be noted that the Committee of Ministers in a Resolution has considered that the execution of judgments would be facilitated if the existence of a systemic problem is already identified in the judgment of the Court. Therefore, it invited the Court: 'I. as far as possible, to identify, in its judgments finding a violation ECHR, what it considers to be an underlying

---

[748]   *Velikova v. Bulgaria*, ECtHR 4 October 2000, appl. no. 41488/96, para. 99.
[749]   *Assanidze v Georgia*, *supra* n. 232, paras. 202–203.
[750]   *Ilascu and Others v. Moldova and Russia*, *supra* n. 82, para. 490.

systemic problem and the source of this problem, in particular when it is likely to give rise to numerous applications, so as to assist states in finding the appropriate solution and the Committee of Ministers in supervising the execution of judgments;

II. to specially notify any judgment containing indications of the existence of a systemic problem and of the source of this problem not only to the state concerned and to the Committee of Ministers, but also to the Parliamentary Assembly, to the Secretary General of the Council of Europe and to the Council of Europe Commissioner for Human Rights, and to highlight such judgments in an appropriate manner in the database of the Court.'[751]

In the Explanatory Report to Protocol No. 14 it is indicated that it would be useful if the Court and, as regards the supervision of the execution of judgments, the Committee of Ministers, adopt a special procedure so as to give priority treatment to judgments that identify a structural problem capable of generating a significant number of repetitive applications, with a view to securing speedy execution of the judgment.[752]

In virtue of Protocol No. 14, paragraphs 4 and 5 of Article 46 ECHR accordingly empower the Committee of Ministers to bring infringement proceedings in the Court (which will sit as a Grand Chamber), having first served the state concerned with notice to comply. The Committee of Ministers' decision to do so requires a qualified majority of two-thirds of the representatives entitled to sit on the Committee. This infringement procedure does not aim to reopen the question of violation, already decided in the Court's first judgment. Nor does it provide for payment of a financial penalty by a High Contracting Party found in violation of Article 46(1). It is felt that the political pressure exerted by proceedings for non-compliance in the Grand Chamber and by the latter's judgment should suffice to secure execution of the Court's initial judgment by the state concerned.[753]

6. REQUEST FOR INTERPRETATION OF A JUDGMENT

Rule 79 of the Rules of Court deals with the possibility to request to the Court the interpretation of a judgment. A party may request such an interpretation within one year following the delivery of the judgment. The request must state precisely the point or points in the operative provisions of the judgment on which interpretation is required. The original Chamber may decide of its own motion to refuse the request on the ground that there is no reason to warrant

---

[751] Committee of Ministers Resolution (2004)3 of 12 May 2004.
[752] *Explanatory Report to Protocol No. 14*, CETS 194, para. 16.
[753] *Ibid.*, para. 98.

considering it. Where it is not possible to constitute the original Chamber, the President of the Court will complete or compose the Chamber by drawing lots. If the Chamber does not refuse the request, the Registrar will communicate it to the other party or parties and will invite them to submit any written comments within a time-limit laid down by the President of the Chamber. The President of the Chamber will also fix the date of the hearing should the Chamber decide to hold one. The Chamber will decide by means of a judgment. A request for interpretation will be dealt with, according to Rule 102 of the Rules of Court, in proceedings largely resembling the normal proceedings before the Court.

At present (November 2016), the Court has decided on a request for interpretation on three occasions only. On 21 December 1972, on the basis of a letter from the original individual applicant, the Commission submitted to the Court a request for interpretation of the Court's second judgment in the *Ringeisen* case of 22 June 1972. By this judgment Ringeisen had been awarded a compensation of DM 20,000. The question whether this amount would have to be paid directly to Ringeisen or whether it might be claimed by the trustee in the bankruptcy of Ringeisen, had been left by the Court to the discretion of the Austrian Government. In this connection, however, the Court had referred to the Austrian legislation concerning compensation on account of detention under remand, which implied that no attachment or seizure may be made against such compensation. The money was, however, sent by the Austrian authorities on consignment to a judicial tribunal. The latter decided that upon request of the persons entitled to it or after a final judicial decision the money was to be paid. The Commission asked the Court what was meant by the order to pay compensation, in particular with respect to the currency and the place of the payment, and whether the term 'compensation' was to be understood as an amount that was exempt from any judicial claims under Austrian law, or on the contrary was subject to such claims. The Court replied that the compensation was to be paid in German Marks and was to be made payable in the Federal Republic of Germany. Further the Court ruled that the money was to be paid to Ringeisen personally, exempt from any claim or title to it. This ruling, therefore, implied disapproval of the position taken by the Austrian authorities. Austria had called into question the competence of the Court in the matter, stating that 'the competence of the (…) Court (…) for interpretation of its judgments (…) is based solely on the Rules of the Court. Therefore in the light of Article 52 of the (…) Convention, the well-founded question may even be raised whether this legal institution is compatible at all with the Convention.'

The Court pointed out that the sole purpose of Article 52 [the present Article 42] is to exclude appeal to another authority from decisions of the Court. It submitted that there is no question of appeal when the Court deals with a request for interpretation. In such a case the Court exercises inherent jurisdiction, because such a request concerns only elucidation of the purport and scope of a preceding judgment. Furthermore, the Court pointed out that Rule 56 (the present Rule 57) had been submitted to the Contracting States at the time of its adoption and that no objections had been raised against it by those States.[754]

In its judgment of 10 February 1995 in the *Allenet de Ribemont* case, the Court awarded the applicant under Article 50 an overall sum of FRF 2,000,000 for pecuniary and non-pecuniary damage, together with FRF 100,000 for costs and expenses. In response to the applicant's request for a ruling that France should guarantee him against any application for enforcement of a judgment delivered by the Paris *tribunal de grande instance* on 14 March 1979, the Court said that 'under Article 41 it does not have jurisdiction to issue such an order to a Contracting State'.[755] In July-August 1995, the applicant was informed that an attachment of the sums awarded to him by the Court had been effected at the request of the parties in whose favour the judgment of the Paris *tribunal de grande instance* had been given. Following a request from Mr Allenet de Ribemont, the Commission submitted to the Court a request for interpretation of the judgment of 10 February 1995. The request was worded as follows: '*Firstly*: Is it to be understood that Article 50 ECHR, which provides for an award of just satisfaction to the injured party if the domestic law of the High Contracting Party allows only partial reparation to be made for the consequences of the decision or measure held to be in conflict with the obligations arising from the Convention, means that any sum awarded under this head must be paid to the injured party personally and be exempt from attachment? *Secondly*: In respect of sums subject to legal claims under French law, should a distinction be made between the part of the sum awarded under the head of pecuniary damage and the part awarded under the head of non-pecuniary damage? and *Thirdly*: If so, what were the sums which the Court intended to grant the applicant in respect of pecuniary damage and non-pecuniary damage respectively?'

The Court observed, first, that when considering a request for interpretation, it is exercising inherent jurisdiction: it goes no further than to clarify the meaning and scope which it intended to give to a previous decision which issued from its own deliberations, specifying if need be what it thereby decided with binding force. The Court understood the first question put by the Commission as an invitation to interpret Article 50 in a general, abstract way. That, however, went outside not only the bounds laid down by Rule 57 of Rules of Court 'A' but also those of the Court's contentious jurisdiction under the Convention. At all events, the Court had not in the instant case ruled that any sum awarded to Mr Allenet de Ribemont was to be free from attachment. The applicant had asked the Court to hold that the State should guarantee him against any application for enforcement of the judgment delivered by the Paris *tribunal de grande instance* on 14 March 1979. In response, the Court had said that 'under Article 50 it does

---

[754] *Ringeisen v. Austria, supra* n. 618, paras. 12–15.
[755] *Allenet de Ribemont v. France*, ECtHR 10 February 1995, appl. no. 15175/89, para. 23.

not have jurisdiction to issue such an order to a Contracting State'. Accordingly, the question had been left to the national authorities acting under the relevant domestic law. In short, the Court had no jurisdiction to answer the first question put by the Commission. As to the Commission's second and third questions, the Court said that in its judgment of 10 February 1995 it had awarded the applicant FRF 2,000,000 'for damage' without distinguishing between pecuniary and non-pecuniary damage. In relation to the sum awarded, the Court had considered that it did not have to identify the proportions corresponding to pecuniary and non-pecuniary damage respectively. It was not bound to do so when affording 'just satisfaction' under Article 50 ECHR. In point of fact, it was often difficult, if not impossible, to make any such distinction. The Court held that the judgment it had delivered on 10 February 1995 was clear on the points in the operative provisions on which interpretation had been requested. To hold otherwise would not be to clarify 'the meaning and scope' of that judgment but rather to modify it in respect of an issue which the Court had decided with binding force. Accordingly, it was unnecessary to answer the Commission's second and third questions.[756]

In the case of *Hentrich*, the Court had ruled in its judgment of 3 July 1995 on just satisfaction, that the French Government should pay a specified amount of money. In her request for interpretation the applicant complained of the delay in paying the just satisfaction – payment being made on 1 December 1995 – and she claimed default interest on the sums awarded. This was not considered a matter for interpretation.[757]

Protocol No. 14 amended Article 46(3) to empower the Committee of Ministers to ask the Court to interpret a final judgment, for the purpose of facilitating the supervision of its execution. The Committee of Ministers' experience of supervising the execution of judgments shows that difficulties are sometimes encountered due to disagreement as to the interpretation of judgments. The Court's reply will settle any argument concerning a judgment's exact meaning. The qualified majority vote required by the last sentence of paragraph 3 shows that the Committee of Ministers should use this possibility sparingly, to avoid overburdening the Court.

No time-limit has been set for making requests for interpretation, since a question of interpretation may arise at any time during the Committee of Ministers' examination of the execution of a judgment. The Court is free to decide on the manner and form in which it wishes to reply to the request. Normally, it would be for the formation of the Court which delivered the original judgment to rule on the question of interpretation. More detailed rules governing this new procedure may be included in the Rules of Court.[758]

---

[756]   *Allenet de Ribemont v. France*, ECtHR (interpretation) 7 August 1996, appl. no. 15175/89, para. 23.

[757]   *Hentrich v. France* ECtHR (interpretation) 3 July 1997, appl. no. 13616/88, paras. 14–16.

[758]   Explanatory Report to Protocol No. 14, CETS 194, paras. 96–97.

7. REQUEST FOR REVISION OF A JUDGMENT

The competence of the Court to deal with requests for revision of its judgments is likewise not regulated by the Convention. Like the competence to give an interpretation of a judgment at the request of a party, the competence to revise a judgment may also be considered as inherent in the jurisdiction of the Court. The procedure to be followed in connection with a request for revision is also to be found in the Rules of Court, *viz.* in Rule 80.

A party may, in the event of the discovery of a fact which might by its nature have a decisive influence and which, when a judgment was delivered, was unknown to the Court and could not reasonably have been known to that party, request the Court, within a period of six months after that party acquired knowledge of the fact, to revise that judgment. The original Chamber may decide of its own motion to refuse the request on the ground that there is no reason to warrant considering it. Where it is not possible to constitute the original Chamber, the President of the Court will complete or compose the Chamber by drawing lots. If the Chamber does not refuse the request, the Registrar will communicate it to the other party or parties and invite them to submit any written comments within a time-limit laid down by the President of the Chamber. The President of the Chamber will also fix the date of the hearing should the Chamber decide to hold one. The Chamber decides by means of a judgment. A request for revision will be dealt with, according to Rule 102 of the Rules of Court, in proceedings largely resembling the normal proceedings before the Court.

Up to the time of writing (November 2016) eight requests for revision have been honoured by the Court,[759] while four requests have been dismissed.[760] This rather low figure is not astonishing. In general, cases in which after the final judgment an originally unknown fact of decisive importance is discovered are very rare. It is even less likely that such a situation will occur after lengthy local proceedings and the elaborate proceedings before the Court.

In the *Pardo* case, the applicant complained, *inter alia,* of a breach of his right to a fair trial. He claimed that, as a party in commercial litigation in the Aix-en-Provence Court of Appeal, he had not had the opportunity to present oral

---

[759] *E.P. v. Italy,* ECtHR (revision) 3 May 2001, appl. no. 31127/96; *Tripodi v. Italy,* ECtHR (revision) 23 October 2001, appl. no. 40946/98; *Viola v. Italy,* ECtHR (revision) 7 November 2002, appl. no. 44416/98; *Frattini v. Italy,* ECtHR (revision) 26 November 2002, appl. no. 52924/99; *Perhirin and 29 Others v. France,* ECtHR (revision) 8 April 2003, appl. no. 44081/98; *Grasso v. Italy,* ECtHR (revision) 29 April 2003, appl. no. 48411/99; *Karagiannis v. Greece* ECtHR (revision) 8 July 2004, appl. no. 51354/99; *Stoiescu v. Romania,* ECtHR (revision) 21 September 2004 appl. no. 31551/96.

[760] *Pardo v. France,* ECtHR (revision) 10 July 1996, appl. no. 13416/87; *Gustafsson v. Sweden,* ECtHR (GC) (revision) 30 July 1998, appl. no. 15573/89; *McGinley and Egan v. United Kingdom,* ECtHR (revision) 28 January 2000, appl. nos. 21825/93 23414/94; *Corsi v. Italy,* ECtHR (revision) 2 October 2003 appl. no. 42210/98.

arguments on the merits, despite the fact that the President had announced that there would be a further hearing at a later date. In its judgment, the Court held that there had been no violation of Article 6(1).[761] At Mr Pardo's request the Commission submitted to the Court a request for the revision of that judgment. The Commission noted that the Court, prior to its hearing on 22 March 1993, had asked the participants in the proceedings to produce certain documents. For the reasons given at the hearing, these requests were not complied with. Since then the applicant had been able to obtain certain of these documents and, in particular, the letter from Mr de Chessé to Mr Davin (both lawyers) of 25 March 1985 and the list of documents contained in the appeal file. The Commission took the view that, as the Court had asked for these documents to be produced, they might by their nature have had a decisive influence on its judgment. The Court took the view that the two documents submitted in support of the Commission's request (the letter from Mr de Chessé to Mr Davin of 25 March 1985 and the list of documents in the appeal file), documents to which Mr Pardo did not have access until after the delivery of the judgment of 20 September 1993, could be regarded as facts for the purposes of Rule 80(1). The Court noted that, under the terms of the second sentence of Rule 58(4) [the present Rule 80(4)], the Chamber constituted to consider the request for revision could only determine the admissibility of that request. It had, accordingly, to confine itself to examining whether, *prima facie,* the facts submitted were such as 'might by [their] nature have a decisive influence'. The task of considering whether they actually had a 'decisive influence' lay in principle with the Chamber which gave the original judgment. A decision on the admissibility of the request, therefore, in no way prejudged the merits of the request. However, in carrying out its examination the Court had to bear in mind that, by virtue of Article 52 [(the present Article 42)] ECHR, its judgments were final. Inasmuch as it called into question the final character of judgments, the possibility of revision, which was not provided for in the Convention but had been introduced by the Rules of Court, was an exceptional procedure. That was why the admissibility of any request for revision of a judgment of the Court under this procedure was subject to strict scrutiny. In order to establish whether the facts on which a request for revision were based 'might by [their] nature have a decisive influence', they had to be considered in relation to the decision of the Court the revision of which was sought. The Court observed in this connection that a request to those appearing before the Court for documents to be produced was not in itself sufficient to warrant the conclusion that the documents in question 'might by [their] nature have a decisive influence'. On the other hand, the Court could not exclude the possibility that the documents in question 'might by [their] nature have a decisive influence'. It fell to the Chamber which gave the original judgment to determine whether those documents actually cast doubt on the conclusions

---

[761] *Pardo v. Italy,* ECtHR 20 September 1993, appl. no. 13416/87, para. 29.

it reached in 1993. The Court accordingly declared the request for revision admissible and referred it to the Chamber which gave the original judgment.[762] In its judgment of 29 April 1997, the Court decided that the documents in question did not provide any information on the proceedings concerned whose course had been in dispute before the Court. The documents would not have had a decisive influence on the original judgment and did not constitute any grounds for revision. Therefore, the request was dismissed.[763]

In the *Gustafsson* case, the applicant complained that the lack of state protection against industrial action conducted by the Hotel and Restaurant Workers' Union (HRF) against his restaurant, gave rise to a violation of his right to freedom of association as guaranteed by Article 11 ECHR. The Court concluded that Article 11 ECHR was applicable in the applicant's case but that there had been no violation of this Article.[764] In requesting the Court to revise its judgment of 25 April 1996, the applicant adduced evidence in relation to two allegations advanced by the Government for the first time in its memorial to the Court during the main proceedings. This concerned, first, its assertion that in 1986 one of his employees, who was also a member of the HRF, had contacted the HRF to complain about the terms of employment. Secondly, it concerned the Government's allegation that the applicant could not substantiate his own assertion that the employment terms which he offered were, as regards salaries, equal to or better than required under a collective agreement with the HRF. The Court held that, although the judgment referred to the additional information in question, this only disposed of a point of procedure in reply to the applicant's contention that the Government were estopped from changing the stance it had adopted before the Commission and from adducing the evidence before the Court. The Court's answer that it was not prevented from taking the information into account if it considered it relevant could not of its own be taken to mean that the Court actually did have regard to the information. The reasons stated in the ensuing part of the original judgment were sufficient to support, and were decisive for, the Court's conclusion that there had been no violation of Article 11 ECHR. It contained no mention of the additional evidence and arguments submitted by Government. Nor was there anything to indicate that the evidence had been relied on here. Nor did other parts of the Court's reasoning and conclusions mention the first set of facts in dispute, namely the Government's allegation that the trade union action had its background in a complaint in 1986 by an HRF member employed by the applicant. Only the second set of disputed facts, concerning the terms and conditions of employment, was alluded to. However, the reasons contained in the relevant part of the judgment were merely accessory to those mentioned above. Furthermore, the Court

---

[762]   *Pardo v. France, supra* n. 762, paras. 24–25.
[763]   *Pardo v. France*, ECtHR (revision merits) 29 April 1997, appl. no. 13416/87, paras. 20–22.
[764]   *Gustafsson v. Sweden* ECtHR (GC) 25 April 1996, appl. no. 15573/89, paras. 51–55.

did not state anything suggesting an acceptance on its part of the arguments and evidence advanced by the Government in rebuttal. It did not regard the additional facts submitted by them as established facts. Rather than determining the disagreement between the applicant and the Government as to the terms and conditions of employment, the Court had regard to the general interest sought to be achieved through the union action, in particular the special role and importance of collective agreements in the regulation of labour relations in Sweden. It followed that the evidence adduced by the applicant would not have had a decisive influence on the Court's judgment of 25 April 1996 in as far as concerned the applicant's complaint under Article 11 ECHR. Nor would it have had any such bearing on its conclusions with respect to his complaints under Article 1 of Protocol No. 1 or Article 6 or 13 ECHR. Accordingly, the evidence did not offer any ground for revision.[765]

Most of the requests for revision have concerned the issue of just satisfaction under Article 41 ECHR. In a number of cases, the applicant had died before the Court had taken a decision in his case, where it found a violation of the Convention and had awarded the applicant compensation under Article 41. Subsequently, the respondent state requested revision of the principal judgment concerning Article 41 ECHR. The Court found that it had not been informed to whom it could legitimately award the just satisfaction due, and decided to revise its principal judgment so that no amount be awarded for non-pecuniary damage.[766] In the case of *E.P. v. Italy*, the Court decided to revise its principal judgment and not to award costs and expenses, because the applicant's lawyer had not provided the information requested.[767] In the *Grasso* case, the Court revised it principal judgment concerning Article 41 in the sense that the payment for moral damage should be paid to the legitimate heirs of the deceased applicant.[768] In the *Viola* case, the applicant's lawyer informed the Court that he had been late informed that the applicant had deceased. He, therefore, requested the Court to take the necessary steps in order to pay the just satisfaction to the applicant's widow. The Court agreed and revised its principal judgment in that sense.[769] In the *Corsi* case, the applicant requested revision of the judgment previously delivered by the Court concerning his application, in which the Court found a violation of Article 6(1) on account of the length of the proceedings but made no financial award in respect of damage. Noting that no sum had been

---

[765] *Gustafsson v. Sweden, supra* n. 762, paras. 27–32.

[766] *McGinley and Egan v. the United Kingdom, supra* n. 762, para. 36; *E.P. v. Italy, supra* n. 761, para. 6; *Tripodi v. Italy supra* n. 761, para. 5; *Metalco Bt. v. Hungary*, ECtHR (revision) 26 June 2012, appl. no. 34976/05, para. 14. See also *Frattini v. Italy, supra* n. 761, para. 3, and *Perhirin and 29 Others v. France, supra* n. 761, para. 5, where the Court revised the judgment concerning Art. 41 with respect the moral damage awarded to the deceased applicants and their heirs.

[767] *E.P. v. Italy, supra* n. 761, para. 7.

[768] *Grasso v. Italy, supra* n. 761, para. 7.

[769] *Viola v. Italy, supra* n. 761, paras. 5–10.

awarded to the applicant because no claim had reached the Registry within the time allowed, and that no new information warranting revision of the earlier judgment had been received, the Court decided to dismiss the application for revision.[770]

In the *Stoiescu* case, the Court had held that there had been a violation of Article 6(1) on account of the lack of a fair hearing and the denial of access to court, and a violation of Article 1 of Protocol No. 1. The Court had ordered the Romanian State to return the property in question to the applicant or, failing that, to pay him EUR 270,000 for pecuniary damage. It also awarded him EUR 6,000 for non-pecuniary damage.[771] The Romanian Government requested revision of the Court's judgment on account of the discovery of a new fact, namely that the applicant had lost his status as heir when his certificate of inheritance was declared null and void following an application by a third party who inherited under the terms of a will. The Court noted that following proceedings in the Romanian courts between 1995 and 1999 the applicant's certificate of inheritance, which formed the basis of his claim for the return of the property, had been declared null and void. That decision could decisively have affected the admissibility decision and the judgment that had been handed down by the Court in the case in 2000 and 2003.The Court considered that, owing to the lack of a computerised database of pending cases in Romania at the material time, the Romanian Government could not reasonably have been aware of events. However, the applicant had been involved in the proceedings concerning the validity of his certificate of inheritance for over seven years and could have informed the Court of the position before it gave its judgment, but had knowingly declined to do so. Since 20 May 1999, when the Bucharest Court of Appeal declared his certificate of inheritance null and void, the applicant had lost his status as his aunt's heir and his right to the return of the property. In those circumstances, he could no longer claim to be a victim, within the meaning of the Convention, of a violation of his rights. Accordingly, the Court unanimously declared the Government's application for revision admissible. Consequently, it declared Mr Stoicescu's application inadmissible and revised the judgment of 4 March 2003 in full.[772] In the case of *Baumann v. Austria*, the Court in its judgment of 7 October 2004, awarded the applicant EUR 2,906.91 in order to cover the costs for two applications made under section 91 of the Courts' Act, and a lump sum of EUR 2,000 as regards the costs of the proceedings before the Court. In its request for revision the Government suggested that the cost award for the two applications under section 91 of the Courts' Act should be reduced to EUR 335, corresponding to the amount chargeable for such applications under applicable domestic law. Having regard

---

[770] *Corsi v. Italy, supra* n. 762, para. 10.
[771] *Stoiescu v. Romania, supra* n. 761.
[772] *Ibid.*, para. 33.

to the parties' submissions the Court awarded the applicant the sum of EUR 335, in respect of the two applications filed under section 91 of the Courts' Act. The Court considered that this sum correctly reflected the costs incurred for the applicant in her attempts to accelerate the domestic proceedings.[773] In the case of *Bajrami v. Albania*, the applicant died before the judgment had been adopted. The Court considered that the award made to the deceased applicant should be paid to his heir or heirs as identified in his will.[774] In the case of *Eremiášová and Pechová v. the Czech Republic*, the second applicant died before the judgment had been adopted but neither the representative nor the first applicant had informed the Court of the death. No information was provided concerning any heirs or whether the first applicant wished to pursue the application. The Court recalled that it has been its practice to strike applications out of the list of cases in the absence of any heir or close relative who has expressed a wish to pursue the application.[775] In the case of case of *Naumoski v. the former Yugoslav Republic of Macedonia*, the Government requested revision of the judgment of 27 November 2012 alleging that the Court had wrongly established that the Supreme Court's decision dismissing the applicant's appeal on points of law had been rendered on 27 March 2003, instead of 27 November 2003. The Court observed that it had indeed wrongly established the date and revised it accordingly. The Court considered that the length of the impugned proceedings, as revised, was excessive and failed to meet the 'reasonable-time' requirement of Article 6(1) ECHR.[776]

8. ADVISORY JURISDICTION OF THE COURT

Since the entry into force of Protocol No. 2 on 21 September 1970, the Court has jurisdiction to give advisory opinions on legal questions concerning the interpretation of the Convention and of the Protocols thereto (Article 1(1) of Protocol No. 2).

Properly speaking, this jurisdiction falls outside the scope of the present chapter, which deals with the consideration of complaints or requests connected with them. The matter is, nevertheless, discussed in this chapter, since it is the chapter devoted to the functioning of the Court.

---

[773] *Baumann v. Austria*, ECtHR (revision) 9 June 2005, appl. no. 76809/01, para. 15.

[774] *Bajrami v. Albania*, ECtHR (revision) 18 December 2007, appl. no. 35853/04, para. 7; *Kulikowski v. Poland*, ECtHR (revision) 21 December 2010, appl. no. 18353/03, para. 8; *Meryem Çelik and Others v. Turkey*, ECtHR (revision) 16 September 2014, appl. no. 3598/03, para. 15.

[775] *Eremiášová and Pechová v. the Czech Republic*, ECtHR (revision) 20 June 2013, appl. no. 23944/04, para. 10.

[776] *Naumoski v. the former Yugoslav Republic of Macedonia*, ECtHR 5 December 2013, appl. no. 25248/05, para. 10.

The advisory jurisdiction of a court may be of great importance for a uniform interpretation and the further development of the law. With regard to international law, this is quite evident from the practice of the International Court of Justice and the Court of Justice of the European Communities. Via its advisory opinions the International Court of Justice has made an important contribution to the interpretation and the progressive development of particularly the law of the United Nations.[777] The advisory jurisdiction of the International Court of Justice is formulated very broadly, without any conditions being made as to the scope of such advisory opinions. According to Article 96 of the Charter of the United Nations in conjunction with Article 65 of the Court's Statute, the Court may give advisory opinions 'on any legal question', so that the most varied issues of international law may be submitted to the Court. The jurisdiction of the Court of Justice of the European Communities is very limited as to its scope, but still comprises the field of the conclusion of treaties, which is of great importance for the Communities.[778]

The practical importance of the advisory jurisdiction of the European Court of Human Rights, on the other hand, has been reduced to a minimum from the outset because of the restrictions which are put on it in the said Protocol. In fact, Article 1(2) provides that advisory opinions of the European Court 'shall not deal with any question relating to the content or scope of the rights or freedoms defined in Section I of the Convention and in the Protocols thereto, or with any other question which the Commission, the Court, or the Committee of Ministers might have to consider in consequence of any such proceedings as could be instituted in accordance with the Convention.'

A request for an advisory opinion must indicate in precise terms the question on which the opinion of the Court is sought, and in addition the date on which the Committee of Ministers decided to request an advisory opinion, as well as the names and addresses of the person or persons appointed by the Committee to give the Court any explanations which it may require (Rule 83 of the Rules of Court). A copy of the request is transmitted to the members of the Court (Rule 84 of the Rules of Court). The President lays down the time-limits for the filing of written comments or other documents (Rule 85 of the Rules of Court). He also decides whether after the closure of the written procedure an oral hearing is to be held (Rule 86 of the Rules of Court).

---

[777] In this context, see in particular the advisory opinions of the Court in: 'Injuries suffered in the service of the United Nations' *ICJ Reports* 1949, p. 174; 'Certain Expenses of the United Nations', *ICJ Reports*, 1962, p. 151; and 'Legal Consequences for States of the Continued Presence of South Africa in Namibia notwithstanding Security Council Resolution 276 (1970)' *ICJ Reports* 1971, p. 6.

[778] See Art. 228 of the EEC Treaty. See, *e.g.*, the important advisory opinion of the Court of Justice of the European Communities 1/76, *Jur.* 1977, p. 741, which partly laid the basis for the present conception of the external powers of the EEC.

Advisory opinions are given by majority vote of the plenary Court. They mention the number of judges constituting the majority, while any judge may attach to the opinion of the Court either a separate opinion, concurring with or dissenting from the advisory opinion, or a bare statement of dissent (Rule 88 of the Rules of Court).

The advisory opinion is read out by the President or his delegate at a public hearing, and certified copies are sent to the Committee of Ministers, the Contracting States, the Commission and the Secretary General of the Council of Europe (Rules 89 and 90 of the Rules of Court).

If the Court considers that the request for an advisory opinion is not within its consultative competence, it so declares in a reasoned decision (Rule 87 of the Rules of Court).

It is obvious that a high degree of inventiveness is required for the formulation of a question of any importance which could stand the test of Article 1(2) of Protocol No. 2 and could therefore be submitted to the Court.

8.1. ADVISORY OPINIONS

So far, at any rate, in June 2004 the Court delivered its first decision on its competence to give an advisory opinion. The request concerned the Commonwealth of Independent States (CIS) which was established in 1991 by a number of former Soviet Republics and at present comprises 12 States. It provides for the establishment of a Human Rights Commission of the Commonwealth of Independent States (the CIS Commission) to monitor the fulfilment of the human rights obligations entered into by States. The CIS Convention entered into force on 11 August 1998. In May 2001, the Parliamentary Assembly of the Council of Europe adopted a Recommendation that the Committee of Ministers request the Court to give an advisory opinion on the question whether the CIS Commission should be regarded as 'another procedure of international investigation or settlement' within the meaning of Article 35(2)(b) ECHR. The Parliamentary Assembly referred to 'the weakness of the CIS Commission as an institution for the protection of human rights' and expressed the view that it should not be regarded as a procedure falling within the scope of Article 35(2)(b).[779] The Committee of Ministers followed the recommendation and requested the Court to give an advisory opinion on 'the co-existence of the Convention on Human Rights and Fundamental Freedoms of the Commonwealth of Independent States and the European Convention on Human Rights'. The Court considered that the request for an advisory opinion related essentially to the specific question whether the CIS Commission could be regarded as 'another procedure of international investigation or settlement' within the meaning of Article 35(2)(b) ECHR and was satisfied that the request

---

[779] Recommendation 1519(2001).

related to a legal question concerning the interpretation of the Convention, as required by Article 47(1). It was, however, necessary to examine whether the Court's competence was excluded by Article 47(2), on the ground that the request raised a 'question which the Court or the Committee of Ministers might have to consider in consequence of any such proceedings as could be instituted in accordance with the Convention'. The Court considered that 'proceedings' in this context referred to proceedings relating to applications lodged with it by states or individuals under Articles 33 and 34 ECHR respectively and that the term 'question' extended to issues concerning the admissibility of applications under Article 35 ECHR. It observed that the question whether an individual application should be declared inadmissible on the ground that the matter had already been submitted to 'another procedure of international investigation or settlement' had been addressed in a number of concrete cases in the past, in particular by the former European Commission of Human Rights. In that connection, the Court endorsed the Commission's approach, which showed that the examination of this question was not limited to a formal verification of whether the matter had been submitted to another procedure but extended, where appropriate, to an assessment of the nature of the supervisory body concerned, its procedure and the effect of its decisions. The question whether a particular procedure fell within the scope of Article 35(2)(b) was therefore one which the Court might have to consider in consequences of proceedings instituted under the Convention, so that its competence to give an advisory opinion was in principle excluded. As far as the CIS Convention procedure was concerned, the Court noted that several States Parties to the European Convention on Human Rights were members of the CIS and that three had signed and one had ratified the CIS Convention. Moreover, the rights set out in the CIS Convention were broadly similar to those in the European Convention on Human Rights. It could not therefore be excluded that the Court might have to consider, in the context of a future individual application, whether the CIS procedure was 'another procedure of international investigation or settlement'. The Court concluded that the request for an advisory opinion did not come within its advisory competence.[780]

The first advisory opinion concerned certain legal questions concerning the lists of candidates submitted with a view to the election of judges to the European Court of Human Rights. The request for an opinion arose out of the following correspondence between the Maltese authorities and the Parliamentary Assembly concerning the composition of the Maltese list of candidates for the post of judge at the Court. The questions asked in the request for an advisory opinion were worded as follows: (1) can a list of candidates for the post of judge at the European Court of Human Rights, which satisfies the criteria listed in Article 21 ECHR, be refused solely on the basis of gender-related issues? (2) are Resolution 1366 (2004) and Resolution 1426 (2005) in breach of the Assembly's

---

[780] Decision ECtHR (GC) 2 June 2004 on the competence of the Court to give an advisory opinion.

responsibilities under Article 22 ECHR to consider a list, or a name on such list, on the basis of the criteria listed in Article 21 ECHR? The Court found that the first question concerned the rights and obligations of the Parliamentary Assembly in the procedure for electing judges, as derived from Article 22 in particular and from the Convention system in general. Accordingly, whatever its implications, it was of a legal character and as such fell within the scope of the Court's jurisdiction under Article 47(1) ECHR. The Court then considered that in view of its reply to the first question, it was not necessary to answer the second question. In relation to the first question, the Court observed that there was nothing to prevent Contracting Parties from, for instance, attempting to achieve a certain balance between the sexes or between different branches of the legal profession on a particular list or within the Court. Nevertheless, while considerations of that kind were legitimate, they could not release the country concerned from its obligation to present a list of candidates each of whom fulfilled all the moral qualities and professional qualifications laid down in Article 21(1). For the Court, it was vital to its authority and the quality of its decisions that it be made up of members of the highest legal and moral standing. Further, while it was clear that the Assembly was required to elect judges on the basis laid down by Article 22, it also had a certain latitude when it came to establishing the procedure for the election of judges, although it was bound first and foremost by Article 21. It was obvious too that the Assembly might take account of additional criteria which it considered relevant for the purposes of choosing between the candidates put forward and might, as it had done in a bid to ensure transparency and foreseeability, incorporate those criteria in its resolutions and recommendations. Indeed, neither Article 22 nor the Convention system set any explicit limits on the criteria which could be employed by the Assembly in choosing between the candidates put forward. The Court noted that the inclusion of a member of the under-represented sex was not the only criterion applied by the Assembly which was not explicitly laid down in Article 21(1). The Assembly also required candidates to have 'sufficient knowledge of at least one of the two official languages'. However, a sufficient knowledge of at least one of the official languages was necessary in order to make a useful contribution to the Court's work, given that the Court worked only in those two languages. The criterion relating to a candidate's sex lacked an implicit link with the general criteria concerning judges' qualifications laid down in Article 21(1). The Court observed that the criterion in question derived from a gender-equality policy which reflected the importance of equality between the sexes in contemporary society and the role played by the prohibition of discrimination and by positive discrimination measures in attaining that objective. There was far-reaching consensus as to the need to promote gender balance at national level and in the national and international public service, including the judiciary. Although only a minority of countries had adopted specific rules aimed at ensuring a certain balance between the sexes in the courts, a great many of them sought to promote such a balance through appropriate policies. The same trend could be observed in the international courts and was also reflected in the European Court of Human Right's own Rules of Court. However, it was essential that such a policy did not make it more difficult for the countries which had ratified the Convention to put forward candidates who also satisfied all the requirements of Article 21(1), which were to be given primary consideration. The principle of nominating candidates of the under-represented sex at the Court was generally accepted, but not without provision being made for derogations from the rule. The obligation was therefore one of means, not of outcome. Such a situation might arise, in particular, for a country where the number of people working in the legal profession was small. Those states had not to be placed in a position where, in order to fulfil the criterion concerning the sex of candidates, they could only nominate candidates who satisfied the criteria of Article 21(1) if they chose non-nationals. It would be unacceptable for a state to be forced to nominate non-national candidates solely to satisfy the criterion relating to a candidate's sex, which was not enshrined in the Convention. Furthermore, it would be liable to produce a situation where the elected candidate did not have the same knowledge of the legal system, language or indeed cultural and other traditions of the country concerned as a candidate from that country. Indeed, the main reason why one of the judges hearing a case had to be the 'national judge' was precisely to ensure that the judges hearing the case were fully acquainted with the relevant domestic law of the country concerned and the context in which it was set. It would therefore be incompatible with the Convention to require a country to nominate a candidate of a different nationality solely to achieve gender balance. Accordingly, although the aim of ensuring a certain mix in the composition of the lists of candidates was legitimate and generally accepted, it might not be pursued without provision being made for some exceptions designed to enable each country to choose national candidates who satisfied all the requirements of Article 21(1). The precise nature and scope of such exceptions had still to be defined. The Court concluded that, in not allowing any exceptions to the rule that the under- represented sex must be represented, the current practice of the Assembly was not compatible with the Convention: where the country concerned had taken all the necessary and appropriate steps with a view to ensuring that the list contained a candidate of the under-represented sex, but without success, and especially where it had followed the Assembly's recommendations advocating an open and transparent procedure involving a call for candidates, the Assembly might not reject the list in question on the sole ground that no such candidate featured on it. Accordingly, exceptions to the principle that lists must contain a candidate of the under-represented sex should be defined as soon as possible.[781]

---

[781] ECtHR 12 February 2008, Advisory Opinion on certain legal questions concerning the lists of candidates submitted with a view to the election of judges to the European Court of Human Rights.

The second advisory opinion arose out of an exchange of letters between the Ukrainian authorities and the Parliamentary Assembly on the composition of the list of candidates for election as a judge of the Court in respect of Ukraine. Following the withdrawal of one of Ukraine's three candidates for personal reasons in September 2007, the Ukrainian authorities announced the withdrawal of the entire list. In October 2007 the Parliamentary Assembly, concluding that there were no 'exceptional circumstances' justifying the withdrawal of the list, requested that Ukraine submit a replacement candidate and not an entirely new list. That request was reiterated in December 2007. Against that background, on 15 July 2009, the Committee of Ministers, the Council of Europe's executive arm, asked the Court to give its opinion on the following questions:

1.
    (a) Can a list of three candidates, nominated by a state for election as a judge to the European Court of Human Rights in respect of that state and submitted to the Parliamentary Assembly, be withdrawn and replaced with a new list of three candidates? If yes, is there any time-limit?
    (b) Can candidates on a withdrawn list be considered as nominated by a state within the meaning of Article 22 ECHR?
    (c) Is the Parliamentary Assembly obliged to consider a new list of candidates submitted by a state in replacement of its withdrawn list?

2.
    (a) If one or more candidates on a list submitted to the Parliamentary Assembly by a state withdraws before the Assembly has voted on the list, is that state obliged under the Convention to submit an additional candidate or candidates to complete the list or is it entitled to submit a new list?
    (b) Are the conditions in paragraphs 1 and 2 of the Appendix to Resolution 1432 (2005) of the Parliamentary Assembly of the Council of Europe in breach of the Assembly's responsibilities under Article 22 ECHR to consider a list, or a name on such a list?[782]

First, the Court observed that its jurisdiction under Article 47 was confined to 'legal questions concerning the interpretation of the Convention and the protocols thereto'. Questions 1(a) through to 2(a), concerning the rights and obligations of the Parliamentary Assembly in the procedure for electing judges, were of a legal character and as such fell within the scope of its jurisdiction under Article 47. On the other hand, question 2(b), which concerned the compatibility with the Convention of a Parliamentary Assembly resolution, and certain of its provisions, fell outside the Court's advisory jurisdiction. The Court considered

---

[782]   AS/Jur (2010)12 rev3 of 11 October 2010.

that states could, in exercising their sovereign power, decide – for reasons of their own – to withdraw lists of candidates for the post of judge at the Court. It would not, however, be compatible with the normal conduct of the election procedure to allow member states to withdraw a list, without any restrictions or conditions, once submitted to the Parliamentary Assembly. Indeed, before submitting their lists, member states would presumably have organised their own selection procedures in such a way as to allow them to choose suitably qualified candidates. Any later possibility of withdrawal could hinder the normal course and timing of the procedure for election by the Parliamentary Assembly. In the Court's opinion, it was thus reasonable for the time-limit for withdrawal of a list to coincide with the deadline set for the member states to submit the lists to the Parliamentary Assembly. In conclusion, member states could withdraw and replace a list of candidates for the post of judge at the Court, but only on condition that they did so before the deadline set for submission of the list to the Parliamentary Assembly (question 1(a)). After that date, the member states would no longer be entitled to withdraw their lists. By the same logic, if the withdrawal occurred before that time-limit: candidates on a list withdrawn by the member state could no longer be regarded as nominated (question 1(b)); candidates on a new list had to be considered by the Parliamentary Assembly (question 1(c)); and, the member state concerned could either replace any absent candidates or submit a new list of three candidates (question 2(a)). If, however, the withdrawal occurred after that date, the member state concerned had to be restricted to replacing only absent candidates (question 2(a)).[783]

8.2. PRELIMINARY QUESTIONS BY NATIONAL COURTS

On 2 October 2013, Protocol No. 16 to the Convention was opened for ratification and will enter into force after 10 ratifications. This treaty was the result of work carried out on the reform of the European Court of Human Rights. Protocol 16 allows the States Parties' highest courts to ask the Court for an advisory opinion on questions of principle relating to the interpretation or application ECHR or its protocols relevant to cases before them.[784] Paragraph 1 of Article 1 sets out three key parameters of the new procedure:

1. the procedure is optional;
2. the request may be made by the 'highest court or tribunal';
3. the nature of the request must relate to the interpretation or application of the rights and freedoms defined in the Convention or the protocols thereto.

---

[783] ECtHR 22 January 2010, Advisory Opinion on certain legal questions concerning the lists of candidates submitted with a view to the election of judges to the European Court of Human Rights (No. 2).
[784] Council of Europe, ETS No. 214 of 2 October 2013.

Paragraph 2 of Article 1 requires the request for an advisory opinion to be made in the context of a case pending before the requesting court or tribunal. Paragraph 3 of Article 1 sets out certain procedural requirements that must be met by the requesting court or tribunal. They reflect the aim of the procedure is to give the requesting court or tribunal guidance on Convention issues when determining the case before it. In providing the relevant legal and factual background, the requesting court or tribunal should present the following:

– the subject matter of the domestic case and relevant findings of fact made during the domestic proceedings, or at least a summary of the relevant factual issues;
– the relevant domestic legal provisions;
– the relevant Convention issues, in particular the rights or freedoms at stake;
– if relevant, a summary of the arguments of the parties to the domestic proceedings on the question;
– if possible and appropriate, a statement of its own views on the question, including any analysis it may itself have made of the question.

Requesting courts or tribunals may address the Court in the national official language used in the domestic proceedings. Paragraph 1 of Article 2 sets out the procedure for deciding whether or not a request for an advisory opinion is accepted. The Court has a discretion to accept a request or not, although it is to be expected that the Court would hesitate to refuse a request that satisfies the relevant criteria by

(i) relating to a question as defined in paragraph 1 of Article 1; and
(ii) the requesting court or tribunal having fulfilled the procedural requirements as set out in paragraphs 2 and 3 of Article 1.

The decision on acceptance is taken by a five-judge panel of the Grand Chamber. The panel must give reasons for any refusal to accept a domestic court or tribunal's request for an advisory opinion. Paragraph 3 of Article 2 states that the panel and the Grand Chamber shall include *ex officio* the judge elected in respect of the High Contracting Party to which the requesting court or tribunal pertains. Paragraph 3 also establishes a procedure for circumstances where there is no such judge, or that judge cannot sit. Article 3 gives to the Council of Europe Commissioner for Human Rights and to the High Contracting Party whose domestic court or tribunal has requested the advisory opinion the right to submit written comments to and take part in any hearing before the Grand Chamber in proceedings concerning that request. The President of the Court may invite any other High Contracting Party or person to submit written comments or take part in any hearing, where to do so is in the interest of the proper administration of justice. It will be for the Court to decide whether or not to hold a hearing on an accepted request for an advisory opinion. Paragraph 1 of Article 4 requires the Court to give reasons for advisory opinions delivered under this Protocol; paragraph 2 of Article 4 allows for judges of the Grand Chamber to deliver a separate (dissenting or concurring) opinion. Paragraph 3 of Article 4 requires the Court to communicate advisory opinions to both the requesting court or tribunal and the High Contracting Party to which that court or tribunal pertains. It is expected that the advisory opinion would also be communicated to any other parties that have taken part in the proceedings in accordance with Article 3. Paragraph 4 of Article 4 requires the publication of advisory opinions delivered under this Protocol. Article 5 states that advisory opinions shall not be binding. They take place in the context of the judicial dialogue between the Court and domestic courts and tribunals. Accordingly, the requesting court decides on the effects of the advisory opinion in the domestic proceedings. The fact that the Court has delivered an advisory opinion on a question arising in the context of a case pending before a court or tribunal of a High Contracting Party would not prevent a party to that case subsequently exercising their right of individual application under Article 34 ECHR. Advisory opinions under this Protocol would have no direct effect on other later applications. Article 6 reflects the fact that acceptance of the Protocol is optional for High Contracting Parties to the Convention. It thus does not have the effect of introducing new provisions into the Convention, whose text remains unchanged.[785]

---

[785] Council of Europe, Explanatory Report on Protocol No. 16 to the European Convention on Human Rights and Fundamental Freedoms, ETS No. 214.

CHAPTER 3

SUPERVISION

Leo Zwaak and Clara Burbano Herrera[*]

CONTENTS

1. SUPERVISORY TASK OF THE COMMITTEE OF MINISTERS

1.1. INTRODUCTION

Unlike the Court, the Committee of Ministers was not set up in connection with the adoption of the European Convention. It is the policy-making and executive organ of the Council of Europe.

One of the tasks of the Committee of Ministers concerning human rights results directly from the Statute of the Council of Europe, *viz.* from Article 8. By virtue of this article the Committee supervises the observance of the obligation contained in Article 3 of the Statute, according to which every

---

[*]   In the fourth edition this chapter was revised and updated by Leo Zwaak. Section 1 of this chapter is written by Leo Zwaak. Section 2 of this chapter is written by Clara Burbano Herrera.

member of the Council of Europe 'must accept the principles of the rule of law and of the enjoyment by all persons within its jurisdiction of human rights and fundamental freedoms'. The more specific tasks of the Committee of Ministers with regard to human rights, however, have been laid down in the Convention. Since the entry into force of Protocol No. 11 the Committee of Ministers performs only a supervisory task under the European Convention in connection with decisions of the Court. In this respect, the Committee has begun producing annual reports on the execution of judgments.[1] In practice, the Committee only meets once a year at ministerial level. Most of the Committee's work is carried out by the Ministers' Deputies who are the permanent representatives of the member states at the Council of Europe. Hereafter the role of the Committee of Ministers, its procedures and the developments in the execution process will be considered.

Article 46(1) ECHR provides that the Contracting Parties 'undertake to abide by the final judgment of the Court in any case to which they are parties'. This undertaking entails precise obligations for respondent states which are found to be in violation of the Convention. On the one hand, they must take measures in favour of the applicants to put an end to these violations and, as far as possible, erase their consequences (*restitutio in integrum*), and, on the other hand, they must take the measures needed to prevent new, similar violations. A primary obligation is the payment of just satisfaction (normally a sum of money), which the Court may award the applicant under Article 41 ECHR and which covers, as the case may be, pecuniary and/or non-pecuniary damage and/or costs and expenses. The payment of such compensation is a strict obligation which is clearly defined in each judgment.

According to Article 46(2) ECHR, once the Court's final judgment has been transmitted to the Committee of Ministers, the latter invites the respondent state to inform it of the steps taken to pay the amounts awarded by the Court in respect of just satisfaction and, where appropriate, of the individual and general measures taken to abide by the judgment.[2] Once it has received this information, the Committee examines it closely. According to Rule 1(c) of the Rules of the Committee of Ministers for the application of Article 46(2) ECHR, in case the chairmanship of the Committee of Ministers is held by the representative of a state which is a party to a case referred to the Committee of Ministers under Article 46(2), that representative shall relinquish the chairmanship during any discussion of that case.

Article 16 of Protocol No. 14 gave new powers to the Committee of Ministers which are designed to make the execution of judgments of the Court more

---

[1]   Committee of Ministers, *Supervision of the Execution of Judgments of the European Court of Human Rights* Council of Europe Publishers 2008.

[2]   See the Rules of the Committee of Ministers for the application of Article 46(2) ECHR; <https://rm.coe.int/16806eebf0>. Unless indicated otherwise, in this chapter the Rules refer to this set of Rules.

effective by adding three new paragraphs to Article 46. The first two paragraphs of Article 46 repeat the two paragraphs of the former Article 46; paragraphs 3, 4 and 5 are new. The new Article 46, in its paragraph 3, empowers the Committee of Ministers to ask the Court to interpret a final judgment, for the purpose of facilitating the supervision of its execution. The Committee of Ministers' experience of supervising the execution of judgments shows that difficulties are sometimes encountered due to disagreement as to the interpretation of judgments. The Court's reply settles any argument concerning a judgment's exact meaning. The qualified majority vote required by the last sentence of paragraph 3 shows that the Committee of Ministers should use this possibility sparingly, to avoid overburdening the Court.[3] Paragraphs 4 and 5 of Article 46 accordingly empower the Committee of Ministers to bring infringement proceedings in the Court (which shall sit as a Grand Chamber), having first served the state concerned with notice to comply. The Committee of Ministers' decision to do so requires a qualified majority of two-thirds of the representatives entitled to sit on the Committee. This infringement procedure does not aim to reopen the question of violation, already decided in the Court's first judgment. Nor does it provide for payment of a financial penalty by a High Contracting Party found in violation of Article 46, paragraph 1. It is felt that the political pressure exerted by proceedings for non-compliance in the Grand Chamber and by the latter's judgment should suffice to secure execution of the Court's initial judgment by the state concerned.[4] They should bring infringement proceedings only in exceptional circumstances. Nonetheless, it appeared necessary to give the Committee of Ministers, as the competent organ for supervising execution of the Court's judgments, a wider range of means of pressure to secure execution of judgments. The procedure's mere existence, and the threat of using it, should act as an effective new incentive to execute the Court's judgments. It is foreseen that the outcome of infringement proceedings would be expressed in a judgment of the Court.[5]

The Directorate General of Human Rights helps the Committee of Ministers to carry out this responsibility under the Convention. In close co-operation with the authorities of the state concerned, it considers what measures need to be taken in order to comply with the Court's judgment. At the Committee of Ministers' request, it supplies opinions and advice based on the experience and practice of the Convention bodies.

In accordance with Rule 3(b), the Committee of Ministers shall examine whether any just satisfaction awarded by the Court has been paid, including, as the case may be, default interest. If required, the Committee shall also take into account the discretion of the state concerned to choose the means

---

[3]   Explanatory Report to Protocol No. 14, para. 96.
[4]   *Ibid.*, para. 99.
[5]   *Ibid.*, para. 100.

necessary to comply with the judgment. In all cases it will strive to ascertain whether individual measures have been taken to ensure that the violation has ceased and that the injured party is put, as far as possible, in the same situation as that party enjoyed prior to the violation of the Convention, and/or, whether general measures have been adopted, preventing new violations similar to that or those found or putting an end to continuing violations. It is the Committee of Ministers' well-established practice to keep cases on its agenda until the states concerned have taken satisfactory measures, and to continue to require explanations or action.[6] When there is a delay in the execution of a judgment, the Committee of Ministers may adopt an interim resolution assessing the progress towards execution. As a rule, this type of interim resolution contains information about any interim measures taken and indicates a timetable for the reforms designed to resolve the problem or problems raised by the judgment once and for all. If there are obstacles to execution, the Committee will adopt a more strongly worded interim resolution urging the authorities of the respondent state to take the necessary steps in order to ensure that the judgment is complied with.

According to Rule 4(b), if the state concerned informs the Committee of Ministers that it is not yet in a position to inform the Committee that the general measures necessary to ensure compliance with the judgment have been taken, the case will be placed again on the agenda of a meeting of the Committee of Ministers taking place no more than six months later, unless the Committee decides otherwise; the same rule applies when this period expires and for each subsequent period. The Committee may bring its full weight to bear in order to induce the state concerned to comply with the Court's judgment. In practice, the Committee of Ministers rarely resorts to political and diplomatic pressure but tends, instead, to function as a forum for constructive dialogue enabling states to work out satisfactory solutions with regard to the execution of judgments. On a number of occasions, however, interim resolutions have been drafted and adopted in order to pressurise states that have refused to afford applicants just satisfaction or to take specific measures in compliance with judgments. Under the Statute of the Council Europe, tougher political sanctions could be considered such as suspension or termination of membership of the Council of Europe under Article 8 of the Statute, but obviously these are ultimate remedies that will be considered in very exceptional circumstances only.

The Committee of Ministers is entitled to consider any communication from the injured party with regard to the payment of the just satisfaction or the taking of individual measures.[7]

---

[6] Rule 4(a) provides that, until the State concerned has provided information on the payment of the just satisfaction awarded by the Court or concerning possible individual measures, the case will be placed on the agenda of each human rights meeting of the Committee of Ministers, unless the Committee decides otherwise.

[7] Rule 6(a).

With respect to access to information Rule 5 provides as follows: 'Without prejudice to the confidential nature of Committee of Ministers' deliberations, in accordance with Article 21 of the Statute of the Council of Europe, information provided by the State to the Committee of Ministers in accordance with Article 46 ECHR and the documents relating thereto shall be accessible to the public, unless the Committee decides otherwise in order to protect legitimate public or private interests. In deciding such matters, the Committee of Ministers shall take into account reasoned requests by the State or States concerned, as well as the interest of an injured party or a third party not to disclose their identity.'

In accordance with Rule 7, the Committee of Ministers may in the course of its supervision of the execution of a judgment adopt interim resolutions in order to provide information on the state of progress of the execution or, where appropriate, to express concern and/or to make relevant suggestions with respect to the execution. There may be situations in which the adverse consequences of the violation suffered by an injured party are not always adequately remedied by the payment of just satisfaction. Depending on the circumstances, the execution of the judgment may also require the respondent state to take individual measures in favour of the applicant, such as the reopening of unfair proceedings if domestic law allows for such reopening, the destruction of information gathered in breach of the right to privacy or the revocation of a deportation order issued despite of the risk of inhumane treatment in the country of destination. It may also require general measures – such as an adaptation of legislation, rules and regulations, or of a judicial practice – to prevent new, similar violations.

After having established that the state concerned has taken all the necessary measures to abide by the judgment, the Committee adopts a resolution concluding that its functions under Article 46(2) ECHR have been exercised.

Finally, Article 17 of the Statute of the Council of Europe provides for yet another tool for the Committee in fulfilling its supervisory powers. According to that article, the Committee of Ministers may set up advisory or technical committees or commissions if it deems this desirable. The Committee of Ministers might proceed to do so for the purpose of taking evidence and other tasks within the context of its function under the Convention.

1.2. SCOPE OF OBLIGATIONS TO COMPLY WITH JUDGMENT

A judgment of the Court does not expressly order the respondent state to take specific measures to rectify the applicant's situation and prevent further violations. Under the Convention, states are free to choose the means whereby they implement individual or general measures.

This is not to say, however, that the payment of just satisfaction is the only obligation that may derive from a judgment of the Court. To execute a judgment finding one or more violations of the Convention the respondent state may, depending on the circumstances, also be required to take certain measures. This may be, first, individual measures for the applicant's benefit, so as to end an unlawful situation, if that situation still continues, and to redress its consequence (*restitutio in integrum*),[8] and secondly, general measures to prevent further violations of a similar nature.[9]

This has been stressed by the Court, for example, in the *Papamichalopoulos* case, where the applicants had alleged that their land had been unlawfully occupied by the Navy Fund since 1967 and that they had not been able either to enjoy their possessions or to obtain compensation. The Court pointed out that from the obligation under Article 46 ECHR it follows, *inter alia*, that a judgment in which the Court finds a breach, imposes on the respondent state a legal obligation not only to pay those concerned the sums awarded by way of just satisfaction, but also to choose, subject to supervision by the Committee of Ministers, the general and/or, if appropriate, individual measures to be taken in their domestic legal order to put an end to the violation found by the Court and to redress so far as possible its effects.[10] This may involve assistance in the preparation or implementation of legislation. It may also include the organisation of seminars to discuss the underlying issues more broadly.[11]

1.3. JUST SATISFACTION

If the Court has decided that the respondent state has to pay just satisfaction under Article 41 ECHR within three months of the delivery of its judgment, the Committee of Ministers will examine the case at its meeting following the delivery of that judgment.[12] In a number of cases against Italy concerning violations of the requirement of a reasonable length of proceedings, the Committee had recommended that the Government pay, within a time-limit of three months, just satisfaction to the applicants. The Italian Government

---

[8]   E.g., the striking out of an unjustified criminal conviction from the criminal records, the granting of a residence permit or the re-opening of impugned domestic proceedings: Recommendation No. R (2000) 2 of the Committee of Ministers to the member States on the re-examination or reopening of certain cases at domestic level following judgments of the European Court of Human Rights, of 19 January 2000.

[9]   E.g., legislative or regulatory amendments, changes of case law or administrative practice or publication of the Court's judgment in the language of the respondent state and its dissemination to the authorities concerned.

[10]   *Papamichalopoulos and Others v. Greece*, ECtHR 31 October 1995, appl. no. 14556/89, para. 34; see also *Scozzari and Giunta v. Italy*, ECtHR (GC) 13 July 2000, appl. nos. 39221/98 and 41963/98, para. 249; *Aleksanyan v. Russia*, ECtHR 22 December 2008, appl. no. 46468/06, para. 238; *Kurić and Others v. Slovenia*, ECtHR (GC) 26 June 2012, appl. no. 26828/06, para. 406.

[11]   CM/Inf/DH(2010)45, final 7 December 2010.

[12]   The 3-month time-limit has become standing practice since *Moreira de Azevedo v. Portugal*, ECtHR 28 August 1991, appl. no. 11296/84, under 1 of the operative part of the judgment.

disagreed with the proposals of the Committee of Ministers and refused to pay the applicants. The Committee subsequently noted at its next meeting that, although the time-limit had been extended, the Government still had not paid the sums it had agreed to pay following the Committee's recommendation. It decided to strongly urge the Government to proceed without delay to pay the specified amount to the applicants. It further decided, if need be, to resume consideration of these cases at each of its forthcoming meetings.[13] In its subsequent session, the Committee of Ministers once again adopted resolutions in the Italian cases and now firmly stated that, in accordance with (former) Article 32(2) ECHR, the Government of Italy was to pay the applicants before a fixed date a certain amount in respect of just satisfaction. The Committee of Ministers invited the Government to inform it of the measures taken in consequence of its decision, having regard to the Government's obligations under (former) Article 32(4) ECHR to abide by it.[14] Finally, on 17 September 1992, the Committee of Ministers ended the consideration of these cases by declaring, after having taken note of the measures taken by the Italian Government, that it had exercised its functions under (former) Article 32 of the Convention.[15]

In case the respondent state is unable to prove the payment, the case will stay on the agenda of the Committee of Ministers and will be dealt with at every subsequent meeting of the Committee until it is satisfied that the payment has been made in full.

It has become practice that, from the expiry of the initial three-month period set for the payment until the final settlement, interest should be payable on the amount at a rate equal to the marginal lending rate of the European Central Bank during the default period.[16]

On the whole, the respondent states are willing to pay the compensation awarded by the Court to the applicant. However, apart from the above-mentioned reasonable-time cases concerning Italy, in a few instances, such as in the *Stran Greek Refineries and Stratis Andreas* case and the *Loizidiou* case, *Garabayev and 33 Others v. Russia* and the case of *Khashiyev and Akayeva*

---

[13]   *Azzi v. Italy*, Res. DH(91)12 of 6 June 1991; *Lo Giacco*, Res. DH(91)13 of 6 June 1991; *Salvoldi v. Italy*, Res. DH(91)21 of 27 September 1991; *Van Eesbeeck v. Italy*, Res. DH(91)22 of 27 September 1991; *Sallustio v. Italy*, Res. DH(91)23 of 27 September 1991; *Minitti v. Italy*, Res. DH 91(24) of 27 September 1991.

[14]   *La Giacco v. Italy*, Res. DH(92)3 of 20 February 1992; *Savoldi v. Italy*, Res. DH92(4) of 20 February 1992; *Van Eesbeeck v. Italy*, Res. DH(92)5 of 20 February 1992; *Sallustio v. Italy*, Res. DH(92)6 of 20 February 1992; *Minitti v. Italy*; Res. DH(92)7 of 20 February 1992.

[15]   *Azzi v. Italy*, Res. DH(92)45 of 17 September 1992; *Lo Giacco v. Italy*, Res. DH(92)46 of 17 September 1992; *Savoldi v. Italy*, Res. DH(92)47 of 17 September 1992; *Van Eesbeeck v. Italy*, Res. DH(92)48 of 17 September 1992; *Sallustio v. Italy*, Res. DH(92)49 of 17 September 1992; *Minnitti v. Italy*, Res. DH(92)50 of 17 September 1992.

[16]   *Öneryildiz v. Turkey*, ECtHR 18 June 2002, appl. no. 48939/99, para. 168; *Gumusten v. Turkey*, ECtHR 30 November 2004, appl. no. 47116/99, para. 34; *Klyakhin v. Russia*, ECtHR 30 November 2004, appl. no. 46082/99, para. 134; *Yaroslavtsev v. Russia*, ECtHR 2 December 2004, appl. no. 42138/02, para. 42.

and 220 Others v. Russia, the Committee of Ministers had to deal with the unwillingness of the respondent state to pay compensation.

After delivery of the judgment of the Court in the *Stran Greek Refineries and Stratis Andreas* case,[17] the Greek Government informed the Committee of Ministers that, considering the size of the just satisfaction awarded to the applicants and the economic problems in Greece, it was not able to make immediate full payment. The Committee of Ministers strongly urged the Greek Government to pay the amount corresponding to the value of just satisfaction as of March 1995 and decided, if need be, to resume consideration of the case at each of its forthcoming meetings.[18] Subsequently, in September 1996, the Chairman of the Committee of Ministers wrote to the Minister of Foreign Affairs of Greece underlining the fact that the credibility and effectiveness of the mechanism for the collective enforcement of human rights established under the Convention is based on the respect of the obligations freely entered into by the Contracting Parties and in particular on respect of the decisions of the supervisory bodies. In its Final Resolution of 20 March 1997, the Committee of Ministers was informed that the Greek Government had transferred US$ 30,863,828.50 to the applicants, which sum the applicants were entitled to enjoy without any interference whatsoever. The Committee, having satisfied itself that the amount paid, increased in order to provide compensation for the loss of value caused by the delay in payment, corresponded to the just satisfaction awarded by the Court, declared that it had exercised its supervisory function under the Convention.[19]

In its interim resolution concerning the judgment in the *Loizidou* case, the Committee of Ministers noted that the Government of Turkey had indicated that the sums awarded by the Court could only be paid to the applicant in the context of a global settlement of all property cases in Cyprus. It concluded that the conditions of payment envisaged by the Government of Turkey could not be considered to be in conformity with the obligations flowing from the Court's judgment. It strongly urged Turkey to review its position and to pay the just satisfaction awarded in this case in accordance with the conditions set out by the Court so as to ensure that Turkey, as a High Contracting Party, met its obligations under the Convention.[20]

In its second interim resolution, the Committee once more stressed that Turkey had had ample time to fulfil in good faith its obligations in the case concerned. It emphasised that the failure on the part of a High Contracting Party to comply with a judgment of the Court is unprecedented. It declared that the refusal of Turkey to execute the judgment of the Court demonstrated a manifest disregard for its international obligations, both as a High Contracting Party to the Convention and as a member state of the Council of Europe. In view

---

[17]   *Stran Greek Refineries and Stratis Andreadis v. Greece*, ECtHR 9 December 1994.
[18]   Interim Resolution of 15 May 1996, DH (96) 251.
[19]   Final Resolution of 20 March 1997, DH (97) 184.
[20]   Interim Resolution of 6 October 1999, DH (99) 680.

of the gravity of the matter, it strongly insisted that Turkey comply fully and without any further delay with the Court's judgment of 28 July 1998.[21] At its subsequent meeting, on 26 June 2001, the Committee declared that it very deeply deplored the fact that Turkey still had not complied with its obligations under the judgment of the Court.[22]

At its meeting on 12 November 2003, the Committee urged the Turkish Government to reconsider its position and to pay without any conditions whatsoever the just satisfaction awarded to the applicant by the Court, within one week at the latest. It declared the Committee's resolve to take all adequate measures against Turkey, if the Turkish Government failed once more to pay the just satisfaction to the applicant.[23] On 12 December 2003, the Chairman of the Committee of Ministers announced that the Turkish Government had executed the judgment of 28 July 1998 in the *Loizidou* case by paying to the applicant the sum which had been awarded to her by the Court in respect of just satisfaction.[24]

In a number of cases the Committee dealt with the unwillingness of the Russian Federation to take the necessary measures. In the case of *Garabayev and 33 Others v. Russia,* the Committee noted that the Russian authorities have taken a number of general measures to prevent abductions and illegal transfers from the Russian territory of persons in respect of whom extradition requests were filed and the Court has indicated an interim measure under Rule 39 of its Rules. The Committee deeply regretted that these measures did not appear to have been sufficient to address the need for urgent adoption of special preventive and protective measures that are effective and called upon the Russian authorities to further develop without further delay an appropriate mechanism tasked with both preventive and protective functions to ensure that applicants, in particular in respect of whom the Court has indicated an interim measure, benefit (following their release from detention) from immediate and effective protection against unlawful or irregular removal from the territory of Russia and the jurisdiction of the Russian courts.[25] In the case of *Khashiyev and Akayeva and 220 Others v. Russia*, the Committee, having regard to the numerous judgments of the European Court finding grave violations of the Convention resulting from actions of the security forces during anti-terrorist operations which took place in the North Caucasus, mainly in the Chechen Republic between 1999 and 2006, the great majority of which concern enforced disappearances, deeply regretted that the measures taken did not bring any significant results in the establishment of the fate of the applicants' missing relatives and strongly urged the Russian authorities to take the measures necessary to create a single and high-level body

---

21   Interim Resolution of 24 July 2000, DH (2000) 105.
22   Interim Resolution of 26 June 2002, DH (2001) 80.
23   Interim Resolution of 12 November 2003, DH (2003) 174.
24   Press Release Council of Europe: < www.mfa.gov.cy/mfa/mfa2016.nsf/CC8E93A64DF9F2FFC 2257F9C00386EA3/$file/The%20Committee%20of%20Ministers-Resolution%20(2003).pdf>.
25   Interim Resolution of 26 September 2013 DH (2013) 200.

mandated with the search for persons reported as missing as a result of counter-terrorist operations in the North Caucasus.[26] In the *Catan and Others* case, Russia refused to fulfil the payment of just satisfaction for more than three years. The Committee urged the Russian authorities to explore all appropriate avenues for the full and effective implementation of this judgment and decided to resume the consideration at the next meeting.[27]

1.4. INDIVIDUAL MEASURES

The need to take individual measures at the domestic level, in addition to the payment of pecuniary compensation if determined by the Court, is considered by the Committee of Ministers where the established breach continues to have negative consequences for the applicant, which cannot be redressed through pecuniary compensation.

The reopening of proceedings at the domestic level may constitute an important means of redressing the effects of a violation of the Convention, where there were serious shortcomings in the procedure followed by the national court. In fact, the reopening of domestic proceedings was also within the powers of the Committee of Ministers to suggest during the period before the entry into force of Protocol No. 11, in cases which had not been referred to the Court and where the Committee of Ministers acted under the former Article 32 as the final arbiter.

In the *Daktaras* case, the Court held that there were insufficient guarantees to exclude all reasonable doubt as to the impartiality of the composition of the Supreme Court which had examined the applicant's cassation petition.[28] The Government informed the Committee of Ministers that the domestic proceedings had been reopened on 29 January 2002 by a decision of the Criminal Chamber of the Supreme Court. This reopening was made possible by the application of the new section of the Code of Criminal Procedure called 'Re-opening of criminal cases following a judgment of the European Court of Human Rights', which entered into force on 15 October 2001. Following the reopening of the national proceedings, on 2 April 2002 a plenary session of the Criminal Chamber of the Supreme Court annulled the previous cassation judgment. According to the new judgment, the cassation petition submitted by the President of the Criminal Chamber of the Supreme Court was not taken into account. The cassation petition submitted by Mr Daktaras, as well as that of his legal representative, were rejected.[29]

Sometimes, reopening of the domestic proceedings is the only form of *restitutio in integrum* regarding a violation of Article 6 by previous proceedings.

---

[26] Interim Resolution of 12 March 2015 DH (2015) 45.
[27] Interim Resolution of 24 September 2015, DH (2015) 157.
[28] *Daktaras v. Lithuania*, ECtHR 10 October 2000, appl. no. 42095/98, para. 38.
[29] Resolution of 6 July 2004, DH(2004)43.

In view of the problem raised in certain cases of the lack of appropriate national legislation, the Committee of Ministers has adopted a recommendation to member states on the re-examination or reopening of certain cases at the domestic level following judgments of the Court.[30] In the recommendation, the Committee of Ministers invites the Contracting Parties to ensure that there exist at national level adequate possibilities to achieve, as far as possible, *restitution in integrum*. In the explanatory memorandum to this recommendation it is indicated that, as regards the terms, the recommendation uses 're-examination' as the generic term. The term 'reopening of proceedings' denotes the reopening of court proceedings, as a specific means of re-examination. Violations of the Convention may be remedied by different measures ranging from administrative re-examination of a case (e.g. granting a residence permit previously refused) to the full reopening of judicial proceedings (e.g. in cases of criminal convictions). The recommendation applies primarily to judicial proceedings where existing law may pose the greatest obstacles to reopening. The recommendation is, however, also applicable to administrative or other measures or proceedings, although legal obstacles will usually be less serious in these areas.

As appears from the text of the recommendation, any such shortcomings must be of such gravity that serious doubt is cast on the outcome of the domestic proceedings. The recommendation does not deal with the problem of who ought to be empowered to ask for reopening or re-examination. Considering that the basic aim of the recommendation is to ensure adequate redress for the victims of certain grave violations of the Convention found by the Court, the logic of the system implies that the individuals concerned should have the right to submit the necessary requests to the competent court or other domestic organ. Considering the different traditions of the Contracting Parties, no provision to this effect has, however, been included in the recommendation. The recommendation also does not address the special problem of 'mass cases', i.e. cases in which a certain structural deficiency leads to a great number of violations of the Convention.[31] It was considered preferable to leave it to the state concerned to decide whether in such cases reopening or re-examination is a realistic solution or other measures are more appropriate.

Another example of an individual measure that may be called for following a judgment is cancellation of a person's criminal record in respect of a conviction

---

[30] Recommendation of 19 January 2000, on the re-examination or reopening of certain cases at domestic level following judgments of the European Court of Human Rights, R (2000) 2.

[31] See in this respect the question of prisoner's right to vote: *Hirst v. the United Kingdom (No. 2)*, ECtHR (GC) 6 October 2005, appl. no. 74025/01; *Greens and M.T. v. United Kingdom*, ECtHR, 23 November 2010, appl. no. 60041/08 60054/08; *McLean and Cole v. United Kingdom*, ECtHR 11 June 2013, appl. nos. 12626/13 and 2522/12; *Dunn and Others v. United Kingdom*, ECtHR 13 May 2014, appl. nos. 7408/09, 566/10, 578/10 et al; *First and Others v. United Kingdom*, ECtHR 12 August 2014, appl. nos. 47784/09, 47806/09, 47812/09, 47818/09, 47829/09, 49001/09, 49007/09, 49018/09, 49033/09 and 49036/09; *McHugh and Others v. United Kingdom*, ECtHR 10 February 2015, appl. no. 51987/08.

that led to a violation of the Convention. Such a measure may be taken, for instance, where the applicant has already served a sentence and the reference to his conviction in his judicial record is the only remaining consequence of the violation.

In the *Van Mechelen* case, the Court had found a violation of Article 6(3)(d) on the ground that the applicants' conviction was based to a decisive extent on statements given by unidentified witnesses who were members of the police and whose reliability could not be tested by the defence.[32] During the examination of the case by the Committee of Ministers, the Government of the Netherlands gave the Committee information about the measures taken with a view to remedying the applicants' situation and preventing new violations. The applicants were provisionally released on 25 April 1997 on the orders of the Minister of Justice, and were subsequently, by letter of 22 July 1997, informed that they would not be required to serve the remainder of their sentences. Furthermore, the reasons why the sentences were not executed in their entirety were mentioned in their criminal records.[33]

In the *Vasilescu* case relating to, first, the unlawful seizure and the continued retention of valuables with respect to which the domestic courts had accepted the applicant's property rights and, secondly, the lack of access to an independent tribunal that could order their return, the Court had found a violation of Article 6(1) and Article 1 of Protocol No. 1.[34] The Romanian Government informed the Committee of Ministers that the Constitutional Court of Romania had rendered a decision declaring that, in order to comply with the Constitution, Article 278 of the Code of Criminal Procedure – concerning the right to appeal decisions of the public prosecutor – would be interpreted to the effect that a person who had an interest could challenge before a court any measure decided by the prosecutor. This decision became final and binding under Romanian law with its publication in the Official Journal of Romania and accordingly enforceable *erga omnes*. The Government considered that similar cases – where the valuables in question had been confiscated without any order from a competent judicial authority – were not likely to recur. The Committee of Ministers decided to resume consideration of the case until legislative reforms had been carried out, or at the latest at one of its meetings at the beginning of 2001.[35]

In the *Kalashnikov* case, concerning the poor conditions in which the applicant was held in detention before trial between 1995 and 2000, due in particular to severe prison overcrowding and to an insanitary environment, and concerning the excessive length of both this detention and the criminal proceedings, the Court had found a violation of Articles 3, 5(1) and 6(1).[36] The

---

[32] *Van Mechelen and Others v. the Netherlands*, ECtHR (GC) 23 April 1997, appl. nos. 21363/93, 21364/93, 21427/93, para. 66.
[33] Resolution 19 February 1999, DH (99) 124.
[34] *Vasilescu v. Romania*, ECtHR 22 May 1998, appl. no. 27053/95, paras. 41 and 54.
[35] Interim Resolution of 8 October 1999, DH (99) 676.
[36] *Kalashnikov v. Russia*, ECtHR 15 October 2002, appl. no. 47095/99, paras. 103, 121 and 135.

Russian Government, in its information to the Committee of Ministers, referred in particular to two major reforms which had already resulted in significant improvement of the conditions of pre-trial detention and their progressive[37] alignment with the Convention's requirements. The Committee of Ministers decided to examine at one of its meetings not later than 2004, further progress achieved in the adoption of the general measures necessary to effectively prevent these kinds of violation of the Convention.[38]

With respect to the fourth inter-state case of *Cyprus against Turkey*, the Committee of Ministers had noted that after a period of some years during which progress seemed rare, at recent meetings concrete information had been presented making it possible to register progress towards the execution of this complex and controversial judgment. In particular, the Committee of Ministers had been informed that a school had opened for Greek Cypriot pupils in the north of the island and that the Committee on Missing Persons had taken steps to bring its terms of reference further into line with the requirements of the Court judgment. That said, there were obviously still serious issues to be resolved.[39]

In the *Dorigo* case, where the applicant was convicted in 1994 for his part in a terrorist attack on a NATO military base and sentenced to over 13 years' imprisonment, the European Court found a violation of Article 6(1) and 6(3)(d) since he had been unable to examine witnesses against him.[40] It took several interim resolutions of the Committee, two resolutions of the Parliamentary Assembly, a lengthy enquiry into the possibility of a presidential pardon, failed legislation in the Italian Parliament, and two separate sets of legal proceedings before the Italian judiciary finally concluded that the applicant's continued detention was illegal, by virtue of the need to give direct effect to the Convention, and ordered his release in 2006. It was not until 2007, more than eight years after the former Commission's finding and 13 years after the initial trial, that the Committee of Ministers closed the examination of the case by which point the applicant had served virtually his entire sentence.[41]

1.5. GENERAL MEASURES

In certain cases it is clear from the circumstances that the violation resulted from particular domestic legislation or from the absence of legislation. In such cases, in order to comply with the Court's judgments, the state concerned must either amend existing law or introduce an appropriate new one. In many cases, however, the structural problem that led to a violation, lies not in an obvious

---

[37]   *Ibid.*
[38]   Interim Resolution of 4 June 2003, DH (2003) 123.
[39]   *Ibid.*
[40]   *Dorigo v. Italy*, ECtHR 16 November 2000, appl. 46520/99.
[41]   Resolution of 20 June 2007 DH (2007) 83.

conflict between domestic law and the Convention but rather in case law of the national courts. In that situation, a change of case law of the national courts may preclude possible future violations. When courts adjust their legal stance and their interpretation of national law to meet the demands of the Convention, as reflected in the Court's judgments, they implement these judgments by virtue of their domestic law. In this way, further similar violations may be effectively prevented. Precondition is, however, that the judgment is published and circulated among the national authorities, including the courts, accompanied, where appropriate, by an explanatory circular. Another group of cases poses problems for the Committee's supervisory function of general measures concerning the failure or serious delays of the domestic authorities to implement final decisions of domestic courts.[42] The problems arising from the execution of both groups of cases are examined by the Committee where it noted that in cases where a violation has been established on account of the failure to enforce a domestic judgment, *restitutio in integrum* cannot be achieved unless and until this judgment is executed. The Committee noted however with concern that in a number of cases, domestic judicial decisions delivered in the applicants' favour remain unexecuted until now and stressed that this situation was incompatible with the respondent's obligation under Article 46 of the Convention to abide *by* the Court's judgments.[43]

In its interim resolution in the *Zhovner* case in respect of 324 cases against Ukraine concerning the failure or serious delay in abiding by final domestic courts' decisions delivered against the state and its entities as well as the absence of an effective remedy the Committee noted that noted that, notwithstanding a number of initiatives reported by the Ukrainian authorities to the Committee since the beginning of its supervision, no satisfactory results had been achieved in their implementation and decided to resume the consideration of the case until the next meeting.[44] And again in its interim resolution of 2010 the Committee noted with deep concern that notwithstanding the Committee's repeated calls, the Ukrainian authorities had failed since 2004 to give priority to devising a comprehensive strategy to bring their legislation and administrative practice into line with the Convention requirements, thus generating new massive applications before the Court and strongly urged once again the Ukrainian authorities at the highest political level to hold to their commitment to resolving the problem of non-enforcement of domestic judicial decisions and to adopt as a matter of priority the specific reforms in Ukraine's legislation

---

[42]   *Timofeyev v. Russia*, ECtHR 23 October 2003, appl. no. 58363/00; *Zhovner v. Ukraine*, ECtHR 29 June 2004, appl. no. 56848/00.

[43]   Interim Resolution of 6 March 2008, DH (2008) 1; see also execution of the pilot judgment of the European Court of Human Rights in the case *Yuriy Nikolayevich Ivanov v. Ukraine and of 386 cases against Ukraine* concerning the failure or serious delay in abiding by final domestic courts' decisions delivered against the state and its entities as well as the absence of an effective remedy Interim Resolution of 30 November 2010 DH(2010) 222.

[44]   Interim Resolution of 3 December 2009 DH (2009)159.

and administrative practice required by the pilot judgment.[45] The Committee decided to resume the consideration of the case at their next meeting.

The *Sylvester v. Austria* case concerned the Austrian authorities' failure to enforce a court decision rendered in December 1995 (and final two months later) under the 1980 Hague Convention on the Civil Aspects of International Child Abduction. This decision ordered that the first applicant's daughter (the second applicant, born in 1994), unlawfully taken away by her mother, should be returned to him in the United States. After an unsuccessful attempt to enforce that decision in May 1996, the mother lodged an appeal before the Austrian courts which set aside the enforcement of the return order by decision of August 1996 (final in October 1996) on the grounds that, due to the considerable lapse of time since the two-year-old child had lost contact with her father, there would be a risk of grave psychological harm if she was separated from her mother, who had become her main person of reference. Subsequently, the second applicant's mother was awarded sole custody of the second applicant.[46] The Austrian authorities informed the Committee of Ministers that according to section 271(1) of the Civil Code, a guardian was to be appointed *ex officio* during the proceedings in the case of a conflict between the interests of the child and her/his legal representative and in case the interests of the child could not be taken care of by the court itself pursuant to its general duty to mediate between the parties in cases of this kind. The authorities underlined that proceedings could be resumed on one party's request, in particular to address the additional grievances made by the applicant, and that in this context, the wishes of the second applicant, now 16 years old, would be taken into consideration (see section 148(1) of the Civil Code, read in conjunction with Article 12 of the 1989 UN Convention on the Rights of the Child). In view of the situation, and taking into account in particular the measures taken by the Austrian authorities in order to ensure that Mr Sylvester had, if he so wished, adequate access to court in order to protect his and his child's interests under the Convention, it seemed that no further individual measure was required for the execution of the present judgment.[47]

It took the United Kingdom seven years to execute the judgment in the *Matthews* case, where the Grand Chamber had found a violation of Article 3 of Protocol 1 because Gibraltarians could not vote in the elections to the European Parliament.[48] Finally, the United Kingdom Parliament adopted the European Parliament (Representation) Act which received the Royal Assent on 8 May 2003. This Act provided for the entirety of UK electoral law, as it applied to European Parliamentary elections, to be applied to Gibraltar for those purposes. Pursuant to its provisions, Gibraltar was to be combined with an existing electoral region in England and Wales to form a new electoral region ('the combined region')

---

[45] Interim Resolution of 30 November 2010 DH (2010)222.

[46] *Sylvester v. Austria*, ECtHR 24 April 2003, appl. no. 36812/97.

[47] Resolution CM/ResDH(2010)84 of 15 September 2010.

[48] *Matthews v. United Kingdom*, ECtHR (GC) 15 July 2002, appl. no. 40302/98.

for the purposes of European Parliamentary elections taking place after 1 April 2004.[49] Since the continuing dispute in the UK over prisoners' voting rights, neither the *Hirst* case[50], nor the *Greens* case[51] have been fully implemented. In its interim resolution of 2015 the Committee recalled that at its last examination of the cases, in September 2015, the Committee reiterated its serious concern about the ongoing delay in the introduction of a Bill to Parliament and expressed profound regret that, despite its repeated calls, the blanket ban on the right of convicted prisoners in custody to vote remains in place.[52]

According to the Committee on Legal Affairs and Human Rights in its report on the Implementation of judgments of the European Court of Human Rights of 2013, since 1996 the number of cases requiring oversight by the Committee of Ministers has been on the rise, making it more and more difficult for the supervisory body to effectively exercise its functions. The future report is to cover eight states which have the highest number of judgments pending execution before the Committee of Ministers, according to the statistics presented by the latter in its annual report for the year of 2012. These states are, in descending order: Italy (2,569 cases), Turkey (1,861 cases), the Russian Federation (1,211 cases), Ukraine (910 cases), Poland (908 cases), Romania (667 cases), Greece (478 cases) and Bulgaria (366 cases).[53]

It is sometimes that general measures must first be adopted to allow individual measure to be taken, for example, where a new remedy is created as a general measure which the applicant than can use. Thus, in the case of *M.D. v. Malta* a new remedy was created as a general measure the Committee considered the case after the general measures was adopted.[54]

Following the judgment of the Court in the *Jersild* case, the Danish Supreme Court acquitted, in a judgment of 28 October 1994, a journalist who had been charged with invasion of privacy by entering without permission an area that was not accessible to the public. In the City Court of Copenhagen and in the Eastern Division of the High Court the journalist had been found guilty as charged. However, the Supreme Court acquitted the journalist as it found that this result was most in keeping with the jurisprudence of the European Court of Human Rights concerning Article 10. In this connection, the Supreme Court made a special reference to the *Jersild* judgment as the latest authority. Moreover, following the *Jersild* judgment of the Court, the Special Court of Revision

---

49 Final Resolution Res DH(2006)57 of 2 November 2006.
50 *Hirst v. United Kingdom*, ECtHR judgment of 6 October 2005, appl. no. 74025–01.
51 *Greens and MT v. United Kingdom*, ECtHR judgment of 23 November 2010, appl. nos. 60041/00 and 60054/08.
52 Interim Resolution CM Res DH (2015)251.
53 Parliamentary Assembly, AS/Jur(2013)14.
54 Resolution of 4 December 2014 DH (2014)265; ECtHR (GC) judgment of 6 October 2005, appl. no. 74025/01.

decided on 24 January 1995 to allow the case against, *inter alia*, Mr Jersild to be reopened.[55]

In the *Gaygusuz* case, a Turkish national complained about a violation of Articles 6(1), 8 and 14 ECHR and of Article 1 of Protocol No. 1 by the Austrian authorities' refusal to grant emergency assistance to the applicant, an unemployed man who had exhausted entitlement to unemployment benefit, on the ground that he did not have Austrian nationality. The Court found a violation of Article 14 in conjunction with Article 1 of Protocol No. 1.[56] The Austrian Government informed the Committee of Ministers that the Austrian Constitutional Court, which was seized with several complaints regarding the constitutionality of the discrimination against foreigners provided for in Articles 33 and 34 of the Unemployment Insurance Act, had changed its earlier jurisprudence according to which benefits such as the emergency assistance did not fall under Article 1 of Protocol No. 1, and had aligned it with that of the Court in the *Gaygasuz* case. In consequence thereof, the Austrian Constitutional Court had annulled with immediate effect the two provisions in question insofar as they reserved the right to emergency assistance to Austrian nationals. It had found it appropriate in the circumstances to deviate from its usual practice of postponing the full effects of its judgment to a future date. Immediately after this judgment, the Austrian Parliament had adopted a new law providing that the amendments to the Unemployment Insurance Act entered into force on 1 April 1998 and not on 1 January 2000.[57]

With respect to the length of proceedings in Italy the Court has been faced with continuous problems. In the *Bottazzi* case, the Court drew attention to the fact that since 25 June 1987, the date of the *Capuano* case, it has delivered 65 judgments in which it had found violations of Article 6(1) in proceedings exceeding a 'reasonable time' in the civil courts of the various regions of Italy. This accumulation of breaches accordingly constituted a practice that was incompatible with the Convention.[58] In its interim resolution, the Committee of Ministers recalled that excessive delays in the administration of justice constitute an important danger, in particular for the respect of the rule of law. The Committee further noted that the question of Italy's adoption of general measures to prevent new violations of the Convention of this kind had been before the Committee of Ministers since the judgments of the Court in the 1990s, and therefore highlighted the existence of serious structural problems in the functioning of the Italian judicial system.[59] At its session in October 2000, the

---

[55]   Resolution of 11 September 1995, DH(95)212.

[56]   *Gaygusuz v. Austria*, ECtHR 16 September 1996, appl. no. 17371/90, para. 52.

[57]   Resolution of 12 November 1998, DH(98)372.

[58]   *Bottazzi v. Italy*, ECtHR (GC) 28 July 1999, appl. no. 34884/97, para. 22; see also *Capuano v. Italy*, ECtHR 25 June 1987, appl. no. 9381/81; *Di Mauro v. Italy*, ECtHR 28 July 1999 appl. no. 34258/96, para. 23.

[59]   See in this respect Resolution of 11 July 1997, DH(97)336; Interim Resolutions of 15 July 199, DH (99) 436 and DH (99) 437.

Committee of Ministers noted with satisfaction that recently the highest Italian authorities had manifested – both at the national level and before the organs of the Council of Europe – their solemn commitment to finding eventually an effective solution to the situation. It decided to continue the attentive examination of this problem until the reforms of the Italian judicial system would become thoroughly effective and a reversal of the trend at domestic level would be fully confirmed.

Meanwhile, the Committee of Ministers resumed its consideration of the progress made, at least at yearly intervals, on the basis of a comprehensive report to be presented each year by the Italian authorities.[60] In concluding its examination of the third annual report presented by the Italian authorities, on 29 September 2004, the Committee of Ministers noted with concern that an important number of reforms announced since 2000 were still pending for adoption and/or for effective implementation, and reminded the Italian authorities of the importance of respecting their undertaking to maintain the high priority initially given to the reforms of the judicial system and to continue to make rapid and visible progress in the implementation of these reforms. As regards the effectiveness of the measures adopted so far, the Committee of Ministers deplored the fact that no stable improvement could be seen yet: with a few exceptions, the situation generally worsened between 2002 and 2003[61] with an increase in both the average length of the proceedings and the backlog of pending cases. The Committee of Ministers accordingly confirmed its willingness to pursue the monitoring until a reversal of the trend at the national level would be fully confirmed by reliable and consistent data. In the light of this situation, the Committee of Ministers took note of the information provided by Italy concerning a follow-up plan aimed at ensuring the respect of the expected execution objectives. It invited Italy to submit rapidly complementary information requested as well as to complete the above-mentioned follow-up plan by an action plan. It also decided to examine the fourth report at the latest in April 2005.[62]

In the cases of *Akdivar, Aksoy, Çetin, Aydin, Mentes, Kaya, Yilmaz, Selçuk and Asker, Kurt, Tekin, Güleç, Ergi* and *Yasa*, the Court had found various violations of the Convention by Turkey, which all resulted from the actions of its security forces in the south-east of the country, a region subject to a state of emergency for the purposes of the fight against terrorism. The Turkish Government informed the Committee of Ministers that it had engaged in an important process, including notably the drafting of measures in respect of regulations and training, in order to implement fully and in all circumstances the constitutional and legal prohibition of the use of torture and ill-treatment. The Committee of Ministers

---

60   Interim Resolution DH(2000)135 of 25 October 2000.
61   See CM/Inf(2004)23 rev.
62   Documents of the Committee of Ministers, CM/AS (2004)9 of 4 October 2004.

noted that the actions of the security forces challenged in these cases took place in a particular context, i.e. the rise of terrorism during the years 1991–93.

The Committee of Ministers called upon the Turkish authorities rapidly to complete the announced reform of the existing system of criminal proceedings against members of the security forces, in particular by abolishing the special powers of the local administrative councils in engaging criminal proceedings, and to reform the prosecutor's office in order to ensure that prosecutors would in the future have the independence and necessary means to ensure the identification and punishment of agents of the security forces who abuse their powers so as to violate human rights.[63]

In its follow-up resolution, the Committee of Ministers noted with satisfaction that Turkey had pursued and enhanced its reform process with a view to ensuring that its security forces and other law enforcement authorities respect the Convention in all circumstances and thus prevent new violations. The Committee of Ministers expressed, however, concern about the continuing existence of new complaints of alleged torture and ill-treatment as evidenced notably through the new applications lodged with the Court. It noted with concern that, three years after the adoption of Interim Resolution DH(99)434, Turkey's undertaking to engage in a global reform of basic, in-service and management training of the Police and *Gendarmerie* remained to be fulfilled and stressed that concrete and visible progress in the implementation of the Council of Europe's Police Training Project was very urgent. The Committee of Ministers urged Turkey to accelerate without delay the reform of its system of criminal prosecution for abuses by members of the security forces, in particular by abolishing all restrictions on the prosecutors' competence to conduct criminal investigations against state officials, by reforming the prosecutor's office and by establishing sufficiently deterring minimum prison sentences for persons found guilty of grave abuses such as torture and ill-treatment. It called upon the Turkish Government to continue to improve the protection of persons deprived of their liberty in the light of the recommendations of the Committee for the Prevention of Torture (CPT) and decided to pursue the supervision of the execution of the judgments concerned until all necessary measures had been adopted and their effectiveness in preventing new similar violations had been established.[64]

In the case of the *Socialist Party v. Turkey*, relating to the dissolution of this party on account of certain statements made in 1991 by one of the applicants, the Party's chairman, Mr Perinçek, the Court had found a violation of Article 11.[65] The Committee of Ministers noted that it had been informed that by judgment of 8 July 1998 – i.e. after the judgment of the Court – the Court of Cassation of Turkey had confirmed a criminal conviction imposed on Mr Perinçek by the

---

[63]   Interim Resolution of 9 June 1999, DH (99) 434.
[64]   Interim Resolution of 10 July 2002, DH (2002) 98.
[65]   *Socialist Party v. Turkey*, ECtHR (GC) 25 May 1998, appl. no. 21237/93, para. 54.

First State Security Court of Ankara on 15 October 1996, according to which the sanction of dissolution of the party also carried with it personal criminal responsibility. It noted, furthermore, that by virtue of this conviction, Mr Perinçek had been sentenced to a 14-month prison sentence, which he started to serve on 29 September 1998. He had furthermore been banned from further political activities. The Committee of Ministers insisted on Turkey's obligation under Article 53 (the present Article 46) ECHR to erase, without delay, through action by the competent Turkish authorities, all the consequences resulting from the applicant's criminal conviction on 8 July 1998 and decided, if need be, to resume consideration of the case at each forthcoming meeting.[66] In its next session, the Committee of Ministers noted with regret that action had still not been taken by the Turkish authorities to give full effect to the judgment of the Court and to the Committee's interim resolution. It urged Turkey, without further delay, to take all the necessary action to remedy the situation of the former Chairman of the Socialist Party, Mr Perinçek.[67]

In 27 judgments against Turkey, the Court had found that the criminal convictions of the applicants on account of statements contained in articles, books, leaflets or messages addressed to, or prepared for, a public audience, had violated their freedom of expression guaranteed by Article 10 ECHR. In its interim resolution on violations of the freedom of expression in Turkey, the Committee of Ministers encouraged the Turkish authorities to bring to a successful conclusion the comprehensive reforms planned to bring Turkish law into conformity with the requirements of Article 10 ECHR.[68] At its subsequent meeting, having examined the significant progress achieved in a series of reforms undertaken with a view to aligning Turkish law and practice with the requirements of the Convention in the field of freedom of expression, the Committee of Ministers welcomed the changes made to the Turkish Constitution, in particular to its Preamble, to the effect that only anti-constitutional activities instead of thoughts or opinions could be restricted, as well as to Articles 13 and 26, which introduced the principle of proportionality and indicated grounds for restrictions of the exercise of freedom of expression, similar to those contained in paragraph 2 of Article 10 ECHR. It noted also the recent, important legislative measures adopted as a result of these reforms, in particular the repeal of Article 8 of the Anti-terrorism Law and the modification of Articles 159 and 312 of the Turkish Criminal Code. The Committee of Ministers welcomed in this context the 'train the trainers' programme currently being carried out within the framework of the 'Council of Europe/ European Commission Joint Initiative with Turkey: to enhance the ability of

---

[66]   Interim Resolution of 4 March 1999, DH (99) 245.
[67]   Interim Resolution of 28 July 1999, DH (99) 529.
[68]   Interim Resolution of 23 July 2001, DH(2001) 106.

the Turkish authorities to implement the National Programme for the adoption of the Community acquis (NPAA) in the accession partnership priority area of democratization and human rights', noting that this programme aimed, among other things, at devising a long-term strategy for integrating Convention training into the initial and in-service training of judges and prosecutors. The Committee of Ministers expressed appreciation in this context of the recent establishment of the Judicial Academy, as well as many Convention awareness-raising and training activities for judges and prosecutors initiated by the Turkish authorities. It welcomed furthermore the amendment of Article 90 of the Constitution, recently adopted by the Turkish Parliament, aimed at facilitating the direct application of the Convention and case law in the interpretation of Turkish Law. It encouraged the Turkish authorities to consolidate their efforts to bring Turkish Law fully into conformity with the requirements of Article 10 ECHR and invited them to ensure, by appropriate means, that statements or accusations falling under Article 6 of the Anti-terrorism Law which serve the public interest and in respect of which the proof of truth is offered, or in respect of which the person concerned is in good faith about the truth, are not punishable and nor indeed the printing of other statements covered by this article which do not incite to violence. The Committee of Ministers decided to resume consideration of the general measures in these cases within nine months, and outstanding individual measures concerning the respective applicants at its 897th meeting (September 2004), it being understood that the Committee's examination of those cases involving applicants convicted on the basis of former Article 8 of the Anti-terrorism Law would be closed upon confirmation that the necessary individual measures had been taken.[69]

In the *Scozzari and Giunta* case, the Court found two violations of Article 8 ECHR by Italy on account, on the one hand, of the delays in organising contact visits and the limited number of such visits between the first applicant and her children, after they had been taken into public care and, on the other hand, of the placement of the children in a community among whose managers were persons convicted for ill-treatment and sexual abuse of handicapped persons placed in the community.[70] The Committee of Ministers noted that, following Ms Scozzari's taking up residence in Belgium, the Belgian Government had approached the Italian authorities in order to examine the possibilities of organising, by judicial means, the placement of the children in Belgium, near the mother's place of residence, under the guardianship of the competent youth court. It found that such a proposal could provide the basis for a solution respecting the Court's judgment. Considering the urgency of

---

[69]   Interim Resolution of 2 June 2004, DH(2004)38.
[70]   *Scozzari and Giunta v. Italy*, ECtHR (GC) 13 July 2000, appl. nos. 39221/98, 41963/98, paras. 183 and 216.

the situation, the Committee of Ministers encouraged the Belgian and Italian authorities to implement without delay the proposal so as to put an end to the violations found.[71] At its next session, the Committee of Ministers expressed regret that, more than one year after the Court's judgment, the latter had still not been fully executed; in fact, several problems at the basis of the Court's finding of a violation in respect of the placement in the *Forteto* community had not been remedied. It invited the Italian authorities rapidly to take concrete and effective measures in order to prevent that the children be irreversibly separated from their mother and to ensure that their placement respected the superior interests of the children and the mother's rights, as defined by the Court in its judgment.[72] The Committee of Ministers noted that certain general measures remained to be taken and that further information and clarifications were outstanding with regard to a number of other measures, including, where appropriate, information on the impact of these measures in practice. It recalled that the obligation to take all such measures is all the more pressing in cases where procedural safeguards surrounding investigations into cases raising issues under Article 2 ECHR are concerned. The Committee of Ministers decided to pursue the supervision of the execution of the judgments concerned until all necessary general measures would have been adopted and their effectiveness in preventing new, similar violations had been established and the Committee of Ministers had satisfied itself that all necessary individual measures had been taken to erase the consequences of the violations found for the applicants. It resumed consideration of these cases, as far as individual measures were concerned, at each of its DH meetings, and, as far as outstanding general measures were concerned, it decided to review their adoption at the latest within nine months from the date of its interim resolution.[73]

Following the idea submitted in the context of the Committee of Ministers' supervision of the implementation of the *Ryabykh v. Russia* judgment, a high-level seminar was held with participation of the Russian highest judiciary, *prokuratura*, executive authorities and advocacy to discuss the prospects for further reforms of the supervisory review procedure, one of the topics at the heart of the Russian judicial reform. The violation of the Convention found in the *Ryabykh* case was due to the quashing by the Presidium of the Belgorod Regional Court in March 1999 of a final judicial decision in the applicant's favour, following an application for supervisory review lodged by the President of the same court under Articles 319 and 320 of the Code of Civil Procedure as they were then in force. The latter gave the President discretionary powers to challenge at any moment final court decisions. The Court found that this

---

[71]   Interim Resolution of 29 May 2001, DH (2001) 65.
[72]   Interim Resolution of 3 October 2001, DH (2001) 151.
[73]   Interim Resolution of 23 February 2005, DH(2005)20.

supervisory review by the Presidium infringed the principle of legal certainty and thus the applicant's right to a court.[74] Subsequently, the Russian Federation adopted some general measures with a view to remedying the systemic problem at the basis of the violation. According to the new Code of Civil Procedure, the time period for lodging an application for supervisory review is limited to one year (Article 376) and the list of state officials empowered to lodge such an application is significantly narrowed (Article 377).

While these measures were welcomed by the Committee of Ministers, doubts were expressed as to whether the measures taken were sufficient to prevent new similar violations of the principle of legal certainty. The Russian authorities were thus invited to continue the reform of the supervisory review procedure, bringing it in line with the Convention's requirements, as highlighted, *inter alia*, by the *Riabykh* judgment. Given the complexity of the issue and the ongoing reflection on the matter in Russian legal circles, it was suggested, at the Committee of Ministers' meeting (8–9 December 2004) to hold a high-level seminar with a view to taking stock of the current *nadzor* practice and to discussing prospects for further reform of this procedure in conformity with the Convention's requirements.

As a result, the Directorate General of Human Rights organised a seminar in Strasbourg, in close co-operation with the Russian authorities. The participants in the Conference welcomed the reforms of the supervisory review procedure adopted by the Russian Federation through the new Codes of Criminal, Commercial (Arbitration) and Civil Procedure (in force respectively since 1 July 2002, 1 January 2003 and 1 February 2003). It was notably suggested by many participants that the supervisory review in its amended form was closer to respecting the legal certainty principle enshrined in the Convention, especially in criminal and commercial matters. More reservations were, however, expressed, from the Convention viewpoint, as to the existing supervisory review procedure in civil matters. The conclusions of the seminar will be reported to competent Russian authorities with a view to contributing to their reflection on possible further reforms of the *nadzor* procedure. The Committee of Ministers will be also informed of the seminar in the context of its supervision of the execution of the Court's judgment in the *Riabykh* case.[75] Given the time needed for the enactment of the new legislative measures, the Committee of Ministers decided to postpone its examination of the case until the legislative reforms had been carried out, or at the latest, until its first meeting in 2006.[76]

---

[74]   *Ryabykh v. Russia*, ECtHR 24 July 2003 (dec.), appl. no. 52854/99, paras. 57– 58.
[75]   Seminar held in Strasbourg, 21–22 February 2005.
[76]   CM/Inf/DH(2005)20 of 23 March 2005.

2. SUPERVISORY FUNCTION OF THE SECRETARY-GENERAL

2.1. INTRODUCTION

In addition to the complaint procedure, the Convention provides for yet another procedure for supervising the observance by the Contracting States of their obligations under the Convention. This form of supervision is based on Article 52 (formerly Article 57) of the Convention and is entrusted to the Secretary-General of the Council of Europe. Article 52 reads as follows: 'On receipt of a request from the Secretary General of the Council of Europe any High Contracting Party shall furnish an explanation of the manner in which its internal law ensures the effective implementation of any of the provisions of this Convention.'

This provision originates from the work of the United Nations. In 1947, within the context of the *travaux préparatoires* of what later developed into the Universal Declaration and the two Covenants on Human Rights, a text was drawn up which related to civil and political rights. This text contained a provision according to which the Secretary-General of the United Nations would have the right to request states, after they had become parties to the treaty then under preparation, to report on the manner in which the effective implementation of the provisions of the treaty was ensured in their internal law. During the preparation of the European Convention this idea was adopted in a British proposal to the Committee of Experts and accepted by that Committee.

Under international law there are several examples of procedures in which states have to submit reports to make possible the assessment of the observance of their obligations. This system of supervision, which in general is referred to as the reporting procedure, may also constitute an effective instrument of control in the field of the protection of human rights.

Overall, states are likely to lodge an application against another state only in very exceptional cases. In this respect, the practice with regard to Article 33 (formerly 24) of the European Convention is self-explanatory. As a result of the lack of initiative on the part of states to start a complaint procedure, a gap in the supervision of the treaty concerned may readily arise, which can, however, be filled by a reporting procedure, such as is provided for in Article 52, because the initiative for the reporting procedure may be taken by an international organ and is not dependent on a decision of one of the Contracting States.

Moreover, even in the case of treaties providing for an individual right of complaint, situations which allegedly conflict with the Convention but have not yet created any victims in the sense of Article 34, can be submitted for review by the Court only by Contracting States. In such cases the supervision of the observance of the obligations under the Convention, therefore, is again dependent on the lodging of a complaint by a state, with all the disadvantages and restrictions involved, and here again, a reporting procedure may have an important supplementary value. Moreover, there may be situations where there *are* victims, who, however, for one reason or another, do not take the initiative to lodge a complaint.

Even apart from the question of whether the complaint procedure provided for in a human rights treaty functions effectively or not and whether or not the initiative has been laid also in the hands of the individual concerned, the existence of a reporting procedure side by side with a complaint procedure may be of great value. A reporting procedure may, precisely because its character differs from that of a complaint procedure, enhance the effectiveness of the international supervision in a number of respects. Thus, via a reporting procedure all the Contracting States can be supervised at the same time, while in a complaint procedure usually the acts or omissions of only one state are examined. The first advantage of this is that the resistance to the supervision may be less if all the states are equally subjected to examination. Further, because of the possibility of comparison, a more balanced picture may be obtained of the state of affairs with respect to the implementation of the treaty in question within the whole group of Contracting States, which may facilitate the taking of measures for the improvement of the situation. In addition, the reporting procedure makes it possible to complete the picture of implementation, because this form of supervision may comprise all the provisions of the treaty in question simultaneously, while in a complaint procedure only one, or at best a few of the provisions at a time will be examined. Furthermore, a reporting procedure has the advantage that the international organ concerned may assure a certain continuity in the supervision, because it can itself decide which aspects are to be examined and when, while in the case of a complaint procedure one must wait until a complaint is submitted, in which case the supervision has more of an *ad hoc* character. The continuity of the reporting procedure allows a comparison with the situation in the past and may thus greatly enhance the effectiveness of the supervision. Finally, the reporting system will in general assume a form that is more flexible than the much more formal complaint procedure.

In view of the above-mentioned advantages it is not surprising that many international instruments for the protection of human rights, both those concerning civil and political rights and those concerning economic, social and cultural rights, provide for a reporting procedure.[77]

---

[77] See, e.g., Arts. 22 and 23 of the Constitution of the International Labour Organisation; Art. 9 of the Convention on the Elimination of All Forms of Racial Discrimination; Arts. 40 et seq. of the International Covenant on Civil and Political Rights; Arts. 16 et seq. of the International Covenant on Economic, Social and Cultural Rights; Art. 19 of the Torture Convention; Art. 18 of the Convention on the Elimination of all forms of Discrimination against Women; Art. 44 of the Convention on the Rights of the Child; Art. 73 of the International Convention on the Protection of the Rights of All Migrant Workers and Members of Their Families; Art. 35 of the Convention on the Rights of Persons with Disabilities; Art. 29

2.2. REPORTING PROCEDURE UNDER ARTICLE 52

In comparison with most other human rights treaties that contain reporting obligations for the Contracting States the provision of Article 52 of the European Convention is very concise and legal practice has clarified how the provision has to be interpreted. At any rate, it is clear from the text of the article that the Secretary-General has the power to request the Contracting States to furnish an explanation of the manner in which in their internal law the effective implementation of the provisions of the Convention is ensured, and that the Contracting States have the duty to provide him with this information. For the remainder, little can be inferred with certainty from the article itself and it is thus important to look at the practice which has developed under this provision.

To date, the Secretary-General has used the power under Article 52 on only nine occasions.

On six occasions, all Contracting States were invited to submit reports on the application of the rights laid down in the Convention,[78] while on three occasions one state has been singled out. Indeed, an important development of the practice was initiated in December 1999, when for the first time the Secretary-General addressed a request to a single Contracting Party, namely the Russian Federation, asking it 'to furnish, in the light of the case-law of the European Court of Human Rights, explanations concerning the manner in which the Convention is currently being implemented in Chechnya, and the risks of violation which may result therefrom'. And the next recourse to the Article 52 procedure (in February 2002) also concerned a single state: Moldova was requested to provide explanations about the implementation of the Convention in the light of certain recent developments in that country (see *infra*). In turn, the November 2005 request to explain the possible presence of so-called black sites on their territory where suspected terrorists were transported and kept in detention, was directed to all Contracting Parties, while the latest, 2015, request has only targeted the Azerbaijani Government.[79]

As regards the subject matter of the request for explanations under Article 52, the Secretary-General has, on some occasions, referred to all or to a few of the provisions of the Convention, and in others to only one of them. In 1964, the Contracting States were requested to furnish information on the question of 'how their laws, their case-law and their administration practice give effect to

---

of the International Convention for the Protection of all Persons from Enforced Disappearance. At the European level, see, e.g., Art. 21 of the European Social Charter and Arts. 24–26 of the Framework Convention for the Protection of National Minorities.

[78]   In 1964, 1970, 1975, 1983, 1988 and 2005, respectively.

[79]   *Address by Mr Thorbjørn Jagland, Secretary General of the Council of Europe before the General Assembly of the Council of Europe*, 2017 Ordinary Session (First part) Report, Fourth sitting, 24 January 2017, AS (2017) CR 04. See also 'Secretary General launches inquiry into respect for human rights in Azerbaijan', *Newsroom*, 16 December 2015, <www.coe.int/en/web/portal/full-news>.

the fundamental rights and freedoms guaranteed by the Convention and its first Protocol'. In that case, therefore, they had to report on all the rights set forth in the Convention and the Protocol. In 1970, on the other hand, the request of the Secretary-General concerned only Article 5(5), while in 1975 information was required on the application of Articles 8, 9, 10 and 11. Moreover, on the latter occasion the Secretary-General reserved for himself the right to ask for a further explanation of certain points in connection with the reports submitted by the states. In 1983, the Secretary-General carried out an enquiry into the implementation of the Convention 'in respect of children and young persons placed in care or in institutions following a decision of the administrative or judicial authorities', while in 1988 the request concerned Article 6(1).[80] The aforementioned 1999 enquiry concerning the Russian Federation referred to recent developments in Chechnya (notably the armed intervention by Russian forces in the autumn of 1999) which raised serious questions concerning the effective implementation of the Convention. The request was not limited to one or more specific provisions of the Convention.[81] The use of the Article 52 procedure in relation to Moldova was prompted by the decision of the Moldovan authorities to suspend for one month the activities of a political opposition party and to lift the administrative parliamentary immunity of three leaders of that party. The request concerned all provisions of the Convention and additional Protocols, but fixed a shorter deadline for the explanations to be given concerning Articles 9–11, 13 and 14 of the Convention.[82] The 2005 enquiry directed to all Contracting States was prompted by allegations in the context of media and NGO reports about operations conducted by foreign agencies on the territory of Contracting Parties involving unacknowledged deprivation of liberty and transport of individuals suspected of terrorist activities. While the request referred in a general way to the domestic implementation of the provisions of the Convention and its additional Protocols, it also referred to a number of rights and freedoms which are particularly relevant to the issue of unacknowledged deprivation of liberty (namely Articles 2, 3, 5, 6, 8, 13 of the Convention and Article 2 of Protocol No. 4 to the Convention).[83]

Lately, in the March 2015 Brussels Declaration, participants to the High Level Conference, essentially consisting of government representatives of the

---

[80] Council of Europe, *Information Sheet*, No. 21, Strasbourg, 1988, p. 95.

[81] *Request for explanations concerning the manner in which the Convention is implemented in Chechnya and the risks of violation which may result therefrom, Report by the Secretary General on the use of his powers under Article 52 of the European Convention on Human Rights in respect of the Russian Federation*, Council of Europe document SG/Inf (2000) 21 and Addendum of 10 May 2000.

[82] *Report by the Secretary General on the use of his powers under Article 52 of the European Convention on Human Rights in respect of Moldova*, Council of Europe document SG/Inf (2002) 20 of 6 May 2002.

[83] *Report by the Secretary General under Article 52 ECHR on the question of secret detention and transport of detainees suspected of terrorist acts, notably by or at the instigation of foreign agencies*, Council of Europe document SG/Inf (2006) 5 of 28 February 2006.

Contracting States, when underlining 'the importance of the efficient supervision of the execution of judgments [of the European Court]' to guarantee the long-term existence of the European Convention system, for this aim 'encourage[d] [...] the Secretary-General to continue, on a case-by-case basis, to use his/her authority in order to facilitate the execution of judgments raising complex and/ or sensitive issues at the national level, including through the exercise of the powers entrusted to him/her under Article 52 of the Convention.'[84]

This recommendation seems to be rather innovative, as it seems to be an incentive from the Contracting States to the Secretary-General to use his powers under Article 52 in a broader way than he has used them until today, namely to make sure that European Court judgments which at the domestic level raise complex and/or sensitive issues, be properly implemented. Finally, in December 2015, the Secretary-General decided to make use of his competence under Article 52 to start an investigation into the way in which Azerbaijan effectively implements the provisions of the European Convention. The investigation aims to obtain explanations regarding the implementation of the judgment of the Strasbourg Court on the detention of Ilgar Mammadov (case of *Ilgar Mammadov v. Azerbaijan*) concerning multiple violations of the European Convention. Mammadov is a political opposition activist, arrested and detained in 2013 following his denouncement of the authorities' official version of the 2013 Ismayilli riots.[85] Meanwhile, in January 2017 a delegation appointed by the Secretary-General, and led by the Director of the Legal Department of the Council of Europe Secretariat Philip Buayai and Director of Political Affairs Alexander Gessel, discussed the *Mammadov* case judgment and other issues related to this with government officials in Baku.

The Article 52 practice shows that, compared to traditional reporting procedures provided for under human rights treaties, the Article 52 procedure is unique in that the Secretary-General's power is of a discretionary nature.

As early as 1964, before the first use was made of this procedure, then under Article 57 of the Convention, the Secretary-General expressed this view in a statement made before the Legal Committee of the Parliamentary Assembly: 'The Secretary-General in making a request under Article 57 is acting under his own responsibility and at his own discretion, in virtue of powers conferred upon him by the Convention independently of any powers he may have in virtue of the Statute of the Council of Europe. His power under Article 57 is not subject to control or instruction.'[86]

---

84   *High-level Conference on the 'Implementation of the European Convention on Human Rights, our shared responsibility',* Brussels Declaration of 27 March 2015.

85   *Address by Mr Thorbjørn Jagland, Secretary General of the Council of Europe before the General Assembly of the Council of Europe, supra* n. 79.

86   *Statement by the Secretary General on Art. 57 of the European Convention on Human Rights made before the Legal Committee of the Consultative Assembly in Oslo on 29 August 1964,* Council of Europe, *Collected Texts,* Strasbourg, 1994, pp. 235–236.

To date not a single Contracting State has officially objected to this interpretation by the Secretary-General of his supervisory powers. It may, therefore, be assumed that the above-mentioned statement constitutes a generally accepted interpretation of Article 52. This is not to say, however, that the Secretary-General's actions in this field are always welcomed by the Contracting States.[87] The sixth request has not been met by adequate explanations from the Russian authorities.[88] It should be noted, however, that the more recent practice of using Article 52 powers in respect of a single state has not been contested by any Contracting Party.

It follows from the discretionary nature of this power that the Secretary-General has discretion notably in deciding whether and when to issue the request, in choosing the state or states to which it will be addressed, in determining the subject matter of the request, and in fixing time-limits for the submission of the explanations. This also appears from the above-mentioned practice under Article 52.

An interesting development occurred in the context of the 1999 request to the Russian Federation about Chechnya. The Secretary-General considered that the lengthy initial reply from the Russian authorities only referred to the Convention in a general and summary way and that it did not contain the explanations requested. He sent a second letter to clarify his request, referring *inter alia* to the requirement of strict proportionality of the use of force set out in Article 2 of the Convention and asking for precise details of precautions taken by the authorities in the choice of means and methods of the operation of the federal forces in Chechnya so as to respect the obligations under Article 2. The second reply was still not considered satisfactory and a subsequent reply to a third and last letter of the Secretary-General did not add much either. In a report transmitted to the Committee of Ministers and the Parliamentary Assembly,[89] the Secretary-General, therefore, concluded that the 'affirmations of a general nature' contained in the replies 'cannot be considered as satisfactory "explanations" for the purposes of Article 52 of the Convention'. He requested a team of recognised experts in international human rights law to analyse the correspondence in greater depth 'in the light of the obligations incumbent on a High Contracting Party which is the recipient of a request under Art 52'.

---

[87] E.g., 3 States have refused to furnish a reply to his fourth request: the Federal Republic of Germany, Iceland and Malta.

[88] The request about detention and transport of suspects of terrorism has not met with any refusal, but some of the reactions led to a second round.

[89] Copies were sent, for information, to the European Court of Human Rights, the Council of Europe Commissioner for Human Rights and the United Nations High Commissioner for Human Rights.

The report submitted by the three experts opens with a general analysis of the legal framework of the Secretary-General's request set out in Article 52.[90] They affirmed the discretionary nature of the power (which includes the possibility of requesting information from one specific Contracting Party in a specific context), but added that this does not mean that there are no guiding principles at all for the exercise of this discretionary power.[91] The experts' report listed six principles derived from the effectiveness principle, which is the principle according to which the provisions of the Convention shall be interpreted and applied in such a manner as will make them effective. These principles are:

– the Secretary-General's choice of the state and of the occasion must be obvious or based on sound arguments;
– the request for explanations must be as specific as possible;
– the Article 52 procedure must be exercised in an objective manner;
– the answer(s) must be adequate and sufficiently detailed; if necessary, additional information must be requested and provided;
– channels for dialogue must be open;
– the Secretary-General must draw conclusions from the outcome of the procedure and submit these to the political and legal bodies within the framework of the Council of Europe.[92]

As regards the obligations of a recipient state, the experts stressed that such a state has the obligation to provide truthful explanations about the effective implementation of the Convention in its internal law. This is an obligation of result: the state cannot limit itself to giving explanations of a formal nature. Bearing in mind also the obligation to execute treaty obligations in good faith (Article 26 of the 1969 Vienna Convention on the Law of Treaties), the state must provide precise and adequate explanations which make it possible to verify whether the Convention is actually implemented in its internal law. According to the experts, this necessarily implies that sufficiently detailed information must be provided about national law and practice, particularly about judicial authorities, and about their conformity with Convention and the case law of its supervisory organs.[93]

---

[90] *Consolidated report containing an analysis of the correspondence between the Secretary General of the Council of Europe and the Russian Federation under Article 52 of the European Convention on Human Rights*, prepared by Tamas Ban, Frédéric Sudre and Pieter van Dijk, Council of Europe document SG/Inf (2000) 24 of 26 June 2000. The 3 individual reports which formed the basis for this consolidated report are contained in document SG/Inf (2000) 24 Addendum of the same date.
[91] *Ibid.*, paras. 4 and 5.
[92] *Ibid.*, para. 7.
[93] *Ibid.*, para. 6.

After having analysed the correspondence under Article 52 in light of these requirements, the experts concluded that the replies were not adequate and that the Russian Federation had failed in its legal obligations as a Contracting State under Article 52 of the Convention.[94]

2.3. FOLLOW-UP TO EXPLANATIONS RECEIVED UNDER ARTICLE 52

Practice under Article 52 has also produced some clarity concerning the question about what is to be done with the reports submitted by the Contracting States and what consequences, if any, may be attached to a violation of the Convention discovered in this way. The Secretary-General compiles the answers of the Contracting States to his requests in a document which is subsequently brought to the notice of all the Contracting States and of the Parliamentary Assembly of the Council of Europe.[95]

Therefore, the answers of the Contracting States are made public. This in itself may already constitute an element of sanction for those cases in which, according to those answers, there has been a violation of the Convention. For that purpose, some kind of (comparative) analysis with the assistance of independent experts might be desirable, as was done with the results of the third inquiry by the Secretary-General.

In this way, the defaulting state is exposed to criticism of the other states, the Parliamentary Assembly and public opinion. However, it is doubtful whether, when serious violations have been found, this sanction will be sufficiently effective to put an end to the violation. The Secretary-General has not been empowered to refer a case via a complaint procedure to the Court. Such a possibility might enhance the effectiveness of the supervision under Article 52, although one may wonder whether this power would not place the Secretary-General too far outside his proper function. It would seem more appropriate to place such a right of application in the public interest with a separate institution. During the drafting of Protocol No. 14 to the Convention (opened for signature on 13 May 2004) the Council of Europe Commissioner for Human Rights suggested that he be given such a right of application. The drafting body, the Steering Committee for Human Rights, considered that such an 'accusatory' role could easily interfere with the Commissioner's main tasks defined in Committee of Ministers Resolution (99) 50, which are based on a co-operative relationship between the Commissioner and the member states. However, the Steering Committee did agree that it would be useful to give the Commissioner

---

[94]   *Ibid.*, para. 32.
[95]   The more recent reports were also transmitted, for information purposes, to other bodies, including the Court.

a right (as opposed to merely the option of asking to be invited, which already existed) to intervene as third party in proceedings before a Chamber or Grand Chamber of the Court, as a way of strengthening the general interest factor in Convention proceedings.[96] This resulted in Article 13 of Protocol No. 14, which introduces a new third paragraph in Article 36 of the Convention, granting the Commissioner such a right of intervention, which he has meanwhile used on several occasions.[97]

Under the present circumstances, in many cases a violation found via the reporting procedure can be subjected to a further examination resulting in a binding decision only if one of the other states is prepared – perhaps also on the basis of the information obtained by means of Article 52 – to make use of its right under Article 33, provided that the admissibility conditions of Article 35(1) are fulfilled. It should be noted, however, that, as concerns the compliance with the Convention by Russia in the context of its actions in Chechnya, no inter-state application was brought during or following the conclusion of the Article 52 procedure, despite clear appeals from the Parliamentary Assembly.[98]

Currently, and next to this, in individual cases before the European Court, information provided by Contracting States in the ambit of a request under Article 52 ECHR may be used by the European Court in order to establish the facts and assess the evidence. For example, in *El-Nashiri v. Poland* and *Husayn (Abu Zubaydah) v. Poland*, the information given by Poland under Article 52 in relation to allegations of secret detention sites operated by the CIA in European states, in which it had held that the findings of the Polish Government's internal enquiry into the alleged existence in Poland of secret detention centres and related overflights, fully denied the allegations in the debate,[99] were picked up by the European Court to slam the respondent State. The Court first confirmed that Poland's lack of co-operation in the course of the international inquiries into the CIA rendition operations was an element that was relevant for its assessment of Poland's alleged knowledge of and complicity in the CIA rendition operations. It then held that the Polish Government, in its 10 March 2006 response to the Secretary-General questions in the ambit of the Article 52 procedure, 'fully denied' the allegations of 'the alleged existence in Poland of secret detention centres and related over-flights, relying on the findings of the Polish Government's internal inquiry", to come to the conclusion that the Government could not have been unaware of the CIA operations in the country

---

[96] Explanatory Report to Protocol No. 14, paras. 86–88.
[97] See, e.g., *Bagirov v. Azerbaijan*, ECtHR communicated on 24 June 2016, appl. no. 28198/15; *Estemirova v. Russia*, ECtHR communicated on 16 November 2015, appl. no. 42705/11.
[98] Parliamentary Assembly Resolution 1221 (2000) on the conflict in the Chechen Republic, para. 22.
[99] *Al-Nashiri v. Poland*, ECtHR 24 July 2014, appl. no. 28761/11, para. 242; *Husayn (Abu Zubaydah) v. Poland*, ECtHR 24 July 2014, appl. no. 7511/13, para. 236.

in 2002–03.[100] Finally, and on the basis of abundant and coherent circumstantial evidence, the Court held that Poland knew of the nature and purposes of the CIA's activities on its territory at the material time and that Poland co-operated in the preparation and execution of the CIA rendition, secret detention and interrogation operations on its territory.[101]

The Secretary-General himself can do little else but bring the issue, if there has been a very serious violation, to the notice of the Committee of Ministers. Under a political monitoring procedure created by the Committee of Ministers' Declaration on compliance with commitments accepted by member states of the Council of Europe (10 November 1994), member states, the Secretary-General or the Parliamentary Assembly may refer matters to the Committee of Ministers regarding 'questions of implementation of commitments concerning the situation of democracy, human rights and the rule of law in any member State'. This is in fact what the Secretary-General did in June 2000, after having received the expert analysis of his correspondence with the Russian Federation under Article 52. In October 2000, the Committee of Ministers decided to deal with this matter as part of the regular discussions on the Council of Europe's contribution to re-establishing the rule of law, respect for human rights and democracy in Chechnya.[102] No measures were taken on the ground of Article 8 of the Statute of the Council of Europe.

By contrast, there was specific follow-up to the next Article 52 enquiry. The replies received from the Moldovan authorities not only indicated that the decision to suspend the activities of the opposition party in question had been revoked but also that they recognised that there were numerous elements of Moldovan law which raised serious questions as to their conformity with the Convention. In his report, the Secretary-General also noted some essential additional problems of compatibility and stated that he expected the Moldovan authorities to conduct a thorough review of domestic law and practice and to take steps rapidly to rectify the shortcomings already found. Furthermore, he expected the authorities to provide him with further information resulting from these actions. This indicates that the Article 52 procedure in respect of Moldova was left open, pending receipt of information about such domestic follow-up measures.[103] The Committee of Ministers subsequently adopted a targeted co-operation programme which was partly designed to assist the Moldovan authorities in conducting the necessary reviews of domestic law and practice in areas identified in the Article 52 procedure. The Council of Europe has on many

---

[100]   *Al-Nashiri v. Poland, supra* n. 100, paras. 429–430; *Husayn (Abu Zubaydah) v. Poland, supra* n. 100, 431–432.

[101]   *Al-Nashiri v. Poland, supra* n. 100, para. 442; *Husayn (Abu Zubaydah) v. Poland, supra* n. 100, para. 444.

[102]   See *Council of Europe monitoring procedures: an overview*, Council of Europe document Monitor/Inf (2004) 2 of 5 April 2004, para. 12.

[103]   See *supra* n. 82, paras. 35–36.

occasions provided comments by Convention experts on existing and draft legislation.

The comparison with the follow-up given to the Article 52 procedure in respect of the Russian Federation concerning Chechnya indicates that, especially in cases of allegations of massive and serious human rights violations, recourse to Article 52 will not bring any practical results if the state concerned is not willing to fulfil its obligations under Article 52 and if the procedure's outcome is not backed up by political support, notably from the Committee of Ministers. On the other hand, where the state co-operates in the procedure, and if the Committee of Ministers is willing to act, the procedure has the potential to lead to concrete steps to improve compliance with the Convention.

CHAPTER 4
SYSTEM OF RESTRICTIONS

Laurens Lavrysen[*]

CONTENTS

1. INTRODUCTION

This chapter deals with the nature and scope of restrictions of Convention rights. With the exception of absolute rights, the rights guaranteed under the Convention can under certain conditions be justifiably restricted by the state. This chapter deals with the nature and scope of such restrictions. It focuses, in particular, on the express limitations clauses attached to Articles 8–11 of the Convention and Article 2 of Protocol No. 4. These are discussed together with Articles 6(1) (right of access to court) and 14 of the Convention and Articles 1–3 of Protocol No. 1, which the Court has interpreted as being subject to implied limitations if a number of criteria resembling those of the express limitations clauses are met. The general restriction clauses of Articles 15–18 of the

---

[*]   In the fourth edition this chapter was revised and updated by Yukata Arai.

Convention are not addressed here, but will rather be discussed in the respective chapters focusing on these provisions. The present chapter also focuses on the scope and limits of positive obligations under the Convention. Finally, the margin of appreciation doctrine, which determines the intensity of the Court's scrutiny in both negative and positive obligations cases, will be discussed.

2. CONDITIONS FOR RESTRICTING CONVENTION RIGHTS

2.1. INTRODUCTION

With the exception of Articles 3, 4 and 9 (the 'internal' dimension of freedom of religion),[1] the rights set forth in the Convention are non-absolute. With respect to some non-absolute rights, the text of the Convention expressly provides for the possibility to restrict these rights. The structure of the second paragraphs of Articles 8–11 of the Convention and the third paragraph of Article 2 of Protocol No. 4 is almost identical, with these paragraphs designed to qualify the exercise of the rights guaranteed under the first paragraph of those provisions.[2] Similarly worded limitations are also found under the second sentence of Article 6(1) relating to the right to a public trial, and Article 1 of the Seventh Protocol which guarantees the right of an alien lawfully resident in the territory of a member state not to be expelled. Despite the variety of denominations used to describe the possibilities of qualifying the exercise of Convention rights in these paragraphs, such as 'interference',[3] 'limitations',[4] 'restrictions',[5] 'formalities, conditions, restrictions or penalties',[6] 'depriv[ation]'[7] and 'control',[8] they can all be categorised as 'limitations'.

With respect to the limitation clauses under Articles 8–11 of the Convention and Article 2 of the Fourth Protocol, the same principles apply when assessing the compliance of interference with the requirements of the Convention provisions. When the Court identifies an interference with a right provided in these provisions, a further examination is required to determine whether such

---

[1] While Art. 9 guarantees both the right to freedom of thought, conscience and religion (the internal dimension) and the freedom to manifest one's religion or belief (the external dimension), the second paragraph only allows room for interferences with the latter freedom.

[2] In the case of Art. 2(3) of the Fourth Protocol, this clause qualifies the rights under the first paragraph and the second paragraph.

[3] Art. 8(2) of the Convention.

[4] Art. 9(2) of the Convention.

[5] First and second sentences of Art. 11(2) of the Convention; and Art. 2(3) and (4) of the Fourth Protocol.

[6] Art. 10(2) of the Convention.

[7] Second sentence of Art. 1(1) of the First Protocol.

[8] Art. 1(2) of the First Protocol.

interference can be justified on the basis of the three standards laid down in the Convention and elaborated through the case law. The first standard demands that any interference with the Convention right must be 'in accordance with law' or 'prescribed by law'. Second, such interference must pursue any of the legitimate aims that are exhaustively laid down in the second paragraphs of Articles 8–11. Third, an interfering measure must be considered 'necessary in a democratic society'. The methodology established in the case law is to examine the three standards in sequence. In case of any finding of a breach of the first or the second standard, this will obliterate the need for evaluations based on the third standard,[9] save in very special circumstances where the Court considers the nature of issues relating to these standards to be such as to require a separate examination.[10] A survey of the case law reveals the tendency of the Court to focus its rigorous scrutiny on the third standard.[11] As regards cases relating to the second paragraphs of Articles 8–11, the Court has repeatedly stressed that exceptions to these rights must be 'narrowly interpreted'[12] and that any restriction 'must be convincingly established'.[13]

With respect to other non-absolute rights that do not contain an express limitations clause, the Court has considered there to be room for so-called 'implied limitations'. The Court has, in particular, accepted such 'implied relations' in relation to the right of access to court, encompassed by Article 6(1),[14] the right of access to education under Article 2 of the First Protocol[15] and the right to vote and to stand for election under Article 3 of the First Protocol.[16] The application of implied limitations can also be seen in respect of limitations of the right to property under Article 1 of Protocol No. 1. The second sentence of the first paragraph and the second paragraph of Article 1 Protocol No. 1, respectively, expressly provide that the state may under certain conditions justifiably take measures that amount to deprivations of possessions or to the control of the use of property. The first sentence of the first paragraph of Article 1 of Protocol No. 1, which sets out the overarching right to the peaceful enjoyment of one's

---

[9]   See, e.g., *Malone v. the United Kingdom*, ECtHR (GC) 2 August 1984, appl. no. 8691/79, para. 82 (legality); and *Nolan and K. v. Russia*, ECtHR 12 February 2009, appl. no. 2512/04, paras. 73–75 (legitimate aim).

[10]   See, e.g., *Baka v. Hungary*, ECtHR (GC) 23 June 2016, appl. no. 20261/12, para. 157.

[11]   See, e.g., *Wille v. Liechtenstein*, ECtHR (GC) 28 October 1999, appl. no. 28396/95, paras. 55–56.

[12]   *Silver and Others v. the United Kingdom*, ECtHR 25 March 1983, appl. nos. 5947/72 etc., para. 97. See also *Klass and Others v. Germany*, ECtHR (GC) 6 September 1978, appl. no. 5029/71, para. 42.

[13]   See, e.g., *Funke v. France*, ECtHR 25 February 1993, appl. no. 10828/84, para. 55.

[14]   See, e.g., *Golder v. the United Kingdom*, ECtHR (GC) 21 February 1975, appl. no. 4451/70, para. 38.

[15]   *Leyla Sahin v. Turkey*, ECtHR (GC) 10 November 2005, appl. no. 44774/98, para. 154.

[16]   See, e.g., *Hirst v. the United Kingdom (No. 2)*, ECtHR (GC) 6 October 2005, appl. no. 74025/01, para. 60.

possessions,[17] however, does not expressly provide for the possibility to restrict this right. The Court has nonetheless interpreted this provision as allowing room for limitations if a number of conditions are met.[18] These implied limitations will be discussed along with the express limitations clauses, since the criteria applied to determine whether the state has justifiably interfered with these rights mirror the three-pronged test contained in Articles 8–11 and Article 2 of Protocol No. 4. The Court has for instance held that, in order for an interference with Article 1 of Protocol No. 1 to be deemed compatible with this provision, it should be 'lawful', pursue a 'legitimate aim' and respect a 'fair balance' between the demands of the general interest of the community and the requirements of the protection of the individual's fundamental rights.[19] While not applying a legality test under these provisions, the Court does require interferences with the right of access to court (Article 6(1)) and Articles 2–3 of Protocol No. 1 to pursue a legitimate aim and to comply with the proportionality test.[20] Moreover, in order to determine whether there is an objective and reasonable justification for a difference in treatment on the basis of certain proscribed grounds, the Court similarly applies a legitimacy and proportionality test under Article 14, which for this reason will therefore be discussed hereunder together with the already-mentioned provisions.

Finally, it must be stressed that restrictions of Convention rights may ensue from the way in which a right has been formulated, with a clause or phrase delimiting the scope of protection of certain rights and explicitly excluding specific areas or persons from their scope of protection, or 'delegating' to state authorities the responsibility of regulating the exercise of certain rights. First, such 'limitations by delimitation' can be seen in the case where provisions expressly refer to certain areas or subject matters as not encompassed by their scope of application *ratione materiae*. Article 2(2) expressly rules out three circumstances as not constituting a violation of Article 2, subject to the condition that the use of force that results in deprivation of life is no more than absolutely necessary. Similarly, Article 4(3) excludes four types of services or work from the notion of 'forced or compulsory labour' within the meaning of the second paragraph, whereas Article 5(1) envisages six exhaustive cases of lawful arrest or detention as exceptions to the right to liberty and security as provided in the first sentence. These 'limitations by delimitation' are not governed by the three-

---

[17] In *James and Others v. the United Kingdom*, ECtHR (Plenary) 21 February 1986, appl. no. 8793/79, para. 37, the Court held that '[t]he three rules are not, however, "distinct" in the sense of being unconnected. The second and third rules are concerned with particular instances of interference with the right to peaceful enjoyment of property and should therefore be construed in the light of the general principle enunciated in the first rule.'

[18] See, e.g., *Sporrong and Lönnroth v. Sweden*, ECtHR (Plenary) 23 September 1982, appl. nos. 7151/75 and 7152/75.

[19] See, e.g., *Beyeler v. Italy*, ECtHR (GC) 5 January 2000, appl. no. 33202/96, paras. 107–114.

[20] See, e.g., *Baka v. Hungary, supra* n. 10, para. 120 (Art. 6(1)); *Leyla Sahin v. Turkey, supra* n. 15, para. 154 (Art. 2 of Protocol No. 1); and *Hirst v. the United Kingdom (No. 2), supra* n. 16, para. 62 (Art. 3 of Protocol No. 1).

pronged test and will therefore not be addressed in this chapter, but rather when discussing the scope of the respective Convention rights concerned.

2.2. PRESCRIBED BY LAW; IN ACCORDANCE WITH THE LAW

The English text of the Convention uses the different terms 'in accordance with the law'[21] 'prescribed by law',[22] as well as 'subject to the conditions provided for by law',[23] but it has been established in the case law that all of them must be interpreted in the light of the same general principles.[24] The French text, which is equally authentic, uses the same expression, *'prévue(s) par la loi'*, in the second paragraphs of Articles 8–11 of the Convention and Article 2(3) of the Fourth Protocol. The Court has similarly required interferences with Article 1 of Protocol No. 1 to be 'lawful', a requirement which it has interpreted in the same sense as the legality requirement under Articles 8–11 and Article 2 of Protocol No. 4.

In the first place, the legality test requires that interferences by state authorities must be in conformity with domestic law. In determining whether the state has complied with this test, the Court will look at the law in its 'substantive', not in its 'formal' sense. Law in the 'substantive' sense includes both 'written' law, encompassing enactments of lower ranking statutes[25] and regulatory measures taken by professional regulatory bodies under independent rule-making powers delegated to them by Parliament,[26] and 'unwritten' law.[27] It includes both statutory law and judge-made law.[28] In short, according to the Court, law in its 'substantive' sense must be understood as 'the provision in force as the competent courts have interpreted it'.[29]

In addition, the Court also scrutinises whether the law is of sufficient 'quality'. The case law reveals three essential components of the notion of 'quality of law'.[30]

---

[21] Art. 8(2) of the Convention, Art. 2(3) and (4) of Protocol No. 4 and Art. 1(1) of Protocol No. 7.

[22] Arts. 9(2), 10(2), 11(2) of the Convention as well as Art. 2(2) of Protocol No. 7.

[23] Art. 1 of Protocol No. 1.

[24] *Silver and Others v. the United Kingdom, supra* n. 12, para. 85; and *Malone v. the United Kingdom, supra* n. 9, para. 66. See also *The Sunday Times v. the United Kingdom (No. 1)*, ECtHR (Plenary) 26 April 1979, appl. no. 6538/74, paras. 47 and 49.

[25] See *De Wilde, Ooms and Versyp v. Belgium ('Vagrancy' Cases)*, ECtHR (Plenary) 18 June 1971, appl. nos. 2832/66, 2835/66 and 2899/66, para. 93.

[26] See *Barthold v. Germany* ECtHR 25 March 1985, appl. no. 8734/79, para. 46.

[27] See *Leyla Sahin v. Turkey, supra* n. 15, para. 88.

[28] *Idem.*

[29] *Idem.*

[30] See, e.g., *The Sunday Times v. the United Kingdom (No. 1), supra* n. 24, para. 49; *Silver and Others v. the United Kingdom, supra* n. 12., paras. 86–88; *Olsson v. Sweden (No. 1)*, ECtHR (Plenary) 24 March 1988, appl. no. 10465/83, para. 61; and *Rekvényi v. Hungary*, ECtHR (GC) 20 May 1999, appl. no. 25390/94, para. 34.

First, the national legal provision that provides for an interfering measure must be accessible to citizens, which means that 'the citizen must be able to have an indication that is adequate, in the circumstances, of the legal rules applicable to a given case'.[31] The test of accessibility does not require states to codify every law, allowing room for common law.[32] It is sufficient that the law is at the reasonable disposal of the citizens with the advice of legal experts. The test of adequate accessibility has not given rise to serious problems for national authorities, and the Strasbourg organs' assessment based on this test has remained relatively brief.

Second, the law must be formulated in such a way as to enable citizens to foresee with precision the exact scope and meaning of the provision so as to enable them to regulate their conduct. The Court has noted that a citizen 'must be able – if need be with appropriate advice – to foresee, to a degree that is reasonable in the circumstances, the consequences which a given action may entail'.[33] This foreseeability or precision test has been deployed as a crucial interpretive device to heighten the standard of review. It furnishes a crucial safeguard for the citizen, requiring the law at issue to be 'sufficiently clear' and precise, with 'adequate indication' as to the conditions under which any intrusive measures, such as secret surveillance and interception, are to be employed.[34] The Court has, however, recognised the relative nature of the level of precision required, which depends on three factors: the content of the legislative instrument, the field it is designed to cover, and the number and status of addressees.[35] On this matter, the Court has consistently recognised that 'many laws are inevitably couched in terms which, to a greater or lesser extent, are vague and whose interpretation and application are questions of practice',

---

[31]   See, *inter alia*, *The Sunday Times v. the United Kingdom (No. 1)*, *supra* n. 24, paras. 47 and 49; *Hashman and Harrup v. the United Kingdom*, ECtHR (GC), 25 November 1999, appl. no. 25594/94, para. 31 (Art. 10); *Silver and Others v. the United Kingdom*, *supra* n. 12, paras. 86–88 (Art. 8); *Larissis and Others v. Greece*, ECtHR 24 February 1998, appl. no. 23372/94, para. 40 (Art. 9); *Maestri v. Italy*, ECtHR (GC) 17 February 2004, appl. no. 39748/98, para. 30 (Art. 11); and *Landvreugd v. the Netherlands*, ECtHR 4 June 2002, appl. no. 37331/97, para. 54 (Art. 2 of Protocol No. 4).

[32]   E.g. in *The Sunday Times v. the United Kingdom (No. 1)*, *supra* n. 24, paras. 46–53, the issue was the common law notion of contempt of court.

[33]   See, *inter alia*, *The Sunday Times v. the United Kingdom (No. 1)*, *supra* n. 24, paras. 47 and 49 (Art. 10); *Silver and Others v. the United Kingdom*, *supra* n. 12, paras. 86–88 (Art. 8); *Larissis and Others v. Greece*, *supra* n. 31, para. 40 (Art. 9); *Maestri v. Italy*, *supra* n. 31, para. 30 (Art. 11); *Landvreugd v. the Netherlands*, *supra* n. 31, para. 54 (Art. 2 of Protocol No. 4).

[34]   See, e.g., *Halford v. the United Kingdom*, ECtHR 25 June 1997, appl. no. 20605/92, para. 49; and *Kopp v. Switzerland*, ECtHR 25 March 1998, appl. no. 23224/94, paras. 64 and 72. See also *Kruslin v. France*, ECtHR 24 April 1990, appl. no. 11801/85, para. 33; and *Hurvig v. France*, ECtHR 24 April 1990, appl. no. 11105/84, para. 32.

[35]   *Chorherr v. Austria*, ECtHR 25 August 1993, appl. no. 13308/87, para. 25. See also *Silver and Others v. the United Kingdom*, *supra* n. 12, para. 88; *Groppera Radio AG and Others v. Switzerland*, ECtHR (Plenary) 28 March 1990, appl. no. 10890/84, para. 68; and *Herczegfalvy v. Austria*, ECtHR 24 September 1992, appl. no. 10533/83, para. 89·

referring to the impossibility of attaining absolute certainty in framing laws and the risk that the search for certainty may entail excessive rigidity.[36]

Third, as enunciated in the *Olsson v. Sweden (No. 1)* case,[37] the notion of 'quality of the law' requires that, as a corollary of the foreseeability test, adequate safeguards against abuses must be proffered in a manner that would clearly demarcate the extent of the authorities' discretion and define the circumstances in which it is to be exercised.[38] The Court has continuously stressed the importance of such safeguards, linking the notion of 'in accordance with law' with the overarching principle of the rule of law. According to the Court, a law that confers discretion is not in itself contrary to the requirement of foreseeability. However, such a law must satisfy the condition that 'the scope of the discretion and the manner of its exercise are indicated with sufficient clarity, having regard to the legitimate aim of the measure in question, to give the individual adequate protection against arbitrary interference'.[39] The need for legal safeguards against arbitrary intrusions is all the more important where the executive exercises a power in secret.[40] In this respect, the Court in *Al-Nashif v. Bulgaria* held that '[e]ven where national security is at stake, the concepts of lawfulness and the rule of law in a democratic society require that measures affecting fundamental human rights must be subject to some form of adversarial proceedings before an independent body competent to review the reasons for the decision and relevant evidence, if need be with appropriate procedural limitations on the use of classified information.'[41]

The principle of legality can also be found in Articles 5(1) and Article 7 of the Convention. The Court has interpreted the expressions 'lawful' and 'in accordance with a procedure prescribed by law' in Article 5(1) as encompassing a foreseeability test. According to the Court, 'given the importance of personal liberty, it is essential that the applicable national law meet the standard of 'lawfulness' set by the Convention, which requires that all law, whether written or unwritten, be sufficiently precise to allow the citizen – if need be, with appropriate advice – to foresee, to a degree that is reasonable in the circumstances, the consequences which a given action may entail.'[42]

---

[36] See, *inter alia*, *The Sunday Times v. the United Kingdom (No. 1)*, *supra* n. 24, para. 49; *Rekyényi v. Hungary*, *supra* n. 30, para. 34; *Busuioc v. Moldova*, ECtHR 21 December 2004, appl. no. 61513/00, para. 52. See *Landvreugd v. the Netherlands*, *supra* n. 31, para. 61 (Art. 2 of the Fourth Protocol).

[37] *Olsson v. Sweden (No. 1)*, *supra* n. 30, para. 61.

[38] See, *inter alia*, *Malone v. the United Kingdom*, *supra* n. 9, para. 67; *Olsson v. Sweden (No. 1)*, *supra* n. 30, para. 61; and *Valenzuela Contreras v. Spain*, ECtHR 30 July 1998, appl. no. 27671/95, paras. 59–60.

[39] See, e.g., *Gillow v. the United Kingdom*, ECtHR 24 November 1986, appl. no. 9063/80, para. 51; *Olsson v. Sweden (No. 1)*, *supra* n. 30, para. 61.

[40] See, *inter alia*, *Kruslin v. France*, *supra* n. 34, para. 25.

[41] *Al-Nashif v. Bulgaria*, ECtHR 20 June 2002, appl. no. 50963/99, para. 123; see also *Hasan and Chaush v. Bulgaria*, ECtHR (GC) 26 October 2000, appl. no. 30985/96, para. 85.

[42] *Steel and Others v. the United Kingdom*, ECtHR 23 September 1998, appl. no. 24838/94, para. 54.

The Court has similarly interpreted Article 7 – which embodies the principle that only the law can define a crime and prescribe a penalty (*nullum crimen, nulla poena sine lege*) and its derivative principle that criminal law must not be extensively construed to the detriment of the accused, for instance, by analogy, as encompassing the requirements of accessibility and foreseeability. In particular, the Court has held that the requirements of Article 7 are satisfied 'where the individual can know from the wording of the relevant provision and, if need be, with the assistance of the courts' interpretation of it, what acts and omissions will make him liable'.[43]

2.3. LEGITIMATE AIM

States may invoke legitimate aims or purposes laid down in the limitation clauses under Articles 8–11 of the Convention and Article 2 of Protocol No.4. The catalogue of such aims includes interests of national security, territorial integrity or public safety, the prevention of disorder or crime, the protection of health or morals, the interest in the well-being of the country, the protection of public order, the maintenance of *ordre public*, the protection of the reputation and the rights and freedoms of others, the prevention of the disclosure of information received in confidence, and the maintenance of the authority and impartiality of the judiciary. The list of legitimate purposes enumerated under the second paragraphs of Articles 8–11 and the third paragraph of Article 2 of Protocol No. 4 is exhaustive. The Court similarly requires the state to pursue a legitimate aim when examining interferences with the right of access to court under Article 6(1) and Articles 1–3 of Protocol No. 1 or when examining whether the state can provide an objective and reasonable justification for a difference of treatment under Article 14.[44] Under these provisions, unlike in the case of Articles 8–11 and Article 2 of Protocol No. 4, the Court is not bound by an exhaustive list of legitimate aims[45] – in other words, any aim that can be considered legitimate will do.

Traditionally, the Court's practice is to be rather succinct during the legitimacy stage, easily accepting that a restriction pursues a legitimate aim.[46] Instead, the Court places the main focus of its enquiry on the proportionality stage, where the weight of the invoked aim will be an important factor in the

---

[43] *Kokkinakis v. Greece*, ECtHR 25 May 1993, appl. no. 14307/88, para. 52.
[44] See, e.g., *Baka v. Hungary*, *supra* n. 10, para. 120 (Art. 6(1)); *Beyeler v. Italy*, *supra* n. 19, para. 111 (Art. 1 of Protocol No. 1); *Leyla Sahin v. Turkey*, *supra* n. 15, para. 154 (Art. 2 of Protocol No. 1); *Hirst v. the United Kingdom (No. 2)*, *supra* n. 16, para. 62 (Art. 3 of Protocol No. 1); and *Konstantin Markin v. Russia*, ECtHR (GC) 22 March 2012, appl. no. 30078/06, para. 125 (Art. 14).
[45] See, e.g., *Leyla Sahin v. Turkey*, *supra* n. 15, para. 154 (Art. 2 of Protocol No. 1).
[46] See, e.g., *Leyla Sahin v. Turkey*, *ibid.*, para. 99; *Maslov v. Austria*, ECtHR (GC) 23 June 2008, appl. no. 1638/03, para. 67; *S. and Marper v. the United Kingdom*, ECtHR (GC) 4 December 2008, appl. nos. 30562/04 and 30566/04, para. 100.

proportionality analysis. Arguably, this practice may be undergoing change, as in a number of more recent cases, the Court has put more emphasis on the legitimacy stage. The Court has, for example, done so by providing a lengthy discussion of this question before accepting the legitimacy of the invoked aim;[47] by raising doubts as to the legitimacy of the invoked aim, nonetheless deciding not to take a firm stance on this question as the challenged interference failed the proportionality test anyway;[48] by filtering out some of the invoked aims for failing to satisfy the legitimacy standard, but nonetheless accepting another legitimate aim for the interference;[49] or by finding a violation on account of a failure to comply with the legitimacy standard.[50]

2.4. NECESSITY; PROPORTIONALITY; FAIR BALANCE

The main focus of the Court's analysis of whether a restriction is justified typically lies on the third standard, the proportionality test. The second paragraph of Articles 8–11 and the third paragraph of Article 2 of Protocol No. 4 require an interference to be 'necessary in a democratic society', which implies that 'there must always be a proportionate relationship between the aims pursued by the interference and the Convention right at stake.'[51] The Court has similarly applied the principle of proportionality in order to determine whether the state could justifiably restrict those rights that can be subjected to implied limitations. In order to determine whether the state has justifiably restricted the right of access to court (Article 6(1) or Articles 1 and 2 of Protocol No. 1), or whether there is an objective and reasonable justification for a difference of treatment under Article 14, the Court has required there to be 'a reasonable relationship of proportionality between the means employed and the aim sought to be realised'.[52] Similarly, under Article 3 of Protocol No. 1, the Court has required 'that the means employed are not disproportionate'.[53] In the context of positive obligations, discussed hereunder, the Court applies a fair

---

[47] See, e.g., *Vintman v. Ukraine*, ECtHR 23 October 2014, appl. no. 28403/05, paras. 94–99.

[48] See, e.g., *Khoroshenko v. Russia*, ECtHR (GC) 30 June 2015, appl. no. 41418/04, paras. 114–115; and *Zaieţ v. Romania*, ECtHR 24 March 2015, appl. no. 44958/05, para. 42.

[49] *S.A.S. v. France*, ECtHR (GC) 1 July 2014, appl. no. 43835/11, paras. 113–120.

[50] See, e.g., *Baka v. Hungary, supra* n. 10, paras. 156–157; *Emel Boyraz v. Turkey*, ECtHR 2 December 2014, appl. no. 61960/08, paras. 52–56; *Dimitrovi v. Bulgaria*, ECtHR 3 March 2015, appl. no. 12655/09, paras. 51–55. Also, the older case of *Nolan and K. v Russia*, ECtHR 12 February 2009, appl. no. 2512/04, paras. 73–75.

[51] J. Gerards, 'How to Improve the Necessity Test of the European Court of Human Rights', 11 *International Journal of Constitutional Law*, 2013, p. 466 at p. 467.

[52] See, e.g., *Baka v. Hungary, supra* n. 10, para. 120 (Art. 6(1)); *Beyeler v. Italy, supra* n. 19, para. 114 (Art. 1 of Protocol No. 1); *Leyla Sahin v. Turkey, supra* n. 15, para. 154 (Art. 2 of Protocol No. 1); and *Konstantin Markin v. Russia, supra* n. 44, para. 125 (Art. 14).

[53] E.g. *Hirst v. the United Kingdom (No. 2), supra* n. 16, para. 62.

balance test in order to determine whether the state has discharged its positive obligations.

Whether the Court resorts to the fair balance or to the proportionality language mostly depends on the area of the case law concerned – the Court is for example more likely to use the proportionality language in the context of negative obligations and the fair balance language in the context of positive obligations. However, the fair balance and proportionality language are often used interchangeably by the Court, indicating that they can be considered to be synonymous.[54] The relevance of the principle of proportionality/fair balance moreover transcends the above-mentioned contexts, the Court having elevated it to the level of a general principle of Convention law, holding that 'inherent in the whole of the Convention is a search for a fair balance between the demands of the general interest of the community and the requirements of the protection of the individual's fundamental rights'.[55]

Broadly speaking, the principle of proportionality/fair balance can be considered a decision-making procedure and an analytical structure employed by courts to deal with tensions between two or more legally protected rights or interests.[56] Balancing as applied by the Court consists of a process of comparing the strength of reasons in favour of the different competing rights and interests in order to determine whether the right invoked should prevail over the countervailing rights and interests.[57]

a. Necessary in a democratic society

In the leading case of *The Sunday Times v. the United Kingdom (No. 1)*, the Court clarified what it considers under the notion of 'necessary in a democratic society'. According to the Court, 'whilst the adjective "necessary" [...] is not synonymous with "indispensable", neither has it the flexibility of such expression

---

[54] Similarly, A. Mowbray, 'A Study of the Principle of Fair Balance in the Jurisprudence of the European Court of Human Rights', 10 *Human Rights Law Review*, 2010, p. 289 at pp. 308–310, considering the fair balance test as the basis for the Court undertaking a proportionality analysis. Mowbray gives the example of *Hutten-Czapska v. Poland*, ECtHR (GC) 19 June 2006, appl. no. 35014/97, para. 167, in which the Court mentioned both concepts in the same breath: 'Not only must an interference with the right of property pursue, on the facts as well as in principle, a "legitimate aim" in the "general interest", but there must also be a reasonable relation of proportionality between the means employed and the aim sought to be realised by any measures applied by the State, including measures designed to control the use of the individual's property. That requirement is expressed by the notion of a "fair balance" that must be struck between the demands of the general interest of the community and the requirements of the protection of the individual's fundamental rights.'

[55] *N. v. the United Kingdom*, ECtHR (GC) 27 May 2008, appl. no. 26565/05, para. 44.

[56] A. Stone and J. Mathews, 'Proportionality Balancing and Global Constitutionalism', 47 *Colombia Journal of Transnational Law*, 2008–09, p. 72 at p. 75.

[57] S. Smet, 'Resolving Conflicts between Human Rights: a Legal Theoretical Analysis in the Context of the ECHR', PhD dissertation, Ghent University, 2014, pp. 145–146.

as '"admissible", "ordinary", "useful", "reasonable" or "desirable" (…)'.[58] The Court further held that 'the notion of "necessity" implies that the interference corresponds to a pressing social need and, in particular, that it is proportionate to the legitimate aims pursued'.[59] While the Court takes into account the state's margin of appreciation, discussed hereunder, when determining whether an interference was 'necessary in a democratic society', 'it remains incumbent on the respondent State to demonstrate the existence of the pressing social need behind the interference'.[60] The 'pressing social need' standard relates to the weight and importance of the aims pursued: 'it is not sufficient that the interests served by a limitation of a Convention right are legitimate, they should also be "pressing".'[61] The Court has, however, refrained from defining the notion of a 'pressing social need', which for this reason has been labelled to be 'highly confusing' in the literature.[62] As the 'pressing social need' standard is not applied outside the sphere of the necessity test, arguably this implies that this test encompasses a more demanding standard of proportionality than the one applied in the context of other areas of Convention law.

In addition, the Court has held that, in order for an interference to be considered 'necessary in a democratic society', the reasons adduced by the national authorities to justify it must be 'relevant and sufficient'.[63] The 'relevant and sufficient reasons' standard is another way for the Court to put that an interference must be proportionate to the legitimate aim pursued, a failure to adduce 'relevant and sufficient reasons' resulting in a failure to comply with the principle of proportionality.[64] The 'relevant reasons' test is typically easily met, since it merely requires there to be reasons for the interference that can be linked to the invoked legitimate aim.[65] In this respect, Tümay considers the 'relevant reasons' test to be 'a transposition of the formal requirement of legitimacy on the factual, specific, situation obtained in the case'.[66] The 'sufficient reasons' test, in contrast, constitutes the core of the Court's proportionality assessment, since it

---

[58]   *The Sunday Times v. the United Kingdom (No. 1)*, *supra* n. 24, para. 59.

[59]   See, e.g., *Khoroshenko v. Russia*, ECtHR (GC) 30 June 2015, appl. no. 41418/04, para. 118.

[60]   *Idem.*

[61]   Gerards, *supra* n. 51, at p. 467.

[62]   *Ibid.*, 482.

[63]   See, e.g., *Nada v. Switzerland*, ECtHR (GC) 12 September 2012, appl. no. 10593/08, para. 181. It must be noted that the Court does not systematically apply the 'relevant and sufficient reasons' standard as part of its necessity test; see Gerards, *supra* n. 51, at p. 468.

[64]   See, e.g., *Karhuvaara and Iltalehti v. Finland*, ECtHR 16 November 2004, appl. no. 53678/00, para. 54; and *Halis v. Turkey*, ECtHR 11 January 2005, appl. no. 30007/96, paras. 38–39.

[65]   See, e.g., *Observer and Guardian v. the United Kingdom*, ECtHR (Plenary) 26 November 1991, appl. no. 13585/88, para. 62. Also see a number of cases in which the Court found that the state 'did adduce relevant but not sufficient reasons' to justify the interference, e.g., *Krone Verlag GmbH & Co. KG v. Austria*, ECtHR 14 November 2008, appl. no. 9605/03, para. 45.

[66]   M. Tümay, 'The Concept of "Necessary in a Democratic Society" in Restriction of Fundamental Rights: a Reflection from European Convention on Human Rights', <www.taa.gov.tr>, at p. 4.

is here that the Court examines the relationship between the legitimate aim and the harm inflicted on the Convention right, examining whether one outweighs the other. This test requires a careful analysis of factors including the nature, severity and effects of obstructing measures in tandem with any expected harm caused to the rights of a citizen.[67] In addition, according to Gerards, this test 'seems to contain some requirement of effectiveness', since the reasons for introducing a measure will typically not be 'sufficient' if that measure 'does not substantially contribute to the achievement of a certain goal'.[68]

b. Relevant factors in the Court's proportionality analysis

The proportionality/fair balance test applied by the Court is characterised by its flexible and open-ended nature,[69] 'which allows for the representation of all interests and arguments at stake'.[70] According to Mowbray, '[w]hen assessing if a fair balance has been achieved in specific cases the Court has had to take account of a myriad of competing individual and community interests asserted by applicants and respondent States'.[71] Viljanen suggests that '[m]aybe it is not even possible to find one definitive answer to the proportionality test, because the test is so multi-shaped and related to the context under which the examination is undertaken'.[72] He adds that '[t]he assessment leads to different results in different contexts, because the weight of factors is different in different contexts'.[73] According to Christoffersen, the 'multipolar balancing exercise comprises a variety of considerations that pull the decision-maker in different directions'.[74]

Given this diversity of contexts, one can at best give an overview of some rules of thumb that explain the Court's application of the principle of proportionality. Christoffersen considers as a rule of thumb that '[t]he greater intensity of an interference increases, *ceteris paribus*, the demand for weighty counter-weighing considerations'.[75] Viljanen in turn considers the main factors determining the Court's proportionality analysis to be the nature of the right in question, the

---

[67] See, e.g., *Ceylan v. Turkey*, ECtHR (GC) 8 July 1999, appl. no. 23556/94, para. 37; *Tammer v. Estonia*, ECtHR 6 February 2001, appl. no. 41205/98, para. 69; *Lešnik v. Slovakia*, ECtHR 11 March 2003, appl. no. 35640/97, para. 63; *Selistö v. Finland*, ECtHR 16 November 2004, appl. no. 56767/00, paras. 63–70; *Busuioc v. Moldova*, *supra* n. 36, para. 95.

[68] Gerards, *supra* n. 51, at p. 467.

[69] S. Sottiaux and G. van der Schyff, 'Methods of International Human Rights Adjudication: Towards a More Structured Decision-Making Process for the European Court of Human Rights', 31 *Hastings International and Comparative Law Review*, 2008, p. 115 at p. 131.

[70] B. Pirker, *Proportionality Analysis and Models of Judicial Review*, Groningen, 2013, p. 228.

[71] Mowbray, *supra* n. 54, at pp. 315–316.

[72] J. Viljanen, 'The European Court of Human Rights as a Developer of the General Doctrines of Human Rights Law', PhD dissertation, University of Tampere, 2003, p. 271.

[73] *Idem.*

[74] J. Christoffersen, *Fair Balance: Proportionality, Subsidiarity and Primarity in the European Convention on Human Rights,* Leiden: Martinus Nijhoff Publishers, 2009, p. 76.

[75] *Ibid.*, 208.

area of the right at which the interference is aimed – in particular whether it is explicitly or implicitly related to the core or the periphery of the right – the legitimate aim involved and the severity of the interference.[76] Another factor is whether the restrictive measures have any deterrent effect on the general public. This is particularly evident through the operation of the 'chilling effect' doctrine in the Court's Article 10 and 11 jurisprudence,[77] which 'seems to be based on the idea that certain interferences with freedom of expression must be considered not only in the light of the individual applicant, but also the broader effect this interference has on freedom of expression generally'.[78]

Another important general characteristic of the Court's proportionality analysis is that not only the substantive but also the procedural aspects of the case are material to the determination of whether a fair balance has been struck.[79] On the one hand, the Court has used the principle of proportionality as a vehicle to inject procedural guarantees into substantive human rights provisions,[80] such as the requirement that decision-making processes leading to the adoption of measures interfering with Convention rights must be fair.[81] On the other hand, the Court increasingly applies a procedural type of review that focuses on the quality of the proportionality assessment undertaken at the domestic level.[82] The impact of such review is that the Court will draw substantive inferences from whether or not such proportionality analysis has been adequately conducted by the domestic authorities.[83] If the domestic authorities have done so, the Court will usually grant some deference to how the balance was struck at the domestic level. If, on the other hand, the domestic authorities have not done so, this will shift the balance in the opposite direction. This was the case, for instance, in *Hirst v. the United Kingdom (No. 2)*, in which the Court found a violation of Article 3 of Protocol No. 1, *inter alia* because 'there is no evidence that Parliament has ever sought to weigh the competing interests or to assess the proportionality of a blanket ban on the

---

[76]   Viljanen, *supra* n. 72, at p. 340.

[77]   See, e.g., *Morice v. France*, ECtHR (GC) 23 April 2015, appl. no. 29369/10, para. 127 (Art. 10); and *Frumkin v. Russia*, ECtHR 5 January 2016, appl. no. 74568/12, para. 141 (Art. 11).

[78]   R. Ó Fathaigh, 'Article 10 and the Chilling Effect Principle', *European Human Rights Law Review*, 2013, p. 304 at p. 312.

[79]   S. Van Drooghenbroeck, *La proportionalité dans le droit de la convention européenne des droits de l'homme*, Brussels, 2001, pp. 313–326.

[80]   More elaborately, see E. Brems, 'Procedural Protection – An examination of procedural safeguards read into Substantive Convention Rights', in E. Brems and J. Gerards (eds.), *Shaping Rights in the ECHR*, Cambridge: Cambridge University Press, 2013, p. 137.

[81]   See, e.g., *W. v. the United Kingdom*, ECtHR (Plenary) 8 July 1987, appl. no. 9749/82, para. 62 (measures taking children into public care); and *Yordanova and Others v. Bulgaria*, ECtHR 24 April 2012, appl. no. 25446/06, para. 118.

[82]   See, more elaborately, E. Brems, 'The "Logics" of Procedural-type Review by the European Court of Human Rights', paper presented at the Expert Seminar on Procedural Review and the European Court of Human Rights, Ghent, 21–22 May 2015.

[83]   *Idem.*

right of a convicted prisoner to vote'.[84] This type of procedural review is also increasingly used by the Court as a method to resolve conflicting rights cases.[85] For example, in the case of *Aksu v. Turkey*, concerning the publication of a book and a dictionary containing stereotypes about Roma which were offensive and discriminatory, involving a conflict between the Romani applicant's Article 8 right and the author's Article 10 right, the Court held that '[i]f the balance struck by the national judicial authorities is unsatisfactory, in particular because the importance or the scope of one of the fundamental rights at stake was not duly considered, the margin of appreciation accorded to the decisions of the national courts will be a narrow one. However, if the assessment was made in the light of the principles resulting from its well-established case-law, the Court would require strong reasons to substitute its own view for that of the domestic courts, which consequently will enjoy a wider margin of appreciation.'[86]

c.   Less restrictive means versus general measures

In its proportionality analysis, the Court often, but far from consistently, takes into account the possibility for the state to achieve the invoked aim using means which are less restrictive than the challenged interference.[87] The Court set out the 'less restrictive means' test in the case of *Nada*, holding that 'for a measure to be regarded as proportionate and as necessary in a democratic society, the possibility of recourse to an alternative measure that would cause less damage to the fundamental right in issue whilst fulfilling the same aim must be ruled out.'[88]

In this case, the Court found a violation of the Convention because the Swiss authorities had failed to show that they had taken – or at least had attempted to take – all possible measures to implement a travel ban under a UN sanctions regime in such a way that the particular situation of the applicant – resident in an Italian enclave in Switzerland – was taken into account.[89]

The 'less restrictive means' test, which requires states to tailor restrictive measures to the particular situation of the individual affected, stands in stark contrast with a number of cases in which the Court has accepted that 'general

---

84   *Hirst v. the United Kingdom (No. 2)*, *supra* n. 16, para. 79.

85   See O. Arnardóttir, 'Rethinking the Two Margins of Appreciation', 12 *European Constitutional Law Review*, 2016, p. 27 at pp. 47–50. On conflicting rights in the case law of the ECtHR, see S. Smet, *Resolving Conflicts between Human Rights: The Judge's Dilemma*, Abingdon: Routledge, 2016.

86   *Aksu v. Turkey*, ECtHR (GC) 15 March 2012, appl. nos. 4149/04 and 41029/04, para. 67. Similarly, *Axel Springer AG v. Germany*, ECtHR (GC) 7 February 2012, appl. no. 39954/08, para. 88.

87   For an overview, see E. Brems and L. Lavrysen, '"Don't Use a Sledgehammer to Crack a Nut": Less Restrictive Means in the Case Law of the European Court of Human Rights', 15, *Human Rights Law Review*, 2015, p. 139.

88   *Nada v. Switzerland*, *supra* n. 63, para. 183. Similarly, see *Mouvement Raëlien Suisse v. Switzerland*, ECtHR (GC) 13 July 2012, appl. no. 16354/06, para. 75.

89   *Ibid.*, para. 196.

measures', 'which apply to pre-defined situations regardless of the individual facts of each case', can be compatible with the Convention.[90] The Court has for example accepted 'general measures' in the context of assisted suicide[91] and the destruction of frozen embryos.[92] The Court has clarified its approach to 'general measures' in the case of *Animal Defenders International*, concerning the application of a blanket ban on political advertising to a non-governmental organisation, holding that a general measure may be 'a more feasible means of achieving the legitimate aim than a provision allowing a case-by-case examination, when the latter would give rise to a risk of significant uncertainty [...], of litigation, expense and delay [...] as well as of discrimination and arbitrariness.'[93]

In such cases, 'in order to determine the proportionality of a general measure, the Court must primarily assess the legislative choices underlying it'.[94]

According to the Court, 'the more convincing the general justifications for the general measure are, the less importance the Court will attach to its impact in the particular case'.[95] Under the 'general measures' approach, the possibility of adopting less restrictive rules is not considered to be relevant by the Court, the central question rather being 'whether, in adopting the general measure and striking the balance it did, the legislature acted within the margin of appreciation afforded to it'.[96]

3. POSITIVE OBLIGATIONS

So far, this chapter has focused on negative obligations, being obligations on the state to refrain from interfering with individuals' Convention rights, unless such interference can be justified in the light of the relevant limitation grounds discussed above. In addition to these negative obligations, the Convention also imposes positive obligations on the state to take action to secure the rights guaranteed by the Convention. While the content of these positive obligations will be further discussed hereunder in connection with the respective rights and freedoms that give rise to them, this section provides a bird's eye view of the Court's positive obligations case law and of the general principles of how the Court delimits the scope of positive obligations under the Convention.[97]

---

[90]   *Animal Defenders International v. the United Kingdom*, ECtHR (GC) 22 April 2013, appl. no. 48876/08, para. 106–107, with references to other cases.

[91]   *Pretty v. the United Kingdom*, ECtHR 29 April 2002, appl. no. 2346/02.

[92]   *Evans v. the United Kingdom*, ECtHR (GC) 10 April 2007, appl. no. 6339/05.

[93]   *Animal Defenders International v. the United Kingdom*, *supra* n. 90, para. 108.

[94]   *Idem.*

[95]   *Ibid.*, para. 109.

[96]   *Ibid.*, para. 110.

[97]   See more elaborately L. Lavrysen, *Human Rights in a Positive State: Rethinking the Relationship between Positive and Negative Obligations under the European Convention on Human Rights*, Cambridge-Antwerp-Portland: Intersentia, 2016.

The breakthrough case for the concept of positive obligations was the 1979 *Marckx v. Belgium* case, in which the Court held that 'the object of [Article 8] is "essentially" that of protecting the individual against arbitrary interference by the public authorities [...]. Nevertheless it does not merely compel the State to abstain from such interference: in addition to this primarily negative undertaking, there may be positive obligations inherent in an effective "respect" for family life.'[98]

In this case, the Court considered the fact that the legal bond between an unmarried mother and her child was not established from the mere fact of birth – in line with the maxim *mater semper certa est* – to be incompatible with the State's positive obligation to provide legal safeguards under domestic law 'that render possible as from the moment of birth the child's integration in his family'.[99] Since *Marckx v. Belgium*, the Court has found positive obligations to exist under every Convention right.[100] Because of the open-ended character of the concept of positive obligations, such obligations can be claimed in virtually any context.[101] The Court itself has held that it 'does not have to develop a general theory of the positive obligations which may flow from the Convention'.[102]

3.1. TYPES OF POSITIVE OBLIGATIONS

Positive obligations can be either horizontal or vertical in nature. In the case of *X and Y v. the Netherlands*, the Court for the first time applied the concept of positive obligations to horizontal relations, finding that '[t]hese obligations may involve the adoption of measures designed to secure respect for private life even in the sphere of relations of individuals between themselves'.[103] Horizontal positive obligations are typically triangular in character, since the individual invokes them against the state to oblige state authorities to intervene in horizontal relations. These positive obligations in the first place oblige the state to put in place a legal framework protecting individuals against violations of their human rights by other private actors.[104] The state is obliged to criminalise the most serious human rights violations. For example, in *X and Y v. the*

---

[98]   *Marckx v. Belgium*, ECtHR (Plenary) 13 June 1979, appl. no. 6833/74, para. 31.

[99]   *Idem.*

[100]   For an overview, see A. Mowbray, *The Development of Positive Obligations under the European Convention on Human Rights by the European Court of Human Rights*, Oxford: Hart Publishing 2004.

[101]   D. Xenos, *The Positive Obligations of the State under the European Convention on Human Rights*, Abingdon: Routledge 2012, p. 4.

[102]   *Plattform 'Ärzte für das Leben' v. Austria*, ECtHR 21 June 1988, appl. no. 10126/82, para. 31.

[103]   *X and Y. v. the Netherlands*, ECtHR 26 March 1985, appl. no. 8978/80, para. 23.

[104]   More elaborately, see L. Lavrysen, 'Protection by the Law: the Positive Obligation to Put in Place a Legal Framework to Adequately Protect ECHR Rights', in Y. Haeck and E. Brems (eds.), *Human Rights and Civil Liberties in the 21st Century*, Dordrecht, 2014, p. 69.

Netherlands, the Court held that Article 8 ECHR requires the criminalisation of rape, since rape touches upon 'fundamental values and essential aspects of private life' and because '[e]ffective deterrence is indispensable in this area and it can be achieved only by criminal-law provisions'.[105] With respect to less serious acts between individuals, the Court does not necessarily require criminalisation. In such cases, the Court has held that '[t]he legal framework could also consist of civil-law remedies capable of affording sufficient protection'.[106]

Positive obligations can also be vertical in nature, in the sense that they directly regulate the relations between the individual and the state. Such cases do not involve claims of protection against third-party interference, but rather concern claims that the state should otherwise enable the individual to effectively enjoy his or her human rights. Such effective enjoyment may for example depend on the state conferring a particular legal status to the individual. This was for example the case in *Marckx v. Belgium*, discussed above, in which the Court required the State to automatically recognise the legal bond between an unmarried mother and her child. Another example is the case of *Christine Goodwin v. the United Kingdom*, in which the Court held that the right to respect for private life requires that a transsexual must be able to obtain legal recognition of his or her gender re-assignment.[107] In addition to conferring a particular legal status on an individual, the state will for example also be directly called upon to assist individuals in enjoying their human rights insofar as there is a 'direct and immediate link between the measures sought by an applicant and the latter's private and/or family life'.[108]

Many of these positive obligations are substantive in nature, in the sense that they are directly concerned with ensuring states of affairs that are conducive to the effective enjoyment of human rights. However, the Court has also recognised positive obligations of a procedural nature that are more concerned with considerations of procedural fairness than with substantive outcomes – even though fair processes may of course facilitate fair outcomes. In a number of areas, the Court has for example held that the state is under a procedural obligation to provide the individual with access to an effective remedy in order to challenge a human rights violation. According to the Court, 'the concepts of lawfulness and the rule of law in a democratic society command that measures affecting fundamental rights be, in certain cases, subject to some form of procedure before an independent body competent to review the reasons for the measures and the relevant evidence'.[109] For example, in the abortion case of *A, B and C v. Ireland*, the Court found a violation of Article 8 ECHR because the 'the

---

[105]   *X and Y v. the Netherlands, supra* n. 103, para. 27.
[106]   *Söderman v. Sweden*, ECtHR (GC) 12 November 2013, appl. no. 5786/08, para. 85.
[107]   *Goodwin v. the United Kingdom*, ECtHR (GC) 11 July 2002, appl. no. 28957/95.
[108]   *Botta v. Italy*, ECtHR 24 February 1998, appl. no. 21439/93.
[109]   *Tysiac v. Poland*, ECtHR 20 March 2007, appl. no. 5410/03, para. 117.

lack of effective and accessible procedures to establish a right to an abortion (...) [had] resulted in a striking discordance between the theoretical right to a lawful abortion in Ireland on the ground of a relevant risk to a woman's life and the reality of its practical implementation.'[110]

Another set of procedural obligations consists of those that require a careful decision-making process leading to the adoption of measures by state authorities in fulfilment of their positive obligations. The Court, for example, consistently examines whether the decision-making process was fair and whether due weight was given to the interests of the individuals concerned in the area of access to abortion,[111] in cases concerning enforcement of custody, access or parental responsibility rights, as required under the positive obligation to facilitate family reunion,[112] and in cases dealing with planning[113] and environmental issues.[114] A good example of the latter type is the case of *Hatton and Others v. the United Kingdom*, concerning the night flight schedule at Heathrow airport, in which the Court held that 'a governmental decision-making process concerning complex issues of environmental and economic policy such as in the present case must necessarily involve appropriate investigations and studies in order to allow them to strike a fair balance between the various conflicting interests at stake.'[115]

3.2. DETERMINING THE SCOPE OF POSITIVE OBLIGATIONS

In order to determine whether a state has discharged its positive obligations, the Court typically does not use the same methodology as when a case involves negative obligations. This is particularly evident with respect to Articles 8–11 ECHR, all of which contain a second paragraph that sets out the conditions under which a state can justifiably interfere with these Convention rights. Instead of verifying whether an alleged failure to comply with a positive obligation is 'in accordance with the law' or 'prescribed by law', whether it serves a 'legitimate aim' set out in the second paragraph and whether it is 'necessary in a democratic society' in order to achieve such aim, the Court has devised a separate test. This test was first set out in the case of *Rees v. the United Kingdom*[116] and has since slightly evolved, the current version being: 'In both contexts [i.e. positive and negative obligations] regard must be had to the fair balance that has to be struck

---

[110]   *A, B and C v. Ireland*, ECtHR (GC) 16 December 2010, appl. no. 25579/05, para. 264.

[111]   E.g., *Tysiac v. Poland*, *supra* n. 109, para. 113.

[112]   E.g., *X v. Latvia*, ECtHR (GC) 26 November 2013, appl. no. 27853/09, para. 102.

[113]   E.g., *Chapman v. the United Kingdom*, ECtHR (GC) 18 January 2001, appl. no. 27238/95, para. 92.

[114]   E.g., *Hatton and Others v. the United Kingdom*, ECtHR (GC) 8 July 2003, appl. no. 36022/97, para. 99.

[115]   *Ibid.*, para. 128.

[116]   *Rees v. the United Kingdom*, ECtHR (Plenary) 17 October 1986, appl. no. 9532/81, para. 34.

between the competing interests of the individual and of the community as a whole; and in both contexts the State enjoys a certain margin of appreciation in determining the steps to be taken to ensure compliance with the Convention. Furthermore, even in relation to the positive obligations flowing from the first paragraph of Article 8, in striking the required balance the aims mentioned in the second paragraph may be of a certain relevance.'[117]

While the Court considers this test to be 'broadly similar' to the one applied when it examines a case from the viewpoint of a negative obligation,[118] notable differences are evident. First of all, the three-pronged test used when examining negative obligations has collapsed into a single overall determination of whether a fair balance has been struck. While the Court is willing to take into account the legitimacy of the invoked aim and the domestic legality of the state's alleged failure to comply with a positive obligation, these questions are not in themselves decisive in order to determine whether the state has complied with its positive obligations. As explained by the Court in the environmental case of *Fadeyeva v. Russia*, 'domestic legality should be approached not as a separate and conclusive test, but rather as one of many aspects which should be taken into account in assessing whether the State has struck a "fair balance"'.[119] Another notable difference lies in the fact that the Court does not stick to the exhaustive list of legitimate aims listed in paragraph 2 – although it somewhat enigmatically considers these aims to be 'of certain relevance' – but rather applies a 'second, more ill-defined "general interest" test'.[120] The less rigorous methodological approach applied in cases involving positive obligations was considered to be problematic by Judge Wildhaber in the case of *Stjerna v. Finland*, since 'the dividing line between negative and positive obligations is not so clear-cut'.[121] For this reason, he proposed a unified approach, considering it 'preferable to construct the notion of 'interference' so as to cover facts capable of breaching an obligation incumbent on the State under Article 8 para. 1, whether negative or positive'.[122] Wildhaber's proposal has so far, however, not been followed in the case law.

As far as the scope of positive obligations is concerned, the Court has recognised that the state cannot guarantee absolutely that a human right is not affected, since a positive obligation 'is an obligation as to measures to be taken and not as to results to be achieved'.[123] When determining the scope of positive obligations, the Court has been mindful to take into account the position of

---

[117] *Hatton and Others v. the United Kingdom, supra* n. 114, para. 98.

[118] See, e.g., *Powell and Rayner v. the United Kingdom*, ECtHR 21 February 1990, appl. no. 9310/81, para. 41.

[119] *Fadeyeva v. Russia*, ECtHR 9 June 2005, appl. no. 55723/00, para. 98.

[120] C. Forder, 'Legal Protection under Article 8 ECHR: Marckx and Beyond', 37 *Netherlands International Law Review*, 1990, p. 162 at p. 179.

[121] *Stjerna v. Finland*, ECtHR 25 November 1994, appl. no. 18131/91, Concurring Opinion of Judge Wildhaber.

[122] *Idem.*

[123] *Plattform, 'Ärzte für das Leben' v. Austria, supra* n. 102, para. 34.

the State, considering as relevant the question 'whether the alleged obligation is narrow and defined or broad and indeterminate [...] and the extent of any burden the obligation would impose on the State'.[124] With respect to the latter factor, the Court has held that 'a positive obligation must be interpreted in a way which does not impose an impossible or disproportionate burden on the authorities'.[125]

The principle of effectiveness is another important consideration taken into account by the Court when undertaking to determine the scope of positive obligations. According to this principle, '[t]he Convention is intended to guarantee not rights that are theoretical or illusory but rights that are practical and effective'.[126] In general terms, the principle of effectiveness in principle requires the existence and implementation of measures that are capable of providing the individual with the necessary protection of his or her human rights.[127] On the other hand, the state cannot be blamed for failing to adopt a measure in fulfilment of its positive obligations that would not have been effective anyway in protecting the applicant's Convention right in practice.[128] According to Xenos, 'the choice of measures is reviewed against the standard of effectiveness, which aims, consciously or unconsciously, at an end/complete result', in particular the end result 'not to suffer a violation of human rights by a given activity'.[129]

In a number of cases, the Court has expressed this preference for effective protection in practice by holding that the principle of effectiveness requires the Court to 'look behind appearances and investigate the realities of the situation complained of'.[130] As explained by the Court in the case of *Georgel and Georgeta Stoicescu v. Romania*, '[t]hat assessment may also involve the conduct of the parties, including the means employed by the State and their implementation'.[131] In this case, the Court found a violation of Article 8 because the authorities had failed to take effective measures to properly implement the existing legal framework with a view to protecting the physical integrity of the population at large against the threat represented by the large number of stray dogs in the city of Bucharest.[132] In other words, it held that it is not sufficient to have a legal framework in place if it is not effectively implemented 'in good time, in an appropriate and consistent manner'.[133]

---

[124] *A, B and C v. Ireland, supra* n. 110, para. 248.
[125] See, e.g., *K.U. v. Finland*, ECtHR 2 December 2008, appl. no. 2872/02, para. 48.
[126] *Airey v. Ireland*, ECtHR 9 October 1979, appl. no. 6289/73, para. 24.
[127] See, e.g., *Fadeyeva v. Russia*, ECtHR 9 June 2005, appl. no. 55723/00, para. 133. See also *I. v. Finland*, ECtHR 17 July 2008, appl. no. 20511/03, para. 105.
[128] *Mosley v. the United Kingdom*, ECtHR 10 May 2011, appl. no. 48009/08, paras. 126–127.
[129] Xenos, *supra* n. 101, at pp. 102 and 118.
[130] See, e.g., *Georgel and Georgeta Stoicescu v. Romania*, ECtHR 26 July 2011, appl. no. 9718/03, para. 59.
[131] *Idem.*
[132] *Ibid.*, para. 61.
[133] *Ibid.*, para. 59.

4. MARGIN OF APPRECIATION DOCTRINE

In order to fully understand the Court's practice in determining whether a State has justifiably interfered with a human right or whether it has discharged its positive obligations, it is necessary to introduce the doctrine of the margin of appreciation. The margin of appreciation has been defined as the label used by the Court 'to indicate the measure of discretion allowed to the Member States in the manner in which they implement the Convention's standards, taking into account their own particular national circumstances and conditions'.[134] While the notion of the margin of appreciation has been used by the Court in a number of areas of its case law,[135] it has been most commonly applied when determining whether or not a fair balance was struck between a Convention right and other rights or the public interest.[136] In this sense, the notion of the margin of appreciation indicates that the Court generally does not consider there to be a single right answer as to how to strike a fair balance and that it will accordingly refrain from imposing a particular answer. Instead, it will merely examine whether the way the state has struck the balance amounts to one of the possibly many answers that are acceptable from the viewpoint of the Convention[137] – in other words, whether the State has remained within its margin of appreciation.

The Court has justified the margin of appreciation doctrine by reference to the principle of subsidiarity, which holds that the primary responsibility for respecting the rights guaranteed by the Convention lies with the member states, whereas the Court has the subsidiary task of intervening where violations have not been remedied at the national level.[138] In the Court's words, 'a margin of appreciation must, inevitably, be left to the national authorities, who by reason of their direct and continuous contact with the vital forces of their countries are in principle better placed than an international court to evaluate local needs and conditions.'[139] However, '[t]his margin of appreciation goes hand in hand with European supervision embracing both the law and the decisions applying it'.[140]

---

[134] Y. Arai-Takahashi, *The Margin of Appreciation Doctrine and the Principle of Proportionality in the Jurisprudence of the ECHR*, Antwerp: Intersentia, 2002, p. 2.

[135] E.g., in the context of Art. 15, discussed *infra*, the Court has granted states a (wide) margin of appreciation in assessing whether the life of their nation is threatened by a public emergency; see *A. and Others v. the United Kingdom*, ECtHR (GC) 19 February 2009, appl. no. 3455/05, para. 180.

[136] S. Greer, *The Margin of Appreciation: Interpretation and Discretion under the European Convention on Human Rights,* Human Rights Files, No. 17, Strasbourg, 2000, p. 5.

[137] See, e.g., *Evans v. the United Kingdom, supra* n. 92, para. 91.

[138] See, e.g., Declaration adopted at the High Level Conference on the Future of the European Court of Human Rights, Brighton, 19–20 April 2012, para. 3.

[139] E.g. *Chapman v. the United Kingdom*, ECtHR (GC) 18 January 2001, appl. no. 27238/95, para. 91.

[140] See *Bayatyan v. Armenia*, ECtHR (GC) 7 July 2011, appl. no. 23459/03, para. 121.

The Court uses the margin of appreciation doctrine as a 'sliding scale model of intensity of review', distinguishing between a 'wide', a 'certain' and a 'narrow' margin of appreciation.[141] These labels respectively correspond with a light, intermediate and strict level of scrutiny applied by the Court. When invoked in relation with the fair balance test, these labels form a sliding scale from a 'lax standard of proportionality' to an 'intense proportionality appraisal'.[142] Where the margin of appreciation is wide, the Court 'usually only superficially and rather generally examines the choices made by the national authorities',[143] often confining itself to merely verifying whether the conduct or decisions by these authorities were 'manifestly without reasonable foundation'.[144] Also, where the margin of appreciation is wide, the Court often applies a procedural approach, refraining from substituting its own view for those of the national authorities where they have carefully assessed and decided the case at the domestic level.[145] Where the margin of appreciation is narrow, on the other hand, 'the Court generally closely considers the facts of the case, carefully determining the interests at stake',[146] often requiring 'convincing and compelling reasons'[147] or 'very weighty reasons'[148] to be adduced by the state as justification.[149] The Court is also more likely to take into account the possibility of applying 'less restrictive means' or to criticise the lack of possibilities for individualised judgments at the domestic level where the margin of appreciation is narrow.[150]

The Court takes into account a number of factors in order to determine the width of the margin of appreciation. Gerards has clustered these factors in three broad categories: the common ground factor (or consensus argument), the better placed argument and the nature of the affected right or interest.[151] The first factor implies that where 'there is no consensus within the member States of the Council of Europe either as to the relative importance of the interest at

---

[141] J. Gerards, 'Pluralism, Deference and the Margin of Appreciation Doctrine', 17 *European Law Journal*, 2011, p. 80 at p. 105.

[142] Arai-Takahashi, *supra* n. 134, at p. 204.

[143] Gerards 2011, *supra* n. 141, at p. 105.

[144] See, e.g., *Dickson v. the United Kingdom*, ECtHR (GC) 4 December 2007, appl. no. 44362/04, para. 78.

[145] Gerards 2011, *supra* n. 141, at pp. 105–106. See, e,g., *Aksu v. Turkey*, *supra* n. 86, para. 67.

[146] *Idem*, 106.

[147] See, e.g., *United Communist Party of Turkey and Others v. Turkey*, ECtHR (GC) 30 January 1998, appl. no. 19392/92, para. 46.

[148] See, e.g., *Abdulaziz, Cabales and Balkandali v. the United Kingdom*, ECtHR (Plenary) 28 May 1985, appl. nos. 9214/80; 9473/81; 9474/81, para. 78.

[149] J. Kratochvíl, 'The Inflation of the Margin of Appreciation by the European Court of Human Rights', 29 *Netherlands Quarterly of Human Rights*, 2011, p. 324 at pp. 347–350.

[150] Gerards 2011, *supra* n. 141, at p. 106, with references to *Informationsverein Lentia and Others v. Austria*, ECtHR 24 November 1993, appl. nos. 13914/88 etc.; *Fuentes Bobo v. Spain*, ECtHR 29 February 2000, appl. no. 39293/98; and *S. and Marper v. the United Kingdom*, *supra* n. 46.

[151] Gerards, *supra* n. 141, at pp. 107–113.

stake or as to how best to protect it, the margin will be wider'.[152] In determining whether or not such consensus exists, the Court also takes into account 'the provisions in specialised international instruments and evolving norms and principles of international law'.[153] The Court has held the consensus argument to be particularly relevant where a case raises 'sensitive moral or ethical issues'[154] or 'complex issues and choices of social strategy'.[155]

The second factor consists of a cluster of areas in which the Court has indicated that the state is presumed to be particularly better placed than the Court and consequently should be left a wide margin of appreciation. According to Gerards, this factor 'is of special relevance with respect to measures based on complex social or economic assessments or measures relating to particularly sensitive or difficult issues'.[156] The Court has, for example, also invoked this rationale as a reason to grant a wide margin of appreciation in cases where a fair balance must be struck between competing Convention rights.[157] In other cases, the Court has framed this requirement in an even broader way, by holding that a wide margin of appreciation must be allowed to the state where a fair balance must be struck between 'competing private and public interests or Convention rights'.[158]

The third factor concerns the importance of the affected right. Gerards holds that 'the margin will be narrow if the essence or 'core' of one of the Convention rights is affected'.[159] The Court has, for example, considered that the margin must be narrow where 'a particularly intimate aspect of an individual's private life' is concerned,[160] such as is the case with respect to a person's sexuality or identity.[161] According to Gerards, this factor also explains why the Court generally only allows a narrow margin of appreciation in cases concerning political expression given the importance of freedom of expression (Article 10)

---

[152] E.g. *Dickson v. the United Kingdom*, ECtHR (GC) 4 December 2007, appl. no. 44362/04, para. 78.

[153] E.g. *A, B and C v. Ireland*, *supra* n. 110, para. 174.

[154] E.g. *Evans v. the United Kingdom*, *supra* n. 92, para. 77.

[155] E.g. *Dickson v. the United Kingdom*, ECtHR (GC) 4 December 2007, appl. no. 44362/04, para. 78.

[156] Gerards, *supra* n. 141, at p. 110, with reference to, e.g., *James and Others v. the United Kingdom*, ECtHR (GC) 21 February 1986, appl. no. 8793/79, para. 46 (complex social or economic assessments) and *Maurice v. France*, ECtHR (GC) 6 October 2005, appl. no. 11810/03, paras. 116–117 (particularly sensitive or difficult issues).

[157] E.g. *Eweida and Others v. the United Kingdom*, ECtHR 15 January 2013, appl. nos. 48420/10 etc., para. 106.

[158] E.g. *Evans v. the United* Kingdom, *supra* n. 92, para. 77.

[159] Gerards, *supra* n. 141, at p. 112.

[160] *Hatton and Others v. the United Kingdom*, *supra* n. 114, para. 103.

[161] Gerards, *supra* n. 141, at p. 113, with reference to *Dudgeon v. the United Kingdom*, ECtHR (GC) 22 October 1981, appl. no. 7525/76, para. 52 (sexuality) and *Jäggi v. Switzerland*, ECtHR 13 July 2006, appl. no. 58757/00, para. 37 (identity).

for a well-functioning democracy.[162] This rationale similarly explains the narrow margin of appreciation under Article 14 (the prohibition of discrimination) in relation to a number of 'suspect' discrimination grounds.[163]

---

[162] Gerards, *supra* n. 141, at p. 112, with reference to, *inter alia*, *Incal v. Turkey*, ECtHR (GC) 9 June 1998, appl. no. 22678/93, para. 46.

[163] In these cases, the Court applies strict scrutiny, requiring 'very weighty reasons' to be adduced to justify such distinction; see O. Arnardóttir, 'The Differences that Make a Difference: Recent Developments on the Discrimination Grounds and the Margin of Appreciation under Article 14 of the European Convention on Human Rights', 14 *Human Rights Law Review*, 2014, p. 647 at pp. 649–654.

CHAPTER 5

RELATIONSHIP BETWEEN THE CONVENTION AND THE EU

Janneke GERARDS

CONTENTS

1. INTRODUCTION

In 2016, 28 of the 47 States Parties to the ECHR were also Member States of the European Union (EU).[1] This means that there is considerable overlap between the two European systems. Indeed, the relationship between the ECHR and

---

[1] Given the 'Brexit' referendum in the United Kingdom on 23 June 2016, the United Kingdom may no longer be an EU Member State in the future.

the EU treaties has been described as that of 'twins separated at birth', which are now growing increasingly together.[2] The Preambles of the original EEC and ECSC Treaties make clear that these treaties aimed at bringing European states together to maintain peace and stability, just like the Preamble of the Statute of the Council of Europe states that its aim is to pursue peace based upon international co-operation, and to achieve a greater unity in Europe. The one main difference between the systems is that the EU and its predecessors have always focused on economic co-operation and the creation of a common market, while the Council of Europe has concentrated on the further realisation of the rule of law, human rights and fundamental freedoms.[3] Owing to various developments, however, fundamental rights have become increasingly important to the EU. Fundamental rights have since long been recognised as general principles of EU law and since 2009, with the Treaty of Lisbon, the EU has a binding catalogue of fundamental rights in the shape of the EU Charter of Fundamental Rights.[4]

The existence of the EU and the availability of an increasing body of EU fundamental rights legislation and case law are of great relevance to the Convention and the ECtHR. Many administrative acts and legislative measures in the EU Member States are no longer purely national in nature, as they are the result of the implementation of EU policies or execution of EU legislation and decisions. This raises a variety of practical and legal questions as to the applicability of the Convention to such acts and the protection of fundamental rights. Moreover, the co-existence of two overlapping, yet different supranational systems protecting fundamental rights incurs the risk of inconsistencies.

The development, scope and meaning of EU fundamental rights are left out of consideration in this chapter; they have been elaborately discussed elsewhere.[5] Instead, this chapter focuses on a number of issues regarding the ECHR-EU relationship from the perspective of the Convention. Section 2 explains how and to what extent the ECHR applies to EU acts and national acts of implementation or execution of EU law; it also discusses the so-called *Bosphorus* doctrine. Subsequently, section 3 addresses the interaction between the ECtHR and the Court of Justice of the EU (CJEU). Finally, section 4 discusses the intended accession of the EU to the ECHR and the procedures and mechanisms which have been drafted to make such accession possible, as well the rejection of those mechanisms by the CJEU in 2014.

---

[2]   G. Quinn, 'The European Union and the Council of Europe on Human Rights Issues: Twins Separated at Birth?', 46 *McGill Law Journal*, 2001, pp. 849–874.

[3]   Quinn, *supra* n. 2, p. 856.

[4]   On these developments, see, e.g., S. Greer, J.H. Gerards and R. Slowe, *Human Rights in the Council of Europe and the European Union. Achievements, Trends, and Challenges*, Cambridge: Cambridge University Press 2018, chs. 4 and 5.

[5]   See *inter alia*, with many references to relevant literature and case law, Greer et al., *supra* n. 4.

2. APPLICABILITY OF THE CONVENTION TO EU ACTS AND IMPLEMENTATION OF EU LAW

2.1. APPLICABILITY TO ACTS OF EU INSTITUTIONS

The EU is an autonomous international organisation that is not a party to the Convention. For that reason, the Strasbourg organs have always held that it is not possible to bring an individual complaint to it when this concerns an alleged violation of the Convention by the EU – such complaints invariably are declared inadmissible *ratione personae*.[6] This would change if the EU were to accede to the Convention, since this would mean that the EU would become a full-fledged party to the Convention. The EU institutions then would become directly accountable for their acts under the ECHR and individual applications could be brought against the EU. As is further discussed in section 3, however, the prospects for such accession to take place in the near future are rather poor.

2.2. APPLICABILITY TO PRIMARY EU LAW

As such, the ECHR clearly does not apply to EU law directly – as mentioned above, the EU simply is not a party to the Convention. Nevertheless, this does not mean that there is no indirect protection against certain EU acts and omissions. In the *Matthews* case, the ECtHR has held that the EU Member States remain fully responsible for the compatibility of EU primary law with the Convention, which includes the EU Treaty (TEU) and the Treaty on the Functioning of the European Union (TFEU).[7] The Court's reason for this is that the EU Treaties cannot be regarded as acts of the EU as such, but they are the direct product of political choices made by the Member States. Since the Member States were free to enter into these Treaties, the Court reasoned, they remain liable for the consequences of doing so under Article 1 ECHR. Consequently, cases brought against one of the Member States concerning the compatibility of primary EU law with the Convention will be admissible *ratione personae*. When the

---

[6]   See *Confédération Française Democratique du Travail v. the European Communities*, EComHR 10 July 1978 (dec.), appl. no. 8030/77, as confirmed in *Bosphorus Hava Yolları Turizm ve Ticaret Anonim Şirketi v. Ireland*, ECtHR (GC) 30 June 2005, appl. no. 45036/98, para. 152. Nevertheless, in some cases the Court still seems to provide for some minimal substantive assessment of such a case to see whether there is no 'manifest deficiency' of the legal protection offered in the EU; see, e.g., *Andreasen v. the United Kingdom and 26 other member States of the European Union*, ECtHR 31 March 2015 (dec.), appl. no. 28827/11, para. 70. See also S. Douglas-Scott, 'The Court of Justice of the European Union and the European Court of Human Rights after Lisbon', in S. de Vries, U. Bernitz and S. Weatherill (eds.), *The Protection of Fundamental Rights in the EU after Lisbon*, Oxford: Hart Publishing, 2013, pp. 153–179 at p. 154.

[7]   *Matthews v. the United Kingdom*, ECtHR (GC) 18 February 1999, appl. no. 24833/94, para. 33.

other admissibility requirements are met, this means that the Court can deal with such complaints on their merits. At the same time, given the sensitive relationship between the EU and the ECHR system, the Court may be reluctant to very strictly assess the compatibility of provisions of primary EU law with the Convention. It is quite likely that it would adopt an approach similar to that taken in relation to secondary EU legislation, as is discussed hereafter.

2.3. APPLICABILITY TO SECONDARY EU LAW

a. Bosphorus doctrine

In practice, cases on primary EU law are only rarely presented to the ECtHR. Many more cases relate to secondary EU law, which is drafted by the EU institutions in the exercise of their competences under the TEU and the TFEU, and which may take the form of legislation (Directives, Regulations) and administrative decisions. As mentioned in section 2.1, when someone feels that his Convention rights have been violated by EU secondary law, he cannot lodge a complaint with the ECtHR against the EU. A typical characteristic of EU law, however, is that secondary EU law can be given practical effect in the EU Member States only if they are implemented or executed by means of national legislation, administrative acts and adjudication. Moreover, the EU Member States have an important say in the drafting of EU legislation. This means that the responsibility for EU legislation and decisions is often shared between the EU institutions and the authorities of the EU Member States. It therefore may rather easily occur that a complaint is brought before the ECtHR against a Member State, for example when it concerns the effects of an EU Directive which has been implemented in national law, or an EU decision which has been executed by national administrative bodies.

For a rather long time there has been some uncertainty as to how such complaints should be dealt with.[8] Only in 2006, in its landmark judgment in the *Bosphorus* case, did the ECtHR clarify its position on the applicability of the ECHR to national acts implementing EU law.[9] The *Bosphorus* doctrine, named after the judgment, takes as its point of departure that all EU Member States have remained fully responsible under Article 1 ECHR for all their acts and omissions, even if they have transferred part of their sovereign powers to an international organisation like the EU. The ECtHR therefore will declare all applications admissible *ratione personae* when they are directed against one or

---

[8] For an overview, see e.g., C. Costello, 'The *Bosphorus* Ruling of the European Court of Human Rights: Fundamental Rights and Blurred Boundaries in Europe', 6 *Human Rights Law Review*, 2006, pp. 87–130.

[9] *Bosphorus Hava Yolları Turizm ve Ticaret Anonim Şirketi v. Ireland*, *supra* n. 6.

more of the EU Member States and when they concern national acts, decisions or omissions. This is true even if the national authorities were obliged under EU law to adopt such measures or take such decisions.

This first part of the test only concerns the admissibility, however. As far as the assessment of the merits of applications concerning national implementation or execution of EU law is concerned, the *Bosphorus* doctrine entails an essential distinction between, on the one hand, interferences with Convention rights that result from *non-discretionary* implementation or execution of EU law and, on the other hand, interferences that are caused by purely national acts or *discretionary exercise of powers* by the national authorities. Put shortly, if a case against an EU Member State concerns *non-discretionary* national (in)action, the ECtHR accepts that the state has acted merely as an agent of the EU and, in fact, it is the EU that is responsible for the contested act or omission. Because the Court does not want to get too much involved in reviewing the reasonableness of acts of another international organisation, it will not examine such a concrete case in detail if it appears that the general level of protection within that international organisation is equivalent to that offered by the Convention (both in substance and procedurally). If such a presumption of equivalence can be made, the Court will only further investigate the complaint when the concrete facts of the case disclose a manifest deficiency of fundamental rights protection, which can clearly serve to rebut the presumption. By contrast, in cases where the national authorities had *discretion* in the implementation of EU law or the exercise of competences within the scope of EU law, the EU Member States remain fully responsible for their own actions and omissions. Accordingly, there is then no need for application of the *Bosphorus* doctrine of equivalent protection.

b. *Bosphorus doctrine and non-discretionary national (in)action*

For the purposes of the *Bosphorus* doctrine, the first question that arises is whether the EU Member States had any discretion in the exercise and implementation of EU law. In by far the majority of cases, the Court will assume that the states still have some latitude, which means that they remain fully responsible for the use of it under the Convention (see hereafter). Only if the EU Member States purely act as EU-agents, without any discretion whatsoever, will the Court apply the 'equivalent protection' doctrine.[10] The Court especially seems to accept that such discretion is lacking when the secondary legislation is very detailed and precise and there is, in addition, a fairly intensive body of

---

[10] See, e.g., *Coopérative des agriculteurs de la Mayenne and Coopérative laitière Maine-Anjou v. France*, ECtHR 10 October 2006, appl. no. 16931/04; see further T. Lock, 'Beyond *Bosphorus*: The European Court of Human Rights' Case Law on the Responsibility of Member States of International Organisations under the European Convention on Human Rights', 10 *Human Rights Law Review*, 2010, pp. 529–545 at p. 544.

case law of the CJEU in which the obligations on the Member States are detailed even further.[11] For example, in the case of *Bosphorus*, the Court accepted that the respondent State, Ireland, had no discretion whatsoever to decide on the imposition of sanction measures on the applicant airline company, as the sanction regime had been laid down in great detail in an EU Regulation which had been specified even further in the case law of the CJEU.[12]

When it is sufficiently clear that the respondent EU Member State had no discretion, under the *Bosphorus* doctrine, the Court must continue to consider if there can be a presumption that the EU generally offers a level of protection of fundamental rights that is equivalent to that offered by the Convention. In *Bosphorus*, the Court noted in general terms that, although the founding treaties of the European Community had not contained any fundamental rights provisions, respect for fundamental rights had gradually developed in the EU and had arrived at a level where the substantive protection of fundamental rights was comparable to that offered by the ECHR.[13] To that extent, equivalent protection therefore could be presumed. The ECtHR also noted, however, that such a presumption can be warranted only when there are sufficiently effective procedural mechanisms of control to ensure the observance of fundamental rights.[14] In the light of this criterion, the Court has showed itself rather cautious as regards the procedural protection offered in the EU system.[15] Although the Court acknowledged in *Bosphorus* that the system overall could be seen to offer adequate judicial protection,[16] in later judgments it has held that an important question to be answered is whether, in a concrete case, 'the full potential of the supervisory mechanism provided for by European Union law' has been deployed.[17] In 2016, in the *Avotiņš* case, the ECtHR dealt at length with the question whether the EU procedure of preliminary rulings sufficiently meets this criterion for the *Bosphorus* presumption of equivalent protection to arise.[18] It considered that the system of preliminary rulings of Article 67 TFEU leaves it fully to the national courts to decide whether or not they want to refer certain issues of compatibility with fundamental rights to the CJEU. Potentially, such discretion could lead to a lack of effective access to justice, especially when the national court would refuse a request for a reference for no good reason, or when it would

---

[11]   *Cf. Avotiņš v. Latvia*, ECtHR (GC) 23 May 2016, appl. no. 17502/07, para. 106.

[12]   *Bosphorus Hava Yolları Turizm ve Ticaret Anonim Şirketi v. Ireland*, *supra* n. 6, paras. 143–148.

[13]   *Ibid.*, para. 159.

[14]   *Ibid.*, para. 160.

[15]   See in particular *Michaud v. France*, ECtHR 6 December 2012, appl. no. 12323/11, paras. 110 and 111.

[16]   *Bosphorus Hava Yolları Turizm ve Ticaret Anonim Şirketi v. Ireland*, *supra* n. 6, para. 165.

[17]   *Michaud v. France*, *supra* n. 15, paras. 113–115; *Avotiņš v. Latvia*, *supra* n. 11, para. 105.

[18]   *Avotiņš v. Latvia*, *supra* n. 11, paras. 109–112.

do so without providing any sound reasoning.[19] Such a refusal would not only raise an issue from the perspective of Article 6 ECHR (the right of access to court and to a fair trial), but it also could detract from the reasonableness of accepting an overall presumption of equivalent protection of fundamental rights in the EU.[20] In the end, however, in *Avotiņš* the Court did not find reason in these concerns to turn away from its original position in *Bosphorus* that the legal remedies available to individuals within the EU system are sufficient to render the EU's protection of fundamental rights generally equivalent to that under the Convention.

The consequence of this general presumption of equivalence for the EU is that the Court will normally accept that a Member State has not departed from the requirements of the Convention when it has done no more than implement EU legal obligations.[21] Hence, the Court will not substantively assess the restrictions and limitations an individual has complained about, and it will simply not find a violation of the Convention, or even declare the case manifestly ill-founded.

However, the Court has built in a check on the general presumption of equivalent protection. When in the circumstances of a particular case it is clear that the protection of Convention rights was manifestly deficient, the presumption can be rebutted and a violation of the Convention can be found.[22] It appears from the ECtHR's case law that, as far as the EU is concerned, the threshold for such rebuttal is high. In the few cases in which the manifest deficiency test has been applied, the Court has adopted a strongly procedural approach. In the original case of *Bosphorus*, for example, the Court restricted itself to mentioning that the facts of the case did not disclose any dysfunction of the mechanisms of control of the observance of Convention rights. Seven years later, in the *Povse* case, the Court considered that the CJEU had held that fundamental rights should be taken into account in the national judgments in the case.[23] Based on this, and without looking at the merits of the case, it again held that there had been no dysfunction in the control mechanisms and accordingly the presumption of equivalent protection had not been rebutted.[24]

---

[19]   See the ECtHR's earlier judgments in *Ullens de Schooten and Rezabek v. Belgium*, ECtHR 20 September 2011, appl. nos. 3989/07 and 38353/07 and *Dhahbi v. Italy*, ECtHR 8 April 2014, appl. no. 17120/09.

[20]   *Avotiņš v. Latvia*, *supra* n. 11, para. 111; indeed, the Court mentioned that if, in a concrete case, an issue were to arise as to an unreasonable refusal to refer preliminary questions or a lack of reasoning for such a refusal, the individual concerned could bring a case against the state under Art. 6 ECHR, which would likely be effective (para. 109); see also *Dhahbi v. Italy*, *supra* n. 19.

[21]   *Bosphorus Hava Yolları Turizm ve Ticaret Anonim Şirketi v. Ireland*, *supra* n. 6, para. 156.

[22]   *Idem.*

[23]   *Povse v. Austria*, ECtHR 18 June 2013 (dec.), appl. no. 3890/11.

[24]   Sometimes the test is a bit more elaborate, yet it remains deferential; see e.g. *Coöperatieve Producentenorganisatie van de Nederlandse Kokkelvisserij U.A. v. the Netherlands*, ECtHR 20 January 2009 (dec.), appl. no. 13645/05.

Only in rare cases has the Court also looked into the substantive proportionality of the interference, but even then the review is superficial and deferential.[25] An exceptional case in which the Court showed more bite, is *Avotiņš*.[26] This case concerned the recognition and execution of judgments in Latvia that had been rendered by a Cypriot court, a situation to which the EU's Brussels I Regulation pertains.[27] The Brussels I Regulation is based on the EU mechanism of mutual recognition and the principle of mutual trust. This mechanism relies on the assumption that procedures conducted in all EU Member States comply with procedural rights and, consequently, judgments can be enforced in all other Member States without there being a need for additional checks on procedural fairness. The ECtHR acknowledged the great importance of this mechanism of EU law for the well-functioning and effectiveness of the EU system as a whole, but it also held that it should not infringe fundamental rights.[28] In the ECtHR's view, the system of mutual recognition could too easily 'run counter to the requirement imposed by the Convention according to which the court in the State addressed must at least be empowered to conduct a review commensurate with the gravity of any serious allegation of a violation of fundamental rights in the State of origin, in order to ensure that the protection of those rights is not manifestly deficient.'[29]

All national courts therefore should be willing to make an exemption to their EU obligations if a serious and substantiated complaint would be raised before them to the effect that the protection of a Convention right had clearly missed the mark.[30] If they would refrain from doing so, that in itself could be reason for the Court to find the presumption of equivalent protection to be rebutted. In the case at hand, the ECtHR indeed found that the applicant had raised cogent arguments alleging the existence of procedural defects in Cyprus, which probably should have precluded the enforcement of the Cypriot judgment under Article 6 ECHR.[31] Surely this might have been cause for the ECtHR to find that the protection of procedural rights had been manifestly deficient and the presumption of equivalent protection had been effectively rebutted. Eventually, however, the Court once again showed considerable deference towards the EU and its Member States, and it concluded that the shortcomings had not be so important as to warrant that far-reaching conclusion.[32] Nevertheless, the

---

[25]   *Coopérative des agriculteurs de la Mayenne and Coopérative laitière Maine-Anjou v. France*, *supra* n. 10; see also Lock, *supra* n. 10, at p. 541.

[26]   *Avotiņš v. Latvia, supra* n. 11.

[27]   EU Council Regulation No. 44/1001 of 22 December 2000 on jurisdiction and the recognition and enforcement of judgments in civil and commercial matters.

[28]   *Ibid.,* para. 114.

[29]   *Idem.*

[30]   *Ibid.,* para. 116.

[31]   *Ibid.,* para. 120.

[32]   *Ibid.,* paras. 121–125.

judgment in *Avotiņš* evidences that the 'manifest deficiency test' cannot be regarded as a test without teeth and it shows that, in future cases, the ECtHR really could find a violation of the ECHR when an EU Member State does no more than directly execute EU law and there is insufficient procedural or substantive protection of fundamental rights.

c. Discretionary implementation of EU law

In situations concerning discretionary implementation of EU law or national exercise of competences within the scope of EU law, there is no need for application of the *Bosphorus* doctrine. The Court has held that the EU Member States remain fully responsible for their own actions and discretionary choices under the Convention, even if the exercise of their discretionary powers may be strongly coloured by EU law or policy.[33] In *Michaud*, the Court noted, for example, that there may be considerable room for manoeuvre in the implementation of EU Directives, which are binding as to the result to be achieved, but leave much latitude as to the means to be chosen to do so.[34] For that reason it assessed the merits of the case in the same manner as it would have done if the case had concerned a purely national act. It will take the same approach if the alleged violation results from the application of an EU Regulation, for example if the Regulation offers the choice to take up a certain responsibility to the authorities of the Member States.[35]

The ECtHR also has considered it relevant whether a national court has referred a preliminary question to the CJEU in a case relating to EU law. If the national court has refused to do so, this is its own, autonomous choice.[36] For that reason the ECtHR has held that a national court which applies EU law, yet refrains from referring questions to the CJEU, remains fully liable for the protection of fundamental rights under the Convention in the exercise of its own discretion.[37] Moreover, as mentioned before, such a refusal implies that the national court withholds from an applicant the possibility to present a certain issue to the CJEU. Although the Court has accepted that this may be in line with EU law, the national courts should provide good reasons for keeping a case away from the CJEU, and the Court will find a violation of Article 6 ECHR when a national court has not done so.[38]

---

[33] *Cf.* Douglas-Scott 2013, *supra* n. 6, at p. 156.

[34] *Michaud v. France, supra* n. 15, para. 113.

[35] *M.S.S. v. Belgium and Greece*, ECtHR (GC) 21 January 2011, appl. no. 30696/09, paras. 339–340.

[36] *Ullens de Schooten and Rezabek v. Belgium, supra* n. 19.

[37] *Idem.*

[38] See in particular *Ullens de Schooten and Rezabek v. Belgium, supra* n. 19 and *Dhahbi v. Italy, supra* n. 19.

3. INTERACTION BETWEEN THE CONVENTION AND THE COURT OF JUSTICE OF THE EU

Although there is currently no formal relationship between the ECtHR and the EU, the ECtHR and the EU are clearly willing to take account of one another's case law and legal systems.[39] This is for good reason, since especially in fields where there is considerable possibility for overlap between the two systems, such as migration and asylum law or data protection, a lack of co-operation between the ECtHR and the CJEU might easily result in inconsistent case law and even in imposing conflicting obligations on the states.[40] In practice, such inconsistencies are avoided as much as possible by means of informal mechanisms, such as meetings between judges of the two Courts to discuss common problems and approaches and by taking close account of the other Court's interpretations and application of fundamental rights norms.[41] The more formal solution for this problem – accession of the EU to the ECHR – is discussed in section 4; the current section focuses on harmonisation through case law.

Particularly good examples of such harmonisation through case law can be found in relation to the Dublin Regulation, which forms the basis for a uniform system for dealing with asylum applications throughout the EU.[42] One of the central principles of the Dublin Regulation is that an asylum application is dealt with by the authorities of the Member State where the asylum seeker has entered the EU. If the asylum seeker has travelled on to another EU Member State, the authorities of that state are competent to transfer the asylum seeker to the state of first entry to have his asylum request dealt with. The Dublin Regulation is based on the principle of mutual trust regarding the level of protection of the fundamental rights of asylum seekers in the EU. In the case of *M.S.S. v. Belgium and Greece*, however, the question was raised before the ECtHR

---

[39] As was expressed in a joint declaration by Presidents of the 2 Courts: Joint Communication Presidents Costa and Skouris, <http://curia.europa.eu/jcms/upload/docs/application/pdf/2011–02/cedh_cjue_english.pdf>. See further, e.g., S. Douglas-Scott, 'A Tale of Two Courts: Luxembourg, Strasbourg and the Growing European Human Rights *Acquis*', 43 *Common Market Law Review*, 2006, pp. 629–665.

[40] See, e.g., S. Morano-Foadi and S. Andreadikis, 'The Convergence of the European Legal System in the Treatment of Third Country Nationals in Europe: The ECJ and ECtHR Jurisprudence', 22 *European Journal of International Law*, 2011, pp. 1071–1088.

[41] See, e.g., G. Harpaz, 'The European Court of Justice and its Relations with the European Court of Human Rights: the Quest for Enhanced Reliance, Coherence and Legitimacy', 46 *Common Market Law Review*, 2009, pp. 105–141 and C. Van de Heyning and R. Lawson, 'The EU as a Party to the European Convention of Human Rights. EU Law and the European Court of Justice Case Law as Inspiration and Challenge to the European Court of Human Rights jurisprudence', in P. Popelier et al. (eds.), *Human Rights Protection in the European Legal Order: The Interaction between the European and the National Courts*, Antwerp: Intersentia, 2011, pp. 35–64.

[42] Regulation No. 343/2003.

---

whether the application of the Dublin Regulation and the principle of mutual trust is compatible with the Convention if it is obvious that the fundamental rights protection in a certain Member State has fallen below any acceptable standard.[43] While this case was pending before the ECtHR, a similar question was raised before the CJEU through the preliminary reference procedure in the *NS* case.[44] Obviously, giving different answers to the same legal question would have given rise to serious problems in the national application of the Dublin Regulation. This was solved by informal harmonisation of judgments: the ECtHR gave judgment in *M.S.S.* first, answering all the substantive questions raised in the case and carefully applying EU law. The CJEU then followed the ECtHR's lead in its judgment in the *NS* case, elaborately referring to the judgment in *M.S.S.* and taking the same approach as the ECtHR had done. In turn, in subsequent cases, the ECtHR has made careful references to the CJEU's case law in the area.[45] Thus, it is ensured as much as possible that no (new) inconsistencies arise.[46]

In other cases, harmonisation of interpretation and application of fundamental rights is less ostentatious, but it is still there. In particular, both Courts frequently refer to one another's judgments. In more recent years the CJEU appears to be doing so less often; instead, it increasingly refers to its own fundamental rights case law and it has expressly stated that, within the EU context, the EU Charter of Fundamental Rights is the primary instrument to be taken into consideration.[47] Nevertheless, the CJEU continues to refer to ECtHR case law when this seems useful to it, for example in judgments regarding fundamental rights issues it has not dealt with before and on which there are relevant ECtHR precedents.[48]

The other way around, the ECtHR often refers to relevant CJEU case law, as well as to EU legislation and policy instruments more generally. It not only uses these instruments as a source of inspiration or as mere support for

---

[43]   *M.S.S. v. Belgium and Greece, supra* n. 35.

[44]   CJEU 21 December 2011, Joined Cases C-411/10 and C-493/10.

[45]   In *Tarakhel v. Switzerland*, e.g., the Court quoted the *NS* judgment at length and it also expressly mentioned it as part of its reasoning; see ECtHR (GC) 4 November 2014, appl. no. 29217/12, paras. 33 and 103.

[46]   Similar approaches are taken in other areas of law, such as extradition of criminal suspects; here, too, the CJEU appears to try to reconcile its own case law and that of the ECtHR, although its own requirements seem rather stricter than those commonly applied by the ECtHR; *cf. Aranyosi and Caldararu*, CJEU 5 April 2016, Joined Cases C-404/15 and C-659/15 PPU.

[47]   *Cf.* G. de Búrca, 'After the EU Charter of Fundamental Rights: The Court of Justice as a Human Rights Adjudicator?', 20 *Maastricht Journal of European and Comparative Law*, 2013, pp. 168–184; J. Krommendijk, 'The Use of ECtHR Case Law by the Court of Justice after Lisbon: the View of Luxembourg Insiders', 22 *Maastricht Journal of European and Comparative Law*, 2015, pp. 812–835.

[48]   For an example, see *Abdida*, CJEU 18 December 2014, Case C-542/13. See further in particular Krommendijk, *supra* n. 47.

---

its reasoning,[49] but also actively aims to align its own approach to that of the CJEU where such appears desirable. In particular, the ECtHR tends to take special account of the particular EU background in assessing the justification for a limitation of fundamental rights that has occurred in an EU legal context or in reviewing the effectiveness of national remedies.[50] In the case of *S.A. Dangeville*, for example, the Court found a violation of the Convention partly because the national authorities had not complied with the principles of direct effect and supremacy of EU law.[51] Similarly, in *Laurus Invest Hungary*, in relation to the requirement of exhaustion of domestic remedies of Article 35 ECHR, it reiterated the obligation of EU Member States to provide for a system for individuals to claim state liability and compensation for damages suffered as a result of a clear violation of EU law by the state.[52] Since such system according to well-established case law of the CJEU has to exist in all EU Member States and it has to be fully effective, the Court held that it ought to be exhausted by the applicant and it therefore declared his complaint inadmissible.

Nevertheless, although the ECtHR generally follows the lead of the CJEU, it does not do so uncritically. As was already shown in the previous section and is also borne out by the *M.S.S.* judgment, the Court is wary of the principle of mutual trust and mutual recognition that is central to EU law, and it may set a fundamental rights check on it. In addition, the Court sometimes may set supplementary requirements for the national interpretation of EU secondary legislation where such is needed for an effective protection of the Convention rights.[53]

---

[49] For an example, see *Parrillo v. Italy*, ECtHR (GC) 27 August 2015, appl. no. 46470/11, paras. 180–182.

[50] See further Van de Heyning and Lawson, *supra* n. 41, at pp. 42–45. For another, more recent example, see *Satakunnan Markkinapörssi Oy and Satamedia Oy v. Finland*, ECtHR (GC) 27 June 2017, appl. no. 931/13.

[51] *S.A. Dangeville v. France*, ECtHR 16 April 2002, appl. no. 36677/97. See similarly, e.g., *Othymia Investments BV v. the Netherlands*, ECtHR 15 June 2015 (dec.), appl. no. 75292/10; *Arlewin v. Sweden*, ECtHR 1 March 2016, appl. no. 22302/10.

[52] *Laurus Invest Hungary KFT and Continental Holding Corporation v. Hungary*, ECtHR 8 September 2015 (dec.), appl. no. 23265/13.

[53] See, e.g., *J.N. v. the United Kingdom*, ECtHR 19 May 2016, no. 37289/12, where the ECtHR rather pointedly remarked that:
'(…) it is true that in accordance with the Returns Directive, which is not binding on the United Kingdom …, the majority of EU Member States may not detain third-country nationals for the purposes of a returns procedure for more than eighteen months …, and that there has been some criticism of the United Kingdom's decision not to adopt a time-limit for the detention of immigrants … However, while the Returns Directive may be regarded by such critics as reflecting a preferable approach to the detention of immigrants than that currently available in the United Kingdom, that does not mean that the system set up under the Returns Directive, including in particular its provision of time-limits, is to be taken as being imposed by sub-paragraph (f) of Article 5 §1 of the Convention or as representing the only system conceivable in Europe as being compatible with sub-paragraph (f)'.

Generally, however, the ECtHR shows considerable deference towards EU law and its aim is one towards comity and co-operation. It even may come to the assistance of the EU institutions if the unwillingness of national authorities to comply with their EU obligations also comes into conflict with their obligations under the ECHR. As was discussed in section 2.2.c., for example, the Court has held that an insufficiently reasoned refusal by a national court to refer a preliminary question to the CJEU might come into conflict with the right of access to a court under Article 6(1) ECHR.[54] The Court's deferential attitude towards the EU is further apparent from a number of cases concerning the question whether the parties to a case before the CJEU should be given the opportunity to give observations about the opinion of the Advocate General. For national legal systems, the ECtHR has consistently held that the right to be given that opportunity follows from the principle of equality of arms, protected by Article 6 ECHR.[55] For the particular context of the CJEU, however, the Court has decided differently. Applying a test of 'manifest deficiency' similar to that developed later in the *Bosphorus* case, it has held that the EU legal system is significantly different from that in the Member States and, for that reason, different procedural rules can reasonably apply.[56] The standards it uses in relation to the Luxembourg procedure thereby are clearly lower than those for the Convention States.

Hence, the ECtHR clearly makes an effort to avoid inconsistencies and discrepancies of fundamental rights case law, and it respects the autonomous and special position of the EU as much as it can. Nevertheless, it is not impossible that inconsistencies arise. The ECtHR may not be aware of a certain line of case law of the CJEU, or it may take a different perspective on a certain issue than the CJEU has done.[57] The informal mechanisms of harmonisation then may be insufficient to avoid and solve such inconsistencies. Indeed, the continuous risk of diverging or even conflicting case law is one of the main reasons for the intended accession of the EU to the ECHR, which is the last topic to be discussed in this chapter.

---

[54] See *Ullens de Shooten and Rezabek v. Belgium*, *supra* n. 19; in that case the Court in the end did not find a violation, but this was different in *Dhahbi v. Italy*, *supra* n. 19.

[55] See, e.g., *Reinhardt and Slimane Kaïd v. France*, ECtHR (GC) 31 March 1998, appl. nos. 23043/93 and 22921/93.

[56] *Coöperatieve Producentenorganisatie van de Nederlandse Kokkelvisserij U.A. v. the Netherlands*, *supra* n. 24.

[57] See e.g. Morano-Foadi and Andreadakis, *supra* n. 40. For an example of case law where different views seem to be taken by both courts on a similar issue, *cf. X, Y and Z*, CJEU 7 November 2013, Joined Cases C-199/12, C-200/12 and C-201/12 and *M.E. v. Sweden*, ECtHR 26 June 2014, appl. no. 71398/12. Also, it seems that in *Tarakhel v. Switzerland*, *supra* n. 45, the ECtHR takes a somewhat different view on the exceptions in the Dublin regulation than are usually accepted by the CJEU (see, e.g., *Abdullahi*, CJEU 10 December 2013, Case C-394/12); on this, see further S. Peers, 'Tarakhel v Switzerland: Another Nail in the Coffin of the Dublin System?', *EU Law Analysis Blogspot* 5 November 2014, <http://eulawanalysis. blogspot.co.uk/2014/11/tarakhel-v-switzerland-another-nail-in.html>.

4. ACCESSION OF THE EU TO THE CONVENTION

4.1. BACKGROUND AND REASONS FOR ACCESSION

The accession of the EU to the ECHR has been contemplated for a very long time.[58] Already in 1979, the first ideas and views on accession were presented,[59] but they were put on hold when it appeared that a legal basis for such accession in the EC Treaties and the ECHR was lacking.[60] The idea resurfaced in the 2000s, even though, by then, the need for accession had become less urgent. In the 1970s it still could be said that the EEC was lacking a fundamental rights catalogue and the recognition and protection of fundamental rights in the EEC were incomplete.[61] This changed significantly over time, however, as a result of the CJEU's acceptance of fundamental rights as general principles of European law and by the proclamation of the EU Charter of Fundamental Rights in 2000. It may therefore seem surprising that the debate on accession intensified in the 2000s. This may be explained, however, by the continued existence of two problems concerning the protection of fundamental rights in the EU, which have not been removed by the development of EU fundamental rights.

First, the ECtHR presently cannot deal with individual applications concerning acts or omissions of the EU institutions.[62] Individuals whose fundamental rights have been breached by EU acts or omissions therefore cannot find a remedy in Strasbourg. Legal protection against such acts on the EU level is also lacking in strength, given the very restrictive case law of the CJEU on the standing of individuals in cases about EU legislation.[63] Although the CJEU has always defended the EU system of legal remedies and the ECtHR has accepted this system as generally offering 'equivalent protection' to the Convention, it may be argued that there is still a gap in the legal protection of individuals. The accession of the EU to the ECHR would fill this gap, since individuals then would be able to lodge complaints against the EU institutions at the ECtHR.

The second reason for accession can be found in the current risk of divergent interpretation of fundamental rights norms and the resulting risk of conflicting

---

58 For an overview, see e.g. J.P. Jacqué, 'The Accession of the European Union to the European Convention on Human Rights and Fundamental Freedoms', 48 *Common Market Law Review*, 2011, pp. 995–1023 and Douglas-Scott, *supra* n. 6, at p. 165.

59 Memorandum of the European Commission on the Accession of the Communities to the European Convention for the Protection of Human Rights and Fundamental Freedoms, Bull. EC Supp. 2/79, part I.

60 Opinion 2/94 of the European Court of Justice of 28 March 1996, [1996] ECR I-17/59.

61 E.g. K. Economides and J.H.H. Weiler, 'Accession of the Communities to the European Convention on Human Rights: Commission Memorandum', 42 *Modern Law Review*, 1979, pp. 683–695.

62 See above, section 2.1.

63 E.g. *Inuit*, CJEU 3 October 2013, Case C-583/11 P, not yet reported.

obligations for the EU Member States.[64] For this problem, accession clearly would be a solution, since upon accession, all EU institutions, including the CJEU, would be bound to comply with the Convention as it is interpreted and applied by the ECtHR. The current situation of two supranational courts co-existing on the same hierarchical level then would be replaced by a situation where the ECtHR is hierarchically positioned above the CJEU. The ECtHR thereby would become the final arbiter in fundamental rights cases and its interpretations would be leading. Even though divergent case law then still might occur, for example because the CJEU would pronounce itself on a fundamental rights matter differently from the ECtHR, this would be a merely temporary matter, since the ECtHR might correct the interpretation of the CJEU in a later case and the CJEU would be bound to comply with the ECtHR's judgment.

These two reasons, as well as a general desire for bolstering fundamental rights protection in Europe, have formed the basis for intergovernmental discussions in the 2000s of the possibilities for accession.[65] These led to the insertion of a provision allowing for the EU to become a party to the Convention in Protocol 14 to the ECHR, which was opened for signature in 2004 and entered into force in 2010.[66] A provision stating that the EU 'shall accede' to the ECHR was added to the TEU by the Treaty of Lisbon in 2009.[67] According to its formulation, this provision contains a legal obligation for the EU to do so.[68] For the accession to be effected, however, such legal bases are not enough. In particular, an international agreement has to be drafted to further detail the conditions for accession and to arrange a number of practical and procedural matters.[69] Moreover, a large set of internal (working) rules have to be devised within the EU legal system and the Council of Europe to facilitate accession.

In 2013, negotiations between the 47 member states of the Council of Europe and the EU resulted in the adoption of the necessary accession agreement (AA).[70] Before the procedure for the EU to accede to the Convention could be continued, however, the CJEU had to give its opinion on the compatibility of the AA with EU law. In its Opinion 2/13 of 18 December 2014, it held that the

---

[64]   See section 3.
[65]   For an overview, see the Explanatory Memorandum to the Accession Agreement, contained in the Final Report of the CDDH ad hoc Negotiation Group and the European Commission (47+1 Group) on the Accession of the European Union to the European Convention on Human Rights, 47+1(2013)008rev2.
[66]   Art.59 (2) ECHR.
[67]   Art. 6 (2) TEU.
[68]   *Cf.* para. 2 of the Explanatory Memorandum to the AA, *supra* n. 65.
[69]   *Ibid.*, paras. 3 and 21.
[70]   For the text of the AA, see 'Fifth negotiation meeting between the CDDH Ad Hoc Negotiation Group and the European Commission on the Accession of the European Union to the European Convention on Human Rights – Final report to the CDDH', Strasbourg, 10 June 2013, 47+1(2013)008rev2.

AA cannot be reconciled with (the general principles of) EU law in a variety of respects. In particular, the CJEU found that the AA adversely affected the special characteristics and the autonomy of the EU and it did not contain sufficient guarantees to respect the nature and effectiveness of the procedures before the CJEU as envisaged in the TFEU. According to Article 218(11) TFEU, the opinion of the CJEU means that the AA, as an international agreement, 'may not enter into force unless it is amended or the Treaties are revised'. At the time of writing of this chapter,[71] no public information was available yet as to whether and how such amendment or revision would be undertaken, nor when negotiations on the AA would be resumed.[72] It is therefore difficult to foresee whether and when accession will take place, and under which conditions.

It is unknown if the original AA will ever enter into force – it may well be radically changed as a result of further negotiations. Nevertheless, the remainder of this section discusses the most important changes it would make to the ECtHR's procedures. The reason for doing so is that there was broad agreement on the need to adopt such procedural changes within both the EU and the Council of Europe. The criticism of the CJEU notwithstanding, at the least some of these mechanisms are therefore likely to find a place in any new arrangements regarding the EU's accession. Moreover, it is only possible to understand the current situation of uncertainty, as well as the criticism of the CJEU in its opinion 2/13, when it is clear what the debate was really all about. Based on the AA as it has been rejected by the CJEU, attention is therefore paid hereafter to the co-respondent mechanism, the prior involvement procedure, the election of judges, and the consequences the AA would have had for the supervision on the execution of judgments. Just as in earlier sections of this chapter, the AA is discussed from the perspective of its relevance to the Convention system, rather than that of the EU or the CJEU.[73]

---

[71]   I.e., by 15 November 2016.

[72]   See further, with references, T. Lock, 'The Future of the European Union's Accession to the European Convention on Human Rights after Opinion 2/13: is it still Possible and is it still Desirable?', 11 *European Constitutional Law Review*, 2015, pp. 239–273.

[73]   Elsewhere, many discussions of the CJEU's opinion and its reasoning can be found; see, e.g., L. Halleskov Storgaard, 'EU Law Autonomy versus European Fundamental Rights Protection – On *Opinion 2/13* on EU Accession to the ECHR', 15 *Human Rights Law Review*, 2015, pp. 485–521; P. Eeckhout, 'Opinion 2/13 on EU Accession to the ECHR and Judicial Dialogue: Autonomy or Autarky?', 38 *Fordham International Law Journal*, 2015, pp. 955–992; F. Cherubini, 'The Relationship between the Court of Justice of the European Union and the European Court of Human Rights in the View of the Accession', 16 *German Law Journal*, 2015, pp. 1375–1386; D. Halberstam, '"It's the Autonomy, Stupid!", A Modest Defense of Opinion 2/13 on EU Accession to the ECHR, and the Way Forward', 16 *German Law Journal*, 2015, pp. 105–146; F. Fabbrini and J. Larik, 'The Past, Present and Future of the Relation between the European Court of Justice and the European Court of Human Rights', *Yearbook of European Law*, 2016, pp. 28–29.

4.2. CO-RESPONDENT MECHANISM

In order to understand the co-respondent procedure and the possibilities for prior involvement of the CJEU, it is important to recall that accession of the EU to the ECHR would bring about a hierarchical relationship between the CJEU and the ECtHR. This could put the autonomy of EU law under strain, in particular if a complaint were brought to the ECtHR about a violation by one of the institutions on which the CJEU never has been able to express itself.[74] Moreover, EU law is characterised by a division of competences between the EU and its Member States, which means that EU law is usually implemented by national authorities and the EU institutions can only act upon the express approval of the Member States (e.g. by means of laying down a competence to act in the EU Treaties).[75] As a result, a case concerning EU law may be as relevant to the EU Member States as it is to the EU institutions. For individual applicants, moreover, it might be difficult to make out whether their application should be directed towards the EU, to one or more of the EU Member States, or to both the EU and its Member States.[76] For such reasons, the AA introduced a procedural mechanism – the 'co-respondent mechanism' – to make sure that the EU Member States and the EU institutions always would be involved in relevant cases dealing with EU law.[77] Before discussing this mechanism in more detail, it is important to stress that it would be relevant only in cases involving both the EU and its Member States. If the EU alone would be responsible (e.g. if a case were brought against the EU concerning an EU decision) or if only the EU Member States would be responsible (e.g. if a case were brought against a Member State relating to its discretionary exercise of powers), the co-respondent mechanism would not come into play.[78]

Presently, under Articles 33 and 34 ECHR, only the State Party to which an application is directed may be considered a respondent state in the procedure before the ECtHR. Other states may become involved only as third-party interveners, which means they are allowed to offer their observations and they are not bound by the eventual judgment.[79] The co-respondent mechanism would open up the possibility for either an EU Member State or the EU to really become a party to the case. This would not merely be a privilege offering additional procedural protection, but it would result in important responsibilities if,

---

[74] Douglas-Scott, *supra* n. 6, at p. 169. This point has been strongly emphasised by the CJEU in its Opinion 2/13 of 18 December 2014 regarding the AA.

[75] *Cf.* Explanatory Memorandum to the DAA, para. 38; see also Opinion 2/13 of the CJEU of 18 December 2014.

[76] *Cf.* T. Lock, 'End of an Epic? The Draft Agreement on the EU's Accession to the ECHR', 31 *Yearbook of European Law*, 2012, pp. 162–197.

[77] See Art.3 AA.

[78] Lock, *supra* n. 76.

[79] Explanatory Memorandum to the AA, *supra* n. 65, para. 45.

eventually, a violation of the Convention is found.[80] In that case the respondent and the co-respondent would become jointly responsible for the violation, unless the Court were to decide differently.[81] This would be important for the action to be taken in execution of the Court's judgments, e.g. the payment of just satisfaction or the amendment of national or EU legislation.

According to the AA, the EU would become a co-respondent if a complaint were brought against one or more EU Member States concerning the compatibility with the Convention of primary or secondary EU law. The drafters of the AA appear to have thought here mainly of the situation where the EU Member States have no discretion, which would mean they could only comply with the Convention by violating their obligations under EU law, or the other way around.[82] However, the text of the AA is not limited to such non-discretionary exercise of powers, so it may be supposed that the EU also could become a co-respondent in other cases concerning EU law where this would be considered useful.[83]

The other way around, the AA states that the EU Member States could become co-respondents only where an application would be directed against the EU and would concern the compatibility of primary EU law with the Convention. The reason for this is that the Member States are directly responsible for primary EU law, which means their involvement would be essential in order for the procedure before the ECtHR to be effective.[84] If only the EU were to be a respondent party, it would not be able to execute the judgment if a violation were found, because the EU cannot itself make changes to primary EU law. By contrast, if a case were to concern secondary EU law and the application were to be directed towards the EU, the AA would not allow the Member States to become a co-respondent.[85]

Under the AA, it would be the ECtHR's role to decide whether the EU or (one or more of) its Member States could become co-respondents, either on their request or on its own invitation. The ECtHR could make such an invitation or request as soon as the case would be notified to the EU or the respondent state and the communication would be published. An invitation by the ECtHR would not be binding on the EU or a Member State; becoming a co-respondent would be an autonomous choice to be made by them.[86] In case a request were to be made to the Court to become co-respondent, the Court would base its decision

---

[80]   *Cf.* Explanatory Memorandum to the AA, *supra* n. 65, para. 39.

[81]   Art. 3(7) AA.

[82]   Explanatory Memorandum to the AA, *supra* n. 65, para. 48.

[83]   *Cf.* X. Groussot, T. Lock and L. Pech, 'EU Accession to the European Convention of Human Rights: A Legal Assessment of the Draft Accession Agreement of 14th October 2011', Fondation Robert Schuman Policy Paper, *European Issues* no. 218, p. 12.

[84]   *Cf.* Groussot, Lock and Pech, *supra* n. 83, p. 12; Lock, *supra* n. 76.

[85]   Explanatory Memorandum to the AA, *supra* n. 65, para. 50.

[86]   *Ibid.*, para. 53.

on the reasons set out in the request, which it would have to assess in the light of the criteria set out above (i.e. the question if primary or secondary EU law is involved in a case).

4.3. PRIOR INVOLVEMENT OF THE CJEU

In practice, the co-respondent mechanism could have the consequence that the EU would be admitted as a co-respondent in a certain case, without the CJEU previously having been offered the opportunity to pronounce on the fundamental rights issues arising in the case. This could have occurred when no preliminary references had been made by the national courts, either because the preliminary questions related to other issues than fundamental rights matters, or because the CJEU did not have jurisdiction to decide on certain matters, such as on the EU's common foreign and security policy.[87] The lack of a possibility for the CJEU to pronounce on such matters would hardly be in line with the notion of subsidiarity governing the ECHR system. Moreover, it would be very difficult to reconcile this with the autonomy of the EU.[88] For that reason, the drafters of the AA envisaged a special 'prior involvement procedure'.[89] According to this procedure, the ECtHR would suspend its examination of the case to allow the CJEU sufficient time to make an assessment of the fundamental rights issues involved in the case and, thereafter, for the parties to make their observations on the judgment of the CJEU. Only after this, the Court would assess the case on its merits.

The actual prior involvement procedure has not been given a clear shape in the AA. It is merely stated that the EU should ensure that a quick assessment of the case is possible so as not to delay the procedure before the ECtHR. Also, it is mentioned that the parties to the case before the ECtHR (including the individual applicant) should have the opportunity to make observations in the procedure before the CJEU.[90] Now that the CJEU has held the AA to be incompatible with EU law, it is uncertain if and how a prior involvement procedure before the CJEU eventually would be designed.[91]

---

[87] See Art. 275 TFEU; on the latter issue, see also Opinion 2/13 of the Court of 18 December 2014.

[88] Both arguments have been questioned as to their validity, especially if compared to the position of national constitutional courts. For a further analysis, see, e.g., Lock *supra* n. 76. Nevertheless, the CJEU has stressed the importance of these points in its Opinion 2/13 of 18 December 2014, holding that the arrangements made in the AA do not sufficiently solve them; accordingly, the AA in the CJEU's view is not compatible with the fundamental principles of EU law.

[89] Art. 3(6) AA.

[90] Explanatory Memorandum to the AA, *supra* n. 65, para. 66.

[91] For some suggestions, see T. Lock, 'Walking on a Tightrope: the Draft ECHR Accession Agreement and the Autonomy of the EU Legal Order', 48 *Common Market Law Review*, 2011, pp. 1025–1054 at pp. 1049–1053.

4.4. ELECTION OF JUDGES

The (rejected) AA confirms that the EU will be allowed to elect one judge. This is in line with Article 20 ECHR, which states that the Court shall consist of a number of judges equal to that of the High Contracting Parties. It is also arranged that a delegation of the European Parliament would participate in the sittings of the Parliamentary Assembly when matters would be discussed and decided relating to the election of judges.[92]

4.5. PARTICIPATION IN THE COMMITTEE OF MINISTERS

Given that the EU would become a High Contracting Party to the ECHR upon accession, it would also play a role in the exercise of the supervisory tasks of the Committee of Ministers (CoM). Not only would it thereby be subjected to CoM supervision in cases in which the EU would be a party, but also would it be able to participate in the supervision of the execution of judgments against the states. Consequently, the EU would play a role also in the supervision of judgments against non-EU member states and it would be able to do so on an equal footing with the other contracting parties.[93] The other way around, it could imply that the 28 EU Member States and the EU would be able to act together in supervising the execution of judgments on EU topics. Effectively this could mean that the supervision would not so much be conducted by the CoM, as well as by the EU, since the EU and its Member States together would hold an absolute majority of 29 of the 48 votes in the CoM. The risk was seen that this could paralyse the functioning of the supervisory system as a whole.[94]

To avoid undue exercise of influence of the EU and reduce the risk of 'block voting' by the Member States and the EU, a number of measures were included in the rejected AA. First, the AA stipulates that the votes of the EU and the EU Member States should be co-ordinated in all matters concerning the fulfilment of obligations by the EU (either alone or jointly with the Member States). By contrast, it is also expressly stated that the EU Member States would remain free to express their own position and exercise their right to vote on topics unrelated to EU matters.[95] Furthermore, an intricate system of specified majority and minority voting was proposed with an eye to cases where there could be a risk of unwarranted block voting.[96] These new voting rules do not form part of the AA itself, but they would be adopted as part of the internal working rules of

---

[92] Art. 6 DAA.
[93] *Cf.* Explanatory Memorandum to the AA, *supra* n. 65, para. 79.
[94] See further Lock, *supra* n. 76.
[95] Art. 7(4)(b) AA. See further Lock, *supra* n. 76.
[96] See Explanatory Memorandum to the AA, *supra* n. 65, paras. 84–90; Lock, *supra* n. 76.

the CoM upon accession.[97] It was proposed in this regard that, for example, a final resolution of the CoM, which formally ends the procedure of supervision because the execution obligations have been complied with, could only be adopted with a qualified majority of four-fifths of the representatives casting a vote, which would mean that always more votes would be needed than only those of the EU and its Member States.[98] For other relevant decisions it has been suggested that they could be taken with a 'hyper-minority' if needed.[99] These compromises have been heavily fought for in the process of drafting the AA. Nevertheless, given that accession has been postponed by the CJEU's rejection of the AA, it is uncertain if they will be re-negotiated in the future and if they ever will enter into force in the shape as proposed in the AA.

---

[97]   Explanatory Memorandum to the AA, *supra* n. 65, para. 90.
[98]   App. III DAA.
[99]   See App. III DAA and the Explanatory Memorandum, *supra* n. 65, para. 87.

CHAPTER 6

RIGHT TO LIFE

(Article 2)

Janneke Gerards*

GUIDING PRINCIPLE

The right to life is one of the most essential human rights. After all, one is only able to enjoy and exercise any human rights when one is alive. Nonetheless, the right to life raises many questions and controversies. When does life begin and who may decide to end it? How far should states go in protecting people against murder or death by natural disasters? And when may the use of violence by state agents be justified?

ARTICLE 2

1. Everyone's right to life shall be protected by law. No one shall be deprived of his life intentionally save in the execution of a sentence of a court following his conviction of a crime for which this penalty is provided by law.
2. Deprivation of life shall not be regarded as inflicted in contravention of this Article when it results from the use of force which is no more than absolutely necessary:
   (a) in defence of any person from unlawful violence;
   (b) in order to effect a lawful arrest or to prevent the escape of a person lawfully detained;
   (c) in action lawfully taken for the purpose of quelling a riot or insurrection.

---

* This chapter is an elaborated and updated version of a chapter published earlier by the author in the book *Grondrechten. De Europese, internationale en nationale dimensie* [*Fundamental rights. The European, international and national dimension*], Nijmegen: Ars Aequi Publishers 2013. In the fourth edition this chapter was revised and updated by Leo Zwaak.

CONTENTS

1. NATURE AND ESSENCE

The Court has frequently mentioned that the right to life 'enshrines one of the basic values of the democratic societies making up the Council of Europe'.[1]

---

[1] *McCann and Others v. the United Kingdom*, ECtHR 27 September 1995, appl. no. 18984/91, para. 147. This phrase is quoted in many later judgments of the Court and clearly expresses a general principle the Court embraces.

Because of its importance, the right warrants special protection, as is reflected in the text of the Convention. Different from many other Convention articles, Article 2 expressly stipulates that this right 'shall be protected by law', thereby providing a special and articulate basis for imposing positive obligations on the states. Nevertheless, infringements of the right are not inconceivable and they can sometimes be justifiable. One can think of a policeman shooting a suspect in self-defence, or the deployment of weapons during armed conflict. Thus, it cannot be said that the right to life is an 'absolutely absolute right' that does not allow for any exceptions whatsoever. Given the importance of the right, however, the possibilities for the justifiable use of lethal violence by the state obviously are very limited. Article 2(2) provides for a limited and exhaustive list of exemptions to the right to life which put very high demands on their justification.

Many important issues have surfaced in relation to the protection of the right to life, such as euthanasia, abortion, enforced disappearances and the death penalty. Moreover, the Court has to deal with many issues of state responsibility and positive obligations. The question has arisen, for example, to what extent the national authorities can be held responsible for the protection of the life of their citizens, not only against the use of force by state agents, but also against other individuals. This chapter focuses on how the Court has dealt with such issues. In section 2, the scope of the right to life is discussed. Attention is paid to the question at what point in time 'life' is considered to begin, the question whether applicability of Article 2 requires that someone has really been deprived of his or her life, as well as questions of state responsibility, burden of proof and causation. Section 3 explains the specific exemptions to the right to life allowed by Article 2, which relate to the death penalty and the legitimate use of lethal force. Finally, section 4 highlights the various positive obligations the European Court of Human Rights has recognised in its case law. This section discusses both the positive obligations intended to actively protect the right to life and the positive obligations to investigate suspicious deaths and provide for effective remedies to the next-of-kin.

2. SCOPE OF APPLICATION

2.1. BEGINNING AND END OF LIFE – ABORTION AND EUTHANASIA

a. Beginning of life

The applicability of Article 2 ECHR is closely related to the question when 'life' can be considered to begin. This question is clearly relevant in relation to issues concerning the protection of unborn life. The Court was confronted with this issue in the case of *Vo*,[2] where the applicant had claimed that the right to life of unborn children was insufficiently protected by French law. The French Government argued in response that Article 2 ECHR did not apply to this type of case, since, according to the French text of the Convention, only the right to life of 'persons' is protected ('Le droit de toute personne à la vie est protégé par la loi'), while a foetus could not yet be considered a 'person'. This case presented the Court with the question if the right to life begins at birth, or rather at conception or perhaps when the foetus is viable. The Court did not venture to provide a conclusive answer to this question; it merely held that this is an issue which falls within the margin of appreciation of the states.[3] Hence, rather differently than for most Convention rights, the scope of application of the right to life is not established autonomously, but it depends on national definitions.

The consequences of this are evident from later case law, such as *Evans*, which concerned an English statutory obligation to destroy embryos that could not be used for IVF-treatment.[4] The applicant argued that such destruction would violate the embryos' right to life, but the Court noted that, under English law, an embryo did not have independent rights or interests. Applying the *Vo* line of reasoning, it held that, in the United Kingdom, 'an embryo cannot claim – or have claimed on its behalf – a right to life under Article 2'.[5] Clearly, however, the Court could arrive at the opposite conclusion for a state with different legislation on the matter. Moreover, even if Article 2 ECHR does not apply to such cases, the Court may still decide to deal with them under Article 8, the right to respect for one's private life.[6]

b. End of life

The question as to the applicability of the right to life may arise also in the context of euthanasia and assisted suicide. In that context, the question takes the form of whether the right to life encompasses a right to die. In the case of *Pretty*, the Court decided that Article 2 cannot have this meaning.[7] It explained that this provision is 'unconcerned with issues to do with the quality of living or what a person chooses to do with his or her life'.[8] Moreover, it held that Article 2 'cannot, without a distortion of language, be interpreted as conferring the diametrically opposite right, namely a right to die; nor can it create a right to self-determination in the sense of conferring on an individual the entitlement to choose death rather than life'.[9] However, in the same *Pretty* case, the Court

---

[2] *Vo v. France*, ECtHR (GC) 8 July 2004, appl. no. 53924/00.
[3] *Ibid.*, para. 82.
[4] *Evans v. the United Kingdom*, ECtHR (GC) 10 April 2007, appl. no. 6339/05.
[5] See the Grand Chamber judgment in the *Evans* case, *idem*, para. 56, in which reference is made to the Chamber's judgment in the case.
[6] *Parrillo v. Italy*, ECtHR (GC) 27 August 2015, appl. no. 46470/11.
[7] *Pretty v. the United Kingdom*, ECtHR 29 April 2002, appl. no. 2346/02.
[8] *Idem*, para. 39.
[9] *Ibid.*

considered that it could not be excluded that a choice for assisted suicide is covered by the right to respect for one's private life (Article 8 ECHR).[10] In later case law, the Court has confirmed this finding, holding 'an individual's right to decide by what means and at what point his or her life will end, provided he or she is capable of freely reaching a decision on this question and acting in consequence, is one of the aspects of the right to respect for private life within the meaning of Article 8 of the Convention'.[11]

The Court has not yet pronounced itself on the question whether legislation permitting active euthanasia would come into conflict with the right to life.[12] The Court has given an opinion, however, on a national court's decision to permit discontinuation of a life-sustaining treatment. In *Lambert*, medical experts had requested such permission for a patient whose life fully depended on artificial nutrition and hydration.[13] The Court considered that withdrawal of such treatment – even if it results in death – cannot be regarded as an active and intentional taking of life by the state.[14] It did involve, however, the state's positive obligation to protect an individual's life which follows from Article 2.[15] The Court further noted the absence of a common approach among the European states on this topic.[16] Given that the national decision-making process in *Lambert* had been very careful and there had been sound judicial remedies, the Court concluded that the judicial order to stop the treatment fell within the state's margin of appreciation.[17]

2.2. LOSS OF LIFE AND LIFE-THREATENING SITUATIONS

For Article 2 ECHR to be applicable, the facts of a case must, in principle, disclose a loss of life. That this is not always the case can be illustrated by the *Tzekov* case.[18] The applicant complained of being seriously wounded by a bullet

---

[10] *Idem*, paras. 65–67.
[11] *Haas v. Switzerland*, ECtHR 20 January 2011, appl. no. 31322/07, para. 51. *Cf.* also *Gross v. Switzerland*, ECtHR 14 May 2013, appl. no. 67810/10, para. 60, where the Court held that 'the applicant's wish to be provided with a dose of sodium pentobarbital allowing her to end her life falls within the scope of her right to respect for her private life under Article 8 of the Convention'.
[12] See, however, the Commission decision in the *Widmer* case, in which it held that Art. 2 does not require criminalisation of passive euthanasia (EComHR 10 February 1993, appl. no. 20527/92).
[13] *Lambert and Others v. France*, ECtHR (GC) 5 June 2015, appl. no. 46043/14.
[14] *Ibid.*, para. 141.
[15] *Ibid.*, para. 124. This is significant, since Art. 2(2) ECHR would not provide for an exemption for this type of situation if the Court were to have qualified the case as one about negative obligations; see further s 3 on the exemption clauses.
[16] *Ibid.*, paras. 144–148.
[17] *Ibid.*, para. 181.
[18] *Tzekov v. Bulgaria*, ECtHR 23 February 2006, appl. no. 45500/99, para. 40.

that had been fired during his arrest. His injuries had caused him permanent disabilities, although they had not been life-threatening. Consequently, the Court was not persuaded that the force used had been of such a nature or degree as to infringe the rights protected under Article 2, and it decided not to examine the case under that provision. Instead, as is common in such cases, the Court continued to consider the case under Article 3, the prohibition of inhuman or degrading treatment.[19]

However, even if no loss of life has actually occurred, the Court may still decide to apply Article 2 if the case concerns the use of potentially lethal violence under life-threatening circumstances. An example is a case where police officers pursued someone driving a car, who had accelerated when the police tried to stop him.[20] The police officers had started firing at the car and they had continued doing so even when the driver had stopped his car. The driver was injured, but still alive. The Court acknowledged that the force used had not been deadly, but it held that this did not exclude an examination of the complaints under Article 2. It thereby reasoned that the text of Article 2 'demonstrates that it covers not only intentional killing but also situations where it is permitted to use force which may result, as an unintended outcome, in the deprivation of life or in the event that there was an unequivocal intention or aim behind the use of force to cause someone's death, even though the person involved did not actually come to die.'[21]

Thus, the Court has applied Article 2 in various cases where there is a life-threatening situation, rather than an established death. It has done so, first, in cases where an applicant suffers from a terminal illness or disease and the claim concerns medical negligence or a lack of medical care.[22] Secondly, the Court has examined cases under Article 2 where the lives of individuals are critically endangered by natural disasters or dangerous activities.[23] And finally, the Court has applied Article 2 in the context of (enforced) disappearances. This last category of cases is special, because of the uncertainty that is involved: when someone has disappeared in suspicious circumstances, it may be impossible for family members to know if their relative is still alive or whether he or she has died.[24] This may make it difficult for the Court to conclusively hold that the right to life has been breached. In *Varnava*, the Court has solved this problem by shifting the burden of proof to the state if a person has disappeared in an area within the exclusive control of the authorities of the state and there is

---

[19]   *İlhan v. Turkey*, ECtHR (GC) 27 June 2000, appl. no. 22277/93, para. 77.

[20]   *Makaratzis v. Greece*, ECtHR 20 December 2004, appl. no. 50385/99.

[21]   *Idem*, para. 49.

[22]   *Colak and Tsakiridis v. Germany*, ECtHR 5 March 2009, appl. nos. 77144/01 and 35493/05, para. 29.

[23]   *Kolyadenko and Others v. Russia*, ECtHR 28 February 2012, appl. nos. 17423/05 et al.

[24]   This normally is the standard required by the Court; see, e.g., *Varnava and Others v. Turkey*, ECtHR (GC) 18 September 2009, appl. nos. 16064/90 and Others, para. 182.

prima facie evidence that the state may be involved.[25] If the state is not able to account for someone's whereabouts and for what has happened to him or her, the Court will hold that Article 2 applies, even if there is no conclusive evidence that the disappeared person has died. In this regard, it is important for the Court to establish that the disappeared person is likely to find himself in a life-threatening situation. The Court may thereby take account of general contextual evidence, such as information that the conduct of military operations in a certain area is accompanied by widespread arrests and killings.[26] In cases relating to disappearances in Russia's Northern Caucasus, for example, the Court has established, based on such contextual evidence, that there is a life-threatening situation – and Article 2 applies – as soon as it is clear that a person has been detained by unidentified state agents without any subsequent acknowledgement of the detention.[27] Another factor of relevance may be the passage of time. For example, the Court has made a presumption of death in the absence of any reliable news of disappeared persons for a period of four and a half years.[28]

2.3. STATE RESPONSIBILITY

a. State obligations in horizontal situations

The Court can only declare an Article 2 complaint admissible if it is directed against the state.[29] Consequently, it may seem difficult to invoke Article 2 successfully if a death is not directly caused by state action, but rather by an individual or a group of individuals (e.g. in the event of murder or of a terrorist attack); if it is the effect of a lack of medical care in a private hospital; if it is the result of suicide or a fatal accident; and so on. The Court can still assess such cases, however, if it is clear that the state bears a certain responsibility for someone's death. In this regard, it is of particular relevance that Article 2 expressly states that the states 'shall protect' the right to life. This means that the state may be held responsible not only if it actively violated the right to life, but also when it falls short of the obligation to protect individuals' lives. For example, if a state has refrained from taking action to prevent lethal domestic violence or murder, a complaint under Article 2 can be made against it, even if the death in such cases is caused by a third party. This means that the positive

---

25   *Ibid.*, para. 184. For an application of this division of the burden of proof in relation to Russia (particularly for disappearances in the Chechen Republic), see (amongst many other authorities) e.g. *Turluyeva v. Russia*, ECtHR 20 June 2013, appl. no. 63638/09, paras. 83–85.

26   *Ibid.*

27   E.g. *Turluyeva v. Russia*, *supra* n. 25, para. 85.

28   *Idem*, para. 86.

29   Art. 34 ECHR.

obligations developed under Article 2 ECHR are of particular importance. They therefore are discussed separately and in more detail below, in section 4.

b.   Burden of proof

Complex evidentiary issues as to the applicability of Article 2 may arise if a state denies responsibility for, for example, a suicide in a prison or a death that has occurred during an arrest. To deal with these issues, the Court has accepted that, if the events to which the complaint pertains 'lie wholly, or in large part, within the exclusive knowledge of the authorities, as in the case of persons within their control while in custody, strong presumptions of fact will arise in respect of injuries and death occurring during that detention'.[30] The state then can escape its responsibility under Article 2 only if the authorities provide for a satisfactory and convincing explanation for the situation.[31] In the absence of such an explanation, the Court may draw inferences which may be unfavourable for the respondent state.[32]

Similarly, in cases about (mass) killings and enforced disappearances, a recurrent defence by some states is that they have been caused by armed groups, terrorists or civilian militias. It may be difficult for the next-of-kin of the deceased to prove state responsibility in such cases, because they usually have little evidence available to prove beyond reasonable doubt that the death of their relative has been brought about by state agents. The Court has adopted a special approach in such cases to ensure the effectiveness of the right to individual complaint. The applicant has to make out a *prima facie* case by adducing sufficient information to persuade the Court that it is likely that someone has died either by the hand of state agents or in a situation for which the state can be held responsible.[33] If such a *prima facie* case has been made, the Court will conduct an elaborate factual investigation of its own.[34] Moreover, if a state has refused access to the complete files of a certain case, or if it has provided only partial information, it has to explain conclusively how, in reality, the events in question occurred.[35] The Court is further prepared to make negative inferences from the failure or refusal of a respondent government to provide for the

---

[30]   *Velikova v. Bulgaria*, ECtHR 18 May 2000, appl. no. 41488/98, para. 70. More recently this was confirmed by the Grand Chamber in *Hassan v. the United Kingdom*, ECtHR (GC) 16 September 2014, appl. no. 29750/09, paras. 47–49.

[31]   *Ibid.* See also the sources mentioned below in relation to the burden of proof in cases about disappearances.

[32]   *Hassan v. the United Kingdom, supra* n. 30, para. 49.

[33]   *Cf.*, e.g., *Khashiyev and Akayeva v. Russia*, ECtHR 24 February 2005, appl. nos. 57942/00 and 57945/00, paras. 144 et seq.

[34]   *Ibid.*

[35]   E.g. *Akkum and Others v. Turkey*, ECtHR 24 March 2005, appl. no. 21894/93, paras. 211 et seq. and *Estamirov and Others v. Russia*, ECtHR 12 October 2006, appl. no. 60272/00, paras. 112–114.

necessary documentation.[36] This almost invariably means in such cases that the Court holds the state responsible for a breach of the right to life.[37]

c. Causality

One further requirement for admissibility of an Article 2 complaint is that there must be a causal relationship between acts or omissions of the state and a person's death (or the immediate threat thereof). The issue of causation was central to the *Finogenov* case, which concerned the taking of hostages at the Moscovian Nord-Ost theatre in 2002.[38] The Russian authorities had tried to rescue the hostages by pumping a narcotic gas into the theatre through the ventilation system. As a result of the rescue operation, the majority of hostages were released, but a large number of them were affected by the gas. About 125 hostages died in the operation. The Russian Government argued that there was no causal relationship between the use of the narcotic gas and the decease of the hostages, since the gas had been of a harmless type. The official explanation was that the deceased had been weakened by the siege or had been seriously ill.[39] The Court reasoned, however, that 'it is unthinkable that 125 people of different ages and physical conditions died almost simultaneously and in the same place because of various pre-existing health problems'.[40] Although the Court accepted that the gas was probably not intended to kill the terrorists or hostages, 'it was, at best, potentially dangerous for an ordinary person, and potentially fatal for a weakened person'.[41] For that reason, it was 'safe to conclude that the gas remained a primary cause of the death of a large number of the victims'. This meant that it could accept state responsibility for the alleged violation and the case could be examined for compliance with the requirements of Article 2 of the Convention.[42]

d. Extraterritorial application

The state's responsibility to protect individuals' lives may also pertain to situations where military or arrest operations have taken place outside the state's own territory, such as in the case of the British military actions in

---

36   *Cf. Timurtaş v. Turkey*, ECtHR 13 June 2000, appl. no. 23531/94, para. 66.
37   Originally the burden of proof was a different one, which was more difficult to meet for applicants; see, e.g., *Kurt v. Turkey*, ECtHR 25 May 1998, appl. no. 24276/94, para. 107/108. See in more detail J. Kratochvíl, 'The Right to Life in the Perspective of the Human Rights Committee and the European Court of Human Rights', working paper December 2006, <http://ssrn.com/abstract=951225>, pp. 17–18.
38   *Finogenov and Others v. Russia*, ECtHR 20 December 2011, appl. nos. 18299/03 and 27311/03. For an example of a case in which the Court did not find causality sufficiently established, see *V.M. and Others v. Belgium*, ECtHR 11 July 2015, no. 60125/11.
39   *Idem*, para. 201.
40   *Idem*, para. 201.
41   *Idem*, para. 202.
42   *Idem*, paras. 198–203.

Iraq.[43] The extent to which the ECHR is applicable to this kind of situation is not determined by Article 2 ECHR, however, but it is an issue of jurisdiction that is determined by Article 1 ECHR. This issue therefore is addressed more fully in Chapter 1 of this volume. Importantly, however, as soon as the state's responsibility is accepted in such cases, it incurs all positive obligations that follow from Article 2. For example, when a case concerns the death of a sailor on a ship anchored in a far-away country, the state where the ship has been registered should provide for an effective investigation into the circumstances of death.[44] Similarly, an investigation may be needed when a civilian in a third country has died of gunshot wounds in an incident involving military personnel of the respondent state.[45] The nature and extent of these obligations are then the same as for deaths which occur on the state's own territory. They are further discussed in section 4.

3. EXEMPTIONS

3.1. INTRODUCTION

Article 2(1) and (2) ECHR contain an exhaustive list of situations in which a death caused by the state does not contravene the Convention. Article 2(1) allows for the death penalty to be imposed, while Article 2(2) exempts three situation types where lethal force legitimately can be used by state agents. In addition, Article 15(2) ECHR – which allows for special derogations from fundamental rights in times of emergency – stipulates that no derogation shall be made from Article 2, except in respect of deaths resulting from lawful acts of war. Besides these limited possibilities for exemption, the ECtHR has not accepted any 'implied' limitations; to that extent, the provision is non-derogable.

In applying the exemptions contained in Article 2 ECHR, the Court takes due account of the paramount importance of the right to life, which it has held to constitute 'the supreme value in the hierarchy of human rights'.[46] This is also reflected in the text of Article 2(2), which states that deprivation of life can be accepted only if it 'results from the use of force which is no more than absolutely necessary'. The proportionality requirement is thus formulated much more strictly than it is in, for example, Articles 8–11 of the Convention.[47]

---

[43] *Al-Skeini and Others v. the United Kingdom*, ECtHR (GC) 7 July 2011, appl. no. 55721/07; see also, however, *Behrami and Behrami v. France* and *Saramati v. France, Germany and Norway*, ECtHR (GC) 2 May 2007, appl. nos. 71412/01 and 78166/01.

[44] *Bakanova v. Lithuania*, ECtHR 31 May 2016, no. 11167/12.

[45] *Jaloud v. the Netherlands*, ECtHR (GC) 20 November 2014, no. 47708/08.

[46] *K.-H.W. v. Germany*, ECtHR (GC) 22 March 2001, appl. no. 37201/97, para. 66.

[47] See, e.g., *McCann v. the United Kingdom*, *supra* n. 1, paras. 149–150; *Gül v. Turkey*, ECtHR 14 December 2000, appl. no. 22676/93, para. 77; *Aydan v. Turkey*, ECtHR 12 March 2013, appl. no. 16281/10, para. 65.

Consequently, the Court will only accept limitations to this right in very special circumstances and it does not allow a margin of appreciation to the states.[48] This may be different for cases which are not concerned with the states' negative obligations, but their positive obligations. Since the requirement to effectively protect individuals' lives is generally regarded as an obligation of means and not of result, the states may be given some leeway as to how they want to comply with it. This is further addressed in section 4.

Hereafter the four different exemptions of Article 2 are discussed separately. It should be noted, however, that the three exemption clauses of Article 2(2) are very closely related.[49] This means the Court will not always as strictly distinguish between the different clauses of Article 2(2) as is done in this section.[50]

3.2. DEATH PENALTY

The drafters of the original text of the ECHR regarded the death penalty as an acceptable punishment: Article 2(1) ECHR states that a deprivation of life will not be held to contravene the Convention if it occurs in 'the execution of a sentence of a court following [a person's] conviction of a crime for which this penalty is provided by law'. However, over time, opinions have changed. In 1983, Protocol 6 ECHR was adopted, Article 1 of which states that 'the death penalty shall be abolished' and that 'no one shall be condemned to such penalty or executed'.[51] According to Article 2 of Protocol No. 6, this is only different if a state 'has made provision in its law for the death penalty in respect of acts committed in time of war or of imminent threat of war'. With the exception of Russia, all States Parties to the Convention have ratified this Protocol, thereby indicating their support for the abolition of the death penalty. This support is even more clearly stressed by the states' adoption of Protocol No. 13 (signed in 2002), which abolishes the exception for imposition of the death penalty in times of war. In 2016, this Protocol was ratified by 44 of the 47 Convention states.[52]

In 2005, in the *Öcalan* case, the Court held that the strong ratification record of Protocols No. 6 and No. 13 could be regarded as proof that the states in fact have chosen to amend the text of Article 2(1) ECHR.[53] In 2010, in *Al-Sadoon and Mufdhi*, the Court confirmed that the European consensus means that

---

[48]   E.g. *Shchiborshch and Kuzmina v. Russia*, ECtHR 16 January 2014, appl. no. 5269/08, para. 204.

[49]   E.g. *Finogenov and Others v. Russia*, *supra* n. 38, paras. 217–218.

[50]   See, e.g., *Cangöz and Others v. Turkey*, ECtHR 26 April 2016, appl. no. 7469/06, paras. 105 et seq.

[51]   CETS-appl. no. 114; see <https://conventions.coe.int>.

[52]   CETS-appl. no. 187; see <https://conventions.coe.int>; Armenia has signed, but not ratified the Protocol; Azerbaijan and Russia have neither signed nor ratified it.

[53]   *Öcalan v. Turkey (No. 1)*, ECtHR (GC) 12 May 2005, appl. no. 46221/99, paras. 162 et seq. See also *Bader and Kanbor v. Sweden*, ECtHR 8 November 2005, appl. no. 13284/04, para. 42.

---

the second sentence of Article 2(1) can no longer be read as a justification for the imposition or execution of the death penalty.[54] Presently, therefore, the exemption of Article 2(1) can be regarded as a dead letter. This is true even for Russia, which at the time of writing had ratified Protocol No. 13 nor Protocol No. 6.[55]

This is important mainly for cases relating to expulsion or extradition. As a consequence of the Court's holding in *Al-Sadoon and Mufdhi*, it would run counter to the state's obligations under Article 2 to expel or extradite someone to a third country where they are exposed to a real and concrete risk of being subjected to a trial where the death penalty can be imposed.[56] Exceptions to the prohibition of expulsion or extradition can be made only if sufficiently reliable and concrete guarantees have been provided that the sentence will not be executed.[57]

3.3. LEGITIMATE (SELF-)DEFENCE

According to Article 2(2)(a) ECHR, interferences with the right to life will not contravene the Convention if they are absolutely necessary 'in defence of any person from unlawful violence'. This exemption is mainly applied in cases where police officers or soldiers have used violence in self-defence or in defence of bystanders, such as happened in the *Ramsahai* case.[58] This case concerned a young man who had stolen a scooter and was pursued by two policemen. When the policemen had finally caught up with the man, they saw him take a pistol from under his belt and warned him not to shoot. When one of the policeman drew nearer, however, the man raised his gun and pointed it to the policeman. Feeling threatened, the policeman also drew his pistol and fired. The man was hit in the neck and died shortly after the incident. In this case the Court found it sufficiently established that the police officer had acted from legitimate self-defence. He had drawn his pistol only after the man had neglected a prior warning, and he had fired a single shot only when the man had directly pointed his pistol to him. The Court also stressed that both policemen had acted in accordance with the official instructions for the use of firearms. In those circumstances, the Court held, the violence used could be considered to be justified.

The test applied in *Ramsahai* is part of the Court's well-established case law on Article 2(2)(a) ECHR.[59] The standards developed in this case law can be

---

54 *Al-Saadoon and Mufdhi v. the United Kingdom*, ECtHR 2 March 2010, appl. no. 61498/08.
55 *A.L. (X.W.) v. Russia*, ECtHR 29 October 2015, appl. no. 44095/14.
56 *Ibid.*
57 *Bader and Kanbor v. Sweden, supra* n. 53, para. 48.
58 *Ramsahai and Others v. the Netherlands*, ECtHR (GC) 15 May 2007, appl. no. 52391/99.
59 For an overview, see, e.g., *Giuliani and Gaggio v. Italy*, ECtHR (GC) 24 March 2011, appl. no. 23458/02.

summarised as follows. First, unwarranted use of (potentially lethal) violence must be avoided as much as possible by careful training of state agents, such as police officers and military personnel, and by putting in place an appropriate legal and administrative framework defining the circumstances in which officials may use force and firearms.[60] Secondly, Article 2(2) states that violence may be resorted to only if this is strictly necessary in the circumstances of the case. The Court has explained this standard as indicating 'that a stricter and more compelling test of necessity must be employed than that normally applicable when determining whether State action is "necessary in a democratic society" under paragraphs 2 of Articles 8 to 11 of the Convention. In particular, the force used must be strictly proportionate to the achievement of the aims set out in sub-paragraphs 2 (a), (b) and (c) of Article 2.'[61]

The Court therefore subjects deprivations of life in the context of self-defence or defence of third parties to the most careful scrutiny and does not allow a margin of appreciation to the states. At the same time, the Court has acknowledged that it may be difficult for it to second-guess the necessity of the use of lethal violence in (self-)defence, especially because of the risks of hindsight bias. In the classic case *McCann*, the Court has therefore emphasised that the use of force by agents of the State may be justified 'where it is based on an honest belief which is perceived, for good reasons, to be valid at the time but which subsequently turns out to be mistaken'.[62] The Court thus will not substitute its own assessment of the situation for that of the police officers who were required to act in the heat of the moment.[63] Nevertheless, the Court has set high standards for police officers. They must be well-prepared, they must remain quiet and they should not easily panic.[64] Moreover, the Court does not accept it if direct and lethal use has been made of firearms if there would have been an opportunity to give a warning or if there was a possibility of using a non-lethal shot.[65]

Finally, the Court has emphasised that the use of lethal force by the state needs to be followed by an effective investigation. The investigation must comply with the general criteria it has formulated in its case law, which are further explained in section 4.[66]

---

[60]   *Idem*, para. 209.
[61]   *Idem*, para. 176.
[62]   *McCann v. the United Kingdom, supra* n. 1, para. 200.
[63]   *Armani da Silva v. the United Kingdom*, ECtHR (GC) 30 March 2016, appl. no. 5878/08, para. 245.
[64]   See, e.g., *Haász and Szabó v. Hungary*, ECtHR 13 October 2015, appl. nos. 11327/14 and 11613/14.
[65]   *Aydan v. Turkey, supra* n. 47.
[66]   See, e.g., *Armani da Silva, supra* n. 63.

3.4. LAWFUL ARREST AND PREVENTION OF ESCAPE

Some suspects try to escape arrest by running away, by using physical violence or by threatening the police with a firearm. Article 2(2)(b) ECHR may allow for the use of (lethal) violence to enable an arrest to be made in such cases, but only if such violence is absolutely necessary. More specifically, the Court has held that potentially lethal methods of arrest may be relied on only if the individual's resistance or escape causes a 'particular risk of irreparable harm'.[67] When the person to be arrested does not appear to bear arms, an escape has been non-violent and there is no apparent risk to the life and limb of police officers or bystanders, it is not acceptable to have recourse to potentially deadly violence.[68] This is true even if a failure to use such force may result in the loss of the opportunity of arrest.[69]

The Court also has made clear that arrest operations normally must be carefully planned in order to avoid unnecessary use of (potentially) lethal violence. As it held in *Nachova*, 'a crucial element in the planning of an arrest operation ... must be the analysis of all the available information about the surrounding circumstances, including, as an absolute minimum, the nature of the offence committed by the person to be arrested and the degree of danger – if any – posed by that person. The question whether and in what circumstances recourse to firearms should be envisaged if the person to be arrested tries to escape must be decided on the basis of clear legal rules, adequate training and in the light of that information.'[70]

In addition, the violence used must be strictly proportionate to the level of risk incurred. It was not acceptable, for example, to fire about 50 shots with an automatic gun at the door of a house which was about to be searched, while the suspect was still unlocking the door and there was no reason for the officers to believe that their lives were at risk.[71] The Court further needs to be convinced that alternative and non-lethal means have been considered and used before the state agents resorted to lethal force.[72] Finally, just as in the case of legitimate self-defence, the use of lethal force obliges the state to provide for an effective investigation.[73]

---

[67] See, e.g., *Nachova v. Bulgaria*, ECtHR 26 February 2004, appl. nos. 43577/98 and 43579/98, para. 100, as confirmed by the Grand Chamber in its judgment in the case of 6 July 2005.

[68] *Ibid.*, para. 95.

[69] *Ibid.*, para. 106.

[70] *Idem*, para. 103, referring to the Chamber judgment in the case of 26 February 2004, para. 110.

[71] *Gül v. Turkey*, *supra* n. 1, para. 82. See similarly, e.g., *Dimov and Others v. Bulgaria*, ECtHR 6 November 2012, appl. no. 30086/05.

[72] *Cangöz and Others v. Turkey*, ECtHR 26 April 2016, appl. no. 7469/06, para. 113.

[73] *Ibid.*, para. 114.

3.5. ACTION FOR THE PURPOSE OF QUELLING A RIOT OR INSURRECTION

Finally, the use of violence can be justified if this is absolutely necessary to quell a riot or insurrection (Article 2(2)(c) ECHR). The requirements of proportionality and subsidiarity are of great importance to the application of this provision. In the *Şimşek* case, for example, the Court held that it is not acceptable to open fire as soon as a demonstration appears to get out of hand. It is necessary to have recourse to less dangerous methods first, such as the use of tear gas, water cannons or rubber bullets.[74] Moreover, careful planning of riot control operations is essential.[75] Police officers engaged in operations to end riots and disturbances should be put in a position to evaluate all parameters and carefully organise their operations.[76] To that end, states should undertake to provide effective training to the police force and police officers should receive clear and precise instructions as to the manner and circumstances in which they should make use of firearms.[77]

4. POSITIVE OBLIGATIONS

4.1. INTRODUCTION

The right to life primarily entails a negative obligation for the states, which should refrain from acts that would deprive individuals of their lives. The Court has acknowledged, however, that this negative obligation does not suffice to effectively protect the right to life. After all, individuals' lives may be put at risk in many ways – by acts of other individuals, by explosions of dangerous installations, by traffic accidents, etc. To protect the right to life to the fullest extent possible, the Court has recognised a great many positive obligations for the states. In addition to a range of obligations to prevent violations of the right to life, which are discussed in section 4, these include procedural obligations to investigate suspicious deaths and provide for an effective remedy, as is explained in section 4.

4.2. OBLIGATIONS TO PROTECT THE RIGHT TO LIFE

a. Training and instructions for using violence

If it is necessary for state agents to have recourse to potentially lethal force, for example to overpower a violent person, they must be able do so in a cautious

---

[74] *Şimşek and Others v. Turkey*, ECtHR 26 July 2005 (dec.), appl. nos. 35072/97 and 37194/97, para. 108.

[75] *Güleç v. Turkey*, ECtHR 27 July 1998, appl. no. 21593/93, para. 71.

[76] *Şimşek v. Turkey*, *supra* n. 74, para. 109.

[77] *Idem*, paras. 109/110; see more recently also *Kavaklıoğlu and Others v. Turkey*, ECtHR 6 October 2015, appl. no. 15397/02.

and well-considered manner. The Court therefore has held that they should not be left in a vacuum when exercising their duties.[78] A legal and administrative framework should define the limited circumstances in which law enforcement officers may use force and firearms.[79] Policemen or military personnel should receive clear and precise instructions regarding the manner and circumstances in which they might make use of firearms and states should provide effective training to the police force with the objective of complying with international standards for human rights and policing.[80]

In its case law, the Court has set increasingly high demands for law enforcement officers. This can be illustrated by the case of *Saoud*.[81] Police officers had endeavoured to overpower a man suffering from schizophrenia who had attacked his mother and sisters and who was violently resisting his arrest. Unable to handcuff his arms behind his back, the policemen handcuffed them in front of his body, pushed him to the ground, and used their body weight to keep him pinned down. They called the emergency medical service to administer a tranquilliser, but by the time the medical services arrived, the man had died. The investigating judge confirmed that the death was caused by the way the man had been held down, in combination with his medical condition. Although the Court acknowledged that the violence used to overpower the man had been necessary to defend the lives of others, it held that the police officers had not complied with the positive obligation to safeguard the man's life. They could have known about the man's vulnerable condition, about which they were informed by one of the man's sisters, and they therefore should have exercised particular care not to use the particular immobilisation technique applied. Consequently, even if they have to act in a split second, law enforcement officers must be sufficiently well-trained to be capable of estimating the risks and consequences of their behaviour.

b. Preparation for potentially life-threatening operations

The Court has recognised a general obligation to carefully plan and control any law enforcement operations in which force is likely to be used, such as in the event of liberation of hostages, anti-terrorist operations, public order operations during demonstrations and manifestations, suppression of prison riots, military action or large-scale arrest operations.[82] The Court has held that 'the more predictable a hazard, the greater the obligation to protect against it', in particular by taking measures to minimise the risk of harm.[83]

---

[78]   *Idem*, para. 105.

[79]   *Ibid.*

[80]   See, amongst many other authorities, *Şimşek v. Turkey*, *supra* n. 74, para. 109 and see more elaborately Kratochvil, *supra* n. 37, p. 5. See also, e.g., *Leonidis v. Greece*, ECtHR 8 January 2009, appl. no. 43326/05.

[81]   *Saoud v. France*, ECtHR 9 October 2007, appl. no. 9375/02.

[82]   The classic case on the issue is *McCann v. the United Kingdom*, *supra* n. 1.

[83]   *Finogenov and Others v. Russia*, *supra* n. 38, para. 243.

The *Isayeva* case may help to illustrate what kind of obligations are meant here.[84] This case concerned the bombardment of a village in Chechnya, which was followed by heaving fighting in the streets. During the events, allegedly 150 civilians were killed. According to the Russian Government, the bombardment was necessary to suppress an illegal armed insurgency. The Court accepted that the situation had called for exceptional measures by the State, including deployment of army units equipped with combat weapons and the use of military aviation and artillery.[85] However, the Court also noted that the military operation had not been spontaneous.[86] The fact that the operation had been planned some time in advance had allowed the military officers sufficient time for preparation and for considering the dangers of methods such as bombing.[87] The Court considered it highly problematic that there was no evidence that any serious calculations had been made about the evacuation of civilians, no precautions had been taken to ensure their safety, no steps had been taken to assist the vulnerable and the infirm, and so on.[88] For that reason, the Court held that the authorities had not complied with their positive obligation of planning and executing the operation with the requisite care for the lives of the civilian population.

The Court arrived at a similar conclusion in the case of *Finogenov*, which concerned the hostage liberation drama in the Nord-Ost theatre in Moscow.[89] The Court noted that the Russian authorities had had about two days to reflect on the situation, which had put them in a position to prepare an emergency plan for the evacuation and medical assistance of the hostages. However, the plan of the rescue and evacuation of the hostages had been flawed in many respects, and there had been major problems of information exchange and co-ordination, lack of appropriate medical equipment, and inadequate logistics.[90] The Court therefore concluded that the State had breached its positive obligations under Article 2.

The Court sets lower standards for planning and control if there is hardly any time for preparations or the use of violence is spontaneous. *Giuliani and Gaggio*, for example, concerned a lethal accident that occurred in a clash between law enforcement officers and demonstrators during mass demonstrations at a G8-summit in Genova.[91] The Court considered that the Italian Government had made sufficient preparations for riot control, e.g. by deploying well-trained personnel to police the event. It noted that the clash between demonstrators and law enforcement officers had occurred suddenly and no previous operational decisions could have taken account of the unforeseeable events that occurred.[92]

---

84 *Isayeva and Others v. Russia*, ECtHR 24 February 2005, appl. no. 57950/00.
85 *Idem*, para. 180.
86 *Idem*, para. 188.
87 *Idem*, para. 189.
88 *Ibid.*
89 *Finogenov and Others v. Russia*, *supra* n. 38, paras. 237–266.
90 *Idem*, para. 266.
91 *Giuliani and Gaggio v. Italy*, *supra* n. 59.
92 *Idem*, para. 254.

Consequently, the Italian authorities had not failed in their obligation to do all that could reasonably be expected of them to avoid the accident.[93]

Thus, although a high level of planning and organisation is required and high demands are set on the training of police officers, the Court will not find a violation of positive obligations if the use of deadly violence resulted from the exigencies of the situation.

c. Persons in vulnerable situations and persons under control of the state

The state has a special responsibility to protect the lives of individuals over which it exercises a certain degree of control or who find themselves in a vulnerable position, such as prisoners or military conscripts. This special responsibility means, of course, that the state should prevent that they are killed by state officials. In addition to this, the state should protect such vulnerable individuals against the use of violence by other people and against suicide. If the authorities know or ought to know of a real and immediate risk to the life of a prisoner from the acts of a third party, they should take all measures within the scope of their powers which, judged reasonably, might be expected to avoid that risk.[94] This can be illustrated by the *Edwards* case, which concerned a paranoid and schizophrenic prisoner who had assaulted and killed his cell-mate.[95] The Court noted that insufficient information about the prisoner's mental illness had been passed on to the prison authorities and he had not been adequately screened upon his arrival in prison.[96] These failures, which had resulted in the decision to put the prisoner in a cell together with another detainee, constituted a breach of the State's positive obligations under Article 2.

Similarly, in cases of suicide in prison or in the army, the Court examines if the competent authorities took sufficient precautions to recognise the risk of suicide in a timely and appropriate fashion and provided for preventive measures.[97] At the same time, the Court has held that oppressive removal of a person's freedom of choice and action should be avoided and the measures should be compatible with Articles 5 ECHR (right to liberty) and 8 ECHR (right to respect for one's private life).[98] Generally, therefore, only precautions should be taken that do not infringe on personal autonomy. Examples are searching a prisoner for the presence of instruments that can be used to commit suicide and removing them (e.g. a belt or shoe laces), or accompanying a prisoner to the toilet to prevent him from jumping out of a window.[99]

---

[93] *Idem*, para. 262.

[94] *Paul and Audrey Edwards v. the United Kingdom*, ECtHR 14 March 2002, appl. no. 46477/99, para. 57.

[95] *Idem.*

[96] *Idem*, paras. 59–64.

[97] See, e.g., *Perevedentsevy v. Russia*, ECtHR 24 April 2014, appl. no. 39583/05.

[98] *Keenan v. the United Kingdom*, ECtHR 3 April 2001, appl. no. 27229/95, para. 92.

[99] *Tanribilir v. Turkey*, ECtHR 16 November 2000, appl. no. 21422/93, para. 75. Whether any more stringent measures are necessary and whether it is reasonable to apply them will depend

Finally, the responsibility of the state to protect the life of persons in vulnerable positions includes a duty to provide prisoners with sufficient medical care.[100] However, this obligation does not go so far as to require that the state release terminally ill prisoners or force-feed them if they engage in a hunger strike.[101]

d. Dangerous activities, natural disasters and accidents

The explosion of a factory or environmental damage done by industrial activities may give cause to lethal casualties and injuries. A landmark judgment on this issue was rendered in *Öneryildiz*, which concerned the death of 39 persons who had lived in illegally built dwellings on a household refuse-tip.[102] After a methane explosion, the refuse erupting from the pile of waste had engulfed more than 10 of the houses. An expert's report drawn up a few years earlier had already drawn the authorities' attention to the risk of an explosion of the methane generated by the decomposing refuse, but no immediate measures had been taken. The Court held that in the particular context of dangerous activities (such as maintaining a refuse-tip), special measures should be taken for licensing, setting up, operation, security and supervision of the activities.[103] The states also have particular obligations to ensure the compliance with safety measures, e.g. by duly conducting inspections.[104] All concerned further should be compelled to take practical measures to ensure the effective protection of citizens whose lives might be endangered.[105] Among these preventive measures, particular emphasis should be placed on the public's right to information.[106]

Similar obligations have been imposed in relation to natural disasters. Although the Court has emphasised that no impossible or disproportionate burden must be laid on the authorities regarding the operational choices they must make in terms of priorities and use of resources,[107] preventive or mitigating action may be required if the imminence of a natural hazard is clearly identifiable or when it is a recurring calamity affecting a distinct area developed for human habitation or use.[108] The authorities should carefully monitor threats

---

on the circumstances of the case; see, e.g., *Keenan v. the United Kingdom, supra* n. 98, para. 93; *Renolde v. France*, ECtHR 16 October 2008, appl. no. 5608/05; *Keller v. Russia*, ECtHR 17 October 2013, appl. no. 26824/04.

[100] E.g. *Salakhov and Islyamova v. Ukraine*, ECtHR 14 March 2013, appl. no. 28005/08.

[101] *Cf. Rappaz v. Switzerland*, ECtHR 26 March 2013 (dec.), appl. no. 73175/10.

[102] *Öneryildiz v. Turkey*, ECtHR (GC) 30 November 2004, appl. no. 48939/99, para. 90.

[103] *Idem*, para. 90.

[104] See specifically *Cevrioğlu v. Turkey*, ECtHR 4 October 2016, appl. no. 69546/12.

[105] *Öneryildiz v. Turkey, supra* n. 104, para. 90.

[106] *Ibid.*

[107] *Budayeva and Others v. Russia*, ECtHR 20 March 2008, appl. nos. 15339/02, 21166/02, 20058/02, 11673/02 and 15343/02.

[108] *Idem*, para. 137.

and dangers and inform the inhabitants of a certain area about them, and they must provide for evacuation plans.[109] Finally, the authorities have a general obligation to keep the infrastructure intended to protect the population, such as dikes and dams, under good maintenance.[110]

When there is a risk of serious and lethal accidents of which the state has (or ought to have) knowledge, the state may be obliged to take and enforce reasonable precautionary measures. For example, safety regulations need to be in place to prevent that individuals get off the train in such a way that they run a risk of being caught by an oncoming train.[111] Similarly, the Court held a state responsible for the death of a man who had been attacked by stray dogs.[112] It found sufficiently established that the competent authorities had been well aware of the problems caused by the dogs, yet had taken insufficient action to combat it. The Court, in particular, also has recognised preventive obligations in relation to the protection of the lives of children. The Court has held, for instance, that children who play in dangerous environments, such as places where there is a risk of being injured by hidden explosives or of collapse of a building, must be duly warned and protected.[113] Also, school authorities should take good care that children are not allowed to walk home alone during extremely cold and snowy weather.[114]

Such risk-avoiding positive obligations of the state only arise when the state reasonably could have been aware of a risk to the life of an individual. In addition, the state cannot be expected to prevent every possible harm. In a case where a private beach club had allowed both swimming and speed boating in the same bay, for example, the Court found that the state system of regulation and licensing had been generally adequate and the State could not have been expected to take any more concrete action to avoid the death of a swimmer who was overrun by a speedboat.[115] Finally, the state cannot be held responsible under Article 2 of the Convention if the death is really due to the individual's own responsibility.[116]

e. Protection against third parties

Although the Convention primarily protects fundamental rights against state action, the right to life can be put at risk also by the acts of individuals, such

---

109 *Idem*, para. 147. See also *Kolyadenko and Others v. Russia, supra* n. 23.

110 *Ibid.*

111 *Kalender v. Turkey*, ECtHR 15 December 2009, appl. no. 4314/02.

112 *Georgel and Georgeta Stoicescu v. Romania*, ECtHR 26 July 2011, appl. no. 9718/03.

113 *Banel v. Lithuania*, ECtHR 18 June 2013, appl. no. 14326/11; *Oruk v. Turkey*, ECtHR 4 February 2014, appl. no. 33647/04.

114 *Ilbeyi Kemaloğlu and Meriye Kemaloğlu v. Turkey*, ECtHR 10 April 2012, appl. no. 19986/06.

115 *Cavit Tınarlıoğlu v. Turkey*, ECtHR 2 February 2016, appl. no. 3648/04.

116 *Bone v. France*, ECtHR 1 March 2005 (dec.), appl. no. 69869/01.

as murder, domestic violence or assaults by armed groups. Given the state's responsibility to protect the right to life under Article 2, it must provide for effective criminal law provisions to prevent such offences against the person. Such provisions should be backed up by an adequate law enforcement machinery for the prevention, suppression and sanctioning of breaches of such provisions.[117] In addition, in the *Osman* case, the Court has held that Article 2 of the Convention may imply a positive obligation on the authorities to take concrete preventive measures to protect an individual whose life is at risk from the criminal acts of another individual.[118] In its judgment, the Court also emphasised, however, that such an obligation must be interpreted in a way 'which does not impose an impossible or disproportionate burden on the authorities, bearing in mind the difficulties involved in policing modern societies, the unpredictability of human conduct and the operational choices which must be made in terms of priorities and resources'.[119] Hence, when there is an allegation that the authorities have not complied with their duty to prevent and suppress offences against the person, it must be established 'that the authorities knew or ought to have known of the existence of a real and immediate risk to the life of an identified individual or individuals from the criminal acts of a third party and that they failed to take measures within the scope of their powers which, judged reasonably, might have been expected to avoid that risk.'[120]

The state also has a specific duty of care in relation to decisions to allow (potentially dangerous) prisoners or mentally ill persons to go on prison leave or be held in a semi-custodial regime.[121] The Court has acknowledged the value and legitimacy of a policy of progressive social reintegration of persons sentenced to imprisonment, as well as the need for social reintegration measures such as temporary release.[122] Nevertheless, because of the potential risk of such release for the lives and safety of others, such measures must be very carefully considered on the basis of adequate information and the legal system should provide for sufficient protective measures for society.[123] A national judge considering any such measures therefore should be able to take into account, for

---

[117]   *Osman v. the United Kingdom*, ECtHR (GC) 28 October 1998, appl. no. 23452/94, para. 115 and *Mastromatteo v. Italy*, ECtHR 24 October 2002, appl. no. 37703/97, para. 67.

[118]   See in particular *Osman v. the United Kingdom*, *supra* n. 117, para. 116 and, similarly, *Van Coll v. the United Kingdom*, ECtHR 13 November 2012, appl. no. 7678/09.

[119]   *Ibid.*

[120]   *Ibid.* Some recent examples of application of this approach can be found in *Branko Tomašić and Others v. Croatia*, ECtHR 15 January 2009, appl. no. 46598/06; *Kayak v. Turkey*, ECtHR 10 July 2012, appl. no. 60444/08; *Civek v. Turkey*, ECtHR 23 February 2016, appl. no. 55354/11. For a situation in which the Court did not see any cause for state action, see, e.g., *Ivison v. the United Kingdom*, ECtHR 16 April 2002 (dec.), appl. no. 39030/97.

[121]   *Mastromatteo v. Italy*, *supra* n. 117; *Choreftakis and Choreftaki v. Greece*, ECtHR 17 January 2012, appl. no. 46846/08.

[122]   *Ibid.*

[123]   *Ibid.*

example, if the prisoner has served a minimum period of imprisonment, if he has been of good behaviour while in prison, and if his release would not present a danger to society.[124]

Finally, the Court has accepted that the states may have a rather more general obligation to afford protection against harm done by other people.[125] The state has a responsibility, for example, to help avoid fatal traffic accidents by regulations governing road traffic and the safety of road users.[126] Thus, for a positive obligation to arise it is not necessary *per se* that an identifiable person or group pose a concrete threat to another person's life, as perhaps could be gathered from the *Osman* case discussed above. The scope of the positive obligations to be imposed in such a more general fashion will depend on an assessment of what can be reasonably expected of a state, given what is known of the risks to individuals' lives and given the limitations of available resources.

f.   Medical care and negligence

The state incurs important positive obligations under Article 2 to prevent death as a consequence of medical failure, inadequate care or negligence.[127] Regarding medical care (including that offered by private institutions), the Court has held that there should be an adequate system of regulation, guaranteeing, for example, that medical staff meet professional quality standards, that informed consent is given for medical treatment and that medication is carefully administered.[128] By means of such regulation, the state may prevent unnecessary and potentially legal health risks from occurring in the health care sector. Moreover, adequate health care facilities should be provided for, as well as sufficient co-ordination of care between different hospitals and health care institutions.[129] Such positive obligations should not impose an impossible or disproportionate burden on the authorities, however, and some leeway is given to the states to allow for operational choices in terms of priorities and resources.[130] The Court further has held that there is no general obligation on the states to pursue any particular preventive health policy.[131] In *Shelley*, the Court found that '[m]atters of health care policy, in particular as regards general preventive measures, are in principle within the margin of appreciation of the domestic authorities who are best placed

[124]   *Ibid.* See also *Choreftakis and Choreftaki v. Greece, supra* n. 121; and *Maiorano and Others v. Italy*, ECtHR 15 December 2009, appl. no. 28634/06.
[125]   *Bljakaj v. Poland*, ECtHR 18 September 2014, appl. no. 74448/12, para. 108.
[126]   *Rajkowska v. Poland*, ECtHR 27 November 2011 (dec.), appl. no. 37393/02.
[127]   See *Byrzykowski v. Poland*, ECtHR 27 June 2006, appl. no. 11562/05, para. 104 and, earlier, *Powell v. the United Kingdom*, ECtHR 4 May 2000 (dec.), appl. no. 45305/99.
[128]   *Altuğ and Others v. Turkey*, ECtHR 30 June 2015, appl. no. 32086/07, paras. 64–66.
[129]   E.g. *Aydoğdu v. Turkey*, ECtHR 30 August 2016, appl. no. 40448/06.
[130]   *Cf. Watts v. the United Kingdom*, ECtHR 4 May 2010 (dec.), appl. no. 53586/09.
[131]   *Shelley v. the United Kingdom*, ECtHR 4 January 2008 (dec.), appl. no. 23800/06.

to assess priorities, use of resources and social needs'.[132] In the same vein, the Court held that a state could not be obliged to allow the use of an unauthorised experimental drug for medical treatment of terminally ill patients, not even if the drug was permitted for 'compassionate use' in other states.[133]

By contrast, the state does have a duty to ensure that medication is offered free of charge to a needy individual if that individual is entitled to receive that medication according to national law.[134] Moreover, when it is evident that an avoidable medical failure or a lack of medical care has caused the death of an individual, when structural issues of mismanagement or lack of co-ordination exist, or emergency medical care has not been administered for purely financial reasons, a state does not comply with its obligations under Article 2 of the Convention.[135] Finally, the state may be held responsible for protecting the lives of members of vulnerable groups, such as children and young adults held in children's homes, which may include providing them with sufficient nutrition, clothes and fuel.[136]

g. Extradition and expulsion

In relation to Article 3 of the Convention, the Court has for long accepted that it would be incompatible with the underlying values of the Convention if a state would knowingly surrender an individual to another state if there were substantial grounds for believing that he would be in danger of being subjected to torture.[137] It is self-evident that expulsion and extradition are equally prohibited if there is a real and immediate danger to the life of the individual in the receiving state. When the Court finds that there are risks under both Articles 2 and 3 of the Convention, the Court usually decides to examine them together under Article 3.[138] In addition, even if the Court relies on Article 2 rather than Article 3, the set of criteria applied is very similar. For that reason, reference is made here to the discussion of the standards developed in the Court's Article 3 case law in Chapter 7.

Importantly, when a case concerns an intended extradition or expulsion to a state which still accepts the death penalty, such extradition and expulsion are not acceptable under Article 2 if there is a real risk that this sentence will be actually imposed and executed.[139] This will be different only if the receiving state

---

[132]   *Ibid.* See in similar vein *Marro and Others v. Italy*, ECtHR 8 April 2014 (dec.), appl. no. 29100/07.
[133]   *Hristozov and Others v. Bulgaria*, ECtHR 13 November 2012, appl. nos. 47039/11 and 358/12.
[134]   *Panaitescu v. Romania*, ECtHR 10 April 2012, appl. no. 30909/06.
[135]   *Mehmet Sentürk and Bekir Sentürk v. Turkey*, ECtHR 9 April 2013, appl. no. 13423/09; *Asiye Genç v. Turkey*, ECtHR 27 January 2015, appl. no. 24109/07; *Aydoğdu v. Turkey, supra* n. 129.
[136]   *Nencheva and Others v. Bulgaria*, ECtHR 18 June 2013, appl. no. 48609/06.
[137]   *Soering v. the United Kingdom*, ECtHR 7 July 1989, appl. no. 14038/88, para. 88.
[138]   E.g. *A.A. v. Sweden*, ECtHR 28 June 2012, appl. no. 14499/09, para. 52.
[139]   *Al-Saadoon and Mufdhi v. the United Kingdom, supra* n. 54, para. 123.

has made clear and unequivocal assurances that the death penalty will not be imposed and these assurances are sufficiently reliable.[140]

4.3. PROCEDURAL POSITIVE OBLIGATIONS

a. Detachable and independent nature

Next to obligations to protect the right to life in an effective manner, the Court has defined a number of procedural positive obligations under Article 2 ECHR. In particular, it has imposed a duty on the state to effectively investigate cases in which a death has occurred as well as provide for appropriate procedures to bring the responsible persons to justice. These procedural positive obligations have grown to be so important that the Court has held that they constitute autonomous, detachable obligations.[141] This means that an Article 2 complaint and a finding of a violation may purely concern procedural flaws, regardless of the substantive issues at stake.

The detachable nature of procedural obligations has important consequences for the states when a death has occurred before the moment the state has ratified the Convention.[142] Clearly, in such a case, the state cannot be held responsible under the Convention for the substantive events resulting in a person's death. In *Janowiec*, however, the Grand Chamber held that procedural positive obligations may still come into effect if there is a 'genuine connection' between the death (as the 'triggering event') and the entry into force of the Convention.[143] Such a genuine connection exists if much of the investigation into a death took place (or ought to have taken place) in the period following the entry into force of the Convention. Moreover, even when there is no such genuine connection, the Court may have jurisdiction to assess the compliance with procedural obligations if this is needed to ensure that the guarantees and the underlying values of the Convention are protected in a real and effective way. This would be the case if the triggering event is of a larger dimension than an ordinary criminal offence and amounts to the negation of the very foundations of the Convention.[144] Examples the Court has given are serious crimes under international law, such as war crimes, genocide or crimes against

---

[140] *Ibid.*; see also *Harkins and Edwards v. the United Kingdom*, ECtHR 17 January 2012, appl. nos. 9146/07 and 32650/07, paras. 83–86.

[141] *Šilih v. Slovenia*, ECtHR (GC) 9 April 2009, appl. no. 71463/01.

[142] See, e.g., *Crainiceanu and Frumusanu v. Romania*, ECtHR 24 April 2012, appl. no. 12442/04 and *Anca Mocanu and Others v. Romania*, ECtHR 13 November 2012, appl. nos. 10865/09, 45886/07 and 32431/08.

[143] *Janowiec v. Russia*, ECtHR (GC) 21 October 2013, appl. nos. 55508/07 and 29520/09, para. 145.

[144] *Idem*, para. 150.

humanity.[145] The only exception to the need to investigate such crimes concerns events which predate the Convention.[146]

b. Obligations to investigate

The procedural obligations recognised under Article 2 of the Convention entail that there should be some form of effective official investigation.[147] Should no such investigation take place, this could undermine the protective value of the right to life, because it then could be made to seem that perpetrators are immune from punishment.[148] Moreover, in the Court's view, a prompt and effective response by the authorities is essential in maintaining public confidence in their adherence to the rule of law and in preventing any appearance of collusion in or tolerance of unlawful acts.[149]

The obligation to conduct an effective investigation is imposed on the states regardless of whether individuals have been killed as a result of the use of force by state agents or by the hand of third parties. It also arises if a death has occurred in a situation of armed conflict or war, if it has occurred outside the state's own territory or, as explained above, if it has occurred before ratification of the Convention.[150] If a death has been caused in the sphere of (health) care, whether in the public or the private sector, it is equally required that there is an effective independent judicial system in place so that the cause of death of patients can be determined and those responsible can be made accountable.[151]

In a long line of case law, the Court has further detailed and specified this general requirement of an effective investigation.[152] First, it has required that the authorities start an investigation of their own motion once a case has come to their attention.[153] They cannot leave it to the initiative of the next-of-kin either to lodge a formal complaint or to request particular lines of inquiry or investigative procedures.[154] Secondly, the persons responsible for and carrying

---

[145] *Ibid.*

[146] *Idem*, para. 151.

[147] *McCann v. the United Kingdom, supra* n. 1, para. 161.

[148] E.g., *Aydan v. Turkey, supra* n. 47; see also Kratochvil, *supra* n. 37, p. 9.

[149] *Nachova v. Bulgaria, supra* n. 67, para. 118.

[150] *Al-Skeini v. the United Kingdom, supra* n. 43; *Jaloud v. the Netherlands, supra* n. 45; *Janowiec v. Poland, supra* n. 143. It seems that, in the last situation-type, the Court sets slightly lower standards for the quality and effectiveness of the investigation; see *Nježić and Štimac v. Croatia*, ECtHR 9 April 2015, appl. no. 29823/13, paras. 70 et seq.

[151] See *Vo v. France, supra* n. 2, para. 89; for more detail, see, e.g., *Colak and Tsakiridis v. Germany, supra* n. 22; *Z. v. Poland*, ECtHR 13 November 2012, appl. no. 46132/08; *Bajić v. Croatia*, ECtHR 13 November 2012, appl. no. 41108/10.

[152] These requirements are similar to those set out in relation to Art. 6, but there may be differences; see, e.g., *Mustafa Tunç and Fecire Tunç v. Turkey*, ECtHR 25 June 2013, appl. no. 24014/05, in particular also the dissenting opinion.

[153] *Nachova v. Bulgaria, supra* n. 67, para. 111.

[154] *Ibid.*

out the investigation must be hierarchically, institutionally and practically independent from those implicated in the events.[155] The investigation, thirdly, should be effective, meaning that it should be capable of leading to a determination of whether the force used was justified in the circumstances and to the identification, prosecution and punishment of those responsible.[156] As the Court has consistently held, this entails that 'the authorities must have taken the reasonable steps available to them to secure the evidence concerning the incident, including, inter alia, eyewitness testimony, forensic evidence and, where appropriate, an autopsy which provides a complete and accurate record of injury and an objective analysis of clinical findings, including the cause of death.'[157]

In addition, the investigation's conclusions must be based on a thorough, objective and impartial analysis of all relevant elements and must apply a standard comparable to the 'no more than absolutely necessary' standard required by Article 2(2) of the Convention.[158] Any deficiency in the investigation which undermines its capability of establishing the circumstances of the case and identifying the person responsible is liable to fall foul of the required measure of effectiveness.[159] Moreover, when expert reports are provided, these reports should be rigorous and of high quality.[160] Fourthly, the investigation must be prompt; lengthy investigations which do not seem to lead to the establishment of any responsibility are not in compliance with Article 2.[161] Fifthly, there must be a sufficient element of public scrutiny of the investigation or its results to secure accountability in practice as well as in theory, maintain public confidence in the authorities' adherence to the rule of law and prevent any appearance of collusion in or tolerance of unlawful acts.[162] And finally, in all cases, the next-of-kin of the victim must be involved in the procedure to the extent necessary to safeguard their legitimate interests.[163] This means in particular that they must be been granted access to the information yielded by the investigation to a degree sufficient for them to participate effectively in any proceedings, although not all requests for (sensitive) information need to be satisfied.[164]

---

[155] *Cf. Anguelova v. Bulgaria*, ECtHR 13 June 2002, appl. no. 38361/97, para. 138; for examples of a lack of independence and objectivity, see *Ergi v. Turkey*, ECtHR 28 July 1998, appl. no. 23818/94, paras. 83–84, and *Bajić v. Croatia*, *supra* n. 151.

[156] *Nachova v. Bulgaria*, *supra* n. 67, para. 113.

[157] *Anguelova v. Bulgaria*, *supra* n. 155, para. 139 and *Ramsahai v. the Netherlands*, *supra* n. 58, paras. 324 and 326 et seq.

[158] *Nachova v. Bulgaria*, *supra* n. 67, para. 113 and *Anguelova v. Bulgaria*, *supra* n. 155, para. 139.

[159] *Ibid.*

[160] *Aydoğdu v. Turkey*, *supra* n. 129.

[161] See, e.g., *McCaughey and Others v. the United Kingdom*, ECtHR 16 July 2013, appl. no. 43098/09.

[162] *Anguelova v. Bulgaria*, *supra* n. 155, para. 140.

[163] *Ibid.*

[164] *Ramsahai v. the Netherlands*, *supra* n. 58, paras. 347–350. See also, e.g., *Gray v. Germany*, ECtHR 22 May 2014, appl. no. 49278/09.

In *Mustafa Tunç and Fecire Tunç*, the Grand Chamber has explained that these requirements 'call for a concrete examination of the independence and effectiveness of the investigation as a whole'.[165] Where an issue arises under Article 2 concerning the obligation to conduct an effective investigation, for the Court 'the correct approach consists in examining whether and to what extent the disputed circumstance has compromised the investigation's effectiveness and its ability to shed light on the circumstances of the death and to punish those responsible'.[166] Thus, the Court has emphasised that the six sets of requirements described above are interrelated; none of them can be seen as an end in itself.[167] This may imply that a shortcoming as regards one of the elements may be ignored for the overall assessment in the light of Article 2, even if a similar shortcoming (such as a lack of independence of a tribunal) would normally suffice to find a violation of Article 6 if the case would have concerned the fairness of judicial proceedings.[168]

c.   Obligations to provide for an effective remedy

When the persons responsible for a death have been identified as a result of an official investigation, the final positive duty to be discussed in this chapter is for the state to provide for procedural instruments to prosecute them and bring them to justice. This obligation under Article 2 to provide for an effective remedy is rather similar to that under Article 13 ECHR; it can be regarded as a *lex specialis* thereof. The Court therefore often holds that it is not necessary to decide on the merits of complaints related to Article 13 if it has already found a violation of the procedural obligations under Article 2.[169]

In principle, Article 2 requires that criminal proceedings be brought against the persons who are suspected to be responsible for a death, irrespective of any other types of remedy which individuals may exercise on their own initiative.[170] It should not be inferred from this, however, that Article 2 entails a right for an applicant to have third parties prosecuted or sentenced for a criminal offence.[171]

---

[165]   *Mustafa Tunç and Fecire Tunç v. Turkey, supra* n. 152, para. 222.

[166]   *Idem*, para. 224.

[167]   *Idem*, para. 225.

[168]   *Idem*, paras. 232–234.

[169]   The obligations under Art. 13 may be somewhat stronger and broader, but usually there is not much difference; see, e.g., *Kaya v. Turkey*, ECtHR 19 February 1998, appl. no. 22729/93, para. 107. The Court deals in a similar way with complaints about a lack of access to court, made under Art. 6, in connection to a death (see, e.g., *M. Özel and Others v. Turkey*, ECtHR 17 November 2015, appl. nos. 14350/05, 15245/05 and 16051/05), although there are exceptions (see, e.g., *Sefer Yılmaz en Meryem Yılmaz v. Turkey*, ECtHR 17 November 2015, no. 611/12).

[170]   *Vo v. France, supra* n. 2, para. 90; *Öneryildiz v. Turkey, supra* n. 104, para. 93; *Budayeva v. Russia, supra* n. 107, para. 142.

[171]   *Öneryildiz v. Turkey, supra* n. 104, para. 95.

Moreover, the states are allowed to accept a certain threshold evidential test to filter out weak or unmeritorious cases.[172]

In the sphere of unintentional deaths, for example when someone has died as a result of medical acts, it is not always considered necessary to provide for criminal prosecution.[173] The obligations under Article 2 then may also be satisfied if the legal system affords victims a remedy in the civil courts, enabling any liability of the persons concerned to be established and allowing for appropriate civil redress, such as an order for damages and for the publication of the decision.[174] As the Court mentioned in *Calvelli and Ciglio*, disciplinary measures may also be envisaged here.[175] When a death is a result of a flagrant denial of medical care, however, not instituting criminal proceedings against the persons responsible still may amount to a violation of the state's positive obligations under the Convention.[176]

---

[172]   *Armani da Silva, supra* n. 63, paras. 265–270.
[173]   *Calvelli and Ciglio v. Italy,* ECtHR (GC) 17 January 2002, appl. no. 32967/96, para. 51; see also *Vo v. France, supra* n. 2, para. 90.
[174]   *Calvelli and Ciglio v. Italy, supra* n. 173, para. 51.
[175]   *Ibid.*
[176]   *Asiye Genç v. Turkey, supra* n. 135, para. 83.

CHAPTER 7

PROHIBITION OF TORTURE AND OTHER INHUMAN OR DEGRADING TREATMENT OR PUNISHMENT

(Article 3)

Ben Vermeulen and Hemme Battjes[*]

GUIDING PRINCIPLE

Article 3 prohibits treatment and humiliation causing intense physical or mental suffering. It does so in absolute terms – limitations or derogations are not allowed for. The assessment of whether treatment reaches the minimum level of severity required by this provision involves many factors, including the vulnerability of the person concerned and the aim pursued. The provision has important consequences in various areas, diverging from detention conditions to the expulsion of foreigners.

ARTICLE 3

No one shall be subjected to torture or to inhuman or degrading treatment or punishment.

---

[*] In the fourth edition this chapter was revised and updated by Ben Vermeulen. This chapter is a revision and update of the previous chapters.

CONTENTS

1. CHARACTER AND CORE

Article 3 forbids submitting a person to (1) torture, (2) inhuman treatment or punishment and (3) degrading treatment or punishment. The Court has repeatedly emphasised its importance: the provision 'enshrines one of the fundamental values of the democratic societies making up the Council of Europe',[1] and is 'a value of civilisation closely bound up with respect for human dignity, part of the very essence of the Convention'.[2]

1.1. ABSOLUTE CHARACTER

This prohibition on ill-treatment is 'absolute', i.e. the provision does not allow for limitations.[3] The Court has emphasised that the 'philosophical basis underpinning the absolute nature of the right under Article 3 does not allow for any exceptions or justifying factors or balancing of interests'.[4] Thus, if a treatment qualifies as torture or inhuman or degrading treatment or punishment, no balancing with other interests is allowed for. This implies, for instance, that 'it is never permissible to have recourse to punishments which are contrary to Article 3, whatever their deterrent effect may be'.[5] Likewise, the requirements of an effective investigation and the difficulties inherent in the fight against crime

---

[1] *Soering v. United Kingdom*, ECtHR 7 July 1989, appl. no. 14038/88, para. 86.
[2] *Bouyid v. Belgium*, ECtHR (GC) 28 September 2015, appl. no. 23380/09, para. 81.
[3] *Ireland v. United Kingdom*, ECtHR (GC) 18 January 1978, appl. no. 5310/71, para. 163.
[4] *Gäfgen v. Germany*, ECtHR (GC) 1 June 2010, appl. no. 22978/05, para. 107.
[5] *Tyrer v. United Kingdom*, ECtHR 25 April 1978, appl. no. 5856/72, para. 31.

cannot result in limits being placed on the protection afforded by this provision.[6] The provision is furthermore absolute, while pursuant to Article 15(2) ECHR no derogations are allowed for, 'even in the event of a public emergency threatening the life of the nation or in the most difficult circumstances, such as the fight against terrorism and organised crime'.[7]

1.2. MINIMUM LEVEL OF SEVERITY

In *Ireland v. United Kingdom*, the Court stated that 'ill-treatment must attain a minimum level of severity if it is to fall within the scope of Article 3. The assessment of this minimum is, in the nature of things, relative; it depends on all the circumstances of the case, such as the duration of the treatment, its physical or mental effects and, in some cases, the sex, age and state of health of the victim, etc.'[8]

This is not an exhaustive list. In *Soering*, the Court mentioned 'the nature and context of the treatment or punishment, the manner and method of its execution',[9] and in other cases the purpose for which the ill-treatment was inflicted and whether the applicant was in a vulnerable situation are mentioned as relevant aspects.[10]

Hence, treatment that causes physical or mental suffering of a certain degree may amount to a violation. Whether treatment does attain this degree depends on a number of factors, such as the effect on the individual applicant: treatment that may be merely hard for a healthy adult may cause suffering amounting to inhuman or degrading treatment when administered to a child or an ill adult. Furthermore, treatment that does cause considerable suffering may, in the particular circumstances of the case, be justified by, for example, medical necessity, security considerations or the need to obtain evidence (see further *infra* section 2.3).[11] This amounts to application of a proportionality test. Consequently, a certain qualification is introduced in a provision formulated in absolute terms, which is almost inevitable in the case of the application of such an abstract norm, containing subjective concepts, to concrete cases. For instance, the question whether a penalty is inhuman or not may depend on the crime committed: an 'exceptionally harsh punishment for a trivial offence might raise

---

[6]   *Tomasi v. France*, ECtHR 27 August 1992, appl. no. 12850/87, para. 115.
[7]   *Khlaifia and Others v. Italy*, ECtHR 15 September 2015, appl. no. 16483/12, para. 158; *cf.* also *Chahal v. United Kingdom*, ECtHR (GC) 15 November 1996, appl. no. 22414/93, para. 79.
[8]   *Ireland v. United Kingdom*, *supra* n. 3, para. 162; repeated in most cases on Art. 3 decided since, *cf. Khlaifia and Others v. Italy*, *supra* n. 7, para. 117.
[9]   *Soering v. United Kingdom*, *supra* n. 1, para. 100.
[10]   *Khlaifia and Others v. Italy*, *supra* n. 7, para. 160 with further references.
[11]   *Jalloh v. Germany*, ECtHR (GC) 11 July 2006, appl. no. 54810/00, paras. 69–70.

a question under Article 3',[12] whereas the same punishment could be acceptable in case of a more serious crime. Similarly, acts that would otherwise amount to inhuman or degrading treatment do not if medical necessity, or security requirements justify them.[13] As a consequence, it is not possible to draw a list of acts that are and of those that are not prohibited by Article 3. Thus, in *Yankov*, forced head shaving of a prisoner qualified as degrading treatment owing to the circumstances: the detainee was 54 years old, it occurred in public and happened a few days before he had to appear at a court hearing.[14] Conversely, in *Caloc*, the Court ruled that the French police had not violated the provision when they threw the applicant on the ground and hit him, as this appeared necessary to prevent his attempt to escape.[15]

1.3. POSITIVE OBLIGATIONS

The Court has furthermore identified important positive obligations: the obligation to investigate whether torture or inhuman or degrading treatment or punishment has been committed, and the obligation to prevent such treatment from being inflicted, both by state agents and by private parties.[16] The assessment whether these obligations have been complied with involves issues – apart from determining whether an act has transgressed the minimum level of severity – such as whether the state has taken reasonable steps to investigate or prevent; they will therefore be discussed separately (see *infra* section 4). Furthermore, the Court has developed an elaborate case law on treatment of persons during arrest and in detention. The standard for treatment in those situations is informed by a duty to secure the well-being of the persons concerned[17] and hence differs from the tests applied in other cases. Therefore, these cases will be discussed separately (*infra* section 5). Finally, the Court has developed a rich case law on the obligation not to expel a person if ill-treatment is the foreseeable consequence,[18] also involving specific issues (see *infra* section 6).

---

[12] *X. v. United Kingdom*, EComHR 30 September 1974 (dec.), appl. no. 5871/72, Coll. 43 (1973), p. 160.

[13] E.g. forced-feeding of prisoners on hunger strike, see *Nevmerzhitsky v. Ukraine*, ECtHR 5 April 2005, appl. no. 54825/00.

[14] *Yankov v. Bulgaria*, ECtHR 11 December 2003, appl. no. 39084/97.

[15] *Caloc v. France*, ECtHR 20 July 2000, appl. no. 33951/96, para. 101.

[16] E.g. *A. v. United Kingdom*, ECtHR 23 September 1998, appl. no. 25599/94 and *Assenov and Others v. Bulgaria*, ECtHR 28 October 1998, appl. no. 24760/94.

[17] *Kudła v. Poland*, ECtHR (GC) 26 October 2000, appl. no. 30210/96, para. 94.

[18] *Soering v. United Kingdom*, supra n. 1, para. 90.

2. TORTURE; INHUMAN TREATMENT OR PUNISHMENT; DEGRADING TREATMENT OR PUNISHMENT

2.1. CLASSIFICATION

Article 3 ECHR prohibits five types of treatment – torture, inhuman treatment, inhuman punishment, degrading treatment and degrading punishment. Although the Convention attaches identical consequences to inflicting these treatments (they are all forbidden under all circumstances and irrespective of the motives, see *supra* section 1), the Court has identified characteristics distinguishing them from each other. It should be borne in mind, however, that in many cases the Court is satisfied with finding a violation of Article 3, or 'ill-treatment' as a catch-all phrase, or a violation of 'inhuman or degrading treatment'; similarly, in many cases it does not bother to distinguish between 'treatment' and 'punishment'.[19]

The Commission already outlined the distinction between the several types of treatment mentioned in Article 3 ECHR in the *Greek case*, which concerned interrogations and assaults by the security police after the *coup d'état* by the Greek military forces in 1967. Inhuman treatment was treatment that 'deliberately causes severe suffering, mental or physical, which, in the particular situation, is unjustifiable'. A person was submitted to degrading treatment 'if it grossly humiliates him before others or drives him to act against his will or conscience'. Torture is an 'aggravated form of inhuman treatment', and has 'a purpose, such as the obtaining of information or a confession'. The Commission further observed that the qualifications torture, inhuman treatment and degrading treatment are not mutually exclusive: 'It is plain that there may be treatment to which all these descriptions apply, for all torture must be inhuman and degrading treatment, and inhuman treatment also degrading.'[20]

Whether a certain treatment qualifies as torture, inhuman treatment or degrading treatment, or whether it falls outside of the scope of Article 3, may change over time. The Court observed in the *Selmouni* case that 'certain acts which were classified in the past as "inhuman and degrading treatment" as opposed to "torture" could be classified differently in future. It takes the view that the increasingly high standard being required in the area of the protection

---

[19] E.g. *J.K. and Others v. Sweden*, ECtHR (GC) 23 August 2016, appl. no. 59166/12, para. 123: 'treatment contrary to Article'; 'a violation of Article 3'; *El-Masri v. Macedonia*, ECtHR (GC) 13 December 2012, appl. no. 39630/09, para. 204: 'inhuman and degrading treatment'.

[20] *Denmark, Norway, Sweden and the Netherlands v. Greece (the Greek case)*, EComHR 5 November 1969 (rep.), appl. nos. 3321/67, 3322/67, 3323/67 and 3344/67, Yearbook 12, p. 186.

of human rights and fundamental liberties correspondingly and inevitably requires greater firmness in assessing breaches of the fundamental values of democratic societies.'[21]

2.2. TORTURE

The Court addressed the qualification of torture for the first time in *Ireland v. United Kingdom* (1978), concerning the treatment of IRA suspects by security forces in Northern Ireland. It stated that by the term 'torture' a 'special stigma' is attached to treatments that are distinguished from other forms of inhuman treatment: it is 'deliberate' inhuman treatment, and it causes 'very serious and cruel suffering'.[22] Furthermore, in all cases where the Court found that ill-treatment amounted to torture, it was administered by state agents. Thus, in *Aydın*, the Court found that 'the especially cruel act of rape', committed by an official (Turkish security forces in search of PKK members in a Kurdish village) on a detainee, qualified as torture,[23] whereas in *M.C. v. Bulgaria* rape, not committed by a state official, merely qualified as ill-treatment, hence not as torture.[24]

a. Relevant factors

For the assessment of the particular level of severity inherent in the notion of torture, the Court addresses the same aspects as it does in the minimum level of severity test implied in an Article 3 violation: the duration, physical and mental effects of the treatment, and occasionally also the age, sex and health of the applicant.[25] In *Ireland v. United Kingdom*, the Court held that the challenged techniques of interrogation – obliging the interrogated persons to stand for a long period on their toes against the wall, covering their heads with black hoods, subjecting them to constant intense noise, depriving them of sleep and sufficient food and drink – 'did not occasion suffering of the particular intensity and cruelty implied by the word torture as so understood'.[26] But in a considerable number of later cases, it did find that this type of treatment qualified as torture. Persons suffering physical ill-treatment that took such forms as 'Palestinian hanging' (being stripped naked, with the arms tied together behind the back,

---

[21] *Selmouni v. France*, ECtHR (GC) 28 July 1999, appl. no. 25803/94, para. 101.
[22] *Cf.* also *Aksoy v. Turkey*, ECtHR 18 December 1996, appl. no. 21987/93, para. 63.
[23] *Aydın v. Turkey*, ECtHR (GC) 25 September 1997, appl. no. 23178/94, paras. 83 and 86.
[24] *M.C. v. Bulgaria*, ECtHR 4 December 2003, appl. no. 39272/98, para. 149.
[25] *Ireland v. United Kingdom*, *supra* n. 3, para. 162.
[26] *Ibid.*, para. 167.

and suspended by the arms),[27] rape,[28] suspension, being sprayed with water and *falaka* (beating of the soles of the feet),[29] kicking, punching and hitting with a metal object[30] and administering electric burns[31] were regarded as victims of torture.

But the stigma of torture is not restricted to particular types of treatment. As is the case for other forms of ill-treatment (see extensively sections 2.3–2.5), the lack of proportionality as well as other circumstances may be relevant for the qualification of ill-treatment as torture. We give a few examples. *El-Masri* concerned the arrest, detention and removal (rendition) of a German national to Afghanistan by CIA officials on Macedonian territory. At the airport, El-Masri was beaten, stripped naked and sodomised with an object, and then forced to march shackled and hooded to the plane where he was thrown to the floor, chained down and forcibly tranquillised.[32] According to the Court, the 'forcible administration of a suppository while the applicant was held on the ground without any explanation was not based on any medical considerations'; furthermore, 'the applicant did not pose any threat to his captors'; therefore, the physical force used against the applicant at the airport was excessive and unjustified in the circumstances, and amounted to torture.[33] In *Nevmerzhitsky*, the Court considered that the forced feeding of a detainee amounted to torture, owing to the manner in which it was applied and in the absence of any medical justification for such a measure.[34] In *Menesheva*, the applicant during an interrogation of two hours was twice beaten up, the pain and suffering inflicted intentionally to extract information from her. The Court qualified this treatment as torture taking into account, inter alia, that the victim was only 19 years old and a female confronted by several men.[35] In *Ilhan*, the Court deemed a relevant factor for qualifying the treatment as torture that the victim had had to wait for 36 hours before he was brought to a hospital, although he had visible injuries to his head and evident difficulties in walking and talking.[36]

---

[27]   *Aksoy v. Turkey, supra* n. 22, para. 64. The Court's interpretation of the notion of 'torture' probably has been inspired by the definition of 'torture' in Art. 1 of the 1984 UN Convention against Torture. *Cf.* also *Salman v. Turkey,* ECtHR (GC) 27 June 2000, appl. no. 21986/93, para. 114.

[28]   *Aydın v. Turkey, supra* n. 23, paras. 83 and 86.

[29]   *Salman v. Turkey, supra* n. 27, para. 115; *Bati and Others v. Turkey,* ECtHR 3 June 2004, appl. nos. 33097/96 and 57834/00, para. 110.

[30]   *Virabyan v. Armen*ia, ECtHR 2 October 2012, appl. no. 40094/05, para. 157.

[31]   *Mikheyev v. Russia*, ECtHR 26 January 2006, appl. no. 77617/01, para. 129.

[32]   *El-Masri v. Macedonia, supra* n. 19, para. 205.

[33]   *Ibid.*, paras. 207–211.

[34]   *Nevmerzhitsky v. Ukraine, supra* n. 13, para. 98.

[35]   *Menesheva v. Russia*, ECtHR 9 March 2006, appl. no. 59261/00, para. 62.

[36]   *İlhan v. Turkey* (GC) 27 June 2000, appl. no. 22277/93, para. 87.

b. Mental suffering

Mental suffering may be relevant or even decisive for qualifying treatment as torture. In *Dikme*, the Court observed that the applicant lived in a permanent state of physical pain and anxiety owing to his uncertainty about his fate.[37] In *Akkoç*, the Court noted – besides electric shocks and other physical ill-treatment – 'elements of psychological pressure suffered by the applicant, in particular the threats made concerning the ill-treatment of her children, which caused the applicant intense fear and apprehension'.[38]

In *Ilaşcu*, the applicant spent a very long period on death row in uncertainty and fear of execution, and while this sentence had no legal basis or legitimacy, he was detained in very strict isolation, his cell was unheated and had no natural light or ventilation, he was deprived of food as a punishment, he could take showers only very rarely and did not receive appropriate health care. The Court concluded that the death sentence, coupled with the harsh conditions he was living in, were particularly serious and cruel so that they could be considered as torture.[39]

A mere threat of physical torture may lead to inhuman treatment or even mental torture, 'provided it is sufficiently real and immediate'.[40] In *Gäfgen*, the Court found that a threat of torture constituted inhuman treatment. The applicant had abducted and killed a child and hidden the body; after that, he demanded a ransom from the parents, suggesting the child was still alive. When he came to collect the ransom the police arrested him. Gäfgen refused to tell where he had hidden the (supposedly still living) child. The German authorities threatened him with torture, after which Gäfgen told the whereabouts of the child's body. The Court considered that 'a threat of torture can amount to torture, as the nature of torture covers both physical pain and mental suffering'.[41]

c. Lasting effects

The physical and mental effects relevant for assessing whether the level of severity not only concern the (level of) pain suffered during the treatment, but also the duration of the effects. In *Mikheyev*, ill-treatment had driven the applicant to attempt suicide, which had resulted in a general and permanent physical disability.[42] In *Akkoç*, the applicant suffered long-term symptoms

---

[37]   *Dikme v. Turkey*, ECtHR 11 July 2000, appl. no. 20869/92, para. 95.
[38]   *Akkoç v. Turkey*, ECtHR 10 October 2000, appl. nos. 22947/93 and 22948/93, para. 116.
[39]   *Ilaşcu and Others v. Moldova and Russia*, ECtHR (GC) 8 July 2004, appl. no. 48787/99, paras. 435–440.
[40]   *Campbell and Cosans v. United Kingdom*, ECtHR 25 February 1982, appl. nos. 7511/76 and 7743/76, para. 26.
[41]   *Gäfgen v. Germany, supra* n. 4, para. 108.
[42]   *Mikheyev v. Russia, supra* n. 31, para. 135.

of anxiety and insecurity, diagnosed as post-traumatic stress disorder and requiring treatment by medication.[43] But the effects need not to be permanent or even long-lasting in order to qualify the treatment that caused them as torture: in *Aksoy*, the victim suffered paralysis of both arms 'which lasted for some time'.[44] Nevertheless, absence of long-term consequences of ill-treatment may be a relevant factor for not qualifying that treatment as torture.[45]

d. Intent

With regard to the element of 'intent' implied in torture, the Court in *Ilhan v. Turkey* stated that there is 'a purposive element' involved, as Article 1 of the United Nations Convention against Torture and Other Cruel, Inhuman or Degrading Treatment or Punishment 'defines torture in terms of the intentional infliction of severe pain or suffering with the aim, inter alia, of obtaining information, inflicting punishment or intimidating'.[46] So in *Aksoy*, the Court observed that Palestinian hanging 'could have been only deliberately inflicted', and that it 'would appear to have been administered with the aim of obtaining admissions or information'.[47] However, in some cases, such as the *Aydın* case quoted above, the Court does not discuss separately the intent of the perpetrator – possibly, because it considered the deliberate character of the treatment self-evident. That the intent of the perpetrator is decisive for qualifying acts as torture is illustrated by the case of *Krastanov*, in which the Court found that the treatment was inhuman, but that it could not be qualified as torture, because it did not appear to be inflicted on the applicant intentionally for the purpose of, for instance, making him confess or breaking his physical and moral resistance, and because it lasted only for a short period of time.[48]

e. Concluding observations

In sum, in torture cases the Court addresses the factors that are also relevant for qualifying an act as inhuman or degrading: the duration of the treatment, its lasting effects and sex, age and health of the victim. Furthermore, the objective of the treatment such as medical necessity may be relevant. And as in other Article 3 cases, mental suffering may amount to a violation of the prohibition of torture.

Torture is distinguished from inhuman and degrading treatment in that the treatment caused very serious and cruel suffering, and that it was

---

43   *Akkoç v. Turkey, supra* n. 38, para. 116.
44   *Aksoy v. Turkey, supra* n. 22, para. 64.
45   *Denizici and Others v. Cyprus*, ECtHR 23 May 2001, appl. nos. 25316/94, 25317/94 and 25318/94, para. 384.
46   *Ilhan v. Turkey, supra* n. 36, para. 85.
47   *Aksoy v. Turkey, supra* n. 22, para. 64.
48   *Krastanov v. Bulgaria*, ECtHR 30 September 2004, appl. no. 50222/99, para. 53.

inflicted deliberately with a particular purpose such as obtaining information. Furthermore, it appears that only treatment inflicted by a state agent may amount to torture. This may have to do with the 'special stigma' that according to the Court applies to torture.

2.3. INHUMAN TREATMENT

a. Relevant factors

As observed above, the Court stated in *Ireland v. United Kingdom* that 'ill-treatment must attain a minimum level of severity', which 'depends on all the circumstances of the case, such as the duration of the treatment, its physical or mental effects and, in some cases, the sex, age and state of health of the victim, etc.'.[49] In later case law it elaborated on these aspects and mentioned two more factors to be taken into account: the purpose for which ill-treatment was inflicted together with the intention or motivation behind it, and the context in which that treatment was inflicted.[50] These factors will be further discussed below. In order to preclude unnecessary repetition, a number of cases concerning degrading rather than inhuman treatment will be discussed here as well.

As to the distinction between inhuman treatment and other forms of treatment – 'merely' degrading treatment – prohibited by Article 3, the Court stated in *Kudła* that it 'has considered treatment to be "inhuman" because, *inter alia*, it was premeditated, was applied for hours at a stretch and caused either actual bodily injury or intense physical or mental suffering'.[51] It differs from torture as regards the level of intensity (it does not require 'very' serious suffering), and the element of intent and purpose that often is, but need not be present (see below). Treatment qualifies as degrading if it debases an individual or arouses feelings of fear, anguish or inferiority capable of breaking an individual's moral and physical resistance, 'even in the absence of' actual bodily injury or intense physical or mental suffering.[52] As inhuman treatment can debase the victim or arouse feelings of anguish as well, the distinction between inhuman and degrading treatment concerns the severity of the act and its effects. However, it should be noted that in many cases the Court does not address the distinction, qualifying treatment instead as 'inhuman or degrading' or as treatment in violation of Article 3.[53]

---

[49]   *Ireland v. United Kingdom, supra* n. 3, para. 162; repeated in most cases on Art. 3 decided since, *cf. Khlaifia and Others v. Italy, supra* n. 7, para. 117.
[50]   E.g. *Khlaifia and Others v. Italy, supra* n. 7, para. 160.
[51]   *Kudła v. Poland, supra* n. 17, para. 92.
[52]   *Ananyev and Others v. Russia*, ECtHR 10 January 2012, appl. no. 42525/07, para. 140.
[53]   E.g. *J.K. and Others v. Sweden, supra* n. 19, para. 123: 'treatment contrary to Article 3'; 'a violation of Article 3'; *El-Masri v. Macedonia, supra* n. 19, para. 204: 'inhuman and degrading treatment'.

b. Duration

The duration of the treatment is a relevant factor in different types of cases. In *Selmouni*, the circumstance that the applicant had to endure assaults over a number of days was a relevant factor for qualifying the treatment as torture.[54] In *Gäfgen*, the Court mentioned as a relevant circumstance that the interrogation during which the applicant was threatened with torture took only 10 minutes,[55] which seemed relevant for the finding that the threat with torture amounted to inhuman treatment, not torture. In detention cases, the length of the detention counts as 'a major factor'[56] for determining whether detention conditions were acceptable, alongside other factors (see further *infra* section 5).

c. Physical and mental effects

Not only the pain or injury suffered during the treatment, but also its lasting effects are relevant. In *V.C. v. Slovakia*, the Court mentioned as examples treatment by state agents 'such as an injury to a person's leg which caused necrosis and subsequently led to the leg having to be amputated, a gunshot wound to a person's knee, a double fracture of the jaw and facial contusions or an injury to a person's face which required stitches, with three of the person's teeth being knocked out.'[57] Other examples of inhuman treatment are rape and female genital mutilation.[58]

Treatment may also qualify as inhuman due to intense mental suffering. In the *Gäfgen* case, the Court classified the threat of torture by the police in order to get information from the applicant on the whereabouts of a boy he had abducted, as inhuman treatment.[59] Likewise, in the *Selçuk and Asker* case, the Court held that the destruction of the applicants' homes caused them suffering of sufficient severity to be categorised as inhuman treatment. Here, the context and manner in which the authorities handled the matter appeared to be relevant (see below).[60]

A specific form of mental suffering is the anguish experienced by family members of disappeared persons, which may amount to treatment contrary to Article 3.[61] Special factors must exist that give 'the suffering of the applicant a dimension and character distinct from the emotional distress which may be regarded as inevitably caused to relatives of a victim of a serious human rights

---

[54] *Selmouni v. France, supra* n. 21, para. 104.
[55] *Gäfgen v. Germany, supra* n. 4, para. 102.
[56] *Kalashnikov v. Russia*, ECtHR 15 July 2002, appl. no. 47095/99, para. 102.
[57] *V.C. v. Slovakia*, ECtHR 8 November 2011, appl. no. 18968/07, para. 102.
[58] *M.C. v. Bulgaria, supra* n. 24, para. 149, *Collins and Akazibie v. Sweden,* ECtHR 8 March 2007, appl. no. 23944/05 (dec.).
[59] *Gäfgen v. Germany, supra* n. 4, para. 108.
[60] *Selçuk and Asker v. Turkey*, ECtHR 24 April 1998, appl. nos. 23184/94 and 23185/94, paras. 77–79. See also *Ayder and Others v. Turkey*, ECtHR 8 January 2004, appl. no. 23656/94, paras. 109–110.
[61] *Kurt v. Turkey*, ECtHR 25 May 1998, appl. no. 24276/94, para. 133.

violation'.[62] Relevant elements are 'the proximity of the family tie, whether the family member witnessed the events, and whether the family member had attempted to obtain information about the disappeared person and the way in which the authorities responded to those enquiries'.[63] The response of the authorities is crucial, as the 'essence' of such a violation is not the fact of the disappearance, but 'the authorities' reactions and attitudes to the situation'.[64] A violation due to such reactions may be found not only if the state was responsible for the disappearance, but also when its failure to respond to a quest for information by relatives 'may be regarded as disclosing a flagrant, continuous and callous disregard' of its obligation to account for the fate of a disappeared person.[65]

Mental suffering caused by knowledge of the suffering of relatives has been found to amount to inhuman or degrading treatment in a number of situations. In the case of *Akkum*, the anguish caused to the applicant as a result of the mutilation of the body of his son amounted to degrading treatment.[66] In *Elberte v. Latvia*, the Court ruled that emotional suffering caused by the removal of tissue from the applicant's deceased husband's body without her knowledge or consent also amounted to degrading treatment.[67] And in *Mayeka and Mitunga*, the mother of a five-year-old child was considered to be a victim of a violation of Article 3, owing to the detention and subsequent expulsion of her daughter from Belgium to Congo, taking into account that the mother lived in Canada and was given very little information about the procedural steps and intentions of the Belgian authorities.[68]

d. Sex, age and health

In *Ireland v. United Kingdom*, the Court mentioned sex, age and health as relevant factors.[69] The removal of a five-year-old unaccompanied minor dealt with in *Mayeka and Mitunga* may serve as an illustration: it showed 'a lack of humanity to such a degree that it amounted to inhuman treatment', even though detention of adults under the same conditions need not be problematic.[70] Likewise, the medical situation of a detainee may render the detention incompatible with Article 3 (see further section 5).

---

62 *Çakici v. Turkey*, ECtHR (GC) 8 July 1999, appl. no. 23657/94, para. 98.
63 *Ibid.*, para. 98; *Ipek v. Turkey*, ECtHR 17 February 2004, appl. no. 25760/94, para. 181; *Akdeniz v. Turkey*, ECtHR 31 May 2005, appl. no. 25165/94, para. 121.
64 *Tanis and Others v. Turkey*, ECtHR 2 August 2005, appl. no. 65899/01, para. 219.
65 *Varnava and Others v. Turkey*, ECtHR (GC) 18 September 2009, appl. no. 16064/90, para. 201.
66 *Akkum and Others v. Turkey*, ECtHR 24 March 2005, appl. no. 21894/93; see also *Akpinar and Altun v. Turkey*, ECtHR 27 February 2007, appl. no. 56760/00, para. 86.
67 *Elberte v. Latvia*, ECtHR 13 January 2015, appl. no. 61243/08, para. 143.
68 *Mubilanzila Mayeke and Kaniki Mitunga v. Belgium*, ECtHR 12 October 2006, appl. no. 13178/03, paras. 62 and 70.
69 *Ireland v. United Kingdom*, supra n. 3, para. 162.
70 *Mubilanzila Mayeke and Kaniki Mitunga v. Belgium*, supra n. 70, para. 58.

The Court has furthermore characterised groups as 'vulnerable' such as children, or 'asylum seekers'.[71] Thus, vulnerability may be an effect of one's status – once in removal proceedings, a former asylum seeker has no longer that 'specific vulnerability'.[72] The Court has also employed the notion of vulnerability for defining the situation of a person in detention (see *infra*, section *f, Context and manner*).

e. Purpose and intention

Further factors include the purpose (or 'object') together with the intention[73] (although 'the absence of any such purpose cannot conclusively rule out a finding of violation of Article 3'[74]). Thus, a medically necessary operation or treatment, however painful it may be for the patient, is in principle not to be considered as torture or inhuman or degrading treatment. So, in the *Herczegfalvy* case, the Court ruled that the 'established principles of medicine are (…) decisive in such cases; as a general rule, a measure which is therapeutic cannot be regarded as inhuman or degrading'.[75] And even if a medical necessity is absent, a 'forcible medical intervention' in order to obtain evidence (such as blood or saliva samples) from a suspect against his will is allowed for,[76] if it is justified on the facts of the case. Relevant factors are the seriousness of the offence, whether alternative methods of recovering the evidence were available, whether the person concerned experienced serious physical pain or suffering,[77] whether it occurred under medical supervision[78] and whether it had (lasting) consequences for the suspect's health.[79] In the case of forced-feeding of prisoners on hunger strike, the Court stressed that procedural guarantees for the decision to force-feed, exist and are complied with.[80]

Thus, the goals of medical intervention or obtaining evidence, security grounds etc. (e.g. in detention cases, see *infra* section 5) may – if applied proportionally – justify treatment that might otherwise amount to inhuman or degrading treatment. As observed above (section 1), a certain qualification is hence applied to an absolute right. It should be observed, however, that the proportionality test is strict and the number of justifications is fairly limited. As

---

71   E.g. *Z and Others v. United Kingdom*, ECtHR (GC) 10 May 2001, appl. no. 29392/95, para. 73; *M.S.S. v. Belgium and Greece*, ECtHR (GC) 21 January 2011, appl. no. 30696/09, para. 232.
72   *Khlaifia and Others v. Italy*, *supra* n. 7, para. 194.
73   *Gäfgen v. Germany*, *supra* n. 4, para. 88.
74   E.g. *Labita v. Italy*, ECtHR (GC) 6 April 2000, appl. no. 26772/95, para. 120.
75   *Herczegfalvy v. Austria*, ECtHR 24 September 1992, appl. no. 10533/83, para. 82.
76   *X v. the Netherlands*, EComHR 4 December 1978 (dec.), appl. no. 8239/78, and *Schmidt v. Germany*, ECtHR 5 January 2006 (dec.), appl. no. 32352/02.
77   *Nevmerzhitsky v. Ukraine*, *supra* n. 13, paras. 94 and 97.
78   *Ilijkov v. Bulgaria*, EComHR 20 October 1997 (dec.), appl. no. 33977/96.
79   *Ibid.*, and *mutatis mutandis, Krastanov v. Bulgaria*, *supra* n. 48, para. 53.
80   *Nevmerzhitsky v. Ukraine*, *supra* n. 13, para. 94.

the Court stated in the *Tomasi* case, the requirements of the investigation and the undeniable difficulties inherent in the fight against terrorism cannot result in limits being placed on the protection by Article 3 to be afforded in respect of the physical integrity of individuals.[81]

f. Context and manner

In the context of Article 3, the fact that one is held in custody evidently is a very relevant aspect. Indeed, a person in police custody is 'in a vulnerable situation',[82] and the same holds true for persons in detention centres for aliens.[83] This circumstance obviously is a relevant factor, although 'an inevitable element of suffering and humiliation' is involved in custodial measures and this as such, in itself, will not entail a violation of Article 3. But as the Court held in *Ribitsch*, 'in respect of a person deprived of his liberty, any recourse to physical force which has not been made strictly necessary by his own conduct diminishes human dignity and is in principle an infringement of Article 3'.[84]

In the case of *Selçuk and Asker*, the applicants had suffered inhuman treatment due to the destruction of their house. The Court mentioned as relevant circumstances that the applicants were 54 and 60 years old at that time and had lived in the village all their lives. The destruction of their homes and most of their property forced them to leave their village. Their removal was carried out without respect for their feelings: they were taken unprepared, had to watch the burning of their homes, their safety was not adequately secured, their protests were ignored and no assistance was provided afterwards. The Court concluded that even if the destruction had the purpose to prevent their homes being used by terrorists or to discourage others, this would not provide a justification for the ill-treatment.[85] In *Yankov*, relevant circumstances leading the Court to classify the shaving of a prisoner as degrading treatment were that a proper justification was absent, that the victim was 55 years old and that he had to attend a court session within a few days.[86]

An aspect of the context of treatment the Court has taken into account in a number of cases concerning arrest and custody is whether there was 'an atmosphere of heightened tension and emotions'.[87] In *Bouyid*, the Court found that a police officer's exasperation with the conduct of the applicant was 'irrelevant', and in *Selmouni* it found that heightened tension and emotions were

---

[81] *Tomasi v. France, supra* n. 6, para. 115; *cf.* also *Ribitsch v. Austria*, ECtHR 4 December 1995, appl. no. 18896/91, para. 38, and *Gäfgen v. Germany, supra* n. 4, para. 107.

[82] *Salman v. Turkey, supra* n. 27, para. 99.

[83] *Khlaifia and Others v. supra* n. 7, para. 160.

[84] *Ribitsch v. Austria, supra* n. 81, para. 38.

[85] *Selçuk and Asker v. Turkey, supra* n. 60, paras. 77–79.

[86] *Yankov v. Bulgaria, supra* n. 14, paras. 117–119.

[87] E.g. *Selmouni v. France, supra* n. 21, para. 104.

absent during the treatments – 'without this in any way justifying them'.[88] But in *Egmez*, the fact that 'the injuries had been inflicted on the applicant over a short period of heightened tension and emotions' was a mitigating factor, leading the Court to qualify them as inhuman treatment rather than torture.[89]

A particularly relevant, though not decisive element is whether the applicant has given his consent or not. The consent of the person concerned may deprive an act, which otherwise would be inhuman or degrading, of that character. However, there are experiments and treatments so inhuman or degrading that the person involved, in spite of his previous consent, is a victim of a violation of Article 3.[90] On the other hand, the absence of consent does not in itself justify the qualification that an intrusive treatment was inhuman or degrading. Thus, the Commission decided that the enforced administration of medicine to a mentally deranged detainee did not have that character, since it had been declared medically necessary and confirmed by a court decision.[91] The Court endorsed a similar view in the *Herczegfalvy* case.[92]

Consent must be informed in order to be able to count as a real consent. In *V.C. v. Slovakia*, the Court deemed a consent not to be informed: the applicant was asked to sign the typed words 'Patient requests sterilisation' while in a supine position and in pain resulting from several hours' labour giving birth, and told by doctors that 'she or her baby would die in the event of a further pregnancy'.[93] In that same case, the Court stated that 'in the sphere of medical assistance, even where the refusal to accept a particular treatment might lead to a fatal outcome, the imposition of medical treatment without the consent of a mentally competent adult patient would interfere with his or her right to physical integrity'.[94] However, it must be stressed that treatment without consent only amounts to inhuman or degrading treatment if it can be established that it reached the minimum level of severity.[95]

g. *Concluding observations*

Allegations of inhuman or degrading treatment often concern acts by state officials such as the police or army officials (*Ireland v. United Kingdom*, *Selçuk and Asker*), but occasionally also other contexts, such as medical interventions

---

[88] *Bouyid v. Belgium*, supra n. 2, para. 107; *Selmouni v. France*, supra n. 21, para. 104.

[89] *Egmez v. Cyprus*, ECtHR 21 December 2000, appl. no. 30873/96, para. 78; maybe the presence of a similar atmosphere in *Gäfgen* had the same effect on the Court's reasoning (*Gäfgen v. Germany*, supra n. 4, para. 88).

[90] *X. v. Denmark*, EComHR 2 March 1983 (dec.), appl. no. 9974/82.

[91] *X. v. Federal Republic of Germany*, EComHR 2 March 1980 (dec.), appl. no. 8518/79.

[92] *Herczegfalvy v. Austria*, supra n. 75, paras. 82–83.

[93] *V.C. v. Slovakia*, supra n. 57, para. 117.

[94] *Ibid.*, para. 105.

[95] *Akopyan v. Ukraine*, ECtHR 5 June 2014, appl. no. 12317/06, paras. 103–105.

(*Herczegfalvy, V.C. v. Slovakia*). The notion of inhuman treatment encompasses rather evident cases such as severe beating and kicking (*Ireland v. United Kingdom, Bouyid*). But the case law shows that the Court carefully addresses several factors and circumstances, in order to secure that other, possibly less self-evident forms of ill-treatment that cause intense suffering are encompassed as well. Thus, owing to a particular vulnerability, what would for others be just harsh treatment may amount to inhuman treatment (*Mayeka*), and the particular circumstances of the case may render the demolishing of a house likewise inhuman treatment (*Selçuk and Asker*).

But the degree or amount of suffering in itself is not always decisive. Due to circumstances and objective, treatment that in other circumstances might qualify as inhuman were found to be justified, such as treatment inflicted upon medical necessity (*Herczegfalvy*) or for obtaining evidence, provided the treatment is proportionate (*Caloc*).

2.4. INHUMAN PUNISHMENT; LIFE IMPRISONMENT

In the *Tyrer* case, the Court held 'that the suffering occasioned must attain a particular level before a punishment can be classified as "inhuman" within the meaning of Article 3'. The complaint concerned the punishment of caning for certain offences, which was provided by law and actually applied in the Isle of Man to boys between 10 and 17. The Court concluded that this did not constitute torture or inhuman punishment.[96] The assessment whether punishment is to be qualified as inhuman involves the same factors that apply to inhuman treatment (see *supra* section 2.3).[97] Indeed, the Court often does not bother to distinguish inhuman punishment from inhuman treatment, qualifying a violation as 'inhuman treatment or punishment'.

According to standard case law, legitimate punishment as such involves an 'inevitable element of suffering or humiliation', so the suffering in the specific instance must go beyond that threshold in order to qualify as inhuman (or degrading) punishment. Deprivation of liberty based on legitimate grounds in general will not amount to a violation of Article 3, as long as detention conditions are compatible with respect for human dignity (see further section 5).[98]

Furthermore, grossly disproportionate punishment is at variance with Article 3.[99] For example in *Chember*, a conscripted soldier had to do 350 knee bends as he had not cleaned the barracks properly, although he was exempted

---

[96]   *Tyrer v. United Kingdom, supra* n. 5, para. 29.
[97]   E.g. *ibid.*, para. 29; *Mathew v. The Netherlands*, ECtHR 29 September 2005, appl. no. 24919/03, para. 175.
[98]   *Kudła v. Poland, supra* n. 17, paras. 92–100.
[99]   *Vinter and Others v. United Kingdom*, ECtHR (GC) 9 July 2013, appl. no. 66069/09, para. 102.

from physical exercise because of a known knee condition. The conscript collapsed, and despite emergency care in hospital the spine injury caused long-term damage to his health. The Court deemed this punishment to violate Article 3.[100]

As can be digested from the *Weeks* case (1987),[101] life imprisonment in itself is not in breach of Article 3. But in 2008 the Court ruled in *Kafkaris* that an *irreducible* life sentence may raise an issue under Article 3.[102] It must be stressed that imposition of a life sentence does not in itself violate Article 3, nor does the fact that in practice such sentence may have to be served in full. Nevertheless, Article 3 requires that there is a prospect of release and a possibility of review.[103] Both guarantees must exist at the moment of the imposition of the sentence, according to the Court in *Vinter*.[104] The review must allow the domestic authorities to consider in full whether any changes with regard to the life prisoner (including his progress towards rehabilitation that has been made in the course of his sentence), are such that continued detention can no longer be justified on legitimate penological grounds.[105] Compassionate release for the terminally ill or physically incapacitated does not count as a prospect of release.[106] The mere existence of a procedure to review life sentences, providing for *de jure* reducibility, is insufficient when *de facto* such sentences are irreducible.[107]

This reasoning applies to life-long sentences, not to sentences of indefinite duration. In *A. and Others v. United Kingdom*, applicants stated that their indefinite detention in fact amounted to life-long sentences. The detention was based on a measure adopted in the aftermath of 9/11 and applied to foreigners who were 'suspected international terrorists' and could not 'for the time being' be removed. The Court however found they were 'not without any prospect of release'; hence, their situation did not give rise to an issue under Article 3.[108]

2.5. DEGRADING TREATMENT OR PUNISHMENT

Treatment is degrading if it 'humiliates or debases an individual, showing a lack of respect for, or diminishing, his or her human dignity, or arouses feelings of fear, anguish or inferiority capable of breaking an individual's moral

---

[100]   *Chember v. Russia*, ECtHR 3 July 2008, appl. no. 7188/03, para. 57.
[101]   *Weeks v. United Kingdom*, ECtHR 2 March 1987, appl. no. 9787/82, para. 47.
[102]   *Kafkaris v. Cyprus*, ECtHR 12 December 2008, appl. no. 21906/04, para. 97.
[103]   *Ibid.*, para. 98.
[104]   *Vinter and Others v. United Kingdom*, *supra* n. 99, para. 122.
[105]   *Ibid.*, para. 119.
[106]   *Ibid.*, para. 127.
[107]   *Murray v. The Netherlands*, ECtHR (GC) 26 April 2016, appl. no. 10511/10, paras. 125–127.
[108]   *A. and Others v. United Kingdom*, ECtHR (GC) 19 February 2009, appl. no. 3455/05, para. 131.

and physical resistance',[109] or 'when it was such as to drive the victim to act against his will or conscience'.[110] Unlike 'inhuman treatment', causing actual bodily injury or intense physical or mental suffering is not required to qualify as degrading treatment.[111] Hence, the difference between the two is one of focus, on suffering (physical or mental) pain and humiliation, as well as one of severity. It should be kept in mind however, that in several cases the Court does not draw a sharp distinction and often use qualifications such as 'inhuman *and* degrading treatment'.[112]

Like inhuman treatment or punishment, the humiliation involved with degrading treatment or punishment must go beyond the degree of intrusion inevitably connected with a given form of legitimate treatment or punishment.[113] Thus, when deciding that caning amounted to degrading punishment in the particular circumstances in the *Tyrer* case, the Court accorded particular weight to the fact that physical force was used by a complete stranger in an institutionalised form, and for that reason concluded that the punishment concerned was degrading.[114] Hence, publicity can be a relevant factor to assess whether a punishment is degrading. But the absence of publicity will not necessarily mean that the punishment is not degrading, because the victim can be humiliated *in his own eyes*.[115]

Another relevant factor, again as in inhuman treatment or punishment cases, is the question whether the *object* (purpose) of the treatment 'was to humiliate and debase the person concerned'.[116] Thus, in the *Albert and Le Compte* case the Court ruled that while the withdrawal from the register of the *Ordre des médicins* had as its object the imposition of a sanction for misconduct, and not the debasement of his personality, it did not amount to a breach of Article 3.[117] And in the *Peers* case, the Court held that the mere absence of a purpose to humiliate or debase, cannot conclusively rule out a finding of violation of Article 3.[118]

As degrading treatment or punishment is at the lower end of the scale of acts prohibited by Article 3, and given the subjectivity inherent to the notion of humiliation, the dividing line between harsh but legitimate treatment and illegitimate degrading treatment or punishment is contentious. In the case of *Campbell and Cosans*, when the Court had to rule on the application of corporal punishment in British schools, it reached the conclusion that in that case it could

---

[109]   E.g. *Pretty v. United Kingdom*, ECtHR 29 April 2002, appl. no. 2346/02, para. 52; *Svinarenko and Slyadnev v. Russia*, ECtHR (GC) 17 July 2014, appl. no. 32541/08, para. 115.

[110]   E.g. *Jalloh v. Germany*, *supra* n. 11, para. 68.

[111]   *Ananyev and Others v. Russia*, *supra* n. 52, para. 115.

[112]   E.g. *Ilaşcu and Others v. Moldova and Russia*, *supra* n. 39, para. 452.

[113]   *Tyrer v. United Kingdom*, *supra* n. 5, para. 30; *Labita v. Italy*, *supra* n. 74, para. 120.

[114]   *Ibid.*, para. 33.

[115]   *Ibid.*, para. 32.

[116]   *Raninen v. Finland*, ECtHR 16 December 1997, appl. no. 20972/92, para. 55.

[117]   *Albert and Le Compte v. Belgium*, ECtHR (GC) 10 February 1983, appl. nos. 7299/75 and 7496/76, para. 22.

[118]   *Peers v. Greece*, ECtHR 19 April 2001, appl. no. 28524/95, para. 74.

not be concluded that a degrading treatment was involved, because the corporal punishment had not actually been applied to the children of the applicants, and the gravity of the punishment and its degrading effect on the person concerned could not therefore be measured. That the punishment had not been executed did not rule out an infringement as a threat may also amount to inhuman or degrading punishment.[119] But the Court ruled that although the boys might have experienced feelings of apprehension, disquiet or alienation, 'these effects fall into a different category from humiliation or debasement'.[120] And in the *Marckx* case, the Court held that 'while the legal rules at issue probably present aspects which the applicants may feel to be humiliating, they do not constitute degrading treatment coming within the ambit of Article 3'.[121] Thus – once again: – ill-treatment must reach a certain (objective) level of severity in order to fall within the ambit of Article 3.[122] In the case of *Costello-Roberts,* the Court again had to address the issue of corporal punishment in British schools. The applicant was a young boy punished in accordance with the disciplinary rules of his school. The Court distinguished the circumstances of this punishment from those of Tyrer's, which was found to be degrading within the meaning of Article 3. Tyrer was sentenced in a juvenile court to three strokes of the birch on the bare posterior; his punishment was administered three weeks later in a police station where he was held by two policemen whilst a third administered the punishment, pieces of birch breaking at the first stroke. Costello-Roberts' punishment on the other hand amounted to being slippered three times on the buttocks through his shorts with a gym shoe by the headmaster in private. Furthermore, Costello-Roberts did not suffer severe or long-lasting effects. In his case the Court found that the minimum level of severity required to conclude that Article 3 was violated was not attained.[123]

In several other cases, the Court likewise ruled that a treatment, although unpleasant or even harsh, did not amount to inhuman or degrading treatment. The situation of Mr Guzzardi, detained on an island, was 'undoubtedly unpleasant or even irksome'; but nevertheless the way he was treated did not attain the minimum level of severity required to fall within the scope of Article 3.[124] The refusal to grant Mr Berrehab a new residence permit after his divorce and his resulting deportation did not infringe Article 3, while he did not undergo suffering of a degree corresponding to the concepts of 'inhuman' or 'degrading' treatment.[125] The conditions in which Mrs *López Ostra* and her

---

[119]   *Campbell and Cosans v. United Kingdom, supra* n. 40, para. 26.

[120]   *Ibid.*, paras. 25–30.

[121]   *Marckx v. Belgium*, ECtHR 13 June 1979, appl. no. 6833/74, para. 66.

[122]   *Ireland v. United Kingdom, supra* n. 3, para. 162.

[123]   *Costello-Roberts v. United Kingdom*, ECtHR 25 March 1993, appl. no. 13134/87, paras. 31–32. The United Kingdom responded to this judgment by passing legislation to prohibit corporal punishment in schools.

[124]   *Guzzardi v. Italy*, ECtHR 6 November 1980, appl. no. 7367/76, para. 107.

[125]   *Berrehab v. the Netherlands*, ECtHR 21 June 1988, appl. no. 10730/84, paras. 30–31.

family lived – near to a plant for the treatment of liquid and solid waste, that despite its partial shutdown continued to emit fumes, repetitive noise and strong smells – did not amount to degrading treatment within the meaning of Article 3.[126] And the suffering that Mr Popov might have experienced due to the non-execution of the judgment to give him back his parents' house was likewise insufficient to amount to ill-treatment within the scope of Article 3.[127]

2.6. STANDARD AND BURDEN OF PROOF

In principle, it falls upon the applicant to substantiate the allegation of ill-treatment, adducing 'appropriate evidence'.[128] When assessing this evidence, the Court in general applies as a standard of proof that the risk of a violation of Article 3 is 'beyond reasonable doubt'.[129] Such 'proof may follow from the co-existence of sufficiently strong, clear and concordant inferences or of similar unrebutted presumptions of fact. The conduct of the Parties when evidence is being obtained has to be taken into account.'[130] However, this standard of proof is not always applied, for instance in cases involving positive obligations (see section 4.1) and in expulsion cases (see section 6). Furthermore, when events lie 'wholly, or in large part, within the exclusive knowledge of the authorities' as in detention cases, injuries incurred during detention raise the presumption of ill-treatment, and 'the burden of proof may be regarded as resting on the authorities to provide a satisfactory and convincing explanation.'[131] In that same line, it follows from *Tomasi* that if there is no reason to assume that the applicant was scarred before detention and presents marks at the earliest possible occasion, it falls upon the state to provide for an explanation.[132] A similar assumption applies if a person disappears after having been taken in custody.[133] The justification for this reversal of the burden of proof in such cases is that detained persons are 'in a vulnerable position', and the government has the duty to protect them.[134]

When assessing the acts complained of, the Court may rely on all evidence adduced by the parties involved, as well as on materials obtained *proprio motu*.[135] The Court occasionally also takes into account assessments made by other

---

[126]   *López Ostra v. Spain*, ECtHR 9 December 1994, appl. no. 16798/90, para. 60.

[127]   *Popov v. Moldova (No. 1)*, ECtHR 18 January 2005, appl. no. 74153/01, paras. 26–27.

[128]   *Klaas v. Germany*, 22 September 1993, appl. no. 15473/89, para. 30; *Labita v. Italy*, *supra* n. 74, para. 121.

[129]   *Ireland v. United Kingdom*, *supra* n. 3, para. 161 and *Labita v. Italy*, *supra* n. 74, para. 121.

[130]   See, e.g., *Ireland v. United Kingdom*, *supra* n. 3, para. 161; *Aydın v. Turkey*, *supra* n. 23, para. 73; *Selmouni v. France*, *supra* n. 21, para. 88; *Chamaïev and Others v. Georgia and Russia*, ECtHR 12 April 2005, appl. no. 36378/02, para. 338.

[131]   *Salman v. Turkey*, *supra* n. 27, para. 100.

[132]   *Tomasi v. France*, *supra* n. 6, para. 110.

[133]   *Kurt v. Turkey*, *supra* n. 61, para. 124.

[134]   *Ibid.*, para. 99.

[135]   *Ireland v. United Kingdom*, *supra* n. 3, para. 160.

international bodies, such as the Committee Against Torture.[136] Furthermore, in detention cases the findings of the European Committee for the Prevention of Torture and Inhuman or Degrading Treatment or Punishment (CPT) are frequently invoked. The Court is 'attentive' to the standards developed by the CPT, such as regards the minimum space required (see section 5.4), but does not treat them as 'a decisive argument'.[137]

Where it comes to the assessment of facts, it follows from the 'subsidiary nature' of the Court's role *vis-à-vis* domestic courts that it must be 'cautious in taking on the role of a first instance tribunal of fact'[138]: 'as a general rule' it falls upon domestic courts to assess the facts.[139] Still, in Article 3 cases, owing to its subject matter the Court's scrutiny must be 'particularly thorough'.[140] Hence the Court can – and should – depart from the findings by domestic courts[141] if 'cogent elements' require so,[142] for example when domestic investigations were not conducted in an independent manner.[143] The Court likewise ruled in *El-Masri*, concerning the arrest, detention and subsequent rendition by the CIA. The Government denied any involvement of Macedonian officials, and the applicant's criminal complaint had been rejected.[144]

2.7. CONCLUDING REMARKS

The case law discussed above may be characterised as an effort to afford protection against undue suffering without trivialising it by setting too low standards. For all types of prohibited treatment (torture, inhuman and degrading treatment and punishment), the central notion is the minimum level of severity, i.e. the degree of intensity of suffering required. For all types of treatment, the following factors are relevant for assessing whether treatment reaches this minimum: the duration of the treatment, the effects on the victim, his or her age, gender and health, the objective pursued and other circumstances of the case.

Torture, inhuman and degrading treatment differ as regards the severity of the inflicted treatment, in a descending scale. Torture furthermore stands apart

---

[136] See, e.g., *Mamatkulov and Askarov v. Turkey*, ECtHR (GC) 4 February 2005, appl. nos. 46827/99 and 46951/99, para. 115, on diplomatic assurances in extradition cases (see further section 6).

[137] *Muršić v. Croatia*, ECtHR (GC) 20 October 2016, appl. no. 7334/13, paras. 113 and 111.

[138] *El-Masri v. Macedonia*, *supra* n. 19, para. 155.

[139] *Klaas v. Germany*, *supra* n. 128, para. 29.

[140] *Ribitsch v. Austria*, *supra* n. 81, para. 32.

[141] *El-Masri v. Macedonia*, *supra* n. 19, para. 155.

[142] *Gäfgen v. Germany*, *supra* n. 4, para. 93.

[143] *McKerr v. United Kingdom*, ECtHR 4 May 2001, appl. no. 28883/95, para. 157, concerning Art. 2, but frequently referred to in Art. 3 cases, e.g., *El-Masri v. Macedonia*, *supra* n. 19, para. 155.

[144] *El-Masri v. Macedonia*, *supra* n. 19, para. 155.

from the other forms of prohibited treatment in that it is intentionally inflicted in order to obtain evidence or for some other purpose.

The relevance of the different factors in a particular case depends on the circumstances of the case. Thus, they may be relevant for deciding whether the intensity of suffering reaches the threshold, but also justify treatment that might otherwise qualify as treatment prohibited by the provision.

The effort in the Court's case law to secure protection against ill-treatment without trivialising it is also visible in its case law on proof. The standard 'beyond reasonable doubt' that often is used sets a high standard for applicants. But the distribution of the burden of proof is dependent on circumstances of the case and may imply that it shifts to the state.

3. SCOPE

3.1. PERSONAL SCOPE

Article 3 protects human beings regardless of their legal status.[145] It does not protect other legal persons.[146] In *Akpinar and Altun*, the Court ruled that the prohibition does not apply to corpses as 'the human quality is extinguished on death'.[147] Security forces had killed the applicant's brother and son, and after their death cut off their ears. The Court ruled that the sight of the mutilation amounted to degrading treatment, though.[148] Likewise, the Court has ruled that relatives of disappeared persons also can suffer ill-treatment (see *supra* section 2.3).

3.2. TERRITORIAL SCOPE

Article 3 ECHR has found extra-territorial application in several types of cases. First, expelling states are liable for the expected treatment inflicted on foreign territory by agents of another state (or by private persons), if at the time of removal it was foreseeable that such treatment would take place.[149] Strictly speaking, in such a situation Article 3 does not apply extra-territorially, as it is the act of removal for which the state is responsible. In *Al-Adsani*, the Court emphasised that extra-territorial application of Article 3 ECHR on this basis is 'limited'.[150] The case concerned a Kuwaiti who had fallen victim of torture

---

[145]   *Cf.* Art. 3: 'no one'.
[146]   *Verein 'Kontakt-Information-Therapie' (KIT) and Hagen v. Austria*, EComHR 12 October 1988 (dec.), appl. no. 11921/86.
[147]   *Akpinar and Altun v. Turkey, supra* n. 66, para. 82.
[148]   *Ibid.*, para. 86.
[149]   *Soering v. United Kingdom, supra* n. 1, para. 91.
[150]   *Al-Adsani v. United Kingdom*, ECtHR (GC) 21 November 2001, appl. no. 35763/97, para. 39.

during the Iraqi occupation of his country. The Court ruled, that as the torture did not take place 'within the jurisdiction of the United Kingdom' and the UK authorities had no 'causal connection with its occurrence', these authorities had no duty to provide him a civil remedy against Kuwait.[151]

However, in *Hirsi Jamaa* the Court ruled that Italy was responsible for acts aboard of ships that carried its flag,[152] executed outside its territorial waters. This case concerned the transfer to Libya of migrants intercepted at sea, in violation of the prohibition on expulsion with the foreseeable consequence of ill-treatment just mentioned. And in a number of other cases, states were found to be responsible for acts committed by their agents on the territory of another state. Thus, in *Mozer Russia* was held to be responsible for detention in violation of Article 3 ECHR on Moldovan territory, and in *Al-Saadoon and Mufhdi* the transfer of detainees to Iraqi authorities by British forces on Iraqi soil was a violation due to the risk of imposition of the death penalty.[153]

3.3. TEMPORAL SCOPE

Particularities as to the temporal scope apply to complaints concerning events dating from before a state's accession to the Convention. According to well-established case law on Article 2, which applies to Article 3 as well,[154] the Court has held that killing or ill-treatment occurring before that 'critical date' falls outside its jurisdiction.[155] Procedural obligations however fall within that jurisdiction, if there is a 'genuine link' between the 'triggering event' and the accession to the Convention, that is, if the event took place reasonably briefly before the accession and 'a major part of the investigation must have been carried out, or ought to have been carried out, after the entry into force'.[156]

4. POSITIVE OBLIGATIONS

4.1. INTRODUCTION

On top of the obligation of the state not to subject a person to ill-treatment, Article 3 also imposes on the state several obligations to act. The Court in

---

[151]   *Ibid.*
[152]   *Hirsi Jamaa and Others v. Italy*, ECtHR (GC) 23 February 2012, appl. no. 27765/09.
[153]   *Mozer v. The Republic of Moldova and Russia*, ECtHR (GC) 23 February 2016, appl. no. 11138/10, *Al-Saadoon and Mufdhi v. United Kingdom*, ECtHR 2 March 2010, appl. no. 61498/08.
[154]   *Mocanu and Others v. Romania*, ECtHR (GC) 17 September 2014, appl. no. 10865/09, para. 206.
[155]   *Ibid.* para. 206 and *Janowiec and Others v. Russia*, appl. no. 21 October 2013, appl. no. 55508/07, para. 147.
[156]   *Janowiec, supra* n. 155, para. 148.

particular has developed a considerable body of case law as regards the obligation to investigate allegations of ill-treatment and to take measures to prevent ill-treatment, both by state agents as well as by private parties (see below).

The obligations to investigate and to prevent have both been labelled by the Court as positive obligations.[157] In other cases however, the Court has applied (also) other labels, or even has done without. Thus, the Court has considered the obligation to investigate as the 'procedural aspect' of the provision,[158] next to the 'substantive aspect' under which heading it discussed the obligation to prevent.[159] Furthermore, the Court has identified similar obligations in particular areas without labelling them as positive obligations. So, in detention cases the Court has emphasised states' obligations to take various measures (such as providing for health care) in order to 'ensure' the prisoners' well-being (see *infra* section 5). And in expulsion cases, the obligation not to expel (labelled as a negative obligation in – for instance – *Paposhvili*)[160] is narrowly intertwined with the obligation to investigate whether expulsion will result in ill-treatment, which however the Court usually does not label as a positive obligation (see further *infra* section 6).

4.2. DUTY TO INVESTIGATE

The Court formulated a 'duty to investigate' flowing from Article 3 for the first time in the case of *Assenov v. Bulgaria*. That case concerned a 14-year-old boy who was bruised after two hours of detention; it was unclear whether he was hit by the police or his father. The Court ruled that the circumstances raised a 'reasonable suspicion' that the police had done it.[161] As subsequent investigations were cursory, the Court ruled that because of 'the lack of a thorough and effective investigation into the applicant's arguable claim that he had been beaten by police officers', Bulgaria had violated Article 3 ECHR.[162]

The essential purpose of investigating ill-treatment allegedly committed by state agents is securing the implementation of domestic laws prohibiting ill-treatment and ensuring their accountability for ill-treatment committed under their responsibility.[163] Such investigations must be carried out by persons who are independent from those implicated, both institutionally and in practice.[164] The authorities must act of their own motion.[165] Authorities that are confronted

---

157   E.g. *O'Keeffe v. Ireland*, ECtHR (GC) 28 January 2014, appl. no. 35810/09, paras. 144 and 173.
158   *Varnava and Others v. Turkey, supra* n. 65, para. 147; *El-Masri v. Macedonia, supra* n. 19, para. 181.
159   *O'Keeffe v. Ireland, supra* n. 157, paras. 144 et seq.
160   *Paposhvili v. Belgium*, ECtHR (GC) 14 December 2016, appl. no. 41738/10, para. 188.
161   *Assenov v. Bulgaria, supra* n. 16, para. 101.
162   *Ibid.*, para. 106.
163   *Mocanu and Others v. Romania, supra* n. 154, para. 318.
164   *Slimani v. France*, ECtHR 27 July 2004, appl. no. 57671/00, para. 32.
165   *Mocanu and Others v. Romania, supra* n. 154, para. 121.

with clear information in official documents concerning a possible violation of Article 3 but not competent to take any investigative steps, should bring this information to the attention of authorities that are competent in the matter.[166] The obligation to investigate even applies in difficult security conditions, including in a context of armed conflict.[167] The award of a compensation to the victim does not affect the duty to continue an investigation capable of leading to the punishment of those responsible.[168]

The investigation must be thorough. All reasonable steps available should be taken to secure the evidence concerning the incident, including eye-witness testimony and forensic evidence; it should be a prompt response and a reasonable expedition and there must be a sufficient element of public scrutiny.[169] Where relevant, next-of-kin should be involved and the victim should be able to participate effectively in the investigation.[170] Criminal proceedings ought not to be discontinued on account of a limitation period, and amnesties and pardons are not allowed in these cases.[171]

In a number of cases, the Court has addressed the procedural aspect in the context of Article 13 rather than Article 3. In *Ilhan*, the Court explained that Article 3 was phrased 'in substantive terms', lacking the words 'protected by law' in Article 2.[172] In more recent cases, however, the Court no longer seems to apply this distinction, and the obligations from Article 3 are similar to those under Article 2.[173]

4.3. ILL-TREATMENT BY NON-STATE AGENTS

In *M.C. v. Bulgaria*, the Court ruled that the duty to investigate is not 'limited solely to cases of ill-treatment by State agents', but applies as well to the allegation of rape by a private person.[174] This case concerned the allegation of rape of a minor. The authorities had terminated proceedings against the suspects 'in the absence of "direct" proof of rape such as traces of violence and resistance or calls for help'.[175] The Court considered the emphasis on direct proof undue, criticised the authorities for having attached too little weight to the vulnerability of the minor and the undue delays in the investigations, and found a violation.

---

[166] *Ahmet Özkan v. Turkey*, ECtHR 6 April 2004, appl. no. 21689/93, para. 359.
[167] *Al-Skeini and Others v. United Kingdom*, ECtHR (GC) 7 July 2011, appl. no. 55721/07, para. 164.
[168] *Jeronovičs v. Latvia*, ECtHR (GC) 5 July 2016, appl. no. 44898/10, para. 107.
[169] *Slimani v. France, supra* n. 164, para. 32.
[170] *Mocanu and Others v. Romania, supra* n. 154, para. 324.
[171] *Ibid.*, para. 326.
[172] *Ilhan v. Turkey, supra* n. 36, para. 92.
[173] *Cf. Mocanu and Others v. Romania, supra* n. 154, paras. 317 and 319.
[174] *M.C. v. Bulgaria, supra* n. 24, para. 151.
[175] *Ibid.*, para. 179.

Other cases where the Court found a breach of the obligation to investigate ill-treatment by private persons, concerned domestic violence of a minor by her father (hitting and verbal abuse),[176] or continuous harassment of a minor by school children.[177] The requirements as regards the investigation are similar to those for claims of ill-treatment by state agents.[178] The obligation to investigate is not triggered if allegations are (too) vague and unspecified.[179]

4.4. DUTY TO PREVENT

States are required to take measures designed to ensure that individuals within their jurisdiction are not subjected to ill-treatment. This obligation is to be interpreted as not imposing an 'excessive burden' on the authorities; but nevertheless the domestic 'measures should, at least, provide effective protection in particular of children and other vulnerable persons and should include reasonable steps to prevent ill-treatment of which the authorities had or ought to have had knowledge.'[180] In the case of *A. v. United Kingdom,* a nine-year-old boy was hit by his stepfather with a garden cane applied with considerable force on more than one occasion. The stepfather was charged with assault, but the jury did not find him guilty, because the treatment would amount to 'reasonable chastisement'. The Court held that the law did not provide adequate protection to the boy against this ill-treatment, which constituted a violation of Article 3.[181]

The outcome of the *A. v. United Kingdom* case suggests that domestic law should be amended in order to secure compliance with the Convention. In *M.C. v. Bulgaria,* the case of the minor subjected to rape discussed above, the Court even stated that 'the member States' positive obligations under Articles 3 and 8 of the Convention must be seen as requiring the penalisation and effective prosecution of any non-consensual sexual act, including in the absence of physical resistance by the victim'.[182] In the case of *Z. and Others v. United Kingdom,* the four applicant children suffered appalling neglect and physical and psychological injury and had been subjected in their home to horrific experiences. Although the Court acknowledged the difficult and sensitive decisions facing social services and the important countervailing principle of respecting and preserving family life, it was concluded that the failure of the

---

[176]   *M. and M. v. Croatia*, ECtHR 3 September 2015, appl. no. 10161/13, 142.
[177]   *Đorđević v. Croatia*, ECtHR 24 July 2012, appl. no. 41526/10.
[178]   *M. and M. v. Croatia, supra* n. 176, para. 148.
[179]   *Đurđević v. Croatia*, ECtHR 19 July 2011, appl. no. 52442/09, paras. 112 and 118.
[180]   *A. v. United Kingdom, supra* n. 16, para. 22; *Z. and Others v. United Kingdom, supra* n. 71, para. 73; *O'Keeffe v. Ireland, supra* n. 157, para. 144.
[181]   *A. v. United Kingdom, supra* n. 16, paras. 23–24.
[182]   *M.C. v. Bulgaria, supra* n. 24, para. 166.

system to protect these children from serious, long-term neglect and abuse amounted to a violation of Article 3.[183]

Furthermore, although the treatment complained of in the *Costello-Roberts* case was the act of a headmaster of an independent school, the state could be held responsible under the Convention if that treatment would be incompatible with Article 3.[184] Indeed, in *O'Keeffe* the Court ruled that 'the positive obligation of protection assumes particular importance in the context of the provision of an important public service such as primary education, school authorities being obliged to protect the health and well-being of pupils and, in particular, of young children who are especially vulnerable and are under the exclusive control of those authorities.'[185] The Government should, 'at a minimum', have adopted effective mechanisms for the detection and reporting of any ill-treatment by and to a State-controlled body.

All these cases mentioned concern the prevention of intentionally inflicted harm. Hitherto, the Court has shown reluctance to accept obligations to prevent suffering or humiliation in other types of situations. However, it did find that Article 3 does impose obligations as regards securing the well-being of persons in state custody and, in particular circumstances, asylum seekers (see *infra* section 5). In *D v. United Kingdom*, concerning the expulsion of a terminally ill person (see *infra* section 6), the Court stated that the absolute character of Article 3 requires it to scrutinise its application also in 'other contexts' than those where the treatment 'emanates from intentionally inflicted acts of the public authorities' or non-state bodies, i.e. where the suffering was due to the person's medical situation.[186] It concluded, that exceptionally Article 3 prohibits expulsion to the home country.

In *Pretty*, the terminally ill applicant had asked the public prosecutor to declare that her husband would not be prosecuted when he would assist her in committing suicide. The applicant stated that the refusal to declare so or otherwise assist in termination amounted to the State's responsibility for ill-treatment. The Court, referring to *D v. United Kingdom*, observed that 'suffering which flows from naturally occurring illness, physical or mental, may be covered by Article 3, where it is, or risks being, exacerbated by treatment, whether flowing from conditions of detention, expulsion or other measures, for which the authorities can be held responsible', but did not discern a similar act or treatment by the UK authorities in this case; furthermore, Article 3 should be construed in harmony with Article 2 which prohibits conduct which might lead to death rather than conferring any right on an individual to require a state to permit or facilitate his or her death'.[187] Likewise, in *Hristozov*, concerning a

---

[183]   *Z. and Others v. United Kingdom, supra* n. 71, para. 74.
[184]   *Costello-Roberts v. United Kingdom, supra* n. 123, para. 28.
[185]   *O'Keeffe v. Ireland, supra* n. 157, para. 148.
[186]   *D. v. United Kingdom*, ECtHR 2 May 1997, appl. no. 30240/96, para. 49.
[187]   *Pretty v. United Kingdom, supra* n. 109, para. 54.

claim to be provided with a certain medicine, the Court observed that 'suffering which flows from an illness may be covered by Article 3 where it is exacerbated by treatment for which the authorities can be held responsible' but also that 'the threshold in such situations is high because the alleged harm emanates not from the authorities but the illness'. It referred to the case of *N. v. United Kingdom* (see section 6) and concluded that Article 3 had not been violated.[188]

The Court has shown reluctance to extend the scope of positive obligations in other contexts. For instance, in the case of *Al-Adsani*, the Court ruled that the prohibition of torture did not imply that the UK could not uphold the claim of immunity by Kuwait, the State that allegedly had tortured the applicant, in civil proceedings (see also *supra* section 3.2, territorial scope).[189]

4.5. SOCIO-ECONOMIC OBLIGATIONS

When detaining a person, the state has the obligation to ensure that the detainee lives 'in conditions which are compatible with respect for his human dignity';[190] this implies obligations as regards the provision of accommodation, food and health care (see further section 5). Outside that context, state obligations as regards socio-economic claims are fairly limited. Thus, Article 3 does not entail an obligation to give refugees financial assistance to enable them to maintain a certain standard of living,[191] nor does it contain an obligation to provide everyone within the state's jurisdiction with a home.[192] However, in *Budina v. Russia*, the Court ruled that 'where an applicant, in circumstances wholly dependent on State support, found herself faced with official indifference when in a situation of serious deprivation or want incompatible with human dignity', state responsibility under Article 3 could arise,[193] but it did not conclude that there was such state responsibility in the case at hand. It did conclude so however in *M.S.S. v. Belgium and Greece*. That case concerned an Afghan who had been registered as an asylum seeker by the Greek authorities, but in respect of whom they had not issued any reception facilities. The Court ruled that 'in view of the obligations incumbent on the Greek authorities under [Union law], the Court considers that the Greek authorities have not had due regard to the applicant's vulnerability as an asylum-seeker and must be held responsible, because of their inaction, for the situation in which he has found himself for several months, living on the street, with no resources or access to sanitary facilities, and without any means

---

[188]   *Hristozov and Others v. Bulgaria*, ECtHR 13 November 2012, appl. no. 47039/11, para. 113.
[189]   *Al-Adsani, supra* n. 150, para. 67.
[190]   *Kudła v. Poland, supra* n. 17, para. 94.
[191]   *Müslim v. Turkey*, ECtHR 26 April 2005, appl. no. 53566/99, para. 85.
[192]   *M.S.S. v. Belgium and Greece, supra* n. 71, para. 253, referring to *Chapman v. United Kingdom*, ECtHR (GC) 18 January 2001, appl. no. 27238/95, para. 99 which refers to Art. 8 ECHR solely.
[193]   *Budina v. Russia*, ECtHR 18 June 2009 (dec.), appl. no. 45603/05.

of providing for his essential needs', which amounted to 'humiliating treatment' incompatible with Article 3 ECHR.[194] The obligation to provide a person with means to secure their well-being has been circumscribed carefully: it applies only when the state is inactive although being bound by the obligation to provide for such means, when the person concerned is vulnerable, has lived for a considerable time in extremely poor living conditions and in prolonged uncertainty, and in case of a 'total lack of any prospects of his situation improving'.[195]

5. DETENTION

5.1. INTRODUCTION

By taking a person into custody, the government takes upon itself an obligation to secure that person's well-being. Thus, in *Kudła* the Court observed that 'a State must ensure that a person is detained in conditions which are compatible with respect for his human dignity, that the manner and method of the execution of the measure do not subject him to distress or hardship of an intensity exceeding the unavoidable level of suffering inherent in detention and that, given the practical demands of imprisonment, his health and well-being are adequately secured by, among other things, providing him with the requisite medical assistance'.[196]

These obligations apply to all persons deprived of liberty, whether held in remand,[197] detained after conviction, detained in mental asylums or in social care homes,[198] or in aliens detention.[199]

Whether or not a specific treatment amounts to an infringement depends, as in most Article 3 cases, on the circumstances of the case (see extensively *supra* section 2.3). Thus, in the *Kröcher and Möller* case, the Commission assessed in detail all aspects of the measure of solitary confinement – including the particular conditions, the stringency of the measure, its duration, the objective pursued and its effects on the person concerned – in the light of the security requirements.[200] And in *Blokhin*, the Court found a violation of the applicant's rights under Article 3 on account of the lack of necessary medical treatment at the temporary detention centre, having regard to his young age and particularly

---

[194] *M.S.S. v. Belgium and Greece, supra* n. 71, paras. 263–264.
[195] *Ibid.*
[196] *Kudła v. Poland, supra* n. 17, para. 94; *cf. Valašinas v.* Lithuania, ECtHR 24 July 2001, appl. no. 44558/98, para. 102.
[197] E.g. *Ananyev and Others v. Russia, supra* n. 52, para. 141.
[198] E.g. *Stanev v. Bulgaria*, ECtHR (GC) 17 January 2012, appl. no. 36760/06, para. 204.
[199] E.g. *Khlaifia and Others v. Italy, supra* n. 7, paras. 160.
[200] *Kröcher and Möller v. Switzerland*, EComHR 16 December 1982 (rep.), appl. no. 8463/78, para. 62.

vulnerable situation as an ADHD sufferer.[201] Below, the case law as regards arrest and prison regime and detention conditions, including health care and required living space, will be discussed further.

5.2. ARREST AND PRISON REGIME

Handcuffing a detainee is not contrary to Article 3 during a lawful arrest or detention if it 'does not entail use of force, or public exposure, exceeding what is reasonably necessary'.[202] In this regard, it is of importance whether, for instance, there is reason to believe that the person concerned would resist arrest or abscond, cause injury or damage or suppress evidence.[203] However, a heavy-handed arrest of a politician at home in the presence of his wife and minor children was considered degrading treatment.[204]

Likewise, strip-searches of detainees are allowed for if necessary on occasions to ensure prison security or prevent disorder or crime and if carried out in an appropriate manner.[205] In *Lorsé*, routine strip-searches amounted to degrading treatment, convincing security needs being absent.[206] In *Valasinas*, the search was degrading as the applicant had to strip naked before a woman, touch his sexual organs and then his food with bare hands.[207] Conversely, in *Wainwright* the strip-search of a detainee's visiting family members did not reach the minimum level of severity as the suspicion that the detainee used drugs justified it and no verbal abuse or touching took place.[208] Furthermore, to keep suspects in a cage during trial was found to be a breach of Article 3, especially where the suspect had no record of violent behaviour.[209]

5.3. CONDITIONS

Each Contracting State is required 'to organise its penitentiary system in such a way as to ensure respect for the dignity of detainees, regardless of financial or logistical difficulties'.[210] That the detention centre is not adequately funded is hence no justification: 'lack of resources cannot in principle justify prison conditions which are so poor as to reach the threshold of treatment contrary

---

201   *Blokhin v. Russia*, ECtHR (GC) 23 March 2016, appl. no. 47152/06, para. 148.
202   *Raninen v. Finland*, *supra* n. 116, para. 57.
203   *Ibid.*, para. 56.
204   *Gutsanovi v. Bulgaria*, ECtHR 15 October 2013, appl. no. 34529/10, paras. 131–137.
205   *Valašinas v. Lithuania*, *supra* n. 196, para. 117.
206   *Lorsé and Others v. The Netherlands*, ECtHR 4 February 2003, appl. no. 52750/99, para. 74.
207   *Valašinas v. Lithuania*, *supra* n. 196, para. 117.
208   *Wainwright v. United Kingdom*, ECtHR 26 September 2006, appl. no. 12350/04, para. 46.
209   *Svinarenko and Slyadnev v. Russia*, *supra* n. 109, para. 138.
210   *Mamedova v. Russia*, ECtHR 1 June 2006, appl. no. 7064/05, para. 63.

to Article 3.'[211] However, in *Khlaifia*, concerning detention of immigrants intercepted in the Mediterranean Sea, the Court ruled that the 'undeniable difficulties and inconveniences endured by the applicants stemmed to a significant extent from the situation of extreme difficulty confronting the Italian authorities at the relevant time', and did not find a violation.[212]

The Court further stated, that when assessing conditions of detention, account has to be taken of the cumulative effects of these conditions, as well as the applicant's specific allegations.[213] Attention should be paid to 'all the circumstances, such as the size of the cell and the degree of overcrowding, sanitary conditions, opportunities for recreation and exercise, medical treatment and supervision and the prisoner's state of health'.[214] Finally, the length of the period during which a person is detained in the particular conditions is a relevant factor.[215]

Furthermore, exceptional detention conditions may in the specific circumstances be justified. In the *Kröcher and Müller* case, the prison conditions including isolation, constant artificial lighting, permanent surveillance by closed-circuit television, denial of access to newspapers and radio and the lack of physical exercise did not amount to inhuman or degrading treatment, as they were necessary to ensure security inside and outside the prison.[216] Other factors that have been accepted by the Commission to justify stringent measures are the dangerous or unco-operative behaviour of the prisoner, 'ability to manipulate situations and encourage other prisoners to acts of indiscipline', the safety of the applicant, and the use of firearms at the time of arrest.[217] Finally, the effect on the applicant remains a relevant factor. Thus, in *Van der Graaf* permanent camera surveillance for four and a half months during remand detention was not at odds with Article 3, as it was insufficiently established that the suffering caused amounted to inhuman or degrading treatment.[218]

5.4. OVERCROWDING

A detention cell may not be overcrowded, and must have sufficient sanitary and sleeping facilities.[219] In the *Muršić* case, the Grand Chamber decided that

---

211   *Poltoratskiy v. Ukraine*, ECtHR 29 April 2003, appl. no. 38812/97, para. 148.

212   *Khlaifia and Others v. Italy*, *supra* n. 7, para. 185.

213   *Dougoz*, ECtHR 6 March 2001, appl. no. 40907/98, para. 46.

214   *Assenov v. Bulgaria*, *supra* n. 16, para. 135.

215   *Ananyev and Others v. Russia*, *supra* n. 52, para. 142.

216   *Kröcher and Möller*, *supra* n. 200, paras. 63–77.

217   *M. v. United Kingdom*, EComHR 12 December 1983 (dec.), appl. no. 9907/82; *X. v. United Kingdom*, EComHR 6 March 1982 (dec.), appl. no. 8231/78; *Ensslin, Baader and Raspe v. Federal Republic of Germany*, EComHR 8 July 1978 (dec.), appl. no. 7572/76.

218   *Van der Graaf v. The Netherlands*, ECtHR 1 June 2004 (dec.), appl. no. 8704/03.

219   *Dougoz*, *supra* n. 213, para. 45. The Court, concluding that Art. 3 was violated, observed that 'it was even impossible for him to read a book because his cell was so overcrowded'!

personal space less than three square metres provides a 'strong presumption' of a violation,[220] which can 'normally' be rebutted only if that 'reduction' is short and occasional, accompanied by sufficient freedom of movement outside the cell and when there are no other aggravating aspects of the conditions of his or her detention.[221] Personal space measuring between three and four square metres is 'a weighty factor' in considering the prison conditions, to be assessed alongside 'access to outdoor exercise, natural light or air, availability of ventilation, adequacy of room temperature, the possibility of using the toilet in private, and compliance with basic sanitary and hygienic requirements'.[222] Thus, in the *Valašinas* case, no violation of Article 3 was found, because the restricted space in the sleeping facilities was counterbalanced by the unlimited freedom of movement during the day.[223] But in *Peers*, the Court concluded that there was a violation of Article 3 because the applicant had to share a cell of approximately seven square metres with another inmate, had to use the toilet in the presence of the other inmate, and had to spend almost the whole 24-hour period practically confined to his bed, in a cell where there was neither ventilation nor a window.[224] The Court has deemed relevant an array of other factors, such as leaving on the light all day and night[225] and providing 'repulsive and virtually inedible' food.[226] Taken alone, these factors usually are not sufficient to amount to an infringement, as the Court ruled on insufficient separation of sanitary facilities from the remainder of the prison cell.[227]

5.5. HEALTH CARE

Article 3 imposes an obligation on the state to protect the physical well-being of persons deprived of their liberty. Health, age and severe physical disability are amongst the most relevant factors to be taken into account.[228] In relation to the medical condition of a detainee and prison facilities that need to be in place in order to accommodate him, the Court distinguishes three different aspects: '(a) the medical condition of the prisoner, (b) the adequacy of the medical assistance and care provided in detention; and (c) the advisability of maintaining the detention measure in view of the state of health of the applicant.'[229] These aspects

---

[220] *Muršić v. Croatia*, *supra* n. 137, para. 124.
[221] *Ibid.*, para. 138.
[222] *Ibid.*, para. 139.
[223] *Valašinas v. Lithuania*, *supra* n. 196, paras. 103 and 107.
[224] *Peers v. Greece*, *supra* n. 118, para. 75.
[225] *Kalashnikov v. Russia*, *supra* n. 56, para. 97.
[226] *Modarca v. Moldova*, ECtHR 10 May 2007, appl. no. 14437/05, para. 67.
[227] *Szafrański v. Poland*, ECtHR 15 December 2015, appl. no. 17249/12, para. 28. The circumstance did amount to a breach of Art. 8 ECHR, though.
[228] *Mouisel v. France*, ECtHR 14 November 2002, appl. no. 67263/01, paras. 38–40.
[229] *Khudobin v. Russia*, ECtHR 26 October 2006, appl. no. 59696/00, para. 92.

are assessed in combination. Thus, in the *Khudobin* case, the Court found that 'the applicant was HIV-positive and suffered from a serious mental disorder. This increased the risks associated with any illness he suffered during his detention and intensified his fears on that account. In these circumstances the absence of qualified and timely medical assistance, added to the authorities' refusal to allow an independent medical examination of his state of health, created such a strong feeling of insecurity that, combined with his physical sufferings, it amounted to degrading treatment within the meaning of Article 3.'[230]

The obligation to ensure the physical well-being may require (temporary) release of the detainee. In the *Keenan* case, the Court held that treatment of a mentally ill person could be incompatible with Article 3, even though the person may not be able to point to any specific ill-effects.[231] In the *Price* case, the Court concluded that to detain a person who was four-limb deficient, in conditions that were inappropriate to her state of health, constituted degrading treatment.[232] The detention of elderly, sick persons for a prolonged period was discussed in the *Papon* case, where the Court stated that this could amount to a violation of Article 3.[233] In the *Mouisel* case, the Court concluded that the treatment of a detainee suffering from cancer amounted to inhuman and degrading treatment, because the prison was scarcely equipped to deal with his illness, while no special measures were taken and he was handcuffed and kept in chains while taken to a hospital.[234] In *Tekin Yıldız*, the applicant had developed a severe illness as a result of his hunger strike against his detention. He was released to recover. His subsequent detention amounted to a violation of Article 3: his poor health had been consistently found to be incompatible with detention.[235]

In a number of cases, it was not the negative consequences of detention as such on the health of the detainee, but the lack of proper medical care while being detained that was is the main issue.[236] In the *Kudła* case, the Court held that Article 3 cannot 'be interpreted as laying down a general obligation to release a detainee on health grounds or to place him in a civil hospital to enable him to obtain a particular kind of medical treatment'.[237] But in *Xiros v. Greece*, the Court ruled that the domestic authorities should at least have sought expert

---

[230]   *Ibid.*, para. 96. *Cf. Popov v. Russia*, ECtHR 13 July 2006, appl. no. 26853/04, paras. 210–220.
[231]   *Keenan v. United Kingdom*, ECtHR 3 April 2001, appl. no. 27229/95. paras. 111 and 113; see also Judgment of *Aerts v. Belgium*, ECtHR 30 July 1998, appl. no. 25357/94, para. 66, and *Renolde v. France*, ECtHR 16 October 2008, appl. no. 5608/05.
[232]   *Price v. United Kingdom*, ECtHR 10 July 2001, appl. no. 33394/96, para. 30.
[233]   *Papon v. France (No. 1)*, ECtHR 7 June 2001 (dec.), appl. no. 64666/01.
[234]   *Mouisel v. France, supra* n. 234, paras. 46–48.
[235]   *Tekin Yıldız v. Turkey*, 10 November 2005, appl. no. 22913/04, para. 83.
[236]   See *Kotälla*, EComHR 6 May 1978, appl. no. 7994/77, where the Commission followed the view of the Dutch court that the deterioration of the physical and mental condition of the applicant was not due to his detention. See also *Guzzardi v. Italy*, EComHR 7 December 1978 (rep.), appl. no. 7367/76, B.35 (1979–1980), p. 34–35 and *Bonnechaux*, EComHR 5 December 1979 (rep.), appl. no. 8224/78, para. 88.
[237]   *Kudła v. Poland, supra* n. 17, para. 93.

advice on the necessity of bringing the detainee to a civilian hospital. The duty
to offer adequate medical care also encompasses utilities, such as orthopaedic
footwear for a detainee whose toes had suffered from frostbite during detention
as a result of which he had trouble with standing up.[238] Returning his damaged
glasses after five months to a detainee and having him wait for another two
months before issuing new ones also amounted to a violation.[239] Conversely, in
Rehbock v. Slovenia, the Court ruled that the excessive use of force during arrest
amounted to inhuman treatment, but the failure of the prison staff to provide the
detainee with pain-killing medication did not. Deterioration of health during
detention does not in itself lead to the finding that Article 3 has been breached, if
it is not substantiated that this deterioration is attributable to the authorities and
if they have in general provided adequate care.[240]

5.6. SOLITARY CONFINEMENT

In cases where the question was raised whether solitary confinement of
a detainee constituted an inhuman treatment, regard must be had to the
surrounding circumstances, including the particular conditions, the stringency
of the measure, its duration, the objective pursued and its effects on the person
concerned, and also the question of whether a given minimum of possibilities
for human contact has been left to the person in question.[241] Absolute sensory
isolation combined with complete social isolation can destroy the personality
and constitutes an inhuman treatment for which no security requirements can
form a justification in view of the absolute character of the right laid down in
Article 3.[242] The Commission distinguished between absolute sensory and social
isolation on the one hand, and 'removal from association with other prisoners
for security, disciplinary and protective reasons' on the other, and has taken the
view that this form of segregation from the prison community normally does
not amount to inhuman or degrading treatment or punishment.[243] In the latter
case it is still possible to meet prison and medical officers, lawyers, relatives
etc., and to have contact with the outside world through newspapers, radio and
television. In *Öcalan*, the applicant was the only inmate of a facility on an island.

---

[238] *Vladimir Vasilyev v. Russia*, ECtHR 10 January 2012, appl. no. 28370/05, para. 68.

[239] *Slyusarev v. Russia*, ECtHR 20 April 2010, appl. no. 60333/00.

[240] *Sakkopoulos v. Greece*, ECtHR 15 January 2004, appl. no. 61828/00.

[241] *Lorsé and Others v. The Netherlands*, *supra* n. 206, para. 63 with references to earlier case law
and Commission decisions.

[242] *Ensslin, Baader and Raspe v. Federal Republic of Germany*, *supra* n. 217.

[243] *Ireland v. United Kingdom*, EComHR 25 January 1976 (rep.), appl. no. 5310/71, B.23/I, p. 379;
Ensslin, Baader and Raspe, EComHR 8 July 1978 (dec.), *supra* n. 217; *McFeeley and Others
v. the United Kingdom*, EComHR 15 May 1980 (dec.), appl. no. 8317/78; *Kröcher and Möller*,
supra n. 200, paras. 63–77; *R. v. Denmark*, EComHR 11 March 1985 (dec.), appl. no. 10263/83;
Treholt v. Norway, EComHR 9 July 1991 (dec.), appl. no. 14610/89.

The Court ruled in 2005 that this did not amount to sensory isolation or cellular confinement.[244] However, the prolonged social isolation infringed Article 3, amongst other things because of excessive restrictions to access to news and persistent problems with access by visitors to the prison.[245]

As to the duration, it follows from the *Sadak* case and the *Yurttas* case that the duration of the isolation should be taken into account to decide whether this measure is in accordance with Article 3.[246] However, in *Ramirez Sanchez*, where the applicant was subjected to relative social isolation, because otherwise he could use communications inside or outside the prison to re-establish contact with members of his terrorist group, seek to proselytise other prisoners or prepare an escape, the Court held that 'irrespective of its duration (eight years and two months), which in itself is regrettable, the applicant's continued solitary confinement has not, given his age and health, caused him suffering of the level of severity required to constitute a violation of Article 3'.[247]

As to the purpose of the solitary confinement, the Court ruled in *Messina* that prolonged social isolation was justified in order to preclude the detainee from re-establishing links with a criminal organisation.[248] In *Mathew* on the other hand, isolation was imposed because the applicant could not adapt to the detention regime and had attacked the staff. Taking into account the poor conditions in the confinement and the mental health of the applicant, the treatment was found by the Court to be inhuman.[249]

6. ASYLUM, EXPULSION, EXTRADITION

According to well-established case law, Article 3 ECHR prohibits extradition, expulsion of asylum seekers and removal otherwise if the person concerned runs a 'real risk' of being subjected to ill-treatment in the receiving country.[250] Assessment of compliance with Article 3 in removal cases differs in important respects from that in domestic cases. To begin with, the assessment concerns the foreseeable risk at the moment of expulsion. Hence, instead of establishing past events 'beyond reasonable doubt', the 'real risk' of *future* ill-treatment has to be assessed (see in detail below). Furthermore, although responsibility for expulsion rests with the State Party to the Convention, the ill-treatment will be inflicted

---

[244] *Öcalan v. Turkey (No. 1)*, ECtHR (GC) 12 May 2005, appl. no. 46221/99, para. 194.

[245] *Öcalan v. Turkey (No. 2)*, ECtHR 18 March 2014, appl. no. 24069/03, para. 146.

[246] *Sadak v. Turkey*, ECtHR 8 April 2004, appl. no. 25142/94, para. 46; *Yurttas v. Turkey*, ECtHR 27 May 2004, appl. no. 25143/94, para. 48.

[247] *Ramirez Sanchez v. France*, ECtHR (GC) 27 January 2005, appl. no. 59450/00, paras. 113 and 120.

[248] *Messina v. Italy (No. 2)*, ECtHR 28 September 2000, appl. no. 25498/94.

[249] *Mathew v. The Netherlands, supra* n. 97, para. 205.

[250] *Soering v. United Kingdom, supra* n. 1, para. 91, *F.G. v. Sweden*, ECtHR (GC) 23 March 2016, appl. no. 43611/11, para. 111.

by other actors. Nevertheless, certain tenets applying in domestic cases apply to removal cases as well. Thus, the prohibition is absolute: if a person runs a real risk of being subjected to ill-treatment, balancing with public order or other interests is not allowed for, not even when the person concerned is a suspect of terrorism.[251]

6.1. BASIS FOR STATE RESPONSIBILITY

The Court for the first time elaborated on the basis of state responsibility in removal cases in *Soering*. That case concerned the extradition by the UK of a man sought for murder in the USA. Extradition might eventually result in prolonged waiting for execution (on 'death row'), which allegedly would amount to ill-treatment. The UK pointed out that it could not be held responsible: American authorities and not the UK would put Soering on death row, and their acts were outside the scope of British jurisdiction as defined in Article 1 of the Convention. The Court however reasoned that the fact that the ill-treatment would be inflicted outside the UK's jurisdiction is not decisive, as it is the act of removal, the 'action which has as a direct consequence the exposure of the individual to proscribed ill-treatment', for which the state is responsible.[252] That 'the brief and general wording of Article 3' does not refer to extradition or removal does not exclude its applicability.[253] Article 3 of the Convention Against Torture explicitly prohibits expulsion if the foreigner is in danger of being tortured abroad, and it 'would hardly be compatible with the underlying values' of the European Convention if a state would extradite in spite of such danger; rather, extradition in such circumstances 'would plainly be contrary to the spirit and intendment of the Article'.[254] Hence, object and purpose of Article 3 read in the light of the development of international law imply the prohibition on removal.

6.2. EXPULSION AND ASYLUM

The prohibition on extradition as identified in *Soering* applies to expulsion of asylum seekers as well.[255] It should be observed, though, that this does not imply a right to asylum, understood as a right to legal residence and social rights. The Court has frequently emphasised that the Convention does not contain a general right of admission to a certain country, and does not contain an explicit right

---

[251] *Chahal v. United Kingdom*, *supra* n. 7, para. 80; *Saadi v. Italy*, ECtHR (GC) 28 February 2008, appl. no. 37201/06, para. 127.
[252] *Soering v. United Kingdom*, *supra* n. 1, para. 91.
[253] *Ibid.*, para. 88.
[254] *Ibid.*
[255] *Cruz Varas and Others v. Sweden*, ECtHR 20 March 1991, appl. no. 15576/89, para. 70.

to asylum; rather, it repeatedly has recognised 'as a matter of well-established international law' the right of states to control entry, residence and expulsion of aliens.[256] Hence, the prohibition on expulsion is the exception to the rule, and, as the Court observed in *Bonger*, the denial of a residence permit *ratione materiae* falls outside the scope of the Convention.[257] Therefore the situation that Bonger could not be expelled while he did not qualify for a residence permit due to public order reasons was not incompatible with the Convention.

6.3. REAL RISK

The Court has employed the criterion it coined in *Soering* in cases of extradition as well as expulsion of (failed) asylum seekers ever since: expulsion 'may give rise to an issue under Article 3 (…) where substantial grounds have been shown for believing that the person concerned faced a real risk of being subjected to torture or to inhuman or degrading treatment or punishment in the country to which he was returned.'[258] Thus, removal is prohibited in case of a 'real risk' of ill-treatment upon return. In subsequent case law the Court has elaborated on the assessment of risk. In 1991, in *Vilvarajah*, it ruled that a 'mere possibility of ill-treatment (…) is not in itself sufficient to give rise to a breach of Article 3'; rather, 'special distinguishing features' should be demonstrated.[259] This could be understood as a rather strict criterion, requiring the applicant to submit evidence of a highly individualised risk, being personally targeted by the actor of harm. In 2008, in the case of *NA v. United Kingdom,* the Court distinguished three types of situation as regards risk. First, 'a general situation of violence in a country of destination' could be 'of a sufficient level of intensity as to entail that any removal to it would necessarily breach Article 3'.[260] The Court emphasised that it 'would adopt such an approach only in the most extreme cases of general violence', i.e. of a devastating (civil) war.[261] Indeed, the Court has hitherto concluded in only one case that due to a general situation of violence everyone fleeing from the area concerned (Mogadishu in 2014) was at real risk.[262] Secondly, Article 3 ECHR 'exceptionally' prohibits expulsion if an applicant 'is a member of a group

---

[256]   *Vilvarajah and Others v. United Kingdom*, ECtHR 30 October 1991, appl. no. 13163/87, para. 102.

[257]   *Bonger v. The Netherlands*, ECtHR 15 September 2005 (dec.), appl. no. 10154/04.

[258]   *Vilvarajah and Others v. United Kingdom*, *supra* n. 256, para. 103 and repeated with slight variations in all cases on expulsion since. It is respectfully submitted that the application of the criterion 'beyond reasonable doubt' in the extradition case *Chamaïev and Others v. Georgia and Russia*, *supra* n. 130, para. 338 was erroneous.

[259]   *Vilvarajah and Others v. United Kingdom*, *supra* n. 256, paras. 111–112.

[260]   *NA v. United Kingdom*, ECtHR 17 July 2008, appl. no. 25904/07, para. 115.

[261]   *Ibid.*

[262]   *Sufi and Elmi v. United Kingdom*, ECtHR 28 June 2011, appl. nos. 8319/07 and 11449/07, paras. 217 and 218.

systematically exposed to a practice of ill-treatment'.[263] This type of situation was found to exist in one case, *Salah Sheekh*. The applicant belonged to a Somali minority whose members were exposed to harassment and who could not find protection.[264] All other cases brought before the Court thus far have fallen into the third category: the applicant has to show 'further special distinguishing features'.[265] However, the special distinguishing features test may be relaxed in the light of the general perils in the country of origin from which the asylum seeker is fleeing.[266]

The finding by the Court in *NA v. United Kingdom* that a real risk of ill-treatment can be due to an individual being exposed to a general situation of violence on return seems a bold step after years of avoiding general statements on risk assessment. An explanation may be that the Court strove to fill the possible gap between the interpretation of Article 3 in the case law of the Court so far, and the reference to the situation of indiscriminate violence, mentioned in Article 15, under (c), of the EU Qualification Directive. At any rate, the Court concluded that the protection afforded by Article 3 and Article 15(c) of the said directive was 'comparable'.[267]

6.4. PROTECTION

The ill-treatment to which an applicant may be exposed after removal may stem from state authorities, as in *Soering*. In *H.L.R. v. France*, concerning a drugs trafficker fearing reprisals from other traffickers, the Court ruled that Article 3 'may also apply where the danger emanates from persons or groups of persons who are not public officials' if 'the authorities of the receiving State are not able to obviate the risk by providing appropriate protection'.[268] In later cases, it ruled that the risk could be obviated also by other actors of protection than state authorities, such as a 'male network' that could provide protection of a woman against alleged honour-related persecution by her husband whom she wanted to divorce.[269] Furthermore, the Court has ruled that if an applicant runs a real risk of ill-treatment in a part of the country, expulsion is nevertheless allowed if in another part of the country no such risk is incurred.[270] In *Salah Sheekh*, it ruled

---

[263]   *NA v. United Kingdom*, *supra* n. 260, para. 116.

[264]   *Salah Sheekh v. The Netherlands*, ECtHR 11 January 2007, appl. no. 1948/04.

[265]   *NA v. United Kingdom*, *supra* n. 260, para. 117.

[266]   *J.K. and Others v. Sweden*, *supra* n. 19, paras. 80–105, in which the Grand Chamber elucidates issues concerning the distribution of the burden of proving a 'real risk' of treatment prohibited by Art. 3 in the case of expulsion.

[267]   Directive 2004/83 (now replaced by Directive 2011/95); *cf. Sufi and Elmi v. United Kingdom*, *supra* n. 262, para. 226.

[268]   *H.L.R. v. France*, ECtHR (GC) 29 April 1997, appl. no. 24573/94, para. 40. *Cf.* also *J.K. and Others v. Sweden*, *supra* n. 19, para. 80.

[269]   *A.A. v. Sweden*, ECtHR 28 June 2012, appl. no. 14499/09, para. 90.

[270]   *Hilal v. United Kingdom*, ECtHR 6 March 2001, appl. no. 45276/99, paras. 67–68.

that expulsion to the 'relatively safe areas' of Puntland was allowed for only if the applicant could safely travel to the area, gain admittance and settle there.[271]

6.5. PROCEDURAL ASPECTS

As observed above, the prohibition on expulsion in case of a real risk of ill-treatment has been labelled as a negative obligation. In *F.G. v. Sweden*, in which case the applicant only at a late stage in the domestic asylum proceedings alleged that he risked ill-treatment in Iran due to his conversion to Christianity after arriving in Sweden, the Court ruled that expulsion without assessment of (that part of) the claim amounted to a violation.[272] Thus, the prohibition on expulsion implies a procedural obligation.

As to the burden of proof, it is in principle for the applicant to adduce evidence showing that he runs a real risk of being subjected to treatment contrary to Article 3.[273] But the Court acknowledges that 'it is frequently necessary to give [asylum seekers] the benefit of the doubt when it comes to assessing the credibility of their statements and the documents submitted in support thereof'.[274] Thus, in principle statements by the applicant must be accepted. But 'when information is presented which gives strong reasons to question the veracity of an asylum-seeker's submissions, the individual must provide a satisfactory explanation for the alleged discrepancies'.[275]

The division of the burden of proof as described above applies in claims based on individual risk ('special distinguishing features'). It suffers exception if the claim for protection is based on 'a well-known general risk' (a general situation of violence as meant in *NA v. United Kingdom*) or if 'the asylum seeker may, plausibly, be a member of a group systematically exposed to a practice of ill-treatment': then, the risk must be assessed by the authorities 'on their own motion'.[276]

Risk assessment concerns the foreseeable consequences of the applicant's removal to the country of destination. Hence, if the applicant has been removed by the time the Court decides the case, the relevant moment in time is that of the removal.[277] Accordingly, the fact that some of the applicants in *Vilvarajah* had been ill-treated upon return was not decisive as the UK authorities could not have foreseen that.[278] In many cases however, removal has not yet taken

---

[271]   *Salah Sheekh v. The Netherlands, supra* n. 264, para. 141.
[272]   *F.G. v. Sweden, supra* n. 250, para. 158.
[273]   *N. v. Finland*, ECtHR 26 July 2005, appl. no. 38885/02, para. 167.
[274]   E.g. *F.G. v. Sweden, supra* n. 250, para. 113.
[275]   *Ibid.*
[276]   *Hirsi Jamaa and Others v. Italy, supra* n. 152, paras. 131–133.
[277]   *Vilvarajah and Others v. United Kingdom, supra* n. 256, para. 108.
[278]   *Ibid.*, para. 112.

place; then the Court itself performs an *ex nunc* scrutiny, and demands that the domestic authorities also do so.[279]

6.6. EXPULSION TO UNSAFE THIRD COUNTRIES

In *T.I. v. United Kingdom*, the Court decided that obligations under Article 3 ECHR may be engaged when a state (the second country, the country of reception) expels an applicant to another country (the third country) than the country of origin where the applicant allegedly runs a real risk of ill-treatment (the first country).[280] It concerned the transfer of an asylum seeker from Sri Lanka by the UK to Germany. As the applicant had 'an arguable claim' that ill-treatment would take place if returned to Sri Lanka, the UK should be satisfied that 'effective procedural safeguards of any kind protecting the applicant from being removed from Germany to Sri Lanka'. It turned out such safeguards were in place. That was not the case in *M.S.S. v. Belgium and Greece*, concerning the transfer of an asylum seeker by Belgium to Greece; the Court had established that due to, *inter alia*, the complete absence of an adequate procedure Greece would violate Article 3. Here, the Court found that 'numerous reports' showed 'the deficiencies of the asylum procedure and the practice of direct or indirect *refoulement* on an individual or a collective basis' by the Greek authorities, and the Belgian authorities knew or ought to have known that.[281] So the Court concluded that the transfer to Greece by Belgium was a violation of Article 3 ECHR.[282] The same principle, *a fortiori* applies to removals to intermediary countries that are not bound by the European Convention.[283]

The Court addressed the issue of the reception of asylum seekers once again in *Tarakhel*. This case concerned the transfer to Italy of a family who had sought asylum in Switzerland. Although the Italian reception facilities could 'in no way be compared' with those in Greece,[284] there appeared to be a shortage of facilities adapted to young children. Hence, a transfer would be allowed only after the Swiss received 'detailed and reliable information concerning the specific facility, the physical reception conditions and the preservation of the family unit[y]'.[285]

---

[279] *Chahal v. United Kingdom, supra* n. 7, para. 86; *Salah Sheekh v. The Netherlands, supra* n. 264, para. 136.

[280] *T.I. v. United Kingdom*, ECtHR 7 March 2000 (dec.), appl. no. 43844/98.

[281] *M.S.S. v. Belgium and Greece, supra* n. 71, paras. 347 and 359.

[282] *Ibid.*, para. 360.

[283] *Hirsi Jamaa and Others v. Italy, supra* n. 152, paras. 153 and 158.

[284] *Tarakhel v. Switzerland*, ECtHR (GC) 4 November 2014, appl. no. 29217/12, para. 114.

[285] *Ibid.*, para. 121.

6.7. DIPLOMATIC ASSURANCES

In order to reconcile the absolute protection of Article 3 ECHR with the exigencies of national security, states can preclude possible ill-treatment through obtaining diplomatic guarantees from the receiving state, ascertaining that the person to be extradited will be treated in accordance with the standards set by Article 3 ECHR. In *Othman*, regarding the extradition of a terrorism suspect convicted *in absentia* in Jordan 'of conspiracy to cause explosions',[286] the Court summed up the factors relevant for assessing the quality of these assurances it had identified in an array of earlier cases. Assurances should, amongst other things, be public, specific and issued by a person that binds the receiving state, including local authorities. Furthermore, the strength of the relations between both states is relevant, as well as whether NGOs, diplomats and local courts can in fact monitor compliance.[287] The assurances as regards ill-treatment issued by Jordan turned out to be sufficient (although expulsion would violate Article 6 as in a retrial the authorities were likely to use evidence previously obtained by torture).

6.8. DEATH PENALTY

In the *Soering* case, the Court ruled that the death penalty cannot, in itself, raise an issue under Article 3 of the Convention, since Article 2 of the Convention expressly permits its imposition.[288] But in *Al-Saadoon* the Court observed that most states had signed and ratified Protocol No. 13 (which provides for the abolition of the death penalty in times of peace as well as in times of war), so that the wording of Article 2 no longer is a bar to the interpretation that the death penalty constitutes 'inhuman or degrading treatment or punishment'.[289]

6.9. SOCIO-ECONOMIC FACTORS AND MEDICAL CASES

In *D. v. United Kingdom*, the Court concluded that the removal of a terminally ill person (in the final stage of AIDS) to a country where there was no adequate medical care would expose him to a real risk of dying under most distressing circumstances and would thus amount to inhuman treatment (see also *supra* section 4.4).[290] The case differed from usual removal cases, in that the risk did not stem from factors emanating directly or indirectly the responsibility of the authorities of the receiving state, St. Kitts; rather, it concerned a disease and

---

[286] *Othman (Abu Qatada) v. United Kingdom*, ECtHR 17 January 2012, appl. no. 8139/09, para. 9.
[287] *Ibid.*, para. 184.
[288] *Soering v. United Kingdom, supra* n. 1, para. 103.
[289] *Al-Saadoon and Mufhdi v. United Kingdom, supra* n. 153, para. 120.
[290] *D. v. United Kingdom, supra* n. 186, para. 53.

the absence of medical and social support. The Court emphasised that such an obligation applies only in 'exceptional circumstances'; furthermore, instead of a real risk of suffering, certainty of imminent death was required. In *N. v. United Kingdom*, concerning an HIV-infected mother of two who allegedly could not in fact obtain medication once expelled, the Court explained its rigorous approach by pointing out that '[a]dvances in medical science, together with social and economic differences between countries, entail that the level of treatment available in the Contracting State and the country of origin may vary considerably … Article 3 does not place an obligation on the Contracting State to alleviate such disparities through the provision of free and unlimited health care to all aliens without a right to stay within its jurisdiction. A finding to the contrary would place too great a burden on the Contracting States.'[291]

In *Paposhvili v. Belgium*, the Court somewhat relinquished its approach. The case concerned the decision to expel a person suffering from leukaemia to Georgia. The Court ruled that the (very) exceptional circumstances required in *D. v. United Kingdom* also refer to the removal of a person who, 'although not at imminent risk of dying, would face a real risk, on account of the absence of appropriate treatment in the receiving country or the lack of access to such treatment, of being exposed to a serious, rapid and irreversible decline in his or her state of health resulting in intense suffering or to a significant reduction in life expectancy.'[292] It further stated that the real risk standard applies.[293]

Already before *Paposhvili*, the Court had accepted exceptions to the rigid stance in *N. v. United Kingdom*. In *Sufi and Elmi*, concerning expulsion to Somalia, it ruled that if very dire 'humanitarian conditions were solely or even predominantly attributable to poverty or to the State's lack of resources to deal with a naturally occurring phenomenon, such as a drought', the *N. v. United Kingdom* test would apply, but because the humanitarian 'crisis is predominantly due to the direct and indirect actions of the parties to the conflict' that counts as a 'treatment', just as it did in *M.S.S. v. Belgium and Greece* (see *supra* section 4.5, Socio-economic obligations for a discussion of the case). And in the extradition case of *Aswat v. United Kingdom*, the Court ruled that the applicant's extradition to the United States, where he was being prosecuted for terrorist activities, would entail ill-treatment, because the conditions of detention in the maximum security prison where he would be placed were liable to aggravate his paranoid schizophrenia.[294]

---

291   *N. v. United Kingdom*, ECtHR (GC) 27 May 2008, appl. no. 26565/05, para. 44.
292   *Paposhvili v. Belgium*, *supra* n. 160, paras. 177 and 183.
293   *Ibid.*, para. 186.
294   *Aswat v. United Kingdom*, ECtHR 16 April 2013, appl. no. 17299/12, para. 57.

CHAPTER 8

PROHIBITION OF SLAVERY AND FORCED LABOUR

(Article 4)

Leo Zwaak[*]

GUIDING PRINCPLE

Article 4 enshrines one of the most fundamental values of a democratic society. Article 4(1) requires that 'no one shall be held in slavery or servitude'. Unlike most of the substantive clauses of the Convention, Article 4(1) makes no provision for exceptions and no derogation from it is permissible under Article 15 (2) even in the event of a public emergency threatening the life of the nation. Article 4(2) prohibits forced or compulsory labour. Article 4(3) delimits the very content of that right, for it forms a whole with paragraph 2 and indicates what the term 'forced or compulsory labour' is not to include.

ARTICLE 4

1. No one shall be held in slavery or servitude.
2. No one shall be required to perform forced or compulsory labour.
3. For the purpose of this Article the term `forced or compulsory labour' shall not include:
    a) any work required to be done in the ordinary course of detention imposed according to the provisions of Article 5 of this Convention or during conditional release from such detention;
    b) any service of a military character or, in case of conscientious objectors in countries where they are recognised, service exacted instead of compulsory military service;
    c) any service exacted in case of an emergency or calamity threatening the life or well-being of the community;
    d) any work or service which forms part of normal civic obligations.

---

[*]   In the fourth edition this chapter was revised and updated by Leo Zwaak.

CONTENTS

1. INTRODUCTION

In Article 4 slavery and servitude are dealt with separately from forced and compulsory labour. The first two terms refer to the status or situation of the person concerned. In considering the scope of the notion of 'slavery' under Article 4, the Court refers to the classic definition of slavery contained in the 1926 Slavery Convention, which defines slavery as 'the status or condition of a person over whom any or all of the powers attaching to the right of ownership are exercised'.[1] Forced labour and compulsory labour, on the other hand, do not refer to the entire situation of the person concerned, but exclusively to the involuntary character of the work and services to be performed by him, which may, and usually will, also have a temporary or incidental character. Together with Articles 2 and 3, Article 4 of the Convention enshrines one of the basic values of the democratic societies making up the Council of Europe.[2] In the *Rantsev* case, the Court held that, like slavery, trafficking in human beings is, by its very nature and aim of exploitation, based on the exercise of powers attaching to the right of ownership. It treats human beings as commodities to be bought and sold and put to forced labour and implies close surveillance of the activities of victims, whose movements are often circumscribed. Also, it involves the use of violence and threats against victims. Accordingly, trafficking itself is prohibited by Article 4 ECHR. The Court concluded that as with Articles 2 and 3 of the Convention, Article 4 may in general, in certain circumstances, require a state to take operational measures to protect victims, or potential victims, of treatment

---

[1]   *Siliadin v. France*, ECtHR 26 July 2005, appl. no. 73316/01, para. 122.
[2]   *Stummer v. Austria*, ECtHR (GC) 7 July 2011, appl. no. 37452/02, 116; *Siliadin v. France, supra* n. 1, para. 82; *C.N and V v. France*, ECtHR 11 October 2012 appl. no. 67724/09, para. 65.

in breach of that article.[3] In order to comply with this obligation, member states are required to put in place a legislative and administrative framework to prohibit and punish human trafficking. The Court observed that the Palermo Protocol and the Anti-Trafficking Convention refer to the need for a comprehensive approach to combat trafficking which includes measures to prevent trafficking and to protect victims, in addition to measures to punish traffickers. It was clear from the provisions of these two instruments that the Contracting States, including almost all of the member states of the Council of Europe, have formed the view that only a combination of measures addressing all three aspects could be effective in the fight against trafficking. Accordingly, the duty to penalise and prosecute trafficking is only one aspect of member states' general undertaking to combat trafficking. Under Article 15(2) no derogation from the first paragraph of Article 4 is permitted under any circumstances. Derogations from the second paragraph, apart from the cases mentioned in the third paragraph, are allowed only under the conditions and restrictions mentioned in Article 15. The specific structure of Article 4, paragraph 3 is not intended to 'limit' the exercise of the right guaranteed by paragraph 2, but to 'delimit' the very content of that right, for it forms a whole with paragraph 2 and indicates what the term 'forced or compulsory labour' is not to include. This being so, paragraph 3 serves as an aid to the interpretation of paragraph 2. The four subparagraphs of paragraph 3, notwithstanding their diversity, are grounded on the governing ideas of general interest, social solidarity and what is normal in the ordinary course of affairs.[4]

2. POSITIVE OBLIGATIONS

In the *Siliadin* case, the Court considered that limiting compliance with Article 4 of the Convention only to direct action by the state authorities would be inconsistent with the international instruments specifically concerned with this issue and would amount to rendering it ineffective. Accordingly, it necessarily follows from this provision that states have positive obligations, in the same way as under Article 3 for example, to adopt criminal law provisions which penalise the practices referred to in Article 4 and to apply them in practice.[5] The extent of the positive obligations arising under Article 4 must be considered within this broader context.[6]

In the case of *C.N. v. United Kingdom*, the Court held that in order for a positive obligation to take operational measures to arise in the circumstances

---

3   *Rantsev v. Cyprus and Russia*, ECtHR 7 January 2010, appl. no. 25965/04, paras. 200–282.
4   *Karlheinz Schmidt v. Germany,* ECtHR 18 July 1994, appl. no. 13580/88, para. 22; *Zarb Adami v. Malta*, ECtHR 20 June 2006, appl. no. 17209/02, para. 44.
5   *Siliadin v. France, supra* n. 1, para. 89.
6   *Ibid.*, para. 285.

of a particular case, it must be demonstrated that the state authorities were aware, or ought to have been aware that an identified individual had been, or was at real and immediate risk of being subjected to such treatment. In the case of an answer in the affirmative, there will be a violation of Article 4 where the authorities fail to take appropriate measures within the scope of their powers to remove the individual from that situation or risk.[7] In interpreting the concepts under Article 4, the Court relied on international instruments such as the ILO Convention No. 29 (Forced Labour Convention),[8] the 1926 Slavery Convention,[9] the Supplementary Convention on the Abolition of Slavery, the Slave Trade and Institutions and Practices Similar to Slavery,[10] and Council of Europe Convention on Action against Trafficking in Human Beings and the Protocol to Prevent, Suppress and Punish Trafficking in Persons, especially Women and Children supplementing the United Nations Convention against Transnational Organised Crime, 2000.[11] In the *Rantsev* case, the Court held that Cyprus violated Article 4 ECHR as it failed to meet its positive obligations arising under that article on two counts: first, its failure to put in place an appropriate legal and administrative framework to combat trafficking as a result of the existing regime of artiste visas, and, second, the failure of the police to take operational measures to protect Ms Rantseva from trafficking, despite circumstances which had given rise to a credible suspicion that she might have been a victim of trafficking.[12]

3. HUMAN TRAFFICKING

Article 4 makes no mention of trafficking, proscribing only 'slavery', 'servitude' and 'forced and compulsory labour'.[13] According to the Court, the absence of an express reference to trafficking in the Convention was unsurprising. The Convention was inspired by the Universal Declaration of Human Rights, proclaimed by the General Assembly of the United Nations in 1948, which itself made no express mention of trafficking. In its Article 4, the Declaration prohibited 'slavery and the slave trade in all their forms'. However, in assessing the scope of Article 4 of the Convention, sight should not be lost of the Convention's special features or of the fact that it is a living instrument which must be interpreted in the light of present-day conditions. The increasingly high standards required in the area of the protection of human rights and

---

7   *C.N. v. United Kingdom,* ECtHR 13 November 2012, appl. no. 4239/08, para. 67.
8   *Van der Mussele v. Belgium,* ECtHR 23 October 1983, appl. no. 8919/80, para. 32.
9   *Siliadin v. France, supra* n. 1, para. 122.
10   *C.N. and V. v. France, supra* n. 2, para. 90.
11   *Rantsev v. Cyprus and Russia, supra* n. 3, para. 282.
12   *Ibid.,* paras. 293 and 298.
13   *Ibid.,* para. 272.

fundamental liberties correspondingly and inevitably require greater firmness in assessing breaches of the fundamental values of democratic societies.[14] In the *Rantsev* case, the Court held that trafficking in human beings, by its very nature and the aim of exploitation, is based on the exercise of powers attaching to the right of ownership. Human trafficking treats human beings as commodities to be bought and sold and put to forced labour, often for little or no payment, usually in the sex industry but also elsewhere. It implies close surveillance of the activities of victims, whose movements are often circumscribed. It involves the use of violence and threats against victims, who live and work under poor conditions. In the Court's view, there could therefore be no doubt that trafficking threatened the human dignity and fundamental freedoms of its victims and could not be considered compatible with a democratic society and the values expounded in the Convention. The Court concluded that trafficking itself, within the meaning of Article 3(a) of the Palermo Protocol and Article 4(a) of the Anti-Trafficking Convention, falls within the scope of Article 4 of the Convention.[15]

4. SLAVERY

The first paragraph of Article 4 has been invoked mainly in connection with complaints of detainees against the obligation to perform work in prison. In those cases the Commission took the position that the terms 'slavery' and 'servitude' are not applicable to such a situation, while from the third paragraph under (a) of Article 4 it is evident that the drafters of the Convention did not wish to prohibit the imposition of such an obligation.[16] In the Siliadin case, the applicant arrived in France from Togo at the age of 15 years with a person who had agreed with her father that she would work until her air ticket had been reimbursed, that her immigration status would be regularised and that she would be sent to school. In reality, it appeared from the evidence that she worked in their house without respite for approximately 15 hours per day, with no day off, for several years, without ever receiving wages or being sent to school, without identity papers and without her immigration status being regularised. She was accommodated in their home and slept in the children's bedroom. The Court found that the treatment suffered by her amounted to servitude and forced and compulsory labour, although it fell short of slavery. It held that, although the applicant was clearly deprived of her personal autonomy, she was

---

14   *Ibid.*, para. 277.
15   *Ibid.*, paras. 281–282. See also *M. and Others v. Italy and Bulgaria*, ECtHR 31 July 2012, appl. no. 40020/03, para. 151.
16   *Twenty-one detainees v. Federal Republic of Germany*, EComHR 6 April 1968 (dec.), appl. nos. 3134/67, 3172/67, 3188 – 3206/67, Yearbook XI (1968), p. 528 (552).

not held in slavery as there was no genuine right of legal ownership over her, thus reducing her to the status of an 'object'.[17] In the case of *M. and Others v. Italy and Bulgaria*, concerning alleged trafficking of a minor girl, the Court also considered that there was no sufficient evidence indicating that she was held in slavery. It held that, even assuming that the applicant's father received a sum of money in respect of the alleged marriage, in the circumstances of that case, such a monetary contribution could not be considered to amount to a price attached to the transfer of ownership, which would bring into play the concept of slavery. In this connection, the Court reiterated that marriage has deep-rooted social and cultural connotations which may differ largely from one society to another and that therefore this payment could reasonably be accepted as representing a gift from one family to another, a tradition common to many different cultures in today's society.[18]

5. SERVITUDE

In the *Siliadin* case, the Court held that for Convention purposes 'servitude' means an obligation to provide one's services that is imposed by the use of coercion, and is to be linked with the concept of slavery.[19] The Court held that with regard to the concept of 'servitude', what is prohibited is a 'particularly serious form of denial of freedom'. It includes, 'in addition to the obligation to perform certain services for others (…) the obligation for the "serf" to live on another person's property and the impossibility of altering his condition'.[20] In the *C.N* case, the Court noted that servitude was a specific form of forced or compulsory labour, or, in other words, 'aggravated' forced or compulsory labour. In the instant case, the essential element distinguishing servitude from forced or compulsory labour within the meaning of Article 4 was the victims' feeling that their condition could not be altered and that there was no potential for change. In this respect, it was enough that that feeling was based on objective elements created or maintained by those responsible.[21] Domestic servitude is a specific offence, distinct from trafficking and exploitation, which involves a complex set of dynamics, involving both overt and more subtle forms of coercion, to force compliance.[22]

---

17 *Siliadin v. France, supra* n. 1, para. 122.
18 *M. and Others v. Italy and Bulgaria, supra* n. 15, para. 151.
19 *Siliadin v. France, supra* n. 1, para. 124; *Sequin v. France*, ECtHR 7 March 2000 (dec), appl. no. 42400/98.
20 *Siliadin v. France, supra* n. 1, para. 123.
21 *C.N. and V. v. France, supra* n. 2, para. 91.
22 *C.N. v. United Kingdom, supra* n. 7, para. 80.

6. FORCED OR COMPULSORY LABOUR

The Court has refrained from giving a definition of the term 'forced or compulsory labour'. However, in the *Karlheinz Schmidt* case, the Court reiterated that 'paragraph 3 of Article 4 is not intended to "limit" the exercise of the right guaranteed by paragraph 2, but to "delimit" the very content of that right, for it forms a whole with paragraph 2 and indicates what "the term 'forced or compulsory labour' shall not include" (ce qui "n'est pas considéré comme 'travail forcé ou obligatoire'"). This being so, paragraph 3 serves as an aid to the interpretation of paragraph 2. The four subparagraphs of paragraph 3, notwithstanding their diversity, are grounded on the governing ideas of the general interest, social solidarity and what is normal in the ordinary course of affairs.'[23]

The first adjective '*forced*' brings to mind the idea of physical or mental constraint. As regards the second adjective '*compulsory*', it cannot refer just to any form of legal compulsion or obligation. For example, work to be carried out in pursuance of a freely negotiated contract cannot be regarded as falling within the scope of Article 4 on the sole ground that one of the parties has undertaken with the other to do that work and will be subject to sanctions if he does not honour his promise.[24] As to the second criterion, namely whether the applicant offered himself voluntarily for the work in question, the Court took into account but did not give decisive weight to the element of the applicant's prior consent to the tasks required.[25] Having held that there existed a risk comparable to 'the menace of [a] penalty' and then that relative weight is to be attached to the argument regarding the applicant's 'prior consent', the Court had regard to all the circumstances of the case in the light of the underlying objectives of Article 4 in order to determine whether the service required of Mr. Van der Mussele fell within the prohibition of compulsory labour. This could be so in the case of a service required in order to gain access to a given profession, if the service imposed a burden which was so excessive or disproportionate to the advantages attached to the future exercise of that profession, that the service could not be treated as having been voluntarily accepted beforehand; this could apply, for example, in the case of a service unconnected with the profession in question.[26]

In the *Van der Mussele* case, the Court used as a starting point for the interpretation of 'compulsory labour' the definition given in Article 2 of ILO Convention No. 29:[27] 'all work or service which is exacted from any person

---

[23]   *Karlheinz Schmidt v. Germany, supra* n. 4, para. 22; *Zarb Adami v. Malta, supra* n. 4, para. 44.

[24]   *Van der Mussele v. Belgium, supra* n. 8, para. 34.

[25]   *Van der Mussele v. Belgium, supra* n. 8, para. 36; *Graziani-Weiss v. Austria,* ECtHR 18 October 2011, appl. no. 31950/06, para. 40.

[26]   *Van der Mussele v. Belgium, supra* n. 8, para. 37.

[27]   International Labour Office, *Conventions and Recommendations 1919–1966* (1966), p. 155.

under the menace of any penalty and for which the said person has not offered himself voluntarily'.[28]

Although a refusal to act as a free legal aid counsel was not punishable by any sanction of a criminal law character, the Court concluded that there was a 'menace of any penalty', since with such a refusal the applicant would run the risk of his name being struck off the roll of pupils or of a rejection of his application for entry in the register of advocates.[29] The Court subsequently observed that the applicant had to accept the requirement concerned, whether he wanted to or not, in order to become an *avocat* and that his consent was determined by the normal conditions of exercise of the profession at the relevant time. Moreover, according to the Court, it should not be overlooked that the acceptance by the applicant was the acceptance of a legal regime of a general character. To decide whether the service required fell within the prohibition of compulsory labour, the Court held that it should have regard to all the circumstances of the case in the light of the underlying objectives of Article 4.[30]

However, the Court also fails to give clear guidelines with respect to the interpretation of 'forced or compulsory labour'. It restricts itself to an investigation of all the circumstances of the case, each of which, according to the Court, 'provides a standard of evaluation'.[31] These standards were in this case the following: the services did not fall outside the ambit of the normal activities of an *avocat*; a compensatory factor was to be found in the advantages attaching to the profession; the services contributed to the professional training of the applicant; the service was a means of securing the benefit, laid down in Article 6(3)(c), and could be seen as a 'normal civic obligation' as referred to in Article 4(3)(d); and, lastly, the burden imposed was not disproportionate, since it only took about 18 hours of the working time.[32] The Court concluded that, although the situation could be characterised as unsatisfactory because of the absence of any fee and the non-reimbursement of incurred expenditure, it did not constitute a violation of Article 4 of the Convention.[33]

The standards developed by the Court for evaluating what could be considered normal in respect of duties incumbent on members of a particular profession take into account whether the services rendered fall outside the ambit of the normal professional activities of the person concerned; whether the services are remunerated or not or whether the service includes another compensatory factor; whether the obligation is founded on a conception of social solidarity; and whether the burden imposed is disproportionate.[34] In

---

[28] *Van der Mussele v. Belgium, supra* n. 8, paras. 32–33.
[29] *Ibid.,* para. 35.
[30] *Idem.*
[31] *Ibid.,* para. 39.
[32] *Ibid.,* para. 39.
[33] *Ibid.,* para. 40.
[34] *Graziani-Weiss v. Austria, supra* n. 25, para. 38.

the case of *Graziani-Weiss*, the refusal to act as a guardian can give rise to disciplinary sanctions for practising lawyers and public notaries.[35] In the case of *Siliadin,* the Court considered that, although the applicant, a minor, was not threatened by a '*penalty*', the fact remained that she was in an equivalent situation in terms of the perceived seriousness of the threat as she was an adolescent girl in a foreign land, unlawfully present on French territory and in fear of arrest by the police. Her fear was nurtured and she was led to believe that her status would be regularised.[36]

In the *Schuitemaker* case, the applicant contended that she was forced to seek and take up employment which was deemed 'generally accepted' as opposed to 'suitable', and that this might result in her having to accept employment unsuitable to her. She submitted that the introduction of such a new requirement compelled her to perform forced or compulsory labour. The Court noted that the obligation of which the applicant complained was in effect a condition for the granting of benefits pursuant to the Work and Social Assistance Act. In the view of the Court, it must in general be accepted that where a state has introduced a system of social security, it is fully entitled to lay down conditions which have to be met for a person to be eligible for benefits pursuant to that system. In particular, a condition to the effect that a person must make demonstrable efforts in order to obtain and take up generally accepted employment cannot be considered unreasonable in this respect. This is the more so given that Dutch legislation provides that recipients of benefits pursuant to the Work and Social Assistance Act are not required to seek and take up employment which is not generally socially accepted or in respect of which they have conscientious objections. Therefore, the condition at issue could not be equated with compelling a person to perform forced or compulsory labour within the meaning of Article 4(2) of the Convention.[37]

More recently, the Court concluded that a physician's obligation to participate in emergency medical service did not amount to compulsory or forced labour for the purposes of Article 4(2) and declared the relevant part of the application inadmissible as being manifestly ill-founded. The Court observed that the services to be rendered did not fall outside the ambit of a physician's normal professional activities. Notwithstanding the fact that the applicant, in his private practice, did not perform services which were remunerated under the public health insurance scheme, it could not be said that the service differed from a physician's usual work. Secondly, it should be noted that the services performed during emergency services were remunerated. A further compensatory factor was to be found in the advantage that the emergency service in principle freed the

---

[35]   *Ibid.*, para. 39.
[36]   *Siliadin v. France, ECtHR 26* July 2005, appl. no. 73316/01, para, 118.
[37]   *Schuitemaker v. the Netherlands*, ECtHR 4 May 2010, appl. no. 15906/08, para. 33.

applicant from the obligation to be *available* for his patients outside consultation hours, notwithstanding the fact that the applicant had chosen not to make use of this option. Moreover, the obligation to which the applicant objected was part of a scheme which is devised to unburden all practising physicians from the obligation to be available during night-time and at weekends and to ensure the availability of medical services during these times. To this extent, it was founded on a concept of professional and civil solidarity and was aimed at averting emergencies. Finally, the burden imposed on the applicant was not disproportionate.[38]

In order to clarify the notion of 'labour' within the meaning of Article 4(2), the Court specified that not all work exacted from an individual under threat of a 'penalty' is necessarily 'forced or compulsory labour' prohibited by this provision. Factors that must be taken into account include the type and amount of work involved. These factors help distinguish between 'forced labour' and a helping hand which could reasonably be expected of other family members or people sharing accommodation.[39] No issue was found to arise under Article 4 in cases where an employee was not paid for work done but the work was performed voluntarily and entitlement to payment was not in dispute[40]

7. EXCEPTIONS

7.1. WORK DURING DETENTION OR CONDITIONAL RELEASE

With respect to the exceptions mentioned in the third paragraph, the following observations may be made. The exception formulated under (a) for the work of detainees and conditionally released persons is put in quite general terms and – unlike Article 2(2)(c) of ILO Convention No. 29 – includes work on behalf of private enterprises and foundations. Complaints with respect to work of such a character have therefore been declared inadmissible by the Commission.[41]

The exception under (a) applies only to work 'in the ordinary course of detention'. In *Steindel v. Germany*[42], the classic *Vagrancy* cases, these words

---

[38] According to the findings of the Administrative Court of Appeal, it is merely envisaged to oblige the applicant to serve on 6 days during a 3-months-interval. This would leave the applicant ample time to take care of his patients in his private practice. Furthermore, his private patients are free to consult him when he is on service; *Steindel v. Germany*, ECtHR 14 September 2010 (dec.), appl. no. 29878/07.

[39] *C.N. and V. v. France*, *supra* n. 2, para. 74.

[40] *Sokur v. Ukraine*, ECtHR 26 November 2002 (dec.), appl. no. 29439/02.

[41] *Twenty-one detainees v. Germany*, *supra* n. 16 (552–558). In some of the Contracting States, however, the courts will have to apply that restriction on the ground of the direct applicability of Convention No. 29, ratified by those states.

[42] *Steindel v. Germany*, *supra* n. 38.

were interpreted by the Court to mean that it must be work directed at the rehabilitation of the prisoner.[43] Moreover, the Court's judgment would seem to imply that Article 4 is violated if the detention itself, in the course of which the work must be performed, conflicts with the first paragraph of Article 5.[44]

Article 4(3)(a) authorises work required to be done in the ordinary course of detention which has been imposed in a manner that does not infringe paragraph 1 of Article 5 or during conditional release from such detention.[45] In the *Stummer* case, the Court held that in establishing what is to be considered 'work required to be done in the ordinary course of detention', the Court will have regard to the standards prevailing in member states[46] The noted that while an absolute majority of Contracting States affiliate prisoners in some way to the national social security system or provides them with some specific insurance scheme, only a small majority affiliate working prisoners to the old-age pension system. Thus, Austrian law reflects the development of European law in that all prisoners are provided with health and accident care and working prisoners are affiliated to the unemployment insurance scheme but not to the old-age pension system.[47] The Court therefore considered that there was no sufficient consensus on the issue of the affiliation of working prisoners to the old-age pension system. It held that Rule 26.17 of the European Prison Rules, which provides that as far as possible, prisoners who work shall be included in national social security systems, reflects an evolving trend. However, this trend cannot be translated into an obligation under Article 4 of the Convention. Consequently, in the Court's view, the obligatory work performed by the applicant as a prisoner without being affiliated to the old-age pension system had to be regarded as 'work required to be done in the ordinary course of detention' within the meaning of Article 4(3)(a).[48]

It should finally be pointed out with respect to the exception under (a) that this exception does not relate exclusively to convicts – such as is the case in ILO Convention No. 29 – nor exclusively to persons whose detention is based on a judicial order – as Article 8 of the UN Covenant on Civil and Political Rights provides – but to all the situations of lawful deprivation of liberty mentioned in the first paragraph of Article 5.[49]

---

[43]   *De Wilde, Ooms and Versyp v. Belgium ('Vagrancy' Cases),* ECtHR 18 June 1971, appl. nos. 2832/66, 2835/66 and 2899/66, para. 90.

[44]   *Ibid.,* para. 89.

[45]   *Van Droogenbroeck v. Belgium,* ECtHR 24 June 1982, appl. no. 7906/77, para. 59.

[46]   *Stummer v. Austria, supra* n. 2, para. 128.

[47]   *Ibid.,* para. 131.

[48]   *Ibid.,* para. 132.

[49]   *X v. Switzerland,* EComHR 14 December 1979, appl. no. 8500/79, D&R 18 (1980), p. 238 (248), which was a case under Art. 5(1)(d).

7.2. MILITARY SERVICE OR SUBSTITUTE CIVILIAN SERVICE

The formulation of the exception under (b), concerning any service of a military character or, in case of conscientious objectors in countries where they are recognised, service exacted instead of compulsory military service too, departs from that of ILO Convention No. 29, where Article 2(2)(a) speaks of 'any work or service exacted in virtue of compulsory military service laws for work of a purely military character'. From the fact that in Article 4(3)(b) the confinement to 'compulsory military service' had not been adopted, the Commission originally concluded that 'it was intended to cover also the obligation to continue a service entered into on a voluntary basis'.[50] However, in our opinion in view of the rationale of this exception, as it appears in particular from the reference to the service exacted instead of compulsory military service, such an application is justified only for those cases where this voluntary military service takes the place of compulsory military service. In fact, in other cases it is not self-evident that military service should be entitled to a special position as compared with other public services in the national interest, such as, for instance, service in public medical institutions or for utility companies.

In the *Bayatyan* case, the Court for the first time ruled on the question of the applicability of Article 9 to conscientious objectors. Unlike the Commission, which refused to apply that article to such persons, the Court noted that Article 4(3)(b) excludes from the scope of 'forced or compulsory labour' prohibited by Article 4(2) 'any service of a military character or, in case of conscientious objectors in countries where they are recognised, service exacted instead of compulsory military service'. In this respect the *travaux préparatoires* on Article 4 state that: 'In sub-paragraph [(b)], the clause relating to conscientious objectors was intended to indicate that any national service required of them by law would not fall within the scope of forced or compulsory labour. As the concept of conscientious objection was not recognised in many countries, the phrase "in countries where conscientious objection is recognised" was inserted'.

In the Court's reading, the *travaux préparatoires* confirmed that the sole purpose of sub-paragraph (b) of Article 4(3) is to provide a further elucidation of the notion 'forced or compulsory labour'. In itself, the sub-paragraph neither recognises nor excludes a right to conscientious objection and should therefore not have a delimiting effect on the rights guaranteed by Article 9.[51] The Court

---

[50]   *W, X, Y and Z* v. *United Kingdom*, EComHR 19 July 1968 (dec.), appl. nos. 3435/67, 3436/67 and 3437/67, Yearbook XI (1968), p. 562 (594).

[51]   *Bayatyan v. Armenia*, ECtHR (GC) 7 July 2011, appl. no. 23459/03, paras. 99–100.

therefore held that Article 9 should no longer be read in conjunction with Article 4(3)(b) in such cases.[52]

7.3. SERVICE REQUIRED DURING AN EMERGENCY OR CALAMITY

The exception mentioned under (c) speaks for itself. Here the central issue is, of course, in what situation an 'emergency or calamity threatening the life or well-being of the community' is involved. It would, however, appear to be more in keeping with the terminology used not to think here of structural inconveniences like those concerned in that case, but of an acute emergency with a temporary character. Thus, one should think of services like aid in extinguishing a fire, urgent repairs of transport systems and dams, supply of water and food in case of a sudden shortage, transport of wounded persons or the evacuation of persons threatened by some danger, and similar incidental services which can be required of everyone in the public interest depending on everybody's capabilities and possibilities. There has been, however, considerable dissension within the Commission about the elements of the concept of 'forced' labour. This is evident from the *Iversen* case. In that case, the Norwegian legislation was brought in issue on the basis of which a dentist might be required to fill for some time a vacancy that failed to be filled after having been duly advertised. The complaint was declared by the Commission to be manifestly ill-founded. Two of the members of the Commission belonging to the majority considered the Norwegian measure justified on the basis of the ground mentioned in the third paragraph under (c): 'emergency or calamity threatening the life or well-being of the community'.[53] Four members of the majority of six, however, held that there was no question of forced or compulsory labour, because the service to be rendered was exacted for a limited time, was properly remunerated and was in keeping with the profession chosen by Iversen, while the law in question had not been applied against him in an arbitrary or discriminatory manner.[54] A minority of four members of the Commission, finally, were of the opinion that the above-mentioned circumstances did not exclude the applicability of the second paragraph, and that the possible application of the third paragraph called for a further examination.[55] In the light of this diversity of views within the Commission it is very curious indeed that the complaint was rejected as being manifestly ill-founded, which barred a thorough examination of the facts and a decision of the Court on this evidently controversial interpretation of the second paragraph. To date (December 2016) the Court has not dealt with this issue.

---

52   *Ibid.*, para. 109.
53   *Iversen v. Norway*, EComHR 17 December 1963 (dec.), appl. no. 1468/62, Yearbook VI (1963), p. 278 (328–330).
54   *Ibid.*, pp. 326–328.
55   *Ibid.*, pp. 330–332.

7.4. NORMAL CIVIC OBLIGATIONS

The exception mentioned under (d) refers to 'normal' civic obligations, which means that no urgent and unforeseen calamity is required. It is still restricted, however, to work and services in the general interest. The difference with the provision under (c) is mainly one of gradation: the circumstances do not have to be as serious and urgent, but on the other hand the duties which are imposed may not be as burdensome for the person involved.[56] The formulation of the provision does not exclude special duties for particular professions in the public interest. In fact, the word 'normal' does not necessarily refer to what may be required equally of everyone, but may also relate to what in the given circumstances may be required of the person in question according to general usage.[57] The rationale of the provision implies that it does not refer to the normal obligations resulting from a profession, such as free legal aid given by lawyers, normal night duties for nurses and the like, since no compulsion in the real sense is involved there as the person concerned may quit the job. The Court has found that 'any work or service which forms part of normal civic obligations' included: compulsory jury service.[58]

Finally, it is to be noted that a practice based on any of the above-mentioned exceptions loses its permissible character if it involves discrimination. By virtue of Article 14 it then resumes the character of compulsory labour contrary to the Convention. In the *Karheinz Schmidt* case, the applicant complained about the system which made it compulsory for men, but not women, to serve in the fire brigade or pay a financial contribution in lieu of such service. He claimed to be the victim of discrimination on the ground of sex in breach of Article 14 taken in conjunction with Article 4(3)(d). The Court considered that compulsory fire service constituted 'normal civic obligations' envisaged in Article 4(3)(d). It observed further that the financial contribution which was payable – in lieu of service – was a 'compensatory charge'. The Court therefore concluded that, on account of its close links with the obligation to serve, the obligation to pay also fell within the scope of Article 4(3)(d). However, the Court found a violation of Article 14 taken in conjunction with Article 4(3)(d).[59]

---

[56] In the Strasbourg case law a clear distinction has not yet been made, as appears from the decision on *S v. the Federal Republic of Germany*, EComHR 4 October 1984 (dec.), appl. no. 9686/82.

[57] *Cf. Van der Mussele v. Belgium, supra* n. 8, para. 36.

[58] *Zarb Adami v. Malta, supra* n. 4, para. 40.

[59] *Karlheinz Schmidt v. Germany, supra* n. 4, paras. 23–29.

CHAPTER 9

RIGHT TO LIBERTY AND SECURITY

(Article 5)

Edwin Bleichrodt[*]

GUIDING PRINCIPLE

The aim of Article 5 is to ensure that no one is arbitrarily deprived of his liberty. The article contains an exhaustive enumeration of the cases in which deprivation of liberty is allowed. The article also provides for procedural safeguards, such as the habeas corpus guarantee and the right to be informed promptly of the reasons of the arrest and the charge.

ARTICLE 5

1. Everyone has the right to liberty and security of person. No one shall be deprived of his liberty save in the following cases and in accordance with a procedure prescribed by law:
   (a) the lawful detention of a person after conviction by a competent court;
   (b) the lawful arrest or detention of a person for non-compliance with the lawful order of a court or in order to secure the fulfilment of any obligation prescribed by law;
   (c) the lawful arrest or detention of a person effected for the purpose of bringing him before the competent legal authority on reasonable suspicion of having committed an offence or when it is reasonably considered necessary to prevent his committing an offence or fleeing after having done so;
   (d) the detention of a minor by lawful order for the purpose of educational supervision or his lawful detention for the purpose of bringing him before the competent legal authority;
   (e) the lawful detention of persons for the prevention of the spreading of infectious diseases, of persons of unsound mind, alcoholics or drug addicts or vagrants;
   (f) the lawful arrest or detention of a person to prevent his effecting an unauthorised entry into the country or of a person against whom action is being taken with a view to deportation or extradition.
2. Everyone who is arrested shall be informed promptly, in a language which he understands, of the reasons for his arrest and of any charge against him.
3. Everyone arrested or detained in accordance with the provisions of paragraph 1(c) of this Article shall be brought promptly before a judge or other officer authorised by law to exercise judicial power and shall be entitled to trial within a reasonable time or to release pending trial. Release may be conditioned by guarantees to appear for trial.
4. Everyone who is deprived of his liberty by arrest or detention shall be entitled to take proceedings by which the lawfulness of his detention shall be decided speedily by a court and his release ordered if the detention is not lawful.
5. Everyone who has been the victim of arrest or detention in contravention of the provisions of this Article shall have an enforceable right to compensation.

---

[*] In the fourth edition this chapter was written revised and updated by Edwin Bleichrodt.

CONTENTS

1. INTRODUCTION

In Article 5 the right to liberty of person and that to security of person are mentioned in the same breath, while in the following part of the article it is only the right to liberty of person that is elaborated. The right to security of person must be seen in the light of the right to liberty of person and the protection of the individual against arbitrariness. The right to security of person has played a role in cases where prisoners have disappeared. In the *Kurt* case, the Court observed that the authorities did not conduct any meaningful investigation into the applicant's insistence that the individual concerned was in detention and that she was concerned for his life. The unacknowledged detention in the absence of the safeguards of Article 5 was considered a particularly grave violation of the right to liberty and the right to security of person.[1]

In the *Bozano* case, the Court held as follows: 'The Convention here (…) also requires that any measure depriving the individual of his liberty must be compatible with the purpose of Art. 5, namely to protect the individual from arbitrariness (…). What is at stake here is not only the "right to liberty", but also the "right to security of person".'[2]

The question arises, however, whether the purpose of the inclusion of the right to security of person is thus done justice. After all, the obligation to give legal protection to the right to liberty of person and the prohibition of arbitrariness in the restriction of that right result from Article 5 and the system of the Convention even without the addition of 'and security',[3] while the term 'security', according to normal usage, refers to more than mere protection against limitation of liberty. The Contracting States also have to give guarantees against other encroachments on the physical[4] security of persons and groups by the authorities as well as individuals, for instance, against unnecessary threats to the physical integrity of spectators during police action or against incitement to action against a particular group of persons.

2. DEPRIVATION OF LIBERTY

2.1. DIFFERENCE BETWEEN DEPRIVATION AND RESTRICTION OF LIBERTY

With respect to the right to liberty of person, in the Court's opinion Article 5 affords protection exclusively against *deprivation* of liberty, not against other restrictions of the physical liberty of a person. The Court infers this from the further elaboration of Article 5, where the terms 'deprived of his liberty', 'arrest' and 'detention' are used, and also from the fact that Article 2 of Protocol No. 4

---

[1]   *Kurt v. Turkey*, ECtHR 25 May 1998, appl. no. 24276/94, paras. 124–129. See also *Varnava and Others v. Turkey*, ECtHR (GC) 18 September 2009, appl. nos. 16064/90 et al.
[2]   *Bozano v. France*, ECtHR 18 December 1986, appl. no. 9990/82, para. 54.
[3]   See *Engel and Others v. the Netherlands*, ECtHR (GC) 8 June 1976, appl. nos. 5100/71; 5101/71; 5102/71; 5354/72; 5370/72, para. 58.
[4]   From its inclusion in Art. 5 it follows that, here, 'security' refers exclusively to physical security and not, e.g., to mental, economic, or social security.

contains a separate provision concerning the restriction of freedom of movement.[5] The right to liberty refers to the individual liberty in its classic sense, the physical liberty of the person.

In order to determine whether there has been *deprivation* of liberty the starting point is, in the opinion of the Court, the individual situation of the person concerned. Further, account must be taken of the special circumstances such as the type, duration, effects and manner of implementation of the measure in question. The degree of supervision and the effects on the possibilities of maintaining normal social contacts are also relevant. The underlying public interest motive, for example to protect the community against a perceived threat emanating from an individual, has no bearing on the question whether that person has been deprived of his liberty.[6]

Certain restrictions of the liberty of movement of soldiers – the obligation to be present in the barracks at particular times, also during leisure – which would constitute a deprivation of liberty for civilians, may be permitted if those restrictions are not 'beyond the exigencies of normal military service'.[7] In the *Engel* case, the Court made the following distinction: it held the so-called 'light arrest' and 'aggravated arrest' not to be in violation of Article 5, because the soldiers concerned were not confined, but were able to perform their normal service; this in contrast with 'strict arrest', which did imply confinement and, therefore, had to be reviewed for its justification, by reference to the exceptions of Article 5.[8] In the *Raimondo* case, the person concerned was placed under police supervision. He was also required to lodge a security of 2,000,000 lire as a guarantee to ensure that he complied with the constraints attaching to this measure, for example, an obligation to return to his house by 9 p.m. and not to leave it before 7 a.m. unless he had valid reasons for doing so and had first informed the relevant authorities of his intention. This measure did not, according to the Court, exceed the boundaries of the mere *restriction* of liberty.[9] A different result was reached in the *Guzzardi* case. In this case, a measure of police supervision was combined with enforced stay on an island, where freedom of movement was limited at night to a few buildings and in the

---

[5]   *Ibid.*; *Winterwerp v. the Netherlands*, ECtHR 24 October 1979, appl. no. 6301/73, para. 37; *Guzzardi v. Italy*, ECtHR 6 November 1980, appl. no. 7367/76, para. 39. In its report in *Bozano v. France*, ECtHR 18 December 1986, appl. no. 9990/82, the Commission came to the conclusion that Art. 5 amounts to a *lex specialis* in relation to the freedom of movement; report of 7 December 1984, A.111, p. 35. See also Ch. 21.

[6]   Remarkable in this context is *Austin and Others v. the United Kingdom*, ECtHR (GC) 15 March 2012, appl. nos. 39692/09; 40713/09 and 41008/09, paras. 58–59. In my opinion, the distinction between the nature of the restriction and the purpose of it is confused in this judgment.

[7]   Report of 19 July 1974, *Engel and Others v. the Netherlands*, ECtHR (GC) 8 June 1976, appl. nos. 5100/71; 5101/71; 5102/71; 5354/72; 5370/72, B.20 (1978), para. 69.

[8]   *Engel and Others v. the Netherlands*, ECtHR 8 June 1976, appl. nos. 5100/71; 5101/71; 5102/71; 5354/72; 5370/72, *supra* n. 3, paras. 61–63.

[9]   *Raimondo v. Italy*, ECtHR 22 February 1994, appl. no. 12954/87, paras. 13 and 39.

daytime to a small area of the island, while the possibilities of social contact with other persons apart from the nearest relatives was very limited. The Court held that deprivation of liberty was involved.[10] In the *Lavents* case, a detainee suffered a heart attack and was sent to a hospital. The Court found that the stay in the hospital implied a deprivation of liberty. It took into consideration that the applicant could not leave the hospital and was under constant supervision, while the restrictions were comparable to those in prison.[11] In the *Amuur* case, asylum seekers from Somalia were refused entry to France. They stayed in a transit zone of the airport. The Court held that the possibility to leave the transit zone of an airport is only theoretical if there is no other country that is prepared to grant entrance to the asylum seeker and to offer him protection comparable to the protection that he expects to find in the country where he is seeking asylum.[12] The measures amounted to a deprivation of liberty. On the other hand, in the specific situation in which the police decided to impose a cordon during a demonstration in order to prevent violence and the injury of persons and people were obliged to stay in the cordon for approximately seven hours, the Court held that the people were not deprived of their liberty.[13] A relevant factor was that the police planned to commence a controlled release just five minutes after the cordon was imposed and tried to release people several times, but their attempts failed owing to the violent and unco-operative behaviour of a significant minority both in the cordon and in the surrounding area outside. From the above case law, it appears that the dividing line between deprivation of liberty and other restrictions of liberty is by no means clear-cut; the distinction is one of degree or intensity rather than one of nature or substance.

The mere fact that a person has assented to his detention does not imply that the detention cannot be an unlawful deprivation of liberty. In the 'Vagrancy' cases, the Court held that 'the right to liberty is too important in a "democratic society" within the meaning of the Convention for a person to lose the benefit of the protection of the Convention for the single reason that he gives himself up to be taken into detention'.[14] In relation to the placement of mentally disordered persons in an institution, the Court has held that the notion of deprivation of liberty does not only comprise the objective element of a person's confinement in a particular restricted space for a not negligible length of time. A person can only be considered to have been deprived of his liberty if, as an additional subjective element, he has not

---

[10]   *Guzzardi v. Italy*, ECtHR 6 November 1980, appl. no. 7367/76, para. 95.

[11]   *Lavents v. Latvia*, ECtHR 28 November 2002, appl. no. 58442/00, para. 63. See also *Stanev v. Bulgaria*, ECtHR (GC) 17 January 2012, appl. no. 36760/06, paras. 121–132.

[12]   *Amuur v. France*, ECtHR 25 June 1996, appl. no. 19776/92 para. 48. See also *Shamsa v. Poland*, ECtHR 27 November 2003, appl. nos. 45355/99 and 45357/99, paras. 22–25.

[13]   *Austin and Others v. the United Kingdom*, ECtHR (GC) 15 March 2012, appl. nos. 39692/09; 40713/09 and 41008/09, *supra* n. 6, paras. 62–67.

[14]   *De Wilde, Ooms and Versyp v. Belgium ('Vagrancy' Cases)*, ECtHR 18 June 1971, appl. nos. 2832/66, 2835/66 and 2899/66, para. 65.

validly consented to the confinement in question. The Court has found that there was a deprivation of liberty in circumstances such as the following: (1) where the applicant, who had been declared legally incapable and admitted to a psychiatric hospital at his legal representative's request, had unsuccessfully attempted to leave the hospital; (2) where the applicant had initially consented to her admission to a clinic but had subsequently attempted to escape; and (3) where the applicant was an adult incapable of giving his consent to admission to a psychiatric institution which, nonetheless, he had never attempted to leave.[15, 16]

In some cases, the (delay in the) transition from a stricter form of detention to a more liberal one is at stake. In the *Ashingdane* case, there had been a 19-month-long failure to implement the applicant's transfer from a special psychiatric hospital to an ordinary psychiatric hospital with a more liberal regime. The Court noted that the place and conditions of detention had not ceased to be those capable of accompanying the lawful detention of a person of unsound mind. The delay thus was not a mischief against which Article 5(1) afforded protection. The Court is stricter when the transfer implies a change of the type of deprivation of liberty to which an applicant is subjected. In the *Mancini* case, the District Court had replaced the pre-trial detention of the applicants with the security measure of house arrest. However, owing to an organisational shortcoming that was attributable to the State, the applicants had not been able to leave the prison until six days later. Although the Court considered both imprisonment and house arrest deprivations of liberty, it concluded that the delay complained of constituted a violation of Article 5. Decisive was that the replacement of detention in prison with house arrest entails a change in the nature of the place of detention from a public institution to a private home.[17] Besides the gradual difference between deprivation of liberty and restriction of liberty, the Court introduced change of the type of deprivation of liberty as a possible criterion that may bring a delay of such change within the scope of Article 5. This makes the case law rather casuistic. The place of the detention may also be relevant in connection of Article 5(1) under (e), the lawful detention of persons for the prevention of the spreading of infectious diseases, of persons of unsound mind, alcoholics or drug addicts or vagrants.[18] In that context, its relevance for the applicability of Article 5 is more easily understandable, because the basis of the deprivation of liberty in those cases is often directly related to the place of the detention, often a clinic, and the possibilities of treatment.

---

[15] See, with references, *Stanev v. Bulgaria, supra* n. 11, para. 118.

[16] *H.M. v. Switzerland*, ECtHR 26 February 2002, appl. no. 39187/98, paras. 44–48.

[17] *Mancini v. Italy*, ECtHR 2 August 2001, appl. no. 44955/98, paras. 17–26. See also *Buzadji v. Moldova*, ECtHR 5 July 2016, appl. no. 23755/07, para. 104.

[18] See, e.g., *Morsink v. the Netherlands*, ECtHR 11 May 2004, appl. no. 48865/99 and *Brand v. the Netherlands*, ECtHR 11 May 2004, appl. no. 49902/99.

2.2. DEPRIVATION OF LIBERTY BY PRIVATE PERSONS

Under which circumstances are the Contracting States responsible for a deprivation of liberty that is primarily carried out by private persons? In the *Nielsen* case, the question arose whether a deprivation of liberty was at stake. The case concerned the hospitalisation for approximately six months of a 12-year-old boy in a psychiatric ward at a state hospital against his will, but with the consent of his mother as the sole holder of parental rights. The Court reached the opinion that Article 5 was not applicable in the case, since the hospitalisation was a responsible exercise of custodial rights by the mother.[19] The situation is different when the containment of the juvenile applicant or a legally incapacitated adult is ordered by a court, as in *D.G. v. Ireland* and in *Stanev*. The Court held in both cases that the applicant was deprived of his liberty within the meaning of Article 5.[20]

In the *Riera Blume* case, the applicants were members of a sect, who were arrested and released. After the decision to release them was taken, the applicants were taken by members of the police in official vehicles to a hotel, where they were handed over to their families with a view to their recovering their psychological balance. Once at the hotel, the applicants were subjected to a process of 'deprogramming'. They were taken to individual rooms under the supervision of private persons and they were not allowed to leave their rooms for the first three days. After 10 days, they were allowed to leave the hotel. On the last two days of their stay in the hotel they were questioned by public authorities. The Court considered the transfer to the hotel and the stay in the hotel for 10 days, on account of the restrictions placed on the applicants, as a deprivation of liberty. Since there was no legal basis for the deprivation of liberty, it was relevant to assess whether the detention fell under the responsibility of the State. The Court answered that question in the affirmative. The contribution of the authorities had been so decisive that without it the deprivation of liberty would not have occurred.[21] This criterion implies a causal connection between the part played by the authorities and the deprivation of liberty.

In the *Riera Blume* case, the police had played an active role. The question arises whether Article 5 may also be violated if the authorities merely play a passive role and acquiesce in the loss of liberty. Depending on the circumstances of the case, it is desirable that the guarantees of Article 5 are also applicable in

---

[19] *Nielsen v. Denmark*, ECtHR 28 November 1988, appl. no. 10929/84, paras. 70–72. In the *Ashingdane* case, the Court held that the enforced stay in an ordinary psychiatric hospital amounted to a deprivation of liberty. See *Ashingdane v. the United Kingdom*, ECtHR 28 May 1985, appl. no. 8225/78, para. 42.

[20] *D.G. v. Ireland*, ECtHR 16 May 2002, appl. no. 39474/98, paras. 72–73 and *Stanev v. Bulgaria*, *supra* n. 11, paras. 121–132. See also *Koniarska v. the United Kingdom*, ECtHR 12 October 2000 (dec.), appl. no. 33670/96.

[21] *Riera Blume and Others v. Spain*, ECtHR 14 October 1999, appl. no. 37680/97, paras. 29–30. See also *Storck v. Germany*, ECtHR 16 June 2005, appl. no. 61603/00, paras. 90–91.

situations in which the authorities are fully aware of the deprivation of liberty and in the position to put it to an end but fail to do so. In the *Storck* case, the Court stressed that Article 5(1) implies a positive obligation for the state to protect its citizens. The lack of any effective state control over the lawfulness of the detention in a psychiatric clinic was held not to be in conformity with this positive obligation.[22] Article 5 also requires the authorities to take effective measures to safeguard against the risk of disappearance.[23] Complaints about the investigation after a disappearance in a case where it was not beyond reasonable doubt that the authorities had taken away the persons were, however, examined under Article 13.[24]

In cases where individuals are under control of the authorities, the Court is rather strict. In the *Bilgin* case, the Court held as follows: 'Bearing in mind the responsibility of the authorities to account for individuals under their control, Article 5 requires them to take effective measures to safeguard against the risk of disappearance and to conduct a prompt and effective investigation into an arguable claim that a person has been taken into custody and has not been seen since.'[25]

2.3. EXTRA-TERRITORIALITY

The applicability of Article 5 is not limited to actions of a state within the borders of its own territory.[26] The acts of diplomatic and consular agents, who are present on foreign territory in accordance with provisions of international law, may amount to an exercise of jurisdiction when these agents exert authority and control over others. The Court has also recognised the exercise of extra-territorial jurisdiction by a Contracting State when, through the consent, invitation or acquiescence of the government of that territory, it exercises all or some of the public powers normally to be exercised by that government. In certain circumstances, the use of force by a state's agents operating outside its territory may also bring the individual thereby brought under the control of the state's authorities into the state's Article 1 jurisdiction. In the *Öcalan* case, the Court accepted that an arrest made by the authorities of one state on the territory of another state, without the consent of the latter, affects the person's individual rights to security under Article 5(1). Another exception to the principle that

---

[22] *Storck v. Germany*, ECtHR 16 June 2005, appl. no. 61603/00, *supra* n. 21, paras. 102–107.

[23] *Kurt v. Turkey*, ECtHR 25 May 1998, appl. no. 24276/94, *supra* n. 1, para. 124; *Timurtas v. Turkey*, ECtHR 13 June 2000, appl. no. 23531/94, para. 103.

[24] *Şarli v. Turkey*, ECtHR 22 May 2001, appl. no. 24490/94, para. 69.

[25] *Bilgin v. Turkey*, ECtHR 17 July 2001, appl. no. 25659/94, para. 149. See also *Orhan v. Turkey*, ECtHR 18 June 2002, appl. no. 25656/94, para. 369. See also *Kurt v. Turkey*, *supra* n. 1, para. 124. In the same sense *Timurtas v. Turkey*, *supra* n. 23, para. 103.

[26] See *Al-Skeini and Others v. the United Kingdom*, ECtHR 7 July 2011, appl. no. 55721/07 and *Hassan v. the United Kingdom*, ECtHR 16 September 2014, appl. no. 29750/09.

jurisdiction under Article 1 is limited to a state's own territory occurs when, as a consequence of lawful or unlawful military action, a Contracting State exercises effective control of an area outside that national territory. It is a question of fact whether a Contracting State exercises effective control over an area outside its own territory. In the *Hassan* case, a civilian had been captured by British troops in Iraq and transferred to United States custody in Camp Bucca. The Court held that Hassan was within the physical power and control of the United Kingdom soldiers and therefore fell within United Kingdom jurisdiction, also after entering Camp Bucca.

Article 5 of the Convention should be interpreted insofar as possible in light of the general principles of international law, including the rules of international humanitarian law which play an indispensable and universally-accepted role in mitigating the savagery and inhumanity of armed conflict.[27]

3. EXCEPTIONS TO THE PROHIBITION OF DEPRIVATION OF LIBERTY – ARTICLE 5(1)(a)–(f)

3.1. INTRODUCTION

Article 5(1) contains an enumeration of the cases in which deprivation of liberty is permitted. This is an exhaustive enumeration[28] that must be interpreted narrowly. Only such an approach is consistent with the aim and purpose of Article 5 to ensure that no one is arbitrarily deprived of his liberty.[29]

As appears from the inclusion in the second sentence of the words 'in accordance with a procedure prescribed by law', it is required for all the cases mentioned that the procedure by means of which the deprivation of liberty has been imposed, be regulated in the law of the country in question. That law does not have to be written law. The words 'prescribed by law' do not imply that in all cases a judicial procedure must have been followed, as is evident, in particular, from the cases under (c) and (f).

The question of whether a detention complies with the requirement 'a procedure prescribed by law' is closely related to the question of whether the detention was 'lawful'. These requirements, the latter of which is expressly mentioned in the individual exceptions under (a)–(f), and which are usually bracketed together by the Court, essentially refer back to national law. It means that the deprivation of liberty must be imposed in conformity with the

---

27 See *Hassan v. United Kingdom, supra* n. 26, para. 102.
28 *Ireland v. the United Kingdom*, ECtHR (GC) 18 January 1978, appl. no. 5310/71, para. 194.
29 *Quinn v. France*, ECtHR 22 March 1995, appl. no. 18580/91, para. 24. See also *Winterwerp v. the Netherlands*, ECtHR 24 October 1979, appl. no. 6301/73, para. 37.

substantive and procedural rules of the applicable national law. The Court is competent to review whether this requirement has been complied with, but is not called upon to give its own interpretation of national law.[30] It is also not its role to assess the facts which have led a national court to adopt one position rather than another.[31] The interpretation and application of national law is primarily left to the domestic authorities,[32] but in cases where a failure to comply with domestic law entails a breach of the Convention, the Court exercises a certain power to examine whether national law has been observed.

A period of detention is, in principle, 'lawful' within the meaning of Article 5(1) if it is based on a court order. Even flaws in the detention order do not necessarily render the detention unlawful, since not every defect is of a nature that it deprives the detention of its legal basis under domestic law.[33] Relevant is whether the meaning of the court order may be considered to have been clear to the applicant and whether the domestic court acted in bad faith or failed to apply domestic law correctly.[34] A detention which extends over a period of several months and which has not been ordered by a court or by a judge or any other person 'authorised (…) to exercise judicial power' cannot be considered 'lawful' in the sense of Article 5(1). In the Court's opinion, the protection afforded by Article 5(1) against arbitrary deprivations of liberty would be seriously undermined if a person could be detained by executive order alone following a mere appearance before the judicial authorities referred to in paragraph 3 of Article 5, as happened in the *Baranowski* case.[35] A failure to comply with a procedural rule of national law[36] may lead to a violation of Article 5(1). The latter occurred in the *Wassink* case, where a judge failed to comply with national law inasmuch as he authorised the confinement of the applicant after a hearing held without a registrar.[37]

Moreover, the Court must ascertain whether domestic law is in conformity with the Convention. The answer to the questions of whether the court is competent (under (a), (c) and (d)) and whether the arrest and detention are lawful, is determined essentially on the basis of national law. In that respect Article 5(1) lays down an obligation to comply with the substantive and

---

[30] See, e.g., *Winterwerp v. the Netherlands*, ECtHR 24 October 1979, appl. no. 6301/73, *supra* n. 29, para. 46; *Bozano v. France*, ECtHR 18 December 1986, appl. no. 9990/82, *supra* n. 2, para. 58; *Benham v. the United Kingdom*, ECtHR 10 June 1996, appl. no. 19380/92, paras. 39–47.

[31] *Kemmache v. France (No. 3)*, ECtHR 24 November 1994, appl. no. 17621/91, para. 44.

[32] *Bozano v. France*, ECtHR 18 December 1986, appl. no. 9990/82, *supra* n. 2, para. 58 and *Lukanov v. Bulgaria*, ECtHR 20 March 1997, appl. no. 21915/93, para. 41.

[33] *Douiyeb v. the Netherlands*, ECtHR (GC) 4 August 1999, appl. no. 31464/96, paras. 44–45 and *Nikolov v. Bulgaria*, ECtHR 30 January 2003, appl. no. 38884/97, para. 63.

[34] See, e.g., *Jecius v. Lithuania*, ECtHR 31 July 2000, appl. no. 34578/97, para. 68.

[35] *Baranowski v. Poland*, ECtHR 28 March 2000, appl. no. 28358/95, para. 57.

[36] *Bozano v. France*, ECtHR 18 December 1986, appl. no. 9990/82, *supra* n. 2, para. 54; *Van der Leer v. the Netherlands*, ECtHR 21 February 1990, appl. no. 11509/85, para. 22.

[37] *Wassink v. the Netherlands*, ECtHR 27 September 1990, appl. no. 12535/86, paras. 23–27.

procedural provisions of national law. But lawfulness also requires that any measure depriving the individual of his liberty must be compatible with the purpose of Article 5, namely, to protect the individual from arbitrariness.[38]

The words 'prescribed by law' are not merely a reference to domestic law. They refer also to the 'quality of the law' and require that the law is 'sufficiently accessible and precise'.[39] In addition, as the Court held in the *Kemmache* case, 'The notion underlying the term in question ['in accordance with a procedure prescribed by law'] is one of fair and proper procedure, namely that any measure depriving a person of his liberty should issue from and be executed by an appropriate authority and should not be arbitrary.'[40]

The last-mentioned requirement – the measure should not be taken arbitrarily – as inferred from the terms 'in accordance with a procedure prescribed by law' and 'lawful',[41] can be regarded as the guiding principle for the interpretation of Article 5. In view of that principle it must also be examined whether less severe measures than the deprivation of liberty could have sufficed. The detention of an individual is such a serious measure that it is only justified where other, less severe measures have been considered and found to be insufficient to safeguard the individual or public interest.[42]

The notion 'lawful', which figures in the individual exceptions, may also imply other requirements. These are discussed in the next section.

3.2. ARTICLE 5(1)(a)

The exception under (a) concerns the lawful detention of a person after conviction by a competent court. Three notions are to be discussed: 'competent court', 'lawful' and 'after conviction'.

The word 'court' implies that the conviction must be imposed by a judicial organ. A decision of the police or a public prosecutor is not sufficient,[43] no more

---

[38] See, e.g., *Lukanov v. Bulgaria*, *supra* n. 32, para. 41; *Giulia Manzoni v. Italy*, ECtHR 1 July 1997, appl. no. 19218/91, para. 21 and *K.-F. v. Germany*, ECtHR 27 November 1997, appl. no. 25629/94, para. 63.

[39] *Amuur v. France*, ECtHR 25 June 1996, appl. no. 19776/92, *supra* n. 12, para. 50; *Steel and Others v. the United Kingdom*, ECtHR 23 September 1998, appl. no. 24838/94, paras. 54–65 and *Baranowski v. Poland*, ECtHR 28 March 2000, appl. no. 28358/95, *supra* n. 35, paras. 51–52.

[40] *Kemmache v. France (No. 3)*, ECtHR 24 November 1994, appl. no. 17621/91, *supra* n. 31, para. 34. See also *Winterwerp v. the Netherlands*, ECtHR 24 October 1979, appl. no. 6301/73, *supra* n. 29, para. 45.

[41] See, e.g., *Bouamar v. Belgium*, ECtHR 29 February 1988, appl. no. 9106/80, para. 47; *Wassink v. the Netherlands*, *supra* n. 37, para. 24.

[42] *Witold Litwa v. Poland*, ECtHR 4 April 2000, appl. no. 26629/95, para. 78.

[43] With respect to the Belgian Advocate-Fiscal, see the report of 4 March 1978, *Eggs*, D&R 15 (1979), p. 35 (62).

---

than a decision of a military commander[44] or of an administrative organ. For an organ to be a judicial organ it must be 'independent both of the executive and of the parties to the case'.[45] It is not required that the members be jurists,[46] nor that they have been nominated for an indefinite period.[47] The question of whether the court is competent, is to be answered on the basis of national law.

The requirement that the deprivation of liberty must be lawful means not only that this particular penalty must find a sufficient basis in the conviction by the court concerned, but also – this in connection with Article 7 – that the facts to which the sentence relates constituted under municipal law, at the time the offence was committed, a punishable act for which the imposition of imprisonment was possible. In addition, the sentence on which the deprivation of liberty is based, must satisfy the provisions of the Convention. It must, for instance, have been pronounced on the basis of a fair and public hearing in the sense of Article 6. In the *Drozd and Janousek* case, the applicants were serving a term of 14 years' imprisonment in France, following their conviction by a court of the Principality of Andorra. They claimed a violation of Article 5(1) because the French courts had not carried out any review of the judgment of the foreign court, whose composition and procedure was, according to the applicants, not in conformity with the requirements of Article 6. Thus, the question arose whether the above-mentioned requirement also applies to sentences that have been passed in another country. The Court expressed as its view that the Contracting States are obliged to refuse their co-operation if it emerges that the conviction is the result of a flagrant denial of justice. However, there is no obligation to verify whether the proceedings which resulted in the conviction were compatible with *all* the requirements of Article 6.[48] The application of this standard, which lead to the conclusion, by 12 votes to 11(!), that Article 5(1) was not violated, is criticised by the minority of the Court because of the fact that the French representatives

---

[44]   Report of 19 July 1974, *Engel and Others v. the Netherlands,* ECtHR (GC) 8 June 1976, appl. nos. 5100/71; 5101/71; 5102/71; 5354/72; 5370/72, B.20 (1978), para. 84. A military commander can, however, order custody on remand, which is covered by para. 1(c): *De Jong, Baljet and Van den Brink v. the Netherlands*, ECtHR 22 May 1984, appl. nos. 8805/79, 8806/79 and 9242/81, paras. 43–44.

[45]   *Neumeister v. Austria,* ECtHR 27 June 1968, appl. no. 1936/63, para. 24. See also *De Wilde, Ooms and Versyp v. Belgium ('Vagrancy' Cases)*, ECtHR 18 June 1971, appl. nos. 2832/66, 2835/66 and 2899/66, *supra* n. 14, para. 77; *Ringeisen v. Austria*, ECtHR 16 July 1971, appl. no. 2614/65, para. 95 and *Engel and Others v. the Netherlands*, ECtHR (GC) 8 June 1976, appl. nos. 5100/71; 5101/71; 5102/71; 5354/72; 5370/72, *supra* n. 3, para. 68.

[46]   *X v. Sweden*, EComHR 8 February 1973, appl. no. 5258/71, Coll. 43 (1973), p. 71 (79).

[47]   The Dutch Supreme Military Court was recognised as a judicial organ in the *Engel* case, although the 4 military members could be discharged from their function by the King. In the opinion of the Commission and the Court the fact that these members had taken not only the judicial, but also the military oath also did not bar their independence: *Engel and Others v. the Netherlands,* ECtHR (GC) 8 June 1976, appl. nos. 5100/71, 5101/71, 5102/71, 5354/72 and 5370/72, *supra* n. 3, para. 68; report of 19 July 1974, B.20 (1978), para. 99.

[48]   *Drozd and Janousek v. France and Spain*, ECtHR 26 June 1992, appl. no. 12747/87, paras. 108–110. See *Iribarne Pérez v. France*, ECtHR 24 October 1995, appl. no. 16462/90, paras. 30–32.

---

in Andorra had the power to ensure that the Convention was respected: they had legislative powers and the competence to appoint judges in Andorra.[49]

The mere fact that a judicial sentence is annulled on appeal does not deprive the imprisonment imposed in execution of that sentence of its lawful character.[50] However, the matter may be different if the ground for annulment is precisely a manifest error with respect to municipal law or a violation of one of the provisions of the Convention, in particular of Articles 6 and 7.

The word 'conviction' has to be understood as signifying both a finding of guilt after it has been established in accordance with the law that an offence has been committed, and the imposition of a penalty or other measure involving deprivation of liberty.[51] If a person is not convicted or sentenced in view of his lack of criminal responsibility, his detention comes under Article 5(1) under (e) instead of (a).[52] A person detained on remand is to be considered, from the moment of his conviction by a court of first instance, as a detainee 'after conviction', so that from that moment and during appeal proceedings the lawfulness of that detention must be reviewed by reference to the provision under (a) and no longer by reference to that under (c).[53] This holds true even if under domestic law the person is still considered as a remand prisoner. The word 'after' in Article 5(1)(a) does not, according to the Court, simply mean that 'the "detention" must follow the "conviction" in point of time', but also that 'the detention must result from, follow, and depend or occur by virtue of, the conviction'.[54]

In the *Van Droogenbroeck* case, the applicant was sentenced by a criminal court to two years of imprisonment and was ordered to be 'placed at the Government's disposal' for 10 years. The Court had to decide whether there was sufficient connection, for the purpose of Article 5, between the sentence and the order, and the subsequent deprivation of liberty on two occasions as a result of the decisions by the Minister of Justice, following the applicant's disappearances. According to the Court, the sentence to imprisonment and the order to be placed at the Government's disposal constituted 'an inseparable whole'. The execution of the order could take several forms, which was a matter of discretion of the Minister of Justice. In this case, the way in which this discretion was exercised respected the requirements of the Convention.[55]

---

[49]   *Ibid.*, pp. 40–43.

[50]   *X v. Austria*, EComHR 24 May 1971, appl. no. 3245/67, Yearbook XII (1969), p. 206 (236); report of 9 March 1978, *Krzycki*, D&R 13 (1979), p. 57 (61).

[51]   *Van Droogenbroeck v. Belgium*, ECtHR 24 June 1982, appl. no. 7906/77, para. 35. See also *Guzzardi v. Italy*, ECtHR 6 November 1980, appl. no. 7367/76, *supra* n. 10, para. 100 and *B. v. Austria*, ECtHR 28 March 1990, appl. no. 11968/86, para. 38.

[52]   *Herczegfalvy v. Austria*, ECtHR 24 September 1992, appl. no. 10533/83, paras. 62–64.

[53]   *Wemhoff v. Germany*, ECtHR 27 June 1968, appl. no. 2122/64, para. 9; *Labita v. Italy*, ECtHR (GC) 6 April 2000, appl. no. 26772/95, paras. 145 and 147 and *Klyakhin v. Russia*, ECtHR 30 November 2004, appl. no. 46082/99, para. 57.

[54]   *X. v. the United Kingdom*, ECtHR 5 November 1981, appl. no. 7215/75, para. 39 and *B. v. Austria*, ECtHR 28 March 1990, appl. no. 11968/86, *supra* n. 51, para. 38.

[55]   *Van Droogenbroeck v. Belgium*, ECtHR 24 June 1982, appl. no. 7906/77, *supra* n. 51, paras. 39–40.

In the *Weeks* case, again, the 'sufficient causal connection between conviction and deprivation of liberty' was at issue. Here the applicant was sentenced to life imprisonment, but released on licence some 10 years later. However, the licence was revoked after 15 months by the Home Secretary. The reason for the sentence to life imprisonment was to make the applicant 'subject to a continuing security measure in the interests of public safety'. Since there was no medical evidence justifying an order to send him to a mental institution, this 'indeterminate sentence' would enable the Home Secretary to monitor his progress. The Court took the position that there were several similarities with an order to place someone at the disposal of the Government. However, the Court continued as follows: 'Applying the principles stated in the *Van Droogenbroeck* judgment, the formal legal connection between Mr. Weeks' conviction in 1966 and his recall to prison some ten years later is not on its own sufficient to justify the contested detention under Article 5, para. 1(a). The causal link required by subparagraph (a) (...) might eventually be broken if a position were reached in which a decision not to release or to re-detain was based on grounds that were inconsistent with the objectives of the sentencing court. In those circumstances, a detention that was lawful at the outset would be transformed into a deprivation of liberty that was arbitrary and, hence, incompatible with Article 5.'[56]

The Court reached the conclusion that the sentencing judges must be taken to have known and intended that it was inherent in Mr Weeks' life sentence that his liberty was at the discretion of the executive for the rest of his life, and that it was not for the Court, within the context of Article 5, to review the appropriateness of the original sentence.[57] Thus, the Court accepted a rather loose link between the original sentence and the renewed detention. However, the Court next examined whether the grounds on which the re-detention was based, were sufficient. Although, here again, the Court took as a starting point that a certain discretion has to be left to the national authorities in this matter, it conducted its own examination of the grounds in a rather detailed manner against the background of the original sentence.[58]

In the *Stafford* case, the Court noted that the finding in previous judgments that the mandatory life sentence according to English law constituted punishment for life and had to be distinguished from the discretionary life sentence, could no longer be regarded as reflecting the real position in the domestic criminal justice system of the mandatory life prisoner. That means that, once the punishment element of the sentence (as reflected in the tariff) has been satisfied, continued detention, as in discretionary life and juvenile murderer cases, depends on considerations of risk and dangerousness associated

---

[56]   *Weeks v. the United Kingdom*, ECtHR 2 March 1987, appl. no. 9787/82, para. 49.

[57]   *Ibid.*, paras. 50–51. See also *Ireland v. the United Kingdom*, ECtHR 16 December 1999, para. 118.

[58]   *Ibid.*, paras. 50–51. See also *Waite v. the United Kingdom*, ECtHR 10 December 2002, appl. no. 53236/99, para. 68.

with the objectives of the original sentence. In the applicant's case, the continued detention relied on the risk of non-violent offences, while the original sentence was based on murder. The Court found no sufficient causal connection.[59]

In the *Eriksen* case, which seems to be rather exceptional, the authorisation to use security measures had expired. The applicant, who had become aggressive after suffering brain damage as a result of a traffic accident, stayed in detention on remand pending proceedings instituted in order to have the authorisation extended. The Court stated that the detention in issue was directly linked to the applicant's initial conviction and could thus be regarded as 'lawful detention (…) after conviction by a competent court' for the purposes of Article 5(1) under (a). It considered that the prolonged detention, if granted, would have been based on the offences which had grounded the applicant's initial conviction. Furthermore, the detention was consistent with the objectives of that authorisation, in particular the serious danger that the person concerned would commit further criminal offences.[60]

3.3. ARTICLE 5(1)(b)

The first permissible form of deprivation of liberty mentioned under (b) – on account of non-compliance with a lawful order of a court – is clear. Here one may think, for instance, of non-compliance with orders of the courts to pay a fine,[61] of a refusal to comply with a civil sentence[62] or to submit to a blood test,[63] or of a measure to enforce an injunction concerning a statutory declaration of assets which the applicant had refused to make.[64]

In the *Steel* case, the Court examined whether the binding-over orders to keep the peace and to be of good behaviour that had been applied to the applicants, were specific enough properly to be described as 'lawful order[s] of a court'. In this respect, it noted that the orders were expressed in rather vague and general terms; the expression 'to be of good behaviour' was particularly imprecise and offered little guidance to the person bound over as to the type of conduct which would amount to a breach of the order. However, in each applicant's case the binding-over order was imposed after a finding that she had committed a breach of the peace. Having considered all the circumstances, the Court was satisfied that it was sufficiently clear that the applicants were being

---

[59] *Stafford v. the United Kingdom*, ECtHR (GC) 28 May 2002, appl. no. 46295/99, paras. 79–81.
[60] *Eriksen v. Norway*, ECtHR 27 May 1997, appl. no. 17391/90, paras. 82–84.
[61] *Tyrrell v. the United Kingdom,* ECtHR 4 September 1996 (dec.), appl. no. 28188/95.
[62] In which case Art. 1 of Protocol No. 4 must be observed by those countries which have ratified that Protocol.
[63] *I. v. Austria*, ECtHR 13 December 1979 (dec.), appl. no. 8278/78, D&R 18 (1980), p. 154 (156).
[64] *X. v. Federal Republic of Germany*, appl. no. 9546/81 (not published).

requested to agree to refrain from causing further, similar, breaches of the peace during the ensuing 12 months.[65]

The duration of the detention must be assessed in connection with the specific aim of the order. In the *Gatt* case, the Court held that a period of detention of more than five years and six months for failure to comply with a court order to pay EUR 23,300 as a result of a single breach of curfew imposed as a bail condition cannot be considered to strike a fair balance between the importance in a democratic society of securing compliance with a lawful order of a court and the importance of the right to liberty.[66] In the *Nowicka* case, the applicant's detention was carried out pursuant to a court order to secure the fulfilment of her obligation to submit to a psychiatric examination. The applicant was held in custody during several days before the (brief) examination was conducted and she remained in detention after the examination ended. Article 5(1) under (b) was violated.[67]

The second exception mentioned under (b) – deprivation of liberty in order to secure fulfilment of an obligation prescribed by law – is less clear. In fact, this wide formulation would seem to pave the way for a great many forms of deprivation of liberty without any judicial intervention, simply by the invocation of a legal norm, with the additional possibility of even taking preventive action before a norm has been violated. It is true that in those cases the fourth paragraph allows appeal to a court, but this does not alter the fact that such a wide interpretation of the second limb of paragraph 1(b) would erode many of the guarantees contained in the other provisions of Article 5. In the *Benham* case, the applicant claimed that his detention ordered by a court because he had not paid the Poll Tax owed by him, did not fall under sub-paragraph (b) since he did not have any means to pay the debt and, therefore, the detention could not have been intended 'to secure the fulfilment' of his obligation. The Court rejected this argument by merely stating that sub-paragraph (b) did apply because the purpose of the detention was 'to secure the fulfilment' of the applicant's legal obligations.[68]

In the *Engel* case, the Court held that 'any obligation' must relate to a 'specific and concrete obligation which the applicant has until then failed to satisfy'. In this case, the Supreme Military Court had invoked Article 5(1)(b) in order to justify an imposed 'strict arrest' as a provisional measure. The Court rejected this position, because it considered the general obligation to comply with military discipline not sufficiently specific.[69] The same applies to the duty not to commit a criminal offence in the imminent future.[70] In order to be covered by Article 5(1)(b), the

---

[65]   *Steel and Others v. the United Kingdom*, ECtHR 23 September 1998, appl. no. 24838/94, *supra* n. 39, paras. 75–76.

[66]   *Gatt v. Malta*, ECtHR 27 July 2010, appl. no. 28221/08, para. 43.

[67]   *Nowicka v. Poland*, ECtHR 3 December 2002, appl. no. 30218/96, para. 61.

[68]   *Benham v. the United Kingdom*, ECtHR 10 June 1996, appl. no. 19380/92, *supra* n. 30, para. 39.

[69]   *Engel and Others v. the Netherlands*, ECtHR (GC) 8 June 1976, appl. nos. 5100/71, 5101/71, 5102/71, 5354/72 and 5370/72, *supra* n. 3, para. 69; report of 19 July 1974, B.20 (1978), p. 64. See *Guzzardi v. Italy*, ECtHR 6 November 1980, appl. no. 7367/76, *supra* n. 10, para. 101.

[70]   *Schwabe and M.G. v. Germany*, ECtHR 1 December 2011, appl. nos. 8080/08 and 8577/08, para. 82.

arrest and detention must further aim at or directly contribute to securing the fulfilment of the obligation and not be punitive in character. In the *Ostendorf* case, the police took the applicant into custody in order to prevent him from arranging a brawl between hooligans in the context of the football match. The Court considered that, by certain specific preventive measures, the applicant had been made aware of the fact that the police intended to avert a hooligan brawl and that he was under a specific obligation to refrain from arranging and/or participating in such a brawl. The applicant had shown that he was not willing to comply with his obligation to keep the peace. The applicant's detention, which served the purpose of preventing him from arranging and taking part in a hooligan brawl, was in this circumstances in conformity with Article 5(1)(b).[71]

In the above-mentioned *Steel* case, the applicants argued that Article 5(1)(b) was violated since a requirement in general terms 'to keep the peace' was not sufficiently concrete and specific to amount to an 'obligation prescribed by law'. The Court did not agree. It observed that the elements of breach of the peace were adequately defined by English law. Furthermore, it was clear that where magistrates are satisfied, on the basis of admissible evidence, that an individual had committed a breach of the peace and that there was a real risk that he or she would do so again, the accused may be required to enter into recognisances to keep the peace or be of good behaviour. Finally, it was also clear that, if the accused refuses to comply with such an order, he or she may be committed to prison for up to six months.

A balance must be drawn between the importance in a democratic society of securing the immediate fulfilment of the obligation in question and the importance of the right to liberty. The duration of the detention is a relevant factor in drawing such a balance.[72] Other relevant factors are: the nature of the obligation arising from the relevant legislation, including its underlying object and purpose; the person being detained; and the particular circumstances leading to the detention.[73] In the *Vasileva* case, the applicant had been arrested because she refused to comply with the obligation to disclose her identity to the police. Although the decision to arrest her was in conformity with Article 5(b), the duration of the detention was, in the context of the specific circumstances of the case, not proportionate to the cause of her detention.[74]

3.4. ARTICLE 5(1)(c)

The provision under (c) in Article 5(1) permits arrest or detention if there is a reasonable suspicion that an offence has been committed, or if this measure

---

[71]   *Ostendorf v. Germany*, ECtHR 7 March 2013, appl. no. 15598/08.
[72]   *Nowicka v. Poland*, ECtHR 3 December 2002, appl. no. 30218/96, *supra* n. 67, para. 61; *Epple v. Germany*, ECtHR 24 March 2005, appl. no. 77909/01, paras. 43–45.
[73]   *Vasileva v. Denmark*, ECtHR 25 September 2003, appl. no. 52792/99, para. 38.
[74]   *Ibid.*

is reasonably considered necessary to prevent an offence or to prevent flight after an offence has been committed. First of all, the relation between these three situations will be discussed. Next the terms 'competent legal authority', 'lawful'[75] and 'reasonable suspicion' will be dealt with. The third paragraph of Article 5 requires that everyone who is detained under sub-paragraph (c), shall be brought *promptly* before a judicial authority and is entitled to trial *within a reasonable time* or to release pending trial. These requirements will be discussed in connection with that provision.

Since the three grounds mentioned in paragraph 1 under (c) have been placed side by side and have not been made cumulative, the provision would appear to justify detention as a measure against persons on suspicion that they will commit crimes without their having as yet committed them. This interpretation is also corroborated by the *travaux préparatoires, viz.* in the report of the Senior Officials, in which it is stated as follows: 'it may (…) be necessary in certain circumstances to arrest an individual in order to prevent his committing a crime, even if the facts which show his intention to commit the crime do not of themselves constitute a criminal offence.'[76] That ground of detention does afford the authorities a means of preventing a concrete and specific offence and is not adapted to a policy of general prevention.[77]

One may wonder why the fear that the accused may flee after having committed an offence has been included as a separate ground, if the suspicion that such an offence has been committed or will be committed is in itself already a sufficient ground for arrest. A rational interpretation is reached if it is assumed that in this provision the grounds for arrest and those for continued detention have been joined. This would then produce the following picture: arrest is permitted in case of a reasonable suspicion that the accused has committed an offence or if the arrest may reasonably be considered necessary to prevent his committing an offence that he is reasonably suspected of planning to commit. For continuation of the detention it is additionally required that it is likely that he will abscond or that there are reasonable grounds for assuming that after his release the arrested person will again commit an offence.[78] This poses, however, the problem that it will then also have to be assumed that these latter grounds of continuation do not constitute an exhaustive enumeration, since the Strasbourg

---

75 The French version of Art. 5(1) under (c) makes no express reference to '*regularity*'. This is without importance because the notion 'lawful' is a general one which applies to the whole of Article 5(1); *Guzzardi v. Italy*, ECtHR 6 November 1980, appl. no. 7367/76, *supra* n. 10, para. 102.

76 Council of Europe, *Collected Edition of the 'Travaux Préparatoires' of the European Convention on Human Rights,* Vol. IV, Strasbourg, 1977, p. 260.

77 *M. v. Germany*, ECtHR 17 December 2009, appl. no. 19359/04, para. 89.

78 See Recommendation R(80)11 of the Committee of Ministers of 27 June 1980 on detention on remand, where the grounds are indeed formulated cumulatively in Art. 3, while Art. 4 provides that detention on remand without one of the grounds of the second category presenting itself 'may nevertheless exceptionally be justified in certain cases of particularly serious offences'.

organs have also recognised as such grounds the risk of suppression of evidence[79] and the danger of collusion.[80]

If a person is arrested on reasonable suspicion that he has committed an offence or in order to prevent his committing an offence or to prevent his fleeing after having done so, the conditions of the Convention are only met if the arrest or detention is really aimed at bringing the accused before a competent judicial authority. The list of grounds of permissible detention does not include internment or preventive detention without any intention to bring criminal charges within a reasonable time. The Court took this position as early as 1961 in the *Lawless* case.[81] In the *Brogan* case the applicants alleged that their arrest and detention were not intended to bring them before the competent legal authority; in fact, they were neither charged nor brought before a court. The Court held that the existence of such a purpose must be considered independently of its achievement. There was no reason to believe that the applicants' detention was not intended to further police investigation by way of confirming or dispelling concrete suspicions which grounded their arrest.[82] In this context the very vague term 'legal authority' must, in conformity with the third paragraph of Article 5, be deemed to mean 'judge or other officer authorised by law to exercise judicial power'.[83] The provision under (c) does not require that the warrant of arrest itself must also originate from a judicial authority.

The mere fact that a person detained on remand is later released under a judicial decision does not render the arrest unlawful with retroactive effect. Article 5(1) (c) requires only that there be a 'reasonable suspicion'. At the moment the arrest is made it need not yet be firmly established that an offence has actually been committed or what the precise nature of that offence is. The object of questioning during detention under sub-paragraph (c) is to further the investigation by way of confirming or dispelling the reason for arrest. Whether the mere continuation of suspicion suffices to warrant the prolongation of the detention on remand is covered not by the first but by the third paragraph of Article 5.

---

[79]   *Wemhoff v. Germany*, ECtHR 27 June 1968, appl. no. 2122/64, *supra* n. 53, paras. 13–14.

[80]   *B. v. Austria*, ECtHR 28 March 1990, appl. no. 11968/86, *supra* n. 51, paras. 42–43.

[81]   *Lawless v. Ireland (No. 3)*, ECtHR 1 July 1961, appl. no. 332/57, para. 14. See also *Ireland v. the United Kingdom*, ECtHR 18 January 1978, appl. no. 5310/71, *supra* n. 28, para. 196; *Jecius v. Lithuania*, ECtHR 31 July 2000, appl. no. 34578/97, *supra* n. 34, para. 50 and *Al-Jedda v. the United Kingdom*, ECtHR (GC) 7 July 2011, appl. no. 27021/08, para. 100.

[82]   *Brogan and Others v. the United Kingdom*, ECtHR 29 November 1988, appl. nos. 11209/84, 11234/84, 11266/84 and 11386/85, paras. 52–54. See also *Murray v. the United Kingdom*, ECtHR (GC) 28 October 1994, appl. no. 14310/88, paras. 67–68, where the applicant was arrested for only 3 hours and released without being charged or being brought before the competent legal authority.

[83]   *Ireland v. the United Kingdom*, ECtHR (GC) 18 January 1978, appl. no. 5310/71, *supra* n. 28, para. 199. In *Lawless v. Ireland*, ECtHR 1 July 1961, appl. no. 332/57, *supra* n. 81, para. 14, the Court speaks of 'judicial authority' and of 'judge'. *Cf.* also *Schiesser v. Switzerland*, ECtHR 4 December 1979, appl. no. 7710/76, para. 30.

The term 'reasonable suspicion' presupposes the existence of facts or information which would satisfy an objective observer that the person concerned may have committed or is about to commit the offence. Thus, the reasonableness depends on all the circumstances of the case.[84] The Court must also assess whether the conduct of the detainee can reasonably imply an offence.[85] In the *Fox, Campbell and Hartley* case the special circumstances in Northern Ireland were at issue. The applicants complained that their arrest under criminal legislation enacted to deal with acts of terrorism was not based on a reasonable suspicion. The Court, although acknowledging that terrorist crime falls under a special category, stressed that this cannot justify stretching the notion of 'reasonableness' beyond the point where the essence of the safeguard secured by sub-paragraph (c) is impaired. Scrutiny lead the Court to the conclusion that previous convictions for acts of terrorism cannot constitute the sole basis of a suspicion justifying the arrest some seven years later.[86] In the *Murray* case, the Government of the United Kingdom, without revealing its secret source that formed at least part of the reason of suspicion, succeeded in convincing the Court that there was a 'plausible and objective basis' for the suspicion that the applicant might have committed the offence of involvement in the collection of funds for the IRA.[87]

As discussed above, the detention under Article 5(1) under (c) comes to an end whenever the person on remand is convicted by a court of first instance. His further detention must then be reviewed under sub-paragraph (a). If no conviction or sentencing takes place because of lack of criminal responsibility on the part of the person concerned in view of his mental capacity, the eventually ordered prolonged detention comes under sub-paragraph (e).[88] In the *Quinn* case, the Paris Court of Appeal set aside a judicial order extending the detention on remand of the applicant. It directed that Mr Quinn should be 'released forthwith if he [was] not detained on other grounds'. This decision was not notified to the applicant nor was any step being taken to commence its execution. On the same day, 11 hours after the Court of Appeal delivered its judgment, the applicant, who was still detained in prison, was arrested with a view to extradition. The Strasbourg Court recognised that some delay in execution of a decision ordering release of a detainee is understandable. The continued detention for 11 hours was nevertheless clearly not covered by sub-paragraph (c) and did not fall under the other sub-paragraphs of Article 5(1).[89] In the *Giulia Manzoni* case, there was a period of seven hours between the decision which implied release and the

---

[84] *Fox, Campbell and Hartley v. the United Kingdom*, ECtHR 30 August 1990, appl. no. 12244/86, 12245/86 and 12383/86, para. 32.

[85] *Lukanov v. Bulgaria*, ECtHR 20 March 1997, appl. no. 21915/93, *supra* n. 32, paras. 42–45.

[86] *Fox, Campbell and Hartley v. the United Kingdom*, ECtHR 30 August 1990, *supra* n. 84, paras. 16–18.

[87] *Murray v. the United Kingdom*, ECtHR (GC) 28 October 1994, appl. no. 14310/88, *supra* n. 82, paras. 50–63.

[88] *Herczegfalvy v. Austria*, ECtHR 24 September 1992, appl. no. 10533/83, paras. 62–64.

[89] *Quinn v. France*, ECtHR 22 March 1995, appl. no. 18580/91, *supra* n. 29, para. 42.

moment the applicant left prison. The Courts concluded that Article 5 (c) was not violated. It took into account that some delay in carrying out a decision to release a detainee is often inevitable, although it must be kept to a minimum.[90]

The Court is stricter in cases where the period of detention does not end by a court order, but is laid down by law. In *K.-F. v. Germany*, the maximum period of 12 hours' detention for the purposes of checking identity was exceeded with 45 minutes. Since the maximum period, which was laid down by law and was absolute, was known in advance, the authorities responsible for the detention were under a duty to take all necessary precautions to ensure that the permitted duration was not exceeded. The Court concluded unanimously that Article 5 under (c) was violated.[91]

As a rule, Article 5 under (c) does not provide a justification for the re-detention or continued detention of a person who has served a sentence after conviction of a specific offence where there is a suspicion that he may commit a further similar offence. However, in the Court's opinion the position is different when a person is detained with a view to determining whether he should be subjected, after expiry of the maximum period prescribed by a court, to a further period of security detention imposed following conviction for a criminal offence. In the *Eriksen* case, the authorities were entitled, having regard to the applicant's impaired mental state and aggressive history as well as to his established and foreseeable propensity for violence, to detain the applicant pending the determination by a court of the prosecutor's request for a prolongation of the authorisation to detain him. Relevant was that such a 'bridging' detention was of a short duration, was imposed in order to bring the applicant before a judicial authority and was made necessary by the need to obtain updated medical reports.[92] The Court emphasised the exceptional character of the case, so the implications of the Court's judgment should not be overrated.

Article 6(2) of the Convention provides that a person who is charged with an offence must be presumed innocent until proved guilty. This presumption of innocence should be respected not only during the hearing in court; out of court, too, the accused – and thus also the person detained on remand – should not be treated as if his guilt were already established. The justification of the limitations to be imposed on the person detained on remand should, therefore, be based on other criteria than the limitations which result from a sentence of imprisonment.[93] This may also imply that persons detained on remand should be segregated if possible from convicted persons, although, unlike in the UN Covenant on Civil and Political Rights, this is not explicitly provided for in the Convention.

---

90   *Giulia Manzoni v. Italy*, ECtHR 1 July 1997, appl. no. 19218/91, *supra* n. 38, para. 25.
91   *K.-F. v. Germany*, ECtHR 27 November 1997, appl. no. 25629/94, *supra* n. 38, para. 72.
92   *Eriksen v. Norway*, ECtHR 27 May 1997, appl. no. 17391/90, *supra* n. 60, para. 86.
93   See Res. (65) 11 of the Committee of Ministers of the Council of Europe on detention on remand. In this resolution it is emphasised that detention on remand should be an exceptional measure, which is applied only if 'strictly necessary'.

3.5.   ARTICLE 5(1)(d)

In the first case mentioned under (d) one has to think of an order – judicial or not – to place a minor under supervision, combined with a restriction of freedom, for instance enforced stay in a reformatory institution or in a clinic. Most legal systems permit such restrictions of freedom in the interest of the minor, even if the latter is not suspected of having committed any criminal offence. It is then required that it may reasonably be assumed that the development or the health of the minor is seriously endangered – for instance in the case of drug addiction and/or prostitution – or that he is being ill-treated. The text speaks only of 'lawful order', so that it does not appear to be required that the order emanates from a judicial organ. Under paragraph 4 of Article 5, however, these minors too – or if the law so provides, their legal representatives – are entitled to institute court proceedings in order that the lawfulness of the restriction of their freedom may be reviewed.[94]

The far-reaching powers emanating from Article 5(1)(d) have led the Court to require rather strict guarantees that the educational purpose is indeed served by the detention. Detention for educational supervision pursuant to Article 5(1)(d) must take place in an appropriate facility with the resources to meet the necessary educational objectives and security requirements. In the *Blokhin* case, the Court held that the applicant's placement in a temporary detention centre could not be compared to a placement in a closed educational institution, which is a separate and long-term measure intended to try to help minors with serious problems. Placement in a temporary detention centre is a short-term, temporary solution and the Court failed to see how any meaningful educational supervision, to change a minor's behaviour and offer him or her appropriate treatment and rehabilitation, can be provided during a maximum period of 30 days.[95] In the *Bouamar* case, a minor was repeatedly confined in a remand prison 'for the purpose of educational supervision'. Although the confinements never exceeded the statutory limit of 15 days, the detentions (nine in total) amounted to a deprivation of liberty for 119 days in less than one year. The Court held that, in order to consider the deprivation of liberty lawful for educational supervision, the Belgian Government was under an obligation to put in place appropriate institutional facilities which met the demands of security and educational objectives; the mere detention of a juvenile 'in conditions of virtual isolation and without the assistance of staff with educational training cannot be regarded as furthering any educational aim'.[96] In *D.G. v. Ireland*, the institution where the minor was placed was considered by the Court as a penal institution.

---

[94]   See, e.g., *Bouamar v. Belgium*, ECtHR 29 February 1988, appl. no. 9106/80, *supra* n. 41, paras. 54–64, where a breach of this provision was established.

[95]   *Blokhin v. Russia*, ECtHR (GC) 23 March 2016, appl. no. 47152/06, paras. 164–172.

[96]   *Bouamar v. Belgium*, ECtHR 29 February 1988, appl. no. 9106/80, *supra* n. 41, para. 56.

The educational and other recreational services were entirely voluntary, while the minor was unwilling to co-operate with the authorities. The detention could also not be considered as an interim measure for the purpose of an educational supervisory regime which was followed speedily by the application of such a regime.[97]

When the applicant has passed the school leaving age, but is still a minor, detention 'for the purpose of educational supervision' may still fall within the scope of Article 5(1) under (d).

According to the *travaux préparatoires* the second case mentioned under (d) is concerned with the detention of minors for the purpose of bringing them before the court to secure their removal from harmful surroundings, so that they are not covered by Article 5(1)(c). This would, therefore, seem to be a measure by which the minor is protected against himself in order to prevent his sliding into criminality. It is not clear, however, what specific reason could bring the person concerned before a court, if no crime has been committed. The only case known to the authors relating to such a measure concerned an enforced stay of eight months in an observation centre, while the authorities examined whether theft and traffic offences had been committed.[98] In any case, the measure of bringing a minor before a judicial authority who decides on the prolongation of the detention, must be the purpose of the initial deprivation of liberty; consequently, there must be a sufficient ground for that measure. Which organ is competent to execute this deprivation of liberty is determined by national law ('lawful detention').

Since Article 5(1) under (d) confers such far-reaching powers on the national authorities with regard to minors, the age at which a person attains majority is of the greatest importance. This age is determined by domestic law. In Resolution (72)29 the Committee of Ministers of the Council of Europe has recommended to fix this age at 18.[99] Domestic law also determines whether and in what cases a minor has the legal capacity to institute proceedings himself, so that a minor who has this right in the Strasbourg proceedings may be dependent on his parents or guardian for the exhaustion of the local remedies.

3.6. ARTICLE 5(1)(e)

The provision under (e) deals with widely divergent categories of persons. There is a link between all those persons in that they may be deprived of their liberty either in order to be given medical treatment or because of considerations dictated by social policy, or on both medical and social grounds.[100] A

---

97   *D.G. v. Ireland*, ECtHR 16 May 2002, appl. no. 39474/98, *supra* n. 20, paras. 81–85.

98   *X. v. Switzerland*, EComHR 14 December 1979, appl. no. 8500/79, D&R 18 (1980), p. 238.

99   Res. (72)29 'Lowering of the age of full legal capacity' and Explanatory Memorandum, Council of Europe, Strasbourg, 1972.

100 *Witold Litwa v. Poland*, ECtHR 4 April 2000, appl. no. 26629/95, *supra* n. 42, para. 60.

predominant reason why the Convention allows the persons mentioned in paragraph 1(e) of Article 5 to be deprived of their liberty is not only that they may be dangerous for public safety but also that their own interests may necessitate their detention.[101]

The word 'lawful' constitutes the general criterion, while under the fourth paragraph of Article 5 the categories here referred to are also entitled to have the lawfulness of their detention reviewed by a court in accordance with the legal rules applying in the country concerned. The latter is important in particular for those cases where the detention can be ordered under municipal law by an administrative organ. If and insofar as, in performing this review, the court determines a civil right in the sense of Article 6, the rules for a fair trial set forth therein have to be observed.[102]

The scope of application of sub-paragraph (e) is essentially determined by the terms 'infectious diseases', 'persons of unsound mind', 'alcoholics', 'drug addicts' and 'vagrants'. The Convention does not contain a definition of these concepts. In deciding whether an individual should be detained for one of the reasons stated in sub-paragraph (e), the national authorities do have a certain discretion. However, in reviewing these national decisions the Court is prepared to carry out an independent examination of the question of whether the deprivation of liberty is in conformity with the Convention. In the case law the concepts 'infectious diseases', 'persons of unsound mind', 'alcoholics' and 'vagrants' have been clarified to some extent.

The essential criteria to assess the lawfulness of the detention of a person 'for the prevention of the spreading of infectious diseases' are whether this spreading is dangerous for public health or safety, and whether less severe measures than detention have been considered and found to be insufficient to safeguard the public interest.[103]

In the *Winterwerp* case, the Court emphasised that the term 'of unsound mind' implies that three minimum conditions have to be satisfied: (1) the person concerned must be 'reliably shown' to be of unsound mind (which 'calls for objective medical expertise'), (2) the nature or degree of the mental disorder must be such as to justify the deprivation of liberty, and (3) continued confinement is only valid as long as the disorder persists.[104] In the *Luberti* case, the question of whether the detention had continued beyond the period justified by applicant's mental disorder, was investigated by the Court in great detail.[105] In *R.L. and*

---

[101]   *Guzzardi v. Italy*, ECtHR 6 November 1980, appl. no. 7367/76, *supra* n. 10, para. 98. See also *Hutchison Reid v. the United Kingdom*, ECtHR 20 February 2003, appl. no. 50272/99, para. 51.

[102]   *Winterwerp v. the Netherlands*, ECtHR 24 October 1979, appl. no. 6301/73, *supra* n. 29, para. 73.

[103]   *Enhorn v. Sweden*, ECtHR 25 January 2005, appl. no. 56529/00, para. 44.

[104]   *Winterwerp v. the Netherlands*, ECtHR 24 October 1979, appl. no. 6301/73, *supra* n. 29, para. 39.

[105]   *Luberti v. Italy*, ECtHR 23 February 1984, appl. no. 9019/80, para. 29. See also the report of 7 October 1981, *B. v. the United Kingdom*, D&R 32 (1983), p. 5 (37–38).

M.-J.D. v. France there was no medical reason for the continued detention of the applicant, but the release was postponed because the physician in charge was not allowed to release the detainee. The Court judged that the applicant was held on administrative grounds that were incompatible with Article 5(1) under (e).[106]

No deprivation of liberty of a person considered to be of unsound mind may be deemed in conformity with Article 5(1) under (e) of the Convention if it has been ordered without seeking the opinion of a medical expert. In urgent cases or in cases where a person is arrested because of his violent behaviour, it may be acceptable that such an opinion be obtained immediately after the arrest. In all other cases a prior consultation is necessary. Where no other possibility exists, for instance owing to a refusal of the person concerned to appear for an examination, at least an assessment by a medical expert, based on the actual state of mental health, on the basis of the file must be sought.[107] In the Court's view, it does not automatically follow from a finding by an expert authority that the mental disorder which justified a patient's compulsory confinement no longer persists, that the latter must be immediately and unconditionally released into the community. The authorities should be able to retain some measure of supervision over the progress of the person once he is released into the community and to that end make his discharge subject to conditions. Appropriate safeguards are necessary to ensure that any deferral of discharge is consonant with the purpose of Article 5(1) and with the aim of the restriction in sub-paragraph (e) and that discharge is not unreasonably delayed.[108]

In the *Witold Litwa* case, the Court interpreted the term 'alcoholics' (*d'un alcoolique*) on the basis of the *ratio legis*. The Court considered that the object and purpose of the exception under (e) cannot be interpreted as only allowing the detention of 'alcoholics' in the limited sense of persons in a clinical state of 'alcoholism'. Persons who are not medically diagnosed as 'alcoholics', but whose conduct and behaviour under the influence of alcohol pose a threat to public order or themselves, can be taken into custody under Article 5(1) under (e) for the protection of the public or their own interests, such as their health or personal safety.[109] The mere fact that someone is under influence of alcohol, however, is not a sufficient basis for a deprivation of liberty. The detention must be assessed in the light of the above-mentioned *ratio legis* of the exception under (e). Decisive is whether the person behaves when drunk in such a way as to pose a threat to public order.[110] The purpose of the measure must be to avert that threat. The same will apply to 'drug addicts'.

---

[106] *R.L. and M.-J.D. v. France*, ECtHR 19 May 2004, appl. no. 44568/98, paras. 124–128.

[107] *Varbanov v. Bulgaria*, ECtHR 5 October 2000, appl. no. 31365/96, para. 47 and *R.L. and M.-J.D. v. France*, ECtHR 19 May 2004, appl. no. 44568/98, *supra* n. 106, para. 117.

[108] *Johnson v. the United Kingdom*, ECtHR 24 October 1997, appl. no. 22520/93, paras. 61–63.

[109] *Witold Litwa v. Poland*, ECtHR 4 April 2000, appl. no. 26629/95, *supra* n. 42, paras. 60–63.

[110] *Hilda Hafsteinsdottir v. Iceland*, ECtHR 8 June 2004, appl. no. 40905/98, para. 42.

In the *De Wilde, Ooms and Versyp ('Vagrancy')* cases, the question arose whether the applicants could be considered as 'vagrants'. The Belgian Criminal Code defined vagrants as 'persons who have no fixed abode, no means of subsistence and no regular trade or profession'. According to the Court, this definition did not appear to be in any way irreconcilable with the usual meaning of the term 'vagrant'. A person falling within the definition of the Belgian Criminal Code in principle comes under the exception of Article 5(1) under (e). In addition, the Court held that the national courts could deduce from the information available that the persons concerned met the criteria.[111] The Court, although confining itself to a marginal review of the national law and its application, took a rather active position when it comes to a review of the conformity of that application with the wording and meaning of Article 5(1) under (e). Thus, a guarantee has been created against too wide a national interpretation and application of the categories mentioned under (e).[112] The necessity of a restrictive interpretation was equally emphasised by the Court in the *Guzzardi* case, where it held that it may not be inferred from the exception permitted under Article 5(1) under (e) that the detention of persons who may constitute a greater danger than the categories mentioned in that article, is permitted equally and *a fortiori*.[113]

The involuntary commitment of an accused person in an observation clinic in most cases cannot be brought under paragraph 1 under (e), because as a rule it is not certain in advance that he is of unsound mind. This deprivation of liberty may perhaps find its justification in paragraph 1 under (b), in case the measure is provided for in a judicial decision which may be enforced if it is not complied with voluntarily.

Since paragraph 1(e) does not contain any limitation as to the duration of the detention, in contrast with the other categories of detention regulated in the same paragraph, the question is of great importance whether paragraph 4 confers on the person concerned only the right to have the lawfulness of the deprivation of his liberty as such reviewed by a court, or also the right to have recourse to a court periodically if the detention is prolonged. This question will be discussed under Article 5(4).

In the *Winterwerp* case, it had been argued on behalf of the applicant that Article 5(1)(e) entails for the person detained on one of the grounds mentioned there the right to appropriate treatment in order to ensure that he is not detained longer than absolutely necessary. This submission, however, was rejected by the Court.[114] In the *Ashingdane* and *Aerts* cases the Court further elaborated on

---

[111] *De Wilde, Ooms and Versyp v. Belgium ('Vagrancy' Cases)*, ECtHR 18 June 1971, appl. nos. 2832/66, 2835/66 and 2899/66, *supra* n. 14, para. 68.

[112] See also *Luberti v. Italy*, ECtHR 23 February 1984, appl. no. 9019/80, *supra* n. 105, para. 27; and *Ashingdane v. the United Kingdom*, ECtHR 28 May 1985, appl. no. 8225/78, *supra* n. 19.

[113] *Guzzardi v. Italy*, ECtHR 6 November 1980, appl. no. 7367/76, *supra* n. 10, para. 98.

[114] *Winterwerp v. the Netherlands*, ECtHR 24 October 1979, appl. no. 6301/73, *supra* n. 29, para. 51.

this. According to the Court, the lawfulness of a deprivation of liberty concerns not only the issuance of the order of the liberty-depriving measures, but also its execution. In other words, the measure must not only be in conformity with domestic law, but also with the purposes of the restrictions laid down in Article 5(1). This also follows from Article 18 of the Convention. Therefore, there must be some relationship between the ground of permitted deprivation of liberty relied on and the place and conditions of detention'. In principle, the 'detention' of a person as a mental health patient will only be 'lawful' for the purposes of sub-paragraph (e) of paragraph 1 if effected in a hospital, clinic or other appropriate institution. An ordinary prison regime is not appropriate.[115] Except for this relationship, however, Article 5(1)(e) is not concerned with suitable treatment or conditions.[116]

In the *Morsink* and *Brand* cases, the relationship between the deprivation of liberty and the place of the detention was at stake. During the first period of the execution of the non-punitive measure, the applicants were held in pre-placement detention in an ordinary remand centre until they could be placed in a custodial clinic. The Court noted that it would be unrealistic to expect that a place be immediately available. The Court found a certain friction between available and required capacity in custodial clinics inevitable and acceptable. However, a delay of six months in the admission of a person to a custodial clinic, due to a structural lack of capacity in custodial clinics, is not acceptable in the view of the Court.[117] The specific circumstances and therapeutic needs are relevant to assess whether detention is 'lawful'.[118] In the *Winterwerp* case, the Court considered the interval of two weeks between the expiry of the earlier order and the making of the succeeding renewal order not unreasonable or excessive.[119] In the *Erkalo* case, the applicant was placed by a court at the Government's disposal. The request of the public prosecutor for the extension of the placement order was not received by the competent court until two months after the expiry of the statutory period, and, as a result, for 82 days the placement of the applicant was not based on any judicial decision. The Court noticed that there was a lack of adequate safeguards to ensure that the applicant's release from detention would not be unreasonably delayed. The 'bridging detention' was unlawful and constituted a breach of Article 5(1) of the Convention.[120]

---

[115] *De Donder and De Clippel v. Belgium*, ECtHR 6 December 2011, appl. no. 8595/06, para. 105.

[116] *Ashingdane v. the United Kingdom*, ECtHR 28 May 1985, appl. no. 8225/78, *supra* n. 19, para. 44; *Aerts v. Belgium*, ECtHR 30 July 1998, appl. no. 25357/94, para. 46.

[117] *Morsink v. the Netherlands*, ECtHR 11 May 2004, appl. no. 48865/99, *supra* n. 18, paras. 63–69 and *Brand v. the Netherlands*, ECtHR 11 May 2004, appl. no. 49902/99, *supra* n. 18, paras. 60–66.

[118] *De Schepper v. Belgium*, ECtHR 13 October 2009, appl. no. 27428/07, para. 46–49.

[119] *Winterwerp v. the Netherlands*, ECtHR 24 October 1979, appl. no. 6301/73, *supra* n. 29, para. 49.

[120] *Erkalo v. the Netherlands*, ECtHR 2 September 1998, appl. no. 23807/94, paras. 57–60. See for a justified 'bridging detention' *Rutten v. the Netherlands*, ECtHR 24 July 2001, appl. no. 32605/96, paras. 39–46.

The Court also stresses the importance of an independent psychiatric opinion as a safeguard against possible arbitrariness in the decision-making when the continuation of confinement to involuntary care is concerned.[121]

3.7. ARTICLE 5(1)(f)

The importance of the provision under (f) consists in that, although the Convention does not grant to aliens a right of admission to or residence in any of the Contracting States, Article 5 nevertheless contains certain guarantees in case the authorities proceed to arrest or to detain an alien pending the decision on his admission, deportation or extradition. These consist first of all in the guarantee that such arrest or detention must be lawful and must, therefore, be in conformity with the applicable provisions of both domestic and international law and may not be imposed arbitrarily.[122] This right is coupled with the right of the person in question under paragraph 4 to have this lawfulness reviewed by a court. However, Article 5 does not merely refer back to domestic law but requires also that the applicable national law is 'sufficiently accessible and precise'. Where deprivation is concerned, it is particularly important that the general principal of legal certainty be obliged.[123] The principle that detention should not be arbitrary must apply to detention under the first limb of Article 5(1) under (f) in the same manner as it applies to detention under the second limb.[124] In the *Amuur* case, French national law did not meet this requirement and moreover the Court held, *inter alia*, that the national courts lacked jurisdiction to review the conditions of detention.[125]

Article 5(1) under (f) does not require that the detention of a person against whom action is being taken with a view to deportation or extradition must be reasonably considered necessary, for example to prevent his committing an offence or fleeing. In this respect Article 5(1) under (f) provides a lower level of protection than Article 5(1) under (c): all that is required under (f) is that action is being taken with a view to deportation or extradition. It is, therefore, immaterial whether the underlying decision can be justified under national or Convention law.[126] It is obvious, however, that in reviewing the lawfulness of the detention, the lawfulness of the deportation or extradition will often also be at issue. This is especially the case when, according to national law, the lawfulness of the detention is made dependent on that of the deportation.[127]

---

121   *X v. Finland*, ECtHR 3 July 2012, appl. no. 34806/04.
122   *Bozano v. France*, ECtHR 18 December 1986, appl. no. 9990/82, *supra* n. 2, para. 54.
123   *Medvedyev and Others v. France*, ECtHR (GC) 29 March 2010, appl. no. 3394/03, para. 80.
124   *Saadi v. the United Kingdom*, ECtHR (GC) 29 January 2008, appl. no. 13229/03, para. 73.
125   *Ibid.*, para. 53.
126   *Chahal v. the United Kingdom*, ECtHR (GC) 15 November 1996, appl. no. 22414/93, para. 112 and *Čonka v. Belgium*, ECtHR 5 February 2002, appl. no. 51564/99, para. 38.
127   Report of 11 October 1983, *Zamir*, D&R 40 (1985), p. 42 (55). The fact that a domestic court has found the deportation procedure to be illegal does not deprive the applicant of his claim

In the *Conka* case, the applicants had received orders to leave the territory of Belgium. They did not obey these orders. The Belgian authorities tried to gain the trust of the applicants with an invitation to come to the Ghent police station. The authorities declared that their attendance was required 'to enable the files concerning their applications for asylum to be completed'. In fact, the applicants were on their arrival at the police station arrested with a view to their deportation to Slovakia. The Court emphasised that acts whereby the authorities sought to gain the trust of asylum seekers with a view to arresting and subsequently deporting them may be found to contravene the general principles stated or implicit in the Convention. The narrow interpretation of the exceptions of Article 5(1) must also be reflected in the reliability of communications. Misleading the individuals concerned about the purpose of a notice so as to make it easier to deprive them of their liberty is not compatible with Article 5.[128]

Article 5(1) under (f) implies the guarantee that the detention must have no purpose other than that of preventing the admission of the alien in question to the country or of making it possible to decide on his deportation or extradition. There must be a close connection between the detention and that purpose.[129] Article 18 of the Convention, which prohibits restrictions of the rights and freedoms for any purpose other than that for which they have been prescribed, applies here as well. In the first place, this means that the deprivation of liberty is unlawful if the deportation order, and the way in which it is enforced, constitute a misuse of power.[130] In the second place, it follows that the detention must not be attended with more restrictions for the person concerned and must not last longer than is required for a normal conduct of the proceedings. The place and conditions of the detention must be appropriate as well.[131] In the *Quinn* case, the Court held: 'It is clear from the wording of both the French and the English versions of Article 5 §1(f) that deprivation of liberty under this sub-paragraph is justified only for as long as extradition proceedings are actually taking place. It follows that if such proceedings are not being conducted with due diligence, the detention ceases to be justified under Article 5 §1(f))'.[132]

Thus, although the duration of detention is only mentioned in paragraph 3 of Article 5 and this provision refers only to detentions under (1)(c), the Court

---

to be a victim of a violation of the Convention by reason of his arrest: report of 7 December 1984, *Bozano*, p. 32.

[128] *Čonka v. Belgium*, ECtHR 5 February 2002, appl. no. 51564/99, *supra* n. 126, paras. 41–42.

[129] *Saadi v. the United Kingdom*, ECtHR (GC) 29 January 2008, appl. no. 13229/03, *supra* n 124, para. 74.

[130] Report of 7 December 1984, *Bozano*, para. 69.

[131] *Kanagaratnam and Others v. Belgium*, ECtHR 13 December 2011, appl. no. 15297/09, para. 84.

[132] *Quinn v. France*, ECtHR 22 March 1995, appl. no. 18580/91, *supra* n. 29, para. 48. See also *Chahal v. the United Kingdom*, ECtHR (GC) 15 November 1996, appl. no. 22414/93, *supra* n. 126, paras. 112–113 and *Slivenko v. Latvia*, ECtHR (GC) 9 October 2003, appl. no. 48321/99, para. 146.

stipulates that the period of detention may not exceed a reasonable time.[133] The reasonableness of the length of detention has to be assessed in each individual case. In this respect, not only the length of the extradition or deportation proceedings is properly relevant, but also the length of connected procedures such as, for instance, summary proceedings which may result in a stay of execution of the extradition. If it has been decided to prolong the detention in the interest and at the request of the person concerned, for example. in order to find a suitable country which is prepared to admit him, or in order to obtain certain guarantees from the extradition-requesting state with regard to his treatment,[134] he cannot claim afterwards that he is the victim of this prolonged detention. Thus, in the *Kolompar* case, the Court found the period spent in detention – it lasted for over two years – pending extradition to be unusually long. Nevertheless, it held that it did not amount to a violation of Article 5(1) under (f) because the Belgian State could not be held responsible for the delays to which the applicant's conduct gave rise.[135]

3.8. INTERPLAY OF THE DIFFERENT EXCEPTIONS

A person may be detained under different subparagraphs of Article 5(1) successively. If a person detained on remand is convicted by a court of first instance, his detention falls no longer under sub-paragraph (c) but under sub-paragraph (a). In the *Herczegfalvy* case, the decision by which the applicant was ordered to be placed in an institution for mentally ill offenders, without convicting or sentencing him, was quashed on appeal. From that moment, the deprivation of liberty once more came under paragraph 1(c).[136] It is also possible that the detention falls under more than one sub-paragraph at the same time. In the *Eriksen* case, the 'bridging detention' between the expiry of an authorisation and the decision on a request for prolongation fell under the provisions of Article 5 under (a) and (c) simultaneously.[137] In the *Kolompar* case, the detention of the applicant came successively under Article 5(1)(c) only, under (c) and (f) at the same time, under (f) only, under (f) and (a) at the same time, and finally once more merely under (f).[138]

It appears sometimes to be difficult to determine whether the exception under (a) or under (e) is applicable. In *X v. the United Kingdom*, the applicant

---

[133] See also *Amuur v. France*, ECtHR 25 June 1996, appl. no. 19776/92, *supra* n. 12, para. 53.

[134] *X. v. Federal Republic of Germany*, appl. no. 9706/82 (not published).

[135] *Kolompar v. Belgium*, ECtHR 24 September 1992, appl. no. 11613/85, paras. 40–42.

[136] *Herczegfalvy v. Austria*, ECtHR 24 September 1992, appl. no. 11613/85, *supra* n. 52, para. 22.

[137] *Eriksen v. Norway*, ECtHR 27 May 1997, appl. no. 17391/90, *supra* n. 60, para. 86.

[138] *Herczegfalvy v. Austria*, ECtHR 24 September 1992, appl. no. 11613/85, *supra* n. 52, paras. 35–36.

was convicted, but this conviction contained solely the establishment that he committed the criminal conduct concerned. No punishment was imposed on him. However, his admission to and detention in a mental hospital for insane offenders was ordered. In assessing under which sub-paragraph the detention of the applicant had to be dealt with, the Court came to the conclusion that, although it recognised the differences between the sub-paragraphs 5(1)(a) and 5(1)(e), both sub-paragraphs could be and were applicable to the applicant's deprivation of liberty, at least initially. In the *Erkalo* case, the applicant was placed at the disposal of the Government in a psychiatric institution. The Court considered that the applicant's detention fell within the ambit of Article 5(1)(a) and (e) of the Convention.[139]

4. THE RIGHT TO BE INFORMED PROMPTLY OF THE REASONS FOR ARREST

4.1. INTRODUCTION

Article 5(2) grants to everyone who is arrested the right to be informed promptly, in a language which he understands, of the reasons for his arrest and of any charge against him. If the national authorities fail to do so, the arrest and detention are unlawful, even if they can be brought under one of the cases mentioned in paragraph 1. The rationale of this second paragraph necessarily ensues from the idea underlying Article 5: the liberty of person is the rule and is guaranteed, and an encroachment on this is allowed only in the cases expressly provided for and in conformity with the law as it stands. In order for the person arrested to be able to judge, from the moment of arrest, whether these two conditions have been met and to decide whether there are reasons for recourse to a court, adequate information must be available to him. Three notions are to be discussed successively: the applicability of Article 5(2), the information that should be given to the arrested person and, finally, the requirement of promptness.

A violation of paragraph 2 of Article 5 may also imply a violation of the fourth paragraph of this article. This question will be dealt with in the framework of the discussion of the fourth paragraph.

---

[139] *Erkalo v. the Netherlands*, ECtHR 2 September 1998, appl. no. 23807/94, *supra* n. 120, para. 51. See also *Morsink v. the Netherlands*, ECtHR 11 May 2004, appl. no. 48865/99, *supra* n. 18. para. 62 and *Brand v. the Netherlands*, ECtHR 11 May 2004, appl. no. 49902/99, *supra* n. 18, para. 59.

4.2. APPLICABILITY

The words 'arrest' and 'charge' used in paragraph 2 could create the impression that this provision is only relevant to cases arising under criminal law. However, the Court took a different view: the second paragraph applies not only to the detentions referred to in paragraph 1 under (c), but to any person arrested.[140] Therefore, paragraph 2 applies to all cases mentioned in the first paragraph of Article 5(1). The Court clarified its position by invoking the autonomous meaning of the terms of the Convention and the aim and purpose of Article 5. In addition, according to the Court, the use of the words 'any charge' ('*toute accusation*') showed that the intention of the drafters was not to lay down a condition for the applicability of Article 5(2), but to indicate an eventuality of which it takes account. Finally, the close link between paragraphs 2 and 4 of Article 5 was considered to support this interpretation.[141]

4.3. RELEVANT INFORMATION

Paragraph 2 of Article 5 requires that any arrested person shall be informed of the reasons of his arrest and of any charge made against him. As the Court held in the *Fox, Campbell and Hartley* case he must 'be told, in simple, non-technical language that he can understand, the essential legal and factual grounds for his arrest, so as to be able, if he sees fit, to apply to a court to challenge its lawfulness in accordance with paragraph 4'.[142] Thus, the Court took the position that the information required by Article 5(2) need not be worded in a particular form and need not even be given in writing. Consequently, as the Court held in the *Lamy* case, there exists at this stage of the proceedings no obligation to make the file available to the defence of the accused person for inspection.[143] In assessing whether the applicant is adequately informed, the Court takes into consideration the special features of the case and the person of the detainee.[144] In the *Fox, Campbell and Hartley* case and the *Murray* case

---

[140] *Fox, Campbell and Hartley v. the United Kingdom,* ECtHR 30 August 1990, appl. nos. 12244/86, 12245/86 and 12383/86, *supra* n. 84, para. 40; *Murray v. the United Kingdom,* ECtHR (GC) 28 October 1994, appl. no. 14310/88, *supra* n. 82, para. 72.

[141] *Van der Leer v. the Netherlands,* ECtHR 21 February 1990, appl. no. 11509/85, *supra* n. 36, paras. 27–28.

[142] *Fox, Campbell and Hartley v. the United Kingdom,* ECtHR 30 August 1990, appl. nos. 12244/86, 12245/86 and 12383/86, *supra* n. 84, para. 40; reiterated in *Murray v. the United Kingdom,* ECtHR (GC) 28 October 1994, appl. no. 14310/88, para. 72. See also *H.B. v. Switzerland,* ECtHR 5 April 2001, appl. no. 26899/95, paras. 48–49.

[143] *Lamy v. Belgium,* ECtHR 30 March 1989, appl. no. 10444/83, para. 31.

[144] See, among others, *Fox, Campbell and Hartley v. the United Kingdom,* ECtHR 30 August 1990, appl. nos. 12244/86, 12245/86 and 12383/86, *supra* n. 84, 12245/86 and 12383/86, para. 40; *Murray v. the United Kingdom,* ECtHR (GC), appl. no. 14310/88, *supra* n. 142, para. 72 and *H.B. v. Switzerland,* ECtHR 5 April 2001, appl. no. 26899/95, para. 47.

the persons concerned were questioned about their alleged activities for the IRA. The Court held that the bare indication of the legal basis for the arrest, taken on its own, was insufficient for the purposes of Article 5(2).[145] However, here the obligation of paragraph 2 had been complied with because the persons concerned had been able to infer the reasons for the arrest clearly enough from the content of the interrogations that took place after the arrest.[146] In the *Dikme* case, the Court even took into account the intensity and frequency of the interrogations, from which the applicant could have gained some idea of what he was suspected of.[147] The rationale of paragraph 2 raises the question of whether the Court should not be a little stricter in these respects. The interests of the arrested person which paragraph 2 is designed to protect, are sufficiently guaranteed only if the prescribed information is communicated to him explicitly and unambiguously.

4.4. PROMPTLY

Article 5(2) prescribes that the information about the reasons of arrest and of any charge must be given 'promptly' ('*dans le plus court delai*'). The Court has indicated that it need not be conveyed in its entirety by the arresting officer at the very moment of the arrest. In the *Fox, Campbell and Hartley* case, the applicants were informed sufficiently about the reasons for their arrest during the interrogations. These interviews took place four and a half, six and a half and three hours, respectively, after their arrest. These intervals could not be regarded in the context of those cases as falling outside the constraints of time imposed by the notion of promptness in Article 5(2).[148] In its decision in the *Durgov* case the Court concluded that, in the context of the case, a delay of ten and a half hours did not fall outside the constraints of time imposed by the notion of promptness, while in the *Lowry* case even an interval of 48 hours between the applicant's arrest and his questioning was considered compatible with Article 5(2).[149]

According to the Court, the arresting officer is not obliged to give the full information at the very moment of the arrest. This implies that at least some relevant information should be given at once.

---

[145] *Ibid.*, para. 41 and para. 76, respectively.
[146] In the same sense, see *Dikme v. Turkey*, ECtHR 11 July 2000, appl. no. 20869/92, para. 56.
[147] *Ibid.*, paras. 55–56.
[148] *Fox, Campbell and Hartley v. the United Kingdom*, ECtHR 30 August 1990, appl. nos. 12244/86, 12245/86 and 12383/86, *supra* n. 84, para. 42. In *Murray v. the United Kingdom*, ECtHR (GC) 28 October 1994, appl. no. 14310/88, *supra* n. 82, para. 78, an interval of 1 hour and 20 minutes did not violate the provision of Art. 5(2) either.
[149] *Durgov v. Bulgaria*, ECtHR 2 September 2004 (dec.), appl. no. 54006/00 and *Lowry v. Portugal*, ECtHR 6 July 1999 (dec.), appl. no. 42296/98.

5. THE RIGHT TO BE BROUGHT PROMPTLY BEFORE A JUDGE OR OTHER OFFICER

5.1. INTRODUCTION

Article 5(3) relates exclusively to the category of detainees mentioned in the first paragraph under (c): those detained on remand.[150] The main purpose of this paragraph, in relation to Article 5(1)(c), is to afford to individuals deprived of their liberty a special guarantee: a procedure of a judicial nature designed to ensure that no one should be arbitrarily deprived of his liberty[151] and, furthermore, to ensure that any arrest or detention will be kept as short as possible.

The judicial review of the detention must be an automatic one.[152] It cannot be made to depend on a preceding application by the detained person. Such a requirement would change the nature of the safeguard provided for under Article 5(3), a safeguard distinct from that in Article 5(4).[153] It might even defeat the purpose of the safeguard under Article 5(3), which is to protect the individual from arbitrary detention by ensuring that the act of deprivation of liberty is subject to independent judicial scrutiny.[154] Prompt judicial review of detention is also an important safeguard against ill-treatment of the individual taken into custody.[155]

5.2. PROMPTLY

Paragraph 3 comprises, first of all, in addition to the right to prompt information conferred in the second paragraph, the right to be brought 'promptly' before a judicial authority. It is obvious that a person cannot always be heard by a judge immediately after being arrested. Unlike in the case of the obligation to inform him of the reasons for his arrest, there is a third person involved in his first contact with a judge. The word 'promptly' – the French text speaks of '*aussitôt*' – therefore must not be interpreted so literally that the investigating judge must be virtually dragged out of bed to arraign the detainee or must interrupt urgent activities for this. However, adequate provisions will indeed have to be made in order that the prisoner can be heard as soon as may reasonably be required in view of his interests.

---

[150] See, e.g., *B. v. Austria*, ECtHR 28 March 1990, appl. no. 11968/86, *supra* n. 51, paras. 33–36; *Quinn v. France*, ECtHR 22 March 1995, appl. no. 18580/91, *supra* n. 29, paras. 51–53.

[151] *Schiesser v. Switzerland*, ECtHR 4 December 1979, appl. no. 7710/76, *supra* n. 83, para. 30.

[152] *De Jong, Baljet and Van den Brink v. the Netherlands*, ECtHR 22 May 1984, appl. nos. 8805/79, 8806/79 and 9242/81, *supra* n. 44, para. 51.

[153] *Ibid.*, para. 57.

[154] *Kurt v. Turkey*, ECtHR 25 May 1998, appl. no. 24276/94, *supra* n. 1, para. 123.

[155] *Aksoy v. Turkey*, ECtHR 18 December 1996, appl. no. 21987/93, para. 76.

The Court gave its opinion about the interpretation of the word 'promptly' in the *De Jong, Baljet and Van den Brink* case. The Court had to answer the question of whether the referral to a judicial authority seven, eleven and six days, respectively, after the arrest was in conformity with the requirement of promptness of Article 5(3). Although this question was answered in the negative, the Court refrained from developing a minimum standard. It only noted that 'the issue of promptness must be assessed in each case according to its special features'.[156] In other cases decided by the Court on the same day it also refrained from indicating a minimum standard.[157]

In the *Brogan* case, the Court had to deal with the question of 'promptness' in the case of arrest and detention, by virtue of powers granted under special legislation, of persons suspected of involvement in terrorism in Northern Ireland. The requirements under ordinary law in Northern Ireland for bringing an accused before a court were expressly made inapplicable to such arrest and detention. None of the applicants was in fact brought before a judge or judicial officer during his time in custody ranging from four days and six hours to six days and sixteen and a half hours. The Court accepted that the investigation of terrorist offences presented the authorities with special problems and that, subject to the existence of adequate safeguards, the context of terrorism in Northern Ireland had the effect of prolonging the period during which the authorities may, without violating Article 5(3), keep a person suspected of serious terrorist offences in custody before bringing him before a judge or other judicial officer. However, it also stressed that the scope for flexibility in interpreting and applying the notion of 'promptness' is very limited.; even the shortest of the four periods of detention, namely the four days and six hours spent in police custody, fell outside the strict constraints as to time permitted by the first part of Article 5(3). The Court held as follows: 'To attach such importance to the special features of this case as to justify so lengthy a period of detention without appearance before a judge or other judicial officer would be an unacceptably wide interpretation of the plain meaning of the word "promptly". An interpretation to this effect would import into Article 5 §3 a serious weakening of a procedural guarantee to the detriment of the individual and would entail consequences impairing the very essence of the right protected by this provision.'[158]

In the *O'Hara* case, the Court stated that detention periods exceeding four days for terrorist suspects are not compatible with Article 5(3).[159] In case of

---

[156]   *De Jong, Baljet and Van den Brink v. the Netherlands, supra* n. 44, para. 52. See also *Koster v. the Netherlands*, ECtHR 28 November 1991, appl. no. 12843/87, para. 24.

[157]   *Van der Sluijs, Zuiderveld and Klappe v. the Netherlands*, ECtHR 22 May 1984, appl. nos. 9362/81, 9363/81 and 9387/81, para. 49; and *Duinhof and Duijf v. the Netherlands*, ECtHR 22 May 1984, appl. nos. 9626/81 and 9736/82, para. 41.

[158]   *Brogan and Others v. the United Kingdom, supra* n. 82, para. 62.

[159]   *O'Hara v. the United Kingdom*, ECtHR 16 October 2001, appl. no. 37555/97, para. 46.

deprivation of liberty on the high seas it can take longer to hand over the person to the judicial authorities. In that case a longer period can be justified.[160]

In the *Koster* case, the applicant was not brought before the Military Court until five days after his arrest. According to the Court this period was too long. The fact that the lapse of time had occurred because of the weekend, which fell in the intervening period, and the two-yearly major manoeuvres, in which the members of the court had been participating, did not justify any delay in the proceedings. The demands of military life and justice could not alter this point of view.[161]

5.3. JUDGE OR OTHER OFFICER

Paragraph 3 provides that the accused should be brought before a 'judge' or 'other officer authorised by law to exercise judicial power'. In the *Schiesser* case, the Court laid down criteria for the determination of whether a person can be regarded as such an 'officer'. It expressed that 'officer' is not identical with 'judge', but 'nevertheless must have some of the latter's attributes'. The first condition is independence of the executive and of the parties. This does not mean that the 'officer' may not be to some extent subordinate to other judges or officers provided that they themselves enjoy similar independence. Secondly, there is a procedural requirement: the 'officer' is obliged to himself hear the individual brought before him. Thirdly, there is a substantive requirement which places the 'officer' under the obligation to review 'the circumstances militating for or against detention', and to decide 'by reference to legal criteria, whether there are reasons to justify detention' and, if this is not the case, to order the release of the person.[162] In this case, the complaint concerned the fact that the same authority who was charged in certain cases with the prosecution also had to decide on the lawfulness of the detention. The Court concluded that the provision of paragraph 3 had not been violated. It held, in particular, that in the case under consideration there had been no blending of functions, that the functionary had been able to proceed, and had

---

[160] *Ali Samatur v. France*, ECtHR 4 December 2014, appl. nos. 17110/10 and 17301/10 and *Hassan v. France*, ECtHR 4 December 2014, appl. nos. 46695/10 and 54588/10. See also *Rigopoulos v. Spain*, ECtHR 12 January 1999, appl. no. 37388/97 and *Medvedyev and Others v. France*, *supra* n. 123, para. 131.

[161] *Koster v. the Netherlands*, *supra* n. 156, para. 25.

[162] *Schiesser v. Switzerland*, ECtHR 4 December 1979, appl. no. 7710/76, *supra* n. 83, para. 31. See also, e.g., *Van der Sluijs, Zuiderveld and Klappe v. the Netherlands*, ECtHR 22 May 1984, appl. nos. 9362/81, 9363/81 and 9387/81, *supra* n. 157, para. 46; *Duinhof and Duijf v. the Netherlands*, ECtHR 22 May 1984, appl. nos. 9626/81 and 9736/82, *supra* n. 157, para. 36; and *Aquilina v. Malta*, ECtHR (GC) 29 April 1999, appl. no. 25642/94, paras. 48–55.

proceeded, independently, and that the procedural and substantive guarantees had been observed.[163]

In two of the three cases against the Netherlands,[164] and to a lesser extent also in the *Pauwels* case, the impartiality[165] of the *auditeur-militair* was found open to doubt because he could also be in charge of prosecuting functions in the same case. With this reasoning, the Court implicitly deviated from its judgment in the *Schiesser* case, where it was held that only the effective concurrent exercise of such functions infringed Article 5(3). This development was clearly confirmed by the *Huber* case and the *Brincat* case. In the *Brincat* case, the Court held as follows: 'only the objective appearances at the time of the decision are material: if it then appears that the "officer authorised by law to exercise judicial power" may later intervene, in the subsequent proceedings, as a representative of the prosecuting authority, there is a risk that his impartiality may arouse doubts which are to be held objectively justified.'[166]

In the *Assenov* case, the prisoner was brought before an investigator who questioned him, formally charged him, and took the decision to detain him on remand. Under Bulgarian law, investigators do not have the power to make legally binding decisions as to the detention or release of a suspect. Instead, any decision made by an investigator is capable of being overturned by the prosecutor. It followed that the investigator was not sufficiently independent properly to be described as an 'officer authorised by law to exercise judicial power' within the meaning of Article 5(3).[167]

5.4. TRIAL WITHIN A REASONABLE TIME

Furthermore, the third paragraph contains for the person detained on remand the right to be tried within a reasonable time or otherwise to be released pending trial, if necessary subject to certain guarantees for his appearance at the trial. The way this provision is formulated seems at first sight to leave a free choice to the judicial authorities: either to prolong the detention on remand, provided

---

[163] *Schiesser v. Switzerland*, ECtHR 4 December 1979, appl. no. 7710/76, *supra* n. 83, paras. 32–38. The presence of counsel was not included by the Court among the relevant guarantees; *ibid.*, para. 36.

[164] *De Jong, Baljet and Van den Brink v. the Netherlands*, ECtHR 22 May 1984, appl. nos. 8805/79, 8806/79 and 9242/81, *supra* n. 44, para. 49; *Van der Sluijs, Zuiderveld and Klappe v. the Netherlands*, ECtHR 22 May 1984, appl. nos. 9362/81, 9363/81 and 9387/81, *supra* n. 157, para. 44.

[165] In the cases against the Netherlands the Court used the word 'independent' instead of 'impartial'.

[166] *Brincat v. Italy*, ECtHR 26 November 1992, appl. no. 13867/88, para. 21. See also *Huber v. Switzerland*, ECtHR 23 October 1990, appl. no. 12794/87, para. 43. This case law is closely related to the case law concerning Art. 6(1).

[167] *Assenov and Others v. Bulgaria*, ECtHR 28 October 1998, appl. no. 24760/94, para. 148. See also *Nikolova v. Bulgaria*, ECtHR (GC) 25 March 1999, appl. no. 31195/96, para. 51.

---

that it has been imposed in accordance with paragraph 1(c), up to the moment of the judgment, which must then be given within a reasonable time, or to provisionally release the detainee pending trial, which trial would then no longer be subject to a given time-limit. Such an interpretation has been resolutely rejected by the Court. In the *Neumeister* case, the Court held with regard to Article 5(3) 'that this provision cannot be understood as giving the judicial authorities a choice between either bringing the accused person to trial within a reasonable time or granting him provisional release even subject to guarantees. The reasonableness of the time spent by an accused person in detention up to the beginning of the trial must be assessed in relation to the very fact of his detention. Until conviction he must be presumed innocent, and the purpose of the provision under consideration is essentially to require his provisional release once his continuing detention ceases to be reasonable.'[168]

And in the *Wemhoff* case, the Court held as follows: 'It is inconceivable that they [the Contracting States] should have intended to permit their judicial authorities, at the price of release of the accused, to protract proceedings beyond a reasonable time. This would, moreover, be flatly contrary to the provision in Article 6(1).'[169] The reference to Article 6(1) is indispensable for the Court's interpretation of Article 5(3); the word 'moreover', therefore, might as well have been omitted by the Court. In fact, as soon as the accused has been released, Article 5(3) is no longer applicable.[170] The obligation that in these cases, too, the trial takes place within a reasonable time, can be based only on Article 6(1). But precisely because Article 6(1) applies to all criminal proceedings, it is evident that Article 5(3) does not contain a choice between either release or trial within a reasonable time, but the obligation to keep a prisoner no longer in detention on remand than is reasonable and to try him within a reasonable time.

According to the quotation from the *Neumeister* case, the Court does not associate the word 'reasonable' with the processing of the prosecution and the trial, but with the length of the detention. The long delay of the trial may in itself be reasonable in view, for instance, of the complexity of the case or the number of witnesses to be summoned, but this does not mean that the continued detention is therefore also reasonable. The Court takes the view that Article 5(3) refers to the latter aspect. This implies at the same time that the criteria for 'reasonable' in Article 5(3) are different from those for the same term in Article 6(1) or, at least, have to be applied in a different way.[171] Some delays may in fact violate Article 5(3) and still be compatible with Article 6(1).[172] This is

---

[168] *Neumeister v. Austria*, ECtHR 27 June 1968, appl. no. 1936/63, *supra* n. 45, para. 4.

[169] *Wemhoff v. Germany*, ECtHR 27 June 1968, appl. no. 2122/64, *supra* n. 53, para. 5.

[170] See, e.g., *Van der Tang v. Spain*, ECtHR 13 July 1995, appl. no. 19382/92, para. 58.

[171] The relation between the 2 provisions is dealt with explicitly in *Stögmüller v. Austria*, ECtHR 10 November 1969, appl. no. 1602/62, para. 5 and in *Matznetter v. Austria*, ECtHR 10 November 1969, appl. no. 2178/64, para. 12.

[172] *Matznetter v. Austria*, ECtHR 10 November 1969, appl. no. 2178/64, *supra* n. 171, para. 12.

also corroborated by the view of the Court in the *Wemhoff* case, that 'an accused person in detention is entitled to have his case given priority and conducted with particular expedition'.[173]

With respect to the period that has to be taken into consideration for the determination of whether the trial has taken place within a reasonable time, the Court has taken the position in the *Wemhoff* case that this is the period between the moment of arrest and that of the judgment at first instance.[174] If that judgment implies acquittal or discharge from further prosecution, at all events it will have to be followed by release, while in the case of conviction henceforth it is a matter of 'detention of a person after conviction' in the sense of Article 5(1)(a), to which the provisions concerning detention on remand no longer apply.[175] Later on, the Court reaffirmed its position adopted in the *Wemhoff* case; it may now be taken as established case law that the period to be taken into consideration ends with the pronouncement of the first instance judgment.[176] Two different periods of detention on remand for the same charge, interrupted by a release, may be taken into consideration together when determining the total period and its reasonable character,[177] but they may also be assessed separately.[178] If a detention on remand has been preceded by a detention of another character or in relation to another criminal charge, the latter detention is not taken into consideration when determining the period to be considered in relation to the former one. The continuation of the detention pending appeal falls within the scope of Article 5(1) under (a). This period may not be taken into consideration when assessing whether the period is reasonable within the meaning of Article 5(3). If the first judgment is quashed, the period between the moment when the judgment is quashed and the moment when the second judgment is delivered must be taken into account to assess whether the length of the detention was reasonable.[179]

5.5. CONTINUED DETENTION

The persistence of the 'reasonable suspicion', as mentioned in sub-paragraph 5(1) under (c), is a condition *sine qua non* for the lawfulness of the continued detention.[180] When the 'reasonable suspicion' ceases to exist, the continued

---

[173] *Wemhoff v. Germany*, ECtHR 27 June 1968, appl. no. 2122/64, *supra* n. 53, para. 17.

[174] *Ibid.*, paras. 6–8.

[175] *Ibid.*, para. 9.

[176] See, e.g., *B. v. Austria*, ECtHR 28 March 1990, appl. no. 11968/86, *supra* n. 51, paras. 34–40; *Labita v. Italy*, ECtHR (GC) 6 April 2000, appl. no. 26772/95, *supra* n. 53, para. 147; *Kalashnikov v. Russia*, ECtHR 15 July 2002, appl. no. 47095/99, para. 110.

[177] See, e.g., *Letellier v. France*, ECtHR 26 June 1991, appl. no. 12369/86, para. 34.

[178] *Kemmache v. France*, ECtHR 27 November 1991, appl. nos. 12325/86 and 14992/89, paras. 46–48.

[179] See, among others, *Cesky v. the Czech Republic*, ECtHR 6 June 2000, appl. no. 33644/96, para. 71.

[180] See, e.g., *Stögmüller v. Austria*, *supra* n. 171, para. 4; *Tomasi v. France*, ECtHR 27 August 1992, appl. no. 12850/87, para. 84; *W. v. Switzerland*, ECtHR 26 January 1993, appl. no. 14379/88,

detention becomes unlawful and accordingly the question as to its reasonableness does not arise at all.

When is continued detention on remand to be considered reasonable? This question cannot be answered *in abstracto*; the answer depends on the special features of the case. For each individual case and at each moment the interests of the accused person will have to be weighed against the public interest, with due regard to the principle of the presumption of innocence.[181] The national authorities have to establish those relevant facts. It is not possible to shift the burden of proof to the detained person. That would be contrary to the principle that detention is an exceptional departure from the right to liberty and one that is only permissible in exhaustively enumerated and strictly defined cases.[182]

In the first instance this weighing is in the hands of the national authorities. They must set out the relevant arguments in their decisions on the applications for release.[183] The Court has clearly shown that it considers itself competent, on the basis of the reasons given in these decisions and the statements of the applicant, to review for their compatibility with the Convention the grounds on which a request for release has been rejected by the national authorities.[184] The mere fact that the 'reasonable suspicion' continues to exist is not sufficient, in the Court's opinion, to justify, after a certain lapse of time, the prolongation of the detention. According to the Court's case law, the question whether the period spent in detention on remand is reasonable, consists of two separate questions. The first question to be answered is whether the (other) grounds given by the national judicial authorities are 'relevant and sufficient' to justify the continued detention. If so, the second question to be answered is whether the national authorities displayed 'special diligence' in the conduct of the proceedings. If they did, the period spent in detention can be considered reasonable.[185] However, in case the first or second question is to be answered in the negative, the period of detention on remand did exceed a 'reasonable time'.

Various grounds have been adduced by the national authorities to justify the continued detention. Thus, for example, in the *Neumeister* case, the *Stögmüller*

---

para. 30; *Labita v. Italy*, ECtHR (GC) 6 April 2000, appl. no. 26772/95, *supra* n. 53, para. 152 and *Shishkov v. Bulgaria*, ECtHR 9 January 2003, appl. no. 38822/97, para. 58.

[181]   *W. v. Switzerland*, ECtHR 26 January 1993, appl. no. 14379/88, *supra* n. 180, para. 30; *Labita v. Italy*, ECtHR (GC) 6 April 2000, appl. no. 26772/95, *supra* n. 53, para. 152.

[182]   *Ilijkov v. Bulgaria*, ECtHR 26 July 2001, appl. no. 33977/96, para. 85.

[183]   See, e.g., *Letellier v. France*, ECtHR 26 June 1991, appl. no. 12369/86, *supra* n. 177, para. 35; *Kemmache v. France*, ECtHR 27 November 1991, appl. nos. 12325/86 and 14992/89, *supra* n. 178, para. 45; *Tomasi v. France*, ECtHR 27 August 1992, appl. no. 12850/87, *supra* n. 180, para. 84; and *Mansur v. Turkey*, ECtHR 8 June 1995, appl. no. 16026/90, para. 52.

[184]   *Ibid.*

[185]   See, e.g., *Matznetter v. Austria*, *supra* n. 171, para. 12; *Letellier v. France*, ECtHR 26 June 1991, appl. no. 12369/86, *supra* n. 177, para. 35; *W. v. Switzerland*, ECtHR 26 January 1993, appl. no. 14379/88, *supra* n. 180, para. 30; *Mansur v. Turkey*, ECtHR 8 June 1995, appl. no. 16026/90, para. 52; *Muller v. France*, ECtHR 17 March 1997, appl. no. 21802/93, para. 35; *Labita v. Italy*, ECtHR (GC) 6 April 2000, appl. no. 26772/95, *supra* n. 53, paras. 152–153 and *Shishkov v. Bulgaria*, ECtHR 9 January 2003, appl. no. 38822/97, *supra* n. 180, para. 58.

case and the *Matznetter* case the Court held that the danger of flight, even if it had initially constituted a sufficient ground for the detention on remand, afterwards had ceased to exist as a ground, specifically because of the possibility of bail.[186] The danger of absconding cannot be gauged solely on the basis of the severity of the sentence risked; it must be assessed with reference to a number of other relevant factors, such as the character of the person involved, his morals, his assets and his contacts abroad.[187]

The risk of a further offence is the other ground mentioned in paragraph 1(c). In the *Clooth* case, the danger of repetition was founded on the psychological deficiencies of the applicant. Nine months after the beginning of the detention an expert report described the applicant as dangerous and mentioned the need for him to be taken into psychiatric care. In these circumstances, the national courts should not extend the period of detention on remand without ordering an accompanying therapeutic measure. They did not order such a measure, consequently the risk of repetition was not sufficient to justify the continued detention.[188] The Court considered that the mere reference to a person's antecedents cannot suffice to justify refusing release.[189] When reviewing the lawfulness of the (prolongation of the) detention, the Court does not consider itself confined to the grounds for detention on remand expressly mentioned in paragraph 1(c), but has also accepted as such grounds the risk of suppression of evidence,[190] the seriousness of the offence in connection with the public order,[191] the safety of a person under investigation,[192] (implicitly) the danger of subornation of witnesses,[193] the danger of collusion[194] and the risk of pressure being brought to a witness.[195]

---

[186] *Neumeister v. Austria*, ECtHR 27 June 1968, appl. no. 1936/63, *supra* n. 45, paras. 7–14; *Stögmüller v. Austria*, ECtHR 10 November 1969, appl. no. 1602/62, para. 15 and *Matznetter v. Austria*, ECtHR 10 November 1969, appl. no. 2178/64, *supra* n. 171, para. 11. In *Wemhoff v. Germany*, ECtHR 27 June 1968, appl. no. 2122/64, *supra* n. 53, para. 15, the Court involved in its different finding the fact that on the part of the detainee there was no evident willingness to give bail.

[187] See, e.g., *Letellier v. France*, ECtHR 26 June 1991, appl. no. 12369/86, *supra* n. 177, para. 43; *Tomasi v. France*, ECtHR 27 August 1992, appl. no. 12850/87, *supra* n. 180, para. 98; *W. v. Switzerland*, ECtHR 26 January 1993, appl. no. 14379/88, *supra* n. 180, para. 33; *Muller v. France*, ECtHR 17 March 1997, appl. no. 21802/93, *supra* n. 185, para. 43.

[188] *Clooth v. Belgium*, ECtHR 12 December 1991, appl. no. 12718/87, para. 40.

[189] See also *Muller v. France*, ECtHR 17 March 1997, appl. no. 21802/93, *supra* n. 185, para. 44.

[190] *Wemhoff v. Germany*, ECtHR 27 June 1968, appl. no. 2122/64, *supra* n. 53, para. 14.

[191] *Kemmache v. France*, ECtHR 27 November 1991, appl. nos. 12325/86 and 14992/89, *supra* n. 178, para. 49; *Tomasi v. France*, ECtHR 27 August 1992, appl. no. 12850/87, *supra* n. 180, paras. 86–91, *I.A. v. France*, ECtHR 23 September 1998, appl. no. 28213/95, para. 104; *Gombert and Gochgarian v. France*, ECtHR 13 February 2001, appl. nos. 39779/98 and 39781/98, para. 46.

[192] *I.A. v. France*, ECtHR 23 September 1998, appl. no. 28213/95, *supra* n. 191, para. 108.

[193] See *Ringeisen v. Austria*, ECtHR 16 July 1971, appl. no. 2614/65, *supra* n. 45, paras. 105–106.

[194] *B. v. Austria*, ECtHR 28 March 1990, appl. no. 11968/86, *supra* n. 51, paras. 42–43; *Clooth v. Belgium*, ECtHR 12 December 1991, appl. no. 12718/87, *supra* n. 188, para. 43; *W. v. Switzerland*, ECtHR 26 January 1993, appl. no. 14379/88, *supra* n. 180, para. 35.

[195] *Letellier v. France*, ECtHR 26 June 1991, appl. no. 12369/86, *supra* n. 177, para. 39; *Kemmache v. France*, ECtHR 27 November 1991, appl. nos. 12325/86 and 14992/89, *supra* n. 178,

In the *Letellier* case, the French Government relied among other arguments on the preservation of public order to justify the continued detention. The Court held that, at least for a time, grave offences may give rise to a 'social disturbance' capable of justifying pre-trial detention. However, it added that 'this ground can be regarded as relevant and sufficient only provided that it is based on facts capable of showing that the accused's release would actually disturb public order. In addition detention will continue to be legitimate only if public order remains actually threatened'.[196] This wording, which can be regarded as established case law,[197] places the national courts under the obligation to state their reasons carefully when deciding to prolong the detention on remand. The mere use of stereotype criteria referring to the requirements of public order will not suffice for the purpose of Article 5(3). The extent to which the commission of offences has been given publicity is not decisive. The duration of the pre-trial detention is a relevant factor. The passage of time will generally weaken the justification of pre-trial detention based on these considerations. This conclusion *mutatis mutandis* seems to hold good for the other grounds capable of justifying the continued detention on remand.[198] In the *Labita* case, the grounds of the continued detention were the risk of pressure being brought to bear on witnesses and of evidence being tampered with, the fact that the accused were dangerous, the complexity of the case and the requirements of the investigation. The Court considered the grounds very general, but reasonable, at least initially. The grounds were not considered sufficient, however, to justify the applicant's being kept in detention for two years and seven months. Other grounds, like the risk of tampering with evidence, can lose their strength after a certain lapse of time.[199] In the *Labita* case, the allegations against the applicant came from a single source, a *pentito*. The Court considered that a suspect may validly be detained at the beginning of proceedings on the basis of statements by *pentiti*. Such statements become, because of their ambiguous nature, necessarily less relevant with the passage of time, especially where no further evidence is uncovered during the course of the investigation. The same reservations must be made with respect to hearsay evidence.[200]

---

para. 53; *Tomasi v. France*, ECtHR 27 August 1992, appl. no. 12850/87, *supra* n. 180, para. 95; *Labita v. Italy*, *supra* n. 53, paras. 156–161.

[196] *Letellier v. France*, ECtHR 26 June 1991, appl. no. 12369/86, *supra* n. 177, para. 51.

[197] See *Kemmache v. France*, ECtHR 27 November 1991, appl. nos. 12325/86 and 14992/89, *supra* n. 178, para. 52; *Tomasi v. France*, ECtHR 27 August 1992, appl. no. 12850/87, *supra* n. 180, para. 91; *I.A. v. France*, ECtHR 23 September 1998, appl. no. 28213/95, *supra* n. 191, para. 104; *Gombert and Gochgarian v. France*, ECtHR 13 February 2001, appl. nos. 39779/98 and 39781/98 *supra* n. 191, para. 46.

[198] See, e.g., *Yankov v. Bulgaria*, ECtHR 11 December 2003, appl. no. 39084/97, para. 172.

[199] See also *Letellier v. France*, ECtHR 26 June 1991, appl. no. 12369/86, *supra* n. 177, para. 39; *Clooth v. Belgium*, ECtHR 12 December 1991, appl. no. 12718/87, *supra* n. 188, para. 43; *Tomasi v. France*, ECtHR 27 August 1992, appl. no. 12850/87, *supra* n. 180, para. 95; *W. v. Switzerland*, ECtHR 26 January 1993, appl. no. 14379/88, *supra* n. 180, para. 35; *Vaccaro v. Italy*, ECtHR 16 November 2000, appl. no. 41852/98, para. 38.

[200] *Labita v. Italy*, ECtHR (GC) 6 April 2000, appl. no. 26772/95, *supra* n. 53, paras. 156–161.

Generalisations and Article 5(3) appear not to fit very well together. A system that excludes any possibility of the release of a person against whom more than one investigation is pending, is incompatible with Article 5(3).[201] However, the Court accepted in the *Pantano* case in the specific circumstances of the crimes of the Mafia a legal presumption of dangerousness. It was relevant that this presumption was not absolute.[202]

As has been observed above, if the prolongation of the detention on remand is based on well-founded reasons, the question remains whether the authorities showed 'special diligence' in the conduct of the proceedings. Article 5(3) does not imply a maximum length of pre-trial detention; the reasonableness cannot be assessed in the abstract.[203] Whether it is reasonable for an accused to remain in detention must be assessed in each case according to its special features. The case law shows that even a very long duration of the detention on remand – in *W v. Switzerland* this was slightly more than four years – may still be deemed acceptable. On the other hand, in the *Shishkov* case a period of approximately seven months and three weeks was considered to exceed the reasonable time, while in the *Belchev* case even a period of four months and fourteen days constituted a violation of Article 5(3). The Court reasoned, against the background of the relatively short periods, that justification for any period of detention, no matter how short, must be convincingly demonstrated by the authorities.[204] The Recommendation (2003)20 of the Committee of Ministers of the Council of Europe provides a maximum detention period in custody of juveniles of six months before the commencement of the trial. But in the *Nart* case, even a period of pre-trial detention of seven weeks constituted a violation of Article 5(3). The Court took into account that the applicant was a minor at the time of the detention and was detained together with adults.[205]

With regard to the criteria by which the reasonableness of the duration of the procedure is to be assessed, three factors seem to be of crucial importance: the complexity of the case, the conduct of the detainee and the conduct of the authorities. In case the length of a period spent in detention on remand does not appear to be essentially attributable either to the complexity of the case or to the applicant's conduct[206] and the authorities did not act with the necessary promptness, Article 5(3) is violated.[207] If a detention on remand has been

---

[201] See *Yankov v. Bulgaria*, ECtHR 11 December 2003, appl. no. 39084/97, *supra* n. 199, para. 173.

[202] *Pantano v. Italy*, ECtHR 6 November 2003, appl. no. 60851/00, paras. 69–70.

[203] *Wemhoff v. Germany*, ECtHR 27 June 1968, appl. no. 2122/64, *supra* n. 53, para. 10, and *W. v. Switzerland*, ECtHR 26 January 1993, appl. no. 14379/88, *supra* n. 180, para. 30.

[204] *Shishkov v. Bulgaria*, ECtHR 9 January 2003, appl. no. 38822/97, *supra* n. 180, para. 66; *Belchev v. Bulgaria*, ECtHR 8 April 2004, appl. no. 39270/98, para. 82.

[205] *Nart v. Turkey*, ECtHR 6 May 2008, appl. no. 20817/04, paras. 31–34.

[206] The right of a prisoner on remand 'to have his case examined with particular expedition must not unduly hinder the efforts of the judicial authorities'. See, e.g., *Toth v. Austria*, ECtHR 12 December 1991, appl. no. 11894/85, para. 77.

[207] See *ibid.*, para. 77 and *Tomasi v. France*, ECtHR 27 August 1992, appl. no. 12850/87, *supra* n. 180, para. 102.

preceded by a detention of another character or in relation to another criminal charge, the latter detention is not taken into consideration when determining *the period* to be considered in relation to the former one. However, that preceding detention must be taken into account in assessing the *reasonable character* of the period spent in detention on remand.[208] The Court examines whether there have been periods of inactivity without a justification.[209]

Article 5(3) expressly allows for making the release of the person detained on remand dependent on guarantees to appear for trial. The rationale of this is obvious: if and as long as prolongation of the detention would be allowed, certain guarantees may be asked for release. The provision is important in particular because of the obligation and the limitations resulting from it for the national authorities.

Although Article 5(3) does not guarantee an absolute right to release on bail, the possibility of demanding bail laid down there entails for the judicial authorities the obligation to ascertain whether by means of such a guarantee the same purpose can be achieved as is aimed at by the detention on remand. In the *Jablonski* case, the domestic courts did not take into account any other guarantees that the applicant would appear for trial. The Court concluded that the prolonged detention could not be considered as necessary from the point of view of ensuring the due course of the proceedings.[210]

In the case law four basic acceptable reasons for refusing bail can be distinguished: the risk that the accused will fail to appear for trial and the risk that the accused, if released, would take action to prejudice the administration of justice, commit further offences, or cause public disorder. If there are sufficient indications and guarantees for a bail, but this possibility is not offered to the detainee, the detention loses its reasonable, and as a consequence also its lawful, character. This will be the case in particular if the only ground for the detention is the risk of flight.[211] If the detainee declines the offer without suggesting an acceptable alternative, he has only himself to blame for the continued detention.[212] On the other hand, the guarantee demanded for release must not impose heavier burdens on the person in question than are required for obtaining a reasonable degree of security. If, for instance, the detainee is required to give bail the amount of which he cannot possibly raise, while it may be assumed that a lower sum would also provide adequate security for his compliance with a summons to appear for trial, the prolongation of the

---

208 *Mansur v. Turkey*, ECtHR 8 June 1995, appl. no. 16026/90, *supra* n. 183, para. 51.
209 *Kalashnikov v. Russia*, ECtHR 15 July 2002, appl. no. 47095/99, *supra* n. 176, para. 120.
210 *Jablonski v. Poland*, ECtHR 21 December 2000, appl. no. 33492/96, para. 84.
211 Thus, also the Court in *Wemhoff v. Germany*, ECtHR 27 June 1968, appl. no. 2122/64, *supra* n. 53, para. 15. See further *Letellier v. France*, ECtHR 26 June 1991, appl. no. 12369/86, *supra* n. 177, para. 64 and the report of 11 December 1980, *Schertenleib*, D&R 23 (1981), p. 137 (195).
212 In the Court's opinion that was the situation in *Wemhoff v. Germany*, ECtHR 27 June 1968, appl. no. 2122/64, *supra* n. 53, appl. no. 2122/64.

detention is unreasonable.[213] This also means that the nature and the amount of the security demanded must be related to the grounds on which the detention on remand is based; thus, in the determination of the amount the damage caused by the accused may not be taken into account. On the other hand, the financial situation of the person concerned and/or his relation to the person who stands bail for him must be taken into consideration. The amount of the bail must be assessed principally in relation to the person concerned.[214] The accused must provide the requisite information about this, but this does not relieve the authorities from the duty of making an inquiry into it themselves, in order to be able to decide on the possibility of releasing him on bail.[215] In the *Iwanczuk* case, the inquiry about the sum and form of the bail lasted four months and fourteen days after the competent judicial authority found prolonged detention on remand unnecessary. The applicant had promptly provided the relevant information as to its assets. In view of these facts, the Court concluded that Article 5(3) was violated.

6. HABEAS CORPUS

6.1. INTRODUCTION

Article 5(4) grants to everyone who is deprived of his liberty by arrest or detention the right to take proceedings by which the lawfulness of such deprivation of liberty will be reviewed speedily by a court and his release ordered if the latter decides that the detention is unlawful. This resembles the remedy of habeas corpus, originating from English law.

Article 5(4) provides a *lex specialis* in relation to the more general requirements of Article 13. A former detainee also may have a legal interest in the determination of the lawfulness of the detention even after having been liberated, for example in giving effect to the right to compensation.[216] The fourth paragraph constitutes an independent provision: even if the Court has found that the first paragraph has not been violated and that the detention, accordingly, had a lawful character, an inquiry into the possible violation of the fourth paragraph may nevertheless be made.[217] This implies that even if the review by the Court leads to the conclusion that the detention was lawful, an assessment must be made of whether the detained person at the time had the possibility to have the

---

[213]   *Neumeister v. Austria,* ECtHR 27 June 1968, appl. no. 1936/63, *supra* n. 45, paras. 12–15.

[214]   See, e.g., *Iwanczuk v. Poland,* ECtHR 15 November 2001, appl. no. 25196/94, para. 66 and *Mangouras v. Spain,* ECtHR 28 September 2010, appl. no. 12050/04, para. 80.

[215]   Report of 11 December 1980, *Schertenleib,* D&R 23 (1981), p. 137 (197).

[216]   *S.T.S. v. the Netherlands,* ECtHR 7 June 2011, appl. no. 277–05, paras. 58–59 and 61.

[217]   See, *inter alia, Winterwerp v. the Netherlands,* ECtHR 24 October 1979, appl. no. 6301/73, *supra* n. 29, para. 53 and *Kolompar v. Belgium,* ECtHR 24 September 1992, *supra* n. 135, para. 45.

lawfulness reviewed by a domestic court. The procedure of paragraph 4 must, therefore, also be considered as independent of the possibility of applying for release on bail.[218]

The fourth paragraph of Article 5, like the second paragraph, requires that the arrested person be informed of the reasons of his arrest in order to be in a position to take proceedings with a view to having the lawfulness of his detention determined.[219] In *X. v. the United Kingdom*, the Court considered that the issue under Article 5(2) was absorbed by the fact that a violation was found of Article 5(4).[220] In the *Van der Leer* case, it stated, on the other hand, that it was not necessary to examine the question of information under paragraph 4 because it dealt with it under the second paragraph.[221]

6.2. APPLICABILITY

The habeas corpus guarantees extend to all cases of deprivation of liberty provided for in the first paragraph of Article 5. The content of the obligation is not necessarily the same in all circumstances and as regards every category of deprivation of liberty.[222] Where a national court, after convicting a person of a criminal offence, imposes a fixed sentence of imprisonment for the purposes of punishment, the supervision required by Article 5(4) is incorporated in that court decision. This view is based on the assumption that in those cases the judicial review of the lawfulness of the detention, which is guaranteed by Article 5(4), has already taken place. This situation must be distinguished from situations in which an indeterminate sanction is imposed. In *X. v. the United Kingdom*, the applicant was convicted of causing bodily harm and was committed to a mental hospital for an indefinite period. According to the Court this deprivation of liberty fell, initially at least, within the ambit of both Article 5(1)(a) and Article 5(1)(e). The Court held that 'By virtue of Article 5 §4, a person of unsound mind compulsorily confined in a psychiatric institution for an indefinite or lengthy period is thus in principle entitled, at any rate where there is no automatic periodic review of a judicial character, to take proceedings at reasonable intervals before a court to put in issue the "lawfulness" (…) of his detention, whether that detention was ordered by a civil or criminal court or by some other authority.'[223]

---

[218] Report of 11 October 1983, *Zamir*, D&R 40 (1985), p. 42 (59).

[219] *X. v. the United Kingdom*, ECtHR 5 November 1981, appl. no. 7215/75, *supra* n. 54, para. 66.

[220] *Ibid.*

[221] *Van der Leer v. the Netherlands*, ECtHR 21 February 1990, appl. no. 11509/85, *supra* n. 36, para. 34.

[222] *X. v. the United Kingdom*, ECtHR 5 November 1981, appl. no. 7215/75, *supra* n. 54, para. 52; *König v. Slovakia*, ECtHR 20 January 2004, appl. no. 39753/98, para. 19.

[223] *X. v. the United Kingdom*, ECtHR 5 November 1981, appl. no. 7215/75, *supra* n. 54, para. 52. The Court, moreover, emphasised that given the scheme of Art. 5, read as a whole, the notion

The *Van Droogenbroeck* case concerned the placing of a recidivist at the Government's disposal for 10 years by court order. This order was given together with a sentence to two years' imprisonment. On the completion of his principal sentence Van Droogenbroeck was placed in semi-custodial care, but he disappeared and, after his arrest, was sent to prison by a decision of the Minister of Justice. Although the Court held that the resulting deprivation of liberty occurred 'after conviction' in accordance with Article 5(1)(a), it considered the fourth paragraph of Article 5 to be applicable, which required in the instant case 'an appropriate procedure allowing a court to determine "speedily" (...) whether the Minister of Justice was entitled to hold that detention was still consistent with the object and purpose of the 1964 Act'.[224]

The same line of reasoning was followed in the *Weeks* case. The applicant, at the age of 17, was convicted of armed robbery and sentenced to life imprisonment. This sanction was not imposed because of the gravity of the offence. The sentencing judge took account of the age and dangerous and unstable personality of the convict and decided that he should impose the sentence of life imprisonment to enable the Secretary of State to release him whenever he had become responsible with the passing of years. After nearly 10 years the applicant was released on licence, but subsequently this licence was revoked. He complained that he had not been able, either on his recall to prison or at reasonable intervals throughout his detention, to take proceedings as required by Article 5(4). The Court stated that the decisions of the executive to release or to re-detain the applicant should be consistent with the objectives of the sentencing court. If not, the detention would no longer be lawful for the purposes of sub-paragraph (a). Because the grounds relied on by the sentencing judges for deciding that the length of deprivation should be subject to the discretion of the executive were 'by their nature susceptible of change', the Court concluded that Mr Weeks was entitled to take proceedings as mentioned under paragraph 4.[225]

In the *Thynne, Wilson and Gunnel* case, each of the applicants had committed grave offences and had been sentenced to life imprisonment. The question of whether this sentence should be imposed was at the discretion of the trial judge. In addition to the need of punishment the applicants were considered to be suffering from a mental disturbance and to be dangerous and in need of treatment. The discretionary life sentence was imposed to enable the administration to assess their improvements and to act accordingly. The Court decided, in line with the *Weeks* case, that the applicants were entitled to take proceedings, but it had to establish from what point in time this would

---

of 'lawfulness' implies that the same deprivation of liberty should have the same significance in paras. 1(e) and 4. See also *Ashingdane v. the United Kingdom*, ECtHR 28 May 1985, appl. no. 8225/78, *supra* n. 19, paras. 51–52.

[224]   *Van Droogenbroeck v. Belgium*, ECtHR 24 June 1982, appl. no. 7906/77, *supra* n. 51, para. 49.

[225]   *Weeks v. the United Kingdom*, ECtHR 2 March 1987, appl. no. 9787/82, *supra* n. 56, para. 59.

be the case. To this end it distinguished between the punitive and the security element of the sentence[226] and concluded that the punitive period of the life imprisonment had expired.[227] According to the judgment in the *Stafford* case, this distinction is also applicable to mandatory life sentences.[228] To sum up, in fact the Court distinguishes between 'the conviction by a competent court' in the sense of Article 5(1)(a) as 'the decision depriving a person of his liberty', on the one hand, and the 'ensuing period of detention in which new issues affecting the lawfulness of the detention might subsequently arise', on the other hand. The 'conviction' does not purport to deal with the latter period. Thus, whenever the latter period starts, the lawfulness of the detention is no longer incorporated in the initial conviction.

In connection with the fourth paragraph, the Court takes account not only of the formal existence of remedies in the legal system of the Contracting Party concerned, but also of the context in which they operate and the personal circumstances of the applicant. The domestic remedies have to be sufficiently certain, otherwise the requirements of accessibility and effectiveness are not fulfilled.[229] In *R.M.D. v. Switzerland*, the applicant was in a position of great legal uncertainty. He had to expect to be transferred from one canton to another at any moment, in which eventuality the courts of the transferring canton no longer had jurisdiction to decide the lawfulness of his detention; that rendered any remedy ineffective, which led to a violation of Article 5(4).[230]

Does the fourth paragraph also apply to the detention on remand, now that the third paragraph already prescribes that an accused person, after his arrest, shall be brought promptly before a judge or other officer authorised by law to exercise judicial power? Even in the case that the person in question has thus been brought to trial it can hardly be said that he has been able to exercise the right 'to take proceedings', while moreover not in all cases is there a decision on the lawfulness of the detention by a 'court' in the strict sense. The position would, therefore, appear justifiable that in certain cases Article 5(4) grants to the person detained on remand a right of (periodic) recourse to a court after the (judicial) decision to detain him or to prolong the detention has been taken.[231]

---

[226] This distinction was confirmed by English law, at least according to the Court. The Government took the opposite view.

[227] *Thynne, Wilson and Gunnell v. the United Kingdom,* ECtHR 25 October 1990, appl. nos. 11787/85, 11978/86 and 12009/86, paras. 71–78.

[228] *Stafford v. the United Kingdom*, ECtHR (GC) 28 May 2002, appl. no. 46295/99, *supra* n. 59, paras. 87–89.

[229] See, among others, *Van Droogenbroeck v. Belgium,* ECtHR 24 June 1982, appl. no. 7906/77, *supra* n. 51, para. 54 and *Sakik and Others v. Turkey,* ECtHR 26 November 1997, appl. nos. 23878/94, 23879/94, 23880/94, 23881/94, 23882/94 and 23883/94, para. 53.

[230] *R.M.D. v. Switzerland,* ECtHR 26 September 1997, appl. no. 19800/92, para. 47.

[231] See Recommendation R(80)11 of the Committee of Ministers of 27 June 1980 on detention on remand, Art. 14 of which provides: 'Custody pending trial shall be reviewed at reasonably short intervals which the law or the judicial authority shall fix. In such a review, account shall

In the *De Jong, Baljet and Van den Brink* case, the Court reached the same conclusion by holding that the procedure, prescribed in Article 5(3), 'may admittedly have a certain incidence on compliance with paragraph 4. For example, where that procedure culminates in a decision by a 'court' ordering or confirming deprivation of the person's liberty, the judicial control of lawfulness required by paragraph 4 is incorporated in this initial decision. (…) However, the guarantee assured by paragraph 4 is of a different order from, and additional to, that provided by paragraph 3.'[232]

In the *Toth* case, the Court held that Article 5(4) did not cover proceedings instituted by an investigating judge for the extension of the pre-trial period. The national court that had to decide on the request of the judge, had to confine itself to 'setting out a framework' within which the investigating judge was free to take decisions. The national court itself did not review the 'lawfulness' of the detention, nor did it give a decision on the question of whether the applicant should be released.[233]

6.3. REVIEW OF LAWFULNESS AT REASONABLE INTERVALS

In the *Winterwerp* case, the Court took the view that a case of detention of a person of unsound mind 'would appear to require a review of lawfulness to be available at reasonable intervals'.[234] This requirement was initially solely connected with persons of unsound mind.[235] In the *Bezicheri* case, however, the applicant was detained on remand. Subsequent to a first judicial review of the lawfulness of the detention, he was, according to the Court, entitled 'after a reasonable interval, to take proceedings by which the lawfulness of his continued detention' was decided.[236]

---

be taken of all the changes in circumstances which have occurred since the person concerned was placed in custody.'

[232] *De Jong, Baljet and Van den Brink v. the Netherlands*, ECtHR 22 May 1984, appl. nos. 8805/79, 8806/79 and 9242/81, *supra* n. 44, para. 57. See also *Bezicheri v. Italy*, ECtHR 25 October 1989, appl. no. 11400/85, para. 20.

[233] *Toth v. Austria*, ECtHR 12 December 1991, appl. no. 11894/85, *supra* n. 207, para. 57.

[234] *Winterwerp v. the Netherlands*, ECtHR 24 October 1979, appl. no. 6301/73, *supra* n. 29, para. 55. See also *Luberti v. Italy*, ECtHR 23 February 1984, appl. no. 9019/80, *supra* n. 105, para. 31, and *De Jong, Baljet and Van den Brink v. the Netherlands*, ECtHR 22 May 1984, appl. nos. 8805/79, 8806/79 and 9242/81, *supra* n. 44, para. 57.

[235] See, e.g., *Luberti v. Italy*, ECtHR 23 February 1984, appl. no. 9019/80, *supra* n. 105, para. 31.

[236] *Bezicheri v. Italy*, ECtHR 25 October 1989, appl. no. 11400/85, *supra* n. 233, para. 20. The restriction to 'persons of unsound mind' was reiterated in *Megyeri v. Germany*, ECtHR 12 May 1992, appl. no. 13770/88, para. 22, but, on the other hand, was lacking in *Navarra v. France*, ECtHR 23 November 1993, appl. no. 13190/87, para. 26 (concerning a prisoner on remand).

According to established case law the right to take proceedings exists *at any rate* where there is no 'automatic periodic review of a judicial character'.[237] It is not yet clear if this right also exists in case the national legislation does provide for such a system. Anyway, the wording of paragraph 4 suggests an answer in the affirmative. On the other hand, one might presume that the national authorities must be left the possibility to reject an application for judicial review if no new facts are adduced and if shortly before an automatic periodic review of judicial character amounted to a negative decision for the applicant.[238] In the *Bezicheri* case, the person concerned, detained under Article 5(3), submitted his application for release one month after the first judicial review. The Italian Government argued that this period was too short to be reasonable, but the Court held that 'detention on remand calls for short intervals'. Consequently, in this case a period of one month was not unreasonable. In the *De Jong, Baljet and Van den Brink* case, the applicants were in remand seven, eleven and six days respectively without any remedy against their deprivation of liberty. The Court held that this amounted to be a breach of Article 5(4).[239]

In case of detention of persons of unsound mind, the intervals can be longer than in case of detention under Article 5(3). In the *Herczegfalvy* case, concerning the automatic periodic review of the detention of a person of unsound mind, intervals of fifteen months and two years, respectively, between two judicial decisions were not considered as 'reasonable intervals'. However, a period of nine months was not criticised by the Court and, therefore, seemed to meet the requirements of the fourth paragraph.[240]

Life sentences may be imposed on offenders owing to considerations of mental instability and dangerousness. These circumstances may change over the passage of time. In the *Oldham* case, the applicant, who was sentenced to life imprisonment, complained that a two-year delay between his Parole Board Reviews was unreasonable. The Court shared this opinion. The Court was not satisfied that the period of two years was justified by considerations of rehabilitation and monitoring and took into consideration that the courses that the applicant underwent to address his problems were concluded within eight months of his recall.[241] The Court seems to require a certain flexibility in determining the period, which must reflect the fact that there are significant differences in the personal circumstances of the prisoners under review.

---

[237] See, e.g., *X. v. the United Kingdom*, ECtHR 5 November 1981, appl. no. 7215/75, *supra* n. 54, para. 52; *Megyeri v. Germany*, ECtHR 12 May 1992, appl. no. 13770/88, *supra* n. 237, para. 22.

[238] Compare the report of the Commission of 15 December 1977, *Winterwerp*, B.31 (1983), para. 94 and para. 109.

[239] *De Jong, Baljet and Van den Brink v. the Netherlands*, ECtHR 22 May 1984, appl. nos. 8805/79, 8806/79 and 9242/81, *supra* n. 44, paras. 58–59.

[240] *Herczegfalvy v. Austria*, ECtHR 24 September 1992, appl. no. 10533/83, *supra* n. 52, para. 77.

[241] *Oldham v. the United Kingdom*, ECtHR 26 September 2000, appl. no. 36273/97, paras. 34–35.

6.4. REVIEW BY A COURT

Paragraph 4 entitles the accused to a decision by a 'court'. In the *Neumeister* case, the Court indicated as the decisive criterion that the competent authority 'must be independent both of the executive and of the parties to the case'.[242] Subsequently, the Court added that the right to judicial review is not of such a scope as to empower the national courts to substitute their own discretion for that of the decision-making authority on questions of pure expediency.[243] To satisfy the requirements of the Convention the review of the national court should comply with both the substantial and procedural rules of the national legislation and be conducted in conformity with the aim of Article 5, the protection of the individual against arbitrariness.[244] What guarantees must be attached to the procedure under the fourth paragraph of Article 5 must be judged by the circumstances of each case, in which context in particular the consequences resulting for the person concerned from the decision to be taken in that procedure must be considered.[245] Consequently, the guarantees which the procedure of Article 5(4) must afford need not necessarily be the same as those prescribed in Article 6(1) for a 'fair trial'.[246] Nevertheless, because of the impact of deprivation of liberty on the fundamental rights of the person concerned, proceedings conducted under Article 5(4) should in principle also meet, to the largest extent possible under the circumstances of an ongoing investigation, the basic requirements of a fair trial.[247] The proceeding must have a judicial character and provide guarantees appropriate to the kind of deprivation of liberty in question. The practical realities and the specific circumstances of the detained person must be taken into consideration.[248]

The procedure must be adversarial and must always ensure 'equality of arms' between the parties.[249] Equality of arms is not ensured if counsel is

---

[242] *Neumeister v. Austria*, ECtHR 27 June 1968, appl. no. 1936/63, *supra* n. 45, para. 24. In this case, the procedure itself was not yet considered decisive by the Court. See also *De Wilde, Ooms and Versyp v. Belgium ('Vagrancy' Cases)*, ECtHR 18 June 1971, appl. nos. 2832/66, 2835/66 and 2899/66, *supra* n. 14, para. 78; *Bezicheri v. Italy*, ECtHR 25 October 1989, appl. no. 11400/85, *supra* n. 233, para. 20.

[243] See, e.g., *Van Droogenbroeck v. Belgium*, ECtHR 24 June 1982, appl. no. 7906/77, *supra* n. 51, para. 49; *E. v. Norway*, ECtHR 29 August 1990, appl. no. 11701/85, para. 50; *Thynne, Wilson and Gunnell*, *supra* n. 228, para. 79.

[244] *Koendjbiharie v. the Netherlands*, ECtHR 25 October 1990, appl. no. 11487/85, para. 27, and *Keus v. the Netherlands*, ECtHR 25 October 1990, appl. no. 12228/86, para. 66.

[245] *De Wilde, Ooms and Versyp v. Belgium ('Vagrancy' Cases)*, ECtHR 18 June 1971, appl. nos. 2832/66, 2835/66 and 2899/66, *supra* n. 14, para. 42.

[246] *Winterwerp v. the Netherlands*, ECtHR 24 October 1979, appl. no. 6301/73, *supra* n. 29, para. 60; *Megyeri v. Germany*, *supra* n. 237, ECtHR 12 May 1992, appl. no. 13770/88, para. 24.

[247] *Schöps v. Germany*, ECtHR 13 February 2001, appl. no. 25116/94, para. 44; *Lanz v. Austria*, ECtHR 31 January 2002, appl. no. 24430/94, para. 41.

[248] *Shishkov v. Bulgaria*, ECtHR 9 January 2003, appl. no. 38822/97, *supra* n. 180, para. 85.

[249] See, e.g., *Sanchez-Reisse v. Switzerland*, ECtHR 21 October 1986, appl. no. 9862/82, para. 51; *Nikolova v. Bulgaria*, ECtHR (GC) 25 March 1999, appl. no. 31195/96, *supra* n. 167, paras. 58–59; *Lanz v. Austria*, ECtHR 31 January 2002, appl. no. 24430/94, *supra* n. 28, para. 44.

denied access to those documents in the investigation file which are essential in order effectively to challenge the lawfulness of his client's detention.[250] The authorities should ensure that both parties have the opportunity to be aware that observations have been filed and have a real opportunity to comment thereon.[251] Whether or not a submission by the prosecution deserves a reaction is a matter for the defence to assess.[252] Article 5(4) does not impose an obligation on a court examining an appeal against detention to address every argument contained in the appellant's submissions. However, the court cannot treat as irrelevant, or disregard, concrete facts invoked by the detainee and capable of putting into doubt the existence of the conditions essential for the 'lawfulness', in the sense of the Convention, of the deprivation of liberty.[253] In the *Lamy* case, the applicant's counsel did not have the opportunity to effectively challenge the statements or views which the prosecution based on these documents, while it was essential to inspect the documents in question in order to challenge the lawfulness of the arrest warrant effectively. Article 5(4) was violated.[254]

The Court recognises that the use of confidential material may be unavoidable where national security is at stake. This does not mean, however, that the national authorities are released from effective control by the domestic courts whenever they choose to assert that national security and terrorism are involved. The Court takes into account that techniques may be employed which both accommodate legitimate security concerns about the nature and sources of intelligence information and yet accord the individual a substantial measure of procedural justice.[255] Also in cases in which full disclosure is not possible, Article 5(4) requires that the detainee is provided with sufficient information about the allegations against him in order to enable him to challenge the allegations and to give effective instructions to his representatives.[256] It is for the authorities to prove that an individual satisfies the conditions for detention.[257]

In the case of a person whose detention falls within the ambit of Article 5(1) under (c), a hearing is required.[258] The detainee must have adequate time to

---

[250] *Garcia Alva v. Germany*, ECtHR 13 February 2001, appl. no. 23541/94, para. 39.

[251] *Schöps v. Germany*, ECtHR 13 February 2001, appl. no. 25116/94, *supra* n. 248, para. 44.

[252] *Lanz v. Austria*, ECtHR 31 January 2002, appl. no. 24430/94, *supra* n. 248, para. 44.

[253] *Nikolova v. Bulgaria*, ECtHR 25 March 1999, appl. no. 31195/96, *supra* n. 167, para. 61; *Ilijkov v. Bulgaria*, ECtHR 26 July 2001, appl. no. 33977/96, *supra* n. 182, para. 94.

[254] *Lamy v. Belgium*, ECtHR 30 March 1989, appl. no. 10444/83, *supra* n. 143, para. 29.

[255] *Chahal v. the United Kingdom*, ECtHR (GC) 15 November 1996, appl. no. 22414/93, *supra* n. 126, para. 131; *Al-Nashif v. Bulgaria*, ECtHR 20 June 2002, appl. no. 50963/99, para. 95.

[256] *A. and Others v. the United Kingdom*, ECtHR (GC) 19 February 2009, appl. no. 3455/05, paras. 218–220.

[257] *Hutchison Reid v. the United Kingdom*, ECtHR 20 February 2003, appl. no. 50272/99, *supra* n. 101, para. 70.

[258] *Schiesser v. Switzerland*, ECtHR 4 December 1979, appl. no. 7710/76, *supra* n. 83, paras. 30–31; *Sanchez-Reisse v. Switzerland*, ECtHR 21 October 1986, appl. no. 9862/82, *supra* n. 250, para. 51; *Nikolova v. Bulgaria*, ECtHR (GC) 25 March 1999, appl. no. 31195/96, *supra* n. 167, para. 58.

prepare the hearing.[259] Article 5(4) does not as a general rule require such a hearing to be public.[260]

According to the Court it is possible that the mental condition of the person makes specific restrictions or derogations necessary as to the exercise of this right, but this cannot in any case justify an encroachment on the right in its essence, but on the contrary calls for special procedural guarantees.[261] In the *Megyeri* case, the national court had to assess whether the continued detention of the applicant was necessary. The applicant was heard in person but that did not meet the requirements of Article 5(4). The Court considered it doubtful whether the applicant was capable of adequately presenting the relevant points. It concluded, also taking into consideration the fact that the applicant had spent more than four years in a psychiatric hospital, that a counsel should have been appointed to assist the applicant in the proceedings.[262] The same point of view was adopted by the Court in the *Bouamar* case, taking into consideration, *inter alia,* that the proceedings concerned a juvenile,[263] and in the *Magalhaes Pereira* case. In the last-mentioned case, the decision to continue the detention relied, *inter alia*, on a medical report that had been obtained a year and eight months beforehand that did not necessarily reflect the applicant's condition at the time of the decision. The Court considered that a delay of that length between the preparation of a medical report and the decision whether or not the detention must be continued, in itself can run counter to the principle of protecting individuals from arbitrariness.[264]

In the *Sanchez-Reisse* case, the applicant, against whom action had been taken with a view to extradition, complained about the fact that he had not been able to apply *directly* to a court. However, the Strasbourg Court had no objections to the requirement of a previous administrative procedure, provided that this did not violate the 'speed' requirement.[265] In the *Singh* case and the *Hussain* case, the Court held that the lack of an oral and adversarial hearing in the proceedings before the Parole Board could not be compensated by the possibility of instituting proceedings for judicial review. It was crucial for the Court that the applicants risked a considerable term of imprisonment and that the decision which had to be taken by the Parole Board on the dangerousness of the applicants involved questions with regard to their 'personality and level of maturity'.[266] In the *Wassink* case, a failure to comply with national law

---

[259] *Frommelt v. Liechtenstein,* ECtHR 24 June 2004, appl. no. 49158/99, para. 33.

[260] *Reinprecht v. Austria,* ECtHR 15 November 2005, appl. no. 67175/01, paras. 38–41.

[261] *Winterwerp v. the Netherlands,* ECtHR 24 October 1979, appl. no. 6301/73, *supra* n. 29, para. 60.

[262] *Megyeri v. Germany,* ECtHR 12 May 1992, appl. no. 13770/88, *supra* n. 237, para. 25.

[263] *Bouamar v. Belgium,* ECtHR 29 February 1988, appl. no. 9106/80, *supra* n. 41, paras. 59–60.

[264] *Magalhaes Pereira v. Portugal,* ECtHR 26 February 2002, appl. no. 44872/98, para. 49.

[265] *Sanchez-Reisse v. Switzerland,* ECtHR 21 October 1986, appl. no. 9862/82, *supra* n. 250, paras. 17 and 54.

[266] *Singh v. the United Kingdom,* ECtHR 21 February 1996, appl. no. 23389/94, paras. 68–69; and *Hussain v. the United Kingdom,* ECtHR 21 February 1996, appl. no. 21928/93, paras. 60–61.

(according to the Court the requirement concerned was not an essential one) did not lead to the conclusion that Article 5(4) was violated.[267]

Article 5(4) does not stipulate the requirement of the court's independence and impartiality and thus differs from Article 6(1). However, the Court has held that independence is one of the most important constitutive elements of the notion of a 'court' and that it would be inconceivable that Article 5(4) should not equally envisage the impartiality of that court. In *D.N. v.* Switzerland, the Court assessed the impartiality of a judge in conformity with the jurisprudence concerning Article 6(1). One of the judges – the only psychiatrist of the court – had previously given an expert opinion on the state of health of the detainee. The Court concluded that the circumstances of the case served objectively to justify the applicant's apprehension that the judge lacked the necessary impartiality.[268]

Article 5(4) does not require the institution of a second level of proceedings.[269] The intervention of one organ satisfies Article 5(4), on condition that the procedure has a judicial character and gives to the detainee guarantees appropriate to the kind of deprivation of liberty in question. However, in principle, if the question of whether the detained person should be released will be heard on appeal, then the Contracting States must offer the persons concerned the same guarantees as at first instance.[270]

6.5. SPEEDY DECISION

Paragraph 4 explicitly requires that the judicial review shall take place 'speedily'. Compliance must be assessed in the light of the specific circumstances of the case.[271] The complexity of medical issues involved in a determination of whether a person can be released may be taken into account.[272] With regard to the period that has to be taken into consideration the Court has taken as a starting point the day the application for release has been made. The relevant period comes to an end on the day the court has given judgment.[273] If the proceedings have been conducted at two levels of jurisdiction an overall assessment must be made

---

[267]   *Wassink v. the Netherlands*, ECtHR 27 September 1990, appl. no. 12535/86, *supra* n. 37, paras. 33–34.

[268]   *D.N. v. Switzerland*, ECtHR 29 March 2001, appl. no. 27154/95, paras. 44–56.

[269]   *Jecius v. Lithuania*, ECtHR 31 July 2000, appl. no. 34578/97, *supra* n. 34, para. 100; *Lanz v. Austria*, ECtHR 31 January 2002, appl. no. 24430/94, *supra* n. 248, para. 42.

[270]   *Toth v. Austria*, ECtHR 12 December 1991, appl. no. 11894/85, *supra* n. 207, para. 84, and *Navarra v. France*, ECtHR 23 November 1993, appl. no. 13190/87, *supra* n. 237, para. 28.

[271]   See, e.g., *Sanchez-Reisse v. Switzerland*, ECtHR 21 October 1986, appl. no. 9862/82, *supra* n. 250, para. 55; and *E. v. Norway*, ECtHR 29 August 1990, appl. no. 11701/85, *supra* n. 244, para. 64.

[272]   *Jablonski v. Poland*, ECtHR 21 December 2000, appl. no. 33492/96, *supra* n. 211, para. 92.

[273]   See, e.g., *Sanchez-Reisse v. Switzerland*, ECtHR 21 October 1986, appl. no. 9862/82, *supra* n. 250, para. 54, and *E. v. Norway*, ECtHR 29 August 1990, appl. no. 11701/85, *supra* n. 244, para. 64.

in order to determine whether the requirement of 'speedily' has been complied with.[274]

In assessing the speedy character required by paragraph 4 comparable factors may be taken into consideration as those which play a role with respect to the requirement of trial within a reasonable time under Article 5(3) and under Article 6(1), such as, for instance, the conduct of the applicant and the way the authorities have handled the case.[275] Neither an excessive workload,[276] nor a vacation period[277] can justify a period of inactivity on the part of the judicial authorities.

The notion of 'speedily' ('*à bref délai*') indicates a lesser urgency than that of 'promptly' ('*aussitôt*') in Article 5(3).[278] In the *Sanchez-Reisse* case, the time which elapsed between the lodging of two requests and the decisions thereon, 31 days and 46 days, respectively, did not satisfy the 'speed' requirement of Article 5(4). In the *Rehbock* case, a period of 23 days on remand was not considered 'speedily'.[279] In the *Kadem* case, the same conclusion was reached with respect to extradition proceedings for a period of 17 days.[280] With respect to a period of nearly one year and five months in which six judicial decisions were given[281], the Court expressed certain doubts about the overall length of the period. Nevertheless, it took into consideration the fact that the applicant had retained the right to submit further applications for release, which were all dealt with in short periods,[282] and reached the conclusion that paragraph 4 was not violated.[283] In the *Fox, Campbell and Hartley* case, two applicants instituted proceedings for habeas corpus. They were released 44 hours after their arrest, before judicial control on the lawfulness of their detention had taken place. The Court held that they were released speedily and did not find it necessary to examine their complaint under Article 5(4).[284]

---

[274]   See, e.g., *Luberti v. Italy*, ECtHR 23 February 1984, appl. no. 9019/80, *supra* n. 105, para. 33, and *Navarra v. France*, ECtHR 23 November 1993, appl. no. 13190/87, *supra* n. 237, para. 28.

[275]   See, e.g., *Luberti v. Italy*, ECtHR 23 February 1984, appl. no. 9019/80, *supra* n. 105, paras. 30–37, and *Van der Leer v. the Netherlands*, ECtHR 21 February 1990, appl. no. 11509/85, *supra* n. 36, para. 36.

[276]   See, e.g., *Bezicheri v. Italy*, ECtHR 25 October 1989, appl. no. 11400/85, *supra* n. 233, para. 25.

[277]   *E. v. Norway*, ECtHR 29 August 1990, appl. no. 11701/85, *supra* n. 244, para. 66.

[278]   *Ibid.*, para. 64.

[279]   *Rehbock v. Slovenia*, ECtHR 28 November 2000, appl. no. 29462/95, paras. 85–86.

[280]   *Kadem v. Malta*, ECtHR 9 January 2003, appl. no. 55263/00, paras. 44–45.

[281]   With respect to 1 application for release the applicant appealed 3 times to the Court of Cassation.

[282]   Periods from 8 to 20 days.

[283]   *Letellier v. France*, ECtHR 26 June 1991, appl. no. 12369/86, *supra* n. 177, paras. 56–57. See also *Navarra v. France*, ECtHR 23 November 1993, appl. no. 13190/87, *supra* n. 237, paras. 29–30.

[284]   *Fox, Campbell and Hartley v. the United Kingdom*, ECtHR 30 August 1990, appl. nos. 12244/86, 12245/86 and 12383/86, *supra* n. 84, paras. 45–46.

7. RIGHT TO COMPENSATION

Article 5(5) grants a direct right to compensation if an arrest or detention is found to be in contravention of the preceding provisions of Article 5.[285] At first sight this provision appears superfluous by the side of the general provision concerning just satisfaction in Article 41 of the Convention. The difference, however, is that Article 41 confers a competence on the Court, while Article 5(5) grants an independent right *vis-à-vis* the national authorities, the violation of which right may constitute the object of a separate complaint and may subsequently lead to the Court's application of Article 41. This difference may be illustrated by the following example. If an arrest has been declared unlawful by the national court and the prisoner has subsequently been released under Article 5(4), he can still complain about a violation of Article 5 if his claim for compensation has not been received or has been rejected. If, on the other hand, a given treatment of a detainee has been stopped after having been found by the national court to conflict with Article 3, but no damages are awarded to the injured person, there is no ground for a separate complaint, since Article 3 itself does not grant a right to compensation and Article 41 applies only after the Court has established violation of – in this case – Article 3.

In the *Brogan* case, the Government argued that the aim of paragraph 5 is to ensure that the victim of an 'unlawful' arrest or detention should have an enforceable right to compensation. In this regard, the Government also contended that 'lawful' is to be construed as essentially referring back to domestic law and in addition as excluding any element of arbitrariness. The Government concluded that even in the event of a violation being found of any of the first four paragraphs, there had been no violation of paragraph 5 because the applicants' deprivation was lawful under Northern Ireland law and was not arbitrary. The Court held that such a restrictive interpretation was incompatible with the terms of paragraph 5, which refers to arrest or detention 'in contravention of the provisions of this Article'.[286]

As was pointed out by the Court in the *Ciulla* case, the effective enjoyment of the right guaranteed in paragraph 5 must be ensured in the Contracting States with 'a sufficient degree of certainty'.[287] In the *Sakik* case, the Court assessed the effectiveness of the application of Article 5(5) by the national authorities. In all

---

[285]   *Emin v. the Netherlands*, ECtHR 29 May 2012, appl. no. 28260/07, para. 22–25.

[286]   *Brogan and Others v. the United Kingdom*, ECtHR 29 November 1988, appl. nos. 11209/84, 11234/84 11266/84 and 11385/85, *supra* n. 82, para. 67. See also *Benham v. the United Kingdom*, ECtHR 10 June 1996, appl. no. 19380/92, *supra* n. 30, para. 50.

[287]   *Ciulla v. Italy*, ECtHR 22 February 1989, appl. no. 11152/84, para. 44. See further *Fox, Campbell and Hartley v. the United Kingdom*, ECtHR 30 August 1990, appl. nos. 12244/86, 12245/86 and 12383/86, *supra* n. 84, para. 76, and *Thynne, Wilson and Gunnell v. the United Kingdom*, ECtHR 25 October 1990, appl. nos. 11787/85, 11978/86 and 12009/86, *supra* n. 228, para. 82.

the cases in which compensation was payable under the domestic legal provision concerned, it was required that the deprivation of liberty was unlawful. However, the domestic courts considered the detention in accordance with domestic law and the right to compensation depended on the unlawfulness under domestic law. Under these circumstances the effective enjoyment of the right guaranteed by Article 5(5) of the Convention is not ensured with a sufficient degree of certainty.[288]

The damage to be compensated may be material as well as non-material.[289] However, in the *Wassink* case the Court took the view that the Contracting States are entitled to make the award of compensation dependent on the real existence of any damage resulting from the violation of Article 5.[290] In this case, the detention under Article 5(1) was unlawful because there was no registrar present at the hearing, as was required by national law. For this reason, it was hard for the applicant to prove any damage; it was uncertain if proceedings conducted in conformity with Article 5 would have led to the release of the applicant. The question of whether damage is involved, concerns the merits and will ultimately have to be decided by the Strasbourg Court.

8. DEROGATION

Article 5 is not included in the enumeration of Article 15(2). Under the conditions mentioned in the first paragraph of that article, the Contracting States may, therefore, derogate from the provision of Article 5 if, insofar as, and as long as this is necessary.[291]

---

[288] *Sakik and Others v. Turkey*, ECtHR 26 November 1997, appl. nos. 23878/94, 23879/94, 23880/94, 23881/94, 23882/94 and 23883/94, *supra* n. 230, para. 60 and *Yankov v. Bulgaria*, ECtHR 11 December 2003, appl. no. 39084/97, *supra* n. 99, para. 194.

[289] *Ringeisen v. Austria*, ECtHR 22 June 1972, appl. no. 2614/65, *supra* n. 45, paras. 23–26. See also *Bozano v. France*, ECtHR 2 December 1987, appl. no. 9990/82, *supra* n. 2, paras. 6–9.

[290] *Wassink v. the Netherlands*, ECtHR 27 September 1990, appl. no. 12535/86, *supra* n. 37, para. 38. See also *De Wilde, Ooms and Versyp v. Belgium ('Vagrancy' Cases)*, ECtHR 18 June 1971, appl. nos. 2832/66, 2835/66 and 2899/66, *supra* n. 14, para. 24.

[291] *Brannigan and McBride v. The United Kingdom*, ECtHR 26 May 1993, appl. nos. 14553/89 and 14554/89 and *A. and Others v. The United Kingdom*, ECtHR (GC) 19 February 2009, appl. no. 3455/05.

CHAPTER 10

RIGHT TO A FAIR TRIAL

(Article 6)

Tom Barkhuysen, Michiel van Emmerik,
Oswald Jansen and Masha Fedorova[*]

GUIDING PRINCIPLE

Access to justice forms one of the pillars of the rule of law. The right to a court, as the Strasbourg Court found in its famous *Golder* judgment,[1] is to be read into Article 6 although the text does not explicitly refer to this right. Article 6 guarantees the right to a court in civil, administrative and criminal cases and provides all kinds of safeguards regarding the fairness of the trial. Article 6 is a key human right in the sense that it enables individuals to enforce a wide range of other human rights against the government or other individuals. This chapter elaborates the guarantees of a fair trial both in 'civil' and criminal cases.

ARTICLE 6

1. In the determination of his civil rights and obligations or of any criminal charge against him, everyone is entitled to a fair and public hearing within a reasonable time by an independent and impartial tribunal established by law. Judgment shall be pronounced publicly but the press and public may be excluded from all or part of the trial in the interest of morals, public order or national security in a democratic society, where the interests of juveniles or the protection of the private life of the parties so require, or to the extent strictly necessary in the opinion of the court in special circumstances where publicity would prejudice the interests of justice.
2. Everyone charged with a criminal offence shall be presumed innocent until proved guilty according to law.
3. Everyone charged with a criminal offence has the following minimum rights:
   a) to be informed promptly, in a language which he understands and in detail, of the nature and cause of the accusation against him;
   b) to have adequate time and facilities for the preparation of his defence;
   c) to defend himself in person or through legal assistance of his own choosing or, if he has not sufficient means to pay for legal assistance, to be given it free when the interests of justice so require;
   d) to examine or have examined witnesses against him and to obtain the attendance and examination of witnesses on his behalf under the same conditions as witnesses against him;
   e) to have the free assistance of an interpreter if he cannot understand or speak the language used in court.

---

[*]   In the fourth edition this chapter was revised and updated by Pieter van Dijk and Marc Viering.
[1]   *Golder v. the United Kingdom*, ECtHR (GC) 21 February 1975, appl. no. 4451/70, paras. 34–36.

CONTENTS

1. SCOPE

For the interpretation of Article 6 the Court, in its *Delcourt* judgment, has set forth the following guideline: 'In a democratic society within the meaning of the Convention, the right to a fair administration of justice holds such a prominent place that a restrictive interpretation of Article 6(1) would not correspond to the aim and the purpose of that provision.'[2]

In thus rejecting a restrictive interpretation, the Court has given guidance not only for its own case law, but also to the national authorities, especially the domestic courts. The Court's case law shows that it considers itself competent to examine in-depth the way in which Article 6 has been interpreted and applied at the national level.

The first issue to be discussed is the scope of Article 6. Thereafter, the various express and implied requirements embodied in the three paragraphs of this provision will be outlined.[3]

1.1. DETERMINATION OF CIVIL RIGHTS AND OBLIGATIONS

Unlike the second and the third paragraph of Article 6, which apply exclusively to proceedings concerning criminal charges, the first paragraph also applies to proceedings in which the determination of civil rights and obligations is (also) at issue.

1.2. DRAFTING HISTORY

The meaning of the words 'determination of his civil rights and obligations' (*contestations sur ses droits et obligations de caractère civil*) is rather vague and leaves ample scope for 'creative' interpretation and even 'judicial policy'.[4] If, as is the case here, the ordinary meaning to be given to treaty provisions does not provide a sufficiently clear interpretation, recourse may be had to supplementary means of interpretation, including the preparatory work of the treaty and the circumstances of its conclusion.[5]

---

[2]   *Delcourt v. Belgium,* ECtHR 17 January 1970, appl. no. 2689/65, para. 25.

[3]   See for further (and regularly updated) references: *Guide on Article 6 of the European Convention on Human Rights. Right to a Fair Trial (civil limb), idem criminal limp* (via <www.echr.coe.int>). See also *Handbook on European Law Relating to Access to Justice* (joint publication Council of Europe and European Union Agency for Fundamental Rights, accessible via <www.echr.coe.int>.

[4]   Thus, the representative of the Commission, Fawcett, before the Court in the *König* case, B.25 (1982), p. 179.

[5]   Arts. 31(1) and 32 of the Vienna Convention on the Law of Treaties; 8 *International Legal Materials* (1969), p. 679.

The drafting history of the words 'civil rights and obligations' was studied in depth at an early stage by several authors.[6] These studies indicate that the drafting history of Article 14 of the International Covenant on Civil and Political Rights, which was used as a model by the drafters of Article 6 of the Convention, offers a rather strong indication that it was not the drafters' intention to restrict the scope of the right of access to court, apart from determinations of criminal charges, to determinations of rights and obligations of a private-law character. On the contrary, one is struck by the fact that proposals which might imply the risk of such a restriction, were criticised for that reason and rejected or amended.[7]

The *travaux préparatoires* of the European Convention do not contain an indication of a discussion of the formula here at issue in any of the bodies involved in the drafting. In the French text of Article 6 the formula of Article 14 of the Covenant was adopted without any change. In the English text 'rights and obligations in a suit at law' was altered, at the very last stage of the drafting process, to 'civil rights and obligations'. The reason for this is not traceable, but apparently it was not considered to have any implications for the scope of Article 6. One may assume that the only reason for it was that, in the eyes of continental lawyers (and of the linguists involved), 'suit at law' was not the obvious equivalent for '*de caractère civil*'.[8] In conclusion, there is no indication that a restrictive interpretation of 'civil rights and obligations' can be based upon the drafting history of either Article 14 of the Covenant or Article 6 of the Convention. The Committee of Experts on Human Rights of the Council of Europe, when making a comparison between the two provisions, also reached the conclusion with respect to the words here under discussion that 'in view of the fact that the French texts use identical terms (…) the intention was the same'.[9]

---

[6] See especially, in chronological order: J. Velu, 'Le problème de l'application aux juridictions administratives, des règles de la Convention européenne des droits de l'homme relatives à la publicité des audiences et des jugements', *Revue de Droit International et de Droit Comparé*, 1961, pp. 129–171; K.J. Partsch, *Die Rechte und Freiheiten der europäischen Menschenrechtskonvention*, Berlin, 1966, pp. 143–150; T. Buergenthal and W. Kewenig, 'Zum Begriff der Civil Rights in Artikel 6 Absatz 1 der europäischen Menschenrechtskonvention', *Archiv des Völkerrechts*, 1966/67, pp. 393–411; F.C. Newman, 'Natural Justice, Due Process and the New International Covenants on Human Rights: Prospectus', *Public Law*, Winter 1967, pp. 274–313.

[7] See Velu, *ibid.*, pp. 145–154. See especially his reference, at p. 150, to a statement by the delegate of the USSR, Mr Pavlov. At p. 154 Velu says: 'Au fond, toutes les délégations étaient d'accord pour que les garanties de procédures prévues s'appliquent à toutes les juridictions.' See also P. Lemmens, *Geschillen over burgerlijke rechten en verplichtingen* [Disputes concerning Civil Rights and Obligations], Antwerp, 1989, pp. 218–220, and M.L.W.M. Viering, *Het toepassingsgebied van artikel 6 EVRM* [The Scope of Article 6 ECHR], Zwolle, 1994, pp. 33–49. Both authors also discuss the intervention by the Danish delegate, Mr Sørensen, who proposed to exclude disputes between a private party and a public authority but did not have a decisive impact on the outcome of the debates on that point.

[8] See Velu, *ibid.*, p. 159.

[9] Council of Europe, *Problems arising from the co-existence of the United Nations Covenants on Human Rights and the European Convention on Human Rights; Differences as regards the*

It may be true that the original intention of the drafters of a treaty may become less relevant as time lapses, especially after states have become parties whose representatives did not participate in the drafting, but this argument is less convincing as long as there is no common and unambiguous legal opinion and/or uniform practice which deviates from that original intention.

1.3. AUTONOMOUS MEANING OF RIGHTS AND OBLIGATIONS

In the *Benthem* case the Court did not give an abstract definition of 'civil rights and obligations',[10] but in its case law the Court has drawn the following main lines.

Although for the determination of whether a right or obligation is at stake the domestic legal system concerned has to be taken as a starting point, the Court has made it clear that, as part of a provision of the Convention, the words 'rights and obligations' have an autonomous meaning. Thus, it held in the *König* case: 'The same principle of autonomy applies to the concept in question; any other solution might lead to results incompatible with the object and purpose of the Convention (…). Whilst the Court thus concludes that the concept of "civil rights and obligations" is autonomous, it nevertheless does not consider that, in this context, the legislation of the State concerned is without importance. Whether or not a right is to be regarded as civil within the meaning of this expression in the Convention must be determined by reference to the substantive content and effects of the right – and not its legal classification – under the domestic law of the State concerned. In the exercise of its supervisory functions, the Court must also take account of the object and purpose of the Convention and of the national legal systems of the other Contracting States (…).'[11]

The first question to be answered is whether a certain claim constitutes a 'right' – or 'legitimate interest?'[12] – under the domestic law of the state concerned for the applicability of Article 6. The Court requires that the determination concerns a right that 'can be said, at least on arguable grounds, to be recognised under domestic law'.[13] The words 'on arguable grounds' leave the Court sufficient room to make an assessment independently of the arguments advanced by

---

Rights Guaranteed, Report of the Committee of Experts on Human Rights to the Committee of Ministers, Doc. H(70)7, Strasbourg, September 1970, p. 37.

[10] *Benthem v. The Netherlands*, ECtHR 23 October 1985, appl. no. 8848/80, para. 35.

[11] *König v. Germany*, ECtHR 28 June 1978, appl. no. 6232/73, paras. 88–89.

[12] *Mennitto v. Italy*, ECtHR (GC) 5 October 2000, appl. no. 33804/96, para. 27.

[13] *James and Others v. the United Kingdom*, ECtHR (GC) 21 February 1986, appl. no. 8793/79, para. 81; *Salerno v. Italy*, ECtHR 12 October 1992, appl. no. 11955/86, para. 14; *Z and Others v. the United Kingdom*, ECtHR (GC) 10 May 2001, appl. no. 29392/95, para. 87; *Berkmann v. Austria*, ECtHR 14 November 2002 (dec.), appl. no. 59879/00, para. 2; *Boulois v. Luxembourg*, ECtHR 3 April 2012, appl. no. 37574/04, paras. 90–94.

the defendant state on the issue.[14] In particular, the Court does not have to be convinced that the legal claim is well-founded under domestic law; it is enough for it to determine that the claim is sufficiently tenable.[15] The fact that the claim concerned was addressed as an issue in national proceedings constitutes sufficient ground for the 'arguability' of the existence of a right.[16] A so-called 'toleration decision' (in Dutch a *gedoogbeschikking*: an explicit declaration of the local authorities not to uphold the legal prohibition of the possession of soft drugs) however, was not deemed to constitute a civil right by the Court in the Dutch case *De Bruin*.[17]

The viewpoint that Article 6 implies a right of access to court[18] has as a consequence that the fact that a certain claim is not actionable under domestic law, is not decisive for the applicability of Article 6. As the Court stated in the *Al-Adsani*, *McElhinney* and *Fogarty* cases: 'Whether a person has an actionable domestic claim may depend not only on the substantive content, properly speaking, of the relevant civil right as defined under national law but also on the existence of procedural bars preventing or limiting the possibilities of bringing potential claims to court. In the latter kind of case Article 6 para. 1 may be applicable.[19] Consequently, the doctrine of state immunity does not lead to the conclusion that the person concerned has no right *vis-à-vis* that state; indeed, the state may waive immunity. The grant of immunity does not qualify a substantive right, but constitutes a procedural bar to have the right determined.[20]

In the *Baraona* case, the Court rejected the Government's submission that the impugned measure had no basis in national law at that time and accordingly could not give rise to liability on the part of the State and could not be the subject of a 'dispute'. The Court adopted the position that it was not for the Court to assess either the merits of the applicant's claim under domestic law or the influence of the revolutionary situation in Portugal on the application of domestic law; this belonged to the exclusive jurisdiction of the national courts. The applicant, however, could claim on arguable grounds to have a right that was recognised under national law as he understood it.[21] And in the *Voggenreiter*

---

14   *O. v. the United Kingdom*, ECtHR (GC) 8 July 1987, appl. no. 9276/81, para. 54.

15   *Editions Périscope v. France*, ECtHR 26 March 1992, appl. no. 11760/85, para. 38; *Le Calvez v. France*, ECtHR 29 July 1998, appl. no. 25554/94, para. 56; *Jori v. Slovakia*, ECtHR 9 November 2000, appl. no. 34753/97, para. 47.

16   *Editions Périscope v. France*, supra n. 15, para. 38; *Mennitto v. Italy*, supra n. 12, para. 27: it was deemed sufficient that the issue 'had given rise to jurisdictional dispute'.

17   *De Bruin v. The Netherlands*, ECtHR 17 September 2013, appl. no. 9765/09, paras. 58–59.

18   *Infra*, 3.1.

19   *Al-Adsani v. the United Kingdom*, ECtHR (GC) 21 November 2001, appl. no. 35763/97, para. 47; *McElhinney v. Ireland and the United Kingdom*, ECtHR (GC) 21 November 2001, appl. no. 31253/96, para. 24; *Fogarty v. the United Kingdom*, ECtHR (GC) 21 November 2001, appl. no. 37112/97, para. 25.

20   *Ibid.*, paras. 48, 25 and 26, respectively; *Stichting Mothers of Srebrenica and Others v. the Netherlands*, ECtHR 11 June 2013, appl. no. 65542/12, para. 139.

21   *Baraona v. Portugal*, ECtHR 8 July 1987, appl. no. 10092/82, paras. 40–41.

case, the Court held that, although according to constant case law of the German Constitutional Court the State cannot be held responsible for legislative acts, the applicant, who complained about the fact that as a result of the adoption of a certain law he had to give up his professional activity, was nevertheless claiming a civil right, since the German Constitution guaranteed the right to the free exercise of one's profession and the right to respect of one's property.[22]

On the other hand, if domestic law expressly excludes the claim, the Court takes the position that 'to this extent' there can be no arguable right which would make Article 6 applicable.[23] The Court may not, by interpreting Article 6(1), create a right that has no basis in the domestic legal system concerned.[24] However, the mere fact that a right has been restricted by the legislator has no effect on the applicability of Article 6.[25] And a court decision to the effect that a certain claim does not exist, cannot remove, retrospectively, the arguability of the claim.[26] However, if the domestic court reaches the conclusion that the claimed right does not exist (any more) under domestic law, Article 6 is no longer applicable and does not guarantee any further access.[27] This may amount to a lack of an effective remedy, but that issue falls under Article 13 and not under Article 6.[28] In *Roche*, the Court held that it must have very good reasons to differ from the opinion of the national court on the interpretation of national conditions and use its own interpretation instead when answering the question whether a right exists.[29] In *Vilho Eskelinen and others v. Finland*, the Court was less strict. In this case, it concerned the award of a personal allowance on the salary of police officers. The Court held in this case that the existence of a right was arguable because they had been promised the allowance and it had also been awarded in similar cases.[30] In any case, when answering the question if a right exists it is of no significance whether the right is protected under the Convention.[31]

---

[22] *Voggenreiter v. Germany*, ECtHR 8 January 2004, appl. no. 47169/99, para. 35.

[23] *Powell and Rayner v. the United Kingdom*, ECtHR 21 February 1990, appl. no. 9310/81, para. 36; *Anne-Marie Andersson v. Sweden*, ECtHR 27 August 1997, appl. no. 20022/92, paras. 35–36; *Berkmann v. Austria*, *supra* n. 13, para. 2; *Roche v. the United Kingdom*, ECtHR (GC) 19 October 2005, appl. no. 32555/96, paras. 119–124.

[24] *Z and Others v. the United Kingdom*, *supra* n. 13, para. 98; *Al-Adsani v. the United Kingdom*, *supra* n. 19, para. 47.

[25] *Mats Jacobsson v. Sweden*, ECtHR 28 June 1990, appl. no. 11309/84, para. 31; *Pauger v. Austria*, ECtHR 28 May 1997, appl. no. 16717/90, para. 44.

[26] *Z and Others v. the United Kingdom*, *supra* n. 13, para. 94 and *T.P. and K.M. v. the United Kingdom*, ECtHR (GC) 10 May 2001, appl. no. 28945/95, para. 89.

[27] *Z and Others v. the United Kingdom*, *supra* n. 13, para. 97; *Truhli v. Croatia*, ECtHR of 28 June 2001, appl. no. 45424/99, para. 27.

[28] *Z and Others v. the United Kingdom*, *supra* n. 13, paras. 102–103.

[29] *Roche v. the United Kingdom*, *supra* n. 23, paras. 119–124.

[30] *Vilho Eskelinen and Others v. Finland*, ECtHR (GC) 19 April 2007, appl. no. 63235/00, para. 41.

[31] *Micallef v. Malta*, ECtHR 15 October 2009, appl. no. 17057/06, para. 74.

The fact that the applicant had also instituted the national proceedings to vindicate the public interest does not stand in the way of the applicability of Article 6, provided that at the same time an individual right was at stake.[32]

The mere fact that the authorities enjoy discretion in their decision-making and that, therefore, the person concerned cannot claim a specific outcome, does not in itself mean that no right of the applicant is involved. Other criteria which may in this respect be taken into consideration by the Court include the recognition of the alleged right in similar circumstances by the domestic courts or the fact that the latter assessed the merits of the applicant's request.[33] The person is entitled to the authorities respecting the limits of their discretion. That discretion is not unfettered and has to be exercised within the framework of the applicable law and in conformity with general principles of law and good administration.[34] However, if the award of a claimed entitlement is totally left to the court and the case law has not established an obligation on the part of the authorities in situations like the one at issue, no 'actual' right exists.[35]

The determination of the existence of an 'obligation' will be less problematic; that issue has not played an important role in the case law so far.

1.4. LEGAL DISPUTE ('*CONTESTATION*')

From the use of the word '*contestations*' in the French text of Article 6(1), which has no equivalent in the English text, it has been inferred that for Article 6 to be applicable the settlement of a dispute concerning a right or obligation must be at issue.[36] The concept of 'dispute' should not be construed too technically and should be given a substantive rather than a formal meaning. In the *Boulois* case, the Court stated: 'It is necessary to look beyond the appearances and the language used and concentrate on the realities of the situation according to the circumstances of each case.'[37] A difference of opinion between two or more (legal) persons who have a certain relation to the right or obligation at issue is sufficient,

---

[32]   *Gorraiz Lizarraga and Others v. Spain*, ECtHR 27 April 2004, appl. no. 62543/00, paras. 45–48.

[33]   *Boulois v. Luxembourg*, *supra* n. 13, paras. 90–94.

[34]   *Pudas v. Sweden*, ECtHR 27 October 1987, appl. no. 10426/83, paras. 36–37; *Tre Traktörer Aktiebolag v. Sweden*, ECtHR 7 July 1989, appl. no. 10873/84, paras. 39–40; *Allan Jacobsson v. Sweden (No. 1)*, ECtHR 25 October 1989, appl. no. 10842/84, para. 69.

[35]   *Masson and Van Zon v. the Netherlands*, ECtHR 28 September 1995, appl. nos. 15346/89 and 15379/89, para. 51; *Leutscher v. the Netherlands*, ECtHR 26 March 1996, appl. no. 17314/90, para. 24.

[36]   *Le Compte, Van Leuven and De Meyere v. Belgium*, ECtHR (GC) 23 June 1981, appl. nos. 6878/75 and 7238/75, para. 45. The Court said, however, 'Even if (…)'. See also *Moreira de Azevedo v. Portugal*, ECtHR 23 October 1990, appl. no. 11296/84, para. 66: 'In so far as the French word '*contestation*' would appear to require the existence of a dispute, if indeed it does so at all (…)'.

[37]   *Boulois v. Luxembourg*, *supra* n. 13, para. 92.

provided that it is 'genuine and of a serious nature'.[38] One of the (legal) persons may be a public authority whose act or decision affects the other (legal) person.[39] If the act or decision is a favourable one and is not contested by the addressee, but is challenged by another public authority or another (legal) person, the latter has raised a 'contestation', also in the relation between the former and the competent authority.[40] For the 'contestation' is not required that damages are claimed.[41]

The 'contestation' must be of a legal character: it must concern the alleged violation of a right.[42] This does not exclude cases in which the administrative authority has discretionary powers,[43] provided that the way in which these powers have been exercised is challenged on legal and not only on policy grounds.[44] These legal grounds may relate to the way in which the limits of the discretion set by law have been respected,[45] or to the issue of whether the challenged act is in conformity with generally recognised principles of law and good administration.[46] Article 6 does not apply to a non-contentious and unilateral procedure which does not involve opposing parties and which is available only where there is no dispute over rights.[47]

The legal-character requirement does not mean that the difference of opinion may not relate to facts, provided that they have some implications for the determination of (the scope of) rights or obligations.[48] The fact that the dispute has been 'settled' by a non-judicial procedure, does not mean that the party who is not satisfied with the settlement no has longer a dispute of a serious and genuine nature.[49]

In the *Moreira de Azevedo* case, the Court held that, although the applicant was only *assistente* in criminal proceedings and had not filed a formal claim for damages, there was a *contestation* concerning his civil rights.[50] It seems to have been deemed crucial that the implications of intervening as an *assistente* were not clear under Portuguese law, because in the subsequent *Hamer* case the Court

---

[38]   *Le Compte, Van Leuven and De Meyere v. Belgium, supra* n. 36, para. 45; *Z and Others v. the United Kingdom, supra* n. 13, para. 92; *Kienast v. Austria*, ECtHR 23 January 2003, appl. no. 23379/94, para. 39.

[39]   *Ringeisen v. Austria*, ECtHR 16 July 1971, appl. no. 2614/65, para. 94.

[40]   *Benthem v. The Netherlands, supra* n. 10, para. 33.

[41]   *Pieniazek v. Poland*, ECtHR 28 September 2004, appl. no. 62179/00, para. 20.

[42]   *Le Compte, Van Leuven and De Meyere v. Belgium, supra* n. 36, para. 46; *Kienast v. Austria, supra* n. 38, para. 43.

[43]   *Lambourdiere v. France*, ECtHR 2 August 2000, appl. no. 37387/97, para. 24.

[44]   *Van Marle and Others v. the Netherlands*, ECtHR (GC) 26 June 1986, appl. nos. 8543/79, 8674/79, 8675/79 and 8685/79, para. 35; *Pudas v. Sweden, supra* n. 34, para. 34.

[45]   *Allan Jacobsson v. Sweden (No. 1), supra* n. 25, para. 69.

[46]   *Skärby v. Sweden*, ECtHR 28 June 1990, appl. no. 12258/86, para. 28.

[47]   *Alaverdyan v. Armenia*, ECtHR 24 August 2010, appl. no. 4523/04, para. 35.

[48]   *Van Marle and Others v. the Netherlands, supra* n. 28, para. 31; *Pudas v. Sweden, supra* n. 34, para. 31.

[49]   *Zwiazek Nauczycielstwa Polskiego v. Poland*, ECtHR 21 September 2004, appl. no. 42049/98, paras. 30–34.

[50]   *Moreira De Azevedo v. Portugal, supra* n. 36, para. 67.

reached the conclusion that there had been no 'dispute' over a civil right because of the failure of the applicant to lodge a formal claim for damages.[51]

In most cases, however, where the applicability of Article 6 is at issue the existence of a '*contestation*' is not in dispute.

1.5. DETERMINATION

The (claimed)[52] judicial proceedings must lead to a 'determination' of civil rights or obligations. The mere communication or warning by a public authority that a certain licence has lapsed *de lege*, is not a 'determination'.[53] However, the mere fact that, at a later stage, the applicant withdrew his action which resulted in the discontinuance of the proceedings, does not affect the applicability of Article 6.[54]

Preliminary proceedings, like those concerned with the granting of an interim measure such as an injunction, are not normally considered to determine civil rights and obligations and do not therefore normally fall within the protection of Article 6. In the *Micallef* case, the Court considered: 'Nevertheless, in certain cases, the Court has applied Article 6 to interim proceedings, notably by reason of their being decisive for the civil rights of the applicant (...). Moreover, it has held that an exception is to be made to the principle that Article 6 will not apply when the character of the interim decision exceptionally requires otherwise because the measure requested was drastic, disposed of the main action to a considerable degree, and unless reversed on appeal would have affected the legal rights of the parties for a substantial period of time (...).'[55]

Furthermore, if the determination by a court has taken place but the court decision is not (fully) executed, the claim for (the remainder of the) execution and damages still forms part of the determination and is covered by Article 6.[56]

There must be a connection between the dispute to be solved and a civil right or obligation. A tenuous connection or remote consequence does not suffice.[57] Thus, the Court held that proceedings concerning the licencing of a

---

[51] *Hamer v. France*, ECtHR 7 August 1996, appl. no. 19953/92, paras. 74–79. See also *Garimpo v. Portugal*, ECtHR 10 June 2004 (dec.), appl. no. 66752/01, which also concerned the position of *assistente* under Portuguese law.

[52] As will be discussed under 'access to court', under 3.1 *infra*, according to the Court, Art. 6(1) not only contains procedural guarantees in relation to judicial proceedings, but also grants a right of access to judicial proceedings for the cases mentioned in this article.

[53] *Kervoëlen v. France*, ECtHR 27 March 2001, appl. no. 35585/97, paras. 28–30.

[54] *Ciz v. Slovakia*, ECtHR 14 October 2003, appl. no. 66142/01, para. 61.

[55] *Micallef v. Malta*, *supra* n. 31, para. 75.

[56] *Dybo v. Poland*, ECtHR 14 October 2003, appl. no. 71894/01, paras. 20–22.

[57] *Le Compte, Van Leuven and De Meyere v. Belgium*, *supra* n. 36, para. 47; *Balmer-Schafroth and Others v. Switzerland*, ECtHR 26 August 1997, appl. no. 22110/93, para. 32; *Chevrol v. France*, ECtHR 13 February 2003, appl. no. 49636/99, para. 44; *Pocius v. Lithuania*, ECtHR 6 July 2010, appl. no. 35601/04, para. 38; *Boulois v. Luxembourg*, *supra* n. 13, para. 90.

nuclear power plant did not have a sufficiently direct link with the applicants' rights to adequate protection of their life, physical integrity and property to bring Article 6(1) into play.[582] And proceedings concerning the annulment of a presidential decree by virtue of an agreement between France and Switzerland, which made enlargement of an airport near the border possible, were deemed not to be sufficiently directly linked to the applicants' right and economic interest to construct an industrial area near the airport.[59] This also means that Article 6(1) does not apply to proceedings instituted by way of *actio popularis*.[60] However, the mere fact that the applicant shares the legal connection with several others does not make that connection remote or tenuous.[61]

On the other hand, the 'determination' does not need to form the main point or even the purpose of the proceedings. It is sufficient that the outcome of the (claimed) judicial proceedings may be 'decisive for',[62] or may 'affect',[63] or may 'relate to'[64] the determination and/or the exercise of the right, or the determination and/or the fulfilment of the obligation, as the case may be. The effects need not be legal; they may also be purely factual.[65] And if the proceedings concern the determination of a civil right or obligation, the same applies to subsequent proceedings concerning legal costs incurred.[66]

The civil right or obligation does not have to constitute the object of the proceedings.[67] If, for instance, the object of the proceedings is the annulment of

---

[58]   *Balmer-Schafroth and Others v. Switzerland, supra* n. 57, para. 10; *Athanassoglou and Others v. Switzerland*, ECtHR (GC) 6 April 2000, appl. no. 27644/95, para. 51.

[59]   *S.A.R.L. du Parc d'Activités de Blotzheim et la S.C.I. Haselaecker v. France*, ECtHR 18 March 2003 (dec.), appl. no. 48897/99, para. 9. See also *Zapletal v. the Czech Republic*, ECtHR 30 November 2010, appl. no. 12720/06 (a case concerning limited noise pollution at a factory) and *Ivan Atanasov v. Bulgaria*, ECtHR 2 December 2010, appl. no. 12853/03 (a case about 'the hypothetical environmental impact of a plant for the treatment of mining waste').

[60]   *Athanassoglou and Others v. Switzerland, supra* n. 58, paras. 53–54. See, however, the joint dissenting opinion of Judges Costa, Tulkens, Fischbach, Casadevall and Maruste, who stressed that the decision whether the action had the character of an *actio popularis* required access to a domestic court.

[61]   *Allan Jacobsson v. Sweden (No. 1), supra* n. 25, para. 70.

[62]   *Ringeisen v. Austria, supra* n. 39, para. 94. See also, *inter alia, Neigel v. France*, ECtHR 17 March 1997, appl. no. 18725/91, para. 38; *Stanev v. Bulgaria*, ECtHR (GC) 17 January 2012, appl. no. 36760/00, para. 233.

[63]   *Winterwerp v. the Netherlands*, ECtHR 24 October 1979, appl. no. 6301/73, para. 73. See also, *inter alia, Ettl and Others v. Austria*, ECtHR 23 April 1987, appl. no. 9273/81, para. 32; *Erkner and Hofauer v. Austria*, ECtHR 23 April 1987, appl. no. 9616/81, para. 62; and *Poiss v. Austria*, ECtHR 23 April 1987, appl. no. 9816/82, para. 48.

[64]   *Skärby v. Sweden, supra* n. 46, para. 27; *A.B. v. Slovakia*, ECtHR 4 March 2003, appl. no. 41784/98, paras. 46–48.

[65]   *Sporrong and Lönnroth v. Sweden*, ECtHR (GC) 23 September 1982, appl. nos. 7151/75 and 7152/75, para. 80 in conjunction with para. 63.

[66]   *Robins v. the United Kingdom*, ECtHR 23 September 1997, appl. no. 22410/93, para. 29. See also, *inter alia, Ziegler v. Switzerland*, ECtHR 21 February 2002, appl. no. 33499/96, paras. 24–25.

[67]   See the *Winterwerp* case, where the object was the deprivation of liberty, which had, however, direct consequences for Mr Winterwerp's legal capacity to perform private-law acts; *Winterwerp v. the Netherlands, supra* n. 63, paras. 73–74.

an administrative decision or sanction, the right or obligation may be the object or one of the objects of that decision or may be implied in the sanction. The civil right may also be a right claimed by a third party who intervenes in criminal proceedings to obtain damages.[68] In the same way, if an administrative decision does (also) affect civil rights of third parties, e.g. the neighbours of a piece of land for which a building permit has been granted or the neighbours of a licensed plant, they also have the right of access to court to challenge the decision.[69] Moreover, the determination need not necessarily concern the actual existence of a right or obligation, but may also relate to its scope or modalities,[70] or to the unlawfulness of interferences with the exercise of a right.[71] The bottom line is reached, however, if the right claimed is not at issue at all in the proceedings concerned. Thus, the Court held Article 6 to be not applicable with regard to one of the applicants in the *McMichael* case. Mr McMichael had failed to take the requisite prior steps to obtain legal recognition of his parental rights. Therefore, the care proceedings, instituted by Mr and Mrs McMichael, could not have a connection with the determination of Mr McMichael's rights as a father.[72]

If under domestic law a person may bring a claim for damages incurred by a criminal act in the criminal proceedings, these proceedings are decisive for his 'civil' rights.[73] This also means that the impossibility of taking certain actions to safeguard these rights may amount to lack of access to court.[74] However, if the applicant has failed to lodge a claim in the appropriate proceedings, the proceedings in which he brings the claim cannot be considered to be decisive for the right concerned for the purpose of Article 6(1); consequently, if the latter proceedings are discontinued, the applicant cannot be said to have been denied access to court.[75] Both in the *Hamer* case and in the *Assenov* case the applicants had claimed damages as a civil party in criminal proceedings. In the *Hamer* case, the applicant had failed to claim damages at the right stage of the proceedings, which would then have been dealt with by the court in its civil composition. In the *Assenov* case, the applicant could have brought civil proceedings for damages, the outcome of which was, in the opinion of the Court, not determined

---

[68]   *Moreira De Azevedo v. Portugal, supra* n. 36, paras. 66–67.

[69]   *Athanassoglou and Others v. Switzerland, supra* n. 58, para. 45.

[70]   *Le Compte, Van Leuven and De Meyere v. Belgium, supra* n. 36, para. 49; *Benthem v. The Netherlands, supra* n. 10, para. 32; *Van Marle and Others v. the Netherlands, supra* n. 28, para. 32.

[71]   *Sporrong and Lönnroth v. Sweden, supra* n. 65, para. 80.

[72]   *McMichael v. the United Kingdom,* ECtHR 24 February 1995, appl. no. 16424/90, para. 77; *Mandela v. Greece*, ECtHR 24 June 2004 (dec.), appl. no. 6709/02: the proceedings only concerned a procedural issue and not a determination of the right at issue.

[73]   *Aït-Mouhoub v. France*, ECtHR 28 October 1998, appl. no. 22924/93, para. 44; *Maini v. France*, ECtHR 26 October 1999, appl. no. 31801/96, paras. 28–29; *Anagnostopoulos and Others v. Greece*, ECtHR 3 April 2003, appl. no. 39374/98, para. 32.

[74]   *Sottani v. Italy*, ECtHR 24 February 2005 (dec.), appl. no. 26775/02, para. 2.

[75]   *Hamer v. France, supra* n. 51, paras. 74–78; *Assenov and Others v. Bulgaria*, ECtHR 28 October 1998, appl. no. 24760/94, para. 112.

by that of the criminal proceedings. However, in the *Calvelli and Ciglio* case, the Court decided in respect of Italy that the criminal proceedings were apt to have repercussions on the claims made by the applicants as civil parties.[76] It appears from the facts of the case that there the applicants had also brought a claim in civil proceedings, but the case was struck out of the civil court's list. In any case, if the civil court stays the proceedings to wait for the outcome of the criminal proceedings concerning the criminal issues involved, the Court takes this into account in assessing the reasonableness of the duration of the trial.[77]

In its judgment of 12 February 2004 in the *Perez* case, the Grand Chamber considered that the Court's case law concerning civil claims in criminal proceedings might present a number of drawbacks, particularly in terms of legal certainty for the parties, and tended to over-complicate any analysis of the applicability of Article 6 to civil party proceedings in French law and similar systems. It indicated that it wished to end this uncertainty and held that there can be no doubt that civil party proceedings constitute (in French law) a civil action for reparation of damages caused by an offence. If the civil component remains closely connected with the criminal component to the extent that the criminal proceedings affect the civil component, Article 6 applies to both components of the proceedings. The damages sought may relate to pecuniary damages, even of a symbolic nature, but also, e.g., to the protection of one's reputation. If, however, the civil action is brought for punitive purposes, Article 6 is not applicable to the private component of the proceedings, since the Convention does not confer any right to 'private revenge' or to an *actio popularis*.[78]

If a remedy is not provided for under national law, it is not possible to determine what effect the outcome of the proceedings have had or might have had. In those cases, the Court investigates whether the challenged decision or refusal to decide was decisive for a civil right or obligation and whether the administrative procedure revealed a *contestation* concerning such a right or obligation.[79]

If the outcome of proceedings concerning procedural requirements determines the merits of the case, these proceedings are decisive for a civil right or obligation, if the merits concern such a right or obligation.[80] The same holds good for non-judicial proceedings which take place in the framework of judicial proceedings determining civil rights and are closely linked to the latter.[81]

---

[76]   *Calvelli and Ciglio v. Italy,* ECtHR (GC) 17 January 2002, appl. no. 32967/96, para. 62.

[77]   *Djangozov v. Bulgaria*, ECtHR 8 July 2004, appl. no. 45950/99, para. 38.

[78]   *Perez v. France*, ECtHR (GC) 12 February 2004, appl. no. 47287/99, paras. 54–71. See also *Anagnostopoulos and Others v. Greece, supra* n. 73, para. 32.

[79]   *Bodén v. Sweden*, ECtHR 27 October 1987, appl. no. 10930/84, para. 32; *Skärby v. Sweden, supra* n. 46, para. 28.

[80]   *Paskhalidis and Others v. Greece*, ECtHR 19 March 1997, appl. no. 20416/92 and 22857/93, para. 30.

[81]   *Siegel v. France*, ECtHR 28 November 2000, appl. no. 36350/97, paras. 37–38.

1.6. AUTONOMOUS MEANING OF 'CIVIL'

The words 'civil rights and obligations' have an autonomous meaning in Article 6.[82] To determine whether a certain right or obligation is a 'civil' right or obligation, one must first examine what the nature of the right or obligation at issue is according to the law of the respondent state.[83] If the right or obligation forms part of private law or family law, it is evident that the first paragraph of Article 6 applies.[84] To this extent the autonomy of the interpretation is a one-way autonomy. The same holds good if the features of private law are 'predominant'.[85] In contrast, the mere fact that the right or obligation at issue is governed by public law does not exclude the applicability of the first paragraph of Article 6; what matters are the contents and effect of that right or obligation rather than its legal classification.[86] In that context, the Court also pays attention to the capacity in which a person claims a right and the conditions under which he wishes to exercise it or exercises it.[87] In doing so, it also takes into account the legal systems of the other Contracting States.[88] This approach makes the scope of Article 6(1) less dependent on the national legal system concerned.

It is also not decisive for the 'civil' nature of a right or obligation whether the underlying dispute is one between individuals or one between an individual and a public authority. Even if in the latter case that public authority is involved in the proceedings in a sovereign capacity, those proceedings can relate to the determination of 'civil rights and obligations'.[89] It is equally not decisive whether the proceedings take place before a civil court or before another body vested with jurisdiction.[90] And, finally, the fact that in legal relations between individuals, great public interests may also be involved, does not bar the applicability of Article 6(1).[91]

Up to the present the Court has held the first paragraph of Article 6 applicable, in addition to proceedings with a private-law character, *inter alia*[92] to the following proceedings as determining civil rights or obligations:

---

[82]   *König v. Germany, supra* n. 11, paras. 88–89. See also *Malige v. France,* ECtHR 29 September 1998, appl. no. 27812/95, para. 34; *Maaouia v. France,* ECtHR (GC) 5 October 2000, appl. no. 39652/98, para. 34.

[83]   *König v. Germany, supra* n. 11, para. 89; *Feldbrugge v. the Netherlands,* ECtHR (GC) 29 May 1986, appl. no. 8562/79, para. 28.

[84]   *Rasmussen v. Denmark,* ECtHR 28 November 1984, appl. no. 8777/79, para. 32.

[85]   *Feldbrugge v. the Netherlands, supra* n. 83, paras. 30–40.

[86]   *König v. Germany, supra* n. 11, para. 89.

[87]   *H. v. Belgium,* ECtHR (GC) 30 November 1987, appl. no. 8950/80, paras. 46–47.

[88]   *König v. Germany, supra* n. 11, para. 89; *Feldbrugge v. the Netherlands, supra* n. 83, para. 29.

[89]   *König v. Germany, supra* n. 11, para. 90; *Benthem v. The Netherlands, supra* n. 10, para. 34.

[90]   *Ringeisen v. Austria, supra* n. 39, para. 94. See also, *inter alia, Baraona v. Portugal, supra* n. 21, paras. 42–43.

[91]   *Rasmussen v. Denmark, supra* n. 84, para. 32.

[92]   See also under 2.8.

- proceedings concerning a permit, licence or other act of a public authority which constitutes a condition for the legality of a contract between private parties;[93]
- proceedings which may lead to the cancellation or suspension by the public authorities of the qualification required for practising a particular profession;[94]
- proceedings concerning the refusal by the authorities to appoint the applicant to a post that belongs to the liberal professions, or concerning dismissal from such a post,[95] and concerning a decision which prevents the applicant from taking up a certain position;[96]
- proceedings concerning certain financial aspects of public service,[97] and concerning labour contracts for positions in state-owned enterprises;[98]
- proceedings concerning the grant or revocation of a licence by the public authorities which is required for setting up a certain business or carry out certain economic activities;[99]
- expropriation, consolidation, designation and planning proceedings,[100] proceedings concerning building permits and other real estate

---

[93] *Ringeisen v. Austria, supra* n. 39, para. 94; *Sramek v. Austria*, ECtHR (GC) 22 October 1984, appl. no. 8790/79, para. 34.

[94] *König v. Germany, supra* n. 11, paras. 91–95; *Le Compte, Van Leuven and De Meyere v. Belgium, supra* n. 36, paras. 46–48; *Albert and Le Compte v. Belgium*, ECtHR (GC) 10 February 1983, appl. nos. 7299/75 and 7496/76, para. 28; *H. v. Belgium, supra* n. 87, paras. 45–47; *Kraska v. Switzerland*, ECtHR 19 April 1993, appl. no. 13942/88, para. 25; *Diennet v. France*, ECtHR 26 September 1995, appl. no. 18160/91, para. 27; *Serre v. France*, ECtHR 29 September 1999, appl. no. 29718/96, para. 20; *Bakker v. Austria*, ECtHR 10 April 2003, appl. no. 43454/98, para. 26; *Krokstäde v. Sweden*, ECtHR 28 September 2004 (dec.), appl. no. 63916/00, para. 1.

[95] *Thlimmenos v. Greece*, ECtHR (GC) 6 April 2000, appl. no. 34369/97, para. 58; *Werner v. Poland*, ECtHR 15 November 2001, appl. no. 26760/95, para. 32.

[96] *Kingsley v. the United Kingdom*, ECtHR 7 November 2000, appl. no. 35605/97, paras. 43–45.

[97] *Dimitrios Georgiadis v. Greece*, ECtHR 28 March 2000, appl. no. 41209/98, para. 21; *S.M. v. France*, ECtHR 18 July 2000, appl. no. 41453/98, para. 19.

[98] *Sienkiewicz v. Poland*, ECtHR 30 September 2003, appl. no. 52468/99 impliedly.

[99] *Benthem v. The Netherlands, supra* n. 10, para. 36; *Pudas v. Sweden, supra* n. 34, para. 37; *Tre Traktörer AB Aktiebolag v. Sweden, supra* n. 34, para. 43; judgment of *Fredin v. Sweden (No. 1)*, ECtHR 18 February 1991, appl. no. 12033/86, para. 63; *G.S. v. Austria*, ECtHR 21 December 1999, appl. no. 26297/95, para. 27; *Kingsley v. the United Kingdom, supra* n. 96, paras. 43–45; *Chevrol v. France, supra* n. 57, para. 49.

[100] *Sporrong and Lönnroth v. Sweden, supra* n. 65, para. 80; *Ettl and Others v. Austria, supra* n. 63, para. 32; *Erkner and Hofauer v. Austria, supra* n. 63, para. 62; and *Poiss v. Austria, supra* n. 63, para. 48; *Bodén v. Sweden, supra* n. 63, para. 32; *Oerlemans v. the Netherlands*, ECtHR 27 November 1991, appl. no. 12565/86, para. 48; *De Geouffre de la Pradelle v. France*, ECtHR 16 December 1992, appl. no. 12964/87, para. 28 (impliedly); *Varipati v. Greece*, ECtHR 26 October 1999, appl. no. 38459/97, para. 21; *Aldo and Jean-Baptiste Zanatta v. France*, ECtHR 28 March 2000, appl. no. 38042/97, para. 24; *Hutten v. the Netherlands*, ECtHR 11 May 2004 (dec.), appl. no. 56698/00.

permits,[101] proceedings concerning orders specifying the use of land,[102] proceedings concerning restoration of ownership as a rehabilitation measure[103] and concerning compensation for forfeited property,[104] proceedings concerning the ownership and use of a religious building,[105] and more in general proceedings the outcome of which has direct consequences for the right of ownership or has an impact on the use or the enjoyment of property;[106]

- proceedings concerning discrimination when bidding for a public works contract[107] and in access to the civil service;[108]
- proceedings in which a decision is taken on entitlement, under a social security scheme, to health insurance benefits,[109] to industrial-accident insurance benefits or payment of compensation for a work-related illness or accident,[110] to welfare (disability) allowances,[111] to state pensions,[112] to invalidity pensions,[113] to survivor pensions,[114] and to old-age pensions;[115]
- proceedings to obtain allowances under a national health service programme;[116]

---

[101] *Allan Jacobsson v. Sweden (No. 1)*, *supra* n. 25, para. 73; *Håkansson and Sturesson v. Sweden*, ECtHR 21 February 1990, appl. no. 11855/85, para. 60; *Mats Jacobsson v. Sweden*, *supra* n. 25, para. 34; *Skärby v. Sweden*, *supra* n. 46, para. 29; *Allan Jacobsson v. Sweden (No. 2)*, ECtHR 19 February 1998, appl. no. 16970/90, para. 42.

[102] *Fredin v. Sweden*, *supra* n. 99, para. 63; *Alge v. Austria*, ECtHR 22 January 2004, appl. no. 38185/97, para. 20.

[103] *Jori v. Slovakia*, *supra* n. 15, paras. 48–49.

[104] *Cegielski v. Poland*, ECtHR 21 October 2003, appl. no. 71893/01, para. 24.

[105] *Sâmbata Bihor Greco-Catolic Parish v. Romania*, ECtHR 12 January 2010, appl. no. 48107/99, para. 65.

[106] *Ruiz-Mateos v. Spain*, ECtHR (GC) 23 June 1993, appl. no. 12952/87, paras. 51–52; *Zander v. Sweden*, ECtHR 25 November 1993, appl. no. 14282/88, para. 27; *Ludescher v. Austria*, ECtHR 20 December 2001, appl. no. 35019/97, para. 16; *Achleitner v. Austria*, ECtHR 23 October 2003, appl. no. 53911/00 impliedly.

[107] *Tinnelly & Sons Ltd and Others and McElduff and Others v. the United Kingdom*, ECtHR 10 July 1998, appl. nos. 20390/92 and 21322/92, paras. 61–62; but see *I.T.C. Ltd v. Malta*, ECtHR 11 December 2007, appl. no. 2629/06 (dec.).

[108] *Devlin v. the United Kingdom*, ECtHR 30 October 2001, appl. no. 29545/95, para. 23.

[109] *Feldbrugge v. the Netherlands*, *supra* n. 83, paras. 26–40; *De Haan v. the Netherlands*, ECtHR 26 August 1997, appl. no. 22839/93, para. 44.

[110] *Deumeland v. Germany*, ECtHR (GC) 29 May 1986, appl. no. 9384/81, paras. 62–74; *Chaudet v. France*, ECtHR 29 October 2009, appl. no. 49037/06, para. 30.

[111] *Salesi v. Italy*, ECtHR 26 February 1993, appl. no. 13023/87, para. 19; *Stamoulakatos v. Greece (No. 2)*, ECtHR 26 November 1997, appl. no. 27159/95, para. 31; *Bogonos v. Russia*, ECtHR 5 February 2004 (dec.), appl. no. 68798/01, para. 1.

[112] *Giancarlo Lombardo v. Italy*, ECtHR 26 November 1992, appl. no. 12490/86, para. 16 and *Francesco Lombardo v. Italy*, ECtHR 26 November 1992, appl. no. 11519/85, para. 17; *Massa v. Italy*, ECtHR 24 August 1993, appl. no. 14399/88, para. 26.

[113] *Schuler-Zgraggen v. Switzerland*, ECtHR 24 June 1993, appl. no. 14518/89, para. 46; *Paskhalidis and Others v. Greece*, *supra* n. 80, para. 30.

[114] *Pauger v. Austria*, *supra* n. 25, para. 45.

[115] *Paskhalidis and Others v. Greece*, *supra* n. 80, para. 30.

[116] *Mennitto v. Italy*, *supra* n. 12, para. 27.

- proceedings against public authorities in which rights and obligations concerning family law are at issue;[117]
- proceedings concerning the change of a surname;[118]
- proceedings against the public administration concerning contracts,[119] concerning damages in administrative proceedings[120] or in criminal proceedings,[121] concerning negligence on the part of the authorities[122] and concerning any (other) tort committed by a person or institution for which the state is responsible;[123]
- proceedings concerning damages as a result of the effects of a land consolidation project;[124]
- proceedings concerning damage caused to one's reputation;[125]
- proceedings relating to compensation for unjustified conviction or detention;[126]

---

[117] *Rasmussen v. Denmark, supra* n. 84, para. 32; *O. v. the United Kingdom, supra* n. 14, paras. 54–60 and *H. v. the United Kingdom*, ECtHR 8 July 1987, appl. no. 9580/81, paras. 69; *W. v. the United Kingdom*, ECtHR (Plenary) 8 July 1987, appl. no. 9749/82, paras. 73–79; *B. v. the United Kingdom*, ECtHR 8 July 1987, appl. no. 9840/82, paras. 73–79; *R. v. the United Kingdom*, ECtHR 8 July 1987, appl. no. 10496/83, paras. 78–84; *Eriksson v. Sweden*, ECtHR (GC) 22 June 1989, appl. no. 11373/85, para. 73; *Olsson v. Sweden (No. 2)*, ECtHR 27 November 1992, appl. no. 13441/87, para. 97; *Keegan v. Ireland*, ECtHR 26 May 1994, appl. no. 16969/90, para. 57; *Paulsen-Medalen and Svensson v. Sweden*, ECtHR 19 February 1998, appl. no. 16817/90, paras. 38–42; *Glaser v. the United Kingdom*, ECtHR 19 September 2000, appl. no. 32346/96, para. 91.

[118] *Petersen v. Germany*, ECtHR 6 December 2001 (dec.), appl. no. 31178/96, para. 4: 'the Court starts with the assumption that Article 6 para. 1 in principle applies.'

[119] *Philis v. Greece*, ECtHR 27 August 1991, appl. nos. 12750/87, 13780/88 and 14003/88, para. 65 (impliedly).

[120] *Baraona v. Portugal, supra* n. 21, para. 44; *Neves e Silva v. Portugal*, ECtHR 27 April 1989, appl. no. 11213/84, para. 37; *H. v. France*, ECtHR 24 October 1989, appl. no. 10073/82, para. 47; *Editions Périscope v. France, supra* n. 15, para. 40; *X v. France*, ECtHR 31 March 1992, appl. no. 18020/91, para. 30; *Racinet v. France*, ECtHR 23 September 2003, appl. no. 53544/99, impliedly.

[121] *Moreira De Azevedo v. Portugal, supra* n. 36, para. 66; *Casciaroli v. Italy*, ECtHR 27 February 1992, appl. no. 11973/86, para. 19 (impliedly); *Werner v. Austria*, ECtHR 24 November 1997, appl. no. 21835/93, para. 39; *Lamanna v. Austria*, ECtHR 10 July 2001, appl. no. 28923/95, para. 29.

[122] *Kaya v. Turkey*, ECtHR 19 February 1998, appl. no. 22729/93, para. 104; *Osman v. the United Kingdom*, ECtHR (GC) 28 October 1998, appl. no. 23452/94, paras. 136–139; *Z and Others v. the United Kingdom, supra* n. 13, para. 89.

[123] *Chaineux v. France*, ECtHR 14 October 2003, appl. no. 56243/00, para. 12; *Broca and Texier-Micault v. France*, ECtHR 21 October 2003, appl. nos. 27928/02 and 31694/02, para. 26; *Mianowski v. Poland*, ECtHR 16 December 2003, appl. no. 42083/98 (impliedly).

[124] *Van Vlimmeren and Van Ilverenbeek v. the Netherlands*, ECtHR 26 September 2000, appl. no. 25989/94, para. 37 (impliedly).

[125] *Werner v. Poland, supra* n. 95, para. 33.

[126] *Georgiadis v. Greece*, ECtHR 29 May 1997, appl. no. 21522/93, para. 34; *Szücs v. Austria*, ECtHR 24 November 1997, appl. no. 20602/92, paras. 36–37; *Humen v. Poland*, ECtHR (GC) 15 October 1999, appl. no. 26614/95, para. 57; *Karakasis v. Greece*, ECtHR 17 November 2000, appl. no. 38194/97, para. 25.

- proceedings concerning public assistance in evicting tenants from a house;[127]
- proceedings concerning the obligation to pay contributions under a social security scheme;[128]
- proceedings concerning the payment of levies for public services;[129]
- patent application proceedings;[130]
- proceedings concerning the right to register as an association;[131]
- proceedings to have one's legal capacity restored; and[132]
- civil party complaints in criminal proceedings.[133]

1.7. PUBLIC LAW PROCEEDINGS OUTSIDE THE SCOPE OF CIVIL RIGHTS AND OBLIGATIONS

There are still certain administrative proceedings where individual rights or obligations are at stake, with respect to which the Court so far has held that Article 6(1) is not applicable.

a. Tax duties

In the *Schouten and Meldrum* case, the Court held in an *obiter dictum* that obligations which derive from tax legislation or are otherwise part of normal civic duties in a democratic society, do not fall under the notion of 'civil obligations'.[134] Almost three years before, in the *Editions Périscope* case, the Court had attributed a decisive meaning to the pecuniary character of the rights and obligations involved rather than to the fact that the dispute concerned damage resulting from the allegedly discriminatory application of tax regulations.[135] And in its judgment in the *National & Provincial Building Society* case, the Court held, referring to its judgment in the *Editions Périscope* case, that the restitution proceedings were decisive for the determination of private-

---

[127] *Immobiliare Saffi v. Italy*, ECtHR (GC) 28 July 1999, appl. no. 22774/93, paras. 62–63; *G.L. v. Italy*, ECtHR 3 August 2000, appl. no. 22671/93, para. 30.

[128] *Schouten and Meldrum v. the Netherlands*, ECtHR 9 December 1994, appl. no. 19005/91 and 19006/91, paras. 49–60.

[129] *Klein v. Germany*, ECtHR 27 July 2000, appl. no. 33379/96, para. 29.

[130] *British-American Tobacco Company Ltd v. the Netherlands*, ECtHR 20 November 1995, appl. no. 19589/92, para. 67.

[131] *APEH Üldözötteinek Szövetsége and Others v. Hungary*, ECtHR 5 October 2000, appl. no. 32367/96, para. 36.

[132] *Matter v. Slovakia*, ECtHR 5 July 1999, appl. no. 31534/96, para. 51; *Stanev v. Bulgaria, supra* n. 62, para. 233.

[133] See, e.g., *Perez v. France, supra* n. 78, paras. 70–71 and *Gorou v. Greece (No. 2)*, ECtHR (GC) 20 March 2009, appl. no. 12686/03, para. 20.

[134] *Schouten and Meldrum v. the Netherlands, supra* n. 128, para. 50.

[135] *Editions Périscope v. France, supra* n. 15, para. 40.

law rights and that the applicability of Article 6(1) was not affected by the fact that these rights had their background in tax legislation and the obligation of the applicant to account for tax under that legislation.[136] The latter judgment, in particular, cast doubt on the precise direction of the case law.

The *Schouten and Meldrum* line of reasoning was confirmed in the *Ferrazzini* case by the Grand Chamber, albeit by eleven votes to six. There the Court started its considerations by observing that pecuniary interests are clearly at stake in tax proceedings. However, merely showing that a dispute is pecuniary in nature is not in itself sufficient to attract the applicability of the first paragraph of Article 6 under its 'civil head'. In examining whether interpreting the Convention as a living instrument should lead to the conclusion that developments have occurred in democratic societies that have affected the fundamental nature of the obligation to pay tax, the Court reached the conclusion that 'tax matters still form part of the hard core of public-authority prerogatives, with the public nature of the relationship between the taxpayer and the tax authority remaining predominant. (...). It considers that tax disputes fall outside the scope of civil rights and obligations, despite the necessary pecuniary effects which they necessarily produce for the taxpayer.'[137]

It is hard to understand why tax procedures, which in all member states of the Council of Europe are governed by rather strict legal rules, should not meet the minimum standards of fair trial of Article 6. As Judge Lorenzen observed in his dissenting opinion, 'it is now recognised at least in the vast majority of the Contracting Parties that disputes in fiscal matters can be decided in ordinary proceedings by a court or tribunal. It is therefore difficult to see why it is still necessary to grant to the States a special prerogative under the Convention in this field and thus deny litigants in tax proceedings the elementary procedural guarantee of Article 6 para. 1'.[138]

In the same dissenting opinion, it is stated that the criterion 'normal civic duties in a democratic society', used by the Court, is not suitable to form the basis for a general distinction between 'civil' and 'non-civil' rights and obligations. 'Thus it is difficult to see why, for example, the obligation to hand over property for public use in return for compensation is not a 'normal civic duty' whereas

---

136 *National & Provincial Building Society and Others v. the United Kingdom,* ECtHR 23 October 1997, appl. nos. 21319/93, 21449/93 and 21675/93, para. 97.

137 *Ferrazzini v. Italy,* ECtHR (GC) 12 July 2001, appl. no. 44759/98, para. 29. See the dissenting opinion of Judge Lorenzen, joined by Judges Rozakis, Bonello, Stráznická, Bîrsan and Fischbach, where it is stated: 'It is not open to doubt that the obligation to pay taxes directly and substantially affects the pecuniary interest of citizens and that in a democratic society taxation (...) is based on the application of legal rules and not on the authorities' discretion. Accordingly (...) Article 6 should apply to such disputes (...)'. See also *Chambaz v. Switzerland,* ECtHR 5 April 2012, appl. no. 11663/04.

138 Dissenting opinion of Judge Lorenzen, joined by Judges Rozakis, Bonello, Stráññická, Bîrsen and Fischbach, para. 8.

the obligation to tolerate tax-based reductions of the compensation is? (…) Or how can it be explained that an obligation to pay contributions under a social-security scheme is 'civil', but an obligation to pay wage-taxes is not?'[139]

The fact that disputes concerning the obligation to pay taxes are not considered to be 'civil' for the purpose of Article 6 leaves, of course, open the question of the applicability of Article 6 to administrative fines, including fines imposed on taxpayers, under the 'criminal' head.[140] That issue will be discussed at a later stage. It is pointed out in the present context, however, that this applicability under the criminal head has as a result that the protection under Article 6 depends on how the legal framework for tax proceedings is organised in the different legal systems, while even within one and the same legal system it may be coincidental whether penalty proceedings and tax assessment proceedings are joined or not.[141] And why should a person who is charged with a fine for not complying with his tax duties, enjoy more legal protection than those who appeal against a tax duty imposed upon them?

b. Admission and expulsion of aliens

In the *Maaouia* case, the Grand Chamber took a principled position in the matter of the applicability of the first paragraph to proceedings concerning admission and expulsion of aliens. There the Court concluded from Article 1 of Protocol No. 7, which contains procedural guarantees for the expulsion of aliens, that 'the States were aware that Article 6 para. 1 did not apply to procedures for the expulsion of aliens and wished to take special measures in that sphere'.[142] This led the Court to hold that 'the proceedings for the rescission of the exclusion order, which form the subject-matter of the present case, do not concern the determination of a "civil right" for the purposes of Article 6 para. 1. The fact that the exclusion order incidentally had major repercussions on the applicant's private and family life or on his prospects of employment cannot suffice to bring those proceedings within the scope of civil rights protected by Article 6 para. 1 of the Convention.'[143]

To indicate that the case was meant to be a 'pilot case' the Court reached the following general conclusion, which extended beyond the facts of the case before it: 'Decisions regarding the entry, stay and deportation of aliens do not concern the determination of an applicant's civil rights or obligations or of

---

[139] *Ibid.*, para. 6.
[140] *Bendenoun v. France*, ECtHR 24 February 1994, appl. no. 12547/86, para. 52; *Faivre v. France (No. 2)*, ECtHR 16 December 2003, appl. no. 69825/01, para. 21.
[141] Thus, also the dissenting opinion, para. 8.
[142] *Maaouia v. France, supra* n. 82, para. 36.
[143] *Ibid.*, para. 38.

a criminal charge against him, within the meaning of Article 6 para. 1 of the Convention.'[144]

It is not self-evident, to put it mildly, that for the interpretation of a provision of the Convention conclusions may be drawn from an instrument which was adopted more than 30 years later and has not yet been ratified by all the States Parties to the Convention. It is even less evident, from the text of Article 1 of Protocol No. 7 and its Explanatory Note, that Protocol No. 7 may be considered a *lex specialis* with respect to (all) the procedural guarantees of the first paragraph of Article 6.[145] Indeed, 'Protocols add to the rights of the individual; they do not restrict or abolish them'.[146] The Explanatory Note states that Article 1 of the Protocol 'does not affect' the position adopted by the Commission that Article 6 does not apply to deportation procedures,[147] which does not imply that, according to the drafters of the Protocol, the said position was the only correct interpretation of Article 6. Moreover, the statement in the Explanatory Note only refers to deportations and, thus, does not give ground for any conclusion as to alien procedures in general.[148]

Moreover, in the light of the observation by the Court that the exclusion order incidentally had major repercussions on the applicant's private and family life or on his prospects of employment, it is difficult to understand how the Court's conclusion is to be reconciled with its case law that for the applicability of the first paragraph of Article 6 it is sufficient that the dispute concerned 'relates' to the scope of a civil right and the manner of its exercise.[149]

In *F. v. the United Kingdom*, the Court observed that an issue may exceptionally be raised under Article 6 by an expulsion order in circumstances where the person being expelled has suffered or risks suffering a flagrant denial of fair trial in the receiving country.[150] This, of course, is a different issue from that here under discussion.

c. Civil servants' employment rights

For a long time, the Court took the view that Article 6(1) did not apply to cases involving civil servants, or at any rate when these civil servants fulfilled tasks typically governed by public law.[151] This case law was controversial because the

---

[144] *Ibid.,* para. 40. The position adopted is still standing case law: *Taheri Kandomabadi v. the Netherlands*, ECtHR 29 June 2004 (dec.), appl. no. 6276/03 and 6122/04.

[145] See the concurring opinion of Judge Costa and the dissenting opinion of Judge Loucaides joined by Judge Traja.

[146] Dissenting opinion of Judge Loucaides joined by Judge Traja.

[147] Explanatory Note, para. 16.

[148] Thus, also Judge Costa in his concurring opinion.

[149] *Skärby v. Sweden, supra* n. 46, para. 27.

[150] *F. v. the United Kingdom,* ECtHR 22 June 2004, appl. no. 17341/03, para. 2.

[151] *Pellegrin v. France,* ECtHR (GC) 8 December 1999, appl. no. 28541/95, paras. 60–66.

exception could not be clearly justified.[152] Moreover, the line the Court took led to legal uncertainty: when does a civil servant perform tasks typically governed by public law and when not?[153] Partly on the grounds of this criticism, the Court has changed direction and has now taken as a starting point that Article 6(1) does apply to cases involving civil servants. Therefore, only in special circumstances is an exception permitted. There are only two cumulative conditions under which the state may exclude civil servants from the effect of Article 6 (known as the 'Eskelinen-test'): (1) access for the category of civil servants in question must be explicitly excluded in national legislation; and (2) the exclusion must be justifiable on objective grounds that are derived from the national interest.[154] On the basis of this test, the Court held, for example, that Article 6(1) is applicable to judicial officers.[155]

1.8. APPLICABILITY

Unlike Article 13, Article 6 does not refer to the 'rights and freedoms as set forth in this Convention' but to 'civil rights and obligations'. The two concepts are not co-extensive, although there may be some overlapping.[156]

It is self-evident that the rights laid down in the Convention are 'rights' in the sense of Article 6. But are they also 'civil' rights in that sense? They certainly do have that character to the extent that they have a 'horizontal effect' within the domestic legal order, since rights and obligations between private parties are 'civil' in character. Thus, an individual's right to respect for his reputation by a private person was considered to be a 'civil right'.[157]

However, the civil rights protected in the Convention may also come under Article 6 if they are vindicated *vis-à-vis* a public authority. Thus, in the *Werner* case the right of protection of one's good reputation against the public authorities, including the courts, was recognised as a 'civil right' in the sense

---

[152] See joint dissenting opinion of Judges Tulkens, Fischbach, Casadevall and Thomassen in *Pellegrin v. France.*

[153] E.g. *Fogarty v. the United Kingdom, supra* n. 19, para. 28.

[154] *Vilho Eskelinen and Others v. Finland, supra* n. 30, para. 62.

[155] *Olujić v. Croatia*, ECtHR 5 February 2009, appl. no. 22330/05; *Harabin v. Slovakia*, ECtHR 20 November 2012, appl. no. 58688/11; *Oleksandr Volkov v. Ukraine*, ECtHR 9 January 2013, appl. no. 21722/11.

[156] *Golder v. the United Kingdom, supra* n. 1, para. 33; *Voggenreiter v. Germany, supra* n. 22, para. 35.

[157] *Helmers v. Sweden*, ECtHR (GC) 29 October 1991, appl. no. 11826/85, para. 29; *Tolstoy Miloslavsky v. the United Kingdom*, ECtHR 13 July 1995, appl. no. 18139/91, para. 58; *Werner v. Poland, supra* n. 95 para. 33; *De Jorio v. Italy*, ECtHR 3 June 2004, appl. no. 73936/01, para. 18; *Djangozov v. Bulgaria, supra* n. 77, para. 41; *Pieniazek v. Poland, supra* n. 41, para. 18. If statements made in Parliament are involved, Art. 6 is also applicable but access to court may be blocked by the principle of 'parliamentary immunity'.

of Article 6.[158] The same was held in the *Ciz* case with respect to an alleged defamation by a member of Parliament.[159]

In the *Balmer-Schafroth* case and the *Athanassoglou* case, the right to have one's physical integrity adequately protected from the risks entailed by the use of nuclear energy was recognised as a right in the sense of Article 6, since it was regulated in the Swiss Nuclear Energy Act and emerged from the constitutional right to life; however, the link between the proceedings concerned and that right was considered to be insufficiently direct to make Article 6 applicable.[160] The right to life also constitutes a civil right for the relatives of the deceased in combination with a claim for damages.[161]

In the *Aerts* case, the Court adopted the position that the right to liberty is a 'civil' right.[162] In the *Paulsen-Medalen and Svensson* case, the right to respect of family life was dealt with as a 'civil' right,[163] as was in the *Petersen* case (on assumption) the claim relating to a change of a child's surname, as being an element of family life.[164] And in the *Ganci* case, the Court held that complaint procedures against a special detention regime with severe restrictions as to visits by relatives, use of telephone and conduct of financial transactions, concerned the detainee's civil rights.[165] In the *APEH Üldözötteinek Szövetsége* case, the right to register as an association, as part of the right to freedom of association, was held to be a 'civil' right, since 'it was (…) the applicant association's very capacity to become a subject of civil rights and obligations (…) that was at stake in the registration proceedings'.[166] In the *Tinnelly & Sons Ltd and McElduff* case, the right not to be discriminated against on grounds of religious belief or political opinion when bidding for a public works contract was held to be a 'civil' right.[167] The same position was taken with respect to discrimination in the area of recruitment for the civil service.[168]

As far as the right to the peaceful enjoyment of possessions is concerned, in the case of expropriation and consolidation decisions and in the case of

---

[158]   *Werner v. Poland, supra* n. 95, para. 33. See also *Bartre v. France,* ECtHR 12 November 2003, appl. no. 70753/01, impliedly.

[159]   *Ciz v. Slovakia, supra* n. 54, para. 61.

[160]   *Balmer-Schafroth and Others v. Switzerland, supra* n. 57, paras. 33–34; *Athanassoglou and Others v. Switzerland, supra* n. 58, para. 44.

[161]   *Sekin and Others v. Turkey,* ECtHR 22 January 2004, appl. no. 26518/95 (impliedly).

[162]   *Aerts v. Belgium,* ECtHR 30 July 1998, appl. no. 25357/94, para. 59. See also *Fabre v. France,* ECtHR 18 March 2003 (dec.), appl. no. 69225/01 (impliedly).

[163]   *Paulsen-Medalen and Svensson v. Sweden, supra* n. 117, paras. 38–42.

[164]   *Petersen v. Germany, supra* n. 118, para. 4: 'the Court starts with the assumption that Article 6 para. 1 in principle applies.'

[165]   *Ganci v. Italy,* ECtHR 30 October 2003, appl. no. 41576/98, paras. 23–26; *Musumeci v. Italy,* ECtHR 11 January 2005, appl. no. 33695/96, para. 36.

[166]   *APEH Üldözötteinek Szövetsége and Others v. Hungary, supra* n. 131, para. 36.

[167]   *Tinnelly & Sons Ltd and Others and McElduff and Others v. the United Kingdom, supra* n. 107, paras. 61–62.

[168]   *Devlin v, the United Kingdom, supra* n. 108, paras. 25–26.

forfeiture of property, the proceedings in which the legitimacy and/or the damages are determined, are considered to be a 'determination of a civil right'.[169] Equally, the decision to place a bank in compulsory administration, which has a decisive impact on the right of the bank to administer its own property and assets, concerns a civil right of the bank.[170] And if a certain claim is combined with a claim for damages, the Court is inclined to consider the proceedings as being closely connected to a claim of a pecuniary nature and as decisive for the determination of civil rights.[171]

For the rights and freedoms laid down in the Convention that are of a political character the situation is less clear. In the *Pierre-Bloch* case, the Court held that the right to stand for elections is a 'political' and not a 'civil' one and that, therefore, disputes concerning the exercise of that right lie outside the scope of Article 6, even if economic interests are involved.[172] The mere fact that in the dispute concerned the applicant's pecuniary interests were also at stake, did not make Article 6 applicable, because these interests were closely connected with the exercise of the political right.[173]

A claim which has a certain connection with the Convention but is not guaranteed as a right there, does not, on that sole basis, come under the protection of Article 6. If the claim concerned is also not recognised as a right under the applicable domestic law, Article 6 is not applicable. Thus, in the *Gutfreund* case, the Court held Article 6 to be not applicable to proceedings concerning legal aid in a civil case, because the right to legal aid in civil cases is not recognised in French law nor, in the circumstances of the case, in Article 6 of the Convention.[174] It reached the same conclusion with respect to proceedings relating to the decision to subject a detainee to a high-security regime.[175]

Thus, it may be concluded that most of the rights and freedoms laid down in the Convention, also in relation to the public authorities, have been recognised by the Court as 'civil' rights unless their political character prevails. Also, where freedom of expression is concerned, and in particular the aspect of access to documents, it is possible that Article 6(1) will not apply.[176] To the extent that the

---

[169]   *Ettl and Others v. Austria*, *supra* n. 63, para. 32; *Erkner and Hofauer v. Austria, supra* n. 63, para. 62; and *Poiss v. Austria, supra* n. 63, para. 48; *Bodén v. Sweden, supra* n. 79, para. 32; *Ruiz-Mateos v. Spain, supra* n. 106, paras. 58–59; *Cegielski v. Poland, supra* n. 104, para. 24; *Beneficio Cappella Paolini v. San Marino*, ECtHR 13 July 2004, appl. no. 40786/98, para. 28.

[170]   *Credit and Industrial Bank v. Czech Republic*, ECtHR 21 October 2003, appl. no. 29010/95, paras. 64–67.

[171]   *Napijalo v. Croatia*, ECtHR 13 November 2003, appl. no. 66485/01, paras. 47–50.

[172]   *Pierre-Bloch v. France,* ECtHR 21 October 1997, appl. no. 24194/94, paras. 50–51; *Guliyev v. Azerbaijan*, ECtHR 27 May 2004 (dec.), appl. no. 35584/02, para. 3; *Krasnov and Skuratov v. Russia*, ECtHR 14 December 2004 (dec.), appl. no. 17864/04 and 21396/04, para. 1; *Geraguyn Khorhurd Patgamavorakan Akum v. Armenia*, ECtHR 11 May 2009, appl. no. 11721/04.

[173]   *Ibid.*, para. 51.

[174]   *Gutfreund v. France*, ECtHR 12 June 2003, appl. no. 45681/99, paras. 31–43.

[175]   *Lorsé and Others v. the Netherlands*, ECtHR 28 August 2001 (dec.), appl. no. 52750/99, para. 3.

[176]   *Shapovalov v. Ukraine*, ECtHR 31 July 2012, appl. no. 45835/05.

applicability of Article 6 is (still) not recognised, Article 13 of the Convention does, of course, apply.[177]

1.9. CONCLUDING OBSERVATIONS

The Strasbourg case law concerning 'civil rights and obligations' is still lacking clarity and certainty in certain respects in spite of several praiseworthy efforts of the Court to draw some general lines. It lacks clarity because no general definition of 'civil rights and obligations' can still be inferred from it, while the criteria developed by the Court, such as that of the effect which the outcome of the proceedings may have for a right or obligation of a civil character, are not very specific and sometimes difficult to apply. It lacks certainty because the lines drawn in the case law curve rather frequently and appear still to lead within the Court to different views in concrete cases. In our opinion this lack of clarity and certainty, which constitutes an undesirable situation not only for the individual seeking justice, but also for the public authorities and the courts in the Contracting States, which are called upon to apply Article 6, can only be eliminated if the Court departs from its present casuistic approach and develops a general and readily applicable definition of 'civil rights and obligations', thus fulfilling its function to give direction to the interpretation and application of the Convention.[178] Its judgments in the *Ferrazzini* and *Maaouia* cases, although one may not agree with the line of reasoning adopted, are a step in the right direction from that perspective, but even these judgments do not yet offer the clarity and certainty required. More clarity about the scope of Article 6 is urgently needed.

It is submitted that the most satisfactory way to end legal uncertainty and maximise effective legal protection is to recognise – as an example of 'evolutive interpretation' – that the first paragraph of Article 6 is applicable to all cases in which a determination by a public authority of the legal position of a private party is at stake, regardless of whether the rights and obligations involved are of a private character and regardless of whether the claim concerns a public law relationship. The basic principle of the rule of law would seem to require that in all cases of government interference with the legal position of a private party the latter has a right of access to court and to a fair trial.[179] As the Court held

---

[177] See for a case of privacy affected by aircraft noise, which was not protected under domestic law, *Hatton and Others v. the United Kingdom*, ECtHR (GC) 7 August 2003, appl. no. 36022/97, paras. 137–142.

[178] For this 'constitutional' function, see *Ireland v. the United Kingdom*, ECtHR (GC) 18 January 1978, appl. no. 5310/71, para. 154.

[179] Dissenting opinion of Judge Loucaides joined by Judge Traja in *Maaouia v. France, supra* n. 82.

in the *Klass* case, 'The rule of law implies, *inter alia*, that an interference by the executive authorities with an individual's rights should be subject to an effective control which should normally be assured by the judiciary, at least in the last resort, judicial control offering the best guarantees of independence, impartiality and a proper procedure.'[180]

2. CRIMINAL CHARGE

2.1. DETERMINATION OF A CRIMINAL CHARGE

The words 'determination of (...) any criminal charge' ('*décidera (...) du bien-fondé de toute accusation en matière pénale*') also raise problems of interpretation.

From the term 'determination' it follows that the 'criminal' limb of Article 6 is not applicable to every procedure in which an accused or detained person is involved, but only to those proceedings in which the well-foundedness of a charge is at stake. Thus, in the *Ganci* case the Court held that complaint procedures against restrictions imposed upon a detainee did not concern the determination of a criminal charge, but did indeed concern the determination of the detainee's civil rights.[181]

More problematic is the term 'criminal charge'. On this point the legal systems of the Contracting States show many variations. To avoid differences in the scope of application of Article 6 in the different national legal orders, and also the risk of this application being eroded by the introduction of legal norms and procedures outside the sphere of criminal law, the adoption of an autonomous meaning, independent of the national legal systems, was necessary here as well. In the *Adolf* case, the Court held with respect to 'criminal charge' in so many words: 'These expressions are to be interpreted as having an "autonomous" meaning in the context of the Convention and not on the basis of their meaning in domestic law.'[182]

In many cases the criminal character of the proceedings involved is clear, either because of their characterisation under the applicable domestic law or in view of their character and purpose, and the terminology used for their regulation.[183] However, there are several cases in which the Court had to draw lines on the basis of an autonomous interpretation.

---

[180]   *Klass and Others v. Germany,* ECtHR (GC) 6 September 1978, appl. no. 5029/71, para. 55.
[181]   *Ganci v. Italy, supra* n. 165, para. 22.
[182]   *Adolf v. Austria,* ECtHR 26 March 1982, appl. no. 8269/78, para. 30.
[183]   *Gradinger v. Austria,* ECtHR 23 October 1995, appl. no. 15963/90, para. 36; *Pullar v. the United Kingdom,* ECtHR 10 June 1996, appl. no. 22399/93, para. 29.

2.2. AUTONOMOUS CONCEPT OF 'CHARGE'

The general point of departure defined in the *Delcourt* case 'that a restrictive interpretation of Article 6 para. 1 would not correspond to the aim and purpose of that provision',[184] also applies here. In addition, in the *Deweer* case, the Court adopted a guideline for the autonomous interpretation of 'charge'. It held that 'the prominent place held in a democratic society by the right to a fair trial (…) prompts the Court to prefer a "substantive", rather than a "formal", conception of the 'charge' contemplated by Article 6 para. 1.'[185] Consequently, the concept is to be understood 'within the meaning of the Convention and not solely within the meaning under national law'.[186]

In the *Deweer* case, the Court gave the following description of the concept of 'charge' in the sense of Article 6: 'the official notification given to an individual by the competent authority of an allegation that he has committed a criminal offence.'[187] This 'notification' marks the beginning of the 'charge' and, consequently, is also relevant with respect to the period of the procedure to which Article 6 applies, for instance for determining whether the reasonable-time requirement has been met. The relevant period starts with the notification, even if it is formulated in a language which the person concerned does not understand[188] or if it did not reach him.[189]

However, a formal notification is not always required. Examples of possible measures other than an official notification are the search of the person's home and/or the seizure of certain goods,[190] the request that a person's immunity be lifted,[191] and the confirmation by the court of the sealing of a building.[192] In the *Corigliano* case, the Court summarised its case law as follows: 'In criminal matters, in order to assess whether the 'reasonable time' requirement contained in Article 6 para. 1 has been complied with, one must begin by ascertaining from which moment the person was "charged"; this may have occurred on a date prior to the case coming before the trial court (…), such as the date of the arrest, the date when the person concerned was officially notified that he would be prosecuted or the date when the preliminary investigations were opened (…). Whilst "charge", for the purpose of Article 6 para. 1, may in general be defined as

---

184 *Delcourt v. Belgium, supra* n. 2, para. 25.
185 *Deweer v. Belgium*, ECtHR 27 February 1980, appl. no. 6903/75, para. 44.
186 *Tejedor García v. Spain*, ECtHR 16 December 1997, appl. no. 25420/94, para. 27.
187 *Deweer v. Belgium, supra* n. 185, para. 46.
188 *Brozicek v. Italy*, ECtHR (GC) 19 December 1989, appl. no. 10964/84, paras. 41–42.
189 *Pugliese v. Italy (No. 1)*, ECtHR 19 February 1991, appl. no. 11840/85, para. 14 in conjunction with para. 10. For possible consequences of notification not in person, see *Colozza v. Italy*, ECtHR 12 February 1985, appl. no. 9024/80, paras. 26–28.
190 *Eckle v. Germany*, ECtHR 15 July 1982, appl. no. 8130/78, para. 74 in conjunction with para. 12.
191 *Frau v. Italy*, ECtHR 19 February 1991, appl. no. 12147/86, para. 14.
192 *Venditelli v. Italy*, ECtHR 18 July 1994, appl. no. 14804/89, para. 21.

"the official notification given to an individual by the competent authority of an allegation that he has committed a criminal offence", it may in some instances take the form of other measures which carry the implication of such an allegation and which likewise substantially affect the situation of the suspect (...).'[193]

From this 'definition' it follows that Article 6 also applies to the pre-trial phase,[194] but only from the moment a charge has been brought. The mere fact that the police are carrying out an investigation or witnesses are being heard, or that a judicial organ is making a preliminary inquiry, does not necessarily mean that a 'criminal charge' exists.

In the *Deweer* case, the Court held that a 'charge' may exist at the stage in which the prosecuting authorities make a proposal for settlement, even if that proposal is made in the framework of an inspection that is not performed within the context of the repression of crime and even if there is no notification of impending prosecution, while the settlement will prevent such prosecution.[195] And even a summons to appear as a witness may mark a criminal charge, if the person concerned may deduce from the circumstances that there is incriminating evidence also against him.[196]

In the *Escoubet* case, the Court adopted the opinion that Article 6 does not apply to the various preliminary measures which may be taken as part of a criminal investigation before bringing a 'criminal charge', "'such as the arrest or interviewing of a suspect (...), measures which may, however, be governed by other provisions of the Convention, in particular Articles 3 and 5.'"[197] This reasoning makes the criteria of 'charge' rather difficult to apply. Indeed, in case of the arrest or interviewing of a *suspect*, the latter may very well experience this as implying an allegation which substantially affects his situation and may be in need of the guarantees of Article 6 from that moment on in order to make these guarantees effective.[198]

Article 6 is also applicable to proceedings by which a detention on remand is reviewed or prolonged on the ground of an existing suspicion, although these proceedings themselves are not directed at the determination of the charge,[199] as well as to proceedings which ended with the conclusion that the offence was not punishable.[200] On the other hand, the refusal to pay compensation for damages caused by a public authority in the course of criminal proceedings which are

---

[193]   *Corigliano v. Italy*, ECtHR 10 December 1982, appl. no. 8304/78, para. 34.

[194]   *Tejedor García v. Spain*, *supra* n. 186, para. 27.

[195]   *Deweer v. Belgium*, *supra* n. 185, paras. 42–45.

[196]   *Serves v. France*, ECtHR 20 October 1997, appl. no. 20225/92, para. 42.

[197]   *Escoubet v. Belgium*, ECtHR (GC) 28 October 1999, appl. no. 26780/95, para. 34.

[198]   See the joint dissenting opinion of Judges Tulkens, Fischbach and Casadevall, attached to the *Escoubet* judgment.

[199]   *Luedicke, Balkacem and Koç v. Germany*, ECtHR 28 November 1978, appl. nos. 6210/73, 6877/75 and 7132/75, para. 49. See also *Reinhardt & Slimane-Kaid v. France*, ECtHR (GC) 31 March 1998, appl. nos. 23043/93 and 22921/93, para. 93; *Lietzow v. Germany*, ECtHR 13 February 2001, appl. no. 24479/94, para. 44.

[200]   *Adolf v. Austria*, *supra* n. 182, paras. 31–33.

subsequently discontinued, does not amount to a penalty,[201] but may involve a 'civil' right. The mere fact that a criminal prosecution is terminated or results in dismissal of the case does not mean that, in retrospect, Article 6 was not applicable, particularly when the person who was originally accused may have left the prosecution with certain prejudicial consequences.[202]

Whether the criminal proceedings were instituted by a private party or by a public authority is irrelevant to the question of whether a 'charge' was brought, and thus for the applicability of Article 6.[203] However, the private party who takes the initiative to start criminal proceedings is not himself entitled to a determination of the charge by a court; he may be entitled to the determination of his civil rights if a civil claim can be, and actually has been submitted in the criminal proceedings.[204] On the other hand, if a third person's rights are affected adversely by measures consequential upon the prosecution of others, no criminal charge can be said to have been brought against the former, who therefore cannot invoke the guarantees of Article 6 concerning the determination of a criminal charge. This approach, adopted in the *Agosi* case,[205] led to the conclusion in the *Air Canada* case that the seizure of an aircraft in which drugs had been brought into the United Kingdom, could not be considered as a 'criminal charge' brought against the airline company. The fact that the company regained the aeroplane only after it had paid an amount of $50,000, did not alter this conclusion.[206] Article 6 may, of course, be applicable under its civil limb.

A tariff-fixing decision by a public authority that determines the period of detention, is itself a sentencing exercise and must comply with the guarantees of Article 6.[207]

2.3. AUTONOMOUS CONCEPT OF 'CRIMINAL'

a. *Applicability to disciplinary procedures and administrative sanctions*

The question of whether Article 6 is applicable to disciplinary procedures was answered in the negative by the Commission for a long time.[208] In the *Engel* case, however, both the Commission and the Court took the position that the

---

[201] *Van Leeuwen BV v. the Netherlands*, ECtHR 25 January 2000 (dec.), appl. no. 32602/96, para. 1.

[202] Appl. no. 8269/78, *X v. Austria*, Yearbook XXII (1979), p. 324 (340–342). See also *Adolf v. Austria, supra* n. 182, para. 33, concerning a decision that an offence was not punishable.

[203] *Minelli v. Switzerland*, ECtHR 25 March 1983, appl. no. 8660/79, para. 28.

[204] *Moreira De Azevedo v. Portugal, supra* n. 36, para. 67; *Calvelli and Ciglio v. Italy, supra* n. 76, para. 62.

[205] *AGOSI v. the United Kingdom*, ECtHR 24 October 1986, appl. no. 9118/80, para. 65.

[206] *Air Canada v. the United Kingdom*, ECtHR 5 May 1995, appl. no. 18465/91, paras. 52–53.

[207] *T. v. the United Kingdom*, ECtHR (GC) 16 December 1999, appl. no. 24724/94, paras. 106–110; *Easterbrook v. the United Kingdom*, ECtHR 12 June 2003, appl. no. 48015/99, para. 26.

[208] See the case law mentioned in the report of 19 July 1974, *Engel and Others*, B.20 (1978), pp. 68–69.

character of a procedure under domestic law cannot be decisive for the question of whether Article 6 is applicable, since otherwise the national authorities would be able to evade the guarantees of that provision by introducing disciplinary procedures with respect to offences which, in view of their nature or the character of the sanction imposed, are very similar to criminal offences.[209] As the Court stated in its judgment: 'The Convention without any doubt allows the States (…) to maintain or establish a distinction between criminal law and disciplinary law, and to draw the dividing line, but only subject to certain conditions. (…) If the Contracting States were able at their discretion to classify an offence as disciplinary instead of criminal or to prosecute an author of a mixed offence on the disciplinary rather than on the criminal plane, the operation of the fundamental clauses of Articles 6 and 7 would be subordinated to their sovereign will. (…) The Court therefore has jurisdiction, under Article 6 (…), to satisfy itself that the disciplinary does not improperly encroach upon the criminal.'[210] The same reasoning was followed in respect of administrative procedures which lead to the imposition of a sanction.[211]

For an answer to the question of whether disciplinary and administrative procedures imply a 'criminal charge' in the sense of Article 6, the Court developed the following criteria in its *Engel* judgment.[212]

b.   Classification under domestic law

The first criterion to be applied is the classification of the allegedly violated norm under the applicable domestic legal system. Does it belong to criminal law or to disciplinary or administrative law? If the former is the case, the matter is settled, since the autonomy of the interpretation of 'criminal charge' is a one-way autonomy. Domestic law is decisive to the extent that, if an act or omission *is* designated as a criminal offence by domestic law, Article 6 is applicable to the proceedings in which the charge related to such act or omission is determined.[213] Criminalisation of certain behaviour may be reviewed for its conformity with other provisions of the Convention,[214] but its justification is not an issue under Article 6.

Only if an offence is not classified as criminal by the relevant legal system or is decriminalised, is there the danger of evasion of the guarantees

---

[209]   *Ibid.*, p. 70 and *Engel and Others v. the Netherlands,* ECtHR (GC) 8 June 1976, appl. nos. 5100/71, 5101/71, 5102/71, 5354/72 and 5370/72, para. 81.

[210]   *Ibid.*

[211]   *Öztürk v. Germany,* ECtHR (GC) 21 February 1984, appl. no. 8544/79, paras. 47–49.

[212]   *Ibid.*, para. 82.

[213]   *Engel and Others v. the Netherlands, supra* n. 209, para. 81; *Pierre-Bloch v. France, supra* n. 172, para. 60.

[214]   See *Dudgeon v. the United Kingdom,* ECtHR (GC) 22 October 1981, appl. no. 7525/76, paras. 60–61, where the legislation in Northern Ireland, prohibiting homosexual intercourse between consenting male persons over 21 years of age, was held to violate Art. 8.

of Article 6 which makes a further examination of the applicability of that provision necessary. This may require some investigation and interpretation by the Court of the relevant domestic law,[215] its legal history or the case law in relation thereto.[216] Even if Article 6 is found to be applicable, that does not mean that the disciplinary or administrative procedures have to be changed into criminal procedures; the only requirement is that they offer the guarantees of Article 6.

In view of the danger of evasion by defining an offence as 'disciplinary' or 'administrative' under national law, the criterion of the classification serves only as a preliminary point of departure for the ultimate assessment of the applicability of Article 6. This assessment has to be made on the basis of objective principles. For that purpose, the Court has developed the following two additional criteria.

c. Scope of the norm and purpose of the penalty

The scope of the norm concerns the circle of its addressees: is the norm only addressed to a specific group or is it a norm of a generally binding character? A provision of disciplinary law only addresses persons belonging to the disciplinary system. Therefore, as a starting point the circle of addressees offers a useful indication, but the same conduct that constitutes an offence under disciplinary law may also amount to an offence under criminal law.[217] On the other hand, there are several criminal law prohibitions which can only apply to certain persons: minors or adults, parents and guardians, spouses, captains, civil servants etc. Therefore, the distinguishing feature implied in this criterion is not the number of addressees, but their quality as members of a particular group, combined with the interests protected by the rule.

The indeterminate character of the criterion came clearly to the fore in the *Weber* case. The applicant had filed a criminal complaint of defamation against the author of a 'reader's letter' in a newspaper. Pending the proceedings he held a press conference to inform the public about his complaint. In summary proceedings he was fined for breaching the secrecy of the investigation. Since his appeal against the conviction was dismissed without public hearing, he claimed that Article 6 had been violated. The Commission had adopted the view that the violated rules were disciplinary rules and that neither the penalty imposed nor the maximum penalty could by their nature make the offence a criminal one.[218] The Court, however, made the following distinction: 'Disciplinary

---

215   *Minelli v. Switzerland, supra* n. 203, para. 28; *Campbell and Fell v. the United Kingdom*, ECtHR 28 June 1984, appl. no. 7819/77 and 7878/77, para. 70.

216   *Öztürk v. Germany, supra* n. 211, para. 51; *Demicoli v. Malta*, ECtHR 27 August 1991, appl. no. 13057/87, para. 32.

217   *Campbell and Fell v. the United Kingdom, supra* n. 215, para. 71.

218   Report of 16 March 1989, paras. 100–111.

sanctions are generally designed to ensure that the members of particular groups comply with the specific rules governing their conduct. Furthermore, in a great majority of the Contracting States disclosure of information about an investigation still pending constitutes an act incompatible with such rules and punishable under a variety of provisions. As persons who above all others are bound by the confidentiality of an investigation, judges, lawyers and all those closely associated with the functioning of the courts are liable in such an event, independently of any criminal sanction, to disciplinary measures on account of their profession. The parties, on the other hand, only take part in the proceedings as people subject to the jurisdiction of the courts, and they therefore do not come within the disciplinary sphere of the judicial system. As Article 185 [of the relevant Swiss Code], however, potentially affects the whole population, the offence it defines, and to which it attaches a punitive sanction, is a 'criminal' one for the purposes of the second criterion.'[219]

That this aspect of the second criterion is not an easy one to apply became even clearer when the Court, in the not so dissimilar *Ravnsborg* case[220] and *Putz* case,[221] reached the opposite conclusion.[222]

In the *Campbell and Fell* case, the Court, moreover, indicated that the distinction between disciplinary and criminal offences is also a relative one. Thus, misconduct by a prisoner is usually no more than a question of internal discipline, but violations of the prison rules may also amount to criminal offences. Relevant indicators are the seriousness of the matter and whether the illegality of the act concerned turns on the fact that it is committed in prison.[223]

The fact that the nature of the offence is only of a minor character is of no relevance under the second criterion. According to the Court, the criminal nature of an offence does not require a certain degree of seriousness.[224]

The purpose of the penalty, as the other aspect of the second criterion, mainly serves to distinguish criminal sanctions from purely reparatory or compensatory sanctions. This sub-criterion was introduced in the *Öztürk* case to determine whether the decriminalisation of certain offences under domestic law had as a consequence that Article 6 would no longer be applicable. The Court held this not to be the case as long as the sanction that could be applied had kept

---

[219]   *Weber v. Switzerland*, ECtHR 22 May 1990, appl. no. 11034/84, para. 33. See also *Demicoli v. Malta, supra* n. 216, para. 33.

[220]   *Ravnsborg v. Sweden*, ECtHR 23 March 1994, appl. no. 14220/88, para. 34.

[221]   *Putz v. Austria*, ECtHR 22 February 1996, appl. no. 18892/91, paras. 34–38.

[222]   *Cf.* also *S.C. IMH Suceava S.R.L. v. Romania*, ECtHR 29 October 2013, appl. no. 24935/04, para. 51 in which the Court found the scope of the norm (prohibition to sell non-registered petrol in order to protect consumers) to be limited to distributors of petrol and therefore in its view the second 'Engel'-criterion had not been met.

[223]   *Campbell and Fell v. the United Kingdom, supra* n. 215, para. 71; *Ezeh and Connors v. the United Kingdom*, ECtHR (GC) 9 October 2003, appl. nos. 39665/98 and 40086/98, para. 101.

[224]   *Öztürk v. Germany, supra* n. 211, para. 53; *Ezeh and Connors v. the United Kingdom, supra* n. 223, para. 104.

its 'deterrent' and 'punitive' character.[225] In the case of fines a clear criterion is whether the fine is merely intended as pecuniary compensation for damage caused or is punitive or deterrent in nature.[226] The fact that an administrative sanction is imposed on a person who has no personal guilt in the matter does not exclude the sanction from having a punitive character.[227] The criterium of guilt plays a role only in determining the classification of the proceedings under domestic law.[228]

Whereas the three criteria developed by the Court are not cumulative, the two aspects of the second criterion are. This means that an offence which is not criminal under national law, may only be considered criminal in the sense of Article 6 by its nature, if both the scope of the violated norm is of a general character and the purpose of the sanction is deterrent and punitive.[229]

The violation of one and the same legal provision may lead to the imposition of measures which are partly compensatory and partly punitive. Only the latter aspect of the measure brings the proceedings under the category of 'criminal charge'. Thus, under taxation law, if a person has failed to pay the taxes imposed upon him, proceedings instituted against him may result in the decision that he still has to pay a certain amount as compensation for his failure, and a surcharge as a sanction on tax evasion. The latter part is of a punitive character.[230]

The mere fact that a sanction or other measure imposed by the administration or the court is of a severe character with far-reaching consequences for the person concerned, does not mean that the sanction or measure is of a punitive character.[231] If the sanction or measure is only meant to restore, or compensate for, the failure on the part of the person concerned, its character is reparatory rather than punitive,[232] even if full 'reparation' is not brought about and is not possible.[233] However, if the sanction or measure is of such a character and severity that it is covered by the third criterion, to be discussed hereafter, Article 6 may still be applicable. This will very rarely be the case, because the person concerned can hardly complain about a measure the only purpose of which is to bring about or promote as closely as possible the situation which he was obliged to create or maintain himself. Possible examples of such severity

---

[225] *Öztürk v. Germany, supra* n. 211, para. 53. See also *Lauko v. Slovakia*, ECtHR 2 September 1998, appl. no. 26138/95, para. 58.

[226] *E.L., R.L. and J.O.-L. v. Switzerland*, ECtHR 29 August 1997, appl. no. 20919/92 and *A.P., M.P. and T.P. v. Switzerland*, ECtHR 29 August 1997, appl. no. 19958/92, paras. 46 and 42.

[227] *E.L., R.L. and J.O.-L. v. Switzerland, supra* n. 226, paras. 42 and 46.

[228] *A.P., M.P. and T.P. v. Switzerland, supra* n. 226, para. 42.

[229] *Öztürk v. Germany, supra* n. 211, para. 53; *Bendenoun v. France, supra* n. 140, para. 47.

[230] *Bendenoun v. France, supra* n. 140, para. 47; *E.L., R.L. and J.O.-L. v. Switzerland, supra* n. 226, para. 46; *J.B. v. Switzerland*, ECtHR 3 May 2001, appl. no. 31827/96, paras. 47–49.

[231] See, e.g., *Bingöl v. The Netherlands*, ECtHR 20 March 2012, appl. no. 18450/07 (dec.): the refusal of an operating licence under the Public Administration (Probity Screening) Act because of criminal antecedents does not involve the determination of a criminal charge.

[232] *Tre Traktörer AB Aktiebolag v. Sweden, supra* n. 34, para. 46.

[233] *Pierre-Bloch v. France, supra* n. 172, para. 58.

would be detention to induce the person concerned to fulfil his obligations ('civil detention') and measures of a repetitive character or of such a long duration that the reparatory character will be overshadowed by the punitive side-effects.[234]

The lack of clarity of the (application of the) second criterion and its relation to the third criterion may be illustrated by the *Pierre-Bloch* case. There the Court examined three kinds of possible sanctions as to their purpose, which surprisingly the Court did under the heading 'nature and degree of severity of the penalty' and not under that of 'nature of the offence'. First, the candidate who violated the Elections Code might be disqualified from standing for election for one year. That sanction was considered not to be 'criminal' since its purpose was to compel candidates to respect the maximum limit of election expenditure and was thus 'designed to ensure the proper conduct of parliamentary elections'. The severity of the sanction did not make it criminal either, because it was limited to a period of one year.[235] Secondly, the penalty to pay an amount equal to the amount by which the candidate had exceeded the ceiling of election expenditure was considered not to be 'criminal', because it was also 'designed to ensure the proper conduct of parliamentary elections'.[236] As to its severity the Court observed, *inter alia*, that the penalty was not entered into the criminal record and that in case of failure to pay no imprisonment could be imposed. A fine of FRF 25,000 could be imposed with as an alternative a year's imprisonment, but that eventuality was not considered relevant as no proceedings were brought against the applicant in connection with that possibility.[237] In particular the criterion used by the Court that the penalty concerned had as its purpose to compel the person concerned to respect the law and was therefore not 'criminal', is convincing only if meant in a reparatory or corrective sense. The punitive elements of a penalty also have the aim of compelling respect for the law, but in a preventive way in respect of the future. Indeed, in the *Lauko* case, the Court held the sanction imposed to be punitive, because 'it was intended as a punishment to deter reoffending'.[238]

To conclude, it is worth mentioning that a complaints procedure to bring about criminal proceedings in the Netherlands (Article 12 of the Code of Criminal Procedure) does not fall within the scope of the notion of a criminal charge.[239]

d.   Nature and severity of the penalty

The third, and in certain cases ultimately decisive criterion is that of the nature and the severity of the penalty with which the violator of the norm is threatened.

---

[234]   *Ibid.*, para. 57.
[235]   *Ibid.*, para. 56.
[236]   *Ibid.*, para. 58.
[237]   *Ibid.*, para. 60.
[238]   *Lauko v. Slovakia, supra* n. 225, para. 58. See also *Bendenoun v. France, supra* n. 140, para. 47: 'the tax surcharges are intended not as pecuniary compensation for damage but essentially as a punishment to deter reoffending.'
[239]   *Ramsahai and Others v. the Netherlands*, ECtHR (GC) 15 May 2007, appl. no. 52391/99.

The element of the 'nature' of the penalty should not be confused with that of the 'purpose' of the penalty, discussed under the second criterion.[240] If the purpose of the sanction (i.e. deterrence and punishment) does not make the second criterion applicable, the nature and severity of the penalty may still bring the procedure under Article 6.[241] On the other hand, if on the basis of the second criterion the proceedings must be deemed to clearly be of a criminal character, the nature and severity of the penalty are not relevant any more. The second and third criterions are alternative and not cumulative.[242] For some time there was uncertainty on this point and in particular about the question whether small fines were not a criminal charge for that reason.[243] In its *Jussila* judgment, the Court ended this uncertainty: small fines also form a criminal charge within the scope of Article 6.[244] However, the Court does subsequently differentiate between classic 'hard core' criminal law and areas that do not fall within this category such as tax law, traffic law, penitentiary law and competition law. In these areas, the criminal charge requirements of Article 6 do not have to apply in full. In the case at hand (a dispute concerning a small tax fine), this means that no public hearing had to be held. The Court found: 'While it may be noted that the above-mentioned cases in which an oral hearing was not considered necessary concerned proceedings falling under the civil head of Article 6 §1 and that the requirements of a fair hearing are the most strict in the sphere of criminal law, the Court would not exclude that in the criminal sphere the nature of the issues to be dealt with before the tribunal or court may not require an oral hearing. Notwithstanding the consideration that a certain gravity attaches to criminal proceedings, which are concerned with the allocation of criminal responsibility and the imposition of a punitive and deterrent sanction, it is self-evident that there are criminal cases which do not carry any significant degree of stigma. There are clearly "criminal charges" of differing weight. What is more, the autonomous interpretation adopted by the Convention institutions of the notion of a "criminal charge" by applying the Engel criteria have underpinned a gradual broadening of the criminal head to cases not strictly belonging to the traditional categories of the criminal law, for example administrative penalties (…), prison disciplinary proceedings (…), customs law […], competition law (…) and penalties imposed by a court with jurisdiction in financial matters (…). Tax

---

[240]   That the Court brings the element of the purpose of the sanction under the second rather than the third criterion is clear from *Weber v. Switzerland, supra* n. 219, para. 33: 'As article 185, however, potentially affects the whole population, the offence it defines, and to which it attaches a punitive sanction, is a "criminal" one for the purposes of the second criterion.'

[241]   *Engel and Others v. the Netherlands, supra* n. 209, para. 85.

[242]   *Öztürk v. Germany, supra* n. 211, para. 54; *Lutz v. Germany*, ECtHR (GC) 25 August 1987, appl. no. 9912/82, para. 55.

[243]   See *Morel v. France*, ECtHR 3 June 2003 (dec.), appl. no. 54559/00.

[244]   See *Jussila v. Finland* ECtHR 23 November 2006, appl. no. 73053/01.

surcharges differ from the hard core of criminal law; consequently, the criminal-head guarantees will not necessarily apply with their full stringency (…).'

In the *Suhadolc* and *Berdajs* cases (concerning minor traffic offences), the Court concluded in line with *Jussila* that no public hearing was required.[245] The case law gives no further indication of what the *Jussila* line means when it comes to the review of legally fixed fines in tax law[246] and (high) fines in competition law.[247] We will return to this when considering the requirement of full jurisdiction in section 3.2.b.

Imprisonment is considered to be the criminal penalty *par excellence*. Unless it is, by its nature, duration or manner of execution 'not appreciably detrimental', it gives an otherwise disciplinary or administrative procedure a criminal character to such an extent that Article 6 must be held applicable.[248] Thus, in the *Engel* case, although the Court reached the conclusion that the offences at issue were against norms regulating the functioning of the Dutch armed forces, and therefore they could justly form the object of disciplinary procedures, it held that, since for some of these offences an imprisonment of considerable duration could be imposed, the conditions of Article 6(1) ought to have been observed in the disciplinary procedures in question.[249]

This judgment makes it clear, first of all, that in the opinion of the Court not every limitation of liberty is a deprivation of liberty. This depends on the factual conditions.[250] Moreover, the deprivation of liberty must be 'liable to be imposed as a punishment',[251] which excludes deprivations of liberty such as the detention of mentally ill people or the detention of aliens with a view to deportation or expulsion. Detention to induce the person concerned to fulfil his obligations ('civil detention') would seem to meet the elements of the third criterion, if of a sufficiently long duration.

In the *Kiss* case, which concerned disciplinary measures against a prisoner, the Commission concluded that Article 6 was not applicable, because it did not consider the possible penalty, loss of the prospect of reduction of the

---

245   *Suhadolc v. Slovenia*, ECtHR 17 May 2011, appl. no. 57655/08; *Berdajs v. Slovenia*, ECtHR 17 May 2012, appl. no. 10390/09.

246   *Segame S.A. v. France*, ECtHR 7 June 2012, appl. no. 4837/06.

247   *Menarini Diagnostics S.R.L. v. Italy*, ECtHR 27 September 2011, appl. no. 43509/08.

248   *Engel and Others v. the Netherlands*, *supra* n. 211, para. 82; *Ezeh and Connors v. the United Kingdom*, *supra* n. 223, para. 126.

249   *Engel and Others v. the Netherlands*, *supra* n. 211, para. 85.

250   In the *Engel* case, the Commission and the Court differed of opinion as far as the penalty of 'aggravated arrest' was concerned. In the course of its opinion that no deprivation of liberty was at issue, the Court held it to be decisive that, although under that regime the soldiers, in off-duty hours, had to serve their arrest in a specially designated place which they were not allowed to leave for recreational purposes, they were not 'kept under lock and key'; judgment of 8 June 1976, para. 62.

251   *Ibid.*, para. 82. This would seem to indicate that a certain link may exist between the nature and the purpose of the sanction.

penalty, a deprivation of liberty.[252] However, in the *Campbell and Fell* case, where the procedure could have resulted in refusal of remission of part of the imprisonment, the Court held that the practice of remission of the penalty creates for the detainee the justifiable expectation that he will be released before the end of the detention period. The procedure might therefore, in the Court's opinion, have such serious consequences for the person concerned as to the duration of his detention that it was to be considered of a criminal character.[253] It reached the same conclusion in the *Ezeh and Connors* case, where it also held that the question whether the resulting longer duration of loss of liberty is 'appreciably detrimental' should not be determined by reference to the length of the sentence already being served.[254] In its decision in *X v. Switzerland*, the Commission came to the conclusion that isolated confinement of a person who is already detained, as a penalty for late return from leave of absence, is a purely disciplinary matter for which the procedural guarantees of Article 6(1) need not be complied with.[255] The Commission here took into consideration that for a person already deprived of his liberty such a confinement is not of a 'severity' as envisaged in the Court's case law.

The *Engel* judgment also makes clear that not every deprivation of liberty renders Article 6 applicable. Its effects on the person concerned must be of a certain severity, *inter alia*, due to its duration. Thus, although the 'strict arrest' was held a deprivation,[256] in this case the maximum duration of two days was considered insufficient by the Court for it to be regarded as a criminal penalty,[257] whereas the Court took a different position with regard to the detention of some months to which the applicants De Wit, Dona and Schul could have been sentenced.[258]

In the *Olivieira* case and the *Landvreugd* case, the order imposed by the *Burgomaster* to the effect that the applicant was not allowed to enter parts of the city centre for 14 days, was considered to be of a preventive character and not of such a severity to give it a 'criminal' character.[259]

It is submitted that it would be desirable and create the required clarity if the third criterion were applied in such a way that in any case where the penalty may consist of a deprivation of liberty in the sense assigned thereto in the case

---

[252] Appl. no. 6224/73, Yearbook XX (1977), p. 156.
[253] *Campbell and Fell v. the United Kingdom, supra* n. 215, para. 72.
[254] *Ezeh and Connors v. the United Kingdom, supra* n. 223, paras. 121–124. The application of this criterion can be found in *Payet v. France*, ECtHR 20 January 2011, appl. no. 19606/08.
[255] Appl. no. 7754/77, D&R 11 (1978), p. 216 (218).
[256] *Engel and Others v. the Netherlands, supra* n. 209, para. 63.
[257] *Ibid.*, para. 85.
[258] *Ibid.* See also *Smith and Ford v. the United Kingdom*, ECtHR 29 September 1999, appl. no. 37475/97 and 39036/97, para. 19 and *Moore and Gordon v. the United Kingdom*, ECtHR 29 September 1999, appl. no. 36529/97 and 37393/97, para. 18; *Wilkinson and Allen v. the United Kingdom*, ECtHR 6 February 2001, appl. nos. 31145/96 and 35580/97, para. 19; *Mills v. the United Kingdom*, ECtHR 5 June 2001, appl. no. 35685/97, para. 20.
[259] Judgments of 6 June 2000, paras. 3 and 2, respectively.

law concerning Article 5, the guarantees of Article 6 should be observed in the procedure that may result in such a deprivation.[260]

It is not yet very clear to what extent disciplinary penalties other than deprivations of liberty may be considered severe enough to make Article 6 applicable. In the *Weber* case, which concerned proceedings where the fine could amount to 500 Swiss francs and could be converted into a term of imprisonment in certain circumstances, the Court held, with a general reference to its third criterion and without further reasoning, that what was at stake was 'sufficiently important to warrant classifying the offence as a criminal one under the Convention',[261] leaving it unclear to what extent the fact that the fine could be converted into imprisonment was decisive. The same lack of clarity was left in the *Demicoli* judgment.[262] The more recent *Ravnsborg* case, *Schmautzer* case and *Putz* case seem to make it even more difficult to fathom the Court's case law on this point. In the *Ravnsborg* case, the imposed maximum fine of 1,000 Swedish crowns did not make the sanction a 'criminal' one. In addition to the amount, the Court took into account that the fine was not registered in the police records and that conversion into a term of imprisonment could take place only if a special procedure, including an oral hearing, was followed.[263] This term of imprisonment amounted to at least two weeks. In the subsequent *Schmautzer* case, the Court held that driving without wearing a seat-belt, an administrative offence under Austrian law, was criminal in nature. It used as an additional argument that the imposed fine (of 200 Austrian schillings) had been accompanied by an order for committal to prison in case of non-payment. The maximum term of imprisonment was only 24 hours.[264] In the *Putz* case, however, the Court held with reference to its reasoning in the *Ravensborg* case that a possible maximum penalty of 20,000 Austrian schillings, that could have been converted into a term of imprisonment of 10 days, did not come within the ambit of Article 6.[265]

The Court went rather far in attributing a decisive character to the severity of a penalty that did not consist in deprivation of liberty in the *Garyfallou AEBE*

---

[260]   Thus, Judge Cremona in his separate opinion in the *Engel* Case, A.22, pp. 52–53.

[261]   *Weber v. Switzerland, supra* n. 219, para. 34.

[262]   *Demicoli v. Malta, supra* n. 216, para. 34.

[263]   *Ravnsborg v. Sweden, supra* n. 220, para. 35.

[264]   *Schmautzer v. Austria*, ECtHR 23 October 1995, appl. no. 15523/89, para. 28. See also, of the same date, 5 other cases against Austria: *Umlauft v. Austria*, ECtHR 23 October 1995, appl. no. 15527/89, para. 31; *Gradinger v. Austria, supra* n. 183, para. 36; *Pramstaller v. Austria*, ECtHR 23 October 1995, appl. no. 16713/90, para. 33; *Palaoro v. Austria*, ECtHR 23 October 1995, appl. no. 16718/90, para. 35; *Pfarrmeier v. Austria*, ECtHR 23 October 1995, appl. no. 16841/90, para. 32. In these cases the imposed fines varied from 5,000 Austrian schillings (in the event of default of payment 200 hours of imprisonment) in the *Pfarrmeier* case to 50,000 schillings (50 days of imprisonment) in the *Pramstaller* case. The maximum penalties that could have been imposed varied from 300 schillings (24 hours of imprisonment) in the *Pfarrmeier* case to 100,000 schillings (3 months of imprisonment) in the *Pramstaller* case.

[265]   *Putz v. Austria, supra* n. 221, para. 37.

case. However, even there the Court took into consideration, in addition to the maximum of the fine and the risk of the company's assets being seized, as 'more importantly, for the purposes of the Court's examination' that, in the event of non-payment of the fine, the directors risked detention of up to one year.[266]

The *Malige* case concerned the measure of docking of points from driving licences after a conviction for a traffic offence. No possible detention as an alternative was involved. The Court found the measure to be of a severity to make it a criminal sanction. However, in its reasoning the Court seems to have mixed the purpose of the sanction with its severity: 'the deduction of points may in time entail invalidation of the licence. It is indisputable that the right to drive a motor vehicle is very useful in everyday life and for carrying on an occupation. The Court, like the Commission, accordingly infers that, although the deduction of points has a preventive character, it also has a punitive and deterrent character and is accordingly similar to a secondary penalty.'[267]

The judgment in the *Escoubet* case suggests that, in the case of two different measures of comparable impact, the connection which a certain measure has with the outcome of criminal proceedings may be decisive for the applicability of Article 6. The Court held with respect to the measure of withdrawal of a driving licence after a road accident: 'The immediate withdrawal of a driving licence is a precautionary measure; the fact that it is an emergency measure justifies its being applied immediately and there is nothing to indicate that its purpose is punitive. Withdrawal of a driving licence is distinguishable from disqualification from driving, a measure ordered by the criminal court at the end of criminal proceedings. In such a case, the criminal court assesses and classifies the facts constituting the offence which may give rise to disqualification.'[268]

The same kind of reasoning was followed in the *Blokker* case. The applicant, who had been stopped by the police driving a car with too high an alcohol level in his blood, had been ordered, *inter alia*, to subject himself to an Educational Measure Alcohol and Traffic, the costs of which he had to pay himself. The Court found the measure not to be of a severity and character to make it a criminal sanction. In the Court's opinion it should be compared with the procedure of issuing a driving licence, aimed at ensuring that the driver possesses the required skills and knowledge of the relevant traffic rules. The costs and time which the applicant had to spend for the Measure were to be compared with the time and costs spent for obtaining a driving licence. The fact that in case of failure to comply with the Measure the driving licence could be declared invalid, did not change the character, since that was to be compared with the consequences of failing to pay for or take an examination for a driving licence,

---

[266] *Garyfallou AEBE v. Greece*, ECtHR 24 September 1997, appl. no. 18996/91, para. 34.

[267] *Malige v. France, supra* n. 82, para. 39.

[268] *Escoubet v. Belgium, supra* n. 197, para. 37. See *Duteil v. France*, ECtHR 20 April 2010, appl. no. 3221/10 for a case in which it was accepted that declaring a driving licence invalid on the basis of a points system could be considered a criminal charge.

and not with disqualification for driving as a measure in the context of criminal proceedings.[269]

2.4. FISCAL PENALTIES

With respect to 'fiscal penalties' the Court has adopted the position that those fiscal penalties which are not compensatory in nature, but are of a punitive character, such as fines, disqualifications and settlements of penalties, give the proceedings a criminal character for the purposes of Article 6.[270]

This was further elaborated upon in the *Bendenoun* case. Although the tax surcharges imposed upon the applicant were, in the Government's submission, to be considered 'administrative' and not 'criminal' penalties under the applicable French law, the Court did not consider this to be decisive. On the basis of the other criteria of its *Engel* judgment it reached the conclusion that the criminal connotation was predominant, since the surcharges were 'intended not as pecuniary compensation for damages but essentially as a punishment to deter reoffending, they were imposed under a general rule, the purpose of which was both deterrent and punitive, and they were very substantial'.[271] In the *Jussila* case already mentioned above, the Court made it clear that small fines can also form a criminal charge in the sense of Article 6. The case in question concerned a slight increase in taxes. The Court does not include tax law, for example, under the classic 'hard core' criminal law, so that not all requirements of Article 6 have to apply in full.[272]

2.5. ADMISSION, EXPULSION AND EXTRADITION PROCEDURES

The prohibition to enter a country does not amount to a criminal penalty. The same holds good for the removal or expulsion of aliens from the territory, although such measure may be experienced by the person concerned as a penalty. In the *Maaouia* case, the Court recognised that such measures may be characterised differently in different domestic legal orders and that their characterisation as a penalty is not decisive for determining whether or not the penalty is criminal in nature. In that respect the Court noted that, in general,

---

[269]   *Blokker v. the Netherlands,* ECtHR 7 November 2000, appl. no. 45282/99, para. 1.
[270]   *Salabiaku v. France,* ECtHR October 1988, appl. no. 10519/83, para. 24; *J.B. v. Switzerland, supra* n. 230, paras. 47–49.
[271]   *Bendenoun v. France, supra* n. 140, para. 47; *J.B. v. Switzerland, supra* n. 230, para. 48; *Västberga Taxi Aktiebolag and Vulic v. Sweden,* ECtHR 23 July 2002, appl. no. 36985/97, paras. 78–82.
[272]   See *Jussila v. Finland, supra* n. 244.

the measure is not characterised as criminal within the member states of the Council of Europe: 'Such orders, which in most States may also be made by the administrative authorities, constitute a special preventive measure for the purpose of immigration control and do not concern the determination of a criminal charge against the applicant for the purposes of Article 6 para. 1. The fact that they are imposed in the context of criminal proceedings cannot alter their essentially preventive nature.'[273]

The *Maaouia* case concerned an exclusion order imposed on the applicant by a criminal court in addition to the imprisonment conviction. The Court does not seem to distinguish this order from expulsion orders. However, Judge Costa, in his concurring opinion, defined the order as an 'ancillary penalty' which comes within criminal law. He nevertheless agreed with the majority that Article 6 was not applicable, but for the reason that the charge forming the basis of the order was not challenged by the applicant in the proceedings for the rescission of the order.

Extradition proceedings are also held not to be covered by Article 6, on the ground that a 'determination' involves the full process of the examination of an individual's guilt or innocence, and not the process of determining whether a person can be extradited to another country.[274]

2.6. CONCLUDING OBSERVATIONS

As in the case of 'civil rights and obligations', the Court should make further efforts to lift the uncertainty and ambiguity with respect to 'criminal charge' which its case law still leaves, in particular with regard to the distinction it made in the *Jussila* case. Although the Court in this judgment finally made clear that small fines also form a criminal charge within the scope of Article 6,[275] it added new uncertainty by differentiating between classic 'hard core' criminal law and areas that do not fall within this category such as tax law, traffic law, penitentiary law and competition law. In these areas, the criminal charge requirements of Article 6 ECHR do not have to apply in full, but the case law until now does not clarify the exact scope of this distinction.

As to the nature of the penalty, Article 6 should be held applicable to all those proceedings which may result in the imposition of a punitive sanction that as to its nature and/or its consequences is so similar to criminal sanctions that there is no justification for excluding judicial review, except by free and unambiguous waiver. This includes in particular deprivation of liberty and the imposition of fines, but could also concern restrictions of economic or professional

---

273 *Maaouia v. France, supra* n. 82, para. 39.
274 Appl. no. 10227/82, *H v. Spain*, D&R 37 (1984), p. 93 (94).
275 See *Jussila v. Finland, supra* n. 244.

freedom of a punitive character (which, moreover, could affect civil rights and obligations). Since the Court has adopted the position that Article 6 makes no distinction between serious and less serious offences and that it may even apply to proceedings which lead to no penalty at all, the severity of the penalty cannot be a decisive element for its 'punitive' character.

As far as the severity of a non-criminal sanction is concerned, there would seem to be no convincing reason to distinguish between detentions of short and of longer duration, since deprivation of liberty has by definition severe consequences. As to fines, it makes sense to distinguish between small and large amounts. However, the financial situation of the person concerned should then be relevant and, in connection therewith, the possibility that, if the fine is not paid, an alternative detention may be imposed.

3. ACCESS TO COURT

3.1. INTRODUCTION

Article 6(1) not only contains procedural guarantees in relation to judicial proceedings, but also grants *a right to* judicial proceedings for the cases mentioned there: the right of access to court. This right has not been laid down in express terms in Article 6. Its first paragraph only refers to entitlement to a fair and public hearing by a court, leaving it unclear whether this entitlement only exists in cases where judicial proceedings have been provided for under domestic law, or that provision implies – or rather presupposes – a right to such judicial proceedings.

This unclarity was lifted by the Court in its *Golder* judgment. The Court referred to the reference in the Preamble of the Convention to the rule of law 'as one of the features of the common spiritual heritage of the member States of the Council of Europe'. According to the Court that reference had to be taken into account when interpreting the terms of Article 6(1) according to their context and in the light of the object and purpose of the Convention. In doing so the Court made the observation that 'in civil matters one can scarcely conceive of the rule of law without there being a possibility of having access to the courts'. The Court further reasoned that Article 6 must be read in the light of the following two legal principles: (1) the principle whereby a civil claim must be capable of being submitted to a judge, as one of the universally recognised fundamental principles of law; and (2) the principle of international law which forbids the denial of justice[276]: 'Taking all the preceding considerations together, it follows that the right of access constitutes an element which is inherent in the right stated by Article 6 para. 1. This is not an extensive interpretation forcing

---

[276]   *Golder v. the United Kingdom, supra* n. 1, paras. 34–35.

new obligations on the Contracting States: it is based on the very terms of the first sentence of Article 6 para. 1 read in its context and having regard to the object and purpose of the Convention, a lawmaking treaty (...), and to general principles of law. The Court thus reaches the conclusion (...) that Article 6 para. 1 secures to everyone the right to have any claim relating to his civil rights and obligations brought before a court or tribunal.'[277]

In conclusion, Article 6(1) also applies to determinations of civil rights and obligations, and of criminal charges, for which domestic law does not provide for judicial proceedings.[278] It does not, however, imply a guarantee against the striking out of a case by the court if there is no sustainable cause of action.[279]

With this extensive, teleological interpretation the Court intended to prevent the states from eroding the guarantees of Article 6 by restricting, or even abolishing, judicial proceedings in some areas and omitting its introduction in others.[280] For the same reason the Court adopted the view that Article 6 also applies to the (non-)implementation of a judicial decision: 'to construe Article 6 as being concerned exclusively with access to a court and the conduct of proceedings would be likely to lead to situations incompatible with the principle of the rule of law.'[281] Where the competent authorities refuse or fail to comply, or even delay doing so,[282] the guarantees under Article 6 enjoyed by a litigant during the judicial phase of the proceedings, are rendered devoid of purpose. Consequently, the power of the Procurator-General to apply for a final judgment to be quashed infringes the principle of legal certainty and the right of access to court.[283] And the same holds good if private parties refuse to execute a judgment and the judgment is not enforced against them.[284] Execution of a judgment given by a court must, therefore, be regarded as an integral part of the 'trial' for the purposes of Article 6.[285] A stay of execution must itself be subject to effective judicial review.[286] Lack of financial means is no justification for non-

---

[277] *Ibid.*, para. 36. See, however, the dissenting opinion of Judge Fitzmaurice, para. 40.

[278] This was the case, e.g., with the Crown appeal procedure in the Netherlands: *Benthem v. The Netherlands*, *supra* n. 10, paras. 41–44. For a specific administrative review procedure in Sweden that did not meet the requirements, see *Sporrong and Lönnroth v. Sweden*, *supra* n. 65, para. 86; *Mats Jacobsson v. Sweden*, *supra* n. 25, para. 36.

[279] *Z and Others v. the United Kingdom*, *supra* n. 13, para. 97.

[280] *Golder v. the United Kingdom*, *supra* n. 1, para. 35.

[281] *Hornsby v. Greece*, ECtHR 19 March 1997, appl. no. 18357/91, para. 40; *Immobiliare Saffi v. Italy*, *supra* n. 127, para. 63; *Antonakopoulos, Vortsela and Antonakopoulou v. Greece*, ECtHR 14 December 1999, appl. no. 37098/97.

[282] Here, the Court judges on the reasonableness of the delay: *Ganenko v. Ukraine*, ECtHR 11 January 2005 (dec.), appl. no. 27184/03.

[283] *Brumarescu v. Romania*, ECtHR (GC) 28 October 1999, appl. no. 28342/95, para. 62.

[284] *Pini and Others v. Romania*, ECtHR 22 June 2004, appl. no. 78028/01 and 78030/01, paras. 174–189.

[285] *Kyrtatos v. Greece*, ECtHR 22 May 2003, appl. no. 41666/98, para. 30; *Timofeyev v. Russia*, ECtHR 23 October 2003, appl. no. 58263/00, para. 40.

[286] *G.L. v. Italy*, *supra* n. 127, para. 40; *Edoardo Palumbo v. Italy*, ECtHR 30 November 2000, appl. no. 15919/89, para. 45.

execution,[287] and even if there are compelling reasons for a stay of execution, the authorities must take speedy and adequate measures to create a situation that allows for execution.[288] Consequently, allowing for a final judgment to be quashed at the Procurator-General's application without any time-limit, was considered by the Court to violate the principle of legal certainty and, consequently, the right to a fair hearing.[289] Access to court is also made illusory if the applicant has the possibility of bringing legal proceedings, but is prevented by operation of the law from pursuing his claim.[290]

Interpreted in this way paragraph 1 of Article 6 takes over to a considerable extent the function of Article 13, which guarantees a right to an effective remedy. Article 6 goes even further. Firstly, because it implies a right of recourse to a *court or tribunal* 'characterised in the substantive sense of the term by its judicial function, that is to say determining matters within its competence on the basis of rules of law and after proceedings conducted in a prescribed manner'.[291] And secondly, because it applies to all determinations of civil rights and obligations and not only to those which are related to one of the rights and freedoms laid down in the Convention. However, Article 13 remains important for cases of violation of rights which according to the Strasbourg case law are not 'civil rights' in the sense of Article 6(1)[292] and, indeed, for cases of violation of (the reasonable-time requirement of) Article 6 itself.[293]

The access guarantee of Article 6 covers all the issues related to the dispute concerning civil rights or obligations, including issues concerning the costs involved in having those rights and obligations determined.[294] Domestic law or case law may not exclude these issues from appeal to a court, not even if, in an indirect way, they depend on issues which themselves may be subjected to judicial examination.[295] For the same reason, the possibility of instituting judicial proceedings for damages does not substitute for the right to refer the underlying dispute to a court.[296]

---

[287]   *Piven v. Ukraine*, ECtHR 29 June 2004, appl. no. 56849/00, para. 40; *"Amat-G" Ltd and Mebaghishvili v. Georgia*, ECtHR 27 September 2005, appl. no. 2507/03, para. 48.

[288]   *Lunari v. Italy*, ECtHR 11 January 2001, appl. no. 21463/93, para. 45.

[289]   *Brumarescu v. Romania*, *supra* n. 283, para. 62.

[290]   *Kutic v. Croatia*, ECtHR 1 March 2002, appl. no. 48778/99, paras. 25–33.

[291]   *Geouffre de la Pradelle v. France*, *supra* n. 100, paras. 36–37; *Cyprus v. Turkey*, ECtHR (GC) 10 May 2001, appl. no. 25781/94, para. 233; *Baumann v. France*, ECtHR 22 May 2001, appl. no. 33592/96, para. 39.

[292]   Thus, the Court in *Golder v. the United Kingdom*, *supra* n. 1, para. 33.

[293]   *Kudla v. Poland*, ECtHR (GC) 26 October 2000, appl. no. 30210/96, paras. 147–149.

[294]   *Robins v. the United Kingdom*, *supra* n. 66, para. 28; *Beer v. Austria*, ECtHR 6 February 2001, appl. no. 30428/96, paras. 12–13.

[295]   *Eriksson v. Sweden*, *supra* n. 66, paras. 80–81; *Keegan v. Ireland*, *supra* n. 118, para. 59.

[296]   *Tre Traktörer AB Aktiebolag v. Sweden*, *supra* n. 34, para. 49.

3.2. REQUIREMENT OF EFFECTIVENESS

a. Introduction

As holds good for all rights laid down in the Convention, the right of access to court must not be theoretical or illusory, but practical and effective.[297] This means that the person concerned not only has a right to apply to a court for the determination of his rights or obligations, but must also be enabled to present his case properly and satisfactorily,[298] which also requires that the proceedings are organised and conducted in a way that takes into account the intellectual abilities of the parties.[299] It further means that the right of access includes the right to obtain a 'determination' of the dispute by the competent court.[300] It also means that there has to be an independent and impartial court with the required jurisdiction to make this determination; otherwise his right of access is not secured.[301] Thus, in its judgments in *W., B.* and *R. v. the United Kingdom*, the Court held that, although the parents could apply for judicial review or institute wardship proceedings, and thereby have certain aspects of the authority's access decisions examined by an English court, during the currency of the parental resolutions the court's powers were not of sufficient scope to fully satisfy the requirements of Article 6, as they did not extend to the merits of the matter.[302]

In the *Obermeier* case, the Court held that there had been a violation of the right of access to court, since the court in question could only determine whether the administrative authorities had exercised their discretionary power in a way compatible with the object and purpose of the applicable law.[303] And in the *Tinnelly* case and the *Devlin* case, the Court adopted the position that the fact that, for national security reasons, the court could not determine the merits of the applicant's complaint concerning discrimination, made the remedy ineffective to an extent that was not justified by the security considerations; it took into consideration that in other contexts it had been found possible to modify judicial proceedings in such a way as to safeguard national security concerns and yet accord the individual a substantial degree of procedural justice.[304]

---

[297]   *Airey v. Ireland*, ECtHR 9 October 1979, appl. no. 6289/73, para. 24; *Kutic v. Croatia, supra* n. 290, para. 25; *Multiplex v. Croatia*, ECtHR 10 July 2003, appl. no. 58112/00, para. 44.

[298]   *Ibid.*

[299]   *S.C. v. the United Kingdom*, ECtHR 15 June 2004, appl. no. 60958/00, para. 36.

[300]   *Multiplex v. Croatia, supra* n. 297, para. 45.

[301]   *Le Compte, Van Leuven and De Meyere v. Belgium, supra* n. xxx, para. 44; *Sporrong and Lönnroth v. Sweden, supra* n. 65, para. 80; *Ashingdane v. the United Kingdom*, ECtHR 28 May 1985, appl. no. 8225/78, para. 55.

[302]   *W. v. the United Kingdom, supra* n. 117, paras. 81–82; *B. v. the United Kingdom, supra* n. 117, paras. 81–82; *R. v. the United Kingdom, supra* n. 117, paras. 86–87.

[303]   *Obermeier v. Austria*, ECtHR 28 June 1990, appl. no. 11761/85, paras. 69–70.

[304]   *Tinnelly & Sons Ltd and Others and McElduff and Others v. the United Kingdom, supra* n. 107, paras. 77–78; *Devlin v. the United Kingdom, supra* n. 108, para. 31.

Consequently, there is a close link between the requirement of effective access to court and the requirement of exhaustion of local remedies, laid down in Article 35(1); if the Court concludes that the local remedies available were not effective it means at the same time, in cases to which Article 6(1) applies, that the applicant did not have effective access to a court.[305]

b. Full jurisdiction

For the right of access to be effective it is not sufficient that the court has jurisdiction to judge on the merits of the case. The court must have full jurisdiction. This means that the court must have competence to judge both on the facts and on the law as a basis for its 'determination'.[306]

However, the Court recognises that especially in procedures of judicial review of administrative decisions it is a common feature that the courts take a somewhat reserved position in reviewing the establishment of the facts by the administration. In judging on whether that approach is sufficient from the perspective of effective access to court, the Court has regard to such aspects as the subject matter of the decision appealed against, the manner in which and the procedure according to which that decision was arrived at, and the contents of the dispute. Especially if the subject matter concerns a specialised area of the law and the facts have been established in the course of a quasi-judicial procedure governed by several of the safeguards required by Article 6, a restricted jurisdiction to re-examine the facts will be acceptable.[307] Thus, on the one hand, in the *Schmautzer* case the Court held that the appeal from the administrative authorities to the administrative court did not satisfy the requirements of Article 6, since the latter did not have full jurisdiction to review and quash the decision of the administrative body both on questions of fact and of law.[308] There the Court took into consideration that the administrative court was sitting in proceedings that were of a criminal nature for the purposes of the Convention. On the other hand, the judgments in the *Bryan* case, the *Chapman* case and the *Jane Smith* case suggest that in more typically administrative proceedings, if a

---

[305] *Baumann v. France, supra* n. 291, para. 48.

[306] *Le Compte, Van Leuven and De Meyere v. Belgium, supra* n. 36, para. 51; *Zumtobel v. Austria*, ECtHR 21 September 1993, appl. no. 12235/86, para. 29; *Fischer v. Austria*, ECtHR 26 April 1995, appl. no. 16922/90, para. 28; *Umlauft v. Austria, supra* n. 264, para. 37; *Van Kück v. Germany*, ECtHR 12 June 2003, appl. no. 35968/97, para. 48 and *Beneficio Cappella Paolini v. San Marino, supra* n. 169, paras. 28–29. See, however, *Bryan v. the United Kingdom*, ECtHR 22 November 1995, appl. no. 19178/91, paras. 44–47, and *Potocka and Others v. Poland*, ECtHR 4 October 2001, appl. no. 33776/96, paras. 52–59, where the Court held that a somewhat restricted jurisdiction could also meet the requirements of Art. 6(1) in specific circumstances.

[307] *Bryan v. the United Kingdom, supra* n. 306, paras. 45–47; *Potocka and Others v. Poland, supra* n. 306, para. 53.

[308] *Schmautzer v. Austria, supra* n. 264, para. 36; *Mauer v. Austria (No. 2)*, ECtHR 20 June 2000, appl. no. 35401/97, para. 16.

---

full review of the facts has been performed by the administrative body, a more restricted jurisdiction may suffice.[309]

This case law has once more been summarised in the *Sigma* judgment, where the Court also indicates the lower limit again: 'Where, however, the reviewing court is precluded from determining the central issue in dispute, the scope of review will not be considered sufficient for the purposes of Article 6 (…). The Court has therefore found violations of Article 6 §1 in cases where the domestic courts considered themselves bound by the prior findings of administrative bodies which were decisive for the outcome of the cases before them, without examining the issues independently (…). In addition the Court has found a violation of Article 6 where a ground of challenge has been upheld by the reviewing court but it was not possible to remit the case for a fresh decision by the same or a different body (…).'[310]

Effective access to a court for a determination also means that the final judgment concerning legal issues relevant for the determination rests with the court. Consequently, the practice of the French *Conseil d'État* to ask the Minister of Foreign Affairs for a preliminary opinion about the reciprocal character of a treaty, which opinion is then followed by the *Conseil d'État* without any possibility for the parties to challenge that opinion, is in violation of the right of access to court.[311]

Finally, it cannot be concluded from the judgments in the cases of *Menarini* and *Segame*, in areas that are not part of the hard core of criminal law (competition law and tax law respectively), that in line with the aforementioned judgment in *Jussila* the Court sets lower requirements in the light of the right to *full jurisdiction*. In *Menarini*, the Court reviewed whether national legal protection from a high administrative fine in competition law met the requirements for *full jurisdiction* (without success for the applicant, by the way). On the one hand, in the *Segame* case, the Court seemed to pay serious attention to the review of the requirements for *full jurisdiction*. On the other hand, it caused confusion when in its review of the statutory tax penalty it referred explicitly to *Jussila*, stating in particular that tax law is not part of the hard core of classical criminal law. This would appear to indicate that in the case of a legally fixed fine in an area on the periphery of criminal law, the Court chooses to leave room for less strict requirements on grounds for *full jurisdiction*, but this is by no means certain.[312]

---

[309]   *Bryan v. the United Kingdom, supra* n. 306, paras. 34–47; *Chapman v. the United Kingdom,* ECtHR (GC) 18 January 2001, appl. no. 27238/95, para. 124 and *Jane Smith v. the United Kingdom,* ECtHR (GC) 18 January 2001, 25154/94, para. 133.

[310]   *Sigma Radio Television Ltd. v. Cyprus,* ECtHR 21 July 2011, appl. no. 32181/04, para. 157.

[311]   *Chevrol v. France, supra* n. 57, paras. 83–84.

[312]   *Menarini Diagnostics S.R.L. v. Italy, supra* n. 247; *Segame S.A. v. France, supra* n. 246.

c. Legal aid

In the *Airey* case, it was held that, although the right of access to court does not imply an automatic right to free legal aid in civil proceedings, it may imply the obligation on the part of the state to provide for the assistance of a lawyer to persons in financial need. This is the case when legal aid proves indispensable for an effective access to court, either because legal representation is rendered compulsory or by reason of the procedural complexity of the case. The state may also, if appropriate and possible, opt for abolition of compulsory representation and simplification of procedure to the effect that effective access to the court no longer requires a lawyer's assistance.[313] Moreover, a certain financial threshold for the legal costs to be incurred may be acceptable.[314]

In the *Aerts* case, the Court adopted the opinion that legal aid may not be refused by the competent authority on the sole basis of the latter's assessment of the prospects of success of the review, unless the assessment is made by a court.[315] In the *Gnahore* case, the Court specified this by stating that the fact that representation by a lawyer was obligatory, had been decisive. It accepted the refusal of legal aid for reason of lack of any serious cassation ground in a case where legal representation was not required and the procedure of selection offered several guarantees.[316] The same position was adopted in the *Essaadi* and *Del Sol* cases.[317] If an *ex gratia* offer has been made, but is refused by the applicant, the latter cannot complain about lack of effective access.[318]

d. Other aspects of effectiveness

In the *De Geouffre de la Pradelle* case, the Court held that if the law regulating the access to court is so complex and unclear that it creates legal uncertainty, access to court cannot be said to be effective.[319]

In the *Golder* case, the Court attached to its view that Article 6 implies a right of access to court and that 'hindering the effective exercise of a right may amount to a breach of that right, even if the hindrance is of a temporary character', the consequence that a refusal to permit detainees to correspond with persons providing legal aid or their counsel is contrary to this provision.[320] Moreover,

---

[313] *Airey v. Ireland, supra* n. 297, paras. 24–26.

[314] *Glaser v. the United Kingdom, supra* n. 117, para. 99.

[315] *Aerts v. Belgium, supra* n. 162, para. 60.

[316] *Gnahore v. France,* ECtHR 19 September 2000, appl. no. 40031/98, paras. 40–41.

[317] *Essaadi v. France,* ECtHR 26 February 2002, appl. no. 49384/99, paras. 33–36 and *Del Sol v. France,* ECtHR 26 February 2002, appl. no. 46800/99, paras. 23–26.

[318] *Andronicou and Constantinou v. Cyprus,* ECtHR (GC) 9 October 1997, appl. no. 25052/94, para. 200.

[319] *De Geouffre de la Pradelle v. France, supra* n. 100, paras. 33–34.

[320] *Golder v. the United Kingdom, supra* n. 1, para. 40. See also *Silver and Others v. the United Kingdom,* ECtHR 25 March 1983, appl. nos. 5947/72, 6205/73, 7052/75, 7061/75, 7107/75,

the detainee has a right to have contact with counsel or a person providing legal aid without the presence of a prison authority.[321]

Effective access to a court also requires that the applicant has access to the judgment. However, if a copy of the judgment is sent to the applicant in a normal way, the fact that he lives far away and has not indicated his intention to receive the copy at a certain address is at his own risk.[322]

3.3. ACCESS TO COURT IN CRIMINAL CASES

For criminal cases and for cases with criminal features which make Article 6 applicable, the right of access to court implies that the person who is 'charged', has the right that any ultimate determination of that charge is made by a court which fulfils the requirements of Article 6(1). It does not imply that the person 'charged' may demand the continuation of the prosecution and an ultimate trial by a court, but only that, when a determination is made, this is done by a court.[323] However, if the charge is dropped on the basis of a financial transaction between the accused and the prosecuting authority, without a free choice on the part of the accused, he is actually denied access to court contrary to Article 6.[324] In other situations, too, a waiver of the right of access by an accused should not be assumed lightly and may be overruled by an important public interest.[325] And if the case is dropped under circumstances in which the odium of guilt would continue to cling to the person in question, Article 6 has nevertheless been violated; this also in the light of the presumption of innocence of the second paragraph.[326]

The right of access to court does not imply the right for the victim of a criminal offence to institute criminal proceedings himself or to claim prosecution by the public prosecutor.[327] However, if the criminal proceedings

---

7113/75 and 7136/75, para. 82; *Campbell and Fell v. the United Kingdom*, *supra* n. 215, paras. 106–107.

[321] *Campbell and Fell v. the United Kingdom*, *supra* n. 215, paras. 111–113.

[322] *Bogonos v. Russia*, *supra* n. 111, para. 1.

[323] Report of 18 October 1985, *Lutz*, para. 48.

[324] *Deweer v. Belgium*, *supra* n. 185, paras. 49–54. In this case, the person in question was subject to the threat that his shop would be closed if he did not agree to the transaction.

[325] *Thompson v. the United Kingdom*, ECtHR 15 June 2004, appl. no. 36256/97, para. 43.

[326] *Minelli v. Switzerland*, *supra* n. 203, paras. 34–41. See, however, *Leutscher v. the Netherlands*, *supra* n. 35, paras. 30–32: The applicant had been tried at first instance *in absentia*. He instituted an appeal, but the appeal proceedings ended in the court of appeal declaring the prosecution time-barred. The applicant's request for reimbursement of legal costs was refused on the ground that suspicion still weighed against the applicant. In the opinion of the Court the result was not a violation of Art. 6(2), since the applicant had been able to exercise the rights of the defence and the decision on reimbursement did not involve a reassessment of the applicant's guilt.

[327] *Helmers v. Sweden*, *supra* n. 157, para. 29.

are the only possibility for him to vindicate his civil right to damages as a civil party, this may be different.[328]

The decision in the *Golder* judgment, that the right of access to court implies the right of free correspondence and consultations in private with a lawyer,[329] also holds good for criminal cases, to the extent that this guarantee does not already follow from the third paragraph under (b). Moreover, the right of (effective) access to court may also play a role in assessing whether free legal aid should have been granted under paragraph 3(c)[330] and whether the state should be held responsible for a manifest failure by a legal aid counsel to provide effective representation.[331]

3.4. ACCESS TO JUDICIAL APPEAL PROCEEDINGS

The possibility of appeal to a higher court constitutes a domestic remedy that has to be previously exhausted according to Article 35. In fact, an appeal court may remedy the fact that the proceedings in the first instance were not in conformity with Article 6 in all respects.[332] A breach of Article 6, however, cannot be remedied by a higher court if the consequences of the previous judgment have since become irreversible.[333]

The right of appeal to a higher court is not laid down, and is also not implied, in Article 6(1).[334] However, if appeal *is* provided for and has been lodged, and the court in that instance is called upon to make a 'determination', Article 6(1) applies.[335] This also means that, if domestic law provides for the remedy of appeal, access to that remedy may not be limited in its essence or in a disproportionate way.[336] If its limitation has a discriminatory effect, this also amounts to a violation of Article 6 in addition to Article 14.[337]

---

[328]   *A contrario*, see *Assenov and Others v. Bulgaria*, *supra* n. 75, paras. 111–112.

[329]   *Golder v. the United Kingdom*, *supra* n. 1, para. 40.

[330]   *Granger v. the United Kingdom*, ECtHR 28 March 1990, appl. no. 11932/86, paras. 44–48.

[331]   *Kamasinski v. Austria*, ECtHR 19 December 1989, appl. no. 9783/82, para. 65.

[332]   *Edwards v. the United Kingdom*, ECtHR 16 December 1992, appl. no. 13071/87, paras. 38–39; *De Haan v. the Netherlands*, *supra* n. 109, para. 54; *Mirilashvili v. Russia*, ECtHR 11 December 2008, appl. no. 6293/04.

[333]   *Mercieca and Others v. Malta*, ECtHR 14 June 2011, appl. no. 21974/07, para. 49; see also *Micallef v. Malta*, *supra* n. 31, para. 75 *vis-à-vis* interim measures ordered by a judge.

[334]   *Belgian Linguistics Case v. Belgium (No. 2)*, ECtHR 23 July 1968, para. 9, Series A no. 6; *Delcourt v. Belgium*, *supra* n. 2, para. 25; *Hoffmann v. Germany*, ECtHR 11 October 2001, appl. no. 34045/96, para. 65 and *Sommerfeld v. Germany*, ECtHR 11 October 2001, appl. no. 31871/96, para. 64.

[335]   See, e.g., *Delcourt v. Belgium*, *supra* n. 2, para. 25 and *Belziuk v. Poland*, ECtHR 25 March 1998, appl. no. 23103/93, para. 37.

[336]   *Poitrimol v. France*, ECtHR 23 November 1993, appl. no. 14032/88, paras. 35–38.

[337]   *Hoffmann v. Germany*, *supra* n. 334, para. 66.

The same holds good for appeal to a constitutional court,[338] unless its review concerns exclusively the constitutionality of the previous judicial decision and not a full 'determination'.[339] It is not easy to understand how and in what situations such a distinction may be made. In fact, the decisive criterion is whether there is a close link between the subject matter of the proceedings before the constitutional court and that of the proceedings which led to the referral of the matter to the constitutional court.[340]

Article 6 may also be applicable to proceedings concerning a so-called 'special remedy'. Thus, the Court held Article 6 applicable to the proceedings concerning a request for revision and retrial.[341] However, the Court took into consideration that the request for revision could also relate to the way the domestic court had applied the law, and in fact replaced the appeal for cassation. As a rule, Article 6 does not apply to requests for revision or reopening.[342]

Article 6 does not debar states from laying down regulations governing the access to an appellate or cassation court, provided that their purpose is to ensure the proper administration of justice. Consequently, there is no violation of Article 6 where an applicant is refused access to such a court due to his own procedural mistake. If the rejection of a petition for review or cassation is, however, the result of an omission on the part of the court, the right of access is violated by that rejection.[343]

The decision of the appellate court declaring the appeal inadmissible on the ground that the appellant no longer had a legal interest, does not limit the right of access in its essence, especially not if he has had the full benefit of a first (and possibly second) instance that was in conformity with Article 6(1).[344]

If Article 6 is applicable, the specific characteristics of the appeal proceedings in question must be taken into account with regard to the question of whether Article 6 has been complied with.[345] Thus, for instance, it must be examined

---

[338] *Süssmann v. Germany*, ECtHR (GC) 16 September 1996, appl. no. 20024/92, para. 41; *Pammel v. Germany*, ECtHR 1 July 1997, appl. no. 17820/91, para. 53; *Pierre-Bloch v. France*, supra n. 172, para. 48; *Trickovic v. Slovenia*, ECtHR 12 June 2001, appl. no. 39914/98, para. 39; *Mianowicz v. Germany*, ECtHR 18 October 2001, appl. no. 42505/98, para. 45; *Kind v. Germany*, ECtHR 20 February 2003, appl. no. 44324/98, para. 43.

[339] *Sramek v. Austria*, supra n. 93, para. 35.

[340] *Ruiz-Mateos v. Spain*, supra n. 106, para. 59.

[341] *S.L. Band Club v. Malta*, ECtHR 29 July 2004, appl. no. 77562/01, paras. 40–48. See, however, *Jussy v. France*, ECtHR 8 April 2003, appl. no. 42277/98, para. 18.

[342] *'Energia' Producers' Cooperative v. Armenia*, ECtHR 9 December 2004, appl. no. 31769/04 (adm. decision).

[343] Report of the Commission of 21 October 1998, *Bogdanska Dimova*, paras. 52–59.

[344] *Venema and Others v. the Netherlands*, ECtHR 29 January 2002 (dec.), appl. no. 35731/97, para. 3.

[345] *Delcourt v. Belgium*, supra n. 2, para. 26; *Pakelli v. Germany*, ECtHR 25 April 1983, appl. no. 8398/78, para. 29; *Pretto and Others v. Italy*, ECtHR (GC) 8 December 1983, appl. no. 7984/77, para. 23; *Granger v. the United Kingdom*, supra n. 330, para. 44; *Brualla Gómes de la Torre v. Spain*, supra n. 99, para. 37.

whether the requirement of publicity of the trial in appeal proceedings[346] and in cassation proceedings[347] has the same fundamental importance as is the case for first instance proceedings. The same even applies to the strict requirement of publicity of the judgment,[348] and the requirement of the presence in person of the person charged.[349] However, the principle of equality of arms has to be respected at every instance.[350]

The former Commission has held a few times that Article 6 was not applicable to proceedings in which a decision is taken about leave of appeal, for instance the procedure by which three judges of the *Bundesverfassungsgericht* take a decision about the admission of a *Verfassungsbeschwerde*.[351] It is disputable, however, whether this view is correct in its generality, since in these proceedings a negative decision may also be based on the manifestly ill-founded nature of the appeal, which in fact implies a 'determination'.[352] A more correct view was adopted by the Commission in the *Monnell and Morris* case, in which Article 6 was deemed to be applicable on account of the close connection of the decision about admission of the appeal with the merits of the appeal proceedings themselves, and because these preliminary proceedings may already lead to an extension of the detention.[353]

In some legal systems the person who has been convicted at first instance, but for whom some remedies against this sentence are still available, is no longer regarded as one against whom a charge is pending, but as a convicted person, so that in such a case, strictly speaking, Article 6 would not be applicable. However, in the *Delcourt* case, in which the Court stressed the desirability of an extensive interpretation of Article 6, it held that the charge has not yet been determined in the sense of Article 6 as long as the verdict of acquittal or conviction has not become final.[354] On the one hand this means that, although Article 6 does not grant a right of appeal for criminal cases[355] (Protocol No. 7 contains such a right in Article 2 with regard to those states which have ratified that Protocol), the

---

[346] *Ekbatani v. Sweden,* ECtHR (GC) 26 May 1988, appl. no. 10563/83, paras. 27–28; *Helmers v. Sweden, supra* n. 157, para. 36; *Jan-Åke Andersson v. Sweden,* ECtHR (GC) 29 October 1991, appl. no. 11274/84, para. 27 and *Fejde v. Sweden,* ECtHR (GC) 29 October 1991, appl. no. 12631/87, para. 31.

[347] *Sutter v. Switzerland,* ECtHR (GC) 22 February 1984, appl. no. 8209/78, para. 30.

[348] *Lamanna v. Austria, supra* n. 121, para. 32.

[349] *Kremzow v. Austria,* ECtHR 21 September 1993, appl. no. 12350/86, para. 58; *Belziuk v. Poland, supra* n. 335, para. 37; *Dondarini v. San Marino,* ECtHR 6 July 2004, appl. no. 50545/99, para. 27.

[350] *Lobo Machado v. Portugal,* ECtHR (GC) 20 February 1996, appl. no. 15764/89, para. 31; *Belziuk v. Poland, supra* n. 335, para. 37; *Beer v. Austria, supra* n. 294, paras. 17–18.

[351] Appl. no. 9508/81, *X v. Federal Republic of Germany* (not published); appl. no. 6916/75, *X, Y and Z v. Sweden,* D&R 6 (1977), p. 101 (107); appl. no. 10663/83, *X v. Denmark* (not published).

[352] *Cf.* the report of 15 March 1985, *Adler,* paras. 48–50.

[353] Report of 11 March 1986, paras. 125–127, followed by the Court in *Monnell and Morris v. the United Kingdom,* ECtHR 2 March 1987, appl. no. 9562/81 and 9818/82, para. 54.

[354] *Delcourt v. Belgium, supra* n. 2, paras. 25–26.

[355] *Ibid.*

proceedings in appeal and in cassation do form part of the 'determination', and, therefore, must equally satisfy the minimum standard laid down in Article 6.[356] The fact that in its examination the court of cassation is confined to the legal grounds on which the lower court has based its sentence, does not stand in the way of applicability of Article 6,[357] nor does the circumstance that in some cases appeal and cassation no longer relate to the validity of the criminal prosecution as such, but exclusively to the penalty imposed.[358] On the other hand, procedures in which a decision is taken on requests for conditional release, revision, pardon or mitigation of penalty are not covered by Article 6, since in those cases there has already been a determination which has acquired the force of *res judicata*.[359] However, in the case of a revocation of a conditional release there is the question of 'determination of a criminal charge' in the sense of Article 6, because such a procedure may result in a renewed imposition of a penalty.[360] And in the above-mentioned cases Article 6 *is* of course applicable if the proceedings also involve civil rights or obligations.[361]

3.5. NO RIGHT OF ACCESS TO COURT IN EACH STAGE OF THE PROCEDURE

In its judgment in the *Le Compte, Van Leuven and De Meyere* case, the Court held that Article 6(1) does not prescribe the Contracting States 'to submit "*contestations*" (disputes) over "civil rights and obligations" to a procedure conducted at each of its stages before "tribunals" meeting the Article's various requirements. Demands of flexibility and efficiency, which are fully compatible with the protection of human rights, may justify the prior intervention of administrative or professional bodies and, *a fortiori*, of judicial bodies which do not satisfy the said requirements in every respect.'[362]

In the *Albert and Le Compte* case, the Court elucidated this as follows: 'in such circumstances the Convention calls at least for one of the two following systems: either the jurisdictional organs themselves comply with the requirements of Article 6, paragraph 1, or they do not so comply but are subject

---

[356]   *Ibid.*

[357]   *Ibid.*, paras. 24–25; *Sutter v. Switzerland, supra* n. 347, para. 30.

[358]   Appl. no. 4623/70, *X v. the United Kingdom*, Yearbook XV (1972), p. 376 (394–396).

[359]   Appl. no. 1760/63, *X v. Austria*, Yearbook IX (1966), p. 166 (174) and the case law mentioned there. See also appl. no. 9813/82, *X v. the United Kingdom* (not published), concerning a change of prison location, and appl. no. 10733/84, *Asociación De Aviadores de La República, Mata and Others*, D&R 41 (1985), p. 211 (224): a decision concerning an amnesty after conviction does not determine a 'criminal charge'.

[360]   Appl. no. 4036/69, *X v. the United Kingdom*, Coll. 32 (1970), p. 73 (75).

[361]   Thus, implicitly also the Commission: appl. no. 1760/63, *X v. Austria*, Yearbook IX (1966), p. 166 (174).

[362]   *Le Compte, Van Leuven and De Meyere v. Belgium, supra* n. 36, para. 51.

to subsequent control by a judicial body that has full jurisdiction and does provide the guarantees of Article 6, paragraph 1.'[363]

This means that, for instance, the situation where objection or appeal against administrative action lies with an administrative body does not conflict with Article 6, also not if this objection or appeal procedure amounts to a determination of civil rights and obligations or a criminal charge, provided that there is in the last resort access to review by a court with full jurisdiction. It was precisely that last requirement which, in the opinion of the Court,[364] had not been fulfilled in the Dutch procedure of Crown appeal.[365] It also means that in the case of a criminal charge the penalty may be determined by an administrative body, e.g., the Revenue,[366] the public prosecutor,[367] local or regional authorities,[368] or the Minister of the Interior,[369] provided that from this decision appeal lies to a court with full jurisdiction. In those cases, it has to be examined whether appeal is effectively open in all cases to the appellate body that is indicated by the respondent government as satisfying Article 6 and whether this is a full appeal.[370]

In the *De Cubber* case, the Court qualified its viewpoint that only the last stage of the proceedings has to fulfil all the requirements of Article 6. It adopted the position that this holds good only for those cases in which under domestic law the proceedings are not of a civil or criminal but, e.g., of a disciplinary or administrative character, and moreover the decision is not in the hands of what within the domestic system are considered 'courts of the classic kind'. If, on the contrary, proceedings are concerned which are to be classified as 'civil' or 'criminal', both in virtue of the Convention and under domestic law, and if the 'determination' is made by a body that is a 'proper court in both the formal and the substantive meaning of the term', Article 6 applies to this body irrespective of whether its decision is open to appeal. The flexible standpoint with regard to disciplinary and administrative proceedings, according to the Court, 'cannot justify reducing the requirements of Article 6, paragraph 1 in its traditional and

---

[363]   *Albert and Le Compte v. Belgium, supra* n. 94, para. 29.

[364]   The Dutch Government had argued that, if one looked 'beyond the appearances', the Administrative Litigation Division of the Council of State in fact acted as a court.

[365]   *Benthem v. The Netherlands, supra* n. 10, paras. 38–43. See, however, *Oerlemans v. the Netherlands, supra* n. 100, paras. 53–57, where the Court accepted the argument of the Dutch Government that, since the *Benthem* judgment, the procedure of Crown appeal left open access to review by a civil court on the basis of the latter's supplementary jurisdiction.

[366]   *Bendenoun v. France, supra* n. 140, para. 46.

[367]   *Hennings v. Germany,* ECtHR 16 December 1992, appl. no. 12129/86, para. 26 in conjunction with para. 10.

[368]   *Lauko v. Slovakia, supra* n. 225, para. 64.

[369]   *Malige v. France, supra* n. 82, para. 45.

[370]   See in particular the report of 3 July 1985, *Ettl and Others,* paras. 76–90. In *Ettl and Others v. Austria, supra* n. 63 paras. 42–43, the Court held that there was no question of violation of Art. 6, since Austria had made a reservation in this respect upon ratification of the Convention.

natural sphere of application. A restrictive interpretation of this kind would not be consonant with the object and purpose of Article 6, paragraph 1'.[371]

This position, which did not receive sufficient attention in legal practice and literature, was reconfirmed in the *Findlay* case with respect to the requirement of independence and impartiality,[372] and in the *Riepan* case with respect to the requirement of publicity.[373] In proceedings before courts 'of the classic kind' the parties are entitled to a first instance tribunal that fully meets the requirements of Article 6(1).

3.6. LIMITATIONS

a. Introduction

The right of access to court laid down in Article 6 is not an absolute right. First of all, it may be waived, provided that this has been done unambiguously.[374] That waiver may concern the right of access as such or certain of its elements, e.g., the publicity of the proceedings[375] – provided that the public interest of publicity does not overrule the interests of the parties in this respect – or the applicant may have limited the judicial review as *dominus litis*.[376] There are also certain implicit restrictions, for instance in the sense that a criminal prosecution may also be terminated without intervention of the court, provided that this does not lead to a formal or factual 'determination'. Moreover, there may be procedural limitations such as time-limits,[377] provided that they are not unreasonably short,[378] the requirement of an interest to sue,[379] court fees that are not excessive,[380] security

---

[371] *De Cubber v. Belgium,* ECtHR 26 October 1984, appl. no. 9186/80, para. 32.

[372] *Findlay v. the United Kingdom,* ECtHR 25 February 1997, appl. no. 22107/93, para. 79.

[373] *Riepan v. Austria,* ECtHR 14 November 2000, appl. no. 35115/97, para. 18.

[374] *Neumeister v. Austria,* ECtHR 7 May 1974, appl. no. 1936/63, paras. 33–36.

[375] *Le Compte, Van Leuven and De Meyere v. Belgium, supra* n. 36, para. 59; *Albert and Le Compte v. Belgium, supra* n. 94, para. 35; *Colozza v. Italy, supra* n. 189, para. 28.

[376] *Air Canada v. the United Kingdom, supra* n. 189, paras. 61–62.

[377] Including civil limitation periods: *Stubbings and Others v. the United Kingdom,* ECtHR 22 October 1996, appl. no. 22083/93 and 22095/93, paras. 51–57; *Howald Moor and Others v. Switzerland,* ECtHR 11 March 2014, appl. nos. 52067/10 and 41072/11 (time-limit of 10 years in case of asbestos-related work disease infringes the right to a court protected by Art. 6), paras. 70–80.

[378] A time-limit of 1 week was not considered by the Court to amount to a denial of access; *Hennings v. Germany, supra* n. xxx, paras. 26–27. See also *Rodriguez Valin v. Spain,* ECtHR 11 October 2001, appl. no. 47792/99, para. 28. See, however, *Pérez de Rada Cavanilles v. Spain,* ECtHR 28 October 1998, appl. no. 28090/95, paras. 46–49 and *Tricard v. France,* ECtHR 10 July 2001, appl. no. 40472/98, paras. 30–33, where a time-limit of 3 and 5 days, respectively, was found to be too short.

[379] *Obermeier v. Austria, supra* n. 303, para. 68; *Venema and Others v. the Netherlands, supra* n. 344, para. 3.

[380] *Kreuz v. Poland (No. 1),* ECtHR 19 June 2001, appl. no. 28249/95, paras. 58–66.

for costs to be incurred by the other party,[381] the obligatory assistance of a lawyer[382] and other admissibility requirements, and even prior authorisation to proceed with the claim.[383] As the Court held in the *Ashingdane* case: 'Certainly, the right of access to the courts is not absolute but may be subject to limitations; these are permitted by implication since the right of access "by its very nature calls for regulation by the State, regulation which may vary in time and in place according to the needs and resources of the community and of individuals". (…) In laying down such regulation, the Contracting States enjoy a certain margin of appreciation. Whilst the final decision as to the observance of the Convention's requirements rests with the Court, it is no part of the Court's function to substitute for the assessment of the national authorities any other assessment of what might be the best policy in this field. (…).'[384]

b. Limitation must not impair the essence of access

The limitations prescribed by law or applied by the courts must not restrict or reduce the access in such a way or to such an extent that the very essence of the right is impaired.[385] They must also be sufficiently clear or the provisions concerned must contain safeguards against misunderstanding.[386] In that context, too, the Court's scrutiny is based on the principle that the Convention is intended to guarantee not rights that are theoretical or illusory but rights that are practical and effective.[387]

Thus, in the *Canea Catholic Church* case, the Court held that an unforeseeable calling into question of the legal personality of the applicant church imposed

---

[381] *Ibid.*, para. 54.

[382] *Gillow v. the United Kingdom*, ECtHR 24 November 1986, appl. no. 9063/80, para. 69.

[383] *Ashingdane v. the United Kingdom*, *supra* n. 301, para. 59; *Kreuz v. Poland (No. 1)*, *supra* n. 380, para. 54.

[384] *Ashingdane v. the United* Kingdom, *supra* n. 301, para. 57. See also, *inter alia*, *Khalfaoui v. France*, ECtHR 14 December 1999, appl. no. 34791/97, paras. 35–36; *Z and Others v. the United Kingdom, supra* n. 13, para. 93; *Pages v. France*, ECtHR 25 September 2003, appl. no. 50343/99, para. 30; *Stone Court Shipping Company S.A. v. Spain*, ECtHR 28 October 2003, appl. no. 55524/00, para. 34; *Zwiazek Nauczycielstwa Polskiego v. Poland*, *supra* n. 49, para. 28; *Stanev v. Bulgaria, supra* n. 62, para. 230.

[385] *Ashingdane v. the United Kingdom, supra* n. 301, para. 57; *Holy Monasteries v. Greece*, ECtHR 9 December 1994, appl. no. 13092/87 and 13984/88, para. 83; *Stubbings and Others v. the United Kingdom, supra* n. 377, para. 52; *Canea Catholic Church v. Greece*, ECtHR 16 December 1997, appl. no. 25528/94, para. 41; *Yagtzilar and Others v. Greece*, ECtHR 6 December 2001, appl. no. 41727/98, para. 23 and *Tsironis v. Greece*, ECtHR 6 December 2001, appl. no. 44584/98, para. 26; *Stone Court Shipping Company S.A. v. Spain, supra* n. 384, para. 35.

[386] *Bellet v. France*, ECtHR 4 December 1995, appl. no. 23805/94, paras. 36–37; *Geouffre de la Pradelle v. France, supra* n. 100, paras. 31–35; *F.E. v. France*, ECtHR 30 October 1998, appl. no. 38212/97, para. 47; *Lagrange v. France*, ECtHR 10 October 2000, appl. no. 39485/98, paras. 40–42.

[387] *Airey v. Ireland, supra* n. 380, para. 24. See also, *inter alia*, *Kreuz v. Poland (No. 1), supra* n. 297, para. 57; *Prince Hans-Adam II of Liechtenstein v. Germany*, ECtHR 12 July 2001, appl. no. 42527/98, para. 45.

a limitation upon the latter that impaired the very substance of its right to a court.[388]

A special category of restrictions is that of immunities. Although immunity does not affect the applicability of Article 6, it may block access to court to a very large extent. For that reason, the Court emphasises that the states must observe restraint in granting and honouring immunity. In the first place, the persons and organs who enjoy immunity must be narrowly defined. In the *Al-Adsani* case, the Court made it clear that conferring, without restraint or control, immunity on large groups or categories of persons would be inconsistent with the basic principle underlying Article 6.[389]

In the second place, the acts in respect of which immunity is claimed must directly relate to the function for which immunity is granted. Thus, a member of Parliament may enjoy immunity in direct relation to his parliamentary work,[390] but not for acts committed outside that specific context.[391] In the third place, the Court examines whether a fair balance has been struck between the public interests which the grant of immunity serves and the interest of unrestricted access to court. Thus, in the *Osman* case, the Court reached the conclusion that the automatic application of a rule which amounts to the grant of immunity to the police, without having regard to competing public-interest considerations, amounted to an unjustifiable restriction.[392]

Parliamentary immunity as such is considered not to constitute a disproportionate restriction of access to court, since it reflects a principle that has been generally recognised in the member states of the Council of Europe.[393] The same holds good for restrictions to bring a civil action against judges, since these serve the proper functioning of the judiciary and are common in domestic and international legal systems.[394] Recognition of immunity to states and state organs in accordance with international treaty law and customary law, even when the civil action concerns *jus cogens*, was deemed proportionate by the Court on the ground that the state concerned is in compliance with the international requirement of good inter-state relations.[395] However, the Court indicates in its case law that in assessing the proportionality of restrictions resulting from immunity, it takes into consideration whether and to what extent reasonable alternatives were available to the applicant to have his claim examined.[396]

---

[388]   *Canea Catholic Church v. Greece, supra* n. 385, para. 41.

[389]   *Al-Adsani v. the United Kingdom, supra* n. 19, para. 47.

[390]   *A. v. the United Kingdom*, ECtHR 17 December 2002, appl. no. 35373/97, paras. 66–89.

[391]   *Kreuz v. Poland (No. 1), supra* n. 380, para. 56; *Cordova v. Italy (No. 1)*, ECtHR 30 January 2003, appl. no. 40877/98, paras. 62–63; *De Jorio v. Italy, supra* n. 157, paras. 29–30.

[392]   *Osman v. the United Kingdom, supra* n. 122, paras. 151–153.

[393]   *A. v. the United Kingdom, supra* n. 16, paras. 78–83.

[394]   *Ernst and Others v. Belgium, supra* n. 304, para. 50.

[395]   *Al-Adsani v. the United Kingdom, supra* n. 19, paras. 54–56; *Fogarty v. the United Kingdom, supra* n. 19, paras. 35–39; *McElhinney v. Ireland, supra* n. 19, paras. 36–40.

[396]   *Waite and Kennedy v. Germany*, ECtHR (GC) 18 February 1999, appl. no. 26083/94, para. 68 *Ernst and Others v. Belgium, supra* n. 304, para. 54; *De Jorio v. Italy, supra* n. 157, para. 32.

The availability (at a later moment) of alternatives also played an important role in assessing the proportionality of the restriction in the *Klass* case. There the Court made the following observation in respect of the complete exclusion of judicial review: 'As long as it [i.e. the security control] remains validly secret, the decision placing someone under surveillance is thereby incapable of judicial control on the initiative of the person concerned, within the meaning of Article 6; as a consequence, it of necessity escapes the requirements of that Article.'[397]

However, the Court added the following observation: 'According to the information supplied by the Government, the individual concerned, once he has been notified of such discontinuance [of the security control], has at his disposal several legal remedies against the possible infringements of his rights; these remedies would satisfy the requirements of Article 6.'[398]

Access to court may also be unduly restricted or taken away by the court itself or by a higher court. In the *Todorescu* case, the courts of first and second instance had examined the applicants' claim for restitution of confiscated property. The court of second instance had decided in favour of the applicants, which decision was upheld by the court of appeal. However, the Supreme Court, at the request of the Procurate General, annulled the second instance judgment and decided that the courts did not have jurisdiction to review the constitutionality of the decree by which the confiscation was ordered. This judgment amounted to barring access to court for the applicants to have their civil right determined. The Court held that the annulment by the Supreme Court of a final judgment was in contravention of the principle of legal certainty and violated the right of access to court.[399]

These cases indicate that the Court is not inclined to leave a very broad margin of appreciation to the national authorities and courts in restricting access to court. In addition, although the Court has repeatedly stated that 'its task is not to substitute itself for the competent domestic authorities in determining the most appropriate means of regulating access to justice, nor to assess the facts which led those courts to adopt one decision rather than another',[400] it does consider it to be its task to examine errors of fact or law allegedly committed by a national court, if these may have resulted in denial of access to court.[401] This may be the case, for instance, if the applicable time-limit for instituting proceedings has not been correctly applied by the court.[402] The Court goes very far in examining

---

[397] *Klass and Others v. Germany, supra* n. 180, para. 75.

[398] *Ibid.*

[399] *Todorescu v. Romania,* ECtHR 30 September 2003, appl. no. 40670/98, paras. 37–40. The line for this case law was set by the Grand Chamber in *Brumarescu v. Romania, supra* n. 283, paras. 61–62.

[400] *Kreuz v. Poland (No. 1), supra* n. 380, para. 56.

[401] *Prince Hans-Adam II of Liechtenstein v. Germany, supra* n. 387, para. 49; *Falcon Rivera v. Italy,* ECtHR 2 December 2004 (dec.), appl. no. 46080/99, para. 1.

[402] *Leoni v. Italy,* ECtHR 26 October 2000, appl. no. 43269/98, paras. 25–27.

whether the procedural rule concerned is reasonable in itself and has been applied in a reasonable way, taking into account such factors as the strictness of the rule, whether or not the applicant had the assistance of a lawyer, and whether the applicant has taken the necessary precautions.[403] The Court, although recognising the appropriateness of the rule concerned, is even prepared to substitute its own assessment for that of the domestic court and conclude that the rule has been applied in such a strict way that the applicant was in fact deprived of his access to court.[404] In this way the Court approaches the role of a fourth instance.

c. Legitimate aim and proportionality

A limitation is not compatible with Article 6(1) if it does not pursue a legitimate aim and if there is no reasonable relationship of proportionality between the means employed and the aim sought to be achieved.[405]

Examples of a legitimate aim are the good or fair administration of justice,[406] limitations aimed at preventing the courts from becoming overloaded,[407] proper functioning of the judiciary,[408] legal certainty,[409] good international relations which may require the grant of state immunity[410] and the public interest in regaining sovereignty.[411] Even if the limitation serves a legitimate aim, its application must not be arbitrary[412] nor be disproportional.[413]

The proportionality of a limitation depends on many aspects. The Court has recognised that limitations on access to court may be more extensive when regulation of activities in the public sphere is at stake than in relation to litigation

---

[403] *Rodriguez Valin v. Spain, supra* n. 378, paras. 23–28.

[404] *Miragall Escolano and Others v. Spain*, ECtHR 25 January 2000, appl. no. 38366/97; 38688/97; 40777/98; 40843/98; 41015/98; 41400/98; 41446/98; 41484/98; 41487/98 and 41509/98, para. 38 (see also the critical dissenting opinion of Judge Pellonpää); *Société Anonyme 'Sotiris and Nikos Koutras Attee' v. Greece*, ECtHR 16 November 2000, appl. no. 39442/98, paras. 21–23; *Platakou v. Greece*, ECtHR 11 January 2001, appl. no. 38460/97, paras. 32–49; *Tsironis v. Greece, supra* n. 385, paras. 27–30.

[405] *Ashingdane v. the United Kingdom, supra* n. 301, para. 57. For a comprehensive review of these criteria, see *Fayed v. the United Kingdom*, ECtHR 21 September 1994, appl. no. 17101/90, paras. 68–83.

[406] *Tolstoy Miloslavsky v. the United Kingdom, supra* n. 157, para. 61; *Annoni di Gussola and Others v. France*, ECtHR 14 November 2000, appl. no. 31819/96 and 33293/96, para. 51; *Rodriguez Valin v. Spain, supra* n. 378, para. 22; *Stone Court Shipping Company S.A. v. Spain, supra* n. 384, para. 34.

[407] *Brualla Gómes de la Torre v. Spain, supra* n. 99, para. 36.

[408] *Ernst and Others v. Belgium, supra* n. 304, para. 50.

[409] *Tricard v. France, supra* n. 378, para. 29; *Rodriguez Valin v. Spain, supra* n. 378, para. 22.

[410] *Al-Adsani v. the United Kingdom, supra* n. 19, para. 54; *Fogarty v. the United Kingdom, supra* n. 19, para. 34; *McElhinney v. Ireland, supra* n. 19, para. 35.

[411] *Prince Hans-Adam II of Liechtenstein v. Germany, supra* n. 387, para. 69.

[412] *Tolstoy Miloslavsky v. the United Kingdom, supra* n. 157, para. 65.

[413] *Zwiazek Nauczycielstwa Polskiego v. Poland, supra* n. 49, para. 38. For an example of clear disproportionality, see *Mortier v. France*, ECtHR 31 July 2001, appl. no. 42195/98, paras. 36–39.

over the conduct of persons acting in their private capacity.[414] It has also held that measures which reflect generally recognised rules of public international law on state immunity cannot in principle be regarded as imposing a disproportionate restriction on the right of access to court.[415] International standards may also be a yardstick for the proportionality of statutes of limitation.[416]

In the *Al-Adsani* case, the argument put forward by a minority of the Court, that rules concerning state immunity must yield for provisions of the Convention that reflect *jus cogens* on the basis of the 'normative hierarchy theory', and, consequently, in such cases do not serve a legitimate aim, was not followed by the majority.[417] However, the Court *did* stress that because immunity rules result in removal from the jurisdiction of the courts of a group of civil claims, the states must exercise restraint in claiming immunity, and such claims must be subject to control by the Court.[418]

Although Article 6 does not guarantee a right of appeal, if a limitation rule amounts to taking away the right of appeal, that effect may well be disproportionate. This is the case, for instance, if appeal is not open to an accused who has failed to surrender to custody, notwithstanding the existence of a warrant for his arrest,[419] or who has failed to pay a bail instead.[420] It may also be the case if the appeal is only admissible if the appellant has deposited the amount for which he was convicted at first instance and the court has not taken into consideration the actual financial situation of the appellant.[421]

In the *Sejdovic* case, where the complaint concerned the refusal of a new trial after conviction *in absentia*, the Court held that a person convicted *in absentia* who could not be considered to have unequivocally waived the right to appear, should in all cases be able to obtain a new ruling by a court.[422]

A short time-limit for bringing an action may be proportionate under normal circumstances, but disproportionate in cases where there are special complications[423] or if the applicant lives far away.[424] If in setting the amount

---

[414] *Fayed v. the United Kingdom, supra* n. 405, para. 75.

[415] *Al-Adsani v. the United Kingdom, supra* n. 19, para. 54; *Fogarty v. the United Kingdom, supra* n. 19, paras. 35–39; *McElhinney v. Ireland, supra* n. 19, paras. 36–40; *Kalogeropoulou and Others v. Greece and Germany,* ECtHR 12 December 2002, appl. no. 59021/00, para. 1.

[416] *Stubbings and Others v. the United Kingdom, supra* n. 385, para. 53.

[417] Dissenting opinion of Judges Rozakis, Caflisch, Wildhaber, Costa, Cabral Barreto and Vajić.

[418] *Al-Adsani v. the United Kingdom, supra* n. 19, para. 47.

[419] *Poitrimol v. France, supra* n. 336, paras. 35–38; *Omar v. France,* ECtHR (GC) 29 July 1998, appl. no. 24767/94, paras. 41–42 and *Guérin v. France,* ECtHR (GC) 29 July 1998, appl. no. 25201/94, para. 43; *Khalfaoui v. France, supra* n. 384, paras. 42–54; *Goedhart v. Belgium,* ECtHR 20 March 2001, appl. no. 34989/97, paras. 31–32 and *Stroek v. Belgium,* ECtHR 20 March 2001, appl. nos. 36449/97 and 36467/97, paras. 29–30; *Skondrianos v. Greece,* ECtHR 18 December 2003, appl. nos. 63000/00, 74291/01 and 74292/01, para. 27.

[420] *Walser v. France,* ECtHR 1 July 2004, appl. no. 56653/00, para. 29.

[421] *Garcia Manibardo v. Spain,* ECtHR 15 February 2000, appl. no. 38695/97, paras. 44–45.

[422] *Sejdovic v. Italy,* ECtHR 10 November 2004, appl. no. 56581/00, para. 30.

[423] *Pérez de Rada Cavanilles v. Spain, supra* n. 378, paras. 45–49.

[424] *Tricard v. France, supra* n. 378, paras. 30–34.

of security for the payment of a possible fine the court has not taken into account that the person concerned had no financial resources, this may in practice amount to depriving him of his recourse before that court.[425] And if, in connection with the amount of court fees to be paid, the domestic court relied on the fact that the applicant was a businessman and should have taken into account the need to secure in advance sufficient funds for court fees, without taking into account the link of the proceedings to the business activity and the actual financial situation of the applicant, the fees may be disproportionate.[426]

If the domestic court applies a certain admissibility requirement in a too formalistic way, this may amount to a disproportionate restriction ('excessive formalism'), especially if the applicant is not given the opportunity to correct his mistake.[427]

d. Retrospective legislation with effect on access

In the case of retrospective legislation which has the effect of influencing the judicial determination of a dispute to which a state is a party, respect for the rule of law requires that any reason adduced to justify such measure be treated with the greatest possible degree of circumspection.[428] Even the fact that access to court is restored by subsequent legislation does not put an end to the violation of the right of access to court if that access was stayed for a considerable period of time.[429] Exceptionally, however, a retrospective limitation may be justified if the legislative action is intended to put an end to the efforts of the applicants to frustrate the clear intention of the legislature,[430] or serves other 'compelling grounds of the general interest'.[431] However, a mere financial risk on the part of

---

[425]   *Aït-Mouhoub v. France, supra* n. 73, paras. 57–61. See also *Tolstoy Miloslavsky v. the United Kingdom, supra* n. 157, paras. 59–67: in the circumstances of the case, even the obligation to pay an amount of GBP 124,900 English as security for costs to pursue an appeal did meet the requirement of proportionality.

[426]   *Kreuz v. Poland (No. 1), supra* n. 380, paras. 62–63.

[427]   *Stone Court Shipping Company S.A. v. Spain, supra* n. 384, paras. 36–43; *Bulena v. Czech Republic,* ECtHR 20 April 2004, appl. no. 57567/00, para. 35; *Masirevic v. Serbia,* ECtHR 11 February 2014, appl. no. 30671/08, paras. 51–52. See also *Tence v. Slovenia,* ECtHR 31 May 2016, appl. no. 37242/14, paras. 35–38: in this case the national court followed a too formalistic approach by declaring inadmissible an appeal submitted by fax but received one day out of time owing to technical problems attributable to the court.

[428]   *Stran Greek Refineries and Stratis Andreadis v. Greece,* ECtHR 9 December 1994, appl. no. 13427/87, para. 49; *Zielinski and Pradal & Gonzalez and Others v. France,* ECtHR (GC) 28 October 1999, appl. nos. 24846/94, 34165/96, 34166/96, 34167/96, 34168/96, 34169/96, 34170/96, 34171/96, 34172/96 and 34173/96, paras. 57–61; *Anagnostopoulos and Others v. Greece, supra* n. 73, paras. 20–21; *Agoudimos and Cefallonian Sky Shipping Co. v. Greece,* ECtHR 28 June 2001, appl. no. 38703/97, para. 30.

[429]   *Kutic v. Croatia, supra* n. 290, paras. 30–33; *Multiplex v. Croatia, supra* n. 297, paras. 49–55; *Acimovic v. Croatia,* ECtHR 9 October 2003, appl. no. 61237/00, para. 42.

[430]   *National & Provincial Building Society and Others v. the United Kingdom, supra* n. 136, para. 112.

[431]   *Zielinski and Pradal & Gonzalez, supra* n. 428, para. 57; *Agoudimos and Cefallonian Sky Shipping Co. v. Greece, supra* n. 428, para. 30; *Multiplex v. Croatia, supra* n. 297, para. 52.

the government cannot warrant such legislative interference.[432] Even though a situation where a significant number of legal suits claiming large sums of money are lodged against the state may call for some further legislation, the measures taken must be compatible with Article 6(1).[433]

Procedural law amendments which limit the right of appeal may have some retroactive effect for pending cases. According to the Court this is in conformity with a generally recognised principle that, save where expressly provided to the contrary, procedural rules apply immediately to proceedings that are under way. Here the same test applies that such a limitation must serve a legitimate aim, may not impair the very essence of the right of access and must be proportionate; and here again less strict criteria apply if the limitation concerns access to a court of appeal or a court of cassation.[434]

e. Limitations with respect to specific groups

The authorities may lay down specific restrictive rules for access to court with regard to, for instance, minors, prisoners or persons of unsound mind,[435] but in those cases as well the 'special status' of the individual concerned cannot warrant the total absence of access.[436]

f. Limitations warranted by security reasons

In the *Klass* case, a drastic restriction was imposed on the right of access to court. Article 6 was invoked by the applicants because the challenged legislation, which permitted interference with correspondence and wire-tapping for security reasons without the knowledge of the person concerned, excluded the normal recourse to a court and replaced it by supervision by a parliamentary committee. Leaving open the question of whether this case concerned civil rights or a criminal charge, the Court held that a distinction should be made between two stages. In the first stage, the measures are still applied without the person's knowledge and as a consequence are incapable of judicial control on the initiative of the person concerned and, thus, of necessity escape the requirements of Article 6. In the stage in which the measures have been terminated and in which, consequently, there is no longer any ground for secrecy, they come within the ambit of Article 6.[437]

The Court was faced here with the dilemma between, on the one hand, the guarantee of effective access to court and, on the other hand, the necessity for

---

432   *Zielinski and Pradal & Gonzalez, supra* n. 428, paras. 58–59.
433   *Multiplex v. Croatia, supra* n. 297, para. 52.
434   *Brualla Gómes de la Torre v. Spain, supra* n. 99, paras. 35–39.
435   *Golder v. the United Kingdom, supra* n. 1, paras. 37–40; *Z and Others v. the United Kingdom, supra* n. 13, para. 93.
436   *Winterwerp v. the Netherlands, supra* n. 63, para. 75.
437   *Klass and Others v. Germany, supra* n. 180, para. 75.

the national authorities to be able to carry out an effective security control for the protection of the democratic values underlying the Convention. The Court observed with respect to the alleged violation of Article 8: 'The rule of law implies, *inter alia*, that an interference by the executive authorities with an individual's rights should be subject to an effective control which should normally be assured by the judiciary, at least in the last resort, judicial control offering the best guarantees of independence, impartiality and a proper procedure.'[438] Nevertheless, the Court opted for the security interest, imposing restrictions on the effective access to court via what might be called a systematic interpretation of the first paragraph of Article 6 in connection with the second paragraph of Article 8. But the Court also emphasised – as had been done by the German *Bundesverfassungsgericht* – that the secrecy *vis-à-vis* the person concerned must not last any longer than is required for the protection of the interest envisaged by the measures, after which period access to court must be fully open again for the person in question.[439] The said parliamentary committee will then have to take particular care that the person in question is indeed informed as soon as the situation permits, since otherwise national judicial review as well as the Strasbourg review might be rendered completely illusory.

In the *Leander* case, which also concerned secret surveillance, the Commission had declared the complaint concerning Article 6 incompatible with the Convention *ratione materiae* on the basis of its case law that litigation concerning access to or dismissal from the civil service falls outside the scope of Article 6.[440] Consequently, the Court could not pronounce on the issue. However, it nevertheless gave a clear indication of its point of view by following, with respect to Article 13, its *Klass* judgment in holding that 'an effective remedy under Article 13 must mean a remedy that is as effective as can be, having regard to the restricted scope for recourse inherent in any system of secret surveillance for the protection of national security'.[441]

In its report in *R.V. v. the Netherlands*, which concerned a request of access to information held by the Dutch Military Intelligence Services (MIS), although no complaint under Article 6 had been lodged but only under Article 8, the Commission based its conclusion that the interference was not 'in accordance with the law', *inter alia*, on the fact that the Royal Decree governing the activities of the MIS did not contain any safeguard mechanism, thus leaving it open whether the safeguards referred to in the Government's observations, which were provided for in a broader framework (investigation by a parliamentary committee and by the National Ombudsman), were sufficiently effective.[442]

---

[438]   *Ibid.*, para. 55.
[439]   *Ibid.*, para. 75 in conjunction with para. 71.
[440]   Appl. no. 9248/81, D&R 34 (1983), p. 78 (83).
[441]   *Klass and Others v. Germany, supra* n. 180, para. 84.
[442]   Report of 3 December 1991, paras. 45–46.

4. THE RIGHT TO A FAIR TRIAL

4.1. INTRODUCTION

Article 6 requires a 'fair hearing'. The notion of 'hearing' may be equated with that of 'trial' or 'trial proceedings'. This follows firstly from the French wording of the provision: *'toute personne a droit à ce que sa cause*(!) *soit entendue'*. Secondly, the right to be heard within a reasonable time, embodied in the first paragraph, refers to the proceedings as a whole[443] and, thirdly, the second sentence of the first paragraph allows the exclusion of the public and the press from all or part of the *trial*. Thus, the notion of 'hearing' should not be seen as equivalent to 'hearing in person' or 'oral hearing', although these two aspects may be elements of the notion of 'fair and public hearing' as contained in Article 6.[444]

When is a hearing 'fair'? In the *Kraska* case, the Court took as a starting point that the purpose of Article 6 is, *inter alia*, 'to place the "tribunal" under a duty to conduct a proper examination of the submissions, arguments and evidence adduced by the parties, without prejudice to its assessments of whether they are relevant to its decision'.[445]

However, the Court has avoided giving an enumeration of criteria in the abstract. In each individual case the course of the proceedings has to be assessed to decide whether the hearing concerned has been a fair one. What counts is the picture which the proceedings as a whole present,[446] although certain aspects *per se* may already conflict with the principle of a fair hearing in such a way that an opinion can be given about the fairness of the trial irrespective of the further course of the proceedings, e.g., the way in which the evidence is collected during a preliminary hearing. Depending on the stage of the proceedings and its special features, the manner of application of Article 6 may differ.[447] The publicity requirement, for example, may be less strict as far as cassation proceedings are concerned.[448]

Certain aspects of a 'fair hearing' are expressly outlined for criminal cases in paragraphs 2 and 3 of Article 6. These aspects in principle also apply to civil cases (and to administrative cases if covered by Article 6). However, from the lack of such an enumeration with regard to civil cases, the Court has concluded that the requirements inherent in the notion of a 'fair hearing' in civil cases are not necessarily identical to the requirements in criminal cases and that there

---

[443] See *infra* 6.2.
[444] See *infra* 4.4.
[445] *Kraska v. Switzerland*, *supra* n. 94, para. 30. See also, e.g., *Barberà, Messegué and Jabardo v. Spain*, ECtHR (GC) 6 December 1988, no. 10590/83, para. 68.
[446] See, e.g., *Barberà, Messegué and Jabardo v. Spain*, *supra* n. 445, para. 68; *Kostovski v. the Netherlands*, ECtHR (GC) 20 November 1989, appl. no. 11454/85, para. 39.
[447] See, e.g., *Ekbatani v. Sweden*, *supra* n. 346, para. 27; *Helmers v. Sweden*, *supra* n. 157, para. 36.
[448] See *infra* 5.

exists a 'greater latitude' for the national authorities when dealing with civil cases than when dealing with criminal procedures.[449]

Although the enumeration in the third paragraph might create a different impression, the content of the term 'fair hearing' in 'criminal' cases is not confined to the provisions of paragraph 3 of Article 6.[450] The guarantees implied in the requirement of a 'fair hearing' in paragraph 1 fully apply to criminal proceedings as well. Consequently, the finding that the proceedings are in conformity with the requirements of the third paragraph does not make a review for their conformity with the 'fair-hearing' principle superfluous in all cases. The proceedings as a whole may, for instance, create the picture that the accused has had insufficient opportunity to conduct an optimal defence, although none of the explicitly granted minimum guarantees has been violated. As the Commission observed in the *Adolf* case: 'Article 6(3) merely exemplifies the minimum guarantees which must be accorded to the accused in the context of the 'fair trial' referred to in Article 6(1).'[451] This implies, on the one hand, that a negative answer to the question of whether the first paragraph has been violated renders an investigation of an alleged infringement of the third paragraph superfluous,[452] while, on the other hand, the investigation of a possible violation of the fair trial principle laid down in the first paragraph must not be confined to an examination of the third paragraph. As a result of an extensive and functional interpretation of the third paragraph in the Strasbourg case law, however, examination for compatibility with the third and with the first paragraph is in fact likely to more or less coincide.

Various aspects of the right of a 'fair trial' are discussed in the following sections. Sometimes it is very difficult to distinguish those aspects, since they are often closely connected. In criminal cases, the Court regularly uses the rather vague notion of 'rights of the defence'. This wording seems equal to the concept of a 'fair trial'.[453]

4.2. EQUALITY OF ARMS

An important element of the fair hearing requirement is the principle of equality of arms. This principle implies, as the Court held in the *Dombo Beheer B.V.* case, with regard to civil proceedings 'that each party must be afforded a reasonable

---

[449] *Dombo Beheer B.V. v. the Netherlands*, ECtHR 27 October 1993, appl. no. 14448/88, paras. 32–33; *Pitkänen v. Finland*, ECtHR 9 March 2004, appl. no. 30508/96, para. 59.

[450] See, e.g., *Funke v. France*, ECtHR 25 February 1993, appl. no. 10828/84, para. 44; *Zoon v. the Netherlands*, ECtHR 7 December 2000, appl. no. 29202/95, paras. 32–50.

[451] Report of 8 October 1980, B.43 (1985), p. 29.

[452] *Ibid.* See also *Deweer v. Belgium, supra* n. 185, para. 56.

[453] See, e.g., *Bendenoun v. France, supra* n. 140, para. 52.

opportunity to present his case – including his evidence – under conditions that do not place him at a substantial disadvantage *vis-à-vis* his opponent.'[454]

For criminal cases, where the very character of the proceedings involves a fundamental inequality of the parties, this principle of 'equality of arms' is even more important, and the same applies, though to a lesser degree, to administrative procedures.[455] The principle can play a role in every stage of the proceedings and with regard to many issues.

The principle of 'equality of arms', that is closely connected to the right to adversarial proceedings, entails that the parties must have the same access to the records and other documents pertaining to the case, at least insofar as these may play a part in the formation of the court's opinion.[456] However, the access to the file may be restricted to an accused's lawyer.[457] A particular way in which the information from the file must be given or be available does not follow from this principle, provided that no insuperable obstacles are created which in fact amount to withholding information.[458] The parties should in principle have the opportunity to make copies of the relevant documents belonging to the case file. The case law on this point is not clear, although the Court in the *Schuler-Zgraggen* case, when deciding the question of whether the access of the applicant to the case file did meet the requirements of Article 6, expressly mentioned the ability of the applicant to make copies.[459] A lack of access to the case file may be remedied by an appeal court.[460]

Each party must be given the opportunity to oppose the arguments advanced by the other party.[461] In the *Feldbrugge* case, for example, the Court came to the conclusion that Article 6(1) had been violated, since the applicant had not been given the opportunity to comment upon the report of a medical expert, which was of decisive importance for the outcome of the proceedings.[462] In the *Hentrich* case, the Revenue exercised the right of pre-emption because it held the sale price of a piece of land contained in the contract of sale to be too low. The applicant did not get a real opportunity to challenge the decision

---

[454] *Dombo Beheer B.V. v. the Netherlands, supra* n. 449, para. 33. See also *Hentrich v. France*, ECtHR 22 September 1994, appl. no. 13616/88, para. 56, and *Stran Greek Refineries and Stratis Andreadis v. Greece, supra* n. 428, para. 46.

[455] *Feldbrugge v. the Netherlands, supra* n. 83, para. 44.

[456] *Ernst and Others v. Belgium, supra* n. 304, paras. 60–61.

[457] *Kamasinski v. Austria, supra* n. 331, para. 88; *Kremzow v. Austria, supra* n. 349, para. 52.

[458] Appl. no. 8289/78, *X v. Austria*, D&R 18 (1980), p. 160 (167–168).

[459] *Schuler-Zgraggen v. Switzerland, supra* n. 113, paras. 50–52.

[460] *Ibid. Cf.* also *Zumtobel v. Austria, supra* n. 306, para. 35.

[461] See, e.g., *Ruiz-Mateos v. Spain, supra* n. 106, para. 63; *Werner v. Austria, supra* n. 121, para. 65; *Beer v. Austria, supra* n. 294, para. 17; *Buchberger v. Austria,* ECtHR 20 December 2001, appl. no. 32899/96, para. 50; *Hrdalo v. Croatia*, ECtHR 27 September 2011, appl. no. 23272/07, para. 38.

[462] *Feldbrugge v. the Netherlands, supra* n. 83, para. 44. See also, e.g., *Ruiz Mateos v. Spain, supra* n. 106, paras. 61–68; *Van de Hurk v. the Netherlands*, ECtHR 19 April 1994, appl. no. 16034/90, paras. 56–57.

of the Revenue, because the tribunals, on the one hand, refused her the possibility to prove that the sale price corresponded to the real market value of the land and, on the other hand, allowed the Revenue to give a meaningless motivation for its decision to exercise the right of pre-emption.[463] These facts amounted to a breach of Article 6(1).[464] In the *Yvon* case, the applicant claimed that the principle of equality of arms had been breached in the proceedings to determine compensation before the expropriation judge. In the proceedings, the expropriated party was not only faced by the expropriating authority but also by the Government Commissioner, who was competent to present oral observations and file submissions, that must include a reasoned valuation of the compensation. The Court took into account that the Government Commissioner and the expropriating authority had full access to the land charges register, which listed all property transfers, where the expropriated parties had only limited access. Moreover, the Government Commissioner's submissions seemed to be of particular significance where they tended towards a lower valuation than proposed by the expropriating authority. If that was the case, the judge who rejected the Government Commissioner's submissions must specifically state the reasons for such a rejection. Therefore, the principle of equality of arms had been breached.[465]

A difference in the compensation of legal costs can also lead to a breach of the principle of equality of arms. In the *Stankiewicz* case, the applicant had won his (civil) case but had received no compensation for the legal costs, while the public prosecutor did not have to pay legal costs.[466]

In many cases the Court has had to deal with the question of whether the participation of the Advocate General or a similar officer in the deliberations of the Court of Cassation or Supreme Court had constituted a violation of the principle of equality of arms. Initially, in the *Delcourt* case, the Court answered the question in the negative, because of the independent position of the *Procureur général* in relation to the Minister of Justice and the fact that the latter cannot give orders or instructions to the *Procureur général* in concrete cases.[467] The Court changed its view in the *Borgers* case. It emphasised the correctness of the *Delcourt* judgment in as far as the independence and impartiality of the Court of Cassation and its *Procureur général* are concerned, but nevertheless concluded that the *Procureur général*, in recommending that an appeal on points of law should be allowed or dismissed, appeared to be an ally or opponent of one of the parties. Therefore, his participation in the deliberations had constituted

---

[463]   The Revenue confined its motivation to stating that the price was too low.
[464]   *Hentrich v. France, supra* n. 454, para. 56.
[465]   *Yvon v. France*, ECtHR 24 April 2003, appl. no. 44962/98, paras. 29–37.
[466]   *Stankiewicz v. Poland*, ECtHR 2 April 2006, appl. no. 46917/99, paras. 68–69.
[467]   *Delcourt v. Belgium, supra* n. 1, para. 32.

a violation of the principle of equality of arms.[468] This point of view may be regarded as settled case law in criminal[469] as well as in civil cases.[470]

On the other hand, in the *Marc-Antoine* case the Court did not find a violation of the equality of arms requirement. This case concerned the communication of the reporting judge's draft decision to the 'public rapporteur' in proceedings before the French *Conseil d'État*. The draft decision of the reporting judge, who was a member of the court responsible for examining the case, was not a document submitted by a party that might influence the court's decision but rather an element produced within the court in the process of preparing the final decision. The adversarial principle enshrined in Article 6(1) of the Convention could not apply to an internal working document of that nature, which was confidential.[471]

A different, although connected issue, namely the impossibility for the parties to reply to the Advocate General's submissions, is discussed regularly under the head of the adversarial principle. However, in the *Apeh Üldözötteinek Szövetsége* (Alliance of APEH's persecutees) case that impossibility amounted to a breach of the equality of arms requirement. The case concerned non-contentious proceedings with a view to registering the applicants' association. The Hungarian Tax Authority (APEH), who learnt about the founding of the association from the press, complained that the name of the association was defamatory for APEH. The public prosecutor's office intervened in the registration proceedings and proposed that the request for registration be rejected because there was no approval of APEH for the use of its name. The Court held that the failure of the national courts to notify the applicants of this intervention and likewise of the submissions of the Attorney General's Office to the Supreme Court had violated the principle of equality of arms.[472]

Another inequality occurred in the *Platakou* case. The Greek code of civil procedure provided that all statutory time-limits were suspended in favour of the State during the holiday season from 1 July until 15 September. The Court held that this provision placed the applicant, whose claim for indemnification after expropriation proceedings had been belated and, therefore, declared inadmissible, at a substantial disadvantage to the opposing party.[473]

---

[468] *Borgers v. Belgium*, ECtHR (GC) 30 October 1991, appl. no. 12005/86, para. 26.

[469] See, e.g., *Bulut v. Austria*, ECtHR 22 February 1996, appl. no. 17358/90.

[470] See, e.g., *Vermeulen v. Belgium,* ECtHR (GC) 20 February 1996, appl. no. 19075/91, para. 34 and *Lobo Machado v. Portugal, supra* n. 350, para. 32; *Kress v. France*, ECtHR (GC) 7 June 2001, appl. no. 39594/98, paras. 82–87; *Immeubles Groupe Kosser v. France*, ECtHR 21 March 2002, appl. no. 38748/97, para. 27.

[471] *Marc-Antoine v. France*, ECtHR 4 June 2013, appl. no. 54984/09 (adm. Dec.): the Court declared the application under Art. 6 inadmissible.

[472] *APEH Üldözötteinek Szövetsége and Others v. Hungary, supra* n. 131, paras. 39–44. See also, with regard to criminal proceedings, *Bulut v. Austria, supra* n. 469, para. 49; *Lanz v. Austria*, ECtHR 31 January 2002, appl. no. 24430/94, paras. 55–60; *Josef Fischer v. Austria*, ECtHR 17 January 2002, appl. no. 33382/96, paras. 16–22.

[473] *Platakou v. Greece, supra* n. 404, paras. 45–48. See also *Dacia S.R.L. v. Moldova*, ECtHR 18 March 2008, appl. no. 3052/04, paras. 73–78: equal time-limits must apply to all parties

The principle further entails that the parties are afforded the same opportunity to summon witnesses. In the *Dombo Beheer B.V.* case, the central question in the national proceedings was whether a certain agreement had been concluded between the applicant company and its bank. The person who represented the bank at the meeting where the alleged agreement was concluded, was allowed to testify before the court. The person who represented the applicant company, however, could not give evidence, because the national court identified him with the company itself. Thus, there was 'a substantial disadvantage' for the company *vis-à-vis* the bank in breach of Article 6.[474] In many legal systems, persons closely related to parties in civil proceedings cannot be heard as witnesses under oath. In the *Ankerl* case, the inability of Mrs Ankerl to give evidence under oath on the allegedly agreed lease between her husband and another party did not amount to a breach of Article 6. The Court held that under national law the court could freely assess the results of the 'measures taken to obtain evidence'. Furthermore, the national court did not attach any particular weight to the testimony of the other party on account of his having given evidence on oath and the court had relied on evidence other than just the statements in issue.[475] Therefore, the giving of evidence on oath by Mrs Ankerl could not have influenced the outcome of the proceedings.

In the *Pisano* case, the applicant claimed that the refusal of the national courts to summon a witness had violated the applicants' right to a fair trial. Italian law legally restricted the possibility to summon witnesses *à decharge* who had not been listed seven days before the first court hearing, to cases in which the judge considered their citation as absolutely necessary. The same limitation did not apply to witnesses *à charge*. Owing to the fact that the applicant did not contest the legitimacy of the refusal, but its correctness, it appeared to the Court not to be necessary to give its express view about this difference. It limited itself to the assessment that the applicant had the opportunity to present his arguments before the courts and that the reasoning in the judgments made clear why the witness had not been summoned. Therefore, Article 6 had not been violated.[476] In the *Vidal* case, the request of the applicant to hear four persons as defence witnesses had been rejected implicitly. The complete silence of the judgment on the request did violate Article 6.[477]

In addition, the parties must have the same possibility to call experts and these should in turn receive the same treatment. In the *Bönisch* case, the Court

---

who wish to submit a complaint unless there are *compelling reasons* that justify a more advantageous position for the state.

[474] *Dombo Beheer B.V. v. the Netherlands*, *supra* n. 449 paras. 33–35. *Cf. Gillissen v. the Netherlands* ECtHR 15 March 2016, appl. no. 39966/09, para. 56 in which the Court found a violation of the fair trial requirement because of the unmotivated refusal of the Dutch administrative courts not to hear a witness in a social security dispute.

[475] *Ankerl v. Switzerland*, ECtHR 23 October 1996, appl. no. 17748/91, para. 38.

[476] *Pisano v. Italy*, ECtHR 27 July 2000, appl. no. 36732/97, paras. 22–29.

[477] *Vidal v. Belgium*, ECtHR 22 April 1992, appl. no. 12351/86, para. 34.

found that the expert involved in the proceedings and the powers given to him insufficiently guaranteed the latter's neutrality, so that he had to be considered as a witness for the prosecution rather than as an expert. Since the accused had not been given the same opportunity to call such an 'expert', the principle of 'equality of arms' had been violated.[478]

Phases in the examination during which neither of the parties was present fulfil the principle of 'equality of arms'. In the *Nideröst-Huber* case, the Court established that the observations of the cantonal court had not been communicated to either of the parties to the dispute before the Federal Court. As the cantonal court could not be regarded as the opponent of either of the parties, the requirement of equality of arms had not been infringed.[479] However, a problem did arise with regard to the right to adversarial proceedings, which is discussed further in the following section.

4.3. ADVERSARIAL PROCEEDINGS AND EVIDENCE

The right to adversarial proceedings entails in principle the opportunity for the parties to have knowledge of and comment on all evidence adduced or observations filed, even those coming from an independent member of the national legal service.[480] It may be deduced from the extensive case law that it is immaterial whether a person has chosen not to be legally represented,[481] whether the documents or observations in issue are important for the outcome of the proceedings,[482] whether the omission to communicate the document in issue has caused any prejudice,[483] or whether the observations present any fact or argument which already appeared in the impugned decision. It is a matter for the parties to assess whether a submission deserves a reaction.[484] In the

---

[478]   *Bönisch v. Austria*, ECtHR 6 May 1985, appl. no. 8658/79, paras. 33–35. The mere fact that an expert is a member of the staff of an institute which reported the initial suspicions, does not suffice to constitute the expert as a 'witness for the prosecution': *Brandstetter v. Austria*, ECtHR 28 August 1991, appl. no. 11170/84, 12876/87 and 13468/87, para. 45.

[479]   *Nideröst-Huber v. Switzerland*, ECtHR 18 February 1997, appl. no. 18990/91, para. 23. See also *Kress v. France, supra* n. 470, para. 73; *Immeubles Groupe Kosser v. France, supra* n. 470, para. 23.

[480]   See, e.g., *Vermeulen v. Belgium, supra* n. 470, para. 33; *Van Orshoven v. the Netherlands,* ECtHR 25 June 1997, appl. no. 20122/92, para. 41; *K.D.B. v. the Netherlands,* ECtHR 27 March 1998, appl. no. 21981/93, para. 44 and *Uzukauskas v. Lithuania,* ECtHR 6 July 2010, appl. no. 16965/04, paras. 45–51.

[481]   See, e.g., *Voisine v. France,* ECtHR 8 February 2000, appl. no. 27362/95, para. 33; *Adoud and Bosoni v. France,* ECtHR 27 February 2001, appl. no. 35237/97 and 34595/97, para. 20.

[482]   See, e.g., *Kerojärvi v. Finland,* ECtHR 19 July 1995, appl. no. 17506/90, paras. 39–42; *F.R. v. Switzerland,* ECtHR 28 June 2001, appl. no. 37292/97, para. 37; *Ziegler v. Switzerland, supra* n. 66, para. 38.

[483]   *Walston v. Norway (No. 1),* ECtHR 3 June 2003, appl. no. 37372/97, para. 58.

[484]   See, e.g., *Nideröst-Huber v. Switzerland, supra* n. 479, para. 29, and, *mutatis mutandis, Bulut v. Austria, supra* n. 469, para. 49; *Lanz v. Austria, supra* n. 472, para. 58; *Fortum Corporation v. Finland,* ECtHR 15 July 2003, appl. no. 32559/96, para. 42.

Reinhardt and Slimane-Kaïd case concerning French cassation proceedings, the Court found a twofold breach of the adversarial requirement: neither the reporting judge's report, which had been disclosed to the Advocate General, nor the submissions of the latter had been communicated to the parties.[485] However, the Court also held that the subsequent changed French practice did meet the requirements of Article 6.[486] This practice implies that the parties and the Advocate General receive only the first section of the reporting judge's report, which includes an analysis of the case, while on the day preceding the hearing the Advocate General informs the parties' lawyers of the tenor of his submissions.[487] They are entitled to reply by means of a memorandum for the deliberations and in cases where there is an oral hearing they may reply to his submissions orally. In the *Kress* case, with regard to a similar practice before the French *Conseil d'État*, the Court reached the same conclusion.[488] In the *Immeubles Groupe Kosser* case, the Court held that the fact that the memorandum was received the day after the public hearing, whilst the deliberations of the *Conseil d'État* took place directly after the hearing, did not constitute a breach of the adversarial principle.[489]

Evidence obtained contrary to the norms laid down in the Convention itself, such as statements extracted via torture or other inhuman treatment contrary to Article 3, or evidence collected by means of encroachment on privacy contrary to Article 8, conflicts on that ground alone with the Convention. However, the Convention does not lay down rules on evidence as such. The Court, therefore, does not exclude as a matter of principle and in the abstract that evidence obtained in breach of provisions of domestic law may be admitted. It is a matter for the national courts to assess the obtained evidence and its relevance.[490] Nevertheless, the Court has adopted the view that the principle of 'fair hearing'

---

485   *Reinhardt & Slimane-Kaid v. France, supra* n. 199, paras. 105–106; see also, *e.g., K.D.B. v. the Netherlands, supra* n. 480, para. 44 and *J.J. v. the Netherlands,* ECtHR 27 March 1998, appl. no. 21351/93, para. 43; *Berger v. France,* ECtHR 3 December 2002, appl. no. 48221/99, paras. 42–43. In *Slimane-Kaïd v. France (No. 2),* ECtHR 27 November 2003, appl. no. 48943/99, para. 17, the omission to communicate the draft judgment, which had been communicated to the Advocate General, to the party also amounted to a breach of Art. 6.

486   *Reinhardt & Slimane-Kaid v. France, supra* n. 199, para. 106; *Fabre v. France, supra* n. 162, paras. 31–32.

487   In *Meftah and Others v. France,* ECtHR 26 July 2002, appl. no. 32911/96, 35237/97 and 34595/97, paras. 49–52, the Court reached the conclusion that a person who has chosen to defend himself without representation should benefit from the same practice.

488   *Kress v. France, supra* n. 470, para. 76; see also *APBP v. France,* ECtHR 21 March 2002, appl. no. 38436/97, paras. 23–27; *Theraube v. France,* ECtHR 10 October 2002, appl. no. 44565/98, paras. 31–32.

489   *Immeubles Groupe Kosser v. France, supra* n. 470, para. 26.

490   See, e.g., *Schenk v. Switzerland,* ECtHR 12 July 1988, appl. no. 10862/84, para. 46; *Miailhe v. France (No. 2),* ECtHR 26 September 1996, appl. no. 18978/91, para. 43; *Mantovanelli v. France,* ECtHR 18 March 1997, appl. no. 21497/93, para. 34; *Ivan Stoyanov Vasilev v. Bulgaria,* ECtHR 4 June 2013, appl. no. 7963/05, para. 30.

may entail specific requirements with respect to evidence. In the *Gäfgen* case, a statement had been obtained that was in violation of Article 3. But in the specific circumstances of this case, not excluding the evidence did not lead to a breach of Article 6: 'The Court concludes that in the particular circumstances of the applicant's case, the failure to exclude the impugned real evidence, secured following a statement extracted by means of inhuman treatment, did not have a bearing on the applicant's conviction and sentence. As the applicant's defence rights and his right not to incriminate himself have likewise been respected, his trial as a whole must be considered to have been fair.'[491]

The notion of a fair criminal trial implies that the public interest in the fight against crime cannot justify the use of evidence obtained as a result of police incitement.[492] From the fact that an accused person is entitled in principle to 'take part in the hearing and to have his case heard', the Court has deduced that 'all the evidence must in principle be produced in the presence of the accused (...) with a view to adversarial argument'.[493] The principle of immediacy is a guarantee of fairness as the observations made by the court about the credibility of a witness may have important consequences for an accused. A change in the composition of the trial court after the hearing of an important witness should, therefore, normally lead to a rehearing of that witness.[494] The evidence produced must be sufficiently ‹direct› to actually make refutation possible during the public hearing.[495] In the *Bricmont* case, the lack of confrontation between the accused persons and a member of the Belgian royal family, as the party seeking damages, amounted to a breach of paragraphs 1 and 3 of Article 6 taken together.[496]

The case law with regard to the opportunity of the accused to challenge and question a witness is further discussed in subsection 9.5. As will be seen, it may be concluded from this case law that a court decision which is exclusively

---

[491] *Gäfgen v. Germany*, ECtHR (GC) 1 June 2010, appl. no. 22978/05, para. 187. *Cf. Kaçiu and Kotorri v. Albania*, ECtHR 25 June 2013, appl. no. 33194/07, para. 120, where the Court accepted a breach of Art. 6, since the statement which led to the conviction had been unlawfully obtained (it was in breach of Art. 6(3) as legal assistance had not been available).

[492] *Teixeira de Castro v. Portugal*, ECtHR 9 June 1998, appl. no. 25829/94, paras. 34–36; *Edwards and Lewis v. the United Kingdom*, ECtHR 22 July 2003, appl. nos. 39647/98 and 40461/98, para. 49 and *Edwards and Lewis v. the United Kingdom*, ECtHR (GC) 27 October 2004, appl. nos. 39647/98 and 40461/98.

[493] *Barberà, Messegué and Jabardo v. Spain*, *supra* n. 445, para. 78. See also *Kostovski v. the Netherlands*, *supra* n. 446, para. 41; *Windisch v. Austria*, ECtHR 27 September 1990, appl. no. 12489/86, para. 26.

[494] *Pitkänen v. Finland*, *supra* n. 449, para. 58. The same rule seems to hold good in civil cases: *Ibid.*, para. 62.

[495] In the *Kamasinski* case, the Commission held it to be in violation of Art. 6(1) that no note had been given to the applicant or his representative of the contents of the information which the judge, acting as rapporteur, had obtained by telephone from the judge of the regional court who had presided over the trial; report of 5 May 1988, paras. 188–195.

[496] *Bricmont v. Belgium*, ECtHR 7 July 1989, appl. no. 10857/84, paras. 78–85.

or almost exclusively based upon indirect evidence of witnesses, has not been taken in accordance with the fair trial requirement, unless in some way or another an adequate possibility for contradiction and counter-evidence has been afforded. The same holds good with respect to other evidence, such as tape recordings; defence against its contents must be allowed and still be practicable. According to the Court, Article 6(1) does not require access to the tape itself. Its relevance for the fairness of the trial depends, *inter alia*, on the vital character of the contents of the tape for the evidence, while it is also relevant whether the transcript of the tape has been verified by an independent person.[497] Although the national authorities have greater latitude when dealing with civil cases than they have when dealing with criminal cases, as a rule the principle of immediacy also seems to apply to civil cases.[498]

In the *Mantovanelli* case, the applicants applied to the administrative courts for a ruling that the hospital where their daughter had received medical treatment, was liable for her death. In Strasbourg, they complained that the procedure followed in preparing the expert medical opinion ordered by the national administrative court had not been in conformity with the adversarial principle. The Court firstly concluded that it was not disputed that the 'purely judicial' proceedings had complied with the adversarial principle. The applicants could have made submissions to the national court on the content and findings of the report of the expert. Nevertheless, the Court doubted whether they had had a real opportunity to comment effectively on it. The question that had to be answered by the expert concerned a technical field that was not within the judge's knowledge and, therefore, the report was likely to have a preponderant influence on the assessments of the facts by that court. The Court further took into account that no practical difficulties stood in the way of the applicants being associated in the process of producing the report, and the fact that the people to be interviewed by the expert were employed by the hospital, the opposing party in the proceedings. Finally, the Court concluded that the applicants had not been able to comment effectively on the main piece of evidence and therefore Article 6 had been breached.[499] The more recent judgment in the *Sara Lindt* case demonstrates that in cases where expert advice can weigh heavily on the legal decision, on the basis of Article 6 requirements can be set on the impartiality of an expert or committee of experts. Or at any rate a situation can arise in which there can be objective legitimate grounds for doubt on the (objective) impartiality of a judge when the advice of an expert or committee of experts

---

[497] *Gillow v. the United Kingdom, supra* n. 382, para. 71. See also *Schenk v. Switzerland, supra* n. 490, paras. 39–49, and *S.N. v. Sweden*, ECtHR 2 July 2002, appl. no. 34209/96, paras. 46–52, with regard to a recorded interview of a minor who was the perceived victim of a sexual offence; *cf. Bykov v. Russia* ECtHR (GC) 10 March 2009, appl. no. 4378/02.

[498] *Pitkänen v. Finland, supra* n. 449, paras. 59–65.

[499] *Mantovanelli v. France, supra* n. 490, paras. 35–36.

with close ties to one of the parties in a legal action is relied upon. Although an expert in such a case does not have to meet the same requirements as the judge, when it comes to advice of a substantial nature he must be sufficiently neutral.[500]

The (unequal) access to medical information which can be of crucial significance in a court judgment can also lead to a violation of the principle of equality of arms. In the *Augusto* case, the request by the complainant for early retirement due to work-related disability was rejected on the grounds of a doctor's report. The complainant had no access to this report. The Court held that this was a violation of Article 6 since the report was of overriding importance. Both parties should have had the opportunity to comment on the report in an efficient manner.[501] However, in the *Eternit* case, the fact that an employer had no access to the medical file of its sick employee was not deemed to be a violation of Article 6. According to the Court, a correct balance between the right of the employer to adversarial proceedings and the right of the employee to the confidentiality of his medical file had already been achieved because the employer can request that a court appoints a medical expert in order to compile a medical file.[502]

The prosecuting authorities are obliged 'to disclose to the defence all material evidence for or against the accused',[503] but the right to disclosure is not an absolute one. In criminal proceedings there may be competing interests, such as national security, the need to protect witnesses or keep secret police methods of investigation of crime.[504] However, only such restrictions as are strictly necessary, are permissible and any difficulties caused to the defence by a limitation of its right must be sufficiently counterbalanced.[505] In principle it is a matter for the national courts to decide whether the non-disclosure of evidence was strictly necessary.[506] The Court scrutinises whether the decision-making procedure applied in each case complied, as far as possible, with the adversarial principle and the principle of equality of arms, and incorporated adequate safeguards to protect the rights of the accused. In this regard, it seems crucial whether the defence is informed, can make submissions and can participate in the decision-making process. The Court further attaches great importance to the fact that the need for disclosure is under constant assessment of the judge,

---

[500] *Sara Lind Eggertsdóttir v. Iceland*, ECtHR 5 July 2007, appl. no. 31930/04. See also *Korosec v. Slovenia*, ECtHR 8 October 2015, appl. no. 77212/12, paras. 52–57.

[501] *Augusto v. France*, ECtHR 11 January 2007, appl. no. 71665/01.

[502] *Eternit v. France*, ECtHR 27 March 2012, appl. no. 20041/10.

[503] *Edwards v. the United Kingdom*, *supra* n. 332, para. 36.

[504] See, e.g., *Doorson v. the Netherlands*, ECtHR 26 March 1996, appl. no. 20524/92, para. 70; *Rowe and Davis v. the United Kingdom*, ECtHR (GC) 16 February 2000, appl. no. 28901/95, para. 61.

[505] *Van Mechelen and Others v. the Netherlands*, ECtHR (GC) 23 April 1997, appl. no. 21363/93, 21364/93, 21427/93 and 22056/93, para. 58; *Rowe and Davis v. the United Kingdom*, *supra* n. 504, para. 61.

[506] *Rowe and Davis v. the United Kingdom*, *supra* n. 504, para. 61.

who may monitor throughout the trial the fairness or otherwise of the disclosed evidence.[507]

According to the Court, security reasons do not constitute a blank cheque for refusing suspects access to certain evidence. There may be sufficient measures available to achieve the correct balance between safeguarding national security and taking account of the legal rights of the individual.[508] In the *A. v. United Kingdom* case, the Court held 'that, even in proceedings under Article 6 for the determination of guilt on criminal charges, there may be restrictions on the right to a fully adversarial procedure where strictly necessary in the light of a strong countervailing public interest, such as national security, the need to keep secret certain police methods of investigation or the protection of the fundamental rights of another person. There will not be a fair trial, however, unless any difficulties caused to the defendant by a limitation on his rights are sufficiently counterbalanced by the procedures followed by the judicial authorities.'[509]

In the *Fitt* case, the Court concluded, by nine votes to eight, that there had not been a violation of Article 6. In the national proceedings the prosecution had made an *ex parte* application to the trial judge for an order authorising non-disclosure. The defence were told that the material in question related to sources of information and they were able to make submissions to the judge outlining the defence case. The Court based its conclusion *inter alia* on the facts that the material formed no part of the prosecution case and was never put to the jury and that the need for disclosure was at all times under the assessment of a judge. The minority, however, took the view that the surveillance of the judge could not remedy the unfairness created by the defence's absence from the *ex parte* proceedings.[510] In the *Jasper* case, the defence were not (even) told of the category of material that the prosecution sought to withhold, but here again, by nine votes to eight, the Court held that Article 6 had not been violated.[511] A different conclusion was reached in the *Rowe* and *Davis* case. During the applicant's trial at first instance the prosecution withheld, without notifying the judge, certain relevant evidence on grounds of public interest. The absence of any scrutiny of the undisclosed evidence by the trial judge could not be remedied in the appeal proceedings. The Court held that the trial judge was fully versed in all the evidence, saw witnesses give their testimony and would have

---

[507] See, e.g., *Rowe and Davis v. the United Kingdom, supra* n. 504, paras. 62–67; *P.G. and J.H. v. the United Kingdom*, ECtHR 25 September 2001, appl. no. 44787/98, paras. 69–71.

[508] *Dagtekin and Others v. Turkey*, ECtHR 13 March 2008, appl. no. 70516/0, para. 34.

[509] *A. and Others v. the United Kingdom*, ECtHR (GC) 19 February 2009, appl. no. 3455/05, para. 205; *cf. A. v. the Netherlands*, ECtHR 20 July 2010, appl. no. 4900/06.

[510] *Fitt v. the United Kingdom*, ECtHR (GC) 16 February 2000, appl. no. 29777/96, paras. 47–50; see also *P.G. and J.H. v. the United Kingdom, supra* n. 507, paras. 70–73.

[511] *Jasper v. the United Kingdom*, ECtHR (GC) 16 February 2000, appl. no. 27052/95, paras. 54–58.

been in a position to monitor the need of disclosure throughout the trial. The judges in the Court of Appeal however, were dependent for their understanding of the relevance of the undisclosed evidence on the transcripts of the hearing of the court in first instance and on the information of the prosecuting counsel. Therefore, the lack of scrutiny of the withheld material deprived the applicants of a fair trial.[512] In the *Edwards* and *Lewis* case, the applicants complained that the undisclosed evidence substantiated their claim that they had been the victims of entrapment. Since they were denied access to the evidence, they were not able to argue the case in full before the judge. According to the Court the matters raised by the applicants were of determinative importance to the applicants' trials. The Court reached the conclusion that the trial had not been fair, taking into account that the judge, who subsequently rejected the defence submissions on entrapment, had already seen prosecution evidence which may have been relevant to the issue, and also the lack of adequate safeguards to protect the interests of the accused.[513]

4.4. PRESENCE AT TRIAL AND ORAL HEARING

The precept of a 'fair hearing' in principle entails the right of the parties to be present in person at the trial. This right is closely connected to the right to defend oneself in person as stipulated in Article 6(3) sub-paragraph (c),[514] the right to an oral hearing[515] and the right to be able to follow the proceedings.[516] In the *Colozza* case, the Court held that, 'although this is not expressly mentioned in para. 1 of Article 6, the object and the purpose of the Article as a whole show that a person 'charged with a criminal offence' is entitled to take part in the hearing'.[517]

There may be exceptions to this principle as far as trials at second or third instance are concerned. However, an exception is not allowed where

---

[512] *Rowe and Davis v. the United Kingdom, supra* n. 504, paras. 65–69. See also *Edwards v. the United Kingdom, supra* n. 332, paras. 35–39; *I.J.L., G.M.R. and A.K.P. v. the United Kingdom,* ECtHR 19 September 2000, appl. no. 29522/95, 30056/96 and 30574/96, para. 118; *Atlan v. the United Kingdom,* ECtHR 19 June 2001, appl. no. 36533/97, paras. 41–46.

[513] *Edwards and Lewis v. the United Kingdom, supra* n. 492, paras. 50–59, confirmed by the Court in *Edwards and Lewis v. the United Kingdom, supra* n. 492, para. 47. See also *Papageorgiou v. Greece,* ECtHR 9 May 2003, appl. no. 59506/00, paras. 30–40, where essential items of evidence had not been produced or adequately examined at the trial.

[514] See, e.g., *Zana v. Turkey,* ECtHR (GC) 25 November 1997, appl. no. 18954/91, para. 68. See on the right to defend oneself in person *infra* 9.4.

[515] See *Fredin v. Sweden (No. 2),* ECtHR 23 February 1994, appl. no. 18928/91, para. 21, and *Fischer v. Austria, supra* n. 472, para. 44.

[516] *Stanford v. the United Kingdom,* ECtHR 23 February 1994, appl. no. 16757/90, para. 26. In this case the applicant complained about the poor acoustics of the courtroom.

[517] *Colozza v. Italy, supra* n. 189, para. 27. See also, e.g., *Monnell and Morris v. the United Kingdom, supra* n. 353, para. 58; *Brozicek v. Italy, supra* n. 186, para. 45.

an appellate court has to examine a case both as to the facts and the law and make a full assessment of the issue of guilt or innocence. In that case the direct assessment of the evidence given in person by the accused for the purpose of proving that he did not commit the alleged offence, is required.[518] Moreover, in principle an exception is permissible only if the accused was entitled to be present at the hearing at first instance.[519] In addition, the Court takes into account the nature of the national (appeal) system,[520] the scope of the powers of the national (appeal) court[521] and the 'manner in which the applicant's interests were actually presented and protected' before the national (appeal) court.[522] In the appeal proceedings in the *Kremzow* case the accused risked a serious increase in sentence. Therefore, the Court held that the gravity of what was at stake implied that the applicant ought to have been able to defend himself in person.[523] A different conclusion was reached in the *Jan Åke Andersson* and *Fejde* cases. The Court attached importance to the fact that the appeal raised questions which could be decided on the basis of the case file, to the minor character of the offence and to the prohibition against the increase of the sentence on appeal.[524]

In the *Jussila* case previously referred to, the Court accepted that in the case of a criminal charge that does not fall under hard core criminal law, not

---

[518] *Tierce and Others v. San Marino*, ECtHR 25 July 2000, appl. no. 24954/94, 24971/94 and 24972/94, para. 95; *Dondarini v. San Marino*, *supra* n. 349, para. 27. However, in *Botten v. Norway*, ECtHR 19 February 1996, appl. no. 16206/90, para. 39 and paras. 48–53, and *Sigurthor Arnarsson v. Iceland*, ECtHR 15 July 2003, appl. no. 44671/98, paras. 30–38, the Court chose a different approach, where it stated that 'even if the court of appeal has full jurisdiction to examine both points of law and of fact, Article 6 para. 1 does not always require a right to a public hearing or, if a hearing takes place, a right to be present in person'.

[519] In many judgments, the Court stated that the notion of a 'fair trial' implies that persons charged with a criminal offence, *as a principle*, are entitled to be present at the first instance trial. See, e.g., *Ekbatani v. Sweden*, *supra* n. 346, para. 25; *Belziuk v. Poland*, *supra* n. 395, para. 37; *Pobornikoff v. Austria*, ECtHR 3 October 2000, appl. no. 28501/95, para. 24. However, there does not seem to be much room for an exception to this principle. In cases where the Court accepted the non-entitlement for the accused to be present at the second or third instance trial, the accused had in fact been present at first instance.

[520] See, e.g., *Monnell and Morris v. the United Kingdom*, *supra* n. 353, paras. 56–70; *Kremzow v. Austria*, *supra* n. 349, para. 63; *Josef Prinz v. Austria*, ECtHR 8 February 2000, appl. no. 23867/94, paras. 36–37.

[521] See, e.g., *Josef Prinz v. Austria*, *supra* n. 520, para. 43; *Pobornikoff v. Austria*, *supra* n. 519, paras. 29–33; *Richen and Gaucher v. France*, ECtHR 23 January 2003, appl. no. 31520/96 and 34359/97, paras. 35–36.

[522] See, e.g., *Helmers v. Sweden*, *supra* n. 157, paras. 36–39; *Michael Edward Cooke v. Austria*, ECtHR 8 February 2000, appl. no. 25878/94, paras. 38 and 43. *Josef Prinz v. Austria*, *supra* n. 520, paras. 37 and 44.

[523] *Kremzow v. Austria*, *supra* n. 349, para. 67. See also *Botten v. Norway*, *supra* n. 518, paras. 48–53, concerning a judgment of the Norwegian Supreme Court in which it had made its own assessment of the facts without hearing the applicant; and *Michael Edward Cooke v. Austria*, *supra* n. 522, para. 42.

[524] *Jan-Åke Andersson v. Sweden*, *supra* n. 346, paras. 29–30; *Fejde v. Sweden*, *supra* n. 346, para. 33.

all requirements of Article 6 have to apply in full (in the present case the right to an oral hearing.[525]) In non-criminal cases this exception had previously been accepted. But the *Milenović* case makes clear that strict conditions are attached to this exception in criminal cases. In this case, the refusal to hold a public hearing did lead to a violation of Article 6(1).[526]

The rule that the person concerned is entitled to be present at the hearing at first instance seems less strict in civil proceedings.[527] However, in the *Helmers* case, concerning the 'civil' right to enjoy a good reputation, the Court developed with regard to the entitlement of the applicant to be present at the appeal hearing the same line of reasoning as in criminal cases.[528] The seriousness of what was at stake – the professional career of the applicant – did not justify an encroachment on the right to be present.[529]

In civil proceedings the right to be present at the trial may be waived, although the waiver must be made in an unequivocal manner.[530] The same holds good for criminal cases.[531] In case the accused has not been notified in person of a hearing, particular diligence is required in assessing whether the accused has waived his right to be present.[532] In the *Sejdovic* case, the Italian authorities took the view that the applicant had waived his right to appear at his trial because he had become untraceable after the allegedly committed crime. However, according to the Court there was nothing to prove that the applicant knew of the proceedings against him and even supposing that he knew, it could not be concluded that he had unequivocally waived his right to appear at his trial. In these circumstances, the applicant should have been able to obtain a new ruling by a court on the charges brought against him. Since Italian law did not guarantee with sufficient certainty that the applicant would have the opportunity to appear at a new trial to present his defence, Article 6 had been violated.[533] Moreover, the Court held that the violation of the Convention was the result of the shortcoming in the Italian legal system, which meant that every person

---

[525] See *Jussila v. Finland, supra* n. 244.

[526] See *Milenović v. Slovenia*, ECtHR 28 February 2013, appl. no. 11411/11.

[527] See *Fredin v. Sweden (No. 2), supra* n. 515, para. 22; *Allan Jacobsson v. Sweden (No. 2), supra* n. 101, para. 49. *Cf.* also *Valová, Slezák and Slezák v. Slovakia*, ECtHR 1 June 2004, appl. no. 44925/98, paras. 63–69.

[528] In particular, *Jan Åke Andersson v. Sweden, supra* n. 346 and *Fejde v. Sweden, supra* n. 346.

[529] *Helmers v. Sweden, supra* n. 157, paras. 36–39. See also, e.g., *Fredin v. Sweden (No. 2), supra* n. 515, para. 22; *Malhous v. Czech Republic*, ECtHR (GC) 12 July 2001, appl. no. 33071/96, para. 60.

[530] See, e.g., *Schuler-Zgraggen v. Switzerland, supra* n. 113, para. 58; *Zumtobel v. Austria, supra* n. 306, para. 34.

[531] *Colozza v. Italy, supra* n. 189, para. 29; *Kremzow v. Austria, supra* n. 349, paras. 66 and 68; *Josef Prinz v. Austria, supra* n. 520, para. 33 in conjunction with para. 44; *Krombach v. France*, ECtHR 13 February 2001, appl. no. 29731/96, para. 85; *Medenica v. Switzerland*, ECtHR 14 June 2001, appl. no. 20491/92, para. 54.

[532] *Yavuz v. Austria*, ECtHR 27 May 2004, appl. no. 46549/99, paras. 49–51, where the accused had been summoned via counsel.

[533] *Sejdovic v. Italy, supra* n. 422, paras. 34–42.

---

convicted *in absentia* could be deprived of a retrial.[534] National legislation may discourage the unjustified absence of an accused at the trial, although there are important restrictions. The right of counsel who attends the trial to conduct the defence in absence of the accused[535] may not be impaired[536] and the measures taken may not be disproportionate otherwise.[537] In the *Medenica* case, where the absence of the accused, who had received the summons to appear, without a valid excuse barred the rehearing of the case, this requirement of proportionality had been met.[538]

The foregoing, of course, does not bar judgment by default, provided that the person in question has been summoned by the prescribed procedure and sufficient guarantees are attached to this procedure. If it is not certain whether the accused was really aware that proceedings against him were taking place and that he had been summoned for a hearing, the Court examines the carefulness of the procedure by means of which contact with him was sought.[539] In any case, the fact that the accused is detained, is no reason for his not being heard, at least not at a first instance trial.[540]

4.5. OTHER REQUIREMENTS

While in criminal matters the *nulla poena sine lege* rule applies, in civil matters, in principle, the legislature is not precluded from adopting new retrospective provisions to regulate rights arising under existing laws. However, the principle of the rule of law and the notion of fair trial embodied in Article 6 preclude any interference by the legislature with the administration of justice designed to influence the judicial determination of the dispute. For this reason the Court held in the *Stran Greek Refineries and Stratis Andreadis* case that Greece had violated the applicants' rights under Article 6 by enacting a law that influenced the proceedings already pending before the courts, between the applicants and the Greek State, in a way favourable to the State.[541] Such interference by the

---

[534] *Ibid.*, para. 44.
[535] See *infra* 9.4.c.
[536] *Van Geyseghem v. Belgium*, ECtHR (GC) 21 January 1999, appl. no. 26103/95, para. 34; *Van Pelt v. France*, ECtHR 23 May 2000, appl. no. 31070/96, para, 67; *Krombach v. France, supra* n. 531, para. 89.
[537] *Poitrimol v. France, supra* n. 336, para. 35.
[538] *Medenica v. Switzerland, supra* n. 531, para. 57. See also *Eliazer v. the Netherlands,* ECtHR 16 October 2001, appl. no. 38055/97, paras. 30–36.
[539] *Colozza v. Italy, supra* n. 189, paras. 27–28; *T v. Italy,* ECtHR 12 October 1992, appl. no. 14104/88, paras. 27–30; *Somogyi v. Italy,* ECtHR 18 May 2004, appl. no. 67972/01, paras. 66–76.
[540] *Kamasinski v. Austria, supra* n. 331, paras. 104–108, seems to indicate a different point of view with regard to appeal proceedings.
[541] *Stran Greek Refineries and Stratis Andreadis v. Greece, supra* n. 428, paras. 42–50.

legislature can only be justified on compelling grounds of interest.[542] In many cases this requirement had not been met,[543] but things turned out differently in the case of *The National & Provincial Building Society*. The effect of the British Finance Act 1992 was to deprive building societies of their chances of winning already pending proceedings against the Inland Revenue. Amongst other arguments, the Court took into account the fact that the interference caused by the Act was of a much less drastic nature than the interference in the *Stran Greek Reference* case, in which the applicants and the State had been engaged in litigation for many years and the applicants had an enforceable judgment against the State. The judicial proceedings by the building societies had just been started. Furthermore, the intervention of the legislature had been foreseeable and the Finance Act 1992 concerned the tax sector, an area where recourse to retrospective legislation was not confined to the United Kingdom. The Court concluded that there had been no violation of Article 6.[544]

The 'fair hearing' requirement implies the right of the accused 'not to contribute to incriminating himself'.[545] This right is focused on respecting the will of an accused person to remain silent. It does not extend to the use in criminal proceedings of material which may be obtained from the accused through the use of compulsory powers, but which has existence independent of the will of the suspect.[546] It applies to criminal proceedings in respect of all types of criminal offences without distinction, from the most simple to the most complex.[547] Although the right not to incriminate oneself and to remain silent lie at the heart of the notion of a fair hearing,[548] these rights are not absolute

---

[542]   See, e.g., *Zielinski and Pradal & Gonzalez and Others v. France*, *supra* n. 428, para. 57; *Agoudimos and Cefallonian Sky Shipping Co. v. Greece*, *supra* n. 428, para. 30; *Smokovitis v. Greece*, ECtHR 22 April 2002, appl. no. 46356/99, para. 23.

[543]   See, e.g., *Papageorgiou v. Greece*, ECtHR 22 October 1997, appl. no. 24628/94, paras. 37–40, where the Greek Government took the position that the dispute in issue, whose outcome had been influenced by the contested Act, was not a dispute between the applicants and the State, because the party in the proceedings was a private-law, not a public-law, entity. However, the Court rejected this argument (para. 27). In this respect, see also *Zielinski and Pradal & Gonzalez and Others v. France*, *supra* n. 428, para. 60; *Agoudimos and Cefallonian Sky Shipping Co. v. Greece*, *supra* n. 428, para. 34.

[544]   Judgment of 23 October 1997, paras. 105–113. See also *OGIS-Institut Stanislas, OGEC St. Pie X and Blanche de Castille and Others v. France*, ECtHR 27 May 2004, appl. no. 42219/98 and 54563/00, paras. 61–72, and *Gorraiz Lizarraga and Others v. Spain*, *supra* n. 32, paras. 64–73, where the Court held that, although the enactment of the law in issue had indisputably been unsupportive of the applicants' submissions, it could not be said to have been intended to circumvent the principle of the rule of law.

[545]   *Funke v. France*, *supra* n. 450, para. 44.

[546]   *Saunders v. the United Kingdom*, ECtHR (GC) 17 December 1996, appl. no. 19187/91, para. 69. See also *Coëme and Others v. Belgium*, ECtHR 22 June 2000, appl. nos. 32492/96, 32547/96, 32548/96, 33209/96 and 33210/96, para. 128.

[547]   *Saunders v. the United Kingdom*, *supra* n. 546, para. 74. See also *Heaney and McGuiness v. Ireland*, ECtHR 21 December 2000, appl. no. 34720/97, para. 57 and *Quinn v. Ireland*, ECtHR 21 December 2000, appl. no. 36887/97, para. 58.

[548]   *Funke v. France*, *supra* n. 450, para. 44.

rights.[549] However, the very essence of these rights may not be destroyed. Therefore, the threat and imposition of a criminal sanction on the accused, such as accumulating fines[550] or a prison sentence,[551] because he fails to supply information to the authorities investigating the alleged commission of crimes, violates the fair hearing requirement.[552]

In the *Saunders* case, the applicant, who had not been charged (yet), had been legally obliged under the Companies Act to give evidence to the inspectors appointed by the Secretary of State for Trade and Industry. The function of the inspectors was an inquisitorial and not a judicial function. It was their task 'to conduct an investigation designed to discover whether there are facts which may result in others taking action'. The applicant, who risked the imposition of a fine or a prison sentence in case of non-compliance with the obligation, did give evidence. In the subsequent criminal proceedings the transcripts of the interviews which he gave to the inspectors were read out to the jury by the prosecution over a three-day period. In these circumstances, the Court held that the subsequent use of the statements was intended to incriminate the applicant and constituted an infringement of the right not to incriminate oneself.[553] However, the use of compulsory powers to obtain information against the person concerned outside the context of criminal proceedings is in itself not prohibited.[554]

In the *John Murray* case, the Court sought to strike the balance between the right to remain silent and the circumstances in which an adverse inference, regulated by law, may be drawn from silence. In its lengthy reasoning the

---

[549]   *Heaney and McGuiness v. Ireland, supra* n. 547, para. 47 and *Quinn v. Ireland, supra* n. 547, para. 47, respectively. In these judgments the Court referred to *John Murray v. the United Kingdom*, ECtHR (GC) 8 February 1996, appl. no. 18731/91, para. 47, in which case the Court held explicitly that the right to remain silent is not absolute, which would seem to imply that the right not to incriminate oneself is also not absolute. In *Saunders v. the United Kingdom, supra* n. 546, para. 74, the Court explicitly refused to answer the question of whether the right not to incriminate oneself is absolute or not.

[550]   *Funke v. France, supra* n. 450, para. 44.

[551]   *Heaney and McGuiness v. Ireland, supra* n. 547, paras. 47–56 and *Quinn v. Ireland, supra* n. 547, paras. 47–56.

[552]   Although not clear, this might be different if statements made by the accused will not be admissible in evidence against him. See *Heaney and McGuiness v. Ireland, supra* n. 547, paras. 52–55 and *Quinn v. Ireland, supra* n. 547, paras. 52–54.

[553]   *Saunders v. the United Kingdom, supra* n. 546, paras. 67–75. See also *I.J.L., G.M.R. and A.K.P. v. the United Kingdom, supra* n. 512, paras. 79–83, concerning 3 persons who were tried together with the applicant in the *Saunders* case and *Kansal v. the United Kingdom*, ECtHR 27 April 2004, appl. no. 21413/02, para. 29.

[554]   *Allen v. the United Kingdom*, ECtHR 10 September 2002 (dec.), appl. no. 76574/01, with regard to the requirement to make a declaration of assets to the tax authorities; *Weh v. Austria*, ECtHR 8 July 2004, appl. no. 38544/97, paras. 47–57, where the Court by 4 votes to 3 held that the obligation of the registered car owner to provide information about who had driven a motor vehicle identified by the number plate at a certain time, did not violate Art. 6. It appeared crucial that the link between the applicant's obligation to disclose the driver of the car and possible criminal proceedings for speeding against him was remote and hypothetical.

Court took account of several safeguards designed to respect the rights of the defence. For instance, the fact that the applicant had been warned that adverse inferences might be drawn from this silence, and the fact that the adverse inferences could only be drawn if a failure to express oneself might 'as a matter of common sense' lead to the conclusion that the accused had been guilty and if there existed very strong other evidence against the accused.[555] The Court concluded that there had been no violation of Article 6.[556] Things were different in the *Condron* case, in which the Court held that the trial judge's omission to direct the jury that it could only draw an adverse inference if satisfied that the applicants' silence at the police interview could only sensibly be attributed to their having no answer or none that would stand up to cross-examination, was incompatible with the exercise of their right to remain silent.[557]

A fair trial may imply the right to have the assistance of a lawyer, including during the phase preceding the trial. This aspect will be discussed under paragraph 3(c) of Article 6. Is it also possible to infer a right to free legal aid from the principle of fair hearing? From paragraph 3(c) it might be concluded *a contrario* that this is not the case.[558] In fact, paragraph 3(c) only guarantees this right for criminal proceedings, and even then only 'when the interests of justice so require'. However, if one party does have the means to secure legal aid and the other does not, there is no 'equality of arms' if the latter does not obtain the assistance of a lawyer as well.[559] Above, in section 3.2.c, the view of the Court was mentioned that the mere right of 'access to court' which is implied in Article 6(1), entails the obligation for the Contracting States to make legal aid available, or at least financially possible, if the person in question would otherwise be faced with an insuperable barrier to defend himself adequately. In that context, the Court will make an independent examination of the complexity of the case and other relevant factors such as the applicable rules of evidence and the emotional involvement of the applicant in the outcome of the proceedings.[560] Other expenses, too, for instance those for a translator or an interpreter, may be so onerous that the principle of 'fair trial' is at stake.[561]

The same applies to the question of whether under Article 6(1) the parties are entitled to have witnesses and experts summoned and examined. From

---

[555] *John Murray v. the United Kingdom, supra* n. 82, paras. 44–58. In *Telfner v. Austria*, ECtHR 20 March 2001, appl. no. 33501/96, paras. 15–20, the drawing of adverse inferences was not allowed under Art. 6(2) because there was no other strong evidence.

[556] The same conclusion was reached in *Averill v. the United Kingdom*, ECtHR 6 June 2000, appl. no. 36408/97, paras. 38–52.

[557] *Condron v. the United Kingdom*, ECtHR 2 May 2000, appl. no. 35718/97, paras. 55–62.

[558] See, e.g., appl. no. 6202/73, *X and Y v. the Netherlands*, D&R 1 (1975), p. 66 (71).

[559] See, *mutatis mutandis, A.B. v. Slovakia, supra* n. 64, para. 61.

[560] Appl. no. 9353/81, *Webb v. the United Kingdom*, D&R 33 (1983), p. 133 (138–141).

[561] Report of 18 May 1977, *Luedicke, Belkacem and Koç*, B.27 (1982), p. 26.

the fact that Article 6(3)(d) contains explicit provisions about this for criminal cases, it might be inferred *a contrario* that such a right does not hold good for the parties in civil proceedings. However, here again, the case law recognises the possibility that the court's refusal to have a particular witness summoned by a party to a dispute, or to hear him, constitutes an encroachment on the right to a fair hearing.[562] That right does not require, however, that a national court appoints, at the request of the defence, another expert when the opinion of the court-appointed expert supports the prosecution case.[563]

Finally, an additional element of 'fair hearing' is the requirement that the judicial decision must state the reasons on which it is based. The extent to which the requirement applies depends on 'the nature of the decision' and can only be assessed in the circumstances of each individual case.[564] According to the Court it is, moreover, necessary to take into account the differences existing in the Contracting States with regard to, *inter alia*, the presentation and drafting of judgments.[565] It is clear that the court is not obliged to give a detailed answer to every argument.[566] When a motivation is lacking altogether, the remedies provided for are likely to become illusory.[567] The detail into which the statement of the reasons must go is, therefore, determined by what an effective remedy against the decision requires in each particular case.[568] Noteworthy is also that under Article 6 judges have to motivate their decision not to ask for a preliminary ruling by the Court of Justice of the European Union, even in cases in which they are not obliged to ask for such a ruling.[569]

From this point of departure the practice existing in some countries to provide certain judgments in criminal cases with a motivation only after an appeal has been instituted, seems questionable. However, in the *Zoon* case,

---

[562]   *Sigurthor Arnarsson v. Iceland, supra* n. 518, paras. 31–38. *Cf. Gillissen v. The Netherlands, supra* n. 474, para. 56.

[563]   *Brandstetter v. Austria, supra* n. 478, 12876/87 and 13468/87, para. 46. *G.B. v. France*, ECtHR 2 October 2001, appl. no. 44069/98, paras. 64–70, constitutes an exception, where the court-appointed expert at the trial, to the detriment of the accused, changed his point of view radically after a brief examination of a prior psychiatric report written by another expert.

[564]   See, e.g., *Ruiz Torija v. Spain*, ECtHR 9 December 1994, appl. no. 18390/91, para. 29 and *Hiro Balani v. Spain*, ECtHR 9 December 1994, appl. no. 18064/91, para. 27; *Higgins and Others v. France*, ECtHR 19 February 1998, appl. no. 20124/92, para. 42; *Ajdarić v. Croatia*, ECtHR 13 December 2011, appl. no. 20883/09, para. 34; *cf. Hansen v. Norway*, ECtHR 2 October 2014, appl. no. 15319/09, para. 83.

[565]   *Jokela v. Finland*, ECtHR 21 May 2002, appl. no. 28856/95, para. 72.

[566]   See, e.g., *Van de Hurk v. the Netherlands, supra* n. 462, para. 61; *Ruiz Torija v. Spain, supra* n. 564, para. 29 and *Hiro Balani v. Spain, supra* n. 564, para. 27; *Garcia Ruíz v. Spain, supra* n. 402, para. 26.

[567]   See *Hadjianastassiou v. Greece*, ECtHR 16 December 1992, appl. no. 12945/87, paras. 34–36.

[568]   See *Suominen v. Finland*, ECtHR 1 July 2003, appl. no. 37801/97, paras. 37–38.

[569]   *Ullens de Schooten and Rezabek v. Belgium*, ECtHR 20 September 2011, appl. nos. 3989/07 and 38353/07, para. 62; *Dhahbi v. Italy*, ECtHR 8 April 2014, appl. no. 17120/09, para. 33.

the Court held that it cannot be said that the applicant's rights were unduly affected by the absence of a complete judgment or by the absence from the judgment in abridged form of a detailed enumeration of the items of evidence relied on to ground his conviction.[570] In case a judgment only refers to the wording of the law without any detailed reasons Article 6 may be violated.[571] In dismissing an appeal an appellate court may, in principle, simply endorse the reasons of the lower court's decision. However, in such a case Article 6 requires that the court 'did in fact address the essential issues which were submitted to its jurisdiction and did not merely endorse without further ado the findings reached by the lower court'.[572] In the *Hirvisaari* case, the endorsement by the national court of the reasoning of the Pension Board, which had found the applicant partly capable of working, violated Article 6. Since the applicant's main complaint in his appeal had been the inadequacy of the Pension Board's reasoning, the court should have given proper reasons of its own.[573]

A remarkable situation occurred in the *Schuler-Zgraggen* case. The national court based its decision with regard to the alleged entitlement of the female applicant to an invalidity pension on the mere assumption that 'women give up work when they give birth to a child'. This reasoning amounted to a breach of Article 6 in conjunction with Article 14.[574] In the *Van Kück* case, the applicant claimed that the German court proceedings concerning her claims for reimbursement of medical expenses in respect of gender re-assignment measures had been unfair. In the special circumstances of the case the Court held that the interpretation by the national court of the term 'medical necessity' and evaluation of evidence in this respect had not been reasonable and that the approach in examining the question of whether the applicant had deliberately caused her transsexuality, had not been appropriate. Therefore, the proceedings in question did not satisfy the requirements of a fair hearing.[575]

---

[570] *Zoon v. the Netherlands, supra* n. 450, paras. 32–50 and *infra* 9.3.

[571] *Georgiadis v. Greece, supra* n. 136, paras. 41–43; *Sakkopoulos v. Greece,* ECtHR 15 January 2004, appl. no. 61828/00, paras. 50–52; *Yiarenios v. Greece,* ECtHR 19 February 2004, appl. no. 64413/01, paras. 21–23.

[572] *Helle v. Finland,* ECtHR 19 December 1997, appl. no. 20772/92, para. 60; *Hirvisaari v. Finland,* ECtHR 27 September 2001, appl. no. 49684/99, para. 30.

[573] *Hirvisaari v. Finland, supra* n. 572, paras. 31–32. See also *H.A.L. v. Finland,* ECtHR 7 July 2004, appl. no. 38267/97, paras. 49–52.

[574] *Schuler-Zgraggen v. Switzerland, supra* n. 113, paras. 66–67.

[575] *Van Kück v. Germany, supra* n. 306, paras. 46–64.

5. PUBLIC TRIAL AND PUBLIC PRONOUNCEMENT OF THE JUDGMENT

Article 6(1) requires that the hearing shall be public. In the *Pretto* case, the Court set forth the rationale of this requirement as follows: 'The public character of proceedings before the judicial bodies referred to in Article 6 para. 1 (…) protects litigants against the administration of justice in secret with no public scrutiny; it is also one of the means whereby confidence in the courts, superior and inferior, can be maintained. By rendering the administration of justice visible, publicity contributes to the achievement of the aim of Article 6 para. 1 (…) namely a fair trial, the guarantee of which is one of the fundamental principles of any democratic society, within the meaning of the Convention.'[576]

In addition to the interest which the parties to the dispute may have in a public hearing, it serves a public interest as well: verifiability of and information about, and thus confidence in the administration of justice. This also means that clear reasons must be given for exceptions to providing public access, for example owing to national security or the protection of victims and witnesses.[577] Furthermore, the question arises whether the parties can waive their right to a public hearing to an unlimited degree or, on the contrary, the court may only comply with a request to that effect if one of the grounds explicitly mentioned for this in Article 6 presents itself. In *Le Compte, Van Leuven and De Meyere*[578] and in *H v.* Belgium,[579] the Court seemed to have taken the first position. This was confirmed by the *Håkansson and Sturesson* judgment, where the Court held that 'neither the letter, nor the spirit' of the provision oppose an express or tacit waiver of the right to a public hearing, although the waiver must be made in an unequivocal manner and 'must not run counter to any important public interest'.[580] In this case the Court concluded that a tacit waiver had occurred. The proceedings concerning the lawfulness of an auction sale usually took place *in camera*. For this reason, in the Court's view, the omission of the applicants to ask the competent authorities for a public hearing could be regarded as a waiver of their entitlement to have their case heard in public.[581] The Court has elucidated its point of view in its subsequent case law. A failure to request a hearing is not to be considered a

---

[576]   *Pretto and Others v. Italy, supra* n. 345, para. 21. See also, e.g., *Axen v. Germany*, ECtHR (GC) 22 February 1984, appl. no. 8273/78, para. 25; *Diennet v. France, supra* n. 94, para. 33; *Werner v. Austria, supra* n. 131, para. 45; *Malhous v. Czech Republic, supra* n. 529, para. 55; *Fazliyski v. Bulgaria*, ECtHR 16 April 2013, appl. no. 40908/05, para. 64.

[577]   See, e.g., *Belashev v. Russia*, ECtHR 4 December 2008, appl. no. 28617/03, para. 86.

[578]   *Le Compte, Van Leuven and De Meyere v. Belgium, supra* n. 36, para. 59.

[579]   *H. v. Belgium, supra* n. 87, para. 54.

[580]   *Håkansson and Sturesson v. Sweden, supra* n. 101, para. 66.

[581]   *Ibid.*

waiver, where the law explicitly excludes a hearing,[582] or where, though the law does not contain a special rule, the court's practice is never to hold one.[583] In case the court's practice is not to hold one of their own motion, but where the law explicitly provides for the possibility to request one,[584] or where it is at least the practice to hold one upon a party's request,[585] a failure to request a hearing is considered an unequivocal waiver.

With a view to the public interest which is served by publicity, in particular in criminal cases, it will, however, have to be assumed that there is merely a possibility of waiving the right to a public hearing, not a right to a hearing *in camera*, and that, if a request for a hearing *in camera* is made, the court may refuse this on the ground of the weighing of the interest of the party concerned against the public interest.[586] The court then will, of course, also have to take into account the protection of the private life of the party concerned, as one of the explicitly mentioned grounds of restriction, and also the danger which publicity may constitute for the presumption of innocence protected in the second paragraph.

The text of Article 6 does not contain any qualification of the right to a public hearing as far as the phase of the proceedings is concerned. However, the Court makes a distinction between a trial before a court at first instance and a trial before an appeal court, also with respect to the public interests involved: 'The Court fully recognises the value attaching to the publicity of the proceedings such as those indicated by the Commission (...). However, even where a court of appeal has jurisdiction to review the case both as to facts and as to law, the Court cannot find that Article 6 always requires a right to a public hearing irrespective of the nature of the issues to be decided. The publicity requirement is certainly one of the means whereby confidence in the courts is maintained. However, there are other considerations, including the right to trial within a reasonable time and the related need for expeditious handling of the court's case-load, which must be taken into account in determining the necessity of a public hearing at stages in the proceedings subsequent to the trial at first instance. Provided a public hearing has been held at first instance, the absence of such a hearing before a second or third instance may accordingly be justified by the special features of the proceedings at issue. Thus, leave to appeal proceedings and proceedings involving only questions of law, as opposed to

---

[582] *Diennet v. France, supra* n. 94, para. 34; *A.T. v. Austria*, ECtHR 21 March 2002, appl. no. 32636/96, para. 37.

[583] *Werner v. Austria, supra* n. 131, para. 48; *Gautrin and Others v. France*, ECtHR 20 May 1998, appl. nos. 21257/93, 21258/93, 21259/93 and 21260/93, paras. 38 and 42; *Rushiti v. Austria*, ECtHR 21 March 2000, appl. no. 28389/95, para. 22.

[584] *Zumtobel v. Austria, supra* n. 306, para. 34; *Schuler-Zgraggen v. Switzerland, supra* n. 113, para. 58; *Rolf Gustafson v. Sweden*, ECtHR 1 July 1997, appl. no. 23196/94, para. 47.

[585] *Pauger v. Austria, supra* n. 25, paras. 60–61.

[586] *Håkansson and Sturesson v. Sweden, supra* n. 101, para. 67.

questions of fact, may comply with the requirements of Article 6, although the appellant was not given an opportunity of being heard in person by the appeal or cassation court.'[587]

In the *Tierce and Others* case, the Court added: 'However, where an appellate court has to examine a case to the facts and the law and make a full assessment of the issue of guilt or innocence, it cannot determine the issue without the direct assessment of the evidence given in person by the accused for the purpose of proving that he did not commit the act allegedly constituting a criminal offence. The principle that hearings should be held in public entails the right for the accused to give evidence in person to an appellate court.'[588]

As far as the publicity requirement is concerned, these quotations do *per se* not raise any difficulty. However, the last clause in the Swedish cases, 'although the appellant was not given an opportunity of being heard in person by the appeal or cassation court', and the statement in the *Tierce and Others* case that the right to a public hearing entails the right to give evidence in person to an appellate court, may cause confusion. The question whether a person should be heard in person has strictly speaking nothing to do with the publicity requirement. In fact, the Court confuses the right to a public hearing – that means a public *trial* – with the right to be heard in person. In fact, in these cases the crucial question did not concern the publicity requirement but appeared to be whether the court of appeal could properly decide to examine the case without the applicants having a right to present their arguments at a hearing.[589]

The form of publicity to be given to the judgment under domestic law must be assessed in the light of the special features of the proceedings.[590] For pragmatic reasons the opinion would seem to be justified that the requirement of a public judgment has been complied with if during a public session the reading is confined to that of the operational part of the judgment,[591] and that even this may be omitted if the operational part contains no more than the determination that the appeal has been rejected or the case is referred back.[592] In that case the parties must receive a copy of the text of the judgment as soon as possible,

---

[587] *Helmers v. Sweden, supra* n. 157, para. 36; *Jan-Åke Andersson v. Sweden, supra* n. 346, para. 27 and *Fejde v. Sweden, supra* n. 346, para. 31. See further, e.g., *Bulut v. Austria, supra* n. 469, paras. 41–42.

[588] *Tierce and Others v. San Marino, supra* n. 518, para. 95.

[589] *Helmers v. Sweden, supra* n. 157, para. 38; *Jan-Åke Andersson v. Sweden, supra* n. 346, para. 29; and *Fejde v. Sweden, supra* n. 346, para. 33; *Tierce and Others v. San Marino, supra* n. 518, paras. 99–102; the question whether a person has the right to be present at the trial is discussed *supra* 4.4.

[590] See, e.g., with regard to cassation proceedings and proceedings before the supreme court *Pretto and Others v. Italy, supra* n. 345, para. 27 and *Axen v. Germany, supra* n. 576, para. 31; *Sutter v. Switzerland, supra* n. 347, para. 34 (proceedings before the Swiss Military Court of Cassation).

[591] *Pretto and Others v. Italy, supra* n. 345, paras. 25–28.

[592] Report of 14 December 1979, *Le Compte, Van Leuven and De Meyere*, B.38, p. 24; report of 15 March 1985, *Adler*, D&R 46 (1986), p. 36 (45).

while the publication of those judgments in which legal questions of a more public interest are at issue, is also of special importance for the verifiability.[593] In case proceedings have been conducted in chambers in order to protect the privacy of children and parties, the pronouncement of the judgment in public may to a large extent frustrate these aims. Despite the fact that Article 6 permits restrictions exclusively with respect to the public nature of the proceedings, not with respect to the public nature of the judgment, the Court has held that in such a case it suffices that anyone who can establish an interest may consult or obtain a copy of the judgment, as long as cases of special interest are routinely published, to enable the public to study the judgments.[594] A failure to deliver the judgment publicly may be remedied on appeal.[595]

In the *Biryukov* case, the Court reiterates clearly the importance of pronouncing a judgment in open court: 'The Court considers that the object pursued by Article 6 §1 in this context – namely, to ensure scrutiny of the judiciary by the public with a view to safeguarding the right to a fair trial – was not achieved in the present case, in which the reasons which would make it possible to understand why the applicant's claims had been rejected were inaccessible to the public.'[596]

Only pronouncing the operative part in public and not the considerations that led to the judgment, constitutes a violation of Article 6. In the case in question, however, it was of significance that third parties were unable to examine the judgment and that during the public hearing only the operative part was read out.

With respect to the possibilities of restricting publicity the following observations may be made. Although in some cases the Court has examined *ex officio* whether one of the exceptions had been applicable,[597] it may be presumed that it is for the national authorities to invoke explicitly the exceptions of Article 6.[598] On the one hand, the Court has shown to be willing to leave the national authorities, and specifically the national courts, a certain 'margin of appreciation' in the assessment of the question whether there is any reason for application of one of the restrictions, as is the case with respect to the grounds of restriction included in other provisions of the Convention.[599] On the other

---

[593] See *ibid.*, p. 24 and p. 45, respectively.

[594] *B. and P. v. the United Kingdom*, ECtHR 24 April 2001, appl. nos. 36337/97 and 35974/97, paras. 45–49.

[595] *Lamanna v. Austria, supra* n. 121, paras. 30–34, and implicitly *Werner v. Austria, supra* n. 131, paras. 54–60 and *Szücs v. Austria, supra* n. 126, paras. 43–48.

[596] *Biryukov v. Russia*, ECtHR 17 January 2008, appl. no. 14810/02, para. 45.

[597] See *Serre v. France, supra* n. 94, para. 22; *Stefanelli v. San Marino*, ECtHR 8 February 2000, appl. no. 35396/97, para. 21.

[598] This point of view seems to be confirmed by *Stallinger and Kuso v. Austria*, ECtHR 23 April 1997, appl. nos. 14696/89 and 14697/89, para. 51; *Gautrin and Others v. France, supra* n. 583, para. 42.

[599] See also *supra* 3.6.c.

hand, the Court has also itself shown to be prepared to make an independent examination of the reasons for the restriction,[600] in which context the Court is not prepared to accept simply a developed practice, but requires that it be set forth specifically for each case which ground of restriction is invoked.[601] However, in principle, it is not inconsistent with Article 6 for a state to designate an entire class of cases, e.g., proceedings concerning minors, as an exception to the general rule.[602] In fact the opposite problem occurred in *T. and V. v. the United Kingdom*, concerning two 11-year-old boys who had been accused of abduction and murder. The applicants complained that they had been deprived of the opportunity to participate effectively in the criminal proceedings because of the massive press attention in and outside court and the fact that the trial had been conducted with the formality of an adult criminal trial, albeit modified to a certain extent in view of the defendants' age. The Government disputed that the public nature of the trial breached the applicants' rights and stressed that the publicity of the trial ensured the fairness of the proceedings. The Court took into account that, according to psychiatric evidence, the ability of the applicants to understand the proceedings in court and to instruct their lawyers was limited and held it 'highly unlikely that the applicants would have felt sufficiently uninhibited in the tense courtroom and under public scrutiny' to consult with their lawyers during the trial or that they would have been capable outside the courtroom to cooperate with them and give them relevant information for the defence. Thus, the defendants' rights to participate effectively in the proceedings had been violated.[603]

In relation to the restriction ground of the protection of public order one is inclined to think of the prevention of disorder. When Article 14 of the International Covenant on Civil and Political Rights was drafted, this interpretation was indeed advocated, on the part of Great Britain, and on that ground objections were raised – in vain – to the addition of the French term *ordre public* in the English text.[604] Now that the text of Article 6 in its present form has been adopted in terms equal to those of Article 14 of the Covenant, a comparison with Articles 10(2) and 11(2), where for the protection of public order the English text has 'the prevention of disorder' and the French text '*la*

---

[600] See, e.g., *Le Compte, Van Leuven and De Meyere v. Belgium, supra* n. 36, paras. 59–61; *Albert and Le Compte v. Belgium, supra* n. 94, paras. 34–37.

[601] *Engel and Others v. the Netherlands, supra* n. 209, para. 89. See also *Eisenstecken v. Austria*, ECtHR 3 October 2000, appl. no. 29477/95, paras. 34–35.

[602] *B. and P. v. the United Kingdom, supra* n. 594, para. 39.

[603] Judgments of 16 December 1999, paras. 80–89 and paras. 81–91, respectively. See also *S.C. v. the United Kingdom, supra* n. 299, paras. 27–37, concerning an 11-year-old boy with limited intellectual capacity, where the Court held that he should have been tried in a specialist tribunal which was able to give full consideration to and make proper allowance for the handicaps under which he laboured and to adapt its procedure accordingly.

[604] See E/CN.4/SR.318, p. 10: 'the proper conception was that closed hearings could be held with a view to preventing disorder'.

défense de l'orde', renders it difficult to maintain the British interpretation, although, on the other hand, the English and the French text of Article 9(2) show that the drafters have not been very consistent in this matter. However, this may be, the prevention of disorder in the courtroom may in any case be brought under the ground 'the interests of justice'.[605] What then does 'public order' mean in this context? In the *Le Compte, Van Leuven and De Meyere* Case, the Belgian Government invoked this ground, alleging that publicity of the medical disciplinary cases might lead to violation of medical professional secrecy. The Commission indeed examined this aspect under that denominator.[606] This seems to point in the direction of public order in the sense of *ordre public*. Medical professional secrecy was also invoked in the *Diennet* case, where the French Government tried to justify the fact that disciplinary proceedings against a medical practitioner had been held *in camera*. However, according to the Court the proceedings in question concerned only 'the method of consultation by correspondence' adopted by the applicant and thus, in principle, not the private life of patients of the applicant.[607]

So far, the interest of national security has hardly played a part, if at all, in the Strasbourg case law with respect to the public nature of the trial, but it is easy to conceive of situations in which proceedings deal with state secrets or other information that is security-sensitive. The court will then have to form an independent opinion about this. Everything that the authorities prefer to be kept secret does not for that reason alone concern national security.

Cases involving the protection of the private life of the parties, except for cases in which the interests of minors are involved,[608] require proceedings *in camera* only if the parties appear to appreciate such protection.[609]

The last ground of restriction – the interests of justice – is explicitly left to the opinion of the domestic court concerned. On occasion it may be necessary to limit the public nature of the proceedings to protect, for instance, the safety and privacy of witnesses; they, too, can claim a 'fair trial'.[610] Here again, however, an ultimate supervision by the Strasbourg Court is fitting. The interests of justice may also require that the space available for the public does not become overcrowded and that agitators are excluded. But, on the other hand, the interest of publicity requires that the administration of justice takes place at locations where reasonable accommodation for the public is available.

---

[605] See *Riepan v. Austria, supra* n. 373, para. 34, where the Court held that in exceptional cases the public may be excluded from the trial for security concerns.

[606] See the report of 14 December 1979, B.38 (1984), pp. 43–44. See also the report of 14 December 1981, *Albert and Le Compte*, B.50 (1986), pp. 40–41.

[607] *Diennet v. France, supra* n. 94, para. 34.

[608] *B. and P. v. the United Kingdom, supra* n. 594, paras. 35–41.

[609] Thus, apparently also the Commission in its report in the *Albert and Le Compte* Case, B.50, pp. 40–41.

[610] See on this *infra* 9.5.

If the trial takes place outside a regular courtroom, to which the general public in principle has no access (e.g. a prison), the national authorities have to take compensatory measures in order to ensure that the public and the media are duly informed about the place of the hearing and are granted effective access.[611]

6. REASONABLE-TIME REQUIREMENT

6.1. INTRODUCTION

Article 6 stipulates in its first paragraph that the hearing of the case by the court must take place 'within a reasonable time' (*dans un délai raisonnable*). Just as with regard to these same words in Article 5(3) this raises the difficult question as to what criteria have to be applied for the assessment of what is reasonable and also what period has to be taken into account in this respect.

In the case of Article 5(3) it is in any event clear what is to be considered as the beginning of the relevant period: this is the moment of the arrest. The rationale of that provision is that the detention on remand does not last longer than is strictly necessary. The purpose of the reasonable-time requirement of Article 6(1), however, is to guarantee that within a reasonable time, and by means of a judicial decision, an end is put to the insecurity into which a person finds himself as to his civil-law position or on account of a criminal charge against him; in the interest of the person in question as well as of legal certainty. This rationale entails that the provision also applies in cases where there is no question of detention on remand.[612]

The judgments with regard to the reasonable-time requirement are quite numerous. However, around the middle of the 1980s the main lines seem to have been charted.

6.2. RELEVANT PERIOD

a. Dies a quo

In the determination of the relevant period the jurisdiction *ratione temporis* must be taken into account. Thus, in the case of an individual complaint concerning proceedings which were already in progress at the moment the state concerned became a party to the Convention – or recognised the individual's

---

[611] *Riepan v. Austria, supra* n. 373, paras. 28–31.
[612] For the relationship between the two provisions, see *Stögmüller v. Austria*, ECtHR 10 November 1969, appl. no. 1602/62, paras. 4–5.

right of complaint under former Article 25 – only the length of the period from that moment can be taken into account. However, for the assessment of the reasonableness of that period the stage at which the proceedings were at that moment is also taken into consideration.[613]

With respect to the determination of civil rights and obligations, the beginning of the period is in general taken to be the moment at which the proceedings concerned are instituted[614] or at which, within the framework of other proceedings, such a right or obligation is put forward in a defence. If prior to the judicial proceedings another action, such as an administrative objection[615] or a request for formal confirmation,[616] must have been brought, the beginning is shifted to the moment of that action.[617] A negotiation phase preceding the proceedings, however, is not counted as part of the relevant period.[618]

With respect to criminal cases the Court has held that the beginning of the relevant period must be taken as the moment at which a 'criminal charge' is brought, since it is only from that moment that the 'determination of (…) any criminal charge' can be involved.[619] However, the rationale mentioned above implies that the period does not in all cases begin at the moment at which the person in question is officially indicted. Even before that he may have been aware of the fact that he is suspected of a criminal offence, so that from that moment he has an interest in a speedy decision about this suspicion being made by the court. This is quite evident in those cases where an arrest precedes the moment of the formal charge.[620] It is, therefore, important here as well that in

---

[613]   See, e.g., *Foti and Others v. Italy*, ECtHR 10 December 1982, appl. nos. 7604/76, 7719/76, 7781/77 and 7913/77, para. 53; *Martins Moreira v. Portugal*, ECtHR 26 October 1988, appl. no. 11371/85, para. 43; *Mitap and Müftüoglu v. Turkey*, ECtHR 25 March 1996, appl. nos. 15530/89 and 15531/89, para. 31; *Kalashnikov v. Russia*, ECtHR 15 July 2002, appl. no. 47095/99, para. 124.

[614]   See, e.g., *Scopelliti v. Italy*, ECtHR 23 November 1993, appl. no. 15511/89, para. 18; *Muti v. Italy*, ECtHR 23 March 1994, appl. no. 14146/88, para. 12; *Katte Klitsche de la Grange v. Italy*, ECtHR 27 October 1994, appl. no. 12539/86, para. 50.

[615]   *König v. Germany, supra* n. 11, paras. 28 and 101.

[616]   *Schouten and Meldrum v. the Netherlands, supra* n. 128, paras. 61–62.

[617]   *Cf.* the *Vallee* Case, *Vallee v. France,* ECtHR 26 April 1994, appl. no. 22121/93, para. 133, where the submission of the preliminary claim for compensation to the administrative authority, required under national law, constituted the starting point of the relevant period. See also *Cazenave de la Roche v. France*, ECtHR 9 June 1998, appl. no. 25549/94, para. 46; *Kress v. France, supra* n. 470, para. 90.

[618]   *Lithgow and Others v. the United Kingdom*, ECtHR (GC) 8 July 1986, appl. nos. 9006/80, 9262/81, 9263/81, 9265/81, 9266/81, 9313/81 and 9405/81, para. 199. See, however, also *Phocas v. France*, ECtHR 23 April 1996, appl. no. 17869/91, para. 69, concerning, *inter alia*, negotiations, expressly recognised by law, prior to formal expropriation proceedings before a court. The Court did assess whether the duration of the preliminary proceedings was reasonable.

[619]   *Neumeister v. Austria, supra* n. 374, para. 18; *Deweer v. Belgium, supra* n. 185, para. 46.

[620]   In *Wemhoff v. Germany*, ECtHR 27 June 1968, appl. no. 2122/64, para. 19, the Court assumed that the 2 moments coincided. See further, e.g., *B v. Austria*, ECtHR 28 March 1990, appl. no. 11968/86, paras. 9 and 48; *Alimena v. Italy*, ECtHR 19 February 1991, appl. no. 11910/85, para. 15; *Dobbertin v. France*, ECtHR 25 February 1993, appl. no. 13089/87, paras. 9 and 138. In the

the Strasbourg case law an autonomous meaning is assigned to the concept of 'charge', the starting point being that a substantive and not a formal concept of 'charge' must be used because of the great importance of the principle of a fair trial for a democratic society.[621] As the Court held in the *Foti* case and in the *Corigliano* case: 'Whilst "charge" (…) may in general be defined as the official notification given to an individual by the competent authority of an allegation that he has committed a criminal offence, it may in some instances take the form of other measures which carry the implication of such an allegation and which likewise substantially affect the situation of the suspect.'[622]

Thus, the existence of a 'charge' is not always dependent on an official act.[623] Examples of such 'other measures' are the search of the person's home,[624] the request that a person's immunity be lifted[625] and the moment the person concerned is informed by the tax authority of its intention to impose additional taxes and tax surcharges on him.[626] However, the imposition of fiscal penalties on companies does not imply that the managing director of the companies is charged personally.[627] In some cases the 'charge' does not constitute the *dies a quo* of the relevant period: if the accused did not receive the official notification and was tried in absence, one has to presume that there exists a 'charge',[628] but the reasonable-time requirement is not at stake (yet), because the accused did not live under the pressure of being prosecuted.[629] The period that an accused, who is aware of the 'charge', is on the run, is excluded from the calculation of the relevant period.[630] If a criminal act is of an ongoing nature, the reasonable time period starts from the time the crime was discovered and/or from the time when the suspect becomes aware that the authorities are considering him. The

---

latter case, there seems to be a clear difference between the moment of arrest and the formal 'charge'. The Court took the moment of arrest as a starting point.

[621] See *supra* 2.1.

[622] *Foti and Others v. Italy, supra* n. 613, para. 52 and *Corigliano v. Italy, supra* n. 193, para. 34.

[623] Initially the Court took a formal criterion to determine the starting point of the relevant period: *Neumeister v. Austria, supra* n. 374, para. 18. Subsequently, it developed a substantive approach in *Eckle v. Germany, supra* n. 190, para. 73, which culminated in *Foti and Others v. Italy, supra* n. 613, para. 52 and *Corigliano v. Italy, supra* n. 613, 8304/78, para. 34.

[624] See, e.g., *Diamantides v. Greece*, ECtHR 23 October 2003, appl. no. 71563/01, para. 21; *Lopez Sole y Martin de Vargas v. Spain*, ECtHR 28 October 2003, appl. no. 61133/00, para. 26.

[625] *Frau v. Italy, supra* n. 191, para. 14.

[626] *Västberga Taxi Aktiebolag and Vulic v. Sweden, supra* n. 271, para. 104 and *Janosevic v. Sweden*, ECtHR 23 July 2002, appl. no. 34619/97, para. 92.

[627] *Hozee v. the Netherlands*, ECtHR 22 May 1998, appl. no. 21961/93, paras. 44–45.

[628] *Colozza v. Italy, supra* n. 189, para. 29. The applicant was sentenced by default and did have, according to the Court, a right to a 'fresh determination of the merits of the charge'. *Cf.* also *S.H.K. v. Bulgaria*, ECtHR 23 October 2003, appl. no. 37355/97, para. 26.

[629] This consequence does not fully correspond with the definition of 'charge' as cited from the *Foti* judgment. The contradiction can be lifted by deleting the word 'likewise'.

[630] *Girolami v. Italy*, ECtHR 19 February 1991, appl. no. 13324/87, para. 15; *Boddaert v. Belgium*, ECtHR 12 October 1992, appl. no. 12919/87, para. 35; *Bunkate v. the Netherlands, supra*, n. 430, para. 21.

uncertainty, after all, commences from the time the suspect becomes aware of the criminal proceedings.[631]

b. Dies ad quem

The above-mentioned rationale of the reasonable-time requirement of Article 6 entails that the end of the period to be taken into consideration is the moment at which the uncertainty concerning the legal position of the person in question has ended. In civil proceedings that is the moment the asserted legal position is determined in a final way.[632] That is not, therefore, the moment at which the hearing in court starts, but the moment at which the decision is taken at highest instance[633] or has become final through the expiration of the time-limit for appeal.[634] Thus, as far as appeal or cassation proceedings 'are capable of affecting the outcome of the dispute', these proceedings must be taken into account in determining the relevant period.[635] Moreover, even stages subsequent to a judgment on the merits, such as enforcement proceedings[636] and proceedings concerning costs,[637] fall under the scope of the reasonable-time requirement. However, the lapse of time caused by preliminary proceedings under Article 267 of the Treaty on the Functioning of the European Union (TFEU) before the Court of Justice of the European Union is not taken into consideration in the assessment of the length of the proceedings.[638] The same holds good for the institution of extraordinary remedies.

The Court has chosen the same approach in 'criminal' cases. As the Court held in its *Wemhoff* judgment: 'there is (…) no reason why the protection given to the persons concerned against the delays of the courts should end at the first

---

[631] *Hamer v. Belgium*, ECtHR 27 November 2007, appl. no. 21861/03, para. 61. See also *Mathy v. Belgium*, ECtHR 24 April 2008, appl. no. 12066/06.

[632] See, e.g., *Di Pede v. Italy*, ECtHR 26 September 1996, appl. no. 15797/89, para. 22 and *Zappia v. Italy*, ECtHR 26 September 1996, appl. no. 24295/94, para. 18; *Pérez de Rada Cavanilles v. Spain*, *supra* n. 378, para. 39.

[633] See, e.g., *Vocaturo v. Italy*, ECtHR 24 May 1991, appl. no. 11891/85, para. 14; *Salerno v. Italy*, *supra* n. 13, para. 18.

[634] See, e.g., *Pugliese v. Italy (No. 2)*, ECtHR 19 February 1991, appl. no. 11671/85, para. 16; *Diana v. Italy*, ECtHR 27 February 1992, appl. no. 11898/85, para. 14.

[635] See, e.g., *Poiss v. Austria*, *supra* n. 63, para. 52; *Acquaviva v. France*, ECtHR 21 November 1995, appl. no. 19248/91, para. 52. The same holds good with regard to proceedings before a Consitutional Court: see, e.g., *Ruiz-Mateos v. Spain*, *supra* n. 106, para. 35; *Probstmeier v. Germany*, ECtHR 1 July 1997, appl. no. 20950/92, paras. 46 and 48 and *Pammel v. Germany*, *supra* n. 338, paras. 51 and 53.

[636] See, e.g., *Silva Pontes v. Portugal*, ECtHR 23 March 1994, appl. no. 14940/89, paras. 35–36; *Hornsby v. Greece*, *supra* n. 281, para. 40; *Nuutinen v. Finland,* ECtHR 7 June 2000, appl. no. 32842/96, para. 109.

[637] *Robins v. the United Kingdom*, *supra* n. 66, para. 28.

[638] *Pafitis v. Greece*, ECtHR 26 February 1998, appl. no. 20323/92, para. 95.

hearing in a trial: unwarranted adjournments or excessive delays on the part of trial courts are also to be feared.'[639]

The determination of the charge, also that by, for example, acquittal or dismissal, must be final.[640] As far as convictions are concerned the determination of the penalty affords certainty to the accused,[641] and then only at the moment at which he can reasonably be assumed to have been informed of the final verdict and its motivation.[642] The decision to refrain from further prosecution may also imply the final determination of the 'charge'.[643]

6.3. REASONABLE TIME

After the length of the relevant period has been established, it must be determined whether this period is to be regarded as reasonable. In many cases the Court only makes an overall assessment,[644] while in other cases it assesses the lapse of time in each stage of the proceedings.[645] The reasonableness cannot be judged in the abstract but has to be assessed in view of the circumstances of each individual case.[646] The interests of the person concerned in as prompt a decision as possible will have to be weighed against the demands of a careful examination of the case and a proper conduct of the proceedings.[647]

According to established case law, when assessing the reasonableness of the relevant period the Court applies, in particular, three criteria: (1) the complexity of the case; (2) the conduct of the applicant; and (3) the conduct of the authorities concerned. However, in an increasing number of cases the Court applies, in connection with the conduct of the authorities, a fourth criterion: (4) the importance of what is at stake for the applicant.[648]

---

[639] *Wemhoff v. Germany, supra* n. 620, para. 18.

[640] See, e.g., *Pugliese v. Italy (No. 1), supra* n. 189, para. 18; *Viezzer v. Italy,* ECtHR 19 February 1991, appl. no. 12598/86, para. 17; *Angelucci v. Italy,* ECtHR 19 February 1991, appl. no. 12666/87, para. 15.

[641] *Eckle v. Germany, supra* n. 190, para. 77.

[642] Report of 8 May 1984, *Vallon,* pp. 22–23.

[643] *S.H.K. v. Bulgaria, supra* n. 628, para. 27.

[644] See, e.g., *Colacioppo v. Italy,* ECtHR 19 February 1991, appl. no. 13593/88, para. 15; *Venditelli v. Italy, supra* n. 192, para. 22; *G.J. v. Luxembourg,* ECtHR 26 October 2000, appl. no. 21156/93, paras. 28–36; *Janssen v. Germany,* ECtHR 20 December 2001, appl. no. 23959/94, paras. 40–53.

[645] See, e.g., *Scopelliti v. Italy, supra* n. 614, paras. 22–26; *Silva Pontes v. Portugal, supra* n. 636, paras. 40–41; *Comingersoll S.A. v. Portugal,* ECtHR 6 April 2000, appl. no. 35382/97, para. 22.

[646] See, e.g., *Santilli v. Italy,* ECtHR 19 February 1991, appl. no. 11634/85, para. 20 and *Maj v. Italy,* ECtHR 19 February 1991, appl. no. 13087/87, para. 15; *Rajcevic v. Croatia,* ECtHR 23 July 2002, appl. no. 56773/00, para. 36.

[647] See, e.g., *H v. the United Kingdom, supra* n. 117, paras. 71–86; *X v. France, supra* n. 120, para. 32; *Silva Pontes v. Portugal, supra* n. 636, para. 39.

[648] See, e.g., *Abdoella v. the Netherlands,* ECtHR 25 November 1992, appl. no. 12728/87, para. 24; *Styranowski v. Poland,* ECtHR 30 October 1998, appl. no. 28616/95, para. 47; *Humen v. Poland, supra* n. 136, para. 60; *Niederböster v. Germany,* ECtHR 27 February 2003, appl. no.

The question of whether a case is complex is, in general, hard to answer. The Court has attached importance to several factors such as the nature of the facts to be established;[649] the number of accused persons[650] and witnesses;[651] the number of defendants and voluminous evidence;[652] the need to obtain the file of a trial conducted abroad;[653] the joinder of the case to other cases;[654] the intervention of other persons in the procedure;[655] and the need to create a special computer program.[656] The complexity may concern questions of fact as well as legal issues.[657] For example, an investigation into a criminal organisation can complicate a case,[658] or the fact that items in a file have to be translated all the time.[659] The difficult estimation of the damage, on the other hand, only contributes to a small extent to the complexity of the case.[660]

An attitude or behaviour of the party in question which led to a delay, weakens his complaint about that delay.[661] However, an accused person is not required to cooperate actively in expediting the proceedings which may lead to his own conviction.[662] This may be different for parties to civil proceedings.[663] A party to proceedings cannot be blamed for making use of his right to lodge an appeal.[664] It is evident that this prolongs the proceedings, but this prolongation, too, must stand the test of reasonableness.[665]

39547/98, para. 39; *Jablonska v. Poland*, ECtHR 9 March 2004, appl. no. 60225/00, para. 39; *Tsikakis v. Germany*, ECtHR 10 February 2011, appl. no. 1521/06, paras. 64 and 68.

[649] See, e.g., *Triggiani v. Italy*, ECtHR 19 February 1991, appl. no. 13509/88, para. 17; *Wiesinger v. Austria*, ECtHR 30 October 1991, appl. no. 11796/85, para. 55; *Vorrasi v. Italy*, ECtHR 27 February 1992, appl. no. 12706/87, para. 17; *Dobbertin v. France, supra* n. 620, para. 42.

[650] *Angelucci v. Italy, supra* n. 640, para. 15.

[651] *Andreucci v. Italy*, ECtHR 27 February 1992, appl. no. 12955/87, para. 17.

[652] *Maton v. Poland*, ECtHR 9 June 2009, appl. no. 30279/07, para. 25.

[653] *Manzoni v. Italy*, ECtHR 19 February 1991, appl. no. 11804/85, para. 18.

[654] *Diana v. Italy, supra* n. 634, para. 17.

[655] *Manieri v. Italy*, ECtHR 27 February 1992, appl. no. 12053/86, para. 18.

[656] *Rösslhuber v. Austria*, ECtHR 28 November 2000, appl. no. 32869/96, para. 27.

[657] *Lorenzi, Bernardini, and Gritti v. Italy*, ECtHR 27 February 1992, appl. no. 13301/87, para. 16; *Katte Klitsche de la Grange v. Italy, supra* n. 614, para. 55.

[658] *Sevim v. Turkey*, ECtHR 5 January 2010, appl. nos. 7540/07 and 7859/07; *Yeşilmen v. Turkey*, ECtHR 16 February 2010, appl. no. 41481/05; and *Celik and Abatay v. Turkey*, ECtHR 29 November 2011, appl. no. 45490/05.

[659] *Amurchanian v. Poland*, ECtHR 19 June 2007, appl. no. 8174/02.

[660] *Tănase v. Romania*, ECtHR 12 May 2009, appl. no. 5269/02.

[661] See, e.g., *Ringeisen v. Austria, supra* n. 39, para. 110; *Eckle v. Germany, supra* n. 190, para. 82; *I.A. v. France*, ECtHR 23 September 1998, appl. no. 28213/95, para. 121; *Barfuss v. Czech Republic*, ECtHR 31 July 2000, appl. no. 35848/97, para. 81.

[662] See, e.g., *Eckle v. Germany, supra* n. 190, para. 82; *Dobbertin v. France, supra* n. 620, para. 43; *Zana v. Turkey, supra* n. 514, para. 79; *Veliyev v. Russia*, ECtHR 24 June 2010, appl. no. 24202/05, para. 177.

[663] *Muti v. Italy, supra* n. 614, para. 16.

[664] See, e.g., *Eckle v. Germany, supra* n. 190, para. 82. *Cf.* also *Katte Klitsche de la Grange v. Italy, supra* n. 614, para. 56. The applicant had applied to the Court of Cassation for a preliminary ruling on jurisdiction of the lower court. Although he could have made a subsequent appeal, his conduct was not open to criticism.

[665] *Lechner and Hess v. Austria*, ECtHR 23 April 1987, appl. no. 9316/81, para. 59.

With regard to the third criterion, the conduct of the authorities, only delays attributable to the state may cause a violation of the reasonable-time requirement.[666] In particular, the efforts the judicial authorities have made to expedite the proceedings as much as possible are an important factor.[667] A special duty rests upon the court concerned to see to it that all those who play a role in the proceedings do their utmost to avoid any unnecessary delay. This holds good as well in criminal as in civil cases, where the initiative in the proceedings in principle may be left to the parties.[668] In the *Capuano* case, the Italian Government drew attention to the fact that the delays in the proceedings at first instance, which lasted for more than six years, were attributable to the experts, who filed their opinions too late. The Court held the court concerned responsible for the delays in preparing expert opinions in proceedings under the court's supervision.[669] In the *Idrocalce* and *Tumminelli* cases, the Court reached the same conclusion with reference to the delays in hearing witnesses.[670] If in a criminal case with two accused persons one of them retards the case, the prosecutor must separate the cases, if possible, in order that the other accused does not become the victim of the delay.[671] Legislation or a judicial practice placing obstacles in the way of a plaintiff for a prompt institution of proceedings, as well as legislation enabling him to leave the other party for a long time in uncertainty as to whether or not an action will be brought, without a reasonably short term of limitation preventing this, does not satisfy Article 6(1). On the other hand, the mere fact that the national authorities fail to comply with legal time-limits is in itself not contrary to Article 6(1).[672]

Under the fourth criterion, the importance of what is at stake for the applicant, the Court pays attention to special interests which may be involved. Thus, in *H v. the United Kingdom*, which concerned the length of the proceedings instituted by the applicant regarding her claimed access to her child, who had been entrusted to the care of a local authority, the Court put special emphasis on the importance of what was at stake for the applicant in the proceedings in question. Not only were these proceedings decisive for her future relations with

---

[666] See, e.g., *Vernillo v. France*, ECtHR 20 February 1991, appl. no. 11889/85, para. 14; *Proszak v. Poland*, ECtHR 16 December 1997, appl. no. 25086/94, para. 40; *Humen v. Poland, supra* n. 136, para. 66.

[667] See, e.g., *König v. Germany, supra* n. 11, paras. 104–105; *B. v. Austria, supra* n. 194, para. 54; *Silva Pontes v. Portugal, supra* n. 636, para. 39; *Sociedade de Construcoes Martins & Vieira Lda. and Others v. Portugal*, appl. nos 56637/10, 59856/10, 72525/10, 7646/11 and 12592/11, paras. 53–59.

[668] *Vernillo v. France, supra* n. 666, para. 30.

[669] *Capuano v. Italy*, ECtHR 25 June 1987, appl. no. 9381/81, para. 30. See also *Nibbio v. Italy*, ECtHR 26 February 1992, appl. no. 12854/87, para. 18; *Scopelliti v. Italy, supra* n. 614, para. 23.

[670] *Idrocalce S.R.L. v. Italy*, ECtHR 27 February 1992, appl. no. 12088/86, para. 18 and *Tumminelli v. Italy*, ECtHR 27 February 1992, appl. no. 13362/87, para. 17. See also *Cooperativa Parco Cuma v. Italy*, ECtHR 27 February 1992, appl. no. 12145/86, para. 18.

[671] Appl. no. 6541/74, *Bonnechaux*, D&R 3 (1976), p. 86 (87).

[672] *G. v. Italy*, ECtHR 27 February 1992, appl. no. 12787/87, para. 17.

her child, but they also had a particular quality of irreversibility, involving as they did what the High Court graphically described as the 'statutory guillotine' of adoption. In these circumstances the Court expected exceptional diligence on the part of the authorities.[673] Subsequently the Court has held that a particular diligence is required in cases concerning civil status and capacity,[674] employment disputes,[675] including pension disputes,[676] and determinations of compensation for the victims of road accidents[677] and for persons infected with HIV as the result of blood transfusion at hospitals.[678] Moreover, the (old) age of the person concerned may urge for swift proceedings.[679] Special diligence is also required in cases where a person is detained pending the determination of the criminal charge against him.[680]

Overburdening of the judiciary in general is not recognised as an excuse, since the Contracting States have the duty to organise the administration of justice in such a way that the various courts can meet the requirements of Article 6.[681] According to constant case law Contracting States are not liable in the event of a temporary backlog of business in their courts, provided that they take, with the requisite promptness, remedial action to deal with an exceptional situation of this kind. The measures taken are assessed as to their effectiveness and it is also ascertained whether they have been taken in good time;[682] measures

---

[673] *H. v. the United Kingdom, supra* n. 117, para. 85. See also in a child abduction case *Hoholm v. Slovakia*, ECtHR 13 January 2015, appl. no. 35632/13, para. 51.

[674] *Bock v. Germany*, ECtHR 29 March 1989, appl. no. 11118/84, para. 49. See also, e.g., *Taiuti v. Italy*, ECtHR 27 February 1992, appl. no. 12238/86, para. 18; *Maciariello v. Italy*, ECtHR 27 February 1992, appl. no. 12284/86, para. 18; and *Gana v. Italy*, ECtHR 27 February 1992, appl. no. 13024/87, para. 17.

[675] See, e.g., *Obermeier v. Austria, supra* n. 303, para. 72; *Vocaturo v. Italy, supra* n. 633, para. 17; *Davies v. the United Kingdom*, ECtHR 16 July 2002, appl. no. 42007/98, para. 26.

[676] *Nibbio v. Italy, supra* n. 669, para. 18 and *Borgese v. Italy*, ECtHR 26 February 1992, appl. no. 12870/87, para. 18; *Ruotolo v. Italy*, ECtHR 27 February 1992, appl. no. 12460/86, para. 17; *H.T. v. Germany*, ECtHR 11 October 2001, appl. no. 38073/97, para. 37.

[677] See, e.g., *Martins Moreira v. Portugal, supra* n. 613, para. 46; *Silva Pontes v. Portugal, supra* n. 636, para. 39; *Signe v. France*, ECtHR 14 October 2003, appl. no. 55875/00, paras. 28 and 38.

[678] See, e.g., *X. v. France, supra* n. 120, para. 32; *A. and Others v. Denmark*, ECtHR 8 February 1996, appl. no. 20826/92, para. 78. *Cf.* also *Dewicka v. Poland,* ECtHR 4 April 2000, appl. no. 38670/97, paras. 55–56, with regard to the installation of a telephone line in the apartment of an old, disabled woman.

[679] *Jablonska v. Poland, supra* n. 648, para. 43; *Krzak v. Poland*, ECtHR 6 April 2004, appl. no. 51515/99, para. 42.

[680] Initially, the Court took this position with regard to the reasonable-time requirement of Art. 5(3). See, e.g., *Tomasi v. France*, ECtHR 27 August 1992, appl. no. 12850/87, para. 84; *Herczegfalvy v. Austria*, ECtHR 24 September 1992, appl. no. 10533/83, para. 71. However, the same holds good for Art. 6(1). See, e.g., *Abdoella v. the Netherlands, supra* n. 648, para. 24; *Jablonski v. Poland*, ECtHR 21 December 2000, appl. no. 33492/96, para. 102; *Kreps v. Poland*, ECtHR 26 July 2001, appl. no. 34097/96, paras. 52–54.

[681] See, e.g., *De Cubber v. Belgium, supra* n. 371, para. 35; *Francesco Lombardo v. Italy, supra* n. 112, para. 17, para. 23; *G.S. v. Austria, supra* n. 99, para. 35; *Ludescher v. Austria, supra* n. 106, para. 23.

[682] *Zimmermann and Steiner v. Switzerland*, ECtHR 13 July 1983, appl. no. 8737/79, paras. 29–32; *Baggetta v. Italy*, ECtHR 25 June 1987, appl. no. 10256/83, paras. 22–25; *Martins Moreira v. Portugal, supra* n. 613, paras. 53–61.

---

taken afterwards cannot make up for the fact that the reasonable period has been exceeded.[683] When making this assessment the Court is prepared to take into consideration the political and social background in the country concerned.[684] In the *Bottazzi* case, the Court drew attention to the fact that it had found numerous violations of the reasonable-time requirement concerning civil proceedings before the civil courts of the various regions of Italy. Therefore, it concluded 'that there is an accumulation of identical breaches which are sufficiently numerous to amount not merely to isolated incidents. Such breaches reflect a continuing situation that has not yet been remedied and in respect of which litigants have no domestic remedy (...). This accumulation of breaches accordingly constitutes a practice that is incompatible with the Convention.'[685]

Subsequently, with reference to its *Bottazzi* judgment, the Court held many complaints against Italy to be well-founded without making a case-to-case assessment on the merits.[686]

The application of the criteria – the complexity of the case, the conduct of the applicant, the conduct of the authorities and what was at stake for the applicant – separately or in combination, may lead to different conclusions. In the *Bunkate* case, for instance, a criminal case, the relevant period lasted two years and ten months. This lapse of time was amongst other factors caused by a period of total inactivity of fifteen and a half months between the filing of the appeal on points of law and the reception of the case file by the registry of the Supreme Court. This period in itself infringed the reasonable-time requirement.[687] On the other hand, in the *Boddaert* case it took slightly more than six years to determine the 'criminal charge'. This lapse of time did not violate Article 6.[688] Comparable differences may be noted as far as civil proceedings are concerned. In the *Ciricosta and Viola* case an overall period of more than 15 years did meet the

---

683   Report of 12 March 1984, *Marijnissen*, D&R 40 (1985), p. 83 (90).

684   See, e.g., *Milasi v. Italy*, ECtHR 25 June 1987, appl. no. 10527/83, paras. 17–20, where the Court took into account the disturbances in the Region concerned, and *Unión Alimentaria S.A. v. Spain*, ECtHR 7 July 1989, appl. no. 11681/85, para. 40. In *Maltzan and Others v. Germany*, ECtHR 2 March 2005 (dec.), appl. no. 71916/01, 71917/01 and 10260/02, paras. 133–134, the Court (Grand Chamber) took into account the wish of the Federal Constitutional Court to group together all cases on similar issues so as to obtain a comprehensive view of the matter, as well as the large flux of constitutional applications following German reunification.

685   *Bottazzi v. Italy*, ECtHR (GC) 28 July 1999, appl. no. 34884/97, paras. 22–23. Moreover, in its subsequent case law the Court has added that such a practice constitutes an aggravating circumstance of the violation of Art. 6 (1). See, e.g., *Giomi v. Italy*, ECtHR 5 October 2000, appl. no. 53361/99, para. 12 and *Mennitto v. Italy, supra* n. 12, para. 30; *Cristina Cardo v. Italy*, ECtHR 28 February 2002, appl. no. 51134/99, para. 10; *Fragnito v. Italy*, ECtHR 9 July 2002, appl. no. 44349/98, para. 14. Under certain circumstances such a practice may also violate Art. 13. See *Kudla v. Poland, supra* n. 293, paras. 146–160.

686   See, e.g., *Dorigo v. Italy*, ECtHR 16 November 2000, appl. no. 46520/99, paras. 9–10; *Vanzetti v. Italy*, ECtHR 11 December 2001, appl. no. 51707/99, paras. 10–11; *Nazzaro and Others v. Italy*, ECtHR 9 July 2002, appl. no. 44348/98, paras. 14–15.

687   *Bunkate v. the Netherlands, supra* n. 630, paras. 20–23.

688   *Boddaert v. Belgium, supra* n. 630, paras. 35–40.

requirements of Article 6(1),[689] but a lapse of time that lasted four years and five months in the *Pugliese II* case did not pass muster.[690]

The requirement of a trial within a reasonable time equally entails that this time may not be unreasonably short, in consequence of which it is not possible for the parties to prepare the case properly. What is expressly provided in paragraph 3(b) for criminal proceedings by virtue of the general requirement of a fair hearing in the first paragraph, applies to civil proceedings as well.

Article 6(1) does not stipulate what the consequences for the proceedings are, if the reasonable-time requirement has not been met. It would seem to ensue from this provision that, if the reasonable time has been exceeded and, consequently, the determination can no longer be made within a reasonable time, the proceedings would have to be stopped and the civil action or criminal charge to be declared inadmissible. However, in the Strasbourg case law a more flexible view has been adopted: 'an excessive length of criminal proceedings can in principle be compensated for by measures of the domestic authorities, including in particular a reduction of the sentence on account of the length of procedure.'[691]

Although this point of view does not easily fit into the text of Article 6(1), it offers the most appropriate solution in certain cases. In civil proceedings the applicant, who has an interest in a final determination, should not become the victim of an unreasonable delay for which the public authorities are to be blamed; both parties can be victims of the delay and be entitled to some form of just satisfaction. And in criminal procedures the public interest in the prosecution and conviction of the criminal may be so great that the prosecution should not be stopped for the sole reason that the reasonable time has been transgressed; another, more proportionate compensation should be awarded to the victim of that transgression. In administrative procedures the interests of third parties may also have to be taken into account.

A more recent trend in the case law is that, when the reasonable-time requirement of Article 6 has been exceeded, on the basis of Article 13 it is required that an effective remedy exists at national level to compensate for this. This is sufficient when it is possible at national level to receive compensation for moral damage caused by the tension and frustration as a result of the reasonable time-limit being exceeded. This tension and frustration is presumed to exist.[692] It should be noted in this regard that when more than one party is involved in proceedings that exceed the time-limits, the Court presumes that the related damages are divided among all concerned and thus also the

---

[689]   *Ciricosta and Viola v. Italy,* ECtHR 4 December 1995, appl. no. 19753/92, paras. 23–32.

[690]   *Pugliese v. Italy (No. 2), supra* n. 634, paras. 50–63.

[691]   Report of 12 December 1983, *Neubeck,* D&R 41 (1985), p. 13 (34). See also *Eckle v. Germany, supra* n. 190, paras. 87 and 94. In *Majaric v. Slovenia,* ECtHR 8 February 2000, appl. no. 28400/95, paras. 47–48, the Court rejected the request of the applicant to order a retrial, because it has no jurisdiction under the Convention to order such a measure.

[692]   *Kudla v. Poland, supra* n. 293; *Scordino v. Italy (No. 1),* ECtHR (GC) 29 March 2006, appl. no. 36813/97.

compensation concerned in this case.[693] The requirement mentioned above to provide an effective remedy is fully addressed when, besides the possibility of compensation at the national level, a remedy also exists to enforce an acceleration in proceedings. However, no legal obligation exists to do so.[694] If such compensation does not occur at national level, the Court can award a comparable compensation on the grounds of Article 41.

7. INDEPENDENT AND IMPARTIAL TRIBUNAL

7.1. INTRODUCTION

The first paragraph of Article 6 provides that the determination there referred to, be made by an independent and impartial tribunal, established by law. The tribunal need not be 'a court of law of the classic kind, integrated within the standard judicial machinery of the country'.[695] For the notion of 'tribunal' it is essential that there exists a power to decide matters 'on the basis of rules of law, following proceedings conducted in a prescribed manner',[696] and that the judicial body has 'full jurisdiction, including the power to quash in all respects, on questions of fact and law, the challenged decision'.[697] The latter requirement had not been met in the *Chevrol* case, concerning the practice of the French *Conseil d'État* to ask preliminary questions to the Minister of Foreign Affairs with regard to international treaties. In the instant case, the position taken by the minister that the treaty in issue was not of a reciprocal character, was decisive for the outcome of the proceedings. The applicant did not have any opportunity to give her opinion on the use of the referral procedure or the wording of the question, or to submit a reply to the minister's point of view. The *Conseil d'État* based its decision solely on the opinion of the minister and, in so doing, considered itself to be bound by that opinion. Thus, according to the Court, the *Conseil d'État* voluntarily deprived itself of the power to examine and take into account factual evidence that could have been crucial for the practical resolution of the dispute before it. In these

---

693   *Arvanitaki v. Greece*, ECtHR 15 February 2008, appl. no. 27278/03.
694   *Mifsud v. France*, ECtHR (GC) 11 September 2002, appl. no. 57220/00.
695   *Campbell and Fell v. the United Kingdom*, supra n. 215, para. 76; *Sramek v. Austria*, supra n. 93, para. 36. See also *McMichael v. the United Kingdom*, supra n. 72, para. 80, with regard to an adjudicatory body composed of 3 'specially trained persons with substantial experience of children' and *British-American Tobacco Company Ltd v. the Netherlands*, supra n. 130, para. 77, concerning patent application proceedings.
696   *Sramek v. Austria*, supra n. 93, para. 36 and the report of 8 December 1982 in this case, p. 31. See also *Benthem v. The Netherlands*, supra n. 10, para. 40; *H. v. Belgium*, supra n. 87, para. 50; *Demicoli v. Malta*, supra n. 216, para. 39.
697   *Västberga Taxi Aktiebolag and Vulic v. Sweden*, supra n. 271, para. 93 and *Janosevic v. Sweden*, supra n. 626, para. 81. See also, e.g., *Bendenoun v. France*, supra n. 140, para. 46; *Schmautzer v. Austria*, supra n. 264, para. 36 and *Pfarrmeier v. Austria*, supra n. 264, para. 40.

circumstances, the Court considered that the applicant did not have access to a tribunal with full jurisdiction.[698] Inherent in the very notion of a 'tribunal' is also that the decision taken by the tribunal may not be deprived of its effect by a non-judicial authority to the disadvantage of the individual party.[699] Moreover, Contracting States' domestic legal systems must guarantee the implementation of judicial decisions, otherwise the right of access to a court would be illusory.[700]

The adjectives 'independent' and 'impartial' are the expression of two different concepts. The notion of 'independence' refers to the lack of any connection between the tribunal and other parts of government, whereas the 'impartiality' must exist in relation to the parties to the suit and the case at issue. However, the Court has not always drawn a clear borderline between the two concepts, and often considers both concepts together, as will be seen in the next sections.[701]

The principles established in the Court's case law with regard to the notions of independence and impartiality apply to professional judges as well as to lay judges and jurors.[702] Where a complaint concerns lack of impartiality on the part of the decision-making body, the concept of full jurisdiction demands that the reviewing court not only considers the complaint but also has the power to quash the impugned decision and either take a new decision or remit the case for a new decision by an impartial body.[703]

If a judicial authority in the first instance does not provide the guarantee of independence and impartiality, in certain cases this can be redressed on appeal by a court that does meet these requirements: 'The Court recalls that even where an adjudicatory body determining disputes over "civil rights and obligations" does not comply with Article 6 §1 in some respect, no violation of the Convention can be found if the proceedings before that body are "subject to subsequent control by a judicial body that has full jurisdiction and does provide the guarantees of Article 6 §1".'[704]

---

[698] *Chevrol v. France, supra* n. 37, paras. 76–84. See also *Terra Woningen B.V. v. the Netherlands,* ECtHR 17 December 1996, appl. no. 20641/92, para. 54.

[699] See, e.g., *Van de Hurk v. the Netherlands, supra* n. 462, paras. 45–52; *Brumarescu v. Romania, supra* n. 283, para. 61; *Morris v. the United Kingdom,* ECtHR 26 February 2002, appl. no. 38784/97, para. 73.

[700] See, *supra*, 3.

[701] See, e.g., *Findlay v. the United Kingdom, supra* n. 372, para. 73; *Incal v. Turkey,* ECtHR (GC) 9 June 1998, appl. no. 22678/93, para. 65; *Agrokompleks v. Ukraine,* ECtHR 6 October 2011, appl. no. 23465/03, para. 128: 'The Court observes that the concepts of independence and objective impartiality are closely linked'.

[702] *Langborger v. Sweden,* ECtHR 22 June 1989, appl. no. 11179/84, para. 30; *Remli v. France,* ECtHR 23 April 1996, appl. no. 16839/90, paras. 46–48; *Pullar v. the United Kingdom, supra* n. 183, paras. 31–32; *Gregory v. the United Kingdom,* ECtHR 25 February 1997, appl. no. 22299/93, paras. 43–50; *Sander v. the United Kingdom,* ECtHR 9 May 2000, appl. no. 34129/96, paras. 22–35.

[703] *Kingsley v. the United Kingdom, supra* n. 96, para. 58, in which the Court held that the High Court and the Court of Appeal did not have full jurisdiction with regard to the decision taken by the Panel of the Gaming Board.

[704] *Crompton v. United Kingdom,* ECtHR 27 October 2009, appl. no. 42509/05, para. 70.

It appears, however, that in cases involving criminal law everybody must itself meet the obligation in full.[705]

7.2. INDEPENDENCE

In the *Ringeisen* case, the Court held that the Regional Commission could be regarded as a 'tribunal' as it was 'independent of the executive and also of the parties'. The latter element, however, refers in fact not to the independence but to the impartiality of the court. The Court added that the members of the Regional Commission had been appointed for five years and the proceedings before it did offer the necessary guarantees.[706] A comparable line of reasoning was developed in the *Langborger* case: 'In order to establish whether a body can be considered "independent" regard must be had, *inter alia*, to the manner of appointment of its members and their term of office, to the existence of guarantees against outside pressures and to the question whether the body presents an appearance of independence.'[707]

These various characteristics of the notion of independence seem to fall into three categories. Firstly, the tribunal must function independently of the executive (and the legislature) and base its decisions on its own free opinion about facts and legal grounds. Secondly, there must be guarantees to enable the court to function independently.[708] As far as the latter requirement is concerned, it is not necessary that the judges have been appointed for life, provided that they cannot be discharged at will or on improper grounds by the authorities.[709] The appointment of judges by parliament is not in breach of Article 6.[710] The absence of a formal recognition of the irremovability of judges during their terms of office does not imply a lack of independence as long as it is recognised

---

[705]   *Cf. Findlay v. United Kingdom*, EComHR 5 September 1995 (rep.), appl. no. 22107/93, para. 107.

[706]   *Ringeisen v. Austria, supra* n. 39, para. 95.

[707]   *Langborger v. Sweden, supra* n. 702, para. 32. See also, e.g., *Procola v. Luxembourg*, ECtHR 28 September 1995, appl. no. 14570/89, para. 43; *Bryan v. the United Kingdom, supra* n. 307, para. 37; *Morris v. the United Kingdom, supra* n. 699, para. 73.

[708]   In *Lauko v. Slovakia, supra* n. 225, paras. 63–65 and *Kadubec v. Slovakia*, ECtHR 2 September 1998, appl. no. 27061/95, paras. 56–58, the administrative authorities who had been entrusted with the prosecution and punishment of minor offences, appeared not to be independent of the executive because of the manner of appointment of the officers of the local and district offices and the lack of guarantees against outside pressures. Other state authorities must also demonstrate that the Convention is observed on this point. *Agrokompleks v. Ukraine, supra* n. 701.

[709]   Implicitly *Ringeisen v. Austria, supra* n. 39. With regard to military tribunals, see *Engel and Others v. the Netherlands, supra* n. 209, para. 89.

[710]   *Sacilor-Lormines v. France*, ECtHR 9 November 2006, appl. no.65411/01.

in fact and the other necessary guarantees are present.[711] A statutory power for the executive authority to dismiss judges will therefore not easily be accepted by the Court.[712] Thirdly, even a semblance of dependence must be avoided. In the *Bryan* case, the Court held that the very existence of the power of the Secretary of State to revoke the power of an inspector to decide an appeal under the Town and Country Planning Act, was enough to deprive the inspector of the appearance of independence.[713] And in the *Sramek* case, where a member of the court was hierarchically subordinate to one of the parties to the suit, the Court held: 'Litigants may entertain a legitimate doubt about his independence. Such a situation seriously affects the confidence which the courts must inspire in a democratic society.'[714] However, strictly speaking, the latter aspect no longer refers to the independence, but to the impartiality of the court.

As to the independence of the tribunal *vis-à-vis* the legislature, the fact that the Council of State of the Netherlands – like similar institutions in other member states – has an advisory function in the legislative process, does not in general affect its independence as a judicial body, although it cannot be excluded that because of the (previous) personal involvement of one of the judges there is an Article 6 problem.[715]

Furthermore, the fact that a body such as the French Council of State is part of the executive according to national law, does not automatically imply that it cannot act independently of the executive in the execution of judicial duties.[716]

Finally, the illegal influence of a judge can also come from within the judiciary itself: 'However, judicial independence demands that individual judges be free not only from undue influences outside the judiciary, but also from within. This internal judicial independence requires that they be free from directives or pressures from the fellow judges or those who have administrative responsibilities in the court such as the president of the court or the president of a division in the court (…). The absence of sufficient safeguards securing the independence of judges within the judiciary and, in particular, vis-à-vis their judicial superiors, may lead the Court to conclude that an applicant's doubts as to the (independence and) impartiality of a court may be said to have been objectively justified.'[717]

---

[711] *Campbell and Fell v. the United Kingdom, supra* n. 215, para. 80; *Morris v. the United Kingdom, supra* n. 699, para. 68.

[712] See, e.g., *Henryk Urban and Ryszard Urban v. Poland*, ECtHR 30 November 2010, appl. no. 23614/08, para. 53.

[713] *Bryan v. the United Kingdom, supra* n. 307, para. 38.

[714] *Sramek v. Austria, supra* n. 93, para. 42.

[715] *Kleyn and Others v. the Netherlands*, ECtHR (GC) 6 May 2003, appl. no. 39343/98, 39651/98, 43147/98 and 46664/99, paras. 193–195.

[716] *Sacilor-Lormines v. France, supra* n. 710.

[717] *Parlov and Tkalic v. Croatia*, ECtHR 22 December 2009, appl. no. 24810/06, para. 86.

7.3. IMPARTIALITY

For impartiality it is required that the court is not biased with regard to the decision to be taken, does not allow itself to be influenced by information from outside the courtroom, by popular feeling, or by any pressure whatsoever, but bases its opinion on objective arguments on the ground of what has been put forward at the trial. Although a judge, as a matter of course, has personal emotions, including during the proceedings, he must not allow himself to be led by them during the hearing of the case and in the formation of his opinion.[718] And although judges may have a political preference and/or adhere to a specific religion or philosophy of life, and although it is right that the various political streams, religions and philosophies of life are also 'represented' within the judiciary, it must not make any difference for the person involved whether he is tried by a judge with one or other preference.

Publicity surrounding a criminal case, where the difference between 'suspected of' and 'guilty of' is not always taken into account, in addition to putting at issue the presumption of innocence principle of the second paragraph of Article 6, may constitute a threat to the right to a fair and impartial trial, in particular also when this publicity proceeds from the authorities, e.g., from the public prosecutor charged with the examination.[719] The judge must duly take this risk into account when forming his opinion. In cases with a markedly political background the said risk and the necessity for the court to be on the alert against improper influences applies to an even higher degree.[720] In the Strasbourg case law it is assumed, however, that a professional judge will in general be aware of these external factors and will not readily allow himself to be influenced thereby,[721] while moreover on appeal the higher court, in this respect, too, may control and compensate for the attitude of the lower court. Thus, in the *Menten* case the former Commission held that the great publicity and the utterance of hostile feelings in this case could not be avoided, but that the Supreme Court had accurately ascertained on what testimony the lower courts had based their considerations.[722] In cases of trial by jury the risk of the jury being influenced by public opinion or by biased statements of witnesses or experts is more likely.[723]

---

[718] See appl. no. 1727/62, *Boeckmans*, Yearbook VI (1963), p. 370 (416–420), where the complaint concerned a judge who, in his indignation about a specific defence, uttered a warning that its upholding might lead to an increase of the penalty. Later on this case was settled: report of the subcommittee of 17 February 1965.

[719] Appl. no. 8403/78, *Jespers*, D&R 22 (1981), p. 100 (127).

[720] Appl. nos. 8603, 8722, 8723 and 8729/79, *Crociani and Others*, D&R 22 (1981), p. 147 (222–223 and 227).

[721] *Craxi v. Italy*, ECtHR 5 December 2002, appl. no. 34896/97, para. 104.

[722] Appl. no. 9433/81, *Menten*, D&R 27 (1982), p. 233 (238).

[723] This risk was emphasised several times by the Commission. See, e.g., appl. no. 7542/76, *X v. the United Kingdom* (not published), where in a case which attracted much publicity the Commission attached great importance to the fact that the judge had drawn the jury's attention to the risk of prejudice.

The requirement of Article 10(2) that the freedom of expression may be restricted 'for maintaining the authority and impartiality of the judiciary' is closely connected with the point of publicity surrounding a trial. This restriction, which relates to the prohibition of 'contempt of court' embedded in Anglo-American law, was discussed at length in Strasbourg in the *Sunday Times* case. The complaint concerned the prohibition, imposed by the English courts up to the highest instance, on publishing during a given time an article about the so-called 'thalidomide children', who had been born with serious physical deformities in consequence of the use of the sedative thalidomide by their mothers during pregnancy. The prohibition had been imposed because, at that moment, various proceedings against the manufacturer of thalidomide were pending and the publication might have led to 'contempt of court'. The Court, although by a narrow majority, came to the conclusion that in this case the prohibition was not justified. They took into account, *inter alia*, that a court is not readily influenced by publications of this kind.[724]

In testing whether a 'tribunal' or judge has been prejudiced, the Court makes a distinction between a subjective and an objective approach to impartiality. The subjective approach refers to the personal impartiality of the members of the tribunal involved; this impartiality is presumed as long as the contrary has not been proved.[725] The establishment of a personal bias is difficult. Even when a judicial decision has been amply reasoned, it is difficult to ascertain by what motives a court was led. It will, therefore, only be possible to conclude that a judge is biased when this is evident from his attitude during the proceedings or from the content of the judgment.[726] It will be even more difficult to prove the prejudice of (members of) a jury, because a decision of the jury does not include a written statement of reasons.[727]

The objective approach refers to the question of whether the way in which the tribunal is composed and organised, or a certain coincidence or succession of functions of one or more of its members, may give rise to doubt as to the impartiality of the tribunal or that member. If there is justified reason for such doubt, even if subjectively there is no concrete indication of bias of the person in question, this already amounts to an inadmissible jeopardy of the confidence

---

[724]   *The Sunday Times v. the United Kingdom (No. 1)*, ECtHR (GC) 26 April 1979, appl. no. 6538/74, paras. 65–68.

[725]   See, e.g., *Piersack v. Belgium*, ECtHR 1 October 1982, appl. no. 8692/79, para. 30; *Hauschildt v. Denmark*, ECtHR (GC) 24 May 1989, appl. no. 10486/83, para. 45; *Thorgeir Thorgeirson v. Iceland*, ECtHR 25 June 1992, appl. no. 13778/88, para. 49; *Fey v. Austria*, ECtHR 24 February 1993, appl. no. 14396/88, para. 28; *Saraiva de Carvalho v. Portugal*, ECtHR 22 April 1994, appl. no. 15651/89, para. 33.

[726]   See, e.g., *Kyprianou v. Cyprus*, ECtHR 27 January 2004, appl. no. 73797/01, paras. 38–42. See also *Kleyn and Others v. the Netherlands*, *supra* n. 715, para. 195.

[727]   *Cf. Pullar v. the United Kingdom*, *supra* n. 183, paras. 31–32; *Gregory v. the United Kingdom*, *supra* n. 702, para. 44; *Sander v. the United Kingdom*, *supra* n. 702, paras. 25–26.

which the court must inspire in a democratic society.[728] The fear that the tribunal or a particular judge lacks impartiality must be such that it can 'be held to be objectively justified'; consequently, the standpoint of the accused on this matter, although important, is not decisive.[729]

This objective-approach test has been applied in several cases so far. Despite the casuistic case law some main lines can be discerned. As the Court held in the *Buscemi* case, the judicial authorities are required to exercise maximum discretion with regard to the cases with which they deal in order to preserve their image as impartial judges and, therefore, they should not make use of the press, even when provoked. Accordingly, the fact that the president of the court publicly used expressions which implied that he had already formed an unfavourable opinion of the applicant's case before presiding over the court that had to decide it, clearly violated the requirement of impartiality.[730] And in the special circumstances of the *Sigurdsson* case Article 6 had been violated because of, in short, the existence of strong financial links between the judge's husband and one of the parties to the suit, the National Bank of Iceland.[731] It can be added to this that if the parties have not been informed of the composition of a court, it is certain that a violation of the requirement of objective impartiality has occurred.[732]

The fact that a judge has taken decisions in the case prior to the trial and subsequently officiates as a trial judge is in itself not incompatible with the requirement of impartiality. What matters is the 'scope and nature' of the measures or decisions taken prior to the trial.[733] The fear of prejudice cannot, for instance, be justified solely by the fact that the judge has taken decisions on the prolongation of the detention on remand. Only special circumstances can give rise to a different conclusion.[734] Such special circumstances did occur in the *Hauschildt* case. In ordering the continued pre-trial detention the judge had to be convinced that there was 'a very high degree of clarity as to the question of guilt'.

---

[728] See, e.g., *Piersack v. Belgium, supra* n. 725, para. 30, para. 31; *De Cubber v. Belgium, supra* n. 371, para. 30; *Saraiva de Carvalho v. Portugal, supra* n. 725, para. 35; *Morris v. the United Kingdom, supra* n. 699, para. 58; *Kleyn and Others v. the Netherlands, supra* n. 715, para. 191.

[729] See, e.g., *Hauschildt v. Denmark, supra* n. 725, para. 48; *Padovani v. Italy,* ECtHR 26 February 1993, appl. no. 13396/87, para. 27; *Saraiva de Carvalho v. Portugal, supra* n. 725, para. 35; *Gautrin and Others v. France, supra* n. 583, para. 58; *Incal v. Turkey, supra* n. 701, para. 71; *Kleyn and Others v. the Netherlands, supra* n. 715, para. 194.

[730] *Buscemi v. Italy,* ECtHR 16 September 1999, appl. no. 29569/95, paras. 67–69; *Lavents v. Latvia,* ECtHR 28 November 2002, appl. no. 58442/00, paras. 119–120.

[731] *Sigurdsson v. Iceland,* ECtHR 10 April 2003, appl. no. 39731/98, paras. 37–41. See also *Pescador Valero v. Spain,* ECtHR 17 June 2003, appl. no. 62435/00, paras. 23–29.

[732] *Vernes v. France,* ECtHR 20 January 2011, appl. no. 30183/06, paras. 42–44.

[733] *Nortier v. the Netherlands,* ECtHR 24 August 1993, appl. no. 13924/88, para. 33; *Saraiva de Carvalho v. Portugal, supra* n. 725, para. 35. In *Fey v. Austria, supra* n. 725, para. 30, the Court held 'the extent and nature' to be decisive.

[734] *Hauschildt v. Denmark, supra* n. 725, para. 50; *Sainte-Marie v. France,* ECtHR 16 December 1992, appl. no. 12981/87, para. 32.

The difference between this assessment and the assessment that had to be made when giving judgment thus became (too) tenuous.[735] On the contrary, in case the prolongation of the detention on remand may be ordered if the judge is convinced that there exists '*prima facie* evidence', no problem with regard to the impartiality arises.[736] In the *Piersack* case the fact that the president of the tribunal had been involved in an earlier phase of the case as a public prosecutor amounted to a violation of Article 6.[737] In the *De Cubber* case, a judge was involved who had previously in the same case acted as an investigating judge and as a president of a chamber respectively. The Court held that these facts created too much doubt about the impartiality of the judge concerned in an objective sense.[738]

Doubt about impartiality is also justified in case a judge who participated in a judgment at first instance also participates in the hearing of an appeal against the same judgment.[739] The requirement of impartiality does not imply, however, that a superior court which quashes the decision of a lower court, is obliged to refer the case to another court or to a differently composed chamber of the lower court.[740] In the *Rojas Morales* case, the written statements of a judgment concerning a co-accused created the impression that the applicant was guilty. Therefore, the participation of the same judges in the applicant's trial created objectively justified doubts with regard to their impartiality.[741] In the *Werner* case, the requirement of impartiality had been violated because the judge who submitted to the court a motion for the applicant to be dismissed as a liquidator subsequently participated in the court's decision on this motion.[742]

The consecutive carrying out of an advisory and a judicial function in the same case was at stake in the *Procola* case. Procola, an association under Luxembourg law, challenged the lawfulness of four ministerial orders for

---

[735] *Hauschildt v. Denmark, supra* n. 725, paras. 51–53. See also *Perote Pellon v. Spain*, ECtHR 25 July 2002, appl. no. 45238/99, paras. 46–52 and *Cianetti v. Italy*, ECtHR 22 April 2004, appl. no. 55634/00, paras. 41–45.

[736] *Nortier v. the Netherlands, supra* n. 733, para. 35; *Saraiva de Carvalho v. Portugal, supra* n. 725, paras. 38–40; *Padovani v. Italy, supra* n. 729, paras. 28–29; *Bulut v. Austria, supra* n. 469, para. 34; *Depiets v. France*, ECtHR 10 February 2004, appl. no. 53971/00, paras. 37–43.

[737] *Piersack v. Belgium, supra* n. 725, para. 30, paras. 30–32. See also *Tierce and Others v. San Marino, supra* n. 518, paras. 78–81.

[738] *De Cubber v. Belgium, supra* n. 699, paras. 29–30; The Court reached the same conclusion in *Kyprianou v. Cyprus, supra* n. 726, paras. 34–37, where a charge of contempt of court had been tried by the same judges before whom the contempt allegedly had been committed. See also, e.g., *Belilos v. Switzerland*, ECtHR (GC) 29 April 1988, appl. no. 10328/83, para. 67, and *Ferrantelli and Santangelo v. Italy*, ECtHR 7 August 1996, appl. no. 19874/92, paras. 53–59.

[739] *Oberschlick v. Austria*, ECtHR (GC) 23 May 1991, appl. no. 11662/85, paras. 50–52; *De Haan v. the Netherlands, supra* n. 100, paras. 47–51; *Castillo Algar v. Spain,* ECtHR 28 October 1998, appl. no. 28194/95, paras. 46–51; *S.L. Band Club v. Malta, supra* n. 341, paras. 61–66.

[740] *Ringeisen v. Austria, supra* n. 39, para. 97; *Diennet v. France, supra* n. 94, paras. 36–39. See also *Thomann v. Switzerland*, ECtHR 10 June 1996, appl. no. 17602/91, paras. 27–37, concerning a criminal trial *in absentia* and retrial in the presence of the accused by the same judges.

[741] *Rojas Morales v. Italy*, ECtHR 16 November 2000, appl. no. 39676/98, paras. 33–35.

[742] *Werner v. Poland, supra* n. 95, paras. 41–47. In *Morel v. France*, ECtHR 6 June 2000, appl. no. 34130/96, paras. 42–50, the insolvency judge did meet the requirements of impartiality.

the Judicial Committee of the *Conseil d'État*. In deciding the case the Judicial Committee also had to give its opinion on the lawfulness of a regulation that had been the subject of an advisory opinion of the *Conseil d'État*. In fact, the *Conseil d'État* had recommended the inclusion of the very provision that was challenged by Procola. The Judicial Committee was composed of five members. The fact that four of them had pronounced on the lawfulness of the regulation in their advisory capacity, was, according to the Court, sufficient reason for casting doubt on the structural impartiality of the Luxembourg *Conseil d'État*.[743] The Court reached the same conclusion in the *McGonnell* case. It held that the mere fact that the deputy Bailiff presided over the States of Liberation when the draft developing plan in issue was adopted, was capable of casting doubt on his impartiality when he subsequently determined, as the sole judge of the law in the case, the applicant's planning appeal.[744]

In the *Kleyn* case, the applicants claimed that the institutionalised simultaneous exercise of both advisory and judicial functions by the Dutch Council of State was incompatible with the required objective impartiality, since no separation was made between the members involved in the exercise of the advisory functions and those involved in the exercise of the judicial functions. However, the Court distinguished that case from the *Procola* case, because the advisory opinions on the Transport Infrastructure Planning Act and the subsequent judicial proceedings concerning the appeals against the railway routing decision, which was based on the Planning Act, did not concern 'the same case' or 'the same decision'.[745] The Court made, however, the observation, as a warning for possible complaints in the future, that it was not as confident as the Dutch Government that the arrangements made by the Council of State with a view to giving effect to the *Procola* judgment, were such as to ensure that the Administrative Jurisdiction Division of the Council of State would constitute in all cases an 'impartial tribunal' for the purposes of Article 6(1) of the Convention.[746]

The independence and impartiality of the members of the *Procureur général*'s department of the Belgian Court of Cassation was tested in the *Borgers* case. The Court concluded, affirming its previous case law, that on this point no violation of Article 6 arose. A similar conclusion was reached with regard to the *Commissaire du Gouvernement* in French administrative proceedings.[747]

---

[743] *Procola v. Luxembourg, supra* n. 707, paras. 44–45.
[744] *McGonnell v. the United Kingdom*, ECtHR 8 February 2000, appl. no. 28488/95, paras. 49–58.
[745] *Kleyn and Others v. the Netherlands, supra* n. 715, paras. 195–202. See also *Pabla Ky v. Finland*, ECtHR 22 June 2004, appl. no. 47221/99 paras. 31–35, concerning a member of Parliament who participates as an expert lay member in the decision-making in a court. See also *Sacilor-Lormines v. France, supra* n. 710.
[746] *Kleyn and Others v. the Netherlands, supra* n. 715, para. 198.
[747] *Borgers v. Belgium, supra* n. 468, para. 26, and *Kress v. France, supra* n. 470, para. 71. See, on the position of the *Avocat général* and similar officers and the (im)possibility to react to their submissions, *supra*, 4.2.

In the *Daktaras* case, the Court reached the opposite conclusion with regard to the role of the president of the criminal division of the supreme court of Lithuania, who was in effect taking up the case of the prosecution and also constituted the court which had to decide the case.[748]

The practice of having courts composed in whole or in part by the military to try members of the armed forces is not contrary to the notion of an independent and impartial tribunal, as long as sufficient safeguards are in place to guarantee the compliance with these concepts.[749] In a series of cases the Court had to deal with the independence and impartiality of British courts-martial convened pursuant to the Army and Air Force Acts 1955. In these cases the role of the convening officer appeared to be crucial. This officer had the final decision on the nature and detail of the charges to be brought and was responsible for convening the court-martial, whose members were subordinate in rank to him. Moreover, the convening officer acted as a confirming officer: the decision of the court-martial was not effective until confirmed by him. According to the Court, these fundamental flaws in the court-martial system were not remedied by the presence of safeguards and, therefore, it held the misgivings of the accused persons about the independence and impartiality of the tribunals which dealt with their cases to be objectively justified.[750] Subsequently, the British legislator changed the impugned provisions. In the *Cooper* case, concerning an air-force court-martial, the Court held that the Armed Forces Act of 1996 did meet the requirements of Article 6. In particular, the presence in a court-martial of the Judge Advocate, a legally qualified civilian, constituted a significant guarantee of the independence of the court-martial proceedings. The Judge Advocate sums up the evidence and delivers further directions to the other members of the court-martial beforehand and he can refuse to accept a verdict if he considers it 'contrary to law' in which case he gives the members of the court-martial further directions in open court, following which those members retire again to consider the verdict.[751] Moreover, with regard to the ordinary members of the court-martial,[752]

---

[748] *Daktaras v. Lithuania*, ECtHR 10 October 2000, appl. no. 42095/98, paras. 33–38.

[749] *Morris v. the United Kingdom, supra* n. 699, para. 59.

[750] See, e.g, *Findlay v. the United Kingdom, supra* n. 372, paras. 73–80; *Coyne v. the United Kingdom*, ECtHR 24 September 1997, appl. no. 25942/94, paras. 56–58; *Cable and Others v. the United Kingdom*, ECtHR 18 February 1999, appl. nos. 24436/94, 24582/94, 24583/94, 24584/94, 24895/94, 25937/94, 25939/94, 25940/94, 25941/94, 26271/95, 26525/95, 27341/95, 27342/95, 27346/95, 27357/95, 27389/95, 27409/95, 27760/95, 27762/95, 27772/95, 28009/95, 28790/95, 30236/96, 30239/96, 30276/96, 30277/96, 30460/96, 30461/96, 30462/96, 31399/96, 31400/96, 31434/96, 31899/96, 32024/96 and 32944/96, paras. 20–22; *Mills v. the United Kingdom, supra* n. 258, paras. 22–27.

[751] *Cooper v. the United Kingdom*, ECtHR (GC) 16 December 2003, appl. no. 48843/99, para. 117.

[752] Those members, who were appointed on an *ad hoc* basis and had no legal qualifications and relatively little court-martial experience, remained subject to RAF discipline in a general sense since they remained RAF officers. However, they could not be reported upon in relation to their judicial decision-making.

the Court considered that the so-called Briefing Notes not only instructed members of the need to function independently, but also provided a significant impediment to any inappropriate pressure being brought to bear.[753] In the *Grieves* case, the Court concluded that the Judge Advocate in a naval court-martial, who is not a civilian but a serving naval officer who, when not sitting in a court-martial, carries out regular naval duties, cannot be considered a strong guarantee of the independence of a naval court-martial.[754]

In several cases the composition of the Turkish National Security Courts has been at issue. These courts are composed of three judges, one of whom is a regular officer and member of the Military Legal Service. In the *Incal* case, the applicant had been convicted by the Izmir Security Court for disseminating leaflets capable of inciting people to resist the Government and to commit criminal offences. The applicant submitted that his conviction had infringed Article 10 and Article 6 of the Convention. As far as Article 6 was concerned, the Court, taking the concepts of independence and impartiality together, firstly took stock of the legal system. It noted that the status of military judges as members of the Security Courts did provide certain guarantees of independence and impartiality. They underwent the same professional training, when sitting enjoyed the same constitutional safeguards as their civilian counterparts and, according to the Turkish Constitution, had to be free from the instructions of public authorities. However, other aspects made the independence and impartiality of military judges questionable: the judges concerned belonged to the army, which takes its orders from the executive; they remained subject to military discipline and assessment reports; decisions pertaining to their appointment were to a great extent taken by the administrative authorities and the army, and, finally, their term of office as National Security Court judges was only four years and could be renewed.[755] The Court further attached special importance to the fact that a civilian had to appear before a court partly composed of members of the armed forces. The Court concluded that because one of the judges of the National Security Court was a military judge, the applicant could legitimately fear that it might allow itself to be unduly influenced by considerations which had nothing to do with the nature of the case. Therefore, he had legitimate doubts about the independence and impartiality of the court.[756] As far as the composition of the

---

[753] *Cooper v. the United Kingdom, supra* n. 751, para. 117. In *Morris v. the United Kingdom, supra* n. 699, paras. 66–79, the Court has reached a different conclusion. In that case the United Kingdom Government had omitted to submit to the Court important information with regard to the practice of court-martial. This new information appeared to be crucial in the *Cooper* case.

[754] *Cooper v. the United Kingdom, supra* n. 751, paras. 82–91. See also *G.W. v. the United Kingdom*, ECtHR 15 June 2004, appl. no. 34155/96, paras. 43–49 and *Le Petit v. the United Kingdom*, ECtHR 15 June 2004, appl. no. 35574/97, paras. 21–24.

[755] *Incal v. Turkey, supra* n. 701, para. 68.

[756] *Ibid.*, paras. 65–73.

Turkish National Security Courts is concerned the *Incal* case may be regarded as standing case law.[757]

The requirement of impartiality may under circumstances restrict the participation of substitute judges, especially in view of any other profession exercised by them, e.g., that of a practising lawyer. In the *Wettstein* case, the applicant was confronted with a substitute judge who had acted in a similar procedure as the legal representative of the opposing party. Although no material link existed between these two cases, in view of the fact that the proceedings partly overlapped in time, the Court concluded that the applicant could have had reason for concern that the judge would continue to see in him the opposing party.[758]

The mere fact that lay assessors also sit on a tribunal, as is frequently the case in disciplinary tribunals, does not mean on this ground alone that they are not impartial, even in cases where they constitute a majority.[759] But if persons are involved who are closely allied to one of the parties, which is often the case in arbitration tribunals, their impartiality may be open to doubt. An issue under Article 6(1) will then arise only when not all the parties or their interests are equally represented in the tribunal in question. Thus, in the *Le Compte, Van Leuven and De Meyere* case, where three medical practitioners had been summoned before a disciplinary tribunal on account of their opposition to the obligatory membership of a professional association of medical practitioners, the Commission reached the conclusion that there was no impartial course of proceedings, since the tribunal judging at first instance, the Provincial Council, was composed largely of persons who had been elected by members of the professional association, while the Appeal Council consisted of medical practitioners and judges on a fifty-fifty basis. The fact that appeal to the Court of Cassation was also possible did not, in the Commission's opinion, eliminate this defect, because review was possible only on the ground of procedural errors or misapplication of the law.[760] The Court, however, did not follow the Commission. Since an appeal had been lodged with the Appeal Council, in the Court's view the impartiality of the Provincial Council did not require examination. With regard to the Appeal Council, the Court held that the impartiality of such a

---

[757] See, e.g., *Çiraklar v. Turkey*, ECtHR 28 October 1998, appl. no. 19601/92, paras. 38–41; *Sürek v. Turkey (No. 1)*, ECtHR (GC) 8 July 1999, appl. no. 26682/95, paras. 66–76; *Yanikoglu v. Turkey*, ECtHR 14 October 2004, appl. no. 46284/99, paras. 23–25. See, with regard to a Turkish Martial Law Court, e.g., *Sahiner v. Turkey*, ECtHR 25 September 2001, appl. no. 29279/95, paras. 33–47; *Ahmet Koc v. Turkey*, ECtHR 22 June 2004, appl. no. 32580/96, paras. 30–32.

[758] *Wettstein v. Switzerland*, ECtHR 21 December 2000, appl. no. 33958/96, paras. 44–50. In *Puolitaival and Pirttiaho v. Finland*, ECtHR 23 November 2004, appl. no. 54857/00, paras. 45–54, the Court reached a different conclusion, taking into account, *inter alia*, the fact that the functions of the person concerned as counsel and judge had not overlapped in time, and the remoteness in time and subject matter of both sets of proceedings.

[759] See, e.g., *Ettl and Others v. Austria*, supra n. 63, para. 38; *Stallinger and Kuso v. Austria*, supra n. 508, para. 37.

[760] Report of 14 December 1979, B.38 (1984), pp. 40–42.

tribunal must be presumed, unless the contrary can be proved, which had not been done in the present case in the Court's opinion.[761]

In the *AB Kurt Kellermann* case, the applicant company claimed that the Swedish labour court could not be composed of members representing the industrial union, since the court had to examine the applicant company's argument that the industrial union action, including a possible blockade of the company, had to be proportionate and socially relevant. The Court applied the objective-impartiality test and held that the deciding issue was whether the balance of interests in the composition of the labour court was upset, and, if so, whether any such lack of balance would result in unfair proceedings. In the circumstances of the case, with five votes to two, the Court answered the first question in the negative and, therefore, a violation of Article 6 did not occur.[762] A comparable line of reasoning lead in the *Holm* case to the conclusion that the impartiality (and independence) of the jury was open to doubt,[763] but in the *Pullar* case the fact that a member of the jury was a junior employee in the firm of one of the witnesses for the prosecution, could pass the objective-impartiality test: Article 6 had not been violated.[764] When serious allegations are made that racist comments have been made by jurors, called upon to try a person of different ethnic origin, the court should take sufficient steps to check whether, as constituted, it is 'an impartial tribunal' within the meaning of Article 6. In the *Remli* case[765] and the *Sander* case,[766] the reaction of the judge concerned appeared not to be sufficient. However, in the circumstances of the *Gregory* case, where the allegation of racial bias was vague and imprecise, the Court held that the redirection of the jury did constitute a sufficient reaction.[767]

In the *Bulut* case, the question arose whether the applicant had waived his right under domestic law to object to the participation of a judge in a criminal trial, who had taken part previously in the questioning of two witnesses. The approach of the Court in this case seems to be ambiguous. On the one hand, it held that it was irrelevant whether a waiver had been made or not, because it was anyhow incumbent on the Court to assess whether the composition of the trial court could cast doubt on its impartiality.[768] On the other hand, however, it

---

[761]   *Le Compte, Van Leuven and De Meyere v. Belgium, supra* n. 36, para. 58; *Albert and Le Compte v. Belgium, supra* n. 94, para. 32; *Campbell and Fell v. the United Kingdom, supra* n. 215, para. 84.

[762]   *AB Kurt Kellermann v. Sweden*, ECtHR 26 October 2004, appl. no. 41579/98, paras. 60–69. The Court reached a different conclusion in *Langborger v. Sweden, supra* n. 702, paras. 31–36.

[763]   *Holm v. Sweden*, ECtHR 25 November 1993, appl. no. 14191/88, paras. 30–33.

[764]   *Pullar v. the United Kingdom, supra* n. 183, paras. 33–41. See also *Hanif and Khan v. United Kingdom*, ECtHR 20 December 2011, appl. no. 52999/08, para. 148: in this case a police officer was a member of the jury. The Court held that the requirements of Art. 6 had not been met.

[765]   *Remli v. France, supra* n. 702, paras. 46–48.

[766]   *Sander v. the United Kingdom, supra* n. 702, paras. 22–35.

[767]   *Gregory v. the United Kingdom, supra* n. 702, paras. 43–50.

[768]   *Bulut v. Austria, supra* n. 469, para. 30.

concluded that the objective approach could offer the applicant no success, since he had refrained from his right to challenge the composition of the Court.[769] In the *McGonnell* case, the Court held that the question of whether the applicant ought to have taken up his complaint with regard to the lack of independence and impartiality with the national judicial authorities, depended on what was reasonable in the circumstances of the case. With reference to the national case law and taking into account the fact that the argument of waiver was not raised before the Commission but for the first time before the Court, the latter concluded that the failure to challenge the domestic tribunal could not be said to have been unreasonable and could not amount to a tacit waiver of the right to an independent and impartial tribunal.[770]

7.4.   ESTABLISHED BY LAW

The prescription that the tribunal must be 'established by law' implies the guarantee that the organisation of the judiciary in a democratic society is not left to the discretion of the executive, but is regulated by law. The phrase covers not only the legal basis for the very existence of a 'tribunal'. In the opinion of the Commission the organisation and functioning of the tribunal must also have a legal basis.[771] The Court left the issue undecided in the *Piersack* case,[772] but in the *Posokhov* case it held that the requirement also covers the composition of the bench in each case.[773] As a rule, the Court takes the interpretation of national law by the domestic judicial authorities more or less for granted,[774] unless there appears to be a flagrant breach of the law.[775]

In the *Coëme and Others* case, four people had been accused of, in short, forgery and fraud. The criminal proceedings took place before the Belgian court of cassation as court of first instance, because the charges against them were closely linked to the prosecution of a former minister before the same court. Since Article 103 of the Belgian Constitution provided only for jurisdiction of the court of cassation as court of first instance in case of the prosecution of (former) ministers, the Court held, with regard to the proceedings against the four, that the court of cassation had not been established by law.[776] In the *Posokhov* case, the failure to compile a list of lay judges implied the lack of any

---

[769]   *Ibid.*, para. 34.
[770]   *McGonnell v. the United Kingdom, supra* n. 744, paras. 44–45; *Thompson v. the United Kingdom, supra* n. 325, paras. 44–45. See, *mutatis mutandis*, also *Pescador Valero v. Spain, supra* n. 731, paras. 23–26.
[771]   Report of 13 May 1981, *Piersack*, B.47 (1986), p. 23.
[772]   *Piersack v. Belgium, supra* n. 725, para. 30, para. 33.
[773]   *Posokhov v. Russia*, ECtHR 4 March 2003, appl. no. 63486/00, para. 39.
[774]   See, e.g., *Bulut v. Austria, supra* n. 469, para. 29.
[775]   *Lavents v. Latvia, supra* n. 730, para. 114.
[776]   *Coëme and Others v. Belgium, supra* n. 546, paras. 105–108. This trend is confirmed in *Savino and Others v. Italy,* ECtHR 28 April 2009, appl. no. 17214/05, para. 107.

legal grounds for the participation of the lay judges in the administration of justice on the day of the applicant's trial and, therefore, amounted to a violation of Article 6.[777]

The assignment of cases does not fall under 'establishment by law' in principle, but in special cases arrangements concerning the assignment of cases can lead to a violation of Article 6 on this point.[778]

8. THE PRESUMPTION OF INNOCENCE

8.1. INTRODUCTION

Article 6(2) sets forth that the person who is charged with a criminal offence, has to be presumed innocent until proved guilty according to law. The principle '*in dubio pro reo*' constitutes a specific expression of the presumption of innocence.[779] As in the case of the third paragraph, this paragraph deals with a special aspect of the general concept of 'fair trial' in criminal cases. The presumption of innocence is one of the elements of the fair criminal trial that is required by Article 6(1).[780] For that reason no further inquiry is made as to a possible violation of this provision when a violation of the first paragraph has already been found.[781] However, in the *Delta* case the Court suggested that in special circumstances there is room for a separate investigation under paragraph 2, despite the fact that a violation of the first paragraph has been established already.[782]

From the case law concerning the autonomous meaning of the concept of 'criminal charge' in the first paragraph it follows that the second and third paragraphs are also applicable to proceedings other than criminal proceedings – e.g., disciplinary proceedings[783] and administrative proceedings[784] – which

---

[777] *Posokhov v. Russia, supra* n. 773, paras. 41–42. See also *Jorgic v. Germany*, ECtHR 12 July 2007, appl. no. 74613/01, para. 65.

[778] *DMD group v. Slovakia*, ECtHR 5 October 2010, appl. no. 19334/03, paras. 65–72.

[779] *Cleve v. Germany*, ECtHR 15 January 2015, appl. no. 48144/09, para. 51; *Vassilios Stavropoulos v. Greece*, ECtHR 27 September 2007, appl. no. 35522/04, para. 39 and *Tendam v. Spain*, ECtHR 13 July 2010, appl. no. 25720/05, para. 37.

[780] *Allenet de Ribemont v. France*, ECtHR 10 February 1995, appl. no. 15175/89, para. 35; *Vassilios Stavropoulos v. Greece, supra* n. 779, para. 35 and *Virabyan v. Armenia*, ECtHR 2 October 2012, appl. no. 40094/05, para. 185; *Mokhov v. Russia*, ECtHR 4 March 2010, appl. no. 28245/04, para. 28; *Cleve v. Germany, supra* n. 779, para. 28; and *El Kaada v. Germany*, ECtHR 12 November 2015, appl. no. 2130/10, paras. 52–55.

[781] *Deweer v. Belgium, supra* n. 185, para. 56.

[782] *Delta v. France*, ECtHR 19 December 1990, appl. no. 11444/85, para. 38.

[783] *Albert and Le Compte v. Belgium, supra* n. 94, paras. 38–42.

[784] See with regard to tax penalties *A.P., M.P. and T.P. v. Switzerland, supra* n. 226, paras. 37–43 and *E.L., R.L. and J.O.-L. v. Switzerland, supra* n. 226, paras. 42–48. In *Hentrich v. France, supra* n. 454, paras. 62–64, the exercise of the right of pre-emption by the French

are to be equated with criminal proceedings by means of the criteria developed in the *Oztürk* case. In the *Phillips* case, the Court held that Article 6(2) was not applicable to confiscation proceedings pursuant to the British Drug Trafficking Act 1994. The scope of Article 6(2) is not limited to pending criminal proceedings, but extends to judicial decisions taken after a prosecution has been discontinued[785] or after an acquittal.[786] Article 6(2) does not prohibit two judicial procedures, e.g., a criminal procedure and an administrative procedure, following one similar forbidden conduct.[787]

In the important *Allen* case,[788] the Court held that the object and purpose of the Convention, as an instrument for the protection of human beings, requires that its provisions be interpreted and applied so as to make its safeguards practical and effective.[789] This applies to Article 6(2) as well.[790] Viewed as a procedural guarantee in the context of a criminal trial itself, the presumption of innocence imposes requirements in respect of, *inter alia*, the burden of proof,[791] legal presumptions of fact and law,[792] the privilege against self-incrimination,[793]

---

tax authorities because the sale price of land declared in the contract of sale was too low, was deemed not to imply an accusation of tax evasion and, accordingly, could not lead to a violation of Art. 6(2).

[785] *Melo Tadeu v. Portugal*, ECtHR 23 October 2014, appl. no. 27785/10, para. 46 offers a concise overview of the Court's case law regarding subsequent procedures in relation to the presumption of innocence. This overview involves the following case law: *Minelli v. Switzerland*, ECtHR 25 March 1983, appl. no. 8660/79; *Lutz, Englert and Nölkenbockhoff v. Germany*, ECtHR 25 August 1987, appl. no. 9912/82; *Sekanina v. Austria*, ECtHR 25 August 1993, appl. no. 13126/87; *Lamanna v. Austria, supra* n. 121; *Leutscher v. the Netherlands, supra* n. 35, para. 29; *Del Latte v. the Netherlands*, ECtHR 9 November 2004 appl. no. 44760/98, para. 30; *Vanjak v. Croatia*, ECtHR 14 January 2010, appl. no. 29889/04, para. 41; *Šikić v. Croatia*, ECtHR 15 July 2010, appl. no. 9143/08, para. 47; *Vassilios Stavropoulos v. Greece*, ECtHR, *supra* n. 779, para. 39; *Tendam v. Spain, supra* n. 779, para. 37; *Lorenzetti v. Italy*, ECtHR 10 April 2012, appl. no. 32075/09, para. 46.

[786] *Capetti and Maimut v. Romania* ECtHR 15 January 2013 (dec.), appl. no. 13043/05 and 23408/08, para. 77; *Rushiti v. Austria, supra* n. 583; and *Lamanna v. Austria, supra* n. 121.

[787] *Kapetanios and Others v. Greece*, ECtHR 30 April 2015, appl. no. 3453/12, 42941/12 and 9028/13, para. 80; *Hrdalo v. Croatia, supra* n. 461; *Vanjak v. Croatia, supra* n. 785.

[788] *Allen v. the United Kingdom, supra,* n. 554, paras. 93–94. See for a few examples of recent summaries of the Court's case law: *Dicle and Sadak v. Turkey*, ECtHR 16 June 2015, appl. no. 48621/07, paras. 50–54; *Kapetanios and Others v. Greece, supra* n. 787, paras. 82–85 and *Cleve v. Germany, supra* n. 779, paras. 32–37.

[789] *Soering v. The United Kingdom*, ECtHR 7 July 1989, appl. no. 14038/88, para. 87; *Al-Skeini and Others v. The United Kingdom*, ECtHR (GC) 7 July 2011, appl. no. 55721/07, para. 162.

[790] *Allenet de Ribemont v. France, supra* n. 780, para. 35; *Capeau v. Belgium*, ECtHR 13 January 2005, appl. no. 42914/98, para. 21; *Nešťák v. Slovakia*, ECtHR 27 February 2007, appl. no. 65559/01, para. 88.

[791] See *Barberà, Messegué and Jabardo v. Spain, supra* n. 445, para. 77, Series A no. 146, and *Telfner v. Austria, supra* n. 555, para. 15.

[792] *Salabiaku v. France, supra* n. 270, para. 28; *Radio France and Others v. France*, ECtHR 30 March 2004, appl. no. 53984/00, para. 24.

[793] *Saunders v. The United Kingdom, supra* n. 546, para. 68; *Heaney and McGuinness v. Ireland, supra* n. 547, para. 40.

pre-trial publicity[794] and premature expressions, by the trial court[795] or by other public officials,[796] of a defendant's guilt.[797]

However, in keeping with the need to ensure that the right guaranteed by Article 6(2) is practical and effective, the presumption of innocence also has another aspect. Its general aim, in this second aspect, is to protect individuals who have been acquitted of a criminal charge, or in respect of whom criminal proceedings have been discontinued, from being treated by public officials and authorities as though they are in fact guilty of the offence charged. In these cases, the presumption of innocence has already operated, through the application at trial of the various requirements inherent in the procedural guarantee it affords, to prevent an unfair criminal conviction being imposed. Without protection to ensure respect for the acquittal or the discontinuation decision in any other proceedings, the fair trial guarantees of Article 6(2) could risk becoming theoretical and illusory.[798] What is also at stake once the criminal proceedings have concluded is the person's reputation and the way in which that person is perceived by the public. To a certain extent, the protection afforded under Article 6(2) in this respect may overlap with the protection afforded by

---

[794] *Akay v. Turkey*, ECtHR 19 February 2002, appl. no. 34501/97; *G.C.P. v. Romania*, ECtHR 20 December 2011, appl. no. 20899/03, para. 46.

[795] *Vakhitov and Others v. Russia*, ECtHR 31 January 2017, appl. no. 18232/11, para. 70; *Mugosa v. Montenegro*, ECtHR 21 June 2016, appl. no. 76522/12, para. 67; *Karaman v. Germany*, ECtHR 27 February 2014, appl. no. 17103/10, para. 63; *Perica Oreb v. Croatia*, ECtHR 31 October 2013, appl. no. 20824/09, para. 140; *Finster v. Poland*, ECtHR 8 February 2011, appl. no. 24860/08, paras. 51–55; *Garycki v. Poland*, ECtHR 6 February 2007, appl. no. 14348/02, para. 66; *Minelli v. Switzerland*, supra n. 203, paras. 27, 30 and 37; *Allenet de Ribemont v. France*, supra n. 780, paras. 35–36; *Matijašević v. Serbia*, ECtHR 19 September 2006, appl. no. 23037/04, para. 45; *Phillips v. the United Kingdom*, ECtHR 5 July 2001, appl. no. 41087/98; *Engel and Others v. the Netherlands*, supra n. 209.

[796] A short overview of the Court's case law can be found in *Popovi v. Bulgaria*, ECtHR 9 June 2016, appl. no. 39651/11, para. 85. See also, e.g., *Toni Kostadinov v. Bulgaria*, ECtHR 27 January 2015, appl. no. 37124/10, paras. 113–115; *Ilgar Mammadov v. Azerbaijan*, ECtHR 22 May 2014, appl. no. 15172/13, para. 126; *Lizaso Azconobieta v. Spain*, ECtHR 28 June 2011, appl. no. 28834/08, para. 37; *Viorel Burzo v. Romania*, ECtHR 30 June 2009, appl. nos. 75109/01 and 12639/02, para. 156; *Gutsanovi v. Bulgaria*, appl. no. 34529/10, paras. 191 and 193 and *Lavents v. Latvia*, supra n. 730, para. 126. These public officials can be the president of Parliament (*Butkevičius v. Lithuania*, appl. no. 48297/99, paras. 50 and 53), the prosecutor (*Daktaras v. Lithuania*, supra n. 748, para. 44) or the State Secretary of Internal Affairs (*Allenet de Ribemont v. France*, supra n. 780, para. 37).

[797] *Allenet de Ribemont v. France*, supra n. 780, paras. 35–36; *Daktaras v. Lithuania*, supra n. 748, para. 41; *Y.B. and Others v. Turkey*, ECtHR 28 October 2004, appl. nos. 48173/99 and 48319/99, para. 44; *A.L. v. Germany*, ECtHR 28 April 2005, appl. no. 72758/01, para. 31; *Nestak v. Slovakia*, supra n. 790, para. 88; *Moullet v. France*, ECtHR 13 September 2007 (dec.), appl. no. 27521/04; *Peltereau-Villeneuve v. Switzerland*, ECtHR 28 October 2014, appl. no. 60101/09, para. 31; *Caraian v. Romania*, ECtHR 23 June 2015, appl. no. 34456/07, para. 74; *Kolomenskiy v. Russia*, ECtHR 13 December 2016, appl. no. 27297/07; *Kemal Coskun v. Turkey*, ECtHR 29 March 2017, appl. no. 45028/07, paras. 41 and 42.

[798] *Alkasi v. Turkey*, ECtHR 18 October 2016, appl. no. 21107/07, paras. 22–29.

Article 8.[799] In short, the Court emphasises that the purpose of the right to be presumed innocent until proven guilty is not only to guarantee the fairness of the criminal trial from undue influences but also to protect a person's reputation from unjustified brandings of guilt.[800] There is a fundamental distinction to be made though, between a statement that someone is merely suspected of having committed a crime and a clear judicial declaration, in the absence of a final conviction, that the individual has committed the crime in question.[801] Officials should refrain from declaring a person guilty before conviction by a court. However, they may tell the public about criminal investigations by, for example, reporting suspicions, arrests and confessions, if they do it discreetly and circumspectly.[802] Choice of words matters.[803]

8.2. WITH RESPECT TO EVIDENCE

The most important aspect of the presumption of innocence concerns the foundation of the conviction. This aspect is very closely connected with the requirement of the court's impartiality discussed above.[804] The court has to presume the innocence of the accused without any prejudice and may sentence him only on the basis of evidence put forward during the trial, which moreover has to constitute 'lawful' evidence recognised as such by law. The Court has formulated the essence of the principle as follows: 'Paragraph 2 embodies the principle of the presumption of innocence. It requires, *inter alia*, that when carrying out their duties, the members of a court should not start with the preconceived idea that the accused has committed the offence charged; the burden of proof is on the prosecution, and any doubt should benefit the accused. It also follows that it is for the prosecution to inform the accused of the case that will be made against him, so that he may prepare and present his defence accordingly, and to adduce evidence sufficient to convict him.'[805]

---

[799] *Zollman v. The United Kingdom*, ECtHR 27 November 2003, appl. no. 62902/00; *Taliadorou and Stylianou v. Cyprus*, ECtHR 16 October 2008, appl. nos. 39627/05 and 39631/05, paras. 27 and 56–59; *Cleve v. Germany, supra* n. 779, para. 35.

[800] *Kemal Coskun v. Turkey, supra* n. 797; *El Kaada v. Germany, supra* n. 780, para. 42 and *Allen v. the United Kingdom supra* n. 554, para. 94.

[801] *Dicle and Sadak v. Turkey, supra* n. 788, para. 52; *Garycki v. Poland, supra* n. 795, para. 71; *Nešták v. Slovakia, supra* n. 790, para. 89; *Wojciechowski v. Poland*, ECtHR 9 December 2008, appl. no. 5422/04, para. 54; *Leutscher v. the Netherlands, supra* n. 35, para. 31.

[802] *Krause v. Switzerland*, appl. no. 7986/77, Commission decision of 3 October 1978, Decisions and Reports 13, p. 73 and *Allenet de Ribemont, supra* n. 780, para. 38.

[803] *Daktaras v. Lithuania, supra* n. 748, para. 41; *Turyev v. Russia*, ECtHR 11 October 2016, appl. no. 20758/04, para. 19; *Slavov and Others v. Bulgaria*, ECtHR 10 November 2015, appl. no. 58500/10, paras. 116–118.

[804] *Cf.*, e.g., *Lavents v. Latvia, supra* n. 730, paras. 119–121 and 125–128, and *Kyprianou v. Cyprus, supra* n. 726, paras. 51–58.

[805] *Barberà, Messegué and Jabardo v. Spain, supra* n. 445, paras. 67–68; see also, *Janosevic v. Sweden, supra* n. 626, para. 97.

The presumption of innocence is closely linked to the right not to incriminate oneself.[806]

The presumption of innocence will be infringed where the burden of proof is shifted from the prosecution to the defence.[807] In the *Capeau*[808] case, the court reviewed an act which expressly provides that a person against whom proceedings have been discontinued must establish his innocence by adducing factual evidence or submitting legal argument to that effect; such a requirement, without qualification or reservation, casts doubt on the applicant's innocence. According to the Court the burden of proof cannot simply be reversed in compensation proceedings brought following a final decision to discontinue proceedings. Requiring a person to establish his or her innocence, which suggests that the court regards that person as guilty, is unreasonable and discloses an infringement of the presumption of innocence. In the *Ringvold*[809] case, the Court considered that, while exoneration from criminal liability ought to stand in the compensation proceedings, it should not preclude the establishment of civil liability to pay compensation arising out of the same facts on the basis of a less strict burden of proof.[810] However, in order to comply with the right guaranteed under Article 6(2), the national courts in the subsequent proceedings need to stay within the bounds of a civil forum and refrain from suggesting criminal characterisation of the applicant's conduct.[811] Any statement or reasoning by a civil court calling into question the applicant's established innocence would be incompatible with the requirements of Article 6(2).

The evidence put forward at the trial may refer back to statements previously made by the accused or testimony by witnesses, provided that the latter can be revoked or refuted during the trial.[812] If a witness does not wish to act as a witness during the trial and can advance a legitimate reason for it, there is no objection to a reading of previous testimony, provided that the right of the defence to question witnesses is sufficiently upheld, e.g., by having provided the opportunity to interrogate and contradict that witness in an earlier phase of the

---

806   *Heaney and McGuinness v. Ireland, supra* n. 547, para. 40.
807   *Telfner v. Austria, supra* n. 555, para. 15.
808   *Capeau v. Belgium, supra* n. 790.
809   *Ringvold v. Norway*, ECtHR 11 February 2003, appl. no. 34964/97. See also *Y. v. Norway*, ECtHR 11 February 2003, appl. no. 56568/00, para. 41; *Lundkvist v. Sweden*, ECtHR 13 December 2003, appl. no. 48518/99; *Vella v. Malta*, ECtHR 11 February 2014, appl. no. 69122/10, para. 56; *Alkasi v. Turkey, supra* n. 798, para. 30.
810   See, *mutatis mutandis*, *X v. Austria*, EComHR 6 October 1982, no. 9295/81, Decisions and Reports (DR) 30, p. 227, and *C. v. The United Kingdom*, EComHR 7 October 1987, appl. no. 11882/85, DR 54, p. 162.
811   *Alkasi v. Turkey, supra* n. 798, para. 30; *Teodor v. Romania*, ECtHR 4 June 2013, appl. no. 46878/06, para. 44; *N.A. v. Norway*, ECtHR 18 December 2014, appl. no. 27473/11, para. 46.
812   See *infra* 9.5.

proceedings. If this condition has not been met, the verdict must not be based exclusively or largely on such testimony.[813]

Every instance giving rise to the least doubt with regard to the evidence has to be construed in favour of the accused.[814] This does not necessarily mean that the evidence put forward must be absolutely conclusive – in several legal systems ultimately the conviction on the part of the court is the point that matters – but it does mean that the court must base its conviction exclusively on the evidence put forward during the trial. A sentence may of course also be based on a confession of guilt on the part of the accused. In that case, however, the court will have to ascertain thoroughly that this confession has been made in complete freedom.[815] From a statement of the accused which is not intended to be a confession of guilt, no such confession may be inferred. Article 6(1) embodies the right of the accused not to incriminate himself and the right to remain silent, which is closely linked to the presumption of innocence. In the *John Murray* case, in which the prosecution had built up a 'formidable' case against the applicant, the Court held that the drawing of adverse inferences from the applicant's silence had not violated Article 6(1).[816] In the *Telfner* case, however, it reached a different conclusion. The drawing of inferences from the applicant's silence had constituted a violation of Article 6(2) because the prosecution had not been able to establish a convincing *prima facie* case against the applicant.[817]

In the *Zollmann* decision,[818] the Court considered that the presumption of innocence prohibits the premature expression by the tribunal itself of the opinion that the person charged with the criminal offence is guilty before he has been so proved according to law.[819] It also covers statements made by other public officials about pending criminal investigations which encourage the public to believe the suspect guilty and prejudge the assessment of the facts by the competent judicial authority. It suffices, in the absence of a formal finding, that there is some reasoning suggesting that the court or the official in question regards the accused as guilty, while a premature expression of such an opinion by the tribunal itself will inevitably run afoul of the presumption of innocence.[820]

---

[813] *Unterpertinger v. Austria*, ECtHR 24 November 1986, appl. no. 9120/80, A.110, paras. 31–33. On the issue of anonymous witnesses, see *infra* 9.5.

[814] *Barberà, Messegué and Jabardo v. Spain, supra* n. 445, para. 77.

[815] Insofar as the confession has been extorted by illegal means, such as physical or mental torture, this follows already from the words 'according to law'; *Austria v. Italy*, EComHR 31 March 1963, appl. no. 788/60, Pfunders, Yearbook VI (1963), p. 784.

[816] *John Murray v. The United Kingdom, supra* n. 549, paras. 44–58.

[817] *Telfner v. Austria, supra* n. 555, paras. 17–20. See on the right to remain silent *supra* 4.5.

[818] *Zollman v. The United Kingdom, supra* n. 799. See also in relation to extradition procedures *Eshonkulov v. Russia*, ECtHR 15 January 2015, appl. no. 68900/13, paras. 74 and 75 and *Ismoilov and Others v. Russia*, ECtHR 24 April 2008, appl. no. 2947/06.

[819] *Minelli v. Switzerland, supra* n. 785.

[820] *Ibid.*, para. 37; *Nerattini v. Greece*, ECtHR 18 December 2008, appl. no. 43529/01, para. 23; *Didu v. Romania*, ECtHR 14 April 2009, appl. no. 34814/02, para. 41; *Nestak v. Slovakia, supra*

What counts, is the true meaning and not the literal meaning of the statement.[821] Article 6(2) is aimed at preventing the undermining of a fair criminal trial by prejudicial statements made in close connection with those proceedings. Where no such proceedings are, or have been in existence, statements attributing criminal or other reprehensible conduct are relevant rather to considerations of protection against defamation and adequate access to court to determine civil rights and raising potential issues under Articles 8 and 6 of the Convention.[822] The fact that the accused was ultimately found guilty does not touch his initial right to be presumed innocent until proved guilty.[823]

In the *Minelli* case, the Court had to review the apportionment of the costs of a private prosecution for defamation. The national court decided not to proceed further with the complaint and to order the applicant to pay part of the court costs and compensation in respect of the prosecutors' expenses. According to the Court, Article 6(2) governs criminal proceedings in their entirety, 'irrespective of the outcome of the prosecution'.[824] Furthermore, the Court emphasises that a fundamental distinction must be made between a statement that someone is merely suspected of having committed a crime, merely describing 'a state of suspicion' and a clear judicial declaration, in the absence of a final conviction, that an individual has committed the crime in question.[825] The latter infringes the presumption of innocence, whereas the former is unobjectionable according to the Court.[826] The principle of the presumption of innocence may be infringed not only by a judge or court but also by other public authorities, including prosecutors. According to the Court in the *Daktaras* case,[827] this is particularly so where a prosecutor performs a quasi-judicial function when ruling on the request of the accused to dismiss the charges at the stage of the pre-trial investigation, over which he has full procedural control. Nevertheless, whether a statement of a public official is in breach of the principle of the presumption of innocence must be determined in the context of the particular circumstances in which the statement was made.[828] However, statements by judges are subject to stricter scrutiny than those by investigative authorities.[829] In the *Sekanina*

n. 790, paras. 88 and 89; *Garycki v. Poland, supra* n. 795, para. 66; *Deweer v. Belgium, supra* n. 185, paras. 56 and 37; *Allenet de Ribemont v. France, supra* n. 780, paras. 35–36.

[821] *Lavents v. Latvia, supra* n. 730, para. 126.

[822] *Zollman v. The United Kingdom, supra* n. 799; *Ismoilov and Others v. Russia, supra* n. 818, para. 160; *Allenet de Ribemont v. France, supra* n. 780, para. 41.

[823] *Matijašević v. Serbia, supra* n. 795, para. 49; *Nestak v. Slovakia, supra* n. 790, para. 90.

[824] *Minelli v. Switzerland, supra* n. 785, paras. 27 and 30; *Adolf v. Austria, supra* n. 182, para. 30.

[825] *Neagoe v. Romania*, ECtHR 21 July 2015, appl. no. 23319/08, para. 42; *Nestak v. Slovakia, supra* n. 790, para. 89; *Matijašević v. Serbia, supra* n. 795, para. 48; *Marziano v. Italy*, ECtHR 28 November 2002, appl. no. 45313/99, para. 31.

[826] *Garycki v. Poland, supra* n. 795, para. 67; *Lutz v. Germany, supra* n. 242, para. 62; *Leutscher v. The Netherlands, supra* n. 35, para. 31.

[827] *Daktaras v. Lithuania, supra* n. 748, para. 42.

[828] *Adolf v. Austria, supra* n. 182, paras. 36–41.

[829] *Pandy v. Belgium*, ECtHR 21 September 2006, appl. no. 13583/02, para. 43.

case,[830] the national courts which had to rule on the claim for compensation undertook an assessment of the applicant's guilt on the basis of the contents of the file. According to the Court the voicing of suspicions regarding an accused's innocence is conceivable as long as the conclusion of criminal proceedings has not resulted in a decision on the merits of the accusation. However, it is no longer admissible to rely on such suspicions once an acquittal has become final.[831]

If during the trial statements are made or produced by the prosecutor, witnesses or experts from which bias on their part is evident, the court has to make a stand against those statements if it is to avoid the semblance of being biased as well. If the court does so, the accused can no longer complain of such bias on the part of the first-mentioned persons.[832] The same holds good if a sentence which the accused alleges to have been dictated by bias, has been upheld on appeal, while the court of appeal has made an inquiry into this very matter. In that case the accused will be able to complain only of bias on the part of this court of appeal or of the fact that the injury caused by the bias of the lower court has not been redressed by the higher court.[833]

In a democratic society it is sometimes inevitable that the press strongly and intensively comments.[834] A virulent press campaign can adversely affect the fairness of a trial by influencing public opinion and, consequently, jurors called upon to decide the guilt of an accused.[835] National courts which are entirely composed of professional judges generally pose, unlike members of a jury, appropriate experience and training enabling them to resist any outside influence.[836] The publication of photographs of suspects does not in itself breach the presumption of innocence,[837] whereas broadcasting of the suspect's images on television may raise an issue.[838]

---

[830]   *Sekanina v. Russia*, ECtHR 25 August 1993, appl. no. 13126/87, para. 30.

[831]   *Rushiti v. Austria*, *supra* n. 583, para. 31; *O. v. Norway*, ECtHR 11 February 2003, appl. no. 29327/95, para. 39; *Geerings v. The Netherlands*, ECtHR 1 March 2007, appl. no. 30810/03, para. 49; *Paraponiaris v. Greece*, ECtHR 25 September 2008, appl. no. 42132, para. 32; *Vlieeland Boddy and Marcelo Lanni v. Spain*, ECtHR 16 February 2016, appl. no. 53465/11 and 9634/12, para. 39.

[832]   *Austria v. Italy*, EComHR 31 March 1963, appl. no. 788/60, Pfunders, Yearbook VI (1963), p. 740 (784); *Nielsen v. Denmark*, EComHR 15 March 1961, appl. no. 343/57, Yearbook IV (1961), p. 490 (568). See also *Bernard v. France*, ECtHR 23 April 1998, appl. no. 22885/93, paras. 37–41, where the Court held that the psychiatric experts appointed by the investigating judge logically had to start from the working hypothesis that the applicant had committed the crimes, which had given rise to the prosecution.

[833]   Report in *Austria v. Italy*, EComHR 31 March 1963, appl. no. 788/60, Pfunders, Yearbook VI (1963), p. 740 (784), *ibid.*

[834]   *Viorel Burzo v. Romania*, *supra* n. 796, para. 160; *Akay v. Turkey*, ECtHR 24 October 2006, appl. no. 58539.

[835]   *Kuzmin v. Russia*, ECtHR 18 March 2010, appl. no. 58939/00, para. 62.

[836]   *Craxi v. Italy*, *supra* n. 721, para. 104; *Mircea v. Romania*, ECtHR 29 March 2007, appl. no. 41250/02, para. 75.

[837]   *Y.B. and Others v. Turkey*, *supra* n. 797, para. 47.

[838]   *Rupa v. Romania*, ECtHR 16 December 2008, appl. no. 58478/00, para. 232.

The practice where during the trial the criminal record, if any, of the accused is brought to the notice of the court, does not constitute a conflict with Article 6(2).[839] It is obvious, however, that such information may promote a presumption of guilt on the part of the court or the jury, so that the person in question has at least to be given an opportunity to advance evidence that the criminal record has unduly influenced the court.

The presumption of innocence requires that criminal liability does not survive the person who has allegedly committed the criminal act.[840]

8.3. WITH RESPECT TO TREATMENT OF THE ACCUSED

In addition to the establishment of guilt, Article 6(2) also has consequences for the treatment of the accused; in this respect, too, his innocence must be presumed. This applies to the treatment of the accused during the preliminary examination and the trial, as well as to the treatment of a person detained on remand: that treatment may not have a punitive character.[841] However, as the Court held in the *Peers* case, Article 6 does not require separate treatment for convicted and accused persons in prisons.[842]

8.4. WITH RESPECT TO THE PRESUMPTION OF ACCOUNTABILITY

The principle embodied in paragraph 2 also applies in those criminal cases where the issue of guilt is not a central issue. In the leading *Salabiaku* case, the Court held that the Contracting States are in principle free, subject to certain conditions, to establish an offence on the basis of an objective fact as such, irrespective of whether it results from criminal intent or from negligence. The applicant was convicted for smuggling prohibited goods, while the legal presumption of accountability was inferred from the proven fact of possession of such goods. The Court stressed the relative nature of the distinction between presumption of accountability and presumption of guilt. Presumptions of fact or of law operate in every legal system; in principle, this is not contrary to the Convention. The Contracting States are, however, under the obligation to remain within reasonable limits in this respect as regards their criminal law provisions, taking into account the importance of what is at stake, and to maintain the

---

[839]   *Albert and Le Compte v. Belgium, supra* n. 94, para. 40.

[840]   *A.P., M.P. and T.P. v. Switzerland, supra* n. 226, paras. 44–48 and *E.L., R.L. and J.O.-L. v. Switzerland, supra* n. 226, paras. 49–53.

[841]   *Erdem v. Germany*, ECtHR 5 July 2001, appl. no. 38321/97, para. 49, where the Court held, however, that is was not necessary to investigate the complaint under Art. 6(2), because it had already found a violation of the reasonable-time requirement of Art. 5(3).

[842]   *Peers v. Greece*, ECtHR 19 April 2001, appl. no. 28524/95, para. 78.

rights of the defence. Indeed, the guarantee of Article 6(2) must also be respected by the legislature while, according to the Court, the words 'according to law' are not to be construed exclusively with reference to domestic law but contain a reference to the fundamental principle of the rule of law.[843]

In other cases, the Court has found that rebuttable presumptions of accountability are not incompatible with Article 6(2) as long as states remain within reasonable limits. In the *Phillips* case, the Court found no unfairness in confiscation proceedings where national law required, in short, the court sentencing a person of a drug trafficking offence to assume that any property appearing to have been held by him during the period of six years prior to the commencement of the criminal proceedings, was received as a payment or reward in connection with drug trafficking. Although the assumption was mandatory, the legal system was not without safeguards, especially because the assumption could have been rebutted if the defendant had shown, on the balance of probabilities, that he had acquired the property other than through drug trafficking.[844]

In the *Radio France and Others* case, the applicants complained that the Audiovisual Communication Act created an irrefutable presumption that the editorial director of the radio station was criminally liable for the defamatory statements made on air. The Court held that the presumption was not completely irrebuttable and that, taking into account what was at stake, i.e. the need to prevent the broadcasting of damaging statements in the media by obliging the editorial director to exercise prior control, it remained within the requisite 'reasonable limits'.[845] In the *Klouvi* case, however, the Court found that the statutory presumption that, in case no charges were brought against a suspect, the accusation made against that suspect should be considered false and malicious, which presumption lead to an automatic conviction for false accusation of the person who complained of a sexual assault, violated Article 6(2).[846]

8.5. WITH RESPECT TO POST-TRIAL DECISIONS

The scope of application of Article 6(2) extends beyond the formal determination of the criminal charge and can be applicable in subsequent proceedings. The Court has examined the application of Article 6(2) to judicial decisions taken following the conclusion of criminal proceedings, for example with regard to an obligation to bear court and prosecution costs, compensation for pre-

---

[843] *Salabiaku v. France, supra* n. 270, para. 28. See also *Pham Hoang v. France*, ECtHR 25 September 1992, appl. no. 13191/87, para. 33; *Falk v. the Netherlands*, ECtHR 19 October 2004, appl. no. 66273/01 (dec.); *Västberga Taxi Aktiebolag and Vulic v. Sweden, supra* n. 613, para. 113.

[844] *Phillips v. the United Kingdom, supra* n. 795, paras. 40–47. The Court discussed the matter under Art. 6(1), because it held Art. 6(2) not to be applicable. See also *Grayson and Barnham v. the United Kingdom*, ECtHR 23 September 2008, appl. no. 19955/05 and 15085/06, paras. 42–50.

[845] *Radio France and Others v. France, supra* n. 792, para. 24.

[846] *Klouvi v. France*, ECtHR 30 June 2011, appl. no. 30754/03, para. 41.

trial detention or other consequences of unlawful or wrongful investigation or prosecution, the imposition of civil liability to compensate the victim, civil claims against insurers, child care orders in cases where the charges against the parent for child abuse have been dropped, disciplinary or dismissal issues, and the revocation of the right to social housing.[847]

In the *Allen* case, the Grand Chamber elaborated on the Court's previous case law on the issue and formulated the principle of presumption of innocence in this context as follows: 'the presumption of innocence means that where there has been a criminal charge and criminal proceedings have ended in an acquittal, the person who was the subject of the criminal proceedings is innocent in the eyes of the law and must be treated in a manner consistent with that innocence. To this extent, therefore, the presumption of innocence will remain after the conclusion of criminal proceedings in order to ensure that, as regards any charge which was not proven, the innocence of the person in question is respected. This overriding concern lies at the root of the Court's approach to the applicability of Article 6 §2 in these cases.'[848]

Importantly, 'there is no single approach to ascertaining the circumstances in which the Article will be violated in the context of proceedings which follow the conclusion of criminal proceedings.'[849] Naturally, much depends on the nature and context of the proceedings. For the assessment whether the decision and its reasoning complied with Article 6(2), the language used by the decision-maker is of critical importance.[850] Having regard to the nature and context of the proceedings, 'even the use of some unfortunate language may not be decisive' to establish a violation of the principle of presumption of innocence.[851]

For the application of Article 6(2) in subsequent proceedings, the applicant must demonstrate the existence of a link between the concluded criminal proceedings and the subsequent proceedings. Such a link can for example be established in cases 'where the subsequent proceedings require examination of the outcome of the prior criminal proceedings and, in particular, where they oblige the court to analyse the criminal judgment, to engage in a review or evaluation of the evidence in the criminal file, to assess the applicant's participation in some or all of the events leading to the criminal charge, or to comment on the subsisting indications of the applicant's possible guilt.'[852]

---

[847] For an elaborate list of references, see *Allen v. the United Kingdom, supra* n. 554, para. 98.

[848] *Ibid.*, para. 103.

[849] *Ibid.*, para. 125.

[850] For examples, see *ibid.*, para. 126. See also *Kemanl Coskun v. Turkey, supra* n. 797, paras. 51–57.

[851] *Allen v. the United Kingdom, supra* n. 554, para. 126. For a recent example, in the context of probationary release proceedings, see *Müller v. Germany*, ECtHR 27 March 2014, appl. no. 54963/08, paras. 46–55.

[852] *Allen v. the United Kingdom, supra* n. 554, para. 104. See also *N.A. v. Norway, supra* n. 811, paras. 31–52 (not violation of presumption of innocence due to absence of a link between proceedings); *Alkasi v. Turkey, supra* n. 798, paras. 30–33 (a violation of presumption of innocence in proceedings before a labour court).

9. MINIMUM RIGHTS FOR THE CRIMINAL SUSPECT

9.1. INTRODUCTION

Article 6(3) contains an enumeration of the minimum rights to which everyone charged with a criminal offence is entitled. This provision, unlike the first paragraph, does not relate to proceedings concerning the determination of civil rights and obligations. On the one hand, however, if a party to civil proceedings is denied the rights mentioned in paragraph 3, under certain circumstances this may entail that there is no 'fair hearing' in the sense of the first paragraph.[853] On the other hand, the fact that 'civil rights and obligations' are at issue does not exclude that the proceedings have a criminal character.[854]

The specific enumeration in the third paragraph for criminal proceedings does not imply that an examination for compatibility with the third paragraph makes an examination for compatibility with the first paragraph superfluous, since the guarantees contained in the third paragraph of Article 6 are constituent elements, *inter alia*, of the general notion of a fair trial.[855] The enumeration of the third paragraph is not limitative in that respect, and it is therefore possible that, although the guarantees mentioned there have been satisfied, the trial as a whole still does not satisfy the requirements of a fair trial. As a result of an extensive and functional interpretation of the third paragraph in the Strasbourg case law, however, examination for compatibility with the third and with the first paragraph is in fact likely to more or less coincide. At all events, in the case of a negative outcome of the examination for compatibility with the first paragraph an examination with regard to the third paragraph is deemed superfluous.[856]

Article 6 – and especially its paragraph 3 – applies not only to the trial court proceedings, but is also relevant to pre-trial proceedings, because an initial failure to comply with the provisions of paragraph 3 before a case is sent for trial, may jeopardise the fairness of the trial as a whole.[857]

---

[853] The lack of free legal aid may, e.g., bar the exercise of the right of 'access to court'.

[854] *Minelli v. Switzerland*, *supra* n. 785, para. 28; *Gäfgen v Germany*, *supra* n. 491, para. 169; *Sakhnovskiy v. Russia*, ECtHR (GC) 2 November 2010, appl. no. 21272/03, para. 94.

[855] *Goddi v. Italy*, ECtHR 9 April 1984, appl. no. 8966/80, para. 28; *Colozza v. Italy*, *supra* n. 189, para. 26.

[856] *Deweer v. Belgium*, *supra* n. 185, para. 56.

[857] See, e.g., *Imbrioscia v. Switzerland*, ECtHR 24 November 1993, appl. no. 13972/88, para. 36; *John Murray v. the United Kingdom*, *supra* n. 549, para. 62; *Berlinski v. Poland*, ECtHR 20 June 2002, appl. nos. 27715/95 and 30209/96, para. 75.

9.2. INFORMATION OF THE ACCUSED

Under paragraph 3(a) the accused is granted the right to be informed promptly, in a language which he understands and in detail, of the nature and cause of the accusation against him. This right, which constitutes an 'essential prerequisite' for a fair trial,[858] is very closely related to the right granted under paragraph 3(b) that he must have adequate time and facilities for the preparation of the defence.[859] As the Court held in the *Pélissier and Sassi* case, the provision implies the right of the accused to be informed of the cause of the accusation, that is to say the acts he is alleged to have committed and on which the accusation is based, but also of the nature of the accusation, that is the legal characterisation given to those acts.[860] This information should be detailed enough for the accused to understand fully the extent of the charges against in order to be able to prepare his defence.[861] However, in this phase it is not yet necessary to furnish any evidence in support of the charge.[862] There are no special requirements as to the manner in which the accused is to be informed of the cause and nature of the charges.[863] The obligation to inform the defendant, which rests entirely on the prosecuting authorities, cannot be complied with passively by making information available without notifying the defence.[864]

The question of whether the required information has been furnished 'promptly' (*dans le plus court délai*), has to be assessed in each individual case on the basis of its specific circumstances. In order to enable the accused to prepare his defence the prosecutor will have to inform him as soon as it has been decided to institute criminal proceedings and, if necessary, make provisions for a translation or for the presence of an interpreter. On that occasion, he will have to provide the relevant data available at that moment, which afterwards are to be supplemented, if need be, particularly when the summons is issued. However, adequate defence may already be of great importance in the phase preceding the

---

[858] See, e.g., *Pélissier and Sassi v. France*, ECtHR (GC) 25 March 1999, appl. no. 25444/94, para. 52; *Dallos v. Hungary*, ECtHR 1 March 2001, appl. no. 29082/95, para. 47; *Sadak and Others v. Turkey (No. 1)*, ECtHR 17 July 2001, appl. nos. 29900/96, 29901/96, 29902/96 and 29903/96, para. 49; *Sejdovic v. Italy, supra* n. 422, para. 90.

[859] See, e.g., *Mattoccia v. Italy*, ECtHR 25 July 2000, appl. no. 23969/94, para. 60.

[860] *Pélissier and Sassi v. France, supra* n. 858, para. 51. See also, e.g., *Dallos v. Hungary, supra* n. 858, para. 47; *Sipavicius v. Lithuania*, ECtHR 21 February 2002, appl. no. 49093/99, para. 27; *Mattocia v. Italy, supra* n. 859, para. 59; *Penev v. Bulgaria*, ECtHR 7 January 2010, appl. no. 20494/04, paras. 33, 42.

[861] *Pélissier and Sassi v. France, supra* n. 858, para. 51; *Mattocia v. Italy, supra* n. 859, para. 60; *Bäckström and Andersson v. Sweden*, ECtHR 5 September 2006, appl. no. 67930/01 (dec.).

[862] *X v. Belgium*, EComHR 9 May 1977, appl. no. 7628/76, D&R 9 (1978), p. 169 (173); *Colozza and Rubinat v. Italy*, EComHR 5 May 1983, appl. no. 9024/80, A.89, p. 28.

[863] *Pélissier and Sassi v. France, supra* n. 858, para. 53; *Drassich v. Italy*, ECtHR 11 December 2007, appl. no. 25575/04, para. 34; *Giosakis v. Greece (No. 3)*, ECtHR 3 May 2011, appl. no. 5689/08, para. 29.

[864] *Mattoccia v. Italy, supra* n. 859, para. 65.

ultimate decision as to whether or not to institute proceedings and it may even affect this decision, so that it results from the rationale of paragraphs 3(a) and 3(b) that even before this formal decision the accused must be kept informed as fully as possible of the suspicion against him.[865]

Paragraph 3(a) requires that the information must be furnished 'in detail', but does not impose any special formal requirement as to the manner in which the defendant is to be informed.[866] The extent of detail depends on the particular circumstances of the case, although it is clear that the information provided must suffice to enable the defendant to understand fully the charges with a view to preparing an adequate defence.[867] An alternative charge satisfies the requirement of specificity.[868]

The reclassification of the charges in the course of the proceedings may impair the accused in his defence. Therefore, he must be made aware that the offence may be reclassified.[869] In case the reclassification concerns only an element intrinsic to the original accusation, the Court holds the view that the accused must be considered to have been aware of the possible reclassification.[870]

From the words 'in a language which he understands' it follows that if the accused has an insufficient mastery of the vernacular, the information must be translated for him. For this no particular form is prescribed, but the Court seems to require a written translation. An oral elucidation by the person who serves the writ of summons upon the accused, or by an interpreter would seem to be

---

[865] In *T. v. Austria*, ECtHR 14 November 2000, appl. no. 27783/95, the Court held Art. 6(1), taken in conjunction with Art. 6(3) sub-paras. (a) and (b), to have been violated. The district court had ordered the applicant to supplement his legal aid request, but it had not informed him of the suspicion that he had made false statements in his previous request. Subsequently the district court imposed a fine for abuse of process. The applicant learned about the accusation only when the district's court decision was served on him.

[866] *Kamasinski v. Austria*, supra n. 331, para. 79; *Pélissier and Sassi v. France*, supra n. 858, para. 53.

[867] *Mattoccia v. Italy*, supra n. 859, para. 60. In this case Art. 6 had been violated *inter alia* because the information in the accusation had been vague on essential points concerning time and place and had been repeatedly contradicted and amended in the course of the trial (paras. 63–72). See also *Kyprianou v. Cyprus*, supra n. 726, paras. 65–68, where the material facts which appeared to be crucial for the court's decision to impose on the applicant the sentence of imprisonment, were not disclosed before that decision, which amounted to a violation of the presumption of innocence.

[868] *X v. The Netherlands*, ECtHR 15 December 1969, appl. no. 3894/68, Coll. 32 (1970), p. 47 (50).

[869] *Pélissier and Sassi v. France*, supra n. 858, para. 56; *Dallos v. Hungary*, supra n. 858, para. 48; *Sadak and Others v. Turkey (No. 1)*, supra n. 858, para. 52. A proposal made by the public authorities, acting as a civil party, to the registry of the Court of Appeal to reclassify the criminal acts, without informing the defendant of this proposal, was considered by the Commission to violate the third paragraph under (a): *Chichlian and Ekindjian v. France*, ECtHR 16 March 1989, appl. no. 10959/84, p. 52. Before the Court gave judgment, a friendly settlement was reached.

[870] *De Salvador Torres v. Spain*, ECtHR 24 October 1996, appl. no. 21525/93, paras. 30–33, with respect to an aggravated circumstance. In *Pélissier and Sassi v. France*, supra n. 858, paras. 57–61, the Court held that 'aiding and abetting criminal bankruptcy' did not constitute an intrinsic element of 'criminal bankruptcy'.

---

an insufficient basis for the preparation of his defence.[871] It also seems dubious whether paragraph 3(a) has been satisfied if the information is sent to counsel who has mastery of the vernacular and may find ways to inform his client, since in this way the authorities shift an obligation resting upon them on to counsel, while it is important for the accused that he himself is also able to follow the defence put forward on his behalf as adequately as possible. In the *Brozicek* case, the Court concluded that, since the applicant was not of Italian origin, did not reside in Italy and informed the judicial authorities that he did not understand the Italian language, it was for the judicial authority to procure a translation unless it could be established that the person concerned was objectively capable of understanding the content of the notification.[872]

9.3. TIME AND FACILITIES FOR THE DEFENCE

Under paragraph 3(b) the accused is guaranteed the right to have adequate time and facilities for the preparation of his defence. Apart from the above-mentioned relation with paragraph 3(a) there is also a close connection with paragraph 3(c), regulating legal aid. In that context, the Commission has emphasised that here not only the rights of the accused are concerned, but equally the rights of counsel, so that for the assessment of the overall situation the position of both of them has to be taken into account.[873] In the *Makhfi* case, after a session that lasted almost 16 hours, counsel for the accused addressed the jury at 4.25 in the morning. The judge and jury, who held their deliberations between 6.15 and 8.15 in the morning, found the applicant guilty and sentenced him to eight years' imprisonment. These facts amounted to a violation of the first paragraph taken together with the third paragraph of Article 6, since the Court considered it essential that not only the accused but also his counsel should be able to make their submissions without suffering from excessive tiredness.[874]

The question of whether the accused has been allowed adequate time for the preparation of his defence will have to be decided afterwards, according to the circumstances in which both the accused and his counsel found themselves, and on the basis of the nature of the case.[875] If the accused has great confidence

---

[871] *Kamasinski v. Austria*, *supra* n. 331, para. 79.
[872] *Brozicek v. Italy*, *supra* n. 188, para. 41.
[873] *Ofner v. Austria*, EComHR 19 December 1960, appl. no. 524/59, Yearbook III (1960), p. 322 (352). The question whether the surveillance of the contacts of a detainee with his lawyer is permissible, will be discussed under para. 3(c).
[874] *Makhfi v. France*, ECtHR 19 October 2004, appl. no. 59335/00, paras. 34–42.
[875] See, e.g., *Öcalan v. Turkey*, ECtHR 12 March 2003, appl. no. 46221/99, paras. 167–169, where Art. 6 was found to have been violated, *inter alia*, because of the fact that the defence received a 17,000-page file approximately 2 weeks before the beginning of the trial and also the fact that the lawyers had only limited access to their client; *X and Y v. Austria*, EComHR 12 October 1978, appl. no. 7909/77, D&R 15 (1979), p. 160 (162–163), where the Commission, notwithstanding the fact that counsel could communicate with his client only with difficulty

in a particular lawyer, who is very occupied at the relevant time, the judicial authorities will have to take this into account as much as possible. On the other hand, in that case the accused cannot advance the resulting delay as a ground for violation of the first paragraph of Article 6. If for one reason or another the accused has to change counsel, the new lawyer will have to be given adequate time to become acquainted with the case.[876] If there is a right to free legal aid, a lawyer has to be assigned in good time.[877] The accused, however, cannot complain if through his own fault he has created a situation in which a lawyer has to be appointed shortly before the hearing is to be held.[878]

The 'facilities' do not include the possibility to choose counsel or have one assigned, since the right to legal aid is separately provided for under paragraph 3(c).

If appeal is open, the time-limit has to be such that a thorough study of the judgment can be made to enable a decision as to whether an appeal should be brought, while the moment of the hearing of the appeal in turn will have to leave adequate time for the preparation of the hearing.[879] The words 'preparation of his defence', therefore, may not be interpreted to mean that the provision of paragraph 3(b) is not applicable to the appeal proceedings in case the accused has been convicted at first instance and, consequently, acts not as defendant but as plaintiff in these proceedings. In the *Hadjianastassiou* case, the applicant had to give notice of appeal on points of law within a time-limit of five days without having the opportunity to take cognisance of the written version of the judgment. The Court took the view that it is essential for the exercise of the defendant's right of appeal that the national courts indicate unambiguously the reasons on which they base their verdicts. As the applicant was barred in the circumstances of the case from submitting an additional memorial, the Court concluded that paragraph 3(b) in conjunction with paragraph 1 had been violated.[880] In the *Zoon* case, the Court held that it had been possible for the applicant, well before the expiry of the 14-day time-limit for lodging an appeal, to take cognisance of the judgment in abridged form of the Dutch regional court.

---

because of her poor psychological and physical condition, held that the time of 10 working days available to him was adequate, considering the complexity of the case.

[876] See, *mutatis mutandis*, *Twalib v. Greece*, ECtHR 9 June 1998, appl. no. 24294/94, para. 40, and, with regard to sub-para. 3(c), *Daud v. Portugal*, ECtHR 21 April 1998, appl. no. 22600/93, para. 38.

[877] Appl. no. 7909/77, *X. and Y. v. Austria*, EComHR 12 October 1978, appl. no. 7909/77, D&R 15 (1979), p. 160 (162), where the Commission stated that the question what period is adequate cannot be answered *in abstracto*.

[878] *X. v. Austria*, EComHR 11 October 1979, appl. no. 8251/78, D&R 17 (1980), p. 166 (169–170).

[879] In *Kremzow v. Austria*, supra n. 349, para. 48, a period of 3 weeks between the receipt of the Attorney General's position paper (the so-called *croquis*) and the hearing of the Supreme Court did suffice to formulate a reply to the *croquis*. For a case where the date for filing the grounds of appeal had not been fixed, but the appellant was informed about the date of the hearing, see *Vacher v. France*, ECtHR 17 December 1996, appl. no. 20368/92, paras. 22–30.

[880] *Hadjianastassiou v. Greece, supra* n. 9, paras. 34–37.

Moreover, in the circumstances of the case the judgment did contain sufficient information. Therefore, the rights of the defence had not been unduly affected by the absence of a complete judgment or a detailed enumeration of the items of evidence relied on to ground the conviction of the applicant.[881]

The reclassification of an offence in the course of proceedings does not violate sub-paragraph (b) as long as the defendant has adequate opportunity to reorganise his defence accordingly.[882]

In the *Bricmont* case, the Commission stated that sub-paragraph (b) recognises the right of the accused to have at his disposal, for the purposes of exonerating himself or obtaining a reduction of his sentence, all relevant elements that can be collected by the competent authorities.[883] The accused cannot complain about lack of facilities if he does not cooperate in producing elements to his defence.[884]

Finally, the possibility of inspection of the files must also be mentioned as an important element of the 'facilities'.[885] The case law of the Court indicates that the right of access is incorporated in the provision under (b), although restriction of this right to the defendant's counsel is not incompatible with Article 6,[886] provided that the evidence is made available to the accused before the hearing and the lawyer of the accused has had the opportunity to comment on it.[887] A lack of adequate time for the preparation of the defence may be cured by way of review proceedings.[888]

9.4. THE RIGHT TO DEFEND ONESELF IN PERSON OR THROUGH LEGAL ASSISTANCE

a. General observations

Paragraph 3(c) guarantees the right of the accused to defend himself in person or through legal assistance of his own choosing or (and), if he has not sufficient means to pay for legal assistance, to be given it free when the interests of justice

---

[881]   *Zoon v. the Netherlands, supra* n. 450, paras. 32–50.

[882]   *Pélissier and Sassi v. France, supra* n. 858, para. 62; *Sadak and Others v. Turkey (No. 1), supra* n. 858, para. 57.

[883]   *Bricmont v. Belgium*, ECtHR 15 October 1987, appl. no. 10857/84, A.158, p. 47. See also *Edwards v. the United Kingdom, supra* n. 332, para. 36.

[884]   *Bricmont v. Belgium*, ECtHR 15 October 1987, appl. no. 10857/84, A.158, p. 49.

[885]   At least from the moment of the charge: *X. v. Austria*, EComHR 22 March 1972, appl. no. 4622/70, Coll. 40 (1972), p. 15 (18).

[886]   *Kamasinski v. Austria, supra* n. 331, para. 88; *Kremzow v. Austria, supra* n. 349, para. 52.

[887]   *Öcalan v. Turkey, supra* n. 875, para. 50.

[888]   *Serves v. France, supra* n. 196, para. 51. *Twalib v. Greece, supra* n. 876, seems to provide another example. See, however, the criticism expressed in the partly dissenting opinion. With respect to complaints against reclassification, see *Dallos v. Hungary, supra* n. 858, paras. 49–52; *Sipavicius v. Lithuania, supra* n. 860, paras. 32–33.

so require. In the *Pakelli* case, the Court, referring to 'the object and purpose of this paragraph, which is designed to ensure effective protection of the rights of the defence', opted for the '*et*' in the French text, and not for the 'or' in the English text. This resulted in the following interpretation by the Court: 'a "person charged with a criminal offence" who does not wish to defend himself in person must be able to have recourse to legal assistance of his own choosing; if he does not have sufficient means to pay for such assistance, he is entitled under the Convention to be given it free when the interests of justice so require.'[889]

There are, therefore, three juxtaposed rights included in this provision, which will be dealt with consecutively hereafter.

Article 6(3) leaves states a margin of appreciation with regard to the choice of the means of ensuring that the right to legal assistance is ensured in their domestic legal order. The Court's task therefore is to ascertain whether the method chosen is consistent with the requirements of a fair trial.[890]

The manner in which the provision applies (in conjunction with the first paragraph of Article 6) in appeal and cassation proceedings or during a preliminary investigation depends on the characteristics of the proceedings in question.[891] The entirety of the proceedings conducted in the domestic legal order and the role of the appellate or cassation court therein must be taken into account and it is necessary to consider matters such as the nature of the procedure, the scope of the powers of the court and the manner in which individuals' interests are actually protected in the procedure.[892] In as far as the rights of the defence have not been irretrievably prejudiced, a failure to comply with the requirement of paragraph 3(c) may in principle be cured in appeal provided that the scope of review of the appellate court is sufficient for that purpose.[893]

The provision under paragraph 3(c) does not contain an '"unlimited right to use any defence arguments"'. It does not in principle offer protection against a subsequent prosecution of the accused because he made '"false suspicions of punishable behaviour"' concerning another person.[894]

---

[889] *Pakelli v. Germany, supra* n. 345, para. 31.

[890] See e.g. *Quaranta v. Switzerland*, ECtHR 24 May 1991, appl. no. 12744/88, para. 30; *Sakhnovskiy v. Russia*, ECtHR (GC) 2 November 2010, appl. no. 21272/03, para. 95; *Mikhaylova v. Russia*, ECtHR 19 November 2015, appl. no. 46998/08, para. 94.

[891] See, e.g., *Meftah and Others v. France, supra* n. 487, paras. 40–48; *Monnell and Morris v. the United Kingdom, supra* n. 353, para. 56; *Tripodi v. Italy*, ECtHR 22 February 1994, appl. no. 13743/88, para. 27; and with regard to the preliminary investigation, see *Imbrioscia v. Switzerland, supra* n. 857, para. 38; *Berlinski v. Poland, supra* n. 857, para. 75.

[892] See e.g. *Monnell and Morris v. the United Kingdom, supra* n. 353.

[893] *Quaranta v. Switzerland, supra* n. 890, para. 37. See also *Toeva v. Bulgaria*, ECtHR 9 September 2004, appl. no. 53329/99; *Khrabrova v. Russia*, ECtHR 2 October 2012, appl. no. 18498/04.

[894] *Brandstetter v. Austria*, ECtHR 28 August 1991, appl. nos. 11170/84, 12876/87 and 13468/87, paras. 50–54.

The Court has noted that even where the applicant suffered no damage, a violation of the Convention is still conceivable.[895]

b. In person

The right for the accused to defend himself in person is closely related to the right to be present at the hearing,[896] which in principle demands that a person charged with a criminal offence is entitled to be present at least at the first instance trial hearing. Therefore, there will normally be a violation of Article 6(3)(c) if an accused is self-represented in accordance with his or her own will, unless the interests of justice require otherwise.[897]

With regard to appeal and cassation proceedings Article 6 does not always entail the right to be present in person.[898] In the *Gillow* case, the Court accepted the requirement of representation by a lawyer to lodge an appeal as 'a common feature of the legal systems in several member States of the Council of Europe'.[899] From paragraph 3(c) it then results that, if the national law stipulates or the judicial authorities decide that the accused must be assisted by a lawyer, he must be able himself to choose this lawyer and, in case of inability to pay for such legal aid, must have a lawyer assigned to him; indeed, in that case such legal aid is evidently considered necessary by national law or the judicial authorities in the interests of justice.

Although some restrictions of the right of the accused to defend himself in person are permitted, these restrictions cannot go so far that the protection offered by the Convention becomes illusory. In the *Kremzow* case, the situation at issue was that national legislation granted the right of a detained person to be present at the hearing of an appeal against his sentence only if the person concerned made a request to this effect in his appeal. The applicant had failed to make such a request. Nevertheless, because the applicant risked a substantial increase of his sentence of imprisonment, the Court held that the national authorities had been obliged to enable the applicant to be present at the hearing and to 'defend himself in person'. The failure to fulfil this duty amounted to a breach of paragraph 6(1) in conjunction with the provision under paragraph 3(c).[900]

---

[895]   *Alimena v. Italy*, ECtHR 19 February 1991, appl. no. 11910/85, para. 20.

[896]   See, e.g., *Zana v. Turkey, supra* n. 514, para. 68; *Yavuz v. Austria, supra* n. 532, paras. 45–52.

[897]   See, e.g., *Galstyan v. Armenia,* ECtHR 15 November 2007, appl. no. 26986/03, para. 91.

[898]   See, e.g., *Kremzow v. Austria, supra* n. 349, para. 58; *Belziuk v. Poland, supra* n. 335, para. 37, *Meftah and Others v. France, supra* n. 487, paras. 40–48.

[899]   *Gillow v. the United Kingdom, supra* n. 382, para. 69.

[900]   *Kremzow v. Austria, supra* n. 349, paras. 65–69; see also *Michael Edward Cooke v. Austria, supra* n. 522, paras. 40–44 and *Josef Prinz v. Austria, supra* n. 520, paras. 39–46. The former judgment is on crucial points almost identical to the *Kremzow* case, but in the latter, concerning proceedings before the Austrian Supreme Court with regard to the question whether the conditions for the applicant's placement in an institution for mentally ill

c. Legal assistance and implied rights

The applicability of the guarantees of Article 6 from the moment that a 'criminal charge' exists, has as a consequence that these guarantees may be relevant during the pre-trial proceedings 'if and in so far as the fairness of the trial is likely to be seriously prejudiced by an initial failure to comply with them'.[901] Prompt access to a lawyer serves as an important counterweight to the suspect's vulnerable position in police custody, protects the suspect against coercion and ill-treatment and contributes to prevention of miscarriages of justice and the fulfilment of the aims of Article 6. In the *John Murray* case, the Court held that Article 6 in principle requires that the accused be allowed to benefit from the assistance of a lawyer already at the initial stages of police interrogation.[902] Subsequently the Court formulated the rule in the *Salduz* case as follows: 'in order for the right to a fair trial to remain sufficiently "practical and effective" (see paragraph 51 above), Article 6 §1 requires that, as a rule, access to a lawyer should be provided as from the first interrogation of a suspect by the police, unless it is demonstrated in the light of the particular circumstances of each case that there are compelling reasons to restrict this right.'[903]

In the *Salduz* case the applicant was denied access to a lawyer during his police custody while he made incriminating statements that were used at trial as main evidence for conviction. The Court, therefore, found a violation of Article 6(3) and (1) of the Convention.

In the landmark *Ibrahim and Others* case, the Grand Chamber reiterated the Court's case law on the issue and specified the test for the justified restriction to this rule.[904] According to the Court, the test for whether a restriction on the access to a lawyer is compatible with the right to a fair trial consists of two stages: first, the existence of compelling reasons for the restriction must be assessed, and second, the prejudice caused to the rights of the defence by the restriction in the case must be evaluated.[905]

The criterion for the assessment of 'compelling reasons' is a stringent one: 'restrictions on access to legal advice are permitted only in exceptional

---

offenders were met, the absence of the applicant had not violated Art. 6. *Cf.* also *Kucera v. Austria*, ECtHR 3 October 2002, appl. no. 40072/98, para. 29.

[901] *Ibrahim and Others v. the United Kingdom*, ECtHR 13 September 2016, appl. no. 50541/08, 50571/08, 50573/08 and 40351/09, para. 253, referring to e.g. *Imbrioscia v. Switzerland*, *supra* n. 857, para. 36.

[902] *John Murray v. the United Kingdom*, *supra* n. 549, para. 63.

[903] *Salduz v. Turkey*, ECtHR (GC) 27 November 2008, appl. no. 36391/02, para. 55. See also e.g. *John Murray v. the United Kingdom*, *supra* n. 549, para. 63. See also *Magee v. the United Kingdom*, ECtHR 6 June 2000, appl. no. 38135/95, para. 41; *Berlinski v. Poland*, *supra* n. 857, para. 75; *Dayanan v. Turkey*, ECtHR 13 October 2009, appl. no. 7377/03, para. 31; *Ibrahim and Others v. the United Kingdom*, *supra* n. 901, para. 256.

[904] *Ibrahim and Others v. the United Kingdom, ibid.*, paras. 257–265.

[905] *Ibid.*, para. 257.

circumstances, must be of a temporary nature and must be based on an individual assessment of the particular circumstances of the case.'[906] When assessing whether compelling reasons have been sufficiently demonstrated it is important to determine whether domestic law provides for a legal basis for the decision to restrict the right to access to legal advice and whether the scope and content of any restriction are sufficiently circumscribed by law in order to guide operational decision-making in practice. According to the Court "the existence of an urgent need to avert serious adverse consequences for life, liberty or physical integrity" can amount to compelling reasons to restrict the access to a lawyer.[907]

However, the Court underlined that the absence of compelling reasons does not in itself lead to the conclusion that there has been a violation of Article 6. Reiterating its general approach to the evaluation of this article, the Court once more stressed that the evaluation of the fairness of the trial has to proceed in view of the proceedings as a whole.[908]

This means that (1) whenever compelling reasons for restricting the right to access to a lawyer are established, 'a holistic assessment of the entirety of the proceedings' must take place in order to determine compliance with Article 6; and (2) whenever there are no compelling reasons for restricting access to legal advice, 'a very strict scrutiny' must be applied to the fairness assessment.[909] The Court moreover provides for a non-exhaustive list of factors that can be taken into account when examining the fairness of the proceedings as a whole:

'(a) Whether the applicant was particularly vulnerable, for example, by reason of his age or mental capacity.

(b) The legal framework governing the pre-trial proceedings and the admissibility of evidence at trial, and whether it was complied with; where an exclusionary rule applied, it is particularly unlikely that the proceedings as a whole would be considered unfair.

(c) Whether the applicant had the opportunity to challenge the authenticity of the evidence and oppose its use.

(d) The quality of the evidence and whether the circumstances in which it was obtained cast doubt on its reliability or accuracy, taking into account the degree and nature of any compulsion.

(e) Where evidence was obtained unlawfully, the unlawfulness in question and, where it stems from a violation of another Convention Article, the nature of the violation found.

---

[906] *Ibid.*, para. 258.
[907] *Ibid.*, para. 259.
[908] *Ibid.*, para. 262.
[909] *Ibid.*, paras. 263–265.

(f) In the case of a statement, the nature of the statement and whether it was promptly retracted or modified.

(g) The use to which the evidence was put, and in particular whether the evidence formed an integral or significant part of the probative evidence upon which the conviction was based, and the strength of the other evidence in the case.

(h) Whether the assessment of guilt was performed by professional judges or lay jurors, and in the case of the latter the content of any jury directions.

(i) The weight of the public interest in the investigation and punishment of the particular offence in issue.

(j) Other relevant procedural safeguards afforded by domestic law and practice.'[910]

Moreover, the Court explicitly underlined another implied right that is inherently connected to the privilege against self-incrimination, the right to silence and the right to legal assistance, namely the right of a person who is charged with a criminal offence to be notified of these rights.[911]

In the *Inbrahim and Others* case the Grand Chamber found that, with respect to three applicants who were suspected of terrorist acts at the time of the safety interviews conducted by national authorities, there were compelling reasons to delay access to a lawyer. This restriction, as well as the admission at trial of statements made in the absence of legal advice, did not render the trial as a whole unfair. The Court did find a violation of Article 6 with regard to the fourth applicant who was initially interviewed as a witness and thus was not cautioned or informed of his right to legal advice, while his right to access to a lawyer was restricted and the incriminating statements made during the interview were later admitted as evidence at trial.[912] In the *Simeonovi* case the accused was denied access to a lawyer for the first three days of police custody. The Court attached decisive importance to the fact that during that period no evidence capable of being used against the applicant was obtained and included in the case file. Although any compelling reasons for the restriction of access to legal advice were lacking, according to the Court the overall fairness of proceedings had not been irretrievably prejudiced in this case.[913]

---

[910] *Ibid.,* para. 274.

[911] *Ibid.,* para. 272.

[912] *Ibid.* Violations of Article 6(1) and (3)(c) were also found in *John Murray v. the United Kingdom, supra* n. 549, paras. 66–70; *Averill v. the United Kingdom, supra* n. 556, paras. 55–62; *Öcalan v. Turkey, supra* n. 875, para. 131; *Magee v. the United Kingdom, supra* n. 903, paras. 42–46; *Sarikaya v. Turkey,* ECtHR 22 April 2004, appl. no. 36115/97, paras. 67–68. No violation was found in e.g. *Brennan v. the United Kingdom,* ECtHR 16 October 2001, appl. no. 39846/98, paras. 44–48.

[913] *Simeonovi v. Bulgaria,* ECtHR 12 May 2017, appl. no. 21980/04, paras. 129–145.

The provision under sub-paragraph (c) also embodies the right of an accused to communicate with his counsel without the presence of a third person. Without this requirement the guarantee offered by the Convention would not be practical and effective, as legal assistance would lose much of its effectiveness whenever a lawyer is not able to confer with his client confidentially.[914] Although some restrictions imposed on lawyer-client contacts can be tolerated,[915] 'the fundamental rule of respect for lawyer-client confidentiality may only be derogated from in exceptional cases and on condition that adequate and sufficient safeguards against abuse are in place.'[916] In the *Öcalan* case, the restriction of the number and length of the visits by the applicant's lawyers to a rhythm of two one-hourly meetings per week, violated the principle of fair trial in view of the highly complex charges and voluminous case file.[917] In the *Lanz* case, the Court held that only 'very weighty reasons' could have justified the surveillance by the investigating judge of the contacts of a detainee with his defence counsel. The mere risk of collusion did not meet the criterion because this was the very reason for which detention had already been ordered.[918] In the recent *M.* case the Court found that as a result of the threat of prosecution should Mr. M. divulge state secrets to his lawyers, communication between him and his lawyers was not free and unrestricted as to its content, thus irretrievably compromising the fairness of the proceedings.[919] However, the 'extraordinary features' of the *Kempers* case, where the defendant had been suspected of being the member of a gang and utmost confidentiality had been necessary in order to catch the other members, justified the restriction in issue.[920]

The Court has attached to the right of access to court, implied in Article 6(1), the consequence that this right has been violated if a detainee is not permitted to correspond with a lawyer or another person giving legal assistance. The Court held that 'hindering the effective exercise of a right may amount to a breach of that right, even if the hindrance is of a temporary character'.[921] Consequently, as soon as a detainee wants to institute an action or wishes to prepare his defence against a criminal charge, such contact must be possible. This may hold

---

[914] *S. v. Switzerland*, ECtHR 28 November 1991, appl. nos. 12629/87 and 13965/88, para. 48; *Öcalan v. Turkey*, *supra* n. 875, para. 133.

[915] See e.g. *Erdem v. Germany*, ECtHR 5 July 2001, appl. no. 38321/97; *Khodorkovskiy and Lebedev v. Russia*, ECtHR 25 July 2013, appl. nos. 11082/06 and 13772/05.

[916] *Erdem v. Germany*, *supra* n. 915, para. 65; *M. v. the Netherlands*, ECtHR 27 July 2017, appl. no. 2156/10, para. 88.

[917] *Öcalan v. Turkey*, *supra* n. 875, para. 154.

[918] *Lanz v. Austria*, *supra* n. 472, para. 52. In *S. v. Switzerland*, *supra* n. 914, para. 49, the fear that the lawyer of the applicant would collude with the lawyer of a co-accused was based on the fact that the lawyers proposed to co-ordinate their defence-strategy. This fact, too, could not justify the restriction on the free communication of the accused and his lawyer.

[919] *M. v. the Netherlands*, ECtHR 27 July 2017, appl. no. 2156/10.

[920] In *Lanz v. Austria*, *supra* n. 472, para. 52, the Court refers to and endorses the decision on admissibility by the Commission in *Kempers v. Austria*, 27 February 1997, appl. no. 21842/93.

[921] *Golder v. the United Kingdom*, *supra* n. 1, para. 26.

good in the pre-trial phase[922] and even with regard to an internal preliminary inquiry.[923]

Searching of counsel and inspection of the correspondence of counsel with his detained client by the prison authorities are in principle also incompatible with the position of counsel. Measures of this kind are justified only in very exceptional circumstances, where the authorities have sound reasons to assume that counsel himself is abusing his position or is allowing it to be abused.[924]

The provision under paragraph 3(c), in conjunction with the first paragraph of Article 6, also implies that counsel who attends the trial must be enabled to conduct the defence also in the absence of the accused, regardless of whether or not there exists an excuse for the latter's absence[925] and whether or not it is possible to apply to have a conviction entered in default set aside.[926] Although in principle national legislation may discourage the unjustified absence of an accused at the trial,[927] this implied aspect of sub-paragraph 3(c) may not be impaired because the legislator 'cannot penalise the accused by creating exceptions to the right of legal assistance'.[928]

d. Legal assistance and the right to choose a lawyer

A person charged with a criminal offence has the right to have legal representation of his own choosing.[929] However, the right of the accused to choose his own lawyer is not an absolute right.[930] It can be subject to certain limitations, such as the national provisions with regard to the question as to who may act as counsel in court, or with regard to the free legal aid system.[931] In the *Croissant* case, the Court held that national courts when appointing defence

---

922   *John Murray v. the United Kingdom, supra* n. 549, paras. 66–70.

923   *Fell v. the United Kingdom*, ECtHR 28 June 1984, appl. no. 7878/77, D&R 23 (1981), p. 102 (113). See also *Campbell and Fell v. the United Kingdom, supra* n. 215, pp. 76–77.

924   See *Campbell and Fell v. the United Kingdom, supra* n. 215, paras. 108–111; *Domenichini v. Italy*, ECtHR 15 November 1996, appl. no. 15943/90, paras. 35–39; *Moiseyev v. Russia*, ECtHR 9 October 2008, appl. no. 62936/00, para. 210.

925   *Lala v. the Netherlands*, ECtHR 22 September 1994, appl. no. 14861/89, para. 33 and *Pelladoah v. the Netherlands*, ECtHR 22 September 1994, appl. no. 16737/90, para. 40.

926   See, e.g., *Krombach v. France, supra* n. 531, para. 85; *Karatas and Sari v. France*, ECtHR 4 May 2000, appl. no. 38396/97, para. 54.

927   See *supra* 4.4.

928   See, e.g., *Van Geyseghem v. Belgium, supra* n. 536, para. 34; *Van Pelt v. France, supra* n. 536, para. 67; *Krombach v. France, supra* n. 531, para. 89.

929   *Ezeh and Connors v. the United Kingdom*, ECtHR (GC) 15 July 2002, appl. nos. 39665/98 and 40086/98, paras. 103–106, 132–134. See also *Berlinski v. Poland, supra* n. 857, paras. 77–78: Art. 6 had been violated because the applicant had no defence council for more than a year, without any justification, and *Thompson v. the United Kingdom, supra* n. 324, para. 47.

930   See e.g. *Croissant v. Germany*, ECtHR 25 September 1992, appl. no. 13611/88, para. 29; *Mefta and Others v. France, supra* n. 487, para. 45; *Pakelli v. Germany, supra* n. 345, par. 31.

931   *X. v. Federal Republic of Germany*, ECtHR 6 March 1962, appl. no. 722/60, Yearbook V (1962), p. 104 (106); *Ensslin, Baader and Raspe v. Federal Republic of Germany*, EComHR 8 July 1978, appl. nos. 7572/76, 7586/76 and 7587/76, Yearbook XXI (1978), p. 418 (464).

counsel must certainly take into account the accused's wishes, although those wishes may be overridden 'when there are relevant and sufficient grounds for holding that this is necessary in the interests of justice'.[932]

In the *Lagerblom* case, for example, the Court considered it not unreasonable, in view of the general desirability of limiting the total costs of legal aid, that national authorities take a restrictive approach to requests to replace public defence counsel once they have been assigned to a case and have undertaken certain activities.[933] Also, refusal to assign an accused's family member instead of a professional lawyer to represent the accused in court was not incompatible with Article 6 requirements. [934]

Furthermore, if such an unsatisfactory relationship between the accused and the lawyer assigned to him is found to exist that an adequate defence is impossible, or if the qualifications of the assigned lawyer are found to be inadequate considering the nature and/or complexity of the case, paragraph 1 and paragraph 3(b) may imply that another lawyer must be assigned to the accused at the latter's request.[935] In the *Kamasinski* case, however, the Court held that the responsibility rests in the first place on the applicant: 'the competent national authorities are required under Article 6(3)(c) to intervene only if a failure by legal aid counsel to provide effective representation is manifest or sufficiently brought to their attention in some other way.'[936]

In this context the Court emphasised in the *Artico* case that the authorities have not complied with their obligation by the mere assignment of a lawyer, since Article 6(3)(c) speaks of 'assistance' and not of 'nomination', so that it must be sufficiently ensured that real assistance is provided.[937] Here again, however, the accused can forfeit his right by personally creating the situation in which at the very last moment before the hearing another lawyer must be nominated.[938]

In the *Dvorski* case the accused was represented by another lawyer than the one chosen by his family during first police interrogation when he made a confession that was used at trial for conviction. The police prevented the chosen lawyer from having access to the accused, while no relevant and

---

[932] *Croissant v. Germany, supra* n. 930, para. 29. See also *Meftah and Others v. France, supra* n. 487, para. 45; *Mayzit v. Russia,* ECtHR 20 January 2005, appl. no. 63378/00, para. 66; *Klimentyev v. Russia,* ECtHR 16 November 2006, appl. no. 46503/99, para. 116; *Zagorodniy v. Ukraine,* ECtHR 24 November 2011, appl. no. 27004/06, para. 52; *Martin v. Estonia,* ECtHR 30 May 2013, appl. no. 35985/09, para. 90; *Dvorski v. Croatia,* ECtHR 20 October 2015, appl. no. 25703/11, para.79.

[933] *Lagerblom v. Sweden,* ECtHR 14 January 2003, appl. no. 26891/95, para. 59.

[934] *Mayzit v. Russia, supra* n. 932, para. 66.

[935] See *Daud v. Portugal, supra* n. 876, paras. 38–43.

[936] See e.g. *Kamasinski v. Austria, supra* n. 331, para. 65. See also *Imbrioscia v. Switzerland, supra* n. 857, para. 41; *Tripodi v. Italy, supra* n. 891, para. 30; *Pavlenko v. Russia,* ECtHR 1 April 2010, appl. no. 42371/02, para. 99.

[937] *Artico v. Italy,* ECtHR 13 May 1980, appl. no. 6694/74, para. 33. See also *Daud v. Portugal, supra* n. 876, para. 38; *Czekalla v. Portugal,* ECtHR 10 October 2002, appl. no. 38830/97, paras. 60–71; *Luchaninova v. Ukraine,* ECtHR 9 June 2011, appl. no. 16347/02, para. 63.

[938] *X. v. Austria,* EComHR 11 October 1979, appl. no. 8251/78, D&R 17 (1980), p. 166 (169–170).

sufficient reasons for this restriction could be established. While there was other incriminating evidence, the Court could not ignore 'the significant likely impact of his initial confession on the further development of the criminal proceedings' against the accused. Thus, the Court held that the fairness of proceedings was undermined in so far as the initial confession was admitted into evidence, while the national courts did not properly address the issue and 'in particular failed to take adequate remedial measures to ensure fairness.'[939]

In light of Court's case law set out above, the Grand Chamber presented an evaluative framework in the *Dvorski* case. The Court, first of all held that a more lenient requirement of 'relevant and sufficient' reasons must be applied in cases where the less serious issue of 'denial of choice' of a counsel is at play, rather than denial of access to counsel.[940] When the accused was assigned a lawyer, but complains that it was not a lawyer of his choosing, the Court must assess, in light of the proceedings as a whole, whether the rights of the defence were 'adversely affected' to the extent that the overall fairness was undermined. Thus, when there are no relevant and sufficient grounds for overriding or obstructing the accused's wishes in relation to the choice of a lawyer, the overall fairness of proceedings must be evaluated taking into account a variety of factors, such as, for example, 'the nature of the proceedings and the application of certain professional requirements; the circumstances surrounding the designation of counsel and the existence of opportunities for challenging this; the effectiveness of counsel's assistance; whether the accused's privilege against self-incrimination has been respected; the accused's age; and the trial court's use of any statements given by the accused at the material time.'[941]

As with other rights, the right to legal assistance can be waived either explicitly or implicitly. Such a waiver of the right must be done unequivocally, voluntary, knowingly and intelligently and must not run counter to any important public interest.[942] Due to the fact that the right to counsel is a fundamental right which ensures effectiveness of the rest of the guarantees set forth in Article 6, it requires special protection of the 'knowing and intelligent waiver' standard.[943] In this context the right to information plays a crucial role.[944]

---

[939]   *Dvorski v. Croatia*, *supra* n. 932, para. 83–113.

[940]   *Ibid.*, para. 81.

[941]   *Ibid.*, para. 82. See also e.g. *Zherdev v. Ukraine*, ECtHR 27 April 2017, appl. no. 34015/07, para. 138.

[942]   *Hermi v. Italy*, ECtHR (GC) 18 October 2006, appl. no. 18114/02, para. 74; *Sejdovic v. Italy*, *supra* n. 422; *Dvorski v. Croatia*, *supra* n. 932, para. 100; *Sakhnovskiy v. Russia*, ECtHR (GC) 2 November 2010, appl. no. 21272/03, para. 90; *Sklyar v. Russia*, ECtHR 18 July 2017, appl. no. 45498/11, par. 22.

[943]   *Pishchalnikov v. Russia*, ECtHR 24 September 2009, appl. no. 7025/04, paras. 77–79; *Dvorski v. Croatia*, *supra* n. 932, para. 82.

[944]   See e.g. *Dvorski v. Croatia*, *supra* n. 932, para. 128; *Simeonovi v. Bulgaria*, ECtHR 12 May 2017, appl. no. 21980/04, para. 128.

e. Free legal assistance

Article 6(3)(c) stipulates that legal assistance should be given free to the accused if (1) he has not sufficient means to pay for it and (2) when the interests of justice so require. This provision does not exclude that an accused is required to pay a contribution to the cost of legal assistance, as long as he has sufficient means to pay.[945] It is the accused who has to show that he lacks sufficient means to pay for legal assistance. Rather than 'beyond a reasonable doubt' the applicable standard is that there are 'some indications' that this is the case.[946] A system that does not contain any obligation for the accused who is acquitted to pay for his defence, but requires the reimbursement of the costs of appointed lawyers in case the person concerned is convicted, is in itself not incompatible with the Convention, as long as the overall fairness of the proceedings is not adversely affected.[947]

The second requirement is that the obligation to provide legal aid only arises 'where the interest of justice so requires'. Whether this is the case has to be assessed, taking into account the facts of the case as a whole, including the facts that can arise in a later stage of the proceedings.[948] Several factors are deemed relevant to establish whether free legal aid is required: the seriousness of the alleged offence in conjunction with the severity of the penalty that the accused risks; the complexity of the case; and the personal situation of the accused including his capacity to present his case.[949] Where deprivation of liberty is at stake the interests of justice in principle call for legal representation,[950] and for the legal representative to be duly heard.[951]

If on the ground of the requirements of a fair hearing of the first paragraph an accused is entitled to free legal aid, that aid will also have to be considered to be required in the interests of justice, while the general interest of the case

---

[945]   *Morris v. the United Kingdom, supra* n. 353, paras. 88–89.

[946]   *Pakelli v. Germany, supra* n. 345, para. 34.

[947]   *Croissant v. Germany, supra* n. 930, paras. 33–38. See also e.g. *Orlov v. Russia*, ECtHR 21 June 2011, appl. no. 29652/04, para. 114; *Chukayev v. Russia*, ECtHR 5 November 2015, appl. no. 36814/06, paras. 116–117.

[948]   *Ibid.*

[949]   See, e.g., *Granger v. the United Kingdom, supra* n. 330, paras. 46–48; *Lagerblom v. Sweden, supra* n. 933, para. 51; *Quaranta v. Switzerland, supra* n. 890, paras. 32–38; *Pham Hoang v. France, supra* n. 843, paras. 39–41; *Benham v. the United Kingdom*, ECtHR 10 June 1996, appl. no. 19380/92, paras. 60–64; *Twalib v. Greece, supra* n. 876, para. 52; *Biba v. Greece*, ECtHR 26 September 2000, appl. no. 33170/96, para. 29; *Artico v. Italy, supra* n. 937, para. 34; *Pakelli v. Germany, supra* n. 345, para. 37–39; *Shabelnik v. Ukraine*, ECtHR 19 February 2009, appl. no. 16404/03, para. 58; *Tsonyo Tsonev v. Bulgaria*, ECtHR 14 January 2010, appl. no. 2376/03, para. 40; *Zdravko Stanev v. Bulgaria*, ECtHR 6 November 2012, appl. no. 32238/04, para. 38.

[950]   *Quaranta v. Switzerland, supra* n. 890, para. 33; *Benham v. the United Kingdom, supra* n. 949, para. 61.

[951]   *Hooper v. the United Kingdom*, ECtHR 16 November 2004, appl. no. 42317/98, para. 20.

exceeding the interests of the accused may also call for legal assistance. If it has been recognised with regard to the written phase of the proceedings that the interests of justice require the assignment of legal aid, as a rule, and even *a fortiori*, this will also apply for the subsequent oral phase.[952]

If a lawyer has been assigned to an accused, but the behaviour of the latter has induced counsel to withdraw, the refusal of the court to assign a new lawyer may be in conformity with the 'interests of justice', provided that from that moment the accused himself is given sufficient opportunity to defend himself in person.[953]

9.5. THE RIGHT TO SUMMON AND EXAMINE WITNESSES

Paragraph 3(d) enshrines the principle that, before an accused can be convicted, all evidence against him must normally be produced in his presence at a public hearing with a view to adversarial argument.[954] The accused should be enabled to examine or have examined witnesses against him and to obtain the attendance and examination of witnesses on his behalf under the same conditions as witnesses against him. The defendant should be given an adequate and proper opportunity to challenge and question a witness against him, either when he makes his statements or at a later stage.[955]

The notion of 'witness' is interpreted autonomously, regardless of classifications under national law.[956] Statements not made in court in person, but for example to the police, are to be regarded as statements of 'witnesses' as far as the national courts take account of these statements.[957] In *Kaste and Mathisen*,[958] the Court underlined that where a deposition may serve to a material degree as the basis for a conviction then, irrespective of whether it was made by a witness in the strict sense or by a co-accused, it constitutes evidence

---

[952]   *Pakelli v. Germany, supra* n. 345, paras. 36–40.

[953]   *X v. the United Kingdom*, EComHR 9 October 1980, appl. no. 8386/78, D&R 21 (1981), p. 126 (130–132).

[954]   *Hümmer v. Germany*, ECtHR 19 July 2012, appl. no. 26171/07, para. 38; *Lucà v. Italy*, ECtHR 27 February 2001, appl. no. 33354/96, para. 41; *Solakov v. The former Yugoslav Republic of Macedonia*, ECtHR 31 October 2001, appl. no. 47023/99, para. 57.

[955]   See, e.g., *Ter-Sargsyan v. Armenia*, ECtHR 27 October 2016, appl. no. 27866/10, para. 45 and *Khodorkovskiy and Lebedev v. Russia*, ECtHR 25 July 2013, appl. nos. 11082/06 and 13772/05, para. 707.

[956]   *Damir Sibgatullin v. Russia*, ECtHR 24 April 2012, appl. no. 1413/05, para. 45; *S.N. v. Sweden, supra* n. 497, para. 45; *Asch v. Austria*, ECtHR 26 April 1991, appl. no. 12398/86, para. 25.

[957]   *Delta v. France, supra* n. 782, para. 34; *Isgrò v. Italy*, ECtHR 19 February 1991, appl. no. 11339/85, para. 33; *Artner v. Austria*, ECtHR 28 August 1992, appl. no. 13161/87, para. 19; *Pullar v. the United Kingdom, supra* n. 183, para. 45.

[958]   *Kaste and Mathisen v. Norway*, ECtHR 9 November 2006, appl. no. 18885/04 and 21166/04, para. 53; see also *Lucà v. Italy, supra* n. 954, para. 41.

for the prosecution to which the guarantees provided by Article 6(1) and 3 (d) apply. The term witness not only includes the co-accused,[959] but also victims[960] and expert witnesses.[961]

The right to examine witnesses not only entails equal treatment of the prosecution and the defence in this matter,[962] but also means that the hearing of witnesses must in general be adversarial. The accused should have an effective opportunity to challenge the evidence against him. Exceptions to this principle are possible but must not infringe the rights of the defence, which, as a rule, require not merely that a defendant should know the identity of his accusers so that he is in a position to challenge their probity and credibility but that the accused should be given an adequate and proper opportunity to challenge and question a witness against him, either when that witness makes his statement or at a later stage of proceedings.[963] Following this general principle, there are two requirements. Firstly, there must be a good reason for the non-attendance of a witness.[964] The Court normally accepts as self-evident that the death of a witness constitutes a good reason for allowing their previously-given statements to be admitted as evidence without the defence being given an opportunity to cross-examine this witness in person.[965] However, as the Court clarifies in the *Dimovic* case[966] this acceptance is not unconditional. The inability of the defence to examine such witnesses should not be related to a lack of diligence on the part of domestic courts, for example. Secondly, when a conviction is based solely or to a decisive degree on depositions that have been made by a person whom the accused has had no opportunity to examine or to have examined, whether during the investigation or at the trial, the rights of the defence may be restricted to an extent that is incompatible with the guarantees provided by Article 6 (the so-called 'sole or decisive rule').[967]

---

[959]   *Trofimov v. Russia,* ECtHR 4 December 2008, appl. no. 1111/02, para. 37.

[960]   *Vladimir Romanov v. Russia*, ECtHR 24 July 2008, appl. no. 41461/02, para. 97.

[961]   *Doorson v. the Netherlands, supra* n. 504, paras. 81–82.

[962]   *Bönisch v. Austria, supra* n. 478, para. 32.

[963]   See, e.g., *Riahi v. Belgium*, ECtHR 14 June 2016, appl. no. 65400/10; *Tseber v. Czech Republic*, ECtHR 22 November 2012, appl. nos. 46203/08, para. 59 and *Sică v. Romania*, ECtHR 9 July 2013, appl. no. 12036/05, para. 69.

[964]   An example of no good reason can be found in *Palchik v. Ukraine*, ECtHR 2 March 2017, appl. no. 16980/06: the repeated attempts of the court to summon witnesses and to order the police to bring them to the hearings failed because the witnesses were on holidays outside the region of the police department's jurisdiction.

[965]   See *Al-Khawaja and Tahery v. the United Kingdom*, ECtHR (GC) 15 December 2011, appl. no. 26766/05 and 22228/06, paras. 103, 121 and 153; *Ferrantelli and Santangelo v. Italy, supra* n. 738, para. 52 and *Mika v. Sweden*, ECtHR 27 January 2009 (dec.), appl. no. 31243/06, para. 37.

[966]   *Dimovic v. Serbia*, ECtHR 28 June 2016, appl. no. 24463/11, para. 37.

[967]   *Al-Khawaja and Tahery v. the United Kingdom, supra* n. 965, para. 119; *Schatschaschwili v. Germany*, ECtHR (GC) 15 December 2015, appl. no. 9154/10, paras. 100–131.

In the case of *Al-Khawaja and Tahery*,[968] the Court clarified the principles to be applied when a witness does not attend a public trial. These principles were summarised by the Court in the *Seton* case[969] as follows:

'(i)   the Court should first examine the preliminary question of whether there was a good reason for admitting the evidence of an absent witness, keeping in mind that witnesses should as a general rule give evidence during the trial and that all reasonable efforts should be made to secure their attendance;

(ii)   typical reasons for non-attendance are, like in the case of Al-Khawaja and Tahery (cited above), the death of the witness or the fear of retaliation. There are, however, other legitimate reasons why a witness may not attend trial;

(iii)   when a witness has not been examined at any prior stage of the proceedings, allowing the admission of a witness statement in lieu of live evidence at trial must be a measure of last resort;

(iv)   the admission as evidence of statements of absent witnesses results in a potential disadvantage for the defendant, who, in principle, in a criminal trial should have an effective opportunity to challenge the evidence against him. In particular, he should be able to test the truthfulness and reliability of the evidence given by the witnesses, by having them orally examined in his presence, either at the time the witness was making the statement or at some later stage of the proceedings;

(v)   according to the "sole or decisive rule", if the conviction of a defendant is solely or mainly based on evidence provided by witnesses whom the accused is unable to question at any stage of the proceedings, his defence rights are unduly restricted;

(vi)   in this context, the word "decisive" should be narrowly understood as indicating evidence of such significance or importance as is likely to be determinative of the outcome of the case. Where the untested evidence of a witness is supported by other corroborative evidence, the assessment of whether it is decisive will depend on the strength of the supportive evidence: the stronger the other incriminating evidence, the less likely that the evidence of the absent witness will be treated as decisive;

(vii)   however, as Article 6 §3 of the Convention should be interpreted in the context of an overall examination of the fairness of the proceedings, the sole or decisive rule should not be applied in an inflexible manner;

---

[968]   *Al-Khawaja and Tahery v. the United Kingdom*, *supra* n. 965.

[969]   *Seton v. the United Kingdom*, ECtHR 31 March 2016, appl. no. 55287/10, para. 58. See also *Asatryan v. Armenia*, ECtHR 27 April 2017, appl. no. 3571/09, paras. 54 and 55. See also *Ter-Sargsyan v. Armenia*, *supra* n. 955, para. 46; *Riahi v. Belgium*, *supra* n. 963, para. 30; *Paić v. Croatia*, ECtHR 29 March 2016, appl. no. 47082/12, paras. 27–31.

(viii) in particular, where a hearsay statement is the sole or decisive evidence against a defendant, its admission as evidence will not automatically result in a breach of Article 6 §1. At the same time, where a conviction is based solely or decisively on the evidence of absent witnesses, the Court must subject the proceedings to the most searching scrutiny. Because of the dangers of the admission of such evidence, it would constitute a very important factor to balance in the scales and one which would require sufficient counterbalancing factors, including the existence of strong procedural safeguards. The question in each case is whether there are sufficient counterbalancing factors in place, including measures that permit a fair and proper assessment of the reliability of that evidence to take place. This would permit a conviction to be based on such evidence only if it is sufficiently reliable given its importance to the case.'[970]

These principles have been further clarified in the *Schatschaschwili* case.[971] Here, the Court confirmed that the absence of good reason for the non-attendance of a witness could not, of itself, be conclusive of the lack of fairness of a trial, although it remains a very important factor to be weighed in the balance when assessing the overall fairness, and one which might tip the balance in favour of finding a breach of Article 6(1) and 3(d). The Court's main concern here is to ascertain whether the proceedings as a whole are fair. The Court will not only review the existence of sufficient counterbalancing factors in cases where the evidence of the absent witness was the sole or the decisive basis for the applicant's conviction, but also in cases where it found it unclear whether the evidence in question was sole or decisive but nevertheless was satisfied that it carried significant weight and its admission might have handicapped the defence. The extent of the counterbalancing factors necessary in order for a trial to be considered fair would depend on the weight of the evidence of the absent witness. The more important that evidence, the more weight the counterbalancing factors would have to carry in order for the proceedings as a whole to be considered fair.[972]

Having regard to the place that the right to a fair administration of justice holds in a democratic society, any measures restricting the rights of the defence should be strictly necessary. If a less restrictive measure can suffice then that measure should be applied.[973]

---

[970] See also *Blokhin v. Russia*, ECtHR (GC) 23 March 2016, appl. no. 47152/06, para. 202.

[971] *Schatschaschwili v. Germany, supra* n. 967, paras. 100–131.

[972] See also *Valdhuter v. Romania*, ECtHR 27 June 2017, appl. no. 70792/10, para. 45 and *Seton v. the United Kingdom, supra* n. 969, para. 59.

[973] *Van Mechelen and Others v. The Netherlands, supra* n. 505, para. 58. The most recent case law of the Court is summarised in *Valdhuter v. Romania, supra* n. 972, paras. 43–45; *Manucharyan v. Armenia*, ECtHR 24 November 2016, appl. no. 35688/11, paras. 47 and 48 (see also *Ter-Sargsyan v. Armenia, supra* n. 955, para. 46). The Court refers to *Al-Khawaja and*

The statement of a witness does not always have to be made in court and in public if it is to be admitted as evidence.[974] The possibility for the accused to confront a material witness in the presence of a judge is an important element of a fair trial though as we have seen above.[975]

According to the Court the admissibility of evidence is a matter for regulation by national law and the national courts.[976] The essential aim of Article 6(3) (d), as is indicated by the words 'under the same conditions', is full 'equality of arms' in the matter. With this proviso, it leaves it to the competent national authorities to decide upon the relevance of the proposed evidence, in so far as this is compatible with the concept of a fair trial, which dominates the whole of Article 6.[977] The Court's only concern is to examine whether the proceedings have been conducted fairly and in particular whether the defendant's rights have not been unacceptably restricted and that he or she remains able to participate effectively in the proceedings.[978]

In the *Blokhin* case,[979] the Court pointed out that as regards juvenile defendants the criminal proceedings must be so organised as to respect the principle of the best interests of the child. According to the Court it is essential that a child charged with an offence is dealt with in a manner which takes full account of his age, level of maturity and intellectual and emotional capacities, and that steps are taken to promote his ability to understand and participate in the proceedings.[980] The right of a juvenile defendant to effective participation in his criminal trial requires that the authorities deal with him with due regard to his vulnerability and capacities from the first stages of his involvement in a criminal investigation and, in particular, during any questioning by the police. The authorities must take steps to reduce as far as possible the child's feelings of intimidation and inhibition and ensure that he has a broad understanding of the nature of the investigation, of what is at stake for him, including the significance of any penalty which may be imposed as well as of his rights of defence and, in particular, of his right to remain silent.[981] In view of his status as a minor, when a

---

       Tahery v. the United Kingdom, supra n. 965, paras. 118–147 and *Schatschaschwili v. Germany, supra* n. 967, paras. 100–131.

[974] *Asch v. Austria, supra* n. 956, para. 27.

[975] *Tarâu v. Romania*, ECtHR 24 February 2009, appl. no. 3584/02, para. 74; *Graviano v. Italy*, ECtHR 10 February 2005, appl. no. 10075/02, para. 38.

[976] See, e.g., *Dimovic v. Serbia*, ECtHR 28 June 2016, appl. no. 24461/11, para. 33 referring to *Gäfgen v. Germany, supra* n. 491, para. 162.

[977] *Topić v. Croatia*, ECtHR 10 October 2013, appl. no. 51355/10, para. 40.

[978] *Stanford v. The United Kingdom, supra* n. 516, para. 26.

[979] *Blokhin v. Russia, supra* n. 970, para. 195.

[980] See *Adamkiewicz v. Poland*, ECtHR 2 March 2010, appl. no. 54729/00, para. 70; *Panovits v. Cyprus*, ECtHR 11 December 2008, appl. no. 4268/04, para. 67; *V. v. the United Kingdom*, ECtHR (GC) 16 December 1999, appl. no. 24888/94, para. 86; *T. v. the United Kingdom, supra* n. 207, para. 84.

[981] See *Martin v. Estonia*, ECtHR 30 May 2013, appl. no. 35985/09, para. 92; *Panovits v. Cyprus, supra* n. 980, para. 67 and *S.C. v. the United Kingdom, supra* n. 299, para. 29.

---

child enters the criminal justice system his procedural rights must be guaranteed and his innocence or guilt established, in accordance with the requirements of due process and the principle of legality, with respect to the specific act which he has allegedly committed. Still according to the Court, on no account may a child be deprived of important procedural safeguards solely because the proceedings that may result in his deprivation of liberty are deemed under domestic law to be protective of his interests as a child and juvenile delinquent, rather than penal. Furthermore, particular care must be taken to ensure that the legal classification of a child as a juvenile delinquent does not lead to the focus being shifted to his status as such, while neglecting to examine the specific criminal act of which he has been accused and the need to adduce proof of his guilt in conditions of fairness. Processing a child offender through the criminal justice system on the sole basis of his status of being a juvenile delinquent, which lacks legal definition, cannot be considered compatible with due process and the principle of legality.[982] Discretionary treatment, on the basis of someone being a child, a juvenile, or a juvenile delinquent, is only acceptable to the Court where his interests and those of the state are not incompatible. Otherwise – and proportionately – substantive and procedural legal safeguards do apply.

In the case of *T. v. UK*,[983] the Court had to consider how the guarantees of Article 6(1) and paragraph 3(d) apply to a young child charged with a grave offence. In this case the Court concluded that the child was unable to participate effectively in the criminal proceedings against him. According to the Court in this case, it was highly unlikely that the child would have felt sufficiently uninhibited, in the tense courtroom and under public scrutiny, to have consulted with his counsel, during the trial or, indeed, that, given his immaturity and his disturbed emotional state, he would have been capable outside the courtroom of co-operating with his lawyers and giving them information for the purposes of his defence.

In the *Blokhin* case court-appointed counsel was present at the hearing to represent the accused, a 12-year-old boy. According to the Court though, it was unclear when she was appointed and to what extent she actually defended the applicant's rights. There was a lack of diligence on the part of counsel and, in the Court's view, also on the part of the judge, who should have ensured that the principle of equality of arms was respected during the proceedings. No efforts were made by the authorities to secure the appearance of the witness, a minor as well, and his mother in court. Considering what was at stake for the accused, the Court considered that it was of utmost importance that the District Court guarantee the fairness of the proceedings. Unfortunately, there were no counterbalancing factors to compensate for the applicant's inability to cross-examine the witness and his mother at any stage of the proceedings. The accused

---

[982] See *Achour v. France*, ECtHR (GC) 29 March 2006, appl. no. 67335/01, paras. 45–47.

[983] *T. v. the United Kingdom, supra* n. 207, para. 83; see also *Blokhin v. Russia, supra* n. 207, para. 195.

was not provided with an opportunity to scrutinise the witnesses' questioning by the investigator, nor was he then or later provided with the opportunity to have his own questions put to them. Furthermore, as the witnesses' statements to the investigator were not recorded on video, neither the applicant nor the judges were able to observe the witnesses' demeanour under questioning and thus form their own impression of their reliability.[984]

The requirement that there be a good reason for admitting the evidence of an absent witness is a preliminary question which must be examined before any consideration is given as to whether that evidence was sole or decisive. Even where the evidence of an absent witness has not been sole or decisive, the Court has still found a violation of Article 6(1) and 6(3)(d) when no good reason has been shown for the failure to have the witness examined.[985] As a general rule, witnesses should give evidence during the trial and all reasonable efforts will be made to secure their attendance. Thus, when witnesses do not attend to give live evidence, there is a duty to enquire whether that absence is justified.[986]

Article 6(1) taken together with paragraph 3 requires the Contracting States to take positive steps, in particular to enable the accused to examine or have examined witnesses against him.[987] Such measures form part of the diligence which the Contracting States must exercise in order to ensure that the rights guaranteed by Article 6 are enjoyed in an effective manner.[988]

In particular, in the event that the witnesses cannot be examined and that this is due to the fact that they are missing, the authorities must make a reasonable effort to secure their presence.[989] However, *impossibilium nulla est obligation;* provided that the authorities cannot be accused of a lack of diligence in their efforts to award the defendant an opportunity to examine the witnesses in question, the witnesses' unavailability as such does not make it necessary to discontinue the prosecution.[990]

---

[984] The Court refers for similar reasoning to *Makeyev v. Russia*, ECtHR 5 February 2009, appl. no. 13769/04, para. 42.

[985] See, e.g., *Lüdi v. Switzerland*, ECtHR 15 June 1992, appl. no. 12433/86, Series A no. 238; *Mild and Virtanen v. Finland*, ECtHR 26 July 2005, appl. nos. 39481/98 and 40227/98; *Bonev v. Bulgaria*, ECtHR 8 June 2006, appl. no. 60018/00; and *Pello v. Estonia*, ECtHR 12 April 2007, appl. no. 11423/03.

[986] *Al-Khawaja and Tahery v. The United Kingdom*, supra n. 965, para. 120; *Gabrielyan v. Armenia*, ECtHR 10 April 2012, appl. no. 8088/05, paras. 78 and 81–84.

[987] *Trofimov v. Russia*, supra n. 950, para. 33; *Sadak and Others v. Turkey (No. 1)*, ECtHR 17 July 2001, appl. nos. 29900/96, 29901/96, 29902/96 and 29903/96, para. 67; *Barberà, Messegué and Jabardo v. Spain*, supra n. 445, para. 78.

[988] *D. v. Finland*, ECtHR 7 July 2009, appl. no. 30542/04, para. 41; *Sadak and Others v. Turkey*, supra n. 858, para. 67; *Colozza v. Italy*, supra n. 189.

[989] *Karpenko v. Russia*, ECtHR 21 October 2010, appl. no. 17444/04, para. 62; *Damir Sibgatullin v. Russia*, supra n. 956, para. 51; *Pello v. Estonia*, supra n. 985, para. 35; *Bonev v. Bulgaria*, supra n. 985, para. 43; *Artner v. Austria*, supra n. 957, para. 21 *in fine*; *Delta v. France*, supra n. 782, para. 37; *Rachdad v. France*, ECtHR 13 November 2003, appl. no. 71846/01, para. 25.

[990] *Gossa v. Poland*, ECtHR 9 January 2007, appl. no. 47986/99, para. 55; *Haas v. Germany*, ECtHR 17 November 2005, appl. no. 73047/01; *Calabrò v. Italy and Germany*, ECtHR 21 March 2002, appl. no. 59895/00, *Ubach Mortes v. Andorra*, ECtHR (dec) 4 May 2000, appl. no. 46253/99;

Paragraph 3(d) does not grant the accused an unlimited right to secure the appearance of witnesses in court. In principle, it is for the national courts to consider whether a particular witness should be heard.[991]

Therefore, it is not sufficient for an applicant to complain in Strasbourg that he has not been allowed to question a certain witness; in addition, he must explain why it is important for the witness concerned to be heard and the evidence must be necessary for the establishment of the truth.[992]

In the *Chap* case,[993] the national Administrative Court refused to grant the application of the accused company to summon witnesses in a case involving tax surcharges, considering that their evidence was not relevant. Although the evidence of these witnesses was not the only evidence against this company, the fact that this evidence was relied upon to establish the company's tax liability brought the Court to the conclusion that the national administrative court's refusal to summon these witnesses meant a violation of Article 6(1) in conjunction with Article 6(3)(d).

In principle, the Court does not assess whether statements of witnesses have been properly admitted as evidence.[994] Thus, it is a matter for the domestic courts to assess whether a statement given by a witness in open court and under oath should be relied on in preference to another statement of the same witness, even when the former is contradictory to the latter.[995]

The Court has deduced from the fact that an accused person is 'entitled to take part in the hearing and to have his case heard in his presence by a tribunal', that all the evidence should 'in principle be produced in the presence of the accused at a public hearing with a view to adversarial argument'.[996] In the *Hulki Günes* case, the lack of any confrontation with the witnesses who had identified the applicant as the person who had taken part in an armed attack during which one soldier died, deprived him of a fair trial, since the judges had not been able to study their demeanour while giving evidence and form a personal opinion as to their credibility.[997] However, it is not inconsistent with paragraph 3(d) and paragraph 1 to use as evidence statements made at the pre-trial stage as long as

---

Artner v. Austria, supra n. 957, para. 21; *Scheper v. the Netherlands*, ECtHR 5 April 2005, appl. no. 39209/02; *Mayali v. France*, ECtHR 14 June 2005, appl. no. 69116/01.

[991] *Vidal v. Belgium, supra* n. 477, para. 33; *Doorson v. the Netherlands, supra* n. 504, para. 82; *Pisano v. Italy, supra* n. 476, para. 23; *Perna v. Italy*, ECtHR (GC) 6 May 2003, appl. no. 48898/99, para. 29; *Laukanen and Manninen v. Finland*, ECtHR 3 February 2004, appl. no. 50230/99, para. 35.

[992] *Perna v. Italy, supra* n. 991, para. 29.

[993] *Chap Ltd. v. Armenia*, ECtHR 4 May 2017, appl. no. 15485/09, paras. 49–53.

[994] See, e.g., *Barberà, Messegué and Jabardo v. Spain, supra* n. 445, para. 68; *Kostovski v. the Netherlands, supra* n. 446, para. 39; *Solakov v. The former Yugoslav Republic of Macedonia, supra* n. 954, para. 57; *Perna v. Italy supra* n. 991; *Topić v. Croatia, supra* n. 977, para. 41; *Poropat v. Slovenia*, ECtHR 9 May 2017, appl. no. 21668/12.

[995] *Doorson v. the Netherlands, supra* n. 504, para. 78.

[996] See, e.g., *Barberà, Messegué and Jabardo v. Spain, supra* n. 445, para. 78; *Lüdi v. Switzerland, supra* n. 186, para. 47; *Van Mechelen and Others v. the Netherlands, supra* n. 505, para. 51.

[997] *Hulki Günes v. Turkey*, ECtHR 19 June 2003, appl. no. 28490/95, paras. 86–96.

the accused has been given 'an adequate and proper opportunity to challenge and question a witness against him, either at the time the witness was making his statement or at some later stage of the proceedings'.[998] If the accused did not have 'an adequate and proper opportunity' to question the witness, his conviction cannot solely or mainly be based on the testimony of the latter.[999] The case law does not seem to leave much room for exceptions to this rule. The use as evidence of a statement made in the pre-trial phase by a person who subsequently, in accordance with national law, refuses to give evidence in court, is in itself not incompatible with the Convention. However, it may lead to a conviction only if there exists evidence that corroborates the statement.[1000] The same holds good for a statement of a witness who has disappeared and, therefore, cannot be summoned to appear in court.[1001]

This approach is also reflected in the case law with regard to the admissibility of the testimony by anonymous witnesses. Both the absence of a witness and the anonymity of a witness result in a potential disadvantage for the accused. The underlying principle is that the defendant should have an effective opportunity to challenge the evidence against him.[1002] First of all, the use of statements by anonymous witnesses is not under all circumstances incompatible with 6(1) and 6(3).[1003] The Contracting States should take into account the interests of witnesses as their life, liberty, security and more generally their interests within the ambit of Article 8. Their criminal proceedings should be organised in a way that the interests of witnesses are not unjustifiably endangered. The principles of a fair trial therefore require that the interests of the defence are balanced against those

---

[998] *Kostovski v. the Netherlands, supra* n. 446, para. 41. See also, e.g., *Unterpertinger v. Austria, supra* n. 813, para. 31; *Asch v. Austria, supra* n. 956, para. 27; *Saïdi v. France*, ECtHR 20 September 1993, appl. no. 14647/89, para. 43; *S.N. v. Sweden, supra* n. 497, para. 44; *Craxi v. Italy, supra* n. 721, para. 86.

[999] *Kostovski v. the Netherlands, supra* n. 446, para. 44; *Windisch v. Austria, supra* n. 493, para. 31; *Isgrò v. Italy, supra* n. 957, para. 35; *Artner v. Austria, supra* n. 957, para. 22; *Saïdi v. France, supra* n. 998, para. 44.

[1000] *Unterpertinger v. Austria, supra* n. 813, paras. 31–33; *Asch v. Austria, supra* n. 956, paras. 28–31.

[1001] *Artner v. Austria, supra* n. 957, paras. 22–24. In *Rachdad v. France, supra* n. 989, paras. 22–25, Art. 6 was deemed to have been violated despite the existing difficulty in ascertaining the whereabouts of the witness and the fact that the applicant had contributed to that difficulty by failing to comply with court summonses and thus causing the courts to convict him in his absence. See also *Destrehem v. France*, ECtHR 18 May 2004, appl. no. 56651/00, paras. 45–47, where the court of first instance acquitted the applicant after the hearing of several witnesses. The court of appeal convicted him grounding its decision on a new interpretation of the evidence given by witnesses it had not itself examined, notwithstanding the applicant's requests to that effect. In these circumstances, the defence rights had been considerably restricted and the refusal to hear the witnesses constituted a violation of Art. 6.

[1002] *Al-Khawaja and Tahery v. the United Kingdom, supra* n. 965, para. 127.

[1003] *Doorson v. the Netherlands, supra* n. 504, para. 69; *Van Mechelen and Others v. the Netherlands, supra* n. 505, para. 52; *Krasniki v. The Czech Republic*, ECtHR 28 February 2006, appl. no. 51277/99, para. 76.

of witnesses and victims called upon to testify.[1004] In the *Riahi* case[1005] the Court concluded that there was a breach of Article 6(1) and 6(3)(d). The victim and only witness was heard by the police and the *juge d'instruction* but never by the court or the accused and his lawyer. They did not have an opportunity to cross-examine and to test the reliability of this witness.[1006] The rigorous and precise examination by the national court of appeal was not enough to counterbalance the lack of confrontation in a public hearing between the accused and the accuser.[1007]

Only in case of relevant and sufficient reasons may the national authorities keep secret the identity of certain witnesses.[1008] The difficulties with which the defence has to work due to the anonymity of the witness should be sufficiently counterbalanced by the procedures followed by the judicial authorities.[1009] In particular, the defence should not be prevented from testing the reliability of the anonymous witness.[1010] At the assessment of the sufficiency of the counterbalancing measures to protect the interests of the accused, due weight should be given to the extent to which the anonymous testimony was decisive in the conviction.[1011]

In case the anonymous witnesses are members of the police force the lack of direct confrontation seems (even) more difficult to repair. In the *Van Mechelen* case, the officers in question had been in a separate room in the presence of the investigating judge, from which the accused and counsel had been excluded. All communication took place by way of a direct communication channel. Since the defence had not only been unaware of the identity of the police officers but also had been prevented from observing their demeanour under direct questioning, the Court held that the handicaps of the defence had not been sufficiently counterbalanced and the Court rejected the argument of the Dutch Government that the anonymity had been justified by operational needs of the police.[1012] In the *Lüdi* case, however, with respect to an undercover agent,

---

[1004] *Doorson v. the Netherlands*, *supra* n. 504, para. 71; *Visser v. the Netherlands*, ECtHR 14 February 2002, appl. no. 26668/95, para. 47.

[1005] *Riahi v. Belgium*, *supra* n. 963, paras. 38–43.

[1006] The Court refers to *Tseber v. Czech Republic*, *supra* n. 963, para. 60; *Sică v. Romania*, *supra* n. 963, para. 70; *Vronchenko v. Estonia*, ECtHR 18 July 2013, appl. no. 59632/09, para. 65; and *Rosin v. Estonia*, ECtHR 19 December 2013, appl. no. 26540/08, para. 62.

[1007] The Court refers here to *Damir Sibgatullin v. Russia*, *supra* n. 956, para. 57 and *Tseber v. Czech Republic*, *supra* n. 963, para. 65.

[1008] *Doorson v. the Netherlands*, *supra* n. 504, para. 71, *Visser v. the Netherlands*, *supra* n. 1004, para. 47; *Sapunarescu v. Germany*, ECtHR 11 September 2006, appl. no. 22007/03; *Dzelili v. Germany*, ECtHR 10 November 2005, appl. no. 65745/01.

[1009] *Doorson v. the Netherlands*, *supra* n. 504, para. 72; *Van Mechelen and Others v. the Netherlands*, *supra* n. 505, para. 54; *Haas v. Germany*, *supra* n. 990.

[1010] *Birutis and Others v. Lithuania*, ECtHR 28 March 2002, appl. nos. 47698/99 and 48115/99, para. 29; *Van Mechelen and Others v. the Netherlands*, *supra* n. 505, paras. 59 and 62; *Kostovski v. the Netherlands*, *supra* n. 446, para. 42.

[1011] *Kok v. the Netherlands*, ECtHR 4 July 2000, appl. no. 43149/98; *Krasniki v. Czech Republic*, *supra* n. 1003, para. 79.

[1012] *Van Mechelen and Others v. the Netherlands*, *supra* n. 505, paras. 56–65. Moreover, the Court held that the conviction was based to a decisive extent on the anonymous statements (para. 63).

a sworn police officer whose function was known to the investigating judge, Article 6 did not object to the examination by the defence of an undercover agent without revealing the *real* identity of the agent, because the accused knew the agent by physical appearance.[1013]

In the *Aigner* case,[1014] the Court stressed the special features of criminal proceedings concerning sexual offences. According to the Court such proceedings are often conceived of as an ordeal by the victim, 'in particular when the latter is unwillingly confronted with the defendant'. These features are even more prominent in a case involving a minor. According to the Court in the assessment of the question whether or not in such proceedings an accused received a fair trial, account must be taken of the right to respect for the private life of the alleged victim. Therefore, the Court accepts that in criminal proceedings concerning sexual abuse certain measures may be taken for the purpose of protecting the victim, provided that such measures can be reconciled with an adequate and effective exercise of the rights of the defence.[1015]

In the case of *S.N. v. Sweden*,[1016] the Court referred to these special features while stating that paragraph 3(d) cannot be interpreted as requiring in all cases that questions be put directly by the accused or his or her defence counsel, through cross-examination or by other means.[1017] According to the Court in the case of *Bocos-Cuesta*,[1018] the applicant was not provided with an opportunity to follow the manner in which the children were heard by the police 'for instance by watching this in another room via technical devices', nor was he then or later provided with an opportunity to have questions put to them. Furthermore, as the children's statements to the police were not recorded on videotape, neither the applicant nor the trial court judges were able to observe their demeanour under questioning and thus form their own impression of their reliability.[1019]

As regards crown witnesses, the Court recognised in the *Cornelis*[1020] decision that the use of statements made by witnesses in exchange for immunity or other

---

[1013] *Lüdi v. Switzerland, supra* n. 186, para. 49. (Art. 6 had nevertheless been violated because the defence did not have any opportunity to question the undercover agent.) *Cf.* also the reference of the Court in *Van Mechelen and Others v. The Netherlands, supra* n. 505, para. 60, to the Dutch Act of 11 November 1993 with regard to the use of make-up or disguise and the prevention of eye contact.

[1014] *Aigner v. Austria*, ECtHR 10 May 2012, appl. no. 28328/03.

[1015] *D. v. Finland, supra* n. 988, para. 43; *F. and M. v. Finland*, ECtHR 17 July 2007, appl. no. 22508/02, para. 58; *Accardi and Others v. Italy*, ECtHR 20 January 2005 (dec.), appl. no. 30598/02; *S.N. v. Sweden, supra* n. 497, para. 47; *Bocos-Cuesta v. the Netherlands*, ECtHR 10 November 2005, appl. no. 54789/00; *Vronchenko v. Estonia, supra* n. 1006, para. 56.

[1016] *S.N. v. Sweden, supra* n. 497, para. 47.

[1017] See also *W.S. v. Poland*, ECtHR 19 June 2007, appl. no. 21508/02, para. 55.

[1018] *Bocos-Cuesta v. the Netherlands, supra* n. 1015.

[1019] See also *P.S. v. Germany*, ECtHR 20 December 2001, appl. no. 33900/96, para. 26; *Accardi and Others v. Italy, supra* n. 1015; *S.N. v. Sweden, supra* n. 497, para. 52; *D. v. Finland, supra* n. 988, para. 50; *A.L. v. Finland*, ECtHR 27 January 2009, appl. no. 23220/04, para. 41.

[1020] *Cornelis v. the Netherlands*, ECtHR 25 May 2004, appl. no. 994/03.

advantages forms an important tool in the fight against serious crime. However, according to the Court the use of such statements may put in question the fairness of the proceedings against the accused 'and is capable of raising delicate issues as, by their very nature, such statements are open to manipulation and may be made purely in order to obtain the advantages offered in exchange, or for personal revenge. The sometimes ambiguous nature of such statements and the risk that a person might be accused and tried on the basis of unverified allegations that are not necessarily disinterested must not, therefore, be underestimated.'[1021]

'However, the use of these kinds of statements does not in itself suffice to render the proceedings unfair.'[1022]

As far as the right to call witnesses for the defence is concerned, the Court considered in the *Perna* case[1023] that 'as a general rule, it is for the national courts to assess the evidence before them as well as the relevance of the evidence which defendants seek to adduce." Paragraph 3(d) leaves it to the courts "to assess whether it is appropriate to call witnesses."[1024] It 'does not require the attendance and examination of every witness on the accused's behalf: its essential aim, as is indicated by the words "under the same conditions", is a full "equality of arms" in the matter'.[1025] It is accordingly not sufficient for a defendant to complain that he has not been allowed to question certain witnesses; he must, in addition, support his request by explaining why it is important for the witnesses concerned to be heard and their evidence must be necessary for the establishment of the truth.[1026]

The second limb of paragraph 3(d) clearly allows for discretion on the part of the national court because its only requirement is that the prosecution and the accused receive equal treatment in this respect. With regard to the summoning of witnesses for the defence and their examination, domestic law and the courts may set conditions and impose restrictions, provided that these equally apply in respect of the witnesses for the prosecution.[1027] Moreover, some initiative on the part of the accused may be required as to the calling of witnesses, as well as, of course, during the examination; the court need not call witnesses of its own accord.[1028] However, here again the fact that paragraph 3(d) has not been violated does not yet mean that the requirements of the first paragraph have been

---

[1021] *Labita v. Italy*, ECtHR (GC) 6 April 2000, appl. no. 26772/95, para. 157.
[1022] *Lorsé v. the Netherlands*, ECtHR 27 January 2004, appl. no. 44484/98; and *Verhoek v. the Netherlands*, ECtHR 27 January 2004, no. 54445/00.
[1023] *Perna v. Italy, supra* n. 991, para. 29.
[1024] *Vidal v. Belgium, supra* n. 477, para. 33.
[1025] *Solakov v. The former Yugoslav Republic of Macedonia, supra* n. 954, para. 57.
[1026] *Perna v. Italy, supra* n. 991, para. 75.
[1027] *Vidal v. Belgium, supra* n. 477, p. 32.
[1028] *X v. the United Kingdom*, EComHR 11 December 1972, appl. no. 5881/72 (not published). In its decision the Commission stated that the calling of witnesses 'was a matter which was within the discretion of the applicant's solicitor and counsel and the fact that they apparently

satisfied. Moreover, the Strasbourg Court has restricted the discretion of the courts somewhat by requiring that the national courts should state the reasons for rejecting a request of the accused to summon a witness.[1029]

9.6. THE RIGHT TO THE FREE ASSISTANCE OF AN INTERPRETER

Paragraph 3(e), finally, grants to the accused the right to have the free assistance of an interpreter if he cannot understand or speak the language used in court. This right applies exclusively in situations where the accused cannot understand or speak the language in court. Hence, an accused who understands the language in court cannot insist on the interpretation of an interpreter to conduct his defence in another language, even if this other language would be the language of the ethnic minority he belongs to.[1030] The fact that the counsel of the accused, but not the accused understands the language used in court does not do away with the latter's right to an interpreter. The right to a fair trial includes the right to participate in the hearing and related to that the right to an interpreter requires that the accused is able to understand the proceedings and to inform his lawyer of any point that should be made in his defence.[1031] In other words, the interpretation assistance should enable the accused to have knowledge of the case against him and to defend himself. The accused should be able to put forward before the court his version of the events.[1032]

The requirements of paragraph 3(e) are particular aspects of the right to a fair trial guaranteed by paragraph 1. Hence, in many cases the Court applies both provisions together.[1033] The Court's considerations in the *Kamasinski* case seem to infer that the right to an interpreter could be waived if it becomes clear that it is the accused himself that took that decision and not his lawyer.[1034]

Paragraph 3(e) guarantees the right to the free assistance of an interpreter for translation or interpretation of all documents or statements in the proceedings

---

chose to call only one medical witness does not suggest in any way that the applicant's rights under this provision [i.e. Art. 6(3)(d)] were not respected'.

[1029] *Vidal v. Belgium, supra* n. 477, para. 34; *Pisano v. Italy, supra* n. 476, para. 24.

[1030] *Lagerblom v. Sweden, supra* n. 933, para. 62. See also *K. v. France*, EComHR 7 December 1983 (dec.), appl. no. 10210/82 and *Bideault v. France*, EComHR 9 December 1987 (dec.), appl. no. 11261/84.

[1031] *Kamasinski v. Austria, supra* n. 331, para. 74; *Cuscani v. the United Kingdom*, ECtHR 24 September 2002, appl. no. 32771/96, para. 38.

[1032] *Baytar v. Turkey*, ECtHR 14 October 2014, appl. no. 45440/04, para. 49; *Protopapa v. Turkey*, ECtHR 24 February 2009, appl. no. 16084/90, para. 80; *Güngör v. Germany*, ECtHR 17 May 2001, appl. no. 31540/96; *Kamasinski v. Austria, supra* n. 331, para. 74; *Luedicke, Belkacem and Koç, supra* n. 561, para. 48.

[1033] See, e.g., *Pala v. France*, ECtHR 30 January 2007, appl. no. 33387/04; *Valentini v. Italy*, ECtHR 18 May 2000, appl. no. 45003/98.

[1034] *Kamasinski v. Austria, supra* n. 331, para. 80.

which the accused should understand or which should be rendered to the court in the language it uses in order for the accused to have a fair trial.[1035]

The right to interpretation is not limited to oral statements at the trial, but also applies to documents and to the pre-trial investigations.[1036] Like the assistance of a lawyer, the assistance of an interpreter should be provided from the investigation stage, unless there are compelling reasons to restrict this right.[1037]

Referring to the *Salduz* case,[1038] the Court emphasises in the *Baytar* case[1039] the importance of the investigation stage for the preparation of the criminal proceedings, as the evidence obtained at this stage may be decisive for the subsequent proceedings. The Court pointed out that an individual held in police custody enjoys a certain number of rights, such as the right to remain silent or to be assisted by a lawyer. The decision to exercise or waive such rights can only be taken if the accused clearly understands the charges, so that he or she can consider what is at stake in the proceedings and assess the advisability of such a waiver. In this case the accused was not placed in a position where she could fully assess the consequences of her alleged waiver of her right to remain silent or her right to be assisted by a lawyer and thus to benefit from the comprehensive range of services that can be performed by counsel. Accordingly, the Court found it questionable whether the choices made by the applicant without the assistance of an interpreter were totally informed. The Court found that this initial defect undermined the fairness of the proceedings as a whole.

In the *Luedicke, Belkacem and Koç* case, the Court held that paragraph 3(e) relates to 'all those documents or statements in the proceedings instituted against him which it is necessary for him to understand in order to have the benefit of a fair trial'.[1040] However, according to the Court, this does not imply that all items of written evidence or official documents have to be translated. Paragraph 3(e) does not go so far as to require a written translation of all items of written evidence or official documents in the procedure. The Courts underlines here that the text of the relevant provisions refers to an 'interpreter' and not to a 'translator'. Therefore, oral linguistic assistance may satisfy the requirements.[1041]

In the *Kamasinski* case, the questions put to the witnesses were not interpreted separately. The interpretation at the trial was 'consecutive and summarising'. This does in itself not amount to a violation of sub-paragraph

---

[1035] *Luedicke, Belkacem and Koç, supra* n. 561, para. 48; *Ucak v. the United Kingdom*, ECtHR 24 January 2002, appl. no. 44234/98; *Hermi v. Italy*, ECtHR (GC) 18 October 2006, appl. no. 18114/02, para. 69; *Lagerblom v. Sweden, supra* n. 933, para. 61.

[1036] *Kamasinski v. Austria, supra* n. 331, para. 74; *Hermi v. Italy, supra* n. 942, para. 70.

[1037] *Baytar v. Turkey, supra* n. 1032, para. 50; *Diallo v. Sweden*, ECtHR 5 January 2010, appl. no. 13205/07, para. 25.

[1038] *Salduz v. Turkey*, ECtHR (GC) 27 November 2008, appl. no. 36391/02.

[1039] *Baytar v. Turkey, supra* n. 1032.

[1040] *Luedicke, Belkacem and Koç, supra* n. 561.

[1041] *Husain v. Italy*, ECtHR 24 February 2005, appl. no. 18913/03; *Hermi v. Italy, supra* n. 942, para. 70.

(e). Neither does the absence of a written translation of the verdict, as long as the accused has sufficient knowledge of the judgment and its reasoning to judge whether he should give notice of appeal.[1042]

Paragraph 3 (e) requires an accused to be given the free assistance of an interpreter. In the *Fedele* case,[1043] the Court ruled that irrespective of the question whether it is a case of criminal or of regulatory proceedings (concerning administrative fines for example), it cannot be inferred from this provision that the treasury has to meet the costs of interpreting where the accused or a person involved in regulatory proceedings fails – in a manner for which he is accountable – to appear at the oral hearing even though he knew that an interpreter would be summoned and that costs would thus be incurred.

The costs of interpretation cannot be claimed back from the accused. In German legal practice paragraph 3(e) was applied in such a way that an interpreter was indeed freely made available to begin with, but the expense involved was ultimately made to fall under the general regulation concerning the costs of the suit. This was considered by the Court to be contrary to the word 'free'.[1044] Moreover, the Court indicated that paragraph 3(e) refers not only to the expenses of an interpreter, but also to translation expenses, and then not only to the expenses relating to the hearing itself, but also to those concerning the translation of the charge brought against the accused, as referred to in Article 6(3)(a), and of the reasons for the arrest and the charges. The *Öztürk* case as well as the *Isyar* case show this is standing case law.[1045]

The obligation to appoint an interpreter rests on the competent authorities, although some personal initiative of the accused may be required.[1046] In the *Cuscani* case, the requirements of Article 6 had not been satisfied by leaving it to the applicant to invoke the untested language skills of his brother. Since the judge had been alerted to counsel's own difficulties in communicating with the applicant, the verification of the applicant's need for interpretation facilities was a matter for the judge to determine in consultation with the accused.[1047]

It should be noted that in this case the accused had legal assistance. However, the Court considers the trial judge as the ultimate guardian of the fairness of the proceedings. Similar wording was used in the *Hermi* case and the *Katritsch* case.[1048]

[1042]   *Kamasinski v. Austria, supra* n. 331, para. 85.

[1043]   *Fedele v. Germany*, ECtHR 9 December 1987, appl. no. 11311/84.

[1044]   *Luedicke, Belkacem and Koç, supra* n. 561, paras. 39–46.

[1045]   *Öztürk v. Germany, supra* n. 211; *Isyar v. Bulgaria*, ECtHR 20 November 2008, appl. no. 391/03. See also *Hovanesian v. Bulgaria*, ECtHR 21 December 2010, appl. no. 31814/03, paras. 48–52.

[1046]   *Delcourt v. Belgium, supra* n. 2, p. 282 (318).

[1047]   *Cuscani v. the United Kingdom, supra* n. 1031.

[1048]   *Hermi v. Italy, supra* n. 942; *Katritsch v. France*, ECtHR 4 November 2010, appl. no. 22575/08.

The language skills of the accused are vital and therefore the nature of the offence the accused is charged of as well as any communications addressed to him by the authorities should be examined in order to assess whether the language skills of the accused match the complexity of the communication.[1049] The obligation to appoint an interpreter is not fulfilled by merely appointing one. If the authorities 'are put on notice in the particular circumstances, [it] may also extend to a degree of a subsequent control over the adequacy of the interpretation provided'.[1050]

In the *Ucak* case,[1051] the Court considered that it is not appropriate under Article 6(3)(e) to lay down any detailed conditions concerning the method by which interpreters may be provided to assist accused persons. An interpreter is not part of the court or tribunal and there is no formal requirement of independence or impartiality as such. According to the Court the services of the interpreter must provide the accused with effective assistance in conducting his defence and the interpreter's conduct must not be of such a nature as to impinge on the fairness of the proceedings.

[1049] *Hermi v. Italy, supra* n. 942; *Katritsch v. France, supra* n. 1048; *Saman v. Turkey,* ECtHR 5 April 2011, appl. no. 35292/05; *Güngör v. Germany, supra* n. 1032.

[1050] *Kamasinski v. Austria, supra* n. 331, para. 74; *Hermi v. Italy, supra* n. 942, para. 70; *Protopapa v. Turkey, supra* n. 1032.

[1051] *Ucak v. the United Kingdom, supra* n. 1035.

CHAPTER 11

NO PUNISHMENT WITHOUT LAW

(Article 7)

Edwin Bleichrodt*

GUIDING PRINCPLE

The *nullum crimen* and *nulla poena sine lege* principles are essential aspects of the rule of law. A criminal conviction is only permitted when it is based on a norm which existed at the time of the incriminating act or omission and no heavier penalty may be imposed than the one that was applicable at the time the offence was committed.

ARTICLE 7

1. No one shall be held guilty of any criminal offence on account of any act or omission which did not constitute a criminal offence under national or international law at the time when it was committed. Nor shall a heavier penalty be imposed than the one that was applicable at the time the criminal offence was committed.

2. This Article shall not prejudice the trial and punishment of any person for any act or omission which, at the time when it was committed, was criminal according to the general principles of law recognised by civilised nations.

---

*   In the fourth edition this chapter was revised by Edwin Bleichrodt.

CONTENTS

1. SCOPE

The first paragraph of Article 7 contains the following two separate and explicit principles, which are essential elements of the rule of law: (1) a criminal conviction can only be based on a norm which existed at the time of the incriminating act or omission (*nullum crimen sine lege*); and (2) on account of the infringement of that norm no heavier penalty may be imposed than the one that was applicable at the time the offence was committed (*nulla poena sine lege*).

The Court has accepted two additional principles: (3) when there are differences between the criminal law in force at the time of the commission of the offence and subsequent criminal laws enacted before a final judgement is rendered, the courts must apply the law whose provisions are most favourable for the defendant (*lex mitior*).[1] Thus, Article 7 intends to offer 'essential safeguards against arbitrary prosecution, conviction and punishment'.[2] In this way, it occupies a primordial place in the Convention system of protection, as is underlined by the fact that no derogation from it is permissible under Article 15 in time of war or other public emergency. Finally, the Court has distinguished as a fourth principle: (4) the authority applying criminal law shall not interpret it extensively, for instance by analogy, to the accused's detriment. From this principle follows, according to the Court, that an offence must be clearly defined in law.[3] It is submitted, however, that this fourth principle is not an entirely separate one, but is embodied in the rationale of the *nullum crimen* and *nulla poena sine lege* principles.

The principles *nulla crimen sine lege* and *nulla poena sine lege* are two separate principles. That means, *inter alia,* that even a purely declaratory

---

[1] *Scoppola v. Italy (No. 2)*, ECtHR 17 September 2009, appl. no. 10249/03, para. 109.

[2] *Kokkinakis v. Greece,* ECtHR 25 May 1993, appl. no. 14307/88, para. 52; *S.W. v. the United Kingdom,* ECtHR 22 November 1995, appl. no. 20166/92, para. 35; *C.R. v. the United Kingdom,* ECtHR 22 November 1995, appl. no. 20190/92, para. 33; *Gabarri Moreno v. Spain,* ECtHR 22 July 2003, appl. no. 68066/01, para. 22.

[3] *Kokkinakis v. Greece, supra* n. 2, para. 52; *Coëme and Others v. Belgium,* ECtHR 22 June 2000, appl. nos. 32492/96, 32547/96, 32548/96, 33209/96 and 33210/96, para. 145.

judgment in which a norm of criminal law is applied with retrospective effect and is declared to have been infringed, but in which no punishment or other measure is imposed on the offender, constitutes a violation of Article 7. This is not without importance, because such a declaratory judgment, when registered, may still have prejudicial consequences for the person in question, even apart from the social repercussions that it may entail.

2. *NULLUM CRIMEN NULLA POENA SINE LEGE*

By virtue of the wording of Article 7 the 'penalty' must be imposed following a conviction for a 'criminal offence'. The Court takes this as a starting-point. It seems to be obvious that the meaning of the words 'criminal offence' is closely related to the notion of 'criminal charge' in Article 6. Thus, it is appropriate to argue that Article 7 is also applicable to those disciplinary and administrative convictions which come within the scope of Article 6. In the *Dogan* case, the Court noted that the alleged eviction of the applicants from their homes and the restrictions on their return to their village did not concern 'a criminal charge' against them within the meaning of Article 6 (1). The Court held that it followed that the events and the measures complained of in the instant case did not concern 'a criminal offence' for the purpose of Article 7 either.[4] It may, therefore, be concluded that the terms 'criminal offence' and 'criminal charge' have the same scope.

The term 'penalty' is autonomous in scope. To render the protection afforded by Article 7 effective the Court can go behind appearances and assess for itself whether a particular measure amounts in substance to a 'penalty' within the meaning of this provision.[5] The text of the Convention is the starting point for such an assessment whether or not Article 7 is applicable. The Court may also use other sources, such as the *travaux préparatoires*. It may, in addition, take into consideration the notions currently prevailing in democratic states.[6] Factors that may be relevant are: the characterisation of the measure under national law, its nature and purpose, the procedures involved in the making and implementation of the measure and its severity.[7] The fact that the applicant feels that the effects of the sanction are punitive, is not sufficient to establish

---

[4]   *Dogan and Others v. Turkey,* ECtHR 29 June 2004, appl. nos. 8803/02–8811/02, 8813/02 and 8815/02–8819/02, para. 126. See also *Tre Traktörer Aktiebolag v. Sweden,* ECtHR 7 July 1989, appl. no. 10873/84, para. 46.

[5]   *Welch v. the United Kingdom,* ECtHR 9 February 1995, appl. no. 17440/90, para. 27.

[6]   See, e.g., *Guzzardi v. Italy,* ECtHR 6 November 1980, appl. no. 7367/76, para. 95 and *Coëme and Others v. Belgium, supra* n. 3, para. 145.

[7]   *Welch v. the United Kingdom, supra* n. 5, para. 28; *Jamil v. France,* ECtHR 8 June 1995, appl. no. 15917/89, para. 31.

that the sanction has a punitive purpose under Article 7.[8] Rather, the purpose of the sanction must be established in an objective way. In the *Welch* case, the Court concluded that a confiscation order imposed in addition to a sentence of imprisonment did constitute a 'penalty'. The fact that the confiscation order had also reparative and preventive aims was not decisive.[9] In view of the combination of punitive elements, the confiscation order turned into a penalty.[10] In the *Jamil* case, the Court held that the prolongation of a term of imprisonment in default resulted in the applicability of Article 7.[11] It took into account that the sanction was ordered by a criminal court, was intended to be deterrent and could have led to a punitive deprivation of liberty. By contrast, a demolition order, which did not depend on any finding of guilt and which had a restorative aim, did not constitute a 'penalty' within the meaning of Article 7.[12]

It follows from Article 7 that an offence must be clearly defined in law. The term 'law' in Article 7 alludes to the same concept as the one to which the Convention refers elsewhere when using that term, a concept which comprises written law as well as unwritten law and which implies qualitative requirements, notably those of accessibility and foreseeability.[13] This requirement serves to avoid a criminal conviction being based on a legal norm of which the person concerned could not, or at least need not, have been aware beforehand. It follows that offences and the connected penalties must be clearly defined by law. This condition is satisfied if the individual may know from the wording of the relevant provision and, if need be, with the assistance of the court's interpretation of it, what acts and omissions will make him criminally liable and what penalty will be imposed.[14] However, it is inevitable for the making of legal provisions that more or less vague wordings are used. The Court accepts that legal provisions must have a certain flexibility to handle changing circumstances and to avoid excessive rigidity. The existence of a 'grey area' does not in itself make a

---

[8]   *Adamson v. the United Kingdom*, ECtHR 26 January 1999 (dec.), appl. no. 42293/98.

[9]   *Welch v. the United Kingdom, supra* n. 5, paras. 27–35; *Jamil v. France, supra* n. 7, para. 32. See also with regards to preventive detention *Glien v. Germany*, ECtHR 28 November 2013, appl. no. 7345/12, paras. 119–131.

[10] *Welch v. the United Kingdom, supra* n. 7, para. 35. The Court distinguished several punitive elements. The combination of these gave the confiscation order the character of a 'penalty'. The Court stressed, however, that the severity of the order was not in itself decisive because 'many non-penal measures of a preventive nature may have a substantial impact on the person concerned'.

[11] *Jamil v. France, supra* n. 7, paras. 34–36.

[12] *Saliba v. Malta*, ECtHR 23 November 2004 (dec.), appl. no. 4251/02.

[13] See, e.g., *Vasiliauskas v. Lithuania*, ECtHR (GC) 20 October 2015, appl. no. 35343/05, para. 154; *Coëme and Others v. Belgium, supra* n. 3, para. 145.

[14] See, e.g., *S.W. v. the United Kingdom, supra* n. 2, para. 35 and *C.R. v. the United Kingdom, supra* n. 2, para. 33; *Veeber v. Estonia (No. 2)*, ECtHR 21 January 2003, appl. no. 45771/99, para. 31; *Radio France and Others v. France*, ECtHR 30 March 2004, appl. no. 53984/00, para. 20; *Cantoni v. France*, ECtHR (GC) 15 November 1996, appl. no. 17862/91, para. 29, *Camilleri v. Malta*, ECtHR 22 January 2013, appl. no. 42931/10, paras. 34–35; and *Ashlarba v. Georgia*, ECtHR 15 July 2014, appl. no. 45554/08, paras. 33–34.

provision incompatible with Article 7, provided that it proves to be sufficiently clear in the large majority of cases. The role of the courts is to dissipate such interpretational doubts as remain, taking into account the changes in everyday practice. The scope of the notion of foreseeability depends to a considerable degree on the content of the text in issue, the field it is designed to cover and the number and status of those to whom it is addressed. Persons carrying on a professional activity can be expected to take special care in assessing the risks that such activity entails.[15] The *Baskaya and Okçuoglu* case was related to the Turkish Prevention of Terrorism Act 1991, in which the 'dissemination of propaganda against the indivisibility of the State' was construed as an offence. The Court recognised that in the area under consideration it may be difficult to frame laws with absolute precision and that a certain degree of flexibility may be called for to enable the national courts to assess whether a publication should be considered separatist propaganda against the indivisibility of the state.[16]

Not only statutory law, but also rules of common law or customary law may provide a sufficient legal basis for a criminal conviction, provided that the law is adequately accessible and is formulated with sufficient precision to enable the person concerned to regulate his conduct.[17] In the *Kokkinakis* case, the Court based its decision on the existence of a constant case law.[18]

Since common law is, by definition, law developed by courts, Article 7(1) may raise special problems there. In *S.W. v. the United Kingdom* and *C.R. v. the United Kingdom*, the Court held that Article 7 'cannot be read as outlawing the gradual clarification of the rules of criminal liability through judicial interpretation from case to case, provided that the resultant development is consistent with the essence of the offence and could reasonably be foreseen'.[19] In these cases, the Court reached the conclusion that the decision of the national courts to lift the immunity of a man from prosecution for rape of his wife constituted a 'reasonably foreseeable development of law'. Moreover, since the 'essentially debasing character of rape' was manifest, the applicants could not claim that they had been subjected to an arbitrary prosecution, conviction and punishment.[20] It seems to have been relevant that values that the Convention tries to protect were at issue. The same approach provides for a clearer understanding of the two

---

[15]   *Cantoni v. France, supra* n. 14, para. 35. See also *K.A. and A.D. v. Belgium*, ECtHR 17 February 2005, appl. nos. 42758/98 and 45558/99, paras. 56–58.

[16]   *Baskaya and Okcuoglu v. Turkey*, ECtHR (GC) 8 July 1999, appl. nos. 23536/94 and 24408/94, para. 39. See also *E.K. v. Turkey*, ECtHR 7 February 2002, appl. no. 53176/99, para. 52.

[17]   For these conditions, *cf. The Sunday Times v. the United Kingdom (No. 1)*, ECtHR 26 April 1979, appl. no. 6538/74, para. 49.

[18]   *Kokkinakis v. Greece, supra* n. 2, para. 52 in conjunction with paras. 37–41. See also *Larissis and Others v. Greece*, ECtHR 24 February 1998, appl. nos. 23372/94, 26377/94 and 26378/94, para. 34.

[19]   *S.W. v. the United Kingdom, supra* n. 2, para. 36 and *C.R. v. the United Kingdom, supra* n. 2, para. 34.

[20]   *Ibid.*, paras. 44–45 and para. 42, respectively.

judgments with regard to the murder of a number of people who had attempted to escape from the former German Democratic Republic (GDR) between 1971 and 1989 by crossing the border between the two German States. The Court considered, in order to assess whether the conviction of murder was lawful, the relevant rules of the GDR's written law and the nature of the GDR's state practice. A complicating factor was that there was a contradiction between the legal provisions on the one hand and the very repressive practice of the border-policy regime on the other. The Court took into account that the state practice not only contradicted the GDR's Constitution and legal provisions, but was also in breach of the obligation to respect human rights, i.e. the right to life. In those circumstances, state practice cannot be considered as 'law' within the meaning of Article 7. A state practice such as the GDR's border-policing policy, which flagrantly infringed human rights and above all the right to life, the supreme value in the international hierarchy of human rights, could not be covered by the protection of Article 7(1) of the Convention. The Court held that, at the time when they were committed, the applicants' acts constituted offences defined with sufficient accessibility and foreseeability by GDR law and by the rules of international law concerning the protection of human rights.[21]

In principle, the national legislature is free to decide what act or omission is to be qualified as an offence and has to be penalised. Article 7 is not in issue there. The European review is confined to the question of whether or not any of the other provisions of the Convention has been violated by that legislation.

The word 'heavier' in the second sentence of Article 7(1) seems to refer merely to the severity of the punishment, but the rationale for this provision entails that also a punishment of a different kind than the one formerly provided for, which reasonably may be felt as more burdensome by the person in question, shall not be applied with retrospective effect.

The *nulla poena* principle with its requirement of legal certainty does not go to such lengths that the exact measure of the penalty, or an exhaustive enumeration of alternatives, must be laid down in the criminal law provision. If, as is customary in several legal systems, only the maxima are indicated, the legal subjects know what is the maximum penalty they may incur upon violation of the norm. The Court examines whether the maximum penalty is not exceeded.[22] If a violation of the norm is penalised without a maximum being laid down, in the literal sense there can be no question of 'a heavier penalty (...) than the one that was applicable at the time the criminal offence was committed', unless at the latter time a different penalty was provided for. In that case, however, the second sentence of Article 7(1) will have to be interpreted

---

[21]　*Streletz, Kessler and Krenz v. Germany*, ECtHR (GC) 22 March 2001, appl. nos. 34044/96, 35532/97 and 44801/98, paras. 53–91; *K.-H.W. v. Germany*, ECtHR (GC) 22 March 2001, appl. no. 37201/97, paras. 48–91.

[22]　See, e.g., *Gabarri Moreno v. Spain, supra* n. 2, para. 33.

to mean that the 'applicable penalty' is the penalty which is usually inflicted for that particular offence within the legal system concerned, or which in any event was reasonably to be expected for the offender. In case the choice of jurisdiction has consequences for the possibility to impose penalties, the relevant provisions must be foreseeable and give sufficient guidance for that choice.[23]

It is possible that the manner of execution of the sentence is heavier than was reasonably foreseeable at the time the sentence was imposed. In general, the manner of execution of a sentence falls beyond the scope of Article 7.[24] In the *Grava* case, the Court held that a system of remission does not influence the heaviness of a penalty because it concerns the execution of the sentence and not the sentence as such.[25] However, the distinction between the penalty and the execution of the penalty is not always as strict as the Court suggests, especially when changes to the applicable law have consequences for the length of the penalty. It is desirable that, just like the interpretation of the term 'criminal charge', not only the classification is considered relevant, but also the assessment of whether or not the nature of the penalty in essence has become heavier.

3. APPLICATION WITH RETROSPECTIVE EFFECT

Article 7 prohibits the retrospective application of criminal law to the detriment of the accused. Even if it cannot be said with certainty that the applicant would have received a lower sentence in case the former provision had been applied, Article 7 can have been violated. That is the case if a real possibility exists that the retroactive application of the provision operates to the applicants' disadvantage as concerns the sentencing.[26] Article 7 clearly does not oppose retrospective application of criminal law in favour of the accused.[27] Accordingly, it also forms part of the review by the Court to examine whether and to what extent the norm of criminal law applied still had effect at the relevant time. Since this is essentially a question of national (constitutional) law, the answer will be guided to a high degree by the opinion of the national courts on the matter.[28] Nevertheless, it is ultimately incumbent upon the Court to decide whether Article 7 has been correctly applied.

---

[23]   *Camilleri v. Malta, supra* n. 14, paras. 39–45.

[24]   *Scoppola v. Italy, supra* n. 1, para. 98. However see *Gouarré Patte v. Andorra*, ECtHR 12 January 2016, appl. no. 33427/10.

[25]   *Grava v. Italy,* ECtHR 10 July 2003, appl. no. 43522/98, para. 51.

[26]   *Maktouf and Damjanovic v. Bosnia and Herzegovina*, ECtHR (GC) 18 July 2013, appl. nos. 2312/08 and 34179/08, para. 70. See for changes in the rules on recidivism *Achour v. France*, ECtHR (GC) 29 March 2006, appl. nos. 67335/01, paras. 44–61.

[27]   *Kokkinakis v. Italy, supra* n. 2, para. 52.

[28]   *Ibid.*

If it is evident from the legal practice in the country concerned that a particular norm of criminal law has fallen completely into desuetude, so that the offender could not reasonably presume that acting contrary to this norm would result in prosecution, it conflicts with Article 7 if that norm is applied in his case. It is, however, obvious that in such a case a heavy burden of proof rests on the applicant.

The words 'be held guilty' and 'be imposed' at first sight point in the direction that Article 7 can only be held to have been violated if a norm of criminal law has actually been applied with retrospective effect, and not merely on the basis of the fact that such a retrospective effect has been made possible by the legislature.[29] However, one should not overlook the fact that the Convention is addressed to the Contracting States and accordingly to all the organs of these states, including the legislature. If the legislature gives retrospective effect to a provision of criminal law, Article 7 of the Convention has been violated. It is true that such a violation in general cannot be the object of an individual complaint, because it is not yet possible to speak of a victim.[30] It is, however, one of the characteristic features of the equally provided possibility of state complaints that legislation may be submitted *in abstracto* for review for its compatibility with the Convention without it being necessary to allege that there are (already) individual victims of the application of that law.

Problems may arise in the case of continuous or continuing offences, i.e. a type of crime committed over a period of time, while the conviction is based on a law that has entered into force in the course of this period. The possibility of the classification of separate acts as a continuous offence should not be used as a way to undermine the guarantees of Article 7.

If an accused is charged with a continuing offence, the principle of legal certainty requires that the acts which make up that offence and which entail his criminal liability, be clearly set out in the bill of indictment.[31] The decision by the domestic court must make it clear that the conviction and sentence are based on evidence concerning the ingredients of a continuing offence. In the *Veeber* case, a considerable number of the acts on the basis of which the applicant was convicted, took place before the extension of the law. The Court observed that it could not be concluded with any certainty that the domestic courts' approach had no effect on the severity of the punishment or did not entail tangible negative consequences for the applicant. Article 7 was violated.[32] In the *Rohlena* case, the applicant was found guilty of the continuous criminal offence

---

[29] This view seems to be implied in the report in the *Greek* case, Yearbook XII (1969), p. 185: 'It is not disputed that the penalties provided (…) have not been imposed in any actual case.'

[30] In specific cases, however, the mere existence of a criminal law provision, even when it has not yet been applied in a concrete case, may hinder a person so much in his freedom of action that he can already be regarded as a victim.

[31] *Ecer and Zeyrek v. Turkey*, ECtHR 27 February 2001, appl. nos. 29295/95 and 29363/95, para. 33.

[32] *Veeber v. Estonia (No. 2), supra* n. 14, para. 36. See also *Rohlena v. Czech Republic*, ECtHR 18 April 2013, appl. no. 59552/08. This case has been referred to the Grand Chamber.

of abusing a person living under the same roof. The Court concluded that the sentence imposed on the applicant was applicable at the time when this offence was deemed to have been completed, was in accordance with a 'law' which was foreseeable as to its effect. The Court took into account that the acts committed would also have been punishable under the older law, the clarity with which the relevant domestic provisions were formulated and elucidated by the national courts' interpretation and the fact that the acts committed before the entry into force of the new law were assessed under the latter did not operate to the applicants' disadvantage as regards sentencing.[33]

In the *Coëme* case, the question arose whether the immediate application of the extension of a limitation period after the prosecution had started, entailed an infringement of Article 7. In the Court's view, Article 7 cannot be interpreted as prohibiting an extension of limitation periods through the immediate application of a procedural law where the relevant offences have never become subject to limitation.[34] The Court did not answer the question whether Article 7 would be infringed if a legal provision would restore the possibility of punishing offenders for acts which were no longer punishable because they had already become subject to limitation.

4.   *LEX MITIOR*

What is the situation if after the time the offence was committed, but before the trial, the norm of criminal law or the penalty has been modified in a sense which is more favourable for the accused? Do the courts then have to apply that modified provision? Article 7 does not expressly mention an obligation for Contracting States to grant an accused the benefit of a change in the law subsequent to the commission of the offence. Article 15 of the UN Covenant on Civil and Political Rights expressly provides as follows: 'If, subsequent to the commission of the offence, provision is made by law for the imposition of a lighter penalty, the offender shall benefit thereby.' Article 49 of the European Union's Charter of Fundamental Rights contains a similar provision. Such a provision is lacking in Article 7 of the Convention. The words 'at the time the criminal offence was committed' suggest that this provision does not confer a right to application of the norm as subsequently alleviated, or of the lowered penalty.[35] However, Article 7 clearly does not prohibit such an application either. In the *Scoppola* case, the Court concluded that a consensus had gradually emerged in Europe and internationally around the view that application of a criminal law

---

[33]   *Rohlena v. the Czech Republic*, ECtHR 27 January 2015, appl. no. 59552/08.

[34]   *Coëme and Others v. Belgium, supra* n. 3, para. 149.

[35]   Appl. 3777/68, *I. v. the United Kingdom*, Coll. 31 (1970), p. 120 (122); Appl. 7900/77, *X v. Federal Republic of Germany*, D&R 13 (1979), p. 70 (71–72).

providing for a more lenient penalty, even one enacted after the commission of the offence, has become a fundamental principle of criminal law. The Court held that Article 7 guarantees not only the principle of non-retrospectiveness of more stringent criminal laws but also, and implicitly, the principle of retrospectiveness of the more lenient criminal law (principle of *lex mitior*). That principle is embodied in the rule that where there are differences between the criminal law in force at the time of the commission of the offence and subsequent criminal laws enacted before a final judgment is rendered, the courts must apply the law whose provisions are most favourable to the defendant.[36]

5. NATIONAL OR INTERNATIONAL LAW

Article 7 refers to 'a criminal offence under national or international law'. The words 'national (...) law' must be understood to mean that a criminal judgment can be based only on the national law of the state in question and not on the law of another state. However, the Court has held it to be legitimate for a state governed by the rule of law to bring criminal proceedings against persons who have committed crimes under a former regime. The courts of such a state, having taken the place of those which existed previously, cannot be criticised for applying and interpreting the legal provisions in force at the material time in the light of the principles governing a state subject to the rule of law.[37]

The reference to international law in the first paragraph of Article 7 raises the question of the internal effect of international law within the national legal order. In those Contracting States where international law has no internal effect, this effect cannot be given in incidental cases to an international criminal law provision. Here again, compliance with Article 7 depends on whether the person concerned could reasonably know that the offence committed by him was prohibited and punishable within the relevant legal system at that time, either by virtue of a national legal provision or by virtue of a directly applicable international legal provision with internal effect.[38]

6. EXCEPTION IN THE SECOND PARAGRAPH

The second paragraph of Article 7 contains an exception to the first paragraph for the case of the trial and punishment of an act or omission which, at the time when it was committed or omitted, was a criminal offence according to

---

[36]   *Scoppola v. Italy, supra* n. 1, para. 109.
[37]   *Streletz, Kessler and Kreuz v. Germany, supra* n. 21, para. 81; *K.-H.W. v. Germany, supra* n. 21, para. 84.
[38]   In *Korbely v. Hungary*, ECtHR (GC) 19 September 2008, appl. no. 9174/02, Art. 3 of the Geneva Convention was at issue.

general principles of law. Although this provision is formulated in a general way, it has evidently been incorporated in particular to enable the application of the national and international legislation, enacted during and after World War II, in respect of war crimes, collaboration with the enemy and treason, to acts committed during the war.[39] In that sense it constitutes a codification of the principles laid down by the tribunals of Nuremberg and Tokyo.[40] The Court has stressed that the two paragraphs of Article 7 are interlinked and are to be interpreted in a concordant manner.[41] The interpretation of Article 7(2) is restrictive. The drafters of the Convention did not intend to allow for any general exception to the rule of non-retroactivity.[42]

However, the second paragraph may also apply to cases other than those mentioned above. In fact, it does not relate exclusively to war crimes, but to all acts and omissions which are criminal 'according to the general principles of law recognised by civilised nations'. Since Article 7(2) does not refer to 'the principles of law common to the Contracting States', but to 'the general principles of law recognised by civilised nations', the Contracting States may not be treated as an isolated group in this respect. The legal rule concerned will also have to be recognised outside this circle by a 'representative' group of states, if the principle of law is to be regarded as a general one. In addition, or frequently also in correlation therewith, general principles of law may emerge from international law as it develops, usually on the basis of a pattern of treaties which have been concluded and/or of an international practice which has been or is in the process of being formed. They can then hardly be distinguished from customary international law. Be this as it may, the concept of general principles of law as here referred to requires that the facts concerned are not only made punishable in the legal systems of nearly all countries and/or under international law, but that their punishable character ensues from a fundamental and generally recognised principle of law. Indeed, otherwise the guarantee of the first paragraph would be seriously jeopardised in all those cases where the legislature deliberately derogates from the criminal law as it applies in most countries in a way which is detrimental for the accused.

All this makes it difficult to establish with any accuracy what offences are meant by Article 7(2). This is particularly the case because here it is not the responsibility of the state but the responsibility of individuals that is at issue, a matter which usually is not regulated by international law. In addition to the above-mentioned war crimes one will have to think, in particular, of the

---

39   Thus, also *Kononov v. Latvia*, ECtHR 17 May 2010 (GC), appl. no. 36376/04, para. 186.
40   See Principle II of the Nuremberg Principles as formulated in 1950 by the International Law Commission, Yearbook I.L.C., 1950, Vol. II, p. 379: 'The fact that international law does not impose a penalty for an act which constitutes a crime under international law does not relieve the person who committed the act from responsibility under international law.'
41   *Kononov v. Latvia, supra* n. 39, para. 186 and *Vasiliauskas v. Lithania, supra* n. 13, para. 188.
42   *Maktouf and Damjanovic v. Bosnia and Herzegovina, supra* n. 10, para. 72.

so-called crimes against peace and crimes against humanity. It seems logical to also link the general principles of law of Article 7(2) with fundamental principles in the field of human rights such as the prohibition of torture and racial discrimination. For the applicability of Article 7(2) it is required that the violation of these principles by individuals is punishable according to the national law of (practically) all countries, or that under international law not only the state but also the individual offender is responsible for it. Only then is it possible to speak of a 'criminal act or omission'.

7. DEROGATION

According to Article 15(2) the guarantee implied in Article 7(1) is non-derogable. As has been observed, however, the consequence of the second paragraph of Article 7 is that with respect to certain offences this guarantee is not an absolute one, neither in the situations referred to in Article 15(1) nor in other cases.

CHAPTER 12

RIGHT TO RESPECT FOR PRIVATE AND FAMILY LIFE

(Article 8)

Karin DE VRIES[*]

GUIDING PRINCIPLE

Article 8 guarantees to everyone a sphere of privacy and personal autonomy generating both positive and negative obligations for the States Parties to the Convention. The scope of Article 8 has expanded substantially over the years as the Court has interpreted the notion of private life to cover a broad range of interests, including informational privacy, personal identity, physical and psychological integrity and relationships with others and the outside world.

ARTICLE 8

1. Everyone has the right to respect for his private and family life, his home and his correspondence.
2. There shall be no interference by a public authority with the exercise of this right except such as is in accordance with the law and is necessary in a democratic society in the interests of national security, public safety or the economic well-being of the country, for the prevention of disorder or crime, for the protection of health or morals, or for the protection of the rights and freedoms of others.

---

[*]   In the fourth edition this chapter was revised and updated by Aalt Willem Heringa and Leo Zwaak. Parts of this chapter have been previously published (in Dutch) in K.M. de Vries, 'Het recht op privéleven en aanverwante rechten', in: J. Gerards (ed.), *Grondrechten. De nationale, Europese en internationale dimensie*, Nijmegen: Ars Aequi Libri 2013, p. 129-161. Thanks are due to Yussef Al Tamimi for his research assistance.

CONTENTS

1. INTRODUCTION

Article 8 protects the right to respect for private life, family life, the home and correspondence. These four elements do not lend themselves to strict separation. The term 'private life' especially is broad and relatively undetermined and partly overlaps with the other rights mentioned. The purpose of this chapter is primarily to provide insight into the scope of Article 8 and to identify the doctrines and criteria developed by the Court in relation to each of the rights and interests covered by this provision. As regards the right to private life, the interests addressed by the Court under this heading are grouped into categories representing more or less self-standing aspects of personhood and the private sphere. These are: 'privacy', 'reputation', 'identity', 'sexual life', 'relationships with others and "the outside world"', 'physical and psychological integrity' and 'reproductive rights'. The same approach is used with regard to the right to family life and respect for the home, although the diversity of interests covered by each of these notions is less extensive. Where necessary sub-categories are used to discuss case law concerning a specific interest within a broader category (e.g. 'gender identity') or a specific context (e.g. 'family life and detention').

The various rights mentioned in Article 8 do not merely protect against interference: the Court has also identified a variety of positive obligations for the States Parties. Although the Court itself does not differentiate between positive obligations to protect individuals against interferences by other private parties (obligation to protect) and positive obligations to act in order to realise a certain result or standard of living (obligation to fulfil), both types of obligations emerge from the case law. The Court further expressly distinguishes between procedural and substantive obligations stemming from Article 8. Whereas the latter concern the material outcome to be reached, the former concern aspects such as the decision-making process followed by the national authorities and the availability of legal remedies. Notwithstanding these categorisations, the content of the obligations imposed on the States Parties tends to be largely specific to the right or interest at stake. The Court itself has, moreover, often stated that the boundary between the positive and negative obligations stemming from a particular right does not lend itself to precise definition. For this reason, this chapter does not contain separate paragraphs dedicated to positive and negative obligations any more. Where the Court expressly qualifies a particular obligation as positive or negative (or procedural or substantive), this is indicated in the discussion of the right or interest concerned. The same applies with regard to criteria relating to the possibility of restriction as mentioned in Article 8, paragraph 2.

2. PRIVATE LIFE

The Court has repeatedly stated that it is neither possible nor necessary to give an exhaustive definition of the notion of private life.[1] However, its case law provides insight into the wide range of rights and interests covered. In its interpretation of the notion of private life the Court is often guided by the principle of personal autonomy.[2] It has moreover stated in several judgments that the right to private life includes a right to personal development, a right to establish relationships with others and a right to self-determination.[3] Neither of these rights has, however, been precisely defined.

2.1. PRIVACY

The term 'privacy' is used here to describe what is perhaps the most traditional aspect of the right to private life: people's interest in not being exposed to unwanted attention from the state or third parties. The right to privacy has particular relevance in relation to criminal investigations. It sets limits to the instruments and methods that the States Parties may use in order to trace crimes and to collect evidence against criminal offenders. This aspect of the right to privacy is also closely related to the right to respect for the home and for one's correspondence. Certain methods of investigation, such as searches or phone tapping, are liable to infringe on each of these rights. A particular type of interference, which the Court has repeatedly dealt with, results from the use of secret surveillance measures such as phone taps and the interception of letters. This issue is discussed in section 2.1(a) below.

Contrary to secret surveillance, the act of monitoring in public places by means of security cameras does not interfere with the rights protected under Article 8, as long as the information gathered through such monitoring is not recorded. This was already decided by the former Commission in the case of *Herbecq and the Association 'Ligue des Droits de l'Homme'*.[4] The applicants claimed that the use of video surveillance might compel individuals to 'censor their own behaviour so as to avoid doing anything or avoid behaving in any way which could be interpreted by observers using such surveillance equipment' and that it might reveal 'certain modes of behaviour or physical attitudes, which the individual in question may not have wished to divulge'. However, the Commission found that the behaviour observed was public behaviour and that

---

[1]   E.g. *Niemietz v. Germany*, ECtHR 16 December 1992, appl. no. 13710/88, para. 29; *S. and Marper v. the United Kingdom*, ECtHR (GC) 4 December 2008, appl. nos. 30562/04 and 30566/04, para. 66.

[2]   *Pretty v. the United Kingdom*, ECtHR 29 April 2002, appl. no. 2346/02, para. 61.

[3]   E.g. *E.B. v. France*, ECtHR (GC) 22 January 2008, appl. no. 43546/02, para. 43.

[4]   *Herbecq and the Association 'Ligue des Droits de l'Homme' v. Belgium*, EComHR 14 January 1998 (dec.), appl. nos. 32200/96 and 32201/96.

the information gathered through monitoring was identical to that which could have been obtained by a person present on the spot. The Commission's stance was subsequently confirmed by the Court.[5]

Also covered by the right to privacy is the storing and processing of personal data, whether in the context of criminal investigations or for other purposes. The Court's case law relating to the storing and processing of data is discussed in section 2.1(b). Section 2.1(c) concerns the unauthorised publication of photographs or other personal information in the media.

a. Secret surveillance

The Court has developed a substantial body of case law concerning the use of secret surveillance measures such as phone tapping, interception of mail and secret recording of conversations. Such measures are normally treated as interferences with the right to respect for private life and correspondence.[6] The Court has held that Article 8 applies to both private and business-related correspondence and regardless of whether the correspondence is conducted from an office or from a private home.[7] A violation of this article may occur even if the information obtained through surveillance measures is not used to prosecute the applicant: it is the surveillance itself that counts as an interference with the applicant's privacy.[8]

Effective protection against unlawful use of secret surveillance measures may be hampered by the fact that applicants often cannot prove that such measures have been used; they may not even know whether or not this has been the case. To address this problem, the Court has accepted that in certain circumstances the mere existence of legislation permitting the interception of communications must be seen as an interference. For example, in the case of *Klass and Others*, the Court found an interference with the right to privacy on the grounds that German law allowed for the interception of the applicants' correspondence without them being informed. Whether interception had actually taken place was not considered relevant.[9] By contrast, where surveillance measures are not permitted by law or policy the applicant will have to adduce evidence to prove that they have in fact been used.[10]

---

[5] E.g. *Peck v. the United Kingdom*, ECtHR 28 January 2003, appl. no. 44647/98, para. 59.

[6] E.g. *Klass and Others v. Germany*, ECtHR (GC) 6 September 1978, appl. no. 5029/71, para. 41. An exception is the case of *Lüdi v. Switzerland*, where the Court held that the use of an undercover agent in a drug deal did not affect the applicant's private life because he must have been aware that the criminal acts in which he was engaged would expose him to the attention of undercover agents (ECtHR 15 June 1992, appl. no. 12433/86, para. 40).

[7] E.g. *Niemietz v. Germany*, supra n. 1, para. 32; *Halford v. the United Kingdom*, ECtHR 25 June 1997, appl. no. 20605/92, para. 44.

[8] *Kopp v. Switzerland*, ECtHR 25 March 1998, appl. no. 23224/94, para. 53.

[9] *Klass and Others v. Germany*, supra n. 6, paras. 34–41.

[10] E.g. *Halford v. the United Kingdom*, supra n. 8, para. 57; *Kennedy v. the United Kingdom*, ECtHR 18 May 2010, appl. no. 26839/05, para. 123.

The Court accepts that secret surveillance measures may be necessary to protect democratic institutions against the threats of terrorism, espionage and more recently corruption. Such measures can therefore serve the legitimate aims of the protection of national security and the prevention of disorder or crime, as mentioned in the second paragraph of Article 8. The Court also recognises, however, that the secret use of power is especially liable to abuse and risks to destroy democracy 'on the ground of defending it'.[11] It tends therefore to carefully assess whether secret surveillance measures are in accordance with the law and whether their application is subject to adequate safeguards. Given the secret nature of these measures, the Court accepts that the requirement of foreseeability does not entail that those who are under surveillance must be informed about this. Nevertheless, the relevant legislation must be formulated in a sufficiently precise way so as to give individuals an 'adequate indication of the circumstances in which and the conditions on which' surveillance can take place.[12] States Parties applying secret surveillance must furthermore arrange for adequate and effective safeguards against abuse, for example in the form of judicial control. The effectiveness of these safeguards will be assessed by the ECtHR taking into account all the circumstances of the case, including the nature and scope of the surveillance measures and the remedies available under national law.[13]

b.   Storing and processing of data

It transpires from the case law on Article 8 that this provision also covers what is often referred to as 'informational privacy' or 'data protection'. While the Court does not usually apply these terms, it has on numerous occasions confirmed that Article 8 protects individuals against the storing and processing of data or information concerning their private life without their consent. A substantial amount of the case law on data protection concerns the use of personal data, such as photographs, fingerprints and DNA profiles, in the course of criminal investigations by the police and the keeping of secret files on individuals by state intelligence agencies.[14] The Court has however also addressed other aspects of data protection, including the confidentiality of medical records and the abuse of identity documents by third parties.[15] In its elaboration of the standards set

---

[11]   E.g. *Klass and Others v. Germany, supra* n. 6, paras. 48–49; *Blaj v. Romania*, ECtHR 8 April 2014, appl. no. 36259/04, paras. 143–144.

[12]   E.g. *Malone v. the United Kingdom*, ECtHR 2 August 1984, appl. no. 8691/79, paras. 67–68.

[13]   E.g. *Klass and Others v. Germany, supra* n. 6, para. 50.

[14]   E.g. *S. and Marper v. the United Kingdom, supra* n. 1 (data processing in criminal investigations) and *Rotaru v. Romania*, ECtHR (GC) 4 May 2000, appl. no. 28341/95 (secret intelligence files).

[15]   E.g. *M.S. v. Sweden*, ECtHR 27 August 1997, appl. no. 20837/92 (confidentiality of medical information); *Romet v. the Netherlands*, ECtHR 14 February 2012, appl. no. 7094/06 (abuse of identity documents).

by Article 8 on data protection the Court is frequently guided by the provisions of the Data Protection Convention,[16] both as regards the determination of which information is protected and as regards the permissibility of restrictions to informational privacy.[17] Conversely, the case law shows little evidence of being influenced by EU data protection law.[18]

The Court has repeatedly stated that the protection of Article 8 extends to information concerning private life.[19] To determine whether the information at stake in a particular case relates to an applicant's private life it takes into account the specific context in which the information has been recorded and retained, the nature of the records, the way in which they are used and processed, the results that may be obtained and the applicant's reasonable expectations as to the private character of the information.[20] It has previously held Article 8 to apply to information concerning a person's telephone calls, e-mail and Internet usage as well as to medical records and banking documents.[21] With regard to data such as photographs, fingerprints and voice samples the Court has stated that they fall within the scope of Article 8 as they constitute personal information directly relevant to the identification of the individual concerned.[22] In the *S. and Marper* case, the Grand Chamber elaborately explained why the storing of cellular samples and DNA profiles also interferes with Article 8. It noted that such materials contain highly personal and sensitive information which may be used to identify family relationships and may disclose information about a person's health or ethnic origin. In addition, it mentioned that 'bearing in mind the rapid pace of developments in the field of genetics and information technology, the Court cannot discount the possibility that in the future the private-life interests bound up with genetic information may be adversely affected in novel ways or in a manner which cannot be anticipated with precision today.'[23]

Article 8 does not only protect information concerning private activities or that has been obtained in private surroundings such as the home. As the notion of private life itself is understood to cover relationships with others, including

---

[16]   Council of Europe Convention for the Protection of Individuals with regard to Automatic Processing of Personal Data, CETS No. 108.

[17]   E.g. *Amann v. Switzerland*, ECtHR (GC) 16 February 2000, appl. no. 27798/95, para.65; *S. and Marper v. the United Kingdom*, *supra* n. 1, paras. 103–104.

[18]   In the *S. and Marper* case, the EU Data Protection Directive (95/46/EC) is listed among the 'relevant national and international materials' (*supra* n. 1, para. 50) but no explicit reference is made to it in the Court's assessment.

[19]   E.g. *Leander v. Sweden*, ECtHR 26 March 1987, appl. no. 9248/81, para. 48.

[20]   *S. and Marper v. the United Kingdom*, *supra* n. 1, para. 67; *P.G. and J.H. v. the United Kingdom*, ECtHR 25 September 2001, appl. no. 44787/98, para. 57.

[21]   *Copland v. the United Kingdom*, ECtHR 3 April 2007, appl. no. 62617/00, para. 44; *Z. v. Finland*, ECtHR 25 February 1997, appl. no. 22009/93, para. 71; *M.N. and Others v. San Marino*, ECtHR 7 July 2015, appl. no. 28005/12, para. 51.

[22]   *S. and Marper v. the United Kingdom*, *supra* n. 1, paras. 83–84.

[23]   *Ibid.*, paras. 70–77.

professional and business relationships (*infra* section 2.5(a)), information pertaining to such relationships can come within the scope of Article 8.[24] In the case of *Rotaru*, the Grand Chamber specified that the systematic collection and storage of public information, such as that relating to the applicant's political activities, comes within the scope of private life especially where it concerns a person's distant past.[25] For Article 8 to be applicable it is moreover not necessary that information relating to a person's private life has been used; the mere storing thereof by public authorities constitutes an interference with that provision.[26] The refusal to inform individuals about the information that is kept about them also constitutes an interference.[27] In its decision in the case of *Reyntjens*, however, the former Commission found that the obligation to carry an identity document and to show it to the police upon request did not interfere with Article 8, provided that the identity card mentions only data such as a person's name, sex and address.[28]

According to the second paragraph of Article 8, interferences with the right to private life must be in accordance with the law. Within the field of data protection this requirement may be interpreted more or less strictly depending on the nature and extent of the interference, as was stated by the Court in the case of *P.G. and J.H.*[29] In that case, the Court found that the practice of 'metering' (whereby information is collected about the numbers dialled from a particular telephone but not about the content of the calls) in itself produced only limited data and was therefore less liable to abuse.[30] By contrast in *S. and Marper*, the Grand Chamber stressed the importance, in sensitive contexts such as covert intelligence-gathering and the retention of DNA samples, of having 'clear, detailed rules governing the scope and application of measures, as well as minimum safeguards concerning, inter alia, duration, storage, usage, access of third parties, procedures for preserving the integrity and confidentiality of data and procedures for its destruction, thus providing sufficient guarantees against the risk of abuse and arbitrariness'.[31]

While recognising that these guarantees concern the quality of the laws allowing for data collection, the Court has previously considered that they are closely related to the question of whether the interference was 'necessary in a democratic society' and has subsumed its assessment of those laws under that heading.[32]

---

[24] E.g. *Amann v. Switzerland*, *supra* n. 17, para.65.
[25] *Rotaru v. Romania*, *supra* n. 14, para. 43. A dissenting opinion was voiced on this point by Judge Bonello.
[26] *Amann v. Switzerland*, *supra* n. 17, para.69.
[27] *Segerstedt-Wiberg and Others v. Sweden*, ECtHR 6 June 2006, appl. no. 62332/00, para. 99.
[28] *Reyntjens v. Belgium*, EComHR 9 September 1992 (dec.), appl. no. 16180/90.
[29] *P.G. and J.H. v. the United Kingdom*, *supra* n. 20, para. 46.
[30] *Ibid.*
[31] *S. and Marper v. the United Kingdom*, *supra* n. 1, para. 99.
[32] *Ibid.*, para. 99; *M.K. v. France*, ECtHR 18 April 2013, appl. no. 19522/09, para. 28.

The Court has accepted that the recording and use of personal information may serve various legitimate aims including national security,[33] the detection and prevention of crime[34] and the economic well-being of the country. The latter aim was at stake in the case of *M.S. v. Sweden*, where the applicants' medical records had been disclosed to a social security agency to determine her eligibility for public benefits.[35] Where the processing of personal data is aimed at the prosecution of crimes committed against other persons, the interest in protecting the confidentiality of personal data has to be carefully balanced against the protection of the rights and freedoms of others.[36]

With regard to the condition that the collection and use of information must be 'necessary in a democratic society', the Court has repeatedly stated that the protection of personal data is of 'fundamental importance' to the enjoyment of private life.[37] The restriction clause of Article 8, paragraph 2, must be interpreted narrowly and the need for restrictions must be convincingly established in a given case.[38] In addition there must exist 'adequate and effective safeguards' against abuse.[39] These requirements are especially salient in case of automatic processing of personal data for police purposes.[40] In the *S. and Marper* judgment, the Grand Chamber found that the British regulation on the storing of DNA samples was disproportionate, especially in view of its 'blanket' and 'open-ended' character which allowed the permanent storing of samples even in case of minor offences or where the person concerned had not been convicted.[41] Given the general consensus existing among the States Parties concerning the restrictions on keeping DNA databases, the Grand Chamber found that there existed only a limited margin of appreciation for the national authorities.[42] The Court has moreover warned that the storing of bodily samples of persons who are not eventually convicted may undermine the presumption of innocence and result in stigmatisation.[43] With regard to medical records, the Court has stressed that the confidentiality of the information contained therein not only serves the patient's sense of privacy but also their trust in the health care system. Where such confidentiality is not guaranteed, this may deter people from seeking medical assistance and thus harm their own health and that of others. There is therefore a strong interest

---

[33] E.g. *Leander v. Sweden, supra* n. 19, para. 59.

[34] E.g. *M.K. v. France, supra* n. 32, para. 29.

[35] *M.S. v. Sweden, supra* n. 15, para. 38.

[36] E.g. *K.U. v. Finland*, ECtHR 2 December 2008, appl. no. 2872/02, para. 49.

[37] E.g. *S. and Marper v. the United Kingdom, supra* n. 1, para. 103.

[38] E.g. *M.N. and Others v. San Marino, supra* n. 21, para. 73.

[39] E.g. *M.S. v. Sweden, supra* n. 15, para. 43; *Rotaru v. Romania, supra* n. 14, para. 59.

[40] E.g. *S. and Marper v. the United Kingdom, supra* n. 1, para. 103.

[41] *Ibid.*, paras. 119–120. See also *M.K. v. France, supra* n. 32, paras. 36–43.

[42] *S. and Marper v. the United Kingdom, supra* n. 1, para. 112.

[43] *Ibid.*, para. 122; *M.K. v. France, supra* n. 32, para. 33.

involved in the protection of the confidentiality of medical files.[44] In particular, the Court noted that the fact of someone being HIV-infected is highly intimate and sensitive information, the disclosure of which may have great impact on that person's private and family life.[45]

The Court's case law offers a few examples of positive obligations in the field of data protection. In the case of *Turek*, the Court found that Article 8 contained a procedural obligation for the Slovakian authorities to ensure that the lustration proceedings concerning the applicant's registration as a collaborator of the former Czechoslovakian security agency were conducted in a fair manner.[46] Two years later, in the case of *I. v. Finland*, the Court held that Finland had failed to comply with its positive obligation under Article 8 to provide practical and effective protection of the applicant's medical records against unauthorised access by third parties. While legislation concerning the confidentiality of medical records was in place, the practical enforcement of this legislation had been lacking.[47] Lastly, in the case of *Romet* the Court did not use the language of positive obligations. However it found that the Netherlands had failed to protect the applicant against identity theft by refusing to annul his driving license after he reported it stolen.[48]

c. *Publication of photographs and other information*

Article 8 covers not only the storing and processing of information relating to a person's private life but also the publication thereof in the media without that person's consent. What is at stake here is again the individual's interest in keeping his or her private life out of the public eye. However, as mentioned elsewhere in this chapter (2.1 and 2.5) the notion of private life can also cover people's activities outside their private surroundings and their relationships with others. The dissemination of photos or other personal information can therefore interfere with Article 8 even if they concern a person acting in a public space. This is clearly illustrated in the case of *Peck*, which concerned the broadcasting of video footage of the applicant that had been recorded in the immediate aftermath of his suicide attempt. The Court pointed out that, although the applicant had been filmed by a security camera in a public space, he had been in a state of distress and the filmed images had been disclosed to the public in a manner which he could not have foreseen. This disclosure therefore constituted a serious interference with the applicant's private life.[49] By contrast, in its

---

[44] E.g. *Z. v. Finland*, *supra* n. 21, para. 95–96.

[45] *Ibid.*

[46] *Turek v. Slovakia*, ECtHR 14 February 2006, appl. no. 57986/00, paras. 111–116. There is, however, no obligation to inform individuals of the information recorded about them, e.g., *Leander v. Sweden*, *supra* n. 19, para. 66.

[47] *I. v. Finland*, ECtHR 17 July 2008, appl. no. 20511/03, paras. 44–48.

[48] *Romet v. the Netherlands*, *supra* n. 15, paras. 37 and 42–43.

[49] *Peck v. the United Kingdom*, *supra* n. 5, paras. 61–63.

judgment in *N.F. v. Italy*, the Court found that the disclosure of the applicant's membership of the freemasons by the press did not interfere with his private life as it concerned information that was already publicly available.[50]

The publication of photos and video footage of individuals has been assessed by the Court in connection with the right to the protection of one's image. This right includes the right to control the use of one's image and to refuse publication thereof.[51] Publication of photographs therefore comes within the scope of private life.[52] The Court found on several occasions that the release of photographs or video footage to the media by police authorities constituted an interference with Article 8. An example is the case of *Khmel*, where the police had invited a local television company to film the applicant's disorderly behaviour at the police station and allowed it to broadcast the images to the public.[53] The scope of protection offered by Article 8 is not reduced where the applicant is the subject of criminal proceedings.[54]

Where photographs or other information concerning a person's private life are disclosed to the media by state authorities, this is considered as an interference with the State Party's negative obligation to respect private life.[55] In the case of *Craxi (No. 2)*, the Court moreover found that the state authorities had a positive obligation to provide appropriate safeguards against the disclosure of personal information about the applicant (transcripts of private phone calls intercepted in the course of a criminal investigation) and to carry out an effective investigation into the matter.[56] In addition, Article 8 entails a positive obligation for the States Parties to protect individuals against interferences by third parties such as privately owned broadcasting and publishing companies. In the Court's view, while 'the boundary between the State's positive and negative obligations under Article 8 does not lend itself to precise definition', similar principles apply.[57]

The Court's approach to cases concerning the publication of photographs or other personal information by third parties was elaborated in the Grand Chamber judgment in *Von Hannover (No. 2)*. In this type of case, the applicant's right to private life must be balanced against the freedom of expression protected by Article 10 and the general principles developed by the Court in respect of both rights must be taken into account.[58] Instead of determining, separately, whether

---

[50]   *N.F. v. Italy*, ECtHR 2 August 2001, appl. no. 37119/97, para. 39.

[51]   E.g. *Reklos and Davourlis v. Greece*, ECtHR 15 January 2009, appl. no. 1234/05, para. 40.

[52]   E.g. *Khuzhin and Others v. Russia*, ECtHR 23 October 2008, appl. no. 13470/02, para. 115.

[53]   *Khmel v. Russia*, ECtHR 12 December 2013, appl. no. 20383/04, para. 44.

[54]   E.g. *Khuzhin and Others v. Russia*, *supra* n. 52, para. 115.

[55]   E.g. *Khmel v. Russia*, *supra* n. 53, para. 41.

[56]   *Craxi v. Italy*, ECtHR 17 July 2003, appl. no. 25337/94, paras. 73–74.

[57]   E.g. *Gurgenidze v. Georgia*, ECtHR 17 October 2006, appl. no. 71678/01, para. 38.

[58]   *Von Hannover v. Germany (No. 2)*, ECtHR (GC) 7 February 2012, appl. nos. 40660/80 and 60641/08, para. 100.

an interference exists and whether it is justified the Court merges both questions in a single 'fair balance' test. In *Von Hannover (No. 2)*, the Grand Chamber formulated five criteria that the national authorities must take into account when conducting this balancing exercise at the national level. It stated that, where these criteria have been applied, it would need 'strong reasons to substitute its view for that of the domestic courts'.[59]

The first and most important criterion is the extent to which the published photos or articles can be said to contribute to a debate of general interest. The second, related criterion is how well known the person concerned is and whether the photos or articles concern activities of a public or private nature. In the Court's view 'public figures', notably politicians, do not enjoy the same amount of protection as private individuals. Nevertheless, publication of photographs may affect a person's private life even where that person is a public figure. The final three criteria concern the prior conduct of the person concerned (whether or not he or she had previously sought media attention), the content, form and consequences of the publication and the circumstances in which the photos were taken (whether or not this occurred surreptitiously).[60]

2.2. REPUTATION

Article 8 does not mention the right to respect for one's honour and reputation. In this respect it differs from Article 12 of the Universal Declaration of Human Rights (UDHR), which served as the main source of reference for the drafting of Article 8 ECHR and is otherwise similar.[61] The Court, though mindful of the difference between the two provisions, has nevertheless accepted that the protection of one's reputation forms part of the right to respect for private life.[62] More specifically, it considers that someone's reputation forms part of their personal identity and psychological integrity.[63] This notwithstanding, Article 8 does not protect individuals against 'a loss of reputation which is the foreseeable consequence of one's own actions such as, for example, the commission of a criminal offence'. For Article 8 to be applicable the attack on someone's reputation must moreover 'attain a certain level of gravity and in

---

[59]   *Ibid.*, para. 107; see also *Lillo-Stenberg and Saether v. Norway*, ECtHR 16 January 2014, appl. no. 13258/09, para. 44.

[60]   *Von Hannover v. Germany (No. 2)*, *supra* n. 58, paras. 109–113.

[61]   O. Diggelmann and M.N. Cleis, 'How the Right to Privacy Became a Human Right', *Human Rights Law Review* (2014) 14 (3): 441–458, at pp. 452–457.

[62]   *A. v. Norway*, ECtHR 9 April 2009, appl. no. 28070/06, para. 63.

[63]   E.g. *Pfeifer v. Austria*, ECtHR 15 November 2007, appl. no. 12556/04, para. 35. See, however, *Karakó v. Hungary*, ECtHR 28 April 2009, appl. no. 39311/05, para. 23, where the Court found that a person's reputation falls to be distinguished from their personal integrity and private life. The Court itself appears to see this judgment as an exception to its doctrine; see *Putistin v. Ukraine*, ECtHR 21 November 2013, appl. no. 16882/03, para. 32.

a manner causing prejudice to personal enjoyment of the right to respect for private life'.[64] In the case of *Lavric*, for example, the Court considered that the accusations of corruption and incompetence made against the applicant were 'of a serious nature and capable of affecting her in the performance of her duties and of damaging her reputation'.[65] It transpires from the judgment in *Putistin* that attacks on the reputation of a deceased family member (*in casu* the applicant's father) can also affect private life and thus come within the scope of Article 8.[66]

An interference with the right to respect for one's reputation may arise directly from an action by the organs of the respondent State Party. This occurred, for example, in the case of *Bălăşoiu (No. 2)*, where defamatory statements concerning the applicant had been included in a report drawn up by the local authorities.[67] In such cases, the Court will assess whether the interference met the requirements set forth in the second paragraph of Article 8. However, in the majority of cases that came before the Court the applicant's loss of reputation resulted from publications by journalists or other third parties. In such cases, the Court will examine whether the respondent State Party has adequately balanced the right to respect for one's reputation against the freedom of expression protected by Article 10. The criteria for this assessment correspond to those applied by the Court in cases involving the publication of photographs or other information relating to a person's private life, as set out in the Grand Chamber judgment in *Von Hannover (No. 2)* (see 2.1(c)).[68] In addition, particular attention is paid by the Court to the distinction between 'statements of fact' and 'value judgements': where the defamatory statements are presented as facts the veracity thereof will have to be demonstrated, whereas 'the truth of value judgments is not susceptible of proof'. Nevertheless, the Court found that even a value judgement will need to be based on a sufficient factual basis, 'failing which it will be excessive'.[69]

Apart from the substantial obligation to protect individuals against attacks on their reputation, by the state or by third parties, Article 8 also contains procedural obligations to ensure that the laws protecting the right to reputation are adequately adjudicated and enforced. For example, in the *Popovski* judgment

---

[64]   E.g. *Axel Springer AG v. Germany*, ECtHR (GC) 7 February 2012, appl. no. 39954/08, para. 83.

[65]   *Lavric v. Romania*, ECtHR 14 January 2014, appl. no. 22231/05, para. 41.

[66]   *Putistin v. Ukraine*, *supra* n. 63, para. 33. See, however, the admissibility decision in *Dzhugashvili v. Russia*, concerning a complaint lodged by a grandson of Stalin. In this decision, the Court specified that a distinction should be drawn between 'defamatory attacks on private persons, whose reputation as part and parcel of their families' reputation remains within the scope of Article 8, and legitimate criticism of public figures who, by taking up leadership roles, expose themselves to outside scrutiny' (ECtHR 9 December 2014 (dec.), appl. no. 41123/10, para. 30).

[67]   *Bălăşoiu v. Romania (No. 2)*, ECtHR 20 December 2011, appl. no. 17232/04.

[68]   E.g. *Mater v. Turkey*, ECtHR 16 July 2013, appl. no. 54997/08, para. 58.

[69]   E.g. *Lavric v. Romania*, *supra* n. 65, para. 39.

the Court found that the legal remedy available to the applicant to contest the defamatory statements published about him had been ineffective.[70] The Court has not ruled on what type of procedure, civil or criminal, would be required to ensure respect for Article 8. Where, however, the protection of someone's reputation must be balanced against the freedom of expression it has warned against the 'chilling effect' that the imposition of criminal sanctions may have on that freedom.[71]

2.3. IDENTITY

The notion of private life, as elaborated by the Court, encompasses aspects relating to personal identity, including one's physical and social identity.[72] It includes elements such as someone's name, family relationships, gender identity, sexual orientation and ethnic identity.[73] The Court has also held 'choices as to an individual's desired appearance, whether in public or in private places,' to come under the notion of private life, including the choice to wear a *burqa* or *niqab*.[74] While all of these elements may be relevant to the shaping by individuals of their own identity, some of them, such as the determination of paternity or the choice of a surname, are also relevant to the development of relationships with others.

A large part of the case law discussed in this section concerns the scope of the obligation of the States Parties to recognise, in law, aspects of an individual's identity, in particular their name, family relationships and gender identity. An example is the obligation to register people by their chosen name or gender or to legally acknowledge their existing family ties. Additionally, in the sphere of family relationships the States Parties have been asked to assist individuals in obtaining information about such relationships, for example in the case of adoption.

Whereas sexual orientation is recognised by the Court as an element of private life (see above) and is likely to form an important aspect of someone's personal identity, it has appeared in the case law mostly in the context of interferences with a person's sexual life (*infra* section 2.4) or as a discrimination ground. It is therefore not treated separately here.

---

[70] *Popovski v. the Former Yugoslav Republic of Macedonia*, ECtHR 31 October 2013, appl. no. 12316/07, para. 91. See also *Kyriakides v. Cyprus*, ECtHR 16 October 2008, appl. no. 39058/05, para. 51.

[71] E.g. *Cumpănă and Mazăre v. Romania*, ECtHR (GC) 17 December 2004, appl. no. 33348/96, para. 114.

[72] E.g. *Mikulić v. Croatia*, ECtHR 7 February 2000, appl. no. 53176/99, para. 53.

[73] E.g. *S. and Marper v. the United Kingdom, supra* n. 1, para. 66.

[74] *S.A.S. v. France*, ECtHR (GC) 1 July 2014, appl. no. 43835/11, para. 107. As the applicant in this case had stated that the wearing of a *burqa* was required by her religion, the Court considered that her complaint mainly raised issues under Art. 9 ECHR.

a. Name

It emerges from the case law that aspects relating to a person's name can come within the scope of the right to private and family life. In the Court's view, a person's name constitutes a means of linking to a family and of personal identification, both by individuals themselves (self-identification) and by society at large.[75] As such, it sits at the very core ('*noyau dur*') of the right to private and family life.[76] The Court found Article 8 to be applicable in cases where the applicants sought to change their own name, including their surname or their patronymic.[77] In the case of *Henry Kismoun*, the applicant was a French and Algerian national who was registered in each of the two countries under a different surname. The Court acknowledged that his request to the French authorities to change his surname reflected his interest in having one single name and in obtaining recognition of his identity as it had been shaped in Algeria, and of which the name Kismoun constituted a major element.[78] Article 8 also covers the choice by parents of their children's first names and of which surname (the father's or the mother's) to pass on to them.[79] This notwithstanding, the impossibility of choosing a particular name or surname will fall within the scope of Article 8 only if it results in a certain degree of inconvenience for the applicant. In the case of *Guillot*, for example, the Court found that the registration of the applicants' daughter as 'Fleur-Marie' instead of 'Fleur de Marie' did not raise an issue under Article 8 as the daughter was able to use that name socially without hindrance.[80]

Whereas the Court has determined that the obligation to change one's name would constitute an interference with the rights protected by Article 8, the refusal to accept the applicant's chosen name is treated as involving a potential positive obligation for the State Party.[81] The Court accepts that there may be legitimate public interests involved in restricting the possibility of changing one's name, such as ensuring an accurate population registration and safeguarding the means of personal identification and establishing family relationships, and that the States Parties have a wide margin of appreciation in this field.[82] They must, however, strike a fair balance between such public interests and the individual interests involved in the choice of one's name. In the cases of *Garnaga* and *Henry Kismoun*, the Court found that Article 8 had been violated because the

---

[75]   *Burghartz v. Switzerland*, ECtHR 22 February 1994, appl. no. 16213/90, para. 24; *Bulgakov v. Ukraine*, ECtHR 11 September 2007, appl. no. 59894/00, para. 51.

[76]   E.g. *Losonci Rose and Rose v. Switzerland*, ECtHR 9 November 2011, appl. no. 664/06, para. 51.

[77]   *Garnaga v. Ukraine*, ECtHR 16 May 2013, appl. no. 20390/07, para. 36.

[78]   *Henry Kismoun v. France*, ECtHR 5 December 2013, appl. no. 32265/10, para. 36.

[79]   *Cusan and Fazzo v. Italy*, ECtHR 7 January 2014, appl. no. 77/07, para. 56.

[80]   *Guillot v. France*, ECtHR 24 October 1996, appl. no. 22500/93, para. 27.

[81]   E.g. *Henry Kismoun v. France*, *supra* n. 78, para. 26.

[82]   E.g. *Garnaga v. Ukraine*, *supra* n. 77, paras. 38–39.

authorities of the respondent States had either failed to advance a public interest justifying the refusal to change the applicant's name or to take the applicant's interests into account.[83]

In addition to the choice of a name, the official spelling of one's name may raise an issue under Article 8. This matter has special relevance for persons belonging to ethnic or national minorities, for whom the spelling of their name in their minority language may differ from the spelling in the official or majority language of the State concerned. Additionally, as the case of *Mentzen aka Mencena* shows, spelling rules may affect migrants whose surname is spelled differently in the host state and in the state of origin.[84] The Court has drawn a distinction between the mere transliteration or grammatical adaptation of someone's name to the phonetics and grammar of the majority language ('Chaikovsky' instead of 'Чайковский'), which does not affect their ethnic and national identity, and its replacement by a different name, with the same historical or etymological roots but belonging to a different cultural context ('John' instead of 'Iwan').[85] While both situations have been brought under the scope of Article 8, the Court has also shown itself sensitive to the historical context of the linguistic policies pursued by respondent States Parties and the individual interests that may be involved in the protection of an official language.[86] Thus, in the cases of *Mentzen aka Mencena* and *Kuharec aka Kuhareca*, it accepted the argument put forward by the Latvian Government that the disputed measures were necessary to protect and develop the Latvian language after the difficulties it had faced while Latvia was under Soviet rule.[87]

Cases involving the choice of a surname after marriage (the husband's or the wife's) or for a newborn child (the father's or the mother's) have been treated by the Court under Article 14 in combination with Article 8.[88] While not prescribing any particular system to be applied to the use of names in family relationships, the Court has determined that in view of the equality of the sexes the same options should be available to men and women. In the *Burghartz* judgment, for example, it found that the rule whereby married couples had to choose a common surname but only the wife was allowed to add her own surname violated the Convention.[89]

---

[83]   *Ibid.*, para. 41; *Henry Kismoun v. France, supra* n. 78, para. 36.

[84]   *Mentzen aka Mencena v. Latvia*, ECtHR 7 December 2004 (dec.), appl. no. 71074/01.

[85]   *Bulgakov v. Ukraine, supra* n. 75, paras. 46–47.

[86]   E.g. *ibid.*, para. 43.

[87]   *Mentzen aka Mencena, supra* n. 84; *Kuharec aka Kuhareca*, ECtHR (dec.) 7 December 2004, appl. no. 71557/01.

[88]   E.g. *Ünal Tekeli v. Turkey*, ECtHR 16 November 2004, appl. no. 29865/96; *Cusan and Fazzo v. Italy, supra* n. 79.

[89]   *Burghartz v. Switzerland, supra* n. 75, paras. 28–29.

b. Personal history and family relationships

The right to private life further encompasses a right for people to obtain information about important aspects of their identity, such as the identity of their biological parents and other family members and the circumstances in which they were raised. In the case of *Odièvre*, the Grand Chamber affirmed that having such information is important to the formation of someone's personality and therefore constitutes an aspect of their private life, even where the right to family life is not at issue.[90] Meanwhile, where individuals seek legal recognition of their actual (social) family ties this will usually come under the heading of both private and family life (see *infra* section 3.2).

The relevance of knowing one's personal history is illustrated in the *Gaskin* judgment, concerning an applicant who had spent most of his youth in foster families. As an adult, he sought access to the files that had been compiled on him by the local authorities to obtain information about his education and development as a child. The Court agreed with the Commission's finding that the files had to be considered as 'a substitute record for the memories and experience of the parents of the child who is not in care' and found that they 'undoubtedly do relate to Mr Gaskin's private and family life in such a way that the question of his access thereto falls within the ambit of Article 8'.[91]

As regards family relationships, Article 8 covers the right of children to know the identity of their biological parents as well as a man's right to establish or contest paternity of a child.[92] In the case of *Mennesson*, the Court moreover recognised the right of children born following a gestational surrogacy agreement concluded abroad (in the United States) to obtain legal recognition of their filiation with their intended parents, of which the father was also their biological father.[93] Such recognition had been refused by the French authorities on the grounds that French law did not permit surrogacy agreements. The Court found, however, that the refusal violated the children's right to private life.

Where it is established that the applicant's interest comes within the scope of Article 8, the Court usually asks whether the respondent State Party had a (positive) obligation to enable them to obtain information about their personal history and family ties. This question is then answered by means of a 'fair balance' test.[94] In the *Mikulić* case, for example, the Court found that Croatia had failed to meet its positive obligation to provide a speedy and effective procedure for the establishment of paternity.[95] Especially where family relationships

---

[90]   *Odièvre v. France*, ECtHR (GC) 13 February 2003, appl. no. 42326/98, paras. 28–29.

[91]   *Gaskin v. the United Kingdom*, ECtHR 7 July 1989, appl. no. 10454/83, paras. 36–37.

[92]   E.g. *Mikulić v. Croatia, supra* n. 72, para. 55; *Ahrens v. Germany*, ECtHR 22 March 2012, appl. no. 45071/09, para. 60.

[93]   *Mennesson v. France*, ECtHR 26 June 2014, appl. no. 65192/11, para. 46.

[94]   E.g. *Gaskin v. the United Kingdom, supra* n. 91, para. 42.

[95]   *Mikulić v. Croatia, supra* n. 72, paras. 57–66.

are at stake, however, the interests of the applicants may need to be balanced against the interests of the other family members involved, who may not wish to be known or have their relationship legally recognised. In cases involving such conflicting interests, the Court will usually grant the States Parties a large margin of appreciation.[96] The same applies when the issue at stake is not subject to consensus within the Council of Europe.[97]

c. Gender identity

The Court has issued a number of important judgments concerning the legal position of transsexuals. Although the Court has consistently shown itself to be sensitive to the psychological, social and legal difficulties faced by many transsexuals, considerable time passed before it saw fit to find that Article 8 entails positive obligations for the States Parties to adjust their legal systems so as to take transsexualism into account. In the landmark judgment in *Christine Goodwin*, however, the Grand Chamber took a principled stance to the effect that it could no longer be considered acceptable to compel post-operative transsexuals to live in an 'intermediate zone' between the sexes. In doing so, it took note of the increased scientific recognition and social acceptance of transsexualism.[98]

It is now established case law that a person's gender identity constitutes a fundamental aspect of the right to private life and that the right to self-identify as male or female is essential to self-determination.[99] In its case law on transsexualism, the Court confirmed that self-determination, or personal autonomy, is an important principle underlying the interpretation of Article 8. It also stated that 'the very essence of the Convention being respect for human dignity and human freedom, protection is given to the right of transsexuals to personal development and to physical and moral security'.[100]

Most of the Court's judgments on transsexualism concern the legal recognition of a person's gender after gender re-assignment surgery. In the *Grant* judgment, the Court found a violation of Article 8 because the respondent State Party had failed to register the post-operative gender of the applicant, who was a male-to-female transsexual, and had not acknowledged the gender re-assignment when determining her eligibility for pension benefits.[101] In the case of *Christine Goodwin*, the Court moreover held that the United Kingdom had violated Article 12 because the applicant was unable to enter into a (heterosexual)

---

[96]   E.g. *Ahrens v. Germany, supra* n. 92, para. 65.
[97]   E.g. *Odièvre v. France, supra* n. 90, para. 46.
[98]   *Christine Goodwin v. the United Kingdom*, ECtHR (GC) 11 July 2002, appl. no. 28957/95, paras. 90–92.
[99]   E.g. *Van Kück v. Germany*, ECtHR 12 June 2003, appl. no. 35968/97, para. 73.
[100]   *Ibid.*, para. 69.
[101]   *Grant v. the United Kingdom*, ECtHR 23 May 2006, appl. no. 32570/03.

marriage on the basis of her post-operative sex.[102] However, in the *Hämäläinen* judgment, the Grand Chamber upheld the disputed Finnish legislation, according to which the applicant could only obtain an identity number and passport matching her post-operative sex if she converted her marriage to a (same-sex) registered partnership (see also Chapter 16 on Article 12).[103]

Other than questions relating to the legal recognition of post-operative gender, the Court has been asked whether Article 8 contains a right to obtain reimbursement of the costs of gender re-assignment surgery. It has held that such a right does not exist. Nevertheless, where the possibility of reimbursement is available the Court will examine whether the applicants' interests relating to their sexual self-determination have been sufficiently taken into account in the assessment of their eligibility.[104]

2.4. SEXUAL LIFE

The Court has repeatedly acknowledged that 'sexual life' forms part of the notion of private life as protected by Article 8.[105] In particular, the freedom to engage in sexual relations in accordance with one's sexual orientation has been marked by the Court as 'a most intimate aspect' of private life. Interferences with this freedom therefore require 'particularly serious reasons' in order to be justified.[106] An exception applies, nevertheless, in situations where sexual activity entails the infliction of physical harm, as in the case of sado-masochism. In such cases it will be up to the national authorities in the first place to balance the public interests involved (such as the protection of public health) against the personal autonomy of the individual consenting to such activity.[107]

The case law shows that interferences with sexual life do not usually occur indiscriminately but that they are related to the sexual orientation of the persons involved. An example is the *Dudgeon* case, where the Court decided that a legal prohibition on homosexual relations between consenting adults was contrary to Article 8. The Court did not consider it relevant to establish whether the applicant had in fact been prosecuted: it found that the mere existence of the criminal legislation formed a continuing interference with the private life of the applicant who was forced to either refrain from entering into homosexual relations or face the risk of prosecution.[108] In subsequent judgments the Court added that the existence of separate ages of consent for homosexual relations

---

[102]   *Christine Goodwin v. the United Kingdom*, *supra* n. 98, para. 103.
[103]   *Hämäläinen v. Finland*, ECtHR (GC) 16 July 2014, appl. no. 37359/09.
[104]   E.g. *Schlumpf v. Switzerland*, ECtHR 8 January 2009, appl. no. 29002/06, para. 115.
[105]   E.g. *S. and Marper v. the United Kingdom*, *supra* n. 1, para. 66.
[106]   *Dudgeon v. the United Kingdom*, ECtHR 22 October 1981, appl. no. 7525/76, para. 52.
[107]   *Laskey, Jaggard and Brown v. the United Kingdom*, ECtHR 19 February 1997, appl. nos. 21627/93, 21826/93 and 21974/93, para. 44.
[108]   *Dudgeon v. the United Kingdom*, *supra* n. 106, para. 41.

between men, as compared to lesbian or heterosexual relations, violated Article 8 read together with Article 14 (the prohibition of discrimination.[109] It also found a violation of these provisions in relation to the Austrian authorities' refusal to clear the applicants' criminal records of their convictions for underage homosexual relations, after the legal provisions prohibiting such relations had been declared unconstitutional and contrary to the Convention.[110]

In addition to legislative restrictions on sexual activity, the Court has decided on a series of complaints concerning official investigations into the applicants' sexual lives surrounding their dismissal from the army. It found that both the dismissals, which were based on the applicants' homosexuality, and the preceding investigations, whereby the applicants had been extensively questioned about their sexual orientation and possible relationships, violated Article 8.[111] While in these cases the dismissal of the applicants on the grounds of their sexual orientation was treated under Article 8 alone, such differences in treatment have also been treated as instances of possible discrimination under Articles 14 and 8 taken together. In those cases, the importance of sexual orientation as an element of private life is reflected in the fact that differences in treatment on this ground require 'very weighty reasons' to be compatible with the Convention.

A final issue relating to sexual orientation is whether homosexual relationships are legally recognised and regulated in the same way as heterosexual relationships including, for example, the possibility to adopt or to exercise shared custody over children. These matters are discussed in section 3 on the right to family life. The Court itself has only recently began to view *de facto* partnerships between same-sex couples as an aspect of family life rather than private life.[112]

2.5. RELATIONSHIPS WITH OTHERS AND 'THE OUTSIDE WORLD'

The right to respect for 'private life', as protected by Article 8, includes the right to enter into relationships with others and with what the Court has termed 'the outside world'. In the *Niemietz* judgment, amongst others, the Court stated that: 'it would be too restrictive to limit the notion [of private life] to an "inner circle" in which the individual may live his own personal life as he chooses and to exclude therefrom entirely the outside world not encompassed within that

---

[109]   E.g. *L. and V. v. Austria*, ECtHR 9 January 2003, appl. nos. 39392/98 and 39829/98, para. 52.

[110]   *E.B. and Others v. Austria*, ECtHR 7 November 2013, appl. nos. 31913/07, 38367/07, 48098/07, 48777/07 and 48779/07, para. 81.

[111]   E.g. *Smith and Grady v. the United Kingdom*, ECtHR 27 September 1999, appl. nos. 33985/96 and 33986/96, para. 71 et seq.

[112]   *Schalk and Kopf v. Austria*, ECtHR 24 June 2010, appl. no. 30141/04, para. 94. See also *infra* section 3.1.

circle. Respect for private life must also comprise to a certain degree the right to establish and develop relationship with other human beings.'[113]

In the case of *Bigaeva*, the Court explained that the right to form and develop relationships with others falls under 'private life' in the broad sense, which includes the right to live a 'social private life', that is the possibility for an individual to develop his or her social identity.[114] While the Court has not provided a definition of 'the outside world' or fully specified the degree to which relationships with others are included in the notion of private life, the case law shows that Article 8 has been successfully invoked for the protection of professional and business relationships (including access to professions). It has also played a role in cases concerning the expulsion of foreign nationals from the States Parties where they held residence and integrated into society. Both strands of case are discussed in more detail below.

a.   Access to profession and professional relationships

In the Court's view, there is 'no reason of principle why [the notion of private life] should be taken to exclude activities of a professional or business nature since it is, after all, in the course of their working lives that the majority of people have a significant, if not the greatest, opportunity of developing relationships with the outside world.'[115] This was stated for the first time in the case of *Niemietz*, to support the Court's finding that the search of the applicant's business premises interfered with his home and private life (see also *supra* section 2.1(a)). However, the Court's statement also indicates that the development of professional and business relationships as such forms part of a person's private life. In the case of *Fernández Martínez*, the Grand Chamber confirmed that 'restrictions on an individual's professional life may fall within Article 8 where they have repercussions on the manner in which he or she constructs his or her social identity by developing relationships with others'.[116]

While the Court has not provided a general definition of which (aspects of) professional and business relationship are covered by Article 8, it has already determined that that provision does not guarantee the right to choose a particular profession or a right of access to the civil service.[117] Nevertheless, it held in the *Sidabras and Džiautas* case that 'a far-reaching ban on taking up private sector employment does affect "private life"'.[118] The applicants in this case were subject to a broadly formulated occupational ban because of their

---

[113]   *Niemietz v. Germany, supra* n. 1, para. 29.

[114]   *Bigaeva v. Greece*, ECtHR 28 May 2009, appl. no. 26713/05, para. 22.

[115]   E.g. *Niemietz v. Germany, supra* n. 1, para. 29.

[116]   *Fernández Martínez v. Spain*, ECtHR (GC) 12 June 2014, appl. no. 56030/07, para. 110.

[117]   E.g. *Sidabras and Džiautas v. Lithuania*, ECtHR 27 July 2004, appl. nos. 55480/00 and 59330/00, para. 46.

[118]   *Ibid.*, para. 47.

previous functions as KGB officers at the time of the Soviet Union. Although the ban did not concern all professional activities, the Court took into account its 'very significant' effect on the applicants' ability to develop relationships with 'the outside world' as well as the difficulties it entailed for them to earn their living, 'with obvious repercussions on the enjoyment of their private lives'. It noted, moreover, that the stigmatisation suffered by the applicants in relation to their association with the Soviet regime might 'in itself be considered an impediment to the establishment of contacts with the outside world, be they employment-related or other'.[119] Similarly, in the above-mentioned *Niemietz* case, the Court considered that the publicity surrounding the search of the applicant's office could have negative repercussions on his professional reputation.[120]

The Court's assertion that Article 8 does not grant the right to choose a particular profession is somewhat mitigated by later judgments, in which it found that restrictions on the possibility to register for certain professions (such as lawyer) can fall within the sphere of private life.[121] Although, in these cases, the Court pointed to the effect of the restrictions on the applicants' ability to develop relationships with 'the outside world', an important consideration in both judgments was that the applicants had been allowed to pursue legal studies and fulfil other requirements for admission to the legal profession (e.g. a traineeship or exam) but were eventually barred from that profession at a final stage. It thus appears that the Court's main concern was in fact that the applicants were precluded from pursuing a particular career after they had been enabled to make substantial efforts to that effect.[122]

Article 8 also covers situations where an employment relationship is terminated because of a person's choices relating to their private life, such as the choice to engage in an extra-marital relationship. In such cases, the right to private life may be at issue both because of the restriction on the person's capacity to engage in professional relationships (see above) and because of the resulting restriction on their freedom to make personal choices concerning their private life.[123] In addition, Article 8 will be engaged where the dismissal is preceded by an investigation into the applicant's private life. In the case of *Özpinar*, for example, the Court found that the investigation leading up to the applicant's dismissal and her revocation as a judge, based *inter alia* on factors

---

[119] *Ibid.*, paras. 48–49.
[120] *Niemietz v. Germany, supra* n. 1, para. 37.
[121] *Bigaeva v. Greece, supra* n. 114; see also, explicitly, *Mateescu v. Romania*, ECtHR 14 January 2014, appl. no. 1944/10, para. 20.
[122] *Bigaeva v. Greece, supra* n. 114, para. 24; *Mateescu v. Romania, supra* n. 121, para. 21.
[123] E.g. *Fernández Martínez v. Spain, supra* n. 116, para. 110. See, however, the dissenting opinion by 8 of the 17 judges stating that 'the applicability of Article 8 is triggered, not by the effects of the decision not to renew the contract, but by the reasons that led to that decision' (Joint dissenting opinion of Judges Spielmann, Sajò, Karakaş, Lemmens, Jäderblom, Vehabović, Dedov and Saiz-Arnaiz, para. 9).

relating to her private life, were not surrounded by sufficient guarantees against arbitrariness, and concluded that there had been a violation of Article 8.[124]

A specific category of cases concerns employment relationships in the religious sphere, for example where a person is employed as a teacher of religion or by a religious organisation, and where the relationship is terminated because the choices made by the person in respect of their private life (e.g. the decision to marry) are incompatible with the precepts of the religion concerned. The Court's approach in such cases, as confirmed by the Grand Chamber in the case of *Fernández Martínez*, is to balance the right to private life against the right of religious organisations to autonomy, as protected by Article 9 of the Convention.[125] It may be noted, however, that in that case the largest possible minority of the judges disagreed with the outcome of the balancing exercise.[126] It follows from other cases, such as *Schüth*, that Article 8 also entails a positive obligation to ensure that appropriate regard is had to the right to private life where the employment relationship was concluded with a private (religious) institution.[127]

b. Ties to country of residence

It is a well-established tenet of the Court's case law that the Convention does not offer non-nationals the right to be admitted to or to reside in a particular State Party.[128] This means that the States Parties are, in principle, not restrained by the Convention in regulating the conditions under which non-nationals may be expelled from their territory. Nevertheless, the Court has acknowledged that the personal, social and economic ties which non-nationals, build up during their stay in the host country, form part of their private life.[129] This includes, for example, the relationships that are created when the non-national attends school or works in the host country. In the case of *Üner*, the Grand Chamber stated that 'the totality of social ties between settled migrants and the community in which they are living constitute part of the concept of "private life".'[130]

The first case in which the Court decided that the expulsion of non-nationals may violate the right to private life was *Slivenko*.[131] The applicants in this case were the family members of former military men who had been stationed in Latvia at the time of the Soviet Union and had created a family there. After Latvia

---

[124] *Özpinar v. Turkey*, ECtHR 19 October 2012, appl. no. 20999/04, para. 79. See also the case of *Smith and Grady v. the United Kingdom*, *supra* n. 111.

[125] *Fernández Martínez v. Spain*, *supra* n. 116, para. 123.

[126] *Ibid.*, Joint dissenting opinion of Judges Spielmann, Sajó, Karakaş, Lemmens, Jäderblom, Vehabović, Dedov and Saiz-Arnaiz.

[127] *Schüth v. Germany*, ECtHR 23 September 2010, appl. no. 1620/03.

[128] E.g. *Üner v. the Netherlands*, ECtHR (GC)18 October 2006, appl. no. 46410/99, para. 54.

[129] *Slivenko v. Latvia*, ECtHR (GC) 9 October 2003, appl. no. 48321/99, para. 96.

[130] *Üner v. the Netherlands*, *supra* n. 128, para. 59.

[131] *Slivenko v. Latvia*, *supra* n. 129. See also *Sisojeva and Others v. Latvia*, ECtHR (GC) 15 January 2007, appl. no. 60654/00.

became independent, their expulsion was ordered as part of the withdrawal of Russian troops as arranged by international agreement. Because the expulsion concerned the family as a whole, the applicants' family life was not at issue (*cp. infra* section 2.5(b)). The Grand Chamber also stated that, in the circumstances of the case, the expulsion had been warranted in principle in the interest of Latvia's national security. Nevertheless, it found that the Latvian authorities had insufficiently taken into account the personal circumstances of the applicants, including the fact that their husband and father had since long retired from the army.[132]

The right to private life has also been invoked before the Court by applicants who were expelled from a State Party after they had been convicted for criminal behaviour. The Court has developed several criteria to be applied in such cases to determine whether the expulsion is justified under the second paragraph of Article 8. These include the nature and seriousness of the offence committed by the applicant, the length of their stay in the country from which they are to be expelled and the best interests and well-being of any children who may be involved.[133] In the *Maslov* judgment, the Grand Chamber specifically stated that 'for a settled migrant who has lawfully spent all or the major part of his childhood and youth in the host country very serious reasons are required to justify expulsion'.[134] On the other hand, where a non-national has built up ties with the host country during a period of unlawful residence, his or her expulsion will violate the right to private life only in exceptional circumstances.[135]

2.6. PHYSICAL AND PSYCHOLOGICAL INTEGRITY

The notion of private life is understood by the Court to encompass a person's physical and psychological integrity.[136] It appears that the terms 'psychological integrity' and 'moral integrity' are used interchangeably.[137] The Court usually refrains from giving any further general definition of these terms. In the case of *Bensaid*, however, it specified that 'mental health must [...] be regarded as a crucial part of private life associated with the aspect of moral integrity'.[138] Additionally, it emerges from the case law that a person's moral or psychological integrity may be affected by well-founded anxiety or fear caused by threats of violence or by harassment against themselves or against close relatives.[139] In

---

132 *Slivenko v. Latvia*, *supra* n. 129, paras. 122–128.
133 *Maslov v. Austria*, ECtHR (GC) 23 June 2008, appl. no. 1638/03, paras. 68–71.
134 *Ibid.*, para. 75.
135 *Butt v. Norway*, ECtHR 4 December 2012, appl. no. 47017/09, paras. 78–79.
136 E.g. *Eremia v. the Republic of Moldova*, ECtHR 28 May 2013, appl. no. 3564/11, para. 73.
137 E.g. *Sandra Janković v. Croatia*, ECtHR 5 March 2009, appl. no. 38478/05, para. 45.
138 *Bensaid v. the United Kingdom*, ECtHR 6 February 2001, appl. no. 44599/98, para. 47.
139 E.g. *Hajduová v. Slovakia*, ECtHR 30 November 2010, appl. no. 2660/03, para. 49.

the case of *Đorđević*, for example, the Court found that the second applicant's moral integrity had been affected by the continuous harassment of her disabled son.[140] Lastly, in the case of *Söderman* the Grand Chamber found that the applicant's 'personal integrity' had been compromised by the actions of her stepfather, who had filmed her by means of a hidden camera as she was about to take a shower.[141]

It can be derived from the early case law of the Convention organs that Article 8 only applies when a person's physical or psychological integrity is adversely affected to a certain degree. Thus, the obligation to wear a seat belt does not come within the scope of the right to private life.[142] Similarly, in the case of *Costello-Roberts*, the Court held that a disciplinary measure taken against a school boy, consisting of 'three "whacks" on the bottom' with a rubber-soled gym shoe did not meet the threshold for the applicability of Article 8.[143] On the other hand, Article 8 may be successfully invoked where the adverse effects of a measure or action on a person's physical or psychological integrity are not of such a serious nature so as to come within the scope of Article 2 or 3 of the Convention.[144] The protection of physical and psychological integrity as part of the right to private life thus has a function independent of the protection offered by the latter Convention articles. The Court has accepted on several occasions that the conditions in which a person is detained may raise an issue under Article 8.[145] However, it held in the case of *D.G. v. Ireland* that the 'normal restrictions and limitations consequent on prison life and discipline during lawful detention are not matters which would constitute a violation of Article 8 either because they are considered not to constitute an interference with the detainee's private and family life [...] or because such interference would be justified.'[146]

The right to physical and psychological integrity, as part of the right to respect for private life, has played a role in a variety of contexts brought before the Court. Specific threads of case law have been developed in relation to violations of a physical or psychological integrity by other individuals, medical treatment or examination without the (informed) consent of the person concerned, the availability of medical treatment and facilities for ill or disabled persons and the

---

[140]   *Đorđević v. Croatia*, ECtHR 24 July 2012, appl. no. 41526/10, para. 97.

[141]   *Söderman v. Sweden*, ECtHR (GC) 12 November 2013, appl. no. 5786/08, para. 86.

[142]   *X. v. Belgium*, EComHR 13 December 1979 (dec.), appl. no. 8707/79.

[143]   *Costello-Roberts v. the United Kingdom*, ECtHR 25 March 1993, appl. no. 13134/87, para. 36. It is doubtful whether, given the diminished acceptance of corporal punishment for children, the Court would still reach the same judgment today.

[144]   E.g. *Juhnke v. Turkey*, ECtHR 13 May 2008, appl. no. 52515/99, para. 71.

[145]   E.g. *Lindström and Mässeli v. Finland*, ECtHR 14 January 2014, appl. no. 24630/10, para. 58. In this judgment the Court noted that 'the concept of private life also comprises of the respect for human dignity'. See also *Szafrański v. Poland*, ECtHR 15 December 2015, appl. no. 17249/12.

[146]   *D.G. v. Ireland*, ECtHR 16 May 2002, appl. no. 39474/98, para. 105.

choice to voluntarily end one's life. These topics are treated in separate sections below.

a. Protection against violations by others

The right to physical and psychological integrity includes the right to be protected against acts of violence or harassment by other individuals. In this regard, the Court has determined that Article 8 encompasses various positive obligations for the States Parties.[147] An overview of these obligations was provided by the Grand Chamber in the above-mentioned *Söderman* judgment.[148] The Grand Chamber reaffirmed that, in principle, it falls within the States Parties' margin of appreciation to choose the means by which they will ensure respect for the right to private life in horizontal relations. However, in case of serious violations such as rape or sexual abuse of children, the States Parties have an obligation to ensure that adequate criminal law provisions are in place and that an effective criminal investigation takes place.[149] In the *Söderman* judgment, the Grand Chamber specified that the criterion applied by the Chamber, namely that there would only be a breach of the State's positive obligation under Article 8 if there had been 'significant flaws in legislation and practice, and their application', could be meaningfully applied to the question of whether there had been an effective investigation. As regards the legal framework, however, the Grand Chamber considered that the relevant criterion was 'whether the law afforded an acceptable level of protection to the applicant in the circumstances'.[150] In case of 'less serious' infringements of psychological integrity between individuals such protection may also consist of the availability of civil remedies.[151] An example is the publication of photographs without the consent of the person concerned. While this matter has been discussed above under the heading of 'privacy', the Court has also related it to the aspect of personal integrity.[152]

The case law shows that the States Parties' positive obligations to protect physical and moral integrity in horizontal relations are especially pronounced where children are concerned, which is related to their 'particular vulnerability'.[153] The Grand Chamber pointed out in the *Söderman* judgment that the obligation to protect children against violence, including sexual abuse, is also included in the United Nations Convention on the Rights of the Child and the Council of Europe Convention on the Protection of Children against

---

[147] E.g. *X. and Y. v. the Netherlands*, ECtHR 26 March 1985, appl. no. 8978/80, para. 23.
[148] *Söderman v. Sweden, supra* n. 141, paras. 78–85.
[149] See also *M.G.C. v. Romania*, ECtHR 15 March 2016, appl. no. 61495/11, para. 59.
[150] *Söderman v. Sweden, supra* n. 141, para. 91.
[151] E.g. *Söderman v. Sweden*, ECtHR (GC) 12 November 2013, appl. no. 5786/08, para. 85.
[152] *Von Hannover v. Germany (No. 2), supra* n. 58, para. 95.
[153] E.g. *Söderman v. Sweden, supra* n.141, para. 81.

Sexual Exploitation and Sexual Abuse.[154] Similarly, in developing its case law on protection against violence by others the Court has taken note of international law instruments requiring state action to eradicate domestic violence.[155] More recently, the Court added racist harassment to the list of actions requiring special vigilance from the authorities, including adequate protection through criminal law mechanisms, especially in situations 'where there is evidence of patterns of violence and intolerance against an ethnic minority'.[156]

b. Medical examination and medical treatment

The right to physical and psychological integrity entails that, exceptional circumstances left aside, medical examinations and medical treatment may not be conducted without the consent of the person concerned. In this respect the Court has determined that 'a person's bodily integrity concerns the most intimate aspects of one's private life, and compulsory medical intervention, even if it is of minor importance, constitutes an interference with this right'.[157] Where a person consents to medical intervention, such consent should moreover be 'free, informed and express'.[158] An example of a case in which a violation of Article 8 was found in connection with forced medical treatment is *Glass*. This case concerned a hospital's decision to treat a seriously ill child with diamorphine against the express wishes of his mother. The Court judged that the hospital should not have continued the treatment without judicial consent.[159] Another example of a violation of Article 8 can be found in the case of *Storck*: the applicant in this case had been treated in a psychiatric hospital for a long time against her will, resulting in serious adverse effects on her health.[160]

In the Court's view, 'the freedom to accept or refuse specific medical treatment, or to select an alternative form of treatment, is vital to the principles of self-determination and personal autonomy'.[161] This was stated in the case of *Jehovah's Witnesses of Moscow and Others*, concerning the applicants' refusal, on religious grounds, to undergo blood transfusions. The Court found that the freedom to make choices concerning medical treatment is only meaningful if patients have the right 'to make choices that accord with their own views and values, regardless of how irrational, unwise or imprudent such choices may appear to others', and that interferences with self-determination in this sphere

---

[154] *Söderman v. Sweden*, *supra* n. 141, para. 82.

[155] E.g. *Eremia v. the Republic of Moldova*, *supra* n. 136, para. 73.

[156] *R.B. v. Hungary*, ECtHR 12 April 2016, appl. no. 64602/12, paras. 83–84.

[157] E.g. *Solomakhin v. Ukraine*, ECtHR 15 March 2012, appl. no. 24420/03, para. 33.

[158] *Juhnke v. Turkey*, *supra* n. 144, para. 76.

[159] *Glass v. the United Kingdom*, ECtHR 9 March 2004, appl. no. 61827/00, paras. 70 and 83.

[160] *Storck v. Germany*, ECtHR 16 June 2005, appl. no. 61603/00.

[161] *Jehovah's Witnesses of Moscow and Others v. Russia*, ECtHR 10 June 2010, appl. no. 302/02, para. 136.

could only 'lessen and not enhance the value of life'.[162] Meanwhile, it indicated that the interest of self-determination would not (necessarily) prevail in cases where there is a need to protect third parties, as in case of mandatory vaccination during an epidemic.[163]

It transpires from the case law that compulsory participation in medical examinations may be justified for certain purposes, for example to obtain information about someone's mental capacity to determine their criminal liability or to obtain evidence in a criminal prosecution. However, such examinations must be conducted in accordance with the law of the respondent state and their necessity will have to be established in light of the specific circumstances of the case.[164] In situations of detention, moreover, the authorities will have to have regard to the vulnerability of the persons concerned and their dependency on the prison staff. In two cases concerning applicants who had been subjected to compulsory gynaecological examinations in prison, the Court held that the fact that the applicants had not or no longer resisted the examinations could not be taken as an expression of their consent.[165]

In addition to the right not to be subjected to medical intervention against one's will, Article 8 guarantees the right to obtain relevant (medical) information enabling individuals to make knowledgeable decisions regarding such interventions. This includes the right of individuals to obtain information about their health and the information needed to assess any risks to their health.[166]

Besides negative obligations, the Court has derived several positive obligations from the right to physical and psychological integrity. These include the obligation to exercise control over the functioning of medical institutions, including hospitals and psychiatric clinics, and to ensure that they take measures to protect the lives and health of their patients.[167] In cases where medical intervention results in the death of a patient, an effective and independent procedure should be in place to establish the cause of death and, where necessary, to impose sanctions on those responsible.[168] It follows from the case law that these obligations apply to public as well as private medical institutions.[169] In cases of medical negligence, the Court has considered that the

---

[162]   *Ibid.*, para. 136.

[163]   *Ibid.*, para. 136.

[164]   E.g. *Worwa v. Poland*, ECtHR 27 November 2003, appl. no. 26624/95, para. 82; *Yuriy Volkov v. Ukraine*, ECtHR 19 December 2013, appl. no. 45872/06, paras. 88–89.

[165]   *Y.F. v. Turkey*, ECtHR 22 July 2003, appl. no. 24209/94, para. 34 and *Juhnke v. Turkey*, *supra* n. 144, para. 76.

[166]   E.g. *Codarcea v. Romania*, ECtHR 2 June 2009, appl. no. 31675/04, paras. 101 and 104; *A.K. v. Latvia*, ECtHR 24 June 2014, appl. no. 33011/08, para. 63.

[167]   E.g. *Storck v. Germany*, *supra* n. 160, para. 150.

[168]   *Trocellier v. France*, ECtHR 5 October 2006 (dec.), appl. no. 75725/01.

[169]   E.g. *Codarcea v. Romania*, *supra* n. 166, para. 102.

availability of a civil remedy to establish liability may be sufficient to fulfil the State Party's positive obligation.[170]

Positive obligations for the States Parties also exist in relation to the right of patients to be informed about the risks involved in medical treatment. In the *Codarcea* judgment, the Court noted that states should adopt regulations to ensure that medical professionals are informed about the health risks involved in the treatment they carry out and that they inform their patients about these risks. Where a foreseeable health risk materialises, in the context of a public hospital, without the patient having been adequately informed, the State Party may be held directly responsible for the failure to provide adequate information.[171] In the case of *A.K. v. Latvia*, the Court found a violation of Article 8 in its procedural aspect because no effective legal proceedings had been available to the applicant in relation to the alleged failure to provide her with adequate medical information and care during her pregnancy.[172]

c. Public funding for health care and mobility

Applicants before the Court have relied on Article 8 in search of protection against compulsory medical interventions or inadequate medical procedures, but also to seek compensation or treatment for disadvantages suffered as a result of illness or disability. While the Court made it clear that Article 8 does not contain a right to free medical care, it did find this provision applicable in cases concerning 'public funding to facilitate the mobility and quality of life of disabled applicants'.[173]

With regard to the private life aspects involved in such cases, a distinction may be drawn between limitations on an applicant's ability to access public places and engage in relationships with others and 'the outside world' (*supra* section 2.5) and impairments to their physical or psychological well-being. In several earlier decisions, the Court appeared to have regard to the former but not the latter.[174] This was especially clear in the case of *Sentges*, concerning a severely disabled applicant who complained of the State's refusal to provide him with a robotic arm to be mounted on his electric wheelchair. While the Court inquired into the disruptions to the applicant's everyday life, it did not address his complaint concerning his lack of independence and the effects thereof on his personal autonomy and quality of life.[175] In the subsequent case of *Mółka*,

---

[170]   E.g. *Trocellier v. France, supra* n. 168.
[171]   *Codarcea v. Romania, supra* n. 166, para. 105.
[172]   *A.K. v. Latvia, supra* n. 166, para. 94. Judge Kalaydjieva, in a separate opinion, questioned whether it would not have been more appropriate to treat the case under Art. 6.
[173]   E.g. *Pentiacova and 48 others v. Moldova*, ECtHR 4 January 2005 (dec.), appl. no. 14462/03.
[174]   E.g. *Zehnalová and Zehnal v. the Czech Republic*, ECtHR 14 May 2002 (dec.), appl. no. 38621/97.
[175]   *Sentges v. the Netherlands*, ECtHR 8 July 2003 (dec.), appl. no. 27677/02.

however, the Court considered that the impossibility for the applicant to access a polling station, due to his disability, 'might have aroused feelings of humiliation and distress capable of impinging on his personal autonomy, and thereby on the quality of his private life'.[176]

More recently, in the *McDonald* judgment, the Court invoked the notions of personal autonomy and of human dignity to interpret Article 8 in relation to the respondent State's decision to provide the applicant, who was unable to visit a commode independently at night, with incontinence pads instead of a night-time carer to support her.[177] Referring to its considerations in the *Pretty* judgment (*infra* section 2.6(d)), the Court found that the applicant was faced with 'the possibility of living in a manner which "conflicted with [her] strongly held beliefs of self and personal identity"' and concluded that the reduction of the care package offered to the applicant fell within the scope of Article 8.[178]

Although the Court has accepted that decisions concerning public funding of medical treatment and facilities for disabled people may raise issues under Article 8 it has not, to date, found any violations in this regard. The Court has repeatedly emphasised that the margin of appreciation afforded to the States Parties is particularly wide when the issues at stake involve 'an assessment of priorities in the allocation of limited State resources', noting also that 'in view of their familiarity with the demands made on the health care system as well as with the funds available to meet those demands, the national authorities are in a better position to carry out this assessment than an international court'.[179] It follows from the decision in *Shelley* that this applies *a fortiori* to measures of preventive health care, at least in the absence of any direct threat to a person's health.[180]

d. Voluntary end to life

The Court has interpreted the right to private life in light of the principle of personal autonomy, so as to include a right for individuals to make choices that may negatively affect their health (*supra* section 2.6(b)). This includes the right to refuse medical treatment, even where such treatment is necessary to save one's life. In the case of *Pretty*, however, the Court had to decide whether the applicant, a terminally ill woman, had to be allowed to actively end her life, with the help of her husband, to save her from further suffering. The Court in *Pretty* did not decide whether the United Kingdom's legislation, which prohibited assisted suicide, constituted an interference with Article 8. However, it acknowledged the seriousness of the applicant's concern about her quality of life, stating that 'in an

---

[176]   *Mółka v. Poland*, ECtHR 11 April 2006 (dec.), appl. no. 56550/00.
[177]   *McDonald v. the United Kingdom*, ECtHR 20 May 2014, appl. no. 4241/12.
[178]   *Ibid.*, para. 47.
[179]   E.g. *ibid.*, para. 54.
[180]   *Shelley v. the United Kingdom*, ECtHR 4 January 2008 (dec.), appl. no. 23800/06.

era of growing medical sophistication combined with longer life expectancies, many people are concerned that they should not be forced to linger on in old age or in states of advanced physical or mental decrepitude which conflict with strongly held ideas of self and personal identity.'[181]

In more recent cases, the Court expressly stated that the right to private life includes the choice of when and how one wants to die.[182] Nevertheless, the Court also held in the *Pretty* judgment that the States Parties may justifiably prohibit or regulate assisted suicide, in particular with a view to the protection of vulnerable individuals who are not capable of taking informed decisions against acts aimed at ending life.[183] While, in the *Haas* judgment, the Court left open the possibility of a positive obligation under Article 8 to enable individuals to end their life in dignity, it did not find that such an obligation existed in that case.[184] It follows from the case of *Gross,* however, that where assisted suicide is permitted in a State Party the relevant legislation should be sufficiently clear and accessible so as to allow individuals to know when its conditions are met.[185]

2.7. REPRODUCTIVE RIGHTS

The Court determined that the right to private life encompasses the possibility of having genetically related children. This includes 'both the decisions to become and not to become a parent'.[186] This choice is of importance to women seeking to avoid or terminate a pregnancy as well as to people wishing to use assisted reproductive technologies, such as in vitro fertilisation (IVF). Both issues are discussed in separate sections below. The Court has moreover received complaints from women who claimed to be victims of forced sterilisation. In the case of *V.C. v. Slovakia* it found that this practice, as such, amounts to a violation of Article 3 of the Convention. However, it also found a violation of Article 8 as regards the respondent State's failure to provide effective safeguards to protect the reproductive health of Roma women as a vulnerable group.[187] As with other medical interventions (*supra* section 2.6(b)), Article 8 obliges the States Parties to ensure that women are adequately informed about and involved in decisions

---

[181] *Pretty v. the United Kingdom, supra* n. 2, para. 65.
[182] E.g. *Haas v. Switzerland,* ECtHR 20 January 2011, appl. no. 31322/07, para. 51.
[183] *Pretty v. the United Kingdom, supra* n. 2, para. 74.
[184] *Haas v. Switzerland, supra* n. 182, para. 61.
[185] *Gross v. Switzerland,* ECtHR 14 May 2013, appl. no. 67810/10. This case was referred to the Grand Chamber, which found that the complaint formed an abuse of the right of application after it came to light that the applicant had died – by means of assisted suicide – one and a half years prior to the Chamber judgment. It appeared that the applicant had taken precautions to avoid the Court being informed of her death and the case being discontinued; see *Gross v. Switzerland,* ECtHR (GC) 30 September 2014, appl. no. 67810/10.
[186] E.g. *Evans v. the United Kingdom,* ECtHR (GC) 10 April 2007, appl. no. 6339/05, para. 71.
[187] *V.C. v. Slovakia,* ECtHR 8 November 2011, appl. no. 18968/07, para. 154.

regarding medical treatment in the reproductive sphere.[188] Cases concerning reproductive rights are often treated by the Court under the heading of private as well as family life.[189]

a. Abortion

The Court has repeatedly held that 'legislation regulating the interruption of pregnancy touches upon the sphere of private life'.[190] Where an abortion is sought for health reasons, the decision to terminate the pregnancy is connected to the mother's right to physical integrity.[191] The Court has however also linked this decision to the notion of personal autonomy, creating a ground for the applicability of Article 8 in cases where the pregnancy does not pose a risk to the mother's health.[192] This notwithstanding, and given that the issue of abortion involves weighing up the rights of the mother and sometimes the father as well as those of the unborn child, the States Parties have a large margin of appreciation to decide in which circumstances abortions are allowed.[193] In the case of *R.R. v. Poland*, the Court nevertheless noted that 'there is indeed a consensus amongst a substantial majority of the Contracting States of the Council of Europe towards allowing abortion and that most Contracting Parties have in their legislation resolved the conflicting rights of the foetus and the mother in favour of greater access to abortion.'[194]

The Court has moreover decided that, where abortion is permitted under domestic law, the State Party concerned must ensure that this right is effective and that the applicable legal framework meets the requirements of the Convention, for example as regards the pregnant women's access to information concerning the foetus' health.[195] This also implies that the possibility for medical professionals to refrain from conducting abortions on religious grounds should not render the possibility of having an abortion inaccessible.[196]

b. Assisted reproduction

The Court has determined that the use of assisted reproduction techniques falls within the scope of the right to private and family life.[197] This does not imply a right to have access to such techniques: as in the case of abortion, the States

---

[188] E.g. *A.K. v. Latvia*, *supra* n. 166, para. 63.
[189] E.g. *Costa and Pavan v. Italy*, ECtHR 28 August 2012, appl. no. 54270/10, para. 51.
[190] E.g. *R.R. v. Poland*, ECtHR 26 May 2011, appl. no. 27617/04, para. 181.
[191] *Tysiąc v. Poland*, ECtHR 20 March 2007, appl. no. 5410/03, para. 107.
[192] E.g. *A., B. and C. v. Ireland*, ECtHR (GC) 16 December 2010, appl. no. 25579/05, para. 216.
[193] E.g. *R.R. v. Poland*, *supra* n. 190, paras. 181 and 187.
[194] *Ibid.*, para. 186.
[195] E.g. *Tysiąc v. Poland*, *supra* n. 191, paras. 116–124.
[196] E.g. *R.R. v. Poland*, *supra* n. 190, para. 206.
[197] E.g. *S.H. and Others v. Austria*, ECtHR (GC) 3 November 2011, appl. no. 57813/00, para. 82.

Parties generally have a large margin of appreciation to decide if and under which circumstances assisted reproduction technology will be available to couples wishing to conceive a child. The width of the margin of appreciation is influenced by the moral and ethical sensitivity of the issue of assisted procreation and by the level of consensus existing amongst the States Parties to the Convention.[198]

The effects of the wide margin of appreciation are clearly illustrated by the case of *Evans*. The applicant, before having her ovaries removed to protect her from cancer, had several eggs fertilised with the sperm of her partner and stored for future use. After the relationship broke down the partner withdrew his consent and the applicant was no longer legally entitled to use the eggs. She claimed that the domestic legislation, requiring the consent of both partners, violated her rights under Article 8. However the Grand Chamber considered that both the applicant and her former partner had a right that was protected by Article 8 and that the United Kingdom legislator, although it could have adopted different rules, had not failed to strike a fair balance between the interests involved.[199]

In the *S.H. and Others v. Austria* judgment, the Grand Chamber found that the respondent State had adequately justified the decision not to allow the donation of egg cells or sperm by third parties for the purpose of in vitro fertilisation.[200] By contrast, in the case of *Costa and Pavan* the Court held that the Italian authorities had violated Article 8 by not allowing the applicants, who were both carriers of cystic fibrosis, to make use of the possibility of preimplantation genetic diagnosis (PGD) to avoid passing on their disease to their child. Taking into consideration that the Italian legislation did allow the termination of a pregnancy in case of a foetus being affected with cystic fibrosis, the Court considered that the question before it was not if the applicants were entitled to opt for a healthy child but rather which means were available to them for that purpose. It then concluded that the disputed legislation was disproportionate, in that it compelled the applicants to risk having to undergo an abortion whereas their wish not to have another child suffering from cystic fibrosis could be reached by other means.[201]

Lastly, in the case of *Parrillo* the applicant challenged the Italian ban on the donation of embryos for the purpose of scientific research. She wished to donate her embryos after her partner died during the IVF trajectory. The Grand Chamber acknowledged that 'the applicant's ability to exercise a conscious and considered choice regarding the fate of her embryos concerns an intimate aspect of her personal life and accordingly relates to her right to self-determination'.[202] However, it also considered that the case did not concern prospective parenthood and therefore the applicant's interest did not fall under the 'core rights' protected

---

[198]   E.g. *ibid.*, paras. 95–97.
[199]   *Evans v. the United Kingdom, supra* n. 186, paras. 90–92.
[200]   *S.H. and Others v. Austria, supra* n. 197, para. 115.
[201]   *Costa and Pavan v. Italy, supra* n. 189, paras. 69–71.
[202]   *Parrillo v. Italy*, ECtHR (GC) 27 August 2015, appl. no. 46470/11, para. 159.

by Article 8. In the absence, moreover, of consensus between the States Parties the Court judged that the ban fell within the wide margin of appreciation existing in this field.[203]

2.8. DECEASED FAMILY MEMBERS

A relatively new development in the Court's case law is the recognition of rights relating to States Parties' treatment of the remains of deceased family members. Although the Court has held Article 8 to be applicable in this area on a number of occasions, it has generally been reticent to qualify the rights at stake and to take a stance on whether they fall under the right to private life or family life. This issue came to the fore in the case of *Petrova*, where the Court found that the removal of organs from the applicant's son's body for transplantation without his or her consent amounted to an interference with the applicant's private life.[204] Judge Wojtyczek, in a separate opinion, argued that there had instead been an interference with the applicant's right to family life and more specifically the right to respect for the dignity of a deceased close relative.[205]

In earlier judgments the Court had already asserted that a delay in returning the body of a deceased person to the family or a failure to do so constitutes an interference with the relatives' right to private and family life. This was first established in the case of *Pannullo and Forte*, where the body of the applicants' daughter had been kept by the State authorities for over seven months after an autopsy had been performed. The Court found that there were no grounds justifying the delay, hence the failure to return the body sooner constituted a violation of Article 8.[206] A violation was found in several other cases, including *Maskhadova and Others* and *Arkeshtov and Others*, where the bodies of the deceased family members had not been returned at all and the applicants had, as a result, been deprived of the opportunity to organise and attend a burial and to know where their family members had been put to rest. In these cases, the Court noted that the interference with the applicants' rights had been 'particularly severe, in that it completely precluded them from any participation in the relevant funeral ceremonies and involved a ban on the disclosure of the location of the grave, permanently cutting the links between the applicants and the location of the deceased's remains.'[207]

---

203 *Ibid.*, paras. 174 et seq.
204 *Petrova v. Latvia*, ECtHR 24 June 2014, appl. no. 4605/05.
205 *Ibid.*, concurring opinion of Judge Wojtyczek, para. 5.
206 *Pannullo and Forte v. France*, ECtHR 30 October 2001, appl. no. 37794/97, paras. 38–39. See also the more recent judgment in *Girard v. France* (ECtHR 30 June 2006, appl. no. 22590/04), concerning a delay in returning samples taken from the applicant's daughter's body.
207 *Maskhadova and Others v. Russia*, ECtHR 6 June 2013, appl. no. 18071/05, para. 228; *Arkeshtov and Others v. Russia*, ECtHR 16 January 2014, 22089/07, para. 93.

The Court showed itself mindful of the fact that the deceased relatives had been involved in insurgent movements and accepted that under the circumstances the States Parties could legitimately take measures to ensure that the burials would not result in disorder or serve as a means of propaganda for terrorist ideas. However, it found no justification for not returning the bodies at all. Also, the decision not to return the bodies could not have been taken automatically, as had been the case, without any assessment by the authorities of the measure's proportionality.[208]

Several other judgments concern the treatment of deceased persons and the regulations adopted by the States Parties in this respect. In *Elli Poluhas Dödsbo*, the Court found that the Swedish authorities had acted lawfully in refusing the relocation of an urn containing the applicant's husband's ashes in the interest of protecting the sanctity of the grave.[209] The cases of *Hadri-Vionnet* and *Marić* concerned the authorities' handling of the burial of the applicants' babies, who had been stillborn.[210] In *Hadri-Vionnet*, the parents complained that they had not been able to attend the child's funeral and that the child's body had been transported in an ordinary delivery van. In *Marić*, the child's remains had been disposed of by the hospital as clinical waste at a location unknown to the parents. In both cases the Court held that there had been an interference with the applicants' rights under Article 8, without specifying whether the right to private or family life had been affected. It noted, however, that 'the management of the death of a close relative' is a 'personal and delicate area', where 'a particularly high degree of diligence and prudence must be exercised'.[211] Nevertheless, in the above-mentioned case of *Arkeshtov and Others*, the Court did not assess whether the storage of the applicants' relatives' bodies in unsuitable conditions constituted an interference with Article 8. The issue was examined under Article 3 but it was found that the threshold of severity pertaining under that provision had not been reached.[212]

3. FAMILY LIFE

While the notion of family life may at first sight appear clear-cut, there are many examples to be found in the Court's case law showing that this is not always so. The Court has been faced with numerous situations in which the legal, biological and social family ties between the persons involved did not coincide. Examples

---

[208] *Maskhadova and Others v. Russia, supra* n. 207, paras. 229–238; *Arkeshtov and Others v. Russia, supra* n. 207, paras. 94–102.

[209] *Elli Poluhas Dödsbo v. Sweden*, ECtHR 17 January 2006, appl. no. 61564/00.

[210] *Hadri-Vionnet v. Switzerland*, ECtHR 14 February 2008, appl. no. 55525/00; *Marić v. Croatia*, ECtHR 12 June 2014, appl. no. 50132/12.

[211] *Hadri-Vionnet v. Switzerland, supra* n. 210, para. 56; *Marić v. Croatia, supra* n. 210, para. 64.

[212] *Arkeshtov and Others v. Russia, supra* n. 207, para. 68.

include the situation where a child is born out of wedlock or raised by adoptive parents.[213] The variety of family formations has moreover expanded over time as a result of increased social acceptance of relationships other than traditional marriages (*de facto* partnerships, same-sex couples) as well as scientific developments enabling, for example, gestational arrangements with surrogate mothers.[214] Also varied are the situations in which the enjoyment of family life is disrupted. Such disruptions may be caused directly by the state authorities, as where a family member is deported or detained or a parent is deprived of custody rights. They may however also result from the behaviour of individuals, in particular other family members, as in the case of child abduction or the refusal of a parent to co-operate with access agreements.

Although the Court does not expressly distinguish between the personal and the material scope of the right to family life, it may be useful to do so here. The issue of personal scope is taken to refer to the question of whether the relationship between the persons involved in a particular case qualifies as 'family life'. The criteria developed by the Court in this respect are discussed in section 3.1. The subsequent sections concern the material scope of the right to family life, i.e. the different forms of interaction between family members that the States Parties should respect or enable. Specific aspects of the right to family life which have been addressed by the Court include the legal recognition of family ties (section 3.2), the award of custody and access rights to parents (section 3.3) and the rights of parents in situations of international child abduction (section 3.3(a)). Section 3.4 discusses the right of family members to live together and enjoy each other's company. With regard to this right, the Court has formulated criteria pertaining to several specific situations including child protection measures (section 3.4(a)), the non-admission or deportation of family members who are not nationals of the respondent state (section 3.4(b)) and the placement of a family member in detention (section 3.4(c)). The Court's case law also addresses the rights of children and their adoptive parents in case of adoption (section 3.5). The right to family life, as protected by Article 8, does not encompass a right to child support or other family benefits. Nevertheless, the Court has found violations of Articles 14 and 8 read together in situations where eligibility for such benefits was determined on the basis of discriminatory criteria.[215]

It is noted, as a general observation, that in cases involving children, the Court is often guided by the provisions of the United Nations Convention on the Rights of the Child (CRC), in particular the principle that in all decisions and actions concerning children the best interests of the child shall be a primary consideration. While this does not imply that those interests are always decisive,

---

[213]　E.g. *Johnston and Others v. Ireland*, ECtHR 18 December 1986, appl. no. 9697/82; *Ageyevy v. Russia*, ECtHR 18 April 2013, appl. no. 7075/10.

[214]　E.g. *Schalk and Kopf v. Austria*, *supra* n. 112; *Mennesson v. France*, *supra* n. 93.

[215]　E.g. *Di Trizio v. Switzerland*, ECtHR 2 February 2016, appl. no. 7186/09.

the Court has emphasised that they must be accorded significant weight.[216] In case of a conflict between the interests of the parent(s) and those of the child, the parents' right to family life does not entitle them to have measures taken that would harm the child's health or development.[217] Another common consideration is that parents and children, to the extent that they are capable of doing so, should be involved in the decision-making process concerning decisions affecting their family life.[218] Lastly, the Court has held in different family life-related contexts that the authorities of the States Parties should exercise due diligence to ensure that actual family relationships are not lost either as a result of inadequate legal procedures or because of obstructive behaviour by another family member, as may be the case for example in child abduction cases.[219]

3.1. DEFINITION

The Court's approach has generally been to define 'family life' as referring to the actual social and emotional ties ('close personal ties') that exist between family members. Although legal and biological ties are not without relevance to determining the existence of family life, they are not in themselves decisive. This was exemplified in the case of *X., Y. and Z. v. the United Kingdom*, concerning the inability of a female-to-male transsexual to be registered as the father of the child born to his partner. The child had been conceived by means of artificial insemination by donor and lived together with her mother and intended father as a family. The Grand Chamber, reiterating the Court's earlier case law, considered that: 'When deciding whether a relationship can be said to amount to "family life", a number of factors may be relevant, including whether the couple live together, the length of their relationship and whether they have demonstrated their commitment to each other by having children together or by any other means.'[220]

In the *Schalk and Kopf* case, the Court established that a *de facto* partnership between a same-sex couple amounts to family life in the same way as a *de facto* heterosexual partnership.[221]

Children born into a relationship between their biological parents are considered to enjoy family life with both parents, also if the relationship ends before or after the birth. While this family tie may cease to exist if there is no

---

[216]   E.g. *Jeunesse v. the Netherlands*, ECtHR (GC) 3 October 2013, appl. no. 12738/10, para. 109.
[217]   E.g. *Buchs v. Switzerland*, ECtHR 27 May 2014, appl. no. 9929/12, para. 51.
[218]   *Idem*, para. 53.
[219]   E.g. *Ignaccolo-Zenide v. Romania*, ECtHR 25 January 2000, appl. no. 31679/96, para. 102.
[220]   *X., Y. and Z. v. the United Kingdom*, ECtHR (GC) 22 April 1997, appl. no. 21830/93, para. 36.
[221]   *Schalk and Kopf v. Austria*, *supra* n. 112, para. 94. As noted in the judgment, the Court previously considered same-sex partnerships to fall under the heading of private life rather than family life.

longer any contact or commitment between the child and a parent, the mere fact that the parents have split up and that one of them has moved out of the family home does not end the family relationship between them and the child.[222] More generally, the Court's approach appears to be that the right to family life can still be invoked where the absence of actual family ties is not attributable to the applicant. Thus, it found that family life between a mother and her child continued to exist after the mother had been divested of her parental rights and the child adopted by others.[223] By contrast, in the case of *I.S. v. Germany* the Court established that a mother who had chosen to give her children up for adoption could no longer rely on the right to family life.[224]

The same approach can be discerned in respect of the relationship between a biological father and his child who are not part of the same *de facto* family. In this context, the Court determined that 'a mere biological kinship between a parent and a child, without any further legal or factual elements indicating the existence of a close personal relationship, is insufficient to attract the protection of Article 8'.[225] Nevertheless, where a father seeks to develop a family relationship with his biological child born out of wedlock he may be able to rely on Article 8, especially where the fact that an actual relationship has not developed is not attributable to him. In this situation, relevant factors for determining the applicability of Article 8 are the nature of the relationship between the parents and a demonstrable interest in and commitment by the father to the child both before and after birth.[226] Lastly, in the case of *I. and U. v. Norway*, the Court assumed that Article 8 applied to the intended family relationship between sisters who had not been able to develop actual family ties because the youngest sister had been placed in a different foster family as from birth.[227]

Relying on its interpretation of family life as the existence of close personal ties the Court has furthermore found family life to exist, *inter alia*, between a child and her grandparents, between a child and her foster parents and between children born out of a gestational arrangement with a surrogate mother and their intended parents.[228] The existence of family life between children and their parents is considered to end when the children reach the age of majority.

---

222 E.g. *Berrehab v. the Netherlands*, ECtHR 21 June 1988, appl. no. 10730/84, para. 21.

223 E.g. *A.K. and L. v. Croatia*, ECtHR 8 January 2013, appl. no. 37956/11, paras. 51–52.

224 *I.S. v. Germany*, ECtHR 5 June 2014, appl. no. 31021/08, para. 69. In the same paragraph, the Court stated that the mother's interests in the determination of her rights *vis-à-vis* her children nevertheless fell within the scope of her private life.

225 E.g. *Schneider v. Germany*, ECtHR 15 September 2011, appl. no. 17080/07, para. 80.

226 E.g. *Ahrens v. Germany*, supra n. 92, para. 58. Where no family life exists, the possibility of establishing biological paternity may still be relevant to the father's private life, see *supra* section 2.3(b).

227 *I. and U. v. Norway*, ECtHR 21 October 2004 (dec.), appl. no. 75531/01.

228 E.g. *Bronda v. Italy*, ECtHR 9 June 1998, appl. no. 22430/93, para. 51; *Moretti and Benedetti v. Italy*, ECtHR 27 April 2010 (dec.), appl. no. 16318/07, paras. 48–52; and *Mennesson v. France*, supra n. 93, para. 87.

However, the Court has determined that family life will continue to exist where the bond between adult children and their parents is characterised by the presence of 'additional factors of dependence other than normal ties of affection'. This will be the case, for example, where the child is disabled or ill and dependent on the care provided by the parents.[229]

With the exception of the above-mentioned case law on intended family life, the Court has interpreted Article 8 so as to protect only family ties that have already been established. By contrast the right to family life does not encompass the right to found a family or create new family relationships, for example through adoption (see *infra* section 3.5). The right to have genetically related children, if needed by means of assisted reproduction, has been addressed as an aspect of the right to private life (*supra* section 2.7).

3.2. RECOGNITION OF EXISTING FAMILY TIES

In line with the Court's understanding of family life as the existence of actual social and emotional ties, the right to family life has been interpreted as including a right to legal recognition of such ties. By contrast, legal rules which have the effect of obstructing or impeding the development of a factual family relationship should be abolished or disapplied. This was first decided in the often-cited *Marckx* judgment, where the Court held that 'when the State determines in its domestic legal system the regime applicable to certain family ties such as those between an unmarried mother and her child, it must act in a manner calculated to allow those concerned to develop a normal family life'.[230]

In the context of paternity proceedings, the Court has held that a man has a family life interest in being legally recognised as the biological father of a child with whom he enjoys an actual or intended family relationship (see also *supra* section 3.1).[231] It is up to the domestic authorities to balance this interest against the other interests involved, especially those of the child concerned.[232]

Where family life exists, the absence of a legal family relationship will often have consequences beyond a mere lack of recognition. This will be the case where, for example, a parent is unable to exercise custody over a child or to be appointed as the child's guardian.[233] In the case of *Mennesson*, the Court established that the applicants (a couple and their two children born from a surrogate mother) faced several practical difficulties as a result of the authorities' refusal to recognise them as a family. The Court also noted the children's inability to obtain

---

[229] E.g. *Emonet and Others v. Switzerland*, ECtHR 13 December 2007, appl. no. 39051/03, para. 37.
[230] *Marckx v. Belgium*, ECtHR (plen.) 13 June 1979, appl. no. 6833/74, para. 31.
[231] E.g. *Różański v. Poland*, ECtHR 18 May 2006, appl. no. 55339/00, paras. 64–65.
[232] *Ibid.*, para. 78.
[233] E.g. *Johnston and Others v. Ireland*, *supra* n. 213, para. 70.

the same nationality as their parents and the legal gap that would ensue if the parents were to divorce or if the father (who was the children's biological father) were to die. Nevertheless, it found that there had not been a violation of the right to family life, as 'they were able to live together in conditions broadly comparable to those of other families and there is nothing to suggest that they are at risk of being separated by the authorities on account of their situation under French law'.[234] By contrast, it held that the failure to recognise the children's affiliation did constitute a violation of their private life (see *supra* section 2.3(b)).

Despite a trend towards increased legal recognition of *de facto* and same-sex relationships, the case law shows that issues still arise under Article 8 because the States Parties' legal systems do not take account of family relationships that differ from the traditional marriage between a man and a woman. This is illustrated by the case of *Taddeucci and McCall*, concerning Italy's refusal to grant a residence permit to the same-sex partner of an Italian national. While it was established that residence permits were only granted to spouses and a non-married heterosexual couple who have been treated the same way, the Court found a violation of Articles 14 and 8 taken together on the grounds that the applicants, unlike heterosexual couples, did not have the possibility to get married under Italian law.[235] Another example is the case of *Gas and Dubois*, where two women in a stable lesbian relationship were denied the possibility to exercise shared parental responsibility over their daughter who had been conceived via artificial donor insemination. As in *Taddeucci and McCall*, the Court examined only whether the applicants had been discriminated against on the grounds of their sexual orientation (which it found not to be the case) and did not assess whether there had been a violation of Article 8 taken alone.[236] Conversely, in *Emonet and Others* the Court found that the Swiss law on adoption, which provided that the legal relationship between a mother and her adult, disabled daughter would be severed as a result of the daughter's adoption by the mother's cohabiting partner, did not meet the standards set by Article 8.[237]

3.3. CUSTODY AND ACCESS

The right to family life encompasses the rights of parents to exercise parental authority or custody over their children, allowing them to decide, for example, where the child shall reside or to consent to medical treatment.[238] It also includes the right of parents to have contact with their children (right of access) and to be

---

234   *Mennesson v. France, supra* n. 93, para. 92.
235   *Taddeucci and McCall v. Italy*, ECtHR 30 June 2016, appl. no. 51362/09.
236   *Gas and Dubois*, ECtHR 15 March 2012, appl. no. 25951/07.
237   *Emonet and Others v. Switzerland, supra* n. 229, paras. 86–88.
238   E.g. *Nielsen v. Denmark*, ECtHR 28 November 1988, appl. no. 10929/84, para. 61.

informed about their well-being.[239] The latter rights come into play where the children and one or both parents no longer live together. This section discusses the Court's case law concerning custody and access in situations where the parents have separated or have never lived together. In such cases, the question before the Court is whether the state authorities have acted in conformity with Article 8 in deciding which parent is awarded custody of the child or children and in determining the access and information rights of the other parent. Access and information rights of parents who have been placed in detention or whose children have been placed into care are discussed in section 3.4 below.

The Court has accepted decisions by national authorities to award parental authority to only one parent after a separation, even where the parents together applied for joint custody.[240] In such cases, the denial of custody to the other parent constitutes an interference with their right to family life. This interference will however be justified if it is established that the exercise of joint custody will not be in the best interests of the child.[241] The Court has found the interests of the child to fall under the legitimate aims of protecting 'health and morals' and 'the rights and freedoms of others' in the second paragraph of Article 8.[242] It also grants a wide margin of appreciation to the States Parties in deciding on custody.[243] In this connection, the Court found in the case of *Buchs* that there existed no consensus amongst the States Parties regarding the refusal of shared custody where one of the parents opposed it. In the same case it also took into account that the applicant enjoyed extensive contact rights.[244]

For parents who do not or no longer have custody over their children, the right to family life still entails a right of access or contact.[245] In this regard, the Court often stated that 'the mutual enjoyment by parent and child of each other's company constitutes a fundamental element of "family life" within the meaning of Article 8'.[246] Although 'family life' is defined by the Court as the existence of 'close personal ties' (*supra* section 3.1), access rights may also be claimed by biological parents who have not, or only very shortly, lived with the child in a family relationship.[247] In some of these cases, however, the Court treated access claims of biological parents under the heading of 'private life' rather than 'family life'.[248]

The denial or limitation of access rights constitutes an interference which must be justified under the second paragraph of Article 8. The Court has

---

[239]   E.g. *Schneider v. Germany, supra* n. 225, para. 90.
[240]   E.g. *Cernecki v. Austria*, ECtHR 11 July 2000 (dec.), appl. no. 31061/96.
[241]   E.g. *Buchs v. Switzerland, supra* n. 217, para. 55.
[242]   E.g. *Elsholz v. Germany*, ECtHR (GC) 13 July 2000, appl. no. 25735/94, para. 47.
[243]   E.g. *Sommerfeld v. Germany*, ECtHR (GC) 8 July 2003, appl. no. 31871/96, para. 63.
[244]   *Buchs v. Switzerland, supra* n. 217, para. 55.
[245]   E.g. *Hendriks v. the Netherlands*, EComHR 8 March 1982, appl. no. 8427/78, para. 94.
[246]   E.g. *Prizzia v. Hungary*, ECtHR 11 June 2013, appl. no. 20255/12, para. 33.
[247]   E.g. *Anayo v. Germany*, ECtHR 21 December 2010, appl. no. 20578/07, para. 62.
[248]   E.g. *I.S. v. Germany, supra* n. 224, para. 69.

repeatedly noted that restrictions on parental access rights 'entail the danger that the family relations between a young child and one or both parents would be effectively curtailed'. Where access rights are concerned, the States Parties' margin of appreciation is therefore smaller than in cases concerning custody.[249] Nevertheless, a restriction or even a denial of access rights will be permitted where it is duly established that this is in the best interests of the child.[250] This includes the situation where the child opposes access arrangements, even where it is established that the child's attitude is influenced by the custodian parent, as was the case in *Süss*.[251] The Court did not, however, accept an access arrangement whereby a father was precluded from seeing both of his children at the same time and the children were denied the possibility of seeing each other.[252] A violation was also found in the case of *Gluhaković*, where the applicant and his daughter were effectively forced to meet each other in a corridor at a counselling centre and no account was taken of the applicant's work schedule.[253]

Where the effectuation of a parent's access rights is obstructed by the other parent (or another person), the States Parties have a positive obligation to take measures aimed at reuniting the parent and his or her child.[254] While this obligation is 'not one of result, but of means' and is subject to the protection of the best interests of the child, the state authorities are required to do 'their utmost to preserve personal relations and, if and when appropriate, to "rebuild" the family'.[255] In this regard, the Court has held that it is especially important for the States Parties to act diligently 'as the passage of time can have irremediable consequences for relations between the child and the parent who does not live with him or her'.[256] A failure to proceed with sufficient diligence or vigour can result in a violation of Article 8.[257] As regards the nature of the measures to be taken, the Court held that 'although coercive measures against children are not desirable in this sensitive area, the use of sanctions must not be ruled out in the event of unlawful behaviour by the parent with whom the children live'.[258] In the case of *Cengiz Kılıç*, it held that the availability of mediation in family matters would have been recommendable.[259]

While Article 8 does not contain explicit procedural requirements, the proceedings relating to the determination of parental authority and access rights must be 'fair and such as to ensure due respect of the interests safeguarded by

---

[249] E.g. *Z.J. v. Lithuania*, ECtHR 29 April 2014, appl. no. 60092/12, para. 97.
[250] E.g. *Süss v. Germany (No. 1)*, ECtHR 10 November 2005, appl. no. 40324/98, para. 91.
[251] *Ibid.*, para. 91.
[252] *Mustafa and Armağan Akın v. Turkey*, ECtHR 6 April 2010, appl. no. 4694/03.
[253] *Gluhaković v. Croatia*, ECtHR 12 April 2011, appl. no. 21188/09.
[254] E.g. *Zawadka v. Poland*, ECtHR 23 June 2005, appl. no. 48542/99, para. 55.
[255] E.g. *Prizzia v. Hungary*, *supra* n. 246, para. 35.
[256] E.g. *Ignaccolo-Zenide v. Romania*, *supra* n. 219, para. 102.
[257] E.g. *Prizzia v. Hungary*, *supra* n. 246, para. 50.
[258] E.g. *ibid.*, para. 37.
[259] *Cengiz Kılıç v. Turkey*, ECtHR 6 December 2011, appl. no. 16192/06, paras. 132–134.

Article 8'.[260] This means that due account must be taken of the interests of the parents as well as those of the children. In the *Elsholz* case, which concerned access rights, the German courts established that the child did not want to see his father and therefore decided that the latter should not be granted access. In the view of the Grand Chamber, the fact that there had been no independent psychological assessment of the child's wishes meant that the father had not been sufficiently involved in the proceedings.[261] Similarly, in the *Antonyuk* case, the Court found that the decision by the Russian authorities refusing a mother to have her son reside with her was not based on sufficient evidence.[262] By contrast, in *Z.J. v. Lithuania* the Court held that the decision-making process concerning the applicant's request for custody of two of his children had been in conformity with Article 8, noting in particular that the applicant as well as the children had been heard and that the applicant had had access to all relevant information relied on by the domestic courts. The Court also noted that the courts had acted promptly and had consistently emphasised that the children would be able to move in with the applicant when their relationship improved.[263]

A State Party's regulations concerning access and custody must respect the prohibition of discrimination as laid down in Article 14 of the Convention. In the cases of *Zaunegger* and *Sporer,* the Court found a violation of Article 8 in combination with Article 14 on the grounds that a father of a child born out of wedlock did not have the same possibilities of exercising custody as a father who had been married to the child's mother.[264] In earlier case law the Court had already established that the decision to award parental rights to one parent rather than the other may not be based on the other parent's religion[265] or sexual orientation.[266]

Child abduction cases

Since 2000, the Court has developed a distinct line of case law relating to situations of international child abduction, where one parent has taken one or more children to another country in breach of the other parent's custody rights. In such cases, the Court interprets Article 8 in the light of the Hague Convention of 25 October 1980 on the Civil Aspects of International Child Abduction (the Hague Convention) as well as the CRC (*supra* section 3).[267] According to

---

[260]   E.g. *Buchs v. Switzerland, supra* n. 217, para. 53.
[261]   *Elsholz v. Germany, supra* n. 242, para. 53.
[262]   *Antonyuk v. Russia*, ECtHR 1 August 2013, appl. no. 47721/10, para. 146.
[263]   *Z.J. v. Lithuania, supra* n. 249, paras. 104–105.
[264]   *Zaunegger v. Germany*, ECtHR 3 December 2009, appl. no. 22028/04, para. 62; *Sporer v. Austria*, ECtHR 3 February 2011, appl. no. 35637/03, paras. 89–90.
[265]   E.g. *Hoffmann v. Austria*, ECtHR 23 June 1993, appl. no. 12875/87, para. 36.
[266]   *Salgueiro da Silva Mouta v. Portugal*, ECtHR 21 December 1999, appl. no. 33290/96, para. 36.
[267]   E.g. *Neulinger and Shuruk v. Switzerland*, ECtHR (GC) 6 July 2010, appl. no. 41615/07, para. 132.

its Preamble, the Hague Convention has as its object and purpose to protect children against the harmful effects of abduction and to establish procedures for their prompt return, as well as to secure protection for rights of access.[268] Exceptions to the obligation of return apply notably where a grave risk exists that the child would be exposed to physical or psychological harm or otherwise placed in an intolerable situation (Article 13 (b) Hague Convention).

In the case of *Neulinger and Shuruk*, the Grand Chamber confirmed that it considers the provisions of the Hague Convention to be in line with its own notion of the child's best interests in custody matters. These include, first, the interest of being able to develop in a sound environment and not being subjected to measures that would harm their health and development and, secondly, to maintain their family ties.[269] The Court has looked to the Hague Convention for guidance on, *inter alia*, the measures to be taken by the States Parties to secure the return of abducted children (Article 7 Hague Convention) and the time-limit within which a decision on return of the child must be reached (Article 11 Hague Convention).[270] It has also made it clear, however, that its task is not to ensure the correct application of the Hague Convention, which it considers to be a procedural instrument rather than a human rights treaty, but to review the States Parties' compliance with Article 8.[271]

In child abduction cases, the applicant may be either the parent who took the child abroad and complains about the return order issued against them or the parent who has been left behind and seeks to be reunited with his or her children. In the former situation the Court qualifies the return order as an interference with the applicant's family life which must be in accordance with the criteria set out in the second paragraph of Article 8. Such interference can be found to exist also if the return order has not yet been executed.[272] Thus far the Court has considered return orders based on the Hague Convention to be 'in accordance with the law' and to pursue the legitimate aim of protecting the rights and freedoms of the child and sometimes the other parent.[273] As regards the question of whether the return order was 'necessary in a democratic society', the criterion applied by the Court is whether the respondent state has, within its margin of appreciation, struck a fair balance between the competing interests at stake, namely those of the child, of the two parents and of public order.[274] The best interests of the child must form a primary consideration and may, depending on their nature and seriousness, override those of the parents.[275] In

---

[268] *Cp. Bianchi v. Switzerland*, ECtHR 22 June 2006, appl. no. 7548/04, para. 83.

[269] *Neulinger and Shuruk v. Switzerland*, *supra* n. 267, paras. 136–137.

[270] E.g. *Ignaccolo-Zenide v. Romania*, *supra* n. 219, para. 113; *Bianchi v. Switzerland*, *supra* n. 268, paras. 93–94.

[271] E.g. *Neulinger and Shuruk v. Switzerland*, *supra* n. 267, para. 145.

[272] E.g. *Šneersone and Kampanella v. Italy*, ECtHR 12 July 2011, appl. no. 14737/09, para. 88.

[273] E.g. *ibid.*, paras. 89–90.

[274] E.g. *ibid.*, para. 91.

[275] E.g. *Neulinger and Shuruk v. Switzerland*, *supra* n. 267, para. 134.

the case of *Šneersone and Kampanella*, for example, the Court concluded that the return order issued by the Italian courts violated Article 8 as the courts had not had regard to the child's psychological health and insufficient safeguards had been provided to ensure his well-being upon return.[276]

If the application is made by the parent whose rights of custody and/or access have been affected by the child's abduction, the Court will assess whether the authorities in the respondent state took all the measures that could reasonably be demanded (*'toutes les mesures que l'on pouvait raisonnablement exiger d'elles'*) to secure the child's return.[277] While the Court usually qualifies the State Party's obligation in such cases as a positive one, it has also contended that the applicable principles in case of both positive and negative obligations are similar and that in both cases a fair balance must be struck between the rights of the individual and those of society as a whole.[278]

The Court's case law on positive obligations in the context of child abductions bears much resemblance to its case law on custody and access rights (*supra* section 3.3). The States Parties have an obligation under Article 8 to reunite parents and their children after an abduction has taken place. This obligation is, however, not absolute: where child and parent have been separated for some time preparatory measures may be needed to facilitate a reunion, with the success of such measures depending on the understanding and co-operation of all concerned.[279] In line with Article 7 (c) of the Hague Convention the Court encourages the States Parties to strive for a friendly settlement and it has repeatedly stated that in general the use of coercion will not be in the best interests of the children involved.[280] However, a failure to take coercive measure against parents who consistently refuse to co-operate can result in a violation of Article 8.[281] As in cases concerning custody and access, the Court considers it very important that the States Parties act swiftly since the parent-child relationship can be irremediably harmed by the passage of time.[282] The strictness of the Court's approach appears clearly from the judgment in *Raw and Others*: despite ample efforts on the part of the French authorities to execute the return order sought by the mother, the Court found a violation of Article 8 because no more significant attempts had been made to return the children after

---

[276] *Šneersone and Kampanella v. Italy, supra* n. 272, paras. 93–98.

[277] E.g. *Raw and Others v. France*, ECtHR 7 March 2013, appl. no. 10131/11, para. 84. In the same consideration the Court also speaks of all necessary and adequate steps (*'les mesures nécessaires et adéquates'*). The 2 criteria appear to be used interchangeably.

[278] E.g. *ibid.*, paras. 77–78.

[279] E.g. *Bianchi v. Switzerland, supra* n. 268, para. 80.

[280] E.g. *Raw and Others v. France, supra* n. 277, paras. 83 and 93.

[281] E.g. *Ignaccolo-Zenide v. Romania, supra* n. 219, paras. 101–113. See *a contrario Maumousseau and Washington v. France*, where the Court found that the use of coercion was justified in view of the mother's unco-operative behaviour (ECtHR 6 December 2007, appl. no. 39388/05, paras. 84–85).

[282] E.g. *Raw and Others v. France, supra* n. 277, para. 83.

a meeting with their mother ended in a physical confrontation. In this case the Court also noted that, although the children's views must be taken into account when deciding upon their return, their resistance does not always constitute an obstacle to the return order being executed.[283]

Lastly, in child abduction cases, as in cases concerning custody and access, the Court has held that Article 8 includes implicit procedural guarantees to the effect that the decision-making process must be fair and conducted in such a way as to allow those concerned to fully present their case. Consequently, the Court's assessment includes whether the domestic courts have 'conducted an in-depth examination of the entire family situation and of a whole series of factors, in particular of a factual, emotional, psychological, material and medical nature, and made a balanced and reasonable assessment of the respective interests of each person, with constant concern for determining what the best solution would be for the abducted child in the context of an application for his return to his country of origin.'[284]

3.4. LIVING TOGETHER

As mentioned above (section 3.2), the Court considers that a fundamental aspect of the right to family life lies in the possibility for people who are in a family relationship to mutually enjoy each other's company. It follows that where family members live together in the same household state authorities should, in principle, refrain from taking measures which temporarily or permanently disrupt this situation. In several cases, all concerning the relationship between parents and their children, the Court has stated that it 'it is an interference of a very serious order to split up a family. Such a step must be supported by sufficiently sound and weighty considerations in the interests of the child'.[285] This notwithstanding, forced separation of family members may be mandated by the public interest. Where one or both parents are incapable of fulfilling their role as carers or their behaviour is even harmful to the child, the state authorities will need to protect the child's well-being even at the expense of the parent-child relationship. The criteria derived by the Court from Article 8 in relation to child protection measures are discussed below in section 3.4(a). The following paragraphs discuss the situations where the separation of a family is the result of immigration measures (section 3.4(b)) or of the fact that a family member is detained following a criminal conviction (section 3.4(c)).

---

[283] *Ibid.*, paras. 85–95.
[284] E.g. *Šneersone and Kampanella v. Italy, supra* n. 272, para. 85.
[285] E.g. *Scozzari and Giunta v. Italy*, ECtHR (GC) 13 July 2000, appl. nos. 39221/98 and 41963/98, para. 148.

a.   Child protection measures

Much of the case law on child protection measures concerns the situation where the state authorities have ordered for a child to be taken away from the parents and placed, temporarily or indefinitely, in the care of a foster family or in a children's home.[286] An even more far-reaching measure is where a child is removed from the parents' home and put up for adoption, with the result that all legal ties between the child and the parents are severed.[287] Both measures constitute interferences with the right to family life, which must be in accordance with the requirements of the second paragraph of Article 8.[288] In assessing whether a child protection measure was justified, the Court carefully scrutinises the actions taken by the respondent state to determine not only whether the measure was necessary but also whether enough was done to mitigate its adverse effects on the family life of the persons involved. Once a child has been placed out of the family home the States Parties have a positive duty to work towards reunification and to in any case ensure that the disruption caused by the separation remains as limited as possible.

Where the decision to place a child into care is concerned, the Court has held that the States Parties have a wide margin of appreciation. It has linked this to varying perceptions in the Contracting Parties 'as to the appropriateness of intervention by public authorities in the care of children', as well as to the fact that the domestic authorities have direct contact with the persons concerned.[289] Nevertheless, and even in the case of urgent protection measures, the Court will assess whether the national authorities have evaluated 'with care' the impact of the care measure and the possibility of other measures.[290] On several occasions the Court found that the grounds adduced by the respondent state did not suffice to justify the care measure. In *Kocherov and Sergeyeva*, for example, the authorities failed to substantiate that the father's (mild) mental disability made him incapable of caring for his daughter.[291] Also, the fact that children could be placed in a more beneficial environment does not as such justify their forced removal from their parents.[292] A clear example is the case of *Wallová and Walla*, where the Court noted that the parents did not lack educational or affective capacity; the main reason for placing the children into care had been that they were not able to provide adequate housing. In those circumstances, the Court found that the authorities could and should have applied less radical measures

---

[286]   E.g. *K. and T. v. Finland*, ECtHR (GC) 12 July 2001, appl. no. 25702/94.
[287]   E.g. *Zhou v. Italy*, ECtHR 21 January 2014, appl. no. 33773/11.
[288]   E.g. *K. and T. v. Finland*, *supra* n. 286, para. 151; *Zhou v. Italy*, *supra* n. 287, para. 44.
[289]   E.g. *Scozzari and Giunta v. Italy*, *supra* n. 285, para. 201.
[290]   E.g. *K. and T. v. Finland*, *supra* n. 286, para. 166.
[291]   *Kocherov and Sergeyeva v. Russia*, ECtHR 29 March 2016, appl. no. 16899/13.
[292]   E.g. *K. and T. v. Finland*, *supra* n. 286, para. 173.

than to separate the family.[293] In the same judgment, the Court contrasted the applicants' situation to that where a child had been abused or where a parent suffered from psychological problems.[294] Where the parents are vulnerable, owing for example to illness or disability, the State Party should exercise special care to ensure adequate protection for their family life.[295] Lastly, in *K. and T. v. Finland*, the Grand Chamber considered that the taking of a baby into emergency care immediately after birth was an 'extremely harsh measure'; it was not satisfied that a less intrusive measure could not have sufficed.[296]

With regard to the determination of access rights after a child has been placed into care and the legal safeguards to ensure effective protection of the family life of the parents and the children, the Contracting States have a narrower margin of appreciation.[297] The State authorities must strike a fair balance between the interests involved; however, where necessary the best interests of the child will override those of the parents.[298] The Court has made it clear that placing a child into care should normally be considered as a temporary measure.[299] Safe for in exceptional circumstances, where the parents are demonstrated to be especially undeserving ('*indignes*') of seeing their children, contact between the family members should be enabled.[300] In *K. and T. v. Finland*, the Court held that: 'the positive duty to facilitate family reunification as soon as reasonably feasible will begin to weigh on the competent authorities with progressively increasing force as from the commencement of the period of care, subject always to its being balanced against the duty to consider the best interests of the child.'[301]

As in cases where one parent's contact with his or her child is obstructed by the other parent (*supra* section 3.3), the Court has warned the states to act swiftly to avoid the relationship disappearing 'through the passage of time alone'.[302] In the case of *Scozzari and Giunta*, amongst others, the Grand Chamber found a violation of Article 8 because the mother had been able to visit her children only a few times over the course of several years.[303] In this judgment, as well as in *K. and T. v. Finland*, the Grand Chamber moreover criticised the negative attitude of the State authorities towards the parents, which had hindered their prospects

---

[293]   *Wallová and Walla v. the Czech Republic*, ECtHR 26 October 2006, appl. no. 23848/04, para. 73.

[294]   *Ibid.*, para. 72.

[295]   E.g. *Zhou v. Italy*, *supra* n. 287, para. 58; see also *K.A.B. v. Spain*, ECtHR 10 April 2012, appl. no. 59819/08, para. 113.

[296]   *K. and T. v. Finland*, *supra* n. 286, para. 168.

[297]   E.g. *Scozzari and Giunta v. Italy*, *supra* n. 285, para. 201.

[298]   E.g. *Zhou v. Italy*, *supra* n. 287, para. 45.

[299]   E.g. *Scozzari and Giunta v. Italy*, *supra* n. 285, para. 169.

[300]   E.g. *Zhou v. Italy*, *supra* n. 287, para. 46.

[301]   *K. and T. v. Finland*, *supra* n. 286, para. 178.

[302]   E.g. *K.A.B. v. Spain*, *supra* n. 295, paras. 96–97.

[303]   *Scozzari and Giunta v. Italy*, *supra* n. 285, para. 183.

of reunification.[304] While the States Parties are thus required to do their utmost to reunite parents and their children, the Court has also acknowledged that such a reunion cannot be successful without the co-operation of all concerned and that the possibilities for the authorities to use coercion are limited in a situation where the rights and interests of all parties, in particular the children, must be taken into account.[305]

In child protection cases, as in other cases where the state interferes in the relationship between children and their parents, the state must ensure that the interests of all persons involved are adequately taken into account (*cf. supra* section 3.3). To this effect the Court has derived several procedural guarantees from Article 8. Notably, parents faced with child protection measures should have the opportunity to voice their interests and to make use of available legal remedies. They are also entitled to have access to the information on which the authorities have based their decision. Where these conditions are not met, the interference in the right to family life cannot be considered as 'necessary in a democratic society'.[306] The obligation to pay special attention to the needs of vulnerable parents also applies to the procedure that is followed; this may imply the need to appoint a legal representative.[307]

b.   Migration cases

In immigration cases, the Court has consistently emphasised that the States Parties have the right to control the entry of non-nationals into their territory and that Article 8 does not impose a general obligation on those states to respect the choice by married couples of their matrimonial residence.[308] This notwithstanding, it holds Article 8 to be applicable to cases where a state's refusal to admit a person to its territory or the decision to deport someone results in a separation from their family members. This was first decided in the case of *Abdulaziz, Cabales and Balkandali*, concerning three women who resided in the United Kingdom and applied for their husbands to join them from abroad. The Court, rejecting the Government's argument that immigration measures fell outside the scope of the Convention, stated that 'the applicants are not the husbands but the wives, and they are complaining not of being refused leave to enter or remain in the United Kingdom but, as persons lawfully settled in that country, of being deprived (...), or threatened with deprivation (...), of the society of their spouses there.'[309]

---

[304]   *Ibid.*, para. 179; *K. and T. v. Finland, supra* n. 286, para. 179.

[305]   *Scozzari and Giunta v. Italy, supra* n. 285, para. 175.

[306]   E.g. *Zambotto Perrin v. France*, ECtHR 26 September 2013, appl. no. 4962/11, para. 93.

[307]   E.g. *A.K. and L. v. Croatia, supra* n. 223, para. 75.

[308]   E.g. *Tuquabo-Tekle and Others v. the Netherlands*, ECtHR 1 December 2005, appl. no. 60665/00, para. 43.

[309]   *Abdulaziz, Cabales and Balkandali v. the United Kingdom*, ECtHR (plen.) 28 May 1985, appl. nos. 9214/80, 9472/81 and 9474/81, para. 60.

In the case of *Berrehab*, the Court confirmed that expulsion or deportation measures can also come within the scope of Article 8.[310] Where a person has lived in the territory of a State Party from a very young age and has built up strong ties within that State, their deportation can also constitute an interference with their right to private life (see *supra* section 2.5(b)).

The Court's general approach in migration cases has been to treat the situation where the applicant has not been legally admitted to the respondent state as involving a potential positive obligation to grant a right of residence, whereas the deportation of a migrant with lawful residence is considered as an interference with the right to family life. This approach was confirmed in the Grand Chamber judgment in *Jeunesse*, concerning an applicant who had lived in the Netherlands for more than 16 years but had never succeeded in obtaining a residence permit.[311] In the same judgment, the Grand Chamber also reiterated the Court's often repeated formula that the boundaries between states' positive and negative obligations do not lend themselves to precise definition and that the applicable principles are similar, as in both cases a fair balance has to be struck between the competing interests of the individual and of the community as a whole.[312] An analysis of the case law shows, however, important differences between the Court's approach depending on whether the case concerns the non-admission or removal of a migrant without lawful residence or the deportation of a legally settled non-national.

In cases where no right of residence has been granted, the Court usually starts its reasoning from the premise that there is no general right for a non-national to be admitted to a State Party for the purpose of enjoying family life. Consequently, family members residing in a State Party are not, in principle, entitled to family reunification in that state. A positive obligation to admit a family member from abroad may, however, exist in some cases, depending on the particular circumstances of the persons involved and the general interest.[313] Relevant factors to be taken into account, as summarised by the Grand Chamber in the *Jeunesse* judgment, are the extent to which family life would effectively be ruptured if admission were refused; the extent of the ties in the Contracting State; whether there are insurmountable obstacles in the way of the family living in the country of origin; whether there are factors of immigration control (such as a history of breaches of immigration law) or considerations of public order weighing in favour of exclusion; and, finally, whether family life was created at a time when the family members were aware that the immigration status of one of them was such that the persistence of family life within the host State would from the outset be precarious, in which case the removal of a non-national family will

---

[310] *Berrehab v. the Netherlands, supra* n. 222, para. 23.
[311] *Jeunesse v. the Netherlands, supra* n. 216, paras. 104–105.
[312] *Ibid.*, para. 106.
[313] E.g. *Rodrigues Da Silva and Hoogkamer v. the Netherlands*, ECtHR 31 January 2006, appl. no. 50435/99, para. 39.

constitute a violation of Article 8 only in exceptional circumstances.[314] Where children are involved, however, the best interests of the child form an important factor to be taken into account.[315]

In the majority of cases before the Court, the application of the above factors has led to the finding that there was no positive obligation to admit the non-national family member because the other family members could have avoided a separation by moving abroad as well. In this respect, cultural differences or a significantly lower standard of living in the country of origin do not qualify as 'insurmountable obstacles'.[316] In several cases, the Court also found that there had been no violation of Article 8 because the family members were not precluded from maintaining the degree of family life which they themselves had chosen when one of the family members opted for migration.[317] It seems, however, that the Court's qualification of the facts in this type of cases is not always consistent. In the case of *Sen*, where the parents also made a conscious decision to leave their daughter in Turkey when they moved to the Netherlands, it found that this decision did not amount to a choice to permanently renounce the possibility of living with her.[318] In the *Sen* case, as in *Tuquabo-Tekle and Others*, the Court found that there was a positive obligation to admit the child who had stayed behind in the country of origin. In both cases it took into consideration that the families included other young children who were born in the host state and had no or very few ties to the country of origin of their parents.[319]

The Court also found a violation of Article 8 in the cases of *Rodrigues Da Silva and Hoogkamer* and *Nunez*.[320] In both cases, the intended removal of the mother would have resulted in their separation from their young children because the parents were separated and custody had been awarded to the father. Although in both cases the mothers had remained in the host state in breach of its immigration rules, the Court found that their deportation would have been contrary to the best interests of the children involved.[321] There were, therefore, 'exceptional circumstances' leading to the conclusion that deportation would not be compatible with Article 8. Meanwhile, the Grand Chamber's approach in the *Jeunesse* judgment appears more lenient compared to the preceding case law. In this case the Grand Chamber found a violation of Article 8 despite the fact that the applicant had always lived irregularly in the host State and that there were no

---

[314] *Jeunesse v. the Netherlands, supra* n. 216, paras. 107–108.
[315] E.g. *Jeunesse v. the Netherlands, supra* n. 216, para. 109; see earlier *Rodrigues Da Silva and Hoogkamer v. the Netherlands, supra* n. 313, para. 44.
[316] E.g. *Darren Omoregie and Others v. Norway*, ECtHR 31 July 2008, appl. no. 265/07, para. 33.
[317] E.g. *Ahmut v. the Netherlands*, ECtHR 28 November 1996, appl. no. 21702/93, para. 70.
[318] *Sen v. the Netherlands*, ECtHR 21 December 2001, appl. no. 31465/96, para. 40.
[319] *Ibid.*, para. 40; *Tuquabo-Tekle and Others v. the Netherlands, supra* n. 308, para. 47.
[320] *Rodrigues Da Silva and Hoogkamer v. the Netherlands, supra* n. 313; *Nunez v. Norway*, ECtHR 28 June 2011, appl. no. 55597/09.
[321] *Rodrigues Da Silva and Hoogkamer v. the Netherlands, supra* n. 313, para. 44; *Nunez v. Norway, supra* n. 320, para. 84.

'insurmountable obstacles' for the family as a whole to move to Suriname.[322] The Court moreover appears increasingly to pay attention to the proportionality of the immigration measures taken by the respondent states. Where a State Party refuses to legally admit a family member for the purpose of family reunion, the Court often accepts without further scrutiny that such a refusal serves the public interest of 'ensuring effective immigration control' and is proportionate to that end.[323] However in several more or less recent cases, including *Nunez* and *Kaplan*, it considered that the state's immigration interest could not weigh too heavily in the balance as the state authorities had failed to act diligently in enforcing the immigration laws.[324]

As stated earlier, the termination of legal residence of a non-national family members is normally regarded as an interference with a negative obligation. The Court's approach is then to assess whether this interference complies with the conditions set out in the second paragraph of Article 8.[325] It follows that in such cases the aim and the necessity of the disputed immigration measure are subject to stricter scrutiny than in cases where the applicant did not have lawful residence.

The Court has accepted that the expulsion of a non-national who has been convicted on criminal charges may serve the legitimate aim of preventing disorder or crime.[326] In the case of *Boultif* and the subsequent Grand Chamber judgment in *Üner*, the Court developed an extensive set of criteria which is used to determine whether a fair balance has been struck between the state's interest in preventing disorder and the individual's interest in the enjoyment of family life. These are:

- the nature and seriousness of the offence committed by the applicant;
- the length of the applicant's stay in the country from which he or she is to be expelled;
- the time elapsed since the offence was committed and the applicant's conduct during that period;
- the nationalities of the applicant and his or her family members;
- the applicant's family situation, such as the length of the marriage, and other factors expressing the effectiveness of the couple's family life;
- whether the spouse knew about the offence at the time when he or she entered into a family relationship;

---

[322] *Jeunesse v. the Netherlands, supra* n. 216, para. 113 et seq. Judges Villiger, Mahoney and Silvis argued in a dissenting opinion that the majority's judgment does not fit in well with the Court's earlier case law. Another example of a more lenient attitude towards family reunion can, however, be found in *Kaplan and Others v. Norway*, ECtHR 24 July 2014, appl. no. 32504/11.

[323] E.g. *Biao v. Denmark*, ECtHR 25 March 2014, appl. no. 38590/10, para. 59.

[324] *Nunez v. Norway, supra* n. 320, para. 82; *Kaplan and Others v. Norway, supra* n. 322, para. 96.

[325] E.g. *Hasanbasic v. Switzerland*, ECtHR 11 June 2013, appl. no. 52166/09, para. 50.

[326] E.g. *Moustaquim v. Belgium*, ECtHR 18 February 1991, appl. no. 12313/86, para. 40.

- whether there are children to the marriage, and if so, their age;
- the seriousness of the difficulties which the spouse is likely to encounter in the country to which the applicant is to be expelled;
- the best interests and well-being of the children, in particular the seriousness of the difficulties which any children of the applicant are likely to encounter in the country to which the applicant is to be expelled; and
- the solidity of social, cultural and family ties with the host country and with the country of destination.[327]

While the above criteria describe the interests and circumstances to be taken into account in deportation cases, they do not indicate the weight to be accorded thereto. Since, in most cases, there will be factors weighing in favour of expulsion and of preserving family life in the host state, the outcome of the balancing exercise remains to a certain extent uncertain. It has been commented that the Court has sometimes tended to lend decisive importance to the nature and seriousness of the crime (the first criterion), while in other cases the difficulties to be experienced by the applicant's family in case of relocation to another country weighed heavily in the balance.[328] In the case of *Maslov*, the Grand Chamber made clear that it attached important weight to the fact that an applicant was born in the host State or arrived there at a very young age, as is the case for second generation immigrants. In such cases 'very serious reasons are required to justify expulsion'.[329] Expulsion decisions are moreover less likely to be justified if the applicant committed the offences before reaching the age of majority.[330] Lastly, in the case of *Emre* the Court considered that medical problems experience by an applicant may form a factor weighing against expulsion.[331]

Besides criminal convictions, other reasons may justify the expulsion of non-national family members. In the *Berrehab* case, the Court noted that the Government's concern had been to regulate the labour market and found that this objective corresponded to the legitimate aim of 'preserving the country's economic well-being'.[332] However, it went on to find that the applicant's expulsion would violate Article 8: here the Court took into account that there were no actual reasons (e.g. criminal convictions or reliance on public means) weighing against the applicant's legal residence.[333] Conversely, in the case of *Hasanbasic*, the Court considered that the respondent State was entitled to hold it against the applicant that he had built up substantial debts and relied on public resources for

---

[327] *Boultif v. Switzerland*, ECtHR 2 August 2001, appl. no. 54273/00, para. 48; *Üner v. the Netherlands, supra* n. 128, paras. 57–58.
[328] P. Boeles et al., *European Migration Law*, Cambridge: Intersentia, 2014, pp. 215–223.
[329] *Maslov v. Austria*, ECtHR (GC) 23 June 2008, appl. no. 1638/03, para. 75.
[330] *Ibid.*, para. 75.
[331] *Emre v. Switzerland*, ECtHR 22 May 2008, appl. no. 42034/04, para. 83.
[332] *Berrehab v. the Netherlands, supra* n. 222, para. 26.
[333] *Ibid.*, para. 29.

more than 10 years. In this regard, the Court expressly noted that 'the economic well-being of the country' is mentioned as a legitimate aim in Article 8, contrary to Articles 9 to 11. Nevertheless, it asserted that the applicant's financial situation was one amongst several factors to be taken into account.[334] Given the long duration of the applicant's residence in the respondent State and his and his wife's social integration there, the Court found that the refusal to renew the applicant's residence permit amounted to a violation of his private and family life.[335]

Lastly, the prohibition of discrimination of Article 14 also plays a role in cases concerning the admission or deportation of non-nationals family members. Even if there is no obligation on a respondent state to allow family members to live together in its territory, the criteria governing admission and residence may not discriminate on the grounds of sex, ethnic origin or the status of being HIV-positive.[336] In the case of *Hode and Abdi*, the Court also found that no reasonable and objective justification had been advanced for distinguishing between applicants for family reunification depending on their residence status (refugees or labour migrants) and, for refugees, depending on whether the family had or had not already been formed in the country of origin.[337] This notwithstanding, the States Parties may legitimately differentiate in their immigration policies between non-nationals of different nationalities.[338] In *Abdulaziz, Cabales and Balkandali*, the Court also allowed more favourable rules for family reunification for persons with strong ties to the host state.[339] However, 20 years later, in the case of *Biao*, it made clear that such rules may not amount to indirect differential treatment of naturalised nationals on the grounds of their ethnic origin.[340]

c. Detention

The Court accepts that detention, despite being lawful for the purposes of Article 5, entails 'by its nature' limitations on the right to family life.[341] Such limitations do not automatically attract the protection of Article 8.[342] However, the Court also held that 'it is an essential part of a prisoner's right to respect for family life that the authorities enable him or, if need be, assist him in

---

[334] *Hasanbasic v. Switzerland, supra* n. 325, para. 59.

[335] *Ibid.*, para. 66.

[336] *Abdulaziz, Cabales and Balkandali v. the United Kingdom*, ECtHR (plen.) *supra* n. 309, para. 83; *Biao v. Denmark, supra* n. 323; *Novruk and Others v. Russia*, ECtHR 15 March 2016, appl. nos. 31039/11, 48511/11, 76810/12, 14618/13 and 13817/14.

[337] *Hode and Abdi v. the United Kingdom*, ECtHR 6 November 2012, appl. no. 22341/09, paras. 54–55.

[338] E.g. *Moustaquim v. Belgium, supra* n. 326, para. 49.

[339] *Abdulaziz, Cabales and Balkandali v. the United Kingdom*, ECtHR (plen.) *supra* n. 309, para. 88.

[340] *Biao v. Denmark, supra* n. 323, paras. 138–139.

[341] E.g. *Messina v. Italy (No. 2)*, ECtHR 28 September 2000, appl. no. 25498/94, para. 61.

[342] *Khodorkovskiy and Lebedev v. Russia*, ECtHR 25 July 2013, appl. nos. 11082/06 and 13772/05, para. 835.

maintaining contact with his close family'.[343] Accordingly, it has found that restrictions such as limitations on the number of family visits allowed, supervision being exercised over those visits or the subjection of detainees to special prison regimes or special visiting arrangements constitute interferences with the right to respect for family life which it will assess in the light of the criteria of the second paragraph of Article 8.[344]

For all practical purposes, family visits require some form of regulation (family members cannot walk in and out of the prison anytime of the day or night) and it is not clear where exactly the Court draws the line between visiting rules that are inherent to the fact of detention and those that interfere with the rights protected by Article 8. Nevertheless, the case law shows that, for example, the refusal of a family visit without any reasons being given constitutes an interference with the applicant's right to family life.[345] The same applies to the physical separation of family members during a visit, to the placement of a person in detention at great distance from the family's place of residence and to the refusal to allow telephone conversations between family members to take place in their preferred language (e.g. Kurdish).[346] In the case of *Varnas*, the Court left open whether the impossibility to receive conjugal visits constitutes an interference with Article 8, stating that the States Parties enjoy a wide margin of appreciation in this regard.[347] It confirmed, however, that the possibility of conjugal visits falls within the ambit of the right to family life, thus rendering applicable the prohibition of discrimination of Article 14 (see below).[348] In the *Dickson* judgment, the Grand Chamber decided that the refusal to grant a detainee access to artificial insemination facilities falls within the scope of the right to private and family life.[349]

As mentioned, the Court's approach in detention cases is normally to assess whether restrictions on the detainee's family life are in accordance with the criteria set out in the second paragraph of Article 8.[350] It has held on several occasions that such restrictions are not 'in accordance with the law' if the

---

[343] E.g. *Khoroshenko v. Russia*, ECtHR (GC) 30 June 2015, appl. no. 41418/04, para. 106.
[344] E.g. *Piechowicz v. Poland*, ECtHR 17 April 2012, appl. no. 20071/07, para. 212. See, however, *Khodorkovskiy and Lebedev v. Russia*, *supra* n. 342, para. 837, where the Court held that the state's duty to assist prisoners in maintaining effective contact with their families constitutes a positive obligation.
[345] *Kurkowski v. Poland*, ECtHR 9 April 2013, appl. no. 36228/06, para. 93.
[346] E.g. *ibid.*, para. 100; *Khodorkovskiy and Lebedev v. Russia*, *supra* n. 342, para. 838; *Nusret Kaya and Others v. Turkey*, ECtHR 22 April 2014, appl. nos. 43750/06, 43752/06, 32054/08, 37753/08 and 60915/08, para. 36.
[347] *Varnas v. Lithuania*, ECtHR 9 July 2013, appl. no. 42615/06, para. 109.
[348] *Ibid.*, para. 110.
[349] *Dickson v. the United Kingdom*, ECtHR (GC) 4 December 2007, appl. no. 44362/04, para. 66.
[350] See, however, the *Dickson* case, where the Grand Chamber confined its assessment to examining whether a fair balance had been struck between the public and private interests involved, *ibid.*, para. 71. Like in many other cases, the Grand Chamber decided to apply this 'fair balance' test after it had determined that in the situation at hand the State's positive and negative obligations could not be clearly separated (*ibid.*, para. 70).

relevant laws do not 'indicate with reasonable clarity the scope and manner of the exercise of any discretion conferred to the relevant authorities to restrict visiting rights'.[351] Meanwhile, the Court has accepted that restrictions on family visits may be necessary to prevent detainees from escaping or maintaining contacts with criminal organisations or armed movements (in the *Öcalan* case). These aims have been related to the protection of 'national security and public safety' and 'the prevention of disorder or crime'.[352] In *Khodorkovskiy and Lebedev*, the Court was also prepared to accept that overcrowded prisons may justify placing detainees further away from their families, in the interest of securing the rights and freedoms of others.[353]

The State Parties must, however, demonstrate the necessity of the interference. In the case of *Khoroshenko*, the Grand Chamber found the very strict regime imposed on the applicant (two short family visits per year for a period of 10 years) to be disproportionate, in view of the fact that it had been made very difficult for the applicant to maintain contact with his close family members and because of the regime's failure to consider the need for socail rehabilitation.[354] In the case of *Moiseyev*, a violation was found because the applicant had been denied physical contact with his family members for over three and a half years, in the absence of a demonstrated security risk.[355] By contrast, in *Messina (No. 2)* the Court accepted that the applicant's subjection to a special prison regime, with only two supervised family visits a month, was justified in view of the need to prevent his maintaining contacts with criminal organisations. In its reasoning, the Court took into account that family links played an important role within the Mafia.[356] It later specified, however, that this situation is to be distinguished from that where there is no actual likelihood of family members being involved in criminal activities or hindering criminal investigations. The States Parties may therefore need to differentiate between categories of detention so as to be able to take into account the circumstances of each prisoner's individual case.[357]

The Court has established that being in custody constitutes an 'other status' for the purpose of Article 14, and that persons placed in pre-trial detention and convicted prisoners find themselves in analogous situations for the purpose of receiving family visits.[358] In the cases of *Laduna* and *Varnas*, it found a violation of Articles 8 and 14 taken together on the grounds that the applicants, who were

---

[351] E.g. *Popenda v. Poland*, ECtHR 9 October 2012, appl. no. 39502/08, para. 72.
[352] *Öcalan v. Turkey (No. 2)*, ECtHR 18 March 2014, appl. nos. 24069/03, 197/04, 6201/06 and 10464/07, para. 160.
[353] *Khodorkovskiy and Lebedev v. Russia, supra* n. 342, para. 845.
[354] *Khoroshenko v. Russia, supra* n. 343, paras. 147–148.
[355] *Moiseyev v. Russia*, ECtHR 9 October 2008, appl. no. 62936/00, paras. 258–259.
[356] *Messina v. Italy (No. 2), supra* n. 341, paras. 66–74.
[357] *Varnas v. Lithuania, supra* n. 347, paras. 119–120.
[358] E.g. *Varnas v. Lithuania, supra* n. 347, paras. 111 and 113.

held in pre-trial detention, had been subject to farther-reaching restrictions on their family contacts than convicted prisoners, without those restrictions being based on a sufficient justification.[359]

3.5. ADOPTION

The right to family life, as defined by the Court, presupposes the existence of a family and does not include the right to adopt a child.[360] Once a family relationship is established, however, family ties between parents and their adopted children are protected in the same way as those between parents and biological children.[361] The Court has moreover accepted that Article 8 can be applicable to a relationship arising from a 'lawful and genuine' adoption even if the adoptive parents have not developed any close personal ties with the child.[362] This is considered as a form of 'intended family life' (see section 3.1).[363] In cases concerning adoption, the Court's interpretation of Article 8 is guided by international legal instruments including the Hague Convention on Protection of Children and Cooperation in respect of Intercountry adoption, the UN Convention on the Rights of the Child (CRC) and the European Convention on the Adoption of Children.[364]

The failure of a State Party to recognise an adoption lawfully enacted abroad constitutes an interference with the right to family life, which must meet the criteria of Article 8 second paragraph.[365] In the case of *Negrepontis-Giannisis*, where the applicant had already reached the age of majority when he was adopted and was not dependent on his adoptive father, the Court noted that the failure to recognise the adoption fell within the scope of the applicant's private and family life.[366] By contrast, the right to family life alone was considered to be at issue in the case of *Emonet and Others*, concerning an adult woman who lived with her mother and adoptive father and depended on their care.[367] In the latter case, the Court found that there had been an unjustified interference with Article 8 on account of the fact that the adoption of the daughter by her mother's partner had automatically resulted in the severance of the legal relationship with her mother.[368]

---

[359] *Laduna v. Slovakia*, ECtHR 13 December 2011, appl. no. 31827/02, para. 69; *Varnas v. Lithuania*, *supra* n. 347, para. 121.

[360] *Moretti and Benedetti v. Italy*, *supra* n. 228, para. 47.

[361] *Negrepontis-Giannisis v. Greece*, ECtHR 3 May 2011, appl. no. 56759/08, para. 55.

[362] *Pini and Others v. Romania*, ECtHR 22 June 2004, appl. nos. 78028/01 and 78030/01, para. 148.

[363] *Ibid.*, para. 143.

[364] E.g. *ibid.*, para. 139.

[365] E.g. *Negrepontis-Giannisis v. Greece*, *supra* n. 361, para. 60.

[366] *Ibid.*, para. 56.

[367] *Emonet and Others v. Switzerland*, *supra* n. 229, para. 37.

[368] *Ibid.*, paras. 86–88.

A somewhat different situation obtained in the case of *Harroudj* where the applicant, a French national, had obtained guardianship of an Algerian child through *kafala*, a legal figure under Islamic law.[369] The applicant sought to have the *kafala* converted into an adoption, which would allow the child to obtain French nationality and entitle her to the applicant's inheritance. French law did not, however, allow the conversion because adoption was prohibited under Algerian law. The Court, in balancing the competing interests, noted that the refusal to grant an adoption was based on a concern to respect international conventions, including the CRC. It also found that French law offered sufficient possibilities to regulate the child's nationality and inheritance in ways comparable to an adoption. Consequently the Court concluded that the French authorities had not failed to strike a fair balance between the public interest and that of the applicant.[370]

State actions to place an adopted child into care and decisions to revoke an adoption are assessed by the Court in the same way as cases involving the separation of children from their biological parents (see section 3.4(a) above).[371] Thus, the measures taken by the state authorities should be aimed at maintaining or rebuilding the unity of the family and ample weight should be attached to the best interests of the child, while the decision-making process should afford due respect to the interests of all persons involved. In the case of *Ageyevy*, the Court found that the Russian authorities had acted in conformity with Article 8 by removing two adopted children from their adoptive parents after one of them sustained injuries at home. However, the subsequent revocation of the adoption was held to be disproportionate and not in the children's interests.[372] By contrast, the case of *Pini and Others* concerned a situation where the adopted children had not yet been placed with their adoptive parents and the children themselves indicated that they were opposed to the enforcement of the adoption order. In its judgment, the Court reiterated that adoption means 'providing a child with a family, not a family with a child'.[373] While noting that it was 'regrettable' that the children had not received psychological support to prepare them for the adoption, which might have avoided the conflict of interests with their adoptive parents, the Court found that the Romanian authorities had been right to enforce the adoption against the children's will.[374]

States Parties which allow adoption by a single parent may not refuse permission for adoption because of the adoptive parent's homosexuality.[375] As regards partner adoptions (adoption by the person with whom one of the child's

---

[369]   *Harroudj v. France*, ECtHR 4 October 2012, appl. no. 43631/09.
[370]   *Ibid.*, paras. 49–51.
[371]   E.g. *Pini and Others v. Romania*, *supra* n. 362, para. 150; *Ageyevy v. Russia*, *supra* n. 213, para. 143.
[372]   *Ageyevy v. Russia*, *supra* n. 213, paras. 131–132 and 154–155.
[373]   *Pini and Others v. Romania*, *supra* n. 362, para. 156.
[374]   *Ibid.*, paras. 163–165.
[375]   *E.B. v. France*, *supra* n. 3, para. 96.

parents is in a relationship), the Court held in *Gas and Dubois* that states may reserve this possibility for married couples even if this means that same-sex couples are precluded from partner adoption.[376] Where, however, unmarried heterosexual couples have access to partner adoption the same should apply to unmarried same-sex couples.[377]

In the case of *Topčić-Rosenberg*, the Court found a violation of Article 8 read together with Article 14 in respect of the refusal of maternity leave to a mother who had adopted a child.[378] While the Croatian legislation did not exclude adoptive parents from maternity leave as such, it allowed parents to take leave only until the child's first birthday whereas the adoption had taken place when the child was already three years old. In the Court's view, the fact that maternity leave allows a mother to stay at home and look after the child meant that an adoptive mother was in a similar situation to a biological mother. In addition, it noted that states should not take measures which could prevent a child's integration in their adoptive family.[379] Lastly, the Court determined on several occasions that adopted children are entitled to the same legal treatment as any biological children of their parents in all respects, including the relations and consequences connected with their family life and the resulting property rights.[380]

4. THE HOME

4.1. INTRODUCTION

Article 8 guarantees the right to respect for the home. To determine the scope of the protection offered by this provision, it is again useful to distinguish between the question of what constitutes 'the home' '(section 4.2) and the question of which uses or activities relating to the home are protected. The Court has consistently held that searches conducted in the course of criminal investigations interfere with the right to respect for the home; the criteria developed in this respect are discussed in section 4.3. Section 4.4 concerns the right to be protected against evictions and forced removals, whereas section 4.5 discusses protection against nuisance and environmental pollution.

It is noted at the outset that Article 8 does not guarantee a right to a home or to housing of a particular standard.[381] Nevertheless, in its decision in *Marzari*

---

[376] *Gas and Dubois v. France, supra* n. 236, para. 68.
[377] *X. and Others v. Austria*, ECtHR (GC) 19 February 2013, appl. no. 19010/07, para. 153.
[378] *Topčić-Rosenberg v. Croatia*, ECtHR 14 November 2013, appl. no. 19391/11, para. 47.
[379] *Ibid.*, para. 42.
[380] E.g. *Pla and Puncernau v. Andorra*, ECtHR 13 July 2004, appl. no. 69498/01, para. 61; *Negrepontis-Giannisis v. Greece, supra* n. 361, para. 82.
[381] *Chapman v. the United Kingdom*, ECtHR (GC) 18 January 2001, appl. no. 27238/95, para. 99; *Bah v. the United Kingdom*, ECtHR 27 September 2009, appl. no. 56328/07, para. 40.

the Court accepted that Article 8 may come into play if a State Party fails to meet the special housing needs of persons who are ill or disabled. In this case Article 8 was held to be relevant in particular because of the effects on the applicant's private life (see also *supra* section 2.6(c)).[382] In the judgment in *Moldovan and Others (No. 2)*, the Court moreover found a violation of Articles 3 and 8 because the State Party had done very little to put an end to the dismal circumstances in which the applicants were forced to live after their houses had been destroyed in a raid involving local police officers.[383]

4.2. DEFINITION

The Court has established that 'the home' constitutes an autonomous concept under the Convention which does not depend on the classification used in domestic law. It is not limited to 'premises which are lawfully occupied or which have been lawfully established'. Instead, the question of whether particular premises constitute a 'home' is determined by the Court on the basis of factual circumstances, in particular 'the existence of sufficient and continuous links with a specific place'.[384] Another relevant factor is whether there is any other place which could qualify as the applicant's home.[385] As a result of the Court's approach, applicants are able to rely on Article 8 also in situations where their right to live in a particular house or place is contested. Article 8 moreover applies to tenants as well as to house owners.

An example of the Court's approach can be found in the case of *Winterstein and Others*, where the applicants were travellers who had lived on a plot of land for five to 30 years. The French authorities contested the lawfulness of the applicants' occupation of the land and had ordered them to move elsewhere. For the Court, the question of whether the land had been lawfully occupied was irrelevant because 'the applicants had sufficiently close and continuous links with the caravans, cabins and bungalows on the land occupied by them for this to be considered their "home"'.[386] A different example is the case of *McCann*, where the applicant continued to live in a flat after his former wife, who was the official tenant, had terminated the rental contract. The Court nevertheless found that the flat qualified as the applicant's home within the meaning of Article 8.[387]

The notion of the home moreover covers business premises as well as private homes. This was decided by the Court in the *Niemietz* case where it held that 'it

---

[382] *Marzari v. Italy*, ECtHR 4 May 1999 (dec.), appl. no. 36448/97.

[383] *Moldovan and Others v. Romania (No. 2)*, ECtHR 12 July 2005, appl. no. 41138/98, paras. 103–114.

[384] E.g. *Brežec v. Croatia*, ECtHR 18 July 2013, appl. no. 7177/10, para. 35.

[385] E.g. *Prokopovitch v. Russia*, ECtHR 18 November 2004, appl. no. 58255/00, para. 38.

[386] *Winterstein and Others v. France*, ECtHR 17 October 2013, appl. no. 27013/07, para. 69.

[387] *McCann v. the United Kingdom*, ECtHR 13 May 2008, appl. no. 19009/04, para. 46.

may not always be possible to draw precise distinctions, since activities which are related to a profession or business may well be conducted from a person's private residence and activities which are not so related may well be carried on in an office or commercial premises.'[388]

The Court also considered that this broad interpretation of the home was consonant with the essential object and purpose of Article 8, to protect the individual against arbitrary interference by the public authorities.[389] Whereas the *Niemietz* case concerned the search of a lawyer's office, the Court has also accepted that a company's business premises fall under the definition of a home. Moreover, where a company's premises are concerned the company itself as a legal person can rely on Article 8 in addition to natural persons.[390]

4.3. SEARCHES

Searches conducted by a state's authorities in the course of a criminal or other investigation constitute an interference with the right to respect for the home.[391] In some cases, searches are found to interfere with the applicants' private life as well.[392] In the case of *Saint-Paul Luxembourg S.A.*, the Court clarified that there had been an interference despite the fact that the applicant had co-operated with the authorities conducting the search. It considered that the authorities had a warrant which they were entitled to execute with or without the applicant's permission; the latter's co-operation therefore did not deprive the search of its intrusive character.[393]

Article 8 requires searches to be conducted in accordance with the law and to be necessary in a democratic society in the interests of at least one of the legitimate aims mentioned in the second paragraph. The Court has accepted that searches may be necessary for the prevention of disorder or crime or for the protection of the rights of others.[394] The relevant legislation and practice must, however, provide 'adequate and effective safeguards against abuse'. In the Court's view, very strict limits on the power to conduct searches are called for to prevent arbitrary interferences with individuals' rights under Article 8. While it is not required that searches are always based on a judicial warrant, the Court has indicated that it will exercise 'particular vigilance' where such a warrant is not needed under domestic law.[395] Generally worded legal provisions cannot serve

---

[388]   *Niemietz v. Germany, supra* n. 1, para. 30.

[389]   *Ibid.*, para. 31.

[390]   E.g. *Saint-Paul Luxembourg S.A. v. Luxemburg*, ECtHR 18 April 2013, appl. no. 26419/10, para. 37.

[391]   E.g. *Vasylchuk v. Ukraine*, ECtHR 13 June 2013, appl. no. 24402/07, para. 77.

[392]   E.g. *Niemietz v. Germany, supra* n. 1, para. 29.

[393]   *Saint-Paul Luxembourg S.A. v. Luxemburg, supra* n. 390, paras. 38–39.

[394]   E.g. *Vasylchuk v. Ukraine, supra* n. 391, para. 78; *Niemietz v. Germany, supra* n. 1, para. 36.

[395]   *Camenzind v. Switzerland*, ECtHR 16 December 1997, appl. no. 21353/93, para. 45.

as a sufficient legal basis for searches in the absence of any individual decision indicating the purpose and scope of the search.[396]

A search will be in violation of Article 8 if the investigation could have been pursued by less intrusive measures.[397] In assessing the proportionality of a search the Court furthermore has regard to a number of criteria, including the severity of the offence in respect of which the search is conducted; the manner and circumstances in which the search order is issued, in particular further evidence available at that time; the content and scope of the order, with particular regard to the nature of the premises searched and the safeguards taken to confine the impact of the search measure and the possible repercussions on the reputation of the person affected by the search.[398] Also relevant is the manner in which the search is conducted: in the case of *Vasylchuk*, the Court concluded that the search carried out by the police had been disproportionate as the applicant's house had been left in a complete mess and some items of furniture had been broken.[399]

4.4. EVICTION AND FORCED REMOVALS

The right to respect for the home also offers protection against the loss of one's home as a result of eviction, forced removal or even destruction of the home. For example, in the case of *Cyprus v. Turkey*, the Grand Chamber found that the Turkish authorities had violated Article 8 by refusing to allow Greek-Cypriot displaced persons to return to their homes in northern Cyprus.[400] In *Akdivar and Others*, a violation was found on account of the deliberate burning of the applicants' houses in the course of conflicts between the Turkish security forces and the PKK.[401] Other situations brought before the Court include the eviction of tenants from rented flats and the forced removal of applicants from unauthorised settlements.[402]

As regards eviction orders, the Court has repeatedly confirmed that the issue of an eviction order constitutes an interference with Article 8, even if the order has not yet been executed or the applicants have subsequently left the home of their own motion.[403] In the case of *Yordanova and Others*, however, the Court did not

---

[396]   *Kilyen v. Romania*, ECtHR 25 February 2014, appl. no. 44817/04, para. 37.

[397]   *Saint-Paul Luxembourg S.A. v. Luxemburg, supra* n. 390, para. 44.

[398]   *Buck v. Germany*, ECtHR 28 April 2005, appl. no. 41604/98, para. 45.

[399]   *Vasylchuk v. Ukraine, supra* n. 391, paras. 79–85.

[400]   *Cyprus v. Turkey*, ECtHR (GC) 10 May 2001, appl. no. 25781/94, para. 175. For a more recent case, see *Chiragov and Others v. Armenia*, ECtHR (GC) 16 June 2015, appl. no. 13216/05, paras. 206–208.

[401]   *Akdivar and Others v. Turkey*, ECtHR (GC) 16 September 1996, appl. no. 21893/93, para. 88.

[402]   E.g. *Yordanova and Others v. Bulgaria*, ECtHR 24 April 2012, appl. no. 25446/06; *Pelipenko v. Russia*, ECtHR 2 October 2012, appl. no. 69037/10.

[403]   E.g. *Ćosić v. Croatia*, ECtHR 15 January 2009, appl. no. 28261/06, para. 18; *Brežec v. Croatia, supra* n. 384, para. 40.

label the removal order issued against the applicants as an interference but stated that a violation of Article 8 would occur if the order were to be enforced.[404] It appears from the judgment in *Brežec* that Article 8 also applies to eviction orders sought by private parties. In this case, the Court did not discuss the position of the flat owner, a private hotel enterprise partly owned by the state.[405]

The Court has dealt on several occasions with cases concerning the eviction or removal of travellers. It recognised that, whether or not a nomadic lifestyle is maintained, the occupation of a caravan is 'an integral part of the identity of travellers'. Measures affecting the possibility for travellers to station their caravans therefore affect not only the right to respect for the home but also the right to private and family life.[406]

The Court has accepted that the eviction of tenants or reclaiming unlawfully occupied land may serve legitimate aims, including the pursuit of urban development and planning policies, the prevention of health and safety hazards and the protection of the rights of house or land owners.[407] It also repeatedly noted that in principle the States Parties have a wide margin of appreciation in the area of housing and planning policy, although this margin will be narrowed where 'the right at stake is crucial to the individual's effective enjoyment of intimate or key rights'.[408]

The Court stated on several occasions that 'the loss of one's home is a most extreme form of interference with the right to respect for the home'.[409] The case law shows that particular emphasis is placed on the availability of procedural safeguards. In the Court's view, respect for the right to the home implies that the proportionality and reasonableness of an eviction or removal must be assessed by an impartial tribunal. This does not have to happen automatically: it is up to the applicant to raise the claim that his or her rights under Article 8 are not adequately protected.[410] The type of proceedings followed is also relevant for the question whether the proportionality of the eviction has been adequately assessed: in the case of *Bjedov* the Court found that the enforcement proceedings instituted against the applicant were 'not properly equipped with procedural tools and safeguards for the thorough and adversarial examination of such complex legal issues'. Instead, it found that the proportionality should have been assessed by the civil court which granted the eviction order.[411]

It appears from the case law that substantive factors to be taken into account in a proportionality assessment at the national level include the length of time

---

404   *Yordanova and Others v. Bulgaria, supra* n. 402, para. 144.
405   *Brežec v. Croatia, supra* n. 384.
406   E.g. *Winterstein and Others v. France, supra* n. 386, para. 70.
407   E.g. *Connors v. the United Kingdom*, ECtHR 27 May 2004, appl. no. 66746/01, para. 69; *Yordanova and Others v. Bulgaria, supra* n. 402, paras. 111–116.
408   E.g. *Connors v. the United Kingdom, supra* n. 407, para. 82.
409   E.g. *Ćosić v. Croatia, supra* n. 403, para. 22.
410   E.g. *Brežec v. Croatia, supra* n. 384.
411   *Bjedov v. Croatia*, ECtHR 29 May 2012, appl. no. 42150/09, para. 71.

during which the applicant lived in the home, whether eviction could have been sought sooner and the availability of alternative accommodation.[412] In addition, the respondent state will need to substantiate the necessity of the eviction in view of the aim pursued (e.g. the protection of property rights). Where such necessity is not demonstrated, the Court will let the applicant's right to respect for the home prevail over the state's interest.[413] In the judgment in *Yordanova and Others*, concerning a removal order issued against the residents of an unauthorised Roma settlement, the Court also put great emphasis on the fact that the applicants belonged to 'an outcast community' and a disadvantaged social group. This should have been taken into account by the Bulgarian authorities when a solution for the unlawful settlement was sought.[414]

4.5. PROTECTION AGAINST NUISANCE

Article 8 not only offers protection against physical breaches of the home, such as searches or evictions, but also against intangible forms of nuisance which affect the activity of living in one's home. In the words of the Court: 'A home will usually be a place, a physically defined area, where private and family life goes on. The individual has a right to respect for his home, meaning not just the right to the actual physical area, but also to the quiet enjoyment of that area. Breaches of the right to respect for the home are not confined to concrete or physical breaches, such as unauthorised entry into a person's home, but also include those that are not concrete or physical, such as noise, emissions, smells or other forms of interference.'[415]

It follows that Article 8 may be relevant to situations of environmental pollution in the broad sense, including noise pollution. This does not mean, however, that the right to respect for the home comprises a general right to environmental protection. This was specified in the case of *Kyrtatos*, where the applicants complained about the destruction of a swamp nearby their property. The Court stated that the applicability of Article 8 is determined by 'the existence of a harmful effect on a person's private or family sphere and not simply the general deterioration of the environment'.[416]

To fall within the scope of Article 8 the alleged environmental pollution must attain a minimum level of severity. The assessment conducted in this respect by the Court is relative and depends on all the circumstances of the case, including the intensity and duration of the nuisance and its physical or

---

[412]   E.g. *Yordanova and Others v. Bulgaria*, supra n. 402, paras. 121–127; *Bjedov v. Croatia*, supra n. 411, paras. 68–69; *Brežec v. Croatia*, supra n. 384, paras. 47–50.

[413]   E.g. *Bjedov v. Croatia*, supra n. 411 para. 70.

[414]   *Yordanova and Others v. Bulgaria*, supra n. 402, paras. 128–133.

[415]   E.g. *Udovičić v. Croatia*, ECtHR 24 April 2014, appl. no. 27310/09, para. 136.

[416]   *Kyrtatos v. Greece*, ECtHR 22 May 2003, appl. no. 41666/98, para. 52.

mental effects.[417] In the *Hatton and Others* judgment, the Grand Chamber found that the noise generated by aircraft from Heathrow airport was susceptible to adversely affecting the applicants' rights under Article 8.[418] Other forms of nuisance which have been found to come within the scope of Article 8 include noise from bars or nightclubs or from a train station,[419] smells, noise and fumes from a waste-treatment plant,[420] toxic emissions from a fertiliser factory[421] and environmental pollution resulting from the use of cyanide in a nearby goldmine.[422] The existence of sufficiently severe effects does not presuppose that there must be serious risks for the applicants' health.[423] The standard of proof applied by the Court is that the adverse effects on the applicants' rights must be established 'beyond reasonable doubt'. Such proof may, however, follow from 'the coexistence of sufficiently, strong, clear and concordant inferences or of similar unrebutted presumptions of fact, and it has been the Court's practice to allow flexibility in that respect, taking into consideration the nature of the substantive right at stake and any evidentiary difficulties involved.'[424]

The right to be protected against nuisance is applicable to nuisance caused directly by the State Party's authorities as well as to the failure of those authorities to adequately regulate the actions of private parties. In this regard the Court has consistently held that, whether the case is analysed in terms of a positive or a negative obligation, the applicable principles are broadly similar. In both cases a fair balance must be struck between the interests of the individual and those of the community as a whole, whereby the aims mentioned in the second paragraph of Article 8 'may be of a certain relevance'.[425] The assessment conducted by the Court moreover includes both the questions of whether the nuisance suffered by applicants is compatible with the rights protected by Article 8 and whether the decision-making process has been such as to accord due weight to the applicants' interests.[426]

The Court in principle grants a wide margin of appreciation to the States Parties to balance the various interests involved in environmental cases.[427] However, where a State Party adopts regulations to ensure protection against nuisance it will have to also ensure effective enforcement of those regulations

---

417   *Oluić v. Croatia*, ECtHR 20 May 2010, appl. no. 61260/08, para. 49.
418   *Hatton and Others v. the United Kingdom*, ECtHR (GC) 8 July 2003, appl. no. 36022/97, para. 118.
419   E.g. *Moreno Gómez v. Spain*, ECtHR 16 November 2004, appl. no. 4143/02, para. 60; *Bor v. Hungary*, ECtHR 18 June 2013, appl. no. 50474/08, para. 26; *Udovičić v. Croatia*, *supra* n. 415, para. 62.
420   *López Ostra v. Spain*, ECtHR 9 December 1994, appl. no. 16978/90, para. 51.
421   *Guerra and Others v. Italy*, ECtHR (GC) 19 February 1998, appl. no. 14967/89, para. 57.
422   *Taşkin and Others v. Turkey*, ECtHR 10 November 2004, appl. no. 46117/99, para. 113.
423   *Ibid.*, para. 113.
424   E.g. *Ivan Atanasov v. Bulgaria*, ECtHR 2 December 2010, appl. no. 12853/03, para. 75.
425   E.g. *Hatton and Others v. the United Kingdom*, *supra* n. 418, para. 98.
426   E.g. *Hatton and Others v. the United Kingdom*, *supra* n. 418, para. 99.
427   E.g. *Taşkin and Others v. Turkey*, *supra* n. 422, para. 116.

to avoid a violation of Article 8.[428] The Court has also repeatedly found violations of the rights protected by Article 8 on the grounds that insufficient procedural guarantees had been available. In the case of *Taşkin and Others*, the Court stated that decision-making processes concerning complex issues of environmental and economic policy should involve appropriate investigations and studies to enable the prediction and evaluation of activities which might infringe individuals' rights and stressed the importance of public access to the information obtained. It also asserted that individuals must have access to a legal remedy before a court if they consider that their interests have been granted insufficient weight.[429] In the case of *Udovičić*, a violation was found on the grounds that none of the legal remedies available to the applicant had been effective.[430] In the case of *Bor*, the Court equally found that the respondent State had not fulfilled its positive obligations under Article 8: although a solution had eventually been found for the noise disturbance suffered by the applicant, it had taken the authorities almost 16 years to do so which the Court considered to be excessive.[431]

5. CORRESPONDENCE

To finish, Article 8 guarantees the right to respect for one's correspondence. The term 'correspondence' has been interpreted by the ECtHR so as to include modern techniques of communication, such as the use of e-mail and Internet.[432] It moreover includes correspondence in professional relationships, for example between lawyers and their clients.[433] The right to respect for correspondence offers protection against the interception and monitoring of correspondence by public authorities without the permission of the person concerned.[434] Interferences with this right often occur in the context of criminal investigations. Where secret surveillance methods are used, the right to private life is often also at stake (see *supra* section 2.1(a)).

The right to respect for one's correspondence is of particularly significance for detainees, for whom letters, e-mail and telephone calls form important means of maintaining contacts without the outside world and providers of legal aid. The same applies to persons who have been forcibly admitted to a psychiatric clinic

---

[428] E.g. *Moreno Gómez v. Spain*, ECtHR 16 November 2004, *supra* n. 419, para. 61.
[429] *Taşkin and Others v. Turkey*, *supra* n. 422, para. 119.
[430] *Udovičić v. Croatia*, *supra* n. 415, para. 159.
[431] *Bor v. Hungary*, ECtHR 18 June 2013, appl. no. 50474/08, para. 28.
[432] E.g. *Copland v. the United Kingdom*, *supra* n. 21, para. 41.
[433] *Niemietz v. Germany*, *supra* n. 1, para. 32.
[434] E.g. *Foxley v. the United Kingdom*, ECtHR 20 June 2000, appl. no. 33274/96, para. 30.

and to minors placed in closed boarding schools.[435] In the case of *Golder*, the applicant wished to submit a complaint against the staff of the prison where he was held but was prevented from contacting his lawyer. The Court found a violation of Article 8.[436] Similarly, in the judgment in *Schönenberger and Durmaz*, a violation was found on account of the fact that the letter sent by a lawyer to a potential client was stopped by the public prosecutor.[437] Detainees suffering from serious illnesses must also be able to correspond with medical specialists without restrictions such as checks by the prison's medical personnel.[438]

It is not the case, however, that Article 8 prohibits the monitoring of detainees' correspondence by prison authorities altogether. The Court has accepted that it may be necessary to monitor the contacts of detainees with the outside world. Such monitoring must, nevertheless, be based on rules that are 'sufficiently clear and detailed to afford appropriate protection against arbitrary interference' with the rights to private life and correspondence.[439] Interferences must moreover be necessary in view of the aim pursued. In the case of *Buglov*, for example, the Court failed to see how the prison authorities' monitoring of the applicant's correspondence with the Court itself was necessary to prevent obstruction of the course of justice.[440] In the same judgment the Court found that it had been disproportionate to place the applicant in a disciplinary cell for bypassing the prison administration when sending a complaint about his detention conditions.[441]

---

[435] E.g. *Koroviny v. Russia*, ECtHR 27 February 2014, appl. no. 31974/11; *D.L. v. Bulgaria*, ECtHR 19 May 2016, appl. no. 7472/14.

[436] *Golder v. the United Kingdom*, ECtHR (GC) 21 February 1975, appl. no. 4451/70, paras. 43–45.

[437] *Schönenberger and Durmaz v. Switzerland*, ECtHR 20 June 1988, appl. no. 11368/85, paras. 24–30.

[438] *Szuluk v. the United Kingdom*, ECtHR 2 June 2009, appl. no. 36936/05, para. 53.

[439] E.g. *Doerga v. the Netherlands*, ECtHR 27 April 2004, appl. no. 50210/99, para. 53.

[440] *Buglov v. Ukraine*, ECtHR 10 July 2014, appl. no. 28825/02, para. 130.

[441] *Ibid.*, para. 132.

CHAPTER 13

FREEDOM OF THOUGHT, CONSCIENCE AND RELIGION

(Article 9)

Ben Vermeulen and Marjolein van Roosmalen[*]

GUIDING PRINCIPLE

The freedom of thought, conscience and religion enshrined in Article 9 of the Convention is one of the foundations of a democratic society. It not only protects individuals but also groups and collectivities. In recent years the number of 'big' issues has grown significantly, regarding especially the multicultural and church and state aspects of this freedom.

ARTICLE 9

1. Everyone has the right to freedom of thought, conscience and religion; this right includes freedom to change his religion or belief and freedom, either alone or in community with others and in public or private, to manifest his religion or belief, in worship, teaching, practice and observance.
2. Freedom to manifest one's religion or belief shall be subject only to such limitations as are prescribed by law and are necessary in a democratic society in the interests of public safety, for the protection of public order, health or morals, or for the protection of the rights and freedoms of others.

---

[*]   In the fourth edition this chapter was revised and updated by Ben Vermeulen.

CONTENTS

1. INTRODUCTION

As the Court has stated in *Kokkinakis* and later judgments, the freedom of thought, conscience and religion enshrined in Article 9 of the Convention is one of the foundations of a democratic society. This freedom is, in its religious dimension, one of the most vital elements that go to make up the identity of believers and their conception of life, but it is also a precious asset for atheists, agnostics, sceptics and the unconcerned. The pluralism indissociable from a democratic society, which has been dearly won over the centuries, depends on it.[1]

The *internal* freedom of thought, conscience and religion – which also includes the right to have and to change one's religion or belief – is guaranteed in Article 9(1) of the Convention without qualification: it is absolute and unconditional. Restrictions are allowed only as to the *external manifestations* of thought, conscience and religion.[2]

Article 9 of the Convention protects the *external manifestations* of religion and belief, expressed through worship, teaching, practice and observance. This right to manifest one's religion or belief is circumscribed in two ways. First, not all opinions, ideas or convictions constitute a religion or belief in the sense protected by Article 9.[3] Religion and belief only denote views that attain a certain level of cogency, seriousness, cohesion and importance.[4] Second,

---

[1] *Kokkinakis v. Greece*, ECtHR 25 May 1993, appl. no. 14307/88, para. 31; *Buscarini and Others v. San Marino*, ECtHR (GC) 18 February, appl. no. 24645/94, para. 34; *S.A.S. v. France*, ECtHR (GC) 1 July 2014, appl. no. 43835/11, para. 124.

[2] *Kokkinakis v. Greece*, supra n. 1, para. 33.

[3] *Pretty v. the United Kingdom*, ECtHR 29 April 2002, appl. no. 2346/02, para. 82.

[4] *Campbell and Cosans v. the United Kingdom*, ECtHR 25 February 1982, appl. no. 7511/76, 7743/76, para. 36.

not every action or omission which is subjectively motivated by a religious conviction or belief may 'count' as a manifestation of religion or belief that falls within the scope of Article 9. Insofar as acts do not directly express the religion or belief concerned[5] or are only remotely connected to a precept of faith, they fall outside the protection of Article 9. In order to qualify as a 'manifestation' within the meaning of this provision the act in question must be intimately linked to a religion or belief.[6]

Article 9 covers actions and omissions irrespective of whether they are individual or collective, whether manifested 'alone or in community with others'. Whereas the inner freedom of thought, conscience and religion only pertains to individual persons,[7] the right to manifest a religion or belief can also be invoked by collectivities – groups, legal persons, churches. Were this collective element – the organisational life of religious or belief communities – not protected by Article 9 of the Convention, all other aspects of the individual's freedom of religion or belief would become vulnerable.[8]

The protection of the freedom to manifest a religion or belief is not absolute and unconditional, because such manifestations may have an impact on others and on society. In order to strike a balance Article 9(2) qualifies this freedom, and allows it to be restricted by law if the restriction is necessary in a democratic society in the interests of public safety, for the protection of public order, health or morals, or for the protection of the rights and freedoms of others.

In principle, there is no interference with the rights under Article 9 when an impediment is the consequence of general legislation which applies on a neutral basis without any specific link to the applicant's belief.[9] For instance, tax legislation applies neutrally and generally in the public sphere, and for that reason conscientious objections against that legislation do not fall within the scope of Article 9.[10]

If there is a restriction of the freedom of religion or belief in Article 9(1), Article 9(2) requires that it is provided for by law, and serves a legitimate aim. The main test, however, is whether the restriction is necessary – that it is proportionate to the aim strived after. The Court, when applying the proportionality test, leaves the state a margin of appreciation. When solely the individual freedom of religion or belief is concerned, the margin is often rather limited. But when the relation between religious communities and other

---

[5]   *Arrowsmith v. the United Kingdom*, EComHR 12 October 1978 (rep.), appl. no. 7050/75, para. 71.

[6]   *Eweida and Others v. the United Kingdom*, ECtHR 15 January 2013, appl. nos. 48420/10, 59842/10, 6167/10 and 36516/10, para. 82.

[7]   *Soukroma v. Czech Republic*, ECtHR 22 November 2011, appl. no. 8314/10.

[8]   *Hasan and Chaush v. Bulgaria*, ECtHR (GC) 26 October 2000, appl. no. 30985/96, para. 62.

[9]   *Tamar Skugar and Others v. Russia*, ECtHR 3 December 2009, appl. no. 40010/04.

[10] *C. v. the United Kingdom*, EComHR 15 December 1983 (dec.), appl. no. 10358/83; *Tamar Skugar and Others v. Russia*, supra n. 9.

organisations (e.g. schools) on the one hand and the state on the other hand also is involved, the latter often enjoys a rather wide margin of appreciation.[11] For instance, Article 9 (in itself as well as read in conjunction with the non-discrimination norm of Article 14) does not postulate a specific model of church-state relations, and allows for different models: a church state system, a secular state or a cooperationist arrangement that lies in between.[12]

For a long time the freedom of religion and belief, protected by Article 9 of the Convention, was not very contentious: it was a safe and secure right, which did not give rise to many cases or conflicts. But in the past 25 years, starting with *Kokkinakis*, the number of 'big' issues that the Court dealt with has grown constantly. The Court has developed a substantial and rich case law, dealing with highly sensitive issues having great social and political impact. This development of case law is reflected in this commentary.

2. THE (INNER) FREEDOM OF THOUGHT, CONSCIENCE AND RELIGION

The inviolability of the *forum internum* – the internal freedom of thought, conscience and religion, which also includes the right to have and to change one's religion or belief – is guaranteed in Article 9(1) of the Convention without qualification: it is absolute and unconditional. Restrictions are allowed only with regard to the *external expressions* of thought, conscience and religion, *viz.* in pursuance of the second paragraph of Article 9 with respect to the *manifestation* of religious and other beliefs.[13]

This *internal* freedom, protecting thoughts, conscience and belief, is not without practical importance. It is true that thoughts, conscientious convictions and religious or non-religious beliefs – as long as they have not been expressed – are intangible and only realise their full potential by their expression in *foro externo*. But that does not render the protection of the *forum internum* useless. This protection guarantees that the state may never interfere in this most intimate and inner sphere, for instance by dictating what a person has to believe, by taking coercive steps to make him change his beliefs[14] ('brain-washing' etc.), or by using inquisitorial methods to discover what his personal thoughts and convictions are.[15] It prohibits any form of compulsion to express thoughts or to divulge a religious or

---

11 *Cha'are Shalom Ve Tsedek v. France*, ECtHR (GC) 27 June 2000, appl. no. 27417/95, para. 84.
12 See 4.3.
13 *Kokkinakis v. Greece, supra* n. 1, para. 33; *Ivanova v. Bulgaria*, ECtHR 12 April 2007, appl. no. 52435/99, para. 79; *Tarhan v. Tukey*, ECtHR 17 July 2012, appl. no. 9078/06, para. 52; *Eweida and Others v. the United Kingdom, supra* n. 6, para. 80.
14 *Ivanova v. Bulgaria, supra* n. 13, para. 79.
15 The fathers of the Convention intended the freedom of thought, conscience and religion to protect the individual against 'ces abominables moyens d'enquête policière ou d'instruction

non-religious conviction, and dictates that no sanction may be imposed either on the holding of a view or on the change of a religion or conviction: it protects against religious indoctrination by the state.[16] It is remarkable that this basic guarantee against such state coercion, indoctrination and inquisition is not included as a non-derogable right in Article 15(2) of the Convention. However, this probably is a theoretical issue: it will be extremely difficult to argue that interfering in this right even in case of emergency is 'strictly required by the exigencies of the situation' in the sense of Article 15(1) of the Convention.

The prohibition of indoctrination is particularly relevant in the sphere of education. This prohibition also follows from Article 2 of Protocol No. 1, which may be regarded as a *lex specialis*, further developing the values of Article 9 for the sphere of education.[17] The Court allows the state discretion in the setting and planning of the curriculum. In general, the subjective views of parents are not decisive in determining whether the content and method of instruction is in line with their religious or philosophical convictions as protected by Article 2 of Protocol No. 1 and Article 9. These provisions will only be violated if the transmission of ideas and knowledge does not take place in an objective, critical and pluralistic way, that is only when it assumes the character of indoctrination. For instance, the Court has ruled that a course of sex education, because of its general and neutral character, did not amount to indoctrination.[18] The obligation to take part in a school parade without military overtones was not such as to offend the parent's religious convictions, and therefore did not constitute an interference with the right to freedom of religion.[19] Ethics classes that did not give emphasis to the Christian religion but made room for different beliefs and convictions were held to be sufficiently neutral.[20] And in *Lautsi* the Court concluded that the mere presence of the Christian crucifix in state schools did not amount to indoctrination and proselytising.[21]

The inner freedom of thought, conscience and religion, including the right to have and to change one's religion or belief, cannot be restricted. This freedom also includes the right *not* to have a religion or belief: 'it is also a precious asset

---

judiciaire qui privent le suspect ou l'inculpé du contrôle de ses facultées intellectuelles et de sa conscience' (*Recueil des 'Travaux Préparatoires'*, Vol. I, The Hague, 1975, p. 223).

[16]   *Angeleni v. Sweden*, EComHR 3 December 1986 (dec.), appl. no. 10491/83; *C.J., J.J. and E.J. v. Poland*, EComHR 16 January 1996 (dec.), appl. no. 23380/94.

[17]   *Lautsi and Others v. Italy*, ECtHR (GC) 18 March 2011, appl. no. 30814/06, para. 59; *Osmanoğlu and Kocabaş v. Switzerland*, ECtHR 10 January 2017, appl. no. 29086/12, para. 90. For further details, see Chapter 18 section 5.1 (Art. 2 of Protocol No. 1; Parental rights; Scope).

[18]   *Kjeldsen, Busk Madsen and Pedersen v. Denmark*, ECtHR 7 December 1976, appl. nos. 5095/71, 5920/72 and 5926/72, paras. 63–64. See also *Willi, Anna and David Dojan v. Germany*, ECtHR 13 September 2011 (dec.), appl. no. 319/08.

[19]   *Valsamis v. Greece*, ECtHR 18 December 1996, appl. no. 21787/93, paras. 34–38; *Efstratiou v. Greece*, ECtHR 18 December 1996, appl. no. 24095/94, paras. 35–39.

[20]   *Appel-Irrgang and Others v. Germany*, ECtHR 6 October 2009 (dec.), appl. no. 45216/07.

[21]   *Lautsi and Others v. Italy*, *supra* n.17, paras. 71–74.

for atheists, agnostics, sceptics and the unconcerned.'[22] Moreover, it also implies that the state is in principle not allowed to interfere in the individuals' freedom of conscience by asking him to reveal his religious beliefs or to force him to manifest these beliefs[23]; nor is it allowed to oblige an individual to act in a way that implies commitment to a church, religion or belief he actually does not have.[24]

In *Alexandridis*, the Court appears to assume that such interferences violate the *forum internum*, and therefore by definition are prohibited.[25] However, in general the Court rules that what is at stake here is a negative aspect of the *freedom to manifest* one's religion or belief, the right not to be obliged to reveal one's religion or belief or to behave in a way which would reveal that conviction, which might be restricted if justified under Article 9(2). But, in general, a restriction will not be justified. For instance, in *Buscarini* and *Dimitras* the Court apparently held that there was a restriction of the freedom to manifest (or not) one's religion or belief, which was disproportionate in the light of Article 9(2) of the Convention and thus violated Article 9.[26] And in *Grzelak* the Court held that the absence of a mark for religion/ethics classes would be understood as an indication that the student was a person without religious beliefs, which in that case amounted to an unjustified difference in treatment, incompatible with Article 14 taken in conjunction with Article 9.[27] However, in *Wasmuth* it was found that a mark on a person's income tax card, indicating that he was not a member of one of the churches or religious organisations for which the State levied a church tax, was a proportionate interference.[28]

It seems that the Commission has deduced from Article 9 the right to have one's religion or belief correctly registered by the authorities. It considered that the complaint that the municipal authorities refused to issue him with a certificate indicating the person's religion fell under the scope of Article 9.[29] And in the *Sinan Işik* case the Court found that the denial of the applicant's request to have the indication 'Islam' on his identity card replaced by the

---

[22] *Kokkinakis v. Greece, supra* n. 1, para. 31; *Buscarini and Others v. San Marino, supra* n. 1, para. 34; *Metropolitan Church of Bessarabia and Others v. Moldova*, ECtHR 13 December 2001, appl. nos. 45701/99 and 45701/99, para. 114.

[23] *Alexandridis v. Greece*, ECtHR 21 February 2008, appl. no. 19516/06, para. 38; *Dimitras and Others v. Greece*, ECtHR 3 June 2010, appl. nos. 42837/06, 3237/07, 3269/07, 35793/07 and 6099/08, para. 78; *Grzelak v. Poland*, ECtHR 15 June 2010, appl. no. 7710/02, para. 87.

[24] *Buscarini and Others v. San Marino, supra* n. 1, para. 39: requiring Members of Parliament to take the oath on the Gospels amounts to requiring 'elected representatives of the people to swear allegiance to a particular religion, a requirement which is not compatible with Article 9'.

[25] *Alexandridis v. Greece, supra* n. 23, paras. 38–41.

[26] *Buscarini and Others v. San Marino, supra* n. 1, paras. 39–40; *Dimitras and Others v. Greece, supra* n. 23, para. 88.

[27] *Grzelak v. Poland, supra* n. 23, paras. 99–101.

[28] *Wasmuth v. Germany*, ECtHR 17 February 2011, appl. no. 12884/03, paras. 58–64.

[29] *H. v. Greece*, EComHR 8 April 1991 (dec.), appl. no. 16319/90.

indication of his faith as 'Alevi', based on an opinion issued by an authority responsible for Islamic religious affairs, was in breach of the State's duty of neutrality and impartiality and thus in violation of Article 9.[30]

3. INDIVIDUAL DIMENSION

3.1. RELIGION OR BELIEF

Article 9 not only protects the (inner) freedom of thought, conscience and religion but also a person's freedom 'to manifest his religion or belief', to express this in *foro externo*. This freedom does not refer to the freedom of expression in general, a right which finds protection in Article 10. Nevertheless, a broad interpretation of the terms 'religion or belief' seems to be called for. A starting point for defining these terms may be the 'self-definition' of the individual (or community) of his religion or belief, but of course the authorities should have the competence to apply some objective, formal criteria to determine if these terms are applicable to the specific case.

There is a great diversity of religions and beliefs. They not only cover the mainstream traditional religions and (non-religious) beliefs, but also various kinds of minority views. For instance, the teachings of Bhagwan Sree Rajneesh, reverend Sun Myung Moon, Mormonism and Santo Daime all are regarded as religions.[31] Pacifism[32] and probably also communism are regarded as a 'belief' falling within the ambit of Article 9.[33] Also veganism (strict vegetarianism) may fall within the scope of this article.[34]

In the absence of a European consensus on the religious nature of the body of beliefs and practices of the Scientology Church, and being sensitive to the subsidiary nature of its role, the Court considered that it must rely on the position of the domestic authorities in this matter and determine the applicability of Article 9 of the Convention accordingly. While the (Russian) national courts qualified Scientology as a religion, the Court saw no reason

---

[30] *Sinan Işık v. Turkey*, ECtHR 2 February 2010, appl. no. 21924/05, para. 46.

[31] *Leela Förderkreis e.V. and Others v. Germany*, ECtHR 6 November 1998, appl. no. 58911/00 (Bhagwan); *Nolan and K. v. Russia*, ECtHR 12 February 2009, appl. no. 2512/04 (Moon's Unification Church); *The Church of Jesus Christ of Latter-Day Saints v. the United Kingdom*, ECtHR 4 March 2014, appl. no. 7552/09 (Mormonism); *Fränklin-Beentjes and CEFLU-Luz da Floresta v. the Netherlands*, ECtHR 6 May 2014 (dec.), appl. no. 28167/07 (Santo Daime).

[32] *Le Court Grandmaison and Fritz v. France*, EComHR 6 July 1987 (dec.), appl. nos. 11567/85 and 11568/85; *Arrowsmith v. the United Kingdom*, supra n. 5.

[33] *N.H., G.H. and R.A. v. Turkey*, EComHR 11 October 1991 (dec.), appl. nos. 16311/90, 16312/90 and 16313/90.

[34] *W. v. the United Kingdom*, EComHR 10 February 1993 (dec.), appl. no. 18187/91. Cf. *Jacóbski v. Poland*, ECtHR 7 December 2010, appl. no. 18429/06, para. 45 (adherence to a vegetarian diet may be regarded as motivated or inspired by a religion).

not to accept that qualification.[35] We respectfully submit that this approach, which primarily is based on the views of the national authorities, undermines the autonomous character of the concepts of 'religion' and 'belief', and has the potential of arbitrarily restricting the scope of protection of Article 9. For instance, it could be that a minority group that unjustly has been branded by the administration as a 'sect' operating under the cloak of religion, thereby is denied its right to freedom of religion, and that what 'counts' as a religion or belief may vary from state to state, or even on a case-by-case basis.

Although the concept of 'religion or belief' must be interpreted broadly, that does not mean that every individual opinion, conviction or preference is to be regarded as such.[36] This concept is akin to that of 'religious and philosophical convictions' which appears in Article 2 of Protocol No. 1, denoting 'views that attain a certain level of cogency, seriousness, cohesion and importance'.[37] Therefore, the preference for a specific language is not a belief in the sense of Article 9.[38] The magic wishes of a 'Wicca' adept were held not to be protected by Article 9, because the applicant failed to specify the content of the Wicca religion,[39] and the same conclusion was reached with regard to the complaint of a 'Lichtanbeter'.[40] With regard to a statement at a private party that the Holocaust was a Zionist lie, the Commission concluded that this 'did not reflect a "belief" within the meaning of Article 9 of the Convention which is essentially destined to protect religions, or theories on philosophical or ideological universal values'.[41] In the *Blumberg* case the applicant doctor's refusal to examine an apprentice for fear of 'a possible bias' was unspecified and unsubstantiated, thus was held not to constitute an expression of a coherent view on a fundamental problem and therefore could not be regarded as a manifestation of personal beliefs in the sense protected by Article 9.[42] And in *Gough*, the Court found that the wish to walk naked in public, based on the conviction that this was, however, socially acceptable behaviour, did not qualify as a religion or belief either.[43]

When the criteria of 'cogency, seriousness, cohesion and importance' are fulfilled, the existence of a religion or belief must be assumed. It is not up to

---

[35] *Kimlya and Others v. Russia*, ECtHR 1 October 2009, appl. no. 76836/01 and 32782/03, para. 79; *cf. Church of Scientology of St Petersburg and Others v. Russia*, ECtHR 2 October 2014, appl. no. 47191/06, para. 32.

[36] *Pretty v. the United Kingdom*, supra n. 3, para. 82.

[37] *Campbell and Cosans v. the United Kingdom*, supra n. 4, para. 36.

[38] *Belgian Linguistics Case v. Belgium (No. 2)*, ECtHR 23 July 1968, appl. nos. 1474/62, 1677/62, 1691/62, 1769/63, 1994/63 and 2126/64.

[39] A contemporary Pagan religious movement.

[40] *X. v. the United Kingdom*, EComHR 7 July 1977, appl. no. 7291/75; *X v. Federal Republic of Germany*, EComHR 1 April 1970 (dec.), appl. no. 4445/70.

[41] *F.P. v. Federal Republic of Germany*, EComHR 29 March 1993, appl. no. 19459/92. The Commission left undecided whether fascist propaganda may fall within the scope of Art. 9: *X v. Italy*, EComHR 21 May 1976 (dec.), appl. 6741/74.

[42] *Blumberg v. Germany*, ECtHR 18 March 2008 (dec.), appl. no. 14618/03.

[43] *Gough v. the United Kingdom*, ECtHR 28 October 2014, appl. no. 49327/11, para. 188.

the state to withhold protection because this religion or belief is regarded as theologically incorrect, untrue or unacceptable. In *Manoussakis*, the Court held that the freedom of religion 'excludes any discretion on the part of the State to determine whether religious beliefs or the means used to express such beliefs are legitimate'.[44]

3.2. FREEDOM TO MANIFEST ONE'S RELIGION OR BELIEF IN PRACTICE

Article 9 protects the freedom to manifest one's religion or belief, in *worship, teaching, practice and observance*. This enumeration suggests that Article 9 primarily concerns the 'traditional' manifestations in religious cults, rites and customs, for example in the observance of regulations concerning worship and devotion, clothing and food.[45] But even with regard to 'traditional' religious manifestations the Court sometimes nevertheless concludes that they fall outside the ambit of Article 9. For instance, in the *Cha'are* case the Court concluded – although recognising that ritual slaughter was a religious act for the purposes of Article 9 – that there would be an interference with the freedom to manifest one's religion only if the prohibition of performing ritual slaughter made it impossible for ultra-orthodox (French) Jews to eat 'glatt' (strictly *kosher*) meat from animals slaughtered in accordance with the religious prescriptions they considered applicable. Because they could obtain such meat in Belgium the Court found that there was no interference.[46] It is submitted here that the Court's reasoning, that the prohibition to perform ritual slaughter (a religious act that it deemed to be covered by Article 9) does not constitute an interference with the freedom of religion because there was an alternative to obtain elsewhere the product of that ritual, is inconsistent. If this type of ritual slaughter 'counts' as a religious act, one according to Article 9(1) in principle is free to perform it, and its prohibition amounts to a restriction that must be justified under Article 9(2).

It might be assumed that the enumeration of protected manifestations in Article 9 (worship, teaching, practice and observance) is not intended to be exhaustive. But in any case, in particular the term 'practice' leaves room for a broad scope, outside the sphere of traditional religious manifestations. However, the Strasbourg case law until recently has followed a rather restrictive

---

44   *Manoussakis v. Greece*, ECtHR 26 September 1996, appl. no. 18748/91, para. 47; see also *Eweida and Others v. the United Kingdom, supra* n. 6, para. 81, with further references.

45   E.g. propagation of religious beliefs, *Kokkinakis v. Greece, supra* n. 1, para. 31; keeping the fast of Ramadan and attending Friday prayers at the mosque, *Kalaç v. Turkey*, ECtHR 1 July 1997, appl. no. 20704/92, para. 29; ritual slaughter, *Cha'are Shalom ve Tsedek v. France, supra* n. 11, para. 74; wearing of the Islamic headscarf, *Leyla Şahin v. Turkey,* ECtHR (GC) 10 November 2005, appl. no. 44774/98, paras. 75–78.

46   *Cha'are Shalom ve Tsedek v. France, supra* n. 11, paras. 74 and 80–83.

interpretation, for the first time formulated explicitly by the former Commission in the *Arrowsmith* case. Arrowsmith had claimed that she was entitled to distribute leaflets (to troops in a British army camp) in which she advocated the view that these troops should not serve in Northern Ireland, as Article 9 gave her the right to express her pacifist belief in this practice. The Commission, however, argued that a subjective criterion would not do: 'the term "practice" as employed in Article 9.1 does not cover each act which is motivated or influenced by a religion or belief'. The Commission applied an objective standard: 'when the actions of individuals *do not actually express the belief concerned* they cannot be considered to be as such protected by Article 9.1, *even when they are motivated by it*' [emphasis added], and concluded that since the pamphlets 'did not express pacifist views', the applicant did not manifest her belief in the sense of Article 9, and therefore could not invoke this provision.[47]

This line of argument has been consistently followed in later decisions of the Commission and in judgments of the Court. The terms 'manifestation' and 'practice' do not cover each act which is motivated by a religion or belief;[48] actions which do not actually express a belief are not protected by Article 9.[49] So the Court, although not doubting the firmness of the applicant's views concerning assisted suicide reflecting her commitment to the principle of personal autonomy, nevertheless found that her seeking the assistance of her husband to commit suicide did not involve a form of manifestation of a religion or belief.[50] Likewise, in *Pichon and Sajous*, it ruled that the refusal of pharmacists to sell contraceptive pills because of their religious convictions could not be regarded as a 'practice of a religion or belief *in a generally accepted form*'[51] [emphasis added].

The same outcome – a narrow interpretation of what 'counts' as a practice of a religion or belief protected by Article 9 – results from the approach which emphasises the general character of the legislation involved and its application on a neutral basis without any link with the applicants' religion or belief, leading to the conclusion that there has not been a restriction of the freedom of religion and belief.[52] For instance, with regard to the obligation to pay taxes the Commission has decided that 'Article 9 does not confer on the applicant the right to refuse,

---

47 *Arrowsmith v. the United Kingdom, supra* n. 5.
48 *C. v. the United Kingdom, supra* n. 10; *Karaduman v. Turkey*, EComHR 3 May 1993 (dec.), appl. no, 16278/90; *Van Dungen v. the Netherlands*, EComHR 22 February 1995 (dec.), appl. 22838/93; *Kalaç v. Turkey, supra* n. 45, para. 27; *Hasan and Chaush v. Bulgaria, supra* n. 8, para. 60; *Pichon and Sajous v. France*, ECtHR 2 October 2001 (dec.), appl. no. 49853/99; *Pretty v. the United Kingdom, supra* n. 3, para. 82; *Eweida and Others v. the United Kingdom, supra* n. 6, para. 82.
49 *B.C. v. Switzerland*, EComHR 30 August 1993 (dec.), appl. no. 19898/92; *Porter v. the United Kingdom*, ECtHR 8 April 2003 (dec.), appl. no. 15814/02; *Skugar and Others v. Russia, supra* n. 9.
50 *Pretty v. the United Kingdom, supra* n. 3, para. 82.
51 *Pichon and Sajous v. France, supra* n. 48. *Cf.* also *Skugar and Others v. Russia, supra* n. 9, with further references.
52 *Valsamis v. Greece, supra* n. 19, paras. 36–37; *Efstratiou v. Greece, supra* n. 19, paras. 37–38.

on the basis of his convictions, to abide by legislation, the operation of which is provided for by the Convention, and which applies neutrally and generally in the public sphere, without impinging on the freedoms guaranteed by that Article.'[53]

In the same way, it was argued that the duty to participate in a pension scheme does not restrict the freedom to manifest one's (anthroposophical) belief: 'the obligation to participate in a pension fund applies to all general practitioners on a purely neutral basis, and cannot be said to have any close link with their religion or beliefs.'[54] The Court has followed a similar reasoning.[55] It has even held that the duty of a citizen to pay a special tax to the Church of Sweden, even though he was not a member, did not violate his right to freedom of religion, because this tax was proportionate to the costs of the Church's purely civil responsibilities.[56]

A restrictive interpretation of the freedom to manifest a religion or belief in general indeed seems to be unavoidable. A legal system consisting of generally binding rules cannot leave the answer to the question whether an act qualifies as a manifestation of a religion or belief – protected by Article 9 – to the subjective conviction and self-definition of the person or group concerned: that would lead to a potentially unlimited scope of this right. Therefore, the legal system itself should provide this answer based on objective criteria, primarily related to the 'outward appearance' of the expression as such and not to the underlying personal motives.

However, for unknown or new minorities which are not to a certain extent affiliated with one of the settled religions or major ideologies, this 'objective' position entails the danger that their actions will only then be considered the expression of a belief when a sufficient resemblance can be found with the known patterns of familiar religions and beliefs. This consequence may be mitigated by giving an applicant who claims that a certain type of behaviour is an expression of his religion or belief, the benefit of the doubt if that claim is not manifestly unfounded.[57] It seems that the Court sometimes is prepared to take this stance, for instance when it accepted that wearing the full-face veil (*burqa*) is a religious expression: the fact that this is only a minority practice (within the minority group of Muslim women) was regarded as irrelevant.[58]

Furthermore, the Court recently has qualified its requirement that the applicant's act, in order to be considered a manifestation in the sense of Article 9,

---

[53] E.g. *C. v. the United Kingdom, supra* n. 10. In the same vein: *Ortega Moratilla v. Spain*, EComHR 11 January 1992 (dec.), appl. 17522/90; *Bouessel du Bourg v. France*, EComHR 18 February 1993 (dec.), appl. 20747/92.

[54] *V. v. the Netherlands*, EComHR 5 July 1984 (dec.), appl. no. 10678/83.

[55] See in particular the well-reasoned decision in *Skugar and Others v. Russia, supra* n. 9, with further references, also to similar US Supreme Court judgments.

[56] *Lundberg v. Sweden*, ECtHR 21 August 2001 (dec.), appl. no. 36846/97; *Bruno v. Sweden*, ECtHR 28 August 2001 (dec.), appl. no. 32196/96.

[57] *Cf. Leyla Şahin v. Turkey, supra* n. 45, para. 78.

[58] *S.A.S. v. France, supra* n. 1, para. 108.

should form part of a practice of a religion or belief *in a generally recognised form.* In *Eweida*, it expounded that '[i]n order to count as a "manifestation" within the meaning of Article 9, the act in question must be intimately linked to the religion or belief. An example would be an act of worship or devotion which forms part of the practice of a religion or belief in a generally recognised form. However, the manifestation of religion or belief is not limited to such acts; *the existence of a sufficiently close and direct nexus between the act and the underlying belief* must be determined on the facts of each case. In particular, there is no requirement on the applicant to establish that he or she acted in fulfilment of a duty mandated by the religion in question'[59] [emphasis added].

The Court thus has expanded the scope of the concept of a 'manifestation of a religion or belief' to those acts that have a sufficiently close and direct nexus with the underlying belief. So, to a certain extent the individual's subjective interpretation of his actions may be relevant in determining whether Article 9 is applicable. The Court not only concluded that wearing a visible Christian cross – which can be regarded as a 'generally recognised form' of a religious practice – but also the refusal of registration of same-sex couples and of psycho-sexual counselling for such couples falls within the ambit of the freedom of religion.[60]

A good example of this more flexible approach is the *Bayatyan* judgment, where the Grand Chamber stated that '(w)hether and to what extent objection to military service falls within the ambit of that provision [Article 9] must be assessed in the light of the particular circumstances of the case. The applicant in the present case is a member of Jehovah's Witnesses, a religious group whose beliefs include the conviction that service, even unarmed, within the military is to be opposed. The Court therefore has no reason to doubt that the applicant's objection to military service *was motivated by his religious beliefs*, which were genuinely held and were in serious and insurmountable conflict with his obligation to perform military service [...]. *Accordingly*, Article 9 is applicable'[61] [emphasis added].

Thus, the subjective religious motivation was decisive in order to conclude that Article 9 applied.

3.3. CONSCIENTIOUS OBJECTIONS TO MILITARY SERVICE

With respect to the exercise of the freedom of religion and belief both in national and in Strasbourg case law the issue of conscientious objections of a religious nature against military service takes a prominent place. Many international

---

59 *Eweida and Others v. the United Kingdom, supra* n. 6, para. 82.
60 *Ibid.*, paras. 89–108.
61 *Bayatyan v. Armenia*, ECtHR (GC) 7 July 2011, appl. no. 23459/03, para. 110.

institutions – including Council of Europe organs – nowadays subscribe to the view that such conscientious objections are covered by Article 9.[62]

The Commission refused to apply this provision to conscientious objectors. The Commission argued that Article 9 should be interpreted in connection with Article 4 (3)(b) of the Convention, finding that the latter provision left the choice whether or not recognise a right to conscientious objection to the Contracting Parties.[63] Consequently, conscientious objectors were excluded from the scope of protection of Article 9, which could not be read as guaranteeing them freedom to refuse to serve.[64] However, Commission and Court were prepared to accept that, notwithstanding the finding that the Convention as such did not guarantee a right to conscientious objection, the case of a conscientious objector could fall 'within the ambit of Article 9', so that the applicants' allegations of discrimination were therefore to be examined under Article 14 of the Convention.[65] For instance, in the *Thlimmenos* case the Court had to deal with a complaint of a Jehovah's Witness who was not appointed as a chartered accountant because of his past conviction for insubordination, due to his refusal – based on religious conscientious objections – to wear the military uniform. Although the Court did not find it necessary to examine the question of applicability of Article 9, it concluded that this case fell within the ambit of Article 9.[66] Since then, in several cases the Court found for conscious objectors relying on Article 14 in conjunction with Article 9 of the Convention.[67]

In the *Bayatyan* case, the Court for the first time ruled on the question of the applicability of Article 9 to conscientious objectors. In this landmark judgment,[68] the Grand Chamber acknowledged that Article 9 does not explicitly refer to a right to conscientious objection. Furthermore, according to the Court it followed from the *travaux préparatoires* that sub-paragraph (b) of Article 4(3) neither recognises nor excludes a right to conscientious objection and should therefore not have a delimiting effect on the rights guaranteed by Article 9. It noted that since the late 1980s there has been an obvious trend among European countries, both existing Council of Europe member States and those that joined the organisation later, to recognise the right to conscientious

---

[62] See the documents mentioned in Bayatyan, *ibid.*, paras. 50–70.

[63] Art. 4(3) as far as it is relevant here reads: 'For the purpose of this Article [forbidding forced or compulsory labour, Article 4(2)] the term "forced or compulsory labour" shall not include:
a. [...]
b. any service of a military character or, *in case of conscientious objectors in countries where they are recognised*, service exacted instead of compulsory military service; [emphasis added]
c. [...]'

[64] *Grandrath v. Germany*, EComHR 12 December 1978 (rep.), appl. no. 2299/64.

[65] *N. v. Sweden*, EComHR 11 October 1984 (dec.), appl. 10410/83.

[66] *Thlimmenos v. Greece*, ECtHR (GC) 6 April 2000, appl. no. 34369/97, para. 42.

[67] See, e.g., *Gütl v. Austria*, ECtHR 12 March 2009, appl. no. 49686/99.

[68] Which has been followed by many other judgments in which the Court has concluded that there was a violation of Art. 9 with respect to Jehovah's Witnesses. See, e.g., *Buldu and Others v. Turkey*, ECtHR 3 June 2014, appl. no. 14017/08, para. 83.

objection, and took notice of similar other important developments concerning the recognition of the right to conscientious objection in various international fora.[69] Relying on its 'living instrument' approach, according to which the Convention has to be interpreted in line with present-day conditions, the Court took the view that nowadays it was not possible anymore to confirm the case law established by the Commission. The Court considered that opposition to military service, where it is motivated by a serious and insurmountable conflict between the obligation to serve in the army and a person's conscience or his deeply and genuinely held religious or other beliefs, constitutes a conviction or belief of sufficient cogency, seriousness, cohesion and importance to attract the guarantees of Article 9. It concluded that the applicant in this case – a Jehovah's Witness – indeed held such beliefs. Accordingly, Article 9 was applicable, and because Bayatyan's criminal conviction for draft evasion was a disproportionate interference with his freedom to manifest his religion there had been a violation of this provision.[70]

As the Court held in *Bayatyan*, whether and to what extent objection to military service falls within the ambit of Article 9 should be assessed in the light of the particular circumstances of the case. This apparently leaves room for a casuistic approach, differentiating between various types of objections. For instance, in the *Aydemir* case it concluded that while the applicant refused to serve in the Turkish army because the Turkish State was founded on laicism and therefore incompatible with the Koran and the Sharia, his objections were not directed against participation in war or bearing arms as such, and therefore were not based on a sincere religious belief coming into a serious and insurmountable conflict with his obligation to serve in the army. Therefore, according to the Court, Article 9 was not applicable.[71]

4. COLLECTIVE DIMENSION

4.1. INDEPENDENT AND LEGAL STATUS OF RELIGIOUS COMMUNITIES

The freedom to manifest a religion or belief is not an exclusively individual right, but also has a collective dimension, explicitly recognised in Article 9 through the

---

[69] *Bayatyan v. Armenia, supra* n. 61, paras. 50–70.

[70] *Ibid.*, paras. 92–128.

[71] *Aydemir v. Turkey*, ECtHR 7 June 2016, appl. no. 26012/11, paras. 79–84. Given the subjective nature of conscience, it is remarkable that the Court assumes that such objections, while they are not directed against war or bearing arms as such, by definition, could not be based on a sincere religious belief. Doesn't the Court pretend here to be allowed to assess the legitimacy of religious beliefs or the way those are expressed (a competence explicitly denied in *Bayatyan v. Armenia, supra* n. 61, para. 120)?

phrase 'in community with others'. It is plausible, therefore, that collectivities such as churches should also be regarded as subjects of this right. Nevertheless, the Commission initially held that a church, 'being a legal and not a natural person, is incapable of having or exercising the rights mentioned in Article 9, paragraph (1) of the Convention', and thus could not claim to be itself the victim of the alleged violation of Article 9.[72]

This position has rightly been criticised, and abandoned. Whereas the inner freedom of thought, conscience and religion – including the freedom to choose a religion or belief – only pertains to individual persons[73], the right to freedom to manifest a religion or a belief does not only have an individual but also a collective dimension, and the entire functioning of churches and other 'belief organisations' depends on respect for this right. These collectivities appear to be eminently deserving in this respect, particularly as Article 34 expressly provides for the possibility of complaints by non-governmental organisations and groups. In later decisions since 1979 the Commission revised its position and characterised the distinction between a church body and its members as artificial.[74] The Court has adopted the same view, *viz.* 'that an ecclesiastical body may, as such, exercise on behalf of its adherents the right guaranteed by Article 9 of the Convention.'[75]

The collective right to manifest a religion is not restricted to churches. Other organisations such as denominational charities may also be capable of possessing and exercising the right to freedom of religion.[76] In certain circumstances even a limited liability company may enjoy this freedom,[77] And in the case *Staatkundig Gereformeerde Partij* the Court was ready to proceed on the presumption that there had been an interference with a political party's rights under *inter alia* Article 9.[78]

---

[72]   *Church of X v. the United Kingdom*, EComHR 17 December 1968 (dec.), appl. no. 3798/68; *X v. Sweden*, EComHR 19 July 1971 (dec.), appl. no. 4733/71.

[73]   *Soukroma v. Czech Republic, supra* n. 7.

[74]   *Pastor X and the Church of Scientology v. Sweden*, EComHR 5 May 1979 (dec.), appl. no. 7805/77. *Cf.* also *Chappell v. the United Kingdom*, EComHR 14 July 1987 (dec.), appl. no. 12587/86; *Finska Församlingen i Stockholm and T. Hautaniemi*, EComHR 11 April 1996 (dec.), appl. no. 24019/94.

[75]   *Cha'are Shalom ve Tsedek v. France, supra* n. 11, para. 72; *Metropolitan Church of Bessarabia and Others v. Moldova, supra* n. 22, para. 101.

[76]   *ISKCON and Others v. the United Kingdom,* EComHR 8 March 1994 (dec.), appl. 20490/92.

[77]   In *Company X v. Switzerland*, EComHR 27 February 1979 (dec.), appl. no. 7865/77, and in *Verein 'Kontakt-Information-Therapie' (KIT) and Hagen v. Austria*, EComHR 12 October 1988 (dec.), appl. no. 11921/86, the Commission held that such a company, given the fact that it concerns a profit-making corporate body, can neither enjoy nor rely on the rights referred to in Art. 9. However, later on in *Kustannus Oy Vapaa Ajattelija and Others v. Finland*, EComHR 15 April 1996 (dec.), appl. no. 20471/92 it ruled otherwise: 'The Commission would therefore not exclude that the applicant association is in principle capable of possessing and exercising rights under Article 9 para. 1.'

[78]   *Staatkundig Gereformeerde Partij v. the Netherlands*, ECtHR 10 July 2012 (dec.), appl. no. 58369/10, para. 68.

It is not sufficient for a Contracting State to guarantee only the right of either the individual or the group to manifest a religion. The Commission rightly endorsed the view that 'the right to manifest one's religion "in community with others" has always been regarded as an essential part of the freedom of religion and finds that the two alternatives "either alone or in community with others" in Article 9(1) cannot be considered as mutually exclusive, or as leaving a choice to the authorities, but only as recognising that religion may be practised in either form.'[79]

The Court has not contested that legislation requesting religious denominations to register may be compatible with Articles 9 and 11 of the Convention. However, this does not imply that it would be compatible with the Convention to sanction individual members of an unregistered religious denomination for prayer or otherwise manifesting their religious beliefs. The freedom of religion or belief, whether alone or in community with others, cannot be made subject to prior public registration or recognition, while that freedom belongs to individuals and communities as rights holders and is not dependent on official authorisation. A contrary view would amount to the exclusion of minority religious beliefs which are not formally registered and would in fact presume that a state may dictate what a person must believe.[80]

In various cases, the Court has emphasised the importance of the collective dimension of the freedom of religion or belief and the principle that the state should not arbitrarily interfere in the organisation of religious communities. As it ruled in *Hasan and Chaush*, '[w]here the organisation of the religious community is at issue, Article 9 of the Convention must be interpreted in the light of Article 11, which safeguards the associated life against unjustified State interference. Seen in this perspective, the believers' right to freedom of religion encompasses the expectation that the community will be allowed to function peacefully, free from arbitrary State intervention. Indeed, the autonomous existence of religious communities is indispensable for pluralism in a democratic society and is thus an issue at the very heart of the protection Article 9 affords. Were the organisational life of the community not protected by Article 9 of the Convention, all other aspects of the individual's freedom of religion would become vulnerable.'[81]

The Court has stressed that one of the means of exercising the right to manifest one's religion, especially for a religious community in its collective

---

[79]   *X v. the United Kingdom*, EComHR 12 March 1981 (dec.), appl. no. 8160/78.
[80]   *Masaev v. Moldova*, ECtHR 12 May 2009, appl. no. 6303/05, para. 26. *Cf.* also *Metropolitan Church of Bessarabia v. Moldova, supra* n. 22, paras. 128–130.
[81]   *Hasan and Chaush v. Bulgaria, supra* n. 8, para. 62. See likewise: *Metropolitan Church of Bessarabia v. Moldova, supra* n. 22, para. 118; *Holy Synod of the Bulgarian Orthodox Church (Metropolitan Inokentiy) and Others v. Bulgaria*, ECtHR 22 January 2009, appl. nos. 412/03 and 35677/04, para. 103; *Sindicatul 'Păstorul cel Bun' v. Romania*, ECtHR (GC) 9 July 2013, appl. no. 2330/09, para. 136; *Fernández Martínez v. Spain*, ECtHR (GC) 12 June 2014, appl. no. 56030/07, para. 127.

dimension, is the legal competence to ensure judicial protection of itself, its members and its assets. Article 9 must therefore not only be seen in the light of Article 11 but also of Article 6 of the Convention.[82] Often the capacity to judicial protection depends on whether the community has legal personality. Therefore, the refusal by the state to accord legal personality status to an association of individuals, based on a religion or belief, amounts to an interference with the exercise of the right to freedom of religion or belief of the community itself as well as of its individual members.[83]

4.2. AUTONOMY AND INTERNAL CONFLICTS

The autonomy of religious communities, which is an inherent aspect of the freedom of religion, implies the duty of state authorities not to intrude in the internal organisation of these communities and to remain neutral and impartial towards them:[84] it is not the role of the authorities to determine whether religious beliefs are legitimate[85] or to interfere with the leadership of a religious community.[86] From these principles follows that the state should not take sides in religious conflicts within and between religious communities. It is 'not the task of the national authorities to act as the arbiter between religious organisations and the various dissident factions that exist or may emerge between them'.[87] For instance, the refusal of legal recognition of a schismatic church for reasons of religious unity must in general be regarded as a disproportionate restriction of religious freedom:[88] a group leaving the community it belonged to thereby exercises the 'freedom to change a religion or belief', explicitly protected by

---

[82] *Canea Catholic Church v. Greece*, ECtHR 16 December 1997, appl. no. 25528/94, paras. 33–45; *Biserica Adevărat Ortodoxă din Moldova and Others v. Moldova*, ECtHR 27 February 2007, appl. no. 952/03, para. 34. See also *Svyato-Mykhaylivska Parafiya v. Ukraine*, ECtHR 14 June 2007, appl. no. 77703/01, para. 152; *Members of the Gldani Congregation of Jehovah's Witnesses and 4 others v. Georgia*, ECtHR 3 May 2007, appl. no. 71156/01, para. 133.

[83] E.g. ECtHR 13 December 2001, *Metropolitan Church of Bessarabia v. Moldova*, supra n. 22, para. 105; ECtHR 31 July 2008, *Religionsgemeinschaft der Zeugen Jehovas and Others v. Austria*, appl. No. 40825/98, para. 66; ECtHR 1 October 2009, *Kimlya and Others v. Russia*, supra n. 35, para. 84; ECtHR 10 June 2010, *Jehova's Witnesses of Moscow and Others v. Russia*, appl. no. 302/02, para. 101.

[84] The state must be the 'neutral and impartial organizer of the exercise of various religions, faiths and beliefs', *Refah Partisi (the Welfare Party) and Others v. Turkey*, ECtHR 13 February 2003, appl. nos. 41340/98, 41342/98, 41343/98 and 41344/98, para. 91.

[85] Constant case law since *Manoussakis v. Greece*, supra n. 44, para. 47.

[86] *Hasan and Chaush v. Bulgaria*, supra n. 8, para. 78. See also *Metropolitan Church of Bessarabia and Others v. Moldova*, supra n. 22, para. 117; *Mirolubovs and Others v. Latvia*, ECtHR 15 September 2009, appl. no. 798/05, para. 80.

[87] *Sindicatul 'Pastorul cel Bun' v. Romania*, supra n. 81, para. 165; *Fernandez Martinez v. Spain*, supra n. 81, para. 128.

[88] *Metropolitan Church of Bessarabia and Others v. Moldova*, supra n. 22, paras. 128–130.

Article 9.[89] And state action favouring one leader or group of a divided religious community, or undertaken with the purpose of forcing the community to come back together under a single leadership against its own wishes, would constitute a very problematic interference with freedom of religion.[90]

The autonomy of religious organisations requires that the state respects their right to preserve the purity of their doctrine and to impose restrictions on their ministers and members in order to guarantee unity in religious profession. As the Commission has argued, churches and other religious communities are free to act out and enforce uniformity in these matters. In other words, these communities are not obliged to provide religious freedom to their servants and members.[91] They are free to determine which new members they admit and which current members they exclude.[92] Article 9 does not enshrine a right of individuals to dissent within religious communities: in the case of disagreement over issues of doctrine or organisation his or her freedom is exercised through the right to freely leave.[93] Nor does it guarantee to believers a right to choose the religious leaders of their community or to oppose decisions by the organisation regarding the election or appointment of ministers.[94]

The degree of loyalty that religious communities may demand of their employees depends on their specific task and position: it varies in accordance with their proximity to the mission of the organisation.[95] Of course, it may be required that they do not become member of another religious community whose teachings are regarded as incompatible with the doctrine of the organisation.[96] Furthermore, from key figures, who are representing the organisation, a *heightened duty of loyalty* may be demanded, even extending to their private lives. This is the case for instance with regard to the clergy,[97]

---

[89] *Mirolubovs and Others v. Latvia, supra* n. 86, para. 93.

[90] *Serif v. Greece*, ECtHR 14 December 1999, appl. no. 38178/97, paras. 36–39; *Hasan and Chaush v. Bulgaria, supra* n. 8, paras. 75–82; *Supreme Holy Council of the Muslim Community v. Bulgaria*, ECtHR 16 December 2004, appl. no. 39023/97, paras. 76–85; *Holy Synod of the Bulgarian Orthodox Church (Metropolitan Inokentiy) and Others v. Bulgaria, supra* n. 81, paras. 105–114.

[91] *X v. Denmark*, EComHR 8 March 1976 (dec.), appl. 7374/76; *Knudsen v. Norway*, EComHR 8 March 1985 (dec.), appl. no. 11045/84; *Karlsson v. Sweden*, EComHR 8 September 1988 (dec.), appl. no. 12356/86. Cf. also *Rommelfanger v. the Federal Republic of Germany*, EComHR 6 September 1989 (dec.), appl. no. 12242/86.

[92] *Svyato-Mikhaylivska Parafya v. Ukraine, supra* n. 82, paras. 146 and 150.

[93] *Holy Synod of the Bulgarian Orthodox Church (Metropolitan Inokentiy) and Others v. Bulgaria, supra* n. 81, para. 137; *Mirolubovs and Others v. Latvia, supra* n. 86, para. 80; *Fernandez Martinez v. Spain, supra* n. 81, para. 128.

[94] *Sotirov and Others v. Latvia*, ECtHR 5 July 2011 (dec.), 13999/05.

[95] *Schüth v. Germany*, ECtHR 23 September 2010, appl. no. 1620/03, para. 69.

[96] *Siebenhaar v. Germany*, ECtHR 3 February 2011, appl. no. 18136/02, paras. 44–46.

[97] *Sindicatul 'Pastorul cel Bun' v. Romania, supra* n. 81, para. 144: 'members of the clergy assume obligations of a special nature in that they are bound by a heightened duty of loyalty, itself based on a personal, and in principle irrevocable, undertaking by each clergyman.'

directors[98] and religious education teachers.[99] On the other hand, the Court found that the dismissal on grounds of adultery of an organist/choirmaster at a Catholic church had not been subjected to a thorough judicial scrutiny of the proportionality required in the light of his rights under Article 8 (private and family life).[100]

4.3. NEUTRALITY OF THE STATE

Article 9, in itself and in conjunction with Article 14, sets certain limitations with regard to the possible models of church and state relations. On the one end of the continuum we find the position of totalitarian secularism, which subscribes to atheism as the official doctrine, and on the other end the theocratic model, where the state relies exclusively on one state religion. Both extremes exclude religious variety, both are incompatible with Article 9 and 14, and with the principles of democracy as set forth in the European Convention.[101] In between these positions basically three European ideal types[102] can be discerned. On the one hand, there is strict secularism that seeks to exclude religion from the government, the (state) school and restrict its presence in the public sphere in general. On the other hand, there is the state church model, in which the state and the dominant majority religion form a close partnership in advancing the causes of both. Finally, there is a middle type, pluralist co-operation, where the state does not take sides among the various religious and secular worldviews, but tries to treat these views on a par, even-handedly. There is no European standard, prescribing a specific model.[103] These three models all in principle are compatible with the Convention,[104] although the state church is specifically vulnerable in that it has an inherent tendency to disregard the rights of religious minorities; we will deal with that shortly.

Of course, the protection of the freedom of thought, conscience and religion requires state neutrality in religious issues, but Article 9 of the Convention can

---

[98] *Obst v. Germany*, ECtHR 23 September 2010, appl. no. 425/03, paras. 50–51.

[99] *Fernandez Martinez v. Spain, supra* n. 81, paras. 137–138.

[100] *Schüth v. Germany, supra* n. 95, paras. 69 and 75.

[101] See in this sense concerning a sharia-based system: *Refah Partisi (Welfare Party) and Others v. Turkey, supra* n. 84, paras. 119 and 123.

[102] In fact, most national systems do not completely fulfil the characteristics of one ideal type, but combine traits of one with those of the other.

[103] *Sindicatul 'Pastorul cel Bun' v. Romania, supra* n. 81, para. 138.

[104] The Court accepted a form of secularism which confined Islam and other religions to the sphere of private practice in *Refah Partisi (Welfare Party) and Others v. Turkey, supra* n. 84, paras. 125–128; *Leyla Sahin v. Turkey, supra* n. 45, para. 108; *cf.* also *Dogru v. France*, ECtHR 4 December 2008, appl. no. 27058/05, para. 72. The co-operation model and the state church model in principle were regarded as acceptable in *Magyar Keresztény Mennonita Egyház and Others v. Hungary*, ECtHR 8 April 2014, appl. nos. 70945/11 et al., paras. 93 and 100 respectively.

hardly be conceived as being likely to diminish the role of a faith or a church with which the population of a country has historically and culturally been associated.[105] Whether or not to continue a traditional arrangement falls within the – large – margin of appreciation of the state,[106] given the great diversity between the European states, particularly in their cultural and historical development.[107] For example, a state church or official church with a special constitutional status is allowed. But such a system must remain within certain limiting conditions. For instance, the freedom of individuals and groups must be safeguarded: in particular no one may be forced to enter or be prevented to leave the state church.[108] Furthermore, the freedom of religion excludes any discretion of the state to determine whether a religious belief or the means used to express it are legitimate,[109] or to what religion an individual or group belongs.[110] And it is also incompatible with Article 9 to make the exercise of the freedom of religion by a community subject to a system of prior authorisation by an ecclesiastical authority of the state church.[111]

In all three models the position of religious minorities – in particular, their equal treatment, especially in the state church type – merits special attention. For instance, the Convention does not require that places of worship are granted a special status, but if that status is offered to established communities, it cannot be denied to minority groups.[112] Although the conclusion of agreements between the state and specific religious communities, establishing a special regime in favour of these communities, does not contravene Article 14 – in conjunction with Article 9 – per se, to refuse certain churches such agreements applying to them criteria that were not upheld with regard to other religious communities violates these provisions.[113] And the imposition of a 10-year waiting period on 'new' religious communities to acquire the status of a 'religious society' offering substantive privileges in general is discriminatory.[114] Finally, it may be that a general regulation which in itself is neutral, nevertheless in its actual application

---

105   *Members of the Gldani Congregation of Jehova's witnesses and Others v. Georgia, supra* n. 82, para. 132.
106   *Cha'are Shalom ve Tsedek v. France, supra* n. 11, para. 84.
107   *Lautsi and Others v. Italy, supra* n. 17, paras. 61 and 68.
108   *Astruarfelagid v. Iceland,* ECtHR 18 September 2012 (dec.), appl. no. 22897/08, par. 27; *cf. Finska församlingen I Stockholm and Hautaniemi v. Sweden, supra* n. 74 (concerning a parish).
109   *Manoussakis v. Greece, supra* n. 44, para. 47; *Hassan and Chaush v. Bulgaria, supra* n. 8, para. 76; *Leyla Sahin v. Turkey, supra* n. 45, para. 107; *Bayatyan v. Armenia, supra* n. 61, para. 120.
110   *Mirolubovs and Others v. Latvia, supra* n. 86, paras. 89–90; *Sinan Işik v. Turkey, supra* n. 30, paras. 45–46.
111   *Manoussakis v. Greece, supra* n. 44, paras. 48–53.
112   *Cumhuriyetçi Eğitim ve Kültür Vakfi v. Turkey,* ECtHR 2 December 2014, appl. no. 32093/10, paras. 48–49; *Izzettin Dogan and Others v. Turkey,* ECtHR 26 April 2016, appl. no. 62649/10, paras. 117–124.
113   *Savez Crkava 'Riječ Života' and Others v. Croatia,* ECtHR 9 December 2010, appl. no. 7798/08, para. 85–93.
114   *Religionsgemeinschaft der Zeugen Jehovas and Others v. Austria, supra* n. 83, paras. 92, 97–98.

is particularly burdensome for a religious minority. This may amount to indirect discrimination, when the state – unjustifiably – fails to treat differently persons whose situations are fundamentally different and violates Article 14 taken in conjunction with Article 9.[115]

5. POSITIVE OBLIGATIONS

The freedom to manifest one's religion or belief does not imply a right to be protected against criticism or ridicule,[116] because such verbal attacks cannot generally be regarded as an interference with this freedom. It is only seldom, in extreme cases, when particular methods of opposing or denying religious or other beliefs may inhibit those who hold those beliefs from exercising their freedom to express them, that the state may be obliged to take repressive and preventive measures in order to guarantee their rights under Article 9. The Court found a violation in *Gldani*, concerning Jehovah's Witnesses who had been attacked, humiliated and beaten by Orthodox extremists during their congregation's meeting. Subsequently they were confronted with total indifference and a failure to act on the part of the authorities who, through their inactivity, failed in their duty to take the necessary measures to ensure that their attackers left the applicants' community at peace, enabling them to exercise freely their right to freedom of religion.[117] In another case, the Court also held that the disruption of a service of worship held by Jehovah's Witnesses and the subsequent detention of the applicants amounted to a violation of Article 9. The assembly in question was not a tumultuous outdoors event but a solemn religious ceremony in an assembly hall which was not shown to create any disturbance or danger to the public order. The intervention of armed riot police with the aim of disturbing the ceremony, followed by the applicants' arrest and a three-hour detention, was disproportionate.[118] And likewise the Court concluded that the lack of adequate measures against and adequate investigation of a violent demonstration against Friday prayers in and outside a mosque amounted to a breach of Article 9.[119]

---

[115] *Thlimmenos v. Greece, supra* n. 66, para. 44. This case concerned a Jehovah's Witness, who for reasons of conscience had refused to wear the military uniform, had to serve a prison sentence and therefore was barred from the profession of chartered accountants.

[116] *Choudhury v. the United Kingdom*, EComHR 5 March 1991, appl. no. 17439/90 (concerning the refusal of the authorities to bring criminal proceedings against the author (Rushdie) and the publisher of Rushdie's *Satanic Verses*); *I.A. v. Turkey*, ECtHR 13 September 2005, appl. no. 42571/98, para. 28.

[117] *Members of the Gldani Congregation of Jehovah's Witnesses and 4 others v. Georgia, supra* n. 82, para. 133.

[118] *Krupko and Others v. Russia*, ECtHR 26 June 2014, appl. no. 26587/07, para. 56. See also *Kuznetsov and Others v. Russia*, ECtHR 11 January 2007, appl. no. 184/02.

[119] *Karaahmed v. Bulgaria*, ECtHR 24 February 2015, appl. no. 30587/1, paras. 101–111.

In the *Otto-Preminger-Institut* case, the Court was prepared to go much further. It ruled that the right to respect for the religious feelings of believers as guaranteed by Article 9 could legitimately be thought to have been violated by *Das Liebeskonzil*, a film supposedly blasphemous in the eyes of the Roman Catholic majority. For this reason, it decided that the seizure and forfeiture of the film was justified under Article 10(2), being necessary for the protection of the right of this majority to respect for their freedom as protected by Article 9.[120] It is submitted here that this judgment was incorrect. The screening of the film in no way would have limited or inhibited Roman Catholics in manifesting their religion and, therefore, did not restrict their rights under Article 9. The Court extended one's right to be protected against vicious attacks by fellow-citizens for a religion or belief that could endanger the actual enjoyment of the freedom to manifest this religion or belief – particularly relevant for minorities – to a general right – even of dominant majorities – not to be insulted in one's religious or non-religious views. But such a right, relied upon 'to sanction improper attacks on objects of religious veneration' and 'to prevent that some people should feel the object of attacks on their religious beliefs in an unwarranted and offensive manner',[121] is not included in Article 9, but on the contrary is inconsistent with the 'pluralism indissociable from a democratic society' that depends on it.[122] It must be noted, however, that in more recent judgments the Court, examining complaints of persons convicted for offending the feelings of believers under Article 10 of the Convention, generally concludes that the freedom of expression had been violated.[123] It may be assumed that *Otto-Preminger* and *Wingrove* are unfortunate 'slips of the pen'.

The Court (and earlier the Commission) on several occasions has had to determine the scope of the positive obligations of public employers to accommodate employees in their rights under Article 9, as well as of national courts in protecting employees against sanctions because of the way they manifested their religion. Article 9 does not necessarily imply that one can back out of one's obligations, consented to or contracted freely and without explicit reservation by claiming the right to manifest one's religion. In the Strasbourg case law these obligations often are not regarded as interfering with the freedom of religion. For instance, in cases of a conflict between an ecclesiastical hierarchy and, on the other hand, a servant of the church who no longer agreed with the hierarchy, the latter had to choose between submitting to ecclesiastical discipline or leaving the

---

[120] *Otto-Preminger-Institut v. Austria*, ECtHR 20 September 1994, appl. no. 13470/87, para. 47; *Wingrove v. the United Kingdom*, ECtHR 25 November 1996, appl. no. 17419/90, para. 48.

[121] *Otto-Preminger-Institut v. Austria, supra* n. 120, paras. 49 and 56.

[122] *Kokkinakis v. Greece, supra* n. 1, para. 31.

[123] *Gündüz v. Turkey*, ECtHR 4 December 2003, appl. no. 35071/97, paras. 42–53; *Gniwieski v. France*, ECtHR 31 January 2006, appl. no. 64016/00, paras. 43–56.

church.[124] In that same vein, the Commission was of the opinion that a Muslim teacher, who regularly neglected his duties in order to participate in the common prayer on Friday afternoon in the mosque near his school, should have made a choice between fulfilling this religious prescription and keeping his position as a teacher.[125] Similarly, the Court concluded that the compulsory retirement of a judge whose conduct and attitude revealed fundamentalist opinions incompatible with the principles of the secular state did not amount to an interference with Article 9.[126] Furthermore, in several decisions the Commission held that the mere possibility of resigning from a job and changing employment that did harmonise with one's religious obligations implied that there was no interference with the employee's religious freedom.[127] Finally in the *Siebenhaar* case, the Court held that the applicant, who was a teacher dismissed by the Protestant Church because he privately attended and undertook activities for a community called 'Universal Church', knew or ought to have known that such activities were incompatible with her contract with the Protestant Church.[128]

However, more recently – in the cases of *Eweida and Others* – the Court has explicitly stated that where an individual complains of a restriction on his freedom of religion in the workplace, rather than holding like the Commission that the possibility of changing job would negate any interference with this right, the better approach would be to weigh that possibility in the overall balance when considering whether or not the restriction was proportionate.[129] In the case of *Eweida* the Court, following this approach, came to the conclusion that the refusal of British Airways to allow the applicant to remain in her post while visibly wearing a cross was disproportionate and therefore in breach of the positive obligation under Article 9.[130]

That does not mean that the claim of an employee based on his freedom of religion will soon prevail. In *Chaplin*, concerning a nurse working on a geriatric ward, the Court ruled that the reason for asking her to remove the cross – protection of health and safety on a hospital ward – was inherently of a greater magnitude, and found that there was no violation of Article 9.[131] In the *Ladele* case, a registrar of marriages who held the view that marriage is the union of one man and one woman for life and believed same-sex civil partnerships to be contrary to God's law, had faced disciplinary action and ultimately lost her job. The Court, examining a complaint under Article 14 in conjunction with

---

[124] *X v. Denmark, supra* n. 91; *Knudsen v. Norway, supra* n. 91; *Karlsson v. Sweden, supra* n. 91. Cf. also *Rommelfanger, supra* n. 91.
[125] *X v. the United Kingdom, supra* n. 79.
[126] *Kalaç v. Turkey, supra* n. 45, para. 30.
[127] *Stedman v. the United Kingdom*, EComHR 3 December 1996 (dec.), appl. no. 29107/95.
[128] *Siebenhaar v. Germany, supra* n. 96, para. 46.
[129] *Eweida and Others v. the United Kingdom, supra* n. 6, para. 83.
[130] *Eweida and Others v. the United Kingdom, supra* n. 6, para. 94.
[131] *Eweida and Others v. the United Kingdom (Chaplin), supra* n. 6, para. 99.

Article 9, made it clear that Ms Ladele, when she entered into her contract of employment, had not waived her right to manifest her religious belief, since this requirement was introduced by her employer at a later date. However, the employer's policy aimed to secure the rights of others which were also protected under the Convention, and therefore the Court did not consider that the national authorities exceeded the margin of appreciation available to them.[132] Finally, the case of *McFarlane* concerned disciplinary proceedings in response to his refusal to provide psycho-sexual counselling to same-sex couples, motivated by his orthodox Christian beliefs about marriage and sexual relationships. The Court concluded that there was no violation of a positive obligation under Article 9, while the employer's action was intended to secure the implementation of his policy to provide a service without discrimination.[133]

6. RESTRICTION CLAUSE

Article 9(2) stipulates that the state may restrict the freedom of religion or belief only when the interference is *prescribed by law*. Such a law must be accessible and foreseeable; it must be formulated with sufficient precision to enable the individual to regulate his conduct.[134] The law must afford a measure of legal protection against arbitrary interferences by public authorities with the freedom of religion or belief: therefore, it must indicate with sufficient clarity the scope of their discretion and the manner of its exercise. For instance, if the law does not provide for any substantive criteria, nor procedural safeguards, state interference with the internal organisation of a religious community cannot be regarded as being 'prescribed by law'.[135] The Court has ruled likewise in cases regarding police intervention during a religious meeting,[136] denial of the right to participate in religious services at a prison's chaplaincy,[137] the power to determine what activities a foreigner in the possession of a residence permit may or may not perform on the state's territory[138] and finally, in relation to the right to manifest one's religion in its collective dimension, refusal to register churches[139] or to provide necessary information for that purpose.[140] On the

---

132 *Eweida and Others v. the United Kingdom (Ladele), supra* n. 6, para. 106.

133 *Eweida and Others v. the United Kingdom (McFarlane), supra* n. 6, para. 109.

134 *Larissis and Others v. Greece*, ECtHR 24 February 1998, appl. no. 23372/94 23372/94, para. 40.

135 *Hasan and Chaush v. Bulgaria, supra* n. 8, paras. 84–86; *cf.* also *Metropolitan Church of Bessarabia and Others v. Moldova, supra* n. 22, para. 109.

136 *Boychev and Others v. Bulgaria*, ECtHR 27 January 2011, appl. no. 77185/01, para. 52.

137 *Igors Dmitrijevs v. Latvia*, ECtHR 30 November 2006, appl. no. 61638/00.

138 *Perry v. Latvia*, ECtHR 8 November 2007, appl. no. 30273/03, para. 65.

139 *Biserica Adevărat Ortodoxă din Moldova and Others v. Moldova, supra* n. 82, para. 36; *Church of Scientology Moscow v. Russia*, ECtHR 5 April 2007, appl. no. 18147/02, para. 97; *Church of Scientology of St Petersburg and Others v. Russia, supra* n. 35, para. 46.

140 *Fusu and Others v. the Republic of Moldova*, ECtHR 17 July 2012, appl. no. 22218/06.

other hand, a requirement of absolute clarity is not realistic, and the Court accepts that a law restricting the freedom of religion or believe sometimes may be couched in rather vague terms in order to avoid excessive rigidity, at least when supplemented by settled national jurisprudence, interpreting that law.[141]

The list of *legitimate aims* enumerated in Article 9(2) is rather short. The freedom to manifest one's religion or belief can only be restricted by such limitations as are prescribed by law and are necessary in a democratic society in the interests of *public safety, for the protection of public order, health or morals, or for the protection of the rights and freedoms of others*. Compared to Article 8(2), 10(2) and 11(2) it is evident that Article 9(2) comprises a relatively small list of interests as grounds for restriction. Furthermore, Article 9(2) refers to 'the protection of public order', whereas the other provisions use the term 'the prevention of disorder'. In its judgment in the *Engel* case the Court held that 'disorder' refers not only to 'public order' but 'also covers the order that must prevail within the confines of a special social group',[142] suggesting that 'public order' in Article 9(2) only refers to the notion of 'order in places accessible to everyone'. However, in more recent cases the Court has used a much broader concept of 'public order', which also comprises the order within a specific group or organisation,[143] the maintenance of a peaceful order between rival religious factions[144] and even constitutional principles such as the secular nature of the state.[145] Furthermore in *S.A.S.* – concerning the prohibition of the full-face veil (*burqa*) – the Court has expanded the scope of the aim of 'protection of the rights and freedom of others' beyond its ordinary meaning, by accepting that it encompasses even so vague a notion as the 'respect for the minimum requirements of life in society'.[146]

It may be assumed, therefore, that in practice there is no fundamental difference between the – extensively interpreted – restriction clause of Article 9 and the restriction clauses of Articles 8, 10 and 11. This is unavoidable. When the case law widens the concept of freedom of religion and belief in Article 9(1) outside of the limited sphere of traditional religious expressions and religious privacy into the broad public sphere, it is logical that the courts also adopt a correspondingly broader interpretation of the limitation grounds in the restriction clause. A theoretical exception might be the ground of 'national security', which is not included amongst the aims in Article 9(2). In *Nolan*, the Court concluded that this implies that this ground cannot be used as a basis for restricting the right to

---

[141] *Kokkinakis v. Greece, supra* n. 1, para. 40; *Dogru v. France, supra* n. 104, paras. 52–59.

[142] *Engel and Others v. the Netherlands*, ECtHR (GC) 8 June 1976, appl. nos. 5100/71, 5101/71, 5102/71, 5354/72 and 5370/72, para. 98.

[143] *Leyla Şahin v. Turkey, supra* n. 45, para. 99.

[144] *Serif v. Greece, supra* n. 90, para. 45; *Supreme Holy Council of the Muslim Community v. Bulgaria, supra* n. 90, para. 92.

[145] *Leyla Şahin v. Turkey, supra* n. 45, paras. 112–116; *Dogru v. France, supra* n. 104, paras. 69–73.

[146] *S.A.S. v. France, supra* n. 1, para. 121.

manifest one's religion or belief.[147] But it is not plausible that in cases of threats to national security which can only be encountered by measures which also restrict the freedom of religion or belief, or when limitations of the right to object to military duties on reasons of religious conscience are necessary, that this motive could not be invoked. In such situations, the administration and the courts probably will resort to a wide interpretation of other aims like 'public safety' and 'public order', that are mentioned in Article 9(2).

So, in fact there is no difference between the way the Strasbourg organs and the national courts will apply the restriction clause of Article 9 compared to the restriction clauses of Article 8, 10 and 11: what interest is involved is of very limited importance. The emphasis is laid on whether a restriction is *proportionate*, that is: whether the limitation is necessary in the light of the legitimate aim(s) pursued.

The Contracting States have a certain *margin of appreciation* in assessing the existence and extent of the necessity of an interference. In delimiting the extent of the margin of appreciation in a given case, the Court must have regard to what is at stake therein. It may also, if appropriate, have regard to any consensus and common values emerging from the practices of the States Parties to the Convention, in which generally only a small margin is left and a strict scrutiny by the Court is called for,[148] or allow for a larger margin when there is a great variety and lack of consensus.[149]

When the issues exclusively concern a conflict between the state and an individual or religious community, in general only convincing and compelling reasons can justify restrictions on these rights,[150] and a strict control by the Court is called for.[151] However, in other cases states are afforded a wide margin of appreciation, especially when various actors are involved, for instance when a whole system of historical church-state relations is at stake (see 5.3), or when the state must balance between conflicting fundamental claims of private and/or public parties.[152]

In various cases the Court concluded that Article 9 had been violated, primarily because of the disproportionality of the interference, often combined with discrimination or lack of neutrality. The case law is casuistic. Only a few examples will be discussed here.

It is rather self-evident that when a religion as such is targeted, in general this will amount to an unjustified – disproportionate – interference. The use of police violence to disrupt peaceful religious meetings is of course disproportionate

---

[147]   *Nolan and K. v. Russia, supra* n. 31, para. 73.

[148]   See, e.g., *Bayatyan v. Armenia, supra* n. 61, paras. 122–128.

[149]   *S.A.S. v. France, supra* n. 1, paras. 129–130, with further references.

[150]   *Jehova's Witnesses of Moscow and Others v. Russia, supra* n. 83, para. 108.

[151]   *Manoussakis v. Greece, supra* n. 44, para. 44. Cf. *Moscow Branch of the Salvation Army v. Russia,* ECtHR 5 October 2006, appl. no. 72881/01, paras. 76–77.

[152]   *Siebenhaar v. Germany, supra* n. 96, para. 39; *Eweida and Others v. the United Kingdom, supra* n. 6, paras. 105 and 109.

and discriminatory, and thus in breach of Article 9 as well as Article 14 in conjunction with Article 9: see section 5. The exclusion of a person from a state's territory,[153] the dismissal from a job,[154] a transfer to a less attractive post,[155] or the order not to host further meetings at home of a small religious community[156] merely on account of the content of one's religion in principle is not necessary, unless a very strong legal and factual justification is put forward.

When the state is not neutral and impartial, but takes sides in order to exclude minority denominations or to (re)enforce religious unity, its interference by definition is not necessary under Article 9(2).[157] For instance, withholding legal recognition of a schismatic church for reasons of religious unity must be regarded as a disproportionate restriction of religious freedom.[158] Likewise, state action favouring one leader or group of a divided religious community, or undertaken with the purpose of forcing the community to come together under a single leadership against its own wishes, is not necessary. In democratic societies, the state should not need to take measures to ensure that religious communities are brought under a unified leadership: its role is not to remove the cause of tension by eliminating pluralism, but to ensure that the competing groups tolerate each other.[159]

A system of prior authorisation (for instance to build a church) depending on the authorisation by an ecclesiastical authority of the dominant religion is irreconcilable with Article 9(2).[160] Denial of legal personality to 'new' religious communities – after a reasonable time – in general is problematic and often disproportionate (see section 4.1). Dissolution of a legally operating religious organisation is a very severe form of interference, and in general is unjustified.[161]

In *Kokkinakis*, the Court decided that the conviction of a Jehovah's Witness for proselytism formed a breach of Article 9 because it was not shown that the applicant's conviction was justified in the circumstances of the case by a pressing social need: the Greek courts had established his liability by merely reproducing the relevant section of the law. Therefore, the measure taken did not appear to be

---

[153] *Nolan and K. v. Austria, supra* n. 31, para. 75.

[154] *Ivanova v. Bulgaria, supra* n. 13, para. 84.

[155] *Sodan v. Turkey*, ECtHR 2 February 2016, appl. no. 18650/05. Remarkably, the Court based its reasoning primarily on Art. 8 (paras. 43–60).

[156] *Dimitrova v. Bulgaria*, ECtHR 10 February 2015, appl. no. 15452/07, paras. 28–31.

[157] *Holy Synod of the Bulgarian Orthodox (Metropolitan Inokentiy) and Others v. Bulgaria, supra* n. 81, para. 107.

[158] *Metropolitan Church of Bessarabia and Others v. Moldova, supra* n. 22, para. 129.

[159] *Serif v. Greece, supra* n. 90, paras. 45–54; *Hasan and Chaush v. Bulgaria, supra* n. 8, paras. 84–99; *Supreme Holy Council of the Muslim Community v. Bulgaria, supra* n. 90, paras. 93–99.

[160] *Manoussakis v. Greece, supra* n. 44, paras. 45–53. Cf. *Church of Scientology of St Petersburg and Others v. Russia, supra* n. 35, para. 47.

[161] *Biblical Centre of the Chuvash Republic v. Russia*, ECtHR 12 June 2014, appl. no. 33203/08, para. 61. See for an exceptional case, in which dissolution of an Islamic association was deemed to be justified: *Kalifatstaat v. Germany*, ECtHR 11 December 2006 (dec.), appl. 13828/04.

proportionate to the aim pursued (the protection of the rights and freedoms of others).[162]

Sometimes a restriction of the freedom of religion or belief in itself may not be unreasonable, but the weight of the interest it pretends to serve may be too slight to justify it. For instance in the *Eweida* case, a job dispute about a practising Christian wearing a discreet cross at work who was no longer allowed to work as a member of the check-in staff for British Airways, the Court took the view that the domestic courts had given too much weight to the wish of the employer to project a certain corporate image which in itself it found legitimate, in relation to the applicant's fundamental right to manifest her religious beliefs.[163] Therefore it found that there had been a violation of Article 9.[164] In the *Ahmet Arslan* case, the Court held that a ban on wearing religious clothing in public spaces outside religious ceremonies, applied to the Aczimendi tarikati group, was in breach of Article 9: although the purpose of the ban was to uphold Turkey's secular and democratic values and as such was legitimate in the light of the aims in Article 9(2), the necessity of this measure to realise those aims had not been established.[165] And in the *Association for Solidarity Witnesses with Jehovah's* case, the Court ruled that a change in planning regulation, making it impossible to continue to use a private apartment for religious meetings because it was too small, was not proportionate and necessary for the maintenance of the public order.[166]

In other cases, however, it will be concluded that the interference is necessary in a democratic society and proportionate to the legitimate aim pursued. For instance, interferences resulting from *prima facie* neutral regulations serving a general interest in principle will be held compatible with Article 9, being necessary in order to pursue that legitimate aim. So, the objective application of general building and housing regulations will often be regarded as justified in the public interest of rational planning.[167] And the requirement that children take part in compulsory mixed-gender swimming lessons is proportionate and justified for reasons of social integration, even though the parents for religious reasons object to these lessons.[168]

---

162 *Kokkinakis v. Greece, supra* n. 1, para. 49. The Court ruled likewise in *Larissis and Others v. Greece, supra* n. 134, para. 59. However, it also found that the conviction of military persons for the proselytism of subordinates was, in view of the special character of the relationship between a superior and a subordinate in the army, not disproportionate to the aim pursued, 'the protection of the rights and freedoms of others' (*ibid.*, para. 54).

163 *Eweida v. the United Kingdom, supra* n. 6.

164 See however *Chaplin v. the United Kingdom, supra* n. 6, para. 99; Ms Chaplin, a Christian state hospital nurse was asked to remove the cross she wore visibly on a chain around her neck as an expression of her belief, as the protection of health and safety on a hospital ward was inherently of a greater magnitude than that which applied in respect of Ms Eweida.

165 *Arslan and Others v. Turkey,* ECtHR 23 February 2010, appl. no. 41135/98, para. 48.

166 *Association for Solidarity Witnesses with Jehovah's and Others v. Turkey,* ECtHR 24 May 2016, appl. no. 36915/10, paras. 104–108.

167 *Vergos v. Greece,* ECtHR 24 June 2004, appl. no. 65501/01, paras. 38–42.

168 *Osmanoğlu and Kocabaş v. Switzerland, supra* n. 17, para. 96–106.

Dress regulations, *de facto* prohibiting wearing Muslim headscarves in public educational institutions, often may be justified by the principle of state neutrality.[169] The requirement to take off head-covering for a security check at an airport may be regarded as necessary in the interest of public safety, also when applied to a Sikh wearing a turban for religious reasons.[170] Likewise the Court did not find a violation of Article 9 in the obligation to appear bareheaded on identity photos for use on official documents.[171] Even a total prohibition to conceal one's face in public places was not held to be disproportionate, as the ban did not specifically target religious clothing (although it had the effect of forbidding the full-face veil, the *burqa*) and was motivated by the respect for the minimum requirements of life in society (that is, living together).[172]

A restriction intending to secure the implementation of a policy of providing a service without discrimination to others may prove to be an important factor to be taken into account, when balancing the individual's right to manifest his religious belief and the employer's interest in securing the rights of others. For instance, in the case of *McFarlane*, who refused to provide psycho-sexual counselling to same-sex couples, motivated by his orthodox Christian beliefs and for that reason was dismissed, the Court concluded that there was no violation of Article 9, while the employer's action was intended to secure the implementation of his policy of providing a service without discrimination.[173]

To conclude, it is submitted that, though for quite some time the freedom of religion and belief protected by Article 9 of the Convention did not seem to be too contentious, in recent years the number of 'big' issues that the Court has dealt with has grown significantly, including quite a number of violations and various well-reasoned, delicate judgments.

---

[169]   *Dahlab v. Switzerland*, ECtHR 15 February 2001 (dec.), appl. no. 42393/98 (concerning a teacher at a state school); *Leyla Şahin v. Turkey, supra* n. 45, paras. 104–114 (concerning a student at a state university); *Köse and 93 Others v. Turkey*, ECtHR 24 January 2006, appl. no. 26625/02; *Kervanci v. France*, ECtHR 4 December 2008, appl. no. 31645/04 and *Dogru v. France, supra* n. 104 (concerning schoolgirls in relation to sports classes); *Aktas v. France*, ECtHR 30 June 2009, appl. no. 43563/08; *Ranjit Singh v. France*, ECtHR 30 June 2009, appl. no. 27561/08. *Cf.* also *Ebrahimian v. France*, ECtHR 15 February 2016, appl. no. 64846/11, paras. 65–72 (concerning an employee in a public hospital, losing her job because of her headscarf).

[170]   *Phull v. France*, ECtHR 11 January 2005 (dec.), appl. no. 35753/03; see also *El Morsli v. France*, ECtHR 4 March 2008 (dec.), appl. no. 15585/06 (concerning a veil).

[171]   *Mann Singh v. France*, ECtHR 11 June 2007, appl. no. 24479/07.

[172]   *S.A.S. v. France, supra* n. 1, paras. 121–122 and 151–159.

[173]   *Eweida and Others v. the United Kingdom (McFarlane), supra* n. 6, para. 109.

CHAPTER 14

FREEDOM OF EXPRESSION

(Article 10)

Arjen VAN RIJN[*]

GUIDING PRINCIPLE

The freedom of expression is considered to be one of the core rights of the Convention because it enables the public debate in matters of public interest, which is vital for the well-functioning of democracy. Although this right is subject to restrictions, as is the case with most of the rights guaranteed by the Convention, those restrictions have to be applied in the light of the special significance of the freedom of expression for the public debate. The search to find a good balance between the freedom of expression and the rights and interests of others manifests itself notably in the case law concerning the private life of public figures.

ARTICLE 10

1. Everyone has the right to freedom of expression. This right shall include freedom to hold opinions and to receive and impart information and ideas without interference by public authority and regardless of frontiers. This Article shall not prevent States from requiring the licensing of broadcasting, television or cinema enterprises.

2. The exercise of these freedoms, since it carries with it duties and responsibilities, may be subject to such formalities, conditions, restrictions or penalties as are prescribed by law and are necessary in a democratic society, in the interests of national security, territorial integrity or public safety, for the prevention of disorder or crime, for the protection of health or morals, for the protection of the reputation or rights of others, for preventing the disclosure of information received in confidence, or for maintaining the authority and impartiality of the judiciary.

---

[*]   In the fourth edition this chapter was revised and updated by Arjen van Rijn.

CONTENTS

1. INTRODUCTION

Article 10 takes up a special position among the rights and freedoms protected by the Convention. The reason is that the freedom of expression has a fundamental significance for the well-functioning of the democratic process. On this basis, the Court has developed a set of principles in order to assess whether Article 10 can be invoked and whether a given expression is permissible or not.

According to the Court's well-established case law freedom of expression 'constitutes one of the essential foundations of a democratic society and one of the basic conditions for its progress and for each individual's self-fulfilment. Subject to paragraph 2 of Article 10, it is applicable not only to information or ideas that are favourably received or regarded as inoffensive or as a matter of indifference, but also to those that offend, shock or disturb. Such are the demands of pluralism, tolerance and broadmindedness without which there is no "democratic society"'.[1]

This freedom is subject to the exceptions set out in the second paragraph of Article 10. As to these exceptions, the Court holds that the need for any restrictions must be established convincingly, which implies the existence of a 'pressing social need'. The authorities have a certain margin of appreciation in assessing whether such a need exists, but it goes hand in hand with a European supervision, embracing both the legislation and the decisions applying it, even those given by an independent court. The Court is, therefore, empowered to give the final ruling on whether a restriction is permissible. In order to be able to do so the Court must look at the impugned interference in the light of the case as a whole, including the content of the alleged expressions and the context in which they were made. In particular, it must be determined whether the interference in issue was 'proportionate to the legitimate aims pursued' and whether the reasons adduced by the national authorities to justify it were 'relevant and sufficient'. In doing so the Court has to satisfy itself that the national authorities applied standards which were in conformity with the principles embodied in Article 10 and, moreover, that they based themselves on an acceptable assessment of the relevant facts.

In this connection, the Court makes reference to the essential function which the press fulfils in a democratic society. Although the press must not overstep certain bounds, particularly as regards the reputation and rights of others and the need to prevent the disclosure of confidential information, its duty is nevertheless to impart – in a manner consistent with its obligations and responsibilities – information and ideas on all matters of public interest. Not only does the press have the task of imparting such information and ideas, with regard to the print media as well as to the audio-visual media,[2] the public also has a right to receive them: 'Were it otherwise, the press would be unable to play its vital role of "public watchdog"'.[3]

Simultaneously the Court is mindful of the fact that journalistic freedom also covers possible recourse to a degree of exaggeration, or even provocation,[4]

---

[1] Since *Handyside v. the United Kingdom*, ECtHR 7 December 1976, appl. no. 5493/72, para. 49. See recently: *Von Hannover v. Germany (No. 2)*, ECtHR (GC) 7 February 2012, appl. nos. 40660/08 and 60641/08, para. 101; *Axel Springer AG v. Germany*, *supra* n. 1, para. 78; *Aksu v. Turkey*, ECtHR (GC) 15 March 2012, appl. nos. 4149/04 and 41029/04, para. 64; *Delfi v. Estonia*, ECtHR 16 June 2015, appl. no. 64569/09, para. 131; *Couderc and Hachette Filipacchi Associés v. France*, ECtHR 10 November 2015, appl. no. 40454/07, para. 88.

[2] *Jersild v. Denmark*, ECtHR (GC) 23 September 1994, appl. no. 15890/89, para. 31.

[3] See, *inter alia*, *Unabhängige Initiative Informationsvielfalt v. Austria*, ECtHR 26 February 2002, appl. no. 28525/95, para. 37; *Perna v. Italy*, ECtHR (GC) 6 May 2003, appl. no. 48898/99, para. 39; *Vides Aizsardzibas Klubs v. Latvia*, ECtHR 27 May 2004, appl. no. 57829/00, para. 42; *Sirbu and Others v. Moldova*, ECtHR 15 June 2004, appl. nos. 73562/01, 73565/01, 73712/01, 73744/01, 73972/01 and 73973/01, para. 17; *Busuioc v. Moldova*, ECtHR 21 December 2004, appl. no. 61513/00, para. 56; *Blaja News Sp. z.o.o. v. Poland*, ECtHR 26 November 2013, appl. no. 59545/10, para. 50; *Couderc and Hachette Filipacchi Associés v. France*, *supra* n. 1, para. 89.

[4] *Prager and Oberschlick*, ECtHR 26 April 1995, appl. no. 15974/90, para. 38. See, *inter alia*, *Gomes da Silva v. Portugal*, ECtHR 28 September 2000, appl. no. 37678/97, para. 34; *Pedersen*

however with the proviso that the limits of permissible criticism are narrower in relation to a private citizen than with respect to politicians and governments. The same applies to the publication of details of a person's private life. In certain special circumstances, the public's right to be informed can even extend to aspects of the private life of public figures, particularly where politicians are concerned. However, this will not be the case – despite the person concerned being well known to the public – where photos and commentaries relate exclusively to details of the person's private life and have the sole aim of satisfying public curiosity in that respect. Since the case of *Von Hannover v. Germany* the Court is demanding a stricter examination relating to the fair balance that has to be struck between a public person's right to respect for his private life guaranteed under Article 8 and the right of the publishing company – also in horizontal relations – to freedom of expression guaranteed under Article 10.[5]

Nevertheless, in general the essential function of the press is always taken into account when an assessment is made whether in the given situation a restriction of the freedom of expression is permissible or not. This also applies to non-governmental organisations which can be characterised as 'social watchdog'. Their activities warrant similar protection to that afforded to the press.[6] Moreover, the press has a valuable secondary role in maintaining and making available to the public archives containing news which has previously been reported.[7]

2. SCOPE

2.1. EVERYONE

Article 10 may be invoked both by natural and legal persons.[8] With regard to the former it is irrelevant for the applicability of Article 10 whether they have a special status like servicemen[9] or civil servants[10], or a special function like police officials[11] or judges.[12] Similarly, it is irrelevant whether the natural or legal

---

[5] *and Baadsgaard v. Denmark*, ECtHR 19 June 2003, appl. no. 49017/99, para. 65; *Perna v. Italy*, supra n. 3, para. 39; *Ukrainian Media Group v. Ukraine*, ECtHR 29 March 2005, appl. no. 72713/01, para. 40.

[5] *Von Hannover v. Germany*, ECtHR 24 June 2004, appl. no. 59320/00.

[6] *Társaság a Szabadságjogokért v. Hungary*, ECtHR 14 April 2009, appl. no. 37374/05, para. 27; *Österreichische Vereinigung zur Erhaltung, Stärkung und Schaffung v. Austria*, ECtHR 28 November 2013, appl. no. 39534/07, para. 34.

[7] *Times Newspapers Ltd v. the United Kingdom (Nos. 1 en 2)*, ECtHR 10 March 2009, appl. nos. 3002/03 and 23676/03, para. 45.

[8] *Autronic AG v. Switzerland*, ECtHR 22 May 1990, appl. no. 12726/87, para. 47.

[9] *Engel and Others v. the Netherlands*, ECtHR (GC) 8 June 1976, appl. nos. 5100/71, 5101/71, 5102/71, 5354/72 and 5370/72, para. 100; *Hadjianastassiou v. Greece*, ECtHR 16 December 1992, appl. no. 12945/87, para. 39; *Vereinigung Demokratischer Soldaten Österreichs and Gubi v. Austria*, ECtHR 19 December 1994, appl. no. 15153/89, para. 27.

[10] *Vogt v. Germany*, ECtHR 26 September 1995, appl. no. 17851/91, para. 43.

[11] *Rekvényi v. Hungary*, ECtHR (GC) 20 May 1999, appl. no. 25390/94.

[12] *Wille v. Liechtenstein*, ECtHR (GC) 28 October 1999, appl. no. 28396/95, para. 42.

person who invokes Article 10 acts as an individual citizen or forms part of the journalistic profession. However, the special status, function or position may be relevant under the second paragraph of Article 10.[13]

It should be noted that the Court holds Article 10 not applicable when the recruitment to the civil service is at stake. In the 1984 case of *Glasenapp v. Germany*, the Court held that under the Land Civil Servants Act the applicant could only become a secondary school teacher with the status of probationary civil servant, if she afforded a guarantee that she would consistently uphold the free democratic constitutional system within the meaning of the Basic Law. This requirement, according to the Court, 'applies to recruitment to the civil service, a matter that was deliberately omitted from the Convention, and it cannot in itself be considered incompatible with the Convention'.[14] In the *Kosiek* case, which was decided on the same day, the Court adopted a comparable reasoning.[15] In both cases, the Court came to the conclusion that in the light of the facts of each case access to the civil service lay at the heart of the issue submitted to it. In refusing such access the authority took account of the applicants' opinions and attitude merely in order to satisfy itself as to whether they possessed one of the necessary personal qualifications for the post in question. There was, therefore, in the Court's view no interference with the exercise of the right protected in paragraph 1 of Article 10.[16]

The Court affirmed this point of view in the *Sidabras and Džiautas* case. Two Lithuanian officials had been dismissed from their position as a tax inspector and a prosecutor, once it was discovered that they were former KGB employees. The Court ruled that Article 10 was not applicable, because the recruitment to the civil service was at stake. The officials had not met the conditions for appointment.[17]

In the latter case, the Court recognised that it does not always seem to follow a consequent line, stating that in the case of *Vogt v. Germany*[18] and the cases of *Volkmer* and *Petersen v. Germany*[19] it indeed held that the dismissal of a civil servant or a state official on political grounds may give rise to a complaint under Article 10 of the Convention. The Court explained the difference in reasoning with the argument that the employment restrictions suffered by the applicants in those cases related to their specific activities as a member of the Communist Party in West Germany (*Vogt*) or as collaborators of the regime in the former German Democratic Republic (*Volkmer* and *Petersen*), while in the *Sidabras and*

---

13   See *infra* 2.6.
14   *Glasenapp v. Germany*, ECtHR (GC) 28 August 1986, appl. no. 9228/80, para. 52.
15   *Kosiek v. Germany*, ECtHR 28 August 1986, appl. no. 9704/82, para. 37.
16   *Ibid.*, paras. 53 and 39, respectively. See also *Leander v. Sweden*, ECtHR 26 March 1987, appl. no. 9248/81, para. 72.
17   *Sidabras and Džiautas v. Lithuania*, ECtHR 27 July 2004, appl. nos. 55480/00 and 59330/00, paras. 68–71.
18   *Vogt v. Germany*, *supra* n. 10, para. 44.
19   *Volkmer v. Germany*, ECtHR 22 November 2001, appl. no. 39799/98 respectively *Petersen v. Germany*, ECtHR 22 November 2001, appl. no. 39793/98.

Dñiautas case both applicants suffered employment restrictions not as a result of the outcome of ordinary labour law proceedings, but as a result of the application to them of special domestic legislation which imposed screening measures on the basis of their former employment with the KGB.[20] Still, considering the cases mentioned, the line of demarcation between a recruitment conflict and a labour conflict does appear to be very clear.

2.2. OPINIONS, INFORMATION AND IDEAS

The freedom of expression covers both the expression of facts and the expression of value judgements. Given the wording of the first paragraph of Article 10 it also includes 'the freedom to hold opinions and to receive and impart information and ideas'. The 'freedom to hold opinions' can hardly be distinguished from the 'freedom of thought' discussed under Article 9 and must be regarded as similar to this term.[21] The freedom to receive information precedes the formation of an opinion by the person who seeks the information, and consequently also its expression. The freedom to impart information and ideas can be regarded as an expression of an opinion, through facts or value judgements, of the informant himself or of a third person. These considerations make it clear why the freedom to hold opinions and to receive and impart information and ideas are indissolubly related with the freedom of expression.

According to the Court the freedom to receive and impart information does not contain a general right for everyone of access to all information, but the Court has recognised that under certain circumstances the public has a right to receive information of general interest.

In the recent case of *Magyar Helsinki Bizottsåag v. Hungary*, the Court, extensively referring to its earlier judgments, clarified the principles which it has developed in its case law so far: 'The Court continues to consider that "the right to freedom to receive information basically prohibits a Government from restricting a person from receiving information that others wish or may be willing to impart to him." Moreover, "the right to receive information cannot be construed as imposing on a State positive obligations to collect and disseminate information of its own motion". The Court further considers that Article 10 does not confer on the individual a right of access to information held by a public authority nor oblige the Government to impart such information to the individual. However, as is seen from the above analysis, such a right or obligation may arise, firstly, where disclosure of the information has been imposed by a judicial order which has gained legal force (which is not an issue in the present case) and, secondly, in circumstances where access to the information

---

[20]   *Sidabras v. Džiautas v. Lithuania, supra* n. 17, paras. 68–71.
[21]   See *supra*, Ch. 13. The correspondence between Art. 9 and Art. 10 will be discussed *infra*, 2.6.

is instrumental for the individual's exercise of his or her right to freedom of expression, in particular "the freedom to receive and impart information" and where its denial constitutes an interference with that right.'[22]

From the case law so far, the Court derives four criteria that ought to be relevant: the purpose of the information request, the nature of the information sought, the role of the applicant and if the information sought is ready and available. In this context, it can be relevant whether a contribution to the public debate is pursued and also whether the applicant is acting as a public watchdog.[23] In the case in question the Court held that the information sought by the applicant NGO from the relevant police departments was necessary for the completion of the survey on the functioning of the public defenders' scheme being conducted by it in its capacity as a non-governmental human-rights organisation, in order to contribute to discussion on an issue of obvious public interest. By denying it access to the requested information, which was ready and available, the domestic authorities impaired the applicant NGO's exercise of its freedom to receive and impart information, in a manner striking at the very substance of its Article 10 rights. There had therefore been an interference with a right protected in this provision.[24] Subsequently, the Court examined whether or not the restrictions criteria of the second paragraph of Article 10 had been met. This was not the case, so accordingly there had been a violation of Article 10.

The Court has so far expressly refused to give a definition of the terms 'information and ideas',[25] but it is clear that the first paragraph of Article 10 offers a broad access to protection. Thus, *inter alia*, photos,[26] medical secrets,[27] the search for the historical truth,[28] factual statements in interviews,[29] television commercials,[30] advertisements in newspapers[31] and television programmes of all kinds received from abroad by satellite[32] fall under information and ideas. The Court has also recognised the important role the Internet plays in enhancing the public's access to news and facilitating the dissemination of information in general.[33]

---

[22] *Magyar Helsinki Bizottság v. Hungary*, ECtHR 8 November 2016, appl. no. 18030/11, para. 156.
[23] *Ibid.*, paras. 157–170.
[24] *Ibid.*, para. 180.
[25] *Groppera Radio AG and Others v. Switzerland*, ECtHR 28 March 1990, appl. no. 10890/84, para. 55.
[26] *Von Hannover v. Germany, supra* n. 5.
[27] *Éditions Plon v. France*, ECtHR 18 May 2004, appl. no. 58148/00.
[28] *Chauvy and Others v. France*, ECtHR 29 June 2004, appl. no. 64915/01.
[29] *Selistö v. Finland*, ECtHR 16 November 2004, appl. no. 56767/00.
[30] *VgT Verein gegen Tierfabriken v. Switzerland*, ECtHR 28 June 2001, appl. no. 24699/94.
[31] *Krone Verlag GmbH & Co KG v. Austria*, ECtHR 11 December 2003, appl. no. 39069/97.
[32] *Khurshid Mustafa and Tarzibachi v. Sweden*, ECtHR 16 December 2008, appl. no. 23883/06.
[33] *Kalda v. Estonia*, ECtHR 19 January 2016, appl. no. 17429/10, para. 44.

The fact that the information concerned is of a commercial nature[34] or that the freedom of expression is not exercised in a discussion of matters of public interest[35] is also irrelevant for the applicability of Article 10. The content of the expressions, with very few exceptions,[36] seems to be irrelevant too, as the Court has held, with reference to the demands of a democratic society, that Article 10 is also applicable to information or ideas that offend, shock or disturb.

However, this principle does not exclude a possibility that certain categories of information and ideas may not be covered by the protection of Article 10 of the Convention. According to the Court, certain classes of speech, such as lewd and obscene speech have no essential role in the expression of ideas. An offensive statement may fall outside the protection of freedom of expression where the sole intent of the offensive statement is to insult. Thus, in the *Rujak* case the Court placed a soldier's remark: 'this is not my State, I am not its national, I don't recognise [respect] you, your rank or the Croatian Army!' outside the ambit of Article 10 and consequently did not examine the proportionality of the given six months' imprisonment.[37] In the case of *Dieudonné M'Bala M'Bala v. France*, the Court found that a performance concerning a degrading portrayal of Jewish deportation victims faced with a man who denied their extermination, was not a performance which, even if satirical or provocative, fell within the protection of Article 10 but was in reality, in the circumstances of the case, a demonstration of hatred and anti-Semitism and support for Holocaust denial, which ran counter to the values of the European Convention.[38] This approach is susceptible to discussion, because it can narrow the scope of protection of Article 10 in an undesirable way. It is not clear, why these kinds of expressions should not be brought under the scope of Article 10 as well and subsequently assessed in accordance with the system of restrictions laid down in the second paragraph.

The fact that Article 10 protects the free expression of opinions implies that a rather strong emphasis is laid on the protection of the specific means by which the opinion is expressed. The Court has expressly upheld that Article 10 protects not only the substance of ideas and information but also the form in which they are conveyed.[39] Even protesting against fox hunting and disrupting the hunt by diverting the dogs' attention with the aid of a hunting horn constitutes an expression of opinion.[40] The same applies to the publication of

---

34   *Markt intern Verlag GmbH and Klaus Beermann v. Germany*, ECtHR 20 November 1989, appl. no. 10572/83, para. 26; *Casado Coca v. Spain*, ECtHR 24 February 1994, appl. no. 15450/89.

35   *Jacubowski v. Germany*, ECtHR 23 June 1994, appl. no. 15088/89; *Diego Nafría v. Spain*, ECtHR 14 March 2002, appl. no. 46833/99.

36   See Ch. 35 on Art. 17.

37   *Vladimir Rujak v. Croatia*, ECtHR 2 October 2012, appl. no. 57942/10, paras. 27–32.

38   *Dieudonné M'Bala M'Bala v. France*, ECtHR 20 October 2015, appl. no. 25239/13, para. 41.

39   See, *inter alia*, *News Verlags GmbH & Co KG v. Austria*, ECtHR 11 January 2000, appl. no. 31457/96, para. 39; *Unabhängige Initiative Informationsvielfalt v. Austria*, *supra* n. 3, para. 38; *Perna v. Italy*, *supra* n. 3, para. 39.

40   *Hashman and Harrup v. the United Kingdom*, ECtHR 25 November 1999, appl. no. 25594/94, para. 28.

photos[41] and news reporting based on interviews.[42] According to the Court it is not for judges 'to substitute their own views for those of the press as to what technique of reporting should be adopted by journalists'.[43] Any restriction of the means will, therefore, imply a restriction of the freedom 'to receive and impart information and ideas'.[44] However, the means by which a particular opinion is expressed are protected only insofar as they are means which have an independent significance for the expression of the opinion.

Also in case the person who provides the means is not the holder of the opinion, he is protected by Article 10. Thus, in the *Müller* case the organisers of the exhibition of Mr Müller's paintings were considered to have exercised their freedom of expression.[45] On the other hand, Article 10 does not bestow any freedom of forum for the exercise of the freedom of expression. Although demographic, social, economic and technological developments are changing the way in which people move around and come into contact with each other, the Court does not consider that this requires unrestricted entry to private property, or even, necessarily, to all publicly owned property. Only if the bar on access to property has the effect of preventing any effective exercise of freedom of expression or if the essence of that right would be destroyed, could a positive obligation arise for the state to regulate property rights, as the Court held in the case of *Appleby*.[46]

On the basis of its liberal approach the Court has been able to assess a wide range of situations. It is once more worth mentioning the *Müller* case, which concerned a conviction for having published obscene material and confiscation of the paintings concerned. In this case, the Court decided that the freedom of artistic expression of a painter, although not mentioned expressly, is also covered by Article 10.[47] Other remarkable cases concern, *inter alia,* the complaint about the conviction of a publisher for having in his possession copies of the 'Little Red School Book' and their destruction as pornography;[48] the injunction of the Irish Supreme Court restraining companies from giving information to pregnant women about the possibility of obtaining abortions abroad;[49] the seizure and subsequent forfeiture of a film;[50] the refusal of the competent authorities to

---

[41]   See, e.g., *Von Hannover v. Germany, supra* n. 5, para. 59.

[42]   *Pedersen and Baadsgaard (No. 2) v. Denmark, supra* n. 4.

[43]   *News Verlags GmbH & Co KG v. Austria, supra* n. 39, para. 39.

[44]   *Autronic AG v. Switzerland, supra* n. 8, para. 47. See also *Jersild v. Denmark, supra* n. 2, para. 31; *Oberschlick v. Austria,* ECtHR (GC) 23 May 1991, appl. no. 11662/85, para. 57.

[45]   *Müller and Others v. Switzerland,* ECtHR 24 May 1988, appl. no. 10737/84, para. 27.

[46]   *Appleby and Others v. the United Kingdom,* ECtHR 6 May 2003, appl. no. 44306/98, para. 47.

[47]   *Müller and Others v. Switzerland,* ECtHR 24 May 1988, *supra* n. 45, para. 27.

[48]   *Handyside v. the United Kingdom, supra* n. 1.

[49]   *Open Door and Dublin Well Woman v. Ireland,* ECtHR 29 October 1992, appl. nos. 14234/88 and 14235/88.

[50]   *Otto-Preminger-Institut v. Austria,* ECtHR 20 September 1994, appl. no. 13470/87. See also *Scherer v. Switzerland,* EComHR 14 January 1993, appl. no. 17116/90, paras. 50–67.

add a magazine to the list of periodicals distributed by the Austrian army,[51] the amount of damages awarded by a court for libel,[52] a ban for a ship chartered by Women on Waves to enter the territorial waters of Portugal,[53] and a ban on speaking Kurdish in an election campaign.[54]

As the *Piermont* case shows, even an expulsion order may come within the ambit of Article 10 if the expulsion order is specifically aimed at the restriction of the freedom of expression. This case concerned an order directing the expulsion of the applicant from the French Polynesia territory and a ban on re-entering as well as an order prohibiting her to enter the territory of New Caledonia. Mrs Piermont had taken part in a demonstration on the territory of French Polynesia in favour of the independence of French Polynesia and during that demonstration had made a speech in which she supported the anti-nuclear and independence positions of some of the local political parties. The orders in question had been imposed by the French authorities and had the clear intention of preventing Mrs Piermont from supporting publicly the opposition against the French authorities in French Polynesia and New-Caledonia. According to the Court, the expulsion order coupled with the prohibition to re-enter French Polynesia as well as the ban on entering New Caledonia constituted an interference with the freedom of expression.[55]

As a consequence of the great weight the Court attaches to the freedom of the press for the concept of a democratic society and to its vital role of public watchdog, it has also brought the protection of journalistic sources under the scope of Article 10. In the *Goodwin* case, a journalist had received information about the financial problems of a company. When he contacted the company to verify the facts, it appeared that the information had been derived from a confidential company report. These events eventually resulted in an injunction restraining the journalist (and the publishers he worked for) from publishing the information and a court order to disclose the identity of Goodwin's source. The Court held that the disclosure order had to be examined under the second paragraph of Article 10 and thus took for granted that the protection of a journalistic source – in itself not an expression of an opinion – comes within the ambit of Article 10.[56]

The right to receive and impart information and ideas also includes the right to do this by means of radio and television. The broadcasting of programmes

---

[51]   *Vereinigung Demokratischer Soldaten Österreichs and Gubi v. Austria, supra* n. 9.
[52]   *Tolstoy Miloslavsky v. the United Kingdom*, ECtHR 13 July 1995, appl. no. 18139/91.
[53]   *Woman On Waves and Others v. Portugal*, ECtHR 3 February 2009, appl. no. 31276/05, para. 30.
[54]   *Şükran Aydin and Others v. Turkey*, ECtHR 22 January 2013, appl. nos. 49197/06, 23196/07, 50242/08, 60912/08 and 14871/09.
[55]   *Piermont v. France*, ECtHR 27 April 1995, appl. nos. 15773/89 and 15774/89, paras. 51 and 80. With regard to the ban on entering New Caledonia, the Commission had reached a different conclusion; *Vella v. Malta*, EComHR 20 January 1994, appl. no. 18420/91, para. 96.
[56]   *Goodwin v. the United Kingdom*, ECtHR 7 March 1996, appl. no. 17488/90, para. 28.

over the air and cable transmissions of such programmes fall within the scope of Article 10,[57] while the same holds good for setting up a radio or television station.[58] However, the extent of this right is subject to a special arrangement, which is laid down in the third sentence of paragraph 1 of Article 10. According to the Court, Article 10(1) makes it clear that states are permitted to regulate by a licensing system the way in which broadcasting is organised in their territories, particularly in its technical aspects but also with regard to other considerations, including such matters as the nature and objectives of a proposed station, its potential audience at national, regional or local level, the rights and needs of a specific audience and the obligations deriving from international instruments. This may lead to interferences whose aim will be legitimate under the third sentence of paragraph 1, even though they do not correspond to any of the aims set out in paragraph 2. Subsequently, the compatibility of such interferences with the Convention must nevertheless be assessed in the light of the other requirements of the second paragraph of Article 10.[59]

Comparatively new means to provide and receive information, for instance over the Internet, are increasingly important. Since the case law attributes a broad effect to the first paragraph of Article 10, these new means, as far as they have an independent significance for the expression of opinions, also come within the ambit of Article 10.[60] In this connection the Court acknowledges 'that the Internet is an information and communication tool particularly distinct from the printed media, especially as regards the capacity to store and transmit information. The electronic network, serving billions of users worldwide, is not and potentially will never be subject to the same regulations and control. The risk of harm posed by content and communications on the Internet to the exercise and enjoyment of human rights and freedoms, particularly the right to respect for private life, is certainly higher than that posed by the press. Therefore, the policies governing reproduction of material from the printed media and the Internet may differ. The latter undeniably have to be adjusted according to technology's specific features in order to secure the protection and promotion of the rights and freedoms concerned.'[61]

---

[57] *Groppera Radio AG and Others v. Switzerland, supra* n. 25, para. 55. See also *X and Y v. Belgium*, EComHR 13 May 1982, appl. no. 8962/80, where the Commission held that a conviction for having used a transceiver for private purposes without the required authorisation constituted an interference with the right to receive and impart information and ideas.

[58] *Informationsverein Lentia and Others v. Austria*, ECtHR 24 November 1993, appl. nos. 13914/88, 15041/89, 15717/89, 15779/89 and 17207/90, para. 26.

[59] *Ibid.*, para. 32. See *infra* 3.5.

[60] *Renaud v. France*, ECtHR 25 February 2010, appl. no. 13290/07; *Ahmet Yildirim v. Turkey*, ECtHR 18 December 2012, appl. no. 3111/10; *Fredrik Neij and Sunde Kolmisoppi v. Sweden*, ECtHR 19 February 2013, appl. no. 40397/12; *Delfi AS v. Estonia, supra* n. 1.

[61] *Wegrzynowski and Smolczewski v. Poland*, ECtHR 16 July 2013, appl. no. 33846/07, para. 58.

In the *Delfi AS* case, the Court held that the liability of an Internet news portal operator for defamatory statements by third persons does not constitute a disproportionate interference with the media's right to freedom of expression.[62] However, the general and complete block of YouTube by the Turkish authorities had to be considered as a disproportionate interference.[63] Last, when prisoners are denied admittance to certain Internet sites, this can only be done on the basis of a detailed analysis, otherwise there is no proof of necessity of this restriction in a democratic society.[64]

Finally, the freedom of expression also entails the right not to express oneself. In the *Young, James and Webster* case, a connection was made by the Court between compulsory membership of a trade union and Article 10: as a result of that compulsory membership the employee in question was no longer free to dissent from a view propagated by the trade union.[65]

2.3. NO INTERFERENCE BY PUBLIC AUTHORITY

Article 10 guarantees the freedom of expression 'without interference by public authority'. In the *Casado Coca* case, the Spanish Government tried to escape from its responsibility by submitting that the disciplinary penalty imposed on a member of the Bar for contravening the ban on advertising, had been imposed by the Barcelona Bar Council and, therefore, not by a 'public authority'. This argument was rejected by the Court. It held that, according to Spanish law, the Bar Council was a public law corporation, that the Bar served the public interest and, moreover, that the penalty had been upheld by the Spanish courts, all of which are state institutions.[66]

2.4. REGARDLESS OF FRONTIERS

The words 'regardless of frontiers' in the first paragraph of Article 10 indicate that the authorities must also admit information from beyond the frontiers of the country and allow the imparting of information from across those frontiers, subject, of course, to the possibilities of restriction laid down in the second paragraph.[67] In this connection, the Court held in the *Association Ekin* case

---

62   *Delfi AS v. Estonia*, *supra* n. 1, para. 92.
63   *Cengiz and Others v. Turkey*, ECtHR 1 December 2015, appl. nos. 48226/10 and 14027/11.
64   *Kalda v. Estonia*, *supra* n. 33, para. 53.
65   *Young, James and Webster v. the United* Kingdom, ECtHR 13 August 1981, appl. nos. 7601/76 and 7806/77, para. 57.
66   *Casado Coca v. Spain*, *supra* n. 34, para. 39.
67   *Groppera Radio AG and Others v. Switzerland*, *supra* n. 25 and *Autronic AG v. Switzerland*, *supra* n. 8, concerning the imparting and receiving of information from abroad.

that the legal obligation to submit publications of foreign origin or written in a foreign language to a public authority before distribution, is not *a priori* incompatible with the Convention, but must be formulated very strictly and scrutinised very thoroughly under the second paragraph of Article 10 in order to prevent arbitrary application.[68]

The applicability of Article 10 to information from beyond the frontiers of a country does, of course, not offer a guarantee that such information is not held back outside the frontiers, since the state concerned bears no responsibility for measures taken to that effect abroad.[69]

2.5. *DRITTWIRKUNG* AND POSITIVE OBLIGATIONS

Article 10 can be invoked before the Court not only in vertical relations but also in horizontal relations, where a state has taken, or has failed to take certain measures, for instance to protect the reputation or the rights of others as referred to in the second paragraph. This opens up a wide range of possibilities to intervene in conflicts between private parties, as a court decision in a conflict between private individuals is also considered as a measure of the state.[70] This especially becomes apparent as regards the collision between the freedom of expression and the right of respect for the private life of individuals, safeguarded by Article 8.[71]

Although the Court has always been hesitant to embrace the *Drittwirkung* of Article 10 in so many words, in the *Fuentes Bobo* case it recognised that a positive obligation can rest with the authorities to protect the freedom of expression against infringements, even by private persons.[72] The applicant, who had been working as a producer with the Spanish public broadcasting company TVE, was fired after having criticised the staff policy of his employer in interviews with another private radio station. The Court held that Article 10 not only applies to relations between employer and employee which are governed by public law, but also to relations which are governed by private law. The Court did not explain which specific obligations the authorities could have had in the concrete situation, but it is evident that in principle the authorities may be held responsible if they do not take appropriate measures to protect freedom of expression in relations governed by private law.

In the *VGT Verein gegen Tierfabriken* case, the Court referred to Article 1 of the Convention and held again that in addition to the primarily negative obligation of a state to abstain from interference in Convention guarantees 'there

---

68   *Association Ekin v. France*, ECtHR 17 July 2001, appl. no. 39288/98, para. 58.
69   *Bertrand Russell Peace Foundation Ltd. v. the United Kingdom*, EComHR 2 May 1978, appl. no. 7597/76.
70   See, e.g., *Bergens Tidende and Others v. Norway*, ECtHR 2 May 2000, appl. no. 26131/95.
71   See *infra* 3.3.
72   *Fuentes Bobo v. Spain*, ECtHR 29 February 2000, appl. no. 39293/98, para. 3.

may be positive obligations inherent' in such guarantees. 'The responsibility of a State may then be engaged as a result of not observing its obligation to enact domestic legislation'.[73] However, the Court 'does not consider it desirable, let alone necessary, to elaborate a general theory concerning the extent to which the Convention guarantees should be extended to relations between private individuals *inter se*'.[74] It was sufficient in the instant case that the refusal of a commercial television company to broadcast a commercial against the ill-treatment of animals was based on a section of the Swiss Federal Radio and Television Act which prohibits 'political advertising' and, therefore, amounted to an interference by 'public authority'.[75]

A positive obligation may not be interpreted in such a way as to impose an impossible or disproportionate burden on the authorities. The need to create an effective system and a favourable climate for the protection of journalists and writers and their participation in the public debate is not seen by the Court beforehand as such an impossible and disproportionate burden. The obligation can even go as far as the need to take steps effectively to investigate and, where necessary, provide protection against unlawful acts involving violence.[76]

As mentioned before, in the *Appleby* case the Court decided that Article 10 does not bestow any freedom of forum for the exercise of that right and that, therefore, it does not automatically create rights of entry to private property or even to all publicly owned property. However, a positive obligation for the state could arise to regulate property rights, where the bar on access to property has the effect of preventing any effective exercise of freedom of expression or where the essence of the right would be destroyed.[77]

In the *Steel and Morris* case, members of a small campaign group had accused McDonald's of abusive and immoral farming and employment practices, deforestation, exploitation of children and their parents through aggressive advertising and the sale of unhealthy food. McDonald's had lodged a claim for defamation. According to the Court it was not in principle incompatible with Article 10 to place on the campaigners in libel proceedings the onus of proving to the civil standard the truth of defamatory statements. The state enjoys a margin of appreciation as to the means it provides under domestic law to enable a company to challenge the truth, and limit the damage, of allegations which risk harming its reputation. In that case, however, it is essential, in order to safeguard the countervailing interests of free expression and open debate, that a measure of procedural fairness and equality of arms is provided for. Because

---

[73]   *Ibid.*, para. 45.
[74]   *VgT Verein gegen Tierfabriken v. Switzerland*, *supra* n. 30, para. 46.
[75]   *Ibid.*, paras. 47–48.
[76]   *Özgür Gündem v. Turkey*, ECtHR 16 March 2000, appl. no. 23144/93, paras. 43–45; *Dink v. Turkey*, ECtHR 14 September 2010, appl. nos. 2668/07, 6102/08, 30079/08, 7072/09 and 7124/09, paras. 106, 137–138.
[77]   *Appleby and Others v. the United Kingdom*, *supra* n. 46, paras. 40 and 47.

the campaigners had no access to free legal aid, the Court held that there was no correct balance between the need to protect the campaigners' rights to freedom of expression and the need to protect McDonald's rights and reputation.[78]

In the *Sirbu* case, the Court took the position that the freedom to receive information 'cannot be construed as imposing on a State, in circumstances such as those of the present case, positive obligations to disclose to the public any secret documents and information concerning its military, intelligence service or police'.[79]Another matter concerns the question of whether the right to receive information calls for pluriformity in imparting information, which then has to be guaranteed by the authorities, for instance by making grants to persons and institutions imparting information, where this is necessary for such pluriformity.[80] In the *Vereinigung Demokratischer Soldaten Österreichs and Gubi* case, the Austrian army had been distributing free of charge its own publications and publications of private associations of soldiers in all the country's barracks, but had refused to distribute *Der Igel*, a magazine published by the first applicant. The Court held that this difference in treatment considerably reduced the chances of *Der Igel* to increase its readership among service personnel and as a result constituted a violation of Article 10.[81] Having regard to this judgment and the fact that the Court regards pluralism as being of particular importance as far as the press is concerned,[82] it is evident that the authorities, once they proceed to subsidise or in any other way support persons and institutions imparting information, have the duty to do so without discrimination.

Finally, the question of whether freedom of expression implies the right of reply or rectification deserves attention. The publications involved will usually originate from a private party and the publication of the reply or rectification will have to be effected in most cases by a private party as well. From Article 10 should then be derived an obligation on the part of the state to create a legal obligation to publish the reply or rectification and to provide for a remedy, either on the ground of a civil claim to that effect or in combination with a criminal conviction for insult. Such an obligation of publication would not constitute an unlawful interference with the freedom of expression laid down in Article 10 for the person on whom it would be imposed, since the justification might be

---

[78]   *Steel and Morris v. the United Kingdom*, ECtHR 15 February 2005, appl. no. 68416/01, para. 95.

[79]   *Sirbu and Others v. Moldova*, *supra* n. 3, para. 18.

[80]   In its decision in *Sacchi v. Italy*, EComHR 12 March 1976, appl. no. 6452/74, the Commission held as regards its previously given opinion that Art. 10(1) does not rule out a government monopoly for TV broadcasts: 'the Commission would not now be prepared purely and simply to maintain this point of view without further consideration.' However, it did not answer the question.

[81]   *Vereinigung Demokratischer Soldaten Österreichs and Gubi v. Austria*, *supra* n. 9, paras. 39–40.

[82]   See, *inter alia*, *Handyside v. the United Kingdom*, *supra* n. 1, para. 49; *Informationsverein Lentia and Others v. Austria*, *supra* n. 58, para. 38.

found in the restriction ground 'protection of the reputation or rights of others'. Meanwhile the Court is of the opinion that a legal obligation to publish a rectification or a reply may be seen as a normal element of the legal framework governing the exercise of the freedom of expression by the print media. It cannot, as such, be regarded as excessive or unreasonable. This flows from the need not only to be able to contest untruthful information, but also to ensure a plurality of opinions, especially on matters of general interest such as literary and political debate.[83]

2.6. RELATION TO OTHER CONVENTION RIGHTS

Article 10 is often invoked in close connection with other articles of the Convention. With respect to Article 6, the *Nikula* case should be mentioned. This case concerned a lawyer who had been convicted for insulting a public prosecutor while defending her client during a court session. The Court held that the right to a fair trial implies a free and even heated exchange of views between the parties. It is the task of counsel to defend the interests of his client fervently. Only in exceptional situations will there be a pressing social need for a restriction of the freedom of expression of counsel during a court session.[84] In the *McVicar* case, the Court concluded in relation to Article 6(1) that the applicant had not been prevented from presenting his defence to a defamation action effectively in the High Court, nor were the proceedings made unfair by reason of his ineligibility for legal aid. Therefore, there was no interference with the applicant's right to freedom of expression.[85] The same applied for the exclusion of evidence. The Court found the rules in this respect clear and unambiguous. The applicant and his legal representative could have taken steps earlier in the proceedings which might have had a bearing on the decision to exclude that evidence, but failed to do so. The exclusion had been ordered following detailed analysis by the trial judge and Court of Appeal of the competing interests at stake and the balance which had to be struck between those interests on the facts of the applicant's case.[86]

Since correspondence, telephone and similar means of communication, protected in Article 8, also constitute means for the expression of an opinion, there is a close connection between that article and Article 10. This connection was put forward in the *Silver* case, which concerned the right of detainees to respect for their correspondence. The Court took the view that in the examination of the

---

[83] *Kaperzyński v. Poland*, ECtHR 3 April 2012, appl. no. 43206/07, para. 66.

[84] *Nikula v. Finland*, ECtHR 21 March 2002, appl. no. 31611/96, para. 55.

[85] In the *Steel and Morris* case, however, the lack of free legal aid led to a breach of the obligation of the authorities to protect the freedom of expression; *Steel and Morris v. the United Kingdom*, *supra* n. 78, para. 95.

[86] *McVicar v. the United Kingdom*, ECtHR 7 May 2002, appl. no. 46311/99, paras. 74–77.

complaints with respect to Article 8, the freedom of expression via correspondence had already been dealt with at such length that a separate examination with regard to Article 10 was not necessary.[87] However, in the subsequent *McCallum* case, also concerning the correspondence of a detainee, the Commission took a somewhat different approach by stating that 'where interference is alleged in the communication of information by correspondence, Article 8 is the *lex specialis* and no separate issues arise under Article 10'.[88] This appears to be too general a statement, since the aim of the two articles is not identical: in Article 8, the main point is the protection of the private character of the means of communication referred to, while in Article 10 its character as a means of expressing an opinion and of providing and receiving information is at issue.

In the *Guerra* case, the applicants complained, *inter alia*, that the authorities had violated Article 10 by failing to inform the public of the risks involved in the operation of the chemical factory in their vicinity, and of what was to be done in the event of an accident connected with the factory's operation. The Court held that the freedom to receive information cannot be construed as imposing on a state, 'in circumstances such as those in the present case', positive obligations to collect and disseminate information of its own motion. It concluded that this part of the complaint had to be considered under Article 8.[89] However, in the *Segerstedt-Wiberg* case, the Court considered that the storage of personal data related to political opinion, affiliations and activities that is deemed unjustified for the purposes of Article 8(2) can have adverse effects on the exercise of political freedoms and therefore *ipso facto* constitutes an unjustified interference with the rights protected by Articles 10 and 11.[90]

Further, the freedom of expression is closely related to the freedom of thought, conscience and religion in Article 9 of the Convention. This is the more so to the extent that in the case of freedom of expression emphasis is laid upon the content of the opinion expressed. This does not alter the fact that Article 10 has a wider scope than Article 9. While for the applicability of Article 9 it is required that the opinion which is expressed reflects the conviction of the person who puts this opinion forward,[91] Article 10 envisages the protection of every expression of an opinion, be it that the measure of protection may vary according to the nature of the opinion expressed.[92]

---

[87]   *Silver and Others v. the United Kingdom*, ECtHR 25 March 1983, appl. nos. 5947/72, 6205/73, 7052/75, 7061/75, 7107/75, 7113/75 and 7136/75, para. 107. See also *Schönenberger and Durmaz v. Switzerland*, ECtHR 20 June 1988, appl. no. 11368/85, para. 71.

[88]   *McCallum v. the United Kingdom*, EComHR 4 May 1989, appl. no. 9511/81, para. 63. The claim under Art. 10 was not pursued before the Court. The Commission had taken the same position in *X v. Federal Republic of Germany*, EComHR 3 October 1979, appl. no. 8383/78.

[89]   *Guerra and Others v. Italy*, ECtHR (GC) 19 February 1998, appl. no. 14967/89, paras. 53–55.

[90]   *Segerstedt-Wiberg and Others v. Sweden*, ECtHR 6 June 2006, appl. no. 62332/00, para. 107.

[91]   *Arrowsmith v. the United Kingdom*, EComHR 12 October 1978 (rep.), appl. no. 7050/75.

[92]   See *supra*, 3.2.

There is also a close connection between Article 10 and the freedom of assembly protected in Article 11. In the *Ezelin* case, concerning a disciplinary penalty imposed on a lawyer because he had participated in a demonstration in which protests were made against judicial decisions and had refused to give evidence to the investigating judge, the Court held that 'the protection of opinions, secured by Article 10, is one of the objectives of freedom of peaceful assembly and freedom of expression as enshrined in Article 11'.[93] Articles 10 and 11 are both applicable in those situations where several persons jointly express a given opinion. Thus, a demonstration always constitutes an expression of opinion, even if it has the character of a silent procession; at the same time there is an assembly. This overlap need not, however, give rise to problems in practice, since the permissible restrictions on the two rights largely coincide, while the specific restrictions of Article 10 clearly refer to the opinion expressed, and not to the question of whether it has been expressed by one person or by several persons jointly.[94]

Principally the Court regards Article 11 as a *lex specialis* in relation to Article 10.[95] However, this does not mean that Article 11 prevails automatically. When both articles apply, it depends on the circumstances, which article stands on the foreground. When the freedom of assembly comes to the fore, Article 11 takes precedence, but must at the same time be read in the light of Article 10.[96] When the freedom of expression is key in a situation, Article 10 takes precedence, but must in turn be read in the light of Article 11. Thus, the Court considered the *Szima* case from the perspective of Article 10 read in the light of Article 11. A chairperson of the Police Trade Union had published a number of writings on the trade union's website. Her critical views about the manner in which police leaders managed the force, and her accusations of disrespect of citizens and of serving political interests in general overstepped the mandate of a trade union leader, because they were not at all related to the protection of labour-related interests of trade union members. Therefore, those statements, being made outside the legitimate scope of trade union-related activities, had to be considered from the general perspective of freedom of expression.[97]

---

[93] *Ezelin v. France*, ECtHR 26 April 1991, appl. no.11800/85, para. 38. See also *Vogt v. Germany*, *supra* n. 10, para. 64.

[94] In *Tatár and Fáber v. Hungary*, ECtHR 24 July 2012, appl. no. 26005/08, the Court considered Art. 11 not to be at stake, although the authorities had treated a gathering as an assembly.

[95] *Ezelin v. France, supra* n. 93, para. 35; *Trade Union of the Police in the Slovak Republic and Others v. Slovakia*, ECtHR 25 September 2012, appl. no. 11828/08, paras. 52–53.

[96] *Berladir and Others v. Russia*, ECtHR 10 July 2012, appl. no. 34202/06; *Trade Union of the Police in the Slovak Republic and Others v. Slovakia, supra* n. 95, paras. 53–76; *Malofeyeva v. Russia*, ECtHR 30 May 2013, appl. no. 36673/04, 128–143.

[97] *Szima v. Hungary*, ECtHR 9 October 2012, appl. no. 29723/11, para. 31. The same in *Fáber v. Hungary*, ECtHR 24 July 2012, appl. no. 40721/08; *Palomo Sánchez and Others v. Spain*, ECtHR (GC) 12 September 2011, appl. nos. 28955/06, 28957/06, 28959/06 and 28964/06, para. 52.

The emphasis on the question of whether the means of expression have an independent significance may delimit the applicability of Article 10 *vis-à-vis* other freedoms, which are related to the possibility of expressing specific opinions but cannot be considered as means which have an independent significance apart from other means available to the person concerned. Thus, in the *Belgian Linguistics* case, the former Commission took the position that freedom of expression does not comprise the right to be offered the opportunity to express one's opinion in a language of one's choice, the consequence of which would be the right to being taught that language.[98] Here, Article 2 of Protocol No. 1 is at issue, not Article 10. This would possibly only be otherwise if, for instance, an immigrant was denied access to being taught the vernacular or if the required facilities for this were not provided, since he would then be deprived of an independent means of expression, i.e. expression in a locally understood language. However, even in such a case it would seem to make more sense to invoke Article 2 of Protocol No. 1.

In the same sense, the right to vote is not protected by Article 10. This observation goes back to established case law of the former Commission and has not been questioned since then.[99] It can hardly be denied that taking part in elections is a form of expressing an opinion. Article 3 of Protocol No. 1 refers to 'the free expression of the opinion of the people'. Nor can it be subject to doubt that it constitutes a means for the expression of that opinion which has an independent character. On the other hand, however, it seems logical to assume that the drafters of Article 10 did not intend to include the right to vote. This may be inferred from the incorporation of a specific provision concerning elections into Protocol No. 1. The duty to vote is not in violation of Article 10 – nor of Article 9 – as long as the secret character is guaranteed; in that case the person concerned is free to express any opinion or no opinion at all.

3. RESTRICTIONS

3.1. INTRODUCTION

The second paragraph of Article 10 explicitly mentions the exceptions to which the freedoms of the first paragraph may be subjected, which are similar (but not completely identical) to the express limitation clauses in Articles 8, 9 and 11. However, while those articles only speak of restrictions or limitations, the second paragraph of Article 10 also mentions formalities, conditions and

---

[98]   *'Relating to certain aspects of the laws on the use of languages in education in Belgium' v. Belgium*, ECtHR 9 February 1967, appl. nos. 1474/62, 1677/62, 1691/62, 1769/63, 1994/63 and 2126/64; *X and Others v. Belgium*, EComHR 26 July 1963, appl. no. 1769/62.

[99]   See, e.g., *X v. the Netherlands*, EComHR 19 December 1974, appl. no. 6573/74 and *Association X, Y and Z v. Federal Republic of Germany*, ECtHR 18 May 1976, appl. no. 6850/74.

penalties as measures to which the freedoms may be subjected.[100] At first sight it is remarkable that specifically with respect to the right to freedom of expression, to which Western democracies attach such great value, the restrictions are formulated more broadly than with respect to other rights and freedoms. However, in practice this broad formulation is of little impact. The imposition of conditions or formalities in fact also amounts to restrictions, while on the other hand the failure to observe a restriction prescribed by law will also be subject to a sanction in most cases. It does not matter much, therefore, whether the complaint is directed against the application of the legal norm restricting the exercise of the freedom or against the penalty imposed for having violated that norm. Indeed, the restriction implied in the imposition of a penalty may therefore not serve the purpose of a retaliation, but should on the contrary be designed to protect the interests enumerated in paragraph 2 in the most comprehensive way.

As is the case with all the rights and freedoms safeguarded by the Convention, also exceptions allowed by Article 10 must be prescribed by law. This requires that the impugned measure should have some basis in domestic law. It also refers to the quality of the law in question, requiring that it should be accessible to the person concerned, who must moreover be able to foresee its consequences for him, and be compatible with the rule of law. Therefore, the law must be formulated with a precision that guarantees a certain foreseeability. A lack of foreseeability can, for example, become evident through contradictory decisions, showing that the law gives no apparent guidance as to how to resolve a conflict between the legislative regimes.[101]

As was pointed out, the Court has taken the position that exceptions to the freedom of expression 'must be narrowly interpreted and the necessity for any restrictions must be convincingly established',[102] which means that an interference is only permissible when it meets a 'pressing social need', it is proportionate to the aims pursued and the reasons to justify it are relevant and sufficient.

This also applies to the full to the exception of 'the protection of the reputation or rights of others', also when these rights concern religions. However, in the context of the reputation or the rights of others national authorities may require that certain 'rules of intellectual battle of ideas' are respected, such as the aspect of fairness and the limits set by criminal law, provided that this does not hamper the right to criticise in even one-sided ways.[103]

Especially in the context of religious opinions and beliefs, the duties and responsibilities may legitimately include avoiding as far as possible expressions

---

[100] See, *inter alia*, *Krone Verlag GmbH & Co KG v. Austria*, ECtHR 6 November 2003, appl. no. 40284/98; *Pakdemirli v. Turkey*, ECtHR 22 February 2005, appl. no. 35839/97.

[101] *Goussev and Marenk v. Finland*, ECtHR 17 January 2006, appl. no. 35083/97, paras. 53–54; *Soini and Others v. Finland*, ECtHR 17 January 2006, appl. no. 36404/97, paras. 54–55; *Delfi v. Estonia*, *supra* n. 1, paras. 71–72.

[102] *The Observer and Guardian v. the United Kingdom*, ECtHR 26 November 1991, appl. no. 13585/88, para. 59. See also *supra* 14.1.

[103] *Tierbefreier e.V. v. Germany*, ECtHR 16 January 2014, appl. no. 45192/09, paras. 47–60.

that are gratuitously offensive to others and thus an infringement of their rights, and which therefore do not contribute to any form of public debate capable of furthering progress in human affairs. The absence of a uniform European conception of the requirements of the protection of the rights of others in relation to attacks on their religious convictions broadens the Contracting States' margin of appreciation when regulating freedom of expression in relation to matters liable to offend intimate personal convictions within the sphere of morals or religion.[104] Still, persons with religious beliefs must tolerate and accept the denial by others of their beliefs and even the propagation by others of doctrines hostile to their faith. Only in extreme cases can the effect of particular methods of opposing or denying religious beliefs be such as to inhibit those who hold such beliefs from exercising their freedom to hold and express them.[105] Within these boundaries an article which stated that certain doctrines of the Catholic Church had 'prepared the ground in which the idea and implementation of Auschwitz took seed' has been considered permissible.[106] On the other hand, in the *PETA* case the Court held the granting of a civil injunction against an advertising campaign against battery animal-farming under the head 'The Holocaust on your plate' permissible, although the campaign undeniably served the public interest. It considered that the facts of the case could not be detached from the historical and social context and that a reference to the Holocaust had also to be seen in the specific historical and social context of the German past and that the German Government's stance concerning a special obligation towards the Jews living in Germany had to be respected.[107]

The Court's strict position towards exceptions to the freedom of expression applies even more to preventive restraints on publications. Such restraints are as such not incompatible with Article 10, but call for the most strict supervision of the Strasbourg organs since, even if they are temporary, they may deprive the information to be published from all its interests.[108] For this reason the relevant law must clearly indicate the circumstances when prior restraints on publications are permissible and, *a fortiori*, when the consequences of the restraint are to block publication of a periodical completely.[109] This most strict supervision of preventive restraints is also reflected in those cases where the Court held that the intended purpose of the ban on publication, the prevention of the disclosure of

---

[104]   *Giniewsky v. France*, ECtHR 31 January 2006, appl. no. 64016/00, paras. 43–44.

[105]   *Otto-Preminger-Institut v. Austria*, *supra* n. 50, para. 47.

[106]   *Giniewsky v. France*, *supra* n. 104, paras. 43–44.

[107]   *PETA Deutschland v. Germany*, ECtHR 8 November 2012, appl. no. 43481/09, paras. 47–49.

[108]   *The Observer and Guardian v. the United Kingdom*, *supra* n. 102 and *The Sunday Times v. the United Kingdom (No. 2)*, ECtHR 26 November 1991, appl. no. 13166/87, para. 51; *Association Ekin v. France*, *supra* n. 68, para. 56; *Cengiz and Others v. Turkey*, *supra* n. 63, para. 62.

[109]   *Gaweda v. Poland*, ECtHR 14 March 2002, appl. no. 26229/95, para. 40.

information, could no longer justify the prohibition because the information had already become public on the basis of another source.[110]

A clear example of the narrow interpretation of the exceptions of the freedom of expression in the second paragraph can be found in the many Turkish cases the Court had to deal with in connection with critical articles in the press and other statements in the public debate. The Court has applied a consistent line. Even when statements paint an extremely negative picture of the Turkish State and thus give the narrative a hostile tone, they can be permissible as long they do not encourage violence, armed resistance or insurrection and do not constitute hate speech.[111] Thus, the Court has been applying a clear and consistent bottom line.

However, more recently the Court has been showing less tolerance towards hostile opinions when it concerns expressions with discriminating content. In this setting, the Court holds that inciting to hatred does not necessarily have to entail a call for an act of violence, or other criminal acts. Attacks on persons committed by insulting, holding up to ridicule or slandering specific groups of the population can be sufficient for the authorities to favour combating racist speech in the face of freedom of expression exercised in an irresponsible manner. In this regard, according to the Court in the *Veideland* case, discrimination based on sexual orientation is as serious as discrimination based on 'race, origin or colour'.[112] This less narrow approach compared to the Turkish cases seems to be justified partially by the 'captive audience' argument. At least, in the *Vejdeland* case the Court took into consideration that the discriminating pamphlets were left in school in the lockers of young people who were at an impressionable and sensitive age and who had no possibility to decline to accept them.

In assessing whether an infringement of the first paragraph has been 'necessary in a democratic society', the Court consistently pays special attention to the essential function the press fulfils in a democratic society and the importance of the freedom of political debate. Central elements of this concept, including the possibility of licensing of audio-visual media, will be discussed in sections 3.2, 3.3, 3.7 and 3.8. Besides, the Court has often referred to the 'duties and responsibilities' mentioned in the second paragraph of Article 10 of those who exercise the freedom of expression. This concept will be discussed in sections 3.4–3.6.

The grounds enumerated in the second paragraph are not entirely identical to the interests mentioned in Articles 8, 9 and 11 of the Convention. Therefore,

---

[110] *The Observer and Guardian v. the United Kingdom*, *supra* n. 102, paras. 66–70 and *The Sunday Times v. the United Kingdom (No. 2)*, *supra* n. 108, paras. 52–56. See also *Weber v. Switzerland*, ECtHR 22 May 1990, appl. no. 11034/84, para. 51, *juncto* para. 13; *Vereniging Weekblad Bluf! v. The Netherlands*, ECtHR 9 February 1990, appl. no.16616/90, para. 45; *Wizerkaniuk v. Poland*, ECtHR 5 July 2011, appl. no. 18990/05, para. 65.

[111] See, *inter alia*, *Dicle v. Turkey*, ECtHR 10 November 2004, appl. no. 46733/99, paras. 12–18.

[112] *Vejdeland and Others v. Sweden*, ECtHR 9 February 2012, appl. no. 1813/07, para. 55; *Féret v. Belgium*, ECtHR 16 July 2009, appl. no. 15615/07, para. 73.

three of the grounds laid down in the second paragraph of Article 10 deserve special attention: 'territorial integrity', 'preventing the disclosure of information received in confidence' and 'maintaining the authority and impartiality of the judiciary'. These grounds will be discussed in sections 3.9–3.11.

3.2. FACTS AND VALUE JUDGEMENTS

According to the Court, in assessing whether there is a pressing social need capable of justifying an interference with the exercise of the freedom of expression, a careful distinction needs to be made between facts and value judgements, because 'The existence of facts can be demonstrated, whereas the truth of value judgments is not susceptible of proof. The requirement to prove the truth of a value judgment is impossible to fulfil and infringes freedom of opinion itself, which is a fundamental part of the right secured by Article 10.'[113] This means that, in general, people may be expected to act more prudently when stating facts than when making value judgements. An interference with the freedom of expression is more likely to be justifiable when it concerns a factual statement which can be proved than when it concerns a value judgement. However, it may sometimes be difficult to distinguish between assertions of facts and value judgements. For this and for other reasons it is also difficult to make an absolute distinction in treatment between the two categories.[114]

Despite of the fact that a value statement cannot be proven, also a value judgment may be impermissible, since even a value judgement without any factual basis to support it may be excessive.[115] In those circumstances an interference by the authorities can be proportionate. In other words, an excessive value judgement needs some kind of factual basis in order to be permissible. However, in the political arena the requirements as to the factual basis of

---

[113]   *Steel and Morris v. the United Kingdom, supra* n. 78, para. 87; *Busuioc v. Moldova, supra* n. 3, para. 61; *Cumpana and Mazare v. Romania*, ECtHR (GC) 17 December 2004, appl. no. 33348/96, para. 98; *Chemodurov v. Russia*, ECtHR 31 July 2007, appl. no. 72683/01, para. 26. See also *Scharsach v. Austria*, ECtHR 13 November 2003, appl. no. 39394/98: the use of the word 'Kellernazi' in relation to an Austrian FPÖ-politician was a permissible value judgement. In *Dichand v. Austria*, ECtHR 26 February 2002, appl. no. 29271/95, para. 50, a journalist had criticised the chairperson of a parliamentary committee who was also a lawyer. The committee dealt with a legislative amendment which was favourable for one of the lawyer's clients. The parliamentarian had omitted to lay down his function as a lawyer. Criticising this was a fair comment, according to the Court.

[114]   Judgment of 27 May 2004, *Vides Aizsardzibas Klubs v. Latvia, supra* n. 3, para. 43.

[115]   *Jerusalem v. Austria*, ECtHR 27 February 2001, appl. no.26958/95, para. 43; *Rizos and Daskas v. Greece*, ECtHR 27 May 2004, appl. no. 65545/01, para. 45; *Vides Aizsardzibas Klubs v. Latvia, supra* n. 3, para. 99; *Hrico v. Slovakia*, ECtHR 20 July 2004, appl. no. 49418/99, para. 40; *Steel and Morris v. the United Kingdom, supra* n. 78, para. 87; *Sokolowski v. Poland*, ECtHR 29 March 2005, appl. no. 75955/01, para. 48; *Ukrainian Media Group v. Ukraine, supra* n. 4, para. 42; *Blaja News Sp. z.o.o. v. Poland, supra* n. 3, para. 52.

an excessive value judgement may again be less than in other situations.[116] It goes too far to require a compelling proof and thereby to apply a degree of precision that comes close to the one usually required for establishing the well-foundedness of a criminal charge by a judicial court. The degree of precision for establishing the well-foundedness of a criminal charge can hardly be compared to that which ought to be observed when expressing someone's opinion on a matter of public concern. The standards applied when assessing someone's political activities in terms of morality are different from those required for establishing an offence under criminal law. Therefore, in the *Brosa* case the Court saw a sufficient factual basis for the applicant's statement in the contribution of a politician to a public debate by way of his letter to the editor emphasising that a local political association had no extreme right-wing tendencies and calling the applicant's statements 'false allegations'.[117]

Besides, requirements as to the proof of factual statements may not be such that these hamper the freedom of the press. In the Court's case law, the starting point is that protection of the right of journalists to impart information on issues of general interest requires that they should act in good faith and on an accurate factual basis and provide reliable and precise information in accordance with the ethics of journalism. This also includes the duty to verify any information before publishing it.[118] Under the terms of Article 10(2) the freedom carries with it duties and responsibilities, which also apply to the press: 'Moreover, these "duties and responsibilities" are liable to assume significance when there is a question of attacking the reputation of a named individual and infringing the "rights of others". Thus, special grounds are required before the media can be dispensed from their ordinary obligation to verify factual statements that are defamatory of private individuals. Whether such grounds exist depends in particular on the nature and degree of defamation in question and the extent to which the media can reasonably regard their sources as reliable with respect to the allegations.'[119]

Thus, the need to verify a factual statement increases with the increase of the defamatory character of the statement.[120]

In the *Colombani* case, the Court found the conviction of the publisher and a journalist of *Le Monde* because of defamation of the Moroccan king impermissible. The newspaper had given an account of a report of the European Commission dealing with drugs trade from Morocco. The Court held that the press must be able to rely on an official report without having the duty to

---

[116] *Lombardo and Others v. Malta*, ECtHR 24 April 2007, appl. no. 7333/06, para. 59.

[117] *Brosa v. Germany*, ECtHR 17 April 2014, appl. no. 5709/09, paras. 41–51.

[118] *Busuioc v. Moldova*, supra n. 3, para. 69. See also *Prager and Oberschlick*, supra n. 4, para. 37; *Belpietro v. Italy*, ECtHR 24 September 2013, appl. no. 43612/10, paras. 51–52.

[119] *Pedersen and Baadsgaard (No. 2) v. Denmark*, supra n. 4, para. 78; *McVicar v. the United Kingdom*, supra n. 86, paras. 74–77, para. 84; *Standard Verlagsgesellschaft mbH v. Austria*, ECtHR 22 February 2007, appl. no. 37464/02, para. 38.

[120] See also *Bjrök Eidsdóttir v. Ireland*, ECtHR 10 July 2012, appl. no. 46443/09, paras. 70–71.

investigate the facts on which the report is based.[121] The Court had come to the same conclusion in the *Tromsø and Stensaas* case. The newspaper and its publisher had based their articles dealing with seal hunting on an official report which had been presented to the Ministry of Fishing. The accusations in the report could not be proved. Nevertheless, the Court considered Tromsø and Stensaas' convictions for defamation disproportionate and, therefore, impermissible, because they had acted in good faith.[122] In this connection the Court also holds that the punishment of a journalist for assisting in the dissemination of statements made by another person in an interview would seriously hamper the contribution of the press to discussion of matters of public interest and should not be envisaged unless there are particularly strong reasons for doing so. In the concrete circumstances of the *Eiðsdóttir* case the Court found that the journalist could not be criticised for having failed to ascertain the truth of the disputed allegations and was satisfied that she acted in good faith, consistently with the diligence expected of a responsible journalist reporting on a matter of public interest.[123]

In the *Pedersen and Baadsgaard* case, the Court also attached importance to the fact that under Article 6(2) individuals have the right to be presumed innocent of any criminal offence until proven guilty. The journalists had made two television documentaries in which they suggested that the police had not correctly judged available evidence in a murder case. As a result, the journalists were convicted of defamation of the Chief Superintendent. After a thorough investigation of all elements of the case, the Court found with the Danish Supreme Court that there was insufficient factual basis for the allegation made by the journalists and that the national authorities thus were entitled to consider that there was a pressing social need to take action against them. Neither were the penalties excessive in the circumstances or of such a kind as to have a chilling effect on media freedom.[124]

An example of close scrutiny is the *Nilsen and Johnsen* case.[125] Trade union officials had accused the independent researcher Mr Bratholm of 'pure misinformation intended to harm the police', 'deliberate lies', 'frivolous allegations' and attempts to undermine the dignity and authority of the police. After having observed that the case had its background in a long and heated

---

[121] *Colombani and Others v. France*, ECtHR 25 June 2002, appl. no. 51279/99, para. 65.

[122] *Bladet Tromso and Stensaas v. Norway*, ECtHR (GC) 20 May 1999, appl. no. 21980/93, para. 65.

[123] *Björk Eidsdóttir v. Iceland, supra* n. 120, paras. 80–81. See also *Wizerkaniuk v. Poland, supra* n. 110: the implementation of a provision in a Press Act which imposed on an editor-in-chief an unequivocal obligation to seek and to obtain the authorisation of the interviewed person before publishing an interview, regardless of the subject matter of that interview and its content, was considered disproportionate.

[124] *Ibid.*, paras. 92–93. See also *McVicar v. the United Kingdom, supra* n. 86, paras. 74–77 and 86–87; *Cumpana and Mazare v. Romania, supra* n. 113, paras. 101–110.

[125] *Nilsen and Johnsen v. Norway*, ECtHR 25 November 1999, appl. no. 23118/93.

public debate in Norway on investigations into allegations of police violence, notably in the city of Bergen, and after having noted that there is little scope under Article 10(2) for restrictions on political speech or on debate on questions of public interest, the Court found that only the accusation of deliberate lies exceeded the limits of permissible criticism. This could be regarded as an allegation of fact susceptible to proof, for which there was no factual basis and which could not be warranted by the researcher's way of expressing himself. The other statements were opinions and thus rather akin to value judgements.[126]

In the *Sokolowski* case, the Court had to decide whether an accusation of theft was a statement of fact or a value judgement. The case concerned the behaviour of the councillors of election committees. The Court noted that the applicant's criticism, couched in ironical language, was meant to stress that the functions in the election committees should have been assigned to those inhabitants of the municipality who were financially worse off than the councillors themselves. The income to be earned for their work in the committees was then compared to the market prices of various goods at that time. It was further suggested that the councillors, by receiving that money paid from the local taxes, would 'take away' these goods from the reader of the leaflet, in which the applicant had written down his criticism. In the Court's view a serious accusation of theft could not be justifiably read into such a statement, particularly when the satirical character of the text and the irony underlying it were taken into account. Therefore, the Court considered that it should be qualified as a value judgement.[127]

3.3. PUBLIC DEBATE, ACTORS AND PRIVATE LIFE

The Court attaches great importance to the freedom of the press.[128] It is the right and task of the press 'to impart information and ideas on political issues just as on those in other areas of public interest,'[129] which also includes those relating to justice and the functioning of the judiciary.[130] This emphasis on the public

---

[126] *Ibid.*, paras. 49–50. See for a differentiated approach also *Busuioc v. Moldova, supra* n. 3, para. 76.

[127] *Sokolowski v. Poland, supra* n. 115, paras. 46–47.

[128] See *supra* 14.1. Which is essentially an external right; it does not dismiss individual journalists from the duty to heed editorial decisions: *Nenkova-Lalova v. Bulgaria*, ECtHR 11 December 2012, appl. no. 35745/05, paras. 50–62.

[129] *Lingens v. Austria*, ECtHR 8 July 1986, appl. no. 9815/82, para. 41. See also *Oberschlick v. Austria, supra* n. 44, para. 58; *Castells v. Spain*, ECtHR 23 April 1992, appl. no. 11798/85, para. 43; *Thorgeir Thorgeirson v. Iceland*, ECtHR 25 June 1992, appl. no. 13778/88, para. 63; *Jersild v. Denmark, supra* n. 2, para. 31; *Fressoz and Roire v. France*, ECtHR 21 January 1999, appl. no. 29183/95, para. 45; *Bergens Tidende and Others v. Norway, supra* n. 70, para. 18; *Sabou and Pircalab v. Romania*, ECtHR 28 September 2004, appl. no.25702/94, para. 33. The wording in these cases is not fully identical.

[130] *Hrico v. Slovakia, supra* n. 115, para. 40; *Rizos and Daskas v. Greece, supra* n. 115, para. 42.

interest is reflected in the case law concerning the restrictions on the freedom of expression.

In the *Lingens* case, the Court stressed the importance of the 'freedom of political debate', which is 'at the very core of the concept of a democratic society', and then held as follows: 'The limits of acceptable criticism are accordingly wider as regards a politician as such than as regards a private individual. Unlike the latter, the former inevitably and knowingly lays himself open to close scrutiny of his every word and deed by both journalists and the public at large, and he must consequently display a greater degree of tolerance.'[131]

In the *Ukrainian Media Group* case, the Court observed that the applicants' publications contained criticism of two politicians in strong, polemical, sarcastic language. Subsequently, the Court stated as follows: 'No doubt the plaintiffs were offended thereby, and may have even been shocked. However, in choosing their profession, they laid themselves open to robust criticism and scrutiny; such is the burden which must be accepted by politicians in a democratic society.'[132] All this applies, in particular, when the politicians themselves make public statements that are susceptible to criticism.[133] In the recent *Ziembinski* case, the Court once more confirmed that in this context the use of sarcasm and irony is fully compatible with the exercise of a journalist's freedom of expression.[134]

On the other hand, when journalists criticise politicians in exaggerating and provocative terms, politicians are in return entitled to reply according to the same principles.[135] Besides, a politician is certainly entitled to have his reputation protected even when he is not acting in a private capacity; however, the requirements of that protection have to be weighed against the interests of open discussion of political issues, since exceptions to freedom of expression must be interpreted narrowly. Moreover, it must be avoided that measures of the national authorities have a chilling effect on the freedom of expression in public debate in general. Therefore, very strong reasons are required to justify restrictions on political speech.[136]

---

[131]   *Lingens v. Austria, supra* n. 129, para. 42. See also, *inter alia, Ukrainian Media Group v. Ukraine, supra* n. 4, para. 39; *Malisiewicz-Gasior v. Poland*, ECtHR 6 April 2006, appl. no. 43797/98, para. 66; *Brosa v. Germany, supra* n. 117, para. 41.

[132]   *Ukrainian Media Group v. Ukraine, supra* n. 4, para. 67; *Vellutini and Michel v. France*, ECtHR 6 October 2012, appl. no. 32820/09, para. 38. See also *Pakdemirli v. Turkey, supra* n. 100, para. 52 and *Otegi Mondragon v. Spain*, ECtHR 15 March 2011, appl. no. 2034/07, para. 55: it is also against the spirit of the Convention to offer increased protection to heads of state as privileged persons. In the same way: *Eon v. France*, ECtHR 14 March 2013, appl. no. 26118/10.

[133]   *Jerusalem v. Austria, supra* n. 115, para. 38; *Mladina d.d. Ljubljana v. Slovenia*, ECtHR 17 April 2014, appl. no. 20981/10, para. 40.

[134]   *Ziembinski v. Poland (No. 2)*, ECtHR 5 July 2016, appl. no. 1799/07, para. 44.

[135]   *Sanocki v. Poland*, ECtHR 17 July 2007, appl. no. 28949/03, para. 65.

[136]   *Malisiewicz-Gasior v. Poland*, ECtHR 6 April 2006, appl. no. 43797/98, para. 68; *Lyashko v. Ukraine*, ECtHR 10 August 2006, appl. no. 21040/02, para. 57; *Krasulya v. Russia*, ECtHR 22 February 2007, appl. no. 12365/03, para. 38. See also *Dabrowski v. Poland*, ECtHR 19 December 2006, appl. no. 18235/02, para. 37: the conviction of a journalist 'amounted to

In the *Castells* case, the Court introduced a further refinement where it held that the bounds of permissible criticism are even wider with regard to the government than in relation to a politician.[137] Similarly, limits of acceptable criticism in respect of civil servants exercising their powers may in some circumstances be wider than those with respect to private individuals. However, civil servants do not knowingly expose themselves to close scrutiny of every word and deed to the same extent as politicians do. Consequently, they should not be treated on an equal footing with politicians when it comes to the criticism of their actions. Moreover, civil servants must enjoy public confidence in conditions free of undue perturbation if they are to be successful in performing their tasks. It may, therefore, prove necessary to protect them from offensive, abusive or defamatory attacks when acting in their official capacity.[138]

For the same reason as politicians who must display a greater degree of tolerance because they enter the public arena voluntarily, private individuals or associations also expose themselves to scrutiny as soon as they enter the arena of public debate.[139]

The Court has taken the position that reporting details of the private life of public figures may contribute to a debate of general interest and may, therefore, be permissible and not constitute a violation of Article 8. This is particularly the case where politicians are concerned. Nevertheless, in balancing the protection of private life against the freedom of expression, in the high-profile *von Hannover* case the Court reached the conclusion that the publishing of photos of Princess Caroline of Monaco was not allowed, because the published photos and accompanying commentaries did not come within the sphere of any political or public debate but related exclusively to details of the princess's private life. The Court noted explicitly that Princess Caroline, although a public figure, did not exercise any function on behalf of the State of Monaco or one of its institutions.[140]

The *von Hannover* case has been a breakthrough in the approach of the Court towards the protection of the privacy of public figures, after the Court had in earlier cases already been cautiously seeking a better balance between the Articles 8 and 10. In the *Plon (société)* case, it had ruled that the proportionality

---

a kind of censorship which was likely to discourage him from making criticisms of that kind again in the future. Such a conviction is likely to deter journalists from contributing to public discussion of issues affecting the life of the community. By the same token, it is liable to hamper the press in the performance of its task of purveyor of information and public watchdog'.

[137] *Castells v. Spain*, supra n. 129, para. 46. In *Karhuvaara and Iltalehti v. Finland*, ECtHR 16 November 2004, appl. no. 53678/00, para. 40, the Court considered politicians and governments as being in the same category.

[138] *Yankov v. Bulgaria*, ECtHR 11 December 2003, appl. no. 39084/97, para. 129; *Rizos and Daskas v. Greece*, supra n. 115, para. 48; *Pedersen and Baadsgaard v. Denmark*, supra n. 4, para. 66; *Thoma v. Luxemburg*, ECtHR 29 March 2001, appl. no. 38432/97, para. 42; *Ziembinski v. Poland II*, supra n. 134, para. 42.

[139] *Jerusalem v. Austria*, supra n. 115, para. 38.

[140] *Von Hannover v. Germany*, supra n. 5, paras. 62–64.

of measures to forbid the publication of details from the medical file of the former President of the French Republic, Mr Mitterand, was influenced by the length of time between the death of Mr Mitterand and the publication of the medical data.[141] In the *Tammer* case, a woman who had had a relationship with, and had a child with the former Minister of the Interior of Estonia, who was married to another woman at that time, had been described as a person breaking up another's marriage and as an unfit and careless mother deserting a child, after she had published her memoirs. The Court held these remarks to be impermissible because they related to aspects of the woman's private life which she described in her memoirs that were written in her private capacity. Although she herself made these details public, the justification of the use of the actual words by the former minister in the circumstances of the case had to be examined against the background which prompted their utterance as well their value to the general public. The Court found that the criticism could have been formulated in a less offensive and insulting manner. It noted that the use of the impugned expressions was not justified by considerations of public concern and that they did not bear on a matter of general importance. Neither had the woman's private life been among the issues that affected the public at the time the former minister's remarks had been made. Those remarks could therefore scarcely be regarded as serving the public interest.[142]

Eventually, the criteria developed in the case law so far that are relevant to answering the question how to balance the freedom of expression against the right to respect for private life, were systematically summarised by the Court in the *Hannover 2* case and the *Axel Springer AG* case. These criteria are: first: the contribution made by photos or articles in the press to a debate of general interest; second: the role or function of the person concerned and the nature of the activities that are the subject of the report and/or photo; third: the prior conduct of the person concerned; fourth: content, form and consequences of the publication; fifth: the circumstances in which the photos were taken; sixth: the severity of the sanction imposed.[143] By means of these criteria the Court examines meticulously the question of whether the public debate on a matter of public interest is at stake. The case law nevertheless shows how difficult it is to predict the outcome of these types of cases.[144] In any case, the Court holds that

---

[141] *Éditions Plon v. France, supra* n. 27, para. 53.

[142] *Tammer v. Estonia*, ECtHR 6 February 2001, appl. no. 41205/98, paras. 66–68.

[143] *Von Hannover v. Germany (No. 2), supra* n. 1. 108–113; *Axel Springer AG v. Germany, supra* n. 1, paras. 89–95; *Delfi AS v. Estonia, supra* n. 1, para. 83; *Couderc and Hachette Filipacchi Associés v. France, supra* n. 1, para. 93.

[144] The right to privacy prevailed in *Egeland and Hanseid v. Norway*, ECtHR 16 April 2009, appl. no. 34438/04; *MGN Limited v. the United Kingdom*, ECtHR 18 January 2011, appl. no. 39401/04, paras. 151–156; *Alkay v. Turkey*, ECtHR 9 October 2012, appl. no. 42811/06; *Print Zeitungsverlag GmbH v. Austria*, ECtHR 10 October 2013, appl. no. 26547/07; *Ruusunen v. Finland*, ECtHR 14 January 2014, appl. no. 73579/10. Aspects of general interest made the publication of photographs permissible in the case of the wedding of an actress and a

Article 8 does not require a legally binding pre-notification requirement. Any restraint which might operate as a form of censorship prior to publication could have a chilling effect and therefore be incompatible with Article 10.[145]

It should be pointed out that not only journalists may claim the high level of protection afforded to the press under Article 10. What counts is the contribution to the public debate on matters of general public interest. Consequently, in a democratic society even small and informal campaign groups may claim this protection, because they must be able to carry out their activities effectively and because there is a strong public interest in enabling such groups and individuals outside the mainstream to contribute to the public debate.[146] The same applies to lawyers because of their central position in the administration of justice.[147] Similarly, the Court also set forth that the freedom of expression is especially important for an elected representative of the people and that, therefore, 'interferences with the freedom of expression of an opposition Member of Parliament call for the closest scrutiny on the part of the Court'.[148]

The safeguard afforded to journalists by Article 10 in relation to reporting on issues of general interest is subject to the proviso that they act in good faith in order to provide accurate and reliable information in accordance with the ethics of journalism. The same principle must apply to others who engage in the public debate.[149]

The case law mentioned so far in this subsection has concerned 'information and ideas' on issues of public interest. The *Markt Intern Verlag and Klaus Beerman* case concerned the question of freedom of the press in business matters. The applicants, a publishing company and its editor, had reported on a dissatisfied client of a mail-order firm. The mail-order firm obtained an injunction, prohibiting publication of the article. According to the Court the

---

musician, because the wedding was organised in a very unusual way and took place in an area that was accessible to the public: *Lillo-Stenberg and Saether v. Norway*, ECtHR 16 January 2014, appl. no. 13258/09.

[145] *Mosley v. the United Kingdom*, ECtHR 10 May 2011, appl. no. 48009/08.

[146] *Steel and Morris v. the United Kingdom*, *supra* n. 78, para. 89.

[147] *Reznik v. Russia*, ECtHR 4 April 2013, appl. no. 4977/05, para. 44. This judgment seems to imply a slight change in approach. In earlier judgments, the Court solely emphasised 'that the special status of lawyers gives them a central position in the administration of justice as intermediaries between the public and the courts. Such a position explains the usual restrictions on the conduct of members of the Bar. Moreover, the courts – the guarantors of justice, whose role is fundamental in a State based on the rule of law – must enjoy public confidence. Regard being had to the key role of lawyers in this field, it is legitimate to expect them to contribute to the proper administration of justice, and thus to maintain public confidence therein (…)'; *Steur v. the Netherlands*, ECtHR 28 October 2003, appl. no. 39657/98, para. 36; *Schmidt v. Austria*, ECtHR 17 July 2008, appl. no. 513/05.

[148] *Piermont v. France*, *supra* n. 55, para. 76; *Jerusalem v. Austria*, *supra* n. 115, para. 36; *Pakdemirli v. Turkey*, *supra* n. 100, para. 33; *Otegi Mondragon v. Spain*, *supra* n. 132, para. 50.

[149] *Steel and Morris v. the United Kingdom*, *supra* n. 78, para. 90; *Selistö v. Finland*, *supra* n. 29, para. 54; *Ringier Axel Springer Slovakia, a.s. v. Slovakia (No. 2)*, ECtHR 7 January 2014, appl. no. 21666/09, para. 53.

contested article did not directly concern the public as a whole and contained information of a commercial nature.[150] This conclusion appeared to be relevant with regard to the margin of appreciation of the national authorities. The Court held as follows: 'Such a margin (...) is essential in commercial matters and, in particular, in an area as complex and fluctuating as that of unfair competition. Otherwise, the European Court of Human Rights would have to undertake a re-examination of the facts and all the circumstances of each case. The Court must confine its review to the question whether the measures taken on the national level are justifiable in principle and proportionate.'[151]

The *Jacubowski* case concerned the prohibition on distributing a circular under the Unfair Competition Act. The supervision of the Court with regard to the question of whether the interference was necessary appeared to be rather loose. Again, the Court left a considerable margin of appreciation to the German courts and based its conclusion that Article 10 had not been violated, amongst other arguments, on the fact that Mr Jacubowski could use other means to express his opinions.[152]

More recently, the Court confirmed its more distanced approach in the *Mouvement raëlien suisse* case. The expression at stake concerned a poster campaign with pictures of extra-terrestrials' faces and a pyramid, together with a flying saucer and the Earth. The authorisation of this campaign was refused by the authorities because the organisation behind it, being a dangerous sect, advocated, among other things, human cloning, 'geniocracy' and 'sensual meditation'. According to the Court the refusal to authorise the poster campaign fell within the margin of appreciation of the national authorities because 'it can be reasonably argued that the poster campaign in question sought mainly to draw the attention of the public to the ideas and activities of a group with a supposedly religious connotation that was conveying a message claimed to be transmitted by extra-terrestrials, referring for this purpose to a website address. The applicant association's website thus refers only incidentally to social or political ideas. The Court takes the view that the type of speech in question is not political because the main aim of the website in question is to draw people to the cause of the applicant association and not to address matters of political debate in Switzerland. Even if the applicant association's speech falls outside the commercial advertising context – there is no inducement to buy a particular product – it is nevertheless closer to commercial speech than to political speech *per se*, as it has a certain proselytising function. The State's margin of appreciation is therefore broader.'[153]

---

[150]   *Markt intern Verlag GmbH and Klaus Beermann v. Germany, supra* n. 34, para. 26.

[151]   *Ibid.*, para. 33. See also *Casado Coca v. Spain, supra* n. 34, paras. 51–55.

[152]   *Jacubowski v. Germany, supra* n. 35; *Diego Nafría v. Spain, supra* n. 35, para. 29.

[153]   *Mouvement Raëlien Suisse v. Switzerland*, ECtHR (GC) 13 July 2012, appl. no. 16354/06, para. 62. Apart from this a private company also has a right to defend itself against defamatory allegations. In addition to the public interest in open debate about business practices, there

It may be concluded that the margin of appreciation of the national authorities increases when commercial speech is involved, while the Strasbourg supervision becomes less strict.

3.4. PROTECTION OF JOURNALISTIC SOURCES

Since the *Goodwin* case the Court has acknowledged the protection of journalistic sources as one of the basic conditions for press freedom. Without such protection, sources may be deterred from assisting the press in informing the public on matters of public interest. As a result, the vital 'public watchdog' role of the press may be undermined and the ability of the press to provide accurate and reliable reporting may be adversely affected. Having regard to the importance of the protection of journalistic sources for press freedom in a democratic society and the potentially chilling effect that an order for disclosure of a source has on the exercise of that freedom, such a measure cannot be compatible with Article 10 unless it is justified by an overriding requirement in the public interest.[154]

The Court's understanding of the concept of journalistic 'source' is 'any person who provides information to a journalist'; it understands 'information identifying a source' to include, as far as they are likely to lead to the identification of a source, both 'the factual circumstances of acquiring information from a source by a journalist' and 'the unpublished content of the information provided by a source to a journalist'.[155] It is clear from the case law that the Convention offers very strong and wide protection for journalistic sources. It does not follow, however, that every individual who is used by a journalist for information is a 'source' in the sense of the case law. In the *Stichting Ostade Blade* case, the magazine's informant was not motivated by the desire to provide information which the public were entitled to know. On the contrary, the informant was claiming responsibility for crimes which he had himself committed; his purpose in seeking publicity through the magazine *Ravage* was to don the veil of anonymity with a view to evading his own criminal accountability. For this

---

is a competing interest in protecting the commercial success and viability of companies, for the benefit of shareholders and employees, but also for the wider economic good. The normal criteria for discussions of matters of public interest apply: *Kuliś and Różycki v. Poland*, ECtHR 6 October 2009, appl. no. 27209/03, paras. 35–37.

154 *Goodwin v. the United Kingdom (No. 1), supra* n. 56, para. 39; *Voskuil v. the Netherlands*, ECtHR 22 November 2007, appl. no. 64752/01, para. 65; *Stichting Ostade Blade v. the Netherlands*, ECtHR 27 May 2014, appl. no. 8406/06, paras. 60–61. An overriding requirement existed in *Sanoma Uitgevers B.V. v. the Netherlands*, ECtHR 31 March 2009, appl. no. 38224/03, paras. 57–60, because there was no alternative possibility to identify a car which had been used for committing a crime.

155 *Telegraaf Media Nederland Landelijke Media B.V. and Others v. the Netherlands*, ECtHR 22 November 2012, appl. no. 39315/06, para. 86.

reason, the Court took the view that he was not, in principle, entitled to the same protection as the 'sources' in foregoing cases.[156]

3.5. LICENSING OF BROADCASTING, TELEVISION OR CINEMA ENTERPRISES

For the most important – at least at the time the Convention was adopted – media in addition to written publications, *viz.* broadcasting, television and cinema, Article 10 provides that they may be subjected to a licensing system. This provision is contained in the first, not the second paragraph. Therefore, at first sight one would expect that when refusing a licence, the authorities are not confined to the restriction grounds mentioned in the second paragraph. However, in the *Groppera Radio AG* case the Court developed a different approach. The case concerned the ban on cable retransmissions in Switzerland of programmes that had been broadcasted by a radio station from Italy. The Court held that the third sentence of the first paragraph permits the Contracting States 'to control the way in which the broadcasting is organised', especially with regard to 'technical aspects', but that otherwise the licensing measures had to comply with the requirements of the second paragraph.[157]

This point of view was further elucidated in the *Informationsverein Lentia* case. The applicants complained that the impossibility of setting up a radio and television station because of the monopoly of the Austrian broadcasting company, constituted a breach of the third sentence of the first paragraph. The Court referred to its judgment in the *Groppera Radio AG* case and held as follows: 'the purpose of that provision is to make clear that States are permitted to regulate by a licensing system the way in which broadcasting is organised in their territories, particularly in its technical aspects. (…) Technical aspects are undeniably important, but the grant or refusal of a licence may also be made conditional on other considerations, including such matters as the nature and objectives of a proposed station, its potential audience and the obligations deriving from international legal instruments. This may lead to interferences whose aims will be legitimate under the third sentence of paragraph 1, even though they do not correspond to any of the aims set out in paragraph 2. The compatibility of such interferences with the Convention must nevertheless be assessed in the light of other requirements of paragraph 2.'[158]

As far as the aims are concerned, the Contracting States do have considerable freedom in setting up a licensing system. Thus, if the licensing system is

---

[156]   *Stichting Ostade Blade v. the Netherlands, supra* n. 154, para. 65.
[157]   *Groppera Radio AG and Others v. Switzerland, supra* n. 25, paras. 59–61. See also *Autronic AG v. Switzerland, supra* n. 8, para. 53.
[158]   *Informationsverein Lentia and Others v. Austria, supra* n. 58, para. 32.

'prescribed by law', the guarantees offered by Article 10 in this respect seem to lie mainly in the necessity test of the second paragraph. The supervision of the Court may be rather strict on this point. In the *Groppera Radio AG* case, the ban on cable transmissions from a foreign radio station was considered permissible because the station was a pirate and wanted to circumvent the rules of the Swiss broadcasting system. In such circumstances, a state has a right to take measures in order to protect its own system.

In the *Autronic AG* case, however, the refusal of the Swiss authorities to authorise a company to receive, by means of a private dish aerial, uncoded, legally broadcast television programmes, in absence of the consent of the broadcasting State, did not meet the requirements of the necessity test.[159]

In the *Informationsverein Lentia* case, the Court held that the impossibility of setting up a radio and television station did not meet these requirements either. The Court referred to the fundamental role of freedom of expression in a democratic society, in particular where, through the press, it serves to impart information and ideas of general interest, which the public moreover is entitled to receive. According to the Court, such an undertaking cannot be successfully accomplished unless it is grounded in the principle of pluralism, of which the state is the ultimate guarantor. This observation holds true particularly in relation to audio-visual media, whose programmes are often broadcasted very widely. Of all the means to ensure that these values are respected, a public monopoly is the one which imposes the greatest restrictions on the freedom of expression. Therefore, these restrictions may only be justified if they correspond to a pressing need. As a result of the technical progress made over the last few decades, justification of these restrictions can no longer today be found in considerations relating to the number of frequencies and channels available.[160]

In the *Tele 1 Privatfernsehgesellschaft mbH* case, the Court held that the refusal to grant a licence for terrestrial television broadcasting is only permissible if cable television broadcasting offers private broadcasters a viable alternative, which is the case when almost all households receiving television in a certain area have the possibility of being connected to the cable network.[161] In the *Demuth* case, the Court accepted the refusal to grant a licence for cable television to a private broadcaster whose programme was mainly aimed at the promotion of automobiles, given the specific Swiss political and cultural context and the requirements which the federal structure sets on a pluralistic programme supply.[162]

Under Article 14 no discrimination is permitted in the granting of licences and, in case of a state monopoly, the broadcasting time granted to a political party, trade union or other institution of a specific political, religious,

---

[159]   *Autronic AG v. Switzerland, supra* n. 8, paras. 60–63.
[160]   *Informationsverein Lentia and Others v. Austria, supra* n. 58, paras. 38–39.
[161]   *Tele 1 Privatfernsehgesellschaft mbH v. Austria*, ECtHR 21 September 2000, appl. no. 32240/96, para. 18.
[162]   *Demuth v. Switzerland*, ECtHR 5 November 2002, appl. no. 38743/97, para. 44.

philosophical or ethical character may not be disproportionate. For the assessment of whether discrimination or disproportionality has occurred, all facets of the political, religious and social climate of the community concerned have to be taken into account. Thus, departure from the arithmetical proportionality on the ground that otherwise a small political party would not be entitled to any broadcasting time at all, or to a uselessly short time only, does not constitute discrimination.

Finally, once a licence has been granted, the authorities have a positive obligation to allocate the corresponding broadcasting frequencies within an appropriate time frame.[163]

The *Jersild* case concerned the criminal liability of a television journalist who had taken the initiative of making a television programme about a group of young people who were known for their racist ideas. Subsequent to the broadcasting of a summary of the interview in which the members of the group ventilated their racist statements and insulted various people, criminal proceedings were instituted and Mr Jersild was convicted and sentenced for aiding and abetting the dissemination of racist statements. According to the national courts, Mr Jersild had not sufficiently counterbalanced the expressed racist views. In assessing the claim of the applicant about violation of Article 10 the Court accepted that the interference pursued 'the protection of the reputation or rights of others'. Next, the Court made a distinction between print media and audio-visual media by explaining that the audio-visual media 'have often a much more immediate and powerful effect'. However, according to the Court, this fact did not justify the Court or the national courts substituting 'their own views for those of the press as to what technique of reporting should be adopted by journalists'.[164] Moreover, the Court seemed to leave no margin of appreciation to the national authorities with regard to evaluating the attitude of the applicant. The Court expressly disagreed with the national courts and held that Mr Jersild clearly dissociated himself from the persons interviewed. Accordingly, Article 10 had been breached.[165]

In the *Murphy* case, a general ban on the broadcasting of any religious advertising was considered permissible. The Court took into account that a provision allowing one religion, and not another, to advertise would be difficult to justify and saw some force in the Irish Government's argument that the exclusion of all religious groupings from broadcasting advertisements generates less discomfort than any filtering of the amount and content of such expressions by such groupings. The Court also observed that there appears to be no clear consensus between the Contracting States as to the manner in which to legislate

---

[163]   *Centro Europa 7 S.r.l. and Di Stefano v. Italy*, ECtHR (GC) 7 June 2012, appl. no. 38433/09, paras. 136–158.

[164]   *Jersild v. Denmark*, *supra* n. 2, para. 31.

[165]   *Ibid.*, paras. 33–37.

for the broadcasting of religious advertisements and that, for example, Greece, Switzerland and Portugal had similar prohibitions.[166] For the same reasons the Court found a general ban on political advertising on television permissible.[167]

3.6. SPECIAL STATUS

It is clear from the text of the second paragraph of Article 10 that everyone – including artists and those who promote their work[168] – who exercises the right contained in the first paragraph bears 'duties and responsibilities'. Those words imply the possibility to differentiate, in assessing the necessity of restricting the freedom of expression, according to 'the particular situation of the person exercising freedom of expression and the duties and responsibilities attaching to that situation'.[169] For the person concerned that special responsibility may lead to a broader or a narrower interpretation of the possibilities to restrict his freedom of expression.

Although the Court has often referred to the 'duties and responsibilities', it appears that this concept plays an important part particularly in three circumstances. First, as discussed in the preceding subsection, if the freedom of the press is involved. Secondly, in case the person who exercises the freedom of expression possesses a special status, such as a serviceman or a civil servant, and thirdly, if the restriction of the protection of morals is involved. The concept of 'duties and responsibilities' of persons with a special status will be discussed below. In subsection 3.8 attention will be paid to the concept in relation to the protection of morals.

First of all, the Court holds that Article 10 applies to members of the armed forces and the police just as it does to other persons within the jurisdiction of the Contracting States. However, the proper functioning of the armed forces and the police is hardly imaginable without legal rules designed to prevent servicemen from undermining the requisite discipline, for example by writings. In this respect, the right to freedom of expression of can be restricted in order to prevent disorder within the organisation, a hierarchically organised body where discipline is quintessential for the carrying out of its functions. Consequently, account must be taken of the need to strike the right balance between the various interests involved.[170]

---

[166] *Murphy v. Ireland*, ECtHR 10 July 2003, appl. no. 44179/98, paras. 77–81.
[167] *Animal Defenders International v. the United Kingdom*, ECtHR (GC) 22 April 2013, appl. no. 48876/08.
[168] *Müller and Others v. Switzerland, supra* n. 45, para. 34.
[169] *Piermont v. France, supra* n. 55, para. 76; *Jerusalem v. Austria, supra* n. 115, para. 36; *Pakdemirli v. Turkey, supra* n. 100, para. 33; *Otegi Mondragon v. Spain, supra* n. 132, para. 50.
[170] *Szima v. Hungary, supra* n. 97, paras. 25–26.

According to the Court, Article 10 applies to the workplace too. Therefore, secondly, also civil servants enjoy the right to freedom of expression. At the same time, the Court is mindful that employees have a duty of loyalty, reserve and discretion to their employer. This is particularly so in the case of civil servants since the very nature of civil service requires that a civil servant is bound by a duty of loyalty and discretion. Since the mission of civil servants in a democratic society is to assist the government in discharging its functions and since the public has a right to expect that they will help and not hinder the democratically elected government, the duty of loyalty and reserve assumes special significance for them.[171]

The special status of civil servants was at issue for the first time in the already mentioned *Glasenapp* case and *Kosiek* case.[172] In these cases Article 10 was not held applicable. The *Vogt* Case concerned the dismissal of a teacher from the civil service because of her political activities on behalf of the German Communist Party. The Court took the position that the Contracting Parties are entitled to require civil servants to be loyal to their constitutional values[173] and held that the 'duties and responsibilities' are 'to a certain extent' also incumbent on teachers outside school.[174] However, in this case the Court found the circumstances adduced by the Government not sufficient to justify the dismissal. The Court referred, *inter alia*, to the fact that Mrs Vogt, in the performance of her duty, had been beyond reproach, that the German Communist Party had not been banned and that there was no evidence, even outside the school, of any anti-constitutional statements on her part. As a result, the dismissal was considered disproportionate to the aim pursued.[175]

In the *Rekvényi* case, the ban contained in the Hungarian Constitution on political activities by police officials was at issue. The Court held this ban to be permissible. Under the given circumstances it found the term 'political activities' clear enough to regulate the behaviour of the police officials. In view of the fact that the police had been an instrument in the hands of the Communist Party until 1989, the purpose of having a politically neutral police force could be considered a pressing social need, which made the interference proportionate.[176]

With respect to judges, their profession does not deprive them of the protection of Article 10 as far as statements or views expressed in the context of a public debate or in the media are concerned. However, when solely

---

171 *Guja v. Moldova*, ECtHR (GC) 12 February 2008, appl. no. 14277/04, paras. 70–71.

172 The Court held Art. 10 not to be applicable because the 'access to the civil service', a right not secured in the Convention, lay at the heart of the case. Judgments *Glasenapp v. Germany*, *supra* n. 14, para. 53 and *Kosiek v. Germany*, *supra* n. 15, para. 39. See also *supra* 2.1.

173 *Vogt v. Germany*, *supra* n. 10, para. 59.

174 *Ibid.*, para. 60.

175 *Ibid.*, para. 61. The Court did not express clearly which aim was involved. The Government relied on the interest of national security, the prevention of disorder and the protection of rights of others; *ibid.*, para. 49.

176 *Rekvényi v. Hungary*, *supra* n. 11, paras. 47–49.

the professional behaviour and the statutory obligations in the context of administration of justice are at stake, again Article 10 is not applicable.[177]

In 1995 the President of the Administrative Court of Liechtenstein gave a lecture on questions of constitutional jurisdiction. His discourse included a statement on the competences of the Constitutional Court under Article 112 of the Liechtenstein Constitution. It was the President's view that the term 'Government' used in this provision included the Prince, an opinion allegedly in conflict with the principle of the Prince's immunity from the jurisdiction of the Liechtenstein judiciary. Subsequently, the Prince sent a letter to the President announcing his decision not to appoint him to a public office in the future anymore. According to the Court this action was disproportionate to the aim pursued and, therefore, impermissible. First, the Court stated: 'Although it is legitimate for a State to impose on civil servants, on account of their status, a duty of discretion, civil servants are individuals and, as such, qualify for the protection of Article 10 of the Convention.'[178] Subsequently, although the Court accepted that the President's lecture inevitably had political implications, it held that this element alone should not have prevented the applicant from making any statement on the matter. The Court stressed that the opinion expressed by the President could not be regarded as an untenable proposition since it was shared by a considerable number of persons in Liechtenstein. Moreover, there was no evidence to conclude that the President's lecture contained any remarks on pending cases, severe criticism of persons or public institutions or insults of high officials or the Prince.[179]

In the *Baka* case, the President of the Supreme Court and the National Council of Justice had expressed his opinion on four legislative reforms affecting the judiciary. The reforms concerned issues related to the functioning and reform of the judicial system, the independent and non-dismissible status of judges and their retirement age. The Court noted that it was not only the applicant's right but also his duty as President of the National Council of Justice to express his opinion on legislative reforms affecting the judiciary, after having gathered and summarised the opinions of different courts. The applicant also used his prerogative to challenge some of the legislation concerned before the Constitutional Court and the possibility to express his opinion directly before Parliament during the relevant parliamentary debate. According to the Court there was no evidence to conclude that the views expressed by the applicant went beyond mere criticism from a strictly professional perspective, or that they contained gratuitous personal attacks or insults. Therefore, the measure to terminate his term of office three and a half years before the end of the fixed term

---

[177] *Harabin v. Slovakia*, ECtHR 20 November 2012, appl. no. 58688/11, paras. 149–151.

[178] *Wille v. Liechtenstein, supra* n. 12, para. 62.

[179] *Ibid.*, para. 67.

applicable under the legislation in force at the time of his election constituted a violation of Article 10.[180]

However, penalties imposed on a former jury member because of the disclosure of the jury's deliberations were justified, although the disclosures did not as such seek to challenge or undermine the verdict in the particular case in question but to contribute to the serious debate concerning the use of expert medical evidence in criminal trials.[181] Here clearly the statutory professional obligations prevailed.

In the *Guja* case, the Court had to deal, for the first time, with a situation in which a civil servant acted as a whistle blower and publicly disclosed internal information. The Court noted that a civil servant, in the course of his work, may become aware of in-house information, including secret information, whose divulgation or publication corresponds to a strong public interest. Thus, the signalling by a civil servant or an employee in the public sector of illegal conduct or wrongdoing in the workplace should, in certain circumstances, enjoy protection. This may be called for where the employee or civil servant concerned is the only person, or part of a small category of persons, aware of what is happening at work and is thus best placed to act in the public interest by alerting the employer or the public at large. Disclosure is only permissible when certain conditions are met: disclosure should be made in the first place to the person's superior or other competent authority or body; there must be an overriding public interest involved in the disclosed information; the information disclosed must be authentic; the damage suffered by the public authority as a result of the disclosure must outweigh the interest of the public in having the information revealed; the employee must act in good faith and in the belief that the information is true, that it is in the public interest to disclose it and that no other, more discreet, means of remedying the wrongdoing is available to him or her; in connection with the review of the proportionality of the interference in relation to the legitimate aim pursued an attentive analysis of the penalty imposed and its consequences is required.[182]

The case law mentioned shows that the Court, as far as servicemen, civil servants and other public officials are concerned, is not inclined to accept automatically that the special 'duties and responsibilities' may lead to a restriction of the freedom of expression.[183]

---

[180] *Baka v. Hungary*, ECtHR 27 May 2014, appl. no. 20261/12, paras. 88–103. In the same sense *Kudeshkina v. Russia*, ECtHR 26 February 2009, appl. no. 29492/05. Restrictions were found justified in *Giovanni v. Italy*, ECtHR 9 July 2013, appl. no. 51160/06 and in *Poyraz v. Turkey*, ECtHR 7 December 2010, appl. no. 15966/06.

[181] *Seckerson and Times Newspapers Limited v. the United Kingdom*, ECtHR 24 January 2012, appl. nos. 32844/10 and 33510/10.

[182] *Guja v. Moldova*, supra n. 171, paras. 73–78; as to the private sector: *Heinisch v. Germany*, ECtHR 21 July 2011, appl. no. 28274/08, paras. 63–70.

[183] See also *Diego Nafría v. Spain*, supra n. 35, in which the dismissal of a high-ranking public bank official was held disproportionate.

3.7. PRISONERS

With regard to Article 10, prisoners stand out as a special group in the case law too, not in connection with the above-mentioned special duties and responsibilities which may be incumbent on a person in a particular capacity, but on the basis of the special requirements assumed to be involved in detention. The Court acknowledges that imprisonment inevitably involves a number of restrictions on prisoners' communications with the outside world. However, also such restrictions must comply with the second paragraph of Article 10 and be necessary in a democratic society in the light of the special situation of prisoners.[184]

The *Yankov* case concerned a prisoner who had criticised the way prisoners were treated by the warders. He had claimed that the prisoners were given very bad and insufficient food, that the warders shouted, cursed and hit prisoners who stayed more than two minutes in the lavatory with truncheons, and that the criminal proceedings against him were unjust and unlawful. The Court considered that, having regard to the particular vulnerability of persons in custody, the punishment of prisoners for having made allegedly false accusations concerning the conditions of detention and acts of the penitentiary authorities require particularly solid justification in order to be considered necessary in a democratic society.[185] The Court added that it was struck by the fact that the prisoner was punished for having written down his own thoughts in a private manuscript which, apparently, he had not shown to anyone at the time it was seized. The prisoner had neither uttered nor disseminated any offensive or defamatory statements. The manuscript was seized when the applicant was about to hand it over to his lawyer to 'impart' its contents. This was the reason the Court did not take the freedom of thought under Article 9 or the prisoner's right for respect of his private life under Article 8 into consideration. Nonetheless, the fact that the prisoner's remarks were never made public was relevant to the assessment of the proportionality of the interference under Article 10: 'The Court notes in this respect, in addition, that the manuscript was not in a form ready for publication and that there was no immediate danger of its dissemination, even if it had been taken out of prison.'[186] The Court found subsequently that the need to ensure that civil servants enjoy public confidence in conditions free of undue perturbation can justify an interference with the freedom of expression only where there is a real threat in this respect. 'The applicant's manuscript obviously did not pose such a threat.'[187] Therefore, the seven days' confinement in a disciplinary cell was disproportionate.

---

[184] *Kalda v. Estonia, supra* n. 33, paras. 45, 48.
[185] *Yankov v. Bulgaria, supra* n. 138, para. 134.
[186] *Ibid.*, para. 141.
[187] *Ibid.*

Although the Court's judgment was favourable to the prisoner, it makes clear that the Court adopts quite a reticent attitude towards the review of interferences of the freedom of expression of prisoners, while there would seem to be room for a stricter necessity test.[188] However, such reticence does not exist when the interest of the media themselves is at stake. Thus, the Court held that the refusal to film and interview a prisoner who had been sentenced for murder inside the prison was not necessary in a democratic society. It accepted that the domestic authorities were better placed to say whether, and to what extent, access to a prison – a closed environment under surveillance – was compatible with order and security in the prison. But in view of the importance of the media in a democratic society and of the reduced margin of appreciation the domestic authorities have in respect of a television programme on a subject of considerable public interest, the Court considered that the domestic authorities had failed to demonstrate convincingly that the absolute refusal of permission to film inside the prison was strictly proportionate to the aims pursued and thus met a 'pressing social need'.[189]

3.8. PROTECTION OF MORALS

The concept of 'duties and responsibilities' also seems to play an important part if 'the protection of morals' has been invoked to justify a restriction of the freedom of expression. In the *Handyside* case, the Government of the United Kingdom relied on this aim to justify the conviction of a publisher for having in his possession copies of the 'Little Red School Book' and their destruction as pornography. The reference to the special responsibility of the publisher constituted an argument for a reserved Strasbourg review.[190]

This case may be compared with the *Otto-Preminger-Institut* case, concerning the seizure and subsequent forfeiture of a film. According to the Austrian authorities this film had disparaged the Roman Catholic religious doctrine. The Government relied on 'the protection of (…) rights of others'. This was accepted by the Court, but it indicated that in this case that aim came very close to the concept of 'morals'. The Court referred to the 'duties and responsibilities'. It held as follows: 'Amongst them – in the context of religious opinions and beliefs – may legitimately be included an obligation to avoid as far as possible expressions that are gratuitously offensive to others and thus an infringement of their rights, and which therefore do not contribute to any form of public debate of furthering

---

[188] *Skalka v. Poland*, ECtHR 27 May 2003, appl. no. 43425/98, in which a prisoner had criticised a judge. The Court found the sentence of 8 months' imprisonment disproportionately severe.

[189] *Schweizerische Radio- und Fernsehgesellschaft SRG v. Switzerland*, ECtHR 21 June 2012, appl. no. 34124/06.

[190] *Handyside v. the United Kingdom*, *supra* n. 1, para. 49. See also, less clear, *Müller and Others v. Switzerland*, *supra* n. 45, para. 33.

progress in human affairs.'[191] The Court concluded that Article 10 had not been violated.

In the *Murphy* case, the Court again pointed out that one of the duties and responsibilities the freedom of expression carries with it is the general requirement to ensure the peaceful enjoyment of the rights guaranteed under Article 9 to the holders of such beliefs, including a duty to avoid as far as possible an expression that is, in regard of objects of veneration, gratuitously offensive to others and profane. The Court held that, therefore, 'a wider margin of appreciation is generally available to the Contracting States when regulating freedom of expression in relation to matters liable to offend intimate personal convictions within the sphere of morals or, especially, religion. Moreover, as in the field of morals, and perhaps to an even greater degree, there is no uniform European conception of the requirements of "the protection of the rights of others" in relation to attacks on their religious convictions. What is likely to cause substantial offence to persons of a particular religious persuasion will vary significantly from time to time and from place to place, especially in an era characterised by an ever-growing array of faiths and denominations. By reason of their direct and continuous contact with the vital forces of their countries, State authorities are in principle in a better position than the international judge to give an opinion on the exact content of these requirements with regard to the rights of others as well as on the "necessity" of a "restriction" intended to protect from such material those whose deepest feelings and convictions would be seriously offended.'[192]

In the same *Murphy* case, the Court held as well that restrictions in the field of morals should in any case be applied in non-discriminatory way. A provision, for example, allowing one religion, and not another, to advertise on radio or television would be difficult to justify and also a provision allowing the filtering by the state or any organ designated by it, on a case-by-case basis, of unacceptable or excessive religious advertising would be difficult to apply fairly, objectively and coherently.[193]

The case law mentioned makes it clear that the reference to 'duties and responsibilities' leads to a broad margin of appreciation if at the same time on good grounds the concept of 'morals' is invoked.

---

[191] *Otto-Preminger-Institut v. Austria, supra* n. 50, para. 49. See also *I.A. v. Turkey*, ECtHR 13 September 2005, appl. no. 42571/98, paras. 28–32.

[192] *Murphy v. Ireland, supra* n. 166, paras. 65 and 67. In *Klein v. Slovakia*, ECtHR 31 October 2006, appl. no. 72208/01, however, the Court held that the publication of an article which sharply criticised the behaviour of the archbishop of Slovakia did not unduly interfere with the right of believers to express and exercise their religion, nor did it denigrate the content of their religious faith. Exclusively the person of the archbishop had been criticised. Furthermore, the archbishop had publicly pardoned Klein.

[193] *Murphy v. Ireland, supra* n. 166, para. 77. See also *supra* 3.5.

3.9. TERRITORIAL INTEGRITY

In the *Piermont* case, the French Government relied on 'territorial integrity' to justify an infringement of the first paragraph of Article 10. Mrs Piermont had taken part in a demonstration on the territory of French Polynesia in favour of the independence of French Polynesia. During that demonstration, she had made a speech in which she supported the anti-nuclear and independence demands of some of the local political parties. The applicant claimed that Article 10 had been violated by the subsequent order by the French authorities, directing her expulsion from the French Polynesian territory coupled with a ban on re-entering, and the order prohibiting her from entering the territory of her next destination, New Caledonia. The Court accepted that the interference pursued two aims, the prevention of disorder and the interest of territorial integrity.[194] With regard to the necessity requirement the Court referred, *inter alia*, to the importance of a free political debate, the fact that the speech had been held during an authorised and non-violent demonstration and that the demonstration had not been followed by any disorder.[195] The Court reached the conclusion that the orders had not been 'necessary in a democratic society'.[196]

3.10. INFORMATION RECEIVED IN CONFIDENCE

The wide formulation of the restriction 'for preventing the disclosure of information received in confidence' overlaps with other grounds. Insofar as it refers to the right of the authorities to take measures against the leakage of state secrets, the ground 'in the interests of national security, territorial integrity or public safety' would appear to sufficiently serve that purpose. And insofar as it refers to the possibility of being exempted from a legal duty to impart information when information received in confidence is involved, for instance as a witness in judicial proceedings, what is involved is not a restriction, but on the contrary a confirmation of the freedom of expression, since the first paragraph entails the right to be silent.[197] And if the protection of a person's privacy is concerned, the restriction 'protection of the reputation or rights of others' will suffice. Nevertheless, cases may occur in which information received

---

[194]   *Piermont v. France, supra* n. 55, para. 70 and (less clear) paras. 82–85.

[195]   In *Chorherr v. Austria*, ECtHR 25 August 1993, appl. no. 13308/87, paras. 32–33, the Court accepted a reference by the Austrian Government to the fear of disorder during a military parade and held that Art. 10 had not been violated.

[196]   *Piermont v. France, supra* n. 55, paras. 73–78 and 86. The Government relied also on Arts. 63 and 16 to justify the interference. The Court rejected these arguments; paras. 23 and 64, respectively.

[197]   This does not hold true if the first paragraph is also taken to contain a right to seek information and accordingly a duty of the authorities to enforce the ('horizontal') obligation to impart information. On this, see *supra* 1.6.

in confidence is revealed without one of the above-mentioned interests being applicable, such as when a civil servant reveals or intends to reveal on his own initiative an official secret which does not affect either national security or the rights of others.[198]

3.11. AUTHORITY AND IMPARTIALITY OF THE JUDICIARY

Another specific feature of the second paragraph of Article 10, in comparison with the restrictions in other articles of the Convention, is the restriction ground 'for maintaining the authority and impartiality of the judiciary'. This ground would seem to have been included mainly with a view to the prohibition, familiar from Anglo-Saxon law, of 'contempt of court', which is intended to prevent the authority and the independence of the court, as well as the rights of the parties to the proceedings,[199] from being impaired by publications and other acts. In the *Weber* case, the Court held that the application of a provision of the criminal code was intended 'to ensure the proper conduct of the investigation' and, therefore, also came within the ambit of this restriction ground.[200]

The restriction was discussed at length in the *Sunday Times* case. In this case the publisher, the editorial staff and the general editor of the *Sunday Times* complained about the ban for a given period, imposed by an English court, on the publication of an article concerning the so-called 'thalidomide children', i.e. children born with serious malformations of limbs, because their mothers had used the sedative thalidomide during pregnancy. The reason given for the prohibition was the prevention of 'contempt of court', because at that time claims for damages were pending before the English courts. In order to be able to answer the question of whether the ban on publication could be justified on this ground, the Commission undertook an independent inquiry into the circumstances under which the prohibition had been imposed. In the final analysis, it concluded that the nature of the prohibited publication did not tend to affect the impartiality of the court, since the article contained only information with which the court had already become familiar from another source. Nor could the authority of the court be impaired by the publication. Moreover, the proposed publication was also specifically meant to protect the interests of those minors. The Commission also took into consideration the circumstance that, although this was a civil action, a public interest was involved in the case as well. Since that public interest had not been brought out, either in

---

[198] See, e.g., *X v. Federal Republic of Germany*, ECtHR 24 July 1970, appl. no. 4274/69. See also *supra* 3.6.

[199] *The Sunday Times v. the United Kingdom (No. 1)*, ECtHR 26 April 1979, appl. no. 6538/74, para. 56; *The Observer and Guardian v. the United Kingdom, supra* n. 102, para. 56.

[200] *Autronic AG v. Switzerland, supra* n. 8, para. 45.

a criminal prosecution or in an inquiry instituted by the authorities, only very compelling reasons could justify a prohibition of information being imparted by private persons. No such compelling reasons existed.[201] With a majority of eleven votes to nine the Court concurred with the opinion of the Commission, amongst others considering that the *Sunday Times* article might have served as a brake on speculative and unenlightened discussion.[202] Thus, the contribution to the public debate was explicitly honoured.

The *Observer and Guardian* case concerned interlocutory injunctions restraining two newspapers from publishing, pending proceedings which had been instituted by the Attorney General to obtain permanent injunctions, details of the manuscript of a book ('Spycatcher') containing the memoirs of a former agent of the British Security Service. The Court held that the injunction had been permissible initially, but could no longer be justified once the book had been published in the United States, because from that very moment the confidentiality of the material had been destroyed.[203]

Ensuring the proper conduct of investigation may not be the only reason for the last restriction of paragraph 2. The aim is wider. According to the Court in the *Skalka* case, the work of the courts, which are the guarantors of justice and which have a fundamental role in a state governed by the rule of law, needs to enjoy public confidence. It should, therefore, be protected against unfounded attacks. However, as with all public institutions, the courts are not immune from criticism and scrutiny. In this respect, a clear distinction must be made between criticism and insult. If the sole intent of any form of expression is to insult a court or members of a court, an appropriate punishment would not, in principle, constitute a violation of Article 10(2).[204] The Court declared the statement in a letter to the President of the Katowice Regional Court that all judges of that court were 'irresponsible clowns' and calling an unnamed judge 'a small-time cretin', 'an illiterate', 'a fool' and 'such a limited individual' impermissible, but nevertheless it considered a prison sentence of eight months disproportionately severe.[205]

In the *Barfod* case, a journalist had been convicted for writing an article of an allegedly defaming character. In his article, he criticised a judgment in a case in which two lay judges had participated, who were both employed as civil servants in the local government, which was the defendant party in that

---

[201] *X. v. the United Kingdom, supra* n. 199, paras. 231–248.

[202] *Ibid.*, paras. 42–68, 66. The issue of 'contempt of court' also arose in *Harmon v. the United Kingdom*, ECtHR 11 May 1984, appl. no. 10038/82, where a lawyer had given access to a journalist to documents which were exclusively meant for purposes of the trial.

[203] *The Observer and Guardian v. the United Kingdom, supra* n. 102, para. 68. See also *The Sunday Times v. the United Kingdom (No. 2), supra* n. 108, para. 54.

[204] *Skalka v. Poland, supra* n. 188, para. 34. See also *Rizos and Daskas v. Greece, supra* n. 115, para. 43.

[205] *Skalka v. Poland, supra* n. 188, para. 41.

case. The applicant's conviction was based on the fact that he suggested that the two lay judges had cast their votes rather as employees of the local government than as independent and impartial judges. The Court held that the interference with the applicant's freedom of expression did not aim at restricting his right under the Convention to criticise publicly the composition of the court in question. It was quite possible to question the composition of that court without at the same time attacking the two lay judges personally. The State's legitimate interest in protecting the reputation of the two lay judges was accordingly not in conflict with the applicant's interest in being able to participate in free public debate on the question of the structural impartiality of the High Court.[206] The Court reached the conclusion that the conviction could not be regarded as disproportionate and that, therefore, Article 10 had not been violated.

Also in the *Prager and Oberschlick* case and in the *Falter Zeitschriften* case, the Court made a clear distinction between the interest of discussing the functioning of the judiciary as such and personal accusations against individual judges. Such accusations need a very solid factual basis in order to be permissible.[207]

In the *Amihalachioaie* case, the Court referred to the right of the public to also be informed about questions which concern the functioning of the judiciary. In an interview, a lawyer had criticised the Constitutional Court of Moldova as being not constitutional and had argued that it was likely that the judges of that court did not recognise the Strasbourg Court's authority. The Constitutional Court had ruled that a legal provision which obliged lawyers to be a member of the national bar association was contrary to the Constitution. The Strasbourg Court held that the statement contributed to a question of general interest, which was the object of a controversial debate and polemic between the members of the legal profession and had been caused by the decision of the Constitutional Court itself. Taking into consideration as well that the lawyer had denied saying everything which had been stated in the interview and that he could not be held responsible for the whole content of that interview, the Court held that the punishment imposed on the lawyer constituted a violation of Article 10.[208]

4. DEROGATION

Article 10 is not mentioned in the enumeration of Article 15(2), and the right to freedom of expression, therefore, is not a non-derogable right. In the 1969 *Greek* case, accordingly, a violation of the Convention on account of a breach

---

[206] *Barfod v. Denmark*, ECtHR 22 February 1989, appl. no. 11508/85, para. 34.
[207] *Prager and Oberschlick*, *supra* n. 4, para. 36; *Falter Zeitschriften GmbH v. Austria*, ECtHR 18 September 2012, appl. no. 3084/07, para. 45.
[208] *Amihalachioaie v. Moldova*, ECtHR 20 April 2004, appl. no. 60115/00, paras. 31–40.

of Article 10 could only be established after the Commission had examined whether the Greek Government had rightly invoked Article 15, and after it had reached a negative conclusion in that respect.[209]

As has been submitted with regard to Article 9, here again it should be noticed that in fact the exceptions provided for in Article 15 can never be applicable to the 'freedom to hold opinions' contained in Article 10, since an exception to that right can in no circumstance be 'strictly required' in the sense of Article 15(1).

---

[209]   Report of 5 November 1969, Yearbook XII (1969), p. 1 (75–76 and 100).

CHAPTER 15

FREEDOM OF ASSEMBLY
AND ASSOCIATION

(Article 11)

Hansko Broeksteeg[*]

GUIDING PRINCIPLE

The freedom of association presupposes the freedom of assembly, as members of an association will have (regular) meetings. Freedom of assembly also contains demonstrations and manifestations. Only peaceful assemblies are protected by Article 11. The Court has taken the view that this right includes several positive obligations for an effective exercise thereof. The freedom of association includes the right to establish and to join political parties and trade unions.

ARTICLE 11

1. Everyone has the right to freedom of peaceful assembly and to freedom of association with others, including the right to form and to join trade unions for the protection of his interests.

2. No restrictions shall be placed on the exercise of these rights other than such as are prescribed by law and are necessary in a democratic society in the interests of national security or public safety, for the prevention of disorder or crime, for the protection of health or morals or for the protection of the rights and freedoms of others. This Article shall not prevent the imposition of lawful restrictions on the exercise of these rights by members of the armed forces, of the police or of the administration of the State.

---

[*]   In the fourth edition this chapter was revised and updated by Aalt Willem Heringa and Fried van Hoof.

CONTENTS

1. INTRODUCTION

In the Convention, the freedom of association and that of peaceful assembly are contained in one and the same provision. Freedom of association in fact presupposes freedom of assembly, since without regular meetings of its members an association cannot lead an effective existence. Freedom of assembly is also important, however, outside the framework of associations, for instance with regard to demonstrations and manifestations. The freedom of association also includes the right to establish and to join a trade union.

Article 11 needs to be interpreted in conjunction with other fundamental rights. Both the freedom of association and the freedom of assembly are closely connected with the freedom of thought, conscience and religion provided for in

Article 9, and with the freedom of expression of Article 10. In fact, the exercise of the right to freedom of association and of the right to freedom of assembly will generally involve the holding and propagation of specific opinions. This was expressly indicated by the Court in the *Young, James and Webster* case.[1] In that case, the Court treated the freedoms set forth in Articles 9 and 10 as elements of Article 11 and considered their violation as constituting an additional argument for the finding of a violation of Article 11. This interpretation is now established case law: the Court invariably repeats its opinion that Article 11 must also be considered in the light of Articles 9 and/or 10.[2] In *Ezelin*, the Court added that '(t)he protection of personal opinions, secured by Article 10, is one of the objectives of freedom of peaceful assembly as enshrined in Article 11'.[3] More recently, in *Schwabe and M.G.*, the Court stressed that '[d]epending on the circumstances of the case, Article 11 has often been regarded as the lex specialis, taking precedence for assemblies over Article 10 (…).'[4]

In some cases, the facts do give rise to a violation of Article 10 as well as of Article 11. In the *Vogt* case, the relevant issue was the compatibility with Articles 10 and 11 of the dismissal of the applicant from her post as a civil servant on the ground of her having persistently refused to dissociate herself from the DKP (the German Communist Party), claiming that membership of that party was not incompatible with her duty of loyalty. The Court first concluded that Article 10 had been violated. It then held that the facts which gave rise to that conclusion also constituted a breach of Article 11. The Court thereby noted that the requirements of paragraph 2 of Article 11 are identical to those laid down in paragraph 2 of Article 10 (with the exception of the last sentence of paragraph 2 of Article 11). Its finding that there had been a disproportionality with respect to the legitimate aim pursued in the context of Article 10, therefore, automatically resulted in the conclusion that there also had been a violation of Article 11.[5]

In some cases, it can be difficult to assess whether Article 10 or Article 11 is applicable. It depends on the circumstances of the case whether the Court scrutinises the case under Article 10 or under Article 11. *Schwabe and M.G.*

---

[1] *Young, James and Webster v. the United Kingdom*, ECtHR 13 August 1981, appl. nos. 7601/76 and 7806/77, para. 57. Other examples of the link between Art. 11 and Art. 10: *Refah Partisi (The Welfare Party) and Others v. Turkey*, ECtHR 13 February 2003, appl. nos. 41340/98, 41342/98, 41343/98 and 41344/98; *Freedom and Democratic Party (Özdep) v. Turkey*, ECtHR (GC) 8 December 1999, appl. no. 23885/94.

[2] An example is the *Chassagnou v. France* case, ECtHR 29 April 1999, appl. nos. 28331/95 and 28443/95, para. 100: an obligation to join an association is an interference with the 'negative' freedom of association and is, therefore, considered by the Court under Art. 11 in the light of Art. 9, since protection of personal opinions is one of the purposes of the freedom of association.

[3] *Ezelin v. France*, ECtHR 26 April 1991, appl. no. 11800/85, para. 37.

[4] *Schwabe and M.G. v. Germany*, ECtHR 1 December 2011, appl. nos. 8080/08 and 8577/08, para. 99. See also explicitly *Trade Union of the Police in the Slovak v. Slovakia*, ECtHR 25 September 2012, appl. no. 11828/08.

[5] *Vogt v. Germany*, ECtHR 26 September 1995, appl. no. 17851/91, paras. 64–65.

concerned a demonstration during a G8 summit in Heiligendamm in 2007. The applicants were arrested, even before they were able to actually participate in the demonstration, and their banners were confiscated. They complained that they had been prevented from participating in and expressing their views during the demonstration. The Court stressed that Article 11 was, in that case, more at issue than Article 10, because the applicants wanted to share their opinions jointly with others.[6] However, since the freedom of demonstration could not be seen as wholly separate from the freedom of expression, the Court interpreted Article 11 in the light of Article 10.[7]

This approach can also work the other way around. In *Tatár and Fáber*, for example, the Court decided that only Article 10 was applicable. The applicants exposed, in the course of an event they termed a 'political performance', several items of dirty clothing on a rope attached to the fence around Parliament in Budapest. They stated that the symbolic meaning of this expression was 'to hang out the nation's dirty laundry'. The applicants spent exactly 13 minutes on the scene. According to the Court it was, among other things, significant that this action was performed by only two persons. Although the Court admitted that a too strict an application of a numerical criterion would go beyond the meaning of the freedom of demonstration, the 'event, irrespective of the characterization attributed to it by the applicants, constituted predominantly an expression (…), all the more so since it involved only two persons and lasted very short time'.[8] This would mean that any common expressive action of two individuals, in principle, does not amount to an assembly, but it could be different when, for example, further participants intend to participate or when the expression is made known for a longer period than in *Tatár and Fáber*. We must conclude that the difference in application, by the Court, of Article 10 and Article 11 is not crystallised once and for all.[9]

In addition to Article 10, the freedom of association and the freedom of assembly can also be related to Article 9, since religious groups can be seen as associations. In the *Moscow Branch of the Salvation Army* case, the refusal to register this branch as a religious association was a violation of Article 11, read in the light of Article 9.[10] Conversely, in a similar case, *Kimlya*, the Court read Article 9 in the light of Article 11. This case concerned the refusal to register the Scientology Church as a non-governmental organisation, which deprived this

---

6   *Schwabe and M.G. v. Germany, supra* n. 4.

7   See for another example: *Navalnyy and Yashin v. Russia*, ECtHR 4 December 2014, appl. no. 76204/11.

8   *Tatár and Fáber v. Hungary*, ECtHR 12 June 2012, appl. nos. 26005/08 and 26160/08, para. 29. The Court scrutinises 1-person demonstrations under Art. 10 and not under Art. 11: *Novikova and Others v. Russia*, ECtHR 26 April 2016, appl. nos. 25501/07, 57569/11, 80153/12, 5790/13 and 35015/13.

9   See for another example: *Taranenko v. Russia*, ECtHR 15 May 2014, appl. no. 19554/05.

10   *Moscow Branch of the Salvation Army v. Russia*, ECtHR 5 October 2006, appl. no. 72881/01, para. 98.

church of several privileges and thereby hindered the church in exercising its freedom of religion.[11] It is, however, difficult to predict what position the Court takes: will Article 9 or will Article 11 prevail?

The *Hasan and Chaush* case concerned state interference in the internal organisation of an Islamic church in Bulgaria. In this case, the Court read Article 9 in the light of Article 11, as a judicial review under Article 11 only 'would take the applicants' complaints out of their context and disregard their substance'.[12] Finally, the example can be mentioned of the *Sindicatul 'Păstoral Cel Bun'* case, in which the Romanian national authorities had refused to register a trade union of priests because the Orthodox Church had declined to approve of such registration. In this case, too, there was a very close interrelatedness of the complaints under Articles 9 and 11. The Court is very reticent in scrutinising trade union freedom and it emphasises the autonomy of the church. It interprets Article 9 in the light of Article 11.[13]

2. PEACEFUL ASSEMBLY

2.1. PEACEFUL

The right to freedom of peaceful assembly is, like the right to freedom of expression, 'a fundamental right in a democratic society and (...) is one of the foundations of such a society'.[14] The adjective 'peaceful' restricts the scope of the protection offered by the first paragraph. If the authorities concerned could reasonably have believed that a planned assembly would not have a peaceful character or if this has become apparent during the assembly, its prohibition or restriction does not conflict with the first paragraph of Article 11. Consequently, the second paragraph need not be relied upon in that case and it is not, for example, required that the prohibition or restriction be 'prescribed by law'. However, a peacefully organised demonstration that runs the risk of resulting in disorder by developments beyond the control of the organisers, for example through a violent counter-demonstration, does not for that reason fall outside the scope of Article 11 of the Convention.[15]

It is the Court itself that examines whether a state can claim that an assembly is or is not peaceful. In *Stankov and the United Macedonian Organisation Ilinden*,

---

[11]   *Kimlya and Others v. Russia*, ECtHR 1 October 2009, appl. nos. 76836/01 and 32782/03. See also *Jehova's Witnesses of Moscow v. Russia and Others*, ECtHR 10 June 2010, appl. no. 302/02.

[12]   *Hasan and Chaush v. Bulgaria*, ECtHR (GC) 26 October 2000, appl. no. 30985/96, para. 65.

[13]   *Sindicatul 'Păstoral cel Bun' v. Romania*, ECtHR (GC) 9 July 2013, appl. no. 2330/09.

[14]   *Rassemblement jurassien et Unité jurassienne v. Switzerland*, ECtHR 10 October 1979, appl. no. 8191/78.

[15]   *Christians against Racism and Fascism v. the United Kingdom*, ECtHR 16 July 1980, appl. no. 8440/78; *Plattform 'Ärzte für das Leben' v. Austria*, ECtHR 21 June 1988, appl. no. 10126/82.

the Government disputed the applicability of Article 11 on the basis of its doubts as to the peaceful character of the applicant association's meetings. The Court dismissed this argument and accepted applicability, since, 'having carefully studied all the material before it, the Court does not find that those involved in the organisation of the prohibited meetings had violent intentions'.[16] It may be safely concluded that the Court relates the applicability of Article 11 to the non-violent intentions of those involved in the assembly, and not of those not involved.

In the *Ezelin* case, the Court was confronted with a demonstration during which some disturbances had occurred. The applicant had been disciplined for not having dissociated himself from offensive and insulting acts committed by other demonstrators.[17] From the position adopted by the Court in that case it may be concluded, in the first place, that an individual participating in an assembly that has not been prohibited cannot afterwards be confronted with allegations that he took part in a non-peaceful assembly that lacked the protection of Article 11. Secondly, the Court's judgment makes clear that an individual participant enjoys the full protection of Article 11 as long as he abstains from non-peaceful behaviour.[18] This was confirmed by the Court's conclusion in the *Gün* case that when a demonstration started peacefully but ended violently, the offenders should be the ones to be prosecuted rather than the organisers.[19]

2.2. ASSEMBLY

An assembly has, according to the Court in continuous case law, as purpose to contribute to a public debate on matters of social importance. The Court therefore assesses whether the participants intend to participate in a debate of matters of public interest.[20] In *Sáska*, the Court stressed that 'the right to freedom of assembly includes the right to choose the time, place and modalities of the assembly, within the limits established in paragraph 2 of Article 11'.[21]

2.3. NOTIFICATION AND IMMEDIATE RESPONSE

In case of a peaceful assembly the question may arise whether the national authorities can require a permit and to what extent spontaneous demonstrations are permitted. In *Berladir*, the Court considered that an obligatory notification

---

[16]   *Stankov and the United Macedonian Organisation Ilinden v. Bulgaria*, ECtHR 20 December 2001, appl. nos. 29221/95 and 29225/95, para. 78.
[17]   *Ezelin v. France, supra* n. 3, para. 53.
[18]   *Ibid.*
[19]   *Gün v. Turkey*, ECtHR 18 June 2013, appl. no. 8029/07. See also *Gülcü v. Turkey*, ECtHR 19 January 2016, appl. no. 17526/10.
[20]   *Schwabe and M.G. v. Germany, supra* n. 4.
[21]   *Sáska v. Hungary*, ECtHR 27 November 2012, appl. no. 58050/08.

does not confine the scope of Article 11, at least as long as the purpose of notification is that the national authorities can take reasonable and appropriate measures to ensure an effortless course of the demonstration.[22] A notification may not represent a hidden obstacle to the freedom of peaceful assembly. The period of notice may not be too short.[23]

Despite a requirement of notification, the Court assumes a breach of the right of assembly when the national authorities terminate a non-notified peaceful demonstration.[24] In this context the Court introduced the doctrine of 'immediate response'. In the *Bukta* case, the Court set forth: 'In the Court's view, in special circumstances when an immediate response, in the form of a demonstration, to a political event might be justified, a decision to disband the ensuing, peaceful assembly solely because of the absence of the requisite prior notice, without any illegal conduct by the participants, amounts to a disproportionate restriction on freedom of peaceful assembly.'[25]

According to the Court, such immediate response can only be accepted in exceptional circumstances, as it stressed in *Eva Molnar*: 'the principle established in the case of *Bukta* and Others cannot be extended to the point that the absence of prior notification can never be a legitimate basis for crowd dispersal. Prior notification serves not only the aim of reconciling, on the one hand, the right of assembly and, on the other hand, the rights and lawful interests (including the right of movement) of others, but also the prevention of disorder or crime. (…) The Court therefore considers that the right to hold spontaneous demonstrations may override the obligation to give prior notification to public assemblies only in special circumstances, namely if an immediate response to a current event is warranted in the form of a demonstration. In particular, such derogation from the general rule may be justified if a delay would have rendered that response obsolete.'[26]

In the more recent *Navalnyy and Yashin* judgment, the Court stressed that the single fact that a demonstration was not notified does not mean that the authorities may intervene, at least not when the demonstration has a peaceful character and does not disturb public life.[27]

3.   RESTRICTIONS

In general, it may be assumed that the more general the ban, the less likely that it will respond to a pressing social need. This is, for example, the case when a

---

[22]   *Berladir and Others v. Russia*, ECtHR 10 July 2012, appl. no. 34202/06.
[23]   *Primov and Others v. Russia*, ECtHR 12 June 2014, appl. no. 17391/06.
[24]   *Gün v. Turkey, supra* n. 19.
[25]   *Bukta v. Hungary*, ECtHR 17 July 2007, appl. no. 25691/04.
[26]   *Eva Molnar v. Hungary*, ECtHR 7 October 2008, appl. no. 10346/05.
[27]   *Navalnyy and Yashin v. Russia, supra* n. 7.

demonstration is prohibited on account of its content. In *Primov.* the Court stressed that: 'Content-based restrictions on the freedom of assembly should be subjected to the most serious scrutiny by this Court, and in the present case the Government did not forward any convincing argument which would justify such a restriction.'[28]

On the other hand, when a demonstration is only prohibited for a certain time or a certain place and the national authorities are willing to deliberate, the complaint is more likely to be declared inadmissible. The Court scrutinises whether the restriction on the freedom of assembly is proportional to the legitimate aims pursued.[29] In *Schwabe and M.G.*, concerning a demonstration regarding a G8 summit, for example, the Court stressed a fair balance between the purpose of the protection of the public order and the prevention of crime on the one hand and the interests of the applicants to demonstrate on the other. The Court takes on board the arguments that the protection of the public order at a G8 summit is a considerable challenge and that decisions with regard thereto must be taken quickly.[30]

The authorities may terminate a demonstration after a certain lapse of time, long enough for the participants to attain their objectives. The *Nosov* case concerned a quasi-permanent demonstration with tents. The closing down thereof after two months 'may be considered to be justified in the interests of public order and the protection of the rights of others in order, for example, to prevent the deterioration of sanitary conditions or to stop the disruption of traffic caused by the assembly'. The Court took account of the tolerance, showed by the authorities, towards the applicants' demonstration. It 'lasted sufficiently long for them to express their position of protest and to draw the attention of the public to their concerns.'[31]

4. POSITIVE OBLIGATIONS

In the light of positive obligations that can derive from the right of peaceful assembly, the Court has taken the view that this right includes the right to protection against counter-demonstrators, because it is only in this way that its effective exercise can be secured to groups wishing to demonstrate with regard to highly controversial issues. If the protection provided by the authorities proves to be insufficient to enable a free exercise of the right to freedom of assembly, this amounts to a restriction which has to be reviewed for its justification on the basis of the second paragraph.

---

[28]   *Primov and Others v. Russia, supra* n. 23.
[29]   E.g., *Kudrevicius v. Lithuania*, ECtHR 15 October 2015, appl. no. 37553/05; *Frumkin v. Russia*, ECtHR 5 January 2016, appl. no. 74568/12.
[30]   *Schwabe and M.G. v. Germany, supra* n. 4.
[31]   *Nosov and Others v. Russia*, ECtHR 20 February 2014, appl. nos. 9117/04 and 10441/04.

Thus, in *Plattform Ärzte für das Leben* the Court reviewed the measures taken to protect the two demonstrations involved against interference by counter-demonstrators for their reasonableness and appropriateness to enable the demonstrations to proceed peacefully. The Court held that the participants of a demonstration must 'be able to hold the demonstration without having to fear that they will be subjected to physical violence by their opponents; such a fear would be liable to deter associations or other groups supporting common ideas or interests from openly expressing their opinions on highly controversial issues affecting the community. In a democracy the right to counter-demonstrate cannot extend to inhibiting the exercise of the right to demonstrate'.

The Court concluded from this that 'genuine, effective freedom of peaceful assembly cannot, therefore, be reduced to a mere duty on the part of the State not to interfere: a purely negative conception would not be compatible with the object and purposes of Article 11. Like Article 8, Article 11 sometimes requires positive measures to be taken, even in the sphere of relations between individuals, if need be'.[32] With respect to the content of these measures, the Court held that the Contracting States have a wide discretion in the choice of the means to be used.[33]

In the *Alekseyev* case, the Court emphasised that participants of a demonstration must not fear physical violence by counter-demonstrators. Therefore, the authorities have the obligation to assess the possibility of a peaceful demonstration and of any (violent) counter-demonstrations: 'the Court concludes that the Government failed to carry out an adequate assessment of the risk to the safety of the participants in the events and to public order. It reiterates that if every probability of tension and heated exchange between opposing groups during a demonstration were to warrant its prohibition, society would be faced with being deprived of the opportunity of hearing different views on any question which offends the sensitivity of the majority opinion'.[34]

In *Promo Lex* and in *Identoba*, the Court applied similar argumentation: the national authorities (which were present in the proximity of both the demonstrations) intervened too late and too little.[35]

The Court also assumes the obligation to communicate properly with the leaders and participants of a demonstration. The authorities should ensure reliable channels of communication and should make clear agreements with the organisers of the demonstration. A severe lack of communication on the part of the authorities means a breach of Article 11.[36]

---

[32] *Plattform Ärzte für das Leben v. Austria, supra* n. 15.
[33] *Ibid.*, para. 34.
[34] *Alekseyev v. Russia*, ECtHR 21 October 2010, appl. nos. 4916/07, 25924/08, 14599/09.
[35] *Promo Lex v. Moldova*, ECtHR 24 February 2015, appl. no. 42757/09; *Identoba and Others v. Georgia*, ECtHR 12 May 2015, appl. no. 73235/12.
[36] *Frumkin v. Russia, supra* n. 29.

5. ASSOCIATION

5.1. AUTONOMOUS MEANING

An autonomous meaning is to be assigned to the word 'association'. The legal form of an association that is chosen and the legal consequences attached thereto by national law cannot be decisive for the Convention context. If that were not the case, the guarantee of Article 11 might be rendered illusory by the national legislature, and great differences in scope of that guarantee might exist among the legal systems of the various Contracting States.[37] The freedom of association means, according to the Court in *Gorzelik*: 'The ability to establish a legal entity in order to act collectively in a field of mutual interest is one of the most important aspects of freedom of association, without which that right would be deprived of any meaning.'[38] Hence, an association is a legal entity intended to operate as such in a specific area. The right to freedom of association implies the right to form one (the 'positive' aspect of the freedom of association) and it includes the right not to be forced to be a member of an association (the 'negative' aspect of the freedom of association).[39] An inherent part of the freedom of association is the recognition of the association as a legal entity. Therefore, refusals of registration are fully covered by the scope of Article 11.

a. Private law and public law associations

The term 'association' presupposes a voluntary, private law organisation.[40] A professional organisation established by the government and governed by public law, which as a rule is intended not only to protect the interests of the members, but also certain public interests, is not an 'association' in the sense of Article 11. So, the Court explicitly makes the distinction between private and public associations. In the *Chassagnou* case, the Court referred to this distinction with regard to a hunters' association. After having noted that the term association has an autonomous meaning, the Court specifically looked into the private law and public law aspects. It remarked in that respect that the hunters' association 'owe their existence to the will of parliament, but (…) that they are nevertheless associations set up in accordance with the Law of 1 July 1901, and are composed of hunters or the owners of land or hunting rights, and therefore of private individuals, all of whom, a priori, wish to pool their land for the purpose of

---

[37]   *Chassagnou and Others v. France, supra* n. 2.
[38]   *Gorzelik v. Poland*, ECtHR 20 December 2001, appl. no. 44158/98, para. 55.
[39]   An example of the latter aspect, outside the area of trade unions, to be discussed *infra*, is *Chassagnou and Others v. France, supra* n. 2, para. 103.
[40]   *Young, James and Webster v. the United Kingdom, supra* n. 1.

hunting. Similarly, the fact that the prefect supervises the way these associations operate is not sufficient to support the contention that they remain integrated within the structures of the State (…). Furthermore, it cannot be maintained that under the Loi Verdell ACCAs [i.e. the hunters' association] enjoy prerogatives outside the orbit of the ordinary law, whether administrative, rule making or disciplinary, or that they employ processes of a public authority, like professional organisations.'[41]

The *Herrmann* case also concerned a hunters' association. The Court considered 'hunting associations are subject to State supervision which goes beyond the supervision normally exercised over private associations'. These associations were established by law in the form of public law associations, were subject to the control of the hunting authority and their internal statutes needed approval by that authority. The Court considered that the hunting associations are sufficiently integrated into state structures in order to qualify them as public law institutions.[42]

This means that the Court carefully examines the dominant features of an association in order to determine its public or private law aspects. In this respect it is an autonomous concept; the Court, as confirmed in the *Chassagnou* and *Herrmann* cases, carefully looks for predominant private law or public law characteristics: was the association founded by individuals or by the legislature; is the association integrated in the structures of the state; is the board of the association appointed by the government; does it pursue an aim which is of general interest; is there any supervision by the state?

b.   Article 17

Not every private law association is, however, an association in the sense of Article 11. The Court has not held this article to be applicable when the organisers and participants of an association have violent intentions or otherwise deny the foundations of a 'democratic society'.[43] Hence, Article 11 is restricted by Article 17 of the Convention. When, for example, an association pursues anti-democratic or anti-Semitic goals, when it pursues the establishment of a caliphate or the introduction of the Sharia, or when the association spreads the destruction of the state of Israel and its population, Article 17 – and not Article 11 – can be[44] applicable.[45]

---

[41]   *Chassagnou and Others v. France, supra* n. 2, paras. 98–101.
[42]   *Herrmann v. Germany*, ECtHR 20 January 2011, appl. no. 9300/07. See also *Karakurt v. Turkey*, ECtHR 20 September 2009, appl. no. 45718/99.
[43]   *Alekseyev v. Russia*, ECtHR 21 October 2010, *supra* n. 34; *Association Nouvelle des Boulogne Boys v. France*, ECtHR 22 February 2011, appl. no. 6468/09.
[44]   Not necessarily: see, e.g., *Refah Partisi v. Turkey* hereafter.
[45]   *Hizb-ut-Tahrir and Others v. Germany*, ECtHR 12 June 2012 (dec.), appl. no. 31098/08; *Kasymakhunov and Saybatalov v. Russia*, ECtHR 14 March 2013, appl. nos. 26261/05 and 26377/06.

c.   Negative freedom of association

The negative freedom of association means that no one may be forced to join an association. Though it cannot be deduced from Article 11 explicitly, the Court acknowledges this negative freedom as a part of the freedom of association. The obligation, for example, of French landowners to join a hunters' association is not compatible with Article 11.[46] The same applies to the obligation to join a co-operative of wine producers on a Greek island, for historical reasons only and for which the authorities could not give any compelling argument.[47]

5.2.   POLITICAL PARTIES

a.   Bans and dissolutions of political parties

That political parties also fall under the term 'association' was implicitly assumed by the Court in the *Vogt* case, in which it found that the dismissal of the applicant from a post as a civil servant on the ground that she had persistently refused to dissociate herself from the KDP, constituted an interference with the right protected by paragraph 1 of Article 11.[48] Moreover, according to the Court in the *United Communist Party of Turkey* case, 'political parties make an irreplaceable contribution to political debate, which is at the very core of the concept of a democratic society'.[49] Over the past decades, the Court has been confronted with many complaints pertaining to bans and dissolutions of political parties. In dealing with these complaints the Court invariably refers to the essential role of political parties in ensuring pluralism and the proper functioning of democracy, and, for that reason, it very strictly assesses the necessity of any restrictions on the freedom of association of political parties protected by Article 11 of the Convention. The basic principles concerning the interpretation of Article 11 with regard to political parties were laid down in several judgments against Turkey in the cases of the *United Communist Party of Turkey*,[50] the *Socialist Party*,[51] the *Freedom and Democracy Party ÖZDEP))*[52] and *Refah Partisi (Prosperity Party)*[53] and they have been applied in a great many cases since (see hereafter). These cases involved sensitive issues

---

46   *Chassagnou and Others v. France, supra* n. 2.

47   *Mytilinaios and Kostakis v. Greece*, ECtHR 3 December 2015, appl. no. 29389/11.

48   *Vogt v. Germany, supra* n. 5, para. 65. The respondent Government had not contested the applicability of Art. 11.

49   *United Communist Party of Turkey and Others v. Turkey*, ECtHR (GC) 30 January 1998, appl. no. 19392/92.

50   *Ibid.*, paras. 42–47.

51   *The Socialist Party v. Turkey*, ECtHR 15 May 1998, appl. no. 21237/93, paras. 41–50.

52   *The Freedom and Democracy Party (ÖZDEP) v. Turkey), supra* n. 1, paras. 37–48.

53   *Refah Partisi and Others v. Turkey, supra* n. 1.

pertaining to considerations of national security, territorial integrity, the protection of minorities and the maintenance of political and social order.

In the *Freedom and Democracy Party (ÖZDEP)* case, the Court held that, although the political design proposed by the party concerned could be considered incompatible with the current principles and structures of the Turkish State, this in itself did not mean that it infringed democratic rules. The Court reasoned that it was the very essence of a democracy to allow diverse political projects to be proposed and debated, even those which called into question the way a state was organised – its constitutional and legal order –, provided they did not harm democracy itself. It further considered that there could be no justification for hindering a political group solely because it sought to initiate dialogue about irksome national issues (i.e. the Kurdish question) as long as the group did not propagate or take recourse to violence.

On similar grounds the Court found a violation of Article 11 in the *United Community Party of Turkey* and the *Socialist Party* cases. It held that only convincing and compelling reasons could justify restrictions on political parties' freedom of association. Such restrictions would not be justified if (1) a party is promoting change, which, although bearing on the existing structures of the state and its established order, is in itself compatible with fundamental democratic principles, and (2) the means proposed to effectuate such change are legal and democratic.

The Court further elaborated these general principles in its seminal judgment in the *Refah Partisi (Prosperity Party)* case. There, it placed great emphasis on the examination of the existence of a 'pressing social need', which it held to be essential to the determination of the necessity of state interference with the freedom of association. The Court considered that in order to establish whether the refusal to register the political party concerned met a pressing social need, it had to examine: '(i) whether there was plausible evidence that the risk to democracy, supposing it had been proved to exist, was sufficiently imminent; (ii) whether the acts and speeches of the leaders and members of the political party concerned were imputable to the party as a whole; and (iii) whether the acts and speeches imputable to the party formed a whole, which gave a clear picture of a model of society conceived advocated by the party which was incompatible with the concept of a "democratic society".'

In light of Refah Partisi's plans to establish a plurality of legal systems in which a Sharia-based regime would be re-introduced in the Turkish State and the failure of Refah's leaders to dissociate themselves from members of the party who publicly called for the use of force, the Court found that the procedure to dissolve the political party served a pressing social need. Although the Court refrained from expressing an opinion in the abstract on the advantages and disadvantages of a plurality of legal systems, it considered that the re-introduction of a Sharia-based regime would be incompatible with the democratic principles on which the Convention is based. Furthermore, taking into account the political momentum

Refah Partisi was gaining, the Court deemed justified the national authorities' restrictions imposed on the party as there was a highly likely prospect that Refah would win the forthcoming general elections.[54]

The standards developed in *Refah Partisi* have been consistently confirmed and applied by the Court in later case law.[55] Put briefly, this case law implies that the national authorities can only decide to dissolve or put a ban on a political party based on the contents of its political program if this political party actively pursues an anti-democratic agenda. Besides, the Court stressed that the political party to be dissolved must be a real danger for democracy. Moreover, in other cases, for example in *Partidul Comunistilor (Nepeceristi) and Ungureanu, Presidential Party of Moldova, Tsnonev* and *Republican Party of Russia*, the Court has applied similar standards in relation to the refusal of the national authorities to register a political party.[56]

b. Political associations

In the *Vona* case, the Court has illuminated the differences between political parties and other associations.[57] Vona used to be the chairman of an association that aimed to guarantee Hungarian culture and traditions. The association established a movement that organised rallies and demonstrations, especially in villages with a large Roma population. The Hungarian authorities decided to dissolve the association and the movement because of the racist and anti-Semitic content of the demonstrations and the paramilitary rituals, which, according to the authorities, were intimidating, promoted segregation, increased social tension and provoked violence. The Court pointed out that political parties and associations 'differ from each other as regards, amongst other elements, the role which they play in the functioning of a democratic society, since many social organisations contribute to that functioning only in an indirect manner'.[58] Social movements, however, contrary to political parties, normally do not enjoy a special legal status and have fewer opportunities to influence political decision-making. 'In the Court's view, the State is also entitled to take preventive measures to

---

[54] *Ibid.*
[55] *Parti Socialiste de Turquie v. Turkey,* ECtHR 12 November 2003, appl. no. 26482/95. See also *Emek Partisi v. Turkey,* ECtHR 31 May 2005, appl. no. 39434/98; *Guneri v. Turkey,* ECtHR 12 July 2005, appl. nos. 42853/98, 43609/98 and 44291/98; *Demokratik Kitle Partisi v. Turkey,* ECtHR 3 May 2007, appl. no. 51290/99; *Kalifatstaat v. Germany,* ECtHR 11 December 2006 (dec.), appl. no. 13828/04; *Herri Batasuna v. Spain,* ECtHR 30 June 2009, appl. nos. 25803/04 and 25817/04; *Hizb-ut-Tahrir v. Germany, supra* n. 45; *Kasymakhunov and Saybatalov v. Russia, supra* n. 45; *DTP and Others v. Turkey,* ECtHR 12 January 2016, appl. nos. 3840/10, 3870/10, 3878/10, 15616/10, 21919/10, 39118/10 and 37272/10.
[56] *Partidul Comunistilor v. Romania,* ECtHR 3 February 2005, appl. no. 46626/99, paras. 50–60. See also *Presidential Party of Moldova v. Moldova,* ECtHR 5 October 2004, appl. no. 65659/01; *Tsonev v. Bulgaria,* ECtHR 13 April 2006, appl. no. 45963/99; *Republican Party of Russia v. Russia,* ECtHR 12 April 2011, appl. no. 12976/07.
[57] *Vona v. Hungary,* ECtHR 9 July 2013, appl. no. 35943/10, paras. 56–58.
[58] *Ibid.,* para. 56.

protect democracy vis-à-vis such non-party entities, if a sufficiently imminent prejudice to the rights of others threatens to undermine the fundamental values on the basis of which a democratic society exists and functions.'

Nevertheless, such measures against non-political associations 'must be supported by relevant and sufficient reasons, just as in the case of dissolution of a political party, although in the case of an association, given its more limited opportunities to exercise national influence, the justification for preventive restrictive measures may legitimately be less compelling than in the case of a political party.'

In conclusion, national authorities can take measures against associations, similar to measures against political parties, but the level of scrutiny will differ. Nevertheless, in *Vona* the Court showed itself convinced that the arguments adduced by the Hungarian authorities were relevant and sufficient to demonstrate that the impugned measure (dissolution) corresponded to a pressing social need.

c.   *Participation in political parties*

The Court has also pronounced on national regulations imposing restrictions on the political activities of civil servants, members of the armed forces and the police, members of the judiciary and other members of the public service (see the last sentence of the second paragraph of Article 11). Unlike the judgments discussed *supra*, these cases concerned general bans on the participation of specific persons or groups in political parties rather than restrictions on the activities of parties themselves. The participation in political parties also forms part of the right of association. For example, the *Ahmed* case concerned a regulation imposing restrictions on civil servants' activities in the political parties of which they were members. The Court found this particular interference with the right protected under Article 11 to be justified and proportionate. It based its conclusion on the fact that the regulation concerned was limited to restricting the extent of the applicants' participation in an administrative and representative capacity in the political parties of which they were members, but it did not restrict their right to join any political party of their choosing.[59] In *Rekvényi*, the Court dealt with a fully-fledged prohibition on members of the army, the police and the security forces from participating in politics and being members of political parties.[60] In this case, the Court reasoned that these restrictions intended to depoliticise the police and security services and thereby contributed to the consolidation and maintenance of a pluralistic democracy. Given these objectives, the Court considered the prohibition to be compatible with democratic principles. In

---

[59]   *Ahmed v. the United Kingdom*, ECtHR 2 September 1998, appl. no. 22954/93, para. 70.
[60]   *Rekvényi v. Hungary*, ECtHR (GC) 20 May 1999, appl. no. 25390/94, paras. 46–50.

this regard, it placed special emphasis on Hungary's totalitarian past where the ruling regime relied to a great extent on the direct commitment of the army, police and security forces. The *Strzelecki* case, finally, concerned the prohibition against police officers becoming members of a political party and participating in political activities. The legitimate aims of this restriction were to guarantee the political neutrality and impartiality of the police and the confidence of citizens in the police. These aims were, according to the Court, legitimate in a country like Poland, where for several decades a totalitarian regime had been in place that had imperilled such confidence and where special measures might be needed to restore it. Besides, there were several exceptions to the prohibitions which mitigated their impact on the freedom of association and their political rights, since police officers still could become a member of a trade union and they had the right to vote and to stand for elections.[61] Redfearn, a taxi driver and a member of the British National Party (an extreme right-wing political party), was fired just after his election as a member of the municipal council. This resignation affected the freedom of association. The Court considered that Redfearn's service was impeccable, no complaint had ever been filed against him and that therefore the respondent State had to take reasonable and appropriate measures to protect employees against unlawful discrimination on the ground of political opinion or affiliation. The Court concluded that there was a violation of Article 11.[62]

5.3. OTHER ASSOCIATIONS

Whilst there is an abundance of case law of the Court with regard to political parties, there is less case law with regard to other associations. It is clear, however, that restrictions related to such associations are subjected to a similar assessment as restrictions related to political parties are. Also concerning these associations, the Court has held, for example, that restrictions 'must be used sparingly, as exceptions to the rule of freedom of association are to be construed strictly and only convincing and compelling reasons can justify restrictions on that freedom'.[63] Such compelling reasons exist, for example, if the association engages in violent behaviour. The Court accepted, for example, the dissolution of an association of supporters of a football club after several violent incidents had occurred in which the association had been involved. Whether such violence actually exists normally remains to be assessed by the national authorities.[64] By contrast, the Court found a violation of Article 11 in relation to the dissolution

---

[61] *Strzelecki v. Poland*, ECtHR 10 April 2012, appl. no. 26648/03.
[62] *Redfearn v. the United Kingdom*, ECtHR 6 November 2012, appl. no. 47335/06.
[63] *Gorzelik v. Poland*, *supra* n. 38, para. 95.
[64] *Association Nouvelle des Boulogne Boys v. France*, *supra* n. 43.

of an association of squatters, since such dissolution was merely intended to guarantee the interests of the owners of the apartments in question and the measure would not even be effective to achieve this objective.[65]

Because of the importance of the freedom of association, the Court has also formulated a number of procedural standards and obligations to be met by the state in registering or dissolving associations. In particular, the prohibition of associations or the refusal to register may not be the result of an arbitrary process of decision-making, especially when the aims of the association are not unconstitutional.[66]

6. TRADE UNIONS

By expressly mentioning trade unions in Article 11, the drafters obviously wanted to put it beyond doubt that the right to trade union freedom falls under the protection of this provision, irrespective of whether, according to national law, a trade union can be considered an association. As the Court puts it: 'the right to form and join trade unions in Article 11 is an aspect of the wider right to freedom of association.'[67]

In *Demir and Baykara*, the Court, in contrast to previous case law, not only recognises trade union freedom as an individual right (for individuals to join a trade union), but at the same time also as a right that can be exercised collectively: 'The development of the Court's case-law concerning the constituent elements of the right of association can be summarised as follows: the Court has always considered Article 11 of the Convention safeguards freedom to protect the occupational interests of trade-union members by the union's collective action, the conduct and development of which the Contracting States must both permit and make possible.'[68] The trade union freedom includes the rights to bargain collectively and the right of collective actions (such as strikes).

6.1. POSITIVE AND NEGATIVE TRADE UNION FREEDOM

In respect of trade unions, the right to *join* and a right to *form* a trade union forms the core of trade union freedom. It is not unusual that employees are discouraged from joining a trade union, candidates are not accepted for a job or that members of a trade union are being harassed. Such proceedings can

---

[65] *Association Rhino v. Switzerland*, ECtHR 11 October 2011, appl. no. 48848/07.
[66] *Association of Victims of Romanian Judges v. Romania*, ECtHR 14 January 2014, appl. no. 47732/06.
[67] See, e.g., *Sigurdur A. Sigurjónsson v. Iceland*, ECtHR 30 June 1993, appl. no. 16130/90, para. 32.
[68] *Demir and Baykara v. Turkey*, ECtHR (GC) 12 November 2008, appl. no. 34503/97.

have a 'chilling effect' on the board and on the members of a trade union.[69] In *Danilenkov* for example, members of a certain trade union were reassigned to financially less attractive working units, were fired unlawfully, were affected by disciplinary sanctions and so forth. The Court established that a criminal conviction could not be achieved because 'it requires proof "beyond reasonable doubts" of direct intent on the part of one of the company's key managers to discriminate against trade-union members', but it deemed Russia responsible for the obligation to protect employees adequately against the practice of discrimination because of a trade union membership.[70] Such discrimination is, however, difficult to prove for employees.[71] In *Wilson*, three employees were offered better working conditions when they would not represent themselves by a trade union in negotiations with their employer. According to the Court, the essence of the right to join a trade union is 'for the protection of their interests that employees should be free to instruct or permit the union to make representation to their employer or to take action in support of their interests on their behalf. If workers are prevented from so doing, their freedom to belong to a trade union, for the protection of their interests, becomes illusory'.[72]

The right *not* to be a member of an association is not explicitly included (see also above regarding other associations). This negative trade union freedom is important in particular with regard to the practice of compulsory trade union membership, the so-called 'closed shop' system. From the *travaux préparatoires* of Article 11 one might conclude that the drafters did not intend to prohibit such a practice.[73] In the seminal *Young, James and Webster* case, the Strasbourg authorities addressed the question of compulsory membership at length. The Court left open the question of whether compulsory membership of a trade union is always contrary to Article 11, but regarded the threat of discharge for those who did not wish to join a given union as a form of coercion which affects the essence of the freedom guaranteed in Article 11. The Court expressed as its opinion that the compulsion imposed on the applicants could not be deemed to be 'necessary in a democratic society' in the sense of the second paragraph.[74]

In 1993, in the *Sigurdur A. Sigurjónsson* case, the Court went beyond its *Young, James and Webster* judgment by concluding that 'Article 11 must be viewed as encompassing a negative right of association'.[75] It, however, did not go so far as to accept a full-blown substantive negative right of association,

---

[69]   *Trade Union of the Police in the Slovak v. Slovakia*, *supra* n. 4.
[70]   *Danilenkov v. Russia*, ECtHR 30 July 2009, appl. no. 67336/01.
[71]   See, e.g., *Palomo Sanchez and Others v. Spain*, ECtHR 12 September 2011, appl. nos. 28955/06, 28957/06, 28959/06 and 28964/06.
[72]   *Wilson and Others v. the United Kingdom*, ECtHR 2 July 2002, appl. nos. 30668/96, 30671/96 and 30678/96.
[73]   See the quotation in *Young, James and Webster v. the United Kingdom*, *supra* n. 1, para. 52.
[74]   *Ibid.*, para. 29.
[75]   *Sigurdur A. Sigurjónsson v. Iceland*, *supra* n. 67, para. 35.

because the Court added that it 'is not necessary for the Court to determine in this instance whether this right is to be considered on an equal footing with the positive right'.[76] The Court concluded that Article 11 had been violated, because the applicant ran a risk of losing his taxi licence as a result of his unwillingness to become a member of a specific private law association.[77]

Summing up, it may be concluded that the Strasbourg case law has now recognised that Article 11 also protects the freedom not to join a trade union. This negative right is not only interfered with after a dismissal, but also when other serious 'sanctions' have been imposed, or in case the individual's refusal to become a member is inspired by personal convictions or opinions. The *Olafsson* case, for example, concerned the obligation for employers of a certain branch to pay tax for employers' organisations. The Court concluded that there was a breach of Article 11, as this tax, although not a big amount, was a disproportionate restriction of the negative freedom of association.[78]

6.2. RIGHTS RELEVANT IN RELATION TO TRADE UNIONS

The case law has gradually refined the trade union freedom in the sense that Article 11 has come to include a variety of rights and freedoms which are important for the enjoyment of the right to join and form trade unions as such.

a. Internal autonomy

In principle, the right to form trade unions involves the right of trade unions to draw up their own rules, to administer their own affairs and to establish and join trade union federations. Such trade union rights are explicitly recognised in Articles 3 and 5 of ILO Convention No. 87, which must be taken into account in the context of Article 11, according to the Court in the *ASLEF* case.[79] Accordingly, in principle trade union decisions in these domains must not be subject to restrictions and control by the state except on the basis of the second paragraph of Article 11.

b. The right to be heard

Article 11 also implies that the trade union must be heard by the authorities in order that it may be able to stand up for those interests, although the Court

---

[76]   *Ibid.*
[77]   See more recently with regard to the negative trade union freedom: *Sørensen and Rasmussen v. Denmark*, ECtHR 11 January 2006, appl. nos. 52562/99 and 52620/99.
[78]   *Olafsson v. Iceland*, ECtHR 27 April 2010, appl. no. 20161/06.
[79]   *ASLEF v. the United Kingdom*, ECtHR 27 February 2007, appl. no. 11002/05.

held that this obligation does not necessarily take the specific form that the authorities have to consult the unions before taking certain decisions,[80] or that the authorities as employers are obliged to conclude a collective agreement with a particular union.[81] In *Wilson*, which is confirmed in *Demir and Baykara*, the Court introduced the right for a trade union 'to seek to persuade the employer to listen to what it has to say on behalf of its members'.[82]

c.   The right to bargain collectively

In the *Demir and Baykara* case, the Court considered 'that, having regard to the developments in labour law, both international and national, and to the practice of Contracting States in such matters, the right to bargain collectively with the employer has, in principle, become one of the essential elements of (...) Article 11 of the Convention, it being understood that States remain free to organise their systems so as, if appropriate, to grant special status to representative trade unions.'

Thus, the right to bargain collectively and to enter into collective agreements is now recognised as an essential element of the right to form and to join trade unions.

In the *Gustafsson* case, the Court referred to Article 6 of the European Social Charter in order to deem protected trade union activities that were aimed at forcing an employer to submit himself to a system of collective agreements.[83] The employer concerned alleged that he had suffered considerable losses because of trade union action, consisting of a boycott. The Court argued that the union action pursued legitimate interests consistent with Article 11. With respect to the right *not* to enter into a collective agreement, alleged by the applicant, the Court held that Article 11 does not as such guarantee the negative right not to participate in collective bargaining.[84] Thus, the Court seemed to draw such conclusions from the fact that, in its opinion, Article 11 does not guarantee a positive right to participate in collective bargaining either.[85] The Court also concluded that the freedom of association had not been significantly affected to such an extent as to conclude that it had been violated.

Furthermore, employers are under no obligation to either recognise a trade union or accept compulsory collective bargaining. Irrespective of the wide

---

[80]   *National Union of Belgian Police v. Belgium*, ECtHR 27 October 1975, appl. no. 4464/70, para. 39.

[81]   *Swedish Engine Drivers' Union v. Sweden*, ECtHR 6 February 1976, appl. no. 5614/72, paras. 39–40.

[82]   *Wilson and Others v. the United Kingdom*, supra n. 72; *Demir and Baykara v. Turkey*, supra n. 68.

[83]   *Gustafsson v. Sweden*, ECtHR (GC) 25 April 1996, appl. no. 15573/89, para. 53.

[84]   *Ibid.*, para. 52.

[85]   See, e.g., *Schettini v. Italy*, ECtHR 9 November 2000, appl. no. 29529/95.

margin of appreciation which states enjoy in deciding how union freedom may be secured, this freedom must, however, be effective. In *Wilson, National Union of Journalists and Others*, the Court held that by permitting employers to use financial incentives to induce employees to surrender union rights, in particular to acquiesce to the termination of their existing collective bargaining agreement, the State has failed in its positive obligation to secure the enjoyment of the rights protected by Article 11.[86]

d.   Collective actions

Collective actions are often seen as an effective method to advocate the interests of employees. These actions aim to exert some constraint on the employer. Collective actions can be the same as a peaceful assembly. An example is the case of *Barraco*, in which truck drivers, in the context of a trade union action, blockaded a motorway by driving very slowly ('operation escargot'). This action was seen by the Court as a peaceful demonstration as well as a collective action.[87]

Strikes are considered by the Strasbourg organs in the *Schmidt and Dahlström* case as a very important, but not an exclusive means for union members to protect their interests: 'The grant of a right to strike represents without any doubt one of the most important of these means, but there are others.' Referring to the European Social Charter, the Court held that a right to strike, assuming that it is protected by Article 11, may be subjected to restrictions by the national legislature.[88] In the case of *Unison* the Court reiterated that strikes are not an exclusive means for union members to protect their interests. In this case, however, the Court also stated that a prohibition to strike qualifies as a restriction of the freedom of association: 'The Court further considers that the prohibition of the strike must be regarded as a restriction on the applicant's power to protect those interests and therefore discloses a restriction on the freedom of association guaranteed under the first paragraph.'[89] This case law had been continued, in for example *National Union of Rail, Maritime and Transport Worker*. The Court accepts collective actions as a part of the trade union freedom, including solidarity strikes. It establishes that restrictions thereof need to abide the scrutiny of paragraph 2 of Article 11. The Court especially takes into account whether a strike causes serious economic damage. Such damage can be a legitimate aim to confine the right to strike.[90]

---

[86]   *Wilson and Others v. the United Kingdom, supra* n. 72, para. 44.

[87]   *Barraco v. France*, ECtHR 5 March 2009, appl. no. 31684/05.

[88]   *Schmidt and Dahlström v. Sweden*, ECtHR 6 February 1976, appl. no. 5589/72, para. 36.

[89]   *Unison v. the United Kingdom*, ECtHR 10 January 2002, appl. no. 53574/99. See also: *Federation of Offshore Workers' Trade Unions v. Norway and Others*, ECtHR 27 June 2002, appl. no. 38190/97; *Enerji Yapi Yol Sen v. Turkey*, ECtHR 21 April 2009, appl. no. 68959/01.

[90]   *National Union of Rail, Maritime and Transport Workers v. the United Kingdom*, ECtHR 8 April 2014, appl. no. 31045/10.

6.3. RESTRICTIONS

In the *Demir and Baykara* case, the Court has defined two general principles with regard to restrictions of the rights of trade unions. First, the Court takes into consideration the totality of the measures taken by the state concerned in order to secure trade union freedom. Secondly, the Court does not accept restrictions that affect the essential elements of trade union freedom, without which that freedom would become devoid of substance. These two principles are not contradictory but are correlated. This correlation implies that the Contracting State in question, whilst in principle being free to decide what measures it wishes to take in order to ensure compliance with Article 11, is under an obligation to take account of the elements regarded as essential by the Court's case law.'[91]

The *Sindicatul 'Păstoral Cel Bun'* case demonstrates however, that the general principles of *Demir and Baykara* are not to be applied always as easily. In this case, priests of the Romanian-Orthodox Church had formed a trade union without the consent of the bishop. Therefore, the national authorities refused to register the trade union. The Court considered Article 11 applicable, noticing the character of the legal relationship between priests and church. It pointed out, however, that the restriction of the trade union freedom was sufficiently foreseeable as it was based on a reasonable interpretation of the churches' Statutes. The Court emphasised the autonomy of the church and that the state may not intervene therein. The national authorities had been consistent in only assessing that the bishop's approval was lacking and that they therefore could not register the trade union. The Court did not consider the restriction disproportionate, since the priests had the possibility to form an association with consent of the bishop and they could join other trade unions.[92]

We have seen before that national regulations can impose restrictions on activities of civil servants, members of the armed forces and the police, members of the judiciary and other members of the public service (see the last sentence of the second paragraph of Article 11). This is also the case for trade union freedom. Restrictions concerning, for example, police officers can meet the legitimate aim of ensuring appropriate behaviour on the part of the police and maintaining public trust in them. Police officers may, on the one hand, join a trade union; they should, on the other hand, act in an impartial manner.[93] In the *Junta Rectora* case, the Court stressed that police officers should be able to intervene at any time, which requires continuous services. This justifies a restriction of trade union freedom.[94] This also applies to the armed forces: there may be legitimate

---

[91]   *Demir and Baykara v. Turkey, supra* n. 68.
[92]   *Sindicatul 'Păstoral Cel Bun' v. Romania, supra* n. 13.
[93]   *Trade Union of the Police in the Slovak v. Slovakia, supra* n. 4.
[94]   *Junta Rectora Del Ertzainen Nazional Elkartasuna v. Spain*, ECtHR 21 April 2015, appl. no. 45892/09.

aims to restrict the freedom of trade union, such as the prevention of disorder, but such restriction may not imply a general ban on forming or joining a trade union.[95]

6.4. POSITIVE OBLIGATIONS AND *DRITTWIRKUNG*

The freedom of trade union can imply positive obligations for the Contracting States. The *Gustafsson* case, for example, concerned an infringement committed by a trade union. The issue in dispute was the permissibility of union action against the applicant's business in order to force him to meet the union's demand to become a party to a collective agreement. The Court laid down some general principles in this respect: 'The matters complained of by the applicant, although they were made possible by national law, did not involve a direct intervention by the State. (…) Although the essential object of Article 11 is to protect the individual against arbitrary interferences by the public authorities with his or her exercise of the rights protected there may in addition be positive obligations to secure the effective employment of these rights.'

The Court emphasised that national authorities may in certain circumstances be obliged to intervene in the relationships between private individuals by taking reasonable and appropriate measures to secure the effective enjoyment of the (negative) right to freedom of association. Yet, the Contracting States should enjoy a wide margin of appreciation in their choice of the means to be employed.[96]

---

[95]   *Adefdromil v. France*, ECtHR 2 October 2014, appl. no. 32191/09; *Matelly v. France*, ECtHR 2 October 2014, appl. no. 10609/10.
[96]   *Gustafsson v. Sweden*, *supra* n. 83, para. 45.

CHAPTER 16

RIGHT TO MARRY

(Article 12)

Arjen van Rijn*

GUIDING PRINCIPLE

Under Article 12 the right to marry and to found a family is guaranteed to persons of the opposite sex only. These rights can be subject to limitations on the national level, as long as the very essence of these rights is not impaired. Therefore, also detained persons must be enabled to marry if they desire to do so.

ARTICLE 12

Men and women of marriageable age have the right to marry and to found a family, according to the national laws governing the exercise of this right.

---

*   In the fourth edition this chapter was revised and updated by Pieter van Dijk.

CONTENTS

1. SCOPE

Article 12 establishes the right to marry and to found a family. As a consequence of its very clear wording this article has to some extent a limited meaning.

In the first place, Article 12 constitutes the right to marry and to found a family as such. Once two persons have become married, interference with their marital and family life does not constitute an issue under Article 12 but under Article 8, which constitutes the right to respect for private and family life.[1] Nevertheless there is a clear connection between the rights protected by Article 12 and Article 8. In practice, the distinction between the protection provided by Article 12 and the protection provided by Article 8 is not always very clear. Reliance by an applicant on the right to marry and to found a family is, therefore, usually combined with reliance on the right to respect for private and family life. Sometimes even the Court itself decides *ex officio* to perform the examination under both articles, although the applicant did not.[2] When Article 8 appears to be at stake, the Court mostly refrains from an examination under Article 12.[3] Nevertheless, in exceptional situations the Court examines the complaint under Article 12 separately after having examined it under Article 8.[4]

In the second place, Article 12 constitutes a right to marry between man and woman only. Same-sex marriages are not protected by this article. The same applies to the right to found a family, which is connected to the right to marry.

---

[1]   See, e.g., *Hämäläinen v. Finland*, ECtHR (GC) 16 July 2014, appl. no. 37359/09, para. 97.

[2]   Appl. no., *ibid.*, para. 4.

[3]   See, e.g., *Dickson v. the United Kingdom*, ECtHR (GC) 4 December 2007, appl. no. 44362/04, para. 86. In *P., C. and S. v. the United Kingdom*, ECtHR 16 October 2002, appl. no. 56547/00, para. 142, the Court regarded Art. 8 as the *lex specialis* in relation to Art. 12 for family life between parents and an existing child. In *Hämäläinen v. Finland*, *supra* n. 1, para. 96, the Court considered Art. 12 as the *lex specialis* in relation to Art. 8 for the right to marry.

[4]   *K.S. v. the United Kingdom*, ECtHR 7 March 2000, appl. no. 45035/98, para. 4.

Thus, until today the article has kept the traditional, limited scope as meant at the time that the Convention was adopted: a union between partners of opposite sex. Admittedly, in 2010 the Court found under Article 12 that it would no longer consider that the right to marry must in all circumstances be limited to marriage between two persons of the opposite sex. However, the question whether or not to allow same-sex marriage is still solely left to regulation by the national law of the Contracting State, as long as there is no consensus between the Contracting States.[5] Nevertheless, as a next step, in 2015 the Court considered that in the absence of marriage, same-sex couples have a particular interest in obtaining the option of entering into a form of civil union or registered partnership, which would guarantee them the relevant protection – in the form of core rights relevant to a couple in a stable and committed relationship – without unnecessary hindrance.[6]

In the third place, although Article 12 does not include a second paragraph laying down possibilities for restrictions, it does not imply an absolute obligation on the part of the authorities to refrain from interfering with the exercise of the right to marry and to found a family, since the exercise of these rights is guaranteed 'according to the national laws governing the exercise of this right'. The national legislature has been left a certain margin for subjecting the exercise of the right laid down in Article 12 to certain conditions. However, this margin is not unlimited. Limitations ensuing from national law must not restrict or reduce the right to marry in such a way or to such an extent that the very essence of the right is impaired[7], nor may they be arbitrary or disproportionate.[8] In the past decades the Court has examined the compliance with these requirements in various cases.

Article 12 does not entail a positive obligation either for the authorities in concrete cases to provide the material means which must enable the persons concerned to marry and to found a family.[9] However, if they proceed to do so, they may not discriminate.[10]

---

5   *Schalk and Kopf v. Austria*, ECtHR 24 June 2010, appl. no. 30141/04, paras. 55–58.
6   *Oliari and Others v. Italy*, ECtHR 21 October 2015, appl. nos. 18766/11 and 36030/11, para. 174.
7   *Rees v. the United Kingdom*, ECtHR 17 October 1986, appl. no. 9532/81, para. 50; *Shalk and Kopf v. Austria*, *supra* n. 5, para. 49; *Jaremowicz v. Poland*, ECtHR 5 January 2010, appl. no. 24023/03, para. 48; *O'Donoghue and Others v. the United Kingdom*, ECtHR 14 December 2010, appl. no. 34848/07, paras. 82–84; *V.C. v. Slovakia*, ECtHR 8 November 2011, appl. no. 18968/07, para. 159.
8   *O'Donoghue and Others v. the United Kingdom*, *supra* n. 7, para. 84.
9   *Cannatella v. Switzerland* (not published), EComHR 7 June 2000, appl. no. 25928/94.
10 With respect to a complaint by a Turkish Cypriot against Cyprus concerning allegedly discriminatory legislation, a friendly settlement was reached after new legislation had been enacted: *Selim v. Cyprus*, ECtHR 16 July 2002, appl. no. 47293/99.

2. THE RIGHT TO MARRY

2.1. INTRODUCTION

Article 12 does not necessarily reflect a concept that must be seen in the same way in all Contracting States. It refers to national law and, consequently, accepts the possibility that, on the issues concerned, the legal systems may vary among the Contracting States. In some Contracting States, for instance, the law attaches to the religious marriage ceremony the legal consequences of matrimony, whereas in other Contracting States this is not the case. The refusal to register a marriage which has not been concluded according to the procedure legally prescribed, does not constitute a violation of Article 12.[11] The question of when a person has reached marriageable age also needs not to be answered the same way in all Contracting States either.

In the *O'Donoghue* case, the Court held that limitations on the right to marry laid down in the national laws may comprise formal rules concerning such matters as publicity and the solemnisation of marriage. They may also include substantive provisions based on generally recognised considerations of public interest, in particular concerning capacity, consent, prohibited degrees of affinity or the prevention of bigamy. However, this does not mean that there are no common minimum norms which national law and those applying it have to respect and against which that law and that application can be reviewed in Strasbourg. The very fact that Article 12 puts the *right* first and foremost, implies that domestic regulations concerning the exercise of that right must not be of such a nature that the right itself would be affected in its essence.[12]

Formalities required by national law for getting married are as a rule accepted as justified, but they may not cause an excessively long delay,[13] nor be applied in a discriminatory way.[14] A provision of domestic law prohibiting marriage between a former parent-in-law and the former child-in-law as long as their former spouses are still alive, was found to violate Article 12, not only

---

[11] *X. v. Federal Republic of Germany*, EComHR 18 December 1974, appl. no. 6167/73, D&R 1 (1975), p. 64 (65). See also *Şerife Yiğit v. Turkey*, ECtHR (GC) 2 November 2010, appl. no. 3976/05, paras. 83–88.

[12] *O'Donoghue and Others v. the United Kingdom*, *supra* n. 7, paras. 83 and 90.

[13] *Sanders v. France*, EComHR 16 October 1996, appl. no. 31401/96, para. 1; *Klip and Krüger v. the Netherlands*, EComHR 3 December 1997, appl. no. 33257/96, para. 2.

[14] *K.M. v. the United Kingdom*, EComHR 9 April 1997, appl. no. 30309/96, para. 2. See also the decisions as to the admissibility of: *Selim v. Cyprus*, *supra* n. 10, where the complaint has been declared admissible concerning a legal regulation in Cyprus that makes contracting a civil marriage impossible for persons professing the Muslim faith. Different: *Muñoz Díaz v. Spain*, ECtHR 8 December 2009, appl. no. 49151/07: it is not discriminatory that Roma marriage has no civil effects, because the regular civil marriage is open to everyone and its regulation does not entail any discrimination on religious or other grounds, but at the same time the refusal to grant a pension on the ground of not being married constitutes a violation of Art. 1 First Protocol in conjunction with Art. 14 because the applicant was in good faith.

because such relationships were not illegal and opinions in this area were divided, but especially so because individuals in a similar situation to the applicants already had been permitted to marry in the past.[15] The prohibition of discrimination does not mean that it principally should not be allowed to make a difference between married and unmarried people, also if they are not able to marry for reasons of family ties, like two sisters living together in one household. The Court finds that the situations of married and unmarried heterosexual cohabiting couples are not analogous for the purposes of survivors' benefits, since 'marriage remains an institution which is widely accepted as conferring a particular status on those who enter it'.[16]

If the right to marry is denied to a person who is already married, this may be justified on the ground that the legislation prohibiting bigamy is so firmly anchored in the national legal order of most of the Contracting States that the Convention was not intended to change this, and that for a person who is already married the essence of the right to marry is not affected by this prohibition.[17] The same holds good for the denial of admission of an alien for family reunion in a situation where his first wife is living in his home state.[18]

Similar reasoning applies with regard to the legislation according to which the right to marry is denied to persons below a given age. As long as there is a reasonable relation between that age limit and the concept of 'marriageable age', the essence of the right is not affected with respect to them. Thus, Article 12 of the Convention cannot be interpreted as imposing on any State Party to the Convention an obligation to recognise a marriage, religious or otherwise, contracted by a 14-year-old child.[19]

If the right to marry is denied to a person because of his limited mental faculties, his state of health, or his financial situation, the relevant national law is considered to affect the essence of that right, assuming of course that such persons can be deemed capable of determining their free will to consent to the marriage.

Further, in the context of immigration laws and for justified reasons, the states may be entitled to prevent marriages of convenience, entered into solely for the purpose of securing an immigration advantage. However, such decisions must be based solely on the genuineness of the proposed marriage. The relevant laws – which must also meet the standards of accessibility and clarity required by the Convention – may not otherwise deprive a person or a category of persons

---

[15]   *B. and L. v. the United Kingdom*, ECtHR 13 September 2005, appl. no. 36536/02, paras. 37–40.

[16]   *Burden v. the United Kingdom*, ECtHR 29 April 2008, appl. no. 13378/05, para. 63.

[17]   In *Johnston and Others v. Ireland*, ECtHR 18 December 1986, appl. no. 9697/82, para. 52, the Court, in general refers to 'a society adhering to the principle of monogamy'. See also *O'Donoghue and Others v. the United Kingdom*, *supra* n. 7, para. 83.

[18]   See *Khan v. the United Kingdom*, EComHR 29 November 1995, appl. no. 23860/94, which was, however, declared inadmissible for non-compliance with the '6 months' rule.

[19]   *Z.H. and R.H. v. Switzerland*, ECtHR 8 March 2016, appl. no. 60119/12, para. 44.

of full legal capacity of the right to marry with the partners of their choice, for example by asking a fee from the immigrant fixed at a level which a needy applicant could not afford, because this could impair the essence of the right to marry.[20]

In general, it must be assumed that an employer is not allowed to discharge an employee on the mere ground that the person has married or has become a parent.[21] However, discharge does not need to constitute a violation when the person concerned has promised in full freedom not to marry, or at least has accepted the consequence that marriage will constitute a ground for discharge. That situation occurs, for example, when a Roman Catholic priest is relieved from his priestly and directly related functions after having given up his celibate status.[22]

The conditions and restrictions set by domestic law may not amount to a violation of any of the other provisions of the Convention and its Protocols either. Reference has already been made to Article 14, which prohibits the national authorities from discriminating in regulating the enjoyment of the rights and freedoms.[23] Another relevant provision is the prohibition of inhuman treatment in Article 3: preventing a married person from founding a family – one may think, for instance, of laws permitting compulsory sterilisation in certain cases – may assume the character of inhuman treatment.[24]

Article 12 does not provide a solution for cases in which the conclusion of a marriage involves links with differing legal systems. The general reference to national law implies that this is left to the rules of private international law (conflicts of law) applying in the country where the marriage is to take place.[25] This means, for instance, that a person whose national law permits polygamy cannot rely on this law under Article 12 in a country where polygamy is prohibited by law and this norm is applied as being one of public policy. Here again, of course, application of a certain rule of private international law may not lead to discrimination. Because of the implications of nationality in this respect, changing a person's nationality may, under certain circumstances, entail restrictions on his possibility of marrying. In the *Beldjoudi* case, the Commission addressed this issue but did not find, on the facts submitted to

---

[20]   *O'Donoghue and Others v. the United Kingdom, supra* n. 7, paras. 87–90.

[21]   See *Staiku v. Greece*, EComHR 2 July 1997, appl. no. 35426/97; the complaint concerned was, however, declared inadmissible *ratione temporis*.

[22]   *Cf. Fernández Martínez v. Spain*, ECtHR (GC) 12 June 2014, appl. no. 56030/07, para. 135; *Schüth v. Germany*, ECtHR 23 September 2010, appl. no. 1620/03, para. 71.

[23]   The equality of the spouses as to marriage, during marriage and in the event of its dissolution is provided for in Art. 5 of Protocol No. 7 and will be discussed *infra*.

[24]   The prohibition imposed on a detainee from marrying during his detention was not considered by the Commission as an inhuman or degrading treatment: *X v. the United Kingdom*, EComHR 21 May 1975, appl. no. 6564/74, D&R 2 (1975), p. 105.

[25]   *X v. Switzerland*, EComHR 5 October 1981, appl. no. 9057/80, D&R 26 (1982), p. 207 (208).

it by the applicants, any appearance of a violation of Article 12.[26] The Court examined the case only from the point of view of respect for the applicant's family life, which encompasses an already existing marriage and is protected under Article 8.[27]

Article 12 does not include the right to marry a deceased person posthumously.[28] Is does imply the right not to marry, although the Court has not seen reason to confirm this with so many words so far.[29]

2.2. TRANSSEXUALS AND PERSONS OF THE SAME SEX

Article 12 guarantees the right to marry to men and women of marriageable age. For many years there has been elaborate discussion, what this limitation to opposite-sex marriages means for persons finding themselves in different constellations, such as transsexuals and same-sex couples.

Until 2002, the Court consequently found that the inability of transsexuals to marry a person of the sex opposite to their re-assigned gender did not constitute a breach of Article 12 of the Convention. These findings were based variously on the reasoning that the right to marry referred to traditional marriage between persons of opposite biological sex, the view that continued adoption of biological criteria in domestic law for determining a person's sex for the purpose of marriage was encompassed within the power of Contracting States to regulate by national law the exercise of the right to marry and the conclusion that national laws in that respect could not be regarded as restricting or reducing the right of a transsexual to marry in such a way or to such an extent that the very essence of the right was impaired. Reference was also made to the wording of Article 12 as protecting marriage as the basis of the family.

However, in the *Christine Goodwin* case the Court observed that Article 12 indeed secures the fundamental right of a man and woman to marry and to found a family, but that the latter is not a condition of the first and the inability of any couple to conceive or parent a child cannot be regarded as *per se* removing their right to enjoy the first limb of Article 12, i.e. the right to marry. The Court noted: 'The exercise of the right to marry gives rise to social, personal and legal consequences. It is subject to the national laws of the Contracting States but the limitations thereby introduced must not restrict or reduce the right in such a way or to such an extent that the very essence of the right is impaired (…). It is true that the first sentence refers in express terms to the right of a man and woman to marry. The Court is not persuaded that at the date of this case it

---

[26]   Report of 6 September 1990, para. 83.
[27]   *Beldjoudi v. France*, ECtHR 26 March 1992, appl. no. 12083/86, paras. 76–80.
[28]   *M. v. Federal Republic of Germany*, EComHR 13 December 1984, appl. no. 10995/84, D&R 41 (1985), p. 259 (261).
[29]   *Marckx v. Belgium*, ECtHR 13 June 1979, appl. no. 6833/74, para. 67.

can still be assumed that these terms must refer to a determination of gender by purely biological criteria (…). There have been major social changes in the institution of marriage since the adoption of the Convention as well as dramatic changes brought about by developments in medicine and science in the field of transsexuality. The Court has found above, under Article 8 of the Convention, that a test of congruent biological factors can no longer be decisive in denying legal recognition to the change of gender of a post-operative transsexual. There are other important factors – the acceptance of the condition of gender identity disorder by the medical professions and health authorities within Contracting States, the provision of treatment including surgery to assimilate the individual as closely as possible to the gender in which they perceive that they properly belong and the assumption by the transsexual of the social role of the assigned gender. The Court would also note that Article 9 of the recently adopted Charter of Fundamental Rights of the European Union departs, no doubt deliberately, departs from the wording of Article 12 of the Convention in removing the reference to men and women (…). The right under Article 8 to respect for private life does not however subsume all the issues under Article 12, where conditions imposed by national laws are accorded a specific mention. The Court has therefore considered whether the allocation of sex in national law to that registered at birth is a limitation impairing the very essence of the right to marry in this case. In that regard, it finds that it is artificial to assert that post-operative transsexuals have not been deprived of the right to marry as, according to law, they remain able to marry a person of their former opposite sex. The applicant in this case lives as a woman, is in a relationship with a man and would only wish to marry a man. She has no possibility of doing so. In the Court's view, she may therefore claim that the very essence of her right to marry has been infringed.'[30]

However, until now the very essence of the right to marry does not mean that this automatically entitles marital partners to continue a marriage which has become a same-sex marriage as a result of change of gender of one of the spouses. This falls within the discretion of the Contracting States.[31]

The latter point of view is in line with the general position which the Court has taken regarding same-sex marriages until today. In the recent *Schalk and Kopf* and *Oliari* cases, the Court kept sticking to the historical context in which the Convention was adopted: 'In the 1950s marriage was clearly understood in the traditional sense of being a union between partners of different sex.'[32] Same-sex

---

[30]   *Goodwin v. the United Kingdom,* ECtHR (GC) 11 July 2002, appl. no. 28957/95, paras. 97–104.

[31]   *Parry v. United Kingdom,* ECtHR 28 November 2006, appl. no. 42971/05, section III.B. See also *Hämäläinen v. Finland, supra* n. 1, paras. 73–74, 96: this case concerned the wish of a transsexual who after surgery wanted to have her marriage changed into a same-sex marriage, although she had the option to remain married according to the pre-existing circumstances. It was also relevant that the applicant and her wife would not lose any other rights if their marriage were converted into a registered partnership.

[32]   *Schalk and Kopf v. Austria, supra* n. 5, para. 55.

couples therefore cannot derive a right to marry from Article 12 yet.[33] However, besides recognising that same-sex couples fall no longer within the notion of private life only but can fall within the notion of family life as protected by Article 8 as well[34], the Court also stated in the same *Schalk and Kopf* case that it 'cannot but note that there is an emerging European consensus towards legal recognition of same-sex couples. Moreover, this tendency has developed rapidly over the past decade. Nevertheless, there is not yet a majority of States providing for legal recognition of same-sex couples. The area in question must therefore still be regarded as one of evolving rights with no established consensus, where States must also enjoy a margin of appreciation in the timing of the introduction of legislative changes'.[35]

The Court noted that marriage has deep-rooted social and cultural connotations which may differ largely from one society to another. It held that it must not rush to substitute its own judgment in place of that of the national authorities, who are best placed to assess and respond to the needs of society.[36]

In the *Oliari* case, however, the Court noted that the number of Contracting States that have recognised same-sex marriages continues to grow.[37] Accordingly, it seems to be a matter of time before the Court will recognise that Article 12 also will apply to same-sex couples, as soon as there will be sufficiently consensus. In the meantime, an option of entering into a form of civil union or registered partnership, which would guarantee them the relevant protection, should be available.[38]

2.3. DIVORCE AND REMARRIAGE

As the exercise of the right to marry always depends on the free consent of the partners, the right to marry cannot be invoked against a law which makes divorce at the request of the other partner possible.[39] But does the right to marry include the right to divorce and to make a new marriage possible?

In the *Johnston* case a complaint had been lodged against Ireland where divorce was not permitted by law. The applicant complained that by this ban he was restricted in his capacity to marry again. The Court held that Article 12 did not oblige the Contracting States to provide the legal possibilities to dissolve a

---

[33]   *Schalk and Kopf v. Austria, supra* n. 5, paras. 61–63; *Hämäläinen v. Finland, supra* n. 1, paras. 73–74, 96; *Oliari and Others v. Italy, supra* n. 6, paras. 191–192; *Chapin and Charpentier v. France*, ECtHR 9 September 2016, appl. no. 40183/07, paras. 36–39.

[34]   *Schalk and Kopf v. Austria, supra* n. 5.

[35]   *Ibid.*, paras. 55–58.

[36]   *Ibid.*, paras. 61–63; *Hämäläinen v. Finland, supra* n. 1, paras. 73–74, 96.

[37]   *Oliari and Others v. Italy*, ECtHR 21 October 2015, *supra* n. 6, paras. 191–192.

[38]   *Ibid.*, para. 174.

[39]   *Slimani v. France*, EComHR 9 April 1997, appl. no. 33597/96, para. 2.

marriage. For an *a contrario* argument the Court referred to Article 16 of the Universal Declaration of Human Rights which, in addition to the right to marry and to found a family, provides for the entitlement to 'equal rights as to marriage, during marriage and at its dissolution', words which were deliberately left out of the Convention. The Court concluded that 'the *travaux préparatoires* disclose no intention to include in Article 12 any guarantee of a right to have the ties of marriage dissolved by divorce'.[40] The applicants had referred to the judgment of the Court in the *Marckx* case, where it was upheld that the Convention is a living instrument which ought to be interpreted in the light of the present-day conditions. To this the Court responded that it could not, 'by means of an evolutive interpretation, derive from these instruments a right that was not included therein at the outset. This is particularly so here, where the omission was deliberate.'[41]

The Court furthermore pointed out that the right to divorce was also not included in Protocol No. 7 to the Convention. According to the Court the Contracting States had not taken the opportunity to deal with this question in Article 5 of that Protocol, which guarantees certain additional rights to spouses, notably in the event of dissolution of marriage, observing that paragraph 39 of the Explanatory Report to the Protocol states that the words 'in the event of its dissolution' in Article 5 'do no imply any obligation on a State to provide for dissolution of marriage or to provide any special forms of dissolution'.[42]

With respect to the applicant's view that the prohibition of divorce was to be seen as a restriction on the capacity to marry the Court held that, even if this was the case, such a restriction could not be regarded as injuring the substance of the right to marry 'in a society adhering to the principle of monogamy'.[43] It might be argued, however, that in many cases the possibility of divorce would precisely serve to avoid situations of factual bigamy.

Since the *F. v. Switzerland* case three decades ago the Court has held that although a right to divorce cannot be derived from Article 12, as soon as national legislation does allow divorce, it secures for divorced persons the right to remarry without unreasonable restrictions. In this respect, the Court has considered that a failure of the domestic authorities to conduct divorce proceedings within a reasonable time could, in certain circumstances, constitute a violation of Article 12. In this respect, three years is too long. Domestic authorities are obliged to conduct the divorce proceedings efficiently and have to take into account the specific circumstances of those proceedings, such as the agreement of the parties to divorce, a possibility of rendering a

---

[40] *Johnston and Others v. Ireland, supra* n. 18, para. 52.
[41] *Ibid.*, para. 54.
[42] *Ibid.*
[43] *Ibid.*, para. 52.

partial decision and the urgent nature of these proceedings under domestic law.[44]

The procedure of separation from bed and board, which exists in several legal systems instead of, or as an alternative to divorce, does not lead to a dissolution of the marriage and, consequently, does not concern the right to remarry. Complaints about the long protraction of the procedure alleging a violation of Article 12 were, therefore, declared manifestly ill-founded.[45]

Article 12 does not deal with the legal consequences attached to the dissolution of marriage such as the right to wardship and to keep contact with the children. Those consequences are considered by the Court to fall within the scope of Article 8.

3. THE RIGHT TO FOUND A FAMILY

As a consequence of the traditional scope of the right to marry, the second aspect of Article 12, the right to found a family, has a limited meaning as well. Although the right to found a family is not a condition for the right to marry, it is true that Article 12 only protects the right to found a family within marriage as guaranteed in Article 12.[46] Certainly, heterosexual couples who are not married and homosexual couples can found a family as well, but this does not fall within the notion of Article 12. Thus, Article 12 also has a limited scope as far as its second aspect is concerned, which differs from the scope of Article 8, since the latter article protects family life regardless of marital status.[47]

But as far as the right to found a family is concerned, this even has a limited meaning for married opposite-sex couples. According to the case law of the Court, Article 12 does not safeguard the desire to found a family and does not guarantee the right to adopt and artificial procreation as such.[48] This also applies to Article 8, which presupposes the existence of a family.[49] However, Article 8 encompasses, *inter alia*, the right to establish and develop relationships with other human beings, the right to 'personal development', or the right to self-determination as such, elements such as names, gender identification, sexual

---

[44]　*F. v. Switzerland*, ECtHR 18 December 1987, appl. no. 11329/85, para. 38; *Aresti Charalambous v. Cyprus*, ECtHR 19 July 2007, appl. no. 43151, para. 56; *V.K. v. Croatia*, ECtHR 27 November 2012, appl. no. 38380/08, paras. 99–107; *Chernetskiy v. Ukraine*, ECtHR 8 December 2016, appl. no. 44316/07, paras. 28–34.

[45]　*D.P. v. Italy*, ECtHR 19 March 1997, appl. no. 27962/95; *Bolignari v. Italy*, EComHR 22 April 1998, appl. no. 37175/97.

[46]　*Goodwin v. the United Kingdom, supra* n. 30, para. 98.

[47]　Since *Marckx v. Belgium, supra* n. 29, para. 31.

[48]　See for adoption *Di Lazzaro v. Italy*, EComHR 10 July 1997, appl. no. 31924/96, p. 139; *Emonet and Others v. Switzerland*, ECtHR 13 December 2007, appl. no. 39051/03, para. 92.

[49]　*Fretté v. France*, ECtHR 26 February 2002, appl. no. 36515/97, para. 41; *S.H. and Others v. Austria*, ECtHR (GC) 3 November 2011, appl. no. 57813/00, paras. 78–120.

orientation and sexual life, and the right to respect for both the decisions to have and not to have a child. Therefore, when a Contracting State has created legal possibilities for artificial procreation or adoption, such measures concern private life and must be implemented in a non-discriminatory way.[50] Thus safeguards for the practical sides of family founding should rather be sought in Article 8 then in Article 12.

Unlike Article 8 the concept of 'family' in Article 12 is confined to the circle of parents and children. A complaint that the applicants were prevented from founding a larger family by having grandchildren, because their children had taken a vow of celibacy, was declared incompatible *ratione materiae*: 'The right to have grandchildren and the right to procreation is not covered by Article 12.'[51]

In the *Abdulaziz, Cabales and Balkandali* case, the Court held that the expression 'family life' as established in Article 8, in the case of a married couple normally comprises cohabitation. In the Court's view this proposition is reinforced by Article 12, 'for it is scarcely conceivable that the right to found a family should not encompass the right to live together'.[52]

With respect to the right to found a family it should be noted that Article 12 neither implies a positive obligation guaranteeing a socio-economic right to, for example, sufficient living accommodation and sufficient means of subsistence to maintain a family.[53] Article 12 primarily contains a prohibition on the authorities from interfering with the founding of a family as defined in that article.

4. DEPORTATION AND EXTRADITION

It is recognised in the case law that from Article 12, too, restrictions may ensue for the authorities of the Contracting States of their power of deportation or extradition, and their power to refuse aliens access to their territory. As regards the right to marry, however, Article 12 can be invoked successfully only against an (imminent) measure of deportation or extradition, or against a refusal of access, if the person in question can make it sufficiently plausible that he or she has concrete plans to marry and cannot reasonably be expected to realise those plans outside the country concerned.[54] With regard to the right to found a family, just as in the case of Article 8, the Commission adopted the view that

---

[50]   *E.B. v. France*, ECtHR (GC) 22 January 2008, appl. no. 43546/02, para. 43.

[51]   *Šijakova and Others v. the Former Yugoslav Republic of Macedonia*, ECtHR 6 March 2003, appl. no. 67914/01, para. 3.

[52]   *Abdulaziz, Cabales and Balkandali v. the United Kingdom*, ECtHR 28 May 1985, appl. nos. 9214/80, 9473/81 and 9474/81, para. 62.

[53]   *Andersson and Kullman v. Sweden*, EComHR 4 March 1986, appl. no. 11776/85, D&R 46 (1986), p. 251 (253).

[54]   *X v. Federal Republic of Germany*, EComHR 12 July 1976, appl. no. 7175/75, D&R 6 (1977), p. 138 (140).

deportation, extradition and refusal of access to the territory of the state do no constitute a violation of Article 12, if the partner is in a position to follow the person concerned to the country of deportation or extradition, or to the country of the latter's residence or any other country, and if this may reasonably be required of the former.[55]

In the *Abdulaziz, Cabales and Balkandali* case, the Court held that, although by guaranteeing the right to respect for family life Article 8 presupposes the existence of a family, 'this does not mean that all intended family life falls entirely outside its ambit'.[56] This implies that couples who apply for admission of one of them in view of their intention to marry, may rely on Article 8 and that, here again, the Court will not be inclined to investigate an alleged violation of Article 12 separately after it has found a violation or non-violation of Article 8. In fact, in the *Abdulaziz, Cabales and Balkandali* case Article 12 was not invoked by the applicants.

If the persons concerned *are* married, the refusal of entry or the expulsion of one of them does not interfere with their right to marry and found a family. Article 12 does not impose a general obligation upon Contracting States to respect a married couple's choice of the place where they wish to found a family or to accept non-national spouses for settlement to facilitate that choice.[57] There may, however, be an issue under Article 8.[58]

On the same ground the refusal of entry for the reason that the alien concerned had the intention of getting married to a partner from her home state and, consequently, was not seeking family reunion in the host state, was not considered to be in violation of Article 12: she could live her marriage with her husband in their home country.[59]

5. DETAINED PERSONS

With regard to detained persons, the Court holds the view that personal liberty is not a necessary precondition for the exercise of the right to marry. In the *Frasik* case, the Court explained to which conditions the exercise of this right may be subjected.[60]

---

[55]   See, e.g., *X v. Federal Republic of Germany,* EComHR 16 July 1965, appl. no. 2535/65, Coll. 17 (1966), p. 28 (30), where the Commission furthermore took into account that the applicant, when she married, knew that her husband did not have a residence permit. For a case of refusal of admission, see *X v. the United Kingdom,* EComHR 3 October 1972, appl. no. 5301/71, Coll. 43 (1973), p. 82 (84).

[56]   *Abdulaziz, Cabales and Balkandi v. the United Kingdom, supra* n. 52, para. 62.

[57]   *Yavuz v. Austria,* EComHR 16 January 1996, appl. no. 25050/94. See also *Abdulaziz, Cabales and Balkandali v. the United Kingdom, supra* n. 52, para. 68 (in relation to Art. 8).

[58]   *Gelaw v. Sweden,* EComHR 21 October 1997, appl. no. 34025/96.

[59]   *K.-V. v. Switzerland,* EComHR 26 June 1996, appl. no. 31042/96, para. 1.

[60]   *Frasik v. Poland,* ECtHR 5 January 2010, appl. no. 22933/02.

Imprisonment deprives a person of his liberty and also – unavoidably or by implication – of some civil rights and privileges. This does not, however, mean that persons in detention cannot, or can only very exceptionally, exercise their right to marry. A prisoner continues to enjoy fundamental human rights and freedoms that are not contrary to the sense of deprivation of liberty, and every additional limitation should be justified by the authorities. While such justification may well be found in the considerations of security, in particular the prevention of crime and disorder, which inevitably flow from the circumstances of imprisonment, there is no question that detained persons forfeit their right guaranteed by Article 12 merely because of their status. The choice of a partner and the decision to marry him or her, whether at liberty or in detention, is a strictly private and personal matter and there is no universal or commonly accepted pattern for such a choice or decision. Under Article 12, the authorities' role is only to ensure that the right to marry is exercised 'in accordance with the national laws', which must themselves be compatible with the Convention; but they are not allowed to interfere with a detainee's decision to establish a marital relationship with a person of his choice, especially on the grounds that the relationship is not acceptable to them or may offend public opinion. What needs to be solved in a situation where a detained person wishes to get married is not whether or not it is reasonable for him to marry in prison but the practical aspects of timing and making the necessary arrangements, which might, and usually will, be subject to certain conditions set by the authorities. Otherwise, they may not restrict the right to marry unless there are important considerations flowing from such circumstances as danger to prison security or prevention of crime and disorder.[61]

The same applies to the right to found a family, with the difference that the Contracting States must be given a wide margin of appreciation, since there is not a common conviction yet, in how far authorities should be willing to facilitate circumstances in which procreation can place. In the *Dickson* case, where artificial insemination facilities were at stake, the Court required at least evidence that the competing individual and public interests are weighed and a proportionality test was performed. Limitations are allowed but they must be reasonable.[62]

6. DEROGATION

Article 12 does not belong to the category of the rights which are non-derogable by virtue of Article 15(2).

---

[61] *Ibid.*, paras. 91–100. See also *Jaremowicz v. Poland, supra* n. 7, paras. 51–61; *Chernetskiy v. Ukraine*, ECtHR 8 December 2016, appl. no. 44316/07, paras. 28–34.

[62] *Dickson v. the United Kingdom, supra* n. 3, paras. 77–85.

CHAPTER 17

PROTECTION OF PROPERTY

(Article 1 of Protocol No. 1)

Maya Beeler-Sigron[*]

GUIDING PRINCIPLE

The protection of property guarantees everyone the peaceful enjoyment of his or her possessions. Over the years the Court has interpreted the concept of 'possessions' to include not only the ownership of physical goods but also certain other rights and interests constituting assets. However, the right to the protection of property is not absolute. The state may control the use of property or deprive a person of his possessions under the conditions prescribed in Article 1 of Protocol No. 1.

ARTICLE 1 OF PROTOCOL No. 1

Every natural or legal person is entitled to the peaceful enjoyment of his possessions. No one shall be deprived of his possessions except in the public interest and subject to the conditions provided for by law and by the general principles of international law.

    The preceding provisions shall not, however, in any way impair the right of a State to enforce such laws as it deems necessary to control the use of property in accordance with the general interest or to secure the payment of taxes or other contributions or penalties.

---

[*]   In the fourth edition this chapter was revised and updated by Arjen van Rijn.

CONTENTS

1. INTRODUCTION

As the Court has often held, Article 1 Protocol No. 1[1] comprises three distinct rules. The first rule, which is expressed in the first sentence and is of a general nature, lays down the principle of peaceful enjoyment of property. The second rule, in the second sentence, covers deprivation of possessions and makes it subject to certain conditions. The third rule, laid down in the second paragraph, recognises that the Contracting States are entitled, amongst other things, to control the use of property in accordance with the general interest, by enforcing such laws as they deem necessary for the purpose. However, these rules are not 'distinct' in the sense of being unconnected. The second and the third rule are concerned with particular instances of interference with the right to peaceful enjoyment of property. They must, therefore, be construed in the light of the general principle laid down in the first rule.[2] Each of the two forms of interference must comply with the principle of lawfulness and pursue a legitimate aim by means that are reasonably proportionate to the aim sought to be realised.[3] An interference must strike a 'fair balance' between the demands of

---

[1]   This Protocol entered into force on 18 May 1954. For the state of ratifications, see App. I.

[2]   See, among others, *Sporrong and Lönnroth v. Sweden*, ECtHR (GC) 23 September 1982, appl. nos. 7151/75 and 7152/75, para. 61; *Broniowski v. Poland*, ECtHR (GC) 22 June 2004, appl. no. 31443/96, para. 134; *Bruncrona v. Finland*, ECtHR 16 November 2004, appl. no. 41673/98, para. 65; *Vistiņš and Perepjolkins v. Latvia*, ECtHR (GC) 25 October 2012, appl. no. 71243/01, para. 93.

[3]   See, *inter alia*, *Beyeler v. Italy*, ECtHR (GC) 5 January 2000, appl. no. 33202/96, paras. 108–114; *Bruncrona v. Finland, supra* n. 2, para. 66.

the general interest of the community and the requirements of the protection of the individual's fundamental rights.[4] '[T]he search for this balance is reflected in the structure of Article 1 of Protocol No. 1 as a whole, regardless of which paragraphs are concerned in each case.'[5]

Before turning to the case law with respect to the above-mentioned three rules, attention will be paid to a particular question related to the applicability of Article 1, that is: the meaning of the term 'possessions'.

2. PEACEFUL ENJOYMENT OF POSSESSIONS

2.1. POSSESSIONS

The Court has repeatedly held that the concept of 'possessions' has an autonomous meaning which is not limited to the ownership of physical goods and is independent from the formal classification in domestic law: certain other rights and interests constituting assets can also be regarded as 'property rights', and thus as 'possessions' for the purposes of Article 1. The issue that needs to be examined in each specific case is whether the circumstances of the case, considered as a whole, conferred on the applicant title to a substantive interest protected by Article 1.[6]

According to constant case law, 'possessions' can be either 'existing possessions' or assets, including claims, in respect of which the applicant can argue that he or she has at least a 'legitimate expectation' of obtaining effective enjoyment of a property right.[7]

---

[4]   *Beyeler v. Italy, supra* n. 3, para. 107.

[5]   *Perdigão v. Portugal,* ECtHR (GC) 16 November 2010, appl. no. 24768/06, para. 67; see also *Air Canada v. the United Kingdom,* ECtHR 5 May 1995, appl. no. 18465/91, para. 36.

[6]   *Depalle v. France,* ECtHR (GC) 29 March 2010, appl. no. 34044/02, para. 62; *Fabris v. France,* ECtHR (GC) 7 February 2013, appl. no. 16574/08, para. 49 et seq.; *Di Marco v. Italy,* ECtHR 26 April 2011, appl. no. 32521/05, para. 50; *Plalam S.P.A. v. Italy,* ECtHR 18 May 2010, appl. no. 16021/02, para. 37; *Bozcaada Kimisis Teodoku Rum Ortodoks Kilisesi Vakfi v. Turkey,* ECtHR 3 March 2009, appl. nos. 37639/03 et al., para. 41; *Anheuser-Busch Inc. v. Portugal,* ECtHR (GC) 11 January 2007, appl. no. 73049/01, para. 63; *Öneryildiz v. Turkey,* ECtHR (GC) 30 November 2004, appl. no. 48939/99, para. 124; *Iatridis v. Greece,* ECtHR (GC) 25 March 1999, appl. no. 31107/96, para. 54; *Gasus Dosier- und Fördertechnik GmbH v. the Netherlands,* ECtHR 23 February 1995, appl. no. 15375/89, para. 53. See further the Commission's decisions in *X. v. Federal Republic of Germany,* EComHR 13 December 1979 (dec.), appl. no. 8410/78, D.R. 18, p. 216, 219–220; *Pudas v. Sweden,* EComHR 5 December 1984 (dec.), appl. no. 10426/83, D.R. 40, p. 234, 241; *Batelaan and Huiges v. the Netherlands,* EComHR 3 October 1984 (dec.), appl. no. 10438/83, D.R. 41, p. 170, 173; *Størksen v. Norway,* EComHR 5 July 1994 (dec.), appl. no. 19819/92, D.R. 78-A, p. 88, 94–95.

[7]   *J.A. Pye (Oxford) Ltd and J.A. Pye (Oxford) Land Ltd v. the United Kingdom,* ECtHR (GC) 30 August 2007, appl. no. 44302/02, para. 61; *Kopecký v. Slovakia,* ECtHR (GC) 28 September 2005, appl. no. 44912/98, para. 35; *Veselinski v. the Former Yugoslav Republic of Macedonia,* ECtHR 24 February 2005, appl. no. 45658/99, para. 75; *Djidrovski v. the Former Yugoslav*

A claim may only be regarded as an 'asset' for the purposes of Article 1 where it has a sufficient basis in national law, for example where there is settled case law of the domestic courts confirming it.[8] Examples of such assets are debts, either recognised[9] or following from the law,[10] claims against fiscal authorities for restitution of tax money[11] and final and binding judgment debts.[12] The quashing or non-enforcement – including the prolonged delays in the enforcement – of a final and binding judgment therefore constitute an interference with the right to property.[13] A mere hope, however understandable that hope may be, cannot be regarded as a form of legitimate expectation for the purposes of Article 1.[14] For

---

Republic of Macedonia, ECtHR 24 February 2005, appl. no. 46447/99, para. 80; *Von Maltzan and Others v. Germany*, ECtHR (GC) 2 March 2005 (dec.), appl. nos. 71916/01, 71917/01 and 10260/02, para. 74. See also *Van der Mussele v. Belgium*, ECtHR 23 November 1983, appl. no. 8919/80, para. 48; *Pine Valley Developments Ltd and Others v. Ireland*, ECtHR 29 November 1991, appl. no. 12742/87, para. 51; *Pressos Compania Naviera S.A. and Others v. Belgium*, ECtHR 20 November 1995, appl. no. 17849/91, para. 31; *Stretch v. the United Kingdom*, ECtHR 24 June 2003, appl. no. 44277/98, para. 35.

[8]   *Maurice v. France*, ECtHR (GC) 6 October 2005, appl. no. 11810/03, para. 66 and *Draon v. France*, ECtHR (GC) 6 October 2005, appl. no. 1513/03, para. 68 both with reference to *Kopecký v. Slovakia*, *supra* n. 7, paras. 35, 48–52; *Vilho Eskelinen and Others v. Finland*, ECtHR (GC) 19 April 2007, appl. no. 63235/00, para. 94. See further *Mottola and Others v. Italy*, ECtHR 4 February 2014, appl. no. 29932/07, para. 44; *Staibano and Others v. Italy*, ECtHR 4 February 2014, appl. no. 29907/07, para. 44.

[9]   *Almeida Garrett, Mascarenhas Falcão and Others v. Portugal*, ECtHR 11 January 2000, appl. nos. 29813/96 and 30229/96, para. 46; *F.L. v. Italy*, ECtHR 20 December 2001, appl. no. 25639/94, para. 23.

[10] *Mora do Vale and Others v. Portugal*, ECtHR 29 July 2004, appl. no. 53468/99, para. 38. For the right to be freed from one's debts, see *Optim and Industerre v. Belgium*, ECtHR 11 September 2012 (dec.), appl. no. 23819/06, para. 35 with reference to *Caisse régionale de crédit agricole mutuel Nord de France v. France,* ECtHR 19 October 2004 (dec.), appl. no. 58867/00.

[11] *S.A. Dangeville v. France*, ECtHR 16 April 2002, appl. no. 36677/97, paras. 44–48; *Buffalo Srl en liquidation v. Italy*, ECtHR 3 July 2003, appl. no. 38746/97, paras. 27–29; *SA Cabinet Diot and SA Gras Savoye v. France*, ECtHR 22 July 2003, appl. nos. 49217/99 and 49218/99, para. 26; *OGIS-Institut Stanislas, OGEC St. Pie X en Blanche de Castille and Others v. France*, ECtHR 27 May 2004, appl. nos. 42219/98 and 54563/00, paras. 77–78; *Aon Conseil and Courtage S.A. and Christian de Clarens S.A. v. France,* ECtHR 25 January 2007, appl. no. 70160/01, paras. 44–45.

[12] *Svetlana Naumenko v. Ukraine*, ECtHR 9 November 2004, appl. no. 41984/98, para. 104; *Pravednaya v. Russia*, ECtHR 18 November 2004, appl. no. 69529/01, para. 39.

[13] *Anghelescu v. Romania*, ECtHR 9 April 2002, appl. no. 29411/95, paras. 63–65; *Ciobanu v. Romania*, ECtHR 16 July 2002, appl. no. 29053/95, paras. 49–52; *Ionescu v. Romania*, ECtHR 2 November 2004, appl. no. 38608/97, paras. 44–46, 48–51; *Chivorchian v. Romania*, ECtHR 2 November 2004, appl. no. 42513/98, paras. 44–46, 48–51; *Tregubenko v. Ukraine*, ECtHR 2 November 2004, appl. no. 61333/00, paras. 50–51; *Popov v. Moldova (No. 1)*, ECtHR 18 January 2005, appl. no. 74153/01, para. 57; *Jeličić v. Bosnia and Herzegovina,* ECtHR 31 October 2006, appl. no. 41183/02, paras. 48–49; *Simaldone v. Italy*, ECtHR 31 March 2009, appl. no. 22644/03, para. 45; *Zaharievi v. Bulgaria,* ECtHR 2 July 2009, appl. no. 22627/03, paras. 35–44; *De Luca v. Italy*, ECtHR 24 September 2013, appl. no. 43870/04, paras. 49–56; *Gerasimov and Others v. Russia,* ECtHR 1 July 2014, appl. nos. 29920/05 et al., paras. 182–183; *Karaivanova and Mileva v. Bulgaria*, ECtHR 17 June 2014, appl. no. 37857/05, paras. 69–82.

[14] *Gratzinger and Gratzingerova v. the Czech Republic*, ECtHR (GC) 10 July 2002 (dec.), appl. no. 39794/98, para. 73, ECHR 2002-VII.

---

example, the mere hope of recognition of the survival of an old property right which has long been impossible to exercise effectively, cannot be considered as a 'possession' within the meaning of Article 1, nor can a conditional claim which lapses as the result of the non-fulfilment of the condition.[15]

A claim as such may constitute a 'possession' in the sense of Article 1,[16] but it should then be a concrete and adequately specified claim. For example, in the *Stran Greek Refineries and Stratis Andreadis* case, the Court examined whether the domestic judgment – i.e. a preliminary decision – and arbitration award concerned had given rise to a debt in the applicants' favour that was sufficiently established to be enforceable. Regarding the judgment, the Court answered the question in the negative. Regarding the arbitration award, the Court concluded that it conferred on the applicants a right in the sums awarded. The award clearly recognised the State's liability. It was final and binding and did not require any further enforcement measure and no ordinary or special appeal lay against it.[17]

In the *Pressos Compania Naviera S.A and Others* case, the Court stated that it may have regard to the domestic law where there is nothing to suggest that that law runs counter to the object and purpose of Article 1. On this basis, the Court accepted that the rules in question were rules of tort. It held that where the domestic law of tort creates a right of compensation as soon as the damage occurs, the resulting claim constitutes an asset and, therefore, amounts to a 'possession' within the meaning of Article 1.[18]

In the context of claims constituting assets, the basic point of departure appears to be the economic value of the right or interest: where state measures do not affect this economic value, no responsibility under Article 1 is engaged. For example, the right to live in a home which one does not own is not as such a 'possession' within the meaning of Article 1.[19] Neither does Article 1 protect a particular quality of living environment, although a high level of noise nuisance may infringe the right to peaceful enjoyment of one's possessions on account of

---

[15] *Prince Hans-Adam II of Liechtenstein v. Germany*, ECtHR 12 July 2001, appl. no. 42527/98, para. 83; *Pistorová v. the Czech Republic*, ECtHR 26 October 2004, appl. no. 73578/01, para. 38; *Anheuser-Busch Inc. v. Portugal, supra* n. 6, para. 64, with reference to *Gratzinger and Gratzingerova v. the Czech Republic, supra* n. 14, para. 69; *Malhous v. the Czech Republic*, ECtHR (GC) 13 December 2000 (dec.), appl. no. 33071/96; *Mühle v. Germany,* ECtHR 10 February 2009 (dec.), appl. no. 21773/05.

[16] See *A., B. and Company A.S. v. Federal Republic of Germany*, EComHR 4 July 1978 (dec.), appl. no. 7742/76, D.R. 14, p. 146, 168.

[17] *Stran Greek Refineries and Stratis Andreadis v. Greece*, ECtHR 9 December 1994, appl. no. 13427/87, paras. 59–62; *Sequaris v. Belgium*, EComHR 14 October 1982 (dec.), appl. no. 9676/82, D.R. 29, p. 245, 249.

[18] *Pressos Compania Naviera S.A. and Others v. Belgium, supra* n. 7, para. 25.

[19] *Durini v. Italy*, EComHR 12 January 1994 (dec.), appl. no. 19217/91, D.R. 76-A, p. 76, 79. See also *Gerasimov and Others v. Russia, supra* n. 13, para. 178 with reference to *H.F. v. Slovakia*, ECtHR 9 December 2003 (dec.), appl. no. 54797/00 and *Kovalenko v. Latvia*, ECtHR 15 February 2001, appl. no. 54264/00.

---

a drop in the value of real property.[20] However, a person who had illegally built a house on state property and had been living in the house for five years, which had been tolerated by the authorities, appeared to have a justified claim under Article 1 that the State would reduce the risks related to an adjoining landfill.[21] Equally, where someone used a cottage in good faith and the authorities tolerated that use for over 10 years while the law recognised that that person's possession of a dwelling in good faith constituted a right of a pecuniary nature, the right to use the cottage as his accommodation was a right that had a clear pecuniary dimension and constituted a possession for the purposes of Article 1 even in the absence of a registered property title.[22]

Claims which a person has as an heir during the testator's lifetime do not fall under the protection of Article 1, because this provision protects existing property and not the right to acquire property.[23] It does of course protect the right of the testator to dispose of his patrimonial rights and the rights which have already been acquired by inheritance even before distribution of assets.[24] In the *Fabris* case, the Court found that the pecuniary interest of the applicant, who was unable to assert his inheritance rights, as he was a child 'born of adultery', fell within the scope of Article 1. The Court held that where the applicant has been denied all or part of a particular asset on a discriminatory ground covered by Article 14 of the Convention, 'the relevant test is whether, but for the discriminatory ground about which the applicant complains, he or she would have had a right, enforceable under domestic law, in respect of the asset in question (…).'[25] In the *Négrépontis-Giannisis* case, concerning an American adoption order, the applicant complained that the Greek courts' refusal to recognise his status as an adopted child, and his entitlement to inheritance, interfered with his property rights.[26] In the case of *Nacaryan and Deryan* the Court held that the refusal of the domestic courts to acknowledge the applicants' title to the deceased's immovable property on the ground that the condition of reciprocity between Greece and Turkey had not been met amounted

---

20   *S. v. France*, ECtHR 17 May 1990 (dec.), appl. no. 13728/88, D.R. 65, p. 250, 261; *Taşkın and Others v. Turkey*, ECtHR 29 January 2004 (dec.), appl. no. 46117/99; *Fägerskiöld v. Sweden*, ECtHR 26 February 2008 (dec.), appl. no. 37664/04; *Galev and Others v. Bulgaria*, ECtHR 29 September 2009 (dec.), appl. no. 18324/04.

21   *Öneryildiz v. Turkey*, ECtHR 18 June 2002, appl. no. 48939/99, paras. 141–142; *Öneryildiz v. Turkey*, ECtHR (GC) 30 November 2004, appl. no. 48939/99, paras. 127–129.

22   *Saghinadze and Others v. Georgia*, ECtHR 27 May 2010, appl. no. 18768/05, paras. 106–108 concerning an internally displaced person (IDP).

23   *Merger and Cros v. France*, ECtHR 22 December 2004, appl. no. 68864/01, para. 37 with reference to *Marckx v. Belgium*, ECtHR 13 June 1979, appl. no. 6833/74, para. 50.

24   *Marckx v. Belgium*, *supra* n. 23, para. 51 and paras. 63–64, respectively, *Inze v. Austria*, ECtHR 28 October 1987, appl. no. 8695/79, para. 43.

25   *Fabris v. France*, *supra* n. 6, paras. 36 and 52, with reference to *Stec and Others v. United Kingdom*, ECtHR (GC) 6 July 2005 (dec.), appl. nos. 65731/01 and 65900/01, para. 55 and *Andrejeva v. Latvia*, ECtHR (GC) 18 February 2009, appl. no. 55707/00, para. 79, ECHR 2009.

26   *Négrépontis-Giannisis v. Greece*, ECtHR 3 May 2011, appl. no. 56759/08, paras. 93–97.

to an interference with the applicants' right to the peaceful enjoyment of their property.[27]

The Court has repeatedly held that Article 1 is not applicable to future earnings, but only to existing possessions, that is to say income once it has been earned or where an enforceable claim to it exists.[28] For instance, the volume of business enjoyed by a liberal profession, which is subject to the hazards of economic life, does not constitute a 'possession' within the meaning of Article 1.[29] Similarly, the Court found in the case of *Voggenreiter* that the applicant was not entitled to believe that the tariff system, which guaranteed his income, would remain in force.[30] However, clientele or 'goodwill' falls within the scope of Article 1.[31] In the *Van Marle* case, the Court stated that it agreed with the Commission that the 'goodwill' relied upon by the applicants may be 'likened to the right of property embodied in Article 1: by dint of their own work, the applicants had built up a clientele; this had in many respects the nature of a private right and constituted an asset and, hence, a possession within the meaning of Article 1.'[32] With respect to the suspension or revocation of licences and permits or the refusal to register a person on a list entitling him or her to practise a particular profession, the Court tends to regard the underlying business or professional practice as a 'possession'.[33] The Convention is applicable to privileges accorded by law where they lead to a legitimate expectation of acquiring certain possessions.[34]

---

[27] *Nacaryan and Deryan v. Turkey,* ECtHR 8 January 2008, appl. nos. 19558/02 and 27904/02, para. 60. See also *Apostolidi and Others v. Turkey,* ECtHR 27 March 2007, appl. no. 45628/99, para. 78; *Yianopulu v. Turkey,* ECtHR 14 January 2014, appl. no. 12030/03, para. 48.

[28] *Van Marle and Others v. the Netherlands,* ECtHR (GC) 26 June 1986, appl. no. 8543/79, paras. 39–41, p. 13; *Anheuser-Busch Inc. v. Portugal, supra* n. 6, para. 64.

[29] *Greek Federation of Customs Officers, Galouris, Christopoulos and 3,333 other customs officers v. Greece,* EComHR 6 April 1995 (dec.), appl. no. 24581/94, D.R. 81-B, p. 123, 124 and 128.

[30] *Voggenreiter v. Germany,* ECtHR 28 November 2002 (dec.), appl. no. 7538/02. See also *Ian Edgar (Liverpool) Limited v. United Kingdom,* ECtHR 25 January 2000 (dec.), appl. no. 37683/97; *Andrews v. United Kingdom,* ECtHR 26 September 2000 (dec.), appl. no. 37657/97, where the applicants had no legitimate expectation that the use of particular types of firearm, including handguns, would continue to be lawful.

[31] *Anheuser-Busch Inc. v. Portugal, supra* n. 6, para. 64; *Malik v. the United Kingdom,* ECtHR 13 March 2012, appl. no. 23780/08, para. 89 (list of persons authorised to practise as doctors for the National Health Service) with reference to *Olbertz v. Germany,* ECtHR 25 May 1999 (dec.), appl. no. 37592/97; *Döring v. Germany,* ECtHR 9 November 1999 (dec.), appl. no. 37595/97; and *Wendenburg v. Germany,* ECtHR 6 February 2003, appl. no. 71630/01; *Buzescu v. Romania,* ECtHR 24 May 2005, appl. no. 61302/00, para. 81 and paras. 88–98, respectively.

[32] *Van Marle and Others v. the Netherlands, supra* n. 28, para. 41; *Malik v. the United Kingdom, supra* n. 31, para. 96. See, however, the decision of the Commission on *Batelaan and Huiges v. the Netherlands, supra* n. 6, p. 170, 173.

[33] *Malik v. the United Kingdom, supra* n. 31, para. 94; *Galina Kostova v. Bulgaria,* ECtHR 12 November 2013, appl. no. 36181/05, paras. 72–75 (concerning removal from list of persons qualified to act as liquidators of insolvent companies).

[34] *Wendenburg v. Germany, supra* n. 31, concerning exclusive rights of audience in German Courts.

In a number of cases the issue was examined whether a licence for carrying out certain activities constitutes a 'possession'. In the case of *Pudas*, the Commission opined as follows: 'the answer will depend *inter alia* on the question whether the licence can be considered to create for the licence-holder a reasonable and legitimate expectation as to the lasting nature of the licence and as to the possibility to continue to draw benefits from the exercise of the licensed activity.'[35]

And indeed, in the *Tre Traktörer Aktiebolag* case, concerning the decision to revoke the applicant's licence to serve alcoholic beverages, the Court held that the withdrawal of the licence had adverse effects on the goodwill and value of the restaurant. It thus constituted an interference with the applicant's right to the peaceful enjoyment of its possessions.[36] In the case of *Centro Europa 7 S.r.l. and Di Stefano*, the Court observed that, in view of the terms of the applicant company's licence for nationwide terrestrial television broadcasting and the legislative framework in place at the time, the applicant company could reasonably have expected the authorities, within the 24 months following of granting the licence, to regulate its terrestrial broadcasting activities. The applicant company therefore had had a 'legitimate expectation' to begin broadcasting. The Court observed that, although the licence was not as such withdrawn, without the allocation of broadcasting frequencies, it was deprived of its substance. It therefore concluded that the applicant company's legitimate expectation constituted a 'possession' within the meaning of Article 1.[37]

With regard to pension schemes and social security systems the Court held – considering that Article 1 does not guarantee as such a right to acquire property – that there is no right under Article 1 to receive a social security benefit or pension payment of any kind or amount, unless national law provides for such an entitlement.[38] In the *Stec and Others* case, the Court abandoned the distinction between contributory and non-contributory benefits for the purposes of the applicability of Article 1. As a result, when a state chooses to set up a pension scheme – there is no obligation on a state under Article 1 to create a welfare or pension scheme –, the individual rights and interests deriving from it fall within the ambit of Article 1, irrespective of the payment of

---

[35] *Pudas v. Sweden, supra* n. 6, p. 234, 241. If a licence-holder no longer meets the conditions for the licence's grant, he cannot be considered to have a legitimate expectation to continue his activities. See *Batelaan and Huiges v. the Netherlands, supra* n. 6, pp. 170, 173. Similarly, a licence-holder cannot be considered to have a reasonable and legitimate expectation to continue his activity if the licence is withdrawn in accordance with the provisions of the law which was in force when the licence was issued. See *Størksen v. Norway, supra* n. 6, p. 88, 94.

[36] *Tre Traktörer Aktiebolag v. Sweden*, ECtHR 7 July 1989, appl. no. 10873/84, para. 53. See also *Bimer S.A. v. Moldova*, ECtHR 10 July 2007, appl. no. 15084/03, para. 49; *Megadat.com SRL v. Moldova*, ECtHR 8 April 2008, appl. no. 21151/04, paras. 62–66.

[37] *Centro Europa 7 S.r.l. and Di Stefano v. Italy*, ECtHR (GC) 7 June 2012, appl. no. 38433/09, paras. 175–179.

[38] *Carson and Others v. the United Kingdom*, ECtHR (GC) 16 March 2010, appl. no. 42184/05, para. 67.

---

contributions and the means by which the pension scheme is funded.[39] In the case of *Béláné Nagy v. Hungary*, the applicant lost her entitlement to a disability pension owing to newly introduced eligibility criteria. The Court held that the expectation of the applicant, as a contributor to the social security scheme who once satisfied the condition of eligibility, was legitimate and continuous in its legal nature. The majority of the Court thus concluded that the applicant had a 'possession'.[40] A minority of three judges considered, however, that in 2012 the applicant did not meet the legal conditions laid down in domestic law for the grant of a pension and thus had no 'possession'.[41] Further, where the amount of a benefit is reduced or discontinued, this may constitute interference with possessions which requires to be justified.[42] Fluctuations in the amount of the benefit may only amount to a violation of Article 1 if a very substantial reduction of the benefit is concerned.[43] And even if the right guaranteed extends, in principle, to periodic increases, it may be subjected to restrictions if the pension is to be paid abroad, since many countries apply specific restrictions to the payment of benefits to foreign countries.[44] However, pension rights, which fall within the scope of Article 1, may not be honoured in a discriminatory way.[45]

---

[39] *Stec and Others v. United Kingdom, supra* n. 25, paras. 47–56, with reference to *Gaygusuz v. Austria,* ECtHR 16 September 1996, appl. no. 17371/90, para. 41; *Andrejeva v. Latvia, supra* n. 25, para. 76; *Torri and Others v. Italy,* ECtHR 24 January 2012 (dec.), appl. no. 11838/07 and 12302/07, paras. 32–35.

[40] *Béláné Nagy v. Hungary,* ECtHR 10 February 2015, appl. no. 53080/13, paras. 47–48 (referral to the Grand Chamber on 1 June 2015).

[41] *Ibid.,* joint dissenting opinion of Judges Keller, Spano and Kjølbro, para. 11.

[42] *Stefanetti and Others v. Italy,* ECtHR 15 April 2014, appl. nos. 21838/10 et al., para. 50 with reference to *Kjartan Ásmundsson v. Iceland,* ECtHR 12 October 2004, appl. no. 60669/00, para. 40. Furthermore, the determination of the starting date for the calculation of entitlement must strike a fair balance. See *Reveliotis v. Greece,* ECtHR 4 December 2008, appl. no. 48775/06, para. 38 (violation).

[43] *Müller v. Austria,* EComHR 1 October 1975 (rep.), appl. no. 5849/72, para. 32, D.R. 3, p. 25. Such a substantial and therefore inacceptable reduction was held to have taken place in *Kjartan Ásmundsson v. Iceland, supra* n. 42, paras. 39–45 (total loss of disability pension). See also *Goudswaard-van der Lans v. the Netherlands,* ECtHR 22 September 2005 (dec.), appl. no. 75255/01 (alleged reduction of widow's pension by no less than 69%); *Apostolakis v. Greece,* ECtHR 22 October 2009, appl. no. 39574/07, paras. 31–43 (total forfeiture of any right to a pension and social cover); *Aizpurua Ortiz and Others v. Spain,* ECtHR 2 February 2010, appl. no. 42430/05, paras. 48–58 (replacement of supplementary annual pension by one-off payment); *Klein v. Austria,* ECtHR 3 March 2011, appl. no. 57028/00, paras. 48–58 (complete loss of pension); *Valkov and Others v. Bulgaria,* ECtHR 25 October 2011, appl. no. 2033/04 et al., paras. 88–101 (capping of retirement pensions); *Lakićević and Others v. Montenegro and Serbia,* ECtHR 11 December 2011, appl. nos. 27458/06 et al., paras. 59–83 (total suspension of pension); *Stefanetti and Others v. Italy, supra* n. 42, paras. 66–67 (loss of 67% of old-age pension); *Torri and Others v. Italy, supra* n. 39, paras. 45–46 (applicants did not claim to have lost substantial amounts).

[44] *J.W. and E.W. v. the United Kingdom,* EComHR 3 October 1983 (dec.), appl. no. 9776/82, D.R. 34, p. 153, 154; *Carson and Others v. the United Kingdom, supra* n. 38, paras. 83–90; *Ramaer and Van Willigen v. the Netherlands,* ECtHR 23 October 2012 (dec.), appl. no. 34880/12.

[45] *Wessels-Bergervoet v. the Netherlands,* ECtHR 4 June 2002, appl. no. 34462/97, para. 43; *Willis v. the United Kingdom,* ECtHR 11 June 2002, appl. no. 36042/97, paras. 48–50; *Stec and Others*

Article 1 also applies to intellectual property, for example trade mark rights,[46] patents,[47] copyrights[48] and domain names.[49] Its applicability further extends to shares which have an economic value.[50] Measures which are taken in order to establish who is entitled to a certain property – for instance seizure[51] – and conditions with regard to the evidence of that entitlement, in themselves do not constitute violations of Article 1, unless such conditions impose an unreasonably heavy burden of proof on the person laying claim to the property.[52]

As pointed out in the beginning, Article 1 does not guarantee the right to acquire property.[53] In the case of *Van der Mussele*, the Court held that the absence of remuneration of relatively small expenses made by the applicant for public services was unrelated to the 'peaceful enjoyment' of the applicant's existing possessions.[54]

---

v. the United Kingdom, supra n. 25, paras. 54–67; *Luczak v. Poland,* ECtHR 27 November 2007, appl. no. 77782/01, paras. 49–60; *Andrejeva v. Latvia, supra* n. 25, paras. 81–92, ECHR 2009; *Muñoz Díaz v. Spain,* ECtHR 8 December 2009, appl. no. 49151/07, paras. 51–71; *Şerife Yiğit v. Turkey,* ECtHR (GC) 2 November 2010, appl. no. 3976/05, paras. 83–88; *Stummer v. Austria,* ECtHR (GC) 7 July 2011, appl. no. 37452/02, paras. 90–111.

[46]   *Anheuser-Busch Inc. v. Portugal, supra* n. 6, paras. 73–78.

[47]   *Smith Kline and French Laboratories Ltd v. the Netherlands,* EComHR 4 October 1990 (dec.), appl. no. 12633/87, D.R. 66, p. 70; *Lenzing AG v. the United Kingdom,* EComHR 9 September 1998 (dec.), appl. no. 38817/97. See further *British-American Tobacco Company Ltd v. the Netherlands,* EComHR 20 November 1995 (opinion), appl. no. 19589/92, paras. 71–72.

[48]   *Melnychuk v. Ukraine,* ECtHR 5 July 2005 (dec.), appl. no. 28743/03; *Balan v. Moldova,* ECtHR 29 January 2008, appl. no. 19247/03, paras. 34–36 (rights in a photograph); *Breierova and Others v. the Czech Republic,* ECtHR 8 October 2002 (dec.), appl. no. 57321/00.

[49]   *Paeffgen GmbH v. Germany,* ECtHR 18 September 2007 (dec.), appl. nos. 25379/04 et al.

[50]   *Sovtransavto Holding v. Ukraine,* ECtHR 25 July 2002, appl. no. 48553/99, para. 51.

[51]   *X v. Belgium,* EComHR 10 December 1976 (dec.), appl. no. 7256/75, D.R. 8, p. 161, 165–166.

[52]   See *De Napoles Pacheco v. Belgium,* EComHR 5 October 1979, appl. no. 7775/77, D.R. 15, p. 143. See further *Tendam v. Spain,* ECtHR 30 July 2010, appl. no. 25720/05, paras. 45–57, where the Court considered that the burden of proof regarding the seized and missing or damaged items had rested with the judicial authorities and not with the applicant.

[53]   *J.A. Pye (Oxford) Ltd and J.A. Pye (Oxford) Land Ltd v. the United Kingdom, supra* n. 7, para. 61; *Kopecký v. Slovakia, supra* n. 7, para. 35; *Veselinski v. the Former Yugoslav Republic of Macedonia, supra* n. 7, para. 75; *Djidrovski v. the Former Yugoslav Republic of Macedonia, supra* n. 7, para. 80. See also *Van der Mussele v. Belgium, supra* n. 7, para. 48; *Pine Valley Developments Ltd and Others v. Ireland, supra* n. 7; *Pressos Compania Naviera S.A. and Others v. Belgium, supra* n. 7, para. 31; *Stretch v. the United Kingdom, supra* n. 7, para. 35.

[54]   *Van der Mussele v. Belgium, supra* n. 7, paras. 25–26. See also *X v. Federal Republic of Germany,* EComHR 17 July 1981 (dec.), appl. no. 8682/79, D.R. 26, p. 97, 99–100, where the Commission held that Art. 1 is not violated when an officially appointed defence counsel is obliged to repay an advance on his fees for not having assured the accused's defence up to the end of the proceedings. See also *Gussenbauer v. Austria,* EComHR 14 July 1972 (dec.), appl. nos. 4897/71 and 5219/71, Coll. 42, pp. 41 and 94, respectively, concerning the obligation to render *pro deo* services as counsel. In these cases, however, a friendly settlement was reached. *Gussenbauer v. Austria,* EComHR 8 October 1974 (rep.), Yearbook XV (1972).

2.2. PEACEFUL ENJOYMENT

Article 1 protects 'peaceful enjoyment'. That implies that this provision may also have been violated when a person has not been affected as to his property or possessions *per se*, but is not accorded an opportunity to use that property, for instance because a necessary permit is refused to him,[55] or because in some other way such restrictions ensue from the legislation or from government measures to the extent that there is no longer any question of a 'peaceful enjoyment'.[56] In the *Loizidou* case, which concerned denial of access to property situated in the area occupied by Turkish Cypriot forces following the civil war in Cyprus, the Court – unlike the Commission – took the position that the applicant's complaint was not limited to the right of freedom of movement and that Article 1 was applicable.[57]

In some cases, the Court appears to have difficulties in bringing the case under either the second sentence of Article 1 (deprivation of possessions) or the second paragraph of that article (control of use of property), although the right to peaceful enjoyment of possessions is clearly affected. In such circumstances, the case is decided on the basis of the 'general rule' laid down in the first sentence.[58] In the *Sporrong and Lönnroth* case, the Court noted that although the expropriation permits left intact in law the owners' right to use and dispose of their possessions, they nevertheless in practice significantly reduced the possibility of its exercise. They also affected the very substance of ownership. In the Court's view, the applicants' right of property thus became precarious and defeasible. With regard to the existence of a deprivation of possessions, the Court considered, *inter alia*, that in the absence of a formal expropriation, i.e. a transfer of ownership, it must investigate the realities of the situation complained of and it has to be ascertained whether that situation amounted to a *de facto* expropriation. The Court concluded that the expropriation permits must

---

55   See, e.g., *Wiggins v. the United Kingdom*, EComHR 8 February 1978 (dec.), appl. no. 7456/76, D.R. 13, p. 40, 46–47, concerning the refusal of a housing licence to the applicant to live in his own house.

56   *Sporrong and Lönnroth v. Sweden*, *supra* n. 2, para. 103, concerning, *inter alia*, restrictions on the possibility to build on land held in freehold. See also *Arrondelle v. the United Kingdom*, EComHR 15 July 1980 (dec.), appl. no. 7889/77, D.R. 19, p. 186, where the complaint concerned the nuisance caused to the owner of a house by the neighbouring airfield; *Satka and Others v. Greece*, ECtHR 27 March 2003, appl. no. 55828/00, paras. 44–50.

57   *Loizidou v. Turkey*, ECtHR 18 December 1996, appl. no. 15318/89, paras. 60–61; see also *Chiragov and Others v. Armenia*, ECtHR (GC) 16 June 2015, appl. no. 13216/05, para. 196 and *Sargsyan v. Azerbaijan*, ECtHR (GC) 16 June 2015, appl. no. 40167/06, para. 218 (property rights of Armenian and Azerbaijani citizens displaced in the context of the Nagorno-Karabakh conflict).

58   See, e.g., *N.K.M. v. Hungary*, ECtHR 14 May 2013, appl. no. 66529/11, para. 43; *R.Sz. v. Hungary*, ECtHR 2 July 2013, appl. no. 41838/11, para. 32; *Ališić and Others v. Bosnia and Herzegovina, Croatia, Serbia, Slovenia and the former Yugoslav Republic of Macedonia*, ECtHR (GC) 16 July 2014, appl. no. 60642/08, paras. 98–99.

---

be examined under the first sentence of the first paragraph of Article 1.[59] In the *Papamichalopoulos and Others* case, concerning the occupation of the applicants' land by the Greek military authorities, the Court concluded that there had been a *de facto* expropriation. It did, however, not specify which sentence of Article 1 applied. Given the circumstances of the case, the Court had little difficulty in finding a violation: 'the loss of all ability to dispose of the land in issue, taken together with the failure of the attempts made so far to remedy the situation complained of, entailed sufficiently serious consequences for the applicants *de facto* to have been expropriated in a manner incompatible with their right to the peaceful enjoyment of their possessions.'[60]

In other cases in which the first sentence was identified as the applicable rule the Court gave some criteria for its choice. In the *Matos e Silva, Lda. and Others* case, the Court held that there was no formal or *de facto* deprivation as the effects of the measures interfering with the applicants' property right were not irreversible as had been the case in *Papamichalopoulos*. The right in question had lost some of its substance but it had not disappeared. Thus, the Court concluded that the second sentence of the first paragraph was not applicable. It examined the measures in the light of the first sentence of the first paragraph of Article 1.[61]

In the *Phocas* case, the Court held the first sentence to be applicable because the applicant did not complain about a deprivation of property or of specific measures restricting the use of it, but of an infringement resulting from the authorities' general conduct.[62] In the *Elia S.r.l.* case, the Court held explicitly that the second sentence of the first paragraph was not applicable, after having observed that the applicant company was not denied access to its land and did not lose control of it and that, although it became more difficult to sell the land, that possibility in principle subsisted. Because the measures did not amount to a control of the use of property within the meaning of the second

---

[59] *Sporrong and Lönnroth v. Sweden, supra* n. 2, paras. 60, 63 and 65. See further *Erkner and Hofauer v. Austria*, ECtHR 23 April 1987, appl. no. 9616/81, para. 74; *Poiss v. Austria*, ECtHR 23 April 1987, appl. no. 9816/82, para. 64 concerning the provisional transfer of the applicants' land.

[60] *Papamichalopoulos and Others v. Greece,* ECtHR 24 June 1993, appl. no. 14556/89, para. 45. Conversely, in *Hentrich v. France*, ECtHR 22 September 1994, appl. no. 13616/88, para. 34, the Court did specify that there had been a deprivation of possessions to which the second sentence applied, but it did not respond to the applicant's contention that there had been a *de facto* expropriation.

[61] *Matos e Silva, Lda., and Others v. Portugal*, ECtHR 16 September 1996, appl. no. 15777/89, para. 85. See also *Hüseyin Kaplan v. Turkey*, ECtHR 1 October 2013, appl. no. 24508/09, paras. 37–48 (assignment of land to public authority 20 years before expropriation combined with restrictions on its use) with reference to *Köktepe v. Turkey*, ECtHR 22 July 2008, appl. no. 35785/03, paras. 81–93 (classification of land as public woodlands rendering the right of property devoid of any substance).

[62] *Phocas v. France*, ECtHR 23 April 1996, appl. no. 17869/91, para. 54 (urban development scheme which impeded the development of the applicant's property without any compensation for more than 16 years).

paragraph either, the situation fell to be dealt with under the first sentence of Article 1.[63] In the case of *Potomska and Potomski*, the applicants complained that they had been prevented from developing their land following the listing as a historic monument and that the authorities had failed to expropriate their land or to provide them with an alternative plot. Having regard to the different facets of the applicants' complaint, the Court examined the complaint under the general rule established in the first sentence of the first paragraph of Article 1.[64] In the case of *Ališić and Others*, concerning the applicants' inability to recover 'old' foreign-currency savings following the dissolution of the former Socialist Federal Republic of Yugoslavia, the Court considered that while, at least in the beginning, the freezing of the bank accounts could be viewed as intended to control the use of the possessions (third rule), it may be questioned whether the fact that their deposits remained unavailable for over 20 years did not amount to a deprivation (second rule). However, the applicable legislation did not extinguish the applicants' claims or otherwise deprive them of legal validity and the respondent States accepted in principle that deposit-holders should be able to dispose of their savings. Thus, the Court found that the applicants were neither formally nor *de facto* deprived of their savings. Consequently, and in view of the complexity of the legal and factual issues involved, the Court held that the alleged violation did not fall into a precise category and that it should thus be examined in the light of the general principle (first rule).[65]

However, the importance of the classification of cases under the three rules of Article 1 should not be exaggerated. As was recalled in section 1 above, the Court has always held that these three rules are not unconnected. This is made clear also by the main test applied for establishing whether or not Article 1 has been violated, which is basically the same in all situations. The Court confirmed this point of view in the *Beyeler* case concerning the question who was the owner of a painting of Vincent van Gogh. The Court did not consider it necessary to decide whether the second sentence of the first paragraph of Article 1 was applicable. It held that the complexity of the factual and legal position prevented the case from being classified in a precise category. It elaborated that the situation envisaged in the second sentence of Article 1 is only a particular instance of interference with the right to peaceful enjoyment of property as guaranteed by the general rule set forth in the first sentence. The Court, therefore, considered that it should examine the situation in the light of that general rule.[66] In recent cases, the Court has refrained from determining the applicable rule on the ground that the principles governing the question of justification are substantially the same,

---

[63]   *Elia S.r.l. v. Italy*, ECtHR 2 August 2001, appl. no. 37710/97, paras. 56–57.

[64]   *Potomska and Potomski v. Poland*, ECtHR 29 March 2011, appl. no. 33949/05, para. 63.

[65]   *Ališić and Others v. Bosnia and Herzegovina, Croatia, Serbia, Slovenia and the former Yugoslav Republic of Macedonia, supra* n. 58, para. 99.

[66]   *Beyeler v. Italy, supra* n. 3, para. 106. See also *Solodyuk v. Russia*, ECtHR 12 July 2005, appl. no. 67099/01, para. 29; *Perdigão v. Portugal, supra* n. 5, para. 62.

involving as they do the legitimacy of the aim of any interference, as well as its proportionality and the preservation of a fair balance.[67]

Under each of the three rules the Court applies a 'fair balance' test: 'The Court must determine whether a fair balance was struck between the demands of the general interest of the community and the requirements of the protection of the individual's fundamental rights. The search for this balance is inherent in the whole of the Convention and is also reflected in the structure of Article 1.'[68]

Here, as with other proportionality tests under the Convention, the Court accepts that a margin of appreciation must be left to the national authorities. In the context of Article 1 this margin of appreciation is usually wide.

The case law with respect to the first sentence shows that there are two – often combined – aspects to the protection offered by the fair balance requirement: (formal) protection against lack of procedural guarantees or against protracted proceedings,[69] and (substantive) protection against arbitrary action by the state,[70] or action which puts an individual and excessive burden on the applicant. The absence of any compensation may also be a relevant factor under the fair balance test.

In order to determine whether a 'fair balance' had been achieved in the *Sporrong and Lönnroth* case the Court examined the possibilities for the applicants to seek a reduction of the time-limits within which the expropriation of their properties might be effected or to claim compensation for the damages suffered during the extremely long period during which the enjoyment of their property right had been impeded. Because remedies to that effect were not available, the Court decided that Article 1 had been violated.[71]

---

[67] *Denisova and Moiseyeva v. Russia*, ECtHR 1 April 2010, appl. no. 16903/03, para. 55; *Ünsped Paket Servisi SaN. Ve TiC. A.Ş. v. Bulgaria*, ECtHR 13 October 2015, appl. no. 3503/08, para. 40.

[68] *Sporrong and Lönnroth v. Sweden, supra* n. 2, para. 69. See, for the second sentence of para. 1, *Holy Monasteries v. Greece*, ECtHR 9 December 1994, appl. nos. 13092/87 and 13984/88, para. 70. For the second para., see *Velosa Barreto v. Portugal*, ECtHR 21 November 1995, appl. no. 18072/91, para. 23. For the requirement of lawfulness and public interest, see *Carbonara and Ventura v. Italy*, ECtHR 30 May 2000, appl. no. 24638/94, para. 63, with reference to *Iatridis v. Greece, supra* n. 6, para. 58; *Hoare v. the United Kingdom*, ECtHR 12 April 2011 (dec.), appl. no. 16261/08, paras. 52 and 59 (revised interpretation of the relevant legislation constituted no more than a reasonably foreseeable development of the law on limitation periods).

[69] See *Wiśniewska v. Poland*, ECtHR 29 November 2011, appl. no. 9072/02, para. 109, where the Court reiterated that although Art. 1 contains no explicit procedural requirements, in order to assess the proportionality of the interference it looks at the degree of protection from arbitrariness that is afforded by the proceedings in the case.

[70] *Veselinski v. the Former Yugoslav Republic of Macedonia, supra* n. 7, paras. 81–82; *Djidrovski v. the Former Yugoslav Republic of Macedonia, supra* n. 7, paras. 86–87.

[71] *Sporrong and Lönnroth v. Sweden, supra* n. 2, paras. 69–74. See also the Court's focus on procedural issues, including the length of the land consolidation proceedings, in *Erkner and Hofauer v. Austria, supra* n. 59, para. 77; *Poiss v. Austria, supra* n. 59, para. 68; likewise, *Wiesinger v. Austria*, ECtHR 30 October 1991, appl. no. 11796/85, para. 77.

Conversely, the fair balance will not be upset where the applicant has failed to make proper use of available procedures for remedying the interferences complained of, even where these interferences were *prima facie* incompatible with the fair balance requirement and even where the conduct of the authorities was not beyond reproach. Thus, in the *Phocas* case the Court first noted that the situation was in principle incompatible with the fair balance required by Article 1. However, the Court then observed that a remedy had been available to the applicant and that – even if the authorities delayed in replying to the applicant's applications – the failure of these proceedings was attributable to the applicant, who first rejected the purchase offer made to him and then applied to the expropriations judge out of time. The Court concluded that Article 1 had not been violated.[72]

The Court reached the opposite conclusion with respect to Article 1 in the above-mentioned *Matos e Silva, Lda. and Others* case. The Court observed that the measures, which did not lack a reasonable basis, had serious and harmful effects that have hindered the applicants' ordinary enjoyment of their rights for more than 13 years. The long period of uncertainty both as to the future of the possessions and the question of compensation further aggravated the measures' detrimental effects. The Court concluded that the applicants had had to bear an individual and excessive burden and that there had been a violation of Article 1.[73] In the *Viaşu* case, the Court concluded in the light of the general rule that the non-enforcement of property decisions in the applicant's favour for several years did not strike a fair balance and that the applicant had had to bear an individual and excessive burden.[74] In the case of *Maria Atanasiu and Others*, concerning restitution and compensation for nationalised property, the Court considered that insufficient legislative and administrative measures, capable of providing all parties to the restitution process with a coherent and foreseeable solution proportionate to the public-interest aims pursued, were adopted. The Court concluded that the non-payment of compensation, up until its judgment, and the uncertainty as to when they might receive it had imposed a disproportionate and excessive burden on the applicants.[75]

---

[72]   *Phocas v. France, supra* n. 62, paras. 59–60, where Judges Foighel and Palm wrote a joint dissenting opinion. Failure to make use of available remedies was also held against the applicant in *Katte Klitsche de la Grange v. Italy*, ECtHR 27 October 1994, appl. no. 12539/86, para. 46.

[73]   *Matos e Silva, Lda., and Others v. Portugal, supra* n. 61, paras. 92–93. The 'individual and excessive burden' criterion was applied by the Court for the first time under the first sentence of para. 1 in *Sporrong and Lönnroth v. Sweden, supra* n. 2, para. 73. As regards the second sentence of para. 1, see *Hentrich v. France, supra* n. 60, para. 49. See also *Elia S.r.l. v. Italy, supra* n. 63.

[74]   *Viaşu v. Romania*, ECtHR 9 December 2008, appl. no. 75951/01, paras. 69–73.

[75]   *Maria Atanasiu and Others v. Romania*, ECtHR 12 October 2010, appl. nos. 30767/05 and 33800/06, paras. 189, 193 and 195 et seq. (application of the pilot-judgment procedure). See also the case of *Lukats v. Romania*, ECtHR 5 April 2016, appl. no. 24199/07, paras. 58, 59 and 62 where the Court concluded that in so far as the state ensures that payment to the applicant

In the *Skibińscy* case, concerning owners who were threatened with expropriation of their property at an undetermined point in the future, the Court reiterated that in the area of land development and town planning the Contracting States should enjoy a wide margin of appreciation in order to implement their town and country planning policy. However, in the Court's view the state of affairs in question – having lasted at least 10 years – disclosed a lack of sufficient diligence in weighing the competing interests. Nor did the applicants have any effective entitlement to compensation throughout this period. Thus, the applicants had had to bear an excessive individual burden and there had been a violation of Article 1.[76] In the case of *Bugajny and Others*, the Court found that the refusal to expropriate privately owned land used as public property, i.e. as roads, did not strike a fair balance between the competing interests and made the applicants bear an excessive individual burden. There had accordingly been a violation of Article 1.[77]

In the above-mentioned *Stran Greek Refineries and Stratis Andreadis* case, the Court noted that Greece was under a duty to pay the applicants the sums awarded by the arbitration award. It concluded that by choosing to intervene at that stage of the proceedings in the Court of Cassation by a law which invoked the termination of the contract in question in order to declare void the arbitration clause and to annul the arbitration award, the legislature upset the fair balance to the detriment of the applicants.[78] The straightforward reasoning of the unanimous Court in this case may be explained by the dubious, *ad hoc* character of the legislation in question. As the Court observed, 'the real objective of the legislature' was to close the domestic proceedings in the present case once and for all.[79]

In the *Mamatas and Others* case, the Court examined the exchange of the applicants' bonds for other securities worth 53.5 per cent less in terms of nominal value. While acknowledging the States' wide margin of appreciation in that sphere, the Court considered *inter alia* that the commercial value of the bonds had already been affected by the reduced solvency of Greece, that the collective action clauses and the restructuring of the public debt were an

---

is made in the conditions prescribed by law – 5 equal annual instalments – the burden imposed on the applicant was not disproportionate or excessive.

[76] *Skibińscy v. Poland*, ECtHR 14 November 2006, appl. no. 52589/99, paras. 88–90 and 97–98. See also *Potomska and Potomski v. Poland, supra* n. 64, paras. 65–80; *Maioli v. Italy*, ECtHR 12 July 2011, appl. no. 18290/02, paras. 50–68. See further *Klaus and Iouri Kiladze v. Georgia*, ECtHR 2 February 2010, appl. no. 7975/06, paras. 71–78, where the Court considered that the complete lack of action over a period of several years, which was attributable to the State and deprived the applicants of effective enjoyment of their right to payment of compensation for non-pecuniary damage within a reasonable time, had imposed a disproportionate and excessive burden on them which could not be justified by the authorities' supposed pursuit of a legitimate general interest in the instant case.

[77] *Bugajny and Others v. Poland*, ECtHR 6 November 2007, appl. no. 22531/05, paras. 67–75.

[78] *Stran Greek Refineries and Stratis Andreadis v. Greece, supra* n. 17, paras. 73–74.

[79] *Ibid.,* para. 66.

appropriate and necessary means of reducing the public debt of Greece and saving it from bankruptcy and that investing in bonds was never risk-free. Accordingly, by taking the contested measures Greece had neither upset the fair balance between the competing interests nor imposed an individual and excessive burden on the applicants.[80]

In the case of *Cindrić and Bešlić*, the applicants had to bear the cost of the State's representation in civil proceedings. The Court considered *inter alia* that the acts at issue bore certain similarities to a terrorist act; that the definition of what constituted a terrorist act was not clarified at the relevant time; that the applicants' opponent was the State represented by the State Attorney's Office; and that the amount of the costs to be reimbursed by the applicants was not insignificant in light of their financial situation. The Court concluded that ordering the applicants to bear the full costs of the State's representation amounted to a disproportionate burden on them.[81]

In the case of *Philippou v. Cyprus*, concerning the forfeiture of the applicant's retirement benefits following his dismissal from the public service, the Court found that, weighing the seriousness of the offences committed by the applicant, including *inter alia* obtaining a substantial amount of money by false pretences, forging cheques, concealment and abuse of office, against the effect of the disciplinary measures, the applicant was not made to bear an individual and excessive burden. Accordingly, there has been no violation of Article 1.[82]

3. DEPRIVATION OF POSSESSIONS

The most important restriction to be imposed by the authorities on the peaceful enjoyment of one's possessions is regulated explicitly in the second sentence: deprivation of property in the public interest. The concept of 'deprivation' covers not only formal expropriations but also *de facto* expropriations, i.e. measures which can be assimilated to a deprivation of possessions.[83] The

---

[80] *Mamatas and Others v. Greece*, ECtHR 21 July 2016, appl. nos. 63066/14, 64297/14 and 66106/14, paras. 94, 112, 116 and 117 (request for referral to the Grand Chamber pending).

[81] *Cindrić and Bešlić v. Croatia*, ECtHR 6 September 2016, appl. no. 72152/13, para. 110.

[82] *Philippou v. Cyprus*, ECtHR 14 June 2016, appl. no. 71148/10, paras. 74–75. See also *Lavrechov v. the Czech Republic*, ECtHR 20 June 2013, appl. no. 57404/08, paras. 47–57, ECHR 2013 (forfeiture of applicant's bail).

[83] *Fredin v. Sweden (No. 1)*, EComHR 6 November 1989 (rep.), appl. no. 12033/86, para. 51; *Fredin v. Sweden (No. 1)*, ECtHR 18 February 1991, appl. no. 12033/86, para. 41; *Brumărescu v. Romania*, ECtHR (GC) 28 October 1999, appl. no. 28342/95, para. 77; *Carbonara and Ventura v. Italy, supra* n. 68, paras. 60 and 61; *Hirschhorn v. Romania,* ECtHR 26 July 2007, appl. no. 29294/02, para. 93, where the Court observed that the applicant's complete inability to enjoy any of the attributes of his ownership rights over the building amounted to *de facto* expropriation for the purposes of the second sentence of the first para. of Art. 1. See

deprivation of an individual's home or property is in principle an instantaneous act and does create a continuing situation of 'deprivation'. In the case of *Blečić*, the termination of the applicant's tenancy occurred prior to the ratification of the Convention by the Contracting State and fell outside the Court's temporal jurisdiction.[84]

Under the second sentence of the first paragraph of Article 1 the Court examines (1) whether the deprivation had a 'public interest' aim, respectively a 'legitimate aim'; (2) whether the measure was proportionate in relation to the aim pursued; and (3) whether the measure was lawful, i.e. 'provided for by law' and by 'the general principles of international law'.[85] Such a test is of course not necessary when the circumstances are clear. Thus, the Court held in the *Sîrbu* case that by failing to comply with the judgments of the Centru District Court, the national authorities prevented the applicants from having their compensation paid and from enjoying the possession of their money: 'The Government have not advanced any justification for this interference and the Court considers that lack of funds cannot justify such an omission.'[86]

3.1. IN THE PUBLIC INTEREST

Whether a particular expropriation has been performed in the public interest will be subjected by the Court to a very limited review only, the main objective being to detect cases of *détournement de pouvoir*[87] or of manifest

---

also *Sarica and Dilaver v. Turkey*, ECtHR 27 May 2010, appl. no. 11765/05, paras. 40, 43–45, where the Court observed that the *de facto* expropriation allowed the authorities to occupy immovable property and change its intended use irreversibly, so that it came to be considered as state property, without any kind of formal declaratory act transferring ownership or prior compensation. A finding of *de facto* expropriation legally endorsed an unlawful situation knowingly created by the authorities and enabled the latter to benefit from their unlawful conduct. The procedure in question put the individuals concerned at risk of unforeseeable and arbitrary outcomes.

84 *Blečić v. Croatia*, ECtHR (GC) 8 March 2006, appl. no. 59532/00, paras. 86 and 92.

85 See *Hentrich v. France, supra* n. 60, where the Court examined all 3 requirements. In most judgments, however, the 'lawfulness' of the deprivation measure is not at issue; in fact, such measures normally take the form of legislation. In *Fotopoulou v. Greece*, ECtHR 18 November 2004, appl. no. 66725/01, para. 38, the Court stated that the legal basis for the demolition of a wall failed. Thus, Art. 1 had been violated.

86 *Sirbu and Others v. Moldova*, ECtHR 15 June 2004, appl. no. 73562/01, para. 32. See also *Timbal v. Moldova*, ECtHR 14 September 2004, appl. no. 22970/02, para. 25; *Tregubenko v. Ukraine, supra* n. 13, para. 54. In *Svetlana Naumenko v. Ukraine, supra* n. 12, para. 104, the Court noted that the impossibility for the applicant to obtain enforcement of the judgment recognising her status of a 'Chernobyl relief worker' for an unreasonably long period of time constituted an interference with her right to the peaceful enjoyment of her possessions.

87 See *A., B., C. and D. v. the United Kingdom*, EComHR 29 May 1967, appl. no. 3039/67, Yearbook X, p. 506, 516–518, where the Commission used the doctrine of the margin of appreciation also on this point. See also *Holy Monasteries v. Greece, supra* n. 68, para. 67 (doubts as to real reasons of a legislative measure; see *infra*).

arbitrariness.[88] As the Commission stated in its report in the *Handyside* case in connection with the fact that the first paragraph speaks of 'in the public interest' and not of 'necessary in a democratic society': 'Clearly the public or general interest encompasses measures which would be preferable or advisable, and not only essential, in a democratic society.'[89]

In the *James* case, the Court held with respect to the state's margin of appreciation as follows: 'Furthermore, the notion of "public interest" is necessarily extensive. [...] the decision to enact laws expropriating property will commonly involve considerations of political, economic and social issues on which opinion within a democratic society may reasonably differ widely. The Court, finding it natural that the margin of appreciation available to the legislature in implementing social and economic policies should be a wide one, will respect the legislature's judgment as to what is "in the public interest" unless that judgment be manifestly without reasonable foundation.'[90]

Regarding the meaning of 'the public interest' the Court held as follows: 'a deprivation of property effected for no reason other than to confer a private benefit on a private party cannot be "in the public interest". Nonetheless, the compulsory transfer of property from one individual to another may, depending upon the circumstances, constitute a legitimate aim for promoting the public interest.'[91]

The Court added that a taking of property effected in pursuance of legitimate, social, economic or other policies may be 'in the public interest', even if the community at large has no direct use or enjoyment of the property taken.[92]

For example, the Court accepted that the prevention of tax evasion is a legitimate objective which is in the public interest.[93] Likewise, the purpose of constructing housing for a category of disadvantaged persons constitutes a public interest aim.[94] In the *Pressos Compania Naviera S.A.* case, the Court accepted that a law depriving the applicants of their property pursued such an aim, without commenting in any specific way on the reasons put forward by

---

[88]   *Handyside v. the United Kingdom*, EComHR 30 September 1975 (rep.), appl. no. 5493/72, para. 163; *James and Others v. the United Kingdom*, ECtHR (GC) 21 February 1986, appl. no. 8793/79, para. 46.

[89]   *Handyside v. the United Kingdom, supra* n. 88, para. 167.

[90]   *James and Others v. the United Kingdom, supra* n. 88, para. 46. See also *Lithgow and Others v. the United Kingdom*, ECtHR (GC) 8 July 1986, appl. nos. 9006/80 et al., para. 122, Series A no. 102; *Pressos Compania Naviera S.A. and Others v. Belgium, supra* n. 7, para. 37; *The former King of Greece and Others*, ECtHR (GC) 23 November 2000, appl. no. 25701/94, para. 87; *Broniowski v. Poland, supra* n. 2, para. 149; *Jahn and Others v. Germany*, ECtHR 30 June 2005, appl. nos. 46720/99, para. 91; *Maurice v. France, supra* n. 8, para. 84; *Draon v. France, supra* n. 8, para. 76; *Vistiņš and Perepjolkins v. Latvia, supra* n. 2, para. 106.

[91]   *James and Others v. the United Kingdom, supra* n. 88, para. 40.

[92]   *Ibid.*, paras. 47–49.

[93]   *Hentrich v. France, supra* n. 60, para. 39.

[94]   *Zubani v. Italy*, ECtHR 7 August 1996, appl. no. 14025/88, para. 45.

the Belgian Government.[95] In two more recent cases, the Court accepted that the 'sense of social justice of the population', in combination with the interest to protect the public purse and to distribute the public burden satisfies the Convention requirement of a legitimate aim, notwithstanding its broadness.[96] The Court further held that the protection of a country's cultural heritage is a legitimate aim and that the conservation of the cultural heritage and, where appropriate, its sustainable use, have as their aim, in addition to the maintenance of a certain quality of life, the preservation of the historical, cultural and artistic roots of a region and its inhabitants.[97]

The Court has a very reticent attitude towards the question of what is in the public interest.[98] It repeatedly held that 'because of their direct knowledge of their society and its needs, the national authorities are in principle better placed than the international judge to appreciate what is "in the public interest". Under the system of protection established by the Convention, it is thus for the national authorities to make the initial assessment as to the existence of a problem of public concern warranting measures of deprivation of property. [...] the national authorities accordingly enjoy a certain margin of appreciation.'[99]

The Court's deference to the national legislature's assessment of what is in the public interest appears very clearly from the judgment in the *Holy Monasteries* case. The Court expressed some doubts on the given public interest (end of illegal land sales, encroachments on it and its abandonment or uncontrolled development) on account of the fact that the law at issue gave the state optional power to transfer the land for use by farmers and that it mentioned also public bodies as possible beneficiaries. Nonetheless, it accepted that the overall objective of the law was legitimate.[100]

However, where the national authorities' assessment was not convincing, the Court found that the deprivation had no 'public interest' aim. In the case of *Tkachevy*, the Court concluded that the public interest underlying the expropriation of the applicants' flat was not clearly and convincingly shown and that there has, accordingly, been a violation of Article 1.[101] In the *Motais de*

---

[95]   *Pressos Compania Naviera S.A. and Others v. Belgium*, *supra* n. 7, para. 34. The Belgian Government had sought to justify the interference (a law which retroactively deprived the applicants of civil law claims against the State) by referring to the need to protect the State's financial interests, the need to re-establish legal certainty and the need to bring Belgian legislation into line with that of neighbouring countries.

[96]   *N.K.M. v. Hungary*, *supra* n. 58, para. 59; *R.Sz. v. Hungary*, *supra* n. 58, para. 48.

[97]   *Kozacıoğlu v. Turkey*, ECtHR (GC) 19 February 2009, appl. no. 2334/03, paras. 53–54. See also *Bogdel v. Lithuania*, ECtHR 26 November 2013, appl. no. 41248/06, paras. 60–62.

[98]   See, e.g., *The former King of Greece and Others*, *supra* n. 90, para. 88.

[99]   *Vistiņš and Perepjolkins v. Latvia*, *supra* n. 2, para. 106; *Ališić and Others v. Bosnia and Herzegovina, Croatia, Serbia, Slovenia and the former Yugoslav Republic of Macedonia*, *supra* n. 58, para. 106; *Broniowski v. Poland*, *supra* n. 2, para. 149.

[100]   *Holy Monasteries v. Greece*, *supra* n. 68, para. 69.

[101]   *Tkachevy v. Russia*, ECtHR 14 February 2010, appl. no. 35430/05, para. 50.

Narbonne case, the Court considered that the placing in reserve of expropriated property does not necessarily breach Article 1. A problem arises if the placing in reserve is not based on grounds of public interest and if, during that time, the respective property experienced a significant increase in value of which the former owners are deprived. This was the case here and the Court found a breach of Article 1.[102] In *Zouboulidis v. Greece (No. 2)*, the Court considered that the mere interest of the State's cash flow or the concern to settle the State's debts promptly could not in themselves be treated as a public or general interest justifying interference with individual rights.[103]

3.2. PROPORTIONALITY OF THE MEASURE

The review by the Court is more extensive as concerns the proportionality requirement, although a wide margin of appreciation for national legislatures is normally also accepted on this score. As was already pointed out in section 2.2 *supra*, the Court assesses the proportionality of the contested measure by determining whether a 'fair balance' has been struck between the interest of the community and the requirements of the protection of the individual's fundamental rights. This means, in particular, that there must be a reasonable relationship of proportionality between the means employed and the aim sought to be realised by any measure depriving a person of his possessions.[104]

According to the Court, compensation terms are material to the assessment of whether the contested measure respects the requisite fair balance and whether or not it imposes a disproportionate burden. In this connection the Court holds that the taking of property without payment of an amount reasonably related to its value will normally constitute a disproportionate interference.[105] However, legitimate objectives of 'public interest may call for less than reimbursement

---

[102]   *Motais de Narbonne v. France,* ECtHR 2 July 2002, appl. no. 48161/99, paras. 21–22. See also *Vassallo v. Malta,* ECtHR 11 October 2011, appl. no. 57862/09, paras. 41–42; *Frendo Randon and Others v. Malta,* ECtHR 22 November 2011, appl. no. 2226/10, paras. 59 and 61; *Beneficio Cappella Paolini v. San Marino,* ECtHR 13 July 2004, appl. no. 40786/98, para. 33.

[103]   *Zouboulidis v. Greece (No. 2),* ECtHR 25 June 2009, appl. no. 36963/06, paras. 35–37.

[104]   See *James and Others v. the United Kingdom, supra* n. 88, para. 50; *Lithgow and Others v. the United Kingdom, supra* n. 90, para. 120; *Holy Monasteries v. Greece, supra* n. 68, para. 70; *Pressos Compania Naviera S.A. and Others v. Belgium, supra* n. 7, para. 33; *The former King of Greece and Others, supra* n. 90, para. 89.

[105]   See, *inter alia, Platakou v. Greece,* ECtHR 11 January 2001, appl. no. 38460/97, para. 55. Furthermore, the fact that compensation for deprivation of property is not paid automatically by the authorities, but must be claimed by the landowner, may prove to be inadequate protection. See *Börekçioğulları (Çökmez) and Others v. Turkey,* ECtHR 19 October 2006, appl. no. 58650/00, para. 42, with reference to *Carbonara and Ventura v. Italy, supra* n. 68, para. 67.

of the full market value'.[106] A total lack of compensation can be considered justifiable only in exceptional circumstances.[107] Such a lack of compensation does not make a deprivation *eo ipso* wrongful, provided that the interference in question satisfies the requirement of lawfulness and is not arbitrary. Decisive is, whether in the context of a lawful expropriation a disproportionate and excessive burden has been imposed on the individual.[108] This requires an overall examination of the various interests in issue, bearing in mind that the Convention is intended to safeguard rights that are 'practical and effective'. Therefore, it is necessary to look behind appearances and investigate the realities of the situation complained of. That assessment may involve not only the relevant compensation terms, but also the conduct of the parties. In that context, uncertainty is a factor to be taken into account in assessing the state's conduct. Public authorities have to act in good time as well as in an appropriate and consistent manner (principle of 'good governance').[109] However, the good governance principle should, as a rule, not prevent the correction of mistakes, even those made by the authorities through negligence. Yet, when correcting such mistakes, the authorities should not disproportionately interfere with new rights that have been acquired by individuals relying on their action in good faith. Thus, states should not be allowed to profit from their mistakes and they must bear the risk of their mistakes.[110]

The Court recognised that the State had to deal with an exceptionally difficult situation in the *Broniowski* case concerning the Polish authorities' obligation to compensate nearly 80,000 people who had lost property as a result of boundary changes after the Second World War. The Court accepted that in the case before it, involving a wide-ranging but controversial legislative scheme with

---

[106]   See *Holy Monasteries v. Greece, supra* n. 68, paras. 70–71; *Papachelas v. Greece,* ECtHR 25 March 1999 (dec.), appl. no. 1423/96, para. 48; *Bruncrona v. Finland, supra* n. 2, para. 68.

[107]   *Holy Monasteries v. Greece, supra* n. 68, para. 73; *Pressos Compania Naviera S.A. and Others v. Belgium, supra* n. 7, para. 31; *The former King of Greece and Others, supra* n. 90, para. 89. In *James and Others v. the United Kingdom, supra* n. 88, para. 54, and in *Lithgow and Others v. the United Kingdom, supra* n. 90, para. 120, the Court had already referred to this practice in terms of a principle applying under the legal systems of the Contracting States, adding that the protection afforded by Art. 1 would be largely illusory in the absence of any equivalent principle. See further *Turgut and Others v. Turkey,* ECtHR 8 July 2008, appl. no. 1411/03, para. 91.

[108]   *The former King of Greece and Others, supra* n. 90, para. 90. See also *James and Others v. the United Kingdom, supra* n. 88, para. 50; *Hentrich v. France, supra* n. 60, para. 49; *Motais de Narbonne v. France, supra* n. 102, paras. 16–23; *Broniowski v. Poland, supra* n. 2, para. 150, ECHR 2004-V; *Yetiş and Others v. Turkey,* ECtHR 6 July 2010, appl. no. 40349/05, paras. 56 and 59.

[109]   *Broniowski v. Poland, supra* n. 2, para. 151; *Sarica and Dilaver v. Turkey,* ECtHR 27 May 2010, appl. no. 11765/05, paras. 43–45.

[110]   *Maksymenko and Gerasymenko v. Ukraine,* ECtHR 16 May 2013, appl. no. 49317/07, para. 64 with reference to *Moskal v. Poland,* ECtHR 15 September 2009, appl. no. 10373/05, para. 73, *mutatis mutandis, Pincová and Pinc v. the Czech Republic,* ECtHR 5 November 2002, appl. no. 36548/97, para. 58; and *Lelas v. Croatia,* ECtHR 20 May 2010, appl. no. 55555/08, para. 74.

significant economic impact for the country as a whole, the choice of measures may necessarily involve decisions restricting compensation for the taking or restitution of property to a level below its market value. Still there should be a reasonable relation to the real value of the property. An earlier compensation to the applicant of 2 per cent did in any case not suffice to cut him off from broader compensation measures, which were to be rewarded to persons who had not yet received any compensation at all.[111]

In *Vistiņš and Perepjolkins v. Latvia*, the compensation awarded to the applicants was less than one-thousandth and respectively some 350 times lower than the cadastral value of the land. The Court held that such disproportionate awards are almost tantamount to a complete lack of compensation. It found that this disproportion – resulting from a retrospective legislative amendment which created an inequality to the State's advantage and to the applicants' disadvantage – was too significant to find that a 'fair balance' had been struck between the competing interests.[112]

After Greece had become a republic in 1974, possessions of the Greek Church and of the former royal family were expropriated without compensation. In the *Holy Monasteries* case, the Court considered that, the State had provided for compensation to the monasteries in an earlier case but that no compensation measures had been taken in the case at hand. The Court concluded that Article 1 had been violated.[113] In the *The former King of Greece* case, the Court pointed out that at least part of the expropriated property was purchased by the applicants' predecessors in title and paid out of their private funds. Moreover, compensation was provided for the last time the property was expropriated. Therefore, the applicants had a legitimate expectation to be compensated. There has been a breach of Article 1.[114]

The judgment in the above-mentioned *Pressos Compania Naviera S.A.* case confirms the Court's critical attitude towards legislative interference with the judicial process and the importance it attaches to rule of law considerations.[115]

---

[111]   *Broniowski v. Poland, supra* n. 2, para. 162–186, ECHR 2004-V. See as to the former German Democratic Republic: *Jahn and Others v. Germany, supra* n. 90, para. 117, where the Court concluded – in view of the circumstances of the case and having regard, in particular, to the uncertainty of the legal position of heirs and the grounds of social justice relied on by the German authorities – that in the unique context of German reunification, the lack of any compensation did not upset the 'fair balance' which had to be struck between the protection of property and the requirements of the general interest. *Străin and Others v. Romania*, ECtHR 21 July 2005, appl. no. 57001/00, paras. 57–59 (total lack of compensation). *Göbel v. Germany*, ECtHR 8 December 2011, appl. no. 35023/04, paras. 44–52, where the loss of shares in land without full compensation in the context of German reunification did not violate Art. 1.

[112]   *Vistiņš and Perepjolkins v. Latvia, supra* n. 2, paras. 119 and 130.

[113]   *Holy Monasteries v. Greece, supra* n. 68, paras. 74–75.

[114]   *The former King of Greece and Others, supra* n. 90, para. 98.

[115]   See also *Stran Greek Refineries and Stratis Andreadis v. Greece, supra* n. 17, discussed *supra* in section 2.2.

The serious financial considerations cited by the government could warrant prospective legislation to derogate from the general law of tort but not legislating with retrospective effect with the aim and consequence of depriving the applicants of their claims for compensation. Such a fundamental interference with the applicants' rights is inconsistent with preserving a fair balance between the interests at stake.[116]

Although legitimate objectives of public interest may call for compensation which does not reflect the full market value, it is self-evident that in less exceptional circumstances reimbursement of the full market value should remain the rule. And even this can turn out to be insufficient in specific situations. In the *Hentrich* case, the Court concluded that, as a selected victim of the exercise of the right of pre-emption, the applicant bore an individual and excessive burden and that there has been a violation of Article 1.[117] A particular feature of this case was the fact that, although compensation had been given to the applicant, the Court found that the French system offered insufficient protection from arbitrary deprivation of property.[118]

In the *Lallement* case, a farmer had lost 60 per cent of his lands, which he used for milk production. He was fully compensated for the expropriation of the land. The Court held that a compensation, which did not cover the loss of his possibilities to continue his milk-producing activities as well, created an excessive burden on the farmer and, therefore, constituted a violation of Article 1.[119]

In the *Kozacıoğlu* case, the Turkish law did not allow the taking into account of the part of a property's value that results from its rarity and its architectural and historical features. The Court held that when determining the compensation for the expropriation of a listed building, it is appropriate to consider, to a reasonable degree, the property's specific features. The Court concluded, accordingly, that there had been a violation of Article 1.[120] In another case concerning prehistoric artworks in a cave, the Court concluded that, given the inherent necessity of protecting the cave and the legal constraints to which it was thus subject, a commercial evaluation *stricto sensu* is not suitable.[121]

---

[116] *Pressos Compania Naviera S.A. and Others v. Belgium, supra* n. 7, paras. 39–44. See also *Scordino v. Italy (No. 1)*, ECtHR 29 July 2004, appl. no. 36813/97, para. 79; *Scordino v. Italy (No. 1)*, ECtHR (GC) 29 March 2006, appl. no. 36813/97, paras. 99–104.

[117] *Hentrich v. France, supra* n. 60, paras. 43–50.

[118] In this connection, it should be noted that the Court also reached a negative conclusion as concerns the lawfulness of the interference. *ibid.*, paras. 40–42. See also *Zubani v. Italy, supra* n. 94, para. 49, where the Court found a violation on account of the way the national authorities had handled the applicants' situation, in spite of the fact that a considerable compensation had been awarded to them.

[119] *Lallement v. France*, ECtHR 11 April 2002, appl. no. 46044/99, para. 24.

[120] *Kozacıoğlu v. Turkey, supra* n. 97, paras. 69–73.

[121] *Helly and Others v. France*, ECtHR 11 October 2011 (dec.), appl. no. 28216/09.

In the case of *Urbárska Obec Trenčianske Biskupice*, the Court accepted the existence of a public interest but it was not persuaded that the declared public interest was sufficiently broad and compelling to justify the substantial difference between the real value of the applicant's land and that of the land which it obtained in compensation.[122] In the *Bistrović* case, concerning the expropriation of parts of the applicants' land with a view to building a motorway in proximity to the house, the Court held that 'by failing to establish all the relevant factors for establishing the compensation for the applicants' expropriated property, and by failing to grant indemnity for the decrease in the value of their remaining estate, the national authorities have failed to strike a fair balance (…).'[123] In the case of *Perdigão*, where the compensation awarded to the applicants was wholly absorbed by the court fees, the Court observed that neither the applicants' conduct nor the procedural activity set in motion could justify such high court fees. Thus, the applicants had to bear an excessive burden.[124]

3.3. PROVIDED FOR BY LAW AND BY THE GENERAL PRINCIPLES OF INTERNATIONAL LAW

Expropriations are permissible only if the conditions provided for by law and by the general principles of international law have been observed. The principle of the rule of law requires, in general, that any interference be based on an instrument of general application. However, in certain exceptional situations the Court has been prepared to accept, albeit implicitly, the existence of special laws laying down specific conditions that apply to one or more named individuals.[125] As regards compliance with national legal conditions, here again the Court does not examine whether national law has been applied correctly. It takes the position that in this matter it has to refer to the judgment of the national court in the case concerned and that it must not function as a 'fourth instance'.[126] Nonetheless, the Court has recalled, also in the context of Article 1, that the notion of 'law' within the meaning of the Convention requires the existence of and compliance with sufficiently accessible, precise and foreseeable domestic

---

[122] *Urbárska Obec Trenčianske Biskupice v. Slovakia,* ECtHR 27 November 2007, appl. no. 74258/01, paras. 120 and 132.

[123] *Bistrović v. Croatia,* ECtHR 31 May 2007, appl. no. 25774/05, para. 44.

[124] *Perdigão v. Portugal, supra* n. 5, 76–79.

[125] *Vistiņš and Perepjolkins v. Latvia, supra* n. 2, para. 99 with references.

[126] It is in the first place for the domestic authorities, notably the courts, to interpret and apply the domestic law and to decide on issues of constitutionality. *The former King of Greece and Others v. Greece, supra* n. 90, para. 82; *Jahn and Others v. Germany, supra* n. 90, para. 86; *Vistiņš and Perepjolkins v. Latvia, supra* n. 2, para. 102. The Court considers, however, whether the interpretation by the domestic authorities was arbitrary or not. See *Jahn and Others v. Germany, supra* n. 90, para. 86, with reference to *Wittek v. Germany,* ECtHR 12 December 2002, appl. no. 37290/97, para. 49.

legal provisions.[127] As to the notion of 'foreseeability', the Court held that its scope depends to a considerable degree on the content of the instrument in issue, the field it is designed to cover and the number and status of those to whom it is addressed.[128] In particular, a rule is 'foreseeable' when it affords a measure of protection against arbitrary interferences by the public authorities.[129] Similarly, the applicable law must provide minimum procedural safeguards commensurate with the importance of the principle at stake.[130]

The fact that the state might have a wide margin of appreciation – for example, as regards general measures of economic or social strategy and the enactment and interpretation of statutes in this field – does not exclude the Court's power to review to what extent such legislation is specific and foreseeable and with what degree of clarity it allows the establishment of whether the applicant's situation falls within the provisions of the relevant law.[131]

With respect to the reference to international legal principles one is inclined to think, first of all, of the obligation to pay damages, as this obligation exists under international law or at all events existed according to the prevalent view at the moment when Protocol No. 1 was drafted. In the *James* case and in the *Lithgow* case the Court held that the reference to the general principles of international law in Article 1 means that those principles are incorporated into that article, but only as regards those acts to which they are normally applicable, that is to say acts of a state in relation to non-nationals.[132] The Court also indicated that the difference in treatment did not constitute discrimination, since the differences in treatment had an 'objective and reasonable justification': 'Especially as regards a taking of property effected in the context of a social reform, there may well be good grounds for drawing a distinction between nationals and non-nationals as far as compensation is concerned.'[133] In the Court's view non-nationals are, first, more vulnerable to domestic legislation since, unlike nationals, they will generally have played no part in the elections.

---

[127] See *Lithgow and Others v. the United Kingdom*, *supra* n. 90, para. 110; *Hentrich v. France*, *supra* n. 60, para. 42; *N.K.M. v. Hungary*, *supra* n. 58, para. 48 with reference to *Guiso-Gallisay v. Italy*, ECtHR 8 December 2005, appl. no. 58858/00, paras. 82–83.

[128] *N.K.M. v. Hungary*, *supra* n. 58, para. 48 with reference to *Sud Fondi S.r.l. and Others v. Italy*, ECtHR 20 January 2009, appl. no. 75909/01, para. 109.

[129] *N.K.M. v. Hungary*, *supra* n. 58, para. 48 with reference to *Centro Europa 7 S.r.l. and Di Stefano v. Italy*, *supra* n. 37, para. 143. See also *Hentrich v. France*, *supra* n. 60, para. 42. Here, the Court criticised the discretionary nature of the exercise of the State's right of pre-emption and the unfairness of the procedure (no adversarial proceedings respecting the principle of equality of arms).

[130] *N.K.M. v. Hungary*, *supra* n. 58, para. 48 with reference to *Vistiņš and Perepjolkins v. Latvia*, *supra* n. 17, paras. 96–98 and *Sanoma Uitgevers B.V. v. the Netherlands*, ECtHR (GC) 14 September 2010, appl. no. 38224/03, para. 88.

[131] *Damjanac v. Croatia*, ECtHR 24 October 2013, appl. no. 52943/10, para. 90.

[132] *James and Others v. the United Kingdom*, *supra* n. 88, para. 61. See also *Lithgow and Others v. the United Kingdom*, *supra* n. 90, para. 114.

[133] *Ibid.*, para. 63 and para. 116, respectively.

Secondly, although the taking of property must always be effected in the public interest, different considerations may apply to nationals and non-nationals and there may well be a legitimate reason for requiring nationals to bear a greater burden in the public interest than non-nationals.[134] Furthermore, the Court pointed to the fact that also the *travaux préparatoires* and Resolution (52)1 of 19 March 1952 approving the text of the Protocol revealed that the reference to the general principles of international law was not intended to extend to nationals.[135] In both cases the Court found that no violation of Article 1 had been established, since in the exercise of its margin of appreciation the United Kingdom was entitled to adopt the compensation provisions as applied to the applicants and these provisions and their application were deemed by the Court not to be unreasonable.

According to this interpretation Article 1 permits a difference in treatment between the state's own nationals and aliens. If any differences on this point still exist at present, developments within international law go into the direction of their minimisation.[136] It should be added that also developments in the case law of the Court as regards compensation for deprivation of property of nationals tend to put these differences into perspective.[137]

4. RESTRICTIONS

4.1. CONTROL OF THE USE OF PROPERTY

The second paragraph of Article 1 allows the national authorities an almost unlimited power to impose restrictions on the use of property in accordance with the general interest. It does not concern the deprivation of property itself

---

[134] *Ibid.*

[135] *Ibid.,* para. 64 and para. 117, respectively.

[136] See the Charter of Economic Rights and Duties of States, adopted by Res. 3281 (XXIX) of the General Assembly of the UN on 12 December 1974, *International Legal Materials* (1975), p. 251.

[137] See the observations made above as concerns the Court's critical attitude in cases where there has been a total lack of compensation. A further way of minimising the differences in protection between nationals and aliens appears from the Commission's report in *Gasus Dosier- und Fördertechnik GmbH v. the Netherlands,* EComHR 21 October 1993 (rep.), appl. no. 15375/89, paras. 57–64. This was a (rare) case of interference with property rights of an alien (a foreign company). The Commission said that this particular form of deprivation of possessions – i.e. seizure of the foreign company's machine in the actual possession of a Dutch company – could not be compared to measures of confiscation, nationalisation or expropriation in regard to which international law provides special protection to foreign citizens and companies. The Court did not pronounce on this aspect of the case, as it examined it under the second para. of Art. 1. See further H. Lambert, *The Position of Aliens in Relation to the European Convention on Human Rights,* Human Rights Files No. 8, Council of Europe Publishing, Strasbourg, 2007, p. 38.

but rather restriction of its use. In this context, it is remarkable that with regard to this restriction it is provided that it must be necessary, while with respect to the expropriation itself it is not.[138] However, the judgment as to what is necessary in the general interest is expressly left to the State: 'as it deems necessary'. Initially, the Court took the view that: 'this paragraph sets the Contracting States up as sole judges of the 'necessity' for an interference. Consequently, the Court must restrict itself to supervising the lawfulness and the purposes of the restriction in question.'[139] However, a more extensive supervision has gradually been developed in the case law. In its report in the *Sporrong and Lönnroth* case the Commission concluded from the slightly modified wording used by the Court in the *Marckx* judgment[140] that the Court recognises the states as the 'sole judges' only with respect to the law on which the restrictions are based, but not in relation to the necessity of the measures themselves. As regards the latter, in the Commission's opinion, the possibility of review by the Strasbourg organs goes further and includes, for instance, the proportionality between those measures and the purpose of the law on which they are based.[141]

In its judgment in the *AGOSI* case, the Court adopted a similar approach, but later judgments show that the Court applies a fair balance test to assess the proportionality of the interference, both as concerns enforcement measures and the underlying legislation.[142] As the Court held in the *Allan Jacobsson* case: 'Under the second paragraph of Article 1 of Protocol No. 1, the Contracting States are entitled, amongst other things, to control the use of property in accordance with the general interest, by enforcing such laws as they deem necessary for the purpose. However, as this provision is to be construed in the light of the general principle enunciated in the first sentence of the first paragraph, there must exist a reasonable relationship of proportionality between the means employed and the aim sought to be realised. In striking the fair balance thereby required between the general interest of the community and the requirements of the protection of the individual's fundamental rights, the authorities enjoy a wide margin of appreciation.'[143]

---

[138] The submission by an applicant that in his case the deprivation of property could not be deemed to have been necessary was not, therefore, examined by the Commission: *A., B., C. and D. v. the United Kingdom, supra* n. 87, p. 506, 516.

[139] *Handyside v. the United Kingdom,* ECtHR 7 December 1976, appl. no. 5493/72, para. 62.

[140] *Marckx v. Belgium, supra* n. 23, para. 64.

[141] *Sporrong and Lönnroth v. Sweden, supra* n. 2, para. 103.

[142] *AGOSI v. the United Kingdom,* ECtHR 24 October 1986, appl. no. 9118/80, para. 52 (distinction between the prohibition of imports as such and the enforcement of this prohibition); *Air Canada v. the United Kingdom, supra* n. 5, paras. 36 et seq.; *Islamic Republic of Iran Shipping Lines v. Turkey,* ECtHR 13 December 2007, appl. no. 40998/98, para. 94; *Perdigão v. Portugal, supra* n. 5, paras. 67 et seq.

[143] *Allan Jacobsson v. Sweden (No. 1),* ECtHR 25 October 1989, appl. no. 10842/84, para. 55. See also *Fredin v. Sweden (No. 1),* ECtHR 18 February 1991, appl. no. 12033/86, para. 51; *Jane Smith v. the United Kingdom,* ECtHR (GC) 18 January 2001, appl. no. 25154/94, paras. 121–125; *Rajnai v. Hungary,* ECtHR 26 October 2004, appl. no. 73369/01, paras. 21–24, in

Given the flexibility of the 'reasonable relationship of proportionality' criterion and the wide margin of appreciation, the Court will not easily conclude that a fair balance has not been achieved, not even when it entertains doubts on this score.[144] Generally speaking, the fair balance will be lacking where the applicant has to bear an individual and excessive burden.[145] Invoking such burden has good chances of success, notably where the applicant can show that the control of the use of his property suffered from procedural irregularities such as non-implementation of recognised claims resulting from expropriation,[146] a legislative amendment which prevented the award of legal costs in pending procedures despite legitimate expectations on the basis of the previous legislation,[147] unreasonable delay in the restitution of tax payments,[148] the excessive term of a court procedure for the benefit of establishing property rights,[149] the six-year long impossibility to get police assistance for the eviction of tenants,[150] contradictory urban planning legislation,[151] non-implementation of domestic court judgments, or (otherwise) a lack of application of domestic law.[152]

---

which the Court approved restrictions on bee-keeping for reasons of public health on the applicant's property. This fair balance test applies also to legislative measures: see *Mellacher and Others v. Austria*, ECtHR 19 December 1989, appl. nos. 10522/83, 11011/84 and 11070/84, para. 48; *Spadea and Scalabrino v. Italy*, ECtHR 28 September 1994, appl. no. 12868/87, para. 40; *Yaroslavtsev v. Russia*, ECtHR 2 December 2004, appl. no. 42138/02, paras. 32–35, in which the Court approved the rule preventing registration of vehicles in respect of which the lawfulness of the acquisition could not be shown.

144   *Allan Jacobsson v. Sweden (No. 1)*, *supra* n. 143, para. 63.

145   *Gasus Dosier- und Fördertechnik GmbH v. the Netherlands*, *supra* n. 6, para. 67. In later judgments, the Court spoke of 'a disproportionate and excessive burden'; see *Beyeler v. Italy*, *supra* n. 3, para. 121. See further *Chassagnou and Others v. France*, ECtHR 29 April 1999, appl. no. 25088/94, 28331/95 and 28443/95, paras. 80–85 and *Herrmann v. Germany*, ECtHR (GC) 26 June 2012, appl. no. 9300/07, paras. 93–94 concerning hunting rights. In *S.A. Dangeville v. France*, *supra* n. 11, paras. 59–61, the fair balance was held to be lacking because of the absence of a sufficient remedy to claim payment of a government debt.

146   *Almeida Garrett, Mascarenhas Falcão and Others v. Portugal*, *supra* n. 9, paras. 49–55; *Ahmet Acar v. Turkey*, ECtHR 30 January 2003, appl. no. 26546/95, paras. 25–29; *Mora do Vale and Others v. Portugal*, *supra* n. 10, paras. 38–45.

147   *Ambruosi v. Italy*, ECtHR 19 October 2000, appl. no. 31227/96, paras. 29–34.

148   *Buffalo Srl en liquidation v. Italy*, *supra* n. 11, para. 39. For delays in implementation of repayment scheme, see also *Suljagić v. Bosnia and Herzegovina*, ECtHR 3 November 2009, appl. no. 27912/02, paras. 55–57.

149   *Tsirikakis v. Greece*, ECtHR 17 January 2002, appl. no. 46355/99, paras. 60–61.

150   *Immobiliare Saffi v. Italy*, ECtHR (GC) 28 July 1999, appl. no. 22774/93, para. 59; *Lunari v. Italy*, ECtHR 11 January 2001, appl. no. 21463/93, paras. 31–34.

151   *Satka and Others v. Greece*, *supra* n. 56, paras. 48–49. See also *Consorts Richet and Le Ber v. France*, ECtHR 18 November 2010, appl. no. 18990/07, paras. 109–125, concerning the adoption of a land use plan and the State's refusal to honour contractual obligations following introduction of new regulations.

152   *Raimondo v. Italy*, ECtHR 22 February 1994, appl. no. 12954/87, para. 36; *Venditelli v. Italy*, ECtHR 18 July 1994, appl. no. 14804/89, para. 40; *Scollo v. Italy*, ECtHR 28 September 1995, appl. no. 19133/91.

As concerns the 'general interest' aim of the interference, the Court, accepting a wide margin of appreciation, has stated that 'it will respect the legislature's judgment as to what is in the general interest unless that judgment be manifestly without reasonable foundation'.[153] Thus, a wide variety of aims have been considered to be in the general interest, such as social and economic policy aims in the fields of housing, town planning and alcohol consumption, but also the protection of the environment, the need to combat international drugs trafficking, the need to preserve evidence of offences and to prevent aggravation of offences, the need to avoid unregulated hunting and encourage the rational management of game stocks and the control by the state of the market in works of art for the purpose of protecting a country's cultural and artistic heritage.[154] In the pursuance of modern social policies the states are entitled even to take measures which affect existing contracts: 'The Court observes that, in remedial social legislation and in particular in the field of rent control, it must be open to the legislature to take measures affecting the further execution of previously concluded contracts in order to attain the aim of the policy adopted.'[155]

With regard to rent control systems, the Court requires that they strike a fair balance between the competing interests. The Court makes an overall assessment which may involve not only the conditions for reducing the rent received by individual landlords and the extent of the state's interference with freedom of contract and contractual relations in the rental market, but also the existence of procedural safeguards ensuring that the operation of the system and its impact on a landlord's property rights are neither arbitrary nor unforeseeable.[156]

---

[153]   *Mellacher and Others v. Austria, supra* n. 143, para. 44; *Spadea and Scalabrino v. Italy, supra* n. 143; *Scollo v. Italy, supra* n. 152, para. 28.

[154]   See, respectively, *Mellacher and Others v. Austria, supra* n. 143, para. 47 (housing); *Allan Jacobsson v. Sweden (No. 1), supra* n. 143, para. 57 (town planning); *Tre Traktörer Aktiebolag v. Sweden, supra* n. 36, para. 56 (alcohol consumption); *Fredin v. Sweden (No. 1),* ECtHR 18 February 1991, appl. no. 12033/86, para. 50 (protection of nature); *Pine Valley Developments Ltd and Others v. Ireland, supra* n. 7 (protection of the environment); *Air Canada v. the United Kingdom, supra* n. 5, para. 39 (combatting international drugs trafficking); *Venditelli v. Italy, supra* n. 152, para. 38 (preservation of evidence of offences and prevention of aggravation of offences); *Chassagnou and Others v. France, supra* n. 145, para. 79 (avoiding unregulated hunting); *Beyeler v. Italy, supra* n. 3, paras. 112–113 (control of the market in works of art); *Longobardi and Others v. Italy,* ECtHR 26 June 2007 (dec.), appl. no. 7670/03 and *Perinelli and Others v. Italy,* ECtHR 26 June 2007, appl. no. 7718/03 (protection of archaeological heritage); *J.A. Pye (Oxford) Ltd and J.A. Pye (Oxford) Land Ltd v. the United Kingdom, supra* n. 7, paras. 67–74 (limitation period and extinguishment of title to land); *Depalle v. France, supra* n. 6, para. 81 (regional planning and environmental conservation); *Brosset-Triboulet and Others v. France,* ECtHR (GC) 29 March 2010, appl. no. 34078/02, para. 84 (protection of the property's designation as public property and of the environment); *Malfatto and Mieille v. France,* ECtHR 6 October 2016, appl. nos. 40886/06 and 51946/07, para. 63 (regional planning and environmental conservation).

[155]   *Mellacher and Others v. Austria, supra* n. 143.

[156]   *Bittó and Others v. Slovakia,* ECtHR 28 January 2014, appl. no. 30255/09, paras. 97–98. See also *Radovici and Stănescu v. Romania,* ECtHR 2 November 2006, appl. no. 68479/01, paras. 88–90 (extension of lease without possibility to claim any rent for several years); *Gauchin v.*

The Court further considers whether there had been a fair distribution of the social and financial burden involved. In a series of cases where the amount of controlled rent had remained considerably lower than the rent for similar housing in respect of which the rent control scheme did not apply, the Court found a violation of Article 1.[157]

When balancing the competing interests, the Court also considers whether the state has taken measures aimed at protecting vulnerable tenants. In the case of *Berger-Krall and Others,* concerning a housing reform resulting in higher rents and reducing security of tenure for tenants, the former holders of a specially protected tenancy had the possibility of purchasing a substitute dwelling from the municipalities under very favourable financial terms. Furthermore, previous owners willing to sell their flats to former holders of occupancy rights were eligible for a public financial reward and tenants who agreed to move out and purchase a flat or build a house were entitled to compensation of up to 80 per cent of the administrative value of the dwelling. In addition to that, rent subsidies were available to tenants in financial difficulties and socially disadvantaged people could apply to obtain another non-profit rental dwelling. Tenants who exercised their right to purchase another dwelling or build a house were entitled to special compensation and a subsidised loan.[158] The Court therefore concluded that the respondent State had ensured a distribution of the social and financial burden involved in the housing reform which had not exceeded its margin of appreciation.[159] By contrast, in the case of *Lindheim and Others* the Court found that the right of ground lease holders to claim an indefinite extension of the lease on the same conditions as previously placed the social and financial burden solely on the applicant lessors.[160] The Court invited the respondent State under Article 46 of the Convention to take appropriate legislative and/or other general measures to ensure the fair balance between the competing interests. It did, however, not specify how these interests should be balanced.[161]

---

[157] *France,* ECtHR 19 June 2008, appl. no. 7801/03, paras. 62–69; (inability to recover land when lease expired); *Almeida Ferreira and Melo Ferreira v. Portugal,* ECtHR 21 December 2012, appl. no. 41696/07, paras. 32–36 (statutory ban on landlord terminating a long lease).

[157] *Bittó and Others v. Slovakia, supra* n. 156, paras. 113 and 119. See also *Hutten-Czapska v. Poland,* ECtHR (GC) 19 June 2006, appl. no. 35014/97, paras. 224–225; *Ghigo v. Malta,* ECtHR 26 September 2006, appl. no. 31122/05, paras. 69–70; *Fleri Soler and Camilleri v. Malta,* ECtHR 26 September 2006, appl. no. 35349/05, paras. 78–80; *Edwards v. Malta,* ECtHR 24 October 2006, appl. no. 17647/04, paras. 78–79; *Urbárska Obec Trenčianske Biskupice v. Slovakia, supra* n. 122, paras. 140–146; *Lindheim and Others v. Norway,* ECtHR 12 June 2012, appl. no. 13221/08, paras. 129–136; *Statileo v. Croatia,* ECtHR 10 July 2014, appl. no. 12027/10, paras. 123–145.

[158] *Berger-Krall and Others v. Slovenia,* ECtHR 12 June 2014, appl. no. 14717/04, paras. 209–210.

[159] *Ibid.,* para. 211.

[160] *Lindheim and Others v. Norway, supra* n. 157, paras. 129–134.

[161] *Ibid.,* para. 137.

Various factors may play a role in the proportionality test.[162] The Court has, for example, on occasion referred to the fact that avenues of judicial review of the contested measures had been available to the applicant.[163] Similarly, the fact that the applicant was engaged in a commercial venture which by its very nature involved an element of risk, the circumstance that the applicant could have sought to reduce this risk, the fact that the applicant must have been aware of the possibility of restrictions on the use of his property, as well as the fact that the duration of a bankruptcy procedure was due to the lack of funds and that the state had no influence as to this aspect.[164] The termination of concession agreements for breach without compensation cannot be described as disproportionate to the control of the use of property in the public interest where it was clear that the applicants could not seek compensation in the event of termination of the contracts for breach and they had been given notice on a regular basis to remedy the breaches.[165] In the case of *OGIS-Institut Stanlislas, OGEC St. Pie X en Blanche de Castille*, the public interest of equal treatment of all schools prevailed over the confidence of some individual schools that overpayments would be restituted.[166]

Although the second paragraph of Article 1 does not explicitly require that the control of use of property be in accordance with the law (as does the second sentence of the first paragraph), the Court has taken the position that it may review the 'lawfulness' of the measures interfering with the use of property. Consequently, even if the Court's review of compatibility with domestic law as such is limited, the usual requirements of foreseeability and accessibility of the law, as well as that of legal protection against interference by public authorities, apply also in the context of the second paragraph.[167] In the case of *R & L, s.r.o. and Others*, the Court found that the rent control scheme lacked a legal basis and that, accordingly, the interference with the applicants' rights could not be considered to be lawful and

---

[162]   See, e.g., *SIA AKKA/LAA v. Latvia*, ECtHR 12 July 2016, appl. no. 562/05, paras. 77–79 (subsidiarity of the mesaure, best interest, limits of measure in scope an time).

[163]   *Gasus Dosier- und Fördertechnik GmbH v. the Netherlands, supra* n. 6, para. 73; *Air Canada v. the United Kingdom, supra* n. 5, para. 46.

[164]   See, respectively, *Pine Valley Developments Ltd and Others v. Ireland, supra* n. 7, para. 59; *Gasus Dosier- und Fördertechnik GmbH v. the Netherlands, supra* n. 6, para. 70; *Fredin v. Sweden (No. 1)*, ECtHR 18 February 1991, appl. no. 12033/86, para. 51; *F.L. v. Italy, supra* n. 9, paras. 29–34.

[165]   *Uzan and Others v. Turkey*, ECtHR 29 March 2011 (dec.), appl. no. 18240/03, paras. 102–110.

[166]   *OGIS-Institut Stanislas, OGEC St. Pie X en Blanche de Castille and Others v. France, supra* n. 11, para. 87.

[167]   *Tre Traktörer Aktiebolag v. Sweden, supra* n. 36, para. 58; *Fredin v. Sweden (No. 1)*, ECtHR 18 February 1991, appl. no. 12033/86, para. 50; *Air Canada v. the United Kingdom, supra* n. 5, para. 46. In *Raimondo v. Italy, supra* n. 152, para. 36, the Court found a violation under this head (unexplained delay in execution of domestic court judgment). See also *Frizen v. Russia*, ECtHR 24 March 2005, appl. no. 58254/00, para. 36, where the legal basis for the decision lacked completely. The Court has treated lack of compliance with domestic law also as being relevant under the proportionality test (see *supra*).

that there had been a violation of Article 1.[168] With regard to obligations flowing from Community law, the Court observed in the case of *Bosphorus Hava Yolları Turizm ve Ticaret Anonim Şirketi* that, once adopted, Regulation (EEC) no. 990/93 was generally applicable and binding in its entirety. Its 'direct applicability' was not disputed. The regulation became part of domestic law without the need for implementing legislation. Thus, the Court found that the impugned interference did not result from an exercise of discretion but from the respondent State's compliance with its legal obligations flowing from Community law.[169]

4.2. SECURE THE PAYMENT OF TAXES OR OTHER CONTRIBUTIONS OR PENALTIES

A broad margin of discretion also applies in the case of the second element of the second paragraph: securing the payment of taxes or other contributions and penalties.

Initially the Commission seemed to read this element as not placing any particular limit on national measures in this area.[170] Later, it accepted that a taxation scheme did not escape its powers of review, notably as concerns the requirements of a 'fair balance' and a 'reasonable relationship of proportionality'. It has taken the position that 'the financial liability arising out of the raising of tax or contributions may adversely affect the guarantee secured under this provision if it places an excessive burden on the person or the entity concerned or fundamentally interferes with his or its financial position'.[171]

Nevertheless, the Contracting States have a wide margin of appreciation in deciding on the type of tax or contribution they wish to levy given the assessment of political economic and social considerations that is involved.[172] A considerable margin of appreciation is also accepted in relation to measures taken by tax

---

[168]   *R & L, s.r.o. and Others v. the Czech Republic*, ECtHR 3 July 2014, appl. nos. 37926/05 et al., paras. 113–127.

[169]   *Bosphorus Hava Yolları Turizm ve Ticaret Anonim Şirketi v. Ireland*, ECtHR (GC) 30 June 2005, appl. no. 45036/98, paras. 143–148, ECHR 2005-VI.

[170]   In its report in the *Greek* case, therefore, the Commission held with regard to this latter provision that it does not prescribe any limitation, either of form or of size; p. 185.

[171]   *Wasa Liv Omsesidigt v. Sweden*, EComHR 14 December 1988 (dec.), appl. no. 13013/87, D.R. 58, p. 163, 188; *Travers and 27 Others v. Italy*, EComHR 16 January 1995 (dec.), appl. no. 15117/89, D.R. 80, p. 5, 11.

[172]   See, e.g., *Azienda Agricola Silverfunghi S.A.S. v. Italy*, ECtHR 24 June 2014, appl. nos. 48357/07 et al., paras. 101–108; *Wallishauser v. Austria (No. 2)*, ECtHR 20 June 2013, appl. no. 14497/06, paras. 63–79; *R.Sz. v. Hungary, supra* n. 58, paras. 54–62. See further *Travers and 27 Others v. Italy, supra* n. 172, p. 5, 12. One may assume that this wide margin of appreciation will apply *a fortiori* in relation to the *level* of taxation. See, however, *Gasus Dosier- und Fördertechnik GmbH v. the Netherlands, supra* n. 6, para. 60, which left open the question of whether the state's right to 'enact […] laws […] to secure the payment of taxes' is limited to procedural tax laws or whether it also covers substantive tax laws (laws that define the circumstances under which tax is due and the amounts payable). This rather mysterious statement could be taken

authorities to enforce tax obligations. In the *Gasus Dosier- und Fördertechnik GmbH* case, the Court held that a system of recovery of tax debts against goods owned by a third party was not uncommon and not incompatible *per se* with the requirements of Article 1. Considering, amongst others, the element of risk involved in the commercial venture, the applicant company's conduct, the fewer possibilities of tax authorities to protect themselves (compared to commercial creditors) and the availability of a legal remedy, the Court concluded that the proportionality requirement had been satisfied in this case.[173] In the case of *OAO Neftyanaya Kompaniya Yukos*, the Court considered that 'the authorities were obliged to take careful and explicit account of all relevant factors in the enforcement process. Such factors were to include, among other things, the character and the amount of the existing debt as well as of the pending and probable claims against the applicant company, the nature of the company's business and the relative weight of the company in the domestic economy, the company's current and probable economic situation and the assessment of its capacity to survive the enforcement proceedings. Furthermore, the economic and social implications of various enforcement options on the company and the various categories of stakeholders, the attitude of the company's management and owners and the actual conduct of the applicant company during the enforcement proceedings, including the merits of the offers that the applicant company may have made in connection with the enforcement were to be properly considered. (...) On the whole, given the pace of the enforcement proceedings, the obligation to pay the full enforcement fee and the authorities' failure to take proper account of the consequences of their actions, the Court finds that the domestic authorities failed to strike a fair balance between the legitimate aims sought and the measures employed.'[174]

In general, enforcement measures that put an individual and excessive burden on the debtor constitute a violation of Article 1.[175]

Outside the area of taxation, as well, enforcement measures such as forfeiture, or even preventive measures such as seizure, have been examined for their compatibility with the second paragraph of Article 1.[176] In the above-mentioned

---

to mean that the Court reserved the question of whether it is competent to review taxation levels under Art. 1.

[173] *Gasus Dosier- und Fördertechnik GmbH v. the Netherlands, supra* n. 6, paras. 67–74.

[174] *OAO Neftyanaya Kompaniya Yukos v. Russia,* ECtHR 20 September 2011, appl. no. 14902/04, paras. 651 and 657.

[175] See, e.g., *Rousk v. Sweden,* ECtHR 25 July 2013, appl. no. 27183/04, paras. 115–127.

[176] As concerns preventive measures, see *Raimondo v. Italy, supra* n. 152, paras. 26–33 (seizure and confiscation not held disproportionate, having regard to the importance of the fight against the Mafia); a violation was found because the confiscation continued even after a domestic court had ordered that the possessions be returned. See also *Venditelli v. Italy, supra* n. 152, paras. 35–40 (sequestration of a flat B to preserve evidence of an offence and prevent any aggravation of the offence B which lasted well beyond the judgment ending the criminal proceedings, placed a disproportionate burden on the applicant); *Microintelect OOD v. Bulgaria,* ECtHR 4 March 2014, appl. no. 34129/03, paras. 38–50 (applicant company's

AGOSI case, concerning the forfeiture of smuggled gold coins, the Commission held that the rule of proportionality requires that the innocent owner be given an opportunity to assert his property right and show that he is an innocent owner.[177] Unlike the Commission, who found a violation of Article 1, the Court concluded that it was not established that the British system failed either to ensure that reasonable account be taken of the behaviour of the applicant company or to afford it a reasonable opportunity to put its case.[178] In the case of *Džinić*, the Court held that, although in principle legitimate and justified, the seizure of the applicant's property without an assessment of whether the value of the seized property corresponded to the possible confiscation claim did not strike a fair balance.[179]

5. POSITIVE OBLIGATIONS

The Court has repeatedly held that genuine, effective exercise of the right protected by Article 1 does not depend merely on the state's duty not to interfere, but may require positive measures of protection, particularly where there is a direct link between the measures an applicant may legitimately expect from the authorities and the effective enjoyment of his or her possessions.[180] In horizontal relations, too, there might be public interest considerations involved, which may impose some obligations on the state.[181] According to the Court, allegations of a failure on the part of the state to take positive action to protect private property should be examined in the light of the general rule in the first sentence of the first paragraph of Article 1, which lays down the right to the peaceful enjoyment of possessions.[182]

---

inability to challenge the measures interfering with its rights under Art. 1, i.e. forfeiture of alcohol, and lack of any safeguards against arbitrariness not necessary in a democratic society for the achievement of the legitimate aim pursued); *Plechkov v. Romania*, ECtHR 16 September 2014, appl. no. 1660/03, paras. 91–93 (confiscation of boat did not satisfy the condition of lawfulness); *Bowler International Unit v. France*, ECtHR 23 July 2009, appl. no. 1946/06, paras. 39–41. Similarly, *Grifhorst v. France*, ECtHR 26 February 2009, appl. no. 28336/02, paras. 85–86.

177   *AGOSI v. the United Kingdom, supra* n. 142, paras. 80–92.
178   *Ibid.*, para. 60.
179   *Džinić v. Croatia*, ECtHR 17 May 2016, appl. no. 38359/13, para. 80.
180   *Hadzhiyska v. Bulgaria*, ECtHR 15 May 2012 (dec.), appl. no. 20701/09, para. 14 (heavy rainfall causing the nearby river to overflow) with reference to *Budayeva and Others v. Russia*, ECtHR 20 March 2008, appl. nos. 15339/02, 21166/02, 20058/02, 11673/02 and 15343/02, para. 172 (maintenance of mud-defence infrastructure); see further *Broniowski v. Poland, supra* n. 2, para. 143.
181   *Kotov v. Russia*, ECtHR (GC) 3 April 2012, appl. no. 54522/00, para. 109. See also *Zolotas v. Greece (No. 2)*, ECtHR 29 January 2013, appl. no. 66610/09, para. 39, ECHR 2013; *Aizpurua Ortiz and Others v. Spain, supra* n. 43, para. 50.
182   *Hadzhiyska v. Bulgaria, supra* n. 180, para. 14 (heavy rainfall causing the nearby river to overflow) with reference to *Budayeva and Others v. Russia, supra* n. 180, para. 172

The applicable criteria to positive and negative obligations do not differ in substance. In both contexts regard must be had to the fair balance to be struck between the interests of the individual and of the community as a whole. In both contexts, the state also enjoys a certain margin of appreciation in determining the steps to be taken.[183]

The nature and extent of the state's positive obligations vary depending on the circumstances.[184] The obligation to protect the right to the peaceful enjoyment of possessions is not absolute, and cannot go further than what is reasonable in the circumstances.[185] With regard to natural disaster the Court considered that 'in deciding what measures to take in order to protect private possessions from weather hazards the authorities enjoy a wider margin of appreciation than in deciding on the measures needed to protect lives. Furthermore, natural disasters, which are as such beyond human control, do not call for the same extent of State involvement as dangerous activities of a man-made nature. Accordingly, the State's positive obligations to protect property against the former do not necessarily extend as far as those in the sphere of the latter.'[186]

In the *Öneryildiz* case, the Court found a causal link between the gross negligence attributable to the State and the engulfment of the applicant's house following a methane explosion at a public rubbish tip. The Court found a breach of a positive obligation, since the State officials and authorities did not do everything within their power to protect the applicant's proprietary interests.[187] In the case of *Hadzhiyska*, the Court held that Article 1 does not require the Contracting States 'to take preventive measures to protect private possessions in all situations and all areas prone to flooding or other natural disasters. In view of the operational choices which must be made in terms of priorities and resources, any obligations arising under this provision must be interpreted in a way which does not impose an impossible or disproportionate burden on the authorities.'[188]

The complaint was manifestly ill-founded and declared inadmissible.

(maintenance of mud-defence infrastructure).

[183] *Broniowski v. Poland, supra* n. 2, paras. 143–144; *Malysh and Others v. Russia,* ECtHR 11 February 2010, appl. no. 30280/03, para. 74; *Archidiocèse catholique d'Alba Iulia v. Romania,* ECtHR 25 September 2010, appl. no. 33003/03, paras. 89–90; *Ališić and Others v. Bosnia and Herzegovina, Croatia, Serbia, Slovenia and the former Yugoslav Republic of Macedonia, supra* n. 58, paras. 100–101.

[184] *Kotov v. Russia, supra* n. 181, para. 111.

[185] *Hadzhiyska v. Bulgaria, supra* n. 180, para. 15.

[186] *Ibid.* See also *Öneryildiz v. Turkey,* ECtHR (GC) 30 November 2004, appl. no. 48939/99, paras. 134–135 (methane explosion at a rubbish tip) with reference to *Bielectric Srl v. Italy,* ECtHR 4 May 2000 (dec.), appl. no. 36811/97 (compliance with the anti-seismic regulations); *Kolyadenko and Others v. Russia,* ECtHR 28 February 2012, appl. nos. 17423/05 et al., para. 213 (overflow of river triggered by the human-controlled release of water).

[187] *Öneryildiz v. Turkey, supra* n. 186, para. 135.

[188] *Hadzhiyska v. Bulgaria, supra* n. 180, para. 16.

By contrast, where the case concerns ordinary economic relations between private parties such positive obligations are much more limited. The Court has repeatedly stressed that Article 1 cannot be interpreted as imposing any general obligation on the Contracting States to cover the debts of private entities[189] nor to maintain the purchasing power of sums deposited with banking or financial institutions.[190] However, when a private individual interferes with another individual's right to peaceful enjoyment of possessions, a positive obligation arises for the state to ensure in its domestic legal system that property rights are sufficiently protected by law and that adequate remedies are provided whereby the victim of an interference can seek to vindicate his rights, including, where appropriate, by claiming damages in respect of any loss sustained.[191] The measures, which the state can be required to take in such a situation, can be preventive or remedial. Remedial measures include an appropriate legal mechanism allowing the aggrieved party to assert its rights guaranteed by Article 1 effectively.[192] The Court has recognised the existence of procedural positive obligations under Article 1 both in cases involving State authorities[193] and in cases between private parties only.[194] In cases belonging to the latter category, the Contracting States are under an obligation to afford judicial procedures that offer the necessary procedural guarantees and therefore enable the domestic courts and tribunals to adjudicate effectively and fairly any disputes between private persons.[195] The state may be held responsible for losses caused by determinations of private-law disputes if court decisions are not given in accordance with domestic law or if they are flawed by arbitrariness or manifest unreasonableness contrary to Article 1.[196] The mere fact that the

---

[189] *Kotov v. Russia, supra* n. 181, para. 111 with reference to *Shestakov v. Russia,* ECtHR 18 June 2002 (dec.), appl. no. 48757/99; *Scollo v. Italy, supra* n. 152, para. 44; *Anokhin v. Russia,* ECtHR 31 May 2007 (dec.), appl. no. 25867/02; *Aizpurua Ortiz and Others v. Spain, supra* n. 43, para. 50.

[190] *Flores Cardoso v. Portugal,* ECtHR 29 May 2002, appl. no. 2489/09, para. 54 with reference to *Rudzińska v. Poland,* ECtHR 7 September 1999 (dec.), appl. no. 45223/99; *Gayduk and Others v. Ukraine,* ECtHR 2 July 2002 (dec.), appl. nos. 45526/99 et al. See also *Ryabykh v. Russia,* ECtHR 24 July 2003 (dec.), appl. no. 52854/99; *Todorov v. Bulgaria,* ECtHR 13 May 2008 (dec.), appl. no. 65850/01.

[191] *Blumberga v. Latvia,* ECtHR 14 October 2008, appl. no. 70930/01, para. 67.

[192] *Shesti Mai Engineering OOD and Others v. Bulgaria,* ECtHR 20 September 2011, appl. no. 17854/04, paras. 79 et seq.

[193] *Jokela v. Finland,* ECtHR 21 May 2002, appl. no. 28856/95, para. 45; see also *Zehentner v. Austria,* ECtHR 16 July 2009, appl. no. 20082/02, para. 73.

[194] *Kotov v. Russia, supra* n. 181, para. 113; *Vrzić v. Croatia,* ECtHR 12 July 2016, appl. no. 43777/13, para. 101.

[195] *Sovtransavto Holding v. Ukraine, supra* n. 50, para. 96; *Ukraine-Tyumen v. Ukraine,* ECtHR 22 November 2007, appl. no. 22603/02, para. 51; *Zagrebačka banka d.d. v. Croatia,* ECtHR 12 December 2013, appl. no. 39544/05, paras. 266 et seq.

[196] *Zagrebačka banka d.d. v. Croatia, supra* n. 195, para. 250 with reference to *Vulakh and Others v. Russia,* ECtHR 10 January 2012, appl. no. 33468/03, para. 44. See also *Melnychuk v. Ukraine, supra* n. 48.

outcome of preventive remedies are not favourable for the applicant, does not mean that the state did not comply with its positive obligation under Article 1, as it is an obligation of means, not of result.[197] In various cases, the Court has discussed the Contracting States' procedural positive obligations.[198] In the case of *Kotov*, the Court concluded, with regard to insolvency procedures, that Russian law provided for a 'deferred' compensatory remedy but the applicant failed to use it when it became available. Thus, Russia complied with its positive obligations under Article 1.[199] When the debtor is a private individual, the state's obligations are limited to providing assistance to the creditor in the enforcement of the respective court awards, for instance, through a bailiff service or bankruptcy procedures.[200] In the case of *Zolotas (No. 2)*, the Court concluded that the State has failed to fulfil its positive obligation to require that banks, in view of the potentially adverse consequences of limitation periods, should inform the holders of dormant accounts when the limitation period is due to expire and thus afford them the possibility to stop the limitation period running.[201] In the *Plechanow* case, the applicants seemed to have fallen victims of the administrative reforms, the inconsistency of the case law and the lack of legal certainty and coherence in this respect and were therefore unable to obtain due compensation for damage suffered. The Court observed that in cases relating to a public entity's liability for damage, the state's positive obligation to facilitate identification of the correct defendant is all the more important and concluded that the state did not comply with its positive obligation.[202]

6. DEROGATION

Since Article 5 of Protocol No. 1 provides on the one hand that 'all the provisions of the Convention shall apply accordingly', while on the other hand no separate mention is made of Article 15(2), it follows from this that none of the rights mentioned in Protocol No. 1 is non-derogable.

---

[197] *Zagrebačka banka d.d. v. Croatia*, *supra* n. 195, para. 274.

[198] For the failure to secure the implementation of a right protected by Art. 1, see *Malysh and Others v. Russia*, *supra* n. 183, paras. 65–76 (failure for years to legislate on the procedure for implementation of entitlement); *Archidiocèse catholique d'Alba Iulia v. Romania*, *supra* n. 183, paras. 89–98 (failure to implement government regulations providing for the restitution of property).

[199] *Kotov v. Russia*, *supra* n. 181, paras. 107 and 132–133. See also *Ceni v. Italy*, ECtHR 4 February 2014, appl. no. 25376/06, paras. 67 et seq., where the Court found that the applicant had no remedy at her disposal to have the opportunity and proportionality of the liquidator's choice examined.

[200] *Anokhin v. Russia*, *supra* n. 189 with reference to *Shestakov v. Russia*, *supra* n. 189; *Krivonogova v. Russia*, ECtHR 1 April 2004 (dec.), appl. no. 74694/01; *Kesyan v. Russia*, ECtHR 19 October 2006, appl. no. 36496/02.

[201] *Zolotas v. Greece (No. 2)*, *supra* n. 181, para. 53–55.

[202] *Plechanow v. Poland*, ECtHR 7 July 2009, appl. no. 22279/04, paras. 109–112.

CHAPTER 18

RIGHT TO EDUCATION

(Article 2 of Protocol No. 1)

Ben Vᴇʀᴍᴇᴜʟᴇɴ and Marjolein ᴠᴀɴ Rᴏᴏsᴍᴀʟᴇɴ[*]

GUIDING PRINCIPLE

Article 2 of Protocol No. 1 comprises two different, though interconnected rights. While its first sentence guarantees a right to education, its second sentence obliges the state to respect the right of parents to ensure education for their children in conformity with their fundamental convictions.

ARTICLE 2 OF PROTOCOL No. 1

No person shall be denied the right to education. In the exercise of any functions which it assumes in relation to education and to teaching, the State shall respect the right of parents to ensure such education and teaching in conformity with their own religious and philosophical convictions.

---

[*]   In the fourth edition this chapter was revised and updated by Ben Vermeulen.

CONTENTS

1. INTRODUCTION

Article 2 of Protocol No. 1 comprises two different, though interconnected rights. While its first sentence guarantees a right to education, its second sentence obliges the state to respect the right of parents to ensure education for their children in conformity with their fundamental convictions. The right to education is the primary right: the article 'constitutes a whole that is dominated by its first sentence (…). The right set out in the second sentence is an adjunct of this fundamental right to education'.[1] The right to education in the first sentence can be invoked by children[2] as well as by their parents representing them.[3] The right in the second sentence can only be invoked by parents.[4]

The first sentence states that the right to education 'shall not be denied', which suggests merely a passive duty of the state not to hinder access to the educational system, rather than the social and cultural right to education entailing a positive obligation on the part of the state. Indeed, in the *Belgian Linguistics cases*, the Court held that Article 2 of Protocol No. 1 does not require that the Contracting States ensure at their own expense, or subsidise, education of a particular type, but merely implies everyone's right 'to avail themselves of the

---

[1] *Kjeldsen, Busk Madsen and Pedersen v. Denmark*, ECtHR 7 December 1976, appl. nos. 5095/71, 5920/72 and 5926/72, para. 52; *Campbell and Cosans v. the United Kingdom*, ECtHR 25 February 1982, appl. nos. 7511/76, 7743/76, para. 40.

[2] E.g. *Townend Sr. and Townend Jr. v. the United Kingdom*, EComHR 23 January 1987 (rep.), appl. no. 9119/80; *Durairaj, Baker (formerly Durairaj) and Durairaj v. the United Kingdom*, EComHR 16 July 1987 (rep.), appl. no. 9114/80; *B. and D. v. the United Kingdom*, EComHR 16 July 1987 (rep.), appl. no. 9303/81.

[3] E.g. *Campbell and Cosans v. the United Kingdom*, *supra* n. 1, para. 39. The Court sees no reason why the position of a separated or divorced parent who does not have custody should be weaker than that of the parent who has custody; see *Vojnity v. Hungary*, ECtHR 12 February 2013, appl. no. 29617/07, para. 37.

[4] *Eriksson v. Sweden*, ECtHR (GC) 22 June 1989, appl. no. 11373/85, para. 93.

means of instruction existing at a given time'.[5] Therefore, its primary objective is to guarantee a right of equal and effective access to the existing educational institutions.[6] As the Grand Chamber held in *Şahin*, this right of access refers to all existing institutions, including higher education.[7] In addition, according to the Court, Article 2 of Protocol No. 1 obliges the state to give official recognition in one form or another (diploma's etc) to those who have completed a given type of studies with good results, since otherwise the exercise of this right would not be effective.[8] Whether this also applies to education pursued abroad has been left open so far. In any case the person in question may be required to undergo an examination in the country where recognition of those studies abroad is requested.[9]

That the right to education in Article 2 of Protocol No. 1 comprises the right to avail oneself of the 'means of instruction existing at a given time' implies that the scope of the right to education may vary from one country to another and may be subject to developments within a particular country. The right to education therefore by its very nature calls for regulation by the state. Regulation may vary in time and place, taking into account the needs and resources of the community and individuals concerned. However, regulation may never be of such a nature and scope that the essence of the right is affected.[10] Of course, it is up to the State to 'strike a balance between on the one hand the educational needs of those under its jurisdiction, and, on the other hand, its limited capacity to accommodate them'.[11] However, it is difficult to accept that a member state of the Council of Europe would not be obliged to ensure the existence of at least a system of elementary education open to all, and would be free to leave it to the 'market' to take care of that (or not). This would injure the essence, the substance of the right to education understood as a right to equal access. This right requires by implication the existence and the maintenance of a minimum of education provided or subsidised by the state, since otherwise that right would be illusory, in particular for those who have insufficient means to maintain their own institutions. Denying a person the possibility to receive primary or secondary education has such far-reaching consequences for his development and for his chances to enjoy the rights and freedoms of the Convention to the full that such treatment is contrary to the object and purpose of the whole system of the Convention, in the light of which Article 2 of Protocol No. 1 has

---

5   *Belgian Linguistics Case v. Belgium (No. 2)*, ECtHR 23 July 1968, appl. nos. 1474/62, 1677/62, 1691/62, 1769/63, 1994/63 and 2126/64, para. 3.

6   *Ponomaryovi v. Bulgaria*, ECtHR 21 June 2011, appl. no. 5335/05, para. 49.

7   *Leyla Şahin v. Turkey*, ECtHR (GC) 10 November 2005, appl. no. 4474/98, para. 134.

8   *Belgian Linguistics cases*, supra n. 5, para. 4; *Leyla Şahin v. Turkey*, supra n. 7, para. 152.

9   *X v. Belgium*, EComHR 9 October 1978 (dec.), appl. no. 7864/77; *Glazewska v. Sweden*, EComHR 10 October 1985 (dec.), appl. no. 11655/85.

10   *Cf. Ali v. the United Kingdom*, ECtHR 11 January 2011, appl. no. 40385/06, para. 62.

11   *Ponomaryovi v. Bulgaria*, supra n. 6, para. 54.

to be interpreted. This interpretation is in line with several judgments in which the Court has stressed the relevance of primary and secondary education. For instance, in the *Timishev* case the Court stated that '(t)here is no doubt that the right to education guarantees access to elementary education which is of primordial importance for a child's development'.[12] And in *Catan* the Grand Chamber has recognised the fundamental importance of primary and secondary education for every child's personal development and future success.[13] Even if access to primary education in specific circumstances has temporarily been denied for sound reasons, the Court urges the state to keep this denial as short as possible. Thus, in *Memlika v. Greece* the Court was not prepared to accept a delay of six months in the establishment of a committee which was to examine whether children, who had been wrongfully diagnosed with lepra, could proceed their education at school.[14]

As the Court ruled in the *Belgian Linguistics cases*, the state has to find a balance between the protection of the general interest of the community and respect of fundamental human rights of individuals, while giving particular importance to the latter.[15] This was confirmed by the Court in its judgment in *Campbell and Cosans*; in that case the parents complained, *inter alia*, that their children were actually denied the right to education because they did not receive the guarantee that at the school in question no corporal punishment would be applied, while there was no alternative for them. Since the refusal to accept corporal punishment in a concrete case had resulted in suspension, and the requirement itself to submit to that kind of punishment conflicted with the parents' right laid down in the second sentence of Article 2 of Protocol No. 1, there was no longer any question of a reasonable regulation of access to education and the Court consequently concluded that the right to education had been violated.[16]

But again: the state has to strike a balance between the individual rights of pupils and parents on the one hand and the public interest on the other. Although Article 2 of Protocol No. 1 does not contain a restriction clause, the state in principle has an inherent, rather wide competence to regulate the educational system through the setting and planning of the curriculum, to formulate disciplinary rules, to lay down criteria concerning access and qualification etc.[17]

For instance, reasonable disciplinary measures are undoubtedly compatible with Article 2 of Protocol No. 1.[18] It is not incompatible with this provision

---

[12]   *Timishev v. Russia*, ECtHR 13 December 2005, appl. nos. 55762/00 and 55974/00, para. 64.
[13]   *Catan and Others v. Moldova and Russia*, ECtHR (GC) 19 October 2012, appl. nos. 43370/04, 8252/05 and 18454/06, para. 144. See also *Ponomaryovi v. Bulgaria*, *supra* n. 6, paras. 56–57.
[14]   *Memlika v. Greece*, ECtHR 6 October 2015, appl. no. 37991/12.
[15]   *Belgian Linguistics cases*, *supra* n. 5, para. 5.
[16]   *Campbell and Cosans v. the United Kingdom*, *supra* n. 1, para. 41.
[17]   *Cf. Kjeldsen, Busk Madsen and Pedersen v. Denmark*, *supra* n. 1.
[18]   *Ali v. United Kingdom*, *supra* n. 10, para. 54.

for pupils who have committed disciplinary offences or who have been caught cheating, to be suspended or expelled from the institute where they study.[19] However, in the absence of any proof of cheating and with regard to an undisputed submission that the applicant had prepared for his entrance exam, the Court has found untenable the conclusion reached by the academic council that his good results could not be explained.[20] The Court also held that there had been a violation in a case in which the applicants were suspended from the university as a result of the exercise of their freedom of expression, as they had petitioned for the introduction of an optional Kurdish language course.[21]

Although Article 2 of Protocol No. 1 in principle confers a right of access to any existing type and any level of available education,[22] the conditions for access and admission as well as the duration of the possibility to study may be regulated.[23] It is an inherent feature of education that one can start or complete a study or course successfully only when the required level has been reached. For instance, conditions of entry referring to an objective assessment of this level are not contrary to the freedom of education.[24] The same holds good for restrictions resulting from admission decisions, fixed numbers of entries, limits as regards the length of the period one is allowed to spend on one's studies and the like, caused by the limited availability of facilities at a given moment in relation to the demand. Since Article 2 of Protocol No. 1 does not imply the obligation to increase this availability, there is no question of violation of the Convention as long as no discrimination or arbitrariness takes place in the admission procedure.[25]

The obligation to wear a school uniform does not violate the right to education.[26] Furthermore, in *Leyla Şahin* the Court concluded that the ban on wearing the Islamic headscarf in higher-education institutions did not contravene Article 9 of the Convention, because the ban was prescribed by law, pursued the legitimate aims of protecting the rights and freedoms of others and protecting public order (secularism, equality) and was necessary in a democratic society, taking into account a (rather wide) margin of appreciation left to the state. Because there was no violation of Article 9, Article 2 of Protocol No. 1 had not been violated either.[27] In the same vein, the Court ruled in *Kervanci* and

---

19   *Yanasik v. Turkey*, EComHR 6 January 1993 (dec.), appl. no. 14524/89; *Sulak v. Turkey*, EComHR 17 January 1996 (dec.), appl. no. 24515/94.

20   *Mürsel Eren v. Turkey*, ECtHR 7 February 2006, appl. no. 60856/00, para. 50.

21   *İrfan Temel and Others v. Turkey*, ECtHR 3 March 2009, appl. no. 36458/02.

22   E.g. *Altinay v. Turkey*, ECtHR 9 July 2013, appl. no. 37222/04, para. 31.

23   *X v. Austria*, EComHR 16 July 1973 (dec.), appl. no. 5492/72.

24   *Lukach v. Russia*, ECtHR 16 November 1999 (dec.), appl. no. 48041/99, para. 3. See also *Tarantino and Others v. Italy*, ECtHR 2 April 2013, appl. nos. 25851/09, 29284/09 and 64090/09, paras. 47–59, in which an entrance examination and a *numerus clausus* did not as such amount to a violation of Art. 2 of Protocol No. 1.

25   *Çam v. Turkey*, ECtHR 23 February 2016, appl. no. 51500/08.

26   *Stevens v. the United Kingdom*, EComHR 3 March 1986 (dec.), appl. no. 11674/85, para. 3.

27   *Leyla Şahin v. Turkey*, supra n. 7, paras. 112–121, 157–162. Cf. also *Köse and 93 Others v. Turkey*, ECtHR 24 January 2006, appl. no. 26625/0226625/02.

Dogru that the French concept of *laïcité* justifies the exclusion of Muslim pupils (from secondary education) who refuse to take off their headscarves.[28] Although these cases only concerned the prohibition to wear headscarves during physical education classes, it may be assumed that a more general prohibition would also be considered not to violate Article 9 or Article 2 of Protocol No. 1.

2. POSITIVE OBLIGATIONS

The primary objective of Article 2 of Protocol No. 1 is to guarantee non-discriminatory access to the existing educational facilities. This provision does not in general – probably apart from primary and secondary education – require that the state establishes or subsidises education of a specific type or level.[29] For instance, the state is not obliged to provide for particular courses of adult education.[30] Moreover, states are not required to establish or subsidise schools in which education is provided in one's own (minority) language,[31] nor is it their duty to guarantee the availability of schools which are in accordance with the religious conviction of the parents.[32] Furthermore, they are not obliged to provide free transport to the school of one's choice where an alternative is available which would involve free transport and which has not been shown to conflict with the parent's convictions[33] or to recognise and subsidise private denominational schools.[34] The state equally is not required to place a dyslexic child in a private specialised school with fees to be paid by the public authorities, when a place is available in an ordinary state school which has special teaching facilities for disabled children.[35] The refusal of a specific school to admit a child diagnosed with autism does not amount to a shortcoming in a State's obligations under Article 2 of Protocol No. 1, though a systematic denial of access may do.[36]

There are certain requirements, demanding that the right to be educated in one of the national languages may not be illusory. Already in the *Belgian*

---

[28] *Kervanci v. France*, ECtHR 4 December 2008, appl. no. 31645/04, paras. 71–72; *Dogru v. France*, ECtHR 4 December 2008, appl. no. 27058/5, paras. 71–72.

[29] *Belgian Linguistics cases*, *supra* n. 5, para. 3, followed by the Commission: *40 Mothers v. Sweden*, EComHR 9 March 1977 (dec.), appl. no. 6853/74; *X and Y v. the United Kingdom*, EComHR 5 July 1977 (dec.), appl. no. 7527/76; *X and Y v. the United Kingdom*, EComHR 7 December 1982 (dec.), appl. no. 9461/81; *Verein Gemeinsam Lernen*, EComHR 6 September 1995 (dec.), appl. no. 23419/94.

[30] *X v. Belgium*, EComHR 29 September 1975 (dec.), appl. no. 7010/75.

[31] *Belgian Linguistics cases*, *supra* n. 5, para. 7.

[32] *X and Y v. the United Kingdom*, *supra* n. 29.

[33] *Cohen v. the United Kingdom*, EComHR 28 February 1996 (dec.), appl. no. 25959/94, para. 1.

[34] *X. v. the United Kingdom*, EComHR 2 May 1978 (dec.), appl. no. 7782/77; *Ingrid Jordebo Foundation of Christian Schools and Ingrid Jordebo v. Sweden*, EComHR 6 March 1987 (dec.), appl. no. 11533/85.

[35] *Simpson v. the United Kingdom*, EComHR 4 December 1989 (dec.), appl. no. 14688/89.

[36] *Sanlisoy v. Turkey*, ECtHR 8 November 2016 (dec.), appl. no. 77023/12.

Linguistics cases, the Court stated that the right to education would be meaningless if it did not at least imply the right to be educated in the national language or in one of the national languages.[37] In *Cyprus v. Turkey*, the Court concluded that the abolition of the facility for children of Greek-Cypriot parents in (occupied) Northern Cyprus wishing to pursue a secondary education in the Greek language constituted an unjustified interference with Article 2 of Protocol No. 1. The children had already received primary education in a Greek-Cypriot school there and for this reason the possibility to continue education in the North (in the Turkish language) was not a viable one. The possibility to transfer the children to the South to pursue education in the Greek language did not fulfil the obligation of Article 2 of Protocol No. 1 because of the impact on family life.[38] And in *Catan v. Moldova and Russia*, the Court found that enforcing the Russification of Moldovan schools in occupied territory, thereby *de facto* denying parents and their children the right to an education in the official national language of their country – which was also their own mother tongue – violated Article 2 of Protocol No. 1.[39]

In *Scozzari and Giunta*, the applicant complained that her children, who were placed in the Il Forteto community in accordance with a care order, did not have adequate schooling, and that the only education they would be receiving was that provided within this community. The Court concluded that there was no violation of Article 2 of Protocol No. 1, because the elder son began school shortly after arriving at the community and the younger son had just reached school age and was attending a nursery school.[40]

In three cases concerning Roma families, the applicants complained that the refusal to allow them to remain on their own land where they lived in a caravan without a planning permission, resulted in their children being denied access to satisfactory education. The Court, however, concluded that the applicants had failed to substantiate their complaints that their children were effectively denied the right to education.[41] In various cases concerning Roma, complaints have been made under Article 2 of Protocol No. 1 read in conjunction with Article 14 of the Convention. In *D.H. and Others v. the Czech Republic*, the Grand Chamber noted that as a result of their turbulent history and constant uprooting the Roma had become a specific disadvantaged and vulnerable minority. The case, dealing with the placement of Roma children in special schools for children with special

---

[37]   *Belgian Linguistics cases*, *supra* n. 5, para. 3.

[38]   *Cyprus v. Turkey*, ECtHR (GC) 10 May 2001, appl. no. 25781/94, paras. 273–280. *Cf.* also *Catan and Others v. Moldova and Russia*, *supra* n. 13, para. 144.

[39]   *Catan and Others v. Moldova and Russia*, *supra* n. 13, paras. 137–150.

[40]   *Scozzari and Giunta v. Italy*, ECtHR (GC) 13 July 2000, appl. nos. 39221/98 and 41963/98, paras. 238–243.

[41]   *Coster v. the United Kingdom*, ECtHR (GC) 18 January 2001, appl. no. 24876/94, para. 137; *Lee v. the United Kingdom*, ECtHR (GC) 18 January 2001, appl. no. 25289/94, para. 125; *Jane Smith v. the United Kingdom*, ECtHR (GC) 18 January 2001, appl. no. 25154/94, para. 129.

needs, warranted particular attention, especially because it concerned minor children for whom the right to education was of paramount importance.[42] The Court found that there had been a violation of Article 14 of the Convention in conjunction with Article 2 of the First Protocol. While recognising the efforts made by the Czech authorities to ensure that Roma children receive schooling, the Court was not satisfied that the difference in treatment between Roma children and non-Roma children was objectively and reasonably justified and that there existed a reasonable relationship of proportionality between the means used and the aim pursued.[43] In *Oršuš*, the Grand Chamber held that it could not ignore that the applicants were members of the Roma minority. Additional steps were needed in order to address a high drop-out rate of Roma pupils.[44] Furthermore, in *Horváth* the Court held that in the context of the right to education of groups which had suffered past discrimination in education with continuing effects, structural deficiencies call for the implementation of positive measures in order, *inter alia*, to assist the applicants with any difficulties they encountered in following the school curriculum.[45]

In *Durmaz, Isik, Unutmaz and Sezal*, a case in which the applicants complained that they had to interrupt their studies in order to serve their prison sentences, the Court concluded that 'the fact that the applicants were only prevented during the period corresponding to their lawful detention after conviction by a court to continue their full-time education, cannot be construed as a deprivation of the right to education within the meaning of Article 2'.[46] From this decision it may be concluded that the right to education at a certain institution can be restricted as a result of a prison sentence after the conviction by a court.[47] But as will be pointed out in section 6, prisoners at least have a right to education that is available for them and which they can follow without unacceptable consequences for the execution of the penalty.

The Court's case law recognises that there is an obligation for the state to guarantee access to the existing educational facilities. But access may not be made illusory by the non-existence of a minimum of educational institutions, the non-continuance of education in a given language, a care order, the refusal of a planning permission or a prison sentence etc. However, there is no obligation

---

[42] *D.H. and Others v. the Czech Republic*, ECtHR (GC) 13 November 2007, appl. no. 57325/00, para. 87.

[43] *Ibid.*, paras. 207–208.

[44] *Oršuš v. Croatia*, ECtHR (GC) 16 March 2010, appl. no. 15766/03, paras. 147 and 177.

[45] *Horváth and Kiss v. Hungary*, ECtHR 29 January 2013, appl. no. 11146/11, para. 104. See also *Sampani and Others v. Greece*, ECtHR 11 December 2012, appl. no. 59608/09, para. 76; *Lavida and Others v. Greece*, ECtHR 30 May 2013, appl. no. 7973/10, para. 62.

[46] *Durmaz, Işik, Unutmaz and Sezal v. Turkey*, ECtHR 4 September 2001 (dec.), appl. nos. 46506/99, 46569/99, 46570/99 and 46939/99, para. 4. See also *Civan Boltan v. Turkey*, ECtHR 27 March 2012 (dec.), appl. no. 32777/09; *Hebun Hakan Akkaya v. Turkey*, ECtHR 27 March 2012 (dec.), appl. no. 32015/09.

[47] See also *Epistatu v. Romania*, ECtHR 24 September 2013, appl. no. 29343/10, paras. 64–65.

for the state to guarantee access to a specific institution. This becomes clear from *Coster*, where the Court concluded that the fact that the children had to change schools did not constitute a substantiated complaint that the children were effectively denied the right to education. Prisoners, too, only have a right to the educational facilities available to them as prisoners. That they have to intermit their studies and change to a school that teaches through correspondence lessons does not constitute a violation of Article 2 of Protocol No. 1.[48]

3. COMPULSORY EDUCATION AND HOME-SCHOOLING

The freedom of education does not imply the freedom not to receive education at all. In *Groza*, the applicant's son remained at home without any form of education for five years, because his father did not want to accept the decisions of the competent authorities to attend a special school more adapted to his special needs. The Court concluded that the Romanian authorities had observed the right of the applicant's son to receive an effective education as far as possible and found the father's complaint manifestly ill-founded.[49]

Another question is whether a system of compulsory education, leaving no room for home-schooling, is contrary to Article 2 of Protocol No. 1. The former Commission had adopted the view that 'it is clear that Article 2 of Protocol No. 1 implies a right for the State to establish compulsory schooling, be it in state schools or private tuition of a satisfactory standard, and that verification and enforcement of educational standards is an integral part of that right.'

In that particular case, the Commission concluded 'that to require the applicant parents to cooperate in the assessment of their children's educational standards by an education authority in order to ensure a certain level of literacy and numeracy, whilst, nevertheless, allowing them to educate their children at home, cannot be said to constitute a lack of respect for the applicant's rights under Article 2 of Protocol No. 1.'[50]

It is interesting to note that the Commission did not attach so much weight to the form of the (primary) education, but rather to the responsibility of the state for its quality: to guarantee a certain level of literacy and numeracy, whilst leaving the rights of the parents unimpaired as much as possible, and allowing for home-schooling. After all, even though compulsory education is not contrary to Article 2 of Protocol No. 1, it is limited by certain rights of the children and their parents, in particular the right to respect for their convictions and family life.

---

48   *Durmaz, Işık, Unutmaz and Sezal v. Turkey*, *supra* n. 46, para. 4.
49   *Groza v. Romania*, ECtHR 21 February 2012 (dec.), appl. no. 31017/05, para. 29.
50   *Family H. v. the United Kingdom*, EComHR 6 March 1984 (dec.), appl. no. 10233/83.

However, the Court has accepted the possibility of a system of compulsory education in schools that excludes any possibility of home-schooling. In *Konrad*, the applicants, who belonged to a Christian community which is strongly attached to the Bible, were refused permission for their children to be exempted from compulsory primary school attendance and to be educated by them at home. The Court observed that there was no consensus among the Contracting States with regard to compulsory attendance of primary schools. While some countries permitted home education, other states provided for compulsory attendance of state or private schools. The Court noted that the German authorities and courts had carefully reasoned their decisions and mainly stressed the fact that not only the acquisition of knowledge but also integration into and experience with society are important goals in primary-school education. The courts found that those objectives could not be met to the same extent by home education, even if that allowed children to acquire the same standard of knowledge as provided by primary-school education. The Court considered that this assumption was not erroneous and fell within the Contracting States' margin of appreciation in setting up and interpreting rules for their education systems. The Federal Constitutional Court had stressed the general interest of society in avoiding the emergence of 'parallel societies' based on separate philosophical convictions and the importance of integrating minorities into society. The Court regarded this motive as being consonant with its own case law on the importance of pluralism for democracy.[51]

4. PRIVATE SCHOOLS

As already discussed in section 1, the Court ruled in the *Belgian Linguistics cases* that Article 2 of Protocol No. 1 does not require that the Contracting States ensure at their own expense, or subsidise, education of a particular type, but merely implies the right 'to avail themselves of the means of instruction existing at a given time'.[52] However, this judgment does not answer the question whether the right to education only comprises the right to receive education or also contains the right to provide for education. Does it, for instance, include the right to provide for private education outside the system of public schools? The freedom of teaching and to organise teaching in the setting of a school – the freedom to establish private schools – is not explicitly contained in Article 2 of Protocol No. 1. However, in its report in the *Kjeldsen, Busk Madsen and Pedersen* case, the Commission took the view that the right to 'the establishment of and access

---

[51]   *Konrad v. Germany*, ECtHR 11 September 2006 (dec.), appl. no. 35504/03. In the same vein: *Sampanis and Others v. Greece*, ECtHR 5 June 2008, appl. no. 32526/05, para. 66.

[52]   *Belgian Linguistics cases*, *supra* n. 5, para. 3. *Cf.* also *Ponomaryovi v. Bulgaria*, *supra* n. 6, para. 49 and *Soukromá základní škola Cesta kúspěchu v. Praze v. the Czech Republic*, ECtHR 22 November 2011 (dec.), appl. no. 8314/10.

to private schools or other means of education outside the public school system' falls under the provision of Article 2 of Protocol No. 1.[53] And in its judgment in that same case the Court, too, by reference to the *travaux préparatoires*, seems to have recognised that the freedom to provide for private education, though not expressly set forth in the text of Article 2 of Protocol No. 1, had been present to the minds of the drafters in the different phases of the drafting process, so that an interpretation which also covers this right is not excluded.[54]

In our opinion, Article 2 of Protocol No. 1 indeed also contains the right of private organisations, groups and individuals to establish and run private educational institutions. Another interpretation, that would exclude such a right, would not be compatible with the principles of religious, philosophical and educational freedom, pluriformity and state neutrality that are enshrined not only in Article 2 of Protocol No. 1, but also in other Convention rights such as the freedoms enshrined in Articles 8–11 and the non-discrimination clause of Article 14. This also implies, that when private schools fulfil the quality conditions and standards that apply to public education, they are entitled to have their diplomas officially recognised. However, of course this right is subject to regulation by the state, in order to ensure a proper educational system as a consistent structure. In *Jordebo*, the Commission found the refusal to permit the Foundation to run the upper stage of the compulsory school compatible with Article 2 of Protocol No. 1, because the education offered did not meet the quality conditions provided in the School Act.[55] And in *Soukromá* the Court decided that the Czech state was not obliged to recognise a private school, because that school did not fulfil specific educational requirements and because there were already sufficient institutions to take care of the demands of the specific category of children.[56] The last-mentioned argument – that there are sufficient public institutions, so it is allowed to exclude private schools from the official education system – in our view is problematic. It seems to suggest that the state is thus allowed to exclude competition by private schools and to maintain a monopoly.

5. PARENTAL RIGHTS

5.1. SCOPE

The second sentence of Article 2 of Protocol No. 1 does not concern the freedom of education of those receiving education, but the right of parents to ensure education for their children in conformity with their own religious and

---

[53] *Kjeldsen, Busk Madsen and Pedersen v. Denmark, supra* n. 1.
[54] *Ibid.,* para. 50.
[55] *Ingrid Jordebo Foundation of Christian Schools and Ingrid Jordebo v. Sweden, supra* n. 34.
[56] *Soukromá základní škola Cesta k úspěchu v. Praze v. the Czech Republic, supra* n. 52.

philosophical convictions. Since Article 2 of Protocol No. 1 in principle also refers to other levels of education to the extent available, it must be assumed that the obligation of the state to ensure pluriformity in religious and philosophical respects in providing for education applies to education for older pupils and adults too.

In *Kjeldsen, Busk Madsen and Pedersen*, the Court rejected the argument of the Danish Government that the second sentence of Article 2 of Protocol No. 1 refers exclusively to specific religious instruction. According to the Court, in all aspects of education in which the Government is involved, the right of parents ensured in Article 2 of Protocol No. 1 has to be respected.[57] The parental right has to be *respected*. The Court rejected the defence of the British Government that it had fulfilled the obligation of Article 2 of Protocol No. 1 with regard to parents who objected to corporal punishment at school since it pursued a policy of gradual abolition of this punishment. Referring to the *travaux préparatoires*, the Court held: 'As is confirmed by the fact that, in the course of the drafting of Article 2, the words "have regard to" were replaced by the word "respect" (…), the latter word means more than "acknowledge" or "take into account"; in addition to a primarily negative undertaking, it implies some positive obligation on the part of the state.'[58]

This demands respect for minority views. As the Court stated in *Valsamis* and *Efstratiou*, reaffirming earlier case law: 'democracy does not simply mean that the views of a majority must always prevail: a balance must be achieved which ensures the fair and proper treatment of minorities and avoids any abuse of a dominant position.'[59]

The right to education in Article 2 of Protocol No. 1 by its very nature calls for regulation by the state.[60] Therefore, as the Court has ruled on several occasions, 'the setting and planning of the curriculum fall in principle within the competence of the Contracting States'. This implies that subjective views of parents are not decisive in determining whether the content of the instruction is in conformity with their religious and philosophical convictions: this question should be examined by reference to objective criteria.[61] The Court held that the

---

[57]   *Kjeldsen, Busk Madsen and Pedersen v. Denmark, supra* n. 1, para. 51.

[58]   *Campbell and Cosans v. the United Kingdom, supra* n. 1, para. 37.

[59]   *Valsamis v. Greece*, ECtHR 18 December 1996, appl. no. 21787/93, para. 27; *Efstratiou v. Greece*, ECtHR 18 December 1996, appl. no. 24095/94, para. 28.

[60]   *Konrad v. Germany, supra* n. 51.

[61]   *Kjeldsen, Busk Madsen and Pedersen v. Denmark, supra* n. 1, para. 53. *Cf. Valsamis v. Greece, supra* n. 59, paras. 28–33, and *Efstratiou v. Greece, supra* n. 59, paras. 29–34: the Court could not discern any military overtones in the school parade, in which the child of Jehovah's Witnesses had to take part, that could possibly offend their pacifist convictions to an extent prohibited by the second sentence of Art. 2 of Protocol No. 1. See also *Lautsi and Others v. Italy*, ECtHR (GC) 18 March 2011, appl. no. 30814/06, in which the personal view of the applicants that the Christian crucifix in public schools amounted to propaganda and indoctrination did not lead the Court to conclude that this symbol was contrary to the principles of educational pluralism and neutrality.

second sentence of Article 2 of Protocol No. 1 'aims in short at safeguarding the possibility of pluralism in education, which possibility is essential for the preservation of the "democratic society" as conceived by the Convention'. And 'in view of the power of the modern State, it is above all through State teaching that this aim must be realized'.[62]

As the government is responsible for the curriculum, it is entitled to include in teaching also the transmission of information of a directly or indirectly religious or philosophical kind, integrated with other subjects, since that will inevitably be implied in the subject matter to be taught. Article 2 of Protocol No. 1 will only be violated if the transmission of ideas does not take place in an objective, critical and pluralistic way, but assumes the character of indoctrination. The issue was carefully examined by the Court in *Kjeldsen, Busk Madsen and Pedersen*; it took into account the purpose of sex education, the general character of the instruction that did not amount to indoctrination, the fact that the instruction did not affect the rights of parents to advise and guide their children in line with their convictions, and the possibility of taking action against abuse at a particular school or by a particular teacher.[63]

Therefore, when the state prescribes a certain subject or curriculum it may not be indoctrinating, but must be objective and pluralistic. When that condition is fulfilled, the Court allows the state a margin of appreciation, for instance when deciding whether exemptions should be allowed. In *Appel-Irrgang*, Protestant applicants had filed constitutional complaints that the ethics classes were not neutral and that their secular nature was contrary to their religious beliefs. The Court, however, found that these classes were neutral, in the sense that they did not give particular weight to a specific religion or faith but made room for different beliefs and convictions. It held that the Berlin legislature's preference for a common compulsory class, instead of separating pupils on the basis of their religious or philosophical background or addressing the subject of ethics during other classes, fell within the State's margin of appreciation and was a question of expediency that in principle was not for the Court to review.[64] A similar reasoning can be found in *Dojan*, a case in which the Court observed that the sex education classes were aimed at a neutral transmission of knowledge and were based on current scientific and educational standards. There was no indication that the education provided had put into question the parent's sexual education

---

[62]   *Kjeldsen, Busk Madsen and Pedersen v. Denmark, supra* n. 1, para. 50.

[63]   *Ibid.*, paras. 53–54. See also *Appel-Irrgang and Others v. Germany*, ECtHR 6 October 2009 (dec.), appl. no. 45216/07 (the German courts had pointed to the fact that the Christian applicant parents complaining of ethics classes were free to educate their children after school and at weekends. Therefore, the parents' right to education in conformity with their religious convictions was not restricted in a disproportionate manner). *Cf. Kose and 93 Others v. Turkey, supra* n. 27: the obligation on the pupils not to cover their heads on school premises, except when attending Koran lessons, did not deprive their parents of their right to enlighten and advise their children.

[64]   *Appel-Irrgang and Others v. Germany, supra* n. 63.

of their children based on their religious convictions, or that the children had been influenced to approve or reject specific sexual behaviour contrary to their parent's convictions. The applicable Schools Act's objectives, stipulating that the aims were to provide pupils with knowledge of biological, ethical, social and cultural aspects of sexuality according to their age and maturity in order to enable them to develop their own moral views and an independent approach towards their own sexuality, were found to be consonant with the principles of pluralism and objectivity embodied in Article 2 of Protocol No. 1. Therefore, the authorities had not overstepped their margin of appreciation.[65]

Religious instruction, primarily based on a particular state religion provided at a public school, is not necessarily contrary to the requirement of pluralism inherent in Article 2 of Protocol No. 1. However, in that case it will be necessary to allow for exemptions which are not burdensome to obtain.[66] In *Folgerø*, the Court found that a system of partial exemption from the subject 'Christianity, religion and philosophy' was capable of subjecting the parents concerned – members of the Norwegian Humanist Association – to a heavy burden with a risk of undue exposure of their private life; there was a potential for conflict, likely to deter them from making such requests. The possibility for the applicant parents to seek alternative education for their children in private schools, heavily subsidised by the respondent State, could not dispense the State from its obligation to safeguard pluralism in state schools which are open to everyone.[67] It has to be noted that the judgment was far from unanimous. In a joint dissenting opinion eight members pointed out that the subject clearly fell within the limits of the margin of appreciation of the Contracting States under Article 2 of Protocol No. 1 and that the refusal to grant the applicant parents a full exemption from the subject for their children did not entail a violation of Article 2 of Protocol No. 1.

In *Zengin*, a case brought against Turkey by parents who adhered to the Alevi faith, the Court considered that the exemption procedure was not appropriate and did not provide sufficient protection to those parents who could legitimately consider that the subject taught – based on Sunni Islam – was likely to bring their children into a conflict of allegiance between the school and their own values. This was especially the case where no possibility for an appropriate alternative had been envisaged for those parents who had another

---

[65]   *Willi, Anna and David Dojan v. Germany*, ECtHR 13 September 2011 (dec.), appl. no. 319/08.

[66]   But although parents thus have the right to keep their children away from religious instruction at a public school, they cannot lay claim to separate instruction as an alternative: *Bulski v. Poland*, ECtHR 30 November 2004 (dec.), appl. nos. 46254/99 and 31888/02.

[67]   *Folgerø v. Norway*, ECtHR (GC) 29 June 2007, appl. no. 15472/02, paras. 100–102. It seems that the Court here departs from *Kjeldsen, Busk Madsen and Pedersen v. Denmark, supra* n. 1, para. 50, where it held that in determining whether Art. 2 of Protocol No. 1 was violated the grant of substantial public assistance to private schools, which could provide an alternative, should be taken into account.

religious or philosophical conviction, because the procedure for exemption was likely to subject the latter to a heavy burden and to disclose their religious or philosophical convictions in order to have their children exempted from religious instruction.[68] In the recent *Mansu Yalçin* case, the Court once again concluded that there was a breach of Article 2 of Protocol No. 1: the changes in the religious instruction curriculum adopted since *Zengin* were insufficient and the exemption procedure still was too burdensome and arbitrary.[69]

In the *Lautsi* judgment, the Court held that the presence of crucifixes in Italian state schools was not associated with compulsory teaching about Christianity. Besides, Italy opened up the school environment to other religions and there was nothing to suggest that the authorities were intolerant of pupils who believed in other religions or who held non-religious philosophical convictions. In addition, the applicants did not assert that the presence of the crucifix in classrooms had encouraged the development of teaching practices with a proselytising tendency. Lastly, the Court noted that the first applicant retained in full her right as a parent to enlighten and advise her children, to exercise in their regard her natural functions as educator and to guide them on a path in line with her own philosophical convictions.[70] These factors, taken together with the margin of appreciation that the states enjoy in these matters, led to the conclusion that there had not been a violation of Article 2 of Protocol No. 1.

The cases discussed here concern public education. It is evident, however, that the state also has competence to set minimum quality and access criteria[71] with regard to private education. However, it is still unclear to what extent the state should leave private schools – in particular those based on a strong ethos or denomination, corresponding to parental wishes – a wider autonomy than public schools in their teachings, organisation and admission policy.

5.2. RELIGIOUS AND PHILOSOPHICAL CONVICTIONS

In *Campbell and Cosans*, the Court gave a description of the concept of 'convictions'. It did not equate these convictions with 'mere' opinions or ideas: 'the word "conviction", taken on its own, is not synonymous with the words "opinions" and "ideas", such as are utilised in Article 10, which guarantees freedom of expression; it is more akin to the term "beliefs" (...) appearing in Article 9 – which guarantees freedom of thought, conscience and religion – and

---

[68] *Hasan and Eylem Zengin v. Turkey,* ECtHR 9 October 2007, appl. no. 1448/04, para. 76.
[69] *Mansu Yalçin and Others v. Turkey,* ECtHR 16 September 2014, appl. no. 21163/11, paras. 75–77.
[70] *Lautsi and Others v. Italy, supra* n. 61, paras. 74–75.
[71] *Ponomaryovi v. Bulgaria, supra* n. 6, para. 49.

denotes views that attain a certain level of cogency, seriousness, cohesion and importance.'[72]

It is evident that when a religion has been recognised by the state, the convictions flowing from that religion in principle fall within the concept of 'religious convictions'. So, in *Valsamis* and *Efstratiou* concerning Jehovah's Witnesses, the Court held that 'Jehovah's Witnesses enjoy both the status of a "known religion" and the advantages flowing from that as regards observance': for this reason, the applicants were entitled to rely on the right to respect for their religious convictions within the meaning of Article 2 of Protocol No. 1.[73]

The Court specified the concept of 'philosophical convictions' in *Campbell and Cosans*: 'Having regard to the Convention as a whole, including Article 17, the expression "philosophical convictions" in the present context denotes, in the Court's opinion, such convictions as are worthy of respect in a "democratic society" (...) and are not incompatible with human dignity; in addition, they must not conflict with the fundamental right of a child to education, the whole of Article 2 being dominated by its first sentence.'[74]

In that context and with respect to objections submitted to corporal punishment, the Court held as follows: 'The applicant's views relate to a weighty and substantial aspect of human life and behaviour, namely the integrity of the person, the propriety or otherwise of the infliction of corporal punishment and the exclusion of the distress which risk of such punishment entails. They are views which satisfy each of the various criteria listed above; it is this that distinguishes them from opinions that might be held on other methods of discipline or on discipline in general.'[75]

Likewise, in *Lautsi*, the Grand Chamber stressed that the views of supporters of secularism must be regarded as 'philosophical convictions' within the meaning of the second sentence of Article 2 of Protocol No. 1, given that they are worthy of 'respect "in a democratic society"', are not incompatible with human dignity and do not conflict with the fundamental right of the child to education.[76]

Until recently, respect for 'philosophical convictions' did not extend to the domain of language. In the *Belgian Linguistics cases*, the Court concluded that Article 2 of Protocol No. 1 'does not require of States that they should, in the sphere of education or teaching, respect parents' linguistic preferences, but only their religious and philosophical convictions. To interpret the terms "religious" or "philosophical" as covering linguistic preferences would amount to a

---

72   *Campbell and Cosans v. the United Kingdom, supra* n. 1, para. 36.

73   *Valsamis v. Greece, supra* n. 59, para. 26; *Efstratiou v.* Greece, *supra* n. 59, para. 27.

74   *Campbell and Cosans v. the United Kingdom, supra* n. 1, para. 36. See also *X, Y and Z v. the United Kingdom,* EComHR 13 October 1982, appl. no. 8566/79.

75   *Campbell and Cosans v. the United Kingdom, supra* n. 1, para. 36.

76   *Lautsi and Others v. Italy, supra* n. 61, para. 58.

distortion of their ordinary and usual meaning and to read into the Convention something which is not there.'[77]

In *Catan*, however, the Court seemed to depart from this view. This case concerned schools that were registered with the Moldovan Ministry of Education, using a curriculum set by that Ministry and providing teaching in the first official language of Moldova. The case concerned Moldovan nationals living in the Moldovan Republic of Transdniestria (MRT). Not only did the Court consider that the forced closure of the schools, based on the MRT law on languages, and the subsequent measures of harassment constituted interferences with the applicant pupils' rights of access to educational institutions existing at a given time and to be educated in their national language. In addition, the Court concluded that these measures amounted to an interference with the applicant parents' rights to ensure their children's education and teaching in accordance with their 'philosophical convictions'.[78]

Although the Court has widened the scope of the concept of 'philosophical convictions', these convictions still do not extend to pedagogical opinions of parents concerning the appropriate school for their disabled child.[79] It has not yet been decided whether opinions of parents about the appropriate school for their disabled child may be said to be based on philosophical convictions. But even assuming that this is the case, the wide measure of discretion left to the authorities implies that the second sentence of Article 2 of Protocol No. 1 does not require the placing of such a child in a regular school with additional facilities rather than in an available place in a special school,[80] nor vice versa.[81]

5.3. EDUCATION AND TEACHING

In its *Campbell and Cosans* judgment, the Court also gave a definition of the words 'education' and 'teaching': 'the education of children is the whole process whereby, in any society, adults endeavour to transmit their beliefs, culture and other values to the young, whereas teaching or instruction refers in particular to the transmission of knowledge and to intellectual development.'[82] Furthermore, it was established that once the government has assumed responsibility for education, no distinction can be made between aspects of education falling under that responsibility and aspects not falling under it, certainly not where

---

[77] *Belgian Linguistics cases, supra* n. 5, para. 6.
[78] *Catan and Others v. Moldova and Russia, supra* n. 13, para. 143.
[79] See, e.g., *Klerks v. the Netherlands*, EComHR 4 July 1995 (dec.), appl. no. 25212/94.
[80] *P.D. and L.D. v. the United Kingdom*, EComHR 2 October 1989 (dec.), appl. no. 14135/88; *Graeme v. the United Kingdom*, EComHR 5 February 1990 (dec.), appl. no. 13887/88; *Klerks v. the Netherlands, supra* n. 79.
[81] *Simpson v. the United Kingdom, supra* n. 35.
[82] *Campbell and Cosans v. the United Kingdom, supra* n. 1, para. 33.

education at public schools is concerned. That responsibility, therefore, extends beyond the curriculum, and for instance also includes the way in which discipline is maintained at the school, even though the government does not concern itself with such maintenance day by day.[83]

In *Lautsi*, the Grand Chamber considered that where the organisation of the school environment is a matter for the public authorities, that task must be seen as a function assumed by the state in relation to education and teaching, within the meaning of the second sentence of Article 2 of Protocol No. 1. It followed that the decision whether crucifixes should be present in state school classrooms forms part of the functions assumed by the respondent state in relation to education and teaching and, accordingly, falls within the scope of the second sentence of Article 2 of Protocol No. 1. Therefore, the state's obligation to respect the right of parents to ensure the education and teaching of their children in conformity with their own religious and philosophical convictions came into play.[84] The Grand Chamber held that the authorities in deciding to keep crucifixes in the classrooms of the state school system had acted within the limits of the margin of appreciation left to the respondent State in the context of its obligation to respect this right of parents.

The broad definition of 'education' set forth in *Campbell and Cosans* implies that the second sentence also applies to situations outside the framework of educational institutions. Previously, the Commission held that a decision to take a child into care did not mean that the right to custody was removed from the parents. However, since a care order temporarily transfers certain parental rights to the public authorities, it is inevitable, according to the Commission, that the contents of the parent's rights in Article 2 of Protocol No. 1 must be reduced accordingly. On the other hand, the responsible authorities must, in the exercise of their rights under a care order, have due regard to these rights. In the case under consideration the Commission, followed by the Court, concluded that there were no serious indications that, prior to the care order, the applicants had been particularly concerned with giving their children a non-religious upbringing and that, moreover, there was no reason to believe that the religious education of their son in the foster home would be in conflict with the education previously given by the applicants.[85]

6. FOREIGNERS AND DETAINEES

A foreigner cannot, by referring to Article 2 of Protocol No. 1, claim admission to a state in order to receive education at one of the existing institutions, since

---

[83]   *Ibid.*, para. 34.
[84]   *Lautsi and Others v. Italy, supra* n. 61, paras. 64–65.
[85]   *Olsson v. Sweden,* EComHR 2 December 1986 (rep.), appl. no. 10465/83, paras. 184–185 and ECtHR 24 March 1988, appl. no. 10465/83 para. 95.

only those who are already under the jurisdiction of the Contracting State may derive rights from this provision. If, however, Article 2 of Protocol No. 1 is interpreted to include the right to give instruction, this may imply that, for instance, a religious group may claim admission for its members to attend a congress, a course of study and the like, or may claim the admission of a person specifically qualified to teach.[86]

Can a foreigner challenge the refusal of the legalisation, or extension of his stay permit, by referring to Article 2 of Protocol No. 1? This was done by 15 foreign students in a complaint against the United Kingdom. The former Commission, however, declared their complaint manifestly ill-founded, holding that the power of the states to decide who may reside in their territory is not limited by Article 2 of Protocol No. 1 – unless perhaps in cases where expulsion might result in the person concerned being deprived of any elementary education.[87] It would seem that with respect to the right to primary education the situation outside the country in question must also be included in the assessment of a possible violation of the Convention, as is the case in expulsion cases where Articles 3, 6, 8 and 12 are invoked. In *Ghali*, a case dealing with a mother seeking asylum with her three-year-old child, it had not been claimed that the child would be refused schooling in Lebanon. Thus, the circumstances of the case did not raise an issue under Article 2 of Protocol No. 1.[88]

As long as a foreigner resides lawfully in a Contracting State, he of course also has a right to education.[89] However, this does not imply the right to receive education in one's home language if that is not already offered by the state concerned; there is only a right of access to the existing educational facilities (cf. section 1). The question remains whether in virtue of the first sentence of Article 2 of Protocol No. 1 it is not at least incumbent on the government to create additional facilities within the existing educational institutions for the benefit of those aliens, having taken up residence in the territory, who do not yet have sufficient command of the language in which education is conducted; otherwise the right to education will remain illusory for them for a long time. At least with regard to elementary education this question may be answered in the affirmative, on the same grounds as have been given for minimum provisions for elementary education in general (section 1).

Article 2 of Protocol No. 1 does not contain a restriction clause, which raises the difficult question as to what extent foreigners without a residence permit can derive from this provision a right to education. As was observed in section 1, this article primarily guarantees a right of equal access to the existing

---

[86]   *Cf. Church of X v. the United Kingdom*, EComHR 17 December 1968 (dec.), appl. no. 3798/68.

[87]   *15 foreign students v. the United Kingdom*, EComHR 19 May 1977 (dec.), appl. no. 7671/76.

[88]   *Abdel Fattah Ghali and Ali Mohammad Ghali v. Sweden*, ECtHR 21 May 2013 (dec.), appl. no. 74467/12, para. 41.

[89]   *Cf. Timishev v. Russia*, *supra* n. 12, para. 66.

educational institutions. Is the fact that these persons do not have a residence permit a sufficient reason for differential treatment by denying them the right of access to educational institutions that nationals and legally residing foreigners have? It seems that at least with regard to primary education this may not be the case[90] as far as it concerns foreigners who, although without legal residence, are likely to stay here for a considerable period of time, for instance because they cannot be expelled for humanitarian reasons. Denying these persons the possibility to receive primary education has such far-reaching consequences, that the fact that they do not legally stay is not a reasonable justification for this differential treatment, which therefore is contrary to Article 2 of Protocol No. 1 in conjunction with Article 14.

With regard to detainees the question of inherent limitations likewise arises, since Article 2 of Protocol No. 1 does not contain a restriction. As was mentioned before, the Court concluded in *Durmaz, Işşik, Unutmaz and Sezal* and other cases that 'the fact that the applicants were only prevented during the period corresponding to their lawful detention after conviction by a court to continue their full-time education, cannot be construed as a deprivation of the right to education within the meaning of Article 2'.[91] However, prisoners too in principle are entitled to make use of the existing educational facilities if this is compatible with the rationale of the detention on remand or the penalty of imprisonment, taking into consideration changing views of penitentiary policy.[92] In *Velev v. Bulgaria*, the Court held that, although Article 2 of Protocol No. 1 does not impose a positive obligation to provide education in prison in all circumstances, where such a possibility is available access should not be subject to arbitrary and unreasonable restrictions. In the instant case, the Court found the refusal to enrol the applicant in the prison school was not sufficiently foreseeable, nor did it pursue a legitimate aim, in a proportionate manner.[93] Thus, correspondence courses or courses via radio, subject to the necessary security measures, must as a rule be permitted, as must also the acquisition of books for purposes of study.

---

[90] See *15 foreign students v. the United Kingdom, supra* n. 87, which points in this direction: expulsion is not limited by Art. 2, unless perhaps in cases where it might result in the person concerned being deprived of any elementary education.

[91] *Durmaz, Işik, Unutmaz and Sezal v. Turkey, supra* n. 46, para. 4. Cf. also *Epistatu v. Romania, supra* n. 47, para. 62.

[92] E.g., the fact that the applicant was prevented, during the period corresponding to his lawful detention after conviction by a competent court, from having access to a portable media player to assist in his English studies could not be construed as a deprivation of the right to education within the meaning of Art. 2 of Protocol No. 1. See *Mehmet Veysi Özel v. Turkey*, ECtHR 22 October 2013 (dec.), appl. no. 4243/09.

[93] *Velev v. Bulgaria*, ECtHR 27 May 2014, appl. no. 16032/07, paras. 34 and 42.

CHAPTER 19

RIGHT TO FREE ELECTIONS

(Article 3 of Protocol No. 1)

Hansko Broeksteeg[*]

GUIDING PRINCIPLE

Article 3 of Protocol No. 1 obliges the states to hold free elections under conditions which will ensure the free expression of the opinion of the people in the choice of the legislature. Article 3 presupposes the existence of a legislature, as the basis of a democratic society. Though the article is formulated as an obligation for the states, it contains the right for individuals to vote and to stand for elections.

ARTICLE 3 OF PROTOCOL No. 1

The High Contracting Parties undertake to hold free elections at reasonable intervals by secret ballot, under conditions which will ensure the free expression of the opinion of the people in the choice of the legislature.

---

[*]   In the fourth edition this chapter was revised and updated by Jeroen Schokkenbroek.

CONTENTS

1. INTRODUCTION

1.1. OBLIGATION TO HOLD ELECTIONS

The main importance of Article 3 does not so much consist of the obligation of the states to hold free elections at reasonable intervals by secret ballot, but lies in the connection between those elections and the composition of the legislature. In fact, this means that Article 3 presupposes the existence of a representative legislature, elected at reasonable intervals, as the basis of a democratic society.[1] Therefore, properly speaking, Article 3 should have preceded the provisions of section I of the Convention as an elaboration of the concept of 'effective political democracy' referred to in the Preamble and of 'democratic society' mentioned in various provisions of the Convention. The centrality of this notion of democracy

---

[1]   See the report of 5 November 1969 in the *Greek* case, Yearbook XII (1969), p. 179.

has always been underlined by the Court. In the first ECtHR judgment with regard to Article 3 the Court emphasised that 'since it enshrines a characteristic principle of democracy, Article 3 of Protocol No. 1 is accordingly of prime importance in the Convention system'.[2] Indeed, given that an important role has been assigned to the national legislature in ensuring the enjoyment of the rights and freedoms set forth in the Convention as well as in subjecting certain of these rights and freedoms to rules which may restrict their enjoyment, it is of eminent importance that this legislature consists of democratically elected representatives of the holders of those rights and freedoms.

With respect to both its formulation and its content Article 3 constitutes an exception among the rights and freedoms laid down in the Convention and its Protocols. It is formulated neither as a right or a freedom nor as an obligation for the national authorities to refrain from interfering with the exercise of a right or freedom, but as an undertaking on the part of the Contracting States to do something; an express and not only an implied positive obligation.

What does that obligation imply for the states? From the text of Article 3 it follows that elections must be held at regular intervals, that those elections must be free, i.e. without any pressure as regards choice, and that the secrecy of the votes cast must be safeguarded.

Moreover, it follows from the word 'choice' in Article 3 that there must be a real choice, which implies that the states must make possible the creation and functioning of political parties and must enable the latter to present candidates for the elections.[3] A one-party system imposed by the state, therefore, would be contrary to Article 3. Indeed, the Court has stressed that there can be no democracy without pluralism and that political parties play an essential role in ensuring such pluralism and the proper functioning of democracy. The obligation under Article 3 to hold elections is an expression of the state's responsibility as the ultimate guarantor of the principle of pluralism. According to the Court the 'free expression of the opinion of the people in the choice of the legislature' is 'inconceivable without the participation of a plurality of political parties representing the different shades of opinion to be found in a country's population'.[4]

1.2. SUBJECTIVE RIGHTS

The formulation of Article 3 as a government undertaking to hold elections rather than as a fundamental right for individuals, might give rise to the assumption that this provision does not imply a right of the individual citizens

---

[2]   *Mathieu-Mohin and Clerfayt v. Belgium*, ECtHR 2 March 1987, appl. no. 9267/81, para. 47.

[3]   Report of 5 November 1969, *Greek* case, *supra* n. 1, p. 180. See also *X v. the United Kingdom*, EComHR 6 October 1976, appl. no. 7140/75, D&R 7 (1977), p. 95 (96).

[4]   *United Communist Party of Turkey and Others v. Turkey*, ECtHR (GC) 30 January 1998, appl. no. 19392/92, paras. 43 and 44.

to vote and to stand for election. For that reason, originally the Commission held that exclusion from the franchise, not only of particular persons,[5] but also of groups of persons,[6] was acceptable, albeit under the condition that 'such exclusion does not prevent the free expression of the opinion of the people in the choice of the legislature'.[7] However, in a decision of May 1975 the Commission clarified that 'it follows both from the preamble and from Article 5 of Protocol No. 1 that the rights set out in the Protocol are protected by the same guarantees as are contained in the Convention itself. It must, therefore, be admitted that, whatever the wording of Article 3, the right it confers is in the nature of an individual right, since this quality constitutes the very foundation of the whole Convention.'[8]

The Commission concluded 'that Article 3 guarantees, in principle, the right to vote and the right to stand for election to the legislature'.[9] Here again, however, the Commission emphasised that this does not mean that it is an absolute or unlimited right. From the words 'under conditions which will ensure the free expression of the opinion of the people in the choice of the legislature' it inferred that the Contracting States are allowed to impose certain restrictions on the right to vote and to stand for election (see hereafter).[10]

By now, the Court has recognised that Article 3 of Protocol No. 1 cannot only be invoked by individuals, but also by political parties.[11] It does, however, not include a right to express political opposition. Such a right must be based on Article 10 and Article 11.[12] Nevertheless, the Court has stressed the importance of accessibility of democracy for opposition parties. That means that restrictions of the right to vote or to stand for elections may not have a disparate impact on opposition parties: '(…), it is important to ensure access to the political arena for opposition parties on terms which allow them to represent their electorate, draw attention to their preoccupations and defend their interests (…). The Court must examine with particular care any measure which appears to operate solely, or principally, to the disadvantage of the opposition, especially where the nature of

---

[5]   Thus, e.g., of a detainee: *X v. Federal Republic of Germany*, EComHR 4 January 1960, appl. no. 530/59, Yearbook III 1960 p. 184 (190), and of a collaborator: *X v. the Netherlands*, EComHR 3 October 1975, appl. no. 6573/74, D&R 1 (1975), p. 87 (8990).

[6]   E.g. the exclusion of Belgian residents in Belgian Congo from the elections in Belgium: *X v. Belgium*, EComHR 30 May 1961, appl. no. 1065/61, Yearbook IV (1961), p. 260 (268).

[7]   *Ibid.*

[8]   *W, X, Y and Z v. Belgium*, EComHR 30 May 1975, appl. nos 6745/74 and 6746/74, Yearbook XVIII (1975), p. 236 (244).

[9]   *Ibid.*

[10]   *Ibid.*

[11]   See, e.g. *Russian Political Party of Entrepreneurs v. Russia*, ECtHR 11 January 2007, appl. nos. 55066/00 and 55638/00; *The Georgian Labour Party v. Georgia*, ECtHR 8 July 2008, appl. no. 9103/04; *Ekoglasnost v. Bulgaria*, ECtHR 6 November 2012, appl. no. 30386/05.

[12]   See, e.g., *Christian Democratic People's Party of Moldova v. Moldova*, ECtHR 14 February 2006, appl. no. 28793/02.

the measure is such that it affects the very prospect of opposition parties gaining power at some point in the future.'[13]

1.3. INHERENT LIMITATIONS

Article 3 does not comprise a limitation clause. In the *Mathieu-Mohin case*, before mentioned, the Court established that the rights that Article 3 comprises, cannot be applied unabbreviated.[14] The rights to vote and to stand for elections cannot be considered as absolute rights; there is room for implied limitations.

As a matter of course, Article 3 does not provide for a specific list of legitimate aims. The states are therefore free to assume the objectives of limitations of universal suffrage, provided that these objectives are compatible with the principles of the rule of law and the general objectives of the Convention.[15] Because of this comprehensive criterion, the Court does not often decide that the objectives, as adduced by the states, are illegitimate. A few examples are *Campagnano*, in which bankrupts were deprived from their right to vote and in which the Court concluded that this measure was only meant as an additional moral reprimand, *Sejdić and Finci* in which the restriction of the right to vote for certain representative bodies to some populations (as a result of the war in former Yugoslavia) had lost its legitimate aim, and *Tănase* in which individuals with a dual nationality were deprived of their right to stand for elections and in which the Court assumed that this measure was suggested by a structural electoral downfall of the major political party.

When scrutinising Article 3 the Court does not use the usual criteria of necessity or pressing social need. Instead, it assesses the question whether the national authorities have acted arbitrarily or disproportionally and whether the restriction is an infringement on 'the free expression of the opinion of the people in the choice of the legislature'. The rights that flow from Article 3 must be concrete and effective and may not be only theoretical or illusory.[16] The Court has to satisfy itself that restriction of the rights of Article 3 do not curtail the rights in question to such an extent as to impair their very essence and deprive them of their effectiveness. The criterion of arbitrariness means, according to the Court, that legislation concerning elections and the right to vote and to stand for elections must be sufficiently clear and precise.[17] In *Grosaru* for example, the Romanian legislation was not clear with regard to the election of minority groups and the electoral committee could not explain why it accepted the one

---

13   *Tănase v. Moldova*, ECtHR (GC) 27 April 2010, appl. no. 7/08.
14   *Mathieu-Mohin and Clerfayt v. Belgium*, *supra* n. 2, para. 52.
15   *Seyidzade v. Azerbaijan*, ECtHR 3 December 2009, appl. no. 37700/05.
16   *Podkolzina v. Latvia*, ECtHR 9 April 2002 appl. no. 46726/99.
17   *Zdanoka v. Latvia*, ECtHR 16 March 2006, appl. no. 58278/00; *Occheto v. Italy*, ECtHR 12 November 2013, appl. no. 14507/07.

interpretation of the legislation instead of the other.[18] The *Kovach* case concerned the way in which the outcome of elections was reviewed by the responsible authorities. The Court found a lack of clarity in the Ukraine Parliamentary Elections Act with regard to the possibility of declaring the outcome of elections in the electoral districts invalid. It concluded a breach of Article 3.[19]

The states have a wide margin of appreciation with regard to the restriction of the rights in Article 3. This wide margin concerns, for example, the electoral system, the organisation of elections and the conditions of eligibility, as the constitutional law of the states is dependent on their political evolution and historical influences and there is a vast variety.[20] As we will see hereafter, it seems to be that the Court assumes a wider margin of appreciation in newly established democracies, compared to older established democracies.

2. LEGISLATIVE BODIES

2.1. LEGISLATURE

Article 3 guarantees free elections by secret ballot for the legislature. The question is then what constitutional bodies belong to the legislature. The Court interprets this term rigorously. It concerns, as a matter of course, bodies with legislative powers. Furthermore, the Court answers the question by reference to the constitutional structure of the state.[21] This means that the Court takes into account the functions that the body in question fulfils in the legislative process. The term 'legislature' means, obviously, the national parliament, but that does not imply all components of parliament. If parliament exists of more than one parliamentary chamber, Article 3 only needs to apply to one of them.[22]

'Legislature', however, infers not only the national parliament. If it follows from the constitutional structure of the state, other legislative bodies with substantial legislative powers can be qualified as 'legislature' within the meaning of Article 3. The Flemish Council, the French Community Council and the Walloon Regional Council, for example, dispose of such powers that the Court designates them as a part of the Belgian legislature. They are vested 'with competences and powers wide enough' to make them 'a constituent part' thereof.[23]

---

[18] *Grosaru v. Romania*, ECtHR 2 March 2010, appl. no. 78039/01.

[19] *Kovach v. Ukraine*, ECtHR 7 February 2008, appl. no. 39424/02.

[20] *Podkolzina v. Latvia*, *supra* n. 16; *Melnychenko v. Ukraine*, ECtHR 19 October 2004, appl. no. 17707/02.

[21] *Mathieu-Mohin and Clerfayt v. Belgium*, *supra* n. 2; *Matthews v. the United Kingdom*, ECtHR (GC) 18 February 1999, appl. no. 24833/94.

[22] *Mathieu-Mohin and Clerfayt v. Belgium*, *supra* n. 2.

[23] *Ibid.*

The Court set out that the legislative body must not only dispose of rule-making power but of autonomous powers as well. This means that the constitution of a state needs to allocate the legislative powers directly to the body concerned. This means, to put it roughly, that the legislative bodies of *Länder* can be qualified as legislature within the meaning of Article 3, while in a unitary state the legislative powers merely are vested in the national parliament.

The regional councils of the autonomous Spanish Communities participate in the exercise of legislative power and are therefore part of the Spanish legislature.[24] Also some Italian regional councils are competent to enact laws in a number of pivotal areas and the Court therefore considers that the Constitution vested competence and powers that are wide enough to make them part of the legislature.[25] The regional council of Brittany, however, only disposes of deliberative powers and does not fall under the scope of Article 3.[26] Provincial or municipal powers are competent to enact by-laws but generally their powers are subordinate to the legislative powers of parliament.[27]

The Court assessed that the election of heads of state or of government leaders falls outside the scope of Article 3. The Court examines the legislative powers of these bodies, but their powers usually are accessory to the parliament's legislative powers.[28] Besides, the Court can test whether the exclusion of the right to vote is compatible with the prohibition of discrimination (Article 1 of Protocol No. 12). Referendums and plebiscites also fall outside the scope of Article 3.[29]

The Court also assessed the question whether the European Parliament is a legislature within the meaning of Article 3. The *Matthews case* concerned Gibraltar citizens that were excluded from the right to vote therefor. The supranational character of the European Parliament is, according to the Court, no reason to except the European Parliament from the scope of Article 3. Indeed, the Court stressed that the European Parliament's powers no longer are advisory and supervisory only and have moved towards being a body with a decisive role

---

24   *Federación Nacionalista Canaria v. Spain*, ECtHR 7 June 2001, appl. no. 56618/00.

25   *Santoro v. Italy*, ECtHR 1 July 2004, appl. no. 36681/97.

26   *Malarde v. France*, ECtHR 5 September 2000, appl. no. 46813/99.

27   *Cherepkov v. Russia*, ECtHR 25 January 2000, appl. no. 51501/99; *McLean and Cole v. the United Kingdom*, ECtHR 11 June 2013, appl. nos. 12626/13 and 2522/12; *Dunn and Others v. the United Kingdom*, ECtHR 13 May 2014, appl. nos. 566/10 etc.; *Uçar v. Turkey*, ECtHR 24 June 2014, appl. no. 4692/09; *Yavaş v. Turkey*, ECtHR 30 August 2016, appl. no. 16576/15.

28   *Baskauskaite v. Lithuania*, ECtHR 21 October 1998, appl. no. 41090/98; *Guliyev v. Azerbaijan*, ECtHR 27 May 2004 (dec.), appl. no. 35584/02; *Boskoski v. the former Yugoslav Republic of Macedonia*, ECtHR 2 September 2004, appl. no. 11676/04; *Paksas v. Lithuania*, ECtHR (GC) 6 January 2011, appl. no. 34932/04; *Krivobokov y. Ukraine*, ECtHR 19 February 2013, appl. no. 38707/04.

29   *Hilbe v. Liechtenstein*, ECtHR 7 September 1999, appl. no. 31981/96; *Santoro v. Italy, supra* n. 25; *McLean and Cole v. the United Kingdom, supra* n. 27.

---

to play in the legislative process of the European Community.[30] Consequently, Article 3 is applicable to the European Parliament's elections.

2.2. ELECTORAL SYSTEM

The Court does not express preference for an electoral system. In *Matthews*, the Court considered that the Convention does not create any obligation to introduce a specific system. Both the constituency voting system of elections within districts and the system of proportional representation are compatible with Article 3.[31] The same must be assumed to apply to a system of indirect elections, since the word 'direct' does not appear in Article 3 and people may be able freely to express their opinion on the ultimate composition of the legislature via an indirect system. In the Court's opinion it does not follow from Article 3 that 'all votes must necessarily have equal weight as regards the outcome of the election or that all candidates must have equal chances of victory. Thus no electoral system can eliminate "wasted votes"'.[32] Whatever the choice for an electoral system, it is consequent jurisprudence of the Court as well, that citizens need to be treated equally in the exercise of their electoral rights. This, however, does not imply that all votes must necessarily carry equal weight as regards the outcome of the election or that all candidates must have equal chances of victory. According to the Court, no electoral system can eliminate wasted votes.[33]

A specific topic concerning the electoral system is the 'reasonable intervals' as mentioned in the text of Article 3. In a case concerning the electoral system of Niedersachsen (Germany), the Commission examined whether a five-year period still constituted a 'reasonable interval' within the meaning of Article 3. It found that this question should be determined by reference to the purpose of parliamentary elections: ensuring that fundamental changes in the prevailing public opinion are reflected in the opinions of the representatives of the people. Too short an interval might impede longer-term planning for the implementation of the will of the people, while too long a period may lead to a composition of a parliament which no longer bears any resemblance to the prevailing will of the electorate. The Commission considered that a five-year interval gave appropriate weight to these various considerations and duly reflected the will of the people.[34] Of course, mid-term elections are allowed, as they are sometimes necessary after a cabinet crisis or a loss of confidence of parliament in the cabinet. A short interval

---

30 *Matthews v. the United Kingdom, supra* n. 21.
31 *Ibid.*
32 *The Liberal Party, Mrs R and Mr P v. the United Kingdom*, EComHR 18 December 1980, appl. no. 8765/79, D&R 21 (1981), p. 211 (224).
33 *Mathieu-Mohin and Clerfayt v. Belgium, supra* n. 2.
34 *Timke v. Federal Republic of Germany*, ECtHR 11 September 1995, appl. no. 27311/95.

due to (for example) a cabinet crisis can be seen as a restriction of Article 3, but as a proportionate one, with a legitimate aim.

It is remarkable that a major part of the Court's jurisprudence on electoral systems concerns the thresholds. The Court allows a wide margin of appreciation in relation to thresholds. Such thresholds exist in a variety of European constitutional systems.[35] Even a relatively high threshold may be regarded as falling within the wide margin of appreciation permitted to states in the choice of electoral system, as is illustrated by the *Yumak and Sadak* case. This case concerned a national threshold of 10 per cent in an electoral system of proportional representation. The political party of the applicants gained, in a certain district, 46 per cent of the vote, but nationwide it obtained only 6 per cent. The Court considered 'that in general a 10% electoral threshold appears excessive. In that connection, it concurs with the organs of the Council of Europe, which have stressed the threshold's exceptionally high level and recommended that it be lowered (…). It compels political parties to make use of stratagems which do not contribute to the transparency of the electoral process.'[36]

Yet, according to the Court it was relevant that political parties could avoid the threshold by submitting lists of candidates jointly with other political parties or by setting up electoral coalitions. The Court was, therefore, not persuaded that the threshold had the effect of impairing in their essence the rights secured by Article 3.

2.3. ORGANISATION OF ELECTIONS

Most states have intricate systems for regulating elections, setting deadlines and conditions for submitting (lists of) candidates, the setting-up of polling stations, counting votes etc. Here, too, the Court generally permits a wide margin of appreciation and allows for the great diversity of the way elections are organised in the various Convention states. In the *Georgian Labour Party* case, the Court considered that the proper management of electoral rolls is a precondition for a free and fair ballot.[37] The national authorities are free in their choice of electoral roll systems. To determine the electoral roll, the national authorities can, for example, use municipal registers or they may ask voters to register themselves. The national authorities are entitled to require a certain amount of signatures when nominating or when submitting a list of candidates. Such a requirement can warrant that only viable political parties, which have sufficient adherents,

---

[35]   *Partei Die Friesen v. Germany*, ECtHR 28 January 2016 (dec.), appl. no. 65480/10 (threshold of 5%).

[36]   *Yumak and Sadak v. Turkey*, ECtHR 8 July 2008, appl. no. 10226/03.

[37]   *The Georgian Labour Party v. Georgia, supra* n. 11.

participate in the elections.[38] Also the requirement of a deposit is compatible with Article 3. The legitimate aim thereof is preventing unreasonable high administrative costs of the registration of political parties and guaranteeing the candidature of viable political parties.[39]

Elections are often organised by electoral committees or councils. These committees and councils need to be sufficiently independent. They need to demonstrate a 'genuine concern for upholding the rule of law and protecting the integrity of the election'.[40] In the *Podkolzina* case, the Court described some requirements for the bodies that have to decide on the election results: '(…) such a finding must be reached by a body which can provide a minimum of guarantees of its impartiality. Similarly, the discretion enjoyed by the body concerned must not be exorbitantly wide; it must be circumscribed, with sufficient precision, by the provisions of domestic law. Lastly, the procedure for ruling a candidate ineligible must be such as to guarantee a fair and objective decision and prevent any abuse of power on the part of the relevant authority.'[41]

In *Ofensiva Tinerilor*, the Court reaffirmed that electoral committees may not enjoy a too wide a discretion and that the composition of such a committee must safeguard impartiality.[42] Electoral committees and councils also must function in a transparent manner; there must be guarantees against the appointment of persons who could reasonably be considered to be involved in an inherent conflict of interests.[43] Decisions concerning the elections and on the election results must be subject to appeal to a court.[44]

---

[38] *Tête v. France*, ECtHR 9 December 1987, appl. no. 11123/84; *Desmeules v. France*, ECtHR 3 December 1990, appl. no. 12897/87; *Mihaela Mihai Neagu v. Romania*, ECtHR 6 March 2014, appl. no. 66345/09; *Soberanía de la Razón v. Spain*, ECtHR 26 May 2015, appl. no. 30537/12.

[39] *Sukhovetskyy v. Ukraine*, ECtHR 28 March 2006, appl. no. 13716/02; *Ekoglasnost v. Bulgaria*, ECtHR 6 November 2012, *supra* n. 11.

[40] *Karimov v. Azerbaijan*, ECtHR 25 September 2014, appl. no. 12535/06.

[41] *Podkolzina v. Latvia*, *supra* n. 16. See also *Gahramanli and Others t. Azerbaijan*, ECtHR 8 October 2015, appl. no. 36503/11; *Shukurov v. Azerbaijan*, ECtHR 27 October 2016, appl. no. 37614/11.

[42] *Ofensiva Tinerilor v. Romania*, ECtHR 15 December 2015, 16732/05.

[43] *The Georgian Labour Party v. Georgia*, *supra* n. 11; *Grosaru v. Romania*, *supra* n. 18; *Tahirov v. Azerbaijan*, ECtHR 11 June 2015, appl. no. 31953/11; *Annagi Hajibeyli v. Azerbaijan*, ECtHR 22 October 2015, appl. no. 2204/11; *Gasimli and Others v. Azerbaijan*, ECtHR 17 December 2015, appl. nos. 25330/11, 25340/11, 25345/11, 25361/11 and 25645/11; *Vugar Aliyev and Others v. Azerbaijan*, ECtHR 17 December 2015, appl. nos. 24853/11, 28465/11, 28502/11 and 31970/11; *Bagirov and Others v. Azerbaijan*, ECtHR 17 December 2015, appl. nos. 17356/11, 30504/11, 31959/11, 31996/11 and 32060/11; *Soltanov and Others v. Azerbaijan*, ECtHR 16 June 2016, appl. nos. 30362/11, 30581/11, 30728/11, 30799/11 and 66684/12; *Gaya Aliyev and Others v. Azerbaijan*, ECtHR 16 June 2016, appl. nos. 29781/11, 29808/11, 30372/11, 30473/11, 30478/11 and 30487/11; *Mammadli and* Others *v. Azerbaijan*, ECtHR 30 June 2016, appl. nos. 2326/11, 8055/11, 25355/11, 30750/11.

[44] *Namat Aliyev v. Azerbaijan*, ECtHR 8 April 2010, appl. no. 18705/06; *Gambar and Others v. Azerbaijan*, ECtHR 9 December 2010, appl. nos. 4741/06, 22457/06, 22654/06, 24506/06, 36105/06, 40318/06.

2.4. CONCLUSION

We can conclude that the Contracting Parties generally have a wide margin of appreciation with regard to the set-up of their electoral system. The Court has shown considerable reticence when it comes to assessing the various aspects thereof such as thresholds, the possibility of preference votes, the reasonable intervals of elections, electoral rolls, the requirement of signatures etc. The margin of appreciation is only exceeded when the electoral system is unclear or arbitrary for voters or for candidates. In the *Grosaru* case, for example, the electoral laws were not sufficiently clear. The electoral committee could not explain sufficiently why it applied the one interpretation of the electoral law and not the other.[45]

3. THE RIGHT TO VOTE AND TO STAND FOR ELECTION

3.1. THE RIGHT TO VOTE

a. Essence

When a complaint concerns the right to vote, the Court continuously scrutinises initially whether the core of this right has been affected. In that case, the Court automatically concludes that there has been a breach of Article 3. The very essence of Article 3 is 'the free expression of the opinion of the people in the choice of the legislature'. Only in a few cases does the Court finds an infringement of the core of Article 3. That is often the case when certain groups of citizens are excluded from the right to vote.

In the *Matthews* case, for example, the Court was faced with a situation where the whole population of a territory (Gibraltar) could not take part in the election for the European Parliament at all. Matthews, as a resident of Gibraltar, was thereby completely denied any opportunity to express her opinion in the choice of the members of the European Parliament. As the legislation which emanates from the European Community forms part of the legislation in Gibraltar, the applicant was, according to the Court, directly affected by the exclusion of her right to vote.[46] After having found that Article 3 applied to these elections (see *infra* section 2.1), the Court held that the very essence of the applicant's right to vote was denied.

---

[45]   *Grosaru v. Romania*, ECtHR 2 March 2010, appl. no. 78039/01. See also *Kovach v. Ukraine*, *supra* n. 19; *Namat Aliyev v. Azerbaijan*, *supra* n. 44; *Kerimova v. Russia*, ECtHR 30 *September* 2010, appl. no. 20799/06; *Melnychenko v. Ukraine*, *supra* n. 20.

[46]   *Matthews v. the United Kingdom*, *supra* n. 21, para. 64.

The Court reached the same conclusion in the *Aziz* case. In this case, the Court criticised the fact that the Cypriot legislature had failed to lay down rules allowing the applicant and other members of the Turkish Cypriot community living in the Government-controlled part of Cyprus to vote in parliamentary elections. The 1960 Cypriot Constitution had provided for two separate electoral lists, one for each community. However, this system had not been applied since the 1960s, owing to the special situation on the island. Members of the Turkish Cypriot community (some 1,000 people) were thereby prevented from voting in the elections, since they could not be registered on the Greek-Cypriot electoral roll. The Court observed that the system envisaged by the Constitution had been rendered ineffective and that there was a manifest lack of legislation to solve the ensuing problems. Consequently, the applicant 'was completely deprived of any opportunity to express his opinion in the choice of the members of the House of Representatives of the country of which he is a national and where he has always lived'.[47] This amounted to both an impairment of the very essence of his right to vote and to discrimination within the meaning of Article 14 of the Convention.[48]

Apart from these cases in which a part of the population was generally excluded from the right of vote, this right can be restricted for specific reasons, such as nationality, residency, imprisonment and the incapacity to vote. We will discuss these specific reasons below.

b.   *Nationality and residency*

Restriction of the franchise to the state's own nationals is very common and to residents is still fairly common. In several states, the law provides that citizens may take part in elections in the country in question only if they also have residence in that country. The Court considered this restriction as being in conformity with Article 3. In the *Doyle* case, it advanced the following justifications for such a restriction: '(…) firstly, the assumption that a non-resident citizen is less directly or less continually concerned with his country's day-to-day problems and had less knowledge of them; secondly, the fact that it is impracticable for the parliamentary candidates to present the different electoral issues to citizens abroad and that non-resident citizens have no influence on the selection of candidates or on the formulation of their electoral programmes; thirdly, the close connection between the right to vote in parliamentary elections and the fact of being directly affected by the acts of the political bodies so elected; and, fourthly, the legitimate concern the legislature may have to limit the influence of citizens living abroad in elections on issues which, while admittedly fundamental, primarily affect persons living in the country.'[49] Consequently, the

---

[47]   *Aziz v. Cyprus*, ECtHR 22 June 2004, appl. no. 69949/01, para. 29.

[48]   *idem*, paras. 30 and 36–38.

[49]   *Doyle v. the United Kingdom*, ECtHR 6 February 2007, appl. no. 30158/06.

applicant's situation was different from that of a resident citizen which justified the residence requirement.

In the *Shindler* case, the Court reassessed these considerations. Since *Doyle*, migration has increased and as a result of new techniques non-residents can more easily keep in touch with their own state. Though states accept more and more legislation whereby non-residents obtain the right to vote, the Court does not accept a general obligation on the part of the state to ensure a right to vote for non-residents.[50]

States can require a duration of residency before granting the right to vote. The Court accepts the requirement of four years of residency[51], but a term of 10 years can only be proportionate where serious circumstances exist, such as a fragile post-war society, after an armed conflict. Such a conflict occurred in New Caledonia, which resulted in (temporary) restrictions of the right to vote.[52]

c. Imprisonment

With regard to the right to vote of prisoners, the Strasbourg case law has long remained restrictive. In the case of a Dutch conscientious objector, who complained about a rule in the Netherlands according to which every prison sentence of more than one year automatically resulted in a suspension of the exercise of the right to vote for three years, the Commission concluded that, taking into account the legislator's margin of appreciation, such a measure did not go beyond the restrictions justifiable in the context of Article 3 of Protocol No. 1.[53] In the case of an Irish prisoner, who was disenfranchised because the law simply did not foresee a right for prisoners to vote, the Commission referred to its case law and held that the fact that all of the convicted prisoner population cannot vote does not affect the free expression of the opinion of the people in the choice of the legislature. It added that the position under Irish law could not be considered to be arbitrary in view of the margin of appreciation and the jurisprudence of the Convention organs.[54]

In the 'famous' *Hirst* case, the Court took a new position. It established some general requirements with regard to the disenfranchisement of prisoners. Such a restriction is, in principle, permitted with 'the aim of preventing crime by sanctioning the conduct of convicted prisoners and also the aim of enhancing civic responsibility and respect for the rule of law'.[55] Restrictions are, however, not always allowed. In brief, the Court considered that a general and automatic

---

50   *Shindler v. the United Kingdom*, ECtHR 7 May 2013, appl. no. 19840/09. See also *Sitaropoulos v. Greece*, ECtHR 15 March 2012, appl. no. 42202/07.
51   *Polacco and Garofalo v. Italy*, ECtHR 15 September 1997, appl. no. 23450/94.
52   *Py v. France*, ECtHR 11 January 2005, appl. no. 66289/01.
53   *H. v. the Netherland*s, EComHR 4 July 1983, appl. no. 9914/82, D&R 33 (1983), p. 242 (245246).
54   *Holland v. Ireland*, EComHR 14 April 1998, appl. no. 24827/94.
55   *Hirst v. the United Kingdom*, ECtHR (GC) 6 October 2005, appl. no. 74025/01.

disenfranchisement of the right to vote of prisoners, thus a general exclusion, is contrary to Article 3. A provision with such a content is, according to the Court, a 'blunt instrument': 'It strips of their Convention right to vote a significant category of persons and it does so in a way is indiscriminate. The provision imposes a blanket restriction on all convicted prisoners in prison. It applies automatically to such prisoners, irrespective of the length of their sentence and irrespective of the nature of gravity of their offence and their individual circumstances. Such a general, automatic and indiscriminate restriction on a vitally important Convention right must be seen as falling outside any acceptable margin of appreciation, however wide that margin may be, and as being incompatible with Article 3 of Protocol No. 1.'[56]

The Court applied and refined these principles in various similar cases. In *Scoppola (No. 3)*, the Court reconsidered the obligatory involvement of a judge. On the one hand, the Court reaffirmed the principles set out in the *Hirst* judgment, in particular the fact that when disenfranchisement affects a group of people generally, automatically and indiscriminately, based solely on the fact that they are serving a prison sentence, irrespective of the length of the sentence and of the nature or gravity of their offence and their individual circumstances, it is not compatible with Article 3. On the other hand, the Court 'points out that the *Hirst* ECtHR makes no explicit mention of the intervention of a Judge among the essential criteria for determining the proportionality of a disenfranchisement measure'. In the Court's opinion not only a judge, but also legislation could sufficiently guarantee the proportionality of restrictions on prisoners' voting rights, since such legislation could distinguish between groups to such an extent that disenfranchisement is no longer a blunt instrument: 'legal provisions (…) defining the circumstances in which individuals may be deprived of the right to vote show the legislature's concern to adjust the application of the measure to the particular circumstances of the case in hand, taking into account such factors as the gravity of the offence committed and the conduct of the offender.'[57]

---

56   See also *Frodl v. Austria*, ECtHR 8 April 2010, appl. no. 20201/04.
57   *Scoppola v. Italy (No. 3)*, ECtHR (GC) 22 May 2012, appl. no. 126/05. See also *Calmanovici v. Romania*, ECtHR 1 July 2008, appl. no. 42250/02; *Cucu v. Romania*, ECtHR 13 November 2012, appl. no. 22362/06; *Anchugov and Gladkov v. Russia*, ECtHR 4 July 2013, appl. nos. 11157/04 and 15162/05; *Söyler v. Turkey*, ECtHR 17 September 2013, appl. no. 29411/07; *Pleş v. Romania*, ECtHR 8 October 2013, appl. no. 15275/10; *Murat Vural v. Turkey*, ECtHR 21 October 2014, appl. no. 9540/07; *Brânduşe v. Romania*, ECtHR 27 October 2015, appl. no. 39951/08; *Leonte v. Romania*, ECtHR 10 November 2015, appl. no. 23931/10; *Kulinski and Sabev v. Bulgaria*, ECtHR 21 July 2016, appl. no. 63849/09. There are several British cases, including a pilot ECtHR procedure: *Greens and M.T. v. the United Kingdom*, ECtHR 23 November 2010, appl. nos. 60041/08 and 60054/08; *McLean and Cole v. the United Kingdom*, supra n. 27; *Dunn and Others v. the United Kingdom*, supra n. 27 (and 130 others); *Firth and Others v. the United Kingdom*, ECtHR 12 August 2014, appl. nos. 47784/09 (and 9 others); *McHugh and Others v. the United Kingdom*, ECtHR 10 February 2015, appl. no. 51987/08 (and 1.014 others); *Millbank and Others the United Kingdom*, ECtHR 30 June 2016, appl. nos. 44473/14 (and 21 others).

In other cases, exclusion of the right to vote is not automatic, but is a specifically imposed sanction. In the *Labita* case, for example, the applicant's voting rights had been automatically suspended as a result of the special police supervision measure that had been imposed on him, even though he had been finally acquitted in the criminal proceedings brought against him. The Court noted that, under Italian law, persons subject to such supervision forfeited their civil rights because they were considered to represent a danger to society or, as in the present case, suspected of belonging to the Mafia. The Government feared that their right to vote might be exercised in favour of other members of the Mafia. The Court had 'no doubt that temporarily suspending the voting rights of persons against whom there is evidence of Mafia membership pursues a legitimate aim'. However, the special supervision measure which had triggered the suspension of voting rights was applied after the applicant had been acquitted on the ground that he had not committed the offence. There was, therefore, no concrete evidence on which a suspicion of Mafia membership could be based and the Court, holding that the removal of the applicant from the electoral register was not proportionate, found a violation of Article 3.[58]

d. Incapacitated

People that are incompetent to vote can be disenfranchised. In *Alajos Kiss*, the Court considered that disenfranchisement of incapacitated pursued the legitimate aim of 'ensuring that only citizens capable of assessing the consequences of their decisions and making conscious and judicious decisions should participate in public affairs'. The Hungarian legislator however, did not make an appropriate difference between persons under whole and under partial guardianship, which resulted in a breach of Article 3: 'The Court cannot accept, however, that an absolute bar on voting by any person under partial guardianship, irrespective of his or her actual faculties, falls within an acceptable margin of appreciation.'

Similar as to prisoners, this restriction needs to be sufficiently individualised: an automatic, general ban is not compatible with Article 3: 'The applicant in the present case lost his right to vote as a result of the imposition of an automatic, blanket restriction on the franchise of those under partial guardianship. (...) The Court therefore concludes that an indiscriminate removal of voting rights, without an individualized judicial evaluation and solely based on a mental disability necessitating partial guardianship, cannot be considered compatible with the legitimate grounds for restricting the right to vote.'[59]

---

[58]   *Labita v. Italy*, ECtHR (GC) 6 April 2000, appl. no. 26772/95, paras. 202–203. See also *Santoro v. Italy*, *supra* n. 25, paras. 58–59, where an excessive delay in executing this special measure (with the result that the applicant missed the opportunity to vote in 2 elections) was held to be neither in accordance with law nor necessary.

[59]   *Alajos Kiss v. Hungary*, ECtHR 20 May 2010, appl. no. 38832/06. See for similar cases *Gajcsi v. Hungary*, ECtHR 23 September 2014, appl. no. 62924/10; *Harmati v. Hungary*, ECtHR 21 October 2014, appl. no. 63012/10.

e. Bankruptcy

Finally, in some Contracting States it was possible for a judge to impose disenfranchisement as an additional punishment on bankruptcy. The Commission accepted such a restriction of the right to vote, but the Court has pointed out that disenfranchisement during the procedure of bankruptcy served no legitimate aim insofar as it was purely meant to be an additional moral reprimand.[60]

3.2. THE RIGHT TO STAND FOR ELECTIONS

a. Essence

As we explained in the previous section, the Court continuously scrutinises initially whether the core of the right to vote has been affected. The same applies to the right to stand for elections. If the core of the right to stand for elections has been affected, the Court automatically concludes that there has been a breach of Article 3. That is regularly the case when certain groups of citizens are excluded from the right to stand for elections. So, the scrutiny of this right resembles very much to the scrutiny of the right to vote.

An example of such an exclusion of groups of citizens from the right to stand for elections (and therefore of a breach of Article 3) is the *Sejdić and Finci* case. In this case the Bosnian legislation made a difference between 'constituent peoples' (Bosniaks, Croats and Serbs) and 'others'. These others were remaining ethnic minorities and persons that would not like to affiliate themselves with the 'constituent peoples'. Only the 'constituent peoples' were represented in the House of the Peoples, a chamber of the bicameral parliament, and in the 'Presidium', the triumvirate that fulfils the Presidency of the State. Applicants, Jewish and Roma, were therefore excluded from their right to stand for elections. This exclusion can, according to the Court, serve a legitimate aim, for example in a very fragile post-war society, in which a balance between population groups has to be found. This aim can, however, not be accepted for too long. After so many years and several positive developments, the Court could not accept that certain ethnic groups were excluded from their right to stand for elections. The Court concluded that there was a violation of Article 3 of Protocol No. 1 in conjunction with Article 14, and, with regard to the right to stand for the so-called Presidium elections, which did not fall within the scope of Article 3 of Protocol No. 1, of Article 1 of Protocol No. 12.[61]

---

[60]   *Campagnano v. Italy*, ECtHR 23 March 2006, appl. no. 77955/01; *Collarile and Others v. Italy*, ECtHR 18 December 2012, appl. nos. 10652/02, 21532/05, 37211/05, 6723/06, 12373/06, 13533/06, 23466/06, 28978/06, 29698/06, 29699/06, 29704/06, 23003/06, 25473/06, 29693/06.

[61]   *Sejdić and Finci v. Bosnia and Herzegovina*, ECtHR (GC) 22 December 2009, appl. nos. 27996/06, 34836/06. See for similar cases *Zornic v. Bosnia and Herzegovina*, ECtHR 15 July

Apart from this case in which a part of the population was generally excluded from the right to stand for elections, this right can be restricted for specific reasons, such as residency, incompatibilities, the fulfilment of previous (political) office or language requirements. We will discuss these specific reasons below.

b. Residency

On the other hand, in the *Melnychenko* case formal application of a residence requirement as ground for refusal to register a candidate having his legal residence in the country but actually living abroad as a refugee, was found to be in breach of Article 3. The Court accepted that stricter requirements may be imposed on the eligibility to stand for election to parliament, as distinguished from voting eligibility (see *infra*); it would not preclude a five-year continuous residence requirement for potential parliamentary candidates as this might be appropriate to enable such persons to familiarise themselves with the issues associated with the parliament's work. Moreover, it would correspond to the interests of a democratic society that the electorate be in a position to assess the candidate's personal qualifications and ability to best represent its interests in parliament. On the specific facts of the case, however, the Court found a violation, since the authorities had applied the residence requirement in a formalistic manner and because it found the applicant's hasty flight from the country and his fear of persecution understandable.[62]

c. Incompatibilities

Certain professions may be incompatible with the fulfilment of a parliamentary mandate. In *Lykourezos*, the Court accepted the incompatibility of the ancillary position as a barrister.[63] The same applies to the profession of prosecutor.[64]

Several cases concerned restrictions of the right to stand for election which applied in respect of civil servants. At issue in the *Gitonas* case was a Greek rule which precluded certain categories of holders of public office from standing for election and being elected in any constituency where they have performed their duties for more than three months in the three years preceding the elections. The Court held that '[s]uch disqualification, for which equivalent provisions exist in several member States of the Council of Europe, serves a dual purpose that is essential for the proper functioning and upholding of democratic regimes, namely ensuring that candidates of different political persuasions enjoy equal

---

2014, appl. no. 3681/06; *Stranka and Others v. Bosnia and Herzegovina*, ECtHR 26 April 2016, appl. no. 414/11; *Šlaku v. Bosnia and Herzegovina*, ECtHR 26 May 2016, appl. no. 56666/12.

62   *Melnychenko v. Ukraine*, *supra* n. 20, paras. 57–58, 63 and 65–66.

63   *Lykourezos v. Greece*, ECtHR 15 June 2006, appl. no. 33554/03.

64   *Barski and Święczkowski v. Poland*, ECtHR 2 February 2016, appl. nos. 13523/12 and 14030/12.

means of influence (since holders of public office may on occasion have an unfair advantage over other candidates) and protecting the electorate from pressure from such officials who, because of their position, are called upon to take many – and sometimes important – decisions and enjoy substantial prestige in the eyes of the ordinary citizen, whose choice of candidate might be influenced.'[65]

While admitting that the Greek system was complex as regards the precise categories of public officials covered by the restriction, the Court did not consider it to be arbitrary or disproportionate. The fact that it was based on objective criteria for disqualification, which prevented the Greek Special Supreme Court from having regard to any special features of each case, was not unreasonable 'having regard to the enormous practical difficulty in proving that a position in the civil service had been used to electoral ends'. The Court also accepted as reasonable the Greek court's assimilation of the applicants' situations (for example, Gitonas had been on secondment from an investment bank to the Prime Minister's office) to the posts explicitly described in the relevant legislation, this being an issue of interpretation of domestic law and thus a matter primarily left to the national authorities.[66]

In the *Ahmed* case, the Court concluded that the restrictions applicable to local civil servants in the United Kingdom (who were prevented from standing for election as long as they held politically restricted posts) did not violate Article 3. The relevant regulations had a legitimate aim, namely to secure the political impartiality of senior officers. Nor could it be maintained that the restrictions limited the very essence of the applicants' rights under Article 3 having regard to the fact that they only operated for as long as the persons concerned occupied politically restricted posts; furthermore, any of the applicants wishing to run for elected office was at liberty to resign from his post.[67]

d. Previous (political) office

Holding or having held a certain office also may be a reason for exclusion from the right to stand for elections, for example when these positions have been held in a former dictatorial (for example communist) regime. In *Ždanoka*, the Court pointed out that active membership of the Communist Party could justify the exclusion of the right to stand for elections. The Court considered it relevant that the legislation on this matter was sufficiently precise and individualised. The Court also held, however, that such exclusion is only permitted in states in transition, i.e. states which have a newly acquired democratic order and need to recover from a former non-democratic regime. By contrast, a provision like

---

[65] *Gitonas and Others v. Greece*, ECtHR 1 July 1997, appl. nos. 18747/91, 19376/92, 19379/92, 28208/95 and 27755/95, para. 40.

[66] *Ibid.*, para. 44.

[67] *Ahmed and Others v. the United Kingdom*, ECtHR 23 September 1998, appl. nos. 22954/93, para. 75.

the one at stake in *Ždanoka* would not be permitted in long vested democracies and even in transition states, they should be of a temporary nature.[68] Moreover, such provisions should be sufficiently clear and precise. In the *Ādamsons* case, for example, the Court did not accept a general exclusion of all former agents of secret services and of security forces from the right to stand for elections, without distinguishing according to the amount of time individuals had been such an agent or the tasks or behaviour of the former agents.[69]

e. Language requirements

In the *Podkolzina* case, which concerned language requirements attached to the right to stand for election to the Latvian Parliament, the Court confirmed that states have a broad latitude to establish constitutional rules on the status of members of parliament, including criteria for declaring them ineligible.[70] The Court accepted that it is in principle for the state alone to choose the working language of the national parliament and that, having regard to their margin of appreciation, requiring candidates in parliamentary elections to have a sufficient knowledge of the official language pursues the legitimate aim of ensuring the normal functioning of the state's institutional system. However, the Court found that, in the absence of any guarantee of objectivity, the procedure followed was incompatible with the requirements of procedural fairness and legal certainty that must be satisfied in relation to candidates' eligibility.[71] The decision to strike Ms Podkolzina off the list of election candidates was, therefore, disproportionate and violated Article 3.

f. Exercising the parliamentary mandate

Quite logically, the Court has interpreted the right to stand for election as also including a right of the person elected to (continue to) exercise the mandate received. This is illustrated by the *Selim Sadak* case, where the applicants, who were elected parliamentarians and members of a pro-Kurdish party, were automatically prohibited from exercising their parliamentary mandates as a result of the dissolution of that party. The Court noted that the dissolution of the political party by the Constitutional Court was based on grounds unrelated to the applicants' personal political activities. In view also of the extreme severity of the measure inflicted upon them the Court found that the sanction was disproportionate and incompatible with the very essence of the right to stand for election and to exercise their mandate which Article 3 granted to them. It added that the measure had also infringed the sovereign power of the

---

[68]   *Ždanoka v. Latvia, supra* n. 17.

[69]   *Ādamsons v. Latvia*, ECtHR 24 June 2008, appl. no. 3669/03.

[70]   *Podkolzina v. Latvia, supra* n. 16, para. 33.

[71]   *Ibid.*, paras. 34 and 36.

electorate that had elected them to parliament.[72] Also in later similar cases the Court considered such measures as disproportionate.[73] In *Paunovic and Milivojevic*, it reaffirmed that a political party cannot submit a resignation letter of a people's representative; only the parliamentarian himself is competent for that purpose.[74]

---

[72] *Selim Sadak v. Turkey (No. 2)*, ECtHR 11 June 2002, appl. nos. 25144/94, 26149-26154/95, 27100/95 and 27101/95, paras. 33 and 37–40.

[73] *Kavakci v. Turkey*, ECtHR 5 April 2007, appl. no. 71907/01; *Silay v. Turkey*, ECtHR 5 April 2007, appl. no. 8691/02; *Ilicak v. Turkey*, ECtHR 5 April 2007, appl. no. 15394/02; *DTP v. Turkey*, ECtHR 12 January 2016, appl. nos. 3840/10, 3870/10, 3878/10, 15616/10, 21919/10, 39118/10 and 37272/10.

[74] *Paunovic and Milivojevic v. Serbia*, ECtHR 24 May 2016, appl. no. 41683/06.

CHAPTER 20

PROHIBITION OF IMPRISONMENT FOR DEBT

(Article 1 of Protocol No. 4)

Sjoerd BAKKER[*]

GUIDING PRINCIPLE

No one shall be deprived of his liberty merely on the ground of inability to fulfil a contractual obligation.

ARTICLE 1 OF PROTOCOL No. 4

No one shall be deprived of his liberty merely on the ground of inability to fulfil a contractual obligation.

---

[*]   In the fourth edition this chapter was revised and updated by Jeroen Schokkenbroek.

CONTENTS

1. SCOPE

Article 5(1) of the Convention contains the following provision: 'Everyone has the right to liberty and security of person. No one shall be deprived of his liberty save in the following cases and in accordance with a procedure prescribed by law:
(…)
(b) the lawful arrest or detention of a person for noncompliance with the lawful order of a court or in order to secure the fulfilment of any obligation prescribed by law (…)'

Article 1 of Protocol No. 4 (which provision corresponds with Article 11 of the International Covenant on Civil and Political Rights)[1] refers to the notion of 'deprivation of liberty' contained in Article 5 above and further restricts the possibility of deprivation of liberty mentioned in that article subparagraph (1) (b) 'for non-compliance with the lawful order of a court in order to secure the fulfilment of any obligation prescribed by law'. The wording 'deprived of his liberty' is designed to cover loss of liberty for any length of time, whether by detention or by arrest.[2]

In those states which have ratified Protocol No. 4, the courts will not be allowed to give such an order for arrest or detention merely on the ground that the person in question is unable to pay a debt or to meet some other contractual obligation, such as non-delivery, non-performance or non-forbearance.[3] Although Protocol No. 4 dates from the late 1960s[4], there have so far been few cases, in which (successful) complaints of a violation of Article 1 have been made. In a number of cases, where an actual complaint was made, the claim for infringement of Article 1 was rejected for the reason that the obligation in question was not of a contractual nature.[5] It should be pointed out, however, that

---

[1]   Art. 11 of said Covenant reads: 'No one shall be imprisoned merely on the ground of inability to fulfil a contractual obligation.'
[2]   See Explanatory Report – ETS 46 – Human Rights (Protocol No. 4), p. 3.
[3]   See Explanatory Report – ETS 46 – Human Rights (Protocol No. 4), p. 3 and D. Harris, M. O'Boyle, E. Bates, and C. Buckley, *Law of the European Convention on Human Rights*, 3rd edn., Oxford: Oxford University Press, 2014, p. 952.
[4]   Protocol No. 4 entered into force on 2 May 1968. For an overview of ratifications, see Appendix I.
[5]   See, e.g., *Göktan v. France*, ECtHR 2 July 2002, appl. no. 33402/96, and *Gatt v. Malta*, ECtHR 27 July 2010, appl. no. 28221/08. See also P. Leach, *Taking a Case to the European Court of*

the classification as chosen by the national legislator of a given custodial measure as being of a penal or other nature, is not in itself decisive. See the *Öztürk* case in which the European Court of Human Rights held: 'The Convention is not opposed to States, in the performance of their task as guardians of the public interest, both creating or maintaining a distinction between different categories of offences for the purposes of their domestic law and drawing the dividing line, but it does not follow that the classification thus made by the States is decisive for the purposes of the Convention.'[6]

Article 1 speaks of 'inability'. If a debtor is reasonably able to fulfil a contractual obligation, but refuses to do so, Article 1 does not exclude deprivation of liberty. As an example, see section 918 of the German code of civil procedure, according to which '(a)rresting a debtor in person is an available remedy (…) if this is required in order to ensure compulsory enforcement against the property of the debtor when such compulsory enforcement is at risk'. Article 585 of the Dutch code of civil procedure contains a similar provision and entails the possibility of detention on the ground that the person in question is unwilling to meet a contractual obligation (other than to pay a debt). Article 588 of the said code, however, forbids such a detention in the case that the debtor is unable to fulfil the obligation, for which detention has been requested.

Moreover, there is the word 'merely'. If a debtor acts in a fraudulent or malicious way, Article 1 does not bar his detention on that ground, even if it is established or it appears afterwards that he was unable to pay his debt.[7] A person whose detention had been ordered by the court because at the request of the creditor he had refused to make an affidavit in respect of his property contrary to the law, was deemed not to be entitled to the protection of Article 1.[8] In its report to the Committee of Ministers, the Committee of Experts gives the following examples of cases to which Article 1 does not apply: a person orders a meal at a restaurant knowing that he is unable to pay; through negligence a person fails to supply goods when he is under a contract to do so; a debtor is preparing to leave the country to avoid meeting his commitments.[9] This emphasis on the word 'merely' seems to be followed in the case law on Article 1, which tends

---

    Human Rights, 3rd edn., Oxford: Oxford University Press, 2011, p. 437; see also the judgment (*supra* 5.4) of the Dutch Supreme Court HR 6 October 1998, *NJ* 1998 no. 880.

6   *Öztürk v. Germany*, ECtHR (GC) 21 February 1984, appl. no. 8544/79.

7   See Explanatory Report – ETS 46 – Human Rights (Protocol No. 4), p. 3 and Explanatory Reports on the Second to Fifth Protocols to the European Convention for the Protection of Human Rights and Fundamental Freedoms, submitted by the Committee of Experts to the Committee of Ministers, H(71)11 (1971), pp. 39–40.

8   See *X v. Federal Republic of Germany*, ECtHR 18 December 1971, appl. no. 5025/71, Yearbook XIV (1971), p. 692 (696 698). See also J.L. Murdoch, Article 5 of the European Convention on Human Rights: The protection of liberty and security of person, *Human rights files* (Issue 12), Council of Europe Publishing, 2002, p. 45.

9   See Explanatory Report – ETS 46 – Human Rights (Protocol No. 4), p. 4.

to conclude to non-applicability of this provision.[10] As a result the prohibition which it contains has only a limited scope.

2. DEROGATION

As to the question of whether the rights and freedoms are non-derogable, for Protocol No. 4 the same reasoning applies as that set out above with regard to Protocol No. 1: since Article 6(1) of Protocol No. 4 declares that all the provisions of the Convention are applicable and does not make any addition to the enumeration of Article 15(2), it must be assumed that, under the circumstances and conditions referred to in Article 15(1), derogations from the provisions of Protocol No. 4 are allowed.

---

[10]   See, e.g., *Ninin v. France*, ECtHR 15 May 1996, appl. no. 27373/95; *Göktan v. France, supra* n. 5
        and *Gatt v. Malta, supra* n. 5.

CHAPTER 21

FREEDOM OF MOVEMENT

(Article 2 of Protocol No. 4)

Janneke Gerards[*]

GUIDING PRINCIPLE

To be able to freely move around, choose one's own place of residence and leave the country whenever one wishes clearly are hallmarks of liberty. These rights are all protected by Article 2 of Protocol No. 4, albeit that there are considerable possibilities for restriction. The liberty of movement complements the prohibition of arbitrary derivation of liberty of Article 5 ECHR, as well as the right to respect for one's private life of Article 8.

ARTICLE 2 OF PROTOCOL No. 4

1. Everyone lawfully within the territory of a State shall, within that territory, have the right to liberty of movement and freedom to choose his residence.
2. Everyone shall be free to leave any country, including his own.
3. No restrictions shall be placed on the exercise of these rights other than such as are in accordance with law and are necessary in a democratic society in the interests of national security or public safety, for the maintenance of ordre public, for the prevention of crime, for the protection of health or morals, or for the protection of the rights and freedoms of others.
4. The rights set forth in paragraph 1 may also be subject, in particular areas, to restrictions imposed in accordance with law and justified by the public interest in a democratic society.

---

[*]   This chapter is an elaborated and updated version of a chapter published earlier by the author in J.H. Gerards et al. (eds.), *Sdu Commentaar EVRM. Deel 1 – materiële bepalingen [Sdu ECHR Commentary. Part 1 – substantive provisions]*, Den Haag: Sdu 2013. In the fourth edition this chapter was revised and updated by Ben Vermeulen.

CONTENTS

1. INTRODUCTION

Article 2 of Protocol No. 4 to the Convention protects three different rights and contains two different exception clauses. The first paragraph of Article 2 of Protocol No. 4 protects the right to liberty of movement and the freedom to choose one's residence. The second paragraph guarantees the freedom to leave any country, including one's own. The first exception clause, laid down in paragraph 3, is applicable to all three rights and is modelled after the exception clauses of Articles 8–11 ECHR. Paragraph 4 lays down the second exception clause, which entails that, in particular areas, the liberty of movement and the freedom to choose one's residence may be subjected to restrictions imposed in accordance with the law and justified by the public interest in a democratic society.

This chapter first pays attention to the scope of protection of Article 2(1) of Protocol No. 4, as well as the interrelationship between the rights protected by this Article and the right to liberty as guaranteed by Article 5 ECHR and the right to respect for one's private and family life of Article 8 ECHR (section 2). Section 3 then discusses five types of situations in which the Court has applied the rights protected by Article 2(1) of Protocol No. 4 in relation to the exception clauses of Article 2(3) and (4) ECHR: obligations to stay in a certain place (e.g. house arrest and the prohibition to leave one's place of residence); prohibitions to enter a certain area and removal orders; restrictions of the freedom to move around in the country; restrictions to the right to choose one's residence; and restrictions in particular areas. Finally, section 4 deals with the right to leave (and return) to one's country as laid down in Article 2(2) of Protocol No. 4, seen in combination with the exception clause of Article 2(3) of Protocol No. 4.

2. SCOPE

2.1. 'LAWFULLY WITHIN THE TERRITORY'

The liberty of movement of Article 2 of Protocol No. 4 needs to be guaranteed only to persons 'lawfully within the territory of a State'. Accordingly, the provision does not prevent the States Parties from setting conditions for the entry or the stay of foreigners, nor does the Court have jurisdiction to decide on the reasonableness of restrictions of the freedom of liberty of immigrants or asylum seekers who have entered the country unlawfully.[1] The limitation to the scope of Article 2 of Protocol No. 4 is particularly relevant where an individual has been granted conditional entry to the state's territory, as was the case in *Omwenyeke*.[2] The applicant in that case had been granted a provisional residence permit which directed that, pending the decision on his asylum request, he should reside and remain within the city of Wolfsburg. The Court accepted that, outside this city, the applicant was not 'lawfully' within German territory, which meant he could not rely on the right to liberty of movement.

The Court's judgment in the *Piermont* case further shows that Article 2 of Protocol No. 4 does not apply if an initially lawful stay is ended by an expulsion or removal order.[3] The applicant, a German national, had visited French Polynesia in her capacity as member of the European Parliament. She had taken part in a demonstration where she had publicly expressed her support for independence of French Polynesia. Shortly afterwards, she was served with an expulsion order that also prohibited her from re-entering the territory. According to the Court, the expulsion and prohibition order meant that Mrs Piermont was no longer lawfully present on Polynesian territory. For that reason, she could not complain about the interference with the exercise of her right to liberty of movement.[4]

The same is true when an exclusion order prohibits an individual from entering the country. This is also illustrated by the case of Mrs Piermont, who wanted to travel to New Caledonia after her visit to Polynesia. There she was served with an order excluding her from the territory, which meant she could not lawfully enter New Caledonia. For that reason, the Court could not hold Article 2 of Protocol No. 4 applicable.[5]

Important to understanding the Court's judgment in *Piermont* is Article 5(4) of Protocol No. 4. This article provides that, if a state has declared the Protocol to be applicable to any territory for whose foreign relations it is responsible, that

---

[1] *Cf.* Explanatory Report to Art. 2 of Protocol No. 4, ETS No. 46, paras. 7–8 and see, e.g., *M.S. v. Belgium*, ECtHR 31 January 2012, appl. no. 50012/08.

[2] *Omwenyeke v. Germany*, ECtHR 20 November 2007 (dec.), appl. no. 44294/04.

[3] *Piermont v. France*, ECtHR 27 April 1995, appl. nos. 15773/89 and 15774/89.

[4] *Ibid.*, para. 44.

[5] *Ibid.*, para. 49.

territory and the territory of the state to which the Protocol already applies by virtue of the ratification shall be treated as separate territories for the application of Article 2 of Protocol No. 4. Given that France has laid down such a declaration in respect of French Polynesia, the Court had to regard French Polynesia as a separate territory, where different rules could apply concerning the entry and residence of aliens as compared to metropolitan France. To give another example, the Kingdom of the Netherlands has declared that the European part of the Kingdom (the Netherlands), the Caribbean part of the Netherlands (the islands Bonaire, Sint Eustatius and Saba), and the self-governing Kingdom countries Aruba, Curaçao and Sint Maarten must be regarded as separate territories for the purposes of Protocol 4.[6] This means that entry to the European part of the Kingdom of the Netherlands may be refused to persons living in the Caribbean entities without there being a need to meet the requirements set by Article 2 of Protocol No. 4.

2.2. RELATION TO OTHER ARTICLES

The liberty of movement guaranteed by Article 2 of Protocol No. 4 is closely related to the right to liberty protected by Article 5 ECHR. In practice, it is not always easy to distinguish between limitations of the liberty of movement and actual deprivation of liberty. This can be illustrated by the first case in which the Court had to express itself on the demarcation of the two provisions: *Guzzardi*.[7] Guzzardi was suspected of being a member of a Mafia group and he had been detained on remand pending criminal proceedings. When his detention on remand could no longer be extended, he was placed under 'special supervision' on the small island of Asinara (about 50 km^2). During his stay on the island, which was to last for three years, Guzzardi was to report to the supervisory authorities twice a day, he was not allowed to return to his residence later than 10 p.m. or could not go out before 7 a.m., he could not frequent bars or night-clubs, and he was to inform the supervisory authorities in advance each time he wished to make or receive a long-distance call. In its judgment in this case, the Court expressly acknowledged that the difference between deprivation of and restriction upon liberty is one of degree or intensity, not one of nature or substance.[8] It held that the applicability of either Article 5 of Article 2 of Protocol No. 4 depends on the concrete situation and on a range of criteria, in particular the type, duration, effects and manner of implementation of the measure in question.[9] Taking such criteria into account, the Court found that in Guzzardi's case, the restrictive regime offered hardly any opportunities for social

---

[6]   Declaration of 27 September 2010 (<http://conventions.coe.int> declarations to Protocol No. 4).
[7]   *Guzzardi v. Italy*, ECtHR 6 November 1980, appl. no. 7367/76.
[8]   *Ibid.*, para. 93.
[9]   *Ibid.*, para. 92.

contacts and supervision was carried out strictly and on an almost constant basis. Although the Court concluded that it might not be possible to speak of 'deprivation of liberty' on the strength of one of these factors taken individually, they cumulatively and in combination raised an issue under Article 5 rather than Article 2 of Protocol No. 4.[10]

Except where a regime is so restrictive in fact that it amounts to deprivation of liberty, as in *Guzzardi*, restrictions such as the requirement to stay at a certain address (house arrest), to report to the police on a regular basis and not to leave a certain place without notifying the police generally have been regarded as restrictions of the liberty of movement.[11] Moreover, the Court tends to apply Article 2 of Protocol No. 4 instead of Article 5 to prohibitions to leave one's place of residence, as it regards these as 'minimal intrusive measures'.[12]

Importantly, this also means that Article 2 of Protocol No. 4 can serve as a kind of 'fall back clause' in cases where a measure does not amount to actual deprivation of liberty and Article 5 does not apply. Rather implicitly this is apparent from the *Austin* case.[13] The applicants had taken part in a demonstration against globalisation in London. At a certain point, they had wanted to go home, but they were not permitted to leave Oxford Circus, where the police had formed a cordon containing the participants for public order reasons and crowd control. They had been free to leave only after a few hours, when the public order risks had decreased. The Court held that the restrictions did not amount to a real deprivation of liberty, but it admitted that the containment had constituted a clear restriction on the freedom of movement. Although it could not further examine the complaint under Article 2 of Protocol No. 4 because the United Kingdom is not party to that Protocol, it is clear that this provision normally would have applied as an alternative to Article 5 ECHR and thereby would have offered some legal protection against arbitrary restrictions.

Article 2 of Protocol No. 4 does not only complement Article 5, but it also stands in a close relationship to the right to respect for one's private and family life (Article 8 ECHR). The case of *Kotiy* is illustrative in this regard. The case concerned a businessman who lived with his family in Germany, but who often travelled to Ukraine for his work. At some point, he was arrested in Ukraine and a prohibition on travelling abroad was imposed on him during the criminal investigations.[14] As a consequence, he was unable to see his wife and children and entertain his professional and personal relationships. The Court found

---

[10]   *Ibid.*, para. 95.
[11]   E.g. *Raimondo v. Italy*, ECtHR 22 February 1994, appl. no. 12954/87, para. 39; *Labita v. Italy*, ECtHR (GC) 6 April 2000, appl. no. 26772/95; *Villa v. Italy*, ECtHR 20 April 2010, appl. no. 19675/06, paras. 41–43.
[12]   *Luordo v. Italy*, ECtHR 17 July 2003, appl. no. 32190/96; *Fedorov and Fedorova v. Russia*, ECtHR 13 October 2005, appl. no. 31008/02, para. 41.
[13]   *Austin and Others v. the United Kingdom*, ECtHR (GC) 15 March 2012, appl. nos. 39692/09, 40713/09 and 41008/09.
[14]   *Kotiy v. Ukraine*, ECtHR 5 March 2015, appl. no. 28718/09.

that the right to private and family life had been violated by the restrictions, and for that reason, it did not see any need to deal with the separate claim concerning the liberty of movement of Article 2 of Protocol No. 4. Thus, similar to the cases overlapping with Article 5, the Court decides on the applicability of either Article 8 or Article 2 of Protocol No. 4 based on the specific facts of each individual case. When the case mainly seems to affect private or family life, it opts for application of Article 8,[15] but when the case in essence relates to the liberty of movement, the Court prefers to apply Article 2 of Protocol No. 4.[16]

3. RESTRICTIONS

3.1. OBLIGATIONS TO STAY IN A CERTAIN PLACE

In several European states it is common to secure the availability of a suspect in a criminal case for interrogation or for court hearings by imposing house arrest or by ordering the suspect not to leave his place of residence without notification. Similar restrictions may be imposed on individuals involved in bankruptcy proceedings in order to facilitate progress in the proceedings and protect the interests of the creditors.[17] Further, as was mentioned in section 2.1, individuals may be subjected to supervision regimes if they are suspected of being involved in criminal organisations. In particular in Italy, restrictions to the freedom of movement are regularly imposed on persons suspected of having connections with the Mafia. Such measures have in common that they include an obligation for the individual to stay in a certain place and thus clearly limit the individual's liberty of movement. The Court has accepted that these kinds of restrictive measure may serve the interests of public order or safety, the prevention or crime or the protection of the rights and freedoms of others.[18] The main question to be answered usually is whether they are in accordance with law as well as necessary in a democratic society, as required by Article 2(3) of Protocol No. 4.

In applying the necessity test the Court tends to leave quite some leeway to the state, even if it does not expressly mention the margin of appreciation doctrine in relation to this provision. A preventive measure restricting the liberty of movement can be justified, for example, if it is based on a reasonable fear that the person concerned may in the future commit criminal offences.[19] Such reasonable fear should be based on concrete evidence, which must relate to objective factors making it likely that the individual is involved in criminal activities.[20]

---

[15] For another example, see *Penchevi v. Bulgaria*, ECtHR 10 February 2015, appl. no. 77818/12.
[16] E.g. *Stamose v. Bulgaria*, ECtHR 27 November 2012, appl. no. 29713/05 and *Kerimli v. Azerbaijan*, ECtHR 16 July 2015, appl. no. 3967/09.
[17] E.g. *Luordo v. Italy, supra* n. 12.
[18] See, e.g., *Labita v. Italy, supra* n. 11; *Luordo v. Italy, supra* n. 12, para. 93.
[19] E.g. *Labita v. Italy, supra* n. 11, para. 195.
[20] *Idem.*

As regards the proportionality of restrictions of movement, the Court has taken account of the particular character and intrusiveness of the measures. A 'minimal intrusive measure' like the requirement not to leave one's place of residence can be justified more easily than a more restrictive supervision regime.[21] The Court also has attached considerable weight to the duration of a restriction of movement. Even the relatively 'light' requirement not to leave one's place of residence may become a disproportionate measure if it is unreasonably protracted. The Court has found a violation of Article 2 of Protocol No. 4, for example, where the applicant was not allowed to move away from his place of residence for a period of 14 years and eight months, even though there was nothing in the case file to suggest that the applicant actually wanted to leave his place of residence or was refused permission to do so.[22] By contrast, a restriction of shorter duration may be justified if there are clear indications of a genuine public interest which outweigh the individual's right to freedom of movement.[23] In its review of these kinds of restriction, the Court will pay particular attention to the question whether the applicants actually sought to leave the area of their residence and, if so, whether permission to do so was refused.[24]

In addition to the necessity and proportionality of restrictive measures, the Court attaches great value to procedural fairness and access to effective remedies. The person concerned should be duly and promptly informed about measures limiting his liberty of movement.[25] Moreover, especially if the measure is of longer duration there must be an accessible and effective remedy for regular re-examination of the necessity and proportionality of the measure, preferably by a court.[26]

3.2. PROHIBITION FROM ENTERING A CERTAIN AREA

If an individual is ordered not to enter a certain area for a certain period of time, this clearly constitutes a limitation of the liberty of movement. Although there is hardly any case law on this type of limitations, an example can be found in the case of *Landvreugd*.[27] The Mayor of Amsterdam had designated the 'Ganzenhoef' area in Amsterdam as a safety risk area. The applicant had been found in the area, using hard drugs, on several earlier occasions, and he had been ordered to leave the area several times. He also had been warned that he would have to

---

[21]   *Fedorov and Fedorova v. Russia*, *supra* n. 12, appl. no. 31008/02, para. 41.
[22]   *Luordo v. Italy*, *supra* n. 12, para. 96. The Court also has held that a measure imposed for a period of 10 years inevitably must be regarded as disproportionate: *Nikiforenko v. Ukraine*, ECtHR 18 February 2010, appl. no. 14613/03, para. 57.
[23]   *Hajibeyli v. Azerbaijan*, ECtHR 10 July 2008, appl. no. 16528/05, para. 63.
[24]   *Antonenkov and Others v. Ukraine*, ECtHR 22 November 2005, appl. no. 14183/02, para. 64.
[25]   *Raimondo v. Italy*, *supra* n. 11, para. 39.
[26]   E.g. *Villa v. Italy*, *supra* n. 11, paras. 51–52.
[27]   *Landvreugd v. the Netherlands*, ECtHR 4 June 2002, appl. no. 37331/97.

either desist from using hard drugs in the area, or stay away.[28] After Landvreugd had neglected the warning on yet a further occasion, a prohibition order was issued for a period of 14 days in order to protect public order.[29] Reviewing the prohibition order in the light of Article 2(3) of Protocol No. 4, the Court held that the warnings had made it sufficiently clear to the applicant what would be the consequences of his acts. Taking into consideration that the applicant could institute objection proceedings and a subsequent appeal to a court, it also accepted that adequate safeguards were afforded against possible abuse.[30] Finally, the Court considered that the prohibition order was not disproportionate, since the applicant did not live or work in the Ganzenhoef area and it had been provided that he could enter the area if that would be necessary, for instance to collect his social security benefits.[31] In such circumstances, the prohibition order was considered to be compatible with Article 2 of Protocol No. 4.

3.3. FREEDOM TO MOVE AROUND

The liberty of movement also encompasses the right to freely move around on the territory of the country where one is lawfully resident. If a citizen is refused entry to a certain region or province or if he is prevented from crossing administrative borders within the state, this constitutes an interference with Article 2(1) of Protocol No. 4.[32] According to the case law available on this topic, restrictions on the freedom to move around may be justified under Article 2(3) of Protocol No. 4 if they are provided for by law, pursue a legitimate aim and are necessary in a democratic society. Orders stopping and refusing someone at an internal administrative border further must be properly formalised and recorded and may not disclose any arbitrariness or discrimination.[33]

It is important to note, however, that not every limitation of one's liberty of movement will require a justification. The case of *Colon*, for example, concerned the entry to an area in the city of Amsterdam which was designated as a safety risk area.[34] One of the consequences of this designation was that any person present in the area might be subjected to a preventive search for weapons. The applicant, who resided in the safety risk area, stated that he felt inhibited in his freedom to move around because of the constant fear of being subjected to the humiliation of a search. The Court held that such subjective feelings alone did not mean that Article 2 of Protocol No. 4 should be held applicable in the case. This only would

---

28   *Ibid.*, para. 63.
29   *Ibid.*, para. 64.
30   *Ibid.*, para. 65.
31   *Ibid.*, paras. 72–73.
32   *Timishev v. Russia*, ECtHR 13 December 2005, appl. nos. 55762/00 and 55974/00, para. 44.
33   *Ibid.*, paras. 48 and 59.
34   *Colon v. the Netherlands*, ECtHR 15 May 2012 (dec.), appl. no. 49458/06.

have been different if there were actual and objective impediments to his exercise of his right to liberty of movement, which in this case it did not find to exist.[35]

3.4. FREEDOM TO CHOOSE RESIDENCE

Article 2(1) of Protocol No. 4 not only safeguards the liberty of movement, but also the freedom to choose residence. A rare example of a case in which the Court applied this freedom is *Tatishvili*, a case in which a stateless person complained about the impossibility to be registered as residing on a certain address.[36] As a consequence, she experienced many practical difficulties in her daily life, such as difficulties in obtaining medical assistance, and she was exposed to administrative penalties and fines.[37] The Court held that the impossibility of having her place of residence registered interfered with the applicant's liberty of movement and her freedom to freely choose residence.[38] The Court also found that the registration had been refused because the application form had not been complete, but the authorities had not indicated to the applicant which documents or information were lacking. As a result, the refusal to register the applicant's place of residence was not in accordance with national law.[39] This judgment confirms that the Court attaches great value to procedural fairness and the presence of sufficient safeguards against arbitrary use of powers.

3.5. RESTRICTIONS IN PARTICULAR AREAS

Article 2(4) of Protocol No. 4 allows for specific restrictions to liberty to be made for particular areas. It allows a rather wide possibility for justification: restrictions need to be 'imposed in accordance with law' and can be 'justified by the public interest in a democratic society'. This special exception clause has been inserted to allow states to conduct specific policies to advance economic welfare or other social objectives, such as preventing overpopulation in certain areas or stimulating an even distribution of certain groups.[40] Because the drafters of the Protocol did not want to include such economic and social welfare considerations as legitimate aims in the general limitation clause of Article 2(3)

---

[35] Previously, the EComHR has held similarly for the obligation to carry an identity card; see *Reyntjens v. Belgium*, EComHR 9 September 1992 (dec.), appl. no. 16810/90.

[36] *Tatishvili v. Russia*, ECtHR 22 February 2007, appl. no. 1509/02.

[37] *Ibid.*, paras. 44 and 46.

[38] *Ibid.*, paras. 46 and 54.

[39] *Ibid.*, para. 54.

[40] Explanatory Report to Art. 2 of Protocol No. 4, *supra* n. 1; see also *Gillow v. United Kingdom*, ECtHR 24 November 1986, appl. no. 9063/80, paras. 54 and 56.

of Protocol No. 4, they decided to devote a separate paragraph to the matter, which was limited to certain 'areas'.[41]

It has long remained unclear in what kind of cases this paragraph could be invoked, but the Court did apply it in its 2016 judgment in *Garib*.[42] This case concerned Dutch legislation which allowed designation of certain urban areas as areas in which it was not permitted to take up new residence without a housing permit. Such a housing permit could be obtained only when certain minimum income requirements were met, such as having a salaried job or a social security allowance. Unemployed persons or those living on social benefits were refused a housing permit. The objective of the system of housing permits was to improve social cohesion and reduce crime in the designated areas. The Court noted that the permit system undoubtedly formed a restriction on the freedom to choose a residence. Because the system did not target any particular individual or individuals, but was of general application in discrete areas, the Court decided to consider the restriction under Article 2(4) ECHR.[43] It then continued to assess the reasonableness of the housing permit system in much the same way as it would have done when it had applied the general exception clause of Article 2(3) ECHR. Allowing a wide margin of appreciation to the state because of the social and economic nature of the measures concerned, and accepting that there were adequate safeguards in the decision-making process, the Court concluded that the measures were not manifestly without reasonable foundation and their application did not amount to a violation of the Convention.

4. FREEDOM TO LEAVE A COUNTRY

Article 2(2) of Protocol No. 4 guarantees the freedom to leave any country, including one's own. An important case in which the Court elucidated the meaning of this freedom is *Baumann*.[44] The case concerned a German national who was staying in a hotel in France, but had temporarily returned to Germany for a hospital visit. During his absence, the French police searched his hotel room because Baumann was suspected of having stolen a car. Amongst other things, they seized his German passport. After his conviction, the applicant lodged an application for the return of the seized goods, including his passport, but this was refused him because the goods had been confiscated. The Court held that the seizure and confiscation of his passport meant that Baumann could no longer use it to leave the country and to go to any other country of the European Union

---

[41]   Explanatory Memorandum to Art 2 of Protocol No. 4, ETS no. 046, paras. 14 et seq.
[42]   *Garib v. the Netherlands*, ECtHR 23 February 2016, appl. no. 43494/09 (notably, at the time of writing, the case was pending before the Grand Chamber).
[43]   *Ibid.*, para. 106.
[44]   *Baumann v. France*, ECtHR 22 May 2001, appl. no. 33592/96.

or to a non-European Union country. It therefore found that the applicant's right to liberty of movement was restricted contrary to Article 2(2) of Protocol No. 4.[45]

More commonly, the freedom to leave the country is restricted by a prohibition on leaving the country. Such prohibitions may be imposed in connection with pending criminal proceedings, pending bankruptcy proceedings and failure to pay taxes or debts, or in relation to the existence of a risk that a parent will abduct a child.[46] Very rarely, a prohibition on leaving the country also may be imposed to fight illegal migration. In Bulgaria, for example, there was an attempt to prevent Bulgarian citizens from entering other EU countries, because this would be in violation of the EU legislation on free movement of persons. If such citizens were to try to re-enter Bulgaria, for example after having been expelled by the EU state they had tried to enter, they were served with a one-year ban on leaving the country. The Court found that such an order would restrict the freedom to leave the country as protected by Article 2(2) of Protocol No. 4.[47]

The Court has accepted that all such bans on leaving the country in principle can be justified under Article 2(3) of Protocol No. 4. Nevertheless, the Court has recognised that travel bans may be particularly restrictive of the liberty of movement if they are imposed on a non-national, since that person may be forced to remain in a foreign country for a relatively long time without having a place to stay and without having an income.[48] They also may be particularly burdensome if the family of the person concerned is living in another country. More generally, for all bans on leaving the country, it must be clear that they are suitable, necessary and proportionate to achieving the legitimate aims pursued.

The Court's judgment in *Bartik* shows that the effectiveness of travel bans is not always accepted.[49] The applicant in this case had worked for a Russian State corporation which developed rocket and space devices. After having resigned from his job, Bartik wanted to travel abroad to visit his father. The authorities refused him a passport, however, because of his knowledge of state secrets and the related safety risks involved in his leaving the country. The Court did not consider this to be an acceptable justification, since a simple ban on international travel would not be able to sufficiently achieve the aim of prevention of disclosure of classified information.[50]

---

[45] *Ibid.*, para. 63. See also *Földes and Földesné Hajlik v. Hungary*, ECtHR 31 October 2006, appl. no. 41463/02; *Sissanis v. Romania*, ECtHR 25 January 2007 (dec.), appl. no. 23468/02; *Kerimli v. Azerbaijan, supra* n. 16, para. 47.

[46] E.g. *Prescher v. Romania*, ECtHR 7 June 2011, appl. no. 6767/04; *Luordo v. Italy, supra* n. 12; *Riener v. Bulgaria*, ECtHR 23 May 2006, appl. no. 46343/99; *Gochev v. Bulgaria*, ECtHR 26 November 2009, appl. no. 34383/03; *Diamante and Pelliccioni v. San Marino*, ECtHR 27 September 2011, appl. no. 32250/08.

[47] *Stamose v. Bulgaria, supra* n. 16.

[48] E.g. *Miażdżyk v. Poland*, ECtHR 24 January 2012, appl. no. 23592/07.

[49] *Bartik v. Russia*, ECtHR 21 December 2006, appl. no. 55565/00.

[50] *Idem,* para. 49.

In addition, the Court has made clear that a restriction on the right to leave one's country can be justified only as long as it serves its aim (e.g. recovering a debt or securing presence during interrogations).[51] If the restriction is of relatively short duration, e.g. only a few months, the Court usually will regard it as permissible.[52] If the restrictions are of longer duration, the proportionality requirement becomes more important.[53] Generally, imposition of an automatic ban for an indefinite time, or for the entire period in which a debt cannot be collected or a procedure is pending, is incompatible with Article 2(3) of Protocol No. 4.[54] A balancing exercise taking into account the 'special features' of the individual case is indispensable, and imposition and continuation of a restriction may be justified only if there are clear indications of a genuine public interest which outweigh the individual's right to freedom of movement.[55] In assessing the reasonableness of the national decisions, the Court also may take account of factors such as whether the proceedings were conducted efficiently and sufficiently speedily, whether the measure was particularly intrusive (e.g. because the individual concerned had a family abroad), whether there were indications that made it likely that the individual would duly return after having left the country, and whether the individual's leaving the country would really undermine the proceedings.[56] The Court may also take account of the individual's willingness to co-operate with the authorities, or of the possibility for the individual to request for the ban to be temporarily lifted in order to visit his family abroad.[57]

Finally, the Court has read certain procedural obligations into Article 2(3) of Protocol No. 4. The relevant criteria to impose a travel ban must be laid down in national legislation with sufficient clarity and detail; a review procedure must be provided for; and there must be a possibility to obtain compensation if the unlawful imposition of a travel ban has caused the individual any damage.[58] Moreover, the Court has recognised an obligation for regular re-examination of the measure, which normally would need to be carried out by a court because of the concomitant guarantees of objectivity, impartiality and independence.[59] The scope of the judicial review should enable the national court to take account of all the factors involved, including those concerning the proportionality of the restrictive measure.[60]

---

51   *Riener v. Bulgaria*, *supra* n. 46, para. 122.
52   E.g. *Diamante and Pelliccioni v. San Marino*, *supra* n. 46, para. 214.
53   *Riener v. Bulgaria*, *supra* n. 46, para. 122; see also *Bessenyei v. Hungary*, ECtHR 21 October 2008, appl. no. 37509/06, para. 24.
54   *Idem*, para. 128; see also *Bessenyei v. Hungary*, *supra* n. 53, paras. 23–24.
55   *Stamose v. Bulgaria*, *supra* n. 16, paras. 34–35; *Miażdżik v. Poland*, *supra* n. 48, para. 35.
56   *Riener v. Bulgaria*, *supra* n. 46, paras. 124 and 126; see also *Kerimli v. Azerbaijan*, *supra* n. 16, para. 59.
57   E.g. *Miażdżik v. Poland*, *supra* n. 48, para. 39; *Pfeifer v. Bulgaria*, ECtHR 17 February 2011, appl. no. 24733/04, para. 56; *Iordan Iordanov and Others v. Bulgaria*, ECtHR 2 July 2009 (dec.), appl. no. 23530/02.
58   *Sissanis v. Romania*, *supra* n. 45, paras. 71–77.
59   *Gochev v. Bulgaria*, *supra* n. 46, para. 50.
60   *Idem*.

CHAPTER 22

PROHIBITION OF EXPULSION OF NATIONALS

(Article 3 of Protocol No. 4)

Janneke Gerards*

GUIDING PRINCIPLE

According to Article 3 of Protocol No. 4, the Convention States are prohibited from expelling their own citizens. Moreover, nationals or citizens of Convention States always should be allowed entry into their own countries. In other words: exile is no longer an acceptable measure.

ARTICLE 3 OF PROTOCOL No. 4

1. No one shall be expelled, by means either of an individual or of a collective measure, from the territory of the State of which he is a national.
2. No one shall be deprived of the right to enter the territory of the State of which he is a national.

---

* In the fourth edition this chapter was revised and updated by Jeroen Schokkenbroek.

CONTENTS

1. PROHIBITION OF EXPULSION OF NATIONALS

Article 3 of Protocol No. 4 concerns the possibility to expel one's own nationals to a third country. The term expulsion is usually used in connection with aliens and not with the state's own nationals. Nevertheless, the drafters of Article 3 of Protocol No. 4 preferred the word 'expelled' to 'exiled', because exile is a word pregnant with meaning. As such, it might raise many interpretation problems. Moreover, the notion of 'expulsion' makes clear that Article 3 not only prohibits exile as a penalty or as a political measure, but any expulsion of a national from the territory. Extradition does not fall under the concept of expulsion, and consequently it does not fall under the prohibition of Article 3 of Protocol No. 4.[1] Nevertheless, extradition – of aliens as well as of nationals – may constitute a violation of one of the other rights and freedoms, specifically of the prohibition of inhuman treatment (Article 3 ECHR) and of the right to respect of family life (Article 8 ECHR).

The Court has qualified the prohibition of Article 3 of Protocol No. 4 as absolute, which means that no restrictions or exceptions are permitted whatsoever.[2]

Case law concerning the prohibition of expulsion of nationals has remained scant. In most cases the Court has not accepted that Article 3 of Protocol No. 4 applies. In *Denizci*, for example, the Court refused to consider the applicants' complaint in the light of Article 3 of Protocol No. 4.[3] The applicants were Cypriot nationals who claimed that they had been forcibly expelled from the territories under the control of the Republic of Cyprus to the northern part of Cyprus, which was under the effective control of Turkey. The Court observed that the applicants thereby did not actually claim that they had been removed to the territory of another state, and that it was not necessary for it to determine whether Article 3 of Protocol No. 4 applied in their case.[4] Similarly, in the case of *Texeira* the Court held that there was no 'expulsion' in a case where a father of a child had moved from Italy to Canada and the domestic court ordered that the

---

[1] Explanatory Report to Protocol No. 4, para. 21.

[2] *Slivenko and Others v. Latvia*, ECtHR (GC) 23 January 2002 (dec.), appl. no. 48321/99, para. 77.

[3] *Deniczi and Others v. Cyprus*, ECtHR 23 May 2001, appl. nos. 25316/94 et al.

[4] *Ibid.*, paras. 407–411.

child should leave the country to stay with him.[5] Moreover, the available case law has made clear that the applicability of the provision is largely dependent on who can be regarded as 'nationals'. The Court has held that such nationality must be determined by reference to national law.[6] If, according to national law, applicants cannot be regarded as 'citizens' or 'nationals', they fall outside the scope of Article 3. This may raise the question if a state can evade its obligations under Article 3 by depriving a person of his nationality for the sole purpose of his expulsion or refusal to admit him.[7] In this respect, the former European Commission of Human Rights (EComHR) has recognised that the existence of a link between the two decisions could create the presumption that the refusal of nationality had the mere purpose of making the expulsion possible.[8] In *Naumov*, the Court confirmed that the revocation of the citizenship followed by expulsion may raise potential problems under Article 3 of Protocol No. 4.[9] However, it may be assumed only in very evident cases that the national authorities intended to evade the operation of the Convention by their measure. In the abovementioned decision the EComHR in fact adopted the view that in this case nothing justified such a conclusion, while in *Naumov* the Court did not substantively deal with the issue because the deportation order never had been executed.

In addition to this, the Court has held that, although a right to nationality or 'citizenship' is guaranteed neither by the Convention nor by its Protocols, an arbitrary denial of nationality may under certain circumstances amount to an interference with the rights under Article 8 of the Convention.[10] It has thus reserved a – modest – possibility to review denials or losses of nationality under that provision.

2. THE RIGHT OF NATIONALS TO ENTER THEIR OWN COUNTRY

The second paragraph of Article 3 contains, without any restriction, the right to be admitted to the state of which one is a national. This provision would seem to be particularly relevant to a state like the United Kingdom, where numerous people have acquired British nationality by birth outside the state, e.g. in the Commonwealth countries. The United Kingdom has avoided the consequences

---

[5]   *Roldan Texeira and Others v. Italy*, ECtHR 26 October 2000 (dec.), appl. no. 40655/98.
[6]   *Slivenko and Others v. Latvia*, *supra* n. 2, para. 62.
[7]   It appears from the Explanatory Report that the drafters were aware of this risk, but they rejected a proposal to include a provision in Art. 3 according to which 'a State would be forbidden to deprive a national of his nationality for the purpose of expelling him' (Explanatory Report to Protocol No. 4, para. 23).
[8]   *X. v. Federal Republic of Germany*, EComHR 15 December 1969 (dec.), appl. no. 3745/68.
[9]   *Naumov v. Albania*, ECtHR 4 January 2005 (dec.), appl. no. 10513/03.
[10] E.g. *Karassev v. Finland*, ECtHR 12 January 1999 (dec.), appl. no. 31414/96.

of Article 3(2) of Protocol No. 4 by not ratifying Protocol No. 4, however. This does not alter the fact that, if that country, in admitting people having its nationality, should discriminate with respect to a particular racial group, it could still come into conflict with its obligations under the Convention. Such discrimination might constitute degrading treatment in the sense of Article 3 ECHR, taken on its own or together with Article 14.[11] The same could apply in relation to a discriminatory denial of the right of entry to a national where the State Party has limited its obligations through a valid reservation to Article 3 of Protocol No. 4.[12]

According to the Explanatory Report, the right of the national to be admitted to his state does not confer on him an absolute right to stay within that state. The Report gives the example of a national who, after having been extradited to another country, takes refuge again in his own state, and of a national who, after having served in the army of another state, wishes to return to his own country.[13] In the first example the state has the right to decide to extradite the person again, and in the second example it has the right to impose the sanction of forfeiture of nationality and of the rights associated with it on service in the army of another state. Moreover, the Court's case law makes clear that this prohibition does not apply to measures that merely diminish one's desire to return to one's own country.[14]

3. TERRITORIAL APPLICATION

With respect to the inhabitants of colonies and other territories for whose international relations a Contracting State is responsible, Article 5 of Protocol No. 4 enables states to indicate to what extent they wish the Protocol to apply to these territories, irrespective of the extent to which they have declared the Convention itself applicable.[15] Thus, they can declare that some articles of the Protocol are applicable to these territories while others are not. Moreover, the fourth paragraph of Article 5 of Protocol No. 4 provides in relation to Article 3

---

[11] See further Chapter 30.

[12] See *HabsburgLothringen v. Austria*, EComHR 14 December 1989, appl. no. 15344/89; even though it accepted the validity of the Austrian reservation with respect to Art. 3 of Protocol No. 4, the Commission went on to examine the complaint about discrimination based on the applicant's family origin under Arts. 3 and 14 of the Convention; it found that the situation complained of had not been shown to constitute a distinction the effects of which were contrary to Art. 3 of the Convention, either alone or taken together with Art. 14.

[13] Explanatory Report to Protocol No. 4, para. 28.

[14] *C.B. v. Germany*, ECtHR 11 January 1994 (dec.), appl. no. 22012/93, holding that an arrest warrant issued against the applicant does not amount to a deprivation within the meaning of Art. 3(2) of Protocol No. 4.

[15] For an overview of the various declarations made in this respect, see <https://conventions. coe.int> ETS No. 46 – Reservations and Declarations.

of Protocol No. 4 that, where there is a reference to 'the territory of a State', the territory of the Contracting State itself and these territories are treated as separate territories.

CHAPTER 23

PROHIBITION OF COLLECTIVE EXPULSION OF ALIENS

(Article 4 of Protocol No. 4)

Cornelis WOUTERS[*]

GUIDING PRINCIPLE

The expulsion of aliens as a group is prohibited except when the particular circumstances of each individual alien in the group are taken into account.

ARTICLE 4 OF PROTOCOL No. 4

Collective expulsion of aliens is prohibited.

---

[*]   In the fourth edition this chapter was revised and updated by Jeroen Schokkenbroek.

CONTENTS

1. INTRODUCTION

Article 4 of Protocol No. 4 prohibits any measure compelling aliens, as a group, to leave a country, except where such a measure is taken on the basis of a reasonable and objective examination of the particular circumstances of each individual of the group.[1]

Article 4 of Protocol No. 4 is particularly important in the context of large refugee and migrant movements, whereby their removal to countries of transit or origin are a means of migratory control for states, combatting irregular migration.[2] The article aims to protect non-nationals from being expelled without their individual circumstances being examined. Article 4 of Protocol No. 4 is not prohibiting the expulsion of aliens per se, but rather their expulsion as a group.[3] The prohibition of collective expulsion would be contrary to the procedural guarantees to which aliens subject to expulsion are entitled.[4] Any Contracting State considering the expulsion of a group of aliens is obliged to consider, with due diligence and in good faith, the full range of individual circumstances that may militate against the expulsion of each individual alien in the group.[5]

---

[1] *Khlaifia and Others v. Italy*, ECtHR 15 December 2016, appl. no. 16483/12, para. 237; *Čonka v. Belgium*, ECtHR 5 February 2002, appl. no. 51564/99, para. 59; *Andric v. Sweden*, ECtHR 23 February 1999 (dec.), appl. no. 45917/99, para. 1. See also *A. and Others v. the Netherlands*, EComHR 16 December 1988 (dec.), appl. no. 14209/88 and *Becker v. Denmark*, EComHR 3 October 1975 (dec.), appl. no. 7011/75. The prohibition of collective expulsion of aliens or mass expulsion of non-nationals is explicitly prohibited under the following human rights instruments and articles: International Convention on the Protection of the Rights of All Migrants Workers and Members of Their Families, Art. 22(1); African Charter on Human and Peoples' Rights, Art. 12(5); American Convention on Human Rights, Art. 22(9); Charter of Fundamental Rights of the European Union, Art. 19.

[2] *Hirsi Jamaa and Others v. Italy*, ECtHR (GC) 23 February 2012, appl. no. 27765/09, para. 176 and *Khlaifia and Others v. Italy, supra* n. 1, para. 241.

[3] See Art. 9 of International Law Commission (ILC) Draft Articles on the expulsion of aliens, Yearbook of the International Law Commission, 2014, Vol. II, Part Two and noted by the United Nations General Assembly, A/RES/69/119 of 10 December 2014. According to the Court these Draft Articles are of great interest; see *Khlaifia and Others v. Italy, supra* n. 1, para. 46.

[4] Human Rights Committee, General Comment No. 16, *The Position of Aliens under the Covenant*, HRI/GEN/1/Rev.9 (Vol. I), para. 10.

[5] ILC commentary para. 4 to Art. 9, International Law Commission (ILC), Draft Articles on the expulsion of aliens, Yearbook of the International Law Commission, 2014, Vol. II, Part Two and noted by the United Nations General Assembly, A/RES/69/119 of 10 December 2014.

Article 4 of Protocol No. 4 is formulated in unlimited terms and may be restricted only in accordance with Article 15(1) by way of derogation in time of war or other public emergency threatening the life of the nation.

2. SCOPE

Article 4 of Protocol No. 4 applies to 'aliens', i.e. all individuals who do not have the nationality of the Contracting State within whose jurisdiction they fall, irrespective of the alien's legal status.[6] The term covers both individuals with a nationality of a – Contracting or Non-Contracting – State and individuals without a nationality of any state, i.e. stateless persons.[7]

The word 'expulsion' has a broad meaning ('to drive away from a place') and refers to any conduct attributable to a state resulting in an alien being forced or coerced to leave, including the refusal of entry resulting in removal.[8]

The notion of 'expulsion' is principally territorial in the sense that expulsions are most often conducted from state territory.[9] However, applying a textual and teleological interpretation and referring to the drafting history as well as the need to interpret the Convention in the light of present-day conditions, the Court, in the case of *Hirsi Jamaa and Others v. Italy*, considered that the wording and object and purpose of the article does not impose an obstacle to its extra-territorial application.[10] As such, collective expulsion can also take place on the

---

[6]   *Georgia v. Russia (No. I)*, ECtHR (GC) 3 July 2014, appl. no. 13255/07, para. 170. The word 'alien' is commonly used in international human rights law and is, e.g., defined in Art. 2(b) of the ILC Draft Articles on the expulsion of aliens as an individual who does not have the nationality of the state in whose territory that individual is present, International Law Commission (ILC), Draft Articles on the expulsion of aliens, Yearbook of the International Law Commission, 2014, Vol. II, Part Two and noted by the United Nations General Assembly, A/RES/69/119 of 10 December 2014. Since Art. 1 of the ECHR obliges Contracting States to secure the rights and freedoms of the Convention to everyone within their jurisdiction, in the context of the ECHR 'aliens' should be defined as an individual who does not have the nationality of the state within whose jurisdiction s/he is. See in this regard: *Hirsi Jamaa and Others v. Italy, supra* n. 2, para. 178.

[7]   Explanatory Report to Protocol No. 4 to the Convention for the Protection of Human Rights and Fundamental Freedoms, securing certain rights and freedoms other than those already included in the Convention and in the first Protocol thereto, Strasbourg, 16 September 1963, ETS No. 46, para. 32.

[8]   *Khlaifia and Others v. Italy, supra* n. 1, paras. 237, 243 and 244. *Hirsi Jamaa and Others v. Italy, supra* n. 2, para. 174. According to the ILC Draft Articles on the expulsion of aliens, Art. 2(a), '"expulsion" means a formal act or conduct attributable to a State by which an alien is compelled to leave the territory of that State; it does not include extradition to another State, surrender to an international criminal court or tribunal, or the non-admission of an alien to a State'. See also Art. 10(2) on 'disguised expulsion', defined as 'the forcible departure of an alien from a State resulting indirectly from an action or omission attributable to the State (…)'.

[9]   *Hirsi Jamaa and Others v. Italy, supra* n. 2, paras. 178 and 167.

[10]   *Ibid.*, paras. 173–175. See also *Sharifi and Others v. Italy and Greece*, ECtHR 21 October 2014, appl. no. 16643/09, para. 212.

high seas. For example, present-day migratory control measures introduced by states, including the interception of refugees and migrants at sea, and returning them to the country of transit or origin they came from, may invoke Article 4 of Protocol No. 4 when individual circumstances are not taken into account.[11]

The effect of Article 4 of Protocol No. 4 depends largely on the interpretation of the word 'collective'. The article does not prohibit the expulsion of aliens *per se*, but rather the expulsion of aliens *as a group* without taking into account individual circumstances.

The Court has only found a violation of the prohibition of collective expulsion of aliens in five cases.[12] The case of *Čonka v. Belgium* concerned a group of Roma from Slovakia who, pending their appeals against the refusals to grant asylum, were detained and issued with deportation orders. The Court noted in particular the absence in the deportation order of a reference to their application for asylum and considered, also in view of the large number of persons who suffered the same fate as the applicants, that the procedure followed did not enable it to eliminate all doubt that the expulsion might have been collective.[13] These doubts were reinforced by a set of circumstances: the fact that the political authorities had announced beforehand that operations of this type would be held and had given instructions for them; the simultaneous convocation to report to the police station; the identical wording of the arrest and expulsion orders; the great difficulty for the persons concerned to contact a lawyer; and the fact that the asylum procedure had not been completed.[14] In the case *Hirsi Jamaa and Others v. Italy*, concerning a group of Somali and Eritrean nationals intercepted by Italy on the high seas and returned to Libya, the Court found a complete absence of any form of identification or individual examination.[15] In the case of *Georgia v. Russia (I)* even though, formally speaking, a court decision was made in respect of each Georgian national, the Court considered that the conduct whereby thousands of expulsion orders expelling Georgian nationals had been made after the issuance of circulars and instructions and followed by a co-ordinated policy of arresting, detaining and expelling Georgian nationals, made it impossible to carry out a reasonable and objective examination of the particular case of each individual.[16] Finally, in the case of *Sharifi and Others v. Italy and Greece*, concerning a group of Afghan, Sudanese and Eritrean asylum-seekers returned from Italy to Greece, the Court noted the absence of any effective possibility to

---

[11]   *Hirsi Jamaa and Others v. Italy, supra* n. 2, paras. 167 and 179. See also *Sharifi and Others v. Italy and Greece, supra* n. 10, paras. 224 and 212.

[12]   *Čonka v. Belgium, supra* n. 1; *Hirsi Jamaa and Others v. Italy, supra* n. 2; *Georgia v. Russia (I), supra* n. 6; *Sharifi and Others v. Italy and Greece, supra* n. 10; *N.D. and N.T. v. Spain*, ECtHR 3 October 2017, appl. nos. 8675/15 and 8697/15.

[13]   *Čonka v. Belgium, supra* n. 1, para. 61.

[14]   *Ibid.*, para. 62.

[15]   *Hirsi Jamaa and Others v. Italy, supra* n. 2, para. 185.

[16]   *Georgia v. Russia (I), supra* n. 6, paras. 175 and 176.

apply for asylum and was particularly concerned about the automatic return, implemented by the Italian border authorities in the ports of the Adriatic Sea, of persons who were handed over to ferry captains with a view of returning them to Greece.[17] In all cases the State had failed to take into account the applicants individual circumstances.

When a state takes expulsion measures affecting a group of aliens based on a reasonable and objective examination of the particular case of each individual alien of the group, there is no collective expulsion within the meaning of Article 4 of Protocol No. 4.[18] Also, when each individual alien of the group is provided with the opportunity to put arguments against her or his expulsion to the competent authorities on an individual basis there is no collective expulsion even when the expulsion for each alien in the group is based on similar or largely identical decisions.[19] Notably, a state cannot be responsible for collective expulsion within the meaning of Article 4 of Protocol No. 4 when the individual alien does not take the opportunity provided by the authorities to have her or his individual circumstances taken into account.[20]

In essence, to ensure the expulsion of a group of aliens does not amount to collective expulsion within the meaning of Article 4 of Protocol No. 4 'sufficient guarantees must be in place allowing personal circumstances of each alien in the group to be genuinely and individually taken into account.'[21] This means the state is required to provide relevant information and allow a reasonable and objective examination of the particular case of each individual alien of the group.[22] It may also include the requirement to provide access to legal assistance and to individual interviews assisted by interpreters.[23] An individual interview is not required in all circumstances, in particular when each alien in the group had the possibility of raising arguments against expulsion in their individual cases and where the authorities had examined those arguments.[24] Further, in the absence of even the slightest factual or legal ground which, under international

---

[17]   *Sharifi and Others v. Italy and Greece*, *supra* n. 10, para. 242.

[18]   See *supra* n. 1.

[19]   *Andric v. Sweden*, *supra* n. 1. Not only was the applicant in this case given the opportunity to put arguments against the expulsion in his individual case to the competent authorities, the authorities took his individual circumstances into account. Therefore, while aliens who were in similar situations as the applicant (i.e. originating from Bosnia-Herzegovina and with both Bosnian and Croatian citizenship) received comparable expulsion decisions, the Court concluded the case did not reveal any appearance of a collective expulsion.

[20]   *Berisha and Haljiti v. 'the former Yugoslav Republic of Macedonia'*, ECtHR 16 June 2005 (partial dec.), appl. no. 18670/03.

[21]   *Čonka v. Belgium*, *supra* n. 1, para. 63. See also *Georgia v. Russia (I)*, *supra* n. 6, paras. 174 and 178.

[22]   *Khlaifia and Others v. Italy*, *supra* n. 1, para. 237.

[23]   *Hirsi Jamaa and Others v. Italy*, *supra* n. 2, paras. 185, 202 and 203. The Court also took into account that the personnel aboard the Italian military ships were not trained to conduct individual interviews. See also *Georgia v. Russia (I)*, *supra* n. 6, para. 175; *Sharifi and Others v. Italy and Greece*, *supra* n. 10, para. 217.

[24]   *Khlaifia and Others v. Italy*, *supra* n. 1, para. 248.

or national law, could have justified a bar on expulsion, the usefulness of an individual interview is questionable.[25] Linking procedural safeguards under Article 4 of Protocol No. 4 to substantive criteria prohibiting expulsion is not without criticism. The article is formulated in unrestricted terms, requiring an individual assessment of every alien's expulsion. Therefore, it is essential that procedural guarantees, such as access to legal assistance and a hearing, are ensured, irrespective of whether the alien has a right to be protected from expulsion.[26]

3. RELATION TO OTHER RIGHTS

Articles 3 and 13 of the Convention further strengthen the obligation for states to ensure sufficient procedural guarantees to avoid collective expulsion of aliens. The expulsion of aliens is often linked to the question whether substantial grounds have been shown for believing the alien would face a real risk of being subjected to treatment prohibited by Article 3 upon return. This question, together with the right to an effective remedy under Article 13, requires independent and rigorous scrutiny and the possibility of suspending the implementation of the expulsion measure.[27] In fact, according to the Court, in an expulsion procedure the possibility of lodging an asylum application is a paramount safeguard.[28] In this regard, Article 4 of Protocol No. 4 strengthens the prohibition of *refoulement* developed under, inter alia, Article 3 of the Convention.

The expulsion of aliens may also constitute a violation of the Convention on other grounds. This may involve cases where expulsion is preceded by the arrest and detention of aliens, affecting Article 5(1), (2) and/or (4) of the Convention,[29] and cases in which the consequences of the expulsion are such that it entails a severance of family ties contrary to Article 8.

Aliens lawfully residing in a Contracting State are also protected by Article 1 of Protocol No. 7, prohibiting their expulsion except when based on a decision reached in accordance with law. In reaching this decision minimum procedural safeguards, including being able to submit reasons against expulsion, the right of review and of representation, must be upheld, except when the expulsion is

---

[25] *Ibid.*, para. 253.

[26] *Ibid.*, partly dissenting opinion of Judge Serghides, paras. 11 and 12. See also S. Zirulia and S. Peers, 'A Template for Protecting Human Rights during the "Refugee Crisis"? Immigration Detention and the Expulsion of Migrants in a Recent ECtHR Grand Chamber Ruling', EU Law Analysis, 5 January 2017, at: <http://eulawanalysis.blogspot.com/>.

[27] *Hirsi Jamaa and Others v. Italy, supra* n. 2, para. 198.

[28] *Khlaifia and Others v. Italy, supra* n. 1, para. 247.

[29] See, e.g., *Čonka v. Belgium, supra* n. 1, paras. 38–46 and 55 and *Khlaifia and Others v. Italy, supra* n. 1, paras. 88–108, 115–122 and 128–135.

necessary in the interests of public order or is grounded on reasons of national security. The above-mentioned case law suggests that, in cases of expulsion of a group of aliens, these procedural safeguards are to some extent already protected by Article 4 of Protocol No. 4 and cannot be restricted in the context of collective expulsion under Article 4 of Protocol No. 4 when issues of public order or national security are at play.

CHAPTER 24

ABOLITION OF THE DEATH PENALTY

(Article 1 of Protocol No. 6)

Edwin BLEICHRODT[*]

GUIDING PRINCIPLE

Every individual has the right not to be condemned to the death penalty or to its not being executed.

ARTICLE 1 OF PROTOCOL No. 6

The death penalty shall be abolished. No one shall be condemned to such penalty or executed.

---

[*]   In the fourth edition this chapter was revised and updated by Jeroen Schokkenbroek.

CONTENTS

1. INTRODUCTION

The abolition of the death penalty has been a matter of concern in and outside the Council of Europe for a long time. As early as 1957 the European Committee on Crime Problems studied the problem of capital punishment in the states of Europe. The Parliamentary Assembly also regularly dealt with this question. In 1980, it adopted two resolutions, in which, on the one hand, it appealed to national parliaments to abolish capital punishment from their penal systems, if they had not already done so,[1] and, on the other hand, called upon the Committee of Ministers to 'amend Article 2 of the European Convention on Human Rights to bring it into line with Resolution 727'.[2] In December 1982, the Committee of Ministers adopted the text of draft Protocol No. 6, prepared by the Steering Committee for Human Rights, and opened it for signature and ratification by the Member States of the Council of Europe on 28 April 1983. The Protocol entered into force on 1 March 1985 after it had received five ratifications.[3]

Until the 1990s no death sentences had been executed in the member States of the Council of Europe for many years. However, the enlargement of this organisation after 1990 made this a matter of topical concern. The Parliamentary Assembly made the willingness to sign Protocol No. 6 within one year and ratify it within three years from the time of accession and to introduce a moratorium upon accession a prerequisite for membership to the Council of Europe on the part of the Assembly. In spite of this some of the new Member States have carried out executions after their accession to the Council of Europe.[4] However, this is no longer the case: all Member States have now abolished the death penalty and ratified Protocol No. 6, with the exception of Russia, where a moratorium has applied since 1996.

---

[1] Res. 727 of the Parliamentary Assembly, 32nd Session, 22 April 1980, Yearbook XXIII (1980), p. 66.

[2] Res. 891 of the Parliamentary Assembly, 32nd Session, 22 April 1980, Yearbook XXIII (1980), p. 66.

[3] For an overview of the Contracting States which have ratified Protocol No. 6, see App. 1.

[4] See *Report on the Abolition of the Death Penalty in Europe* (Committee on Legal Affairs and Human Rights, rapporteur: Mrs Wohlwend) of 25 June 1996, Parliamentary Assembly, Doc. 7589.

2. SCOPE

Article 1 of the Protocol must be read in conjunction with Article 2 of the Convention. It follows from this that a state, which wants to become a party to the Protocol may no longer rely on the exception mentioned in Article 2 and has to delete the death penalty from its criminal law. The second sentence of Article 1 underlines that it contains not only an obligation, but also a right: every individual has the right not to be condemned to the death penalty or to the death sentence not being executed.

However, the scope of the obligation to abolish the death penalty is limited to acts committed in peacetime. Protocol No. 6 does not apply to acts committed in times of war or of imminent threat of war. However, following a proposal of the Parliamentary Assembly that a new additional protocol be drawn up abolishing the death penalty also in wartime,[5] instructions were given by the Committee of Ministers to the Steering Committee for Human Rights which led to the entry into force of Protocol No. 13 to the Convention, on 1 July 2003, providing for the abolition of the death penalty under all circumstances.

There is so far little case law concerning Protocol No. 6, which may be explained by the fact that the States Parties to the Convention refrained from ratifying this Protocol before first abolishing the death penalty within their own legal system. However, Article 1 of Protocol No. 6 may also be relevant in expulsion and extradition cases, on the basis of the reasoning followed by the Court in the *Soering* case.[6] There, the Court accepted that Article 3 of the Convention could not be interpreted as generally prohibiting the death penalty, because the existence of Protocol No. 6 shows that the intention of the drafters was to use the normal method of amendment of the text to introduce an obligation to abolish capital punishment. However, the circumstances relating to a death sentence may be such as to give rise to an issue under Article 3. Article 3 in its turn prohibits expulsion or extradition in case a person would face a real risk of exposure to inhuman or degrading treatment or punishment in the receiving state. The *Soering* case concerned extradition by a state not bound by Protocol No. 6, but where the state is so bound, Article 1 of the Protocol may be violated if the state extradites or expels a person to another state where he is at serious risk that he will be sentenced to death and that sentence will be carried out. In the latter cases, there is no need for the Court to proceed in an indirect manner by examining, under Article 3, the circumstances relating to the death sentence. The key question is whether extradition or expulsion would expose the applicant to a real risk of being subjected to capital punishment.[7] In the *Ilascu* case a Grand Chamber had already held that the anxiety and suffering

---

5   See Recommendation 1246 (1994) on the abolition of capital punishment.
6   *Soering v. United Kingdom*, ECtHR 7 July 1989, appl. no. 14038/88, para. 111.
7   *Aylor-Davis v. France*, EComHR 20 January 1994, appl. no. 22742/93, para. 111.

engendered by a death sentence 'can only be aggravated by the arbitrary nature of the proceedings which led to it, so that, considering that a human life is at stake, the sentence thus becomes a violation of the Convention'. In this case, the Court found a violation of Article 3 in respect of the first applicant on account of the death sentence coupled with the conditions and the treatment suffered during his detention.[8]

Finally, in view of the rejection of the death penalty by the Member States of the Council of Europe,[9] there is consensus that the exception to the right to life made in the second sentence of Article 2, paragraph 1, of the Convention should be deemed to have been abrogated. This question received a provisional answer from the Court in the *Öcalan* case. Put briefly, the extensively reasoned judgment referred to the considerable evolution of the legal position as regards the death penalty (at the time of the judgment: de jure abolition in 43 of the 44 Member States; all Member States having signed Protocol No. 6 and all but one of them having ratified it). Against this consistent background the Court expressed the view that capital punishment in peacetime has come to be regarded as an unacceptable, if not inhuman, form of punishment, which is no longer permissible under Article 2 of the Convention. However, the Court found it unnecessary to reach a firm conclusion on this point since it construed Article 2 of the Convention as prohibiting the *implementation* of the death penalty in respect of a person who has not had a fair trial and Article 3 of the Convention as prohibiting the *imposition* of the death penalty after an unfair trial, as such imposition would amount to inhuman treatment.[10] In the *Al-Saadoon and Mufdhi* case, the Court took note of an evolution towards the complete *de facto* and *de jure* abolition of the death penalty within the Member States of the Council of Europe. When addressing the effect of signature and ratification of Protocol No. 13 on the interpretation of Articles 2 and 3 of the Convention it held, in particular: 'It can be seen, therefore, that the Grand Chamber in Öcalan did not exclude that Article 2 had already been amended so as to remove the exception permitting the death penalty. Moreover, as noted above, the position has evolved since then. All but two of the Member States have now signed Protocol No. 13 and all but three of the States which have signed

---

8   *Ilaşcu and Others v. Moldova and Russia*, ECtHR (GC) 8 July 2004, appl. no. 48787/99, paras. 431 and 440. The Court considered that the facts complained of did not call for a separate examination under Art. 2 of the Convention, since the risk of enforcement of the death penalty was now more hypothetical than real (Mr Ilascu having been released and living in Romania with that country's nationality) (paras. 416–417 of the judgment).

9   See, e.g., the *Guidelines on Human Rights and the Fight against Terrorism*, adopted by the Committee of Ministers on 15 July 2002, Art. X, para. 2, of which provides: 'Under no circumstances may a person convicted of terrorist activities be sentenced to the death penalty; in the event of such a sentence being imposed, it may not be carried out.'

10   *Öcalan v. Turkey*, ECtHR 12 March 2003, appl. no. 46221/99, paras. 195–196, 198 and 202–207. The reasoning was followed by the Grand Chamber, *Öcalan v. Turkey (No. 1)*, ECtHR (GC) 12 May 2005, appl. no. 46221/99, paras. 162–175.

have ratified it. These figures, together with consistent State practice in observing the moratorium on capital punishment, are strongly indicative that Article 2 has been amended so as to prohibit the death penalty in all circumstances. Against this background, the Court does not consider that the wording of the second sentence of Article 2 §1 continues to act as a bar to its interpreting the words "inhuman or degrading treatment or punishment" in Article 3 as including the death penalty.'[11]

In recent case law the close connection between Article 2, Article 3 and Article 1 of the Protocol No. 6 has been emphasised in case of extradition or deportation of an individual to another state where substantial grounds have been shown for believing that he or she would face a real risk of being subjected to the death penalty there. In the *Al Nashiri* case, the applicants had arrived in Poland on board an aircraft of the 'extraordinary rendition' by the United States Central Intelligence Agency (CIA), had been detained in a CIA detention facility and had been transferred from Poland to the United States on a CIA rendition aircraft. The Court held that there had been a violation of Articles 2 and 3 of the Convention taken together with Article 1 of Protocol No. 6 to the Convention on account of the transfer of the applicant from the respondent State's territory despite the existence of a real risk that he could be subjected to the death penalty.[12]

3. DEROGATION

The prohibition of the death penalty is non-derogable.[13] Moreover, according to Article 4 of the Protocol it is not possible to make any reservation in respect of the provisions of the Protocol.

---

[11]   *Al-Saadoon and Mufdhi v. the United Kingdom*, ECtHR 2 March 2010, appl. no. 61498/08, paras. 116 and 119–120.
[12]   *Al-Nashiri v. Poland*, ECtHR 24 July 2014, appl. no. 28761/11, para. 578.
[13]   Art. 3 of the Protocol.

CHAPTER 25

PROCEDURAL SAFEGUARDS RELATING TO EXPULSION OF ALIENS

(Article 1 of Protocol No. 7)

Kees FLINTERMAN[*]

GUIDING PRINCIPLE

Article 1 of Protocol 7 deals with the traditional sovereign power of states to expel aliens. It gives those aliens who are lawful residents certain rights which they may exercise before being expelled and in some situations even after their expulsion.

ARTICLE 1 OF PROTOCOL No. 7

1. An alien lawfully resident in the territory of a State shall not be expelled therefrom except in pursuance of a decision reached in accordance with law and shall be allowed:
   a) to submit reasons against his expulsion,
   b) to have his case reviewed, and
   c) to be represented for these purposes before the competent authority or a person or persons designated by that authority.
2. An alien may be expelled before the exercise of his rights under paragraph 1(a), (b) and (c) of this Article, when such expulsion is necessary in the interests of public order or is grounded on reasons of national security.

---

[*]   In the fourth edition this chapter was revised and updated by Kees Flinterman.

CONTENTS

1. INTRODUCTION

As is clear from the text of the article, and as is emphasised in the Explanatory Report,[1] the guarantees laid down therein only apply to certain categories of aliens, and even then, not in all circumstances. Indeed, Article 1 only concerns aliens lawfully resident in the territory of the state in question. The word 'resident' is intended to exclude any alien who has arrived at the border or the (air)port, but has not yet passed through immigration control. Aliens who have been admitted for the purpose of transit or for other non-residential purposes, or who are waiting for a decision on a request for a residence permit, are also excluded from the scope of this article.

The term 'lawfully' refers to domestic law. It is up to domestic law to determine the conditions for a person's presence in the territory to be considered 'lawful'. As soon as an alien no longer complies with one or more of these conditions, his presence can no longer be considered 'lawful'.

According to the Explanatory Report the phrase 'expulsion' must be considered as an autonomous concept, independent of any domestic definition. It refers to any measure compelling the departure of an alien from the territory except extradition.[2]

2. REQUIREMENTS FOR EXPULSION

The Convention contains implied guarantees in several articles for aliens against whom a measure of expulsion is taken. First of all, Article 4 of Protocol No. 4 contains the prohibition of collective expulsion of aliens. In addition, in individual cases Articles 3, 5(1)(f) and 8, in conjunction with Article 13, do provide some guarantees against measures of expulsion.[3] Article 1 of Protocol No. 7 has been added 'in order to afford minimum guarantees to such persons

---

[1] Explanatory Report on Protocol No. 7 to the Convention for the Protection of Human Rights and Fundamental Freedoms, para. 9.

[2] *Ibid.,* para. 10.

[3] See *supra* for Arts. 3, 5 and 8, and *infra* for Art. 13.

(aliens) in the event of expulsion from the territory of a Contracting Party'.[4] And minimal they are indeed.

Expulsion may take place only 'in pursuance of a decision reached in accordance with law'. The word 'law' refers to domestic law. It is, therefore, up to domestic law to determine which authority is competent to decide on expulsion and the procedure to be followed, provided that the requirement of an effective remedy of Article 13 of the Convention is met. A judicial authority is not required, as Article 6 of the Convention does not apply to cases of expulsion. However, if the domestic law itself requires a judicial decision for the expulsion, then the absence of such decision leads to a violation of Article 1 of Protocol 7.[5] Within the framework of the procedure the alien concerned has further some minimum rights, as set forth in paragraph 1(a)–(c).[6]

As regards the first right – to submit reasons against his expulsion – here again it is up to domestic law to determine the conditions governing the exercise of this right. This right may, however, also be exercised in the first phase of the procedure and not only at the review stage, as is clear from its formulation separately from the right formulated in paragraph 1(b).[7]

As regards the second right – to have his case reviewed – it is emphasised in the Explanatory Report that this does not necessarily imply 'a two-stage procedure before different authorities, but only that the competent authority should review the case in the light of the reasons against expulsion submitted by the person concerned'.[8] This 'competent authority' may be the same authority that took the original decision or a higher authority. The form of the review, again, is determined by domestic law. The review, however, must not be purely formal, but genuine in the light of possible arguments against the expulsion.[9]

The minimalistic approach, which overshadowed the preparation of the Protocol, can be clearly inferred from the Explanatory Report where it expressly states that Article 1 does not relate to the stage of proceedings, existing in some states, in which aliens have the possibility of lodging an appeal against the decision taken following the review of their case: 'The present Article (…) does not therefore require that the person concerned should be permitted to remain in the territory of the State pending the outcome of the appeal introduced against the decision taken following the review of his case.'[10]

Also for the third right – to be represented before the competent authority or a person or persons designated by that authority – it is up to domestic law to determine the form of representation and the competent authority. There

---

4   Explanatory Report, *supra* n. 1, para. 9.
5   *Bolat v. Russia*, ECtHR 5 October 2016, appl. no. 14139/03.
6   See also Art. 5 of the Convention.
7   Explanatory Report, *supra* n. 1, para. 13.1.
8   *Ibid.*, para. 13.2.
9   *Kaushal v. Bulgaria*, ECtHR 2 September 2010, appl. no. 1537/08.
10   Explanatory Report, *supra* n. 1, para. 13.2.

is no requirement for the representative to be a lawyer or for the competent authority to be a judicial organ. The authority is not even required to be the authority which finally decides on the expulsion. In order to comply with this article, it is sufficient that the competent judicial or administrative authority makes a recommendation to an(other) administrative authority, which then decides on the expulsion measure.[11] The provision does not give the alien or his representative the right to be physically present when the case is considered, nor does the procedure have to include an oral hearing; the whole procedure may be a written one.[12]

In the *Maaouia* case,[13] the European Court of Human Rights held that Article 6(1) does not apply to procedures for the expulsion of aliens. According to the Court it was obvious that by adopting Article 1 of Protocol No. 7 the Contracting States had clearly indicated their intention not to include proceedings for the expulsion of aliens within the scope of Article 6. Furthermore, the Court held that proceedings for the rescission of the exclusion order do not concern the determination of a civil right for the purposes of Article 6(1), nor do excluding orders concern the determination of a criminal charge.

3. EXCEPTIONS

As a rule, the alien concerned has the right to make use of the minimum guarantees laid down in the first paragraph of Article 1 before being expelled. The second paragraph, however, allows for exceptions to this rule 'when such expulsion is necessary in the interests of public order or is grounded on reasons of national security'. The words 'in a democratic society', which are part of the necessity requirement in the several provisions of the Convention, which allow for restrictions of the rights embodied therein, are lacking here for unclear reasons. However, Strasbourg case law has not (yet) made these words play a distinctive role. With reference to that case law the Explanatory Report states that the exceptions have to be applied 'taking into account the principle of proportionality as defined in the case law of the European Court of Human Rights'.[14]

When a state relies on the interest of public order, it is up to that state to show why in the particular case or cases that exception was necessary. If, however, a state grounds the exception on reasons of national security, according to the

---

[11] *Ibid.*, para. 13.3.
[12] *Ibid.*, para. 14.
[13] *Maaouia v. France*, ECtHR (GC) 5 October 2000, appl. no. 39652/98.
[14] Explanatory Report, *supra* n. 1, para. 15; see also *C.G. and Others v. Bulgaria*, ECtHR 24 April 2008, appl. no. 1365/07.

Explanatory Report 'this in itself should be accepted as sufficient justification'.[15] Since this view would imply that review by the Strasbourg organs is not possible at all, it would run counter to the purpose of the Protocol to place the rights embodied therein under the supervisory system of the Convention; the necessity requirement in particular must be subject to the review of the Court, albeit that the latter may leave a margin of discretion to the national authorities in that respect. In recent case law,[16] the Court has, however, emphasised that when a state has not submitted any material or evidence corroborating its claim that the interests of national security or public order have been at stake, then the normal procedure of paragraph 1 must be followed. In other cases, it is only scant comfort for the alien concerned to know that he may still exercise his rights under paragraph 1 of this article after his expulsion.

4. DEROGATION

Article 1 is not a non-derogable right under Article 15 of the Convention.

---

[15] *Ibid.*
[16] *Nolan and K. v. Russia*, ECtHR 12 February 2009, appl. no. 2512/04.

CHAPTER 26

RIGHT TO APPEAL
IN CRIMINAL MATTERS

(Article 2 of Protocol No. 7)

Kees Flinterman[*]

GUIDING PRINCIPLE

Article 2 of Protocol No. 7 provides for a right of review for everyone who is convicted of a criminal offence. States parties may however subject this right to some exceptions.

ARTICLE 2 OF PROTOCOL No. 7

1. Everyone convicted of a criminal offence by a tribunal shall have the right to have his conviction or sentence reviewed by a higher tribunal. The exercise of this right, including the grounds on which it may be exercised, shall be governed by law.
2. This right may be subject to exceptions in regard to offences of a minor character, as prescribed by law, or in cases in which the person concerned was tried in the first instance by the highest tribunal or was convicted following an appeal against acquittal.

---

[*]   In the fourth edition this chapter was revised and updated by Kees Flinterman.

CONTENTS

1. SCOPE

The scope of this article is essentially determined by the concepts of 'criminal offence', 'tribunal' and 'conviction or sentence'. It seems to be obvious that the meaning of the words 'criminal offence' is closely related to the notion of 'criminal charge' of Article 6 of the Convention. Thus, it would seem appropriate to argue that Article 2 of Protocol No. 7 also applies to those disciplinary and administrative sanctions that fall within the scope of Article 6. It seems to be inapplicable, however, to preventive measures, deportation orders and decisions concerning extradition as far as no criminal law elements are involved.

Article 2 presupposes the existence of a 'conviction or sentence', which notions are to be interpreted autonomously. Article 2 is to be inapplicable if a person is not convicted and also not sentenced in view of lack of evidence or guilt.

In the first sentence of paragraph 1 it is emphasised that the conviction must have been imposed 'by a tribunal'. According to the Explanatory Report this phrase was added to make it clear that the right laid down in this provision is not applicable to 'offences which have been tried by bodies which are not tribunals within the meaning of Article 6 of the Convention'.[1] At first sight this is a somewhat remarkable restriction, since Article 6 of the Convention requires that the determination of criminal charges be made by an independent tribunal. Therefore, trial of a criminal offence by a non-judicial organ would in itself be a violation of the Convention. However, since Strasbourg case law has accepted the possibility that the determination of a criminal charge is made, in the first instance, by a non-judicial body, provided that from that determination appeal lies to a tribunal, the drafters must be assumed to have intended to make it clear that this first appeal to a tribunal is not a review in the sense of Article 2; its decision on appeal must be open to review by a higher instance, which has to meet the standards of an independent tribunal.

2. CONVICTION OR SENTENCE

The first sentence of paragraph 1 provides that everyone has the right to have the 'conviction or sentence' reviewed. The reason for using the word 'or' instead of 'and' is, again according to the Explanatory Report[1], that it is not required that in every case both the conviction and the sentence should be reviewed. For example, if a person has pleaded guilty and has been convicted, the right of review may be restricted to the review of the sentence. Here, too, the line of reasoning is not very convincing. Although in most cases in which a suspect has pleaded guilty the review will in fact mainly focus on the sentence, it may be necessary also to review the way the confession was obtained, and, therefore, the basis of the conviction. On the other hand, a review of the conviction alone, without the sentence also being reviewed, is only possible in those cases in which the suspect has been found guilty, but no sentence has been imposed. Just as in the corresponding Article 14(5) of the Covenant on Civil and Political Rights, it would, therefore, have been better if the word 'and' instead of 'or' had been used.[2]

3. DOMESTIC MODALITIES

As is made clear in the second sentence of the first paragraph, exercising this right of appeal shall be governed by law. In other words, the modalities of the review are left for determination by domestic law. The Explanatory Report adds to this that the review may either concern a review of findings of facts and questions of law, or be limited to questions of law.[3] According to the Court in the *Krombach* case, states have a wide margin of appreciation to determine how the right secured by Article 2 of Protocol No. 7 to the Convention is to be exercised.[4] The Court set forth that 'thus, the review by a higher court of a conviction or sentence may concern both points of fact and points of law or be confined solely to points of law. Any restrictions contained in domestic legislation on the right to a review guaranteed by this provision must, by analogy with the right of access to a court embodied in Article 6 para. 1 of the Convention, pursue a legitimate aim and not infringe the very essence of that right.'[5]

It may be deduced from this that the Court will not accept a restricted form of review of questions of law which cannot result in an annulment or alteration of the conviction or sentence concerned as sufficient. The Court has indeed emphasised, also in the context of Article 2 of Protocol No. 7, that the Convention is intended to guarantee no rights that are theoretical and illusory but rights that are practical and effective.[6] Thus, the Court has decided, that an

---

[1]   Explanatory Report on Protocol No. 7 to the Convention for the Protection of Human Rights and Fundamental Freedoms, para. 17.

[2]   Art. 14(5) of the Covenant on Civil and Political Rights uses the word 'and'.

[3]   Explanatory Report, *supra* n. 1, p. 17.

[4]   *Krombach v. France*, ECtHR 13 February 2001, appl. no. 29731/96, para. 96.

[5]   *Ibid.*, para. 96; see also *Gurepka v. Ukraine*, ECtHR 6 September 2005, appl. no. 61406/00, para. 59, and *Galstryan v. Armenia*, ECtHR 15 November 2007, appl. no. 26986/03, para. 125.

[6]   *Rusban Yakovenko v. Ukraine*, ECtHR 4 June 2015, appl. no. 5425/11, para. 78.

extra-ordinary review procedure which depends on the domestic authorities' discretionary powers and lacks a clear defined procedure on time-limits represents an ineffective remedy for the purposes of Article 2.[7]

Some countries have a system according to which persons who wish to appeal to a higher tribunal must in certain cases first apply for leave to appeal. According to the Explanatory Report such a procedure is in itself to be regarded as a form of review within the meaning of the present article.[8] Whether this interpretation is in conformity with the text of the article may be doubted. The decision to grant or refuse leave of appeal may be based upon reasons of expediency and does not necessarily imply a substantive review of the conviction or sentence as Article 2 would seem to guarantee, but may rather block such a review. Moreover, one may wonder whether such a decision can be said always to amount to a review 'by a higher tribunal'. It is submitted that the Court should be guided by the text and purpose of Article 2 rather than by the restrictive interpretation given in the Explanatory Report on this point.

4. EXCEPTIONS

The second paragraph of Article 2 contains three exceptions to the right laid down in the first paragraph.

The first exception concerns offences of a minor character. In practice, it will not always be clear where the dividing line between serious and minor offences is to be drawn. The Explanatory Report proposes as an important criterion the question of whether the offence is punishable by imprisonment or not.[9]

Although this criterion is a clear one, it is unlikely to lead to a common scope or autonomous meaning of the concept of 'offences of a minor character'. Since the question of imprisonment is entirely regulated by domestic law, major differences may occur between the Contracting States. More importantly, in several states a great many minor offences, such as infringements of traffic rules, are made punishable by imprisonment, though such sentences are never imposed in practice. It is unlikely that the drafters of the Protocol wished to make the right of review by a higher tribunal also obligatory in such cases.

The second exception concerns cases in which a person has been tried in the first instance by the highest tribunal. This exception refers to situations in which domestic law has assigned the highest tribunal as a court of first instance because of the status of the accused as a minister, judge or other high official, or because of the nature of the offence. It is obvious that in those cases review by a higher tribunal is not even possible.

---

7   *Kakabadze and Others v. Georgia*, ECtHR 2 October 2012, appl. no. 1484/07.
8   Explanatory Report, *supra* n. 1, para. 18.
9   *Ibid.*, para. 19.

The third exception concerns cases where the conviction has been pronounced following an appeal against acquittal. For the person concerned this exception can be very unsatisfactory, especially when he thinks that the court of second instance has made an error of fact or law. In most member states of the Council of Europe, however, the convicted person will normally have the right of appeal in cassation to a third instance. In that case, at least any error of law can be restored. The assumption must be that the third exception does not apply in the case that the acquittal has been pronounced by a non-judicial body. Since Article 6 of the Convention requires that the determination of criminal charges be made by an independent tribunal, no consequences should ensue from a decision of a non-judicial body in this respect.

5. DEROGATION

Article 2 does not belong to the non-derogable rights in the sense of Article 15(2) of the Convention.

CHAPTER 27

COMPENSATION FOR WRONGFUL CONVICTION

(Article 3 of Protocol No. 7)

Kees FLINTERMAN[*]

GUIDING PRINCIPLE

Everyone who is the victim of a miscarriage of justice is entitled to compensation except in situations where the person involved is partly or wholly to blame for such miscarriage.

ARTICLE 3 OF PROTOCOL No. 7

When a person has by a final decision been convicted of a criminal offence and when subsequently his conviction has been reversed, or he has been pardoned, on the ground that a new or newly discovered fact shows conclusively that there has been a miscarriage of justice, the person who has suffered punishment as a result of such conviction shall be compensated according to the law or the practice of that State concerned, unless it is proved that the non-disclosure of the unknown fact in time is wholly or partly attributable to him.

---

* In the fourth edition this chapter was revised and updated by Kees Flinterman.

CONTENTS

1. SCOPE

The right to compensation for miscarriage of justice, which is acknowledged in Article 3 of Protocol 7 should not be confounded with the right to compensation for unlawful detention which is guaranteed by Article 5 of the Convention.[1] Both rights are distinct rights. Under a miscarriage of justice is understood: 'some serious failure in the judicial process involving grave prejudice to the convicted person.'[2] The right to compensation in such a situation can only be exercised if seven preconditions have been fulfilled.

First, Article 3 presupposes the existence of a 'criminal offence'. It seems to be obvious that the notion of 'criminal offence' is closely related to the notion of 'criminal charge' of Article 6 of the Convention. Thus, it is appropriate to argue that Article 3 also applies to those disciplinary and administrative sanctions that fall within the scope of Article 6.

Secondly, the person concerned must have been 'convicted'. Consequently, the article does not apply in cases where the charge is dismissed or the accused is acquitted.[3]

Thirdly, the person concerned must have been convicted by a 'final decision'. A decision is final 'if, according to the traditional expression, it has acquired the force of *res judicata*. This is the case when it is irrevocable, that is to say when no further ordinary remedies are available or when the parties have exhausted such remedies or have permitted the time-limit to expire without availing themselves of them.'[4]

Fourthly, the person concerned must, as a result of this final decision, have suffered punishment. Thus, if the suspect has been found guilty, but no sentence has been imposed or the sentence has not (yet) been executed, Article 3 does not apply.

---

[1]   See Art. 5(5) ECHR.
[2]   Explanatory Report on Protocol No. 7 to the Convention for the Protection of Human Rights and Fundamental Freedoms, para. 23.
[3]   Explanatory Report, *supra* n. 2, para. 22. Under certain circumstances the fifth paragraph of Art. 5 of the Convention may offer compensation.
[4]   *Ibid.*, with reference to the Explanatory Report of the European Convention on the International Validity of Criminal Judgments, Commentary on Article 1(a), Council of Europe, Strasbourg, 1970, p. 22.

Fifthly, the right laid down in this article can only be exercised, if the conviction has been reversed or pardoned. The case law stresses that Article 3 does not apply before the conviction has been reversed or pardoned.[5]

Sixthly, the reversal or pardon must have taken place because of new or newly discovered facts. In the latter case an assessment must moreover be made into whether the circumstance that these facts were not disclosed in time is wholly or partly attributable to the person concerned. It is obvious that if a person is willingly withholding relevant information, he loses his right to compensation because the prejudice suffered is (partly) due to his own conduct. If, besides the convicted person, others are also responsible for the fact that certain relevant facts were not disclosed, it may not always be fair to put the blame solely on the former by fully denying him a right to compensation. In that case a partial compensation may be more appropriate.

Seventhly, the new or newly discovered facts on the basis of which the person's conviction has been reversed or the pardon has been awarded must conclusively show that there has been a miscarriage of justice. Reversal or pardon on other grounds – pardon may often especially be granted on other grounds – does not create a right to compensation. According to the Explanatory Report the intention is that compensation should be paid only in 'clear cases of miscarriage of justice, in the sense that there would be acknowledgement that the person concerned was clearly innocent'.[6] In what follows the Explanatory Report seems to imply that reversal on the ground that new facts have been discovered which introduce a reasonable doubt as to the guilt of the accused is not enough.[7] It is submitted that this interpretation would seem to be too strict, especially in view of the right to be presumed innocent, laid down in Article 6(2) of the Convention, which implies that reasonable doubt and clear innocence should lead to the same result.

2.   STANDARD OF COMPENSATION

If all conditions have been fulfilled, Article 3 provides that the person who has suffered punishment as a result of such conviction shall be compensated according to the law[8] or the practice of the state concerned.

What the phrase 'the practice of the State concerned' means is rather unclear. The Explanatory Report does not clarify it any further than by providing

---

[5]   *Pogkosyan and Baghdasaryan v. Armenia*, ECtHR 12 June 2012, appl. no. 22999/06, para. 49.
[6]   Explanatory Report, *supra* n. 2, para. 23.
[7]   *Ibid.*
[8]   Art. 14(6) ICCPR recognises the same right. According to this article, compensation should be paid by the state according to law. The Human Rights Committee in its General Comment No. 13, para. 18, has made it clear that this means that states must enact laws which provide compensation to victims of miscarriages of justice.

that 'the State should provide for the payment of compensation in all cases to which the Article applies'.[9] It is submitted that this phrase, which does not appear anywhere else in the Convention, is rather unfortunate. It does not add anything to the reference that is already made to national law and it may lead to confusion as to its meaning. Article 5(5) of the Convention, which establishes a right to compensation for victims of arrest or detention in contravention of the provisions of Article 5, uses the words 'an enforceable right to compensation'. This phrase should also have been adopted here.

In the event of absence of a law which provides for compensation for miscarriage of justice, the state must be deemed not to be relieved of its obligation to pay compensation for miscarriage of justice. The state remains bound by international standards.[10] The European Court of Human Rights has recently confirmed this view by deciding that compensation for miscarriage of justice is also payable if the domestic law or practice makes no provision for such compensation. The Court further stated that the purpose of Article 3 of Protocol 7 is 'not merely to recover any pecuniary loss caused by a wrongful conviction but also to provide a person convicted as a result of a miscarriage of justice with compensation for any non-pecuniary damage such as distress, anxiety, inconvenience and loss of enjoyment of life'.[11]

3. DEROGATION

Article 3 does not belong to the non-derogable rights in the sense of Article 15(2) of the Convention.

---

[9] Explanatory Report, *supra* n. 2, para. 25.
[10] See in this regard Art. 27 Vienna Convention on the Law of Treaties, which reads: 'A party may not invoke the provisions of its internal law as justification for its failure to perform a treaty.'
[11] *Pogkosyan and Baghdasaryan v. Armenia, supra* n. 5, para. 51.

CHAPTER 28

RIGHT NOT TO BE TRIED OR PUNISHED TWICE

(Article 4 of Protocol No. 7)

Bas van Bockel[*]

GUIDING PRINCIPLE

The principle of *ne bis in idem* is a fundamental principle of law, which restricts the possibility of a defendant being prosecuted repeatedly on the basis of the same (historical) facts. What the principle requires from judicial and other authorities is that a subject is only confronted with the legal consequences of a single historical event once. This is so regardless of whether this takes place in a single set of proceedings or several well-coordinated sets proceedings forming a 'coherent whole'.

ARTICLE 4 OF PROTOCOL No. 7

1. No one shall be liable to be tried or punished again in criminal proceedings under the jurisdiction of the same State for an offence for which he has already been finally acquitted or convicted in accordance with the law and penal procedure of that State.
2. The provisions of the preceding paragraph shall not prevent the re-opening of the case in accordance with the law and penal procedure of the State concerned, if there is evidence of new or newly discovered facts, or if there has been a fundamental defect in the previous proceedings, which could affect the outcome of the case.
3. No derogation from this Article shall be made under Article 15 of the Convention.

---

[*] Many thanks are owed to Floris Tan and Janneke Gerards for their comments. Any mistakes off course remain my own. In the fourth edition this chapter was revised and updated by Edwin Bleichrodt.

CONTENTS

1. SUBSTANCE AND NATURE OF THE GUARANTEE

A distinction must be made between the right not to be tried, and the right not to be punished again for an offence for which the subject has been finally acquitted, mentioned in the provision. According to the case law, the ne bis in idem principle of Article 4 of Protocol No. 7 primarily sets forth the prohibition of double prosecution. This offers more extensive protection for the subject than the prohibition of double punishment, which merely prohibits the accumulation of penalties in respect of the same offence.[1] The phrase '*ne bis in idem*' is used only in reference to the prohibition of double *prosecution* ('right not to be tried again') and not to that of double *punishment* ('right not to be punished again') throughout this chapter.

The guarantee of *ne bis in idem* bars any further proceedings in respect of the same facts once the outcome of the first set of proceedings has become *final*. This applies regardless of whether a penalty was imposed in the first proceedings, or of the manner in which that penalty was calculated. In the decision of the Grand Chamber in the case of *Zolotukhin*, the ECtHR identified a third 'distinct' guarantee contained in Article 4 of Protocol No. 7: 'that no one shall be (…) liable to be tried' for an offence for which that person has been finally acquitted or convicted.[2] It can be assumed that this means that the protection afforded by Article 4 of Protocol No. 7 extends into the pre-trial stages of the prosecution.[3]

---

[1] The ECtHR has consistently held that Art. 4 of Protocol No. 7 'is not confined to the right not to be punished twice but extends to the right not to be tried twice': *Franz Fischer v. Austria*, ECtHR 29 May 2001, appl. no. 37950/97; *Sergey Zolotukhin v. Russia*, ECtHR (GC) 10 February 2009, appl. no. 1493/03.

[2] *Sergey Zolotukhin v. Russia*, *supra* n. 1, para. 110.

[3] Similarly to that of Art. 6 ECHR.

2. SCOPE

As to the scope of application of Article 4 of Protocol No. 7 four dimensions can be distinguished: the objective and subjective scope, the temporal scope, and the scope of application *ratione materiae*. The subjective and the temporal scope of application of Article 4 of Protocol No. 7 do not appear to raise many issues. Although there has been no case to date before the ECtHR concerning the subjective scope of application of the provision, it follows from its wording that only a subject who has actually been tried and has had his or her case finally disposed of can rely on the provision. As for the temporal scope of application, the ECtHR has consistently held that Article 4 of Protocol No. 7 applies if the second proceedings reached their conclusion in a decision given on a later date than the entry into force of Protocol No. 7 for that member state.[4] In the following, only the scope of application *ratione materiae* and the objective scope of application of the provision will be discussed in more detail.

2.1. *RATIONE MATERIAE*

The ECtHR held in *Zolotukhin v. Russia* that 'the legal characterisation of the procedure under national law cannot be the sole criterion of relevance for the applicability of the principle of *non bis in idem* under Article 4 §1 of Protocol No. 7. Otherwise, the application of this provision would be left to the discretion of the Contracting States to a degree that might lead to results incompatible with the object and purpose of the Convention.'[5]

In the first paragraph, Article 4 of Protocol No. 7 refers to 'criminal proceedings', which echoes the term 'criminal charge' from Article 6 ECHR. The scope of application of Article 4 of Protocol No. 7 is accordingly determined by reference to the three criteria used to determine the existence of a criminal charge in relation to Article 6, which are commonly known as the '*Engel* criteria'.[6] The first criterion is the legal classification of the offence under national law, the second is the nature of the offence and the third is the severity of the penalty that the person concerned risks incurring. According to the Court, '(t)he second and third criteria are alternative and not necessarily cumulative. This, however, does not exclude a cumulative approach where separate analysis of each criterion does not make it possible to reach a clear conclusion as to the existence of a criminal charge'.[7] Applying the *Engel* criteria to the facts of *Zolotukhin v.*

---

[4] *Gradinger v. Austria*, ECtHR 23 October 1995, appl. no. 15963/90; *Margus v. Croatia*, ECtHR 27 May 2014, appl. no. 4455/10.

[5] *Sergey Zolotukhin v. Russia, supra* n. 1, para. 78.

[6] *Idem*; *Engel and Others v. Netherlands*, ECtHR (GC), 8 June 1976, (Series A-22).

[7] *Idem*, para. 53.

Russia, for example, the Grand Chamber found that the administrative offence of 'minor disorderly acts' in the Russian Code of Administrative Offences served to guarantee the protection of human dignity and public order, 'values and interests which normally fall within the sphere of protection of criminal law'. Furthermore, the measures at stake were aimed at punishment and deterrence, forming 'characteristic features of criminal penalties'.[8] The *Engel* rule then leads to a presumption that the charges against a subject are 'criminal', 'a presumption (…), which can be rebutted entirely exceptionally, and only if the deprivation of liberty cannot be considered appreciably detrimental given their nature, duration or manner of execution'.[9] In applying these criteria it is the maximum potential penalty for which the relevant law provides which must be taken into account. The sentence that was actually imposed 'cannot diminish the importance of what was initially at stake'.[10]

However, the Grand Chamber ruled in *A and B v. Norway* that Article 4 of Protocol No. 7 ECHR leaves the member states of the Council of Europe free to choose a combination of complementary legal responses to socially offensive conduct, provided that these responses form a coherent whole so as to address different aspects of the social problem involved, and that the accumulated legal responses do not represent an excessive burden for the subject. Under these conditions, the Grand Chamber does not require that proceedings are conducted entirely 'simultaneously from beginning to end', as long as they are sufficiently connected in time and form a coherent whole. In many jurisdictions, these issues are already adequately dealt with through an *'una via'* rule, requiring the authorities to decide upfront whether to initiate criminal or administrative proceedings, or through a mechanism of prior co-ordination and concentration of proceedings.

2.2. OBJECTIVE SCOPE

Within national systems of law, the scope of application of the *ne bis in idem* principle is traditionally limited to one and the same state. Absent any specific legal basis in international law, states are generally unwilling to accept the negative enforcement consequences of foreign *res iudicata*. Indeed, it is clear from the wording of Article 4 of Protocol No. 7 that the objective scope of application of this provision is limited to the jurisdiction of one and the same state. The scope of application of the provision in the member states is also limited by the fact that not all of the member states of the Council of Europe have ratified Protocol No. 7 ECHR.

---

8   *Idem*, para. 55.
9   *Idem*, para. 56.
10 *Ibid.*

3. *NE BIS IN IDEM*

The guarantee comprises of two main elements: one and the same subject must be tried *twice* (*bis*) for *the same* (*idem*) 'offence'. The interpretation given to these elements in the case law of the ECtHR is discussed in the following paragraphs.

3.1. FINAL OUTCOME

As a general rule, a subject is deemed to be tried 'twice' only from the time that the outcome of the first trial or prosecution is final onwards. As further discussed in the following this requirement is not absolute. According to established case law a judicial decision is *final* when it is has acquired *res iudicata* in reference to the applicable rules under national law, and has become irrevocable.[11] This is the case when: (1) there are no more ordinary remedies available under the law; (2) when all available remedies are exhausted, or (3) when the time-limits for bringing such remedies have expired.[12] Decisions against which an ordinary appeal may still be brought are therefore excluded from the application of the *ne bis in idem* principle. The possibility of bringing extraordinary remedies under national law does *not* affect the final nature of the decision for the purposes of Article 4 of Protocol No. 7.[13] The question whether the decision in question is an acquittal or a conviction is irrelevant in this regard; the ECtHR has emphasised that the *only* relevant question is whether that decision has become 'final'.[14] It follows from this that Article 4 of Protocol No. 7 does not stand in the way of the reopening of a case if there is a legal possibility to resume proceedings. In *A and B v. Norway*, the Grand Chamber ruled that the requirement of finality does not mean that proceedings which are 'sufficiently connected in time' and form a 'coherent whole' must be conducted entirely 'simultaneously from beginning to end'. In the judgment, the ECtHR clarified that Article 4 of Protocol No. 7 leaves the member states of the Council of Europe free to 'choose (a combination of) complementary legal responses to socially offensive conduct', provided however that these responses 'form a coherent whole so as to address different aspects of the social problem involved', and that 'the accumulated legal responses do not represent an excessive burden'. The relevant case law is further discussed below.

In the case of *Nikitin v. Russia*, the applicant was acquitted from charges of 'treason through espionage' and 'aggravated disclosure of an official secret'.[15] The Russian Procurator General filed a request with the presidium

---

[11]   *Sergey Zolotukhin v. Russia, supra* n. 1, para. 107.
[12]   *Ibid.*; see also: *Nikitin v. Russia*, ECtHR 20 July 2004, appl. no. 50178/99, para. 107.
[13]   *Sergey Zolotukhin v. Russia, supra* n. 1, para. 107.
[14]   *Ibid.*, para. 111.
[15]   *Nikitin v. Russia, supra* n. 12.

of the Supreme Court to review the acquittal in supervisory proceedings, but this request was refused. The applicant himself thereupon challenged the Russian legislation which allowed for a re-examination of a closed case and the quashing of an acquittal in supervisory review proceedings before the Russian Constitutional Court. His appeal was successful and the relevant legislation was declared unconstitutional. The applicant also complained to the ECtHR that the request for supervisory review proceedings by the Procurator General breached Article 4 of Protocol No. 7 because it had rendered him *liable* to be tried again by creating the potential for a new prosecution. In the judgment that followed, the ECtHR noted that within the Russian legal system at the time, an acquittal such as that in the case of *Nikitin* did not become 'final' until the time-limit for a request for supervisory review (one year) had expired. However, because supervisory review could be seen as an extraordinary appeal in that it was not accessible to the defendant in a criminal case and its application depended on the discretion of the authorised official, the ECtHR assumed that the actual acquittal had become final for the purposes of Article 4 of Protocol No. 7.[16] The ECtHR observed that Article 4 of Protocol No. 7 'draws a clear distinction between a second prosecution or trial, which is prohibited by the first paragraph of that Article, and the resumption of a trial in exceptional circumstances, which is provided for in its second paragraph. Article 4(2) of Protocol No. 7 expressly envisages the possibility that an individual may have to accept prosecution on the same charges, in accordance with domestic law, where a case is reopened following the emergence of new evidence or the discovery of a fundamental defect in the previous proceedings.'[17]

The ECtHR, however, held that, in this instance, the mere *attempt* by the prosecution to secure a supervisory review was in itself not sufficient to consider that it had rendered the applicant liable to be tried again. After all, this request was refused. Furthermore, the prosecution's request should be seen as an attempt to have the proceedings reopened, rather than an attempt to hold a second trial.[18]

3.2. SAME OFFENCES

Before the judgment of the Grand Chamber in *Zolotukhin*, the case law of the ECtHR on the interpretation of the notion of 'the same offence' contained in Article 4 of Protocol No. 7 ECHR was riddled with questions and uncertainties. Several different approaches to the interpretation of the notion of '*idem*' could be identified in the case law. After some initial, vying judgments in *Gradinger* and *Oliveira*, the ECtHR adopted an autonomous

---

[16] *Idem*, para. 39.
[17] *Idem*, para. 45.
[18] *Idem*, para. 47.

approach to the interpretation of 'the same offence' by taking into account the question whether two or more offences share the same *essential elements* in *Franz Fischer* and several subsequent judgments.[19] This approach however gave rise to considerable legal uncertainty.[20] In the *Zolotukhin* judgment (GC), the Grand Chamber expressly denounced the earlier case law on this point and considered that 'the existence of a variety of approaches to ascertaining whether the offence for which an applicant has been prosecuted is indeed the same as the one of which he or she was already finally convicted or acquitted engenders legal uncertainty incompatible with a fundamental right'.[21] The Grand Chamber changed its course and embraced a broad, objective approach to the interpretation of the element of *idem*: 'Article 4 of Protocol No. 7 must be understood as prohibiting the prosecution or trial of a second "offence" insofar as it arises from identical *facts or facts* which are substantially the same.'[22] It is worth briefly discussing the facts of the case, which concerned a Russian national who had displayed disorderly behaviour towards several public officials. He was placed in detention for three days for the administrative offence of 'minor disorderly acts'. Shortly afterwards, he was prosecuted for the criminal offences of 'disorderly acts', 'use of violence against a public official', and 'insulting a public official' on the basis of substantially the same facts. He lodged an application with the ECtHR, which was declared (partly) admissible and in which a Chamber found a violation of Article 4 of Protocol No. 7.[23] At the request of the Russian Government, the case was referred to the Grand Chamber for review. In the judgment, the Grand Chamber held that: '(…) the use of the word 'offence' in the text of Article 4 of Protocol No. 7 cannot justify adhering to a more restrictive approach. It reiterates that the Convention must be interpreted and applied in a manner which renders its rights practical and effective, not theoretical and illusory. (…)

The Court further notes that the approach which emphasises the legal characterisation of the two offences is too restrictive on the rights of the individual, for if the Court limits itself to finding that the person was prosecuted for offences having a different legal classification it risks undermining the guarantee enshrined in Article 4 of Protocol No. 7 rather than rendering it practical and effective as required by the Convention (¼). Accordingly, the Court takes the view that Article 4 of Protocol No. 7 must be understood as prohibiting

---

[19]   *Gradinger v. Austria, supra* n. 4; *Olivieri v. Switzerland*, ECtHR 30 July 1998, appl. no. 25711/94; *Franz Fischer v. Austria, supra* n. 1.

[20]   See: S. Trechsel, with the assistance of S.J. Summers, *Human Rights in Criminal Proceedings*, Oxford: Oxford University Press, 2005, p. 394. See also UK Law Report Commission, Law Com. No. 267, Cm. 5048, London, 2001, pp. 29–32; and B. van Bockel, *The Ne Bis In Idem Principle in EU Law*, Alphen aan de Rijn: Kluwer Law International, 2010, pp. 191–201.

[21]   *Sergey Zolotukhin v. Russia, supra* n. 1, para. 78.

[22]   *Idem*, para. 82.

[23]   *Sergey Zolotukhin v. Russia, supra* n. 1.

the prosecution or trial of a second "offence" in so far as it arises from identical facts or facts which are substantially the same.'[24]

The Court has thus fundamentally rejected any recourse to more formal (and therefore more arbitrary) criteria that tie in with the legal qualification of the act or facts, such as the 'essential elements' of an offence as defined in national criminal law. This requires a high degree of objectivity in assessing the underlying facts of the case from the judiciary in the Member States of the Council of Europe that are signatories to the Seventh Protocol. This approach offers stronger protection for the individual and strengthens legal certainty. It should, however, not be forgotten that the facts underlying the prosecution of a subject inevitably derive their significance from the constitutive elements of the relevant offence as it is codified in law, so that this the objectivity required by the *Zolotukhin* doctrine is by definition not absolute.

4. EXCEPTIONS

Article 4(2) of Protocol No. 7 allows for 'the reopening of the case (…) if there is evidence of new or newly discovered facts, or if there has been a fundamental defect in the previous proceedings that could affect the outcome of the case'.[25] Case law on this provision is sparse and little can be said about it beyond what is clear from its wording. It is perhaps worth mentioning that in a number of cases concerning 'supervisory review' the ECtHR has examined whether the power to reopen the case 'was exercised by the authorities so as to strike, to the maximum extent possible, a fair balance between the interests of the individual and the need to ensure the effectiveness of the system of criminal justice'.[26] The Court has, however, consistently done so under Article 6, rather than Article 4(2) of Protocol No. 7 ECHR in those cases. Although the logical link between the right to a fair trial and *ne bis in idem* is clear (as was confirmed in the *Nikitin* case, where it was held that Article 4 of Protocol No. 7 'is itself one aspect of a fair trial'), it is therefore not certain whether the same reasoning applies to Article 4(2) of Protocol No. 7 ECHR. Supervisory review creates a particular possibility to reopen a case that is only available to the authorities and has the effect of cancelling out the entire earlier prosecution. It is found in the laws of some of the member states of the Council of Europe that were part of, or within the sphere of influence of, the former Soviet Union.[27] In the *Nikitin* case, the Court held that 'the mere possibility of reopening a criminal case is (…) prima

---

[24]   *Ibid.*, paras. 82 and 83.
[25]   *Nikitin v. Russia supra* n. 12, para. 56.
[26]   *Idem*, para. 57.
[27]   Amongst others: *ibid.*, *Radchikov v. Russia* ECtHR 24 May 2007 appl. no. 65582/01; *Giuran v. Romania* ECtHR 20 June 2011, appl. no. 24360/04.

facie compatible with the Convention, including the guarantees of Article 6 (...) however, certain special circumstances of the case may reveal that the actual manner in which it was used impaired the very essence of a fair trial'.[28] In the *Radchikov* case, the Court further indicated the circumstances that must be taken into account in this regard: 'The relevant considerations to be taken into account in this connection include, in particular, the effect of the reopening and any subsequent proceedings on the applicant's individual situation and whether the reopening resulted from the applicant's own request; the grounds on which the domestic authorities revoked the finality of the judgment in the applicant's case; the compliance of the procedure at issue with the requirements of the domestic law; the existence and operation of procedural safeguards in the domestic legal system capable of preventing abuses of this procedure and other pertinent circumstances of the case (...)'[29]

Other grounds considered by the ECtHR in these cases are whether there is new and previously undiscovered evidence, and whether the reopening of a case was detrimental for the subject.[30]

A different issue is, that systems of judicial administration do not always function perfectly. Article 4(2) of Protocol No. 7 only applies to instances in which proceedings were brought *in the knowledge* that the defendant has already been tried; the bringing of proceedings in error does not infringe the *ne bis in idem* principle if those proceedings are subsequently discontinued.[31]

5. RELATION TO OTHER PROVISIONS

Unlike the International Covenant on Civil and Political Rights (ICCPR), the Convention does not treat the *ne bis in idem* principle as an element or precondition for the right to a fair trial. In *Ponsetti & Chesnel*, the ECtHR held that the *ne bis in idem* principle 'is embodied solely in Article 4 of Protocol No. 7 (and) the other provisions of the Convention do not guarantee compliance with it either expressly or implicitly'.[32] In the case of *Nikitin* however, the Court took the other view and held that 'Article 4 of Protocol No. 7, (...) is itself one aspect of a fair trial'.[33] The case law is therefore inconclusive on this point, and one can

---

[28]   *Nikitin v. Russia, supra* n. 12, para. 57.

[29]   *Radchikov v. Russia, supra* n. 27, para. 147.

[30]   *Savinskiy v. Ukraine*, ECtHR 28 February 2006, appl. no. 6965/02; *Xheraj v. Albania*, ECtHR 29 July 2008, appl. no. 37959/02; *Kiselev v. Russia*, ECtHR 29 January 2009, appl. no. 75469/01; *Eduard Chistyakov v. Russia*, ECtHR 9 April 2009, appl. no. 15336/02.

[31]   *Zigarella v. Italy* (decision on admissibility), ECtHR 3 October 2002, appl. no. 48154/99; *Falkner v. Austria* (decision on admissibility), ECtHR 30 September 2004, appl. no. 6072/02.

[32]   *Ponsetti and Chesnel v. France*, ECtHR, 14 September 1999 (dec.), appl. nos. 36855/97 and 41731/98, para. 6.

[33]   *Nikitin v. Russia, supra* n. 12, para. 107.

only point to the strong logical link between the *ne bis in idem* principle and the right to a fair trial.

6. DEROGATION

The ECHR places the *ne bis in idem* rule amongst those guarantees that cannot be derogated from even in time of war or another public emergency.

CHAPTER 29

EQUALITY BETWEEN SPOUSES

(Article 5 of Protocol No. 7)

Frederik Swennen[*]

GUIDING PRINCIPLE

Article 5 warrants equality between spouses and ex-spouses in the private law relations between themselves, and between them and their children. The article's impact is limited to being invoked as subsidiary, supplementary or additionally violated provision, for a parallel protection is offered under Article 8 of the Convention, Article 14 of the Convention read in conjunction with Article 8, and Article 1, Protocol No. 12. Its added value lies in offering parallel protection to Article 23, paragraph 4, of the International Covenant on Civil and Political Rights (ICCPR), which it mirrors.

ARTICLE 5 OF PROTOCOL No. 7

Spouses shall enjoy equality of rights and responsibilities of a private law character between them, and in their relations with their children, as to marriage, during marriage and in the event of its dissolution. This article shall not prevent States from taking such measures as are necessary in the interests of the children.

---

[*]   In the fourth edition this chapter was revised and updated by Kees Flinterman.

CONTENTS

1. INTRODUCTION

Article 5 of Protocol No. 7 imposes mainly positive obligations on the states to create a legal framework under which spouses have equal rights and obligations,[1] and in which particularly sex discrimination is absent.[2]

The article was introduced with a view to extending the European human rights protection in line with the rights protected in Article 23, paragraph 4, ICCPR.[3] The Human Rights Committee (CCPR) General Comment on Article 23[4] is therefore relevant for the interpretation of Article 5.[5]

Article 5 can be considered the tailpiece of equality protection offered to (future) spouses, and should be read in conjunction with different other provisions. Article 12 of the Convention protects the right to marry and to found a family. Once married, Article 16 of the European Social Charter safeguards the spouses' right to social, legal and economic protection. Article 5 has completed this with equality protection regarding private law relations. Afterwards, Article 4(d) of the European Convention on Nationality extended equality protection with regard to the spouses' nationality.

Almost parallel protection to Article 5 is offered in Article 8 of the Convention, Article 14 of the Convention read in conjunction with Article 8, and Article 1 of Protocol No. 12.[6] The ECtHR often finds that complaints under Article 5 are so closely linked to complaints under Article 8 and 14 of the

---

[1]   *Iosub Caras v. Romania*, ECtHR 27 July 2006, appl. no. 7198/04, para. 56.

[2]   P. Lemmens, 'Het 7e Protocol bij het Europees Verdrag over de Rechten van de Mens: een "discreet" verdrag?', in W. Pintens, A. Alen, E. Dirix and P. Senaeve, *Vigilantibus ius scriptum. Feestbundel voor Hugo Vandenberghe*, Bruges: die Keure, 2007, p. 181.

[3]   Explanatory Report on Protocol No. 7 to the Convention for the Protection of Human Rights and Fundamental Freedoms, para. 3.

[4]   CCPR, General Comment No. 19: Article 23 (The Family) Protection of the Family, the Right to Marriage and Equality of the Spouses, 1990.

[5]   Lemmens, *supra* n. 2, at p. 181.

[6]   C. Pettiti, 'L'égalité entre époux', in F. Krenc and M. Puéchavy (eds.), *Le droit de la famille à l'épreuve de la Convention européenne des droits de l'homme*, Brussels: Anthemis, 2008, p. 37 et seq.

Convention that they do not warrant a separate examination[7] or, as master of the characterisation to be given to the facts of the case, the Court decides to examine them only under those articles[8] or under Article 6.[9] Further, applications that only invoked a violation of Article 5 were declared inadmissible[10] or were struck out.[11] As a result, the Court has not had to assess the merits of applications based solely on Article 5.

2. SCOPE

2.1. SPOUSES

Article 5 applies only to *spouses*. Hence it does not apply to:

- future spouses, in the period preceding marriage;
- the conditions of capacity to enter into marriage, which fall under the scope of Article 12 of the Convention;
- registered or *de facto* partners. Like spouses, those partners can, however, rely on Article 14 of the Convention read in conjunction with Article 8 with a view to enjoying equality of rights and responsibilities,[12] and on Article 1 of Protocol No. 12.[13]

Article 5, however, does apply to:

- both opposite-sex and same-sex spouses.[14] Even if Article 12 of the Convention does not impose an obligation to grant access to marriage to same-sex couples,[15] the Court no longer considers that the right to marry must in all circumstances be limited to opposite-sex couples.[16] In my opinion,

---

[7] E.g. *Docra v. Romania*, ECtHR 15 April 2014 (dec.), appl. no. 59651/13; *Reslová v. The Czech Republic*, ECtHR 18 July 2006, appl. no. 7550/04, para. 68.

[8] E.g. *Capaldo v. Italy*, ECtHR 2 December 2008 (dec.), appl. no. 25846/04.

[9] *Panetta v. Italy*, ECtHR 15 July 2014, appl. no. 38624/07.

[10] *Klöpper v. Switzerland*, EComHR 18 January 1996 (dec.), appl. no. 25053/94; *Frischknecht v. Switzerland*, EComHR 18 January 1996 (dec.), appl. no. 28334/95; *Tews v. Austria*, EComHR 6 September 1995 (dec.), appl. no. 26941/95; *Purtonen v. Finland*, EComHR 9 September 1998 (dec.), appl. no. 32700/96; *Heckl v. Austria*, ECtHR 31 August 1999 (dec.), appl. no. 32012/96; *Cernecki v. Austria*, ECtHR 11 July 2000 (dec.), appl. no. 31061/96; *R.W. and C. T.G.-W. v. Austria*, ECtHR 22 November 2001 (dec.), appl. no. 36222/97.

[11] *D.D. v. France*, ECtHR 8 November 2005, appl. no. 3/02; *Özlen v. Turkey*, ECtHR 17 September 2013, appl. no. 6634/07.

[12] E.g. *Ünal Tekeli v. Turkey*, ECtHR 16 November 2004, appl. no. 29865/96, paras. 57–68.

[13] Pettiti, *supra* n. 6, at pp. 29 and 30.

[14] *Contra*: Pettiti, *supra* n. 6, at p. 32.

[15] *Hämäläinen v. Finland*, ECtHR (GC) 16 July 2014, appl. no. 37359/09, para. 96.

[16] *Schalk and Kopf v. Austria*, ECtHR 24 June 2010, appl. no. 30141/04, para. 61.

Article 5 should therefore apply to all spouses in states that have lawfully extended marriage to same-sex couples, so as also to prohibit discrimination on other grounds than sex;
- ex-spouses, particularly regarding maintenance and regarding their relations with their children.

All private law consequences of marriage, both during marriage and in the event of its dissolution, fall under the scope of this article.

The reference to the dissolution of marriage, however, does not imply a duty for states to provide for (specific forms of) dissolution of marriage.[17] A right to divorce can be derived from neither Article 12 nor Article 8 of the Convention.[18] Importantly however, Article 5 does prohibit discrimination in regard to the grounds and procedures for separation and divorce.[19] This has led the French *Cour de Cassation* to refuse the recognition of foreign repudiations in case the procedural and substantive rights of the woman were not safeguarded.[20]

2.2. PRIVATE LAW RIGHTS

Article 5 only applies to private (family) law rights and obligations and not 'to other fields of law, such as administrative, fiscal, criminal, social, ecclesiastical or labour laws'.[21]

On the one hand, the article applies to rights and obligations between the spouses themselves, both regarding their person and property.[22] Regarding their person, the article, for example, precludes discrimination in the fields of nationality and family names, in the choice of residence and the running of the household. Regarding their property, the article, for example, requires equality in the administration of assets and entitlements to maintenance.[23]

On the other hand, Article 5 applies to rights and obligations between the spouses and their children,[24] such as the passing of family names or the education of the children.[25] It is also interpreted as favouring joint parental responsibility after the dissolution of the marriage.[26] Article 5 does not explicitly

---

[17] Explanatory Report, *supra* n. 3, at para. 39.
[18] *Babiarz v. Poland*, ECtHR 10 January 2017, appl. no. 1955/10, para. 49.
[19] General Comment, *supra* n. 4, at paras. 8–9.
[20] Hereto e.g. L. Gannagé, Case note, *Rev.crit.dr.intern.privé.* 2002, p. 735; Lemmens, *supra* n. 2, at p. 182; Pettiti, *supra* n. 5, at p. 41–45.
[21] Explanatory Report, *supra* n. 3, at para. 35.
[22] *Ibid.*, at para. 35.
[23] General Comment, *supra* n. 4, at paras. 7–9.
[24] Explanatory Report, *supra* n. 3, at para. 35.
[25] General Comment, *supra* n. 4, at paras. 8–9.
[26] J. Hauser, 'L'égalité des parents en cas de separation', in F. Sudre (ed.), *Le droit au respect de la vie familiale au sens de la Convention européenne des droits de l'homme*, Brussels: Anthemis, 2002, p. 324.

limit its scope to the spouses' *common* children, though this would have been self-evident at the time of the preparatory works. One should, however, not exclude that a spouse would rely on Article 5 regarding national provisions regulating, for example, joint responsibility of spouses over non-common children.[27]

3. RESTRICTIONS

Article 5 shall not prevent states from taking such measures as are necessary in the interests of the children. In the application of Article 8 of the Convention, courts need to take into account the best interest of the child. The possible resulting difference in treatment between (ex-)spouses therefore cannot be considered contrary to Article 14 of the Convention.[28] For that reason, applications contending a discrimination violation regarding parental responsibility and custody upon divorce,[29] mostly to the detriment of divorced fathers, are often declared inadmissible as manifestly ill-founded.[30] In one judgment on the merits, the Court found there had been no violation of the father's equal rights in his relation with the child, by allowing the adoption of the child by its stepfather. The father had only infrequent and limited contact with the child even before the divorce from its mother.[31]

The Explanatory Report also adds that Article 5 shall not prevent states from taking due account of all relevant factors when deciding on the division of property upon the dissolution of marriage.[32] One may think of preferential rights to the family home or household assets.

4. DEROGATION

Article 5 does not belong to the non-derogable rights referred to in Article 15(2) of the Convention.

---

27   E.g. the Dutch art. 1:253sa Civil Code.
28   Explanatory Report, *supra* n. 3, at para. 36; Lemmens, *supra* n. 2, at p. 182.
29   General Comment, *supra* n. 4, at paras. 8–9.
30   E.g. *R.R. v. Romania (No. 1)*, ECtHR 12 February 2008 (dec.), appl. no. 1188/05; *(No. 3)*, ECtHR 15 March 2011 (dec.) appl. no. 18074/09, para. 202; *(No. 4)*, ECtHR 6 March 2011 (dec.), appl. no. 3574/11, para. 42.
31   *Chepelev v. Russia*, ECtHR 26 July 2007, appl. no. 58077/00, para. 36.
32   Explanatory Report, *supra* n. 3, at para. 38.

CHAPTER 30

PROHIBITION OF DISCRIMINATION

(Article 14 and Article 1 of Protocol No. 12)

Janneke GERARDS[*]

GUIDING PRINCIPLE

In a democratic society, everyone should be allowed to participate. No groups or individuals should be unduly excluded from important social goods and everyone should be able to take part in public life on an equal footing. Social exclusion, stigmatisation and discrimination therefore are not allowed, as is guaranteed by Article 14 ECHR and Article 1 of Protocol No. 12.

ARTICLE 14 ECHR

The enjoyment of the rights and freedoms set forth in this Convention shall be secured without discrimination on any ground such as sex, race, colour, language, religion, political or other opinion, national or social origin, association with a national minority, property, birth or other status.

ARTICE 1 PROTOCOL No. 12

1. The enjoyment of any right set forth by law shall be secured without discrimination on any ground such as sex, race, colour, language, religion, political or other opinion, national or social origin, association with a national minority, property, birth or other status.
2. No one shall be discriminated against by any public authority on any ground such as those mentioned in paragraph 1.

---

[*]   This chapter is based on the author's earlier writings, in particular in *Sdu Commentaar EVRM. Deel 1 – materiële bepalingen [Sdu ECHR Commentary. Part 1 – substantive provisions]*, Den Haag: Sdu 2013. In the fourth edition this chapter was revised and updated by Aalt Willem Heringa and Fried van Hoof.

CONTENTS

1. INTRODUCTION: TWO PROVISIONS

Two ECHR provisions contain a prohibition of discrimination: Article 14 and Article 1 of Protocol No. 12. These provisions are different in that Article 1 of Protocol No. 12 contains an independent and autonomous non-discrimination guarantee, whilst Article 14 is an accessory provision. The accessory character means that Article 14 can only be invoked in conjunction with a right that comes within the ambit of one of the substantive human rights protected by the Convention. Article 1 of Protocol No. 12 deliberately does not contain such a limitation, but can be invoked as soon as there is a difference in treatment in the enjoyment of 'any right set forth by law'.[1] The drafters of Protocol No.

---

[1] *Cf.* R. Wintemute, '"Within the Ambit": How Big is the "Gap" in Article 14 European Convention on Human Rights? Part 1', 4 *European Human Rights Law Review*, 2004, p. 366 at p. 367. See further section 2.2.

12 considered that such an independent prohibition would strengthen the protection against discrimination.[2]

Protocol 12 has not obtained very wide support: although it entered into force in 2005, by 2016 only 19 of 47 ECHR states had ratified the Protocol. Nine states, amongst which Denmark, France, the United Kingdom, Sweden and Switzerland, had not even signed the Protocol. For this reason, it is not surprising that the ECtHR has so far found little opportunity to explain its meaning. Generally, however, it has held that the two provisions should be interpreted in a similar way. Beyond the issue of scope, there are hardly any differences between the two provisions.[3]

Hence, the two different prohibitions of discrimination can be discussed in one single chapter. The chapter starts by explaining the scope of Article 14 ECHR and the meaning of its accessory character; this is followed by a discussion of the scope of application of Article 1 of Protocol No. 12 (section 2). Section 2 also explores the meaning of the lists of grounds of discrimination provided by both articles. Subsequently, section 3 discusses a number of important discrimination concepts, such as substantive and indirect discrimination. Section 4 discusses discriminatory violence and other discriminatory behaviour, while section 5 deals with positive action and reasonable accommodation. Section 6 highlights the tests of comparability and of justification applied in cases of unequal treatment. Finally, section 7 discusses the 'very weighty reasons test' as a special variant of the margin of appreciation doctrine.

2. SCOPE

2.1. SCOPE AND ACCESSORY CHARACTER OF ARTICLE 14

It can be derived from the text of Article 14 ECHR that the prohibition of discrimination only can be invoked in conjunction with one of the other provisions of the ECHR or its Protocols. For the applicability of Article 14 it is not required, that a substantive provision has actually been breached.[4] Moreover, the Court has given a particularly wide reading to the substantive provisions for the purposes of the application of the non-discrimination clause. Decisive for the applicability of Article 14 is whether the facts of the case 'fall within the ambit' of one of the substantive provisions. This means that it is not necessary

---

[2] See Explanatory Report to Protocol No. 12 of the Convention, CETS No. 177; see also Committee on Legal Affairs and Human Rights of the Parliamentary Assembly of the Council of Europe, Report of 14 January 2000, Doc. 8614, para. 4.

[3] *Sejdić and Finci v. Bosnia and Herzegovina*, ECtHR (GC) 22 December 2009, appl. nos. 27996/04 and 34836/05, para. 55.

[4] See, however, *Prince Hans-Adam II of Liechtenstein v. Liechtenstein*, ECtHR 12 July 2001, appl. no. 42527/98, para. 92.

for Article 14 to apply that the facts of a case fall within the actual scope of a substantive rights provision. Instead, it only needs to be shown that there is an objective connection with the substance of the provision.[5] This flexible 'ambit' test renders the non-discrimination clause of Article 14 applicable in a great many cases, including cases on private employment, planning policy, social security and – to some extent – health care.[6]

Of special relevance to the applicability of Article 14 is the Court's 'in for a penny, in for a pound' approach.[7] The Court has taken this approach, for example, in its admissibility decision in Stec.[8] In this case the Court acknowledged that Article 1 of Protocol No. 1 does not oblige the states to provide for a certain type or amount of social benefits and, as such, such social benefits are not covered by Article 1 Protocol No. 1. If, however, a state has voluntarily undertaken to provide for such benefits, they thereby come within the ambit of Article 1 of Protocol No. 1 for the purposes of the applicability of Article 14 and the state must ensure they are guaranteed without any undue discrimination.[9] The Court has held similarly for other state acts which normally would fall outside the scope of the Convention, such as deciding to grant citizenship,[10] setting up and subsidising of educational establishments,[11] conferring specific rights to immigrants,[12] or establishing special compensation regimes.[13]

Regardless of its flexibility, the Court has not completely deprived Article 14 of its accessory character. If the connection between the alleged discrimination and a substantive provision is too remote, the Court still declares the complaint inadmissible. This is illustrated by the *Haas* case, which concerned the refusal by the authorities to recognise the applicant as the heir of P.[14] The applicant stated that the refusal was due to the fact that he was P's unlawful child, which indicated a discrimination based on birth. It was apparent from the facts of the case, however, that P had always denied being the applicant's biological father

---

5   See classically *Marckx v. Belgium*, ECtHR 13 June 1979, appl. no. 6833/74, para. 31.

6   See, e.g., *Sidabras and Džiautas v. Lithuania*, ECtHR 27 July 2004, appl. nos. 55480/00 and 59330/00, paras. 47–50; *Moreno Gómez v. Spain*, ECtHR 16 November 2004, appl. no. 4143/02; *Pentiacova and 48 Others v. Moldova*, ECtHR 4 January 2005 (dec.), appl. no. 14462/03.

7   Further on this approach, see J.H. Gerards, 'The European Court of Human Rights and the National Courts – Giving Shape to the Notion of "Shared Responsibility"', in: J.H. Gerards & J.W.A. Fleuren (eds.), *Implementation of the European Convention on Human Rights and of the Judgments of the ECtHR in National Case Law. A Comparative Analysis*, Antwerp: Intersentia, 2014, pp. 13–94, at pp. 49–51.

8   *Stec and Others v. the United Kingdom*, ECtHR (GC) 6 July 2005 (dec.), appl. nos. 65731/01 and 65900/01.

9   For a similar approach, see *E.B. v. France*, ECtHR (GC) 22 January 2008, appl. no. 43546/02, para. 49; *Carson and Others v. the United Kingdom*, ECtHR 4 November 2008, appl. no. 42184/05, para. 71.

10   *Genovese v. Malta*, ECtHR 11 October 2011, appl. no. 53124/09.

11   *Ponomaryovi v. Bulgaria*, ECtHR 21 June 2011, appl. no. 5335/05.

12   *Hode and Abdi v. the United Kingdom*, ECtHR 6 November 2012, appl. no. 22341/09.

13   *Raviv v. Austria*, ECtHR 13 March 2012, appl. no. 26266/05.

14   *Haas v. the Netherlands*, ECtHR 13 January 2004, appl. no. 36983/97.

and the contact between P and the applicant had been, at the most, sporadic. In the Court's view, this meant that no family life could be established and the facts of the case therefore could not be brought 'within the ambit' of Article 8 of the Convention.[15] Other cases where the Court has excluded application of Article 14 concern the payment of a salary of a particular amount,[16] the choice of language in parliamentary debates,[17] and claims to have access to certain facilities and premises.[18]

Finally, it is important to note that, in most cases, the Court leaves the non-discrimination case undecided if the case can be readily 'solved' by applying one of the Convention's substantive guarantees. The Court's general position is that all rights protected by the Convention must be guaranteed to everyone in an equal manner: 'It is as though Article 14 formed an integral part of each of the provisions laying down rights and freedoms.'[19] Since the Court usually starts its reasoning by examining the complaints made under the substantive provisions, it often will have dealt with the discrimination aspects of the application already if it reaches the complaints made under Article 14. The Court then usually no longer finds it necessary to examine the complaint under the Article 14 separately.[20] In practice, the Court is inclined to deal with the discrimination complaints only if the difference of treatment is a fundamental aspect of the case; if the discrimination complaint clearly relates to a different aspect of the case than the complaint made under the substantive provisions; or if the complaint relates to an aspect of a substantive right which comes within the (wider) ambit of a substantive provision but not within its (more narrow) scope.[21] Moreover, if the non-discrimination complaint clearly forms the core of the application, the Court may even decide to deal with the case only under Article 14 in conjunction with a substantive provision.[22] Hence, the question whether a non-discrimination complaint will be dealt with separately can be answered only based on the facts of the case.[23]

---

[15] See also *Alboize-Barthes and Alboize Montezume v. France*, ECtHR 21 October 2008 (dec.), appl. no. 44421/04.

[16] *Vilho Eskelinen and Others v. Finland*, ECtHR (GC) 19 april 2007, appl. no. 63235/00, para. 94.

[17] *Birk-Lévy v. France*, ECtHR 21 September 2010 (dec.), appl. no. 39426/06.

[18] *Farcaş v. Romania*, ECtHR 14 September 2010 (dec.), appl. no. 32596/04.

[19] *Marckx v. Belgium, supra* n. 5, para. 32.

[20] E.g. *Kamasinski v. Austria*, ECtHR 19 December 1989, appl. no. 9783/82, para. 65; see more recently, e.g., *Yordanova and Others v. Bulgaria*, ECtHR 24 April 2012, appl. no. 25446/06.

[21] E.g. *Airey v. Ireland*, ECtHR 9 October 1979, appl. no. 6289/73, para. 30; *Oršuš and Others v. Croatia*, ECtHR (GC) 16 March 2010, appl. no. 15766/03, para. 144; *Genovese v. Malta, supra* n. 10, paras. 33–36.

[22] E.g. *L. and V. v. Austria*, ECtHR 9 January 2003, appl. nos. 39392/98 and 39829/98, para. 35; see more recently, e.g., *Özgürlük ve Dayanışma Partisi (ÖDP) v. Turkey*, ECtHR 10 May 2012, appl. no. 7819/03; *The Church of Jesus Christ of Latter-Day Saints v. the United Kingdom*, ECtHR 4 March 2014, appl. no. 7552/09.

[23] *Makhashevy v. Russia*, ECtHR 31 July 2012, appl. no. 20546/07, para. 139.

2.2. SCOPE OF ARTICLE 1 OF PROTOCOL No. 12

Article 1(1) of Protocol No. 12 prohibits discrimination 'in the enjoyment of any right set forth by law', while Article 1(2) of Protocol No. 12 generally prohibits discrimination by any public authority. According to the Explanatory Report, the Article thus covers cases of discrimination:

1. in the enjoyment of any right specifically granted to an individual under national law;
2. in the enjoyment of a right which may be inferred from a clear obligation of a public authority under national law, that is, where a public authority is under an obligation under national law to behave in a particular manner;
3. by a public authority in the exercise of discretionary power (for example, granting certain subsidies);
4. by any other act or omission by a public authority (for example, the behaviour of law enforcement officers when controlling a riot).[24]

It can be expected that the first paragraph of Article 1 of Protocol No. 12 ('The enjoyment of any right set forth by law shall be secured (…)') covers the first two categories of discrimination in legislation and policy measures, whilst the second paragraph ('No one shall be discriminated against by any public authority (…)') pertains to the last two categories of discriminatory use of power and 'other acts and omissions' by public authorities and state agents.

The Court generally has found little need to distinguish between the different paragraphs and categories. In the case of *Sejdić and Finci*, for example, where the complaint related to a difference in treatment in electoral legislation, the Court found that Article 1 of Protocol No. 12 was applicable to the case without indicating which paragraph or category of discrimination was concerned.[25] Only in more complex cases may the categories play a certain role, as the case of *Savez Crkava 'Riječ Života'* can illustrate.[26] Reformist churches had complained about the fact that, contrary to registered religious communities, they had not been granted permission to provide pastoral care in various institutions and religious education in schools and to conclude officially recognised religious marriages. Having assessed the applicable national legislation, the Court concluded that it covered the claimed right to provide pastoral care, but it held differently for the right to provide religious education and to conduct marriages; the latter privileges were granted exclusively on the basis of agreements concluded with the Government. Since the State was not bound to enter into such agreements,

---

24 Explanatory Report to Protocol 12 ECHR, ETS No. 177, para. 22.
25 *Sejdić and Finci v. Bosnia and Herzegovina, supra* n. 3. See similarly *Ramaer and Van Willigen v. the Netherlands*, ECtHR 23 October 2012 (dec.), appl. no. 34880/12.
26 *Savez Crkava 'Riječ Života' and Others v. Croatia*, ECtHR 9 December 2010, appl. no. 7798/08.

the complaint did not concern a 'right specifically granted under national law' (category 1). However, the Court considered that the complaints did fall within the third category specified in the Explanatory Report, as they concerned alleged discrimination 'by a public authority in the exercise of discretionary power'. Consequently, Article 1 of Protocol No. 12 to the Convention was applicable to all complaints, albeit for different reasons.

An important, yet still open question is whether Article 1 of Protocol No. 12 can apply to rights which are laid down in international treaties a state has ratified and is bound to comply with. The text of the Explanatory Report does not rule out that 'the word "law" [in the first paragraph] may also cover international law'.[27] It also states, however, that 'this does not mean that this provision entails jurisdiction for the European Court of Human Rights to examine compliance with rules of law in other international instruments'.[28] The Court has not yet been given the opportunity to elucidate what this means for individual complaints about discrimination in the exercise of rights which have been laid down in binding international treaties, but which do not have direct effect or have not been transposed into national law.[29]

2.3. GROUNDS OF DISCRIMINATION

Article 14 and Article 1 of Protocol No. 12 contain identical lists of grounds of discrimination; both provisions also mention that discrimination on 'other status' is prohibited. According to the Court this addition means that the list of grounds is illustrative rather than exhaustive. Consequently, discrimination on grounds other than those expressly mentioned still may fall within the scope of the prohibition of discrimination.[30] Nevertheless, there is some ambiguity in the Court's case law as to whether the scope of the prohibition of discrimination is limited by the specific mention that such a discrimination should be based on an 'other status'.[31] In one line of case law, the Court has stressed that 'there is no call to determine on what ground [the] difference was based, the list of grounds appearing in Article 14 not being exhaustive'.[32] There

---

[27] Explanatory Report Protocol 12, ETS No. 177, para. 29.

[28] *Ibid.*

[29] See further, e.g., N. Grief, 'Non-Discrimination under the European Convention on Human Rights: A Critique of the United Kingdom Government's Refusal to Sign and Ratify Protocol 12', 27 *European Law Review Human Rights Survey*, 2002, p. HR/10 and U. Khaliq, 'Protocol 12 to the European Convention on Human Rights: A Step Forward or a Step Too Far?', *Public Law*, 2001, p. 458.

[30] Classically, e.g., *Engel and Others v. the Netherlands*, ECtHR (GC) 8 June 1976, appl. nos. 5100/71 et al., para. 72.

[31] For a further analysis see J.H. Gerards, 'The Discrimination Grounds of Article 14 ECHR', 13 *Human Rights Law Review*, 2013, pp. 99–124.

[32] E.g. *Rasmussen v. Denmark*, ECtHR 28 November 1984, appl. no. 9118/80, para. 34.

are also judgments, however, in which the Court has held that the requirement of discrimination based on a 'status' means that a discrimination must be based on 'a personal characteristic by which persons or groups of persons are distinguishable from each other'.[33] In the *Carson* case, the Court has tried to bring these two lines of case law together by noting that the words 'other status' should be given a wide meaning, yet the Convention's prohibition of discrimination should not be applied to differences in treatment resulting from the existence of different legal regimes or geographical differences.[34] The intermediate approach adopted in *Carson* implies that the notion of 'status' has a legal impact on the types of grounds covered by the Convention prohibition of discrimination. Nevertheless, it also suggests that not only 'purely' personal, innate and inherent characteristics are covered by it (such as gender, ethnic origin and age), but also other statuses connected to the person of the applicant, such as his place of residence.[35] The Court's case law since *Carson* is not entirely consistent in the application of this intermediate position, however. In some cases, it still requires that a distinction is based on a really 'personal' characteristic, while in other cases it is prepared to provide a wider definition of 'other status'.[36]

3. CONCEPTS OF NON-DISCRIMINATION LAW

3.1. FORMAL AND SUBSTANTIVE DISCRIMINATION

The ECtHR's case law has long been characterised by a formal understanding of the principles of equal treatment and discrimination. The Court originally only showed itself concerned about cases disclosing an actual difference of treatment. If the same rule was applied to two different cases, it would find no discrimination, even if the applicants maintained that the cases were essentially incomparable and therefore the application of the rule had unfairly unequal

---

[33] E.g. *Kjeldsen, Busk Madsen and Pedersen v. Denmark*, ECtHR 7 December 1976, appl. nos. 5095/71, 5920/72 and 5926/72, para. 56.

[34] *Carson v. the United Kingdom*, *supra* n. 9, paras. 70–71. See also, e.g., *Magee v. the United Kingdom*, ECtHR 6 June 2000, appl. no. 28135/95, para. 50.

[35] E.g. *Clift v. the United Kingdom*, ECtHR 13 July 2010, appl. no. 7205/07, para. 59.

[36] See for the 'personal characteristics' approach, e.g., *Springett and Others v. the United Kingdom*, ECtHR 27 April 2010 (dec.), appl. nos. 34726/04, 14287/05 and 34702/05; *Peterka v. the Czech Republic*, ECtHR 4 May 2010, appl. no. 21990/08; *Raviv v. Austria*, *supra* n. 13; *Zammit and Attard Cassar v. Malta*, ECtHR 30 July 2015, appl. no. 1046/12. For a wider reading, or for a complete lack of attention to the issue, see, e.g., *Chabauty v. France*, ECtHR (GC) 4 October 2012, appl. no. 57412/08; *The Church of Jesus Christ of Latter-Day Saints v. the United Kingdom*, *supra* n. 22; *Berkvens and Berkvens v. the Netherlands*, ECtHR 27 May 2014 (dec.), appl. no. 18485/14.

results.[37] In 2000, however, in *Thlimmenos*, the Court recognised that such substantive inequalities (i.e. inequalities of result) are covered by Article 14.[38] The Court expressly held that 'the right not to be discriminated against (…) is also violated when States without an objective and reasonable justification fail to treat differently persons whose situations are significantly different'.[39] This phrase is now part of the Court's well-established case law. Consequently, applicants can complain about unwarranted equal treatment of dissimilar cases just as easily as about unequal treatment of similar cases.[40]

In some cases, the Court even derives positive obligations from the notion of substantive discrimination, as it did in the case of *Yordanova*.[41] This case concerned the intended expulsion of Roma from their (illegally built) houses. The Government had stated that the expulsion followed from a logical application of the rules on illegal inhabitation. If it would not proceed to expel the Roma group, this would amount to privileged treatment and discrimination against the majority population. According to the Court, this argument failed to recognise the applicants' situation as an outcast community and a socially disadvantaged group. The failure to attempt to correct this inequality through different treatment might in itself give rise to a breach of Article 14. Similarly, the Court has held that the implementation of positive measures can be called for in the context of the right to education of members of groups who have suffered from discrimination with lasting effects.[42] These positive obligations are closely related to the concepts of reasonable accommodation and positive action, which are separately addressed in section 5.

3.2. DIRECT AND INDIRECT DISCRIMINATION

Direct discrimination can be defined as a difference in treatment which is directly based on a prohibited ground of discrimination, such as ethnic origin. By contrast, the notion of indirect discrimination refers to measures or decisions which, at face-value, are based on (relatively) neutral grounds (such as linguistic ability), but which in practice appear to cause a disproportionately disadvantageous effect for a group characterised by a salient ground (e.g. ethnic origin).

The concept of indirect discrimination has long remained unused in the case law of the Court. This can be explained at least partly from the fact that

---

[37] See, e.g., *Stubbings and Others v. the United Kingdom*, ECtHR 22 October 1996, appl. nos. 22083/93 and 22095/93.

[38] *Thlimmenos v. Greece*, ECtHR (GC) 6 April 2000, appl. no. 34369/97.

[39] *Ibid.*, para. 44.

[40] See, e.g., *Taddeucci and McCall v. Italy*, ECtHR 30 June 2016, appl. no. 51362/09.

[41] *Yordanova and Others v. Bulgaria*, *supra* n. 20.

[42] *Horváth and Kiss v. Hungary*, ECtHR 29 January 2013, appl. no. 11146/11.

the Convention's non-discrimination clauses do not contain an exhaustive list of grounds. Since almost any difference in treatment is covered by the prohibition of discrimination (as long as it is based on a 'status'), it is hardly necessary to establish that a difference in treatment is directly or indirectly based on one of the grounds expressly mentioned in the provisions. Nevertheless, recognition of the concepts may be of value even for open-textured prohibitions of discrimination, as the ground of discrimination may influence the intensity of the Court's review. As is discussed in more detail in section 7, the Court has applied a very strict test of justification to discrimination based on certain grounds; it has even stated that discrimination that is purely based on 'suspect' grounds, such as race and colour, will never be acceptable. This strict test stands in sharp contrast to the much more deferential test applied to differences in treatment based on, for example, place of residence or immigration status. This can make it valuable for applicants to try to establish that the difference in treatment they have suffered is based on a 'suspect' ground, albeit only indirectly. Moreover, by taking account of the indirect effects of seemingly neutral classifications, the Court can contribute to fighting structural and hidden differences in treatment.[43]

Against this background and for these reasons, the Court has gradually come to recognise the concept of indirect discrimination.[44] The seminal case in which the Court expressly accepted and developed this concept is *D.H. v. the Czech Republic*.[45] In the Czech Republic, children with special learning needs and learning disabilities were placed in special schools. Clearly, thus, the placement policy was based on neutral and pertinent criteria. It appeared in practice, however, that the number of Roma children placed in special schools was much higher than would be expected statistically. According to the applicants, this meant that the seemingly neutral placement policy resulted in indirect discrimination based on ethnic origin, for which there was no justification. In its judgment in the case the Court elaborately explained how it would deal with indirect discrimination complaints.

As a first step, the Court held that a *prima facie* case of indirect discrimination must be established. The applicant bears the burden of persuading the Court that an otherwise neutrally formulated policy or legislation affects a disproportionate number of members of a group characterised by a 'suspect' ground (in *D.H.*: ethnic origin), thereby placing them at a significant disadvantage. Given the potential difficulties for applicants in making out such a *prima facie* case, the Court held that less strict evidential rules should apply. Generally, reliable and significant statistics are sufficient to constitute the necessary prima facie evidence.[46] Later case law has shown that if such statistics are lacking, the Court may take account

---

43   This also seems to be one of the rationales for its indirect discrimination case law; *cf.*, e.g., *Di Trizio v. Switzerland*, ECtHR 2 February 2016, appl. no. 7186/09.

44   E.g. *Hoogendijk v. the Netherlands*, ECtHR 6 January 2005 (dec.), appl. no. 58641/00.

45   *D.H. and Others v. Czech Republic*, ECtHR (GC) 13 November 2007, appl. no. 57325/00.

46   E.g. *Di Trizio v. Switzerland*, *supra* n. 43.

of other types of evidence and look at all evidence in combination. A *prima facie* case can be based, for example, on limited statistical evidence combined with reports of non-governmental or international organisations supporting the arguments of the applicants,[47] or even on logical derivatives of the facts of a particular case.[48] Moreover, the Court has stressed that it is not necessary to prove any discriminatory intent on the part of the relevant authorities.[49]

Once a *prima facie* case of indirect discrimination has been established, the second step is to shift the burden to the respondent state, which must show that the indirect difference in treatment is not discriminatory. This means that the state should prove that the difference in the impact of the legislation was the result of objective factors unrelated to the 'indirect' ground of discrimination (in *D.H.*: the Roma origin of the children). In the case of *D.H.*, for example, the Court examined if the tests and standards used to place pupils in special schools were sufficiently neutrally formulated and did not disclose any negative bias towards Roma children.[50] As it did not find this to be the case, it found a violation of Article 14 ECHR.

3.3. SEGREGATION

Segregation can be defined as the situation where two groups are treated in the same way, but they are physically separated. One can think of a situation where boys and girls, or Roma and non-Roma children, are placed in separate classes, although they are given an education which is similar in content and quality. The Court has most often dealt with these complaints by applying its indirect discrimination approach. An example is the case of *Sampanis*, which concerned a group of Roma children who followed classes in a regular school, but who were placed in separate classes in a different building upon the request of (and after threats made by) the parents of non-Roma children.[51] The Court recognised that the situation had a disproportionately negative impact on the Roma children and it found that the placement in the separate classes was mainly due to the requests and threats of the parents of non-Roma children. For that reason, it not only held

---

[47] E.g. *Oršuš and Others v. Croatia*, *supra* n. 21; and *Opuz v. Turkey*, ECtHR 9 June 2009, appl. no. 33401/02. For a stricter approach, see *A. v. Croatia*, ECtHR 14 October 2010, appl. no. 55164/08.

[48] E.g. *Biao v. Denmark*, ECtHR (GC) 24 May 2016, appl. no. 38590/10, paras. 111–113.

[49] Also, e.g., *Biao v. Denmark*, *supra* n. 48, para. 103. See, however, the case law on forced sterilisation of Roma women, in which the requirement of discriminatory intent does seem to play a role – e.g. *V.C. v. Slovakia*, ECtHR 8 November 2011, appl. no. 18968/07, para. 177 and *I.G. and Others v. Slovakia*, ECtHR 13 November 2012, appl. no. 15966/04.

[50] See similarly *Oršuš and Others v. Croatia*, *supra* n. 21; and *Horváth and Kiss v. Hungary*, *supra* n. 42.

[51] *Sampanis and Others v. Greece*, ECtHR 5 June 2008, appl. no. 32526/05. For another example, see the follow-up case to *Sampanis*: *Sampani and Others v. Greece*, ECtHR 11 December 2012, appl. no. 59608/09.

---

that the situation disclosed a case of indirect discrimination, but it also held that the Government had not succeeded in persuading the Court that this was the result of objective factors unrelated to the Roma origin of the children.

It can be gleaned from the Court's strict review of the justification offered by the Government that the Court is sensitive to the specific discrimination problems connected to involuntary segregation.[52] Indeed, in a case against Hungary, the Court confirmed that the placement of Roma children in special and physically segregated remedial classes creates a presumption of discrimination 'of a type which of itself may amount to degrading treatment'.[53] More recently, this seems to have led the Court to recognise segregation as a distinct concept of discrimination, which does not necessitate a *prima facie* test of indirect discrimination.[54] Instead, as soon as there is evidence of ethnic segregation, positive obligations arise for the state to correct the situation. If the state does not present very good arguments for not taking sufficient action, the Court will find a violation of Article 14 ECHR.[55]

4. DISCRIMINATORILY MOTIVATED BEHAVIOUR AND VIOLENCE

A special category of discrimination is constituted by discriminatory behaviour, such as racist or xenophobic violence. This type of discrimination is special in that it does not necessarily comprise unequal treatment. Racist, xenophobic or sectarian violence are regarded as unacceptable *per se*, not so much because they cause one person to be treated differently from another, but because of the inherently reprehensible motive. As the Court has explained for racial violence, this entails 'a particular affront to human dignity'.[56]

For all such behaviour, the Court has made clear that it is irreconcilable with Article 14 as soon as it is established that there was a discriminatory motive.[57] Consequently, there is no possibility for justification. Moreover, there is no need to point to a comparator to prove that there is a difference in treatment of comparable cases, as normally would be the case in unequal treatment cases (see *infra*, section 6.2). Instead, the focus is entirely on the motives of those responsible for the violence or other behaviour. This also implies that, if in such cases a discriminatory motive or intent is lacking or it cannot be sufficiently substantiated, Article 14 will not apply.[58] The same is true if no causal

---

[52] *Ibid.*, para. 96.
[53] *Horváth and Vadászi v. Hungary*, ECtHR 9 November 2010 (dec.), appl. no. 2351/06.
[54] *Lavida and Others v. Greece*, ECtHR 30 May 2013, appl. no. 7973/10.
[55] *Ibid.*, para. 73.
[56] *Nachova and Others v. Bulgaria*, ECtHR (GC) 6 July 2005, appl. nos. 43577/98 and 43579/98, para. 145.
[57] On the test applied to discrimination in the form of unequal treatment, see *infra*, section 6.
[58] *Aksu v. Turkey*, ECtHR (GC) 15 March 2012, appl. nos. 4149/04 and 41029/04, para. 45.

relationship can be shown between a specific personal characteristic (e.g. sexual orientation) and the decision or act concerned.[59]

Although many discrimination cases of this category concern violence motivated by ethnic or national origin, sexual orientation or religion,[60] discriminatorily motivated acts may take various forms. Examples of non-violent discriminatory behaviour are highly stereotyped and discriminatory comments about homosexuals made in a television show,[61] or the refusal by a national court to grant parental rights to a single parent because of his sexual orientation or religion.[62] Since most cases on the topic concern the use of force by state agents (e.g. police officers) or a third party, however, this section focuses on the case law developed on discriminatory violence.

The Court has formulated the relevant standards for establishing a case of discriminatorily motivated violence in *Nachova*.[63] The case concerned the pursuit of two Roma men by the police, which resulted in the police shooting and killing them. According to the applicants, racist motives had played an important role in the event. In order to establish whether the case disclosed a violation of Article 14, the Court held it was necessary to determine whether racism was a causal factor in the shooting.[64] It thereby adopted the relatively strict standard of proof 'beyond reasonable doubt', although it stressed that such proof may follow from 'the coexistence of sufficiently strong, clear and concordant inferences or of similar unrebutted presumptions of fact'.[65] It is apparent from *Nachova* as well as subsequent judgments that it is relatively difficult to meet this burden of proof. The Court has found a breach of Article 14 only if it can be proved for the concrete case that prejudice formed the direct motive for a certain act. The victim cannot just provide a general reference to expressions of concern by national and international organisations about allegations of violence against ethnic groups by law enforcement officers.[66] Instead, in order to substantiate a claim that the violence was discriminatory, he must refer to concrete and specific facts and circumstances, supported by

---

59   *Sousa Goucha v. Portugal*, ECtHR 22 March 2016, appl. no. 70434/12, paras. 60 and 66.
60   See, e.g., *Milanović v. Serbia*, ECtHR 14 December 2010, appl. no. 44614/07, paras. 96 and 97; *P.F. and E.F. v. the United Kingdom*, ECtHR 23 November 2010 (dec.), appl. no. 28326/09; *Begheluri and Others v. Georgia*, ECtHR 7 October 2014, appl. no. 28490/02; *Identoba and Others v. Georgia*, ECtHR 12 May 2015, appl. no. 73235/12; *M.C. and A.C. v. Romania*, ECtHR 12 April 2016, appl. no. 12060/12.
61   *Cf. Sousa Goucha v. Portugal*, *supra* n. 59, although the Court dealt with the issue under Art. 8 here rather than Art. 14.
62   E.g. *Hoffmann v. Austria*, ECtHR 23 June 1993, appl. no. 12875/87; *Salgueiro da Silva Mouta v. Portugal*, ECtHR 21 December 1999, appl. no. 33290/96.
63   *Nachova and Others v. Bulgaria*, *supra* n. 56.
64   *Idem*, para. 146.
65   *Idem*, para. 147.
66   *Cobzaru v. Romania*, ECtHR 26 July 2007, appl. no. 48254/99, para. 95; *Mižigárová v. Slovakia*, ECtHR 14 December 2010, appl. no. 74832/01, para. 117.

witness statements and police reports.[67] In more recent cases, however, the Court has accepted that the existence of a systematic practice of discrimination in a state against certain groups, the existence of strongly negative attitudes, or the specific vulnerability and socially disadvantaged position of that group, may be important factors in establishing a *prima facie* case of discrimination.[68]

When a *prima facie* case has been made, the state is asked to rebut the allegations by providing for a plausible alternative explanation of the situation. When no such explanation can be given, the Court will either find a substantive violation of Article 14 directly (in cases where state agents, such as police officers, were directly responsible for the violence), or it may turn to examining whether the state has sufficiently complied with its positive obligations. These positive obligations are twofold: firstly, states incur compelling substantive positive obligations to protect people against discriminatory violence when they are sufficiently aware of the risk of such violence; secondly, they have a procedural positive obligation to carefully investigate instances where such violence appears to have occurred and they need to provide for sufficient remedies.[69]

Many of the cases on substantive, protective and preventive measures focus on whether a state knew or reasonably could have known of the existence of a concrete risk of violence against a particular group or person. Especially in states where a violent religious climate prevails or where strongly negative attitudes towards sexual minorities or other vulnerable groups exist, the responsible authorities should anticipate the use of violence against such groups in case of gatherings, meetings or protests and they should provide for their protection.[70] Such protection may entail concrete action, such as police assistance, but the Court also has held that states more generally must provide for adequate protection against offences with discriminatory motives.[71] Such protection should take the shape of separate criminalisation of discriminatory violence or penalty-enhancing provisions.[72] Specifically for domestic violence, moreover, the Court has held that the national authorities are obliged to fully appreciate the seriousness and extent of the problem of such violence and its discriminatory effect on women. This means that the states need to institute an adequate system of prevention and protection against such domestic violence.[73]

---

[67] *Cobzaru v. Romania, supra* n. 66, para. 94. For successful claims, see *Stoica v. Romania*, ECtHR 4 March 2008, appl. no. 42722/02, paras. 125–130; *Makhashevy v. Russia, supra* n. 23, paras. 176–179; *Begheluri and Others v. Georgia, supra* n. 60, para. 176.

[68] E.g. *Begheluri and Others v. Georgia, supra* n. 60; *Identoba and Others v. Georgia, supra* n. 60; *Balász v. Hungary*, ECtHR 20 October 2015, appl. no. 15529/12; *M.C. and A.C. v. Romania, supra* n. 60.

[69] E.g. *Identoba and Others v. Georgia, supra* n. 60, para. 80.

[70] *Begheluri and Others v. Georgia, supra* n. 60, paras. 119 and 179; *Identoba and Others v. Georgia, supra* n. 60, para. 80.

[71] E.g. *Yotova v. Bulgaria*, ECtHR 23 October 2012, appl. no. 43606/04, paras. 109–110.

[72] *Idem*, para. 104.

[73] *T.M. and C.M. v. Moldova*, ECtHR 28 January 2014, appl. no. 26608/11, para. 62.

When possibly discriminatory acts of violence have occurred, the states have a positive obligation to conduct an effective investigation, regardless of whether it was the state or a third party which has engaged in the violent acts.[74] This obligation will only arise, however, if the state could have had a reasonable suspicion of discriminatory motives. The Court thereby takes account of the special features of the individual case (e.g. racist insults that have been shouted or discriminatory messages that have been posted on social media), as well as of general information about the likelihood of discriminatory motives in a specific context.[75] It is up to the applicant to make out a *prima facie* case of a suspicion of discriminatory motives, but in relation to the positive obligation to investigate, the burden of proof is relatively light.[76] For example, there is no need for the applicant to prove that the behaviour was based on no other motives than his personal characteristics; the Court has recognised that perpetrators may have mixed motives.[77] At the same time, the Court has acknowledged that investigating discriminatory motives may be difficult for the national authorities. For that reason, the obligation to investigate possibly discriminatory overtones to a violent act is an obligation to use best endeavours.[78] Nevertheless, it has held that the investigation must be pursued 'with vigour and impartiality'.[79] In particular if there is evidence of patterns of violence and intolerance in a certain state, a high standard is required of states to respond to alleged bias-motivated incidents.[80] In this regard, the authorities must do what is reasonable in the circumstances to collect and secure the evidence, explore all practical means of discovering the truth and deliver fully reasoned, impartial and objective decisions, without omitting suspicious facts that may be indicative of discriminatory violence.[81] Finally, the state needs to provide for appropriate legal avenues for victims to seek a remedy for discriminatory violence or behaviour.[82]

---

[74]   *Nachova and Others v. Bulgaria, supra* n. 56, para. 161.

[75]   See, e.g., *Dimitrova and Others v. Bulgaria*, ECtHR 27 January 2011, appl. no. 44862/04, para. 98; *M. and Others v. Italy and Bulgaria*, ECtHR 31 July 2012, appl. no. 40020/03, para. 178; *T.M. and C.M. v. Moldova, supra* n. 73, para. 62; *Balász v. Hungary, supra* n. 68; *M.G. v. Turkey*, ECtHR 22 March 2016, appl. no. 646/10.

[76]   The Court relatively frequently finds that the national authorities had a positive obligation to investigate; see, e.g., *Cobzaru v. Romania, supra* n. 66; *Stoica v. Romania, supra* n. 67; *Turan Cakir v. Belgium*, ECtHR 10 March 2009, appl. no. 44256/06; *B.S. v. Spain*, ECtHR 24 July 2012, appl. no. 47159/08.

[77]   *Balász v. Hungary, supra* n. 68, para. 70.

[78]   *Idem.*

[79]   *Nachova and Others v. Bulgaria, supra* n. 56, para. 160.

[80]   *R.B. v. Hungary*, ECtHR 12 April 2016, appl. no. 64602/12, para. 84.

[81]   *Nachova and Others v. Bulgaria, supra* n. 56, para. 160.

[82]   *R.B. v. Hungary, supra* n. 80, para. 90.

5. POSITIVE ACTION AND REASONABLE ACCOMMODATION

Positive action and preferential treatment measures are generally adopted to remove or compensate for factual inequalities in society, or to arrive at a more proportionate representation of certain groups. Thus far, the Court has found little opportunity to develop a doctrine on positive action. The lack of case law on this topic is understandable from the fact that such positive action measures are usually taken in the field of employment law. This field has been brought within the ambit of Article 8 ECHR to a limited extent only, which means that Article 14 can hardly ever be invoked because of its accessory character.

Nevertheless, in different fields, there are some cases from which the Court's views on the topic can be gleaned. The case of *Sejdić and Finci*, for example, concerned the design of the electoral system for Bosnia and Herzegovina. In order to be eligible for the parliamentary and presidential elections, candidates had to declare their affiliation to one of three ethnically defined 'constituencies' (Serbs, Bosniacs and Croats). In the applicants' view this amounted to discrimination, but the Government defended the system by pointing to the necessity to ensure a balanced and proportionate representation of the different ethnic groups in the complicated society of Bosnia and Herzegovina. The Court recognised that the Convention does not prohibit the states 'from treating groups differently in order to correct "factual inequalities" between them'.[83] Apparently, thus, the Court accepted removal of and compensation for inequalities as a reasonable basis for unequal treatment. In this as well as in similar cases on electoral rights, however, the Court also has made clear that there is no positive obligation on the states to actually provide for such compensation.[84] Moreover, the Court has left a wide margin of appreciation to the states as to how they would like to promote effective participation of persons belonging to national minorities in public affairs.[85]

By contrast, the Court has accepted that the states may have a positive obligation to provide for special protection of vulnerable persons and minorities in order to compensate for the special difficulties they are confronted with.[86] The Court has not yet given a concrete elaboration of the notion of positive action, however, nor has it developed any special standards to be used in the particular context of positive action measures.

In recent case law, the Court has started developing a notion that is somewhat related to positive action – the notion of reasonable accommodation. Put shortly, this notion implies that states may be required to make special provision

---

[83]   *Supra* n. 3, para. 44.
[84]   *Partei Die Friesen v. Germany*, ECtHR 28 January 2016 (dec.), appl. no. 65480/10.
[85]   *Idem.*
[86]   E.g. *Yordanova and Others v. Bulgaria*, *supra* n. 20; *Horváth and Kiss v. Hongaria*, *supra* n. 42, para. 104.

for certain groups in order to allow them to fully participate in society. The Court first applied this notion in *Çam*, a case brought by a blind girl who was not admitted to a music conservatory because she could not demonstrate that she would be capable of attending all lessons.[87] The Court held that the State is obliged to take account of the needs of pupils such as Ms Çam and of their particular vulnerability. Although the Court acknowledged that the national authorities are generally better placed than it is itself to estimate which measures may be called for, the State at the least should make an effort to identify the needs of Ms Çam and try to search for facilities to accommodate these needs. In similar vein, in *Guberina* the Court held that the State should have done more to ensure that the father of a severely disabled child could fully participate by allowing him to benefit from a tax exemption for those having difficulties to meet their housing needs.[88] In this respect, the Court has referred to the UN Convention on Disability Discrimination and it aims to align the standards it develops under Article 14 to those laid down in that Convention.[89]

6. REVIEW OF UNEQUAL TREATMENT

6.1. STANDARDS AND ELEMENTS

Article 14 and Article 1 of Protocol No. 12 do not contain express limitation clauses, but it cannot be derived from this that the provisions have an absolute character and no unequal treatment is allowed. Quite to the contrary: the Court mentioned in its landmark judgment in the *Belgian Linguistics* case that reading Article 14 as forbidding every difference in treatment would lead to absurd results.[90] By lack of an express limitation clause, the Court has developed its own standards to assess the justifiability of differences in treatment, in particular in the *Belgian Linguistics* case and in *Marckx*.[91] In this regard, there are no significant differences between the standards used in cases on Article 14 and Article 1 of Protocol No. 12.[92] This is in line with the intentions of the drafters of Protocol 12, who wanted the meaning of the term 'discrimination' of Article 1 of Protocol No. 12 to be identical to that in Article 14 of the Convention.[93]

---

[87]   *Çam v. Turkey*, ECtHR 23 February 2016, appl. no. 51500/08.
[88]   *Guberina v. Croatia*, ECtHR 22 March 2016, appl. no. 23682/13.
[89]   *Idem*, para. 92.
[90]   *Case Relating to Certain Aspects of the Laws on the Use of Languages in Education in Belgium*, ECtHR 23 July 1968, appl. nos. 1474/62 et al.
[91]   *Idem*; *Marckx v. Belgium*, *supra* n. 5, para. 32.
[92]   *Sejdić and Finci v. Bosnia and Herzegovina*, *supra* n. 3, para. 55; *Ramaer and Van Willigen v. the Netherlands*, *supra* n. 25.
[93]   Explanatory Memorandum Protocol 12, ETS No. 177, para. 20.

The standards developed in the Court's case law can schematically be presented as follows:[94]

1. Is the applicant placed in a similar or analogous position as the person or group he refers to?
   a. If no: the difference in treatment is acceptable and does not constitute prohibited discrimination;
   b. If yes:
2. Does the difference in treatment have a reasonable and objective justification?
   a. Does the difference in treatment pursue a legitimate aim?
   b. Is there a reasonable relationship of proportionality between the means employed and the aim sought to be realised?

Especially in regard to the test of justification, the Court often accords a certain margin of appreciation to the state, which will vary in scope according to the circumstances of the case, the subject matter and its background.[95] If a narrow margin of appreciation is accorded, the margin of appreciation formula is often replaced by the so-called 'very weighty reasons test'. This test implies very strict scrutiny of the justification and a difference in treatment subjected to this test is hardly ever sustained. Section 7 further discusses the very weighty reasons test and the circumstances in which it applies.

Finally, it is important to note that the Court will never accept a justification for cases of discriminatory behaviour or acts of violence, as discussed in section 4. This can be explained by the fact that these cases are characterised by a clearly discriminatory motive or intent, of which the Court has held that this is inherently unacceptable and therefore incompatible with the Convention.

6.2. COMPARABILITY

According to the Court's decision model, there is a need for justification only if the facts of the case actually disclose a difference in treatment. This may be either a formal difference in treatment (i.e. unequal treatment of similar cases) or a substantive difference in treatment (i.e. equal treatment of dissimilar cases or inequality of result).[96] This difference in treatment must amount to a real disadvantage in the treatment of one group or person compared to another.[97] Furthermore, it must relate to groups, persons or situations which

---

[94] See J.H. Gerards, *Judicial Review in Equal Treatment Cases*, Leiden: Martinus Nijhoff, 2005, p. 123.

[95] *Rasmussen v. Denemark, supra* n. 32, para. 40.

[96] Next to this it is possible that the case discloses an indirect discrimination on a certain ground, which is a category of cases which has been discussed separately, in section 3.2.

[97] *British Gurkha Welfare Society and Others v. the United Kingdom*, ECtHR 15 September 2016, appl. no. 44818/11, para. 77.

are in a sufficiently analogous position. The Court has indicated that this does not require that the comparator groups be identical or in a fully analogous position.[98] The applicable standard is whether the applicant was in a relevantly similar situation to other persons or groups.[99] This has to be established for each individual case, based on the specific circumstances.[100] To illustrate, in a case concerning a difference in treatment of advertisements placed by animal protection groups and by the meat industry,[101] the Court mentioned that the promotions of the meat industry were economic in nature, whereas the message of the advertisements by the animal protection group were political in nature. Using the yardstick of the nature of the aim of the advertisements, it could establish that the cases were relevantly different and, therefore, the decision did not disclose any prohibited form of discrimination. By contrast, a case about differences in social security benefits for patients detained in a psychiatric hospital concerned as many as four comparator groups.[102] Distinctions were made between 'civil patients' and three groups of convicted prisoners, who had been placed in a psychiatric hospital at different moments and for different reasons. The Court acknowledged that there were significant differences between the four groups of detainees in terms of their criminal law status.[103] Nevertheless, the Court found it established that all groups had in common that their stay in hospital served a curative purpose.[104] It considered those similarities sufficiently relevant as to enable it to proceed to the justification stage of the Article 14 test.

Hence, the application of the test of comparability is strongly dependent on the facts of each individual case. Nevertheless, more generally, it can be seen that the Court does not accept comparability in cases where the state cannot be held responsible for certain differences, because they occurred naturally, they were the result of technical differences, or they were brought about by the existence of separate legal regimes. An example of the first situation is the case of *Schwizgebel*, which concerned a maximum age limit for adoption by single parents.[105] According to the applicant, the age limit resulted in unequal treatment between adoptive parents and women who can give birth to biological children. The Court held that the situations were not relevantly comparable as the state had no influence over the possibility for women to have biological children.[106] An

---

[98]   *Laduna v. Slovakia*, ECtHR 13 December 2011, appl. no. 31827/02, para. 56.

[99]   *Idem*.

[100] Nevertheless, the Court may sometimes assess the reasonableness of a justification in cases where it doubts the comparability of the situations presented to it; see, e.g., *The Church of Jesus Christ of Latter-Day Saints v. the United Kingdom*, *supra* n. 22.

[101] *VgT Verein gegen Tierfabriken v. Switzerland*, ECtHR 28 June 2001, appl. no. 24699/94, para. 86.

[102] *S.S. v. the United Kingdom*, ECtHR 21 April 2015 (dec.), appl. nos. 40356/10 and 54466/10.

[103] *Idem*, para. 40.

[104] *Idem*, para. 41.

[105] *Schwizgebel v. Switzerland*, ECtHR 10 June 2010, appl. no. 25762/07.

[106] *Ibid.*, para. 84.

example of the second situation can be seen in a case about French legislation which authorised the audio-visual media to broadcast motor-sports competitions in France without concealing the cigarette brands displayed on the cars, drivers' suits or tracks.[107] At the same time, the legislation prohibited the publication of photographs of such competitions if the cigarette logos and advertisements were not made invisible or blurred. The Court held that these situations were not sufficiently analogous, as it was not feasible technically to hide the logos and advertisements on audio-visual footage.[108] The third situation can be seen where a state has concluded bilateral social security treaties only with certain states. According to the Court, nationals who live in countries which are not party to such reciprocal social security agreements are not in a relevantly similar position to residents of countries which are party to such agreements.[109]

6.3. OBJECTIVE AND REASONABLE JUSTIFICATION

The first part of the Court's test of justification entails the examination of whether the difference in treatment pursued a legitimate aim. Since Article 14 and Article 1 of Protocol No. 12 do not contain an exhaustive list of acceptable aims, the Court is free to decide whether or not to accept certain objectives as legitimate. In its case law it has held that certain aims or motives for unequal treatment never can be accepted. This is true, firstly, for aims which have been considered impermissible already at the national level, for instance because they cannot be reconciled with domestic law.[110] Secondly, differences in treatment stemming from negative attitudes or a predisposed bias against a certain minority cannot be regarded as legitimate.[111] In the same vein, general and unfounded assumptions, unwarranted generalisations, prevailing social prejudice and stereotypical views on (the behaviour of) certain groups cannot constitute a justifiable basis for a difference in treatment.[112]

The Court's case law is rather ambivalent as to the acceptability of respect for traditional views as a legitimate aim. The Court has rejected this aim in relatively strong wording in several cases,[113] but in other cases it has accepted

---

[107] *Hachette Filipacchi Presse Automobile and Dupuy v. France*, ECtHR 5 March 2009, appl. no. 13353/05.

[108] *Ibid.*, para. 63.

[109] E.g. *Carson v. the United Kingdom*, supra n. 9, paras. 88–90.

[110] *Hode and Abdi v. the United Kingdom*, supra n. 12, paras. 53–54.

[111] *L. and V. v. Austria*, supra n. 22, para. 52; *Alekseyev v. Russia*, ECtHR 21 October 2010, appl. nos. 4916/07, 25924/08 and 14599/09, para. 109.

[112] E.g. *Palau-Martinez v. France*, ECtHR 16 December 2003, appl. no. 64927/01, para. 42; *Kiyutin v. Russia*, ECtHR 10 March 2011, appl. no. 2700/10, para. 68; *Konstantin Markin v. Russia*, ECtHR (GC) 22 March 2012, appl. no. 30078/06, paras. 141 and 143; *Vrountou v. Cyprus*, ECtHR 13 October 2015, appl. no. 33631/06, para. 75; *Biao v. Denmark*, supra n. 49, para. 126.

[113] See in particular *Konstantin Markin v. Russia*, supra n. 112, paras. 127 and 142.

that 'protection of the family in the traditional sense is, in principle, a weighty and legitimate reason which may justify a difference in treatment'.[114] When it turns out that there is a growing awareness at the national level of the discriminatory character of a certain traditional measure, however, it seems that the Court will hold this against the state and will find it more difficult to accept a justification.[115] In addition, it has held that – as such – traditional family values cannot serve to justify a (direct or indirect) discrimination based on a suspect ground such as sexual orientation.[116]

The second part of the Court's justification test entails a review of the proportionality of the difference in treatment. The Court has made clear that proportionality requires that the difference in treatment must in principle be suitable and necessary to realise the aim pursued.[117] In addition, it has held that some objectives which, at face value, constitute a legitimate aim, cannot provide for a justification when a closer look is taken. Although financial or budgetary considerations generally can be reasonable aims, for example, the Court has held that they cannot by themselves constitute a sufficient justification for unequal treatment based on 'suspect grounds', such as nationality or gender.[118] Further, the Court has generally rejected general or blanket rules which do not do justice to the individual circumstances of the case. In the case of *Kiyutin*, for example, the Russian legislation provided that any application for a residence permit would be refused if the applicant was unable to show his HIV-negative status.[119] The Court objected to the indiscriminate nature of the legislation, which did not entail any individualised judicial evaluation and which did not require the national authorities to take into account further information on the health risks and family ties of the individual applicant. An exception to this general line in the Court's case law concerns social security regulations. The Court has accepted that in creating social security schemes it can be necessary to use cut-off points that apply to large groups of people.[120] Generally such broad categorisations, even if they seem rather arbitrary, are considered to fall within the wide margin of appreciation the states are accorded in this field. For the field of social security the Court has also accepted that it may take time to remove disparities

---

114   *Kozak v. Poland*, ECtHR 2 March 2010, appl. no. 13102/02, para. 98. See also, e.g., *Karner v. Austria*, ECtHR 24 July 2003, appl. no. 40016/98, para. 41 and *X. and Others v. Austria*, ECtHR (GC) 19 February 2013, appl. no. 19010/07.

115   *Cf. Di Trizio v. Switzerland*, *supra* n. 43.

116   *Taddeucci and McCall v. Italy*, *supra* n. 40.

117   E.g. *Karner v. Austria*, *supra* n. 114, para. 43; *Kozak v. Poland*, *supra* n. 114, para. 92.

118   E.g. *Dhahbi v. Italy*, ECtHR 8 April 2014, appl. no. 17120/09; *Vrountou v. Cyprus*, *supra* n. 112, para. 79. This may be different, however, in certain social security cases; see, e.g., *British Gurkha Welfare Society and Others v. the United Kingdom*, *supra* n. 97, para. 83.

119   *Kiyutin v. Russia*, *supra* n. 112, paras. 72 and 73; see also e.g. *Zaunegger v. Germany*, ECtHR 3 December 2009, appl. no. 22028/04.

120   *Twizell v. United Kingdom*, ECtHR 20 May 2008, appl. no. 25379/02, para. 24. See also, e.g., *Carson and Others v. the United Kingdom*, *supra* n. 9, para. 62 and *Maggio and Others v. Italy*, ECtHR 31 May 2011, appl. no. 46286/09.

which have been part of the system for a long time, such as differences in the pensionable ages for men and women.[121] As long as there is a gradual change in the system, the Court accepts that remaining inequalities will not easily constitute prohibited discrimination.[122] Only if the developments really are too slow or they are obstructed without there being any good reasons for this, the Court will hold differently.[123]

Finally, the Court sometimes pays attention to the aspect of over-inclusiveness or under-inclusiveness of legislation. Over-inclusiveness means that cases are brought within the scope of legislation which, given the specific aims of the legislation, should not be covered by it. Under-inclusiveness relates to the opposite situation, i.e. the situation in which certain cases fall outside the scope of a certain measure while they actually should be covered in light of the aims pursued. Both situations can be problematic from the perspective of the prohibition of discrimination. Over-inclusiveness may mean that a rule entailing a burden (e.g. a tax measure or a sanction regime) is applied to more persons or groups than is reasonable given its aims. Under-inclusive legislation may be detrimental if it means that persons or groups are unjustifiably excluded from certain benefits. An example of both elements can be found in *Vučković*.[124] The applicants in the case were reservists who were entitled to receiving a *per diem*, yet in practice these were not paid out. After the reservists had objected to this, the state decided that only the reservists residing in a small number of municipalities would be guaranteed gradual payment of their entitlements. According to the state these municipalities were chosen because of their underdeveloped status, which implied the reservists' indigence. The Court held that this classification was not compatible with Article 14 because of its over- and under-inclusiveness. There was no evidence that only the reservists residing in the listed municipalities could be regarded as indigent, while all other reservists without a registered residence in these municipalities could not. The other way around, surely not all reservists living in the municipalities could be considered indigent. Hence, the Court concluded that the classification 'was nothing short of arbitrary'.[125]

---

121 E.g. *Stec v. the United Kingdom*, *supra* n. 8, paras. 61–66. For application in a different context, see *British Gurkha Welfare Society and Others v. the United Kingdom*, *supra* n. 97.

122 *Idem*. See also, in a different context, *Stummer v. Austria*, ECtHR (GC) 7 July 2011, appl. no. 37452/02.

123 E.g. *Konstantin Markin v. Russia*, *supra* n. 112, paras. 139–140; see also *Andrle v. the Czech Republic*, ECtHR 17 February 2011, appl. no. 6268/08, para. 59.

124 *Vučković and Others v. Serbia*, ECtHR 28 August 2012, appl. nos. 17153/11 and Others; the Grand Chamber declared the case inadmissible for non-exhaustion of domestic remedies and therefore did not address the merits of the Art. 14 complaint (see ECtHR (GC) 25 March 2014).

125 *Ibid.*, para. 85. For other examples, see *X. and Others v. Austria*, *supra* n. 114, para. 144; *Vrountou v. Cyprus*, *supra* n. 112, para. 77; *Biao v. Denmark*, *supra* n. 49, para. 125.

7. VERY WEIGHTY REASONS TEST AND 'SUSPECT' GROUNDS OF DISCRIMINATION

7.1. INTENSITY OF REVIEW IN DISCRIMINATION CASES

The Court may accord a certain margin of appreciation to the states in deciding whether a difference in treatment can be regarded as justifiable. In relation to classifications and unequal treatment in social security in particular, the margin of appreciation generally is a wide one and the Court's justification review will be deferential. This is clearly reflected in the social security case law discussed in section 6, where the Court has accepted, for example, general and indiscriminate measures and gradual removal of factual differences.

In relation to Article 14, the scope of the margin of appreciation is not only determined by the usual factors, such as the socio-economic character of the policy area involved. An important, often decisive factor is the ground on which the difference in treatment is based. According to well-established case law of the Court, some grounds of discrimination can be considered to be 'suspicious' or, with an American term, 'suspect'. This is true in particular for grounds which relate to personal characteristics salient to vulnerable, stigmatised groups, or to groups which have for a long time been subjected to discrimination. In the Court's terminology, a discrimination based on such suspect grounds can only be justified by 'very weighty reasons'.

The very weighty reasons requirement corresponds with a very narrow margin of appreciation for the state and, consequently, with very strict review of the justification advanced by the state. In practice, it is rare for differences in treatment to survive the application of the test. Moreover, in many cases the Court will not even get to the stage of reviewing the arguments adduced by the state in justification of the difference in treatment. For example, the applicant in *Timishev* was an ethnic Chechen who had been refused entry to the Kabardino-Balkar Republic of the Russian Federation.[126] The Court found that the refusal was essentially based on the applicant's Chechen origin. After having recalled that discrimination on grounds of origin triggered the application of the very weighty reasons test, it held that 'no difference in treatment which is based exclusively or to a decisive extent on a person's ethnic origin is capable of being objectively justified in a contemporary democratic society built on the principles of pluralism and respect for different cultures'.[127] Hence, if a case is purely or to a decisive extent based on the prohibited or suspect ground, the very weighty reasons test implies that the Court will find a violation of Article 14 without conducting any justification review.

---

[126] *Timishev v. Russia*, ECtHR 13 December 2005, appl. nos. 55762/00 and 55974/00.
[127] *Ibid.*, para. 58.

In other cases, the state may try to argue that the difference in treatment, even if it is based on a suspect ground, can be justified by important objectives of general interest. The very weighty reasons test then implies that the burden of proof for the justification fully lies with the respondent state and that the Court will critically review any of the arguments presented. In particular, the Court will set high demands for the suitability and necessity of the difference in treatment to achieve a compelling general interest.[128] In relation to legislative classifications the Court also requires that the state show it was unavoidable to use the suspect ground (rather than a more objective criterion) to delineate the scope of application of legislation.[129] Perhaps not surprisingly, the Court does not often conclude that Article 14 has not been violated in such cases.[130]

7.2. SUSPECT GROUNDS

Since the very weighty reasons test is only applied to discrimination based on certain grounds, it is important to understand which grounds have been classified as 'suspect' grounds. Thus far the test has been applied in relation to the following grounds:

– Race and ethnicity
– Nationality
– Birth or origin (legitimate/illegitimate; adoption)
– Sexual orientation
– Mental or physical disability, chronic illness, HIV-positive status
– Gender
– Religion.

Hereafter these grounds are briefly discussed, paying attention to the reasons why the Court has accepted the application of the very weighty reasons test in relation to them, to the meaning of these grounds and to some exceptions the Court has accepted.

7.3. RACE AND ETHNICITY

Already in 1973 the former European Commission of Human Rights stressed that discrimination based on race constituted a special form of affront to human dignity and it held that differential treatment of a group of persons on

---

[128] *X. and Others v. Austria, supra* n. 114, para. 140.
[129] *Idem.*
[130] For an exception, see, e.g., *Qing v. Portugal*, ECtHR 5 November 2015, appl. no. 69861/11.

the basis of race might be capable of constituting degrading treatment.[131] It took until 2005 before the Court found the opportunity to expressly embrace this position by applying the very weighty reasons test to discrimination based on ethnic origin.[132] In its judgment in *Timishev*, the Court stressed that racial discrimination is a particularly invidious kind of discrimination and, in view of its perilous consequences, requires from the authorities special vigilance and a vigorous reaction.[133] It is clear from the judgment that the Court will hardly ever accept ethnic origin as a permissible ground for discrimination. If a difference in treatment is based exclusively or to a decisive extent on a person's ethnic origin, it never can be capable of being objectively justified.[134] If there are other grounds and arguments which have been presented as justification, the Court may undertake to review such arguments, yet it sets very high demands and it usually will find a violation of the prohibition of discrimination.[135] Importantly, moreover, also when the case concerns indirect discrimination, it falls to the government to put forward 'compelling or very weighty reasons unrelated to ethnic origin'.[136]

The Court has given a wide definition of the notions of ethnicity and race. In *Timishev*, the Court stressed that ethnicity and race are related and overlapping concepts.[137] It recognised that 'whereas the notion of race is rooted in the idea of biological classification of human beings into subspecies according to morphological features such as skin colour or facial characteristics, ethnicity has its origin in the idea of societal groups marked by common nationality, tribal affiliation, religious faith, shared language, or cultural and traditional origins and backgrounds.'[138]

However, the differences between the concepts are not relevant to the application of the very weighty reasons test, as the Court also held that 'discrimination on account of one's actual or perceived ethnicity is a form of racial discrimination'.[139]

More recently, the Court has accepted that discrimination based on the duration of residency in a certain state, or discrimination based on national origin, may amount to indirect discrimination based on ethnicity and may thereby trigger the very weighty reasons test to apply.[140] Nevertheless, it has also

---

[131] *East African Asians v. the United Kingdom*, EComHR 14 December 1973, appl. nos. 4403-4419/70, 4422/70, 4434/70, 4443/70, 4476-4478/70, 4486/70, 4501/70 and 4526-4530/70, para. 207.

[132] *Timishev v. Russia, supra* n. 126.

[133] *Idem*, para. 56.

[134] *Timishev v. Russia, supra* n. 126, para. 58.

[135] See, e.g., *Sejdić and Finci v. Bosnia and Herzegovina, supra* n. 3.

[136] *Biao v. Denmark, supra* n. 49, para. 114.

[137] *Timishev v. Russia, supra* n. 126, para. 55.

[138] *Ibid.*

[139] *Idem*, para. 56; see also *Sejdić and Finci v. Bosnia and Herzegovina*, ECtHR (GC) 22 December 2009, *supra* n. 3, para. 43.

[140] *Biao v. Denmark, supra* n. 49.

mentioned that race and national origin are clearly distinct grounds, which may deserve a different assessment, although they may be strongly connected.[141]

7.4. NATIONALITY

In the *Gaygusuz* case, decided in 1996, the Court accepted that 'very weighty reasons would have to be put forward before the Court could regard a difference of treatment based exclusively on the ground of nationality as compatible with the Convention'.[142] This may have come as a surprise at the time, as the Court usually left a wide margin of appreciation to the states in cases in which a complaint was made about nationality-based differences in treatment.[143] The earlier cases all related to migration law related issues, however, whilst the *Gaygusuz* case concerned a disparity laid down in a social security measure. The Court has never clearly explained the rationale for the application of the very weighty reasons test to nationality in this context, but it may be that it considers it inherently unfair if national measures related to social security, taxation, detention regimes etc., distinguish between residents purely on basis of their nationality.[144] Moreover, it seems that the consensus rationale plays a certain role here, at the least when the case concerns a difference in treatment between nationals from birth and other nationals, including naturalised persons.[145]

It seems that a difference in treatment should be directly based on nationality in order for the very weighty reasons test to apply. Classifications based on related grounds, such as immigration status, have not as such been regarded as 'suspect'.[146] Indeed, the Court has even chosen to leave the states a wide margin of appreciation as regards differences of treatment based on such grounds.[147] The reason for this seems to be that the Court regards immigration status as a so-called 'choice ground'. Because the individual has deliberately decided to immigrate, while he also could have chosen to avoid the negative consequences of an immigration status by not doing so, the Court seems to see less need for very strict scrutiny than in cases of direct nationality discrimination. By contrast, in *Andrejeva* the Court held that it could not have been expected of the applicant to avoid discrimination by altering her nationality, as this would

---

[141]   *British Gurkha Welfare Society and Others v. the United Kingdom, supra* n. 97, para. 58.
[142]   *Gaygusuz v. Austria*, ECtHR 16 September 1996, appl. no. 17371/90, para. 42.
[143]   E.g. *Moustaquim v. Belgium*, ECtHR 18 February 1991, appl. no. 12313/86.
[144]   See, e.g., *Luczak v. Poland*, ECtHR 27 March 2007, appl. no. 77782/01, para. 52; *Andrejeva v. Latvia*, ECtHR (GC) 18 February 2009, appl. no. 55707/00; *Fawsie v. Greece*, ECtHR 28 October 2010, appl. no. 40080/07, para. 35; *Rangelov v. Germany*, ECtHR 22 March 2012, appl. no. 5123/07; *Dhahbi v. Italy, supra* n. 118.
[145]   *Biao v. Denmark, supra* n. 49, para. 132.
[146]   *Bah v. United Kingdom*, ECtHR 27 September 2009, appl. no. 56328/07.
[147]   *Ibid.*

render Article 14 devoid of substance.[148] The Court has also accepted that the element of choice is less relevant in relation to someone's status as refugee.[149] Finally, the Court has accepted that certain instances of discrimination based on nationality-related factors, such as the length of stay in a certain state after having obtained the nationality of that state, may amount to indirect discrimination based on ethnic origin.[150] If this can be established on the basis of concrete evidence, the very weighty reasons test will apply for that reason.

Finally, it should be stressed that the case law of the Court on nationality discrimination is not entirely consistent. In a variety of cases the Court has mentioned that a distinction (e.g. a distinction in relation to access to education) was based on nationality, yet it did not pay attention to the consequences of this finding for the intensity of its review.[151] In some other cases, the Court has allowed the strongly economic character of certain social security regulations to trump the suspectness of nationality-based discrimination.[152] The case law on this ground therefore still seems to be 'under construction'.

7.5. ILLEGITIMATE BIRTH

In the *Marckx* case, decided in 1979, the Court indicated that the impossibility for illegitimate children to develop legal ties with their mother and have the maternal affiliation established from the moment of birth, constituted a flagrant violation of Article 14.[153] Although the Court did not use the very weighty reasons wording in this case, its review of the justification was very strict. This strictness was motivated in particular by the existence of a European consensus rejecting discrimination based on illegitimate birth. In 1987, in *Inze*, the Court expressly confirmed the applicability of the very weighty reasons test in relation to discrimination based on the illegitimate birth of a child, based on a similar consensus reasoning.[154] The Court has always applied a very strict review in such cases.[155] In other cases, the Court has provided an additional rationale for the recognition of the 'suspectness' of these grounds. In *Mazurek* in particular, the Court stressed that it would be unfair to punish a child for circumstances for which he or she is not responsible.[156] Thus, the Court seemed to attach some value to the fact that birth is not a 'choice ground'.

---

[148] *Andrejeva v. Latvia, supra* n. 144, para. 91.
[149] *Hode and Abdi v. United Kingdom, supra* n. 12.
[150] *Biao v. Denmark, supra* n. 49, para. 130.
[151] *Ponomaryovi v. Bulgaria, supra* n. 11; *Kurić and Others v. Slovenia*, ECtHR (GC) 26 June 2012, appl. no. 26828/06.
[152] *British Gurkha Welfare Society and Others v. the United Kingdom, supra* n. 97, para. 81.
[153] *Marckx v. Belgium, supra* n. 5.
[154] *Inze v. Austria*, ECtHR 28 October 1987, appl. no. 8695/79, para. 41.
[155] *Fabris v. France*, ECtHR (GC) 7 February 2013, appl. no. 16574/08, paras. 57–59 and 68.
[156] *Mazurek v. France*, EHRM 1 February 2000, appl. no. 34406/97, para. 54.

Finally, it is important to note that the Court has widened the applicability of the very weighty reasons test to a number of closely related grounds, such as illegitimacy of the parent (rather than the child)[157] and the status of being an adopted child.[158]

7.6. SEXUAL ORIENTATION

Sexual orientation is a relatively recent addition to the list of suspect grounds. Although the 1999 case of *Salgueiro da Silva Mouta* already made clear that the Court rejected discriminatory treatment purely based on sexual orientation,[159] the Court expressly applied the very weighty reasons test only in 2003, in *L. and V. v. Austria*.[160] Without providing further reasons, the Court held that 'just like differences based on sex, differences based on sexual orientation require particularly serious reasons by way of justification'.[161]

Although the Court has reaffirmed the applicability of the very weighty reasons test in all subsequent judgments on the topic, it has never offered a substantive rationale.[162] Although in *Sousa Goucha* the Court noted that sexual orientation is an intimate characteristic, it did not use this finding as a basis for considering discrimination based on this ground 'suspect'.[163] Moreover, a closer look at the Court's case law demonstrates that the Court's approach is somewhat ambivalent. *Schalk and Kopf*, for example, concerned the impossibility for same-sex couples to marry.[164] In its judgment the Court mentioned the very weighty reasons test, but it also stressed the lack of European consensus as regards the right to marry for same-sex couples. Apparently, thus, the lack of consensus 'overruled' the applicability of the very weighty reasons test and the Court left a margin of appreciation to the State. Given the Court's recognition of the special status of the institution of marriage, it may be concluded that the very weighty reasons test does not apply in this particular context.[165] This appears to be different if the discrimination does not pertain to the institution of marriage, but to other partnership regimes, such as registered partnerships or civil unions. If such regimes are open only to different-sex partners, or if they do not even exist, the Court will leave the states a very narrow margin of appreciation and it is likely to find a violation when same-sex partners are disadvantaged by

---

[157]   *Sahin v. Germany*, ECtHR (GC) 8 July 2003, appl. no. 30943/96, para. 94.
[158]   E.g. *Negrepontis-Giannisis v. Greece*, ECtHR 3 May 2011, appl. no. 56759/08, para. 82.
[159]   *Salgueiro da Silva Mouta v. Portugal, supra* n. 62.
[160]   *L. and V. v. Austria, supra* n. 22.
[161]   *Ibid.*, para. 45.
[162]   For confirmation, see, e.g., *X. and Others v. Austria, supra* n. 114, para. 99.
[163]   *Sousa Goucha v. Portugal, supra* n. 59, para. 27.
[164]   *Schalk and Kopf v. Austria*, ECtHR 24 June 2010, appl. no. 30141/04.
[165]   See also *X. and Others v. Austria, supra* n. 114.

this.[166] Importantly, it thereby recognises that the very weighty reasons test may not only apply in cases of direct discrimination based on sexual orientation, but also in cases of indirect or substantive discrimination.

7.7. DISABILITY, ILLNESS AND HIV-STATUS

Another more recent addition to the list of 'suspect' grounds can be found in the 2010 judgment in *Alajos Kiss*.[167] This case concerned the impossibility for mentally ill persons to cast their vote in parliamentary elections. In its judgment, the Court did not only hold that the very weighty reasons test applied to discrimination based on mental disability, but it also explained the reasons for this. The Court explained that the restriction concerned a particularly vulnerable group in society, who had suffered considerable discrimination in the past.[168] Such groups were historically subject to prejudice with lasting consequences, resulting in their social exclusion.[169] According to the Court, such prejudice may bring about legislative stereotyping which prohibits the individualised evaluation of their capacities and needs.[170]

Although the Court has referred to a European consensus rejecting the acceptability of discrimination based on physical disability and chronic illness and it has recognised that the states' margin of appreciation in this context is narrow, it has not yet used the very weighty reasons wording as such.[171] Nevertheless, it is evident from the case law that discrimination based on disability or chronic illness will be subjected to very strict review.

The Court has granted a special status to discrimination based on HIV-status or aids. In *Kiyutin*, the Court stressed that from the onset of the epidemic in the 1980s, people living with HIV/aids have suffered from widespread stigma and exclusion.[172] It also mentioned that misunderstanding and fear have led to creating a false nexus between the infection and personal irresponsibility, which has reinforced other forms of stigma and discrimination, such as racism, homophobia or misogyny.[173] For that reason the Court considered that people living with HIV are a vulnerable group with a history of prejudice

---

[166]   *X. and Others v. Austria, supra* n. 114, paras. 112 and 140; *Vallianatos and Others v. Greece*, ECtHR (GC) 7 November 2013, appl. nos. 29381/09 and 32684/09, para. 85; *Taddeucci and McCall v. Italy, supra* n. 40, para. 93.

[167]   *Alajos Kiss v. Hungary*, ECtHR 20 May 2010, appl. no. 38832/06.

[168]   *Ibid.*, para. 42.

[169]   *Idem.*

[170]   *Idem.*

[171]   *Glor v. Switzerland*, ECtHR 30 April 2009, appl. no. 13444/04, para. 53; see also, however, *G.N. and Others v. Italy*, ECtHR 1 December 2009, appl. no. 43134/05, where the Court did not apply heightened review although the discrimination was clearly based on health status.

[172]   *Kiyutin v. Russia, supra* n. 112.

[173]   *Ibid.*, para. 64.

and stigmatisation and that the state should be afforded only a narrow margin of appreciation in choosing measures that single out this group for differential treatment.[174] Accordingly, discrimination based on HIV-status (also in horizontal relationships) will be subjected to the strictest possible review.[175] Although the Court has also pointed to the strong European consensus rejecting restrictions based on HIV-status, it seems that the 'stereotyping-rationale' is decisive in this respect.[176]

7.8. GENDER

The 'suspectness' of gender as a ground for discrimination was accepted by the Court in 1985, in the case of *Abdulaziz, Cabales and Balkandali*.[177] The Court stressed that 'the advancement of the equality of the sexes is today a major goal in the member States of the Council of Europe', which meant that 'very weighty reasons would have to be advanced before a difference of treatment on the ground of sex could be regarded as compatible with the Convention'.[178] The existence of a consensus rejecting discrimination based on gender still constitutes an important reason for applying the very weighty reasons test.[179] Only in more recent cases has the Court paid attention to the existence of stereotypical and traditional views on the roles of men and women in society.

The consensus rationale may imply that very weighty reasons are not always required in gender discrimination cases. This is illustrated best by the *Petrovic* case, in which a father complained about the fact that he could not obtain a parental leave allowance, as these were only granted to women.[180] Although the Court admitted that the very weighty reasons test applied in this case, because the discrimination was clearly based on gender, it also noted that at the material time (i.e. the end of the 1980s) 'there was no common standard in this field'.[181] It emphasised that only very few states granted parental leave allowances to fathers,[182] and, for that reason, it concluded that the refusal to do so by the Austrian authorities did not exceed the State's margin of

---

174   *Idem.*
175   See also *I.B. v. Greece*, ECtHR 3 October 2013, appl. no. 552/10.
176   *Cf. Novruk and Others v. Russia*, ECtHR 15 March 2016, appl. nos. 31039/11 and Others, para. 99.
177   *Abdulaziz, Cabales and Balkandali v. the United Kingdom*, ECtHR 28 May 1985, appl. nos. 9214/80, 9473/81 and 9474/81.
178   *Ibid.*, para. 78.
179   E.g. *Staatkundig Gereformeerde Partij v. the Netherlands*, ECtHR 10 July 2012 (dec.), appl. no. 58369/10, paras. 72–73 and 76–77; *Emel Boyraz v. Turkey*, ECtHR 2 December 2014, appl. no. 61960/08, para. 51.
180   *Petrovic v. Austria*, ECtHR 27 March 1998, appl. no. 20458/92.
181   *Ibid.*, para. 39.
182   *Ibid.*, para. 42.

appreciation.[183] Hence, the Court seemed to aim for a certain differentiation as to the applicability of the very weighty reasons test, depending on the context in which gender discrimination would occur and in particular on the existence or lack of European consensus.

The differentiation approach of *Petrovic* can been criticised for entailing the risk that existing inequalities are confirmed and continued. The European consensus itself, after all, may be based on stereotypical and traditional views on the roles of men and women, which the Court's approach would only help to reaffirm. The Court's more recent choice for an anti-stereotyping rationale seems to indicate that the Court has acknowledged this risk. In its 2012 judgment in *Konstantin Markin*, the Grand Chamber expressly held that 'references to traditions, general assumptions or prevailing social attitudes in a particular country are insufficient justification for a difference in treatment on grounds of sex' and that 'States are prevented from imposing traditions that derive from the man's primordial role and the woman's secondary role in the family'.[184] The judgment also shows, however, that the Court still attaches some importance to the consensus argument: the Court also emphasised that the majority of European states had moved towards a more equal sharing between men and women of responsibility for their children.[185] In judgments rendered after *Konstantin Markin* the Court has continued to refer to the consensus rationale rather than the anti-stereotyping rationale.[186] Moreover, there are several (indirect) gender discrimination cases in which the Court did not apply the very weighty reasons test because the case related to the kind of socio-economic policy issues for which the Court usually leaves a wide margin of appreciation,[187] or because the case concerned the protection of 'the integrity and well-being of children'.[188] While normally the 'suspectness' and *prima facie* unacceptability of a certain ground would 'overrule' such factors pointing towards a wider margin of appreciation, it thus appears that the Court has not fully accepted that gender is a really suspect ground. Instead, the 'suspectness' of gender-based discrimination is contextual in nature, which means that the application of the very weighty reasons test depends on the concrete circumstances of the case.

---

[183] *Ibid.*, para. 43.

[184] *Konstantin Markin v. Russia, supra* n. 112, para. 127.

[185] *Ibid.*, para. 140.

[186] E.g. *Staatkundig Gereformeerde Partij v. the Netherlands, supra* n. 179, paras. 72–73 and 76–77.

[187] *Raviv v. Austria, supra* n. 13, para. 48.

[188] *M.D. v. Ireland*, ECtHR 16 September 2014 (dec.), appl. no. 50936/12, para. 37 – the case concerned a complaint of discrimination between underage males and females who were both willing participants in sexual intercourse; according to Irish law, it was only the male party who incurred criminal liability for such sexual acts.

7.9. RELIGION AND BELIEF

It has long remained uncertain if the Court would apply the very weighty reasons test to discrimination based on religion or belief, although a few cases seemed to make clear that the Court regarded religion as a highly objectionable ground for unequal treatment. In particular, the Court has always rejected judicial decisions motivated by considerations and objections directly related to the religion of one of the parties, such as decisions not to grant parental rights to Jehovah's Witnesses.[189] In other cases, the Court has stressed that decisions related to religion call 'for particular scrutiny on the part of the Court'.[190] Nonetheless, it was not until 2013 that the Court expressly mentioned the very weighty reasons test in relation to religion-based discrimination. In *Vojnity*, it held that 'in the light of the importance of the rights enshrined in Article 9 of the Convention in guaranteeing the individual's self-fulfilment, such a treatment will only be compatible with the Convention if very weighty reasons exist'.[191]

It is evident from *Vojnity* that the rationale for the recognition of this ground as 'suspect' is found in the close relation between religion and personal autonomy and self-fulfilment. Importantly, however, *Vojnity* has not fully ended the lack of clarity as regards the applicability of heightened review, as can be seen from the more recent *Eweida* case.[192] The applicants in the case had been dismissed from their functions because of the way they wanted to express their religion (i.e. by wearing a headscarf or a cross) or because of their conscientious objections against certain parts of their jobs (e.g. having to register a same-sex marriage). Although the Court recognised that the employment decisions constituted discrimination based on religion, it did not apply a very weighty reasons test. Quite to the contrary, it left a wide margin of appreciation to the State, because the cases pertained to complex conflicts of rights, the national authorities were better placed than the Court to take decisions in such conflicts and, generally, there was a lack of European consensus to explain the wide margin of appreciation left in cases on displaying religious symbols and wearing religious apparel.[193] Accordingly, it seems likely that religion, just like gender, will be a 'suspect' ground only in specific cases, for example if the discrimination is essentially based on religious convictions rather than on religious expression.

---

[189]   E.g. *Hoffmann v. Austria*, *supra* n. 62, para. 36.

[190]   *Savez Crkava 'Riječ Života' and Others v. Croatia*, *supra* n. 26, para. 88.

[191]   *Vojnity v. Hungary*, ECtHR 12 February 2013, appl. no. 29617/07, para. 36.

[192]   *Eweida and Others v. the United Kingdom*, ECtHR 15 January 2013, appl. nos. 48420/10, 59842/10, 51671/10 and 36516/10.

[193]   See also *Ebrahimian v. France*, ECtHR 26 November 2015, appl. no. 64846/11.

CHAPTER 31

ABOLITION OF THE DEATH PENALTY IN TIME OF WAR

(Article 1 of Protocol No. 13)

Edwin BLEICHRODT[*]

GUIDING PRINCIPLE

This article provides for the abolition of the death penalty in all circumstances, even in case of crimes committed in time of war or of imminent threat of war.

ARTICLE 1 OF PROTOCOL No. 13

The death penalty shall be abolished. No one shall be condemned to such penalty or executed.

---

[*]   In the fourth edition this chapter was revised and updated by Jeroen Schokkenbroek.

CONTENTS

1. INTRODUCTION

Protocol No. 13, concerning the abolition of the death penalty in all circumstances, seeks to remove the last remaining possibility for Contracting States to have recourse to this form of punishment. While Protocol No. 6 went a very long way towards the abolition of the death penalty – thus rendering largely obsolete the second sentence of the first paragraph of Article 2 of the Convention (right to life) – it still contained an exception in Article 2 of the Protocol according to which a state may make provision in its law for the death penalty in respect of crimes committed in time of war or of imminent threat of war. In the light of the strong trend in Europe and beyond in favour of abolition of the death penalty in general, it is hardly surprising that the specific issue of the use of the death penalty in time of war came on the political agenda of the organs of the Council of Europe. It was raised for the first time by the Parliamentary Assembly in Recommendation 1246 (1994), in which it recommended that the Committee of Ministers draw up an additional protocol to the Convention, providing for the abolition of the death penalty both in peace- and in wartime. While a large majority of the Steering Committee for Human Rights at the time advised that a favourable response be given to the recommendation by the Committee of Ministers, the latter considered that the political priority was to obtain and maintain moratoria on executions, to be consolidated by complete abolition of the death penalty.[1] Indeed, as was noted in Chapter 24 above, around the mid-1990s some newer member states still continued to execute death sentences.

Only a few years later almost all Contracting States had ratified Protocol No. 6 and a moratorium on executions was firmly in place in the few states that had not yet done so. The European Ministerial Conference on Human Rights, held in November 2000 on the occasion of the 50th anniversary of the Convention, agreed in its Resolution No. II (para. 14) to invite the Committee of Ministers to consider the feasibility of an additional protocol to the Convention which would exclude the possibility of maintaining the death penalty in respect of acts committed in time of war or of imminent threat of war. In January 2001, the Committee of Ministers gave instructions to the Steering Committee for

---

[1]   See the Explanatory Report on Protocol No. 13, para. 9.

Human Rights to study the proposal and give its views as to the feasibility of a new protocol on this matter. The Steering Committee presented a draft text in November 2001. The Committee of Ministers adopted the text of Protocol No. 13 on 21 February 2002 and opened it for signature on 3 May 2002.[2] It entered into force on 1 July 2003 after it had received ten ratifications.[3]

2. SCOPE

Article 1 of Protocol No. 13 is identical to Article 1 of Protocol No. 6. The additional protection offered by Protocol No. 13 as compared to Protocol No. 6 lies in the fact that the exception provided in Article 2 of Protocol No. 6 (death penalty for acts committed in time of war or of imminent threat of war) is not included in the new Protocol. This means, having regard also to the fact that the Protocol does not allow any reservations or derogations (Articles 2 and 3 of the Protocol), that the prohibition of the death penalty contained in Protocol No. 13 is complete and absolute. The Explanatory Report indicates that, as an additional protocol, it does not, from a technical point of view, supersede Article 2 of the Convention, since the first sentence of paragraph 1 and the whole of paragraph 2 of that article still remain valid, even for States Parties to this Protocol. However, it is clear that the second sentence of Article 2(1) of the Convention is no longer applicable in respect of those states; this holds true also for the possibility provided for in Article 2 of Protocol No. 6.[4]

Most certainly as a reflection of the evolution of the political and legal position on the death penalty in Europe since the 1980s, the Protocol places the abolition of the death penalty squarely in the context of the right to life, much more clearly than Protocol No. 6 did. The Preamble to Protocol No. 13 expresses the conviction that 'everyone's right to life is a basic value in a democratic society and that the abolition of the death penalty is essential for the protection of this right and for the full recognition of the inherent dignity of all human beings'. Noting the exception still permitted by Protocol No. 6, it describes Protocol No. 13 as a 'final step in order to abolish the death penalty in all circumstances'. For this reason it would not be justified to regard the existence of Protocol No. 13 as a valid argument against an evolutive interpretation of Article 2 of the Convention as far as the abolition of the death penalty in time of peace is concerned.[5] On the contrary, the preamble's strong emphasis on the right-to-life context of abolition of the death penalty, as an authoritative

---

2   See paras. 10–13 of the Explanatory Report.
3   For an overview of the Contracting States which have ratified Protocol No. 13, see App. 1.
4   See para. 18 of the Explanatory Report.
5   See the discussion of *Soering v. the United Kingdom*, ECtHR 7 July 1989, appl. no. 14038/88 and *Öcalan v. Turkey*, ECtHR 12 March 2003, appl. no. 46221/99 in Ch. 24, *supra*.

expression of contemporary opinion as to the scope and implications of that right, rather militates in favour of such an evolutive interpretation. In the *Al-Saadoon and Mufdhi* case the Court took note of an evolution towards the complete *de facto* and *de jure* abolition of the death penalty within the Member States of the Council of Europe. The ratifications of Protocol 13, together with consistent state practice in observing the moratorium on capital punishment, are strongly indicative that Article 2 has been amended so as to prohibit the death penalty in all circumstances. Against this background, the Court did not consider that the wording of the second sentence of Article 2(1) continues to act as a bar to its interpreting the words 'inhuman or degrading treatment or punishment' in Article 3 as including the death penalty.[6]

For the same reasons as were expressed in relation to Protocol No. 6, it is unlikely that Protocol No. 13 will give rise to an important case law about the application of the death penalty within the legal orders of the Contracting Parties. However, as with Protocol No. 6, it is not excluded that it may be invoked in relation to measures of extradition or expulsion to states not bound by the Protocol.[7] Article 2 of the Convention and Article 1 of Protocol No. 13 prohibit the extradition or deportation of an individual to another state where substantial grounds have been shown for believing that he or she would face a real risk of being subjected to the death penalty there.[8] In that case the Court can examine the issues under Articles 2 and 3 of the Convention and Article 1 of Protocol No. 13 together, because they can be indissociable.[9]

Finally, mention should be made of the fact that the Protocol takes a very restrictive view as to the possibility for States Parties to withdraw or modify any declarations made concerning the territorial application of Protocol No. 13. While Article 4(3) of the Protocol does allow for such withdrawal or modification (following a similar provision of Article 5 of Protocol No. 6), the Explanatory Report specifies that this is allowed only on formal grounds, in cases where the state concerned ceases to be responsible for the international relations of the territory in question and not in order to permit the re-introduction of the death penalty in such a territory.[10]

---

[6]   *Al-Saadoon and Mufdhi v. the United Kingdom*, ECtHR 2 March 2010, appl. no. 61498/08, paras. 116 and 119–120.

[7]   A first decision of admissibility in a case of this kind was given in *Bader and Others v. Sweden*, ECtHR 26 October 2004 (dec.), appl. no. 13284/04 (expulsion to Syria where the first applicant had been sentenced to death).

[8]   *Hakizimana v. Sweden*, ECtHR 27 March 2008, appl. no. 37913/05 and *Al-Saadoon and Mufdhi v. the United Kingdom*, ECtHR 2 March 2010, appl. no. 61498/08, para. 123.

[9]   *Hakizimana v. Sweden*, ECtHR 27 March 2008, appl. no. 37913/05.

[10]   See para. 17 of the Explanatory Report.

3. DEROGATION

No derogations from the provisions of Protocol No. 13 are permitted. It should be recalled that the very object and purpose of the Protocol are to abolish the death penalty in all circumstances, including in time or war or of imminent threat of war.[11]

---

[11]   See Art. 2 of the Protocol and para. 15 of the Explanatory Report.

CHAPTER 32

RIGHT TO AN EFFECTIVE REMEDY

(Article 13)

Tom Barkhuysen and Michiel van Emmerik[*]

GUIDING PRINCIPLE

Article 13 requires an effective remedy before a national authority in case of an 'arguable claim' of a violation of a Convention right. This remedy needs to be 'effective', both in theory and practice (the Court rejects 'excessive formalism' that hinders access to an effective remedy). Apart from some general observations (about *inter alia* the ancillary character and inherent limitations), this chapter deals with the requirements of the arguability test and the effectiveness of the remedy. It also focuses on the relation with some substantive Convention rights. The general conclusion is on the one hand that there is quite a casuistic approach vis-à-vis, for example the arguability test, but that on the other hand Article 13 has gained autonomous meaning, in particular – but not only – when it comes to effective remedies in case of a violation of the reasonable time requirement of Article 6 ECHR.

ARTICLE 13

Everyone whose rights and freedoms as set forth in this Convention are violated shall have an effective remedy before a national authority notwithstanding that the violation has been committed by persons acting in an official capacity.

---

[*] In the fourth edition this chapter was revised and updated by Yutaka Arai.

CONTENTS

1.   INTRODUCTION

1.1.   ANCILLARY CHARACTER

Ideally, a general guarantee of an effective remedy should be provided for anyone who alleges that one of his or her rights has been violated by the authorities or by another individual. The concept of the rule of law, which along with the idea of democracy constitutes one of the pillars of the Council of Europe,[1] would justify a broader construction of the requirements of Article 13. However, as can be seen from the words 'whose rights and freedoms as set forth in this Convention are violated', Article 13, instead of embodying such a general guarantee, refers exclusively to cases in which the alleged violation concerns one of the rights and freedoms of the Convention.[2] The applicability of Article 13 depends on the finding that the principal complaints are not declared incompatible *ratione*

---

[1]   See in particular, the Preamble and Art. 3 of the Statute of the Council of Europe.
[2]   For the case law of the Commission, see, e.g., *X and Y v. the Netherlands*, EComHR 19 December 1974, appl. no. 6753/74, D&R 2 (1975), p. 118 (119). For the case law of the Court, see, for example, *Ecclestone v. The United Kingdom*, ECtHR 18 May 2004, appl. no. 42841/02 para. 4.

materiae, and that they are arguable. Article 13 cannot be invoked independently from, but only in conjunction with, one or more of the substantive rights and freedoms of the Convention (Articles 2–12, or Article 14),[3] or of its Protocols.

Both the rule on exhaustion of domestic remedies under Article 35(1) and the requirement of effective remedies available at national level under Article 13 embody the principle of subsidiarity, according to which the Convention system is subsidiary to the primary responsibility of national constitutional systems for safeguarding fundamental rights.[4] The fact that the procedural rule under Article 35(1) presupposes the existence of an effective domestic remedy suggests a 'close affinity' between the two provisions, but Article 13 establishes an 'additional guarantee' for an individual.[5] According to the *travaux préparatoires*, Article 13 aims to accord a means whereby individuals can obtain relief at the national level for violations of their Convention rights before having recourse to the European Court of Human Rights.[6]

The development of case law has provided guidelines for the application of this important procedural right. These guidelines concern for example the arguability test, the requirements of effectiveness, possible limitations to the remedy and requirements for the national authority. Apart from this often-casuistic case law, the Court has given clear guidelines *vis-à-vis* the requirements of Article 13 in cases in which the reasonable time has been exceeded contrary to Article 6 ECHR, a field in which Article 13 has proved to be of added value.[7]

1.2. INHERENT LIMITATIONS

The Court has taken the view that the absence of any limitation clauses under Article 13 does not mean that this right is absolute; this provision should be construed as having inherent limitations.[8] The standard of remedy that must be provided is 'a remedy that is as effective as can be having regard to the restricted scope for recourse inherent in [the particular context]'.[9] The theory of inherent limitations has been invoked to support the argument that Article 13 does not

---

3   Though rejected on the specific facts of the case, the Court examined the possibility of a violation of 2 'ancillary' provisions of Arts. 13 and 14 in *Boyle and Rice v. The United Kingdom*, ECtHR 27 April 1988, appl. nos. 9659/82, 9658/82, paras 85–86.

4   *Rachevi v. Bulgaria*, ECtHR 23 September 2004, appl. no. 47877/99, para. 61.

5   *Selmouni v. France*, ECtHR (GC) 28 July 1999, appl. no. 25803/94, para. 74; and *Kudla v. Poland*, ECtHR 26 October 2000, appl. no. 30210/96, para. 152.

6   *Collected Edition of the 'Travaux Préparatoires' of the European Convention on Human Rights*, vol. II, pp. 485 and 490, and vol. III, p. 651; cited in *Kudla, supra* n. 5, para. 152.

7   See for further references *Handbook on European Law Relating to Access to Justice* (joint publication, Council of Europe and European Union Agency for Fundamental Rights, accessible at <www.echr.coe.int>).

8   See, e.g., *Leander v. Sweden*, ECtHR 26 March 1987, appl. no. 9248/81, para. 79.

9   *Klass and Others v. Germany*, ECtHR (GC) 6 September 1978, appl. no. 5029/71, paras. 31 and 69; *Kudla v. Poland*, ECtHR (GC) 26 October 2000, appl. no. 30210/96, *supra* n. 5, para. 151.

---

recognise constitutional judicial review, which would allow a member state's laws to be challenged before a national authority as being incompatible with the Convention.[10] The Court has, however, emphasised the need to minimise such implied restrictions.[11] It is possible to argue that one of the jurisprudential rationales for such inherent limitations lies in the 'positive' nature of the state obligations under Article 13. The scope of positive obligations depends on the nature of the complaint,[12] including the nature of the substantive rights invoked in conjunction, with a more stringent and broader obligation recognised in the case of alleged violations of non-derogable rights, such as the right to life and the freedom from torture or other forms of ill-treatment.

1.3. MEANING OF 'ARE VIOLATED' AND 'HAS BEEN COMMITTED'

The words 'are violated' and 'has been committed' (in French, '*ont été violés*' and '*aurait été commise*') literally denote that a violation of a substantive right or freedom of the Convention has occurred or has been established. However, such interpretation would run afoul of the Convention's underlying objective of establishing an international supervisory system, depriving Article 13 of its meaning, as the very establishment of a violation by a national tribunal may suggest that the applicant has had an effective remedy in the national system. The Court has enunciated that this phrase should be interpreted as 'guaranteeing an 'effective remedy before a national authority' to everyone who *claims* that his rights and freedoms under the Convention have been violated'.[13]

The approach of the Strasbourg organs has been to shift their focus from the literal construction of the phrase 'are violated' and 'has been committed', to the examination of the two following substantive issues: first, the question of the scope of application *ratione materiae* of a claimed right, examining whether the principal complaint as to a substantive right falls within the scope of the Convention;[14] and secondly, the analysis of the arguability of the principal complaint, as discussed below. Even if the Court has found no violation of a substantive right, the Contracting State remains obliged to provide an effective remedy for the

---

[10]   *Kudla v. Poland*, ECtHR (GC) 26 October 2000, appl. no. 30210/96, *supra* n. 5, para. 151. See also *James and Others v. The United Kingdom*, ECtHR (GC) 21 February 1986, appl. no. 8793/79, para. 86; and *Leander v. Sweden*, ECtHR 26 March 1987, appl. no. 9248/81, *supra* n. 8, para. 79.

[11]   *Kudla v. Poland*, ECtHR (GC) 26 October 2000, appl. no. 30210/96, *supra* n. 5, para. 152.

[12]   See, e.g., *Toimi v. Sweden*, ECtHR 31 August 2004, appl. no. 55164/00.

[13]   *Klass and Others v. Germany*, ECtHR (GC) 6 September 1978, appl. no. 5029/71, *supra* n. 9, para. 64 (emphasis added).

[14]   *Pierre-Bloch v. France*, ECtHR 21 October 1997, appl. no. 24194/94, paras. 62–64; *Kaukonen v. Finland*, ECtHR 8 December 1997, appl. no. 24738/94, D&R 91-A (1997), p. 14; *Vjekoslav Banekovic v. Croatia*, ECtHR 23 September 2004, appl. no. 41730/02.

examination of the alleged violation. This means that the Court can find a separate violation of Article 13 without finding a violation of the corresponding substantive Article.[15] In that sense, while being invoked only in conjunction with one of the other Convention rights, Article 13 embodies an independent right.

2. ARGUABILITY TEST

2.1. MEANING

According to the case law, where an individual has an 'arguable claim' to be a victim of a breach of the Convention rights, national authorities must provide him with a remedy that is capable of determining his claim and, if appropriate, of securing redress.[16] The approach of the Court is to avoid an abstract definition of the notion of arguability[17] and to examine this notion on a case-by-case basis, with special regard to the particular facts and the nature of the legal issues raised.[18] A close examination of the case law provides some guidelines for the meaning of this test. The Court has repeatedly emphasised that Article 13 does not require a remedy in domestic law to be established in relation to *any* alleged grievance of a Convention right, irrespective of how unmeritorious such a grievance may be.[19]

2.2. COMPARISON WITH NOTION OF MANIFESTLY ILL-FOUNDEDNESS

The arguability test, which requires assessment of the substance of claims, is closely related to the manifest ill-foundedness test, which is used to screen frivolous cases at the admissibility stage. In the *Boyle and Rice* case the Court held that the notion of non-arguability is not the same as manifest ill-

---

[15] See, e.g., *Lindstrand Partners Advokatbyra AB v. Sweden*, ECtHR 20 December 2016, appl. no. 18700/09: the applicant company had to undergo searches and audits carried out on 2 other companies. Violation of Art. 13 taken in conjunction with Art. 8 caused by a lack of standing in administrative appeal proceedings, but no violation of Art. 8 separately.

[16] See, e.g., *Silver and Others v. The United Kingdom*, ECtHR 25 March 1983, appl. nos. 5947/72, 6205/73, 7052/75, 7061/75, 7107/75, 7113/75, 7136/75, para. 113; *Leander v. Sweden*, ECtHR 26 March 1987, appl. no. 9248/81, *supra* n. 8, para. 77; *Kaya v. Turkey*, ECtHR 19 February 1998, appl. no. 22729/83, para. 106; and *Kudla v. Poland*, ECtHR (GC) 26 October 2000, appl. no. 30210/96, *supra* n. 5, para. 157.

[17] *Boyle and Rice v. The United Kingdom*, ECtHR 27 April 1988, appl. no. 9659/82, *supra* n. 3, para. 55; and *Plattform 'Ärzte für das Leben' v. Austria*, ECtHR 21 June 1988, appl. no. 10126/82, para. 27.

[18] *Ibid.*

[19] *Boyle and Rice v. The United Kingdom*, ECtHR 27 April 1988, appl. no. 9659/82, *supra* n. 3, para. 52.

---

foundedness, suggesting that a complaint declared manifestly ill-founded may retain arguability. Invoking the judgment in the *Airey* case,[20] in which the notion of manifest ill-foundedness was equated to the absence of even a *prima facie* case,[21] the Court conceded that 'it is difficult to conceive how a claim that is "manifestly ill-founded" can nevertheless be "arguable", and vice versa'.[22]

The confusion as to the two concepts has been compounded by the fact that though both notions call for examinations of the merits of the claim, their operational spheres differ, with the notion of manifest ill-foundedness appearing at the admissibility stage and the arguability test being applied at the merit phase. It is submitted that the notion of arguability must be distinguished from that of manifestly ill-founded in that the admissibility decisions as to the latter concept are not confined to determining whether or not the applicant has made a *prima facie* case, but cover a fully-fledged review of the merits. However, analysis of the case law suggests that while the possibility of discrepancy between the two concepts is not ruled out, this is very unlikely in view of the Court's deference to the reasoning of an admissibility decision.[23]

2.3. COMPARISON WITH 'GENUINE AND SERIOUS' REQUIREMENT UNDER ARTICLE 6(1)

The standard of arguability may also be compared with the test of the 'genuine and serious' nature of a claim, which needs to be demonstrated to make Article 6(1) applicable. In the context of Article 6(1) the Court has emphasised that the applicability of this provision requires, *inter alia*, that the dispute in question be 'genuine and serious', which may be related to the existence of a right or to its scope and the manner of its exercise.[24] The Court has held that a claim submitted to a domestic tribunal can be presumed to be both 'genuine and serious', except in case of clear indications to the contrary, as in the case

---

20   *Airey v. Ireland*, ECtHR 9 October 1979, appl. no. 6289/73, para. 18.
21   *Boyle and Rice v. The United Kingdom*, ECtHR 27 April 1988, appl. no. 9659/82, *supra* n. 3, para. 54.
22   *Boyle and Rice v. The United Kingdom*, ECtHR 27 April 1988, appl. no. 9659/82, *supra* n. 3, para. 54. In this regard, the Court recalled the *Airey* case in which it found that the rejection of a complaint as 'manifestly ill founded', amounted to a decision that 'there is not even a *prima facie* case against the respondent State' (*Airey v. Ireland*, ECtHR 9 October 1979, appl. no. 6289/73, para. 18). See also the respondent State's submission in *Plattform 'Ärzte für das Leben' v. Austria*, ECtHR 21 June 1988, appl. no. 10126/82, *supra* n. 17, para. 26.
23   See, e.g., *Powell and Rayner v. The United Kingdom*, ECtHR 21 February 1990, appl. no. 9310/81, para. 33.
24   See, e.g., *Skärby v. Sweden*, ECtHR 28 June 1990, appl. no. 12258/86, para. 27; *Kraska v. Switzerland*, ECtHR 19 April 1993, appl. no. 13942/88, para. 24; *Zander v. Sweden*, ECtHR 25 November 1993, appl. no. 14282/88, para. 22; *Kerojärvi v. Finland*, ECtHR 19 July 1995, appl. no. 17506/90, para. 32; *Acquaviva v. France*, ECtHR 21 November 1995, appl. no. 19248/91, para. 46.

of the claim that is frivolous or vexatious, or lacking in foundation.[25] It is this requirement of a 'genuine and serious' nature of the dispute that raises a question whether its threshold is comparable to that of arguability under Article 13. Two differences between the nature of disputes under Article 6(1) and the nature of complaints under Article 13 must be highlighted. First, Article 6(1) concerns a dispute over any civil right or obligation, the category of which naturally goes beyond the Convention rights. Second, Article 6(1) concerns a dispute that must be raised before a domestic tribunal, whereas a remedy under Article 13 does not have to be judicial in the strict sense. Bearing in mind these differences, one can note that both the literal construction of the 'genuine and serious' nature of the claim and the thorough manner in which the Court examines the genuine and serious nature of a dispute over a civil right,[26] suggest that its threshold may be higher than that of arguability under Article 13.

3. REQUIREMENT OF EFFECTIVENESS

Prior to undertaking detailed examinations of what specific elements the notion of effectiveness has yielded in the development of the case law under Article 13, this sub-section provides two preliminary observations. First, the 'authority' before which an effective remedy must be available within the meaning of Article 13 need not be a judicial authority but, if it is not, both the powers and the procedural guarantees that it affords are considered as 'relevant' factors for determining the effectiveness of the remedy at issue.[27] Second, when ascertaining the effectiveness of remedies, the Strasbourg organs have allowed a cumulative evaluation in favour of national authorities; even when no single remedy may itself entirely satisfy the requirements of Article 13, the aggregate of remedies provided for under domestic law may do so.[28] In addition, the case law demonstrates that Convention states have a degree of freedom when

---

[25]   *Rolf Gustafson v. Sweden*, ECtHR 1 July 1997, appl. no. 23196/94, para. 39; and *Törmälä and Others v. Finland*, ECtHR 18 March 2004, appl. no. 41258/98.

[26]   See, e.g., *Rolf Gustafson v. Sweden*, ECtHR 1 July 1997, appl. no. 23196/94, *supra* n. 25, para. 39.

[27]   *Klass and Others v. Germany*, ECtHR (GC) 6 September 1978, appl. no. 5029/71, *supra* n. 9 para. 67; *Silver and Others v. The United Kingdom*, ECtHR 25 March 1983, appl. nos. 5947/72, 6205/73, 7052/75, 7061/75, 7107/75, 7113/75, 7136/75, *supra* n. 16, para. 113; *Leander v. Sweden*, ECtHR 26 March 1987, appl. no. 9248/81, *supra* n. 8, para. 77; *Kudla v. Poland*, ECtHR (GC) 26 October 2000, appl. no. 30210/96, *supra* n. 5, para. 157; and *Toimi v. Sweden*, ECtHR 31 August 2004, appl. no. 55164/00, *supra* n. 12.

[28]   See, e.g., *Silver and Others v. The United Kingdom*, ECtHR 25 March 1983, appl. nos. 5947/72, 6205/73, 7052/75, 7061/75, 7107/75, 7113/75, 7136/75, *supra* n. 16, para. 113; *Leander v. Sweden*, ECtHR 26 March 1987, appl. no. 9248/81, *supra* n. 8, para. 77; *Chahal v. The United Kingdom*, ECtHR (GC) 15 November 1996, appl. no. 22414/93, para. 145; *Kudla v. Poland*, ECtHR (GC) 26 October 2000, appl. no. 30210/96, *supra* n. 5, para. 157; and *Toimi v. Sweden*, ECtHR 31 August 2004, appl. no. 55164/00, *supra* n. 12.

designing means of redress to satisfy the conditions of Article 13.[29] The central issue must be dealt with within the scope of the means of redress. If this is not the case, for example because an authority is limited in its review and thus the proportionality of a measure cannot be reviewed, this constitutes a violation of Article 13.[30]

In order to flesh out the substance of the requirements under Article 13, the Court has consistently invoked the principle of effective protection, which serves as one of the 'constitutional' underlying principles of the Convention. The application of this principle under Article 13 suggests that the exercise of domestic remedies must not be unjustifiably hindered by acts or omissions of the authorities of the respondent state.[31] Excessive formalism, for example, can result in the use of a remedy no longer being effective and thus leading to a violation of Article 13.[32] In addition, the notion of effectiveness is construed as ensuring either the prevention of the alleged violation, or the provision of adequate redress, including compensation, for a victim of a violation.[33] In the case of asylum proceedings, for example, the remedy would cause proceedings to be suspended. If the party involved could be deported pending the proceedings, then no effective protection exists.[34] In the case of complaints of the length of proceedings, such alternative nature of Article 13 requirements demands that remedies must be capable either of expediting a decision by

---

29   *Čonka v. Belgium*, ECtHR 5 February 2002, appl. no. 51564/99; *Garabayev v. Russia*, ECtHR 7 June 2007, appl. no. 38411/02; *Soldatenko v. Ukraine*, ECtHR 23 October 2008, appl. no. 2440/07.

30   *Stamose v. Bulgaria*, ECtHR 27 November 2012, appl. no. 29713/05.

31   *Aksoy v. Turkey*, ECtHR 18 December 1996, appl. no. 21987/93, para. 95; *Aydin v. Turkey*, ECtHR (GC) 25 September 1997, appl. no. 23178/94, para. 103; *Kaya v. Turkey*, ECtHR 19 February 1998, appl. no. 22729/83, *supra* n. 16, para. 89; *İlhan v. Turkey*, ECtHR (GC) 27 June 2000, appl. no. 22277/93, para. 97; *Kudla v. Poland*, ECtHR (GC) 26 October 2000, appl. no. 30210/96, *supra* n. 5, para. 157; *Ipek v. Turkey*, ECtHR 17 February 2004, appl. no. 25760/94, para. 197; *Özalp and Others v. Turkey*, ECtHR 8 April 2004, appl. no. 32457/96, para. 59; *Dulas v. Turkey*, ECtHR 30 January 2001, appl. no. 25801/94, para. 65; *Yöyler v. Turkey*, ECtHR 24 July 2003, appl. no. 26973/95, para. 87; and *Altun v. Turkey*, ECtHR 1 June 2004, appl. no. 24561/94, para. 70.

32   *G.R. v. the Netherlands*, ECtHR 10 January 2012, appl. no. 22251/07; *Zednik v. Czech Republic*, ECtHR 28 June 2005, appl. no. 74328/01.

33   See, e.g., *Kudla v. Poland*, ECtHR (GC) 26 October 2000, appl. no. 30210/96, *supra* n. 5, paras. 158; and *Toimi v. Sweden*, ECtHR 31 August 2004, appl. no. 55164/00, *supra* n. 12; *Poghosyan & Baghdasaryan v. Armenia*, ECtHR 12 June 2012, appl. no. 22999/06.

34   In particular when there is a threat of a violation of Art. 3: *Conka v. Belgium*, ECtHR 5 February 2002, appl. no. 51564/99, *supra* n. 29. See also *Gebremedhin [Gaberamadhien] v. France*, ECtHR 26 April 2007, appl. no. 25389/05; *M.S.S. v. Belgium and Greece*, ECtHR (GC) 21 January 2011, appl. no. 30696/09; *Hirsi Jamaa and Others v. Italy*, ECtHR (GC) 23 February 2012, appl. no. 27765/09 and *A.M. v. the Netherlands*, ECtHR 5 July 2016, appl. no. 29094/09. But sometimes the Court considers that a claim under Article 13 in conjunction with Article 8 also requires the domestic remedy to have an automatic suspensive effect: *De Souza Ribeiro v. France*, ECtHR (GC) 13 December 2012, appl. no. 22689/07. See more generally A.M. Reneman, *EU Asylum Procedures and the Right to an Effective Remedy*, Oxford, 2014.

the courts, or of providing the litigant with adequate redress for delays in proceedings.[35]

The evolution of effective investigation obligations under Articles 2 and 3 in the case law since the 1990s has provided an impetus for the Court to clarify the corresponding requirement of effective investigations under Article 13. In particular, the parallel relationship between the procedural limb of obligations under Article 2 and Article 13 is readily discernible in the Court's methodology. In order to obtain a useful insight into the notion of effectiveness under Article 13, it is necessary to discuss briefly the effective investigations requirement under Article 2. Since the mid-1990s the Court has elaborated upon the requirement of effective investigations under this provision.[36] For inquiries into an alleged unlawful killing by state agents to be effective for the purposes of Article 2, several subsidiary requirements must be complied with. The first requirement is related to institutional elements, demanding that the persons responsible for and conducting the investigation must be independent from those implicated in the alleged killing or disappearance.[37] The notion of independence goes beyond the mere absence of a hierarchical or institutional connection, calling for 'practical independence'.[38] This requirement is purported to bolster the objective nature of inquiries and the public confidence in their legitimacy.[39] Second, the notion of effectiveness is broadened to include procedural elements, requiring not only the possible determination of the lawfulness of the force used in the impugned fatal incident but also the identification and punishment of those responsible.[40] On this matter, the Court stressed that while this investigative obligation is not that of result, but of means, the procedural duties must be capable of securing the necessary evidence to determine the cause of death or the responsible person,[41] by means of,

---

[35] *Kudla v. Poland*, ECtHR (GC) 26 October 2000, appl. no. 30210/96, *supra* n. 5, para. 159; *Ramirez Sanchez v. France*, ECtHR (GC) 4 July 2006, appl. no. 59450/00.

[36] See, e.g., *Silih v. Slovenia*, ECtHR (GC) 9 April 2009, appl. no. 71463/01, paras. 158–159.

[37] *Güleç v. Turkey*, ECtHR 27 July 1998, appl. no. 21593/93, paras. 81–82; and *Oður v. Turkey*, ECtHR 20 May 1999, appl. no. 21594/93, paras. 91–92; *Kelly and Others v. The United Kingdom*, ECtHR 4 May 2001, appl. no. 30054/96, para. 114; *Orhan v. Turkey*, ECtHR 18 June 2002 appl. no. 25656/94, para. 348; and *Ipek v. Turkey*, ECtHR 17 February 2004, appl. no. 25760/94, *supra* n. 31, para. 170.

[38] *Ergi v. Turkey*, ECtHR 28 July 1998, appl. no. 23818/94, paras. 83–84; and *Kelly and Others v. The United Kingdom*, ECtHR 4 May 2001, appl. no. 30054/96, *supra* n. 37, para. 95.

[39] A. Mowbray, *The Development of Positive Obligations under the European Convention on Human Rights by the European Court of Human Rights*, Oxford, 2004, at pp. 32–33. *Cf.* M. Beijer, *The Limits of Fundamental Rights Protection by the EU: the Scope for the Development of Positive Obligations*, Antwerp, 2017, with also attention to the development of positive obligations in the Strasbourg case law.

[40] *Oður v. Turkey*, ECtHR 20 May 1999, appl. no. 21594/93, *supra* n. 37, para. 88; *Kelly and Others v. The United Kingdom*, ECtHR 4 May 2001, appl. no. 30054/96, *supra* n. 37, para. 96; *Ipek v. Turkey*, ECtHR 17 February 2004, appl. no. 25760/94, *supra* n. 31, para. 170.

[41] *Ipek v. Turkey*, ECtHR 17 February 2004, appl. no. 25760/94, *supra* n. 31, para. 170.

inter alia, eye-witness testimony,[42] forensic tests, ballistic examinations of bullets and autopsy.[43] The third subsidiary requirement implicit in the procedural/ investigative limb of positive duties under Article 2 is that of promptness and reasonable expedition.[44] This requirement is of decisive importance to allegations of disappearance in detention,[45] but it also entails a public dimension in that by averting any appearance of collusion or tolerance of unlawful acts on the part of authorities, it serves to maintain public confidence in the rule of law.[46] Fourth, the Court demands 'a sufficient element of public scrutiny of the investigation or its results', which is designed to 'secure accountability in practice as well as in theory'.[47] The absence of thorough and prompt investigations of alleged detention of family members in life-threatening or inhuman environments may involve a concurrent breach of the parallel, positive obligation to conduct effective investigations under Article 5.[48]

An influx of cases alleging killings, disappearances and ill-treatment committed by Turkish security forces in South-eastern Turkey prompted the Court to formulate a judicial strategy based on the combined strengths of effective investigation obligations under Articles 2 and/or 3 on the one hand, and Article 13 on the other. The Court has repeatedly emphasised that once an individual has an 'arguable claim' relating to the substance of the complaints under Articles 2 or/and 3, the notion of effectiveness under Article 13 entails the institutional and investigative/procedural elements parallel to those established under Article 2 or 3.

First, in relation to the institutional obligations under Article 13, the Court stressed the need not only of the absence of a hierarchical or institutional

---

[42] For witnesses, see *Tanrikulu v. Turkey*, ECtHR (GC) 8 July 1999, appl. no. 23763/94, para. 109; *Güleç v. Turkey*, ECtHR 27 July 1998, appl. no. 21593/93, *supra* n. 37, para. 82; *Akkoç v. Turkey*, ECtHR 10 October 2000, appl. nos. 22947/93, 22948/93, para. 98.

[43] *Kaya v. Turkey*, ECtHR 19 February 1998, appl. no. 22729/83, *supra* n. 16, para. 89; *Mahmut Kaya v. Turkey*, ECtHR 28 March 2000, appl. no. 22535/95, para. 104; *Gül v. Turkey*, ECtHR 14 December 2000, appl. no. 22676/93, para. 89; and judgment of 10 April 2001, *Tanli v. Turkey*, ECtHR 10 April 2001, appl. no. 26129/95, para. 150.

[44] *Yasa v. Turkey*, ECtHR 2 September 1998, appl. no. 22495/93, paras. 102–104; *Çakici v. Turkey*, ECtHR (GC) 8 July 1999, appl. no. 23657/94, paras. 80, 87, 106; *Tanrikulu v. Turkey*, ECtHR 8 July 1999, appl. no. 23763/94, *supra* n. 42, para. 109; *Mahmut Kaya v. Turkey*, ECtHR 28 March 2000, appl. no. 22535/95, *supra* n. 43, paras 106–107; *Kelly and Others v. The United Kingdom*, ECtHR 4 May 2001, appl. no. 30054/96, *supra* n. 37, para. 97; *Ipek v. Turkey*, ECtHR 17 February 2004, appl. no. 25760/94, *supra* n. 31, para. 171; and *Buldan v. Turkey*, ECtHR 20 April 2004, appl. no. 28398/95, para. 84.

[45] *Orhan v. Turkey*, ECtHR 18 June 2002 appl. no. 25656/94, *supra* n. 37, para. 336.

[46] *Kelly and Others v. The United Kingdom*, ECtHR 4 May 2001, appl. no. 30054/96, *supra* n. 37, para. 97; *McKerr v. The United Kingdom*, ECtHR 4 May 2001, appl. no. 28883/95, paras. 108–115; *Avsar v. Turkey*, ECtHR 10 July 2001, appl. no. 25857/94, paras. 390–395; *Ipek v. Turkey*, ECtHR 17 February 2004, appl. no. 25760/94, *supra* n. 31, para. 171; and *Buldan v. Turkey*, ECtHR 20 April 2004, appl. no. 28398/95, *supra* n. 37, para. 84.

[47] *Kelly and Others v. The United Kingdom*, ECtHR 4 May 2001, appl. no. 30054/96, para. 98.

[48] *Ipek v. Turkey*, ECtHR 17 February 2004, appl. no. 25760/94, *supra* n. 31, paras. 189–191; *Scordino v. Italy (No. 1)*, ECtHR (GC) 29 March 2006, appl. no. 36813/97.

connection but also of 'practical independence' of the persons responsible for carrying out the investigations into alleged killings or ill-treatment.[49] In *Khan v. UK*, which involved a complaint about the use of covert listening devices in breach of Article 8, the Court found that recourse to the Police Complaints Authority did not meet the requirement of effectiveness under Article 13 in that this authority lacked the necessary independence, with its members subject to appointment, remuneration and even dismissal by the Secretary of State.[50]

Second, as regards the investigative/procedural limb, the effective inquiries requirement under Article 13 demands 'a thorough and effective investigation' that can lead to the 'identification and punishment of those responsible' for violations of Article 2 or 3 (killings, torture or other proscribed forms of ill-treatment, or destruction of properties) and that ensures 'effective access' by the complainant or the relatives to the investigatory procedure.[51] The effectiveness of a remedy for the purpose of Article 13 does not hinge on the certainty of a favourable outcome for an applicant.[52] Such obligation is deemed as inherent both in the substantive right under Article 2 or 3, and in the general duty under Article 1 of the Convention. The Court held that while lacking a provision calling for the investigative duty akin to Article 12 of the 1984 United Nations Convention against Torture and Other Cruel, Inhuman or Degrading Treatment or Punishment, which imposes a duty to proceed to a 'prompt and impartial' investigation whenever there is a reasonable ground to believe that an act of torture has been committed, such an inquiry requirement is implicit in the notion of an 'effective remedy' under Article 13.[53] Third, the requirement of promptness and reasonable expedition is held as inherent in the notion of effectiveness, so as to call for prompt investigations into alleged killings or ill-treatment contrary to Article 2 or 3.[54] The Court emphasised that the requirement of promptness under Article 13 ensures both the maintenance

---

[49] *Oður v. Turkey*, ECtHR 20 May 1999, appl. no. 21594/93, *supra* n. 37, para. 91; and *Mehmet Emin Yüksel v. Turkey*, ECtHR 20 July 2004, appl. no. 40154/98, para. 37.

[50] *Khan v. The United Kingdom*, ECtHR 12 May 2000, appl. no. 35394/97, para. 47. See also report of *Govell v. The United Kingdom*, ECtHR 15 January 1998, appl. no. 27237/95, paras. 68–70.

[51] See, e.g., *Aksoy v. Turkey*, ECtHR 18 December 1996, appl. no. 21987/93, *supra* n. 31, para. 98; *Aydin v. Turkey*, ECtHR (GC) 25 September 1997, appl. no. 23178/94, *supra* n. 31, para. 103 and *Singh and Others v. Belgium*, ECtHR 2 October 2012, appl. no. 33210/11.

[52] *Vilvarajah and Others v. The United Kingdom*, ECtHR 30 October 1991, appl. no. 13163/87, 13164/87, 13165/87, 13447/87, 13448/87, para. 122. See also *Costello-Roberts v. The United Kingdom*, ECtHR 25 March 1993, appl. no. 13134/87 paras. 37–40.

[53] *Aksoy v. Turkey*, ECtHR 18 December 1996, appl. no. 21987/93, *supra* n. 31, para. 98. Compare this reasoning with that in *Soering*, in which the Court, by way of effective and teleological construction, recognised the obligation of non-refoulement as inherent in Article 3: *Soering v. The United Kingdom*, ECtHR 7 July 1989, appl. no. 14038/88 para. 88.

[54] *Yasa v. Turkey*, ECtHR 2 September 1998, appl. no. 22495/93, *supra* n. 44, paras. 102–104; *Çakici v. Turkey*, ECtHR (GC) 8 July 1999, appl. no. 23657/94, *supra* n. 44, paras. 80, 87 and 105–106; *Mahmut Kaya v. Turkey*, ECtHR 28 March 2000, appl. no. 22535/95, *supra* n. 43, paras. 106–107; and *Çelik and Imret v. Turkey*, ECtHR 26 October 2004, appl. no. 44093/98, para. 59.

of public confidence in the rule of law and the prevention of any appearance of collusion in, or tolerance of, unlawful acts.[55]

The requirement of effectiveness under Article 13 can be usefully compared with the meaning of 'remedies' under Article 35, which need to be exhausted before an applicant brings complaints before the Strasbourg Court. Recognising the 'close affinity' between Articles 13 and 35 (1) of the Convention,[56] the Court emphasised that the concept of an 'effective' remedy as required under Article 35(1) corresponds to the alternative nature of the obligations under Article 13, namely, either the duty to prevent an alleged violation through expediting a decision by the courts, or the duty to provide adequate redress for delays.[57]

The Court has demonstrated that 'remedies' for addressing breaches of the Convention rights under Article 35 must meet the tests of accessibility and effectiveness. The construction of 'remedies' under Article 35 is guided by the principle of effective protection, according to which the existence of such domestic remedies must be 'sufficiently certain not only in theory but also in practice'.[58] The effective protection principle also entails significant implications for the distribution of the burden of proof, which is inherent in Article 35(1). The respondent state needs to establish that 'the remedy was an effective one available in theory and in practice at the relevant time, that is to say, that it was accessible, was one which was capable of providing redress in respect of the applicant's complaints and offered reasonable prospects of success'.[59]

The *Doğan* case illustrates the closely intertwined relationship between issues of exhaustion of domestic remedies under Article 35(1) and the requirement to safeguard an effective remedy under Article 13. In that case, the Court found that the forced eviction of the applicants from their village and the inability to return to their homes and livelihood constituted violations of Article 1 of Protocol No. 1, and of Articles 8 and 13 of the Convention. In relation to the preliminary objection, the Court found that the Government failed to establish the availability of a remedy that could provide redress for the applicants'

---

[55] *Çelik and Imret v. Turkey*, ECtHR 26 October 2004, appl. no. 44093/98, *supra* n. 54, para. 55.

[56] *Kudla v. Poland*, ECtHR (GC) 26 October 2000, appl. no. 30210/96, *supra* n. 5, para. 152.

[57] *Mifsud v. France*, ECtHR (GC) 11 September 2002, appl. no. 57220/00, para. 17; and *Davenport v. Portugal*, ECtHR 29 January 2004, appl. no. 57862/00. See also *Kudla v. Poland*, ECtHR (GC) 26 October 2000, appl. no. 30210/96, *supra* n. 5, para. 158.

[58] See, *inter alia, Vernillo v. France*, ECtHR 20 February 1991, appl. no. 11889/85, para. 27; *Dalia v. France*, ECtHR 19 February 1998, appl. no. 26102/95, para. 38; *Mifsud v. France*, ECtHR (GC) 11 September 2002, appl. no. 57220/00, *supra* n. 57, para. 15; *Akdivar and Others v. Turkey*, ECtHR (GC) 16 September 1996, appl. no. 21893/93, para. 66; *Pihlak v. Estonia*, ECtHR 20 January 2004, appl. no. 73270/01; and *Rachevi v. Bulgaria*, ECtHR 23 September 2004, appl. no. 47877/99, *supra* n. 4, para. 62.

[59] *Vernillo v. France*, ECtHR 20 February 1991, appl. no. 11889/85, *supra* n. 58, para. 27; *Selmouni v. France*, ECtHR (GC) 28 July 1999, appl. no. 25803/94, *supra* n. 5, para. 76; *Zynger v. Poland*, ECtHR 13 July 2004, appl. no. 66096/01, para. 62; and *Yarashonen v. Turkey*, ECtHR 24 June 2014, appl. no. 72710/11, paras. 63–66.

Convention complaints with reasonable prospects of success.[60] This failure was held to constitute a violation of Article 13 as well,[61] with no need for separate reasoning. Similarly, in the *Rachevi* case the Court's appraisal of the exhaustion of domestic remedies in response to the preliminary objections under Article 35(1) was determinative of the conclusion that the remedies under the Bulgarian Code of Civil Procedure were not effective for the purposes of Article 13.[62]

4. RELATIONSHIP WITH SUBSTANTIVE RIGHTS AND FREEDOMS

4.1. INTRODUCTION

In order to shed light on the relationship between Article 13 as an ancillary right and substantive provisions (Articles 2–12 and 14 of the Convention, as well as provisions of the Protocols), the following analysis focuses on three areas: the effective investigation obligations guaranteed under Article 13 and the concomitant obligations derived from non-derogable rights under Article 2 or 3; issues of the length of proceedings discussed under Article 5(4) or Article 6(1) in conjunction with Article 13; and whether or not to dispense with the need to find a separate violation of Article 8 or 10 in tandem with Article 13.

4.2. ARTICLE 13 AND ARTICLE 2 OR 3

When a grievance relates solely to a breach of a substantive duty, i.e. the duty not to commit torture or other proscribed form of ill treatment, it is incumbent on the Court to carry out a separate appraisal under Article 13.[63] In the case

---

[60]   *Dogan and Others v. Turkey*, ECtHR 29 June 2004, appl. no. 8803–8811/02, 8813/02 and 8815–8819/02, para. 110.

[61]   *Ibid.*, para. 164. See also, e.g., *McFarlane v. Ireland*, ECtHR (GC) 10 September 2010, appl. no. 31333/06.

[62]   *Rachevi v. Bulgaria*, ECtHR 23 September 2004, appl. no. 47877/99, *supra* n. 4, paras. 60–68 and 96–104. *Cf. A.M. v. the Netherlands*, ECtHR 5 July 2016, appl. no. 29094/09, *supra* n. 34.

[63]   See, e.g., judgment of 4 February 2003, *Lorsé and Others v. The Netherlands*, ECtHR 4 February 2003, appl. no. 52750/99, paras. 74 and 87–96 (finding of a breach of a 'negative' obligation under Art. 3, in respect of 'inhuman and degrading treatment at the 'Extra Security Institution', but no breach of effective investigation obligations under Art. 13); and judgment of 26 November 2002, *E. and Others v. the United Kingdom*, ECtHR 26 November 2002, appl. no. 33219/96, paras. 101, and 106–116 (breach of a 'positive' obligation, under Art. 3, to protect the applicants from child abuse constituting inhuman and degrading treatment, and a breach of Art. 13 in respect of the lack of means to obtain a determination of alleged failure of the local authorities to protect them). See also the judgment of 13 September 2005, *Ostrovar v. Moldova*, ECtHR 13 September 2005, appl. no. 35207/33, paras 90 and 112;

---

of an alleged breach of the procedural limb of the positive obligations under Article 2 or Article 3 (namely, the effective investigation obligations), there is an overlapping relationship between such procedural obligation and the effectiveness requirements under Article 13. This would raise the question whether holding a respondent state to have breached the procedural obligations under Article 2 or 3 would justify abandoning a separate examination and a finding of a breach of the corresponding obligations under Article 13, or conversely whether such obligations can be ascertained solely in the context of Article 13.

In admissibility decisions, the examinations of whether complaints under Article 2 or 3 are manifestly ill-founded under Article 35(3) are closely intertwined with examinations of Article 13. If complaints under Article 2 or 3 are declared both admissible as well as well-founded, the Court does not engage in detailed examinations of the complaint under Article 13, declaring it admissible for the same reason.[64] The Court may join the question of exhaustion of domestic remedies to the merits of the case on the basis that the grievances concerning effective investigations are closely connected to the substance of the complaints under Articles 2 and 3.[65] Surely, it is also conceivable that issues of non-exhaustion of local remedies in relation to substantive provisions other than Articles 2 and 3 can be joined to the merits of the complaint under Article 13,[66] but such possibility seems more persuasive in the context of Articles 2 and 3. Further, when examining the merits in their admissibility decisions, the Court seems to equate the notion of manifest ill-foundedness to that of 'arguability' under Article 13.[67] Once the complaints are declared admissible, another array of salient features may be revealed at the merits phase. First, even if the Court has found the applicant to fail the test of proof beyond reasonable doubt as to a respondent state's implication in the disappearance, killing or ill-treatment under the heading of 'negative' obligations under Articles 2 and/or 3, this does not detract from the arguable nature of the complaint in relation to these

---

judgment of 21 September 2005, *Dizman v. Turkey*, ECtHR 20 September 2005, appl. no. 27309/95, paras 8586 and 99–100; *Iovchev v. Bulgaria*, ECtHR 2 February 2006, appl. no. 41211/98, paras 135–138 and 146–148; and *Doganay v. Turkey*, ECtHR 21 February 2006, appl. no. 50125/99, paras 33 and 41–42.

64 See, e.g., *Koval v. Ukraine*, ECtHR 30 March 2004 (dec.), appl. no. 65550/01 (complaints relating to the conditions of detention, and insufficient medical treatment and assistance). For such combined assessment of the notion of manifest ill-foundedness under other substantive provisions and Art. 13, see, e.g., *Russian Conservative Party of Entrepreneurs, Zhukov and Vasilyev v. Russia*, ECtHR 18 March 2004, appl. no. 55066/00 (Art. 3 of Protocol I and Art. 13).

65 See, e.g., *Siddik Aslan and Others v. Turkey*, ECtHR 19 October 2004, appl. no. 75307.

66 *Kirilova and Others v. Bulgaria*, ECtHR 5 February 2004, appl. nos. 42908/98, 44038/98, 44816/98 and 7319/02 (the question of exhaustion of domestic remedies in relation to the complaints under Art. 1 of Protocol I joined to the merits of the complaint under Art. 13).

67 See, e.g., *Menesheva v. Russia*, ECtHR 15 January 2004, appl. no. 59261/00 (lack of an effective remedy against ill-treatment); *Siddik Aslan and Others v. Turkey*, ECtHR 19 October 2004, appl. no. 75307, *supra* n. 65.

substantive provisions for the purposes of Article 13.[68] This can be readily explained by the fact that the standard of evidence beyond reasonable doubt[69] is much more onerous than the more 'lax' notion of arguability. Conversely, the 'arguable' nature of grievances concerning alleged killing, disappearance or ill-treatment can be *ipso facto* assumed, once such grievances are found to constitute a violation of Article 2 or 3 of the Convention.[70] Second, according to the Court's reasoning, the scope of positive obligations under Article 13 hinges on the nature and gravity of the interference complained of under the Convention rights, especially the nature of the rights guaranteed under Articles 2 and 3.[71] The non-derogable nature of Articles 2 and 3 rights are more susceptible to a separate and stringent appraisal of the requirements of Article 13 than in instances involving other provisions.[72]

Third, the Court has stated that the requirements of Article 13 are 'broader' than the obligation of investigation imposed by Article 2.[73] This dictum brings

---

[68]   See, e.g., *Orhan v. Turkey*, ECtHR 18 June 2002 appl. no. 25656/94, *supra* n. 37, para. 386; *Kaya v. Turkey*, ECtHR 19 February 1998, appl. no. 22729/83, *supra* n. 16, pp. 330–31, para. 107; and *Yasa v. Turkey*, ECtHR 2 September 1998, appl. no. 22495/93, *supra* n. 44, para. 113; *Tekdag v. Turkey*, ECtHR 15 January 2004, appl. no. 27699/95, para. 97; *Nuray Sen v. Turkey (No. 2)*, ECtHR 30 March 2004, appl. no. 25354, para. 192; *Buldan v. Turkey*, ECtHR 20 April 2004, appl. no. 28398/95, *supra* n. 44, para. 104; *Agdas v. Turkey*, ECtHR 27 July 2004, appl. no. 34592/97, para. 110. This principle can be deduced from the Court's approach in *Boyle and Rice v. The United Kingdom*, ECtHR 27 April 1988, appl. no. 9659/82, *supra* n. 3, para. 52.

[69]   Note that this standard, while being suitable for criminal proceedings, is criticised for being too harsh in a discrimination context. See the applicants' submissions under Art. 14 in: *Nachova and Others v. Bulgaria*, ECtHR 26 February 2004, appl. no. 43577/98 and 43579/98, para. 153.

[70]   *Dulas v. Turkey*, ECtHR 30 January 2001, appl. no. 25801/94, *supra* n. 31, para. 67; *Altun v. Turkey*, ECtHR 1 June 2004, appl. no. 24561/94, *supra* n. 31, para. 72. This dictum is based upon an *a contrario* interpretation that was developed in *Boyle and Rice v. The United Kingdom*, ECtHR 27 April 1988, appl. no. 9659/82, *supra* n. 3, para. 52, and the cases concerning killing: *Kaya v. Turkey*, ECtHR 19 February 1998, appl. no. 22729/83, *supra* n. 16, para. 107, and *Yasa v. Turkey*, ECtHR 2 September 1998, appl. no. 22495/93, *supra* n. 44, para. 113.

[71]   *Chahal v. The United Kingdom*, ECtHR (GC) 15 November 1996, appl. no. 22414/93, *supra* n. 28, paras. 150–51; *Aksoy v. Turkey*, ECtHR 18 December 1996, appl. no. 21987/93, *supra* n. 31, para. 95; *Aydin v. Turkey*, ECtHR (GC) 25 September 1997, appl. no. 23178/94, *supra* n. 31, para. 103; *Tekdag v. Turkey*, ECtHR 15 January 2004, appl. no. 27699/95, *supra* n. 68, para. 95; *Ramirez Sanchez v. France*, ECtHR (GC) 4 July 2006, appl. no. 59450/00, *supra* n. 35, paras. 165–166; and *Budayeva and Others v. Russia*, ECtHR 20 March 2008, appl. no. 15339/02. See also *Mentes and Others v. Turkey*, ECtHR 28 November 1997, appl. no. 23186/94, para. 89 (in the context of Art. 8).

[72]   *Kaya v. Turkey*, ECtHR 19 February 1998, appl. no. 22729/83, *supra* n. 16, para. 107; *Tekdag v. Turkey*, ECtHR 15 January 2004, appl. no. 27699/95, *supra* n. 68, para. 96. In the case of Art. 3, while stressing the 'irreversible nature' of the harm that might occur, the Court demanded an 'independent and rigorous scrutiny' of a complaint of a 'real risk' that an applicant would be subjected to ill-treatment within the meaning of Art. 3: see, *inter alia, Jabari v. Turkey*, ECtHR 11 July 2000, appl. no. 40035/98.

[73]   *Kaya v. Turkey*, ECtHR 19 February 1998, appl. no. 22729/83, *supra* n. 16, para. 107; *Salman v. Turkey*, ECtHR (GC) 27 June 2000, appl. no. 21986/93, paras. 104–109 and 123; *Agdas v. Turkey*, ECtHR 27 July 2004, appl. no. 34592/97, *supra* n. 68, para. 111; *Mehmet Sirin Yilmaz*

us back to the question whether finding a breach of a duty to mount an effective investigation under Article 2 would necessarily entail a concurrent violation of Article 13, or whether such a finding would make a separate examination under Article 13 redundant. The Court has more or less consistently[74] shown a willingness to find concurrent violations of Article 2 and Article 13.[75] The Court's methodology is not to engage in a detailed, separate assessment under Article 13, but to reiterate its findings concerning the lack of effective investigations under a substantive provision (Article 2 or 3) to justify its separate finding of a breach of Article 13.[76] In the *Ipek* case, in view of serious deficiencies of the investigations conducted by the relevant Turkish authorities, which consisted, *inter alia*, of the absence of independence of the body responsible for inquiries, the lack of due diligence and vigour in investigations, and the failure to seek evidence from eye-witnesses, the Court found a breach of the duty to engage in effective investigation under Article 2.[77] Such findings were automatically, and without any further separate examinations, translated into the finding of the absence of a thorough and effective investigation in breach of Article 13.[78] A similar approach can be discerned in other cases involving inadequate inquiries into the death of family members, with the Court holding such investigative defects as amounting to combined violations of Articles 2 and 13.[79]

---

    v. Turkey, ECtHR 29 July 2004, appl. no. 35875/97, para. 94. See also *Orhan v. Turkey*, ECtHR 18 June 2002 appl. no. 25656/94, *supra* n. 37, para. 387; *Kiliç v. Turkey*, ECtHR 28 March 2000, appl. no. 22492/93, para. 93; *Ipek v. Turkey*, ECtHR 17 February 2004, appl. no. 25760/94, *supra* n. 31, para. 198; and *Nuray Sen v. Turkey (No. 2)*, ECtHR 30 March 2004, appl. no. 25354, *supra* n. 68, para. 193.

[74]   So far, there exist only few cases in which the chamber held that the effective investigation obligation under Art. 13 was absorbed into the same obligation under Art. 2, and that a breach of the latter obligation was sufficient: *Nachova and Others v. Bulgaria*, ECtHR 26 February 2004, appl. no. 43577/98 and 43579/98, *supra* n. 69, paras 115–141 and 146; *Makaratzis v. Greece*, ECtHR 20 December 2004, appl. no. 50385/99, paras 71–72, 78–79 and 86 (violation of both substantial and procedural limbs of Article 2); and *Ramsahai and Others v. The Netherlands*, ECtHR 10 November 2005, appl. no. 52391/99, paras 407–408, 430–431 and 437–438 (violation only of a procedural limb under Article 2).

[75]   See, e.g., *Kaya v. Turkey*, ECtHR 19 February 1998, appl. no. 22729/83, *supra* n. 16, para. 107; *Salman v. Turkey*, ECtHR (GC) 27 June 2000, appl. no. 21986/93, *supra* n. 73, para. 123, *Tekdag v. Turkey*, ECtHR 15 January 2004, appl. no. 27699/95, *supra* n. 68, paras. 98–99; *Agdas v. Turkey*, ECtHR 27 July 2004, appl. no. 34592/97, *supra* n. 68, para. 111; *Ikincisoy v. Turkey*, ECtHR 27 July 2004, appl. no. 26144/95, paras. 76–80 and 119–126; *Mehmet Sirin Yilmaz v. Turkey*, ECtHR 29 July 2004, appl. no. 35875/97, *supra* n. 73, para. 94.

[76]   See, e.g., *Kaya v. Turkey*, ECtHR 19 February 1998, appl. no. 22729/83, *supra* n. 16, paras. 89–92 and 108; *Ananyev and Others v. Russia*, ECtHR 10 January 2012, appl. no. 42525/07; *Yefimenko v. Russia*, ECtHR 12 February 2013, appl. no. 152/04.

[77]   *Ipek v. Turkey*, ECtHR 17 February 2004, appl. no. 25760/94, *supra* n. 31, paras. 173–177.

[78]   *Ibid.*, paras. 200–201.

[79]   Apart from the *Ipek* case, which is discussed here, for cases involving such concurrent identification of breaches of Arts. 2 and 13, see, e.g., *Nuray Sen v. Turkey (No. 2)*, ECtHR 30 March 2004, appl. no. 25354, *supra* n. 68, paras. 174–179 and 193–194; *Özalp and Others v. Turkey*, ECtHR 8 April 2004, appl. no. 32457/96, *supra* n. 31, paras. 43–47, and 62–65; *Buldan v. Turkey*, ECtHR 20 April 2004, appl. no. 28398/95, *supra* n. 44, paras. 85–90, 105–106.

The Court's policy remains obscure, however, in respect of the relationship between the requirement to mount an effective investigation into alleged ill-treatment under Article 3 and the corresponding requirement under Article 13.[80] The Court's methodology in respect of alleged violations of both Articles 3 and 13 is distinct from that established in the case of combined assessment of Articles 2 and 13, in that the Court may incorporate examinations of the procedural limb of Article 3 in the context of Article 13. Such a reasoning process has been established since the *Ilhan* judgment, in which the Grand Chamber found that the applicant's complaints concerning the lack of effective investigations by the authorities into the cause of his injuries fell to be dealt with under Article 13.[81] The Court has asserted that in case of alleged breaches of the positive obligations to conduct effective inquiries under Article 3, the examinations of such procedural obligations can be dispensed with, stating that they are subsumed into the appraisal under Article 13.[82] The Chamber's approach in the subsequent case of *Mehmet Emin Yüksel* follows the methodology seen in *Ilhan*. The Chamber dispensed with a separate finding of Article 3 in respect of the absence of effective inquiries, holding that it was satisfied with the finding of a breach of the substantive obligation (to refrain from torture), and that the investigation requirement could be 'more appropriately' dealt with under Article 13.[83] However, in the more recent case of *Menesheva*, another chamber has departed from the Grand Chamber's methodology in *Ilhan* and identified a concurrent violation both of Article 13 and of the procedural limb of Article 3.[84]

Beyond the general and rather obscure statement in the *Ilhan* case that '[w]hether it is appropriate or necessary to find a procedural breach of Article 3 will (...) depend on the circumstances of the particular case',[85] the Grand

---

[80] Under Art. 13, the Court has established virtually the same principles as those that are applicable under Art. 3. The Court held that '[w]here an individual has an arguable claim that he has been tortured or subjected to serious ill-treatment by agents of the State, the notion of an "effective remedy" entails, in addition to the payment of compensation where appropriate, a thorough and effective investigation capable of leading to the identification and punishment of those responsible and including effective access for the complainant to the investigatory procedure': *Aksoy v. Turkey*, ECtHR 18 December 1996, appl. no. 21987/93, *supra* n. 31, para. 98; *Mehmet Emin Yüksel v. Turkey*, ECtHR 20 July 2004, appl. no. 40154/98, *supra* n. 49, para. 36; *Salman v. Turkey*, ECtHR (GC) 27 June 2000, appl. no. 21986/93 *supra* n. 73, para. 121–122.

[81] *Ilhan v. Turkey*, ECtHR (GC) 27 June 2000, appl. no. 22277/93, *supra* n. 31, paras. 92–93.

[82] *Mahmut Kaya v. Turkey*, ECtHR 28 March 2000, appl. no. 22535/95, *supra* n. 43, para. 120; *Mehmet Emin Yüksel v. Turkey*, ECtHR 20 July 2004, appl. no. 40154/98, *supra* n. 49, para. 32; *Balogh v. Hungary*, ECtHR 20 July 2004, appl. no. 47940, para. 60 (in the latter case, while finding a violation of the substantive limb of Article 3, the Court was satisfied that the applicant had an effective remedy within the meaning of Article 13 in relation to his complaint under Article 3); and *Çelik and Imret v. Turkey*, ECtHR 26 October 2004, appl. no. 44093/98, *supra* n. 55, para. 50.

[83] *Mehmet Emin Yüksel v. Turkey*, ECtHR 20 July 2004, appl. no. 40154/98, *supra* n. 49, para. 32.

[84] Judgment of 9 March 2006, appl. no. 59261/00, paras. 68 and 74. In that case, the chamber also found a breach of the substantive limb of Art. 3 (paras. 59–60).

[85] *İlhan v. Turkey*, ECtHR (GC) 27 June 2000, appl. no. 22277/93, *supra* n. 31, para. 92.

Chamber provided neither clear guidelines nor rationales for obliterating the need for separate appraisal and findings of a violation of the procedural/ investigative limb of Article 3, in conjunction with Article 13. This question, which links the procedural duties of Article 3 and Article 13, is closely intertwined with the inconsistency of the approaches followed by the Court in relation to the question whether the finding of a substantive violation of Article 3 (breach of obligations not to commit torture or other maltreatment) can justify the exclusion of determining a breach of the effective investigation obligation under the same provision.[86] In the *Ilhan* case, the Grand Chamber failed to explain why issues of investigative obligations under Article 3 can be so differentiated from the comparable obligations under Article 2 as to exempt an independent finding of a violation under Article 3.[87]

4.3. ARTICLE 13 AND ARTICLE 5(4) AND (5)

The Court has consistently asserted that in the case of deprivation of liberty and compensation for unlawful detention, paragraphs 4 and 5 of Article 5 constitute a *lex specialis* in relation to the more general requirements of Article 13.[88] At the admissibility level the policy of the Court, as in the case of Articles 2 and 3, is that once the complaints under Article 5(4) are declared admissible as being not manifestly ill-founded, the Court, for the same reason and without any separate examinations, tends to admit the complaint under Article 13.[89] However, in the merits phase the tendency is that the finding of a violation of the right to a prompt review of the lawfulness of the detention by a court under Article 5(4) is considered as sufficient to dispense with a separate examination

---

[86] On this matter, compare the Grand Chamber's refusal of a separate finding of the procedural limb under Art. 3 in *Ilhan*, with inconsistent approaches disclosed by Chambers in *Assenov and Others v. Bulgaria*, ECtHR 28 October 1998, appl. no. 24760/94; *Sevtap Veznedaroglu v. Turkey*, ECtHR 11 April 2000, appl. no. 32357/96; *Satik and Others v. Turkey*, ECtHR 10 October 2000, appl. no. 31866/96 (findings of violation of Article 3 in both substantive and procedural limbs); *Denizci and Others v. Cyprus*, ECtHR 23 May 2001, appl. no. 25316–25321/94 and 27207/95 (finding of inhuman treatment but no separate examination of effective inquiries under Article 3).

[87] Evidently, when a grievance relates solely to a breach of substantive duty not to commit torture or other proscribed form of ill treatment, it is incumbent on the Court to carry out a separate appraisal under Article 13. See, e.g., *Lorsé and Others v. The Netherlands*, ECtHR 4 February 2003, appl. no. 52750/99, *supra* n. 63, paras. 74 and 87–96 (finding of inhuman and degrading treatment in breach of Article 3, but no violation of Article 13).

[88] *Stoichkov v. Bulgaria*, ECtHR 9 September 2004, appl. no. 9808/02, para. 5. As to the habeas corpus provision of Article 5(4), see also *M.A. and M.M v. France*, ECtHR 23 November 1999, appl. no. 39671/98. For the right to compensation under Article 5(5), see, e.g., *Tsirlis and Kouloumpas v. Greece*, ECtHR 29 May 1997, appl. nos. 19233/91, 19234/91, para. 73.

[89] See, for instance, *Menesheva v. Russia*, ECtHR 15 January 2004, appl. no. 59261/00, *supra* n. 67, (absence of effective remedies against the imposition of the 'administrative' detention); *Falkovych v. Ukraine*, ECtHR 29 June 2004, appl. no. 64200/00.

under Article 13.[90] In *De Wilde, Ooms and Versyp* (*Vagrancy* Cases), where the vagrants arrested and brought before the police court complained of guarantees inferior to those recognised in criminal proceedings, the Court was satisfied to find a violation only of Article 5(4), to the exclusion of a separate appraisal under Article 13.[91] Similarly, in *De Jong, Baljet and Van den Brink*, the Court, after having found a violation of Article 5(4), decided to abandon the examination of the alleged violation of Article 13 on the basis that Article 5(4) guarantees a right to proceedings before a 'court', which is considered as a *lex specialis* with respect to the general obligation under Article 13 to provide an effective remedy before an authority of unspecified status.[92] In *Brannigan and McBride*, the Court ruled out the examination under Article 13, holding that detainees could challenge the lawfulness of their detention by recourse to habeas corpus proceedings, as found in the *Brogan* case.[93] However, in his dissenting opinion Judge Walsh averred that the habeas corpus remedies, which depended on showing a breach of national laws, did not satisfy the requirements of Article 13, stating that the Court's judgment overlooked the fact that the arrested person was 'held incommunicado and without legal assistance' within the crucial first 48 hours of detention.[94]

As with the complaints of concurrent violations of Articles 6(1) and 13 with respect to the delay in proceedings, the gist of complaints under Article 13 is specifically directed to the absence of an effective remedy, whether judicial or not, which would have allowed a complaint of the absence of a prompt judicial review to be heard. In that sense, a separate appraisal under Article 13 can hardly be considered superfluous.[95]

4.4. ARTICLE 13 AND ARTICLE 6

The Court has consistently held that Article 6 constitutes the *lex specialis* in relation to Article 13 and that the requirements under the latter provision are

---

[90] See, e.g., *Pavletic v. Slovakia*, ECtHR 22 June 2004, appl. no. 39359/98, para. 100; *Kolanis v. The United Kingdom*, ECtHR 21 June 2005, appl. no. 517/02, paras 82 and 86; and *Gorshkov v. Ukraine*, ECtHR 8 November 2005, appl. no. 67531/01, paras 46–47.

[91] *De Wilde, Ooms and Versyp v. Belgium* ('Vagrancy' Cases), ECtHR 18 June 1971, appl. nos. 2832/66, 2835/66, 2899/66, paras. 74–80, and 95.

[92] *De Jong, Baljet and Van den Brink v. The Netherlands*, ECtHR 22 May 1984, appl. nos. 8805/79, 8806/79, 9242/81, para. 60. See also *Bouamar v. Belgium*, ECtHR 29 February 1988, appl. no. 9106/80, para. 65.

[93] *Brannigan and McBride v. The United Kingdom*, ECtHR 26 May 1993, appl. nos. 14553/89, 14554/89, para. 76.

[94] *Ibid.*, dissenting opinion of Judge Walsh, paras. 12–15.

[95] See, e.g., *Ikincisoy v. Turkey*, ECtHR 27 July 2004, appl. no. 26144/95, *supra* n. 75, in which the finding of violations both of Art. 5(4) as regards the dilatory nature of a judicial remedy for determining lawfulness of detention under Art. 5(4) and of Art. 5(5) with respect to the absence of compensation for unlawful arrest or detention, did not stop the Court from making a separate appraisal under, and finding a violation of, Art. 13.

'less strict than', and susceptible to absorption by those of Article 6.[96] In case the Court reaches the conclusion that Article 6 is not violated in view of the absence of the determination of a 'civil right', a separate inquiry into a possible violation of Article 13 may be required. Article 13 grievances would relate specifically to the question of excessive length of proceedings concerning such putative, though rejected, civil rights. On the other hand, if a violation of Article 6 *has* been found, it may be questioned whether a further inquiry under Article 13 is superfluous, to the extent that the guarantees of the two provisions overlap or that the requirements of Article 13 are subordinate to those of Article 6. Even if the Court, after finding a violation of Article 6(1) with respect to effective access to a court and/or length of proceedings, carries out examinations under Article 13, it may find no violation under Article 13.[97] In a number of cases, the Court abandoned the examination of the complaint under Article 13, on the ground that the requirements of Article 13 are absorbed by more stringent obligations under Article 6.[98]

This 'absorption approach' cannot be assumed in relation to all procedural requirements of Article 6. The Court has held that the decision to dispense with a separate examination under Article 13 can be warranted in circumstances where a substantive right in relation to which the right to a fair trial under Article 6(1) is allegedly infringed concerns a 'civil right'.[99] The Court applied the same

---

[96]   *Airey v. Ireland*, ECtHR 9 October 1979, appl. no. 6289/73, para. 35; *Golder v. The United Kingdom*, ECtHR (GC) 21 February 1975, appl. no. 4451/70, para. 33; *Sporrong and Lönnroth v. Sweden*, ECtHR (GC) 23 September 1982, appl. nos. 7151/71, 7152/75, para. 88; *W. v. The United Kingdom*, ECtHR 8 July 1987, appl. no. 9749/82, para. 86; *Pudas v. Sweden*, ECtHR 27 October 1987, appl. no. 10426/83, para. 43; *Tre Traktörer Aktiebolag v. Sweden*, ECtHR 7 July 1989, appl. no. 10873/84, para. 51; *Allan Jacobsson v. Sweden (No. 1)*, ECtHR 25 October 1989, appl. no. 10842/84, para. 78; and *Kamasinski v. Austria*, ECtHR 19 December 1989, appl. no. 9783/82, para. 110. For more recent cases, see, e.g., *Ahlskog and Oy Maple House AB v. Finland*, ECtHR 4 May 2004, appl. no. 75619/01; *Ziliberberg v. Moldova*, ECtHR 4 May 2004, appl. no. 61821/00 and *Krokstäde v. Sweden*, ECtHR 28 September 2004 (dec.), appl. no. 63916/00.

[97]   For admissibility decisions, see, e.g., *Uzkureliene and Others v. Lithuania,* ECtHR 8 January 2004, appl. no. 62988/00 (admissible as to the complaint under Art. 6 of the non-execution of the Supreme Court judgment, but inadmissible as to the same complaint under Art. 13); *Toimi v. Sweden*, ECtHR 31 August 2004, appl. no. 55164/00, *supra* n. 12 (admissible as to the complaints concerning effective access to a court and the length of proceedings under Art. 6(1) but inadmissible with respect to an effective remedy requirement under Art. 13).

[98]   See, *inter alia*, *Sporrong and Lönnroth v. Sweden*, ECtHR (GC) 23 September 1982, appl. nos. 7151/71, 7152/75, *supra* n. 96, para. 88; *Silver and Others v. The United Kingdom*, ECtHR 25 March 1983, appl. nos. 5947/72, 6205/73, 7052/75, 7061/75, 7107/75, 7113/75, 7136/75, *supra* n. 16, para. 110; *Campbell and Fell v. The United Kingdom*, ECtHR 28 June 1984, appl. nos. 7819/77, 7878/77, para. 123; *O. v. The United Kingdom*, ECtHR (GC) 8 July 1987, appl. no. 9276/81, para. 69; *Pudas v. Sweden*, ECtHR 27 October 1987, appl. no. 10426/83, *supra* n. 96, para. 43; and *Hokkanen v. Finland*, ECtHR 23 September 1994, appl. no. 19823/92, para. 74.

[99]   *Sporrong and Lönnroth v. Sweden*, ECtHR (GC) 23 September 1982, appl. nos. 7151/71, 7152/75, *supra* n. 96, para. 88 (in contrast, the Commission found a separate violation of Article 13); *W. v. The United Kingdom*, ECtHR (Plenary) 8 July 1987, appl. no. 9749/82, *supra* n. 96, para. 86; *Pudas v. Sweden*, ECtHR 27 October 1987, appl. no. 10426/83, *supra* n. 96,

reasoning to cases where the complaints relate to the adequacy of an existing appellate or cassation 'criminal' procedure.[100]

As regards the requirement of holding a trial within a reasonable time, in the *Kudla* case the Court made a crucial departure from precedents, considering it necessary to make a further examination under Article 13, as distinct from the finding of a violation of Article 6(1). According to the Court the requirements of Article 13 should be considered as 'reinforcing' those of Article 6(1), rather than being absorbed by the obligation to prohibit inordinate delays in legal proceedings under Article 6(1).[101] In the *Kudla* case, the Court distinguished the complaints under the two headings, holding that while the complaints under Article 6(1) concerned criminal charges, the thrust of the applicant's complaints under Article 13 related to the unreasonable length of proceedings. In the previous cases of a comparable nature the Court, however, evaded a separate evaluation under Article 13 when it already found a breach of the 'reasonable time' requirement under Article 6(1).[102] The Court invoked institutional problems to justify the review of the case law. It pointed out that both the growing accumulation of applications concerning excessive delays in the administration of justice and the absence of domestic remedies for such delays in certain States Parties[103] risked seriously undermining the rule of law.[104] The Court's wariness as to such systematic shortcomings is bolstered by the concern of judicial economy. Unless a violation of Article 13 is established to highlight the absence of domestic remedies to cure those institutional shortcomings, the Court will be inundated with complaints relating to the same matter. The thrust of the argument for a separate appraisal under Article 13 is that there is no overlap between the complaint of the unreasonably dilatory nature of proceedings for determining civil rights and obligations or a criminal charge under Article 6(1) on the one hand, and the grievance concerning the lack of an effective remedy to ventilate a complaint of such undue delays under Article 13 on the other.[105]

---

para. 43; *Tre Traktörer AB v. Sweden*, ECtHR 7 July 1989, appl. no. 10873, para. 51, *supra* n. 96,; *Allan Jacobsson v. Sweden (No. 1)*, ECtHR 25 October 1989, appl. no. 10842/84, para. 78, *supra* n. 96 (the Commission dispensed with a separate finding under Article 13); and *Brualla Gómez de la Torre v. Spain*, ECtHR 19 December 1997, appl. no. 26737/95, para. 41.

[100]   *Kamasinski v. Austria*, ECtHR 19 December 1989, appl. no. 9783/82, *supra* n. 96, para. 110.

[101]   *Kudla v. Poland*, ECtHR (GC) 26 October 2000, appl. no. 30210/96, *supra* n. 5, para. 152.

[102]   See, e.g., *Pizzetti v. Italy*, ECtHR 26 February 1993, appl. no. 12444/86, para. 21; *Bouilly v. France*, ECtHR 7 December 1999, appl. no. 38952/07, para. 27; and *Giuseppe Tripodi v. Italy*, ECtHR 25 January 2000, appl. no. 40946/98 para. 15.

[103]   *Bottazzi v. Italy*, ECtHR (GC) 28 July 1999, appl. no. 34884/97, para. 22; *Di Mauro v. Italy*, ECtHR 28 July 1999, appl. no. 34256/96, para. 23; *A.P. v. Italy*, ECtHR 28 July 1999, appl. no. 35265/97, para. 18; *Ferrari v. Italy*, ECtHR 28 July 1999, appl. no. 33440/96, para. 21. See also the Committee of Ministers of the Council of Europe's Resolution DH (97) 336 of 11 July 1997 (Length of civil proceedings in Italy: supplementary measures of a general character).

[104]   *Kudla v. Poland*, ECtHR (GC) 26 October 2000, appl. no. 30210/96, *supra* n. 5, para. 148.

[105]   *Ibid.*, para. 147.

Ever since, the Court's policy in respect of excessive length in proceedings has generally been to follow the *Kudla* approach with the need to carry out a separate examination under Article 13.[106] At the admissibility level, the general policy seems to be that when complaints about the absence of access to a court under Article 6(1) are declared admissible and well-founded, this would induce the Court to adopt the same conclusion under Article 13 without any separate examination.[107] At the merits phase the Court is very likely to find concurrent breaches of both the 'reasonable time' requirement under Article 6(1) and the requirement to establish an 'effective remedy' within the meaning of Article 13 so as to enforce the rights under Article 6(1). This approach is seen not only in relation to the right to a 'hearing within a reasonable time',[108] but also in relation to the right to secure the execution of a judgment given by a court.[109] This methodology is characterised by the Court as one of adducing the findings under Article 6(1) to support the conclusion under Article 13 with little separate assessment.[110] In some instances, however, the Court felt the need to engage in a thorough appraisal under Article 13, duly separating the length of proceedings under Article 6(1) from the absence of procedures to complain of such delays under Article 13. In this scenario, the appraisal of the issues under Article 6(1) may have little bearing on issues under Article 13 beyond the preliminary question of arguability.[111] Finally, it is interesting to note that the Court has found violations of Article 13 in cases of the non-enforcement of national judicial decisions.[112]

---

[106] See, e.g., *McFarlane v. Ireland*, ECtHR (GC) 10 September 2010, appl. no. 31333/06.

[107] See, *inter alia, Sukhorubchenko v. Russia*, ECtHR 15 January 2004, appl. no. 699315/01; *Jonasson v. Sweden*, ECtHR 30 March 2004, appl. no. 59403/00; and *Romashov v. Ukraine*, ECtHR 27 July 2004, appl. no. 67534/01, paras. 29–35.

[108] See, e.g., *Zynger v. Poland*, ECtHR 13 July 2004, appl. no. 66096/01, paras. 58 and 65.

[109] *Romashov v. Ukraine*, ECtHR 27 July 2004, appl. no. 67534/01, *supra* n. 107, paras. 42–47 and *"Amat-G" Ltd and Mebaghishvili v. Georgia*, ECtHR 27 September 2005, appl. no. 2507/03, paras 49–50. The right to have a final, binding judicial decision executed is recognised on the basis of the effective interpretation of Article 6(1): *Hornsby v. Greece*, ECtHR 19 March 1997, appl. no. 18357/91, para. 40; and *Romashov v. Ukraine*, ECtHR 27 July 2004, appl. no. 67534/01, *supra* n. 107, para. 42.

[110] See, e.g., *Kormacheva v. Russia*, ECtHR 29 January 2004, appl. no. 53084/99, paras. 60–64; *E.O. and V.P. v. Slovakia*, ECtHR 27 April 2004, appl. nos. 56193/00, 5781/00, paras. 83–86, and 97–98; *Plaksin v. Russia*, ECtHR 29 April 2004, appl. no. 14949/02, paras. 37–44, and 49–50. *Cf. Zynger v. Poland*, ECtHR 13 July 2004, appl. no. 66096/01, *supra* n. 59, where the Court undertook a relatively lengthy assessment in response to the Government's submissions under Article 13 (*ibid.*, paras. 62–65).

[111] *Rachevi v. Bulgaria*, ECtHR 23 September 2004, appl. no. 47877/99, *supra* n. 4, para. 99. In that case, the Court's elaborate examinations of the effectiveness of domestic remedies under Article 35(1) in relation to the preliminary objections were decisive for the conclusion as to the issues of Article 13: *ibid.*, paras. 60–68, and 96–104.

[112] See, e.g., *Burdov v. Russia (No. 2)*, ECtHR 15 January 2009, appl. no. 33509/04 (also violations of Article 6 and the right to property of Article 1 of Protocol).

4.5. ARTICLE 13 AND ARTICLE 8

The relationship between Article 13 and Article 8 may provide a basis for surmising how the Strasbourg Court has dealt with the alleged concurrent violations of Article 13 and substantive rights of the Convention, other than non-derogable rights under Articles 2 and 3, or due process rights under Articles 5 and 6. The assessment of the case law reveals a certain unevenness in the Court's methodology. In most cases the Court followed an 'absorption approach', invoking a finding of a violation of a substantive right to justify the exclusion of a separate examination of a grievance under Article 13. Absence of an examination even in a cursory manner under Article 13 may give reason to think that in such circumstances the Court has reduced the independent character of Article 13 to the vanishing point.[113]

In the *Malone* case, where the interception of postal and telephone communications as well as the release of information obtained from the 'metering' of telephones were found to contravene Article 8, the Court dispensed with the need to rule on the alleged breach of Article 13 without any further argument.[114] Such absorption approach was followed in a number of subsequent cases. In *X and Y v. the Netherlands*, the Court justified the exclusion of a separate examination under Article 13 on the ground that its evaluation under Article 8 took into account the absence of adequate means of obtaining a remedy for Ms Y, a mentally handicapped victim of sexual abuse.[115] Similarly, in the *Herczegfalvy* case, the Court did not pursue the issue of the alleged Article 13 violation, stressing that it was sufficient to find violations of Articles 8 and 10 with respect to forced medical treatment and feeding, as well as to the refusal to send on the applicant's correspondence.[116]

Yet, in some cases the Court did not recoil from carrying out a separate appraisal, and even did so in a thorough manner. It is submitted that the ancillary but autonomous character of Article 13 demands a separate appraisal and finding under Article 13. An example of this approach has occasionally surfaced in the case law, albeit without guidelines as to when such concurrent finding was deemed necessary. In the *Campbell and Fell* case, the complaint under Article 8 was mainly directed to two issues: the refusal to allow confidential correspondence by a prisoner with his lawyer and the restrictions on his personal correspondence. The fact that the Court found a violation of

---

[113] With respect to Arts. 8 and 10; see also *Herczegfalvy v. Austria*, ECtHR 24 September 1992, appl. no. 10533/83, paras. 95–96.

[114] *Malone v. The United Kingdom*, ECtHR 2 August 1984, appl. no. 8691/79, paras. 90–91.

[115] *X and Y v. the Netherlands*, ECtHR 26 March 1985, appl. no. 8976/80, paras. 35–36.

[116] *Herczegfalvy v. Austria*, ECtHR 24 September 1992, appl. no. 10533/83, *supra* n. 113, paras. 95 and 96.

Article 8 in these respects[117] did not prevent the Court from examining the alleged violation of Article 13 on both counts.[118]

In other cases, the Court showed a greater willingness to apply the methodology of pursuing separate appraisal, and such tendency can be exemplified, most notably, in two areas of complaints directed against English remedies under Article 8: intrusions into privacy of homosexuals in the army, and use of surveillance devices. On issues of homosexuals the Court justified its progressive construction of Article 8 in tandem with Article 13 on the basis of the emerging European consensus on more tolerant attitudes towards homosexuality. In the *Smith and Grady* case, concerning the privacy of homosexuals in the army, the Court, after finding a violation of Article 8, concluded that the English remedies, including judicial review proceedings, did not satisfy the requirement of effectiveness under Article 13.[119] In *Kahn*, the finding of a violation of Article 8 in respect of the use of covert listening devices did not prevent the Court from thoroughly examining whether the remedies suggested by the United Kingdom Government were effective.[120]

Even with regard to other types of grievances under Article 8 the case law of the Court does not seem to exclude the possibility of separate appraisal under Article 13.[121] Yet, beyond several complaints against English remedies, it is not certain whether the Court has now come to espouse the *general* policy of pursuing separate examinations under Article 13. The Court has failed to provide guidelines as to circumstances that would necessitate the concurrent examinations of Article 13 in tandem with Article 8, beyond its assertion that the scope of obligations under Article 13 depends on the nature of the rights at issue and the particular circumstances of the case. Such an approach can be contrasted to the Court's approach in cases involving alleged violations of Articles 10 and

---

[117]   *Campbell and Fell v. The United Kingdom*, ECtHR 28 June 1984, appl. nos. 7819/77, 7878/77, *supra* n. 98, paras. 110 and 120.

[118]   *Ibid.*, paras. 124–128 (violation of Art. 13 on both accounts).

[119]   *Smith and Grady v. The United Kingdom*, ECtHR 27 September 1999, appl. nos. 33985/96, 33986/96, paras. 135–139. See also the subsequent case of *Beck, Copp and Bazeley v. The United Kingdom*, ECtHR 22 October 2002, appl. no. 48535/99, 48536/99, 48537/99, para. 58.

[120]   *Khan v. The United Kingdom*, ECtHR 12 May 2000, appl. no. 35394/97, *supra* n. 50, paras. 28 and 47 (violation of Article 13 as well). See also the subsequent cases dealing with the use of surveillance measures: *Allan v. The United Kingdom*, ECtHR 5 November 2002, appl. no. 48539/99, paras. 36 and 55; *Chalkley v. The United Kingdom*, ECtHR 12 June 2003, appl. no. 63831/00, paras. 25 and 27 (in those two cases, the Government accepted the violations of Articles 8 and 13, following the judgment in *Kahn*).

[121]   See, e.g., *Maskhadova and Others v. Russia*, ECtHR 6 June 2013, appl. no. 18071/05 (on the refusal to return the bodies of killed terrorists to the families, where the Court found a violation of both Arts. 8 and 13 ECHR). In *G.R. v. the Netherlands*, ECtHR 10 January 2012, appl. no. 22251/07, *supra* n. 32, the Court found it more appropriate to consider the case under Article 13 of the Convention, while the applicant only relied on Article 8 (he complained of the financial threshold preventing him from seeking a residence permit for the purpose of residing with his wife and children).

13. The Court's methodology emerging from a much smaller number of relevant cases seems to be that the finding of a violation of Article 10 does not make it purposeless to engage in a separate appraisal under Article 13.[122] A similar approach was adopted as regards the allegation of concurrent violations of Articles 9 and 13.

5. IN OFFICIAL CAPACITY

5.1. EXCLUSION OF IMMUNITIES AND *DRITTWIRKUNG*

From the words 'notwithstanding that the violation has been committed by persons acting in an official capacity' one can infer that the Convention purports to deny the legal effect of national laws providing public officials with immunity from responsibility of human rights violations under the Convention. Further, this wording may suggest the broader interpretation that an effective legal remedy within the meaning of Article 13 must also, and *a fortiori*, be furnished when the violation has been committed by a private individual, raising the possibility of the indirect *Drittwirkung* (third-party effect) of the Convention rights between citizens. It is possible to find the jurisprudential rationale for *Drittwirkung* to lie in the combined effect of the principle of effective protection and the general obligation to guarantee the rights and freedoms under Article 1 of the Convention. Yet, in view of the principle of subsidiarity underlying the application of Article 13, this possibility should be restricted to cases of positive obligations to protect individuals against risk of serious violations stemming from other individuals, as in the case of the duty to protect individuals against life-threatening risk under Article 2 or risk of ill-treatment under Article 3.

5.2. POSITION OF LEGISLATIVE POWER

The Court's position on the responsibility of the legislator under the ECHR is that national authorities are given a margin of appreciation in assessing the manner in which the Convention rights are secured, including as to the form of remedies in the case of an alleged breach of those rights, with no duty of

---

[122] See, e.g., *Vereinigung Demokratischer Soldaten Österreichs and Gubi v. Austria*, ECtHR 19 December 1994 appl. no. 15153/89, paras. 40 and 53 (violations of both Articles 10 and 13); *Wille v. Liechtenstein*, ECtHR (GC) 28 October 1999, appl. no. 28396/95, paras. 70, 76–78 (violations of both Articles 10 and 13); and *Vgt Verein gegen Tierfabriken v. Switzerland*, ECtHR 28 June 2001, appl. no. 24699/94, paras. 79–83 (violation of Art. 10 but not of Art. 13).

incorporating the Convention into domestic law.[123] According to the Court, Article 13 does not guarantee either a remedy that would allow a Contracting State's laws as such to be challenged before a national authority on the ground of being contrary to the Convention or equivalent domestic norms,[124] or a remedy that would make available a constitutional review allowing an individual to challenge the terms of subordinate legislation.[125] What matters most is that such remedies, whatever form may be secured in domestic legal order, must be able to enforce and claim non-compliance with the substance of the Convention rights and freedoms.[126]

It must be noted that the Court has recognised that in certain circumstances a mere existence of a law as such may constitute a violation of Article 8 of the Convention without any specific application to alleged victims.[127] This means that in contrast to cases where applicants complain of specific measures, applicants claiming to be victims of infringement of their right by virtue of an impugned law in itself are excluded from raising the question of effective remedies under Article 13. Once such a law is applied to the alleged victim, the Court's willingness to review the effectiveness of remedies under Article 13

---

[123] *The Observer and Guardian v. The United Kingdom*, ECtHR 26 November 1991, appl. no. 13585/88, para. 76.

[124] See, e.g., *James and Others v. The United Kingdom*, ECtHR (GC) 21 February 1986, appl. no. 8793/79, *supra* n. 10, para. 85; *Holy Monasteries v. Greece*, ECtHR 9 December 1994, appl. nos. 13092/87, 13984/88, para. 90. See also, *Grant v. the United Kingdom*, ECtHR 19 May 2005, appl. no. 32570/03 (adm.dec.), in which this case law is confirmed in view of the so-called declaration of incompatibility on the basis of the Human Rights Act and *Greens & M.T. v. the United Kingdom*, ECtHR 23 November 2010, appl. nos. 60041/08 and 60054/08.

[125] *Lithgow and Others v. The United Kingdom*, ECtHR 8 July 1986, appl. nos. 9006/80, 9262/81, 9263/81, 9265/81, 9266/81, 9313/81, 9405/81, para. 206; and *Boyle and Rice v. The United Kingdom*, ECtHR 27 April 1988, appl. no. 9659/82, *supra* n. 3, para. 87.

[126] See, *inter alia*, *James and Others v. The United Kingdom*, ECtHR 21 February 1986, appl. no. 8793/79, *supra* n. 10, para. 84; *Lithgow and Others v. The United Kingdom*, ECtHR 8 July 1986, appl. nos. 9006/80, 9262/81, 9263/81, 9265/81, 9266/81, 9313/81, 9405/81, *supra* n. 125, para. 205; *Boyle and Rice v. The United Kingdom*, ECtHR 27 April 1988, appl. no. 9659/82, *supra* n. 3, para. 52; *Chahal v. The United Kingdom*, ECtHR (GC) 15 November 1996, appl. no. 22414/93, *supra* n. 28, para. 145; *Aksoy v. Turkey*, ECtHR 18 December 1996, appl. no. 21987/93, *supra* n. 31, para. 95; *Aydin v. Turkey*, ECtHR (GC) 25 September 1997, appl. no. 23178/94, *supra* n. 31, para. 103; *Kaya v. Turkey*, ECtHR 19 February 1998, appl. no. 22729/83, *supra* n. 16, para. 89; and *Tekdag v. Turkey*, ECtHR 15 January 2004, appl. no. 27699/95, *supra* n. 68, para. 95.

[127] See, e.g., *Dudgeon v. The United Kingdom*, ECtHR 22 October 1981, appl. no. 7525/76; *Norris v. Ireland*, ECtHR 26 October 1988, appl. no. 10581/83; and *Modinos v. Cyprus*, ECtHR 22 April 1993, appl. no. 15070/89 (The mere existence of a law criminalising private homosexual conduct between consenting adults was found to contravene the right to private life of homosexuals, who were recognised as potential victims, irrespective of whether the law has been applied to them). *Cf.* cases concerning secret surveillance in which the Court has accepted the claim of the victim of a violation occasioned by the mere existence of secret measures or of legislation permitting secret measures, without having to allege that such measures had been in fact applied to him. See *Klass and Others v. Germany*, ECtHR (GC) 6 September 1978, appl. no. 5029/71, *supra* n. 9 and, more recently, *Roman Zakharov v. Russia*, ECtHR (GC) 4 December 2015, appl. no. 47143/06.

depends on whether or not it has found the law as such to be in conformity with the substantive provisions of the Convention, such as Articles 6 and 8. If this is the case, the Court tends to conclude that no violation of Article 13 occurred.[128] If not, the Court may set stricter standards under Article 13.[129]

---

[128] See *James and Others v. The United Kingdom*, ECtHR (GC) 21 February 1986, appl. no. 8793/79, *supra* n. 10, para. 86; and *Lithgow and Others v. The United Kingdom*, ECtHR 8 July 1986, appl. nos. 9006/80, 9262/81, 9263/81, 9265/81, 9266/81, 9313/81, 9405/81, *supra* n. 125, para. 207.

[129] *Abdulaziz, Cabales and Balkandali v. The United Kingdom*, ECtHR 28 May 1985, appl. nos. 9214/80, 9473/81, 9474/81 paras. 92–93.

CHAPTER 33

DEROGATION IN TIME OF EMERGENCY

(Article 15)

Stefan Sᴏᴛᴛɪᴀᴜx[*]

GUIDING PRINCIPLE

A properly designed and judicially enforced derogation clause provides the best legal foundation for reconciling the interest in effectively meeting a crisis situation with the rights of the individual. The substantive and procedural requirements governing the use of emergency powers are expected to put a brake on unjustified infringements of fundamental rights.

ARTICLE 15

1. In time of war or other public emergency threatening the life of the nation any High Contracting Party may take measures derogating from its obligations under this Convention to the extent strictly required by the exigencies of the situation, provided that such measures are not inconsistent with its other obligations under international law.
2. No derogation from Article 2, except in respect of deaths resulting from lawful acts of war, or from Articles 3, 4 (paragraph 1) and 7 shall be made under this provision.
3. Any High Contracting Party availing itself of this right of derogation shall keep the Secretary General of the Council of Europe fully informed of the measures which it has taken and the reasons therefore. It shall also inform the Secretary General of the Council of Europe when such measures have ceased to operate and the provisions of the Convention are again being fully executed.

---

[*] In the fourth edition this chapter was revised and updated by Yutaka Arai.

CONTENTS

1. INTRODUCTION

'No doctrine, involving more pernicious consequences, was ever invented by the wit of man than that [constitutional rights] can be suspended during any of the great exigencies of government.'[1] With these words, written in 1866, US Supreme Court Justice Davis strongly rejected the power to derogate from fundamental rights in time of crisis. Like other constitutional documents from that era, the US Constitution makes no express provision of emergency powers.[2] Yet, history has shown that the absence of a derogation clause in domestic constitutions did not stop governments from resorting to emergency measures. The principled rejection of emergency powers has not prevented *de facto* derogation from human rights standards under the pressure of circumstances.[3] It has been argued that a human rights regime with no provisions for emergency derogations leaves political decision-makers and courts with no other choice but to circumvent human rights norms or the legal order as whole. Such systems fail to constrain the state's response to war and emergency situations altogether. Against this background, the derogation provisions which can be found in most international human rights instruments, and of which Article 15 is a prime example, must be seen as an attempt to constrain, rather than broaden, the scope of government action in emergency situations. According to many observers, a properly designed and judicially enforced derogation clause provides the best legal foundation for reconciling the interest in effectively meeting a crisis situation with the rights of the individual. The substantive and procedural requirements governing the use of emergency powers are expected to put a brake on unjustified infringements of fundamental rights.

---

[1] *Ex p Milligan*, 71 US 2, 123–124 (1866).
[2] One important exception is the power to suspend the writ of habeas corpus in Art I, s 9 US Constitution.
[3] See, eg, *Korematsu v. United States*, 323 US 214 (1944).

A study of the state practice and Strasbourg case law in relation to Article 15 allows us to assess the merits of this claim. It is clear that the wording of Article 15 subjects derogations to a number of substantive and procedural requirements. For a derogation to be valid, the following conditions must be met: (1) there must be a war or public emergency threatening the life of the nation; (2) the derogating measures must be strictly required by the exigencies of the situation; (3) the derogating measures must be consistent with other obligations under international law; (4) no derogation is permitted with respect to a number of non-derogable rights, and (5) there must have been a notification to the Secretary-General of the Council of Europe of the measures taken and the reasons for doing so.

The purpose of this chapter is to outline the Court's and the former Commission's general approach to each of these conditions. It should be noted at the outset that only a small number of states have availed themselves of the possibility of derogation of the Convention and that the Strasbourg case law on Article 15 is consequently rather limited. Almost all cases that have reached the Strasbourg organs involved crisis situations caused by continuing campaigns of terrorist violence in the United Kingdom and Turkey. However, before we study these cases in detail, we first consider the preliminary issue of the justiciability of Article 15 and the proper standard of review.

2. JUSTICIABILITY AND STANDARD OF REVIEW

Article 15 can best be seen as a specific limitation clause, allowing restrictions on Convention rights which would not normally be permissible, for instance through the application of the common limitation clauses of Articles 8–11 or the flexible reading of the guarantees of Articles 5 and 6. While the division of labour between the domestic authorities and the Court in reviewing limitations is a contentious issue in any context, this is even more so in relation to Article 15. This is due to the fact that the judicial enforcement of Article 15 at the European level raises serious issues of judicial policy. On the one hand, it is often claimed that the domestic political and judicial authorities are better placed to assess the reality and seriousness of an emergency situation and the necessity of concomitant human rights restrictions than an international court which operates far away from the zone of conflict or turmoil. Sensitive to this fact, judges exercising international supervision over emergency powers are advised to decline jurisdiction or adopt a highly deferential standard of review. On the other hand, it is submitted that the international character of a supervising body – composed of members of many different nationalities – allows it to take a more detached stance from domestic legislative and executive attempts to curb fundamental rights. The argument is often made that a national crisis will result in an increase in the prestige and power of the political branches and that it may well be more difficult for national courts to intervene than it is for an international body. Because domestic judges are part of the national government, they may be more inclined to identify with their government's interests, especially when that government is charged with the defence of the nation. This would be a reason for international courts to closely scrutinise derogating measures.

The position of the Strasbourg organs in this debate can be summarised as follows. From the beginning, the Court and the Commission have declared themselves competent to adjudicate cases involving the application of Article 15. In *Greece v. United Kingdom*, the first case in which Article 15 was at issue, the Commission considered itself 'competent to pronounce on the existence of a public danger (…) [and] to decide whether the measures (…) had been taken to the extent strictly required by the exigencies of the situation' –, the two main substantive requirements for a valid derogation.[4] A few years later, in *Lawless*, the Court took a very similar position: 'it is for the Court to determine whether the conditions laid down in Article 15 for the exercise of the exceptional right of derogation have been fulfilled in the present case.'[5]

However, in these early cases the Convention organs also made it clear that they would take a deferential attitude with respect to applications based on Article 15. In *Greece v. United Kingdom*, the Commission stated that 'the Government should be able to exercise a certain measure of discretion' in the context of Article 15.[6] The notion of a 'certain measure of discretion' later developed into what has become known as the doctrine of the margin of appreciation. The Court's observation in *Lawless* that the existence of a public emergency 'was *reasonably* deduced' by the Irish Government from a combination of factors, is testimony to the same deferential stance.[7] A number of years later, in *Ireland v. UK*, the Court for the first time mentioned the margin of appreciation doctrine in relation to Article 15. It decided that it would grant the domestic authorities a *wide* margin of appreciation in reviewing derogations under Article 15.[8] Since then, the recurring observation in this connection reads as follows: '[I]t falls to each Contracting State, with its responsibility for "the life of [its] nation", to determine whether that life is threatened by a "public emergency" and, if so, how far it is necessary to go in attempting to overcome the emergency. By reason of their direct and continuous contact with the pressing needs of the moment, the national authorities are in principle better placed that the international judge to decide both on the presence of such an emergency and on the nature and scope of the derogations

---

[4] *Greece v. UK*, EComHR 26 September 1958 (dec.), appl. no. 176/56, 2 *Yearbook* 174, 176 (1958–59).

[5] *Lawless v. Ireland (No. 3)*, ECtHR 1 July 1961, appl. no. 332/57, para. 22.

[6] *Greece v. UK, supra* n. 4.

[7] *Lawless v. Ireland, supra* n. 5, para. 28.

[8] *Ireland v. UK*, ECtHR (GC) 18 January 1978, appl. no. 5310/71, para. 207.

necessary to avert it. Accordingly, in this matter a wide margin of appreciation should be left to the national authorities. Nonetheless, Contracting Parties do not enjoy an unlimited discretion. It is for the Court to rule whether, inter alia, the States have gone beyond the "extent strictly required by the exigencies" of the crisis. The domestic margin of appreciation is thus accompanied by a European supervision. In exercising this supervision, the Court must give appropriate weight to such relevant factors as the nature of the rights affected by the derogation and the circumstances leading to, and the duration of, the emergency situation'.[9]

Critics have argued that the discretion left to the Contracting States in Article 15 cases is too broad and amounts to an abdication by the Strasbourg organs of their responsibility to protect fundamental rights and the integrity of the Convention system, especially in view of the often-prolonged nature of emergency situations caused by terrorist violence. These concerns are reflected in several concurring and dissenting opinions. In *Brannigan and McBride*, Judge Pettiti observed that '[e]ven if it is accepted that States have a margin of appreciation (...), the situation relied on must be examined by the European Court'.[10] '[T]he derogation cannot constitute a carte blanche accorded to the State for an unlimited duration, without it having to adopt the measures necessary to satisfy its obligations under the Convention'.[11] Sometimes, a distinction is drawn between the two requirements of Article 15. For instance, Judge Martens opined that as far as the assessment of the existence of an emergency is concerned, '[i]nevitably (...) a certain margin of appreciation should be left to the national authorities'.[12] However, as to the question whether the derogation is 'strictly required by the exigencies of the situation', the 'wording underlined clearly calls for a closer scrutiny than the words "necessary in a democratic society" which appear in the second paragraph of Articles 8–11. Consequently, with respect to this second question there is, if at all, certainly no room for a wide margin of appreciation'.[13] A similar approach can be found in the judgment of the UK House of Lords in *A and others*.[14] The majority showed considerable deference with respect to the existence of an emergency within the territory of the UK in the aftermath of the September 11 attacks. This was regarded as a 'pre-eminently political judgement', which involved 'a factual prediction of what various people around the world might or might not do'.[15]

---

[9]   See, e.g., *Brannigan and McBride v. UK*, ECtHR 26 May 1993, appl. nos. 14553/89 and 14554/89, para. 43; *A and Others v. UK*, ECtHR (GC) 19 February 2009, appl. no. 3455/05, para. 173.

[10]   *Brannigan and McBride v. UK, supra* n. 9, concurring opinion Judge Pettiti.

[11]   *Ibid.*

[12]   *Brannigan and McBride v. UK, supra* n. 9, concurring opinion Judge Martens, para. 4.

[13]   *Ibid.*

[14]   *A and Others v Secretary of State for the Home Department* [2004] UKHL 56.

[15]   *Ibid.*, Lord Bingham, para. 29.

However, when the Law Lords considered the proportionality of the response to the emergency, they took a more activist stance and argued that the margin of appreciation recognised by the European Court precisely assumes that the derogating measures will, at the national level, receive closer scrutiny.[16] When the case reached the Court in Strasbourg, it explicitly endorsed this last point.[17]

3.   SUBSTANTIVE REQUIREMENTS

3.1.   WAR CONDITIONS

The first substantive condition is the existence of a 'war' or 'other public emergency threatening the life of the nation'. So far, none of the Contracting States have invoked a status of 'war' for the purpose of Article 15. Issues pertaining to the interpretation of the notion 'war' are of minor importance, as armed conflicts which would not be covered may still be qualified as 'other public emergencies'.

The meaning of the words 'public emergency threatening the life of the nation' was first clarified in *Lawless v. Ireland*.[18] According to the Court, the 'natural and customary meaning' of the expression is 'sufficiently clear' and refers to 'an exceptional situation of crisis or emergency which affects the whole population and constitutes a threat to the organised life of the community of which the State is composed'.[19] The Commission refined this definition in the *Greek* case. There it held that an emergency must have the following characteristics to be covered by Article 15: (1) it must be actual or imminent; (2) its effects must involve the whole nation; (3) the continuance of the organised life of the community must be threatened; and (4) the crisis or danger must be exceptional, in that the normal measures or restrictions, permitted by the Convention for the maintenance of public safety, health and order, are plainly inadequate.[20] In spite of what these definitions seem to suggest, a crisis limited in scope to a certain part of the territory of a state, may nevertheless amount to an emergency threatening the life of the nation as a whole.[21]

To date, the *Greek* case is only one case in which the Strasbourg organs were not satisfied with the Contracting Party's assessment of the existence of a public emergency. However, since the respondent government in this case had come

---

[16]   *Ibid.*, Lord Bingham, para. 40 and Lord Hope, para. 131.
[17]   *A and Others v. UK, supra* n. 9, para. 184.
[18]   *Lawless v. Ireland, supra* n. 7.
[19]   *Ibid.*, para. 28.
[20]   *Greek Case*, EComHR 5 November 1969 (dec.), appl. nos. 3321/67, 3322/67, 3323/67 and 3344/67.
[21]   See, e.g., *Ireland v. UK, supra* n. 8, para. 205.

to power after a military coup, its precedential value can be considered to be limited.[22] Apart from this case, the Convention organs have generally accepted the Contracting States' reliance on a public emergency. On various occasions, both the Commission and the Court have made it clear that serious terrorist violence may constitute a public emergency threatening the life of the nation. Thus, for instance, in *Lawless* the existence of a public emergency was deduced from a combination of several factors: the existence and violent activities of a 'secret army' within the territory of the country; the operations of the IRA outside of Ireland potentially jeopardising relations with other countries; and the 'steady and alarming' increase in the intensity and scale of the terrorist violence.[23] In *Ireland v. UK*, the existence of a public emergency was not contested by the parties and was 'perfectly clear' to the Court, as terrorism had for a number of years represented 'a particularly far-reaching and acute danger for the territorial integrity of the United Kingdom'.[24] Similar conclusions were reached as regards the continuing security situation in Northern Ireland in the cases of *Brannigan and McBride* and *Marshall v. the UK*.[25] In *Aksoy v. Turkey*, the Court accepted that Kurdish separatist violence (by the PKK) had given rise to a public emergency in Turkey.[26]

Finally, in *A and Others v. UK*, although no Al-Qaeda attack had taken place within the territory of the United Kingdom, the Court agreed with the House of Lords that the domestic authorities could not be criticised for fearing, in the light of the evidence available to them at the time, that such an attack was 'imminent'. The Court held that the 'requirement of imminence cannot be interpreted so narrowly as to require a State to wait for disaster to strike before taking measures to deal with it'.[27] The Court further noted that the danger of an attack had been tragically shown by the bombings which took place in London several years later. Also, the Court stated that it would not require an emergency to be 'temporary', although the duration of the emergency may be relevant in the stage of the assessment of the proportionality of the derogations.[28] Finally, it rejected the applicants' argument, founded on the dissenting opinion of Lord Hoffmann in the House of Lords, that the notion 'life of the nation' would imply a threat to the 'institutions of government or our existence as a civil community'. In the Strasbourg Court's opinion, an emergency can exist even though the institutions of the State do not appear to be imperilled.[29]

---

[22]   *Greek case, supra* n. 20.
[23]   *Lawless v. Ireland, supra* n. 5, paras. 31–32.
[24]   *Ireland v. UK, supra* n. 8, para. 205.
[25]   *Brannigan and McBride v. UK, supra* n. 9, para. 47; *Marshall v. UK*, ECtHR 10 July 2001 (dec.), appl. no. 41571/98.
[26]   *Aksoy v. Turkey*, ECtHR 18 December 1996, appl. no. 21987/93, para. 70.
[27]   *A and Others v. UK, supra* n. 9, para. 177.
[28]   *Ibid.*, para. 178.
[29]   *Ibid.*, para. 179.

It is important to note that in a series of cases against Turkey, the Court declared the derogation inapplicable *ratione loci* to the facts of the case. The reason for this was that the detentions, allegedly violating Article 5 of the Convention, were executed in a part of the Turkish territory which was not explicitly named in in the notice of derogation.[30]

3.2. EXIGENCIES OF THE SITUATION

The second substantive requirement for a valid derogation is that the measures be taken only to 'the extent strictly required by the exigencies of the situation'. This obligation reflects the principle of proportionality which is common to the limitation of rights both in ordinary and emergency situations. Traces can be found of the three components of the proportionality test (effectiveness, necessity and proportionality *stricto sensu*) in the Article 15 jurisprudence. Usually, the first inquiry conducted under the 'strictly required' prong is whether the derogating measures were necessary, in that ordinary limiting measures would not have been adequate to meet the emergency. Thus, for instance, in the *Lawless* case the Court observed that the ordinary law had proved unable to check the growing terrorist danger which threatened the Republic of Ireland.[31] Preventive detention had accordingly been justified as a measure required by the circumstances. Next, the Strasbourg organs will consider the proportionality *stricto sensu* of the derogating measures by weighing the seriousness of the emergency against the gravity of the interference: the greater the danger, the greater the permissible derogation, both as a matter of degree and duration.[32] A significant issue, in this respect, is whether the respondent state has put in place sufficient guarantees against abuse. To take the same example, the Court in *Lawless* had regard to the presence of a number of safeguards designed to prevent abuses in the operation of the system of preventive detention.[33] A full review of the first requirement, i.e. the effectiveness of the measures, is, however, generally absent in the Strasbourg case law. For instance, in *Ireland v. UK*, the Court replied to the Irish Government's contention that measures of preventive detention had proved to be ineffective, that it was not its function 'to substitute

---

30   *Sakik and Others v. Turkey*, ECtHR 26 November 1997, appl. no. 87/1996/706/898–903, paras. 34–39; *Yurttas v. Turkey*, ECtHR 27 May 2004, appl. nos. 25143/94 and 27098/95, paras. 52–59.

31   *Lawless v. Ireland*, *supra* n. 5, para. 36.

32   In *Brannigan and McBride*, the Court stated that it will give appropriate weight to such relevant factors as 'the nature of the rights affected by the derogation, the circumstances leading to, and the duration of, the emergency situation'. See *Brannigan and McBride v. UK*, *supra* n. 9, para. 43.

33   *Lawless v. Ireland*, *supra* n. 5, para. 37.

for the British government's assessment any other assessment of what might be the most prudent or most expedient policy to combat terrorism'.[34]

The measures derogating from the Convention which have been scrutinised by the Court can be divided into two groups. A first line of cases concerns measures of preventive detention, i.e. the incarceration of individuals suspected of no specific crime but (allegedly) involved in dangerous conduct. This practice departs from the normal standards of Article 5(1)(c) of the Convention, which permits detention only with the purpose of initiating criminal proceedings. The second type of cases involves prolonged police custody. This is the prolongation beyond the normal limits of Article 5(3) of the period before which a suspected person is brought before a judicial body.

The central cases of the former group are *Lawless v. UK*, *Ireland v. UK* and *A and others v. UK*. In *Lawless* and *Ireland v. UK*, the Court reached the conclusion that the measures satisfied the 'strictly required' condition. In *Lawless*, particular emphasis was placed on the difficulties of gathering the necessary evidence to convict persons involved in the IRA, owing to the secret character of the organisation and the fear it created among the population.[35] In addition, the Court believed that there were adequate safeguards against abuse, namely regular parliamentary review and the right to refer a case to the Detention Commission, whose opinion, if favourable to the release of the applicant, was binding upon the government.[36] In *Ireland v UK*, which concerned various extra-judicial powers of arrest and detention exercised by the British authorities in Northern Ireland, the Court observed that detention of persons merely for the purpose of obtaining information can be justifiable only in 'very exceptional circumstances'.[37] The situation in Northern Ireland fell in this category. In view of the widespread practice of intimidation of witnesses, the authorities were entitled to confine those witnesses to question them 'in conditions of relative security'.[38] The Court further had regard to the fact that the deprivation of liberty was authorised only for a maximum of 48 hours.

With respect to the second line of cases, mention should first be made of *Brogan and others v. UK*.[39] In this case, the Court found that a period of detention in police custody of four days and six hours without judicial scrutiny breaches the right to be brought promptly before a judge enshrined in Article 5(3) of the Convention. In response to this decision, the United Kingdom lodged a derogation from its Article 5 obligations. The Court had the opportunity to consider that derogation in *Brannigan and McBride v. UK*,

---

[34]   *Ireland v. UK, supra* n. 8, para. 214.
[35]   *Lawless v. Ireland, supra* n. 5, para. 36.
[36]   *Ibid.*, para. 37.
[37]   *Ireland v. UK, supra* n. 8, para. 212.
[38]   *Ibid.*
[39]   *Brogan and Others v. UK*, ECtHR 29 November 1988, appl. nos. 11209/84, 11234/84, 11266/84 and 11386/85.

a case which involved the police detention of two suspected IRA terrorists for respectively six days and 14 hours and four days and six hours.[40] It concluded that the United Kingdom had not overstepped its margin of appreciation in deciding that the measures were strictly required by the exigencies of the situation, taking into account the nature of the terrorist threat in Northern Ireland, the limited scope of the derogation, and the existence of basic safeguards against abuse. As regards the necessity of the measure, the Court accepted the Government's argument that the judiciary in Northern Ireland is 'small and vulnerable to terrorist attacks' and that their involvement in detention procedures 'created a real risk of undermining their independence as they would inevitably be seen as part of the investigation and prosecution process'.[41] It also acceded to the argument that prolonged detention was necessary given the fact that some terrorist suspects are trained in remaining silent under police questioning, which hampers and protracts the investigation.[42] Turning to the safeguards, the Court noted several factors: the remedy of habeas corpus remained available; the detainees were granted the right to consult a solicitor after 48 hours, and they were entitled to inform a relative or a friend about their detention and to have access to a doctor. Taken together, these safeguards were found to provide 'an important measure of protection against arbitrary behaviour and incommunicado detention'.[43]

A different conclusion was reached in *Aksoy v. Turkey*, the second major case in which the Court had to face a derogation from the right to prompt judicial control in Article 5(3).[44] The case involved the incommunicado detention of an individual for at least 14 days on suspicion of aiding and abetting the PKK and being a member of that organisation. This time, the Court was not convinced that the derogating measures were strictly required by the exigencies of the situation. To begin with, the length of unsupervised detention was found to be excessive. The 'exceptional long' period rendered the applicant 'vulnerable not only to arbitrary interference with his right to liberty but also to torture'.[45] As regards the necessity, the Court observed that, in contrast to *Brannigan and McBride*, the respondent government had failed to adduce 'any detailed reasons before the Court as to why the fight against terrorism in South-East Turkey rendered judicial intervention impracticable'.[46] Adding to this, the Court found the safeguards by the Turkish detention scheme to be wholly insufficient: no access to counsel, a doctor, relative or friend had been provided for and there

---

[40] *Brannigan and McBride v. UK, supra* n. 9.

[41] *Ibid.*, paras. 56 and 59.

[42] *Ibid.*, para. 56.

[43] *Ibid.*, para. 62.

[44] *Aksoy v. Turkey, supra* n. 26.

[45] *Ibid.*, para. 78.

[46] *Ibid.*

had been no realistic possibility of challenging the detention before a court.[47] The Court reached similar conclusions in a number of later judgments against Turkey, which all concerned incommunicado detention without access to a court which had lasted 10 days or longer.[48] The Court made it clear that simple assertions about the 'difficulties caused by terrorism' and the 'thorough' and 'careful' nature of the police investigation, did not provide an answer to the central issue, 'namely for what precise reasons relating to the actual facts of the (…) case would judicial scrutiny of the applicants' detention have prejudiced the progress of the investigation'.[49]

3.3. OBLIGATIONS UNDER INTERNATIONAL LAW

The measures taken by the state derogating from Convention obligations must not be 'inconsistent with its other obligations under international law'. This condition has been of little importance in the case law thus far. It can be seen as a confirmation of the principle of Article 53, which holds that the Convention cannot be relied upon by a state to limit or derogate from its other domestic of international human rights obligations. Potentially relevant treaty obligations are the Geneva Conventions on humanitarian law and the United Nations International Covenant on Civil and Political Rights (ICCPR). In this last respect, the applicant in the *Brannigan and McBride* case argued that it was an essential requirement for a valid derogation under Article 4 ICCPR that a public emergency must have been 'officially proclaimed' and that, since such proclamation had never taken place, the derogation was inconsistent with the United Kingdom's other obligations under international law. The Court observed that it is not its role to define authoritatively the meaning of the terms 'officially proclaimed' in Article 4 and that, in any event, the statement to the House of Commons of the Secretary of State, which was formal in character and made public the Government's intentions, was 'well in keeping with the notion of an official proclamation.'[50]

3.4. NON-DEROGABLE RIGHTS

Article 15(2) sets forth a list of rights which are not susceptible to derogation, not even in the exceptional circumstances described in Article 15(1). The non-

---

47   *Ibid.*, para. 83.
48   See, e.g., *Demir and Others v. Turkey*, ECtHR 23 September 1998, appl. nos. 21380/93, 21381/93 and 21383/93; *Sen v. Turkey*, ECtHR 17 June 2003, appl. no. 41478/98; *Bilen v. Turkey*, ECtHR 21 February 2006, appl. no. 34482/97.
49   *Demir and Others v. Turkey, supra* n. 48, para. 52.
50   *Brannigan and McBride v. UK*, ECtHR 26 May 1993, appl. nos. 14553/89 and 14554/89, para. 72.

derogable rights are: the right to life, except in respect of deaths resulting from lawful acts of war (Article 2); the prohibition of torture or degrading treatment or punishment (Article 3); the prohibition of slavery or servitude (Article 4(1)) and the requirement that there be no punishment without law (Article 7). Additional non-derogable rights can be found in the Protocols to the ECHR. For example, Article 4(3) of Protocol No. 7 stipulates that no derogation shall be made from the right not to be tried or punished twice.[51] It can be observed that the derogation clause in Article 4 of the ICCPR contains a longer list which also includes, for instance, freedom of thought, conscience and religion.

On the other hand, the Human Rights Committee made it clear that derogations from other rights not listed in Article 4 may be equally inappropriate.[52] More particularly, the Committee found that certain aspects of the right to a fair trial are not susceptible to derogation: 'Safeguards related to derogation, as embodied in article 4 of the Covenant, are based on the principles of legality and the rule of law inherent in the Covenant as a whole. As certain elements of the right to a fair trial are explicitly guaranteed under international humanitarian law during armed conflict, the Committee finds no justification for derogation from these guarantees during other emergency situations. The Committee is of the opinion that the principles of legality and the rule of law require that fundamental requirements of fair trial must be respected during a state of emergency. Only a court of law may try and convict a person for a criminal offence. The presumption of innocence must be respected. In order to protect non-derogable rights, the right to take proceedings before a court to enable the court to decide without delay on the lawfulness of detention, must not be diminished by a State party's decision to derogate from the Covenant.'[53]

4. PROCEDURAL REQUIREMENTS

A final issue is the procedural conditions for a valid derogation and, more specifically, the notification requirement in Article 15(3). According to this provision, a derogating state is under the obligation to keep the Secretary General of the Council of Europe 'fully informed of the measures which it has taken and the reasons therefor' and to inform the Secretary General when such measures have ceased to operate and the provisions of the Convention are again being fully executed. A preliminary question here is whether Article 15 requires a formal proclamation of the state of emergency. Although there is no requirement

---

[51]   See also Art. 3 of Protocol No. 6 (abolition of the death penalty).
[52]   HRC, General Comment No 29: States of Emergency (Article 4), CCPR/C/21/Rev.1/Add.11 (2001).
[53]   *Ibid.*, para. 16.

of an 'official proclamation' comparable to Article 4 ICCPR, the Commission stated in *Cyprus v. Turkey* that Article 15 requires 'some formal and public act of derogation, such as a declaration of martial law or state of emergency, and that, where no such act has been proclaimed by the High Contracting Party concerned, although it was not in the circumstances prevented from doing so, Article 15 cannot apply'.[54]

However, as the Court noted in *Lawless*, the Convention does not contain any special provision to the effect that the Contracting State must promulgate in its territory the notice of derogation addressed to the Secretary-General of the Council of Europe.[55]

The precise nature of the notification requirement in Article 15(3) was clarified by the Commission and the Court in the *Lawless* case. According to the Commission, no special form is prescribed for the notice of derogation.[56] Nevertheless, the High Contracting Party 'should notify the Secretary-General of the measures in question without any unavoidable delay and must furnish sufficient information concerning them to enable the other High Contracting Parties and the European Commission to appreciate the nature and extent of the derogation'.[57]

In a similar vein, the Court requires 'sufficient information of the measures taken and the reasons therefore'.[58] As regards the timing of the notice of derogation, it follows from the case law that the notification must not necessarily be prior to the date on which the derogating measures are implemented. In *Lawless*, both the Commission and the Court were satisfied that a delay of 12 days after the entry into force of the measures was in conformity with Article 15(3). In the *Greek* case, the Commission decided that a delay of four months was too long.[59]

5. CONCLUDING OBSERVATIONS

As mentioned in the introduction, Article 15 can be seen as an attempt to constrain, rather than broaden, the scope of government action in emergency situations. It is hoped that the substantive and procedural requirements governing the use of emergency help prevent unjustified infringements of fundamental rights. Does the Article 15 case law live up to these expectations? Much depends on the standard of review adopted by the courts, both at the

---

[54]   *Cyprus v. Turkey*, EComHR 10 July 1976 (dec.), appl. nos. 6780/74 and 6950/75, para. 527.
[55]   *Lawless v. Ireland*, *supra* n. 5, para. 47.
[56]   *Lawless v. Ireland*, EComHR 19 December 1959 (dec.), appl. no. 332/57, Report p. 74.
[57]   *Ibid.*, p. 73.
[58]   *Lawless v. Ireland*, *supra* n. 5, para. 47.
[59]   *Greek case*, *supra* n. 20, Report pp. 43–44.

domestic and the European level. Clearly, in the early years of the Convention, the Strasbourg organs took a highly deferential approach. However, an examination of the Court's contemporary Article 15 jurisprudence reveals a gradual tightening of the margin of appreciation in this area. Although the Court remains deferential to the Contracting States' assessment of the existence of a public emergency, it is not willing to simply defer to the respondent government's assessment of the measures required to meet the emergency. The current application of the 'strictly required' test can perhaps best be described as an 'intermediate scrutiny' balancing inquiry. As a result, the Court offers a meaningful degree of human rights protection in emergency situations, while not overstepping the margin left to the domestic authorities. As in other contexts, it is primarily the responsibility of the national authorities, including the national courts, to ensure that the fundamental rights and freedoms enshrined in the Convention are respected.

CHAPTER 34

RESTRICTIONS ON
POLITICAL ACTIVITY OF ALIENS

(Article 16)

Yutaka Arai and Cornelis Wouters[*]

GUIDING PRINCIPLE

The political activity of aliens can be restricted notwithstanding the principle of non-discrimination and aliens' right to freedom of expression and freedom of assembly and association.

ARTICLE 16

Nothing in Article 10, 11 and 14 shall be regarded as preventing the High Contracting Parties from imposing restrictions on the political activity of aliens.

---

[*]   In the fourth edition this chapter was revised and updated by Kees Flinterman.

CONTENTS

1. INTRODUCTION

Article 16 does not contain an individual right. Referring explicitly to the rights to freedom of expression, freedom of assembly and association and the prohibition of discrimination, Article 16 allows states to impose restrictions on the political activities of aliens, without any further qualifications such as the limitation clauses contained in the second paragraphs of Articles 8 to 11 of the Convention. The article forms an exception to the general principle that Convention rights are guaranteed to everyone, within the jurisdiction of a Contracting State, without discrimination.

The short yet broadly formulated text of Article 16 may be read as giving states a wide margin of appreciation allowing restrictions to the political activities of aliens irrespective of the principle of non-discrimination and the safeguards stipulated in the limitation clauses of Article 10(2) and 11(2) respectively. The current text of Article 16, which was initially not included in the draft of the Consultative Assembly, was inserted by the Committee of Experts.[1] According to the Committee, the Consultative Assembly had overlooked the problem that can arise by the political activity of aliens on the territory of Contracting States and that states are free to restrict activities of aliens.[2] While this may have been a predominant notion at the time of drafting, the former European Commission called it outdated.[3] As a consequence, in the case of *Perinçek v. Switzerland* the Court considered that an 'unbridled reliance on [Article 16] to restrain the possibility for aliens to exercise their right to freedom of expression would run against the Court's rulings in cases in which

---

[1]   Council of Europe, *Preparatory work on Article 16 of the European Convention on Human Rights*, Strasbourg, 25 May 1967, CHD (67) 4, available at: <www.echr.coe.int/LibraryDocs/Travaux/ECHRTravaux-ART16-CDH(67)4-BIL1338903.pdf>.

[2]   According to the former European Commission of Human Rights, the *travaux préparatoires* suggest that Art. 16 was included in the Convention to reflect the predominant concept in international law existing at the time of drafting that states are free to restrict the political activity of aliens, see *Piermont v France*, EComHR 20 January 1994 (dec.), appl. nos. 15773/89 and 15774/89, para. 58.

[3]   *Perinçek v. Switzerland*, ECtHR 15 October 2015, appl. no. 27510/08, para. 121. The Court makes reference to a decision of the former European Commission, calling the drafters' understanding 'outdated'; see *Piermont v France*, EComHR 20 January 1994 (dec.), appl. nos. 15773/89 and 15774/89, para. 58.

aliens have found entitled to this right without any suggestion that it could be curtailed by reference to Article 16.'[4]

Nowadays, an unfettered discretion would be difficult to imagine in light of the internationalisation of politics.[5] Further, it would be equally difficult to imagine that the object and purpose of Article 16 can be fully disconnected from the object and purpose of fundamental freedoms and the principle of proportionality required when applying the limitation clauses to the freedom of expression and the freedom of association and assembly.[6] It can be questioned what the added value of Article 16 compared to the limitation clauses of the articles as mentioned in Article 16 is.

Case law on Article 16 is limited, as is evident from this chapter. In no case has the Court concluded that Article 16 could authorise the state to restrict the political activity of aliens.

2. SCOPE

The personal scope (*ratione personae*) of this provision is confined to 'aliens'. In general, this term refers to all individuals who do not have the nationality of the Contracting State within whose jurisdiction they fall, and covers both nationals and stateless persons.[7] Notwithstanding this common interpretation of the word 'alien', in the case of *Piermont v. France* the Court considered that Article 16 could not be raised against the applicant, a German member of the European Parliament, for restricting her political activities in the overseas French territory of Polynesia, even though she was – strictly speaking – an alien within the meaning of Article 16. Hereby the Court referred to the applicant possessing the nationality of a Member State of the European Union, her status as a member of the European Parliament, and the fact that the overseas territory of Polynesia takes part in the European Parliamentary elections.[8] With the establishment of

---

4   *Perinçek v. Switzerland*, *supra* n. 3, para. 121, referring explicitly to *Cox v. Turkey*, ECtHR 20 May 2010, appl. no. 2933/03, para. 31, noting that in this judgment the Court considered 'that no distinction can be drawn between the protected freedom of expression of nationals and that of foreigners'.

5   *Piermont v. France*, ECtHR 27 April 1995, appl. nos. 15773/89 and 15774/89, joint partly dissenting opinion judges Ryssdal, Matscher, Freeland and Jungwiert, para. 5.

6   *Ibid.*, joint partly dissenting opinion judges Ryssdal, Matscher, Freeland and Jungwiert, para. 5.

7   The term 'alien' is commonly used in international human rights and is, e.g., defined in Art. 2(b) of the ILC Draft Articles on the expulsion of aliens, Yearbook of the International Law Commission, 2014, Vol II, Part Two and noted by the United Nations General Assembly, A/RES/69/119 of 10 December 2014.

8   *Piermont v. France*, *supra* n. 5, para. 64. Notably, the Court rejected the idea of European citizenship on the basis that – at the time of its judgment – 'the Community treaties did not at the time recognize any such citizenship'. With the entry into force of the Treaty on the

European Union citizenship in Article 20 of the Treaty on the Functioning of the European Union this issue is no longer relevant.

In terms of the material scope (*ratione materiae*) the article is limited to a specific type of activities, namely, those of 'political' character. In the case of *Perinçek v. Switzerland*, the Court considered the phrase 'political activities' only to apply to '"activities" that directly affect the political process,' without giving any reasoning for this restrictive interpretation.[9] In the *Perinçek* case, the applicant, a Turkish national and chairman of the Turkish Workers' Party, took part in three public events in Switzerland, including a press conference, a conference and a rally of the Turkish Workers' Party. During the events, the applicant denied, both orally and in writing, that the events of 1915 and the following years affecting Armenians had constituted genocide.[10] While dismissing this to be relevant in the context of Article 16, in assessing Article 10(2), the Court considered these events and statements to be political, relating to 'acute sensitivities',[11] but that there was not enough evidence that these events and statements would affect the political agenda.[12] It remains to be seen what the difference is between a political activity not directly affecting a political process (but merely a political agenda) and a political activity that does. Nevertheless, the Court's restrictive interpretation of the terms 'political activity' is understandable in light of its cautious approach towards Article 16 and of academic literature on this point.[13] Moreover, the onus should be placed on a state invoking Article 16 to establish convincingly why specific 'political activities' by aliens are of such nature as to justify restrictions.

Article 16 makes express reference to the right to freedom of expression (Article 10), the right to freedom of assembly and association (Article 11) and the prohibition of discrimination (Article 14). The meaning of the explicit reference to the general prohibition of discrimination and two freedom rights remains unclear. Does explicit reference to Articles 10 and 11 mean that states can only restrict the political activity of aliens in the context of the right to freedom of expression and to freedom of association and assembly, or can a state also invoke Article 16 to justify constraining political activity of aliens in the context of other rights, such as the freedom of thought, conscience and religion under Article 9 and of the right to vote and to stand for election developed under Article 1 of Protocol No. 1? In other

---

Functioning of the European Union (TFEU) Citizenship of the European Union is recognised under Art. 20.

9   *Perinçek v. Switzerland, supra* n. 3, para. 122.

10   *Ibid.*, paras. 12–15.

11   According to the Court, the applicant 'spoke as a politician, not as a historical or legal scholar'. Further, '[h]e took part in a long-standing controversy (...) relating to an issue of public concern', in *Perinçek v. Switzerland, supra* n. 3, paras. 231 and 233.

12   *Ibid.*, paras. 234, 236 and 238.

13   See, e.g., references to various academic writing on this in Y. Haeck, 'Beperkingen op politieke activiteiten van vreemdelingen', in J. vande Lanotte and Y. Haeck (eds.), *Handboek EVRM. Deel 2 Artikelsgewijs Commentaar. Volume II*, Antwerp/Oxford: Intersentia, 2004, p. 236.

words, are the rights for which states can restrict political activities exhaustively listed, or does, for example, the explicit reference to Article 14 imply that a Contracting State is allowed to take discriminatory measures against aliens in relation to the exercise of any Convention right, provided the measure is to restrict political activity?[14] Further, constraining political activity in the context of the freedom of religion, the right to vote, or any other right will likely be able to affect the freedom of expression, assembly and/or association. As such, a far-reaching implication of Article 16 could be that a Contracting State would be allowed to obstruct aliens, including those who are lawful residents of a host state such as refugees and migrant workers, as well as nationals of other Contracting States, from exercising any right, and not just the rights guaranteed by Article 10 and 11, on the pretext that the exercise of those rights entails political ramifications. As a consequence, they could be precluded from participating in demonstrations, publishing political pamphlets criticising not only the policies of the host state, but also policies of their home states, or of third states, or participating in electoral processes in their home state or country of nationality.

One salient feature of the application of Article 16 is that, insofar as political activities are identified, a Contracting State may restrict the rights of aliens under Articles 10 and 11, even without the need for such restrictions at first to be justified under the limitation clauses of those provisions. Put differently, Article 16 may enable a state to bypass what it may perceive as a cumbersome process of having its interfering measure tested in conformity with elaborate sub-tests fleshed out in the case law under the limitation clauses. It should be recalled that the countervailing interests that a state may invoke to justify limitations on the rights under Articles 10 and 11, such as 'the interests of national security and public safety',[15] and 'the prevention of disorder',[16] are comprehensively enumerated in the list of legitimate aims. Problematically, the legal effect of Article 16 is to create an extra possibility of restrictions *outside* such an already tightly knit framework of the limitation clauses. An important way to counter such a tricky outcome is to interpret the scope of Article 16 narrowly as the Court did, as explained above, in the *Piermont* case with regard to the *ratione personae* and in the *Perinçek* case with regard to the *ratione materiae*.

3. RELEVANCE

The very idea underlying Article 16, according to which the political activity of aliens can be restricted unhindered, is not without questions. Article 16 can

---

[14]   *Mathieu-Mohin and Clerfayt v. Belgium,* ECtHR 2 March 1987, appl. no. 9267/81, paras. 51 and 54.

[15]   The second para. of Arts. 10 and 11 of the Convention.

[16]   The second para. of Art. 10 of the Convention.

be challenged for its compatibility with the progressively elaborated standards of the rights of the Convention as a 'living instrument' as well as the general obligation of the Contracting States to secure to everyone the enjoyment of the rights and freedoms of the Convention (Article 1) and the general limitation on the use of restrictions on rights (Article 18).[17]

As early as 1977, the Parliamentary Assembly urged the Committee of Ministers '[t]o instruct the competent committee of experts to make proposals of the amendment of the European Convention for the Protection of Human Rights and Fundamental Freedoms in such a way as to exclude restrictions at present authorised by Article 16 with respect to political activity on the exercise by aliens of the freedoms guaranteed by Article 10 (freedom of expression) and Article 11 (freedom of association).'[18]

Further, in 2001, the Parliamentary Assembly of the Council of Europe adopted Recommendation 1500 (2001) on *Participation of immigrants and foreign residents in political life in the Council of Europe member States*.[19] This document recommends the Committee of Ministers, *inter alia,* to reappraise minimum standards of human rights for non-citizens residing in the member states, 'with a view to granting the right to vote and stand in elections to all legally established migrants irrespective of their origin, and invite member governments to take all appropriate action to ensure their implementation'.[20] It also urges the member states of the Council of Europe 'to grant the right to vote and stand in local elections to all migrants legally established for at least three years *irrespective of their origin*',[21] and to ratify the European Convention on the Participation of Foreigners in Public Life at a Local Level.[22] Article 6(1) of this Convention specifically recognises the duty of the Contracting Parties to grant the right to vote and to stand for election in local authority elections to every foreign resident, subject to the conditions that they have been a lawful and habitual resident in the state for the five years preceding the elections.[23]

---

[17] H. Lambert, *The position of aliens in relation to the European Convention on Human Rights*, Human Rights Files No. 8, Council of Europe, 2007, p. 25.

[18] Recommendation 799 (1977) on the political rights and position of aliens, 25 January 1977; Parliamentary Assembly, 28th Ordinary Session, Third part, Texts Adopted (1977).

[19] Recommendation 1500 (2001), Test adopted by the Assembly on 26 January 2001 (8th Sitting), based on *Participation of immigrants and foreign residents in political life in the Council of Europe member states,* Report by the Committee on Migration, Refugees and Demography (Rapporteur: Mr. Luis), Doc. 8916, 22 December 2000. See also Resolution 141 (2002) on the Participation of Foreign Residents in Local Public Life: Consultative Bodies, adopted by the Council of Europe, Congress of Local and Regional Authorities.

[20] *Ibid.*, para. 11(i).

[21] *Ibid.*, para. 11(iv)(a), emphasis added.

[22] *Ibid.*, para. 11(iv)(e).

[23] However, Art. 6(2) of this Convention allows states parties to make a declaration to the effect that they can be exempted from granting to foreign residents the right to stand for election. Further, the rights guaranteed under Art. 6(1) are subject to greater restrictions in time of war or other public emergency within the meaning of Art. 9. After entering into force in 1997,

Finally, international human rights law, including the International Covenant on Civil and Political Rights, does not contain an exceptional provision such as Article 16.[24]

---

the European Convention on the Participation of Foreigners in Public Life at a Local Level only counts 9 states parties.

[24] Notably, certain states parties to the ECHR have made reservations to Arts. 2(1), 19, 21 and 22 of the ICCPR to ensure consistency with Art. 16 ECHR.

CHAPTER 35

PROHIBITION OF
THE ABUSE OF RIGHTS

(Article 17)

Antoine Buyse[*]

GUIDING PRINCIPLE

Are there limitations to invoking human rights? Article 17 of the Convention posits there are: those who abuse their rights to destroy the rights of others, cannot invoke the Convention's rights in such situations. From incitement to violence or extreme hatred to the denial of the Holocaust, the application of Article 17 has caused controversies that go the core of what human rights should and should not protect.

ARTICLE 17

Nothing in this Convention may be interpreted as implying for any State, group or person any right to engage in any activity or perform any act aimed at the destruction of any of the rights and freedoms set forth herein or at their limitation to a greater extent than is provided for in the Convention.

---

[*] This chapter builds on the author's earlier work 'Contested contours: the limits of freedom of expression from an abuse of rights perspective: Articles 10 and 17 ECHR', in: E. Brems and J. Gerards (eds.), *Shaping Rights in the ECHR. The Role of the European Court of Human Rights in Determining the Scope of Human Rights*, Cambridge: Cambridge University Press 2013, pp. 183–208. In the fourth edition this chapter was revised and updated by Yutaka Arai.

CONTENTS

1. PARADOXICAL CHARACTER

Article 17 is the Convention's clause on the abuse of human rights. As its content reflects, the provision is a microcosm for particular situations of what the European Convention is more generally aiming for: protecting human rights and democracy and preventing totalitarianism. The wording of Article 17 has its roots in Article 30 of the Universal Declaration of Human Rights. Comparable abuse of rights clauses can be found in many global and regional human rights treaties.[1]

The prohibition of the abuse of rights is one of the most paradoxical provisions of the Convention. It reflects two paradoxes, one of function and one of interpretation. First, Article 17 functionally reflects the concept of a democracy that should be able to defend itself against its enemies, a so-called *wehrhafte* or *streitbare Demokratie*. The Court has recognised this concept as a legitimate aim of policies that restrict human rights. The underlying idea is that too much liberty may facilitate the actions of those who aim to destroy democracy and fundamental rights. Thus, a democracy risks handing the tools of its own destruction to totalitarian or anti-democratic groups. However, too many restrictions on rights in turn endanger the core of those rights. In respect of the freedom of expression, for example, the Court has indicated that the free exercise of that right is one of its fundamental aspects and distinguishes a democratic, tolerant and pluralist democracy from a totalitarian or dictatorial regime.[2] Abuse of rights clauses like Article 17 try to wed these two aims – protection of rights for all and protection of democracy against its enemies – into an uneasy marriage.

Secondly, there is a paradox of interpretation. Facts or actions which are deemed to fall within the scope of Article 17 fall outside the protective scope of substantive articles of the Convention, such as the freedom of assembly or the freedom of expression. Those who try to destroy democracy can expect the state to use harsher methods than in ordinary situations. If the Court holds that

---

[1] E.g. Art. 5(1) ICCPR; Art. 5(1) ICESCR; Art. 29(1) American Convention on Human Rights.
[2] *Perinçek v.Switzerland*, ECtHR 17 December 2013, appl. no. 27510/08, para. 52.

Article 17 applies, the application at hand is declared inadmissible by that very fact, excluding an assessment on the merits. This reflects a categorical approach of adjudicating. By contrast, an assessment on the merits under one of the other Convention articles would enable an explicit balancing approach, evaluating for example whether an interference was proportionate. The paradox is that some kind of implicit balancing assumedly must be undertaken by the Court – testing whether the state's action was not grossly disproportionate – before applying Article 17. One cannot imagine, for example, that a sentence of 30 years of imprisonment for denying the Holocaust once would be proportionate.

These two paradoxes have led to difficult dilemmas for the Court on whether and when to apply Article 17. As a result, the use of Article 17 has been both inconsistent and contested. The Court has applied the provision both directly and indirectly. In the latter cases, the abuse clause played a role in the assessment under one of the substantive articles of the Convention.

2. DUAL PURPOSE

The general aim of the abuse clause is to 'prevent totalitarian groups from exploiting in their own interests the principles' of the ECHR.[3] To that purpose, Article 17 addresses states on the one hand and groups and individuals on the other hand. In that sense, it stands out in a human rights treaty that mostly focuses on limits to state actions. Therefore, the provision has been called a special limitation clause.[4] In addressing the state, Article 17 seems largely redundant. If, as the text of the provision states, no greater limitations to rights are allowed than provided under the Convention, then any added value of Article 17 seems absent. The usual grounds of limitation under the substantive rights of the Convention simply apply. The practice of the European Court reflects this: if an interference with a Convention right is justified under a substantive right, then supplementary review of the same situation under Article 17 is unnecessary.[5] When applicants do invoke Article 17 against the state, this is 'essentially an allegation of bad faith against the state'[6] for which it would be extremely difficult to adduce proof. The Court has thus far never sustained such a claim.[7]

---

[3] *W.P. and Others v. Poland*, ECtHR 2 September 2004 (dec.), appl. no. 42264/98, p. 10.

[4] J.A. Frowein and W. Peukert, *Europäische Menschenrechtskonvention. EMRK-Kommentar*, 3rd edn., Kehl am Rhein, 2009, p. 430.

[5] E.g. *Refah Partisi (The Welfare Party) v. Turkey*, ECtHR 13 February 2003, appl. nos. 41340/98 a.o., para. 137.

[6] D.J. Harris, M. O'Boyle, E.P. Bates and C.M. Buckley, *Harris, O'Boyle and Warbrick. Law of the European Convention on Human Rights,* 2nd edn., Oxford: Oxford University Press 2009, p. 652.

[7] See e.g. *Seurot v. France*, ECtHR 18 May 2004 (dec.), appl. no. 57383/00; and *Şimşek and Others v. Turkey*, ECtHR 26 July 2005 (dec.), appl. nos. 35072/97 and 37194/97.

The second aspect of the provision relates to groups and individuals. Whereas the first aspect protects against state abuse, this second aspect rather enables the state to restrict the rights of people more than under the substantive Convention articles. As indicated, this does not mean the state can act without any limitations: an implicit principle of proportionality must be assumed to be part of the application of Article 17.[8] Otherwise it would give states a dangerous *carte blanche* which would undermine rather than defend human rights and democracy. A proportionality analysis has for the most part remained implicit in the Court's case law. Whenever potentially disproportionate state interference with a fundamental right is at stake, the Court has seemed to opt for an assessment on the merits under one of the substantive articles of the Convention.

The dual purpose of Article 17 entails that it can be invoked by both the state and the applicant before the European Court. Notably, the provision enables states to protect democracy but it does not require them to do so. It does not impose positive obligations.[9] Such positive obligations to combat racism, for example, may of course flow from other legal sources.[10]

Article 17 does not figure very prominently in the Court's jurisprudence. This may be explained both by its paradoxical character but also by its contested nature. The provision can be used as a clause to be applied directly. But the abuse of rights clause can also be regarded as a general principle of the Convention, or even as a mere symbolic declaration[11], in the light of which the rest of the ECHR can be interpreted. In practice, the Court has used the clause in both ways, depending on the case at hand.

3. SCOPE

Article 17 addresses specific situations in which the destruction of rights or freedoms is at stake. This distinguishes the provision from single or structural violations of substantive Convention rights, but also from the more severe emergency threats which fall under Article 15 ECHR. Under the latter, derogations from a number of Conventions rights are possible in situations of war or other public emergencies. The abuse clause, by contrast, does not provide states parties to the ECHR with a justification to derogate. The state's arms are still to a certain degree bound, which again points to an implicit proportionality assessment.

---

8   See in this sense the decision of the former European Commission of Human Rights: *De Becker v. Belgium*, EComHR 8 January 1960 (rep.), appl. no. 214/56, para. 279.
9   Harris et al., *supra* n. 6, at p. 652.
10 E.g. the United Nations Convention on the Elimination of Racial Discrimination.
11 H. Cannie and D. Voorhoof, 'The Abuse Clause and Freedom of Expression in the European Human Rights Convention: An Added Value for Democracy and Human Rights Protection?', 29–1 *Netherlands Quarterly of Human Rights* (2011) pp. 54–83, at p. 83.

The wording of the abuse clause reflects that a violation of Article 17 is necessarily connected to one or several of the rights and freedoms in the Convention itself. However, the Court's case law shows that it does not relate to all substantive Convention rights. More procedure-oriented rights such as the key rights to liberty and to a fair trial cannot be encroached upon by invoking Article 17. In its very first case, *Lawless v. Ireland*, the Court ruled that Article 17 'which is negative in scope cannot be construed a contrario as depriving a physical person of the fundamental individual rights guaranteed by Articles 5 and 6 of the Convention'.[12] The same holds for the rights from which one cannot derogate in times of public emergency – exceptions referred to under Article 15(2): the right to life, the prohibitions of torture and slavery and the rule of no punishment without law.[13] By inference, the less serious situations to which Article 17 applies cannot be used to take away the protective scope of those rights. The rights to which Article 17 seems to be most relevant are the right to respect for private life, the freedom of religion, the freedom of expression, the freedom of association, the prohibition of discrimination and the right to free elections.[14] Of these, most cases in Strasbourg so far have related to the freedom of expression and to a lesser extent to the right to peaceful assembly and association.

4. DIRECT APPLICATION

Article 17 is not often invoked by parties in Strasbourg proceedings and the Court's application of the provision has been even rarer, although it can apply the provision *ex officio*.[15] The Court has applied the abuse clause in two different ways: directly and indirectly. The direct approach is considered as the most problematic, as it excludes the possibility to explicitly balance the different interests at stake under the substantive right at stake. Directly applying the abuse clause effectively kills an application, since it enables the Court to declare a complaint inadmissible. Thus, in the Court's own view, this approach should be used only in exceptional circumstances in extreme situations.[16]

In the first few decades of the Convention's existence, until 1998, the European Commission on Human Rights decided on admissibility issues. In the two only instances in which the Commission applied Article 17 directly this meant that the application did not reach the Court. The first decision came

---

12   *Lawless v. Ireland (No. 3)*, ECtHR 1 July 1961, appl. no. 332/57, para. 7. This is a continuous line in the Court's jurisprudence, e.g. the much more recent judgment in *Varela Geis v. Spain*, ECtHR 5 March 2013, appl. no. 61005/09, para. 40.

13   Arts. 2, 3, 4 and 7 ECHR respectively.

14   Arts. 8–11 and 14 ECHR and Art. 3 of the first Additional Protocol to the ECHR.

15   *Perinçek v. Switzerland*, supra n. 2.

16   *Paksas v. Lithuania*, ECtHR (GC) 6 January 2011, appl. no. 34932/04, para. 87.

as early as 1957 in the case of the *German Communist Party*. The Commission dismissed the complaint about the dissolution and prohibition of that party by holding that Article 17 aimed to safeguard the rights and freedoms of the Convention 'by protecting the free operation of democratic institutions'.[17] The Committee held that recourse to a dictatorship (in this case a dictatorship of the proletariat) ran contrary to the ECHR. The second time the Commission directly applied the abuse clause was more than 20 years later, in 1979, in a situation at the other end of the political spectrum. In *Glimmerveen and Hagenbeek* adherents of an extreme-right Dutch Party complained about their conviction for the possession of racist leaflets which they had wanted to spread. The Commission held that the leaflets, with references to 'our Dutch, white people' and calls for the removal of all foreigners, went against the spirit of the ECHR and could contribute to the destruction of rights. In both decisions, the intentions rather than real or possible consequences seem to have been key in the assessment.[18]

After 1998, with the reforms of Protocol 11 ECHR, the Court itself dealt with all incoming applications. Since then it has held Article 17 to be directly applicable in four types of situations: (1) persons or groups espousing totalitarian movements or aims; (2) the denial or (historical) revisionism of Nazi and fascist crimes from World War II; (3) open instances of racism, anti-Semitism, Islamophobia and expressions of hatred against other minorities; (4) and direct calls for violence. Put differently, Article 17 may apply to incitement to hatred or violence, both of which run counter to the underlying values of the Convention. All of these situations are problematic in different ways: does one assess intentions or actual actions? In addition, they pose questions of proof. Furthermore, open racism and calls for totalitarianism have become increasingly rare. Modern forms of these are less open and more implicit. These factors taken together may explain that the Court's direct application of Article 17 has remained inconsistent and sparse. It also reflects a changing consensus in Europe on what is considered dangerous or out of bounds. Communism has faded as a public concern, but the awareness of other dangers has increased.

On the first category of situations, the espousal of totalitarianism, the Court held already in 1998 that 'the justification of a pro-Nazi policy' would not fall under the protection of the freedom of expression.[19] In 2013, in the case of *Vona v. Hungary* – about the dissolution of a movement that organised threatening paramilitary marches through Roma villages – the Court further clarified that Article 17 would apply directly only if there was *prima facie* an act aimed at the destruction of Convention rights or an intention to 'publicly defend of or

---

[17]   *German Communist Party v. Germany*, EComHR 20 July 1957 (dec.), appl. no. 250/57, p. 4.

[18]   *Glimmerveen and Hagenbeek v. the Netherlands*, EComHR 11 October 1979 (dec.), appl. nos. 8348/78 and 8406/79.

[19]   *Lehideux and Isorni v. France*, ECtHR 23 September 1998, appl. no. 24662/94, para. 53.

disseminate propaganda in support of totalitarian views'.[20] In other cases, the applicability of the abuse clause would be decided upon 'in the light of all the circumstances of the case' when reviewing the substantive Convention article concerned.[21] Article 17 may also directly apply to situations of expressed contempt for victims of totalitarianism[22] although the mere and unintended effects on such victims, by contrast, cannot by themselves set the limits of freedom of expression.[23]

The second strand of instances concerns forms of denial or historical revisionism of war crimes. Statements which clearly seek to justify war crimes such as torture or summary executions would deflect Article 10 of its aim and thus call for direct application of Article 17.[24] But statements that deny or give unorthodox views on crimes are less easily categorised. The Court has taken the position that it is not its function to adjudicate on what is the correct historical interpretation of the past.[25] Slightly revisionist views on historical massacres without denying the killings as such or seeking to completely exonerate the perpetrators is not sufficient to trigger direct application of the abuse clause, the Court found in a case about the Azeri-Armenian war of the early 1990s.[26] Typically, it would thus leave the qualification of historical facts to historians. But in the case of the Holocaust, the Court has held in *Garaudy* – an author who claimed the massacre of Jews in World War II was a myth – that denial of 'the reality of clearly established historical facts, such as the Holocaust' has nothing to do with historical research and calls for direct application of Article 17.[27] It has never become clear to what extent other war crimes from the past would trigger the abuse clause directly. In the case of *Perinçek*, about a Swiss conviction of a Turkish political leader who had called the idea of an Armenian genocide an international lie, the Court explicitly refused to apply Article 17 directly. It argued that Perinçek had not denied the fact that massacres and deportations had taken place, but only the legal qualification of these as genocide. Such a denial of the precise label was not of a nature to incite hatred against Armenians in the Court's view nor aimed at denigrating the victims.[28]

Closely connected are the third type of situations, the most heinous expressions of hatred against particular groups. This foremost includes anti-Semitism, but it is not limited to that, as the Court has gradually although not

---

20   *Vona v. Hungary*, ECtHR 9 July 2013, appl. no. 35943/10, para. 38, building on 2 earlier cases: *Sidiropoulos v. Greece*, ECtHR 10 July 1998, appl. no. 26695/95, and *Vajnai v. Hungary*, ECtHR 8 July 2008, appl. no. 33629/06.

21   *Ibid.*

22   *Fáber v. Hungary*, ECtHR 24 July 2012, appl. no. 40721/08, para. 58.

23   *Vajnai, supra* n. 20, para. 57.

24   *Orban and Others v. France*, ECtHR 15 January 2009, appl. no. 20985, para. 35.

25   *Chauvy and Others v. France*, ECtHR 29 June 2004, appl. no. 64915/01, para. 69.

26   *Fatullayev v. Azerbaijan*, ECtHR 22 April 2010, appl. no. 40984/07, para. 81.

27   *Garaudy v. France*, ECtHR 24 June 2003 (dec.), appl. no. 65831/01.

28   *Perinçek, supra* n. 2, paras. 49–54.

consistently expanded this category. In *Ivanov*, the Court applied Article 17 directly to a newspaper editor who had depicted Jews as the cause of evil in Russia.[29] It did the same in *W.P. and others*, which concerned a Polish association that alleged that the Jewish minority in Poland had persecuted the Polish majority – a clear sign of reviving anti-Semitism according to the Court.[30] In *Norwood*, the Court extended the abuse clause's reach to Islamophobia by directly applying it to the case of public display of an anti-Islamic poster which called for 'Islam out of Britain' shortly after the 9/11 terror attacks. The connection of an entire religious group to terrorism was found to be contrary the Convention's values of 'tolerance, social peace and non-discrimination'.[31] As no violence or social tension had ostensibly resulted from the display of the poster, intentions rather than effects seem to have been decisive for the Court's assessment. In *Molnar v. Romania*, a case about right-wing nationalist propaganda posters, the Court further extended this to messages of open hatred towards Roma and homosexual minorities, emphasising the particular national context in which these messages could gravely hurt public order and went against the fundamental values of the Convention.[32]

The fourth and final type of situations relates to open calls for, or espousal of, violence. Such calls run counter to the underlying values of the ECHR including peacefully settling international disputes and the sanctity of life itself, as the Court held in *Hizb Ut-Tahrir*, a case about an association in Germany which had advocated the violent destruction of Israel and its inhabitants and had defended suicide attacks.[33] It applied the same logic of direct Article 17 application in a case concerning two members of the same organisation convicted in Russia.[34] A similar line of argumentation applies to political parties. When their leaders incite to violence or put forward non-democratic policies aimed to destroy democracy itself, such parties lose the protection of the Convention.[35] The Court thus explicitly links the destruction of human rights and of democracy.

5. INDIRECT APPLICATION OF ARTICLE 17

The indirect approach is more often used in the Court's jurisprudence. It entails that Article 17 considerations are integrated in the third prong of the test of limitations of rights, for example under Articles 9, 10 and 11 ECHR:

---

[29]   *Ivanov v. Russia*, ECtHR 20 February 2007 (dec.), appl. no. 35222/04.
[30]   *W.P. and Others v. Poland*, ECtHR 2 September 2004 (dec.), appl. no. 42264/98.
[31]   *Norwood v. the United Kingdom*, ECtHR 16 November 2004 (dec.), appl. no. 23131/03.
[32]   *Molnar v. Romania*, ECtHR 23 October 2012, appl. no. 16637/06 (dec.), para. 23.
[33]   *Hizb Ut-Tahrir and Others v. Germany*, ECtHR 12 June 2012 (dec.), appl. no. 31098/08.
[34]   *Kasymakhunov and Saybatalov v. Russia*, ECtHR 14 March 2013, appl. nos. 26261/05 and 26377/06.
[35]   *Yazar and Others v. Turkey*, ECtHR 9 April 2002, appl. nos. 22723 and Others, para. 49.

was the interference necessary in a democratic society? Applying the indirect approach, the situation under review does not at first sight reflect an abuse of rights but rather requires a substantive, more in-depth assessment. In that assessment, abuse of rights considerations can play a part in the balancing under the necessity test, pointing towards non-violation of the substantive article concerned. The applicant may thus end up with the same result as in a direct application of Article 17, with the key difference that a balancing exercise allows for an assessment of the proportionality of the state interference with the applicant's rights. However, there is no full consistency in this, as an in-depth assessment may also lead to the conclusion that a situation does reflect an abuse of rights after all. The latter happened in *Kaptan*, in which the Court eventually held that certain publications advocated and glorified violence and thus fell outside the substantive scope of Article 10. It concluded this, however, as part of the necessity test of Article 10.[36] In *Schimanek*, a case about an active promoter of National Socialism who had been convicted, the Court likewise concluded under the necessity test that this was an ideology with the aim of destroying fundamental rights and that the conviction had thus been necessary.[37]

In other freedom of expression cases, a proportionality analysis is explicitly applied. *Lehideux and Isorni* was a case about a book trying to positively revise the role of Pétain, the head of the Vichy regime, that had collaborated with the Nazis.[38] The Court held that the criminal conviction which had been imposed on the applicants was disproportionate. As the applicants had not sought to deny or revise Nazi atrocities, but rather discussed a specific version of the role of Pétain in the policies of the Vichy regime, Article 17 did not come into play for the Court as the defining factor. But even Holocaust denial cases as such have at times been assessed by way of a balancing exercise in Strasbourg.[39] The same goes for instances of Islamophobic political speech[40] and racist or xenophobic political utterances.[41]

Article 17 can also be applied indirectly to cases of political parties. In the Grand Chamber judgment of *Refah Partisi and others v. Turkey*, the Court ruled on the dissolution of that country's main Islamic party at that time. In holding that a compromise between defending democracy and upholding individual rights is necessary, the Court dismissed a categorical, direct application of Article 17 and rather went into the merits under the freedom of association (Article 11 ECHR). This shows that the old position of the European Commission

---

36   *Kaptan v. Switzerland*, ECtHR 12 April 2001 (dec.), appl. no. 55641/00.
37   *Schimanek v. Austria*, ECtHR 1 February 2000 (dec.), appl. no. 32307/96.
38   *Lehideux and Isorni v. France*, ECtHR 23 September 1998, appl. no. 24662/94.
39   *Witzsch v. Germany*, ECtHR 20 April 1999 (dec.), appl. no. 41448/98.
40   In *Le Pen v. France*, ECtHR 20 April 2010 (dec.), appl. no. 18788/09, the Court dismissed the complaint of a French politician in an admissibility decision which included a necessity test but which did not explicitly mention Art. 17.
41   *Féret v. Belgium*, ECtHR 16 July 2009, appl. no. 15615/07.

of Human Rights of direct application of Article 17 to dissolution of political parties cases has been abandoned. Under the substantive Article 11 assessment the Court then went on to develop a strict necessity test which included criteria related to imminent threats to democracy and ideas which were incompatible with a democratic society. As the Court noted, it was 'not at all improbable that totalitarian movements, organised in the form of political parties, might do away with democracy, after prospering under the democratic regime, there being examples of this in modern European history'.[42] This thus relates both to intentions and consequences and can be seen as an implicit elaboration of an indirect Article 17 assessment. Whereas in *Refah Partisi* no violation was found eventually, in a range of similar party dissolution cases the Court did conclude that Article 11 had been violated. Turkey had argued for application of Article 17 in vain, as the Court found nothing in the parties' programmes or actions which aimed at the destruction of rights or called for recourse to violence.[43]

---

[42] *Refah Partisi and Others v. Turkey, supra* n. 5, para. 99.
[43] E.g. *United Communist Party of Turkey and Others v. Turkey,* ECtHR (GC) 30 January 1998, appl. no. 19392/92.

CHAPTER 36

PROHIBITION OF
THE MISUSE OF POWER

(Article 18)

Yutaka Arai and Joachim Meese[*]

GUIDING PRINCIPLE

Article 18 generally prohibits the Contracting States from using the restrictions permitted under the Convention for any purpose other than those for which they are intended. Unlike many other Convention provisions, Article 18 is rarely invoked and there have been only a few cases where the Court declared a complaint under Article 18 admissible, let alone found a violation thereof, although the provision seems to have attracted more attention lately. The scarcity of the case law under the provision has also induced the Court to show particular diligence in each new case where allegations of improper motives are made.

ARTICLE 18

The restrictions permitted under this Convention to the said rights and freedoms shall not be applied for any purpose other than those for which they have been prescribed.

---

[*] In the fourth edition this chapter was revised and updated by Yutaka Arai. In the current edition it was revised and updated by Joachim Meese.

CONTENTS

1. SUBSIDIARY CHARACTER

The subsidiary nature of this provision is demonstrated by the fact that its prohibition cannot constitute the object of an independent complaint but may be advanced only in conjunction with one of the Convention rights,[1] including the prohibition of discrimination under Article 14,[2] or the right to individual communication with the Court under Article 34.[3] However, as is the case with Articles 13 and 14, Article 18 has 'limited autonomous' status in that this provision may be violated considered in conjunction with a principal provision, even though the latter is not violated.[4]

In most cases involving an alleged violation of Article 18, the Court has not found it necessary to carry out a separate examination under this provision.[5]

The survey of the case law suggests that there are two scenarios in which a separate examination under Article 18 may be dispensed with. First, an appraisal under Article 18 may be forgone when the Court has carried out detailed examinations of an alleged violation of a substantive right. The Court may consider it sufficient that the principal right invoked has not been violated in order to warrant the conclusion that an alleged violation of Article 18 is

---

[1]   See *Gusinskiy v. Russia*, ECtHR 19 May 2004, appl. no. 70276/01, para. 75 and *Tymoshenko v. Ukraine*, ECtHR 30 April 2013, appl. no. 49872/11, para. 294 (holding that 'Article 18 of the Convention does not have an autonomous role').

[2]   See, e.g., *Hasan İlhan v. Turkey*, ECtHR 9 November 2004, appl. no. 22494/93, paras. 130–132 and *Menteşe and Others v. Turkey*, ECtHR 18 January 2005, appl. no. 36217/97, paras. 90–92. In both cases, which concerned an alleged abuse based on discrimination against the Kurds, the Court found neither Art. 14, taken together with substantive rights, nor Art. 18 to have been violated, on the ground that the allegation was unsubstantiated.

[3]   See, e.g., judgment of *Orhan v. Turkey*, ECtHR 18 June 2002, appl. no. 25656/94, para. 402. However, the Court did not examine the complaints of a violation of Art. 34 in tandem with Art. 18, holding that aspects of Art. 18 were already discussed in the context of Art. 38 of the Convention: *ibid.*, para. 274.

[4]   *Gusinskiy v. Russia, supra* n. 1, para. 73.

[5]   See, e.g., *Bozano v. France*, ECtHR 18 December 1986, appl. no. 9990/82, para. 61. In that case, the applicant alleged that his deportation by the French authorities to Switzerland and the ensuing deprivation of his liberty were, *inter alia*, contrary to Art. 5. The Court dispensed with an auxiliary examination of this issue under Art. 18 taken in tandem with Art. 5(1). It felt no need to go beyond the finding that the deportation procedure was 'abused for objects and purposes other than its normal ones' under the heading of Art. 5(1) alone.

unsubstantiated.[6] Still, in view of the (albeit limited) autonomous nature of Article 18 claims (as noted above), the rationale for this method may be questioned. In contrast, the Court may be satisfied with finding a violation only of that principal provision, obliterating an examination of an ancillary claim based on improper use of restrictions under Article 18.[7] A separate appraisal under Article 18 may be viewed as superfluous, on the ground that the issue of misuse of powers is 'absorbed' into the assessment of encroachments on substantive rights or on the right of individual application.[8]

Second, an ancillary review under Article 18 may be omitted where the considerations of misuse of power are integrated into the appraisal under a limitation clause attached to some substantive rights. The Court's methodology is to infer from the finding that the interfering measure has struck a requisite balance[9] that this does not entail any extraneous motives or improper aims contrary to Article 18.

In a limited number of cases, however, the complaints under Article 18 have not been dismissed out of hand, and the Strasbourg organs have duly carried out a separate assessment of an alleged breach of Article 18 taken together with a substantive provision.[10]

---

[6] See, e.g., *Engel and Others v. the Netherlands*, ECtHR (GC) 8 June 1976, appl. nos. 5100/7, 5101/71, 5102/71 and 5354/72, para. 108 (finding no need to examine the complaints under Art. 11 taken together with Arts. 17 and 18 in view of no 'interference' with the rights under Art. 11). See the Court's observation as to an alleged breach of Art. 6 taken with Art. 18: *ibid.*, para. 93. There, the Court ruled that the examinations of Art. 6 with respect to the choice of disciplinary rather than criminal proceedings against the applicants, which resulted in depriving them of guarantees under Art. 6, would make it superfluous to examine the issue under Art. 18 (a breach only in respect of the duty to provide public proceedings and no violation in respect of other guarantees under Art. 6).

[7] *Bozano v. France, supra* n. 5, para. 61 (finding that the deportation procedure at issue contravened Art. 5(1) and obliterated a separate appraisal under Art. 18 taken in tandem with Art. 5(1)).

[8] *Ibid.* On this matter, see also *Cyprus v. Turkey*, ECtHR (GC) 10 May 2001, appl. no. 25781/94, paras. 206 and 388 (finding violations of the rights of displaced persons to respect for their home and property under Arts. 8 and 13 of the Convention, and Art. 1 of the First Protocol).

[9] See, *inter alia*, *Handyside v. the United Kingdom*, ECtHR 7 December 1976, appl. no. 5493/72, paras. 52 and 62–64 (Art. 10 of the Convention and Art. 1 of the First Protocol); *Engel and Others v. the Netherlands, supra* n. 6, para. 104 (dispensing with an examination of an alleged violation of Art. 10 together with Arts. 17 and 18 in view of the finding of no violation under Art. 10(2); *Şenerv. Turkey*, ECtHR 18 July 2000, appl. no. 26680/95, paras. 61–62 (Art. 10). See also *Dicle v. Turkey*, ECtHR 10 November 2004, appl. no. 46733/99, paras. 24–25. In that case, though finding the criminal convictions based on the publication of an article in a newspaper to be disproportionate and thus a violation of Art. 10, the Court considered the aims pursued to be legitimate, and hence no need for a separate review under Art. 18.

[10] See, e.g., *Ashingdane v. the United Kingdom*, ECtHR 28 May 1985, appl. no. 8225/78, paras. 43–49.

2. GENERAL APPLICABILITY

The text of Article 18 makes it clear that it is purported to cover all restrictions allowed under the Convention. This suggests that the applicability of Article 18 can be contemplated in three situations. First and foremost, Article 18 is applied to the limitation clauses designed to qualify specific substantive rights, such as the second paragraphs of Articles 8–11 of the Convention, the second paragraph of Article 1 of the First Protocol, the third paragraph of Article 2 of the Fourth Protocol and the second paragraph of Article 1 of the Seventh Protocol.

Second, Article 18 should be deemed applicable to cases of so-called 'limitations by delimitation', where certain Convention provisions expressly exclude specific areas or persons from their scope of guarantee. This can be seen in relation to Article 4(3) (exemption of certain work or service from the meaning of 'forced or compulsory labour'), the third sentence of Article 10 (licensing of broadcasting, television or cinema enterprises), the second sentence of Article 11(2) ('lawful restrictions on the freedom of assembly and association exercised by members of the armed forces, of the police or of the administration of the State') and Article 12 (national laws 'governing' the exercise of the right to marry).

Third, Article 18 applies to the general restrictions ensuing from Articles 15, 16 and 17. In the *De Becker* case, the former Commission relied in part on Article 18 to conclude that the measures which were taken in accordance with Article 15 in connection with an emergency situation of the Nazi occupation during World War II were no longer justified if they contravened the requirements of Article 18. The Commission rejected the Belgian Government's submission that derogating measures under Article 15 would not cease to operate merely because the war was over. The Commission was of the view that such an argument was irreconcilable with the proportionality requirement under Article 15 read together with Article 18.[11] Moreover, it should be highlighted that the five non-derogable rights guaranteed under Articles 2–4 and 7 of the Convention and Article 4 of the Seventh Protocol are, by nature, not susceptible to any restrictions, express or implicit. The express wording of Article 18 'The restrictions permitted under this Convention to the said rights and freedoms…' suggests that it is logically impossible to conceive a concurrent violation of Article 18 in relation to any of the five non-derogable rights, the right to security (as opposed to the right to liberty) under Article 5, and the right to conscience under Article 9. Any improper motive or purpose, if ever proven in relation to an interference with a non-derogable right, is an aggravating factor that must be taken into account in assessing the threshold of a violation or otherwise of that 'absolute' right.

---

[11]   *De Becker v. Belgium*, EComHR 9 June 1958 (dec.), appl. no. 214/56.

3.   BURDEN OF PROOF

The analysis of the case law suggests that the Court has generally recoiled from endorsing an ancillary violation of Article 18.[12] *Prima facie*, the dearth of the pertinent case law in the ECHR context, as compared with the doctrine of the prohibition of misuse of power (*détournement de pouvoir*, or the cognates such as the doctrine of *ultra vires* and *excès de pouvoir*) in the settings of national public law, seems inscrutable. One rationale adduced by the Court is that the general structure of the ECHR is built on the assumption that public authorities of the member states operate in good faith,[13] albeit this assumption is rebuttable.[14] This explains why a very exacting[15] standard of proof is imposed on applicants invoking Article 18.[16] They must establish an improper motive or purpose operating behind an interference with a substantive right or with the petition right under Article 34. Moreover, the applicants must prove that such a motive goes beyond the aims envisaged under the limitation clauses of particular provisions. As a consequence, the standard of proof is even higher than 'beyond reasonable doubt', with no burden shifting even after the applicant makes a *prima facie* showing. Unless the malicious intent of the national authorities can be clearly inferred from the nature of the impugned measure, the burden of proof incumbent on an applicant invoking Article 18 is onerous.[17] However, for direct proof such as written evidence, which would clearly facilitate a review under Article 18,[18] the Court is reluctant to recognise contextual evidence that suggests an 'arguable claim' of improper motive as contrary to this provision.[19] Such onus is aggravated by the general reluctance of the Court to rely on Article 18 *proprio*

---

[12]   The Court itself acknowledges this point, although the Court also mentions that it must show particular diligence in each new case where allegations of improper motives are made because of the scarce case law with regard to Art. 18. See, e.g., *Khodorkovskiy and Lebedev v. Russia*, ECtHR 25 July 2013, appl. nos. 11082/06 and 13772/05, para. 898.

[13]   *Khodorkovskiy v. Russia*, ECtHR 31 May 2011, appl. no. 5829/04, para. 255.

[14]   *Khodorkovskiy and Lebedev v. Russia, supra* n. 12, para. 899.

[15]   This term is used in the jurisprudence of the Court; see *Ilgar Mammadov v. Azerbaijan*, ECtHR 22 May 2014, appl. no. 15172/13, para. 138.

[16]   See, e.g., the main cases where Art. 18 claims were rejected: *Sisojeva and Others v. Latvia*, ECtHR (GC) 15 January 2007, paras. 127–129; *Khodorkovskiy v. Russia*, ECtHR 31 May 2011, appl. no. 5829/04, paras. 249–261; *OAO Neftyanaya Kompaniya Yukos v. Russia*, ECtHR 20 September 2011, appl. no. 14902/04, paras. 663–666; *Khodorkovskiy and Lebedev v. Russia*, *supra* n. 12, paras. 886–909. Also see the joint concurring opinion of judges Sajó, Tsotsoria en Pinto de Albuquerque in the *Tchankotadze* case (*Tchankotadze v. Georgia*, ECtHR 21 June 2016, appl. no. 15256/05), where the presumption of good faith is defined as '*extremely strong*' (para. 6).

[17]   Note should be taken of the *Engel* case. In that case, the Court rejected a complaint that the imposition of disciplinary proceedings for writing in a journal in the army had extraneous motives of suppressing trade unions activities in violation of Art. 18 in tandem with Arts. 10 and 11 (*Engel and Others v. the Netherlands, supra* n. 6, paras. 104–108).

[18]   *Gusinskiy v. Russia, supra* n. 1, paras. 76–77.

[19]   *Khodorkovskiy and Lebedev v. Russia, supra* n. 12, paras. 902–903.

motu, even though it is not only competent, but arguably even obliged to do so under Article 19.[20]

The question is whether this *mountain high*[21] standard of proof will not be abandoned in future decisions, because a review of the current standard has been insisted on by various judges of the Court.[22]

4. CASE LAW

In *Khodorkovskiy and Lebedev v. Russia,* the Court was reluctant to accept the serious criticism that the whole machinery of the Russian public authorities was tainted by bad faith and political motives against any opponents, including against the oligarchs.[23] The Court has observed that 'the applicant alleging that his rights and freedoms were limited for an improper reason must convincingly show that the real aim of the authorities was not the same as that proclaimed (or as can be reasonably inferred from the context)'.[24] Unsurprisingly, when faced with a very grave allegation, the Court has used a correspondingly heightened evidentiary threshold, such as 'a very exacting standard of proof'[25] or 'an incontrovertible and direct proof'.[26] But as stated above, a review of the current standard of proof has already been insisted on by various judges of the Court.

Clearly, in the vast majority of the member states of the Council of Europe where liberal democratic values are fully anchored in the political and judicial consciousness, it should be rare that ulterior motives of restricting Convention rights manifest themselves. In this regard, some cases arising from Russia, Ukraine and Moldova form unsavoury exceptions, redolent of their tumultuous transition from communist dictatorships to the Western-style democracies, or their return to reactionary regimes. In *Gusinskiy v. Russia,* the applicant complained that his detention was an abuse of power in that

---

[20] See, however, *X v. Federal Republic of Germany,* EComHR, 11 July 1973 (dec.), appl. no. 6038/73.

[21] The wording is from judge Kūris (joint concurring opinion in *Tchankotadze v. Georgia, supra* n. 16, para. 6).

[22] See the joint concurring opinion of judges Sajó, Tsotsoria en Pinto de Albuquerque in the *Tchankotadze* case (*Tchankotadze v. Georgia, supra* n. 16, para. 7) and the concurring opinion of judge Kūris in the same case (para. 51).

[23] *Khodorkovskiy and Lebedev v. Russia, supra* n. 12, paras. 904–909. See also *Khodorkovskiy v. Russia,* ECtHR 31 May 2011, appl. no. 5829/04, paras. 255–261.

[24] *Khodorkovskiy and Lebedev v. Russia, supra* n. 12, para. 899. See also *Khodorkovskiy v. Russia, supra* n. 23, para. 255.

[25] *Khodorkovskiy and Lebedev v. Russia, supra* n. 12, para. 899. See also *Khodorkovskiy v. Russia, supra* n. 23, para. 255.

[26] *Khodorkovskiy v. Russia, supra* n 23, para. 260 and *OAO Neftyanaya Kompaniya Yukos v. Russia,* ECtHR 20 September 2011, appl. no. 14902/04, para. 663.

the authorities compelled him to sell his media business to a state petroleum company, Gazprom, on unfavourable terms and conditions. While in prison, the applicant was asked to sign an agreement with Gazprom, which was later endorsed by a State Minister. The signature of this agreement led to the charges against him being dropped. The Court found a violation of Article 18 together with Article 5(1)(c).[27] In *Cebotari v. Modova*, a breach of Article 18 was spotted in that the applicant's arrest and detention 'was visibly linked' to the improper purpose of foreclosing the application submitted before the Court.[28] Political motives were found to be preponderant in two Ukrainian cases. In *Lutsenko v. Ukraine*, the Court found evidence of politically motivated prosecution of the opposition leader when he was divested of his liberty in breach of Article 5(1). In that case, the prosecutory authorities made it plain that their avowed aim of arresting the applicant was to punish him for publicly disagreeing with the accusations and asserting his innocence in communication with the public.[29] Similarly, in *Tymoshenko v. Ukraine*, the Court found that the reasoning given by the national authorities was imbued with the nature of politically motivated prosecution, and with an improper purpose, other than that for bringing her before the national judiciary on reasonable suspicion of having committed an offence under Article 5.[30] In *Rasul Jafarov v. Azerbaijan*, an NGO activist was being prosecuted for an alleged failure to comply with legal formalities of an administrative nature while carrying out his work. The Court determined that the case could not be viewed in isolation, because several notable human rights activists who had co-operated with international organisations for the protection of human rights, including, most notably, the Council of Europe, were similarly arrested and charged with serious criminal offences entailing heavy imprisonment sentences. The Court found a violation of Article 18 and concluded that the actual purpose of the impugned measures was to silence and punish the applicant for his activities in the area of human rights.[31] In *Merabishvili v. Georgia*, the Court found that the applicant's pre-trial detention was used not only for the purpose of bringing him before the competent legal authority on reasonable suspicion of abuse of official authority and other offences in public office with which he had been charged, but was also treated by the prosecuting authority as an additional opportunity to obtain leverage

---

27   *Gusinskiy v. Russia, supra* n. 1, paras. 76–77.
28   *Cebotari v. Moldova*, ECtHR 13 November 2007, appl. no. 35615/06, paras. 46–53.
29   *Lutsenko v. Ukraine,* ECtHR 3 July 2012, appl. no. 6492/11, paras. 108–109.
30   *Tymoshenko v. Ukraine*, ECtHR 30 April 2013, appl. no. 49872/11, paras. 299–301. Judges Jungwiert, Nussberger and Potocki, in their joint concurring opinion, forcefully averred that '… in interpreting Article 18 of the Convention the direct link between human rights protection and democracy must be taken into account', and that 'If the human rights of politically active persons are restricted for the purpose of hindering or making impossible their participation in the political life of a country, democracy is in danger'.
31   *Rasul Jafarov v. Azerbaijan*, ECtHR 17 March 2016, appl. no. 69981/14, paras. 153–163.

over the unrelated investigation into the death of the former Prime Minister and to conduct an enquiry into the financial activities of the former head of state. It therefore concluded to a violation of Article 18.[32]

---

[32] *Merabishvili v. Georgia*, ECtHR 14 June 2016, appl. no. 72508/13, paras. 100–107.

CHAPTER 37

RESERVATIONS

(Article 57)

Janneke GERARDS[*]

GUIDING PRINCIPLE

When ratifying the Convention, the States Parties may make reservations as regards specific obligations under the Convention, which they are not (or not yet) able to meet under national law at the time of ratification. Although this is common practice in international law, the European Court of Human Rights has set strict conditions for the validity of such reservations because of the special character of the Convention as a human rights treaty. Appeals to reservations made by respondent states in concrete cases are therefore frequently refused.

ARTICLE 57

1. Any State may, when signing this Convention or when depositing its instrument of ratification, make a reservation in respect of any particular provision of the Convention to the extent that any law then in force in its territory is not in conformity with the provision. Reservations of a general character shall not be permitted under this Article.

2. Any reservation made under this Article shall contain a brief statement of the law concerned.

---

[*] This chapter is a translated and adapted version of J.H. Gerards, 'Artikel 57 – Voorbehouden' [Article 57 ECHR – reservations], in: J.H. Gerards et al. (eds.), *Sdu Commentaar EVRM. Deel 2 – procedurebepalingen [Sdu ECHR Commentary. Part 2 – procedural provisions]*, Den Haag: Sdu 2014. In the fourth edition this chapter was revised and updated by Kees Flinterman.

CONTENTS

1. INTRODUCTION

Under Article 57 of the Convention, States Parties may make reservations to their obligations arising under the Convention.[1] They may only be made in respect of particular provisions of the Convention, however, and only to the extent that a specific national law is not in conformity with the relevant provision. Reservations of a general nature are not permitted and, according to Article 57(2), any reservation made must contain a brief statement of the law concerned.

The possibility of making reservations is important for states, since becoming a party to the Convention means that they undertake binding obligations to respect the ECHR rights and they are subjected to supervision by the Convention authorities.[2] If it would appear that, at the moment of ratification, a state has legislation in place which seems incompatible with the ECHR, a certain delay may be desirable before the obligations under the Convention obtain their full effect so as to allow the state to adapt such legislation. It is for the reason of giving the states some leeway in this regard that Article 57 provides for the possibility for reservations. Indeed, several Contracting States have made such reservations in respect of the Convention.[3] Many of these have been made

---

[1] There is only one exception: according to Art. 4 of Protocol No. 6, states are not allowed to make reservations to that Protocol.

[2] J. van der Velde, *Grenzen aan het toezicht op de naleving van het EVRM [Limits to the supervision of the compliance with the ECHR]* (Dissertation, Leiden University, 1997) pp. 287–288.

[3] A list of declarations and reservations can be found at <http://conventions.coe.int> CETS No. 005 > List of declarations, reservations and other communications.

by the states who became a party to the Convention when it was drafted, but reservations also have been made by states which have accessed the ECHR in more recent times.[4]

At the same time, the inclusion in the Convention of the possibility of making reservations was a controversial matter at the time the Convention was drafted. The Committee on Legal and Administrative Questions of the Consultative Assembly was opposed to giving the states unlimited power to do so, as it considered that such a power would threaten to deprive the Convention of its practical effect and in any case of its moral authority.[5] Indeed, the possibility for states to make reservations would seem to be at odds with the presumption of universality of human rights, since by making such reservations, a state excludes or modifies its obligations under that particular treaty. The consequence is that the acceptance of the human rights standards is not of a common level in all the Contracting Parties. Moreover, the possibility of making reservations is hard to be reconciled with the character and contents of human rights obligations as minimum standards. As the Human Rights Committee, established under the UN Covenant on Civil and Political Rights, stated in its General Comment on Issues Relating to Reservations, 'it is desirable in principle that States accept the full range of obligations, because the human rights norms are the legal expression of the essential rights that every person is entitled to as a human being'.[6] Clearly, this reasoning also applies for the legal system established by the Convention.

Fortunately, the states seem to have been aware of the special nature of the Convention and the objections against making reservations to such a human rights treaty. Most of the reservations which have been made have a fairly limited scope, and overall it can be said that the possibility to make reservations has been used rather sparingly by the states.[7] Moreover, the drafters of Article 57 have tried to avoid the risk that a state escape some of the important obligations under the Convention by using the leeway left by Article 57 by setting strict conditions for reservations to be valid.

These conditions for the validity of reservations are discussed hereafter in section 2. The consequences of the validity or invalidity of reservations are explained in section 3, where also the question is addressed as to when reservations can be held to be applicable in concrete cases. Section 4 deals with the question whether and to what extent reservations can be modified or withdrawn and with the possible retroactive effect of such changes. Finally, it

---

4   Van der Velde, *supra* n. 2, p. 201.

5   Council of Europe, Cons. Ass., Ordinary Session 1950, Documents, Part II, Doc. 6, p. 534.

6   Human Rights Committee, General Comment No. 24 on issues relating to reservations made upon ratification or accession to the Covenant or the Optional Protocols thereto, or in relation to declarations under article 41 of the Covenant, 11 November 1994, para. 4. UN Doc. HRI/GEN/1/Rev.7, p. 161.

7   Van der Velde, *supra* n. 2, p. 299.

should be noted that some states have not (only) made reservations at the time of ratification, but (also) have laid down so-called interpretative declarations in which they state how, in their view, certain ECHR provisions should be understood. The meaning of such declarations and their relationship with reservations is explored in section 5.

Before dealing with these issues, however, it is important to emphasise that a wide body of knowledge is available on the topic of reservations to international treaties.[8] International (customary) law, in particular as codified in Articles 19–24 of the Vienna Convention on the Law of Treaties, thereby deviates from the ECHR practice in important respects. Usually, for example, the States Parties to multilateral treaties can either accept or object to reservations proposed by a state, while for the ECHR, such acceptance and objections are hardly relevant.[9] Specific differences further can be found in regard to the consequences of invalidity of a reservation and as a consequence of the specific formulation of Article 57.[10] Given the specificity of the ECHR system, this chapter does not discuss such aspects of generic international law on reservations, but it focuses on Article 57. Where appropriate, however, the discussion is supplemented by references to the Vienna Convention on the Law of Treaties.

2. REQUIREMENTS FOR VALIDITY

2.1. INTRODUCTION

For a reservation to be valid, it must meet a number of specific requirements. These can be found in Article 57 ECHR, supplemented by the general requirements of Article 19 of the Vienna Convention on the Law of Treaties. The Strasbourg organs – after a certain period of hesitation – have considered themselves competent to decide whether these requirements have been met when reservations are invoked

---

[8] The International Law Commission has even drafted a *Guide to Practice on Reservations to Treaties*; see Report of the ILC on the Work of its 63rd session, General Assembly, Official Records, 66th Session, Supplement n° 10, Addendum 1, UN Doc. A/66/10/Add.1. For an overview, see, e.g., A. Pellet, 'The ILC Guide to Practice on Reservations to Treaties: A General Presentation by the Special Rapporteur', 24 *European Journal of International Law*, 2013, pp. 1055–1059.

[9] S. Marks, 'Reservations Unhinged: The *Belilos* Case before the European Court of Human Rights', 39 *International and Comparative Law Quarterly*, 1990, pp. 300–327 at pp. 317 et seq.; K.L. McCall-Smith, *Reservations to Human Rights Treaties* (Dissertation University of Edinburgh, 2012), <https://www.era.lib.ed.ac.uk/bitstream/1842/6320/3/McCall-Smith2012.pdf>, pp. 144 et seq.

[10] *Cf.* R. Baratta, 'Should Invalid Reservations to Human Rights Treaties be Disregarded?', 11 *European Journal of International Law*, 2000, pp. 413–425; McCall-Smith, *supra* n. 9, pp. 139 et seq.

in concrete cases coming before them.[11] This should not obscure that in many cases the question as to the validity of reservations has remained open, since it is not often raised in individual or inter-state cases, and there may therefore be a protracted uncertainty about the validity of certain reservations. Nevertheless, the applications in which reservations have been questioned so far have enabled the Court to usefully detail the requirements and conditions for validity.

This section first discusses the substantive requirements for validity of reservations as they have been developed in the Strasbourg case law (section 2.2). These are that the requirement that the reservation must concern laws in force at the time of signature or ratification, the requirement of specificity and the prohibition of general reservations and the requirement that a reservation should not be contrary to the aim and purpose of the Convention. In addition to these substantive requirements, two procedural conditions are discussed in section 2.3. These relate to the point in time a reservation must be made and to the statement of reasons for making a reservation.

2.2. SUBSTANTIVE REQUIREMENTS

a. Legislation in force

According to the text of Article 57(1) ECHR, a reservation can be made as regards any law in force at the time of signature or ratification of the Convention that is not in conformity with a specific Convention provision. The requirement that the reservation must concern legislation that is already in force is closely related to the rationale of Article 57. As mentioned in section 1, this rationale is to provide a certain leeway to the states to adapt their national legislation to the obligations resulting from the Convention and to assure that they do not refrain from not signing or ratifying the Convention as a whole because they cannot (or do not want to) comply with certain of its provisions.

In its case law the Court has gradually clarified the precise meaning of the requirement. First, it has made clear that, obviously, reservations cannot pertain to newly introduced legislation, i.e. legislation or other measures which were not yet in force at the time of signature or ratification.[12]

Secondly, the Court has answered the question how existing legislation should be dealt with which has been amended after ratification in such a way as

---

[11] *Temeltasch v. Switzerland*, EComHR 5 March 1983 (Rep.), appl. no. 9116/80, para. 65; see further P.H. Imbert, 'Reservations to the European Convention on Human Rights before the Strasbourg Commission: the *Temeltasch* case', 33 *International and Comparative Law Quarterly*, 1984 pp. 558–595 at pp. 582 et seq.; Marks, *supra* n. 9, pp. 307–308; Van der Velde, *supra* n. 2, p. 311.

[12] *Stallinger and Kuso v. Austria*, ECtHR 23 April 1997, appl. nos. 14696/89 and 14697/89. See also *Dacosta Silva v. Spain*, ECtHR 2 November 2011, appl. no. 69966/01, para. 37.

to add new restrictions to the relevant Convention provision. The Court dealt with this issue in the *Fischer* case,[13] which related to the right to a public hearing as protected by Article 6(1) ECHR. Austria had made the following reservation to this provision: 'The provisions of Article 6 of the Convention shall be so applied that there shall be no prejudice to the principles governing public court hearings laid down in Article 90 of the 1929 version of the Federal Constitutional Law.'[14]

After ratification of the Convention, the Austrian legislation on the right to a public hearing had been changed to the effect of considerably extending the national courts' power to refuse to hold a public hearing. The Court concluded from this that the reservation could not apply, since the provisions on which the refusal to hold such a hearing was based could not be considered to have been in force at the time the reservation was made. It is clear from this that legislation that is introduced at a later point in time, or amendments that are made after ratification, can only be valid if their scope and contents are either identical or narrower than the legislation in force at the time the reservation was made.

Thirdly, the question has arisen if the requirement entails certain temporal restrictions. In the case of *Schädler-Eberle*,[15] the applicant had argued that it would be irreconcilable with the rationale of Article 57 if a reservation would be permitted to continue to exist as long as the legislature would decide not to amend or repeal the relevant laws, which potentially could mean that an exclusion could be maintained indefinitely.[16] The Court acknowledged the pertinence of this argument and it stressed that the Parliamentary Assembly, too, had made clear that reservations should be confined to the period required to bring the legislation in question into conformity with the Convention.[17] Nevertheless, the Court also held that such temporal limitations could not be found in the text of Article 57. For that reason, a reservation made in conformity with Article 57 of the Convention will remain valid as long as it has not been withdrawn by the respondent state.[18]

b. *Prohibition of general reservations*

The first sentence of Article 57 requires that reservations relate to a particular provision of the Convention, while the second sentence states that reservations of a general character are not permitted. These two conditions are closely connected and in the case law they are even sometimes referred to in a single

---

[13] *Fischer v. Austria*, ECtHR 26 April 1995, appl. no. 16922/90.
[14] *Ibid.*, para. 30.
[15] *Schädler-Eberle v. Liechtenstein*, ECtHR 18 July 2013, appl. no. 56422/09.
[16] Judge De Meyer already emphasised this rationale in his concurring opinion to *Belilos v. Switzerland*, ECtHR (GC) 29 April 1988, appl. no. 10328/83. See further Marks, *supra* n. 9, p. 319.
[17] *Schädler-Eberle v. Liechtenstein*, *supra* n. 15, para. 70.
[18] *Ibid.*

sentence.[19] Nevertheless, there is a notable difference between the requirement of specificity and the prohibition of general reservations. While the specificity requirement implies that a reservation must pertain to a particular Convention requirement, the prohibition of general reservations relates to the contents and formulation of the reservation itself.

An example of a case in which the specificity requirement was applied can be found in *Steck-Risch*.[20] The applicants in the case had stated that the right to a fair and public hearing had been breached, but the Liechtenstein Government referred to the following reservation it had made as regards Article 6(1) ECHR: 'In accordance with Article 64 of the Convention [i.e., Article 57 since the entry into force of the Protocol No 11], the Principality of Liechtenstein makes the reservation that the principle that hearings must be held and judgments pronounced in public, as laid down in Article 6, paragraph 1, of the Convention, shall apply only within the limits deriving from the principles at present embodied in the following Liechtenstein laws (…)'.

The Court noted that the reservation made by Liechtenstein referred to a specific provision of the Convention, namely Article 6(1), and more particularly to a specific requirement contained therein, namely that hearings must be held and judgments be pronounced in public. Although the Court criticised the wording of the reservation for being somewhat complicated, it held that the text made it sufficiently clear that publicity would be restricted as provided for in the laws mentioned in the reservation. For that reason, the Court considered that the reservation could be held to be valid.

The prohibition of general reservations has been further detailed by the Court in *Belilos*.[21] The case related to an interpretative declaration the Swiss Government had made in respect to Article 6(1), which was formulated as follows: 'The Swiss Federal Council considers that the guarantee of fair trial in Article 6, paragraph 1 of the Convention, in the determination of civil rights and obligations or any criminal charge against the person in question is intended solely to ensure ultimate control by the judiciary over the acts or decisions of the public authorities relating to such rights or obligations or the determination of such a charge (…).'[22]

After having concluded that the declaration qualified as a reservation,[23] the Court explained that the notion 'reservation of a general character' in Article 57 refers to a reservation 'couched in terms that are too vague or broad for it to be possible to determine their exact meaning and scope'.[24] It may be derived from

---

[19]   *Temeltasch v. Switzerland*, *supra* n. 11, para. 84.
[20]   *Steck-Risch v. Liechtenstein*, ECtHR 14 February 2004 (dec.), appl. no. 63151/00.
[21]   *Belilos v. Switzerland*, *supra* n. 16.
[22]   *Ibid.*, para. 29.
[23]   As is further discussed *infra*, section 5.
[24]   *Belilos v. Switzerland*, *supra* n. 16, para. 55; more recently, see also *Grande Stevens and Others v. Italy*, ECtHR 4 March 2014, appl. nos. 18640/10 and Others, para. 209.

this that the wording of the reservation must be sufficiently clear and precise as to ascertain the exact meaning of the reservation. The Court did not consider it to be of any relevance that the Government had tried to provide for further explanations of the meaning of the reservation in its observations. In the Court's view, only the 'objective reality of the actual wording of the declaration' could be taken into consideration. Examining the text of the Swiss declaration in this light, the Court found it to be rather ambiguous, in particular because it did not clearly state which categories of disputes would be excluded from the applicability of Article 6 ECHR. It therefore concluded that the reservation could not be considered to be valid.

The Court arrived at a similar outcome in the *Eisenstecken* case,[25] which related to the lack of a public hearing in a case about property rights. The Austrian Government invoked the reservation it had made in relation to Article 6 ECHR, which was already quoted above, concerning the right to a public hearing.[26] The reservation referred to Article 90 of the Federal Constitutional Law, which had the following wording: 'Hearings by trial courts in civil and criminal cases shall be oral and public. Exceptions may be prescribed by law.'[27] The Court held that such a reservation, 'which merely refers to a permissive, non-exhaustive, provision of the Constitution and which does not refer to, or mention, those specific provisions of the Austrian legal order which exclude public hearings' could not be considered to be sufficiently precise as to meet the requirements of Article 57.[28]

The prohibition of general reservations does not forbid that reservations exclude a large body of law from the protection of the Convention, as long as it is formulated with sufficient precision. This is apparent from the case of *Kozlova and Smirnova*,[29] in which the Latvian Government invoked its reservation to Article 1 of Protocol No. 1. In this reservation, it had excluded from the scope of application of this provision a long list of laws on property reform. In the applicant's view, this list was so long that the reservation should be regarded as a general reservation, which therefore would need to be held to be invalid. The Court, however, stressed that Article 57 only required that the text of reservations should not be overly vague or broad and that the text should enable it to determine the reservation's exact meaning and scope. In this case, that requirement was met, since the reservation referred to a coherent body of statutory provisions regulating property reform and to a sufficiently precisely defined and strictly limited list of laws.

---

[25] *Eisenstecken v. Austria*, ECtHR 3 October 2000, appl. no. 29477/95.

[26] *Ibid.*, para. 21.

[27] *Ibid.*, para. 18.

[28] *Ibid.*, para. 22.

[29] *Kozlova and Smirnova v. Latvia*, ECtHR 23 October 2001 (dec.), appl. no. 57381/00.

c. Not contrary to aim and purpose of the Convention

Article 57 of the Convention does not set any requirements as to the contents of reservations. It is not stated, for example, that reservations cannot be made in relation to non-derogable ECHR provisions such as Articles 3 or 7.[30] The Vienna Convention on the Law of Treaties, however, provides in Article 19(c) that any reservation must be in conformity with the aim and purpose of a treaty to be valid. Given this requirement, it seems unlikely that the European Court would accept any reservations with respect to, for example, the prohibition of torture and inhuman and degrading treatment of Article 3.[31] It is evident, after all, that this prohibition belongs to the very core of the Convention and the Court has not accepted any exceptions to it in its case law.[32] For the same reason, the Court probably would resist any reservations which outstretch the outer limits of the possibilities for restriction and limitations accepted by the Court in its case law.[33] Finally, in *Zalyan*, the Court has made clear that it is unacceptable for a state to try to avoid its responsibility under the Convention by formally resorting to certain procedures prescribed in domestic law in whose respect a reservation has been made (e.g. disciplinary proceedings), and, by doing so, in reality pursuing aims for which those procedures were not designed (e.g. imposition of a criminal sanction).[34] In that case, the Court even refused to consider the validity of the reservation as such.

2.2. FORMAL AND PROCEDURAL REQUIREMENTS

a. Reservation at time of signature or ratification

Article 57 allows states to make reservations either when they sign the Convention or when they deposit their act of ratification (see Article 59 ECHR). If a state has already made a reservation at the time of signature, it does not need to do so again in the act of ratification. As mentioned in section 1, some of the original Contracting Parties made reservations at the time the Convention entered into force, but also states that have acceded to the Convention at a later point in time have been allowed to add reservations to their acts of ratification.

Although Article 57 in this respect is relatively straightforward, some doubts are possible in regard to its application where it is decided to extend

---

30   Van der Velde, *supra* n. 2, p. 326.
31   Indeed, albeit rather implicitly, the Court mentioned the 'object and purpose' requirement in *Loizidou v. Turkey*, ECtHR (GC) 23 May 1995 (prel. obj.), appl. no. 15318/89, para. 89.
32   See further Ch. 7 on Art. 3.
33   See further Van der Velde, *supra* n. 2, pp. 344–345.
34   *Zalyan and Others v. Armenia*, ECtHR 17 March 2016, appl. nos. 36894/04 and 3521/07, para. 311.

the territorial scope of application of the Convention in line with Article 56 of the Convention.[35] Strictly speaking, there is then no act of ratification, which would mean that no reservations can be made. In light of the rationale of Article 57, however, it can be argued that it is acceptable to make reservations at the time of extension of territorial scope.[36]

b. Statement of the law concerned

Article 57(2) ECHR states that any reservation should contain a brief 'statement of the law concerned'. The question may arise what the consequences are if such a statement is lacking, since full invalidity of the reservation in some cases might seem to be a rather disproportionate consequence of the non-obedience of such a formal requirement. In its classic *Temeltasch*[37] decision, the former EComHR indeed indicated that the consequences should be connected to the rationale of the requirement. An important function of the requirement is that a state would not make reservations of a general nature as is prohibited under Article 57 ECHR.[38] The EComHR derived from this that the lack of a statement of the law concerned is less problematic if it is sufficiently clear from the reservation to what legislation it pertains.[39] It might be concluded that, in that case, the omission of a statement would not lead to invalidity. The requirement further serves the need for legal certainty and clarity for the other Contracting States, who would need to know in relation to what laws states have made a reservation. According to the EComHR, this particular rationale would make the requirement more important in relation to Convention provisions with a very wide scope (such as Article 10 ECHR) than to Convention provisions of which the scope is more narrowly defined (such as Article 6(3)(e) ECHR).[40]

In *Belilos*, the ECtHR confirmed the EComHR's reading of Article 57 in *Temeltasch*.[41] It added to this that also the nature of the reservation may be of consequence. The *Belilos* case related to a reservation that, in the Court's view, had to be regarded as a general reservation in the sense of Article 57(1) ECHR.[42] The Court reasoned that in case of such a generally formulated reservation, the lack of a statement of the laws concerned was problematic, since it meant that there was even less of a guarantee that the reservation would not be overly broad.[43] Given the importance of guaranteeing that the reservation would

---

[35] On the territorial application of the Convention, see further Chapter 1.
[36] Van der Velde, *supra* n. 2, p. 319.
[37] *Ibid.*
[38] See *supra*, section 2.2.a.
[39] *Temeltasch*, *supra* n. 11, para. 89.
[40] *Ibid.*, para. 90.
[41] *Belilos v. Switzerland*, *supra* n. 16.
[42] See *supra*, section 2.2.a.
[43] *Belilos v. Switzerland*, *supra* n. 16, para. 59.

not go beyond the legislation expressly excluded by the state concerned, the combination of a general nature of the reservation and the lack of a statement of reasons had the overall result that the reservation was declared invalid.[44]

It appears from the case law that the Court is otherwise rather flexible as to the level of precision that is required in the statement of laws. It is not necessary, for example, to provide for an exhaustive overview of the relevant legislation or an elaborate indication of its contents. As the Court explained in *Chorherr*,[45] the interests of legal certainty do not even require a concise description of the substance of the texts in question.[46] A reference to the Official Gazette in which the legislation is published, combined with a very brief indication of the subject matter of the relevant provisions, suffices to make it possible to identify the precise laws concerned and to obtain any information regarding them. In *Steck-Risch*,[47] the Court added to this that even a mere mentioning of the titles of the relevant legislation is enough to meet the requirement, as long as the titles provide some indication as to the legislation's contents.

3.   CONSEQUENCES AND INTERPRETATION

The Strasbourg authorities have deemed themselves competent to examine the conformity of reservations with the substantive and formal requirements of Article 57 ECHR.[48] If they have found a reservation to be valid, the consequence is that the concrete provision (or part of the provision) to which the reservation relates does not apply in the case at hand.[49] The Court then will not examine the merits of the case and will declare the case inadmissible.[50]

There also may be cases in which the Court concludes a reservation is valid, yet it still does not declare the case inadmissible. It may want to do so when it has found that, in the concrete circumstances of the case, the specific reservation does not apply. An example of this can be found in the case of *Schädler-Eberle*.[51] The applicant in this case complained about the lack of an oral hearing in his case, in violation of Article 6(1) ECHR, but Liechtenstein had made a reservation to Article 6(1) ECHR to the effect that exceptions could be made to the obligation that hearings should take place in public.[52] The Court considered this a valid reservation, but it went on to examine its applicability in the case at hand. In

---

[44]   See similarly *Grande Stevens and Others v. Italy, supra* n. 24, paras. 208–211.
[45]   *Chorherr v. Austria*, ECtHR 25 August 1993, appl. no. 13308/87.
[46]   *Ibid.*, para. 20.
[47]   *Steck-Risch and Others v. Liechtenstein, supra* n. 20.
[48]   Van der Velde, *supra* n. 2, p. 315.
[49]   *Cf. Temeltasch v. Switzerland, supra* n. 11, para. 93.
[50]   E.g. *Steck-Risch and Others v. Liechtenstein, supra* n. 20.
[51]   *Schädler-Eberle v. Liechtenstein, supra* n. 15.
[52]   *Ibid.*, para. 86.

this respect, it took into account that according to its case law, the right to a fair or oral hearing means that a case is dealt with before the national court in the presence of both parties.[53] Such a hearing can be held in public, but also, occasionally, behind closed doors.[54] The Court remarked that neither the right to a fair hearing, nor the right to an oral hearing had been expressly mentioned in Liechtenstein's reservation. Given the need for strict interpretation of reservations, the Court could not arrive at the clear conclusion that oral hearings as well as public hearings were covered by it. For that reason, even though the reservation was valid, the Court decided not to declare the case inadmissible, but instead continued to examine the case on its merits.

In the opposite situation, i.e. where the reservation is found to be invalid, the Court will reject the respondent state's appeal to the reservation. If the case is not inadmissible for other reasons, it will then normally continue to examine it on its merits.[55] This means that the Strasbourg approach is characterised by the 'severance principle' – the Court is ready to 'severe' the reservation from the remainder of the state's obligations under the Convention. This approach is a rather extraordinary one from the perspective of public international law, since normally, invalidity of a reservation means that the state must modify or withdraw it, or it must consider itself no longer bound by the Treaty.[56] It fits in well, however, with the system of the ECHR and its rationale of effective protection of fundamental rights.[57]

4. MODIFICATION, WITHDRAWAL AND EXPIRY

Article 57 does not contain any express provisions about modification or withdrawal of reservations by the states. Modification can be considered unacceptable, however, if this would have the effect of widening the scope of a reservation, since this would be incompatible with both the rationale of Article 57 and the system and the underlying principles of the Convention.

Given the same rationale of Article 57, it will of course be permitted to modify a reservation in a way that restricts its scope or to withdraw it altogether.[58] Such a withdrawal or a restricting modification can be made at any time, but it is especially likely for a state to do so if a reservation has been found to be invalid.[59]

---

53   *Ibid.*, paras. 82–83.
54   *Ibid.*
55   E.g. *Belilos v. Switzerland, supra* n. 16, para. 60 e.v.; *Weber v. Switzerland*, ECtHR 22 May 1990, appl. no. 11034/84.
56   See Baratta, *supra* n. 10 and, elaborately, McCall-Smith, *supra* n. 9.
57   Indeed, the 'Strasbourg approach' is also followed by international human rights bodies such as the Human Rights Committee; see General Comment No. 24, *supra* n. 6, para. 20.
58   Van der Velde, *supra* n. 2, p. 322.
59   Baratta, *supra* n. 10, p. 420.

A reservation will be held to be withdrawn as soon as the Secretary-General is informed about the withdrawal or, in cases where the reservation is withdrawn or modified because of the entry into force of new legislation, from the moment the new legislation enters into force.[60] In specific cases, a reservation may no longer apply as from a certain date because the text of the reservation itself so provides.

The question if there can be any retroactive effect to a withdrawal of a reservation was raised in the case of *Jecius v. Lithuania*.[61] This case concerned the right of detainees to be brought promptly before a court (Article 5(3) ECHR), to which Lithuania had made the following reservation: 'The provisions of Article 5, paragraph 3, of the Convention shall not affect the operation of Article 104 of the Code of Criminal Procedure of the Republic of Lithuania (amended version No. I-551, July 19 1994) which provides that a decision to detain in custody any persons suspected of having committed a crime may also, by decision of a prosecutor, be so detained. This reservation shall be effective for one year after the Convention comes into force in respect of the Republic of Lithuania.'[62]

It is readily apparent from the text of this reservation that it would only be effective for one year. The question arose, however, whether after that date it could still apply to cases where the detention had already started. The Court answered this question in the positive. A reservation under Article 57 of the Convention would be devoid of purpose if, upon its expiry, the state were required to enforce the right retroactively for the period covered by the reservation.[63] As regards the facts of the *Jēčius* case, the Court noted that the reservation had expired on 21 June 1996. At that moment, the applicant had been held in detention on remand since 14 March 1996. According to the Court it followed that when the reservation expired, Lithuania was no longer under an obligation to bring the applicant promptly before an appropriate officer and there had been no violation of Article 5(3).

Hence, it is clear that a reservation will only lose its force as from the moment of its withdrawal or from the date of its expiry, without any retroactive effect. It is as yet unclear, however, how the Court will decide in cases of continuing violations, i.e., violations that have already started before the moment of repeal and which have continued to exist. Thus far no cases have been presented to the Court on this matter.

---

[60] Van der Velde, *supra* n. 2, p. 322.
[61] *Jēčius v. Lithuania*, ECtHR 31 July 2000, appl. no. 34578/97.
[62] *Ibid.*, 38.
[63] *Ibid.*, 85.

5. INTERPRETATIVE DECLARATIONS

In addition to the possibility of making reservations, states are allowed to make interpretative declarations in which they lay down how, in their view, a certain provision or obligation should be read.[64]

The distinction between interpretative declarations and reservations is highly relevant in practice, because only a reservation can have the result that the Court cannot examine a complaint on its merits and will, if the reservation applies to the facts of the case, declare the case inadmissible *ratione materiae*. In case an interpretative declaration is made, the Court can always deal with the merits of the case. Whether or not the Court then will be guided by the interpretation proposed by the government in its declaration is not entirely clear. It is evident from Article 32 ECHR, however, that the Court has jurisdiction to deal with all aspects regarding the interpretation of the Convention. In all probability, the Court's interpretation of the Convention thereby will prevail over any interpretation given by the states, so in this respect the Court will always have the final say.[65]

In practice, the distinction between reservations and interpretative declarations cannot always be strictly drawn, however, especially since a certain interpretation may lead to the exclusion of certain obligations for a certain state.[66] Yet the Strasbourg organs have always made clear that a state cannot be allowed to escape its obligations and responsibilities under the Convention by presenting a reservation as an interpretative declaration. The Commission stated this in its report in the *Temeltasch* case of 1983.[67] This case related to an interpretative declaration made by Switzerland in relation to Article 6(3) (e) ECHR, in which the right to free assistance by an interpreter is laid down. The interpretative declaration was phrased as follows: '(…) the Swiss Federal Council declares that it interprets the guarantee of (…) the free assistance of an interpreter in Article 6, paragraph 3 (…) (e) of the Convention as not permanently absolving the beneficiary from payment of the resulting costs.'[68]

The Commission considered that a declaration, 'whatever it is called', must be assimilated to a reservation if it is presented as a condition of its consent to be bound by the Convention and if it is intended to exclude or alter the legal effect of some of its provisions.[69] The Commission concluded that it was necessary to interpret the intention of the author of the declaration in order to be able to qualify the declaration as a declaration or as a reservation. Based on an extensive examination of the background and history of the Swiss declaration,

---

[64]   Van der Velde, *supra* n. 2, p. 304.
[65]   *Cf.* Marks, *supra* n. 9, p. 304.
[66]   Van der Velde, *supra* n. 2, p. 299.
[67]   *Temeltasch v. Switzerland, supra* n. 11.
[68]   *Ibid.*, para. 57.
[69]   *Ibid.*, para. 73.

the Commission eventually concluded that the declaration should be regarded as a reservation.[70] The Court in its later judgment in *Belilos*[71] confirmed that 'in order to establish the legal character of such a declaration, one must look behind the title given to it and seek to determine the substantive content'. Just like the Commission, it has held that it is necessary to look for the intentions of the government based on the history and explanations surrounding the declaration.[72]

---

[70] See further elaborately Imbert, *supra* n. 7.
[71] *Belilos v. Switzerland, supra* n. 16.
[72] *Ibid.*, para. 49.

TABLE OF CASES

B

C

E

H

K

O

X

INDEX